FOR REFERENCE

Do Not Take From This Room

T4-ALG-952

Jackson College Library

WITHDRAWN

HG   4009   .H66   2001

Hoover's handbook of world business
  2001

ATKINSON LEARNING RESOURCES CENTER
JACKSON COMMUNITY COLLEGE
2111 EMMONS ROAD
JACKSON, MICHIGAN 49201

We're long on information when you're short on time.

The information you need, when you need it

Hoover's Online has expanded its Web-based service to bring you a broader range of business research tools to complement our high-quality company information. Now you can rely on Hoover's editors to provide a business-oriented perspective on a variety of topics important to business researchers, including...

- Industries: descriptions, analysis and news
- Money: stock quotes, investing strategies, financial news and IPO information
- Career Development: career news, job search tips and tools, conference information and online education
- Business Travel: travel booking, destination guides, tips and special deals
- News: company, market, industry and IPO news

"If *information* is *power*, then **Hoover's Online** is a power tool of the first order. **We can't live without it.**"
— *Fast Company*

Whether you're using Hoover's to get to know your customers, vendors, competitors, investments, or potential employers, finding information on Hoover's Online is easy using Hoover's powerful search tools:

- keyword
- person's name
- company name
- ticker symbol
- ZIP code
- area code

- industry
- location
- annual sales
- company type
- stock performance criteria
- IPO underwriter

www.hoovers.com

To subscribe to the new Hoover's Online, call 800-486-8666.

Hoover's Handbook of World Business

2001

BUSINESS PRESS

Austin, Texas

Hoover's Handbook of World Business 2001 is intended to provide readers with accurate and authoritative information about the enterprises covered in it. Hoover's asked all companies and organizations profiled to provide information. Many did so; a number did not. The information contained herein is as accurate as we could reasonably make it. In many cases we have relied on third-party material that we believe to be trustworthy, but were unable to independently verify. We do not warrant that the book is absolutely accurate or without error. Readers should not rely on any information contained herein in instances where such reliance might cause loss or damage. The publisher, the editors, and their data suppliers specifically disclaim all warranties, including the implied warranties of merchantability and fitness for a specific purpose. This book is sold with the understanding that neither the publisher, the editors, nor any content contributors are engaged in providing investment, financial, accounting, legal, or other professional advice.

The financial data (Historical Financials sections) in this book are from a variety of sources. Media General Financial Services, Inc., provided selected data for the Historical Financials sections for most publicly traded companies. For the remainder of the public companies, for private companies and for historical information on public companies prior to their becoming public, we obtained information directly from the companies or from trade sources deemed to be reliable. Hoover's, Inc., is solely responsible for the presentation of all data.

Many of the names of products and services mentioned in this book are the trademarks or service marks of the companies manufacturing or selling them and are subject to protection under US law. Space has not permitted us to indicate which names are subject to such protection, and readers are advised to consult with the owners of such marks regarding their use. Hoover's is a trademark of Hoover's, Inc.

BUSINESS PRESS

Copyright © 2001 by Hoover's, Inc. All rights reserved. No part of this book may be reproduced or transmitted in any form or by any means, electronic or mechanical, including by photocopying, facsimile transmission, recording, rekeying, or using any information storage and retrieval system, without permission in writing from Hoover's, except that brief passages may be quoted by a reviewer in a magazine, in a newspaper, online, or in a broadcast review.

10 9 8 7 6 5 4 3 2 1

Publishers Cataloging-in-Publication Data

Hoover's Handbook of World Business 2001

Includes indexes.

1. Business enterprises — Directories. 2. Corporations — Directories.

HF3010 338.7

Hoover's Company Information is also available on America Online, Bloomberg Financial Network, EBSCO, Factiva, LEXIS-NEXIS, and on the Internet at Hoover's Online (www.hoovers.com), Alta Vista (www.altavista.digital.com), CBS MarketWatch (cbs.marketwatch.com), MSN MoneyCentral (moneycentral.com), The New York Times, (www.nytimes.com), The Washington Post (www.washingtonpost.com), Yahoo! (www.yahoo.com), and others.

A catalog of Hoover's products is available on the World Wide Web at www.hoovers.com.

ISBN 1-57311-066-3

ISSN 1055-7199

This book was produced for Hoover's Business Press by Sycamore Productions, Inc., Austin, Texas, using Quark, Inc.'s QuarkXPress 4.04; EM Software, Inc.'s Xtags 4.1b25; and fonts from Adobe's Clearface, Futura, and Myriad families. Cover design is by Shawn Harrington. Electronic prepress and printing were done by Edwards Brothers Incorporated, Ann Arbor, Michigan. Text paper is 60# Arbor.

US AND WORLD DIRECT SALES

Hoover's, Inc.
1033 La Posada Drive, Suite 250
Austin, TX 78752
Phone: 512-374-4500
Fax: 512-374-4501
e-mail: orders@hoovers.com

EUROPE

William Snyder Publishing Associates
5 Five Mile Drive
Oxford OX2 8HT
England
Phone & fax: +44-186-551-3186
e-mail: snyderpub@cs.com

HOOVER'S, INC.

Founder: Gary Hoover
Chairman, President, and CEO: Patrick J. Spain
EVP: Carl G. Shepherd

DATABASE EDITORIAL
Managing Editor: Nancy Regent
Assistant Managing Editor: Valerie Pearcy
Editorial Operations Manager: Margaret Duerksen
Director, Financial Information & MasterList: Dennis Sutton
Editorial Strategist: Shaun McDonald
Information Resources Manager: Jen Venable
Senior Editors: Rachel Brush, Scott Farley, Paul Geary, Joe Grey, Mary Mickle, Michael Sims
Contributing Editor: Travis Brown
Senior MasterList Editor: April Karli
Assistant Senior Editors: Larry Bills, Ashley Schrump, Joe Simonetta, David Woodruff
Associate Editors: Joy Aiken, Sally Alt, Graham Baker, Jodi Berls, Margaret Claughton, Bobby Duncan, Carrie Geis, Todd Gernert, Allan Gill, Gregg Gordon, Melanie Hall, Kathleen Kelly, John Mitchell, Jim Moore, Matt Saucedo, Vanita Trippe, Jennifer Westrom, Randy Williams
Senior Writers: David Hamerly, Stuart Hampton, Nancy McBride
Writers: Linnea Anderson, Alexander Blunt, Angela Boeckman, Joe Bramhall, James Bryant, Ryan Caione, Robert Carranza, Jason Cella, Jason Cother, David Crosby, Danny Cummings, Tom Elia, Delia Garza, Dan Gattuso, Michael Gaworecki, Guy Holland, Laura Ivy, Josh Lower, John MacAyeal, Michael Mulcahy, Nell Newton, Sheri Olander, Lynett Oliver, Amanda Palm, Elizabeth Paukstis, Lisa Ramirez, Rob Reynolds, Seth Shafer, Tim Walker, Chris Zappone, Bryan Zilar
Contributing Writer: Diane Lee
Financial Editors: Adi Anand, Dan Cabaniss, Chris Huston, Bill Ramsey, Joel Sensat
MasterList Editors: Anna Porlas, David Ramirez
QC Editor, MasterList: John Willis
Chief Copyeditor: Emily Weida
Assistant Editors: Michaela Drapes, Lesley Epperson, Jeanette Herman, Lavanya Ramanathan, Tami Saldana, Bronwen Taylor, Shannon Timmerman
Editorial Assistants: Tommy Ates, Rachel Carson, Jana Cummings, Travis Irby, Lisa Kean, Jay Koenig, Andreas Knutsen, Julie Krippel, Anne Law, Michael McLellan, Michelle Medina, Erick Olszewski, Lydia Puente, Ismara Quant, Kcevin Rob, Amy Schein, Anne Schroll, Christopher Sovine, Anthony Staats, Daysha Taylor, Leslie Westmoreland
Research Coordinator: Jim Harris
Library Coordinator: Kris Stephenson
Library Assistants: Litto Bacas, Melissa Chinn
Documents Coordinator: Carla Baker
Interns: Daniel Croll, Tom Moore

HOOVER'S, INC. MISSION STATEMENT

1. To produce business information products and services of the highest quality, accuracy, and readability.
2. To make that information available whenever, wherever, and however our customers want it through mass distribution at affordable prices.
3. To continually expand our range of products and services and our markets for those products and services.
4. To reward our employees, suppliers, and shareholders based on their contributions to the success of our enterprise.
5. To hold to the highest ethical business standards, erring on the side of generosity when in doubt.

Abbreviations

AB – Aktiebolag (Swedish)*
ADR – American Depositary Receipts
AG – Aktiengesellschaft (German)*
AFL-CIO – American Federation of Labor and Congress of Industrial Organizations
AMEX – American Stock Exchange
A/S – Aktieselskab (Danish)*
ASA – Allmenne Aksje Selskaper (Norwegian)*
ATM – asynchronous transfer mode; automated teller machine
CAD/CAM – computer-aided design/ computer-aided manufacturing
CASE – computer-aided software engineering
CD-ROM – compact disc – read-only memory
CEO – chief executive officer
CFO – chief financial officer
CMOS – complementary metal oxide semiconductors
COMECON – Council for Mutual Economic Assistance
COO – chief operating officer
DAT – digital audio tape
DOD – Department of Defense
DOE – Department of Energy
DOT – Department of Transportation
DRAM – dynamic random-access memory
DVD – digital versatile disc
EC – European Community
EPA – Environmental Protection Agency
EPS – earnings per share
EU – European Union
EVP – executive vice president
FCC – Federal Communications Commission
FDA – Food and Drug Administration
FDIC – Federal Deposit Insurance Corporation
FTC – Federal Trade Commission
GATT – General Agreement on Tariffs and Trade
GmbH – Gesellschaft mit beschränkter Haftung (German)*
GNP – gross national product
HDTV – high-definition television
HMO – health maintenance organization
HR – human resources
HTML – hypertext markup language
ICC – Interstate Commerce Commission
IMF – International Monetary Fund
IPO – initial public offering
IRS – Internal Revenue Service

KGaA – Kommanditgesellschaft auf Aktien (German)*
LAN – local-area network
LBO – leveraged buyout
LNG – liquefied natural gas
LP – limited partnership
Ltd. – Limited
MFN – Most Favored Nation
MITI – Ministry of International Trade and Industry (Japan)
NAFTA – North American Free Trade Agreement
Nasdaq – National Association of Securities Dealers Automated Quotations
NATO – North Atlantic Treaty Organization
NV – Naamlose Vennootschap (Dutch)*
NYSE – New York Stock Exchange
OAS – Organization of American States
OAO – open joint stock company (Russian)
OECD – Organization for Economic Cooperation and Development
OEM – original equipment manufacturer
OPEC – Organization of Petroleum Exporting Countries
OS – operating system
OTC – over-the-counter
P/E – price-earnings ratio
PLC – public limited company (UK)*
RAM – random-access memory
R&D – research and development
RISC – reduced instruction set computer
ROA – return on assets
ROI – return on investment
SA – Société Anonyme (French)*; Sociedad(e) Anónima (Spanish and Portuguese)*
SA de CV – Sociedad Anónima de Capital Variable (Spanish)*
SEC – Securities and Exchange Commission
SEVP – senior executive vice president
SIC – Standard Industrial Classification
SpA – Società per Azioni (Italian)*
SPARC – scalable processor architecture
SVP – senior vice president
VAR – value-added reseller
VAT – value-added tax
VC – vice chairman
VP – vice president
WAN – wide-area network
WWW – World Wide Web

* These abbreviations are used in companies' names to convey that the companies are limited liability enterprises; the meanings are usually the equivalent of *corporation* or *incorporated*.

Contents

List of Lists

Companies Profiled

ABOUT *HOOVER'S HANDBOOK* OF WORLD BUSINESS 2001

That the world has become a smaller place is indisputable. All one has to do is page through this eighth edition of *Hoover's Handbook of World Business* and read about the many global combinations and cross-border alliances and partnerships that are the rule rather than the exception to business in the 21st century. With the power of today's computer and telecommunications services, anyone with proper access can move money, products, and even services on the other side of the globe.

This book, which features 300 of the world's most influential companies based outside of the United States, is one of the most complete sources of in-depth information on large, non-US-based business enterprises available anywhere.

In addition to this volume, we have other international reference products that you may find useful. *Hoover's MasterList of International Companies* provides basic information on more than 1,600 leading public and private enterprises in the world. And we still make available through our catalog many of the best business reference works from other countries around the world. To see our complete selection, call us at 1-800-486-8666 and request a catalog of our products, or see our catalog online.

Another resource for information on the companies in this book as well as many more is Hoover's Online, which provides coverage of some 50,000 business enterprises. Our goal is to provide one site that addresses all the needs of business professionals. Hoover's has partnered with other prestigious business information and service providers to bring you all the right business information, services, and links in one place. Additionally, Hoover's Company Information is available on more than 25 other sites on the Internet, including The Wall Street Journal, The New York Times, and online services Reuters, Yahoo!, and America Online.

We believe that anyone who buys from, sells to, invests in, lends to, competes with, interviews with, or works for a company should know about that enterprise. If you are an investor, this book offers a chance to look at some of the more than 1,500 foreign companies listed on the US stock exchanges. If you are in sales or marketing, check out the purchasing power of multinational companies such as Toyota or Nestlé. If you are looking for a job, consider the US opportunities available with major manufacturers such as BMW and Samsung

or financial services companies, such as Nomura Securities or Credit Suisse Group. More than ever, the right information at the right time is the key to success in business.

Hoover's Handbook of World Business 2001 is one of a four-title series available as an indexed set. The others are *Hoover's Handbook of American Business* (two volumes), *Hoover's Handbook of Emerging Companies,* and *Hoover's Handbook of Private Companies.* These books, together with our many other Hoover's products, represent the most complete source of basic corporate information readily available to the general public.

This book consists of four sections:

1. Using the Profiles describes the contents of our profiles and explains the ways in which we gather and compile our data.

2. A List-Lover's Compendium contains lists of the largest, most profitable, and most valuable companies in this book, and selected lists from other sources of superlatives related to companies involved in world business.

3. The Profiles — 300 business enterprises of global importance, arranged alphabetically — make up the largest and most important part of the book.

4. Three indexes complete the book: The companies are indexed by industry groups and headquarters location, and there is a main index of all the brand names, companies, and people mentioned in the profiles. To help you find a particular company, a complete list of all profiled companies can be found at the front of the book.

As always, we hope you find our books useful. We invite your comments via telephone (512-374-4500), fax (512-374-4501), mail (1033 La Posada Drive, Suite 250, Austin, TX 78752), or e-mail (info@hoovers.com).

The Editors
Austin, Texas
December 2000

USING THE PROFILES

SELECTION OF THE COMPANIES PROFILED

The 300 profiles in this book include a variety of international enterprises, ranging from some of the largest publicly traded companies in the world — DaimlerChrysler AG, for example — to the largest business entity in New Zealand, Fletcher Challenge Limited. It also includes many private businesses, such as Bertelsmann AG and Dentsu Inc., as well as a selection of government-owned entities, including the British Broadcasting Corporation and Mexico's Petróleos Mexicanos. The companies selected represent a cross-section of the largest, most influential, and most interesting companies based outside the United States.

In selecting these companies, we followed several basic criteria. We started with the global giants, including Toyota and Royal Dutch/Shell Group, and then looked at companies with substantial activity in the US, such as Seagram and Diageo (owner of Burger King). We also included companies that dominate their industries (e.g., Electrolux, the world's #1 producer of household appliances), as well as representative companies from around the world (one Indian conglomerate, Tata; one firm from Finland, Nokia; and two companies from Russia, OAO Gazprom and OAO LUKOIL). Companies that weren't necessarily global powerhouses but had a high profile with consumers (e.g., IKEA) or had interesting stories (Virgin Group) were included. Finally, because of their truly global reach, we added the Big Five accounting firms (even though they are headquartered or co-headquartered in the US).

ORGANIZATION

The profiles are presented in alphabetical order. We have shown the full name of the enterprise at the top of the page, unless it was too long, in which case you will find it above the address in the Locations section of the profile. Also, full names are provided in the Locations section for some companies, primarily Japanese, that are profiled under their more well-known English translations. (The legal name of Nippon Steel Corporation is Shin Nippon Seitetsu Kabushiki Kaisha.) If a company name starts with a person's first name (e.g., George Weston Limited), it is alphabetized under the first name.

We've also tried to alphabetize companies where you would expect to find them – for example, Deutsche Lufthansa is in the L's and Grupo Televisa can be found under T. Company names (past and present) mentioned in the profiles are indexed in the main index of the book.

The annual financial information contained in the profiles is current through fiscal year-ends occurring as late as June 2000. We have included certain nonfinancial developments, such as officer changes, through November 2000.

OVERVIEW

In the first section of the profile, we have tried to give a thumbnail description of the company and what it does. In addition to summarizing the operations and company structure, the description will usually include information on the company's strategy, reputation, and ownership.

HISTORY

This extended section reflects our belief that every enterprise is the sum of its history and that you have to know where you came from in order to know where you are going. While some companies have limited historical awareness and were unable to help us much and other companies are just plain boring, we think the vast majority of the enterprises in this book have colorful backgrounds. We have tried to focus on the people who made the enterprises what they are today. We have found these histories to be full of twists and ironies; they make fascinating reading.

OFFICERS

Here we list the names of the people who run the company, insofar as space allows. We have shown age and pay information where available, although most non-US companies are not required to report the level of detail revealed in the US.

While companies are free to structure their management titles any way they please, most modern corporations follow standard practices. The ultimate power in any corporation lies with the shareholders, who elect a board of directors, usually including officers or "insiders" as well as individuals from outside the company. The chief officer, the person on whose desk the buck stops, is usually called the chief executive officer

(CEO) in the US. In other countries, practices vary widely. In the UK, traditionally, the Managing Director performs the functions of the CEO without the title, although the use of the term CEO is on the rise there. In Germany it is customary to have two boards of directors: a managing board populated by the top executives of the company and a higher-level supervisory board consisting of outsiders.

We have tried to list each company's most important officers, including the chief financial officer (CFO), the chief legal officer, and the chief human resources or personnel officer. For companies with US operations, we have included the names of the US CEO, CFO, and top human resources executive, where available. The Officers section also includes the name of the company's auditing (accounting) firm, where available. The people named in the profiles are included in an index at the back of the book.

LOCATIONS

Here we include the company's headquarters, street address, telephone and fax numbers, and Web site, as available. We also list the same information for the US office for each company, if one exists. Telephone numbers of foreign offices are shown using the standardized conventions of international dialing. The back of the book includes an index of companies by headquarters location.

In some cases we have also included information on the geographical distribution of the company's business, including sales and profit data. Note that these profit numbers, like those in the Products/Operations section below, are usually operating or pretax profits rather than net profits. Operating profits are generally those before financing costs (interest income and payments) and before taxes, which are considered costs attributable to the whole company rather than to one division or part of the world. For this reason the net income figures (in the How Much sections) are usually much lower, since they are after interest and taxes. Pretax profits are after interest but before taxes.

PRODUCTS/OPERATIONS

This section lists as many of the company's products, services, brand names, divisions,

subsidiaries, and joint ventures as we could fit. We have tried to include all its major lines and all familiar brand names. The nature of this section varies by company and the amount of information available. If the company publishes sales and profit information by type of business, we have included it. The brand, division, and subsidiary names are listed in the last index in the book.

COMPETITORS

In this section we have listed enterprises that compete with the profiled company. This feature is included as a quick way to locate similar companies and compare them. Due to the difficulty in identifying companies that only compete in foreign markets, the list of competitors is still weighted to large international companies with a strong US presence.

HISTORICAL FINANCIALS & EMPLOYEES

Here we have tried to present as much data about each enterprise's financial performance as we could compile in the allocated space. While the information varies somewhat from industry to industry, and is less complete in the case of private companies that do not release data (although we have tried always to provide annual sales and employment), the following information is generally present.

A 10-year table, with relevant annualized compound growth rates, covers:

- **Sales** — fiscal year sales (year-end assets for most financial companies)
- **Net Income** — fiscal year net income (before accounting changes)
- **Income as a Percent of Sales** — fiscal year net income as a percent of sales (as a percent of assets for most financial firms)
- **Earnings Per Share** — fiscal year earnings per share (EPS)
- **Fiscal Year Stock Price** — the high, low, and close for the fiscal year.
- **P/E** — high and low price-earnings ratio
- **Dividends Per Share** — fiscal year dividends per share
- **Book Value Per Share** — fiscal year-end book value (common shareholders' equity per share)
- **Employees** — fiscal year-end or average number of employees

The information on the number of employees is intended to aid the reader interested in knowing whether a company has a long-term trend of increasing or decreasing employment. As far as we know, we are the only company that publishes this information in print format.

The year at the top of each column in the Historical Financials & Employees section is the year in which the company's fiscal year actually ends. Thus a company with a June 30, 2000, year-end is shown as 2000.

Key year-end statistics in this section generally show the financial strength of the enterprise, including:

- Debt ratio (total debt as a percent of combined total debt and shareholders' equity)
- Return on equity (net income divided by the average of beginning and ending common shareholders' equity)
- Cash, marketable securities, and short-term investments on hand
- Current ratio (ratio of current assets to current liabilities)
- Total long-term debt (including capital lease obligations)
- Number of shares of common stock outstanding
- Dividend yield (fiscal year dividends per share divided by the fiscal year-end closing stock price)
- Dividend payout (fiscal year dividends divided by fiscal year EPS)
- Market value at fiscal year-end (fiscal year-end closing stock price multiplied by fiscal year-end number of shares outstanding)
- Sales (or assets, where applicable) translated into US dollars at the fiscal year-end exchange rates for those companies with foreign currency-denominated Historical Financials & Employees tables.

Per share data have been adjusted for stock splits and rights issues. The data for public companies with sponsored ADRs have been provided to us by Media General Financial Services, Inc. Other public company information was compiled by Hoover's, which takes full responsibility for the content of this section.

In the case of private companies that do not publicly disclose financial information, we usually did not have access to such standardized data. We have gathered estimates of sales and other statistics from numerous sources.

A NOTE ABOUT THE NUMBERS

Dealing with companies from around the world presents some obvious reporting problems. Here are the guidelines we used:

- If a public company's stock is traded on a US exchange, the numbers are presented in US dollars, using the appropriate exchange rate at fiscal year-end.
- If a public company is not traded in the US, the numbers are presented in the currency in which the stock is traded. However, US dollars are used for the sales and market value in the year-end chart.
- Foreign nonpublic companies are presented in US dollars, using the appropriate exchange rate at fiscal year-end.

As usual, there are some exceptions:

- A few of our profiles cover groups of companies, such as *keiretsu* (e.g., Mitsubishi) in Japan and *chaebol* (e.g., Samsung) in South Korea. For these we have presented group numbers, where available; otherwise, we have used the numbers for the largest entity or for the one that is publicly traded.

CURRENCY SYMBOLS

Country/Region	Currency	Symbol
Australia	dollar	A$
Canada	dollar	C$
European Monetary Union	euro	€
Hong Kong	dollar	HK$
Japan	yen	¥
New Zealand	dollar	NZ$
Singapore	dollar	S$
South Korea	won	won
Sweden	krona	SK
Switzerland	franc	SF
Taiwan	dollar	NT$
UK	pound, pence	£, p
US	dollar	$

THE EURO

Since the adoption of the euro, the common currency of the European Monetary Union, on January 1, 1999, all transfer payments, financial transactions, and market transactions are conducted in euros; circulation of actual euro notes and coins begins on January 1, 2002.

For participating EU public companies (in Austria, Belgium, Finland, France, Germany, Ireland, Italy, Luxembourg, the Netherlands, Portugal, and Spain) not traded in the US, Historical Financial information is presented in euros, using the following conversion rates adopted by the EU on January 1, 1999.

One euro equals:

13.7603	Austrian schilling
40.3399	Belgian franc
5.94573	Finnish markka
6.55957	French franc
1.95583	German mark
.787564	Irish punt
1936.27	Italian lira
40.3399	Luxembourg franc
2.20371	Dutch guilder
200.482	Portuguese escudo
166.386	Spanish peseta

Hoover's Handbook of World Business

A List-Lover's Compendium

The 100 Largest Companies by Sales
in *Hoover's Handbook of World Business 2001*

Rank	Company	Sales ($ mil.)	Rank	Company	Sales ($ mil.)
1	DaimlerChrysler AG	151,035	51	Royal Ahold N.V.	33,811
2	Toyota Motor Corporation	119,656	52	Koninklijke Philips Electronics N.V.	31,748
3	Mitsui Group	117,373	53	Suez Lyonnaise des Eaux	31,682
4	ITOCHU Corporation	116,704	54	BASF Aktiengesellschaft	31,537
5	Mitsubishi Group	115,024	55	Eni S.p.A.	31,225
6	Royal Dutch/Shell Group	105,366	56	BNP Paribas Group	31,050
7	Marubeni Corporation	100,413	57	British American Tobacco p.l.c.	30,374
8	Nippon Telegraph and Telephone	97,956	58	Olivetti S.p.A.	30,157
9	Sumitomo Group	95,532	59	British Telecommunications plc	29,820
10	AXA	92,812	60	ThyssenKrupp AG	29,749
11	BP Amoco p.l.c.	83,566	61	Tesco PLC	29,666
12	Nippon Life Insurance Company	82,860	62	Ito-Yokado Co., Ltd.	29,308
13	Volkswagen AG	75,697	63	Tengelmann Group	28,820
14	Siemens AG	73,049	64	Industrial Bank of Japan, Limited	28,434
15	Daewoo Group	71,526	65	Robert Bosch GmbH	28,103
16	Matsushita Electric Industrial Co., Ltd.	71,118	66	Bayer AG	27,511
17	Allianz AG	70,028	67	France Telecom	27,424
18	Nissho Iwai Corporation	69,012	68	TOMEN Corporation	27,173
19	Sony Corporation	63,082	69	Repsol YPF, S.A.	26,537
20	ING Groep N.V.	59,171	70	UBS AG	26,110
21	Honda Motor Co., Ltd.	57,455	71	Telecom Italia S.p.A.	25,989
22	Samsung Group	57,199	72	Canon Inc.	25,709
23	Nissan Motor Co., Ltd.	56,388	73	J Sainsbury plc	25,681
24	LG Group	55,000	74	Nippon Steel Corporation	25,407
25	Toshiba Corporation	54,493	75	ABB Ltd.	24,681
26	E.ON AG	53,392	76	Petróleos Mexicanos	24,400
27	Prudential plc	52,116	77	Banco Santander Central Hispano S.A.	24,332
28	Deutsche Bank AG	51,491			
29	Fujitsu Limited	49,808	78	Mannesmann AG	23,428
30	Hyundai Group	49,093	79	Alcatel	23,235
31	Fiat S.p.A.	48,741	80	Telefónica, S.A.	23,168
32	NEC Corporation	48,461	81	Compagnie de Saint-Gobain	23,113
33	Credit Suisse Group	47,546	82	Enel S.p.A.	22,918
34	Nestlé S.A.	46,924	83	Telefonaktiebolaget LM Ericsson	22,760
35	METRO AG	44,114	84	The Bank of Tokyo-Mitsubishi Ltd.	22,664
36	Unilever	43,636	85	AEGON N.V.	22,580
37	The Tokyo Electric Power Company, Incorporated	42,720	86	Nortel Networks Corporation	22,217
38	TOTAL FINA ELF S.A.	42,566	87	Barclays PLC	21,097
39	Vivendi	41,914	88	Novartis AG	20,404
40	RWE Aktiengesellschaft	41,772	89	Bridgestone Corporation	20,403
			90	Nokia Corporation	19,954
41	Zurich Financial Services	39,962	91	The Dai-Ichi Kangyo Bank, Limited	19,065
42	HSBC Holdings plc	38,789	92	Pinault-Printemps-Redoute	19,042
43	PSA Peugeot Citroën S.A.	38,072	93	SANYO Electric Co., Ltd.	19,002
44	Renault S.A.	37,851	94	Preussag AG	18,739
45	Carrefour SA	37,622	95	Petróleos de Venezuela S.A.	18,657
46	ABN AMRO Holding N.V.	36,232	96	Otto Versand Gmbh & Co.	18,625
47	Elf Aquitaine	35,797	97	Diageo plc	17,998
48	Deutsche Telekom AG	35,796	98	Kingfisher plc	17,484
49	NTT DoCoMo, Inc.	35,246	99	Roche Holding Ltd.	17,326
50	Bayerische Motoren Werke AG	34,643	100	PricewaterhouseCoopers	17,300

Source: Hoover's, Inc., Database, December 2000

The 100 Most Profitable Companies
in *Hoover's Handbook of World Business 2001*

Rank	Company	Net Income ($ mil.)	Rank	Company	Net Income ($ mil.)
1	Hutchison Whampoa Limited	15,102	51	AEGON N.V.	1,584
2	Cable and Wireless plc	12,905	52	Anglo American plc	1,552
3	Royal Dutch/Shell Group	8,584	53	TOTAL FINA ELF S.A.	1,534
4	DaimlerChrysler AG	5,785	54	Scottish Power plc	1,502
5	HSBC Holdings plc	5,408	55	BNP Paribas Group	1,494
6	Olivetti S.p.A.	4,974	56	Diageo plc	1,480
7	ING Groep N.V.	4,967	57	Vivendi	1,441
8	BP Amoco p.l.c.	4,686	58	Granada Compass PLC	1,425
9	Toyota Motor Corporation	4,540	59	The Nomura Securities Co., Ltd.	1,380
10	Novartis AG	4,185	60	Pohang Iron & Steel Co., Ltd.	1,368
11	UBS AG	3,960	61	Rio Tinto plc	1,282
12	AB Volvo	3,780	62	Deutsche Telekom AG	1,265
13	BCE Inc.	3,773	63	BASF Aktiengesellschaft	1,245
14	Roche Holding Ltd.	3,623	64	Compagnie de Saint-Gobain	1,235
15	Nippon Life Insurance Company	3,594	65	RWE Aktiengesellschaft	1,186
16	Credit Suisse Group	3,356	66	Royal Bank of Canada	1,173
17	British Telecommunications plc	3,274	67	Sony Corporation	1,149
18	Zurich Financial Services	3,260	68	OAO LUKOIL	1,120
19	Unilever	3,165	69	Tesco PLC	1,064
20	Nestlé S.A.	2,969	70	Cadbury Schweppes plc	1,037
21	Glaxo Wellcome plc	2,926	71	Repsol YPF, S.A.	1,020
22	Eni S.p.A.	2,877	72	PETROBRAS	972
23	Barclays PLC	2,842	73	Matsushita Electric Industrial Co., Ltd.	971
24	Nippon Telegraph and Telephone	2,821	74	BHP Limited	971
25	France Telecom	2,788	75	Bank of Montreal	939
26	Suez Lyonnaise des Eaux	2,719	76	British American Tobacco p.l.c.	898
27	E.ON AG	2,693	77	Prudential plc	876
28	Teléfonos de México, S.A. de C.V.	2,656	78	Bridgestone Corporation	868
29	Nokia Corporation	2,601	79	Volkswagen AG	850
30	Enel S.p.A.	2,598	80	Royal KPN N.V.	832
31	ABN AMRO Holding N.V.	2,594	81	Marconi plc	831
32	Deutsche Bank AG	2,589	82	Fuji Photo Film Co., Ltd.	827
33	Honda Motor Co., Ltd.	2,472	83	The Tokyo Electric Power Co., Inc.	818
34	Petróleos de Venezuela S.A.	2,404	84	The Tokio Marine and Fire Ins. Co., Ltd.	797
35	NTT DoCoMo, Inc.	2,390	85	PSA Peugeot Citroën S.A.	779
36	Telstra Corporation Limited	2,304	86	Vodafone Group PLC	776
37	Allianz AG	2,249	87	Carrefour SA	760
38	Elf Aquitaine	2,088	88	Royal Ahold N.V.	758
39	AXA	2,035	89	Nintendo Co., Ltd.	720
40	The Toronto-Dominion Bank	2,026	90	The News Corporation Limited	714
41	Bayer AG	2,016	91	L'Oréal SA	701
42	Siemens AG	1,987	92	Canadian Imperial Bank of Commerce	699
43	National Australia Bank Limited	1,841	93	LVMH Moët Hennessy Louis Vuitton SA	696
44	Telefónica, S.A.	1,821	94	Canon Inc.	689
45	Koninklijke Philips Electronics N.V.	1,816	95	Groupe Danone	688
46	SmithKline Beecham plc	1,781	96	Reuters Group PLC	687
47	Telecom Italia S.p.A.	1,666	97	Singapore Airlines Limited	678
48	ABB Ltd.	1,614	98	Kingfisher plc	677
49	Telefonaktiebolaget LM Ericsson	1,609	99	The Dai-Ichi Kangyo Bank, Limited	671
50	Banco Santander Central Hispano S.A.	1,586	100	Compagnie Générale des Établissements Michelin	669

Source: Hoover's, Inc., Database, December 2000

The 100 Most Valuable Public Companies
in *Hoover's Handbook of World Business 2001*

Rank	Company	Market Value* ($ mil.)	Rank	Company	Market Value ($ mil.)
1	Vodafone Group PLC	340,772	51	Royal Ahold N.V.	19,356
2	Nippon Telegraph and Telephone	249,591	52	Reuters Group PLC	19,161
3	Nokia Corporation	222,259	53	TDK Corporation	17,514
4	Deutsche Telekom AG	215,102	54	Nissan Motor Co., Ltd.	15,960
5	Toyota Motor Corporation	194,969	55	Groupe Danone	15,729
6	BP Amoco p.l.c.	192,600	56	Scottish Power plc	14,638
7	Nortel Networks Corporation	139,093	57	The Toronto-Dominion Bank	14,305
8	France Telecom	136,786	58	Akzo Nobel N.V.	14,224
9	Sony Corporation	127,073	59	Pohang Iron & Steel Co., Ltd.	13,507
10	British Telecommunications plc	122,416	60	Royal Bank of Canada	13,338
11	HSBC Holdings plc	120,748	61	WPP Group plc	12,877
12	Telecom Italia S.p.A.	103,966	62	Cadbury Schweppes plc	12,222
13	Glaxo Wellcome plc	101,724	63	SANYO Electric Co., Ltd.	11,326
14	TOTAL FINA ELF S.A.	96,607	64	Norsk Hydro ASA	11,188
15	Telefónica, S.A.	85,714	65	British American Tobacco p.l.c.	11,157
16	DaimlerChrysler AG	78,254	66	AB Volvo	11,148
17	SmithKline Beecham plc	72,033	67	Kirin Brewery Company, Limited	11,071
18	The Bank of Tokyo-Mitsubishi Ltd.	66,345	68	Fiat S.p.A.	11,070
19	AEGON N.V.	63,835	69	Gucci Group N.V.	10,654
20	Matsushita Electric Industrial Co., Ltd.	62,492	70	Bank of Montreal	10,163
21	ING Groep N.V.	58,985	71	Bass PLC	10,022
22	BCE Inc.	58,065	72	Imperial Oil Limited	9,333
23	NEC Corporation	48,356	73	AB Electrolux	9,200
24	Royal KPN N.V.	46,019	74	Novo Nordisk A/S	9,168
25	Koninklijke Philips Electronics N.V.	45,781	75	Alcan Aluminium Limited	9,034
26	Cable and Wireless plc	45,551	76	Canadian Imperial Bank of Commerce	8,649
27	LVMH Moët Hennessy Louis Vuitton SA	44,571	77	Alcatel	8,353
28	Aventis	44,356	78	Imperial Chemical Industries PLC	7,746
29	Eni S.p.A.	44,105	79	United News & Media plc	6,394
30	STMicroelectronics N.V.	43,889	80	WMC Limited	6,296
31	Barclays PLC	43,030	81	Imperial Tobacco Group PLC	6,120
32	Elf Aquitaine	42,503	82	British Airways Plc	5,813
33	Teléfonos de México, S.A. de C.V.	42,044	83	Pechiney S.A.	5,773
34	Honda Motor Co., Ltd.	39,586	84	Teleglobe Inc.	5,759
35	ABN AMRO Holding N.V.	37,159	85	Hanson PLC	5,256
36	Canon Inc.	35,350	86	Pioneer Corporation	5,242
37	British Sky Broadcasting Group plc	35,340	87	Rogers Communications Inc.	5,012
38	Kyocera Corporation	31,386	88	Kubota Corporation	4,899
39	Diageo plc	30,422	89	Coles Myer Ltd.	4,394
40	Grupo Televisa, S.A.	30,165	90	Compañía de Telecomunicaciones de Chile S.A.	4,367
41	Repsol YPF, S.A.	27,621	91	Inco Limited	4,267
42	The Seagram Company Ltd.	25,732	92	Benetton Group S.p.A.	4,125
43	E.ON AG	25,170	93	Placer Dome Inc.	3,520
44	Rio Tinto plc	25,138	94	Tomkins PLC	2,896
45	Anglo American plc	25,075	95	Gallaher Group Plc	2,546
46	Ito-Yokado Co., Ltd.	24,103	96	The Rank Group PLC	2,371
47	Fuji Photo Film Co., Ltd.	22,644	97	Laidlaw Inc.	2,064
48	National Australia Bank Limited	21,908	98	Ispat International N.V.	2,049
49	SAP Aktiengesellschaft	21,814	99	Creative Technology Ltd.	1,918
50	BHP Limited	21,242	100	Cominco Ltd.	1,807

Source: Hoover's, Inc., Database, December 2000

The 100 Largest Employers
in *Hoover's Handbook of World Business 2001*

Rank	Company	Number of Employees	Rank	Company	Number of Employees
1	DaimlerChrysler AG	466,938	51	George Weston Limited	119,000
2	Siemens AG	443,000	52	Telefónica, S.A.	118,778
3	Hitachi, Ltd.	337,911	53	Kingfisher plc	118,416
4	Royal Ahold N.V.	309,000	54	Ito-Yokado Co., Ltd.	116,636
5	Volkswagen AG	306,275	55	Alcatel	115,712
6	OAO Gazprom	298,000	56	Bayerische Motoren Werke AG	114,874
7	Carrefour SA	297,290	57	Allianz AG	113,584
8	Vivendi	275,000	58	Anglo American plc	113,000
9	Sodexho Alliance	269,973	59	Honda Motor Co., Ltd.	112,400
10	Samsung Group	267,000	60	ABN AMRO Holding N.V.	108,689
11	Daewoo Group	265,044	61	British American Tobacco p.l.c.	107,620
12	Tata Enterprises	255,000	62	BASF Aktiengesellschaft	104,628
13	Unilever	255,000	63	Telefonaktiebolaget LM Ericsson	103,667
14	Nestlé S.A.	230,929	64	KPMG International	102,000
15	Koninklijke Philips Electronics N.V.	226,874	65	Bridgestone Corporation	101,489
16	Nippon Telegraph and Telephone	224,000	66	Aventis	101,000
17	Suez Lyonnaise des Eaux	222,000	67	Ernst & Young International	97,800
18	Fiat S.p.A.	220,000	68	Royal Dutch/Shell Group	96,000
19	METRO AG	216,457	69	Banco Santander Central Hispano S.A.	95,442
20	Toyota Motor Corporation	214,631	70	Deutsche Bank AG	93,232
21	Hyundai Group	200,000	71	AB Electrolux	92,926
22	Tengelmann Group	200,000	72	AXA	92,008
23	Toshiba Corporation	198,000	73	Deloitte Touche Tohmatsu	90,000
24	Robert Bosch GmbH	194,889	74	Karstadt Quelle AG	89,920
25	Sony Corporation	189,700	75	ING Groep N.V.	86,040
26	J Sainsbury plc	189,227	76	Akzo Nobel N.V.	85,000
27	Fujitsu Limited	188,053	77	Enel S.p.A.	84,938
28	France Telecom	174,262	78	BAE SYSTEMS	83,400
29	Deutsche Telekom AG	170,000	79	Novartis AG	81,854
30	PSA Peugeot Citroën S.A.	165,800	80	Tesco PLC	80,650
31	Compagnie de Saint-Gobain	165,000	81	BP Amoco p.l.c.	80,400
32	ABB Ltd.	164,154	82	Canon Inc.	79,800
33	PricewaterhouseCoopers	160,000	83	Granada Compass PLC	78,871
34	Renault S.A.	159,608	84	Pinault-Printemps-Redoute	78,540
35	Coles Myer Ltd.	157,000	85	BNP Paribas Group	77,472
36	RWE Aktiengesellschaft	155,576	86	Nortel Networks Corporation	76,700
37	HSBC Holdings plc	146,897	87	Groupe Danone	75,965
38	Andersen Worldwide	135,000	88	Marks and Spencer p.l.c.	75,492
39	E.ON AG	131,602	89	Bass PLC	74,451
40	Mannesmann AG	130,860	90	Barclays PLC	74,300
41	Olivetti S.p.A.	129,073	91	Casino Guichard-Perrachon	73,468
42	Accor	128,850	92	Diageo plc	72,474
43	TOTAL FINA ELF S.A.	127,252	93	Teléfonos de México, S.A. de C.V.	72,321
44	Compagnie Générale des Établissements Michelin	127,241	94	Eni S.p.A.	72,023
45	Woolworths Limited	125,000	95	Laidlaw Inc.	71,400
46	Delhaize "Le Lion" S.A.	124,933	96	MAN Aktiengesellschaft	71,239
47	Telecom Italia S.p.A.	122,662	97	Wal-Mart de Mexico, S.A. de C.V.	70,700
48	Invensys plc	121,683	98	Tomkins PLC	70,039
49	Bayer AG	120,400	99	Hudson's Bay Company	70,000
50	OAO LUKOIL	120,000	100	Zurich Financial Services	68,785

Source: Hoover's, Inc., Database, December 2000

The Top 100 Companies in Five-Year Sales Growth in *Hoover's Handbook of World Business 2001*

Rank	Company	Annual % Change	Rank	Company	Annual % Change
1	Saatchi & Saatchi	70.1	51	Virgin Group Ltd.	14.6
2	British American Tobacco p.l.c.	60.7	52	British Broadcasting Corporation	14.6
3	Dentsu Inc.	58.8	53	Banco Santander Central Hispano S.A.	14.2
4	Vodafone Group PLC	55.6	54	Wolters Kluwer nv	14.1
5	Teleglobe Inc.	52.8	55	The News Corporation Limited	13.4
6	Olivetti S.p.A.	48.5	56	The Toronto-Dominion Bank	13.3
7	Anglo American plc	44.8	57	Interbrew S.A.	13.2
8	Invensys plc	42.9	58	KPMG International	12.9
9	SANYO Electric Co., Ltd.	40.0	59	BAE SYSTEMS	12.9
10	PricewaterhouseCoopers	36.2	60	Telefónica, S.A.	12.8
11	AXA	35.4	61	Compagnie de Saint-Gobain	12.7
12	The Seagram Company Ltd.	33.0	62	Waterford Wedgwood plc	12.6
13	NTT DoCoMo, Inc.	32.2	63	Tomkins PLC	12.6
14	Prudential plc	30.2	64	CANAL+	12.5
15	SAP Aktiengesellschaft	28.7	65	Suez Lyonnaise des Eaux	12.1
16	Sodexho Alliance	27.2	66	Hutchison Whampoa Limited	12.0
17	Ispat International N.V.	26.5	67	Isuzu Motors Limited	11.6
18	SOFTBANK CORP.	25.9	68	Compañía de Telecomunicaciones de Chile S.A.	11.5
19	Diageo plc	25.5	69	TOTAL FINA ELF S.A.	11.3
20	Gucci Group N.V.	25.4	70	Deutsche Bank AG	11.3
21	Wal-Mart de Mexico, S.A. de C.V.	25.0	71	George Weston Limited	11.0
22	Nokia Corporation	24.1	72	Sema plc	10.6
23	Molson Inc.	24.1	73	BP Amoco p.l.c.	10.5
24	Computacenter plc	23.4	74	VNU N.V.	10.5
25	Credit Suisse Group	23.4	75	Seiko Epson Corporation	10.4
26	ING Groep N.V.	23.3	76	HSBC Holdings plc	10.3
27	adidas-Salomon AG	22.0	77	Acer Inc.	10.2
28	Kingfisher plc	21.7	78	IKEA International A/S	10.1
29	United News & Media plc	20.6	79	Agrium Inc.	10.0
30	Nortel Networks Corporation	20.1	80	Sony Corporation	9.8
31	Hollinger Inc.	19.4	81	Carlsberg A/S	9.8
32	Danka Business Systems PLC	19.1	82	WPP Group plc	9.8
33	Telefonaktiebolaget LM Ericsson	19.0	83	OAO LUKOIL	9.8
34	Andersen Worldwide	19.0	84	Pearson plc	9.7
35	Daewoo Group	18.2	85	UBS AG	9.7
36	Granada Compass PLC	17.3	86	Honda Motor Co., Ltd.	9.5
37	Scottish Power plc	17.3	87	STMicroelectronics N.V.	9.2
38	Teléfonos de México, S.A. de C.V.	17.0	88	Fujitsu Limited	9.2
39	Quebecor Inc.	16.5	89	LVMH Moët Hennessy Louis Vuitton SA	9.1
40	Royal Ahold N.V.	16.4	90	Otto Versand Gmbh & Co.	9.0
41	Bombardier Inc.	16.2	91	Publicis Groupe S.A.	9.0
42	Ernst & Young International	16.2	92	Casino Guichard-Perrachon	9.0
43	British Sky Broadcasting Group plc	15.7	93	Canadian Imperial Bank of Commerce	8.7
44	Dr. Ing. h. c. F. Porsche AG	15.6	94	Reckitt Benckiser plc	8.4
45	Deloitte Touche Tohmatsu	15.5	95	National Australia Bank Limited	8.1
46	Airbus Industrie	15.0	96	ABN AMRO Holding N.V.	8.1
47	Rio Tinto plc	15.0	97	Bacardi Limited	8.0
48	Cable and Wireless plc	14.9	98	Roche Holding Ltd.	8.0
49	Logitech International S.A.	14.8	99	British Telecommunications plc	7.8
50	AEGON N.V.	14.7	100	Fuji Photo Film Co., Ltd.	7.8

Source: Hoover's, Inc., Database, December 2000

The Top 100 Companies in Five-Year Employment Growth in *Hoover's Handbook of World Business 2001*

Rank	Company	Annual % Change	Rank	Company	Annual % Change
1	Acer Inc.	97.6	51	ING Groep N.V.	13.3
2	Vodafone Group PLC	58.0	52	Andersen Worldwide	13.2
3	Olivetti S.p.A.	43.9	53	Allianz AG	13.2
4	Invensys plc	42.4	54	Danka Business Systems PLC	12.8
5	Daewoo Group	42.3	55	Nippon Steel Corporation	12.7
6	Computacenter plc	40.5	56	Nokia Corporation	12.5
7	Diageo plc	35.4	57	Sema plc	12.4
8	Teleglobe Inc.	34.5	58	NTT DoCoMo, Inc.	12.4
9	SAP Aktiengesellschaft	33.4	59	Otto Versand Gmbh & Co.	12.2
10	Ito-Yokado Co., Ltd.	33.3	60	VNU N.V.	12.0
11	Carrefour SA	30.4	61	Kingfisher plc	11.9
12	PricewaterhouseCoopers	30.0	62	George Weston Limited	11.6
13	Ispat International N.V.	29.4	63	Repsol YPF, S.A.	11.6
14	British Sky Broadcasting Group plc	27.8	64	Deloitte Touche Tohmatsu	11.1
15	Virgin Group Ltd.	25.7	65	Tomkins PLC	11.0
16	LVMH Moët Hennessy Louis Vuitton SA	25.0	66	The Nomura Securities Co., Ltd.	10.9
17	Dai Nippon Printing Co., Ltd.	24.9	67	SANYO Electric Co., Ltd.	10.8
18	TOTAL FINA ELF S.A.	24.5	68	Wal-Mart de Mexico, S.A. de C.V.	10.7
19	Sodexho Alliance	23.6	69	Placer Dome Inc.	10.7
20	Hollinger Inc.	23.1	70	Hutchison Whampoa Limited	9.9
21	Banco Santander Central Hispano S.A.	22.7	71	WPP Group plc	9.7
22	Kao Corporation	22.3	72	BNP Paribas Group	9.6
23	Royal Ahold N.V.	21.9	73	Ernst & Young International	9.3
24	Yamaha Corporation	21.6	74	Toyota Motor Corporation	9.2
25	adidas-Salomon AG	21.4	75	BP Amoco p.l.c.	9.1
26	AXA	20.7	76	KPMG International	9.1
27	CANAL+	20.2	77	Pioneer Corporation	9.1
28	Quebecor Inc.	20.0	78	Casino Guichard-Perrachon	9.0
29	Imperial Tobacco Group PLC	19.7	79	YPF, S.A.	8.9
30	Gucci Group N.V.	19.4	80	Laidlaw Inc.	8.9
31	Granada Compass PLC	19.2	81	Bombardier Inc.	8.8
32	METRO AG	18.5	82	Samsung Group	8.7
33	Wolters Kluwer nv	18.0	83	Delhaize "Le Lion" S.A.	8.7
34	Credit Suisse Group	17.5	84	Cable and Wireless plc	8.5
35	The News Corporation Limited	17.1	85	Airbus Industrie	8.3
36	Logitech International S.A.	17.0	86	STMicroelectronics N.V.	8.2
37	Suez Lyonnaise des Eaux	16.9	87	Telefonaktiebolaget LM Ericsson	8.0
38	Formosa Plastics Corporation	16.9	88	Henkel KGaA	7.9
39	IKEA International A/S	16.7	89	HSBC Holdings plc	7.7
40	Interbrew S.A.	16.5	90	Ricoh Company, Ltd.	7.7
41	BAE SYSTEMS	16.4	91	Heineken N.V.	7.6
42	Compagnie de Saint-Gobain	16.4	92	Foster's Brewing Group Limited	7.6
43	SOFTBANK CORP.	16.2	93	Roche Holding Ltd.	7.6
44	Swire Pacific Limited	16.2	94	Norsk Hydro ASA	7.6
45	Cap Gemini Ernst & Young	15.7	95	Pinault-Printemps-Redoute	7.3
46	Seiko Epson Corporation	15.7	96	Woolworths Limited	7.1
47	Publicis Groupe S.A.	15.3	97	Mitsui Group	7.1
48	Telefónica, S.A.	14.3	98	Sharp Corporation	7.0
49	ABN AMRO Holding N.V.	14.3	99	Agrium Inc.	6.8
50	UBS AG	14.0	100	Dr. Ing. h. c. F. Porsche AG	6.2

Source: Hoover's, Inc., Database, December 2000

The World's 100 Largest Public Companies by Market Value

Rank	Company	Country	Market Value ($ mil.)
1	General Electric	US	562,937
2	Intel	US	453,541
3	Cisco Systems	US	432,357
4	Microsoft	US	372,798
5	Exxon Mobil	US	281,469
6	Pfizer	US	265,664
7	Vodafone Group	UK	259,218
8	Citigroup	US	249,292
9	NTT DoCoMo	Japan	242,430
10	Nortel Networks	Canada	233,625
11	Wal-Mart Stores	US	230,481
12	Oracle	US	229,249
13	IBM	US	219,918
14	Royal Dutch/Shell	Netherlands/UK	215,164
15	BP Amoco	UK	204,797
16	American International Group	US	201,320
17	Nokia	Finland	191,041
18	Sun Microsystems	US	186,205
19	EMC	US	182,560
20	Nippon Telegraph & Telephone	Japan	181,883
21	Merck	US	171,216
22	Toyota Motor	Japan	161,642
23	Coca-Cola	US	152,830
24	SBC Communications	US	143,491
25	Ericsson	Sweden	137,446
26	Deutsche Telekom	Germany	134,079
27	Lucent Technologies	US	133,874
28	Johnson & Johnson	US	133,772
29	France Telecom	France	130,334
30	HSBC Holdings	UK	129,949
31	America Online	US	124,784
32	Home Depot	US	123,176
33	AT&T	US	118,545
34	Morgan Stanley Dean Witter	US	115,393
35	Verizon Communications	US	115,183
36	TOTAL FINA ELF	France	114,784
37	Novartis	Switzerland	110,532
38	China Telecom	Hong Kong	110,278
39	Hewlett-Packard	US	110,164
40	Texas instruments	US	107,388
41	Glaxo Wellcome	UK	105,140
42	Bristol-Myers Squibb	US	104,144
43	WorldCom	US	99,697
44	Dell Computer	US	97,636
45	Viacom	US	96,807
46	Telefonica de Espana	Spain	95,262
47	Time Warner	US	92,912
48	Bank of America	US	92,721
49	JDS Uniphase	US	91,854
50	Tyco International	US	91,572

Source: *The Wall Street Journal;* September 25, 2000

The World's 100 Largest Public Companies
by Market Value (continued)

Rank	Company	Country	Market Value ($ mil.)
51	Siemens	Germany	89,689
52	Sony	Japan	88,049
53	Allianz	Germany	86,504
54	Berkshire Hathaway	US	84,159
55	Eli Lilly	US	83,970
56	Walt Disney	US	83,315
57	Alcatel	France	82,272
58	British Telecommunications	UK	81,689
59	Procter & Gamble	US	81,657
60	Nestlé	Switzerland	80,464
61	Qwest Communications	US	80,180
62	American Express	US	79,490
63	Corning	US	78,845
64	AstraZeneca	UK	78,632
65	Motorola	US	75,924
66	Philip Morris	US	75,076
67	American Home Products	US	74,806
68	SmithKline Beecham	UK	73,786
69	Wells Fargo	US	72,979
70	Pharmacia	US	71,242
71	BellSouth	US	71,157
72	Yahoo!	US	69,660
73	Amgen	US	69,208
74	Telecom Italia	Italy	68,109
75	Roche Holding	Switzerland	67,775
76	ING Group	Netherlands	67,537
77	PepsiCo	US	66,871
78	UBS	Switzerland	64,790
79	Medtronic	US	64,198
80	Chase Manhattan	US	64,101
81	Hutchison Whampoa	Hong Kong	63,410
82	United Parcel Service	US	63,315
83	Applied Materials	US	62,397
84	SAP	Germany	61,796
85	Abbott Laboratories	US	61,781
86	Aventis	France	60,628
87	Credit Suisse	Switzerland	60,198
88	AXA	France	60,109
89	Philips Electronics	Netherlands	60,106
90	Schering-Plough	US	59,567
91	Fannie Mae	US	59,053
92	Enron	US	58,770
93	Matsushita Electric Industrial	Japan	56,830
94	DaimlerChrysler	Germany	56,302
95	Deutsche Bank	Germany	55,386
96	Seven-Eleven	Japan	55,312
97	Chevron	US	54,798
98	Fujitsu	Japan	54,584
99	Compaq Computer	US	54,294
100	Aegon	Netherlands	53,868

Forbes' "Richest People in the World" by Net Worth

Rank	Name	Net Worth ($ bil.)	Country	What
1	William H. Gates III	60.0	United States	Microsoft Corp.
2	Lawrence Joseph Ellison	47.0	United States	Oracle Corp.
3	Paul Gardner Allen	28.0	United States	Microsoft Corp.
4	Warren Edward Buffett	25.6	United States	Berkshire Hathaway
5	Theo & Karl Albrecht and family	20.0	Germany	Retail
6	Prince Alwaleed Bin Talal Alsaud	20.0	Saudi Arabia	Investment
7	S. Robson Walton	20.0	United States	Wal-Mart Stores
8	Masayoshi Son	19.4	Japan	Softbank
9	Michael Dell	19.1	United States	Dell Computer Corp.
10	Kenneth Thomson	16.1	Canada	Thomson Corp.
11	Philip F. Anschutz	15.5	United States	Oil, railroad, telecommunications
12	Steven Anthony Ballmer	15.5	United States	Microsoft Corp.
13	Liliane Bettencourt	15.2	France	Cosmetics
14	Silvio Berlusconi	12.8	Italy	Media
15	Johanna Quandt and family	12.8	Germany	BMW
16	Bernard Arnault	12.6	France	Luxury goods
17	Sumner M. Redstone	12.1	United States	Viacom, Inc.
18	John Werner Kluge	11.9	United States	Metromedia Co.
19	Leo Kirch	11.5	Germany	Media
20	Li Ka-shing	11.3	Hong Kong	Real estate, telecomm, diversified
21	Charles Ergen	11.2	United States	EchoStar Communications
22	Thomas J. Pritzker	10.7	United States	Hyatt Corporation
23	Keith Rupert Murdoch	9.4	United States	Publishing
24	Yasuo Takei	9.3	Japan	Consumer finance
25	Ernesto Bertarelli	9.1	Switzerland	Pharmaceuticals
26	Walter, Thomas, and Raymond Kwok	9.0	Hong Kong	Sun Hung Kai Properties
27	Gad Rausing and family	9.0	Sweden	Packaging
28	Lee Shau Kee	8.6	Hong Kong	Henderson Land Development
29	Walter Haefner	8.3	Switzerland	Computer Associates
30	Robert E. (Ted) Turner	8.3	United States	Turner Broadcasting
31	Mehmet Karamehmet and family	8.0	Turkey	Diversified
32	Suliman Olayan	8.0	Saudi Arabia	Investment
33	Carlos Slim Helu	7.9	Mexico	Diversified
34	Francois Pinault	7.8	France	Pinault-Printemps-Redoute, Christie's
35	Stefan Persson	7.7	Sweden	Retail clothing
36	Charles R. Schwab	7.5	United States	Discount stock brokerage
37	Abigail Johnson	7.4	United States	Fidelity Investments
38	Hans Rausing	7.4	Sweden	Investment
39	Nobutada Saji and family	7.1	Japan	Suntory Ltd.
40	Forrest Edward Mars Jr.	7.0	United States	Mars, Inc.
41	Jacqueline Badger Mars	7.0	United States	Mars, Inc.
42	John Franklyn Mars	7.0	United States	Mars, Inc.
43	Azim Premji and family	6.9	India	Information technology
44	Tsai Wan-lin and family	6.7	Taiwan	Insurance
45	Dhirubhai Ambani and family	6.6	India	Petrochemicals
46	David Filo	6.6	United States	Yahoo!
47	Jon Meade Huntsman	6.6	United States	Huntsman Corp.
48	Sanjiv Sidhu	6.5	United States	i2 Technologies
49	Roberto Marinho and family	6.4	Brazil	Media
50	Jerry Yang	6.4	United States	Yahoo!

Source: http://www.forbes.com/worldsrichest; December 6, 2000

The *FORTUNE* Global 500

Rank	Company	Country	1999 Sales ($ mil.)
1	General Motors	US	176,558.0
2	Wal-Mart Stores	US	166,809.0
3	Exxon Mobil	US	163,881.0
4	Ford Motor	US	162,558.0
5	DaimlerChrysler	Germany	159,985.7
6	Mitsui	Japan	118,555.2
7	Mitsubishi	Japan	117,765.6
8	Toyota Motor	Japan	115,670.9
9	General Electric	US	111,630.0
10	Itochu	Japan	109,068.9
11	Royal Dutch/Shell Group	Britain/Netherlands	105,366.0
12	Sumitomo	Japan	95,701.6
13	Nippon Telegraph & Telephone	Japan	93,591.7
14	Marubeni	Japan	91,807.4
15	AXA	France	87,645.7
16	International Business Machines	US	87,548.0
17	BP Amoco	Britain	83,566.0
18	Citigroup	US	82,005.0
19	Volkswagen	Germany	80,072.7
20	Nippon Life Insurance	Japan	78,515.1
21	Siemens	Germany	75,337.0
22	Allianz	Germany	74,178.2
23	Hitachi	Japan	71,858.5
24	Matsushita Electric Industrial	Japan	65,555.6
25	Nissho Iwai	Japan	65,393.2
26	U.S. Postal Service	US	62,726.0
27	ING Group	Netherlands	62,492.4
28	AT&T	US	62,391.0
29	Philip Morris	US	61,751.0
30	Sony	Japan	60,052.7
31	Deutsche Bank	Germany	58,585.1
32	Boeing	US	57,993.0
33	Dai-ichi Mutual Life Insurance	Japan	55,104.7
34	Honda Motor	Japan	54,773.5
35	Assicurazioni Generali	Italy	53,723.2
36	Nissan Motor	Japan	53,679.9
37	E.ON	Germany	52,227.7
38	Toshiba	Japan	51,634.9
39	Bank of America Corp.	US	51,392.0
40	Fiat	Italy	51,331.7
41	Nestlé	Switzerland	49,694.1
42	SBC Communications	US	49,489.0
43	Credit Suisse	Switzerland	49,362.0
44	Hewlett-Packard	US	48,253.0
45	Fujitsu	Japan	47,195.9
46	Metro	Germany	46,663.6
47	Sumitomo Life Insurance	Japan	46,445.1
48	Tokyo Electric Power	Japan	45,727.7
49	Kroger	US	45,351.6
50	TOTAL FINA ELF	France	44,990.3

Source: *FORTUNE;* July 24, 2000

The *FORTUNE* Global 500 (continued)

Rank	Company	Country	1999 Sales ($ mil.)
51	NEC	Japan	44,828.0
52	State Farm Insurance Cos.	US	44,637.2
53	Vivendi	France	44,397.8
54	Unilever	Britain/Netherlands	43,679.9
55	Fortis	Belgium/Netherlands	43,660.2
56	Prudential	Britain	42,220.3
57	CGNU	Britain	41,974.4
58	Sinopec	China	41,883.1
59	Sears Roebuck	US	41,071.0
60	American International Group	US	40,656.1
61	Peugeot	France	40,327.9
62	Enron	US	40,112.0
63	Renault	France	40,098.6
64	BNP Paribas	France	40,098.6
65	Zurich Financial Services	Switzerland	39,962.0
66	Carrefour	France	39,855.7
67	TIAA-CREF	US	39,410.2
68	HSBC Holdings	Britain	39,348.1
69	ABN AMRO Holding	Netherlands	38,820.7
70	Compaq Computer	US	38,525.0
71	Home Depot	US	38,434.0
72	Munich Re Group	Germany	38,400.4
73	RWE Group	Germany	38,357.5
74	Lucent Technologies	US	38,303.0
75	Procter & Gamble	US	38,125.0
76	Elf Aquitaine	France	37,918.3
77	Deutsche Telekom	Germany	37,835.1
78	Albertson's	US	37,478.1
79	WorldCom	US	37,120.0
80	McKesson HBOC	US	37,100.5
81	Fannie Mae	US	36,968.6
82	BMW	Germany	36,695.9
83	State Power	China	36,076.1
84	Kmart	US	35,925.0
85	Koninklijke Ahold	Netherlands	35,798.1
86	Texaco	US	35,690.0
87	Merrill Lynch	US	34,879.0
88	Électricité de France	France	34,146.6
89	ENI	Italy	34,091.0
90	Meiji Life Insurance	Japan	33,966.6
91	Morgan Stanley Dean Witter	US	33,928.0
92	Mitsubishi Electric	Japan	33,896.2
93	Chase Manhattan Corp.	US	33,710.0
94	Target	US	33,702.0
95	Suez Lyonnaise des Eaux	France	33,559.7
96	Royal Philips Electronics	Netherlands	33,556.6
97	Verizon Communications	US	33,174.0
98	Crédit Agricole	France	32,923.5
99	Thyssen Krupp	Germany	32,798.0
100	Merck	US	32,714.0

The *FORTUNE* Global 500 (continued)

Rank	Company	Country	1999 Sales ($ mil.)
101	Chevron	US	32,676.0
102	PDVSA	Venezuela	32,648.0
103	Bank of Tokyo-Mitsubishi	Japan	32,623.6
104	J.C. Penney	US	32,510.0
105	SK	South Korea	31,997.3
106	HypoVereinsbank	Germany	31,868.1
107	Hyundai	South Korea	31,669.4
108	BASF	Germany	31,437.9
109	Motorola	US	30,931.0
110	BT	Britain	30,546.0
111	Tesco	Britain	30,351.9
112	Olivetti	Italy	30,087.8
113	Mitsubishi Motors	Japan	29,951.3
114	Robert Bosch	Germany	29,727.2
115	Samsung	South Korea	29,715.2
116	Intel	US	29,389.0
117	Bayer	Germany	29,141.6
118	France Télécom	France	29,048.8
119	Safeway	US	28,859.9
120	Ito-Yokado	Japan	28,670.9
121	Ingram Micro	US	28,068.6
122	Repsol YPF	Spain	28,048.3
123	E.I. du Pont de Nemours	US	27,892.0
124	Fuji Bank	Japan	27,815.8
125	UBS	Switzerland	27,651.9
126	Johnson & Johnson	US	27,471.0
127	Costco Wholesale	US	27,456.0
128	Time Warner	US	27,333.0
129	Sumitomo Bank	Japan	27,065.2
130	United Parcel Service	US	27,052.0
131	Samsung Electronics	South Korea	26,991.5
132	Allstate	US	26,959.0
133	Industrial Bank of Japan	Japan	26,939.9
134	CNP Assurances	France	26,802.5
135	Prudential Ins. Co. of America	US	26,618.0
136	Aetna	US	26,452.7
137	Asahi Mutual Life Insurance	Japan	26,246.1
138	Commerzbank	Germany	26,221.1
139	J Sainsbury	Britain	26,218.0
140	L.M. Ericsson	Sweden	26,052.3
141	Royal & Sun Alliance	Britain	26,018.0
142	Bank One Corp.	US	25,986.0
143	Mitsubishi Heavy Industries	Japan	25,820.6
144	Pemex	Mexico	25,783.1
145	Tomen	Japan	25,747.6
146	Nichimen	Japan	25,702.7
147	USX	US	25,610.0
148	Santander Central Hispano Group	Spain	25,582.6
149	Lockheed Martin	US	25,530.0
150	MetLife	US	25,426.0

The *FORTUNE* Global 500 (continued)

Rank	Company	Country	1999 Sales ($ mil.)
151	Goldman Sachs Group	US	25,363.0
152	GTE	US	25,336.2
153	Daiei	Japan	25,320.1
154	Dell Computer	US	25,265.0
155	United Technologies	US	25,242.0
156	BellSouth	US	25,224.0
157	Deutsche Post	Germany	25,101.1
158	Cardinal Health	US	25,033.6
159	Mannesmann	Germany	24,816.3
160	ABB	Switerzerland	24,681.0
161	ConAgra	US	24,594.3
162	International Paper	US	24,573.0
163	Alcatel	France	24,558.1
164	Telefónica	Spain	24,487.7
165	Saint-Gobain	France	24,482.4
166	Freddie Mac	US	24,268.0
167	Nippon Mitsubishi Oil	Japan	24,214.8
168	AutoNation	US	24,206.6
169	Westdeutsche Landesbank	Germany	24,079.1
170	Nippon Steel	Japan	24,074.5
171	Berkshire Hathaway	US	24,028.0
172	IRI	Italy	23,944.7
173	Aegon	Netherlands	23,865.8
174	Honeywell International	US	23,735.0
175	Groupe Auchan	France	23,493.6
176	Walt Disney	US	23,402.0
177	Société Générale	France	23,398.6
178	Kansai Electric Power	Japan	23,246.2
179	Dresdner Bank	Germany	23,208.8
180	Canon	Japan	23,062.0
181	Lloyd's TSB Group	Britain	22,836.7
182	Tyco International	US	22,496.5
183	East Japan Railway	Japan	22,478.5
184	Jusco	Japan	22,451.3
185	Rabobank	Netherlands	22,373.6
186	Enel	Italy	22,320.1
187	Mitsui Mutual Life Insurance	Japan	22,223.8
188	First Union Corp.	US	22,084.0
189	Wells Fargo	US	21,795.0
190	Duke Energy	US	21,742.0
191	New York Life Insurance	US	21,679.3
192	Novartis	Switerzerland	21,608.9
193	Barclays	Britain	21,573.0
194	Nortel Networks	Canada	21,287.0
195	American Express	US	21,278.0
196	Nokia	Japan	21,090.4
197	Loews	US	20,952.6
198	PG&E Corp.	US	20,820.0
199	Conoco	US	20,817.0
200	Viag	Germany	20,758.8

The *FORTUNE* Global 500 (continued)

Rank	Company	Country	1999 Sales ($ mil.)
201	Cigna	US	20,644.0
202	Hyundai Motor	South Korea	20,566.3
203	PepsiCo	US	20,367.0
204	Supervalu	US	20,339.1
205	AMR	US	20,262.0
206	Bristol-Myers Squibb	US	20,222.0
207	Groupe Pinault-Printemps	France	20,144.1
208	Industrial & Commercial Bank of China	China	20,130.4
209	Sara Lee	US	20,012.0
210	FleetBoston	US	20,000.0
211	Sanwa Bank	Japan	19,999.9
212	Sprint	US	19,930.0
213	Yasuda Mutual Life Insurance	Japan	19,861.7
214	Raytheon	US	19,841.0
215	Coca-Cola	US	19,805.0
216	Microsoft	US	19,747.0
217	Caterpillar	US	19,702.0
218	Norwich Union	Britain	19,697.5
219	Swiss Reinsurance	Switzerland	19,640.7
220	UnitedHealth Group	US	19,562.0
221	Japan Tobacco	Japan	19,486.5
222	National Westminster Bank	Britain	19,480.7
223	Chubu Electric Power	Japan	19,467.5
224	Mazda Motor	Japan	19,413.0
225	Sakura Bank	Japan	19,372.9
226	British American Tobacco	Britain	19,328.6
227	Skandia Group	Sweden	19,288.6
228	Preussag	Germany	19,280.0
229	Xerox	US	19,228.0
230	Lehman Brothers Holdings	US	18,989.0
231	Dow Chemical	US	18,929.0
232	Indian Oil	India	18,728.6
233	UtiliCorp United	US	18,621.5
234	Daewoo Corp.	South Korea	18,618.7
235	Electronic Data Systems	US	18,534.2
236	China Telecommunications	China	18,484.6
237	AstraZeneca	Britain	18,445.0
238	Tokio Marine & Fire Insurance	Japan	18,363.8
239	Roche Group	Switzerland	18,348.8
240	Bridgestone	Japan	18,343.2
241	J.P. Morgan & Co.	US	18,110.0
242	CVS	US	18,098.3
243	Sanyo Electric	Japan	18,089.9
244	Dai-Ichi Kangyo Bank	Japan	18,065.0
245	UAL	US	18,027.0
246	Banco Do Brasil	Brazil	17,981.9
247	Statoil	Norway	17,945.0
248	Bouygues	France	17,895.3
249	Standard Life Assurance	Britain	17,846.8
250	Walgreen	US	17,838.8

The *FORTUNE* Global 500 (continued)

Rank	Company	Country	1999 Sales ($ mil.)
251	Georgia-Pacific	US	17,796.0
252	AMP	Australia	17,760.3
253	Federated Department Stores	US	17,716.0
254	Groupama-Gan	France	17,655.0
255	Bank of China	China	17,623.8
256	Kingfisher	Britain	17,602.4
257	Samsung Life Insurance	South Korea	17,574.6
258	Japan Postal Service	Japan	17,496.9
259	Foncière Euris	France	17,475.0
260	Sysco	US	17,422.8
261	SNCF	France	17,348.0
262	Franz Haniel	Germany	17,330.2
263	Bergen Brunswig	US	17,244.9
264	TXU	US	17,118.0
265	Abbey National	Britain	17,113.4
266	Tech Data	US	16,991.8
267	TRW	US	16,969.0
268	DENSO	Japan	16,914.8
269	Crédit Lyonnais	France	16,838.0
270	Swiss Life Ins. & Pension	Switerland	16,834.6
271	FedEx	US	16,773.5
272	Alstom	France	16,760.1
273	Deutsche Bahn	Germany	16,672.2
274	Sharp	Japan	16,657.7
275	HCA	US	16,657.0
276	MYCAL	Japan	16,504.1
277	Landesbank Baden-Württemberg	Germany	16,457.7
278	Alcoa	US	16,446.4
279	Legal & General	Britain	16,443.5
280	Petrobrás	Brazil	16,351.0
281	La Poste	France	16,313.5
282	Diageo	Britain	16,309.5
283	Almanij	Belgium	16,243.5
284	Groupe Caisse d'Épargne	France	16,218.8
285	Pfizer	US	16,204.0
286	Johnson Controls	US	16,139.4
287	Lowe's	US	15,905.6
288	KarstadtQuelle	Germany	15,832.7
289	Minnesota Mining & Mfg.	US	15,659.0
290	Idemitsu Kosan	Japan	15,636.2
291	Delhaize "Le Lion"	Belgium	15,562.0
292	Kajima	Japan	15,518.0
293	Liberty Mutual Insurance Group	US	15,499.0
294	Dynegy	US	15,430.0
295	Norinchukin Bank	Japan	15,395.9
296	Akzo Nobel	Netherlands	15,394.3
297	Northwestern Mutual Life Ins.	US	15,306.3
298	Reliant Energy	US	15,302.8
299	Toyota Tsusho	Japan	15,218.9
300	Bayerische Landesbank	Germany	15,203.0

The *FORTUNE* Global 500 (continued)

Rank	Company	Country	1999 Sales ($ mil.)
301	LG International	South Korea	15,177.6
302	Banco Bradesco	Brazil	15,164.3
303	Michelin	France	15,137.5
304	NKK	Japan	15,136.4
305	Volvo	Sweden	15,120.7
306	Taisei	Japan	15,099.8
307	Sinochem	China	15,063.8
308	LG Electronics	South Korea	15,021.1
309	MAN	Germany	15,007.0
310	Mitsubishi Chemical	Japan	14,997.5
311	Petronas	Malaysia	14,943.9
312	Dexia Group	Belgium	14,936.7
313	Electrolux	Sweden	14,914.3
314	Halliburton	US	14,898.0
315	Cable & Wireless	Britain	14,825.9
316	Bertelsmann	Germany	14,810.7
317	Tokai Bank	Japan	14,784.2
318	Delta Air Lines	US	14,711.0
319	Nippon Express	Japan	14,708.7
320	Fleming	US	14,645.6
321	Invensys	Britain	14,556.8
322	Old Mutual	South Africa	14,550.4
323	RAG	Germany	14,541.4
324	Coles Myer	Australia	14,538.2
325	Usinor	France	14,531.4
326	Banco Bilbao Vizcaya Argentaria	Spain	14,485.8
327	Halifax	Britain	14,456.4
328	Coca-Cola Enterprises	US	14,406.0
329	British Airways	Britain	14,405.3
330	Endesa	Spain	14,375.8
331	Dentsu	Japan	14,368.2
332	Tosco	US	14,362.1
333	Japan Airlines	Japan	14,356.2
334	Otto Versand	Germany	14,290.9
335	Archer Daniels Midland	US	14,283.3
336	Emerson Electric	US	14,269.5
337	May Department Stores	US	14,224.0
338	Groupe Danone	France	14,179.3
339	Tohoku Electric Power	Japan	14,166.3
340	Winn-Dixie Stores	US	14,136.5
341	Agricultural Bank of China	China	14,127.8
342	Eastman Kodak	US	14,089.0
343	IBP	US	14,075.2
344	Shimizu	Japan	14,052.7
345	George Weston	Canada	14,033.9
346	Aérospatiale Matra	France	13,991.6
347	Phillips Petroleum	US	13,852.0
348	Broken Hill Proprietary	Australia	13,778.0
349	Glaxo Wellcome	Britain	13,738.0
350	News Corp.	Australia	13,715.2

The *FORTUNE* Global 500 (continued)

Rank	Company	Country	1999 Sales ($ mil.)
351	DDI	Japan	13,704.5
352	Imperial Chemical Industries	Britain	13,671.6
353	Suzuki Motor	Japan	13,661.8
354	Lufthansa Group	Germany	13,629.9
355	Washington Mutual	US	13,571.2
356	SmithKline Beecham	Britain	13,561.6
357	Nationwide Insurance Enterprise	US	13,554.9
358	American Home Products	US	13,550.2
359	Isuzu Motors	Japan	13,531.1
360	Hartford Financial Services	US	13,528.0
361	Canadian Imperial Bank of Commerce	Canada	13,441.2
362	Aventis	France	13,438.0
363	Japan Energy	Japan	13,432.7
364	China Construction Bank	China	13,392.3
365	Dana	US	13,353.0
366	Taiyo Mutual Life Insurance	Japan	13,341.3
367	UniCredito Italiano	Italy	13,335.4
368	McDonald's	US	13,259.3
369	Marks & Spencer	Britain	13,205.7
370	Chiyoda Mutual Life Insurance	Japan	13,198.6
371	US WEST	US	13,182.0
372	Abbott Laboratories	US	13,177.6
373	Atlantic Richfield	US	13,176.0
374	Royal Bank of Canada	Canada	13,146.1
375	Norsk Hydro	Norway	13,130.5
376	Waste Management	US	13,126.9
377	Lagardère Groupe	France	13,103.9
378	Publix Super Markets	US	13,068.9
379	Kimberly-Clark	US	13,006.8
380	Ricoh	Japan	12,996.9
381	Warner-Lambert	US	12,928.9
382	Korea Electric Power	South Korea	12,899.3
383	Goodyear Tire & Rubber	US	12,880.6
384	Daido Life Insurance	Japan	12,873.8
385	Viacom	US	12,858.8
386	Kyushu Electric Power	Japan	12,829.8
387	Sumitomo Metal Industries	Japan	12,789.8
388	Montedison	Italy	12,786.3
389	Rite Aid	US	12,731.9
390	Vodafone Airtouch	Britain	12,686.0
391	Kanematsu	Japan	12,644.5
392	Circuit City Group	US	12,614.4
393	Fuji Photo Film	Japan	12,589.4
394	Best Buy	US	12,494.0
395	National Australia Bank	Australia	12,487.0
396	Migros	Switzerland	12,444.2
397	Lear	US	12,428.0
398	Fluor	US	12,417.4
399	TransCanada Pipelines	Canada	12,415.2
400	Banca Intesa	Italy	12,391.4

The *FORTUNE* Global 500 (continued)

Rank	Company	Country	1999 Sales ($ mil.)
401	DG Bank Group	Germany	12,345.7
402	Safeway	Britain	12,341.5
403	OAO Gazprom	Russia	12,299.5
404	Adecco	Switzerland	12,294.4
405	Yasuda Fire & Marine Insurance	Japan	12,280.9
406	Weyerhaeuser	US	12,262.0
407	Bankgesellschaft Berlin	Germany	12,251.1
408	Royal Bank of Scotland	Britain	12,173.8
409	Cisco Systems	US	12,154.0
410	Associates First Capital	US	12,131.2
411	British Post Office	Britain	12,120.4
412	Henkel	Germany	12,118.5
413	COFCO	China	12,099.2
414	Fuji Heavy Industries	Japan	11,945.8
415	Woolworths	Australia	11,920.9
416	Toys "R" Us	US	11,862.0
417	Corus Group	Britain	11,794.9
418	Seagram	Canada	11,784.0
419	Sekisui House	Japan	11,768.9
420	Sumitomo Electric Industries	Japan	11,752.2
421	Deere	US	11,750.9
422	Sun Microsystems	US	11,726.3
423	Anheuser-Busch	US	11,703.7
424	Centrica	Britain	11,678.1
425	Gap	US	11,635.4
426	Japan Travel Bureau	Japan	11,633.6
427	Southern	US	11,585.0
428	Textron	US	11,579.0
429	Anglo American	Britain	11,578.0
430	Snow Brand Milk Products	Japan	11,565.4
431	Dai Nippon Printing	Japan	11,555.8
432	Kawasho	Japan	11,488.1
433	Telstra	Australia	11,475.3
434	L'Oréal	France	11,451.4
435	BAE Systems	Britain	11,396.5
436	R. J. Reynolds Tobacco	US	11,394.0
437	Arbed	Luxembourg	11,362.7
438	Stora Enso	Finland	11,344.9
439	Kawasaki Steel	Japan	11,292.7
440	Asahi Glass	Japan	11,289.5
441	Union Pacific	US	11,273.0
442	Kobe Steel	Japan	11,248.8
443	Lafarge	France	11,230.0
444	Bank of Montreal	Canada	11,139.3
445	Kyoei Life Insurance	Japan	11,128.8
446	Bank of Nova Scotia	Canada	11,118.6
447	Toppan Printing	Japan	11,110.2
448	Ultramar Diamond Shamrock	US	11,079.2
449	Central Japan Railway	Japan	10,971.4
450	Kyobo Life Insurance	South Korea	10,899.1

The *FORTUNE* Global 500 (continued)

Rank	Company	Country	1999 Sales ($ mil.)
451	Tenet Healthcare	US	10,880.0
452	All Nippon Airways	Japan	10,863.8
453	Oji Paper	Japan	10,826.3
454	CSX	US	10,811.0
455	Lukoil	Russia	10,780.8
456	Mitsui Fudosan	Japan	10,730.8
457	Asahi Chemical Industry	Japan	10,727.4
458	Farmland Industries	US	10,709.1
459	West Japan Railway	Japan	10,696.4
460	Pohang Iron & Steel	South Korea	10,683.8
461	American General	US	10,679.0
462	Jardine Matheson	China	10,674.8
463	Air France Group	France	10,661.9
464	Takashimaya	Japan	10,617.9
465	El Paso Energy	US	10,581.0
466	Sun Life Assurance of Canada	Canada	10,511.1
467	Whirlpool	US	10,511.0
468	Toronto-Dominion Bank	Canada	10,470.3
469	Asahi Bank	Japan	10,420.3
470	Kawasaki Heavy Industries	Japan	10,325.4
471	Northwest Airlines	US	10,276.0
472	Uny	Japan	10,269.9
473	Cosmo Oil	Japan	10,266.0
474	Office Depot	US	10,263.3
475	Kinki Nippon Railway	Japan	10,255.8
476	Nomura Securities	Japan	10,221.8
477	Obayashi	Japan	10,166.7
478	Great Atlantic & Pacific Tea Co.	US	10,151.3
479	Pechiney	France	10,140.9
480	Pharmacia	US	10,126.0
481	Humana	US	10,113.0
482	Teléfonos De México	Mexico	10,076.2
483	Sodexho Alliance	France	10,035.2
484	Onex	Canada	10,007.6
485	Eli Lilly	US	10,002.9
486	PacifiCare Health Systems	US	9,989.1
487	Peninsular & Oriental Steam Nav.	Britain	9,929.8
488	Power Corp. of Canada	Canada	9,920.2
489	Cathay Life	Taiwan	9,904.5
490	Nippon Yusen	Japan	9,900.9
491	Gillette	US	9,897.0
492	Alliance Unichem	Britain	9,860.9
493	Mass. Mutual Life Insurance	US	9,841.0
494	SHV Holdings	Netherlands	9,779.1
495	Manpower	US	9,770.1
496	AmeriSource Health	US	9,760.1
497	San Paolo IMI	Italy	9,738.8
498	Kreditanstalt für Wiederaufbau	Germany	9,737.5
499	Somerfield	Britain	9,725.9
500	Limited	US	9,723.3

Business Week's Information Technology 100

Rank	Company	Revenues* ($ mil.)	Rank	Company	Revenues* ($ mil.)
1	Nokia	21,986.2	51	Computer Associates	6,766.0
2	Siebel Systems	958.7	52	Altera	923.0
3	Oracle	9,699.1	53	SK Telecom	3,771.9
4	Nvidia	452.0	54	Celestica	5,827.7
5	Taiwan Semiconductor Mfg.	2,800.0	55	Nortel Networks	24,121.0
6	CDW Computer Centers	2,885.8	56	Integrated Device Technology	701.7
7	PC Connection	1,157.8	57	Chartered Semiconductor	801.9
8	Legend Holdings	1,501.0	58	Apple Computer	7,182.0
9	Xilinx	1,021.0	59	Asustek Computer	1,600.0
10	Analog Devices	1,881.1	60	Tokyo Electron	4,000.0
11	Sun Microsystems	14,218.8	61	Tech Data	16,991.7
12	Amdocs	853.9	62	Titan	503.4
13	Network Appliance	579.3	63	Atmel	1,469.3
14	Micron Technology	4,921.5	64	ATI Technologies	1,400.3
15	Yahoo Japan	52.7	65	Network Solutions	280.9
16	CTS	761.2	66	Tellabs	2,489.3
17	Broadcom	609.6	67	Citrix Systems	445.8
18	Powerwave Technologies	340.4	68	Nextel Comunications	3,741.0
19	S3	470.0	69	Voicestream Wireless	627.4
20	STMicroelectronics	5,645.2	70	Comverse Technology	872.2
21	China Telecom (Hong Kong)	4,665.7	71	Sprint PCS Group	3,753.0
22	Cypress Semiconductor	818.1	72	BEA Systems	532.5
23	JDS Uniphase	993.5	73	Rational Software	572.2
24	Dell Computer	27,007.0	74	Netcreations	33.4
25	Cisco Systems	16,739.0	75	Microsoft	22,916.0
26	EMC	7,054.9	76	Cognos	385.6
27	Hon Hai Precision	1,898.0	77	Conexant Systems	1,844.2
28	Symantec	704.9	78	America Online	6,301.0
29	Ericsson (LM) Telephone	25,331.4	79	Lexmark International	3,557.0
30	Internet Capital Group	15.3	80	SCI Systems	7,838.3
31	Flextronics International	5,739.7	81	Ciena	608.1
32	Netcom AB	963.3	82	Compuware	2,230.6
33	Amkor Technology	2,044.8	83	Gateway	8,880.0
34	Broadvision	158.6	84	Lattice Semiconductor	395.8
35	Kemet	822.1	85	Sanmina	1,673.1
36	Advanced Micro Devices	3,318.0	86	Solectron	10,172.9
37	LSI Logic	2,241.0	87	Viant	84.0
38	Scientific-Atlanta	1,518.0	88	Art Technology Group	49.2
39	AVX	1,630.3	89	Vignette	135.3
40	NTT Docomo	34,432.0	90	SBC Communications	50,269.0
41	ADC Telecommunications	2,319.9	91	Sapient	319.4
42	Logitech International	615.7	92	Maxim Integrated Products	767.8
43	Veritas Software	768.8	93	Take-Two Interactive Software	360.5
44	I2 Technologies	639.8	94	Yahoo!	713.1
45	Getronics	3,911.1	95	Micromuse	84.1
46	Infineon Technologies	5,017.5	96	Verisign	103.3
47	Murata Manufacturing	4,300.0	97	Worldcom	37,976.0
48	IDT	997.1	98	Hewlett-Packard	45,381.0
49	Jabil Circuit	2,586.4	99	Burr-Brown	321.0
50	Texas Instruments	10,040.0	100	Infospace	50.7

Source: *Business Week;* June 19, 2000
Note: Rank based on shareholder return, return on equity, revenue growth, and total revenues (for the 12-month period ended May 31, June 30, or July 31; most recent FY for those companies that do not report quarterly results).

The World's Top 25 Electronics Companies

Rank	Company	Electronics Revenue* ($ mil.)	Total Revenue* ($ mil.)
1	IBM	87,548.0	87,548.0
2	Matsushita Electric Industrial	63,667.7	63,667.7
3	Fujitsu	49,576.0	49,576.0
4	Hewlett-Packard	45,772.0	45,772.0
5	NEC	40,334.0	40,334.0
6	Compaq Computer	38,525.0	38,525.0
7	Lucent Technologies	38,015.0	38,015.0
8	Siemens	37,907.4	72,898.9
9	Sony	36,269.9	57,571.3
10	Motorola	33,075.0	33,075.0
11	Toshiba	33,064.0	44,504.0
12	Intel	29,389.0	29,389.0
13	Ingram Micro	28,068.6	28,068.6
14	Philips Electronics	26,639.7	33,467.0
15	Hitachi	26,371.6	65,929.0
16	Dell Computer	25,265.0	25,265.0
17	Canon	23,266.2	25,708.5
18	Samsung Electronics	22,810.3	22,810.3
19	Microsoft	22,352.0	22,352.0
20	Ericsson	22,329.1	22,329.1
21	Nortel Networks	22,217.0	22,217.0
22	Nokia	21,034.0	21,034.0
23	Alcatel	20,696.2	24,492.6
24	Electronic Data Systems	18,534.2	18,534.2
25	Tech Data	16,991.8	16,991.8

*For the four quarters ending closest to December 31, 1999
Source: *Electronic Business;* August 2000

Top 10 Japanese Electronics Companies by Revenue

Rank	Company	Sales* ($ mil.)
1	Matsushita Electric Industrial	63,667.7
2	Fujitsu	49,576.0
3	NEC	40,334.0
4	Sony	36,269.9
5	Toshiba	33,064.0
6	Hitachi	26,371.6
7	Canon	23,266.2
8	Sharp	14,655.0
9	Mitsubishi Electric	12,104.1
10	Ricoh	11,972.0

*For the four quarters ending closest to December 31, 1999
Source: *Electronic Business;* August 2000

Top 10 European Electronics Companies by Revenue

Rank	Company	Sales* ($ mil.)
1	Siemens	37,907.4
2	Philips Electronics	26,639.7
3	Ericsson	22,329.1
4	Nokia	21,034.0
5	Alcatel	20,696.2
6	Bosch	14,178.7
7	Marconi	12,299.1
8	Thomson-CSF	7,328.7
9	Thomson multimedia	7,117.0
10	Veba	6,179.8

*For the four quarters ending closest to December 31, 1999
Source: *Electronic Business;* August 2000

The World's Top 20 Electronics and Electrical Equipment Companies

Rank	Company	Country	1999 Revenues ($ mil.)
1	Siemens	Germany	75,337
2	Hitachi	Japan	71,859
3	Matsushita Elec. Industrial	Japan	65,556
4	Sony	Japan	60,053
5	Toshiba	Japan	51,635
6	NEC	Japan	44,828
7	Mitsubishi Electric	Japan	33,896
8	Royal Philips	Netherlands	33,557
9	Motorola	US	30,931
10	Intel	US	29,389
11	Samsung Electronics	South Korea	26,991
12	L.M. Ericsson	Sweden	26,052
13	ABB	Switzerland	24,681
14	Tyco International	US	22,497
15	Nokia	Finland	21,090
16	Sanyo Electric	Japan	18,090
17	Sharp	Japan	16,658
18	LG Electronics	South Korea	15,021
19	Electrolux	Sweden	14,914
20	Emerson Electric	US	14,270

Source: *FORTUNE;* July 24, 2000

The World's Top 25 Motor Vehicle and Parts Manufacturers

Rank	Company	Country	1999 Revenues ($ mil.)
1	General Motors	US	176,558
2	Ford Motor	US	162,558
3	DaimlerChrysler	Germany	159,986
4	Toyota Motor	Japan	115,671
5	Volkswagen	Germany	80,073
6	Honda Motor	Japan	54,773
7	Nissan Motor	Japan	53,680
8	Fiat	Italy	51,332
9	Peugeot	France	40,328
10	Renault	France	40,099
11	BMW	Germany	36,696
12	Mitsubishi Motors	Japan	29,951
13	Robert Bosch	Germany	29,727
14	Hyundai Motor	South Korea	20,566
15	Mazda Motor	Japan	19,413
16	TRW	US	16,969
17	Denso	Japan	16,915
18	Johnson Controls	US	16,139
19	Volvo	Sweden	15,121
20	Man	Germany	15,007
21	Suzuki Motor	Japan	13,662
22	Isuzu Motors	Japan	13,531
23	Dana	US	13,353
24	Lear	US	12,428
25	Fuji Heavy Industries	Japan	11,946

Source: *FORTUNE;* July 24, 2000

The World's Top 20 Telecommunications Companies

Rank	Company	Country	1999 Revenue ($ mil.)
1	Nippon Tel. & Tel.	Japan	93,592
2	AT&T	US	62,391
3	SBC Communications	US	49,489
4	Deutsche Telekom	Germany	37,835
5	WorldCom	US	37,120
6	Verizon Communications	US	33,174
7	BT	Britain	30,546
8	Olivetti	Italy	30,088
9	France Telecom	France	29,049
10	GTE	US	25,336
11	BellSouth	US	25,224
12	Alcatel	France	24,558
13	Telefónica	Spain	24,488
14	Sprint	US	19,930
15	China Telecommunications	China	18,485
16	Cable & Wireless	Britain	14,826
17	DDI	Japan	13,705
18	US WEST	US	13,182
19	Vodafone Airtouch	Britain	12,686
20	Telstra	Australia	11,475

Source: *FORTUNE;* July 24, 2000

The World's Top 25 Petroleum Refining Companies

Rank	Company	Country	1999 Revenues ($ mil.)
1	Exxon Mobil	US	163,881
2	Royal Dutch/Shell	Britain/Netherlands	105,366
3	BP Amoco	Britain	83,566
4	TOTAL FINA ELF	France	44,990
5	Sinopec	China	41,883
6	Elf Aquitaine	France	37,918
7	Texaco	US	35,690
8	ENI	Italy	34,091
9	Chevron	US	32,676
10	PDVSA	Venezuela	32,648
11	SK	South Korea	31,997
12	Repsol YPF	Spain	28,048
13	USX	US	25,610
14	Nippon Mitsubishi	Japan	24,215
15	Conoco	US	20,817
16	Indian Oil	India	18,729
17	Statoil	Norway	17,945
18	Petrobrás	Brazil	16,351
19	Idemitsu Kosan	Japan	15,363
20	Petronas	Malaysia	14,944
21	Tosco	US	14,362
22	Phillips Petroleum	US	13,852
23	Japan Energy	Japan	13,433
24	Atlantic Richfield	US	13,176
25	Ultramar Diamond Shamrock	US	11,079

Source: *FORTUNE;* July 24, 2000

The World's Top 10 Chemical Companies

Rank	Company	Country	1999 Revenue ($ mil.)
1	BASF	Germany	31,438
2	Bayer	Germany	29,142
3	E. I. Du Pont de Nemours	US	27,892
4	Dow Chemical	US	18,929
5	Akzo Nobel	Netherlands	15,394
6	Mitsubishi Chemical	Japan	14,998
7	Imperial Chemical Industries	Britain	13,672
8	Norsk Hydro	Norway	13,130
9	Henkel	Germany	12,119
10	Asahi Chemical Industries	Japan	10,727

Source: *FORTUNE;* July 24, 2000

The World's Top 10 Pharmaceutical Companies

Rank	Company	Country	1999 Revenue ($ mil.)
1	Merck	US	32,714
2	Johnson & Johnson	US	27,471
3	Novartis	Switzerland	21,609
4	Bristol-Myers Squibb	US	20,222
5	Astrazeneca	Britain	18,445
6	Roche Group	Switzerland	18,349
7	Pfizer	US	16,204
8	Glaxo Wellcome	Britain	13,738
9	SmithKline Beecham	Britain	13,562
10	American Home Products	US	13,550

Source: *FORTUNE;* July 24, 2000

The World's Top 10 Metals Companies

Rank	Company	Country	1999 Revenue ($ mil.)
1	Nippon Steel	Japan	24,074
2	Alcoa	US	16,446
3	NKK	Japan	15,136
4	Usinor	France	14,531
5	Sumitomo Metal Industries	Japan	12,790
6	Corus Group	Britain	11,795
7	Arbed	Luxembourg	11,363
8	Kawasaki Steel	Japan	11,293
9	Kobe Steel	Japan	11,249
10	Pohang Iron & Steel	South Korea	10,684

Source: *FORTUNE;* July 24, 2000

The World's Top 7 Energy Companies

Rank	Company	Country	1999 Revenue ($ mil.)
1	Enron	US	40,112
2	RWE Group	Germany	38,358
3	Suez Lyonnaise des Eaux	France	33,560
4	Dynegy	US	15,430
5	TransCanada PipeLines	Canada	12,415
6	OAO Gazprom	Russia	12,300
7	El Paso Energy	US	10,581

Source: *FORTUNE;* July 24, 2000

The World's Top 15 Electric and Gas Utilities

Rank	Company	Country	1999 Revenue ($ mil.)
1	Tokyo Electric Power	Japan	45,728
2	State Power	China	36,076
3	Électricité de France	France	34,147
4	Kansai Electric Power	Japan	23,246
5	Enel	Italy	22,320
6	Duke Energy	US	21,742
7	PG&E Corp.	US	20,820
8	Chubu Electric Power	Japan	19,467
9	Utilicorp United	US	18,622
10	TXU	US	17,118
11	Reliant Energy	US	15,303
12	Endesa	Spain	14,376
13	Tohoku Electric Power	Japan	14,166
14	Korea Electric Power	South Korea	12,899
15	Kyushu Electric Power	Japan	12,830

Source: *FORTUNE;* July 24, 2000

The World's Top 9 Engineering and Construction Companies

Rank	Company	Country	1999 Revenue ($ mil.)
1	Vivendi	France	44,398
2	Bouygues	France	17,895
3	Kajima	Japan	15,518
4	Taisei	Japan	15,100
5	Halliburton	US	14,898
6	Shimizu	Japan	14,053
7	Fluor	US	12,417
8	Sekisui House	Japan	11,769
9	Obayashi	Japan	10,167

Source: *FORTUNE;* July 24, 2000

The World's 50 Largest Public Financial Companies

Rank	Company	Country	Assets ($ mil.)	Net Income ($ mil.)
1	Deutsche Bank	Germany	955,579	2,933
2	Bank of Tokyo-Mitsubishi	Japan	726,286	1,251
3	Citigroup	US	716,937	9,855
4	BNP Paribas	France	703,091	2,632
5	Bank of America	US	632,574	7,876
6	UBS	Switzerland	616,798	3,962
7	HSBC Holdings	UK/Hong Kong	601,847	5,410
8	Fannie Mae	US	575,092	3,843
9	Fuji Bank	Japan	561,345	517
10	Bayerische Hypo Bank	Germany	559,860	417
11	Sumitomo Bank	Japan	519,153	605
12	AXA	France	518,234	2,034
13	Dai-Ichi Kangyo Bank	Japan	503,203	693
14	ING Group	Netherlands	495,968	4,932
15	Sakura Bank	Japan	474,474	612
16	Dresdner Bank	Germany	460,139	1,223
17	ABN Amro	Netherlands	459,574	2,506
18	Sanwa Bank	Japan	453,454	1,169
19	Credit Suisse	Switzerland	452,143	3,283
20	Allianz	Germany	435,602	2,593
21	Commerzbank	Germany	427,896	1,058
22	Industrial Bank of Japan	Japan	415,482	692
23	Barclays	UK	412,412	2,847
24	Societe Generale de France	France	409,140	1,993
25	Fortis Group	Belgium/Netherlands	408,708	2,331
26	Chase Manhattan	US	406,105	5,375
27	Federal Home Loan Mortgage	US	385,387	2,065
28	Morgan Stanley Dean Witter	US	367,022	4,755
29	Merrill Lynch	US	328,071	2,580
30	Gruppo Intesa	Italy	305,538	1,095
31	CGNU	UK	296,510	1,624
32	Tokai Bank	Japan	295,921	407
33	Abbey National	UK	292,561	1,980
34	Lloyds/TSB Group	UK	284,972	4,069
35	Asahi Bank	Japan	281,657	307
36	Bank One	US	269,425	3,473
37	American International Group	US	268,238	5,055
38	Halifax	UK	262,303	1,722
39	J.P. Morgan	US	260,898	2,020
40	Banco Santander Central Hispano	Spain	258,076	1,585
41	First Union	US	253,024	3,217
42	Goldman Sachs	US	250,491	2,708
43	Dexia	Belgium	246,085	766
44	Prudential	UK	243,791	877
45	Aegon	Netherlands	230,272	1,577
46	Bankgesellschaft Berlin	Germany	224,459	174
47	Wells Fargo	US	218,103	3,712
48	Zurich Financial Services	Switzerland	211,771	3,077
49	Munich Reinsurance	Germany	195,728	1,316
50	Lehman Brothers	US	191,463	1,054

Source: *Wall Street Journal;* September 25, 2000

The World's Top 25 Airlines

Rank	Airline	1999 No. of RPKs*
1	United	201,873
2	American	177,334
3	Delta	168,596
4	Northwest	119,336
5	British Airways	117,463
6	Continental	93,367
7	Air France	83,736
8	Japan Airlines	82,904
9	Lufthansa	81,401
10	US Airways	66,875
11	Singapore	64,529
12	KLM	58,903
13	Southwest	58,695
14	Qantas	58,134
15	All Nippon	56,725
16	TWA	41,945
17	Cathay Pacific	41,503
18	Air Canada	39,005
19	Thai International	38,534
20	Alitalia	36,689
21	Korean	36,662
22	Iberia	35,379
23	Swissair	34,670
24	Malaysia	32,238
25	America West	28,497

*Revenue passenger kilometers

Source: *Air Transport World*; July 2000

The Top 25 Airline Fleets

Rank	Airline	No. of Aircraft
1	American	697
2	FedEx	650
3	United	594
4	Delta	584
5	Northwest	423
6	US Airways	398
7	Continental	370
8	Southwest	318
9	British Airways	283
10	Lufthansa	240
10	American Eagle	240
11	Air France	234
12	UPS	231
13	TWA	183
14	Iberia	172
15	Air Canada	157
16	America West	153
17	SAS	152
17	Alitalia	152
18	Continental Express	149
19	All Nippon	141
20	Japan Airlines	138
21	Mesa	135
22	Aeroflot Russian	121
23	Airborne Express	113
24	Comair	109
25	Korean	107

Source: *Air Transport World*; July 2000

The World's Top 50 Advertising Organizations

Rank	Company	Headquarters	Revenue ($ mil.)
1	Omnicom	New York	5,743.4
2	Interpublic Group of Cos.	New York	5,079.3
3	WPP Group	London	4,819.3
4	Havas Advertising	Levallois-Perret, France	2,385.1
5	Dentsu	Tokyo	2,106.8
6	B Com3 Group	Chicago	1,933.8
7	Young & Rubicam Inc.	New York	1,870.1
8	Grey Advertising	New York	1,577.9
9	True North	Chicago	1,489.2
10	Publicis SA	Paris	1,434.6
11	Hakuhodo	Tokyo	827.9
12	Saatchi & Saatchi plc	London	732.2
13	Cordiant Communications Group	London	713.0
14	TMP Worldwide	New York	512.9
15	Carlson Marketing Group	Minneapolis	353.3
16	Asatsu-DK	Tokyo	331.0
17	HA-LO	Niles, IL	251.0
18	Aspen Marketing Group	Los Angeles	225.3
19	MarchFirst	Chicago	209.4
20	Tokyu Agency	Tokyo	199.2
21	Daiko Advertising	Tokyo	198.0
22	Digitas	Boston	190.0
23	Cyrk/Simon Worldwide	Gloucester, MA	172.3
24	Lighthouse Global Network	Chicago	160.0
25	SPAR Group	Tarrytown, NY	153.5
26	Nelson Communications	New York	136.2
27	Deutsch	New York	133.1
28	Cheil Communications	Seoul	130.7
29	Incepta	London	123.0
30	Sapient Corp.	Cambridge, MA	110.8
31	Maxxcom	Toronto	110.0
32	Epb.communications	New York	109.3
33	IXL Enterprises	Atlanta	109.2
34	I&S/BBDO	Tokyo	106.5
35	Clemenger/BBDO	Melbourne	102.4
36	Yomiko Advertising	Tokyo	102.0
37	Doner	Southfield, MI	100.0
38	Harte-Hanks/DiMark	Langhorne, PA	95.1
39	U.S. Marketing & Promotions	Torrance, CA	93.6
40	Asahi Advertising	Tokyo	81.4
41	HMG Worldwide	New York	80.0
42	Cramer-Krasselt	Chicago	79.1
43	Icon Medialab International	Stockholm	72.0
44	Rubin Postaer & Associates	Santa Monica, CA	70.2
45	Richards Group	Dallas	69.0
46	Springer & Jacoby Werbung	Hamburg, Germany	67.9
47	Oricom Co.	Tokyo	67.7
48	Xceed	New York	67.5
49	AppNet	Bethesda, MD	67.4
50	Luminant Worldwide Corp.	Dallas	65.9

Source: *Advertising Age;* April 24, 2000

The World's Top 50 Food and Beverage Companies

Rank	Company	Country	1999 Revenues ($ mil.)
1	Nestlé	Switzerland	49,730
2	Unilever	Netherlands/UK	22,864
3	Diageo	UK	19,540
4	Danone	France	14,170
5	Snow Brand Milk Products	Japan	9,870
6	Suntory	Japan	9,600
7	Eridania Béghin-Say	France	9,010
8	Asahi Breweries	Japan	8,630
9	Kirin	Japan	7,740
10	Heineken	Netherlands	7,360
11	Maruha	Japan	7,300
12	Associated British Foods	UK	7,030
13	Tate & Lyle	UK	6,900
14	Cadbury Schweppes	UK	6,850
15	Nippon Meat Packers	Japan	6,740
16	Allied Domecq	UK	6,700
17	Ajinomoto	Japan	6,360
18	Parmalat Finanziaria	Italy	5,960
19	Meiji Milk Products	Japan	5,410
20	Yamazaki Baking	Japan	5,350
21	Sapporo Breweries	Japan	5,235
22	South African Breweries	South Africa	4,900
23	Groupe Lactalis (Besnier)	France	4,540
24	Carlsberg	Denmark	4,480
25	Nichirei	Japan	4,460
26	Friesland Coberco	Netherlands	4,380
27	Scottish & Newcastle	UK	4,260
28	Interbrew	Belgium	4,129
29	Pernod Ricard	France	3,820
30	Unigate	UK	3,810
31	Itoham Foods	Japan	3,520
32	New Zealand Dairy Board	New Zealand	3,487
33	Nippon Suisan Kaisha	Japan	3,460
34	FEMSA	Mexico	3,330
35	Campina Melkunie	Netherlands	3,316
36	Morinaga Milk Industry	Japan	3,310
37	Antarctica Paulista	Brazil	3,300
38	Glanbia	Ireland	3,280
39	Bongrain	France	3,270
40	Hillsdown Holdings	UK	3,200
41	Danisco	Denmark	2,900
42	Wessanen	Netherlands	2,890
43	Nisshin Flour Milling	Japan	2,840
44	MD Foods	Denmark	2,800
45	Panamco	Mexico	2,773
46	Ceval Alimentos	Brazil	2,750
47	Brahma	Brazil	2,600
48	Kerry Group	Ireland	2,580
49	Bimbo	Mexico	2,543
50	Sadia	Brazil	2,200

Source: *Prepared Foods;* July 2000

Japanese Companies in the Nikkei Index

Advantest
Ajinomoto
All Nippon Airways
Alps Electric
Aoki Corp.
Asahi Bank
Asahi Breweries
Asahi Chemical Industry
Asahi Glass
Bank of Tokyo-Mitsubishi
Bank of Yokohama
Bridgestone
Canon
Casio Computer
Chiyoda Corp.
Chubu Electric Power
Citizen Watch
Clarion
Daiichi Pharmaceutical
Dai Nippon Printing
Dainippon Pharmaceutical
Daiwa House Industry
Daiwa Bank
Daiwa Securities Group
DDI
Denki Kagaku Kogyo
Denso
Dowa Mining
East Japan Railway
Ebara Corp.
Eisai
Fanuc
Fuji Electric
Fuji Heavy Industries
Fuji Photo Film
Fujikura Ltd.
Fujita Corp.
Fujitsu
Furukawa Co.
Furukawa Electric
Hazama
Heiwa Real Estate
Hino Motors
Hitachi
Hitachi Zosen
Hokuetsu Paper Mills
Honda Motor
Iseki & Co.
Ishikawajima-Harima Heavy
Industries
Isuzu Motors
Ito-Yokado
Itochu Corp.
Japan Energy
Japan Steel Works
Japan Tobacco
Jusco
Kajima
Kanebo
Kansai Electric Power
Kao
Kawasaki Heavy Industries

Kawasaki Kisen
Kawasaki Steel
Keihin Electric Express Railway
Keio Electric Railway
Keisei Electric Railway
Kikkoman
Kirin Brewery
Kobe Steel
Komatsu Ltd.
Konica
Koyo Seiko
Kubota
Kumagai Gumi
Kuraray
Kyocera
Kyokuyo
Kyowa Hakko Kogyo
Marubeni Corp.
Marui
Matsushita Communication
Industrial
Matsushita Electric Industrial
Matsushita Electric Works
Mazda Motor
Meidensha
Meiji Milk Products
Meiji Seika
Mercian
Minebea
Mitsubishi Chemical
Mitsubishi Corp.
Mitsubishi Electric
Mitsubishi Estate
Mitsubishi Heavy Industries
Mitsubishi Logistics
Mitsubishi Materials
Mitsubishi Motors
Mitsubishi Paper Mills
Mitsubishi Rayon
Mitsubishi Trust & Banking
Mitsui & Co.
Mitsui Engineering &
Shipbuilding
Mitsumi Electric
Mitsui Fudosan
Mitsui Marine & Fire Insurance
Mitsui Mining & Smelting
Mitsui O.S.K. Lines
Mitsukoshi
Mizuho Holdings
Morinaga & Co.
Nachi-Fujikoshi
NEC
NGK Insulators
Nichirei
Niigata Engineering
Nikko Securities
Nikon
Nippon Express
Nippon Flour Mills
Nippon Kayaku
Nippon Light Metal

Nippon Oil
Nippon Paper Industries
Nippon Sharyo
Nippon Sheet Glass
Nippon Shinpan
Nippon Soda
Nippon Steel
Nippon Suisan
Nippon Telegraph and Telephone
Nippon Yusen
Nissan Chemical Industries
Nissan Motor
Nisshin Flour Milling
Nisshin Oil Mills
Nisshinbo Industries
Nissho Iwai
Nitto Boseki
NKK
Nomura Securities
NSK
NTN
NTT Data
NTT DoCoMo
Obayashi Corp.
Odakyu Electric Railway
Oji Paper
Oki Electric Industry
Okuma Corp.
Osaka Gas
Pioneer Electronic
Ricoh
Sakura Bank
Sankyo Co.
Sanwa Bank
Sanyo Electric
Sapporo Breweries
Sato Kogyo
Secom
Seven-Eleven Japan
Sharp
Shimizu
Shinko Securities
Shin-Etsu Chemical
Shionogi
Shiseido
Shizuoka Bank
Showa Denko
Showa Shell Sekiyu
Sony
Sumitomo Bank
Sumitomo Chemical
Sumitomo Corp.
Sumitomo Electric Industries
Sumitomo Heavy Industries
Sumitomo Marine & Fire
Insurance
Sumitomo Metal Industries
Sumitomo Metal Mining
Sumitomo Osaka Cement
Sumitomo Trust & Banking
Suzuki Motor
Taiheiyo Cement

Source : http://www.nni.nikkei.co.jp/FR/SERV/nikkei_indexes/namecode_225.html; October 2, 2000

Japanese Companies in the Nikkei Index (continued)

Taisei Corp.
Taiyo Yuden
Takara Shuzo
Takeda Chemical Industries
TDK
Teijin
Teikoku Oil
Terumo
Toa Corp.
Toagosei
Tobishima
Tobu Railway
Toei Co.
Toho Zinc
Tokai Bank

Tokai Carbon
Tokio Marine & Fire Insurance
Tokyo Dome
Tokyo Electron
Tokyo Electric Power
Tokyo Gas
Tokyu Corp.
Tokyu Department Store
Tomen Corp.
Toppan Printing
Topy Industries
Toray Industries
Toshiba
Tosoh
Toto

Toyo Seikan
Toyo Trust & Banking
Toyobo
Toyota Motor
Ube Industries
Unitika
Yamaha Corp.
Yamanouchi Pharmaceutical
Yasuda Fire & Marine Insurance
Yasuda Trust & Banking
Yokogawa Electric
Yokohama Rubber
Yuasa

Singapore Companies in the Straits Times Index

Cerebos Pacific Limited
Chartered Semiconductor
    Manufacturing Ltd
Comfort Group Ltd.
Creative Technology Ltd.
Cycle & Carriage Limited
Dairy Farm International Holdings
    Limited
DBS Group Holdings Ltd.
Econ International Limited
Fraser and Neave Limited

GP Batteries International Limited
Hotel Properties Limited
Hwa Hong Corporation Limited
Inchcape Motors Limited
Informatics Holdings Ltd.
Jardine Matheson Holdings
    Limited
Keppel Corporation Limited
Metro Holdings Limited
Neptune Orient Lines Limited
SembCorp Industries Ltd

Shangri-La Hotel Limited
Singapore Airlines Limited
Singapore Press Holdings Limited
Singapore Technologies
    Engineering Ltd.
Singapore Telecommunications
    Limited
United Industrial Corporation
    Limited
Want Want Holdings Ltd.
Wing Tai Holdings Limited

Source: http://www.hoovers.com/company/lists_biggest; December 4, 2000

Hong Kong Companies in the Hang Seng Index

Amoy Properties Limited
Bank of East Asia, Limited
Cathay Pacific Airways Limited
Cheung Kong (Holdings) Limited
Cheung Kong Infrastructure
    Holdings Limited
China Mobile (Hong Kong)
    Limited
China Resources Enterprise,
    Limited
CITIC Pacific Ltd.
CLP Holdings Limited
Dao Heng Bank Group Limited
First Pacific Company Limited

Hang Lung Development
    Company, Limited
Hang Seng Bank Limited
Henderson Investment Limited
Henderson Land Development
    Company Limited
The Hong Kong and China Gas
    Company Limited
Hongkong Electric Holdings
    Limited
HSBC Holdings plc
Hutchison Whampoa Limited
Hysan Development Company
    Limited

Johnson Electric Holdings
    Limited
Legend Holdings Limited
New World Development
    Company Limited
Pacific Century CyberWorks
    Limited
Shanghai Industrial Holdings
    Limited
Sino Land Company Limited
Sun Hung Kai Properties Limited
Swire Pacific Limited
Television Broadcasts Limited
The Wharf (Holdings) Limited
Wheelock and Company Limited

Source: http://www.hoovers.com/company/lists_biggest; December 4, 2000

UK Companies in the FT-SE 100 Index

3i Group plc
Abbey National plc
Alliance & Leicester plc
Allied Domecq PLC
AMVESCAP PLC
Anglo American plc
ARM Holdings plc
AstraZeneca PLC
BAA plc
BAE SYSTEMS
Baltimore Technologies plc
Bank of Scotland
Barclays PLC
Bass PLC
BG Group plc
Billiton Plc
Blue Circle Industries PLC
The BOC Group plc
Bookham Technology plc
The Boots Company PLC
BP Amoco p.l.c.
British Airways Plc
British American Tobacco p.l.c.
British Sky Broadcasting
  Group plc
British Telecommunications plc
Cable and Wireless plc
Cadbury Schweppes plc
Canary Wharf Group plc
The Capita Group Plc
Carlton Communications PLC
Celltech Group plc
Centrica plc
CGNU plc
CMG plc

COLT Telecom Group plc
Daily Mail and General Trust PLC
Diageo plc
Dimension Data Holdings Limited
Dixons Group plc
Electrocomponents plc
EMAP PLC
EMI Group plc
Energis plc
Exel plc
GKN plc
Glaxo Wellcome plc
Granada Compass PLC
Granada Media plc
The Great Universal Stores P.L.C.
Halifax plc
Hays plc
Hilton Group PLC
HSBC Holdings plc
Imperial Chemical Industries PLC
Imperial Tobacco Group PLC
International Power plc
Invensys plc
J Sainsbury plc
Kingfisher plc
Land Securities PLC
Lattice Group plc
Legal & General Group Plc
Lloyds TSB Group plc
Logica plc
Marconi plc
Marks and Spencer p.l.c.
Misys plc
The National Grid Group plc
Nycomed Amersham plc

Old Mutual plc
P&O Princess Cruises plc
Pearson plc
PowerGen plc
Prudential plc
Railtrack Group PLC
Reckitt Benckiser plc
Reed International P.L.C.
Rentokil Initial plc
Reuters Group PLC
Rio Tinto plc
Royal & Sun Alliance Insurance
  Group plc
The Royal Bank of Scotland
  Group plc
The Sage Group plc
Schroders plc
Scottish and Southern Energy plc
Scottish Power plc
Sema Group plc
The "Shell" Transport and Trading
  Company plc
Shire Pharmaceuticals Group plc
SmithKline Beecham plc
South African Breweries plc
Spirent plc
Standard Chartered PLC
Telewest Communications plc
Tesco PLC
Unilever PLC
United News & Media plc
United Utilities PLC
Vodafone Group PLC
WPP Group plc

Source: http://www.hoovers.com/company/lists_biggest; December 4, 2000

German Companies in the DAX

adidas-Salomon AG
Allianz AG
BASF Aktiengesellschaft
Bayer AG
Bayerische Hypo- und
  Vereinsbank Aktiengesellschaft
Bayerische Motoren Werke AG
Commerzbank AG
DaimlerChrysler AG
Degussa-Huls AG
Deutsche Bank AG

Deutsche Telekom AG
Dresdner Bank AG
E.ON AG
EPCOS AG
Fresenius Medical Care
  Aktiengesellschaft
Henkel KGaA
Infineon Technologies AG
Karstadt Quelle AG
Linde AG
Deutsche Lufthansa AG

MAN Aktiengesellschaft
METRO AG
Münchener Rückversicherungs-
  Gesellschaft Aktiengesellschaft
Preussag AG
RWE Aktiengesellschaft
SAP Aktiengesellschaft
Schering AG
Siemens AG
ThyssenKrupp AG
Volkswagen AG

Source: http://www.hoovers.com/company/lists_biggest; December 4, 2000

French Companies in the SBF 120

Accor
Société Air France
Alcatel
ALSTOM
Altadis, S.A.
Altran Technologies
Assurances Générales de France
Atos Origin
Aventis
AXA
Azeo
Société BIC S.A.
BNP Paribas Group
Bouygues Offshore
Bouygues S.A.
Bull
Business Objects S.A.
CANAL+
Cap Gemini Ernst & Young
Carrefour SA
Casino Guichard-Perrachon
Castorama-Dubois
  Investissements
Ciments Français
Clarins
Club Méditerranée S.A.
CNP Assurances SA
Coface
Coflexip, S.A.
CPR
Crédit Lyonnais
Groupe Danone
Dassault Systemes S.A.
Dexia Group
Eiffage S.A.
Equant N.V.
Eramet
Eridania Béghin-Say

Essilor International SA
Eurafrance
Euro Disney S.C.A.
European Aeronautic Defence
  and Space Company EADS N.V.
Eurotunnel S.A.
Faurecia
France Telecom
Galeries Lafayette
Compagnie Générale d'Industrie
  et de Participations
Genset, S.A.
Compagnie Générale de
  Géophysique, S.A.
GrandVision S.A.
Guyenne et Gascogne SA
Havas Advertising
Hermès International
IMERYS
Infogrames Entertainment S.A.
Labinal SA
Lafarge S.A.
Lagardère SCA
L'Air Liquide SA
Lapeyre SA
Le Carbone-Lorraine
Legrand SA
Legris Industries
Liberty Surf Group Sa
L'Oréal SA
LVMH Moët Hennessy Louis
  Vuitton SA
Compagnie Générale des Établissements Michelin
Natexis Banques Populaires
Neopost S.A.
NRJ SA
Pechiney S.A.

Pernod Ricard
PSA Peugeot Citroën S.A.
Pinault-Printemps-Redoute
Compagnie Plastic Omnium
Publicis Groupe S.A.
Rémy Cointreau
Renault S.A.
Rexel S.A.
Rhodia SA
Royal Canin
Sagem S.A.
Compagnie de Saint-Gobain
Sanofi-Synthélabo
Schneider Electric SA
SCOR
SEB S.A.
Sidel SA
Simco SA
Société Générale
Sodexho Alliance
Sommer Allibert
SPIR Communication S.A.
STMicroelectronics N.V.
Suez Lyonnaise des Eaux
Technip
Société Télévision Française 1
THOMSON multimedia S.A.
Thomson-CSF
TOTAL FINA ELF S.A.
Ubi Soft Entertainment S.A.
Unibail
Usinor
Valeo S.A.
Vallourec S.A.
Valtech
VINCI
Vivendi
Zodiac S.A.

Source: http://www.hoovers.com/company/lists_biggest; December 4, 2000

French Companies in the CAC 40 Index

Accor
Alcatel
ALSTOM
Assurances Générales de France
Aventis
AXA
BNP Paribas Group
Bouygues S.A.
CANAL+
Cap Gemini Ernst & Young
Carrefour SA
Casino Guichard-Perrachon
Crédit Lyonnais
Groupe Danone
Dexia Group

Equant N.V.
European Aeronautic Defence
  and Space Company EADS N.V.
France Telecom
Lafarge S.A.
Lagardère SCA
L'Air Liquide SA
L'Oréal SA
LVMH Moët Hennessy Louis
  Vuitton SA
Compagnie Générale des Établissements Michelin
PSA Peugeot Citroën S.A.
Pinault-Printemps-Redoute
Renault S.A.

Compagnie de Saint-Gobain
Sanofi-Synthélabo
Schneider Electric SA
Société Générale
Sodexho Alliance
STMicroelectronics N.V.
Suez Lyonnaise des Eaux
Société Télévision Française 1
THOMSON multimedia S.A.
Thomson-CSF
TOTAL FINA ELF S.A.
Valeo S.A.
Vivendi

Source: http://www.hoovers.com/company/lists_biggest; December 4, 2000

Non-US Company Stocks Available in the US

Company	Exchange	Symbol	Company	Exchange	Symbol
Argentina			Australia & New Zealand		
Alpargatas S.A.I.C.	OTC	ALPAY	Banking Group	NYSE	ANZ
Banco de Galicia			Australian Goldfields Nl	OTC	AUGZY
y Buenos Aires B	NAS	BGALY	Australian Oil and Gas		
Banco Frances Del Rio de La			Corp Ltd	OTC	AUOGY
Plata Common	NYSE	BFR	Barbeques Galore Limited	NAS	BBQZY
Banco Rio de La Plata S.A.	NYSE	BRS	Biota Holdings Limited	OTC	BTAHY
Buenos Aires Embotelladora			Boral Limited	OTC	BORLY
B Shares	OTC	BAE	Boulder Group N.L.	OTC	BDRGY
Cresud Common Shares	NAS	CRESY	Broken Hill Proprietary		
Grupo Financiero Galicia S.A.	NAS	GGAL	Company	NYSE	BHP
Irsa Common Shares	NYSE	IRS	Burns, Philip and		
Metrogas S.A.	NYSE	MGS	Company Ltd	OTC	BPHCY
Nortel Inversora Series B	NYSE	NTL	Cape Range Limited	OTC	CPGEY
Pc Holdings S.A.	NYSE	PC	Centaur Mining and		
Quilmes Industrial			Exploration Ltd	NAS	CTRL
(Quinsa), S.A.	NYSE	LQU	Central Norseman Gold		
Sol Petroleo Common Shares	OTC	SLEOY	Corporation	OTC	CNOGY
Telecom Argentina Stet-			Central Pacific Minerals N.L.	NAS	CPMNY
France Telecom SA	NYSE	TEO	Charter Mining N.L.	OTC	CMNGY
Telefonica de Argentina S.A.	NYSE	TAR	Charters Towers Gold Mines Nl	OTC	CTGLY
Transportadora de Gas			Clyde Industries Limited	OTC	CYDNY
Del Sur, S.A.	NYSE	TGS	Coca-Cola Amatil Limited	OTC	CCLAY
Ypf Sociedad Anonima			Coles Myer Limited	NYSE	CM
D Shares	NYSE	YPF	Computershare Limited	OTC	CMSQY
			Coopers Resources N.L.	OTC	CRNLY
Austria			Crystal Mining N.L.	OTC	CRYOTC
Bank Austria Ag	OTC	BAAGY	Csr Limited	OTC	CSRLY
Boehler-Uddeholm Ag	OTC	BDHHY	Davnet Limited	OTC	DAVNY
Evn Ag	OTC	EVNVY	Deepsky Webmarket Limited	OTC	DSWMY
Julius Meinl International Ag	OTC	JLMXY	Delta Gold Limited	OTC	DGNLY
Lauda Air Luftfahrt Ag	OTC	LAUOTC	Denehurst Limited	OTC	DEHNY
Lenzing Ag	OTC	LNZNY	Digicall Group Limited	OTC	DGCGY
Mayr-Melnhof Karton Ag	OTC	MNHFY	Dioro Exploration N.L.	OTC	DIORY
Omv Ag	OTC	OMVKY	Dominion Mining Limited	OTC	DMNOY
Osterreichische Elek			Email Limited	OTC	EMALY
(Verbund) Ag	OTC	OEZVY	Emperor Mines Limited	OTC	EMPMY
Topcall International Ag	OTC	TPCIY	Erg Limited	OTC	ERGAY
Va Technologie Ag	OTC	VATXY	Euralba Mining Limited	OTC	EUROTC
Vienna International			F.H. Faulding & Co. Limited	OTC	FAFHY
Airport (Via)	OTC	VIAAY	First Australian Resources N.L.	OTC	FAUSY
Wienerberger			Firstpac Limited	OTC	FPCLY
Baustoffindustrie Ag	OTC	WBRBY	Forbio Limited	OTC	FOBLY
Wmp Bank Ag	OTC	WMPBY	Formulab Neuronetics		
Wolford Ag	OTC	WLFDY	Corporation Limited	NAS	FNCYQ
			Forsayth N.L.	OTC	FORNY
Australia			Foster's Brewing Group Limited	OTC	FBWGY
Accor Asia Pacific	OTC	AAPCY	Geo 2 Limited	OTC	GOTWY
Airboss Limited	OTC	AIRBY	Ghana Gold Mines Limited	OTC	GHNMY
Alpha Sensors Limited	OTC	ASORY	Golconda Minerals N.L.	OTC	GOLOTC
Amcor Ltd.	NAS	AMCR	Golden Valley Mines N.L.	OTC	GVYMY
Amrad Corporation Limited	OTC	AMDJY	Goodman Fielder Limited	OTC	GMFIY
Ashton Mining Limited	OTC	AHMNY	Great Fingall Mining Co. Nl	OTC	GRFMY
Asia Oil and Minerals Limited	OTC	AOMLY	Greenvale Mining N.L.	OTC	GVLMY
Astro Mining Nl	OTC	ATRMY	Hallmark Gold N.L.	OTC	HGLOTC
Atlas Pacific Limited	NAS	APCFY	Haoma Mining N.L.	OTC	HONOY
Auridiam Consolidated N.L.	OTC	AURAY	Herald Resources Limited	OTC	HRECY
Australia & New Zealand			Hmc Australasia	OTC	HMCAF
Bank Group Pref	NYSE	ANZXXX	Howard Smith Limited	OTC	HWSMY
Australia & New Zealand			Hoyts Entertainment Limited	OTC	HELOTC
Bank Group Pref	NYSE	ANZXX	Hydromet Corporation Limited	OTC	HYRCY

Source: The Bank of New York (bankofny.com/adr); October 18, 2000

Company	Exchange	Symbol	Company	Exchange	Symbol
Imperial One Limited	OTC	IMWNY	Samson Exploration N.L.	OTC	SAEZY
Indonesian Diamond			Santos Ltd.	NAS	STOSY
Corporation Ltd.	OTC	IDIMY	Sapphire Mines N.L.	OTC	SHRETY
International Mining			Silex Systems Limited	OTC	SILXY
Corporation	OTC	IMCOTC	Simsmetal Limited	OTC	SIMEY
Iron Carbide Australia Limited	OTC	ICAUY	Sons of Gwalia N.L.	OTC	SOGAY
Isis Communications Ltd.	OTC	ISCMY	Southcorp Holdings Limited	OTC	STHHY
James Hardie Industries			Southern Pacific Petroleum	NAS	SPPTY
Limited	OTC	JHINY	Southern Ventures N.L.	OTC	SOVEY
Jimberlana Minerals N.L.	OTC	JBLMY	St. Barbara Mines Limited	OTC	STBRY
Jingellic Minerals N.L.	OTC	JINGY	St. George Bank Limited	OTC	STGKY
Julia Mines N.L.	OTC	JULIY	Star City Holdings Limited	NAS	SCITY
Kern Corporation	OTC	KCTOTC	Striker Resources N.L.	OTC	SKRRY
Kidston Gold Mines Limited	OTC	KSGMY	Tabcorp Holdings Limited	OTC	TABCY
Lend Lease Corporation			Telstra Corporation Ltd -		
Limited	OTC	LLESY	Interim Ads	NYSE	TLSPP
Lightning Jack Film Trust	OTC	LJFTY	Telstra Corporation Ltd.	NYSE	TLS
Lihir Gold Limited	NAS	LIHRY	Tennyson Holdings Ltd.	OTC	TENYY
M.I.M. Holdings Limited	OTC	MIMOY	Terrex Resources N.L.	OTC	TRXRY
Magellan Petroleum			Transcontinental Holdings	OTC	TCOHF
Australia Ltd.	OTC	MAPAY	Trans-Global Interactive		
Mayne Nickless Ltd.	OTC	MAYNY	Limited	NAS	TGBR
Memtec Limited	OTC	MET	Triad Minerals N.L.	OTC	TIDMY
Menzies Gold N.L.	OTC	MZILY	Vanguard Petroleum Ltd	OTC	VGDPY
Meridian Oil N.L.	OTC	MEOLY	Victoria Petroleum N.L.	OTC	VPTOY
Merlin Mining N.L.	OTC	MNNOTC	Village Roadshow Limited	OTC	VLRDY
Metal Storm Limited	OTC	MTSXY	Village Roadshow Ltd.		
Micromedical Industries			Preference Shares	OTC	VLRPY
Limited	OTC	MMIDY	Virotec International Ltd.	OTC	VIROY
Mid-East Minerals N.L.	OTC	MEMIF	Walhalla.Com Limited	OTC	WLHLY
Mincorp Petroleum N.L.	OTC	MRTOTC	Westpac Banking Corporation	NYSE	WBK
Mintaro Slate & Flagstone			Wmc Limited	NYSE	WMC
Co., Ltd.	OTC	MTSKF	Woodside Petroleum Limited	OTC	WOPEY
Mount Burgess Gold Mines N.L.	OTC	MTBGY			
National Australia Bank			**Belgium**		
Limited Pref.	NYSE	NABXX	Gevaert Photo-Production N.V.	OTC	GEVAY
National Australia Bank Ltd.	NYSE	NAB	Solvay S.A.	OTC	SLVYY
New Australia Resources	OTC	NAUSY	Tessenderlo Chemie	OTC	TSDOY
New Tel Limited	NAS	NWLL	Xeikon Nv	NAS	XEIK
Newcrest Mining Limited	OTC	NWCMY			
The News Corporation Limited	NYSE	NWS	**Bermuda**		
News Corporation, Preferred	NYSE	NWSA	China Broadband Corporation		
Normandy Mining Limited	OTC	NMDMY	Limited	NAS	CBBC
Normandy Mt Leyshon			China Rich Holdings Limited	OTC	CRHSY
Mining Limitred	OTC	NMLYY	Ebiz.Hk.Com Limited	OTC	EBZHY
North Broken Hill-Peko			Frontline Ltd.	NAS	FRONY
Limited	OTC	NBHKY	Jinhui Shipping and		
Novogen Limited	NAS	NVGN	Transportation Ltd	OTC	JNSTY
Orbital Engine Corporation			King Pacific International		
Limited	NYSE	OE	Holdings Ltd	OTC	KPCIY
Origin Energy Limited	OTC	OGFGY	Shangri-La Asia Limited	OTC	SHALY
Pacific Capital Limited	OTC	PCFLY			
Pacific Dunlop Limited	NAS	PDLPY	**Bolivia**		
Pacmin Mining Corporation			Banco Bisa S.A.	OTC	BITSY
Limited	OTC	PMMCY	Banco Mercantil		
Petrogulf Resources Limited	OTC	PRLOTC	Common Shares	OTC	BMBVY
Petsec Energy Ltd.	OTC	PSJEY	Banco Nacional de Bolivia	OTC	BNBVY
Placer Pacific Limited	OTC	PLCAY	Banco Santa Cruz	OTC	BSCZY
Range Resources Ltd.	OTC	RGRLY	Seguros Illimani	OTC	SEGUROS
Regent Mining Ltd.	OTC	REGMY			
Resolute Limited	OTC	RSLLY	**Brazil**		
Rio Tinto Limited	OTC	RTOLY	Acesita-Cia.	OTC	ACAIY
Roycol Limited	OTC	ROYCF	Aracruz Celulose	NYSE	ARA
			Bahia Sul Cellulose, S.A. Ords	OTC	BHISY

Non-US Company Stocks Available in the US (continued)

Company	Exchange	Symbol	Company	Exchange	Symbol
Bahia Sul Cellulose, S.A. Pref	OTC	BHIAY	Embratel Participacoes S.A.	NYSE	EMT
Banco Bradesco SA	OTC	BBQCY	Eucatex S.A. Industria E		
Bombril S.A.	OTC	BMBBY	Cornercio	OTC	ECTXY
Bompreco S.A. Supermerca Brasil			Gerdau S.A.	NYSE	GGB
Telecom Participacoes S.A.	NYSE	BRP	Globex Utilidades S.A. Preferred	OTC	GBXPY
Celesc-Centrais Ele.			Globo Cabo S.A.	NAS	GLCBY
da Santa Catarina B	OTC	CAIBY	Industrias Klabin de		
Centrals Geradoras			Papel e Celulose	OTC	IKLBY
(Gerasul) Common	OTC	GESUY	Iochpe-Maxion	OTC	IOCJY
Centrals Geradoras			Lojas Americanas	OTC	LOJAY
(Gerasul) Preffered	OTC	GESXY	Makro Atacadista S.A.	OTC	MKRAY
Cia Energetica de Sao Paulo -			Marcopolo, SA	OTC	MCPOY
Cesp Comm	OTC	CSQSY	Oxiteno S.A.	OTC	OXTIY
Cia Geracao Ener Elet			Perdigao S.A.	OTC	PDGAY
Paranapanema	OTC	CEPWY	Petrobras Distribuidora S.A.	OTC	PTBRY
Cia Geracao Ener Elet			Petroleo Brasileiro S.A.	NYSE	PBR
Paranapanema Pref	OTC	CEPVY	Rossi Residencial S.A.	OTC	RSRZY
Cia Geracao Ener Elet Tiete	OTC	CDEEY	S.A. Fabrica de Produtos		
Cia Geracao Ener Elet			Aliment Vigor	OTC	SFPVY
Tiete Pref	OTC	CDEOY	Sao Paulo Alpargatas S.A.		
Cia Transmissao Ener			Common Shares	OTC	SAALY
Elet Paulista	OTC	CTPTY	Sao Paulo Alpargatas S.A.		
Cia Transmissao Ener Elet			Pref Shares	OTC	SAANY
Paulista Pref	OTC	CTPZY	Saraiva S.A. Common	OTC	SVLOY
Comp. Paranaense de Energia-			Saraiva S.A. Preferred	OTC	SVLSY
Copel Common	OTC	CXBVY	Teka-Tecelagem Kuehnrich S.A.	OTC	TKTPY
Comp. Paranaense de Energia-			Tele Celular Sul		
Copel Pref	NYSE	ELP	Participacoes S.A.	NYSE	TSU
Companhia Brasileira de			Tele Centro Oeste		
Dist.-Cbd	NYSE	CBD	Celular Part S.A.	NYSE	TRO
Companhia de Bebidas Das			Tele Leste Celular		
Americas Comm	NYSE	ABV.C	Participacoes S.A.	NYSE	TBE
Companhia de Bebidas Das			Tele Nordeste Celular		
Americas Pref	NYSE	ABV	Participacoes S.A.	NYSE	TND
Companhia Energ. de Minas			Tele Norte Celular		
Gerais	OTC	CEMFY	Participacoes S.A.	NYSE	TCN
Companhia Energetica de			Tele Norte Leste		
Minas Gerais	OTC	CEMCY	Participacoes S.A.	NYSE	TNE
Companhia Energetica de Sao			Tele Sudeste Celular		
Paulo-Cesp	OTC	CMPSY	Participacoes S.A.	NYSE	TSD
Companhia Fabricadoras de			Telebras Basket Adr (Rctb40)	NYSE	RTB
Pecas-Cofap	OTC	CFPEY	Telebras Holding Company	NYSE	TBH
Companhia Siderurgica			Telebras Preferred Shares	OTC	TBAPY
Belgo-Mineira S.A.	OTC	CSBMY	Telecomunicacoes		
Companhia Siderurgica de			Brasileiras (Rctb31)	OTC	TBASY
Tubarao	OTC	CSTPY	Telecomunicacoes de		
Companhia Siderurgica			Sao Paulo - Telesp	NYSE	TSP
Nacional-Csn	NYSE	SID	Telemig Celular		
Companhia Suzano			Participacoes S.A.	NYSE	TMB
de Papel E Celulose	OTC	CSZPY	Telesp Celular		
Companhia Vale do Rio			Participacoes S.A.	NYSE	TCP
Doce (Cvrd)	NYSE	RIO	Ultrapar Participacoes S/A Pref	NYSE	UGP
Copene Petroquimica			Unibanco-Uniao de		
do Nordeste - Pref	NYSE	PNE	Bancos Brasileiros SA	NYSE	UBB
Ctm Citrus	OTC	CTMMY	Votorantim Celulose		
Electrobras-Centrais			e Papel Pref	NYSE	VCP
Electricas Ord.	OTC	CAIFY			
Electrobras-Centrais			**Cayman Islands**		
Electricas Pref	OTC	CAIGY	Asat Holdings Limited	NAS	ASTT
Electrolux Du Brasil, SA	OTC	EXDBY	Greater China Technology		
Embraer-Empresa Brasileira			Group Ltd.	OTC	GCTGY
de Aeronautic	NYSE	ERJ	Wherever.Net Holding		
			Corporation	NAS	WNET

Non-US Company Stocks Available in the US (continued)

Company	Exchange	Symbol
Chile		
Afp Provida Common Shares	NYSE	PVD
Banco de A. Edwards	NYSE	AED
Banco Santander Chile	NYSE	BSB
Banco Santiago	NYSE	SAN
Bbv Banco Bhif	NYSE	BB
Chilectra S.A.	OTC	CLRAY
Compania Cervecerias Unidas S.A.	NYSE	CU
Compania de Telecom. de Chile A Shares	NYSE	CTC
Cristalerias de Chile, S.A.	NYSE	CGW
Distribucion y Servicio D & S S.A.	NYSE	DYS
Embotelladora Andina, S.A. A Shares	NYSE	AKOA
Embotelladora Andina, S.A. B Shares	NYSE	AKOB
Embotelladora Arica S.A.	OTC	EMAZY
Empresas Telex-Chile S.A. Common Shares	NYSE	TL
Endesa-Empresa Nacional de Electricidad	NYSE	EOC
Enersis S.A.	NYSE	ENI
Gener S.A.	NYSE	CHR
Laboratorio Chile S.A.	NYSE	LBC
Lan Chile S.A.	NYSE	LFL
Madeco Common Shares	NYSE	MAD
Masisa S.A.	NYSE	MYS
Quinenco S.A.	NYSE	LQ
Santa Isabel S.A.	NYSE	ISA
Sociedad Quimica y Minera de Chile A	NYSE	SQMA
Sociedad Quimica y Minera de Chile B	NYSE	SQM
Supermercados Unimarc Common Shares	NYSE	UNR
Vina Concha y Toro Common Shares	NYSE	VCO
China		
Beijing Yanhua Petrochemical Co., Ltd.	NYSE	BYH
China Eastern Airlines Corp. Ltd.	NYSE	CEA
China Shipping Dev Company Ltd	OTC	CSDXY
China Southern Airlines Company Ltd.	NYSE	ZNH
China Unicom Limited	NYSE	CHU
Guangshen Railway Company Limited	NYSE	GSH
Guangzhou Shipyard Int'l.Co.Ltd.HShs.	OTC	GSHIY
Huaneng Power International Inc.	NYSE	HNP
Jilin Chemical Industrial Company Ltd.	NYSE	JCC
Netease.Com, Inc	NAS	NTES
Petrochina Company Limited	NYSE	PTR
Shandong Huaneng Power N Shares	NYSE	SH

Company	Exchange	Symbol
Shanghai Chlor-Alkali Chemical Co., Ltd.	OTC	SLLBY
Shanghai Erfangji Co. Ltd. B	OTC	SHFGY
Shanghai Jinqiao Processing Dev Co. Ltd.	OTC	SJQIY
Shanghai Lujiazui Finance Trade Zone Dev	OTC	SLUJY
Shanghai Outer Gaoqiao Ftz Dev. Co. Ltd.	OTC	SGOTY
Shanghai Petrochemical Company Limited	NYSE	SHI
Shanghai Tyre and Rubber Co. Ltd.	OTC	SIRHY
Shenzhen S.E.Z. Real Estate and Prop.	OTC	SZPRY
Tsingtao Brewery Company Limited	OTC	TSGTY
Yanzhou Coal Mining Company Limited	NYSE	YZC
Colombia		
Banco Ganadero Common Shares	NYSE	BGA
Banco Ganadero Preferred Shares	NYSE	BGA-P
Bancolombia S.A. Preferred	NYSE	CIB
Comunicacion Celular, S.A.	OTC	CMCQY
Corporacion Financiera del Valle	OTC	CFDVY
Occidente y Caribe Celular, S.A.	OTC	OYCCY
Czech Republic		
Komercni Banka A.S.	OTC	KMBNY
Denmark		
Danske Bank A/S	OTC	DEAFY
Euro909.Com	NAS	ENON
Novo Nordisk A/S	NYSE	NVO
Tele Danmark A/S	NYSE	TLD
Dominican Republic		
Tricom S.A.	NYSE	TDR
Ecuador		
Banco de Guayaquil, S. A.	OTC	BGYQY
Banco La Previsora S.A.	OTC	PREVCY
Egypt		
Misr International Bank	OTC	MIBZY
Finland		
Amer Group Ltd.	OTC	AGPDY
Instrumentarium Corporation	NAS	INMRY
Metso Corporation	NYSE	MX
Nokia Corporation	NYSE	NOK
Sonera Corp	NAS	SNRA
Stora Enso Oyj	NYSE	SEO
Upm-Kymmene Corp.	NYSE	UPM
France		
Accor, S.A.	OTC	ACRFY
Activcard SA	NAS	ACTI
Alcatel	NYSE	ALA
Alstom	NYSE	ALS
Aventis S.A.	NYSE	AVE

Non-US Company Stocks Available in the US (continued)

Company	Exchange	Symbol	Company	Exchange	Symbol
AXA	NYSE	AXA	Dialog Semiconductor Plc	NAS	DLGS
Bnp Paribas	OTC	BNDQY	Digitale Telekabel AG	NAS	DTAGY
Bouygues Offshore S.A.	NYSE	BWG	Dresdner Bank AG	OTC	DRSDY
Business Objects S.A.	NAS	BOBJ	E.On AG	NYSE	EON
Canal Plus	OTC	CNPLY	Epcos AG	NYSE	EPC
Ciments Francais	OTC	CIMFY	Fresenius Medical Care AG	NYSE	FMS
Clarins	OTC	CRASY	Fresenius Medical Care Ag Pref	NYSE	FMS+
Club Méditerranée	OTC	CLMDY	Hannover Ruckversicherungs	OTC	HVRRY
Coflexip	NAS	CXIPY	Henkel Kgaa Common Shares	OTC	HENKY
Compagnie de Suez	OTC	CSUZY	Henkel Kgaa Preferred Shares	OTC	HENOY
Compagnie Générale de			Incam AG	NAS	INAGY
Geophysique	NYSE	GGY	Infineon Technologies AG	NYSE	IFX
Dassault Systemes S.A.	NAS	DASTY	Ixos Software AG	NAS	XOSY
Diffusion Internationale	OTC	DFUBY	Jumptec AG	OTC	JMTKY
Edap Technomed S.A.	NAS	EDAYE	Karstadt Ag, Rudolf	OTC	KARDY
Elf Aquitaine	NYSE	ELF	Kloeckner Werke, A.G.	OTC	KKWAY
Fiat France S.A. (Ffsa)	OTC	FFSAY	Lion Bioscience AG	NAS	LEON
Flamel Technologies S.A.	NAS	FLMLY	Mannesmann AG	OTC	MNNSY
France Telecom	NYSE	FTE	New York Broker		
Genset	NAS	GENXY	Deutschland AG	OTC	NYBDY
Groupe AB	NYSE	ABG	Pfeiffer Vacuum Technology AG	NYSE	PV
Groupe Danone	NYSE	DA	Primacom AG	NAS	PCAG
Ilog SA	NAS	ILOG	Prosieben Media Ag Preferred	OTC	PBMGY
Infovista SA	NAS	IVTA	Qs Communications AG	NAS	QSCG
Lafarge S.A.	OTC	LFCPY	Realax Software AG	NAS	RLAXY
Lagardère Groupe S.C.A.	OTC	LGDDY	Rosenthal AG	OTC	ROSLY
L'air Liquide	OTC	AIQUY	Rwe AG	OTC	RWEOY
L'oréal	OTC	LORLY	Rwe Ag Preferred	OTC	RWEPY
LVMH	NAS	LVMHY	Sap Ag Pref	NYSE	SAP
Pechiney	NYSE	PY	Schwarz Pharma AG	OTC	SWTZY
Pernod Ricard S.A.	OTC	PDRDY	Sgl Carbon AG	NYSE	SGG
Peugeot Citroën S.A.	OTC	PEUGY	Siemens AG	OTC	SMAWY
Publicis Groupe S.A.	NYSE	PUB	Singulus Technologies AG	OTC	SGTSY
Rhodia	NYSE	RHA	Stahlwerke Peine		
Scor	NYSE	SCO	Salzgitter, A.G.	OTC	SPSOTC
Sidel SA	OTC	SIELY	Trion Technology AG	NAS	TRIN
Société Genéralé	OTC	SCGLY	Volkswagen AG	OTC	VLKAY
Thomson Multimedia S.A.	NYSE	TMS	Volkswagen Ag Preferred	OTC	VWBP
Thomson-Csf	OTC	TCSFY	Washtec AG	OTC	WHTCY
Total Fina Elf S.A.	NYSE	TOT	Washtec AG	OTC	WSHDY
Transgene S.A.	NAS	TRGNY			
Valeo S.A.	OTC	VLEEY	**Ghana**		
Vivendi	NYSE	V	Ashanti Goldfields		
Wavecom SA	NAS	WVCM	Company Ltd.	NYSE	ASL
Germany			**Greece**		
Basf Aktiengesellschaft AG	NYSE	BF	Antenna Tv	NAS	ANTV
Bayer Ag	OTC	BAYZY	Boutari & Son, S.A.	OTC	BJSWY
Bayerische Hypo-Und			Boutari & Son, S.A. Preferred	OTC	BJSPY
Vereinsbank Ag	OTC	HVMGY	Credit Bank A.E.	OTC	CBAEY
Beta Systems Software A.G.	OTC	BSSWY	Globe Group S.A.	OTC	GLGYP
Beta Systems Software AG	OTC	BSSAG	Hellenic Telecommunication		
Bhf Bank AG	OTC	BHFFY	Org. S.A.	NYSE	OTE
Brokat Infosystems AG	OTC	BROA	M.J. Maillis S.A.	OTC	MJMSY
Bus-Berzilius			National Bank of Greece S.A.	NYSE	NBG
Umwelt-Service AG	OTC	UMWELT	Stet Hellas		
Commerzbank AG	OTC	CRZBY	Telecommunications S.A.	NAS	STHLY
Continental AG	OTC	CTTAY			
Deutsche Bank AG	OTC	DTBKY	**Hong Kong**		
Deutsche Beteiligungs			Akai Holdings Limited	OTC	AKHLY
Holding AG	OTC	DEUBY	Amoy Properties Limited	OTC	AMOPY
Deutsche Lufthansa AG	OTC	DLAKY	Applied International		
Deutsche Telekom AG	NYSE	DT	Holdings Limited	OTC	APIHY
			Apt Satellite Holdings Limited	NYSE	ATS

Non-US Company Stocks Available in the US (continued)

Company	Exchange	Symbol	Company	Exchange	Symbol
Asia Satelite Telecom Holdings	NYSE	SAT	Gzitic Hualing Holdings		
Bank of East Asia, Limited	OTC	BKEAY	Limited	OTC	GZHUY
Brilliance China Automotive			Hang Lung Development		
Holdings Ltd	NYSE	CBA	Company, Limited	OTC	HANLY
C.P. Pokphand Co. Ltd.	OTC	CPPKY	Hang Seng Bank Limited	OTC	HSNGY
Cable & Wireless Hkt	NYSE	HKT	Hanny Holdings Limited	OTC	HNYMY
Cathay Pacific Airways Limited	OTC	CPCAY	Hanny Magnetics		
Cdl Hotels International Limited	OTC	CDLHY	(Holdings) Ltd.	OTC	HMHOTC
Champion Technology			Hb International	OTC	HBIHY
Holding Limited	OTC	CMPLY	Henderson Investments		
Chen Hsong Holdings Limited	OTC	CHHGY	Limited	OTC	HDVTY
Cheung Kong (Holdings)			Henderson Land		
Limited	OTC	CHEUY	Development Co., Ltd	OTC	HLDCY
Chevalier (Oa) Int'l Ltd.	OTC	COAZY	Heng Fung Holdings Co.	OTC	HNFGE
Chevalier International			Hong Kong & China		
Holdings Ltd.	OTC	CHVLY	Gas Co. Ltd.	OTC	HOKCY
China Aerospace			Hong Kong Aircraft		
International Hlds. Ltd.	OTC	CAIHY	Engineering Co. Ltd.	OTC	HKAEY
China Internet Global			Hongkong Construction		
Alliance Limited	OTC	CIGBY	(Holdings) Ltd	OTC	HKGCY
China Mobile (Hong Kong)			Hongkong Electric		
Limited	NYSE	CHL	Holdings, Limited	OTC	HGKGY
China On-Online (Bermuda)			Hongkong Land Holdings Ltd	OTC	HKHGY
Limited	OTC	COBVY	Hopewell Holdings Limited	OTC	HOWWY
China Overseas Land &			Hutchison Whampoa Limited	OTC	HUWHY
Investment Ltd.	OTC	CAOVY	Hysan Development Co., Ltd.	OTC	HYSNY
China Pharmaceutical			I-Cable Communications		
Enterprise Invest.	OTC	CHPTY	Limited	NAS	ICAB
China Resources Enterprise,			Idt International Limited	OTC	IDTTY
Limited	OTC	CREHY	Jardine Matheson		
City E-Solutions Limited	OTC	CTYSY	Holdings Limited	OTC	JARLY
City Telecom (Hk) Ltd.	NAS	CTEL	Jardine Strategic		
Clp Holdings Limited	OTC	CLPHY	Holdings Limited	OTC	JDSHY
Consolidated Electric			Jinhui Holdings		
Power Asia Ltd.	OTC	CWERY	Company Limited	OTC	JHUHY
Dairy Farm International			Johnson Electric		
Holdings Ltd.	OTC	DFIHY	Holdings Limited	OTC	JELCY
Daiwa Associate Holdings Ltd.	OTC	DAWXY	K. Wah Construction		
Eganagoldpfeil (Holdings)			Materials Limited	OTC	IPPEY
Limited	NAS	EGNI	K. Wah International		
Emperor International			Holdings Limited	OTC	KWHAY
Holdings Limited	OTC	EPRRY	Kingboard Chemical		
Emperor(China Concept)			Holdings Limited	OTC	KBDCY
Investments Ltd.	OTC	EPCHY	Legend Holdings Ltd.	OTC	LGHLY
Fairyoung Holdings Limited	OTC	FRYHY	Magician Industries		
First Pacific Company Limited	OTC	FPAFY	(Holdings) Limited	OTC	MGCIY
Frankie Dominion			Mandarin Oriental		
International Limited	OTC	FDKMY	International Ltd.	OTC	MAORY
Giordano Holdings Limited	OTC	GRDHY	New World Development		
Glorious Sun Enterprises			Company Limited	OTC	NDVLY
Limited	OTC	GSUNY	Ngai Hing Hong Company		
Gold Peak Industries			Limited	OTC	NGAKY
(Holdings) Limited	OTC	GPINY	Onfem Holdings Limited	OTC	ONHLY
Golden Resources			Online Credit International		
Development Int'l. Ltd.	OTC	GDRPY	Limited	OTC	OLCIY
Grand Hotel Holdings Limited	OTC	GHOAY	Pacific Century		
Graneagle Holdings Limited	OTC	GEGHY	Cyberworks Ltd	NYSE	PCW
Great Eagle Holdings Ltd.	OTC	GEAHY	Pacific Concord		
Great Wall Cybertech Limited	OTC	GWCBY	Holding Limited	OTC	PFCHY
Guangdong Investment Limited	OTC	GGDVY	Paul Y. - Itc Construction		
Guangnan Holdings Limited	OTC	GUGNY	Holdings Ltd.	OTC	PYCHY
Guangzhou Investment			Pearl Oriental Cyberforce		
Company Limited	OTC	GUAZY	Limited	OTC	POCFY

Company	Exchange	Symbol	Company	Exchange	Symbol
Peregrine Investments			**Ireland**		
Holdings Limited	OTC	PGIQY	Allied Irish Banks, Plc	NYSE	AIB
Recor Holdings Limited	OTC	RCRHY	Anglo Irish Bankcorp	OTC	AGIBY
Shun Tak Holdings Limited	OTC	SHTGY	Arcon International		
Sino Land Company Limited	OTC	SNLAY	Resources Plc	OTC	ARCKY
South China Morning Post			Bank of Ireland	NYSE	IRE
(Holdings) Ltd.	OTC	SCHPY	Crh Plc	NAS	CRHCY
Starlight International			Eircom Plc	NYSE	EIR
Holdings Limited	OTC	SLIEY	Elan Corporation -		
Sun Hung Kai & Co., Limited	OTC	SHGKY	Initial Warrants	NYSE	ELNWSB
Sun Hung Kai Properties Ltd.	OTC	SUHJY	Elan Corporation, Plc	NYSE	ELN
Sunday Communications			Elan Warrants	NYSE	ELNA
Limited	NAS	SDAY	Esat Telecom Group Plc	NAS	ESAT
Swire Pacific Limited A	OTC	SWRAY	Glanbia Plc	OTC	GLANB
Swire Pacific Limited B	OTC	SPCBY	Glencar Mining Plc.	OTC	GCEXY
Tai Cheung Holdings Limited	OTC	TAICY	Greencore Group	OTC	GNCGY
Techtronic Industries Company			Hibernia Foods Plc Adr	NAS	HIBNY
Limited	OTC	TTNDY	Hibernia Foods Plc		
Television Broadcasts Limited	OTC	TVBCY	Class C Warrant	NAS	HIBWF
Theme International Holdings			Hibernia Foods Plc		
Limited	OTC	THIHY	Class D Warrants	NAS	HIBZF
Tomorrow International			Icon Plc	NAS	ICLR
Holdings Limited	OTC	TIHDY	Iona Technologies Ltd.	NAS	IONA
Truly International Holdings			Jefferson Smurfit Group Plc	NYSE	JS
Limited	OTC	TRUCY	Minmet Plc	OTC	MINMY
Tung Fong Hung (Holdings)			Parthus Technologies Plc	NAS	PRTH
Limited	OTC	TGFGY	Riverdeep Group Plc	NAS	RVDP
Udl Holdings Limited	OTC	UDLHY	Ryanair Holdings Plc	NAS	RYAAY
Varitronix International Limited	OTC	VARXY	Smartforce Plc	NAS	SMTF
Vtech Holdings Limited	OTC	VTKHY	Trinity Biotech Plc	NAS	TRIBY
Wah Kwong Shipping Holdings			Trintech Group Plc	NAS	TTPA
Limited	OTC	WKSHY	Warner Chilcott Plc	NAS	WCRX
Welback Holdings Limited	OTC	WELKY	Waterford Wedgwood Plc	NAS	WATFZ
Wing Hang Bank, Ltd.	OTC	WGHGY			
Winsor Industrial Corporation			**Israel**		
Ltd	OTC	WIINY	Blue Square-Israel Ltd.	NYSE	BSI
Wo Kee Hong (Holdings)			Delta-Galil Industries Ltd.	NAS	DELT
Limited	OTC	WKHHY	Elite Industries Limited Nis 1	OTC	ELEIY
Zindart Limited	NAS	ZNDT	Elite Industries Limited Nis 5	OTC	ELEDY
			Formula Systems (1985) Ltd.	NAS	FORTY
Hungary			The Israel Land Development		
Fotex Rt	OTC	FOTXY	Company, Ltd.	NAS	ILDCY
Matav Rt	NYSE	MTA	Isras Investment		
North American Bus			Company Ltd. Nis 1	OTC	ISIMY1
Industries Rt.	OTC	NABHY	Isras Investment		
Pannonplast Rt.	OTC	PNPSY	Company Ltd. Nis 5	OTC	ISIMY5
			Koor Industries Limited	NYSE	KOR
India			Kopel Limited	OTC	KOPLY
Grasim Industries Limited	OTC	GRASM	Matav-Cable Systems Media Ltd.	NAS	MATVY
Icici Bank Ltd	NYSE	IBN	Nice Systems Ltd.	NAS	NICE
Icici Limited	NYSE	IC	Partner Communications		
Infosys Technologies Limited	NAS	INFY	Company Ltd.	NAS	PTNR
Jagatjit Industries			Super-Sol Ltd	NYSE	SAE
Silverline Technologies Ltd	NYSE	SLT	Teva Pharmaceutical		
Videsh Sanchar Nigam Limited	NYSE	VSL	Industries Ltd.	NAS	TEVA
Indonesia			**Italy**		
P.T. Indosat	NYSE	IIT	Bastogi I.R.B.S.	OTC	BATGY
P.T. Inti Indorayon Utama	OTC	PTIDE	Benetton Group S.P.A.	NYSE	BNG
P.T. Telekomunikasi	NYSE	TLK	De Rigo S.P.A.	NYSE	DER
Pasifik Satelit Nusantara	NAS	PSNRY	Ducati Motor Holding S.P.A.	NYSE	DMH
PT Jakarta Int'l Hotels &			Enel Spa	NYSE	EN
Development	OTC	PJIHY	Eni Spa	NYSE	E
			Fiat S.P.A. (Ordinary)	NYSE	FIA

Non-US Company Stocks Available in the US (continued)

Company	Exchange	Symbol	Company	Exchange	Symbol
Fiat S.P.A. (Preference)	NYSE	FIAPR	CSK Corporation	NAS	CSKKY
Fiat S.P.A. (Savings)	NYSE	FIAPRA	Dai Nippon Printing Co., Ltd.	OTC	DNPCY
Fila Holding S.P.A.	NYSE	FLH	Daibiru Corporation	OTC	DIBUY
Gucci Group Nv	NYSE	GUC	Dai'ei, Inc., The	NAS	DAIEY
Industrie Natuzzi S.P.A.	NYSE	NTZ	The Dai-Ichi Kangyo Bank, Ltd.	OTC	DAIKY
Instrumentation Laboratory			Daiwa Danchi Co., Ltd	OTC	DWADY
S.P.A.	OTC	ILABY	Daiwa House Industry Co.,Ltd.	OTC	DWAHY
Interpump Group S.P.A.	OTC	IPGMY	Daiwa Securities Group Inc.	OTC	DSECY
Istituto Bancario San Paolo			Daiwa Seiko, Inc.	OTC	DWASY
Di Torino SA	NYSE	IMI	Denso Corporation	OTC	DNZOY
Istituto Nazionale Delle			Ebara Corporation	OTC	EBCOY
Assicurazioni	OTC	INZAY	Eisai Company	OTC	ESALY
Italcementi Fabriche			Fuji Bank, Ltd., The	OTC	FUJPY
Riunite Cemento Spa	OTC	ILMNY	Fuji Heavy Industries Ltd.	OTC	FUJHY
La Rinascente S.P.A.	OTC	LARCY	Fuji Photo Film Co., Ltd.	NAS	FUJIY
Luxottica Group S.P.A.	NYSE	LUX	Fujita Corporation	OTC	FTACY
Montedison S.P.A.	NYSE	MNT	Fujitsu Limited	OTC	FJTSY
Olivetti & C., S.P.A.			Furukawa Electric Co., Ltd.	OTC	FUWAY
(Ordinary Shares)	OTC	OLVTY	Hachijuni Bank, Ltd., The	OTC	HACBY
Olivetti & C., S.P.A.			Hino Motors, Ltd.	OTC	HINOY
(Preference Shares)	OTC	OLVXY	Hitachi Cable, Ltd	OTC	HCBLY
Pirelli, S.P.A.	OTC	PIREY	Hitachi Koki Co., Ltd.	OTC	HKKIY
Saes Getters S.P.A.			Hitachi Limited	NYSE	HIT
Savings Shares	NAS	SAESY	Hitachi Metals, Ltd.	OTC	HMTLY
Snia Spa	OTC	SBPDY	Hochiki Corporation	OTC	HHKIY
Telecom Italia Savings Shares	NYSE	TIA	Hokuriku Bank, Ltd., The	OTC	HKRBY
Telecom Italia Spa	NYSE	TI	Honda Motor Co., Ltd.	NYSE	HMC
			Industrial Bank of Japan	OTC	ILBKY
Jamaica			Internet Initiative Japan Inc.	NAS	IIJI
Caribbean Cement			Isuzu Motors Ltd.	OTC	ISUZY
Company Ltd.	OTC	CRBNY	Itochu Corporation	OTC	ITOCY
Ciboney Group Ltd.	OTC	CIBOTC	Ito-Yokado Co., Ltd.	NAS	IYCOY
Jamaica Broilers	OTC	JAMB	Japan Airlines Co., Ltd.	NAS	JAPNY
Jamaica Flour Mills Ltd.	OTC	JFLRY	Japan Steel Works	OTC	JPSWY
			Japan Telecom Co., Ltd.	OTC	JPNTY
Japan			Jusco Co., Ltd.	OTC	JUSCY
Aida Engineering	OTC	ADERY	Kajima Corporation	OTC	KAJMY
Ajinomoto Company	OTC	AJINY	Kanebo, Ltd.	OTC	KABOY
Akai Electric	OTC	AKELY	Kao Corporation	OTC	KAOCY
All Nippon Airways Co. Ltd	OTC	ALNPY	Kawasaki Heavy Industries, Ltd.	OTC	KWHIY
Alps Electric Co., Ltd	OTC	APELY	Kawasaki Steel Corporation	OTC	KSKSY
Amada Co., Ltd	OTC	AMDLY	Kirin Brewery Co., Ltd	NAS	KNBWY
Amway Japan Limited	NYSE	AJL	Kobe Steel, Ltd.	OTC	KBSTY
Arisawa Manufacturing Co., Ltd.	OTC	ASWAY	Komatsu Limited	OTC	KMTSU
Asahi Bank, Ltd (The)	OTC	ASIBY	Konica Corporation	OTC	KNCAY
Asahi Chemical Industry	OTC	ASHSY	Kubota Limited	NYSE	KUB
Asahi Glass Company, Limited	OTC	ASGLY	Kumagai Gumi Co., Ltd.	OTC	KUMGY
Ashikaga Bank Ltd.	OTC	AKGBY	Kyocera Corporation	NYSE	KYO
Bandai Co. Ltd.	OTC	BNDCY	Makita Corporation	NAS	MKTAY
Bank of Fukuoka, Ltd.	OTC	BOFLY	Marubeni Corporation	OTC	MARUY
Bank of Tokyo-Mitsubishi, Ltd.	NYSE	MBK	Marui Co., Ltd.	OTC	MAURY
Bank of Yokohama	OTC	BKJAY	Matsushita Electric		
Banyu Pharmaceutical Co., Ltd	OTC	BNYUY	Industrial Co., Ltd.	NYSE	MC
Bodysonic Co., Ltd.	OTC	BDYSY	Matsushita Electric Works	OTC	MSEWY
Bridgestone Corporation	OTC	BRDCY	Meiji Seika Kaisha Limited	OTC	MSIKY
Brother Industries	OTC	BRTHY	Minebea Co., Ltd.	OTC	MNBEY
Calpis Food Industry Co.,Ltd	OTC	CPISY	Mitsubishi Chemical		
Canon Inc	NYSE	CANNY	Corporation	OTC	MUCCY
Casio Computer Company			Mitsubishi Chemical		
Limited	OTC	CSIOY	Machinery Mfg., Co.	OTC	MCMMY
Crayfish Co., Ltd.	NAS	CRFH	Mitsubishi Corporation	OTC	MSBHY
Crosswave			Mitsubishi Electric Corp	OTC	MIELY
Communications Inc.	NAS	CWCI			

Non-US Company Stocks Available in the US (continued)

Company	Exchange	Symbol	Company	Exchange	Symbol
Mitsubishi Estate			Teijin Seiki Co. Ltd.	OTC	TSERY
Company, Ltd.	OTC	MITEY	Toa Harbor Works Company		
Mitsubishi Trust &			Limited	OTC	TOAHY
Banking Corp.	OTC	MITTY	Tokai Bank Limited	OTC	TOKBY
Mitsui & Company Limited	NAS	MITSY	Tokio Marine & Fire Insurance		
Mitsui Marine and Fire I			Company	NAS	TKIOY
nsurance Company	OTC	MMFIY	Tokyo Dome Corporation	OTC	TKDOY
Mitsukoshi, Ltd.	OTC	MKOLY	Tokyu Land Corporation	OTC	TOLAY
Nagoya Railroad Co., Ltd.	OTC	NARRY	Toppan Printing Co., Ltd.	OTC	TONPY
NEC Corp.	NAS	NIPNY	Toray Industries, Inc.	OTC	TRYIY
New Japan Securities Co., Ltd	OTC	NEJSY	Toto Ltd.	OTC	TOTOY
Nifco Inc.	OTC	NIFCY	Toyo Suisan Kaisha Ltd.	OTC	TSUKY
The Nikko Securities Co., Ltd.	OTC	NIKOY	Toyobo Co., Ltd.	OTC	TYOBY
Nikon Corp.	OTC	NINOY	Toyota Motor Corporation	NYSE	TM
Nintendo Co., Ltd.	OTC	NTDOY	Trend Micro Inc.	NAS	TMIC
Nippon Shinpan Co., Ltd.	OTC	NSHPY	Tsubaki Nakashima Co., Ltd.	OTC	TSPRY
Nippon Shokubai Co., Ltd.	OTC	NSHKY	Tsugami Corporation	OTC	TSGMY
Nippon Suisan Kaisha, Ltd.	OTC	NISUY	Victor Company of Japan	OTC	VJAPY
Nippon Telegraph and			Wacoal Corporation	NAS	WACLY
Telephone Corp.	NYSE	NTT	Yamazaki Baking Co., Ltd.	OTC	YMZBY
Nippon Yusen Kabushiki Kaisha	OTC	NYUKY	Yasuda Trust and Banking		
Nissan Motor Co., Ltd.	NAS	NSANY	Co. Ltd.	OTC	YSUTY
Nisshin Steel Co., Ltd.	OTC	NHISY			
Nitto Denko Corp.	OTC	NDEKY	**Jordan**		
Nkk Corporation	OTC	NKKCY	The Housing Bank for		
Nomura Securities Co., Ltd.	OTC	NRSCY	Trade & Finance	OTC	HSBJY
Nsk Limited	OTC	NPSKY			
Ntt Docomo, Inc. Level I	OTC	NTDMY	**Kazakhstan**		
Oji Paper Company Limited	OTC	NOJIY	Kazakhtelecom	OTC	KZHXY
Olympus Optical Co., Ltd.	OTC	OLYOY			
Omega Project Inc.	OTC	OGPJY	**Korea**		
Omron Corporation	OTC	OMTEY	H & CB	NYSE	HCB
Onward Kashiyama & Co. Ltd.	OTC	OKASY	Hanaro Telecom Inc.	NAS	HANA
Orix Corporation	NYSE	IX	Korea Electric Power		
Pioneer Corporation	NYSE	PIO	Corporation	NYSE	KEP
Q.P. Corporation	OTC	QPCPY	Korea Telecom Corporation	NYSE	KTC
Ricoh Company, Ltd.	OTC	RICOY	Korea Thrunet Co., Ltd.	NAS	KOREA
Sakura Bank Limited	OTC	SAKUY	Mirae Corporation	NAS	MRAE
Sanwa Bank Limited	OTC	SANWY	Pohang Iron & Steel		
Sanyo Electric Co., Ltd.	NAS	SANYY	Company Limited	NYSE	PKX
Sanyo Securities Co., Limited	OTC	SSECY	Sk Telecom Co., Ltd.	NYSE	SKM
Sawako Corporation	NAS	SWKOY			
Secom Co., Ltd	OTC	SOMLY	**Luxembourg**		
Sega Enterprise, Ltd.	OTC	SEGNY	Anangel-American		
Sekisui House, Ltd.	OTC	SKIHY	Shipholdings Limited	NAS	ASIPY
Seven-Eleven Japan Co., Ltd.	OTC	SVELY	BT Shipping Limited	NAS	BTBT
Sharp Corporation	OTC	SHCAY	Carrier1 International S.A.	NAS	CONE
Shiseido Co., Ltd.	OTC	SSDOY	Espirito Santo Financial		
Shizuoka Bank, Ltd.	OTC	SHZUY	Holding S.A.	NYSE	ESF
Showa Sangyo Co., Ltd.	OTC	SHSGY	Security Capital Us Realty	NYSE	RTY
Sony Corporation	NYSE	SNE	Societe Europeenne		
The Sumitomo Bank, Limited	OTC	SUBJY	de Comm. S.A. A	NAS	SECAY
Sumitomo Electric Industries	OTC	SMTOY	Societe Europeenne		
Sumitomo Metal Industries, Ltd.	OTC	SMMLY	de Comm. S.A. B	NAS	SECBY
Sumitomo Trust & Banking			Stolt-Nielsen S.A.	NAS	STLBY
Co Ltd	OTC	STBUY			
Suruga Bank Limited	OTC	SUGBY	**Malaysia**		
Taiheiyo Cement Corporation	OTC	THYCY	Amsteel Corporation Berhad	OTC	AMCSY
Taisei Corporation	OTC	TISCY	Angkasa Marketing Berhad	OTC	AKAMY
Taiyo Yuden Co., Ltd.	OTC	TYOYY	Bandar Raya Developments		
TDK Corporation	NYSE	TDK	Berhad	OTC	BRYDY
Teijin Limited	OTC	TINLY	Boustead Holdings Berhad	OTC	BSTHY
			Genting Berhad	OTC	GEBHY

Non-US Company Stocks Available in the US (continued)

Company	Exchange	Symbol	Company	Exchange	Symbol
Genting Berhad	OTC	GEBEY	Grupo Imsa Units	NYSE	IMY
Inter-Pacific Industrial			Grupo Industrial Durango		
Group Berhad	OTC	IPIGY	A Cpo	NYSE	GID
Kesang Corp.			Grupo Industrial Maseca		
(Damansara Realty Bhd)	OTC	KSGCY	S.A. de C.V.	NYSE	MSK
Kuala Lumpur Kepong Berhad	OTC	KLKBY	Grupo Industrial Maseca		
Lion Land Berhad	OTC	LONLY	S.A. de C.V. A	OTC	GRIMY
Malayan United Industries			Grupo Industrial Saltillo		
Berhad	OTC	MYLUY	S.A. Series B	OTC	GISXY
Mbf Holdings Berhad	OTC	MBFHY	Grupo Iusacell, S.A. de C.V.	NYSE	CEL
Patimas Computers Berhad	OTC	PTCBY	Grupo Mexicano de Desarrollo		
Perlis Plantations Berhad	OTC	PPBHY	B Shares	OTC	GMDBY
Resorts World Berhad	OTC	RSWSY	Grupo Mexicano de		
Selangor Properties Berhad	OTC	SGPBY	Desarrollo L Shares	NYSE	GMD
Sime Darby Berhad	OTC	SIDGY	Grupo Minsa, S.A. de C.V.	OTC	GPMNY
Sime Darby Berhad	OTC	SIDBY	Grupo Pypsa B Shares	OTC	GPPSY
Tenaga Nasional Berhad	OTC	TNABY	Grupo Qumma, S.A. de C.V.	OTC	GPQMY
			Grupo Radio Centro,		
Mexico			S.A. de C.V.	NYSE	RC
Altos Hornos de Mexico, SA	NYSE	IAM	Grupo Sidek B Shares	OTC	GPSBY
Apasco, SA de Cv A	OTC	AASAY	Grupo Sidek L Shares	OTC	GPSAY
Apasco, SA de Cv B	OTC	AASBY	Grupo Simec B Shares	AMEX	SIM
Banca Quadrum Units	NAS	QDRMY	Grupo Situr B Shares	OTC	GPSRY
Banpais L Shares	OTC	BPIBY	Grupo Syr, S.A. de C.V.	OTC	GSYOTC
Biper, S.A. de C.V.	NAS	BIPRY	Grupo Televisa, S.A.	NYSE	TV
Bufete Industrial Cpo	OTC	BUFEY	Grupo Tribasa Common Shares	NYSE	GTR
Carso Global Telecom,			Hilasal Mexiciana, S.A. de C.V.	OTC	HLMXY
S.A. de C.V.	OTC	CGTVY	Hylsamex B Shares	OTC	HLETY
Cemex SA de Cv	NYSE	CX	Iem SA (Industria		
Coca-Cola Femsa L Shares	NYSE	KOF	Electrica de Mexico)	OTC	IEMSY
Consorcio G Grupo Dina L	NYSE	DINL	Industrias Bachoco Units	NYSE	IBA
Consorcio G Grupo Dina			Internacional de Ceramica		
SA de Cv	NYSE	DIN	B Shares	OTC	CEROTC
Consorcio Hogar B Shares	OTC	CSHHY	Internacional de Ceramica		
Controladora Commercial			D Shares	NYSE	ICM
Mexicana S.A.	NYSE	MCM	Jugos Del Valle SA de Cv	OTC	JUVAY
Desc, S.A. de C.V. Series C	NYSE	DES	Kimberly Clark de Mexico	OTC	KCDMY
Empaques Ponderosa,			Nadro S.A de C.V. B Shares	OTC	NADBY
S.A. de C.V.	OTC	EPQRY	Nadro S.A de C.V. L Shares	OTC	NADLY
Empresas Ica A Cpo	NYSE	ICA	Pepsi-Gemex S.A. de C.V.	NYSE	GEM
Far-Ben, S.A. de C.V.	OTC	FRBNY	Savia, S.A. de C.V.	NYSE	VAI
Fomento Economico			Telefonos de Mexico A Shares	NAS	TFONY
Mexico S.A. de C.V.	NYSE	FMX	Telefonos de Mexico S.A. de		
G Collado, S.A. de C.V.	OTC	GCLOY	C.V. Ser L	NYSE	TMX
Gruma S.A. de C.V. B Shares	NYSE	GMK	Transportacion Maritima		
Grupo Aeropuerto Del			Mexicana A	NYSE	TMMA
Sureste, SA de Cv	NYSE	ASR	Transportacion Maritima		
Grupo Carso, S.A. de C.V.	OTC	GPOOY	Mexicana L	NYSE	TMM
Grupo Casa Saba, S.A. de C.V.	NYSE	SAB	Tubos de Acero de Mexico, S.A.	AMEX	TAM
Grupo Continental			Tv Azteca, S.A. de C.V.	NYSE	TZA
Common Shares	OTC	GPOCY	Vitro, S.A. de C.V.	NYSE	VTO
Grupo Dataflux, S.A.			Wal-Mart de Mexico S.A.		
de C.V.	OTC	GDFXY	de C.V. Series C	OTC	WMMXY
Grupo Elektra Cpo	NYSE	EKT	Wal-Mart de Mexico S.A.		
Grupo Financiero			de C.V. Series V	OTC	WMMVY
Bancomer O Shares	OTC	GFNSY	Wal-Mart de Mexico S.A.		
Grupo Financiero Bbva			de C.V. Series V	OTC	WMMBY
Bancomer	OTC	GFBVY			
Grupo Financiero Bital,			**The Netherlands**		
S.A. de C.V.	OTC	GFBLY	Abn Amro Holding N.V.	NYSE	ABN
Grupo Financiero Inbursa			Aegon N.V.	NYSE	AEG
S.A. de C.V.	OTC	GPFOY	Akzo Nobel N.V.	NAS	AKZOY
Grupo Herdez B Shares	OTC	GUZBY	Arcadis N.V.	NAS	ARCAF

Non-US Company Stocks Available in the US (continued)

Company	Exchange	Symbol
Asm International	NAS	ASMI
Asm Lithography Holding, NV	NAS	ASML
Baan Company NV	NAS	BAANF
Be Semiconductor Industries NV	NAS	BESI
Buhrmann NV	OTC	BUHRY
Chicago Bridge & Iron NV NY Share	NYSE	CBI
Cnh Global N.V.	NYSE	CNH
Completel Europe N.V.	NAS	CLTL
Docdata N.V. Ny Reg Shares	NAS	DOCD
Dsm N.V.	OTC	DSMKY
Elsevier NV	NYSE	ENL
Equant NV	NYSE	ENT
Fortis N.V.	OTC	FAMVY
Head N.V.	NYSE	HED
Heineken N.V.	OTC	HINKY
Hunter Douglas N.V.	OTC	HDOUY
Ing Groep N.V.	NYSE	ING
Ispat International, N.V. NY Shares	NYSE	IST
Klm Royal Dutch Airlines	NYSE	KLM
Konink. Neder. Vlieg. Fokker N.V.	OTC	FOKKY
Koninklijke Ahold N.V.	NYSE	AHO
Koninklijke Ahold N.V. 3% Conv. Notes	OTC	AHOXX
Koninklijke Bijenkorf Beheer Kbb NV	OTC	KBBNY
Koninklijke Bolswessanen N.V.	OTC	KNKWY
Koninklijke Hoogovens N.V.	OTC	HOGVY
Koninklijke Philips Electronics N.V.	NYSE	PHG
Kpn (Ptt Nederland NV)	NYSE	KPN
Kpnqwest N.V.	NAS	KQIP
Libertel N.V.	OTC	LBTNY
Memorex Telex N.V.	OTC	MEMXY
New Skies Satellites N.V.	NYSE	NSK
Oce NV	NAS	OCENY
Royal Dutch Petroleum Co.	NYSE	RD
Royal Nedlloyd Group N.V.	OTC	RNLGY
Stmicroelectronics N.V.	NYSE	STM
Tnt Post Group N.V.	NYSE	TP
Toolex International N.V	NAS	TLXAF
Trader.Com N.V.	NAS	TRDR
Unilever N.V.	NYSE	UN
United Pan-Europe Communications N.V.	NAS	UPCOY
Van Ommeren NV	OTC	VAOSY
Verenigd Bezit N.V.	OTC	VNUNY
Versatel Telecom International N.V.	NAS	VRSA
Wolters Kluwer NV	OTC	WTKWY

Norway

Company	Exchange	Symbol
Bergesen D.Y. A/S (A Shares)	OTC	BEDAY
Bergesen D.Y. A/S (B Shares)	OTC	BEDBY
DNB Holding ASA	OTC	DNBHY
Kvaerner Asa Class A	OTC	KRVEY
Kvaerner Asa Class B	OTC	KRVBY
NCL Holding ASA	NYSE	NRW
Nera A.S.	NAS	NERAY
Norsk Hydro A/S	NYSE	NHY

Company	Exchange	Symbol
Orkla A.S. A	OTC	ORKLY
Orkla A.S. B	OTC	ORKBY
Petroleum Geo-Services A/S	NYSE	PGO
Skibsaksjeselkapet Storli	OTC	SRLIY
Smedvig A.S. A Shares	NYSE	SMVA
Smedvig A.S. B Shares	NYSE	SMVB
Tomra Systems, A/S	OTC	TOMRA
Unitor A.S.	OTC	UTORY
Viking Media A/S	OTC	VIKMY

New Zealand

Company	Exchange	Symbol
Brierley Investment Ltd.	OTC	BYINY
Evergreen Forests Limited	OTC	EVFSY
Fletcher Challenge Limited Energy	NYSE	FEG
Fletcher Challenge Ltd. Forests Div.	NYSE	FFS
Fletcher Challenge Ltd. Building	NYSE	FLB
Fletcher Challenge Ltd. Paper	NYSE	FLP
Sky Network Television Ltd.	OTC	NZSKY
Telecom Corporation of New Zealand Ltd.	NYSE	NZT
Tranz Rail Holdings Limited	NAS	TNZR

Panama

Company	Exchange	Symbol
Cerveceria Nacional, S.A.	OTC	CVNLY
Grupo Melo, S.A.	OTC	GPMLY

Peru

Company	Exchange	Symbol
Banco Wiese Limitado	NYSE	BWP
Bellsouth Peru S.A.	OTC	BSPUY
Cementos Lima	OTC	CEMTY
Compañía de Minas Buenaventura B Shares	NYSE	BVN
Ferreyros Common Shares	OTC	FERXY
Grana y Montero S.A.	OTC	GRYMY
Peru Real Estate S.A.	OTC	PERUY
Telefónica Del Peru S.A.	NYSE	TDP

Philippines

Company	Exchange	Symbol
Philippine Long Distance Telephone	NYSE	PHI
Philippine Long Distance Telephone Pref	NYSE	PHIPRA
Philodrill Corporation, The	OTC	PHLOY
Psi Technologies	NAS	PSIT
Rfm Corporation	OTC	RFMFY
San Miguel Corp.	OTC	SMGBY
United Paragon Mining Corporation	OTC	UNPGY

Papua New Guinea

Company	Exchange	Symbol
Bougainville Copper Limited	OTC	BOCOY
Oil Search Limited	OTC	OISHY

Poland

Company	Exchange	Symbol
Mostostal Export Corp.	OTC	MECOY
Netia Holdings SA	NAS	NTIA
Universal S.A.	OTC	UVSFY

Portugal

Company	Exchange	Symbol
Banco Comercial Portugues	NYSE	BPC
Cimpor-Cimentos de Electricidade de Portugal	NYSE	EDP

Non-US Company Stocks Available in the US (continued)

Company	Exchange	Symbol	Company	Exchange	Symbol
Engil-Sociedado Gestora de Participacoes	OTC	ESGPY	Bidvest Group Limited	OTC	BDVSY
Inapa-Investimentos, Partic. E Gestao	OTC	IPGXY	C.G. Smith Limited	OTC	CGSMY
Portugal Telecom	NYSE	PT	De Beers Consolidated Mines	NAS	DBRSY
			Durban Roodeport Deep Limited	NAS	DROOY
Russia			East Rand Proprietary Mines Limited	OTC	ERNDY
Bank Vozrozhdeniye	OTC	BKVZY	Egoli Consolidated Mines Limited	OTC	ELCMY
Bashinformsvyaz	OTC	BHFZY	Eskom E167	OTC	ESKA
Buryatzoloto Jsc	OTC	BYZJY	Eskom E168	OTC	ESKB
Chelyabinsk Svyazinform	OTC	CYSZY	Eskom E169	OTC	ESKC
Chernogorneft	OTC	CHRHY	Eskom E170	OTC	ESKD
Gum (A O Torgovy Dom)	OTC	GUMRY	Ettington Investments Limited	OTC	ETNVY
Irkutskenergo (Jsc)	OTC	IKSGY	Federale Mynbou Beperk	OTC	FDMBF
Jsc Rosneftegazstroy	OTC	RFGZY	Fedsure Holdings Limited Ord	OTC	FSURY
Kazan City Telephone Network	OTC	KZCTY	Fedsure Holdings Limited Preference	OTC	FSUPY
Kazanorgsintez	OTC	AKZGY	Foschini Limited	OTC	FHNIY
Khantymansiyskokrtelecom	OTC	KYKTY	Free State Development & Invest Corp.	OTC	FSDIY
Kubanelectrosvyaz (Jsc)	OTC	KBEZY	Genbel South Africa Limited	OTC	GIVLY
Kuzbassenergo (Jsc)	OTC	KZBGY	Gencor Ltd.	OTC	GNCRY
Lukoil	OTC	LUKOY	Gold Fields Limited	NAS	GOLD
Lukoil Pref	OTC	LUKPY	Gold Fields of South Africa	NAS	GLDFY
Mobile Telesystems Ojsc	NYSE	MBT	Harmony Gold Mining Company	NAS	HGMCY
Moscow City Telephone Network	OTC	MWCTY	Highveld Steel and Vanadium Corp.	NAS	HSVLY
Mosenergo (Ao)	OTC	AOMOY	Impala Platinum Holdings Limited	OTC	IMPAY
Nizhnekamskneftekhim Oao	OTC	ONKMY	Imperial Holdings Limited	OTC	IHSAY
Nizhnekamskshina	OTC	NZKMY	Investec Bank Ltd.	OTC	IVBOY
Novgorodtelecom	OTC	NVGTY	Iscor Limited	OTC	ISCRY
Primorsky Shipping Corp.	OTC	APKSY	Jd Group	OTC	JDGRY
Rostelecom	NYSE	ROS	Johnnic Holdings Limited	OTC	JICPY
Rostov Electrosvyaz	OTC	RVESY	Kolosus Holdings Limited	OTC	KOLHY
Rostovenergo	OTC	RTVGY	Liberty Group Limited	OTC	LBYLY
Rostovenergo Preferred	OTC	RTVPY	Mawenzi Resources Limited	OTC	MWZRY
Samaraenergo (Jsc) - Common	OTC	SMRGY	Messina Limited	OTC	MSNAY
Samaraenergo (Jsc) - Preferred	OTC	SMRJY	Metro Cash & Carry Ltd.	OTC	MECCY
Samarasvyazinform	OTC	SVZIY	Nampak Limited	OTC	NMPKY
Seversky Tube Works	OTC	STBWY	Nedcor Limited	OTC	NDCRY
Sibneft	OTC	SBKYY	New Wits Limited	OTC	NWITY
Surgutneftegaz	OTC	SGTZY	Ocean Diamond Mining Holdings Limited	OTC	OCDIY
Surgutneftegaz Preferred	OTC	SGTPY	Palabora Mining Company Limited	OTC	PBOMY
Tatneft (Ao)	NYSE	TNT	Pepkor Limited	OTC	PKRLY
Trading House Tsum	OTC	TDHSY	Rand Mines Limited	OTC	RADMY
Tyumenaviatrans	OTC	TYAVY	Randgold & Exploration Co. Ltd.	NAS	RANGY
Tyumentelecom Ordinary	OTC	TUYMY	Remgro Limited	OTC	RMGOY
Tyumentelecom Preferred	OTC	TUYPY	Sage Group Limited	OTC	SGGRY
Unified Energy Systems	OTC	USERY	Sappi Limited	NYSE	SPP
Unified Energy Systems of Russia	OTC	USEPY	Sasol Limited	NAS	SASOY
Uralsvyasinform (Jsc)	OTC	UVYZY	Simmer and Jack Mines Limited	OTC	SJACY
Vimpelcom (Ojsc)	NYSE	VIP	South African Land & Exploration Co.,Ltd	OTC	STHAY
South Africa			Stilfontein Gold Mining Company	OTC	STILY
Abercom Group Limited	OTC	ABGRY			
Ae and Ci Limited	OTC	AECLY			
Afrikander Lease Limited, The	OTC	AFKDY			
Anglo American Platinum Corp Ltd. 'new'	OTC	AAPTY			
Anglogold Limited	NYSE	AU			
Anglovaal Industries Ltd.	OTC	AOVIY			
Anglovaal Mining Limited	OTC	ANAVY			
Avgold Limited	OTC	AVGLY			
Barlow Limited	OTC	BRRAY			

Non-US Company Stocks Available in the US (continued)

Company	Exchange	Symbol	Company	Exchange	Symbol
Stocks & Stocks Limited	OTC	STKKY	Banco Santander Central		
Sub Nigel Gold Mining Co Ltd	OTC	SUBGY	Hispano S.A.	NYSE	STD
Tiger Brands Limited	OTC	TIOAY	Bankinter, S.A.	OTC	BKNTY
Trans Hex Group Limited	OTC	TRHXY	Corporacíon Mapfre	OTC	CRFEY
Venfin Limited	OTC	VNFNY	Empresa Nacíonal de		
Western Areas Limited	OTC	WARSY	Electricidad, S.A.	NYSE	ELE
Witwatersrand Nigel Limited	OTC	WWRNY	NH Hoteles, S.A.	OTC	NHHEY
Wooltru Limited (Ords)	OTC	WLTUY	Repsol Ypf, S.A.	NYSE	REP
Wooltru Limited Class N	OTC	WLTVY	Telefónica S.A	NYSE	TEF
Woolworths Holdings Ltd.	OTC	WWHZY	Terra Networks S.A.	NAS	TRRA

Company	Exchange	Symbol	Company	Exchange	Symbol
Singapore			**Sweden**		
Allgreen Properties Limited	OTC	AGPSY	AGA AB B Shares	OTC	AGAXY
Asia Pulp & Paper			Atlas Copco AB A Shares	OTC	ATLA
Company, Ltd.	NYSE	PAP	Atlas Copco AB B Shares	OTC	ATLPY
Asia Pulp & Paper Warrants	NYSE	PAP/WS	Biacore International AB	NAS	BCOR
Asti Holdings Limited	OTC	AIHGY	Biora AB	NAS	BIORY
Chartered Semi-Conductor			Electrolux AB	NAS	ELUX
Manufacturing	NAS	CHRT	Ericsson Telephone (LM)		
City Developments Limited	OTC	CDEVY	Debenture	NAS	ERICZ
Cosco Investment (Singapore)			Ericsson Telephone Company		
Ltd.	OTC	CSCMY	B Shares LM	NAS	ERICY
Cycle and Carriage Limited	OTC	CYCRY	Esselte AB B Shares	OTC	ESLTY
DBS Group Holdings Limited	OTC	DBSDY	Foreningssparbanken AB	OTC	FGSKY
DBS Land Limited	OTC	DBSLY	Indigo Aviation AB	NAS	IAAB
Del Monte Pacific Limited	OTC	PDMXY	Industriforvaltnings AB		
Flextech Holdings Limited	OTC	FLXHL	Kinnevik 'A'	NAS	KVIKA
GB Holdings Limited	OTC	GBHLY	Industriforvaltnings AB		
Hai Sun Hup Group Ltd.	OTC	HISHY	Kinnevik 'B'	NAS	KVIKB
IDT Holdings (Singapore)			Lundin Oil AB	NAS	LOILY
Limited	OTC	IDHSY	Modern Times Group Mtg AB	NAS	MTGNY
Inchcape Motors Limited	OTC	INCHY	Netcom AB	NAS	NECS
Keppel Corporation Ltd.	OTC	KPES	Netcom AB Class A	NAS	NECSA
Neptune Orient Lines Ltd.	OTC	NTOLY	Pricer AB	OTC	PCRBY
Overseas Union Bank, Limited	OTC	OUBLY	Sandvik AB	OTC	SAVKY
Raffles Medical Group	OTC	RAFLY	Scania AB A Shares	NYSE	SCVA
Roly International Holdings Ltd.	OTC	RYIHY	Scania AB B Shares	NYSE	SCVB
Singapore Land Limited	OTC	SINPY	Skf AB	NAS	SKFR
Singapore Telecommunications			Svenska Cellulosa		
Limited	OTC	SGTCY	Aktiebolaget (SCA)	OTC	SVCBY
ST Assembly Test Services			Swedish Match AB	NAS	SWMAY
Limited	NAS	STTS	Tele1 Europe Holding AB	NAS	TEUR
United Overseas Bank Limited	OTC	UOVEY	Volvo AB B Shares	NAS	VOLVY
United Overseas Land Limited	OTC	UNOLY			
Want Want Holdings Co., Ltd.	OTC	WWHGY	**Switzerland**		
			ABB AG	OTC	ABBAG
Slovakia			Adecco SA	NYSE	ADO
Slovnaft A.S.	OTC	SLVXF	Ciba Specialty Chemicals		
			Holding Inc.	NYSE	CSB
Spain			Compagnie Financière		
Aceralia Corp Siderurgica, S.A.	OTC	ARAXY	Richemont AG	OTC	RCHMY
Banco Bilbao Vizcaya			Credit Suisse Group	OTC	CSGKY
(Ser A Pref)	NYSE	BVG+	Holderbank Financière		
Banco Bilbao Vizcaya			Glaris Ltd	OTC	HFGCY
(Ser B Pref)	NYSE	BVGB	Logitech International S.A.	NAS	LOGIY
Banco Bilbao Vizcaya			Nestlé S.A. Registered Shares	OTC	NSRGY
(Ser C Pref)	NYSE	BVGC	Novartis AG	NYSE	NVS
Banco Bilbao Vizcaya			Roche Holdings Ltd.	OTC	RHHBY
(Ser E Pref)	NYSE	BVGE	Serono SA	NYSE	SRA
Banco Bilbao Vizcaya			SGS Société Généralé de		
Argentaria, S.A.	NYSE	BBV	Surveillance	OTC	SGSOY
Banco Español de Credito,			Sulzer Medica Ltd.	NYSE	SM
S.A. (Banesto)	OTC	BNSTY	Swiss Reinsurance Company	OTC	SWCEY
			Swisscom AG	NYSE	SCM

Company	Exchange	Symbol	Company	Exchange	Symbol
TFS	OTC	TFSLY	Astrazeneca Plc	NYSE	AZN
Zurich Allied AG	OTC	ZRHAY	Atlantic Caspian Resources Plc	OTC	ALCRE
			Autonomy Corp Plc	NAS	AUTN
Taiwan			BAA Plc	OTC	BAAPY
Macronix International			Bae Systems Plc	OTC	BAESY
Company Limited	NAS	MXICY	Baltimore Technologies Plc	NAS	BALT
Premier Image Technology			Barclays Bank Capital Note		
Corp.	OTC	PITCYP	Unit, Ser E	NYSE	BCB+
Premier Image Technology			Barclays Bank Preferred		
Reg S	OTC	PIT-	(Series C)	NYSE	BCBC
CYPREGS			Barclays Bank Preferred		
Siliconware Precision			(Series D)	NYSE	BCBD
Industries	NAS	SPIL	Barclays Plc	NYSE	BCS
Taiwan Semiconductor			Bass Plc	NYSE	BAS
Manufacturing Co.	NYSE	TSM	Bespak Plc	OTC	BPAKY
			BG Group Plc	NYSE	BRG
Thailand			Billiton Plc	OTC	BLTOY
Advanced Info Service Plc	OTC	AVIFY	Blue Circle Industries Plc	OTC	BCLEY
Asia Fiber Company Limited	OTC	ASFBY	BOC Group Plc	NYSE	BOX
Charoen Pokphand Foods Plc	OTC	CPOKY	Body Shop International Plc	OTC	BDSPY
Delta Electronics Pcl	OTC	DLETY	Booker Plc	OTC	BKERY
Hana Microelectronics Plc	OTC	HANAY	Bookham Technology Plc	NAS	BKHM
Jasmine International Plc	OTC	JASMY	Boots Company Plc, The	OTC	BOOOY
Pae (Thailand) Pcl	OTC	PATFY	BP Amoco Plc	NYSE	BP
Ptt Exploration and			Bright Station Plc	NAS	BSTN
Production Pcl	OTC	PTXPY	British Airways Plc	NYSE	BAB
Sahaviriya Steel Industries Pcl	OTC	SAVXY	British American Tobacco Plc	AMEX	BTI
Shin Corporations Public			British Bio-Technology		
Company Limited	OTC	SHNZY	Group Plc	NAS	BBIOY
Shin Satellite Public Company			British Energy Plc	NYSE	BGY
Ltd	OTC	SHSTY	British Sky Broadcasting		
Swedish Motors Corporation			Group Plc	NYSE	BSY
Public Co Ltd	OTC	SWMTY	British Telecommunications Plc	NYSE	BTY
Thai Telephone &			Bunzl Plc	NYSE	BNL
Telecommunication Pcl	OTC	TTTLY	Burmah Castrol Plc	NAS	BURMY
Total Access			Cable and Wireless		
Communication Pcl	OTC	TACPY	Communications Plc	NYSE	CWZ
Wattachak Pcl	OTC	WAPCL	Cable and Wireless Plc	NYSE	CWP
			Cadbury Schweppes P.L.C.	NYSE	CSG
Trinidad			Cantab Pharmaceuticals Plc	NAS	CNTBY
Trinidad Cement Ltd	OTC	TDDCY	Caradon Plc	OTC	CRDOY
			Carlton Communications Plc	NAS	CCTVY
Turkey			Celltech Group Plc	NYSE	CLL
Demirbank	OTC	DMRFY	Centrica Plc	OTC	CNRKY
Medya Holdings A.S.	OTC	MDYHY	Charterhall Plc	OTC	CTHAY
Net Holding Inc.	OTC	NETHY	Chloride Group Limited	OTC	CDGPY
Turkcell Iletisim			CML Microsystems Plc	OTC	CMLMY
Hizmetleri A.S.	NYSE	TKC	Coats Viyella Plc	OTC	COAVY
Turkiye Garanti Bankasi	OTC	TURKY	Colt Telecom Group Plc	NAS	COLT
			Cookson Group Plc	OTC	CKSNY
United Kimgdom			Cordiant Communications		
Abbey National Plc	OTC	ABYNY	Group Plc	NYSE	CDA
Abbey National Plc-			Corporate Service Group P.L.C.	OTC	CPSVY
Preference Share	NYSE	ANBA	Corus Group Plc	NYSE	CGA
Albert Fisher Group	OTC	AFHGY	Danka Business Systems Plc	NAS	DANKY
Allied Domecq Plc	OTC	ALDCY	Denison Hydraulics Plc	NAS	DENHY
Allied Zurich Plc	OTC	ADZHY	Diageo Plc	NYSE	DEO
Amarin Corporation Plc	NAS	AMRN	Dixons Group Plc	OTC	DXNGY
Amvescap Plc	NYSE	AVZ	Doncasters Plc	NYSE	DCS
Anglo American Plc	NAS	AAUK	Ebookers.Com Plc	NAS	EBKR
Antofagasta Plc	OTC	ANFGY	Ecsoft Group Plc	NAS	ECSG
Arcoplate Holdings Plc	OTC	APHUY	Eidos Plc	NAS	EIDSY
Arm Holdings Plc	NAS	ARMHY			
Associated British Foods Plc	OTC	ADBFY			

Non-US Company Stocks Available in the US (continued)

Company	Exchange	Symbol
Elf Aquitaine Uk (Holdings)		
Series A	OTC	ELAOTC
Series B	OTC	ELBOTC
Series C	OTC	ELCOTC
Series D	OTC	ELDOTC
Series E	OTC	ELFEOTC
Series F	OTC	ELFFOTC
Series G	OTC	ELFGOTC
Series H	OTC	ELFHOTC
Series I	OTC	ELFIOTC
Emi Group Plc	OTC	EMIPY
Energis Plc	NAS	ENGSY
Enodis Plc	NYSE	ENO
Enterprise Oil Plc	NYSE	ETP
Enterprise Oil Plc Pref. Series B	NYSE	ETPZ
Eurotunnell Plc/Eurotunnel S.A.	OTC	ETNLY
Exel Plc	AMEX	XLL
Freeserve Plc	NAS	FREE
Futuremedia Plc	NAS	FMDAY
Galen Holdings Plc	NAS	GALN
Gallaher Group Plc	NYSE	GLH
Gemini Genomics Plc	NAS	GMNI
Gentia Software Plc	NAS	GNTI
Gestetner Holdings Plc (Ordinary)	OTC	GTETY
GGT Group Plc	OTC	GGTRY
GKN Plc	OTC	GKNLY
Glaxo Wellcome Plc	NYSE	GLX
Govett Strategic Investment Trust Plc	OTC	GSVTY
Great Universal Stores Plc	OTC	GUNKY
Hanson Plc	NYSE	HAN
Hartstone Group P.L.C., The	OTC	HSTEY
Henlys Group Plc	OTC	HNLYY
Hillsdown Holdings Plc	OTC	HDWHY
Hilton Group Plc	OTC	HLTGY
HSBC		
10.25% Preferred Series B	NYSE	HBPPRB
8.875% Preferred Series A	NYSE	HBPPRA
9.125% Preferred Series C	NYSE	HBPPRC
9.55% Preferred Series D	NYSE	HBPPRD
HSBC Holdings Plc	NYSE	HBC
Huntingdon Life Sciences Group Plc	NYSE	HTD
Imperial Chemical Industries Plc	NYSE	ICI
Imperial Tobacco Group Plc	NYSE	ITY
Independent Energy Holdings Plc	NAS	INDYY
Innogy Holdings Plc	NYSE	IOG
Insignia Solutions Plc	NAS	INSGY
Interactive Investors International Plc	NAS	IINV
International Power Plc	NYSE	IPR
Invensys Plc	OTC	IVNSY
Jazztel Plc	NAS	JAZZ
JD Wetherspoon Plc	OTC	JDWPY
Johnson Matthey	OTC	JMPLY
Kingfisher Plc	OTC	KNGFY
Lasmo Plc	NYSE	LSO
Lastminute.Com	NAS	LMIN
Laura Ashley Holdings Plc	OTC	LARAY
Legal & General Group Plc	OTC	LGGNY

Company	Exchange	Symbol
Lloyds TSB Group Plc	OTC	LLDTY
London Finance and Investment	OTC	LFVGY
London Pacific Group Limited	NYSE	LDP
Lonmin Plc	OTC	LOMNY
Lonrho Africa	OTC	LNAFY
Marconi Plc	OTC	MONI
Marks & Spencer	OTC	MASPY
Merant Plc	NAS	MRNT
Millennium & Copthorne Hotels Plc	OTC	MLCTY
National Grid Company	NYSE	NGG
National Westminister Bank PrefC Shs	NYSE	NW+C
National Westminster Bank Plc	NYSE	NW
National Westminster Bank Pref B Shs	NYSE	NW+B
NDS Group Plc	NAS	NNDS
Nycomed Amersham Plc	NYSE	NYE
Omnimedia Plc	OTC	OMMDY
Pearson Plc	NYSE	PSO
Pearson Plc	OTC	PRSNY
Pearson Plc Rights	OTC	PRSQF
Peninsular and Oriental Steam Navigation	OTC	POSNY
Pittencrieff Resources Plc	OTC	PTNFY
Powergen Plc	NYSE	PWG
Premier Farnell Plc Ordinary	NYSE	PFP
Premier Farnell Plc Preference	NYSE	PFP+
Premier Oil Plc	OTC	PMOIY
Professional Staff Plc	NAS	PSTF
Proteus International Plc	OTC	POTUY
Provalis Plc	NAS	PVLSE
Prudential Corporation Plc	NYSE	PUK
Qxl.Com Plc	NAS	QXLC
Racal Electronics Plc	OTC	RCALY
Railtrack Group Plc	OTC	RTKHY
Ramco Energy Plc	AMEX	RCO
Rank Group Plc	NAS	RANKY
Redbus Interhouse Plc	OTC	RDBIY
Redland Plc	OTC	REDPY
Redland Plc (Series A)	OTC	REDPYA
Redland Plc (Series B)	OTC	REDPYB
Redland Plc (Series C)	OTC	REDPYC
Redland Plc (Series D)	OTC	REDPYD
Redland Plc (Series E)	OTC	REDPYE
Reed International Plc	NYSE	RUK
Rentokil Initial Plc	OTC	RTOKY
Reuters Group Plc	NAS	RTRSY
Rexam Plc	NAS	REXMY
Rio Tinto Plc	NYSE	RTP
Rodime Plc	OTC	RODMY
Rolls Royce Plc	OTC	RYCEY
Royal & Sun Alliance Insurance Group Plc	OTC	RSAIY
Royal Bank of Scotland Plc,		
Pref B	NYSE	RBSB
Pref C	NYSE	RBSC
Pref D	NYSE	RBSZ
Pref E	NYSE	RBSE
Pref F	NYSE	RBSF
Pref G	NYSE	RBSG
Pref H	NYSE	RBSH

Company	Exchange	Symbol
Royal Bank of Scotland,		
Pref I	NYSE	RBSI
Pref J	NYSE	RBSJ
Royal Bank of Scotland,		
Pref Series 1	NAS	RBSS1
Royal Bank of Scotland,		
Pref Series 2	NAS	RBSS2
Ryan Hotels Plc	OTC	RYHOTC
Saatchi & Saatchi Plc	NYSE	SSA
Sainsbury Plc, J.	OTC	JSNSY
Scoot.Com Plc	NAS	SCOP
Scottish & Southern		
Energy Plc	OTC	SSEZY
Scottish and Universal		
Investments Plc	OTC	SUVLY
Scottish Power Plc	NYSE	SPI
Select Software Tools Plc	NAS	SLCTY
Sema Group Plc	NAS	SEMA
Senetek Plc	NAS	SNTKY
Shell Transport & Trading		
Company Ltd	NYSE	SC
Shire Pharmaceuticals		
Group Plc	NAS	SHPGY
Signet Group Plc	NAS	SIGYY
Skyepharma Plc	NAS	SKYEY
Smallworldwide Plc	NAS	SWLDY
Smith & Nephew Plc	NYSE	SNN
Smithkline Beecham	NYSE	SBH
South African Breweries Plc	OTC	SBWUY
Spirent Plc	OTC	SPNUY
Tate and Lyle P.L.C.	OTC	TATYY
Taylor Nelson Sofres Plc	OTC	TYNLY
Telewest Communications Plc	NAS	TWSTY
Tesco Plc	OTC	TSCPY
TI Group Plc	OTC	TIGUY
Tomkins Plc	NYSE	TKS
Topjobs.Net Plc	NAS	TJOB
Townpagesnet.Com	NAS	TPN
Transport Development		
Group Ltd.	OTC	TDVGY
Trinity Mirror Plc	OTC	TNMRF
Unigate Plc	OTC	UNGAY
Unilever Plc	NYSE	UL
Union American Holdings	OTC	UA
United Biscuits (Holdings) Plc	OTC	UTBCY
United News & Media Plc	NAS	UNEWY
United Utilities Plc	NYSE	UU
Virgin Express Holdings Plc	NAS	VIRGY
Vodafone Group Plc	NYSE	VOD
Wace Group Plc	OTC	WCGRY
Wembley Plc	OTC	WMBYY

Company	Exchange	Symbol
Wiggins Group Plc	OTC	WGGGY
Williams Holdings	OTC	WL
WPP Group Plc	NAS	WPPGY
Xenova Group Plc	NAS	XNVA
Ukraine		
Azovstal	OTC	AZVSY
Dniproenergo	OTC	DNOEY
Khmelnitskoblenergo	OTC	KHMGY
Nyzhniodniprovsky Pipe		
Rolling Plant	OTC	NVTRY
Stirol	OTC	STRLY
Ukrnafta	OTC	UKRNY
Zaporozhtransformator, Ojsc	OTC	ZRTFY
Venezuela		
Banco Venezolano de Credito		
Common	OTC	BVZCY
C.A. La Electricidad de		
Caracas, SACA	OTC	ELDAY
Cantv-Nacional Telefonos		
de Venezuela	NYSE	VNT
Ceramica Carabobo A Shares	OTC	CMCJY
Ceramica Carabobo B Shares	OTC	CMCKY
Corimon C.A. S.A.C.A.	NYSE	CRM
Dominguez y Cia.		
Common Shares	OTC	DCIAY
Dominguez y Cia.		
Preferred Shares	OTC	DCIPY
F.V.I Fondo de Valores I		
nmobiliarios	OTC	FVIMY
Mantex Common Shares	OTC	MTXVY
Manufacturas de Papel,		
C.A. (Manpa)	OTC	MUPAY
Mavesa B Shares	NYSE	MAV
Mercantil Servicios		
Financieros C.A.	OTC	MSVFY
Sivensa A Shares	OTC	SDNZY
Sivensa B Shares	OTC	SDNVY
Sudamtex de Venezuela		
B Shares	OTC	SDXVY
Venepal B Shares	OTC	VNPSY
Zambia		
Zambia Consolidated Copper		
Mines Limited	OTC	ZAMBY
Zambia Copper Investments		
Limited	OTC	ZMBAY
Zimbabwe		
Mhangura Copper Mines		
Limited	OTC	MTDGY

The World's Top 50 Emerging-Market Companies

Rank	Company	Country	Market Value ($ mil.)
1	China Telecom	China	102,464
2	Taiwan Semiconductor Mfg.	Taiwan	50,034
3	Samsung Electronics	Korea	47,453
4	Telefonos de Mexico (Telmex)	Mexico	36,383
5	United Microelectronics	Taiwan	32,954
6	SK Telecom	Korea	30,388
7	Petrobrás	Brazil	24,463
8	Korea Telecom	Korea	23,218
9	Anglo American	South Africa	17,711
10	Korea Electric Power (Kepco)	Korea	17,171
11	Turkiye IS Bankasi	Turkey	15,487
12	Gazprom	Russia	14,796
13	Check Point Software Technologies	Israel	13,632
14	Cathay Life Insurance	Taiwan	12,829
15	Hindustan Lever	India	12,635
16	Hellenic Telecommunications Organization	Greece	12,349
17	Asustek Computer	Taiwan	11,572
18	Tenaga Nasional	Malaysia	11,339
19	Telekom Malaysia	Malaysia	10,984
20	Lukoil Holding	Russia	10,915
21	Telecomunicacoes de Sao Paulo (Telesp)	Brazil	10,670
22	National Bank of Greece	Greece	10,620
23	Winbond Electronics	Taiwan	10,518
24	Nan Ya Plastic	Taiwan	10,421
25	Infosys Technologies	India	10,383
26	Hon Hai Precision Industries	Taiwan	10,068
27	Telekomunikacja Polska (TPSA)	Poland	10,023
28	Malayan Banking	Malaysia	9,769
29	Vale Do Rio Doce	Brazil	9,693
30	Wipro	India	9,526
31	Wal-Mart de Mexico	Mexico	9,364
32	Banco Itau	Brazil	9,026
33	Korea Telecom Freetel	Korea	8,892
34	Eletrobras	Brazil	8,654
35	de Beers Consolidated Mines	South Africa	8,654
36	Grupo Televisa	Mexico	8,622
37	Quanta Computer	Taiwan	8,279
38	Reliance Industries	India	8,125
39	Surgutneftegaz	Russia	7,913
40	Hyundai Electronics Industries	Korea	7,697
41	China Development Industrial Bank	Taiwan	7,667
42	Legend Holdings	China	7,520
43	Formosa Plastics	Taiwan	7,342
44	Pohang Iron & Steel (POSCO)	Korea	7,261
45	Old Mutual	South Africa	7,245
46	Billiton	South Africa	7,183
47	Grupo Modelo	Mexico	7,169
48	Matav	Hungary	7,140
49	Telefonica de Argentina	Argentina	7,066
50	Tele Norte Leste Participacoes	Brazil	6,870

Source: *Business Week*; July 10, 2000

Top 25 US Trade Deficit Countries

Rank	Country	1999 US Deficit Positions ($ bil.)
1	Japan	-73.4
2	China	-68.7
3	Canada	-32.1
4	Germany	-28.4
5	Mexico	-22.8
6	Taiwan	-16.1
7	Malaysia	-12.4
8	Italy	-12.3
9	Thailand	-9.3
10	South Korea	-8.2
11	Indonesia	-7.5
12	France	-6.8
13	Venezuela	-6.0
14	India	-5.4
15	Philippines	-5.1
16	Ireland	-4.6
17	Iraq	-4.2
18	Russia	-3.9
19	Sweden	-3.9
20	Nigeria	-3.8
21	Colombia	-2.7
22	Norway	-2.6
23	Israel	-2.2
24	Angola	-2.2
25	Singapore	-1.9

Source: http://www.ita.doc.gov/td/industry/otea/usfth/-tabcon.html; July 28, 2000

Top 25 US Trade Surplus Countries

Rank	Country	1999 US Surplus Positions ($ bil.)
1	Netherlands	+10.9
2	Australia	+6.5
3	Belgium/Luxembourg	+3.8
4	Egypt	+2.4
5	Argentina	+2.3
6	Hong Kong	+2.1
7	United Arab Emirates	+2.0
8	Brazil	+1.9
9	Panama	+1.4
10	Spain	+1.1
11	Bahamas	+0.6
12	Jamaica	+0.6
13	Turkey	+0.6
14	Paraguay	+0.5
15	Greece	+0.4
16	Leeward & Windward Islands	+0.4
17	Cayman Islands	+0.4
18	Bermuda	+0.3
19	Haiti	+0.3
20	Uzbekistan	+0.3
21	Lebanon	+0.3
22	Uruguay	+0.3
23	Jordan	+0.2
24	Barbados	+0.2
25	Tunisia	+0.2

Source: http://www.ita.doc.gov/td/industry/otea/usfth/-tabcon.html; July 28, 2000

Top 25 US Supplier Countries

Rank	Country	1999 Imports ($ bil.)
1	Canada	198.7
2	Japan	130.9
3	Mexico	109.7
4	China	81.8
5	Germany	55.2
6	United Kingdom	39.2
7	Taiwan	35.2
8	South Korea	31.2
9	France	25.7
10	Italy	22.4
11	Malaysia	21.4
12	Singapore	18.2
13	Thailand	14.3
14	Philippines	12.4
15	Venezuela	11.3
16	Brazil	11.3
17	Ireland	11.0
18	Hong Kong	10.5
19	Israel	9.9
20	Switzerland	9.5
21	Indonesia	9.5
22	Belgium/Luxembourg	9.5
23	India	9.1
24	Netherlands	8.5
25	Saudi Arabia	8.3

Source: http://www.ita.doc.gov/td/industry/otea/usfth/-tabcon.html; July 28, 2000

Top 25 US Export Markets

Rank	Country	1999 Exports ($ bil.)
1	Canada	166.6
2	Mexico	86.9
3	Japan	57.5
4	United Kingdom	38.4
5	Germany	26.8
6	Korea	23.0
7	Netherlands	19.4
8	Taiwan	19.1
9	France	18.9
10	Singapore	16.2
11	Belgium/Luxembourg	13.4
12	Brazil	13.2
13	China	13.1
14	Hong Kong	12.7
15	Australia	11.8
16	Italy	10.1
17	Malaysia	9.1
18	Switzerland	8.4
19	Saudi Arabia	7.9
20	Israel	7.7
21	Philippines	7.2
22	Ireland	6.4
23	Spain	6.1
24	Venezuela	5.4
25	Thailand	5.0

Source: http://www.ita.doc.gov/td/industry/otea/usfth/-tabcon.html; July 28, 2000

The 25 Largest Foreign Investors in the US

Rank	Company	Country	US Investment(s)	% owned	Revenue ($ mil.)
1	DaimlerChrysler AG	Germany	DaimlerChrysler Corp. Freightliner Mercedes-Benz US Intl.	100 100 100	86,071
2	BP Amoco Plc	UK	BP Amoco Atlantic Richfield	100 100	51,841
3	Royal Ahold	Netherlands	Ahold USA US Foodservice	100 100	25,542
4	Sony	Japan	Sony Music Entertainment Sony Pictures Entertainment Sony Electronics	100 100 100	21,117
5	Royal Dutch/Shell Group	Netherlands/UK	Shell Oil	100	18,438
6	Toyota Motor	Japan	Toyota Motor Mfg. New United Motor Mfg.	100 50	17,863*
	Denso	Japan	Denso International America	100	
7	Diageo	UK	Burger King Pillsbury United Distiller & Vintners (US)	100 100 100	17,539
8	ING Group	Netherlands	ING North America Insurance ING Barings (US)	100 100	14,997
9	Deutsche Bank AG	Germany	Deutsche Bank Americas DB Alex Brown	100 100	14,500*
10	Tyco International	Bermuda	Tyco International (US)	100	14,409
11	Siemens AG	Germany	Siemens US	100	14,350
12	Vodafone AirTouch	UK	Verizon Wireless	45	14,000*
13	AXA Group	France	AXA Financial	60	13,371
14	Petróleos de Venezuela	Venezuela	Citgo Petroleum	100	13,317
15	Honda Motor	Japan	Honda of America Mfg.	100	13,100*
16	Nestlé SA	Switzerland	Nestlé USA Alcon Laboratories	100 100	12,799
	L'Oréal	France	Cosmair (US)	100	
17	Nortel Networks	Canada	Nortel Networks (US)	100	12,758
18	Delhaize "Le Lion" SA	Belgium	Delhaize America Super Discount Markets	44 60	11,194
19	E.On	Germany	VEBA (US) Viag (N. America)	100 100	11,132
20	Aegon NV	Netherlands	Aegon USA	100	11,083
21	Zurich Allied/Allied Zurich Zurich Financial Services	Switzerland/UK Switzerland	Zurich Group (US) Farmers Group Scudder Kemper Investments Zurich Reinsurance Centre	100 100 73 100	11,075
22	ABN Amro Holding	Netherlands	ABN Amro (N. America) European American Bank ABN Amro Chicago	100 100 100	10,965
23	Prudential Corp Plc	UK	Jackson National Life Jackson National Life of NY	100 100	10,619
24	News Corp.	Australia	News America	100	10,163
25	Tengelmann	Germany	Great A&P Tea Co.	55	9,993

* Estimate

Source: *Forbes;* July 24, 2000

Hoover's Handbook of World Business

The Company Profiles

ABB LTD.

ABB flexes its abs in energy, engineering, and technology. The diversified company, which is based in Zurich, operates through six segments (power transmission, power distribution, automation, petroleum products, building contracting, and financial services) and owns about 600 facilities in more than 100 countries.

Its automation division develops special products and systems to help customers with their manufacturing and production processes, while its building technologies division creates products and systems for specialized plant design and maintenance. ABB's power transmission and distribution services have been expanding into emerging areas in Africa, Asia, Eastern Europe, and Latin America, where infrastructure and energy plant construction is booming. The petroleum division works with customers such as Chevron, Exxon Mobil, and Shell to develop cleaner fuels. ABB's financial operations provide funding and risk management services for its own companies and for outside customers.

The two holding companies that formerly controlled ABB — ABB AB of Sweden and ABB AG of Switzerland — were combined into one, ABB, in 1999.

HISTORY

Asea Brown Boveri (ABB) was formed in 1988 when two lackluster giants, ASEA AB of Sweden and BBC Brown Boveri of Switzerland, combined their electrical engineering and equipment businesses. Percy Barnevik, head of ASEA, became CEO.

ASEA was born in Stockholm in 1883 when Ludwig Fredholm founded Electriska Aktiebolaget to manufacture an electric dynamo created by engineer Jonas Wenstrom. In 1890 the company merged with Wenstrom's brother's firm to form Allmanna Svenska Electriska Aktiebolaget (ASEA), a pioneer in industrial electrification. Early in the 1900s ASEA began its first railway electrification project. By the 1920s it was providing locomotives and other equipment to Sweden's national railway, and by the next decade ASEA was one of Sweden's largest electric equipment manufacturers. In 1962 it bought 20% of appliance maker Electrolux. ASEA created the nuclear power venture ASEA-ATOM with the Swedish government in 1968 and bought full control in 1982.

BBC Brown Boveri was formed in 1891 as the Brown, Boveri, and Company partnership between Charles Brown and Walter Boveri in Baden, Switzerland. It made power-generation equipment and produced the first steam turbines in Europe in 1900. BBC entered Germany (1893), France (1894), and Italy (1903) and diversified into nuclear power equipment after World War II.

By 1988 BBC, the bigger company, had a West German network that ASEA, the more profitable company, coveted. Both had US joint ventures. In an unusual merger, ASEA (which became ABB AB) and BBC (later ABB AG) continued as separate entities sharing equal ownership of ABB. Barnevik crafted a unique decentralized management structure under which national subsidiaries were closely linked to their local customers and labor forces. In six years ABB took over more than 150 companies worldwide.

In 1995 ABB merged its transportation segment into Adtranz (a joint venture with Daimler-Benz, now DaimlerChrysler) to form the world's #1 maker of trains. Tragedy struck in 1996. Robert Donovan, CEO of ABB's US subsidiary, died in a plane crash along with Commerce Secretary Ron Brown and other executives on a trade mission. Donovan's death hastened the US unit's restructuring.

In 1997 Barnevik gave up the title of CEO, remaining as chairman, and was succeeded by Göran Lindahl, an engineer who had worked his way up the ranks at ASEA. Meanwhile, after 1997 profits dipped drastically, Lindahl scrapped Barnevik's vaunted regional matrix structure in favor of one organized by product areas under a strong central management. Though the Asian financial crisis slowed orders, ABB still pulled in large contracts, including one to build the world's largest cracker plant in Texas in 1998.

In 1999 ABB acquired Elsag Bailey, a Dutch maker of industrial control systems, for about $1.5 billion, and sold its 50% stake in Adtranz to DaimlerChrysler for about $472 million. ABB and France's Alstom combined their power generation businesses to form the world's largest power plant equipment maker. That year ABB AB and ABB AG were at last united under a single stock.

ABB scaled back its power plant-related activities in 2000. The company sold its nuclear power business to BNFL for $485 million and sold its 50% stake in ABB Alstom Power to Alstom for $1.2 billion. Lindahl announced plans to resign that year, and Jörgen Centerman, head of the company's automation business, was named to replace him.

Chairman: Percy N. Barnevik
VC: Robert A. Jeker
President and CEO: Göran Lindahl, age 55
EVP and CFO: Renato Fassbind, age 45
EVP Automation: Jörgen Centerman, age 48
EVP Building Technologies: Armin Meyer, age 51
EVP Financial Services: Jan Roxendal, age 47
EVP Oil, Gas, and Petrochemicals: Gorm Gundersen, age 55
EVP Power Transmission and Power Distribution: Sune Karlsson, age 54
Senior Corporate Officer, Research and Development and Technology: Markus Bayegan
Corporate Communications: Bjorn Edlund
Human Resources: Rene Lichtsteiner
Investor Relations: Manfred Ebling
Auditors: KPMG Klynveld Peat Marwick Goerdeler SA; Ernst & Young AG

HQ: Affolternstrasse 44, CH-8050 Zurich, Switzerland
Phone: +41-1-317-7111   **Fax:** +41-1-317-7321
US HQ: 501 Merritt 7, Norwalk, CT 06851
US Phone: 203-750-2200   **US Fax:** 203-750-2263
Web site: http://www.abb.com

ABB operates through about 600 companies in more than 100 countries.

1999 Sales

	SF mil.	% of total
Europe	22,426	57
North & South America	9,265	24
Asia/Pacific & South Asia	4,535	11
Middle East & Africa	3,219	8
Total	**39,445**	**100**

1999 Sales

	SF mil.	% of total
Automation	13,216	34
Building technologies	10,105	26
Power transmission	5,956	15
Oil, gas & petrochemicals	4,942	13
Power distribution	4,582	11
Financial services	564	1
Other	80	—
Total	**39,445**	**100**

Selected Products and Services
Automation power products (drives, motors, electronics)
Cables
Design, installation, and maintenance of electrical and ventilation systems and complete infrastructure
Flexible automation and robotics products and systems
High-voltage products and substations
Industrial fans and ventilation products and systems
Leasing and financing
Power generation systems
Power network management services
Project management and financing of infrastructure
Refineries and petrochemical plants
Subsea production systems
Transformers

AIG	Hitachi	Nippon Steel
Alstom	Ingersoll-Rand	Peter Kiewit
Bechtel	Johnson Controls	Sons'
BHP	Mannesmann AG	Rolls-Royce
Fluor	Mark IV	Siemens
GE	McDermott	SPX
Halliburton	Mitsubishi	Toshiba

Swiss: ABBN FYE: December 31	Annual Growth	12/90	12/91	12/92	12/93	12/94	12/95	12/96	12/97	12/98	12/99
Sales (SF mil.)	1.6%	34,081	29,768	39,165	42,992	38,887	38,944	45,298	45,705	42,458	39,445
Net income (SF mil.)	14.7%	753	481	866	906	994	1,518	1,654	836	1,795	2,579
Income as % of sales	—	2.2%	1.6%	2.2%	2.1%	2.6%	3.9%	3.7%	1.8%	4.2%	6.5%
Earnings per share (SF)	—	—	—	—	—	—	—	—	—	—	8.90
Stock price - FY high (SF)	—	—	—	—	—	—	—	—	—	—	195.00
Stock price - FY low (SF)	—	—	—	—	—	—	—	—	—	—	135.75
Stock price - FY close (SF)	—	—	—	—	—	—	—	—	—	—	194.75
P/E - high	—	—	—	—	—	—	—	—	—	—	22
P/E - low	—	—	—	—	—	—	—	—	—	—	15
Dividends per share (SF)	—	—	—	—	—	—	—	—	—	—	4.79
Book value per share (SF)	—	—	—	—	—	—	—	—	—	—	29.88
Employees	(3.0%)	215,154	214,399	213,407	206,490	207,557	209,637	214,894	213,057	199,232	164,154

HIGH/LOW/CLOSE

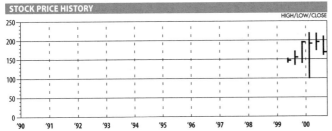

Debt ratio: 35.9%
Return on equity: 29.3%
Cash (SF mil.): 10,049
Current ratio: 1.13
Long-term debt (SF mil.): 5,014
No. of shares (mil.): 300
Dividends
  Yield: 0.0%
  Payout: 0.5%
Market value ($ mil.): 58,425

ABN AMRO HOLDING N.V.

ABN AMRO must be Dutch for banking. Although ING Groep is the #1 financial services company in the Netherlands, Amsterdam-based ABN AMRO is the country's top bank. On its home turf, ABN AMRO provides consumer, corporate, and private banking services through a 900-branch network. Overseas it operates some 2,600 other offices in 75 countries and counting.

The Netherlands' financial giants are victims of their tiny country's success, and have had to move overseas in order to grow. As a result of aggressive expansion in Europe and other regions, ABN AMRO has begun to prune its operations by culling its international retail network. As part of this effort it is reorganizing along business lines to facilitate global seamless service for its multinational clientele.

The company remains undaunted by recent turmoil in emerging markets where other banks now fear to tread — it has a large presence in Brazil through its 88% interest in Banco Real and Malaysia (where it has operated for more than 100 years) and has picked up operations in Manila, India, Singapore, Taiwan, and Thailand.

HISTORY

ABN AMRO comes by its initials honestly. It is the product of a 1991 merger between the Netherlands' #1 and #2 banks — Algemene Bank Nederland (ABN) and Amsterdam-Rotterdam Bank (AMRO), respectively — and a final amalgamation of what were the four top banks in the Netherlands.

The Netherlands Trading Society was founded in 1824 to finance business ventures in the Dutch colonies, operating from an office in what is now Jakarta, Indonesia. The company moved into agricultural financing and commercial banking and acquired several banks in the early 1900s. Although it weathered WWI and the Depression, WWII was catastrophic — Germany occupied the homeland and Japan took over the Dutch East Indies.

The Netherlands Trading Society never recovered and in 1964 it merged with Twentsche Bank (founded in 1861 as an agricultural bank) to form Algemene Bank Nederland. ABN's chief rival was AMRO, product of the 1964 merger of Amsterdam Bank and Rotterdam Bank. Founded in 1863, Rotterdam Bank financed commercial activity in the colonies before refocusing on the shipping business through Rotterdam. The Amsterdam Bank was founded in 1871 by several Dutch and German banks and was the largest Dutch bank when it merged with Incasso Bank in 1948. In 1964 the new entity added the operations of Hollandsche Bank - Unie.

ABN was smaller than AMRO until it bought merchant bank Mees & Hope (1975) followed by the purchase of Chicago-based LaSalle National Bank (1979). ABN had retreated so far from its colonial roots that it was largely unscathed by the mass default of Third World banks in 1987. AMRO followed a different path, financing oil and gas exploration and construction on the English Channel Tunnel.

ABN and AMRO merged in 1991 and the new company turned its attention overseas, concentrating on the American Midwest, where LaSalle National Bank was gobbling up competitors like Talman Home Federal Savings (1991). ABN AMRO also took control of European American Bank (EAB), which had sustained heavy losses on bad real estate and Third World loans. It bought investment banks Chicago Corp. and Alfred Berg in 1995.

Expansion brought internal oversight problems during the next few years: In 1995 Swiss banking authorities asked ABN AMRO to better police its branches there after the bank lost as much as $124 million to embezzlement. In 1997 the firm closed its diamond office after losing about $100 million to fraud.

In 1998 ABN AMRO bought Brazil's Banco Real and Bandepe banks (and then closed their European and US offices). The next year it began buying minority interests in Italian banks. Also in 1999 the company elected to become a major force in European real estate with the acquisition of Bouwfonds Nederlandse Gemeenten, the Netherlands' #5 mortgage lender. As part of this effort, it expanded its mortgage servicing portfolio with the purchase of Pitney Bowes subsidiary Atlantic Mortgage & Investment Corp.

In 2000 ABN AMRO planned to cut 150 branches in its overbanked home market (along with about 10% of its Dutch workforce). It bought the energy-derivative business of Merrill Lynch and agreed to buy 25% of BlueStone Capital Partners, with the intention of boosting its growing Web presence via an Internet brokerage through BlueStone's Trade.com subsidiary. The company also agreed to buy Barclays' Dial car-leasing unit and Alleghany Corporation's asset management unit.

Chairman Supervisory Board: A. A. Loudon, age 63
VC Supervisory Board: Hans van Liemt
Chairman Managing Board: R. W. J. Groenink, age 50
Member Managing Board European Division:
J. M. de Jong, age 54
Member Managing Board International Division:
J. Ch. L. Kuiper, age 53
Member Managing Board Investment Banking Division:
R. W. F. van Tets, age 53
Member Managing Board Investment Banking Division:
W. G. Jiskoot, age 49
Member Managing Board, Risk Management Division
and CFO: T. de Swaan, age 54
Member Managing Board Resources Management
Division: R. G. C. van den Brink, age 52
SEVP Business Development European Division:
C. M. A. Collee
SEVP Operations European Division: G. B. J. Hartsink
SEVP International Branch Network and COO,
International Division: J. J. Oyevaar
CEO North America International Division:
H. F. Tempest
Auditors: Ernst & Young

HQ: Foppingadreef 22, 1102 BS Amsterdam,
The Netherlands
Phone: +31-20-628-9898   Fax: +31-20-628-1229
US HQ: 135 S. La Salle St., Ste. 625, Chicago, IL 60603
US Phone: 312-904-2920   US Fax: 312-606-8425
Web site: http://www.abnamro.com

ABN AMRO Holdings and its subsidiaries have some
3,500 offices, with operations in Africa, the Americas,
Asia, Australia, Europe, and the Middle East.

Selected Subsidiaries
AA Interfinance B. V.
AAGUS Financial Services Group N.V.
ABN AMRO Asia (Hong Kong)
ABN AMRO Asset Management Ltd. (UK)
ABN AMRO Banc (Morocco)
ABN AMRO Bank (Russia)
ABN AMRO Bank (Poland)
ABN AMRO Bank (Kazakstan) Ltd. (51%)
ABN AMRO Corporate Finance (UK)
ABN AMRO France S.A. (88%)
ABN AMRO Lease Holding N. V.
ABN AMRO Leasing (Hellas) S.A. (Greece)
ABN AMRO North America, Inc. (60%)
    LaSalle National Corporation
ABN AMRO Savings Bank, Manila (60%)
ABN AMRO Securities (India) Private Ltd. (75%)
ABN AMRO Yatyrym Menkul Degerter A.S. (Turkey)
ABN AMRO Bouwfonds Nederlandse (50%)
Alfred Berg Holding A/B (Sweden)
Banco ABN AMRO Real S. A. (88%; Brazil)
Hollandsche Bank-Unie N.V.
PT ABN AMRO Financie Indonesia (85%)
Saudi Hollandi Bank (40%, Saudi Arabia)

Banco Bilbao	Dai-Ichi Kangyo
Bank Nederlandse	Deutsche Bank
Gemeenten	Dresdner Bank
Bank of Tokyo-Mitsubishi	Harris Bankcorp
BANK ONE	Heller Financial
Caisse Nationale de Credit	HSBC Holdings
Agricole	ING
CCF	Northern Trust
Citigroup	Rabobank Group
Credit Suisse	Société Générale

NYSE: ABN FYE: December 31	Annual Growth	12/90	12/91	12/92	12/93	12/94	12/95	12/96	12/97	12/98	12/99
Assets ($ mil.)	9.4%	—	—	246,577	252,131	290,936	339,773	344,418	412,867	503,896	462,097
Net income ($ mil.)	15.9%	—	—	926	1,039	1,318	1,626	1,911	1,902	2,132	2,594
Income as % of assets	—	—	—	—	—	—	0.5%	—	0.5%	0.4%	0.6%
Earnings per share ($)	15.8%	—	—	—	—	—	—	—	1.29	1.42	1.73
Stock price - FY high ($)	—	—	—	—	—	—	—	—	24.44	27.56	25.81
Stock price - FY low ($)	—	—	—	—	—	—	—	—	18.25	14.25	19.00
Stock price - FY close ($)	13.9%	—	—	—	—	—	—	—	19.50	21.75	25.31
P/E - high	—	—	—	—	—	—	—	—	19	19	15
P/E - low	—	—	—	—	—	—	—	—	14	10	11
Dividends per share ($)	—	—	—	—	—	—	—	—	0.00	0.29	0.65
Book value per share ($)	(25.2%)	—	—	—	—	—	—	—	14.73	8.67	8.24
Employees	9.0%	—	—	59,639	60,451	62,181	63,694	66,172	74,935	105,826	108,689

HIGH/LOW/CLOSE

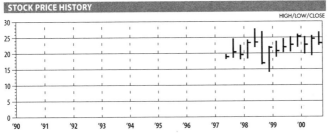

Equity as % of assets: 2.6%
Return on assets: 0.5%
Return on equity: 22.8%
Long-term debt ($ mil.): 115,619
No. of shares (mil.): 1,468
Dividends
  Yield: 2.6%
  Payout: 37.6%
Market value ($ mil.): 37,159
Sales ($ mil.): 36,232

ACCOR

OVERVIEW

Most would agree that A-c-c-o-r spells hospitality in French. Evry, France-based Accor is one of the world's largest hoteliers, with 3,300 hotels in 140 countries. Its hotel brand names include the luxury Sofitel chain; the moderate Novotel and Mercure; and the budget Etap Hotel, Formule 1, Ibis, and US-based Motel 6 and Red Roof Inns.

Accor owns 50% of one of the world's largest travel agency networks, operating as Carlson Wagonlit Travel (the US's Carlson Companies owns the other half). In addition, the firm is a leading distributor of service vouchers, which provide prepaid access to restaurants, transportation, child care, med-

ical care, and other services. Other lines of business include car rentals (Europcar), casino operations (Accor Casinos), catering and restaurants (Lenôtre, Courtepaille), and sleeper car and onboard catering (Wagons-Lits).

With more than one-third of Accor's hotels located in North America, the company is looking to expand in underdeveloped markets, primarily in Asia, South America, and Africa. It also is growing its casino business in Africa, the Mediterranean, and Northern Europe. In its travel sector, the company is investing €100 million to get its Carlson Wagonlit operations online.

HISTORY

Until Gérard Pélisson and Paul Dubrule built their first hotel in 1967, French hotels were generally quaint old inns or expensive luxury hotels. Pélisson and Dubrule's Novotel introduced mid-priced hotels based on the American model. The pair opened the Ibis Hotel in 1973 and bought the Mercure chain in 1975.

By 1979, when it opened its first US hotel in Minneapolis, Novotel was Europe's #1 hotel chain, operating 184 hotels on four continents.

Dubrule and Pélisson married their growing hotel business to Jacques Borel International, forming publicly traded Accor in 1983. Jacques Borel had started out with one restaurant in 1957 and was Europe's #1 restaurateur by 1975, when he took over Belgium's Sofitel chain of luxury hotels. Losses in the hotel game prompted Borel to sell Sofitel to Dubrule and Pélisson in 1980, making their company one of the world's top 10 hotel operators — a list traditionally dominated by US chains. They picked up the rest of Borel's empire in 1983, launching Accor into the restaurant business.

Accor began offering packaged vacations in 1984, after buying a majority stake in Africatours (Africa's largest tour operator), then expanded into the South Pacific, Asia, and the Americas by buying Islands in the Sun (1986), Asia Tours (1987), and America Tours (1987).

The company opened its first budget hotels (Formule 1) in France in 1985. Accor started marketing Paquet cruises in 1986 and formed the Hotelia and Parthenon chains (Brazilian residential hotels) the next year.

Faced with a mature European market and eager to take advantage of favorable exchange rates, Accor bought Dallas-based budget chain Motel 6 (along with its high debts and poor reputation, which Accor began remedying with

an expensive renovation program) in 1990. The next year Accor bought US-based Regal Inns (now part of Motel 6).

Also in 1990 Accor joined Société Générale de Belgique to buy 26.7% of Belgium's Wagons-Lits, owner of about 300 hotels in Europe, Thailand, and Indonesia, as well as restaurants, caterers, and travel agencies in Europe. After a battle involving both Belgian and EC antitrust officials, Accor was allowed to buy a majority stake of Wagons-Lits.

This buy — along with Accor's attempt to increase its share of the luxury market, the continuing burden of its US purchases, and a recession in the travel business — took a financial toll. In response, it began selling assets in 1994, ridding itself of expensive hotel real estate. The company also sold some of its Wagons-Lits operations in the Netherlands.

In 1997 co-chairmen Dubrule and Pélisson retired from active management and were succeeded by Jean-Marc Espalioux, formerly of Générale des Eaux (now Vivendi). As part of its strategy to continue to expand internationally, Accor reached an agreement that year with the Moroccan government to develop that country's hotel industry. In 1999 Accor continued hotel acquisitions with US chain Red Roof Inns and hotels in Holland, Poland, Sweden, Finland, and France. The following year the company opened a luxury Sofitel hotel in downtown Manhattan and began developing other Sofitels in Dallas, Chicago, and Washington, DC.

Co-Chairman, Supervisory Board: Paul Dubrule
Co-Chairman, Supervisory Board: Gérard Pélisson
Chairman, Management Board and CEO: Jean-Marc Espalioux
Member, Management Board Hotel: Sven Boinet
Member, Management Board, Finance and Holdings: Benjamin Cohen
Member, Managment Board, Services and Human Resources: John Du Monceau
President and CEO, Accor North America: John Lehodey
Corporate Secretary: Pierre Todorov
General Controller: Thierry Gaches
Director Human Resources: Volker Buring
Director Communications: Jaques Charbit
Director Financial Resources: Eliane Rouyer
Legal Director: Jean-Paul Ribert
Group Treasury Director: Christian Gary
Auditors: Deloitte Touche Tohmatsu

HQ: 2, rue de la Mare Neuve, 91021 Evry Cedex, France
Phone: +33-1-69-36-80-80   Fax: +33-1-69-36-79-00
US HQ: 245 Park Ave. South, New York, NY 10167
US Phone: 212-949-5700   US Fax: 212-490-0499
Web site: http://www.accor.com

1999 Sales

	% of total
Europe	
France	37
Other countries	34
North America	20
Latin America	7
Other regions	2
Total	**100**

1999 Sales

	% of total
Hotels	62
Restaurants	8
Travel agencies	7
Car rental	6
Corporate services	6
On-board train services	5
Casinos & other	6
Total	**100**

Selected Hotel Chains

Etap Hotel	Motel 6 (US)
Formule 1	Novotel
Ibis	Red Roof Inns (US)
Mercure	Sofitel

Selected Other Activities
Car rentals (Europcar, partnership with Volkswagen)
Casinos (Accor Casinos)
Institutional catering (Gemeaz Cuzin, Lenôtre)
Railway onboard services (Wagons-Lits)
Restaurants (Courtepaille)
Tour operators (Accor Tour, Couleurs Locales, Frantour)
Travel agencies (50%, Carlson Wagonlit Travel)

American Express	Helmsley Hilton	Movenpick Holding
Avis Europe	Hilton Group	Ritz Carlton
Bass	Hyatt	Sixt
Cendant	La Quinta Inns	Starwood Hotels
Euro Disney	Lufthansa	& Resorts
Ford	Marriott	Worldwide
Four Seasons Hotels	International	Thomas Cook

Euronext Paris: AC FYE: December 31	Annual Growth	12/90	12/91	12/92	12/93	12/94	12/95	12/96	12/97	12/98	12/99
Sales (€ mil.)	12.6%	2,100	2,126	4,494	5,006	5,103	4,728	4,315	4,845	5,622	6,101
Net income (€ mil.)	9.7%	153	145	122	48	108	141	161	230	297	351
Income as % of sales	—	7.3%	6.8%	2.7%	1.0%	2.1%	3.0%	3.7%	4.7%	5.3%	5.8%
Earnings per share (€)	5.3%	1.22	1.10	1.10	0.79	0.87	0.98	1.04	1.29	1.66	1.94
Stock price - FY high (€)	—	32.84	25.64	25.37	22.44	23.36	20.73	24.45	36.37	54.42	50.36
Stock price - FY low (€)	—	19.00	17.57	14.45	17.07	15.37	15.89	18.48	19.24	27.47	34.40
Stock price - FY close (€)	9.8%	20.70	19.79	18.75	18.08	17.68	19.33	20.03	34.12	36.89	47.97
P/E - high	—	27	23	23	28	27	21	24	28	33	26
P/E - low	—	16	16	13	22	18	16	18	15	17	18
Dividends per share (€)	7.7%	0.46	0.49	0.55	0.55	0.55	0.61	0.61	0.70	0.70	0.90
Book value per share (€)	4.0%	13.13	17.56	16.71	20.49	19.66	16.95	16.49	16.93	16.97	18.67
Employees	13.3%	41,976	45,743	144,093	143,740	146,931	120,668	124,378	121,396	126,908	128,850

HIGH/LOW/CLOSE

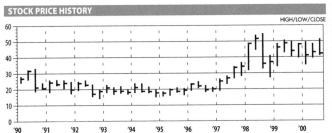

Debt ratio: 0.4%
Return on equity: 10.8%
Cash (€ mil.): 488
Current ratio: 0.88
Long-term debt (€ mil.): 2,633
No. of shares (mil.): 185
Dividends
  Yield: 0.0%
  Payout: 0.5%
Market value ($ mil.): 8,898

ACER INC.

OVERVIEW

Stan Shih has set his Acer on stunned. Hsichih, Taiwan-based Acer is a leading worldwide PC maker. Its business units also make notebooks, computer chips, peripherals, CD-ROM drives, motherboards, and networking products, among others. The company sells under its own brand and derives additional income by making computers for companies such as Compaq, Fujitsu, and Hitachi.

Founder and CEO Shih, long an advocate of using speed to competitive advantage, has been forced to shutter assembly factories, disabling a global manufacturing model that positioned plants next to end markets.

Weakened in a competitive PC market, Acer is restructuring beyond its hardware heritage to become a maker of products for the telecom (digital communications devices) and e-commerce (Internet access appliances) markets, and expanding into Internet start-up funding and other ventures. It has also cut back its retail business in North America (40% of sales) to focus on China and other Asian markets.

HISTORY

Acer founder and chairman Stan Shih, respected enough for his business acumen to once be considered for the premiership of Taiwan, designed that country's first desktop calculator in the early 1970s. The company's precursor, Multitech International, was launched in 1976 with $25,000 by Shih and four others who called themselves the "Gardeners of Microprocessing." In 1980 Multitech introduced the Dragon Chinese-language CRT terminal, which won Taiwan's top design award; in 1983 it introduced an Apple clone and its first IBM-compatible PC. Multitech set up AcerLand, Taiwan's first and largest franchised computer retail chain, in 1985.

The company changed its name to Acer (the Latin word for "sharp, acute, able, and facile") in 1987 and went public on the Taiwan exchange the next year. Acer got into the semiconductor market in 1989 when it entered into a joint venture with Texas Instruments (named TI-Acer) to design and develop memory chips in Taiwan. In 1990 Acer's US subsidiary, Acer America, paid $90 million for Altos Computer Systems, a US manufacturer of UNIX systems.

During the prosperous 1980s Acer increased its management layers and slowed the decision-making process. In late 1990 the company restructured, trimming its workforce by 8% (about 400 employees), including two-thirds of headquarters. The layoff was unprecedented — being asked to resign from a job in Taiwan carries a social stigma. Shih wrote a letter to all those affected, explaining the plight of the company. The following year Acer began its decentralization plan to create a worldwide confederation of publicly owned companies.

Acer suffered its first loss in 1991 on revenues of almost $1 billion, partly because of increased marketing budgets in the US and Europe and continuing investment in TI-Acer.

The company bounced back in 1993, with 80% of its profit coming from that joint venture.

The Aspire PC, available in shades of gray and green, was unveiled in 1995. In 1996 the company expanded into consumer electronics, introducing a host of new, inexpensive videodisc players, video telephones, and other devices in order to boost global market share. In 1997 Acer purchased TI's notebook computer business. A slowdown in memory chip sales, plus a financial slide at Acer America, cost the firm $141 million, but Acer finished the year in the black.

In 1998 Shih stepped down as president to focus on restructuring. The company ended its venture with TI, buying TI's 33% stake and renaming the unit Acer Semiconductor Manufacturing. The company also began making information appliances, introducing a device able to play CD-ROMs via TV sets and perform other task-specific functions. Continued losses due to a highly competitive US market caused a drop in profits for 1998.

In 1999 Acer sold a 30% stake in its struggling Acer Semiconductor Manufacturing (renamed TSMC-Acer Semiconductor Manufacturing) affiliate to Taiwan Semiconductor Manufacturing Corp. (it is buying the rest). The competitive heat and the rise of under-$1,000 PCs took a toll that year when Acer cut US jobs, streamlined operations, and withdrew from the US retail market. The company intensified its focus on providing online software, hardware, and support for users, launching a digital services business and a venture capital operation to invest in promising Internet startups. In 2000 the company suffered a financial blow when large customer IBM cancelled a contract manufacturing order for desktop computers.

OFFICERS

Chairman and CEO; CEO, Acer SoftCapital: Stan Shih
CFO: Philip Peng
CEO, Acer Digital Services: George Huang
CEO, Acer Information Products: Simon Lin
CEO, Acer International Services: William Lu
CEO, Acer Sertek Service: J.T. Wang
President and COO, Acer America: Max Wu
President, Acer Peripherals: K. Y. Lee
Chief Information Officer Acer America: Alex Wei
Executive Director, US Sales, Acer America:
 Gregg Pendergast
Executive Director, North America Marketing, Acer America: Todd Osborne
General Manager Acer America Corp. Canadian Operations: Anthony Lin
Auditors: KPMG Peat Marwick

LOCATIONS

HQ: 21F, 88, Hsin Tai Wu Rd., Sec 1.,
 Hsichih, Taipei Hsien 221, Taiwan
Phone: +886-2-696-1234 **Fax:** +886-2-696-1777
US HQ: 2641 Orchard Pkwy., San Jose, CA 95134
US Phone: 408-432-6200 **US Fax:** 408-922-2933
Web site: http://global.acer.com

Acer has 21 manufacturing sites and 15 assembly plants in 10 countries.

1999 Sales

	% of total
North America	40
Europe	23
Taiwan	12
Other regions	25
Total	**100**

PRODUCTS/OPERATIONS

1999 Sales

	% of total
PCs	58
Peripherals	25
Semiconductors	10
Other	7
Total	**100**

Selected Products
Acer Aspire home computers
AcerAltos servers
AcerPower desktop computers
AcerView monitors
Digital cameras
Fax/modems
Integrated circuits
Internet devices
Keyboards
Motherboards
Multimedia display tools
Network add-on cards
Networking products (switches and routers)
Phones and other digital communications devices
Scanners
Set-top boxes
Software

COMPETITORS

Apple Computer
Compaq
Dell Computer
eMachines
Fujitsu
Gateway
Hewlett-Packard
Hitachi
IBM
Legend Holdings
NEC
Samsung
Sun Microsystems
Toshiba
Unisys

HISTORICAL FINANCIALS & EMPLOYEES

Taiwan: 2306 FYE: December 31	Annual Growth	12/90	12/91	12/92	12/93	12/94	12/95	12/96	12/97	12/98	12/99
Sales (NT$ mil.)	24.5%	25,285	25,123	23,134	34,003	63,017	107,063	115,208	137,345	169,660	181,331
Net income (NT$ mil.)	69.3%	64	(579)	56	1,073	3,152	5,536	3,060	3,740	2,492	7,309
Income as % of sales	—	0.3%	—	0.2%	3.2%	5.0%	5.2%	2.7%	2.7%	1.5%	4.0%
Earnings per share (NT$)	87.1%	—	—	0.03	0.63	1.80	2.95	1.42	1.57	1.01	2.41
Stock price - FY high (NT$)	—	—	—	11.25	25.00	54.13	51.75	56.00	111.50	78.00	97.00
Stock price - FY low (NT$)	—	—	—	6.38	7.38	18.63	35.25	33.60	39.10	28.80	53.00
Stock price - FY close (NT$)	42.6%	—	—	7.88	25.00	42.63	45.38	50.50	50.00	37.30	94.50
P/E - high	—	—	—	375	40	30	18	39	71	77	40
P/E - low	—	—	—	213	12	10	12	24	25	29	22
Dividends per share (NT$)	—	—	—	0.00	0.00	0.00	0.00	0.00	0.00	0.00	0.00
Book value per share (NT$)	21.5%	—	—	4.94	5.62	7.30	12.88	15.34	17.62	18.11	19.30
Employees	47.4%	—	—	—	—	—	—	—	—	23,000	33,912

STOCK PRICE HISTORY 1999 FISCAL YEAR-END

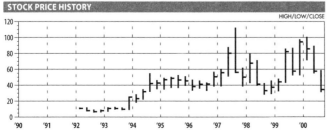

HIGH/LOW/CLOSE

Debt ratio: 0.1%
Return on equity: 13.7%
Cash (NT$ mil.): 11,191
Current ratio: 1.39
Long-term debt (NT$ mil.): 5,321
No. of shares (mil.): 3,108
Dividends
 Yield: —
 Payout: —
Market value ($ mil.): 293,674

ADIDAS-SALOMON AG

OVERVIEW

Call it the wisdom of Salomon. adidas' purchase of France's Salomon has pushed Herzogenaurach, Germany-based adidas-Salomon into the sports equipment market. In addition to its three-striped athletic shoes, the company (the #2 maker of sporting goods worldwide, behind NIKE) makes athletic clothing and gear such as Salomon skis, snowboards, and in-line skates; Taylor Made golf clubs; and Mavic bike components. (adidas products account for nearly 85% of sales.)

adidas-Salomon also makes erima team equipment and Bonfire snowboarding apparel.

Chairman Robert Louis-Dreyfus brought the company back from near bankruptcy in the early 1990s. Although the purchase of Salomon was intended to create economies of scale and an advantage in emerging markets for trendy sports, integrating the company has been difficult. adidas-Salomon also has been hurt by soft demand for Taylor Made's golf products in Asia and the US.

HISTORY

adidas grew out of an infamous rift between German brothers Adi and Rudi Dassler, who created athletic shoe giants adidas and Puma. As WWI was winding down, Adi scavenged for tires, rucksacks, and other refuse to create slippers, gymnastics shoes, and soccer cleats at home. His sister cut patterns out of canvas. By 1926 the shoes' success allowed the Dasslers to build a factory. At the 1928 Amsterdam Olympics, German athletes first showcased Dassler shoes to the world. In 1936 American Jesse Owens sprinted to Olympic gold in Dassler's double-striped shoes.

Business boomed until the Nazis commandeered the Dassler factory to make boots for soldiers. Although both Rudi and Adi were reportedly members of the Nazi party, only Rudi was called to service. Adi remained at home to run the factory. When Allied troops occupied the area, Adi made friends with American soldiers — even creating shoes for a soldier who wore them at the 1946 Olympics. Rudi came home from an American prison camp and joined his brother; together they scavenged the war-torn landscape for tank materials and tents to make shoes.

Soon a dispute between the brothers split the business. Rumors circulated that Rudi resented that Adi had failed to use his American connections to help spring him from prison camp. Rudi set up his own factory facing Adi across the River Aurach. The brothers never spoke to each other again, except in court. Rudi's company was named Puma, and Adi's became adidas. Adi added a third stripe to the Dassler's trademark shoe, while Rudi chose a cat's paw in motion. Thus began one of the most intense rivalries in Europe. The children of Puma and adidas employees attended separate elementary schools, and the employees even distinguished themselves by drinking different beers.

With Adi's innovations throughout the late 1940s and 1950s (such as the replaceable-cleat soccer shoe), adidas came to dominate the world's athletic shoe market. In the late 1950s it capitalized on the booming US market, overtaking the canvas sneakers made by P.F. Flyers and Keds. The company also initiated the practice of putting logos on sports bags and clothing.

In the 1960s and 1970s, adidas continued to expand globally to maintain its dominant position. However, a flood of new competitors following the 1972 Munich Olympics and the death of Adi in 1978 signaled the end of an era. As NIKE and Reebok captured the North American market during the 1980s, adidas made one of its biggest missteps — it turned down a sneaker endorsement offer from a young Michael Jordan in 1984.

French politician and entrepreneur Bernard Tapie bought the struggling company in 1989, but he stepped down in 1992 amid personal, political, and business scandals. The next year Robert Louis-Dreyfus became CEO. He shifted production to Asia, pumped up the advertising budget, and brought in former NIKE marketing geniuses to re-establish the company's identity.

adidas became adidas-Salomon in 1997 with its $1.4 billion purchase of Salomon, a French maker of skis and other sporting goods. The company also opened its first high-profile store in Portland, Oregon, that year. In a 1998 reorganization, Louis-Dreyfus sacked Jean-François Gautier as Salomon's president in the wake of disappointing sales, particularly from Taylor Made Golf, Salomon's golf subsidiary.

Amid a 10% slide in revenue, several key executives decided to leave the company in early 2000, including adidas America CEO Steve Wynne; he was replaced by former Gillette executive Ross McMullin. Claiming poor health, Louis-Dreyfus soon followed (but remained as chairman). In the fall of 2000 the company announced it would consolidate its apparel under the Heritage label to reinforce its position in the burgeoning casual wear market.

Chairman: Robert Louis-Dreyfus
Deputy Chairman and COO, Europe, Africa, and Asia/Pacific Regions: Herbert Hainer
Deputy Chairman: Christian Tourres
CFO: Robin Stalker
SVP Global Marketing, Europe, Africa, and Asia/Pacific Regions: Erich Stamminger
President, adidas America: Ross McMullin, age 43
Director, Human Resources; Director General Administration, Salomon Group and Salomon S.A. France: Michel Perraudin
General Counsel: Manfred Ihle
Auditors: KPMG Deutsche Treuhand-Gesellschaft

HQ: Adi-Dassler-Strasse 1-2,
91074 Herzogenaurach, Germany
Phone: +49-9132-84-2471   **Fax:** +49-9132-84-3127
US HQ: 9605 SW Nimbus Ave., Beaverton, OR 97008
US Phone: 503-972-2300   **US Fax:** 503-797-4935
Web site: http://www.adidas.com

1999 Sales

	$ mil.	% of total
Europe	2,735	51
North America	1,826	34
Asia/Pacific	657	12
Latin America	126	2
Other regions	35	1
Total	**5,379**	**100**

1999 Sales

	$ mil.	% of total
adidas	4,486	83
Salomon	546	10
Taylor Made	293	5
Mavic	44	2
Other	10	—
Total	**5,379**	**100**

Brands
adidas (footwear and apparel for basketball, cycling, running, soccer, and tennis)
Bonfire (snowboarding apparel)
erima (team sports apparel, swimwear, and accessories)
Mavic (bicycle components)
Salomon (ski and snowboard equipment, in-line skates, and hiking boots)
Taylor Made (golf clubs, accessories)

Amer Group	New Balance
Benetton	NIKE
Callaway Golf	Puma
Converse	Reebok
Fila	Rollerblade
Fortune Brands	Schwinn/GT
Head-Tyrolia-Mares	Skis Rossignol
Huffy	Spalding
K-Swiss	Trek
K2	

OTC: ADDDF FYE: December 31	Annual Growth	12/90	12/91	12/92	12/93	12/94	12/95	12/96	12/97	12/98	12/99
Sales ($ mil.)	23.2%	—	—	—	1,539	2,063	2,434	3,055	3,724	5,944	5,379
Net income ($ mil.)	74.7%	—	—	—	8	76	170	204	259	241	229
Income as % of sales	—	—	—	—	0.5%	3.7%	7.0%	6.7%	6.9%	4.0%	4.3%
Earnings per share ($)	3.8%	—	—	—	—	—	—	2.25	2.85	2.65	2.52
Stock price - FY high ($)	—	—	—	—	—	—	—	47.88	73.00	87.00	54.92
Stock price - FY low ($)	—	—	—	—	—	—	—	39.25	42.38	46.00	37.50
Stock price - FY close ($)	(4.5%)	—	—	—	—	—	—	42.88	63.90	48.37	37.33
P/E - high	—	—	—	—	—	—	—	21	26	33	22
P/E - low	—	—	—	—	—	—	—	17	15	17	15
Dividends per share ($)	1.5%	—	—	—	—	—	—	0.44	0.54	0.50	0.46
Book value per share ($)	5.2%	—	—	—	—	—	—	6.47	8.29	6.49	7.53
Employees	16.6%	—	—	—	5,096	5,087	5,730	6,986	7,993	12,036	12,829

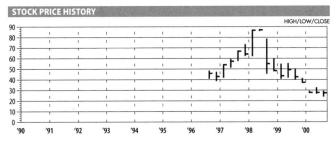
HIGH/LOW/CLOSE

Debt ratio: 31.4%
Return on equity: 36.0%
Cash ($ mil.): 69
Current ratio: 1.88
Long-term debt ($ mil.): 1,492
No. of shares (mil.): 91
Dividends
  Yield: 0.0%
  Payout: 0.2%
Market value ($ mil.): 3,386

AEGON N.V.

OVERVIEW

Not only is AEGON expanding across Europe, it is also spreading Transamerica. The giant Dutch insurer acquired the US-based rival of the San Francisco pyramid headquarters fame (although it plans to sell the Transamerica Finance subsidiary) in a bid to boost its already powerful North American segment.

AEGON is using its expertise in acquisition and consolidation (it is itself the amalgamation of several companies) to build a transnational collection of financial services businesses. Its subsidiaries in Canada, Germany, Hungary, the Netherlands, Spain, the UK, and the US offer personal and commercial life, and accident insurance, as well as retirement and savings advice and management services. Its US operations also offer life and nonmedical health and long-term-care insurance and sell annuities and other retirement products.

Along with Transamerica, AEGON has bought UK-based Guardian Royal Exchange's life, pensions, and unit trust operations as part of its strategy to enlarge its asset management operations.

Vereniging AEGON, an independent trust, owns 30% of AEGON.

HISTORY

AEGON traces its roots to 1844 when former civil servant and funeral society agent J. Oosterhoff founded Algemeene Friesche, a burial society for low-income workers. The next year a similar organization, Groot-Noordhollandsche, was founded. These companies later became insurers and expanded nationwide. Meanwhile, Olveh, a civil servants' aid group, was founded in 1877. The three companies merged in 1968 to form AGO Holding.

AEGON's other operations came from different traditions. Vennootschap Nederland was founded in 1858 as a tontine (essentially a death pool, with the survivors taking the pot) by Count A. Langrand-Dumonceau, an ex-French Foreign Legionnaire from Belgium. In 1913 the company merged with Eerste Nederlandsche, whose accident and health division had been previously spun off as Nieuwe Eerste Nederlandsche.

A year after Vennootschap was founded, C. F. W. Wiggers van Kerchem founded a similar scheme, Nillmij, in the Dutch East Indies. The government promoted Nillmij to colonial civil servants and military people, and for a while the company enjoyed a monopoly in the colony. Nillmij's Indonesian operations were nationalized after independence in 1957, but its Dutch subsidiaries continued to operate. All insurers were hit by fast-growing postwar government social programs. As a result, industry consolidation came early to the Netherlands. In 1969 Eerste Nederlandsche, Nieuwe Eerste Nederlandsche, and Nillmij merged to form Ennia.

The shrinking Dutch insurance market forced companies to look overseas. AGO moved into the US in 1979 by buying Life Investors; by 1982 half of its sales came from outside the Netherlands. Ennia, meanwhile, expanded in Europe (it entered Spain in 1980) and the US (buying Arkansas-based National Old Line Insurance in 1981).

AGO and Ennia merged in 1983 to form AEGON. The company made more purchases at home and abroad and spent much of the rest of the decade assimilating operations.

AEGON's US units accounted for about 40% of sales in the mid-1980s, and the firm increased that figure with acquisitions. In 1986 it bought Baltimore-based Monumental Corp. (life and health insurance) and expanded the company's US penetration.

This left AEGON underrepresented in Europe as deregulation paved the way for economic union, and social service cutbacks spurred opportunities in private financial planning in the region. So in the 1990s AEGON began buying European companies, including Regency Life (UK, 1991) and Allami Biztosito (Hungary, 1992), and formed an alliance with Mexico's Grupo Financiero Banamex in 1994. This reduced its reliance on US sales. It continued buying specialty operations in the US, particularly asset management lines.

In 1997 AEGON began to concentrate on life insurance and financial services and to shed its other operations. It bought the insurance business of Providian and sold noncore lines such as auto coverage. The next year it sold FGH Bank (mortgages) to Germany's Bayerische Vereinsbank (now Bayerische Hypotheken und Vereinsbank) and in 1999 sold auto insurer Worldwide Insurance.

That year AEGON expanded further in the US with the $9.7 billion purchase of Transamerica and bought the life and pensions businesses of Guardian Royal Exchange. In 2000 the company sold Labouchere N.V., a Dutch banking subsidiary, to Dexia.

Chairman, Executive Board: Kees J. Storm
EVP Group Business Development:
Alexander R. Wynaendts
EVP Group Finance: Joseph B.M. Streppel
EVP Group Treasury and Investor Relations:
Robert J. McGraw
SVP Corporate Actuarial Department: Ad A.M. Kok
SVP Group Communications: Gerard van Dongen
SVP Group Finance: Ruurd A. van den Berg
SVP Group Legal: N. Willem van Vliet
SVP Group Tax: Adri D.J. Verzijl
SVP Group Treasury and Treasurer:
C. Michiel van Katwijk
CEO AEGON USA: Donald J. Shepard
EVP and Chief Marketing Officer, AEGON USA:
Bart Herbert Jr.
VP and Corporate Actuary, AEGON USA:
Douglas C. Kolsrud
Director Human Resources AEGON USA:
Pat Wlodarczyk
Auditors: Ernst & Young

HQ: Mariahoeveplein 50, PO Box 202,
2501 CE The Hague, The Netherlands
Phone: +31-70-344-3210   **Fax:** +31-70-344-8445
US HQ: 1111 N. Charles St., Baltimore, MD 21201
US Phone: 410-576-4571   **US Fax:** 410-347-8685
Web site: http://www.aegon.com

1999 Sales

	% of total
The Americas	51
The Netherlands	39
UK	10
Total	**100**

1999 Assets

	$ mil	% of total
Cash & equivalents	973	—
Bonds	57,261	25
Stocks	8,588	4
Other investments	48,180	21
Assets in separate account	109,272	47
Receivables	4,592	2
Other assets	2,047	1
Total	**230,913**	**100**

Selected Subsidiaries
AB-AEGON Altalanos Biztosito (Hungary)
AEGON Bank N.V.
AEGON Lebensversicherung-AG (Germany)
AEGON Nederland N.V.
AEGON UK plc
AEGON Union Aseguradora S.A. de Seguros y
Reaseguros (Spain, 98%)
AEGON USA, Inc.
Guardian Assurance plc (UK)
Seguros Banamex AEGON S.A. (Mexico, 48%)
Scottish Equitable plc (UK)
Transamerica Corporation (US)
Transamerica Life Insurance Company of Canada

AIG	Legal & General	Royal & Sun
Allianz	Group	Alliance
AXA	Merrill Lynch	Insurance
CIGNA	MetLife	Swiss Life
Citigroup	New York Life	Winterthur
Fortis (NL)	Prudential	Zurich Financial
The Hartford	Prudential plc	Services
ING		

NYSE: AEG FYE: December 31	Annual Growth	12/90	12/91	12/92	12/93	12/94	12/95	12/96	12/97	12/98	12/99
Assets ($ mil.)	23.0%	35,861	41,830	46,093	66,002	79,032	93,660	105,027	134,623	153,070	230,913
Net income ($ mil.)	15.2%	444	485	500	517	632	823	929	1,089	1,385	1,584
Income as % of assets	—	1.2%	1.2%	1.1%	0.8%	0.8%	0.9%	0.9%	0.8%	0.9%	0.7%
Earnings per share ($)	13.4%	0.42	0.50	0.48	0.50	0.63	0.76	0.82	0.96	1.26	1.30
Stock price - FY high ($)	—	3.61	3.65	4.28	5.85	6.40	11.19	15.91	22.69	62.88	65.06
Stock price - FY low ($)	—	2.73	2.74	3.30	4.11	4.94	6.39	10.28	15.28	22.22	34.81
Stock price - FY close ($)	35.3%	3.14	3.50	4.16	5.43	6.35	11.00	15.81	22.41	61.13	47.75
P/E - high	—	8	7	8	11	10	14	19	23	50	49
P/E - low	—	6	5	6	8	8	8	12	16	18	26
Dividends per share ($)	16.2%	0.14	0.14	0.18	0.18	0.20	0.20	0.37	0.00	0.69	0.54
Book value per share ($)	14.0%	3.14	3.55	3.53	4.42	4.43	4.85	6.10	7.72	7.94	10.22
Employees	3.8%	—	—	—	19,393	19,713	19,806	19,346	23,429	20,723	24,316

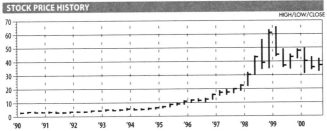

1999 FISCAL YEAR-END
Equity as % of assets: 5.9%
Return on assets: 0.8%
Return on equity: 13.9%
Long-term debt ($ mil.): 2,051
No. of shares (mil.): 1,337
Dividends
Yield: 1.1%
Payout: 41.5%
Market value ($ mil.): 63,835
Sales ($ mil.): 22,580

AGRIUM INC.

AGRIUM INC.

OVERVIEW

Agrium digs the smell of fertilizer in the morning. It smells like — victory. The Calgary, Alberta-based enterprise is among the top producers of nitrogen fertilizer in North America, and it is a major supplier of potash and phosphate fertilizers. Agrium also sells other nutrients such as urea and sulfur. The company sells fertilizers, chemicals, and seed, and provides services, including soil monitoring, through its Crop Production Services and Western Farm Service subsidiaries.

Agrium has nitrogen plants in the US and Canada as well as in South America. Its phosphate and potash production facilities

are located primarily in Canada. The company also operates more than 225 farm retail centers in the US.

Escalating prices for natural gas (a raw material in nitrogen fertilizer), along with low selling prices for phosphate have dogged Agrium. The company also faces a mature market in North America. Agrium hopes to boost profits by expanding its presence in South America. As part of that strategy, it began production at its Profertil nitrogen plant in Argentina in 2000. It has also increased its nitrogen production capacity some 60% with the acquisition of Unocal's agricultural products division.

HISTORY

Agrium was formed in 1992 to facilitate the reorganization of Cominco's fertilizer division and to acquire the fertilizer business of the Alberta Energy Company (1993). Cominco was founded in 1896 as the Smelting and Refining Company when Fritz Heinze fired up his first smelter at Trail Creek Landing, British Columbia. Using the ores of the nearby Rossland mines, the company soon diversified into other products (such as fertilizers) and new metallurgical technologies. In 1906 the Smelting and Refining Company, the Rossland mines, and the St. Eugene Mine merged to form the Consolidated Mining and Smelting Company of Canada Limited.

During WWI the Canadian government conscripted all the company's lead, zinc, and chemical production and instructed the company to make explosive-grade ammonium nitrate at its fertilizer plants.

The company opened a nitrogen plant in Homestead, Nebraska, in 1965. The following year Cominco became the company's official name. In 1968 Cominco further expanded in the US when it opened a nitrogen production facility in Borger, Texas.

Alberta Energy was formed in 1973 to lessen Alberta's dependence on foreign oil, in response to the OPEC oil embargo. In 1989 its petrochemical division established fertilizer (ammonium nitrate) subsidiaries in the United States.

Agrium was established to compete in the rapidly consolidating fertilizer market (the number of North American ammonia producers fell from 55 in 1980 to 26 at the end of 1996). The phosphate and potash industries also consolidated, albeit on a smaller scale.

Between 1993 and 1996 the company

expanded its US operations by acquiring Crop Protection Services and Western Farm Service (both retail operations), AG-BIO (the phosphate-based fertilizer business of Imperial Oil), and Nu-West Industries.

Agrium expanded into South America in 1995 by opening retail sales units for selling fertilizer, agricultural chemicals, and other services in the farming regions of Argentina.

In 1996 Agrium acquired Viridian, a Canadian fertilizer producer with nitrogen- and phosphate-based fertilizer plants in Alberta. Expanding its supply base, the company bought a phosphate mine in Alberta in 1997. The next year Agrium began constructing the largest nitrogen fertilizer production facility in Argentina, where it owns and operates 18 retail farm centers. Also that year Agrium acquired the Rasmussen Ridge phosphate mine in Idaho. The company also bought back 10% of its shares in 1998.

Agrium opened a phosphate rock mine in Ontario in 1999 to replace its reliance on phosphate rock imported from West Africa.

In 2000 Agrium agreed to buy Unocal's nitrogen-based fertilizer operations for approximately $325 million. Also that year Agrium's Profertil nitrogen plant, a joint venture with Spain's industrial giant Repsol-YPF, began production in Argentina, but the plant was shut down by a government agency following an accidental discharge of ammonia. The plant was reopened later in 2000. Agrium also increased its nitrogen production capacity by acquiring Unocal's agricultural products division.

Chairman: Frank W. Proto
President and CEO: John M. Van Brunt, $562,059 pay
EVP and COO: William J. Robertson, $378,513 pay
SVP and CFO: Bruce Waterman
VP, General Counsel, and Corporate Secretary:
Leslie A. O'Donoghue
VP Human Resources: Michael J. Klein
VP Marketing and Distribution: John M. Yokely,
$200,933 pay
VP North American Retail: Richard L. Gearheard,
$235,816 pay
VP Operations: William C. McClung
VP South America: Robert J. Rennie
VP Strategic Development and Planning:
Dorothy E. A. Bower
Auditors: KPMG LLP

HQ: 13131 Lake Fraser Dr. SE,
Calgary, Alberta T2J 7E8, Canada
Phone: 403-225-7000 **Fax:** 403-225-7609
US HQ: 4582 S. Ulster St., Ste. 1400, Denver, CO 80237
US Phone: 303-804-4400 **US Fax:** 303-804-4482
Web site: http://www.agrium.com

Agrium has seven nitrogen fertilizer plants, two
phosphate plants, and one potash mine in the US and
Canada, plus a nitrogen production facility in Argentina.

1999 Sales

	$ mil.	% of total
US	1,167	68
Canada	383	22
Argentina	94	6
Other countries	72	4
Total	**1,716**	**100**

1999 Sales

	$ mil.	% of total
Wholesale		
Nitrogen	422	24
Phosphate	255	14
Potash	145	8
Sulfate & other	65	4
Retail		
Fertilizers	437	25
Chemicals	345	19
Other	106	6
Adjustments	(59)	—
Total	**1,716**	**100**

Subsidiaries and Affiliates
Agrium Argentina SA
Agrium Nitrogen Company (US)
Agrium Partnership
Agrium U.S. Inc.
Agroservicios Pampeanos (Argentina)
Canpotex Limited (33%)
Crop Production Services, Inc. (US)
Nu-West Industries, Inc. (US)
Profertil SA (50%, Argentina)
Viridian Fertilizers Ltd.
Viridian Inc.
Western Farm Service, Inc. (US)

CF Industries
IMC Global
Mississippi Chemical
Norsk Hydro
Phosphate Resource
Partners

Potash Corporation
SQM
Terra Industries
Terra Nitrogen

NYSE: AGU FYE: December 31	Annual Growth	12/90	12/91	12/92	12/93	12/94	12/95	12/96	12/97	12/98	12/99
Sales ($ mil.)	25.9%	—	—	343	396	763	1,171	1,814	1,938	1,805	1,716
Net income ($ mil.)	29.8%	—	—	10	20	62	112	151	185	121	64
Income as % of sales	—	—	—	3.0%	4.9%	8.1%	9.6%	8.3%	9.5%	6.7%	3.7%
Earnings per share ($)	(25.5%)	—	—	—	—	—	1.59	1.07	1.40	0.94	0.49
Stock price - FY high ($)	—	—	—	—	—	—	15.65	16.25	15.88	15.75	10.63
Stock price - FY low ($)	—	—	—	—	—	—	8.66	11.75	9.88	7.88	7.50
Stock price - FY close ($)	(14.9%)	—	—	—	—	—	14.99	13.75	12.19	8.69	7.88
P/E - high	—	—	—	—	—	—	9	15	11	16	22
P/E - low	—	—	—	—	—	—	5	11	7	8	15
Dividends per share ($)	53.1%	—	—	—	—	—	0.02	0.07	0.11	0.11	0.11
Book value per share ($)	2.5%	—	—	—	—	—	6.17	4.99	5.00	6.29	6.82
Employees	14.0%	—	—	—	2,070	2,008	3,481	4,520	4,432	4,530	4,536

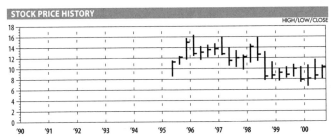

HIGH/LOW/CLOSE

Debt ratio: 39.4%
Return on equity: 11.2%
Cash ($ mil.): 104
Current ratio: 1.37
Long-term debt ($ mil.): 497
No. of shares (mil.): 112
Dividends
Yield: 1.4%
Payout: 22.4%
Market value ($ mil.): 883

SOCIÉTÉ AIR FRANCE

Back in the black and partly privatized, once-stodgy Air France now looks like a bold new airline. Europe's #3 air carrier (behind British Airways and Lufthansa), Roissy-based Air France flies to about 175 destinations in 85 countries. A 1999 IPO was the reward for tough cost-cutting that returned the carrier to profitability.

In an industry increasingly defined by global marketing alliances, Air France, Delta, AeroMexico, and Korean Air Lines have formed SkyTeam to compete with Oneworld (anchored by British Airways and American Airlines) and Star (anchored by United Airlines and Lufthansa). The French carrier's cargo operation has its own coalition, which includes Delta and Korean Air Lines. The airline also owns an interest in the computer reservation system Amadeus.

Increasing the number of flights linking France to the US — at a time when other carriers are abandoning transatlantic routes — accounts for much of Air France's renewed vigor. Meanwhile, Air France has bought stakes in regional carriers at home to consolidate its position in the domestic market.

The French government maintains a 63% stake in Air France.

HISTORY

Société Air France was founded in 1933, the product of consolidation during the adolescence of French aviation. The government that year forced a four-way merger of France's competing airlines: Air Union, Air Orient, Société Générale de Transport Aérien, and Compagnie Internationale de Navigation Aérienne. These carriers, too, had been shaped by mergers; for example, Air Orient had swallowed The Line, which had gained fame on the wings of author/aviator Antoine de St.-Exupery.

Air France expanded during the 1930s to become one of the world's leading airlines, but its ascent was interrupted by World War II, during which the carrier shuttered operations.

Air France resumed flight after the war and added Douglas DC3s and DC4s to its fleet. The French state began nationalizing some industries to quickly rebuild the postwar economy and took control of the airline in 1948. Renamed Compagnie Nationale Air France, the carrier enjoyed government-backed financing that allowed it to launch its expansion.

With the era of big jets dawning, Air France began adding Boeing 707s to its fleet in 1960. Then France and the UK agreed in 1962 to jointly develop a supersonic transport — the Concorde. The next year French authorities realigned France's airline industry: International flights to Africa, Australia, and the Pacific were granted to a private carrier, Union de Transports Aériens (UTA); Air France controlled the remaining international routes. The domestic market was closed to both.

Air France added Boeing 747s and Airbus A300s in the early 1970s, and the airline launched its cargo transport services. The company began flying the Concorde in 1976. Though spiraling development costs had made the Mach 2 jetliner a debatable invest-

ment, the world's only supersonic transport served as a symbol of national pride.

The late 1980s were boom times in the industry, with Air France scoring healthy profits. But its attempt to take control of the domestic market by buying Air Inter was challenged by UTA, which increased its Air Inter stake in opposition. The battle was resolved in 1990: Air France bought control of both airlines.

But this French consolidation came just as the Gulf War, high oil prices, and an economic downturn began to wreak havoc on airlines. Air France fell into a money-losing streak just as deregulation in Europe was about to unleash new levels of competition. The government slapped down management's attempt to cut wages and jobs in 1993 in the face of massive strikes. But as Air France suffered record losses the next year, chairman Christian Blanc gained worker support for a new cost-cutting plan. Blanc, however, resigned in 1997 as the state dragged its feet on privatization.

With the 1998 signing of a US-France open skies agreement, Air France boosted flights to the US and struck code-sharing deals with Continental and Delta. The government finally launched a public offering of the airline in 1999.

To better compete with members of the Star and Oneworld global airline marketing alliances, Air France joined Delta Air Lines, AeroMexico, and Korean Air Lines to form the SkyTeam alliance in 2000. Also that year Air France further consolidated the domestic market by acquiring or upping stakes in Proteus Airlines, Flandre Air, and Regional Airlines.

An Air France Concorde jet crashed shortly after takeoff from Paris in 2000, killing all 109 people on board and four more on the ground. Concorde flights were grounded after the crash pending further investigation.

Chairman and CEO: Jean-Cyril Spinetta
President and COO: Pierre-Henri Gourgeon
CFO: Philippe Calavia
Deputy COO General Coordination: Auguste Gayte
Inspector General: Alain Vidalon
SVP Ground and Flight Operations: Pascal de Izaguirre
SVP Social Policy: Jacques Pichot
SVP International Commercial Affairs:
 Patrick Alexandre
SVP Commercial France: Christian Boireau
SVP Marketing and Development: Marc Lamidey
SVP Network Management: Bruno Matheu
SVP Flight Operations: Gilbert Rovetto
SVP Industrial Resources: Alain Bassil
General Manager Air France Cargo: Marc Boudier
Auditors: Cabinet Constantin; Deloitte Touche
 Tohmatsu

LOCATIONS

HQ: 45, rue de Paris, 95747 Roissy, France
Phone: +33-1-41-56-78-00   **Fax:** +33-1-41-56-56-00
US HQ: 125 W. 55th St., New York, NY 10019
US Phone: 212-830-4000   **US Fax:** 212-830-4244
Web site: http://www.airfrance.net

PRODUCTS/OPERATIONS

1999 Fleet

	No.
Airbus A320	58
Boeing 737	44
Boeing 747	39
Airbus A319	16
Airbus A340	16
Airbus A321	12
Airbus A310	10
Boeing 777	8
Boeing 767	5
Concorde	5
Total	**213**

COMPETITORS

Alitalia
AMR
British Airways
Iberia
KLM
Lufthansa
SAirGroup
SAS
TWA
UAL
Virgin Atlantic Airways

HISTORICAL FINANCIALS & EMPLOYEES

Euronext Paris: AF FYE: March 31	Annual Growth	3/90	3/91	3/92	3/93	3/94	3/95	3/96	3/97	3/98	3/99
Sales (€ mil.)	3.6%	—	—	—	—	—	—	—	8,474	9,253	9,100
Net income (€ mil.)	—	—	—	—	—	—	—	—	(22)	286	249
Income as % of sales	—	—	—	—	—	—	—	—	—	3.1%	2.7%
Earnings per share (€)	—	—	—	—	—	—	—	—	—	—	1.37
Stock price - FY high (€)	—	—	—	—	—	—	—	—	—	—	18.35
Stock price - FY low (€)	—	—	—	—	—	—	—	—	—	—	15.25
Stock price - FY close (€)	—	—	—	—	—	—	—	—	—	—	15.55
P/E - high	—	—	—	—	—	—	—	—	—	—	13
P/E - low	—	—	—	—	—	—	—	—	—	—	11
Dividends per share (€)	—	—	—	—	—	—	—	—	—	—	0.00
Book value per share (€)	—	—	—	—	—	—	—	—	—	—	13.62
Employees	(0.1%)	—	—	—	—	—	—	—	55,269	54,325	55,199

STOCK PRICE HISTORY

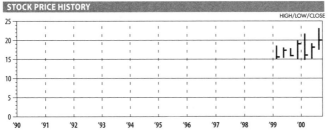

HIGH/LOW/CLOSE

| '90 | '91 | '92 | '93 | '94 | '95 | '96 | '97 | '98 | '99 | '00 |

1999 FISCAL YEAR-END

Debt ratio: 57.8%
Return on equity: —
Cash (€ mil.): 73
Current ratio: 1.38
Long-term debt (€ mil.): 3,704
No. of shares (mil.): 198
Dividends
 Yield: —
 Payout: —
Market value ($ mil.): 3,312
Sales ($ mil.): 9,767

AIRBUS INDUSTRIE

Airbus Industrie, perennial also-ran to Boeing as the world's largest producer of commercial airliners, is betting that size does count. Based in Blagnac, France, Airbus' 109- to 400-passenger, single-aisle and wide-body jets make up about a third of the world's air fleet. Much to Boeing's chagrin, however, Airbus is now neck-and-neck with Boeing in new aircraft orders and will soon begin building the A3XX, a double-decker plane which will carry more than 550 people.

A consortium, Airbus is 80%-owned by the newly formed European Aeronautics Defence & Space Company (EADS), which consists of DaimlerChrysler Aerospace (Germany), Aérospatiale Matra (France), and CASA (Spain).

UK-based BAE SYSTEMS holds the other 20%. Each member company oversees part of the production — for example, aircraft wings come from the UK, cockpits come from France, and interiors come from Germany. Airbus plants in France and Germany assemble the parts.

Airbus is banking on its jumbo A3XX (which received brisk orders even before it was formally approved), a steady increase in passenger air travel and air cargo transport, new flight routes, and the need for more midsized, long-range aircraft for future success. The long-sought restructuring of Airbus into a more competitive single corporate entity (to be named Airbus Intergrated Company) is finally in the offing, hastened by the creation of EADS.

In the 1970s three US companies, Boeing, Lockheed, and McDonnell Douglas, dominated the commercial aircraft market. France and the UK had been discussing an alliance to build competing jets since 1965, but political infighting stalled the talks. Finally, in 1969 France and West Germany committed to building the Airbus A300. Airbus Industrie was born in 1970 as a *groupement d'intérêt économique* (grouping of economic interest, a structure used by allied French vineyards). Seed money came from partners Aérospatiale Matra and Deutsche Airbus. CASA joined in 1971.

The A300 entered service with Air France in 1974, but Airbus had trouble selling it outside member countries. The following year the firm hired former American Airlines president George Warde to help market the A300 in the US. His efforts paid off when Eastern Air Lines decided to buy the A300. Also in 1995 Airbus launched the A310, a smaller, more fuel-efficient version of the A300. The UK joined the consortium in 1979.

By 1980 Airbus trailed only Boeing among the world's commercial jet makers. The A320 was introduced in 1984 — it featured a ground-breaking "fly-by-wire" system that allowed pilots to adjust the aircraft's control surfaces via a computer, helping to make it the fastest-selling jetliner in history. The firm launched the A330 and A340, larger planes designed for medium- and long-range flights, in 1987. Two years later Airbus introduced the A321, an elongated version of the A320, and received a $6 billion order from Federal Express.

The German government sold its 20% stake in Deutsche Airbus to Daimler-Benz (now DaimlerChrysler) in 1992, giving Daimler-

Benz 100% ownership of the German partner (now about 38%).

In 1993 Airbus sold only 38 planes, about one-sixth as many as Boeing. Such dismal results led to the consortium's resolve to build its planes more quickly and less expensively. Sales rebounded in 1995 and 1996. The next year the four Airbus partners agreed to restructure the consortium as a limited liability company, possibly as a first step toward taking Airbus public. Also in 1997 Boeing irked Airbus when the US-based rival won exclusive long-term contracts with Delta, Continental, and American Airlines.

Seeking more customers in Asia, Airbus signed parts contracts with Japanese suppliers in 1999 and launched production of its A318, a 107-seat short-haul passenger jet designed to compete with Boeing's 717. Also that year, for the first time ever, the company recorded more plane orders than Boeing.

In 2000 the UK government pledged $836 million in loans to back consortium partner BAE SYSTEMS' participation in the A3XX project, a plane that would seat more than 550 passengers. The same year the German government announced plans to purchase up to 75 Airbus A400M transports valued at around $9.8 billion. In June the company announced that it had finally inked a deal to turn Airbus into a corporation, to be known as Airbus Integrated Company (AIC). Not surprisingly, it also committed to producing the superjumbo A3XX and soon received 17 firm orders from Air France and Emirates Airline. Around the same time, the European Aeronautic Defence & Space Company (EADS), which owns 80% of Airbus, launched its IPO.

Chairman of the Supervisory Board: Manfred Bischoff
CEO: Noël Foregard
COO: Dietrich Russel
EVP Strategy, Government Relations, and External Affairs: Philippe Delmas
SVP Administration: Adolfo Revuelta
SVP Commercial: John J. Leahy
SVP Customer Service: Bernard Catteeuw
SVP Engineering: Alain Garcia
SVP Large Aircraft Division: Jurgen Thomas
SVP Programmes: Horst Emker
VP Human Relations: Robert Earenfeld
Chairman and CEO, Airbus Industrie of North America: Jonathan M. Schofield
President and COO, Airbus Service: Clyde Kizer
Financial Controller: Ian Massey

LOCATIONS

HQ: 1, Rond Point Maurice Bellonte, BP 33, 31707 Blagnac Cedex, France
Phone: +33-5-61-93-33-87 **Fax:** +33-5-61-93-49-55
US HQ: 198 Van Buren St., Ste. 300, Herndon, VA 20170
US Phone: 703-834-3400 **US Fax:** 703-834-3548
Web site: http://www.airbus.com

Airbus Industrie has offices in China, Russia, North America, and Singapore, and it manufactures airplanes in factories throughout Europe, with final assembly carried out in France and Germany.

PRODUCTS/OPERATIONS

Selected Aircraft

Single-aisle twin-engine jets
A318
A319
A320
A321
Superjumbo four-engine jets
A3XX

Wide-body four-engine jets
A330-200
A340-200
A340-300
Wide-body twin-engine jets
A300-600F
A310-300

Selected Customers

Aer Lingus
Air Canada
Air France
Alitalia
America West
China Southern
Delta
Federal Express
Iberia

Japan Air System
Korean Airlines
Lufthansa
Northwest
SilkAir (Singapore Airlines)
United
US Airways
Virgin Atlantic Airways

COMPETITORS

Boeing
Bombardier
Embraer
Gulfstream Aerospace
Sextant Avionique

HISTORICAL FINANCIALS & EMPLOYEES

Consortium FYE: December 31	Annual Growth	12/90	12/91	12/92	12/93	12/94	12/95	12/96	12/97	12/98	12/99
Sales ($ mil.)	15.2%	4,700	7,500	7,700	8,700	8,500	9,600	8,800	11,600	13,300	16,817
Employees	8.8%	1,400	947	2,700	2,700	1,367	2,182	2,207	2,289	2,700	3,000

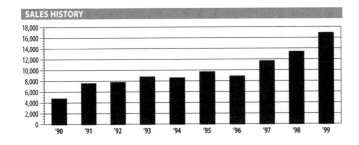

SALES HISTORY

AKZO NOBEL N.V.

OVERVIEW

Akzo Nobel is the world's largest paint maker, but it can do more than paint a pretty picture. The Arnhem, Netherlands-based company is among the world's largest chemical manufacturers and is also a major salt producer. The company is organized along three business lines. Its coatings group makes paints, inks, automotive finishes, and industrial coatings and resins. Its chemical unit produces pulp and paper chemicals, functional chemicals (including flame retardants and animal feed additives), surfactants (used in detergents and industry), polymers, and catalysts. The company's pharmaceuticals unit produces contraceptives and fertility treatments, over-the-counter drugs, and veterinary medicines.

Akzo Nobel exited the fibers business by selling its Acordis unit to CVC Capital Partners. Already an established leader in coatings and chemicals, the company has purchased Hoechst Roussel Vet (animal health) to strengthen its position in pharmaceuticals.

HISTORY

The Akzo side of Akzo Nobel traces its roots to two companies — German rayon and coatings maker Vereinigte Glanzstoff-Fabriken (founded in 1899) and Dutch rayon maker Nederlandsche Kunstzijdebariek (founded in 1911 and known as NK or Enka). In 1928 NK built a plant near Asheville, North Carolina, in what later became the town of Enka. The two companies merged in 1929 to create Algemene Kunstzijde-Unie (AKU).

In 1967 two Dutch companies merged to form Koninklijke Zout-Organon (KZO). In 1969 KZO bought US-based International Salt and merged with AKU to form Akzo. In the 1980s Akzo focused on building its chemicals, coatings, and pharmaceuticals businesses. It then began reorganizing operations, centralizing management, cutting its workforce, and streamlining R&D. Akzo sold its paper and pulp business to Nobel in 1993. A few months later the company reclaimed that business when it bought Nobel.

Best remembered for the prizes that bear his name (which were first awarded in 1901 through a bequest in his will), Alfred Nobel invented the blasting cap in 1863, making it possible to control the detonation of nitroglycerin. He then persuaded Stockholm merchant J. W. Smitt to help him finance Nitroglycerin Ltd. to make and sell the volatile fluid (1864). Nobel's quest to improve nitroglycerin led to his invention of dynamite in 1867.

After Nobel's death in 1896, Nitroglycerin Ltd. remained an explosives maker, and in 1965 it changed its name to Nitro Nobel. In 1978 Swedish industrialist Marcus Wallenberg bought Nitro Nobel for his KemaNord chemical group, known afterward as KemaNobel. Within six years industrialist Erik Penser controlled both Bofors and KemaNobel, and he merged them in 1984 as Nobel Industries.

Risky investments led Penser to ruin in 1991. His holdings, including Nobel, were taken over by a government-owned bank and conveyed into Securum, a government-owned holding company (which owns 18% of Akzo Nobel). In 1992 Nobel spun off its consumer-goods segment.

Akzo bought Nobel in 1994. Although the company had good financial results in 1995, it faced pressure from rising costs for raw materials and a difficult foreign-exchange environment. Akzo announced major closings and layoffs — it sold its polyethylene resin business and moved some clothing-grade rayon operations to Poland. In 1995 the UK and German governments issued health warnings regarding the company's birth-control pills, resulting in lowered sales the next year.

The merger between Akzo and Nobel was legally completed in 1996. That year the company introduced Puregon, a fertility drug, and Remeron, touted as a replacement for Prozac, in the US and other countries. In 1997 Akzo Nobel put most of its worst-performing segment, fibers, into a joint venture with Turkish conglomerate Sabanci. It also sold its North American salt unit to Cargill.

Akzo Nobel acquired Courtaulds (coatings, sealants, and fibers) in 1998 and changed the firm's name to Akzo Nobel UK. Akzo Nobel also bought BASF deco, the European decorative-coatings business of BASF Coatings. Akzo Nobel combined its fiber business with Akzo Nobel UK to form a new division, Acordis. Akzo Nobel then sold Acordis to investment firm CVC Capital Partners in 1999 for $859 million (Akzo Nobel retains a 21% share). Other Akzo Nobel UK units sold include window and high-tech films (to Solutia) and aerospace coating and sealing products to (PPG Industries). Also in 1999 Akzo Nobel bought Hoechst's animal-health unit, Hoechst Roussel Vet, for $712 million. The next year the company agreed to buy Dexter Corporation's coatings business.

Chairman of the Supervisory Board:
Aarnout A. Loudon, age 63
Deputy Chairman of the Supervisory Board:
Frits H. Fentener van Vlissingen, age 66
Chairman of the Board of Management:
Cees J. A. van Lede, age 58
Deputy Chairman and CFO: Fritz W. Frohlich, age 58
Group Director Pharma: Paul K. Brons, age 59
Group Director Coatings: Ove H. Mattsson, age 60
Group Director Chemicals: Rudy M. J. van der Meer, age 55
SVP Finance: Fritz Hensel, age 57
SVP Human Resources: Olle Werner, age 56
Auditors: KPMG Accountants N.V.

LOCATIONS

HQ: Velperweg 76, PO Box 9300,
6800 SB Arnhem, The Netherlands
Phone: +31-26-366-4433   **Fax:** +31-26-366-3250
US HQ: 300 S. Riverside Plaza, Chicago, IL 60606
US Phone: 312-906-7509   **US Fax:** 312-906-7545
Web site: http://www.akzonobel.com

1999 Sales by Country of Origin

	$ mil.	% of total
North America	3,194	22
Europe		
The Netherlands	2,607	18
Germany	1,961	13
UK	1,418	10
Sweden	1,011	7
Other countries	2,840	19
Asia	693	5
Latin America	571	4
Other regions	270	2
Total	**14,565**	**100**

PRODUCTS/OPERATIONS

1999 Sales

	$ mil.	% of total
Coatings	5,555	38
Chemicals	3,870	27
Pharmaceuticals	2,891	20
Acordis/fibers	2,263	15
Adjustments	(14)	—
Total	**14,565**	**100**

Selected Products

Adhesives	Polymer chemicals
Automotive finishes	Prescription drugs
Catalysts	Printing inks
Decorative coatings	Resins
Functional chemicals	Pulp and paper chemicals
Industrial coatings	Salt
Nonprescription drugs	Veterinary products
Plastic additives	

COMPETITORS

Abbott Labs	H.B. Fuller
ALFA, S.A. de C.V.	Hercules
American Home Products	ICI Americas
BASF AG	Merck
Bayer AG	Montedison
Borden	Novartis
Bristol-Myers Squibb	Novo Nordisk A/S
Dow Chemical	PPG
DuPont	Roche Holding
Elf Aquitaine	Rohm and Haas
Eli Lilly	Sabanci Holding
Engelhard	Sherwin-Williams
Ferro	Solutia
Formosa Plastics	Solvay
Glaxo Wellcome	TOTAL FINA ELF

HISTORICAL FINANCIALS & EMPLOYEES

Nasdaq: AKZOY FYE: December 31	Annual Growth	12/90	12/91	12/92	12/93	12/94	12/95	12/96	12/97	12/98	12/99
Sales ($ mil.)	4.0%	10,228	9,871	9,263	8,499	12,794	13,363	12,882	11,872	14,557	14,565
Net income ($ mil.)	(7.6%)	418	340	355	283	680	817	757	797	711	206
Income as % of sales	—	4.1%	3.4%	3.8%	3.3%	5.3%	6.1%	5.9%	6.7%	4.9%	1.4%
Earnings per share ($)	(11.9%)	2.22	1.85	1.93	1.50	2.31	2.88	2.66	2.80	2.49	0.71
Stock price - FY high ($)	—	18.44	19.75	22.69	26.38	31.88	33.69	33.94	47.38	63.69	52.25
Stock price - FY low ($)	—	9.44	10.25	17.69	18.31	24.25	26.25	26.44	31.81	31.56	33.63
Stock price - FY close ($)	18.3%	11.00	19.69	19.31	24.19	29.06	29.00	33.75	43.44	44.63	49.75
P/E - high	—	8	11	12	18	13	12	13	17	26	19
P/E - low	—	4	6	9	12	10	9	10	11	13	13
Dividends per share ($)	9.5%	0.93	0.72	0.77	0.75	0.76	0.83	0.90	0.78	1.06	2.11
Book value per share ($)	(9.1%)	15.49	30.35	30.34	29.34	25.36	28.89	31.07	31.28	7.44	6.57
Employees	2.1%	70,500	65,200	62,500	73,400	70,400	69,800	70,700	68,900	68,900	85,000

STOCK PRICE HISTORY

HIGH/LOW/CLOSE

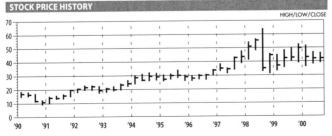

1999 FISCAL YEAR-END

Debt ratio: 59.0%
Return on equity: 10.3%
Cash ($ mil.): 941
Current ratio: 1.09
Long-term debt ($ mil.): 2,703
No. of shares (mil.): 286
Dividends
  Yield: 4.2%
  Payout: 297.2%
Market value ($ mil.): 14,224

ALCAN ALUMINIUM LIMITED

OVERVIEW

Alcan Aluminium's can-do attitude has helped make it the world's second-largest aluminum producer, behind the US's Alcoa. Based in Montreal, Alcan mines bauxite (aluminum ore) and makes aluminum and aluminum products for the container, packaging, transportation, electrical, and construction industries. Alcan is a leading producer of flat-rolled aluminum (sheet and foil), most of which goes into making beverage cans. Other products include cable, extruded products (doors and automotive parts), and aluminum-related specialty chemicals. Its Alcan Global Automotive Products unit coordinates supplying aluminum parts to automakers worldwide. Alcan also generates hydroelectric power and is one of the world's largest aluminum recyclers.

After having reorganized the company into two divisions (global fabrication and primary metals), Alcan has continued to streamline operations through divestitures, mostly in the company's fabrication division. The company had planned to challenge Alcoa by merging with major aluminum manufacturers Pechiney and Alusuisse Lonza Group (Algroup). Antitrust concerns scuttled the initial plan, then Pechiney withdrew leaving Alcan and Algroup to go it alone. Alcan did acquire Algroup, but it's left with a much smaller business combination than it had envisioned. Former Algroup shareholders now own about 34% of Alcan.

HISTORY

In 1886 American chemist Charles Hall and a French chemist simultaneously discovered an inexpensive process for aluminum production. Two years later Hall, with an investor group led by Captain Alfred Hunt, formed the Pittsburgh Reduction Company. It became the Aluminum Company of America (Alcoa) in 1907.

As mandated by a US antitrust divestment order, in 1928 Alcoa organized its Canadian and other foreign operations as a separate company, Aluminium (British spelling for aluminum) Limited. Aluminium Limited retained close ties with Alcoa and appointed Edward Davis, brother of former Alcoa chairman Arthur Davis, as its first.

After narrowly surviving the Depression, Aluminium Limited expanded globally, building plants in Asia and Europe. Aluminum demand during WWII made it the world's largest smelter by war's end.

US courts in 1950 ordered the Mellon and Davis families to end their joint ownership of Alcoa and Aluminium Limited. Both families opted to stay with Alcoa.

In 1961 the company began fabricating its own products in Oswego, New York. Aluminium Limited changed its name to Alcan in 1966. Alcan had to readjust its strategy when Guyana nationalized its raw resources in 1971. Six years later Jamaica (a major bauxite producer) acquired 70% of Alcan's assets, and the two formed joint venture Jamalcan.

David Culver became the company's CEO (the first non-Davis family member to hold the position) in 1979 and led Alcan through an early 1980s recession with a massive cost-cutting campaign. In 1989 Alcan built the world's largest aluminum beverage-can recycling plant in Berea, Kentucky.

The entrance of former Soviet republics and other Eastern Bloc countries into the international aluminum market in 1991 caused a drastic drop in aluminum prices worldwide. By 1994 increased global demand for aluminum and cutbacks in production spurred industry-wide recovery, and Alcan's operations returned to the black for the first time in four years.

In 1998 Alcan signed a 10-year pact to supply aluminum to General Motors. As market conditions in Asia soured, Alcan reduced its ownership of Nippon Light Metal Company from 45% to about 11%. Also that year it sold Handy Chemicals Limited.

Facing tough market conditions in 1999, Alcan restructured into two divisions — primary metals (bauxite and alumina) and fabricated products (fabricated aluminum and recycling). The company also announced the sale of its alumina refinery in Ireland to Glencore and agreed to acquire Pechiney and Alusuisse Lonza Group (Algroup) in a three-way merger to create Alcan-Pechiney-Algroup.

In 2000 the European Commission approved a proposed merger between Alcan and Algroup, but Alcan's plan to include Pechiney in a three-way merger had to be withdrawn due to antitrust concerns. Pechiney pulled out of the deal entirely after Alcan voted against selling its 50% stake in a German aluminum plant (Norf). In the meantime, Alcan and Taihan Electric Wire agreed to acquire 66% and 30%, respectively, of Aluminum of Korea (Koralu) from the Hyundai Group. The same year Alcan acquired Algroup in a $5.3 billion deal.

Chairman: John R. Evans, age 70
President and CEO: Jacques Bougie, age 52,
$740,700 pay
EVP and CFO: Suresh Thadhani, age 60
EVP; President, Alcan Primary Metal Group:
Emery P. LeBlanc, age 58, $812,253 pay
**EVP; President, Aluminum Fabrication, Americas and
Asia:** Brian W. Sturgell, age 50, $879,550 pay
EVP; President, Aluminum Fabrication, Europe:
Richard B. Evans, age 52, $786,807 pay
SVP Human Resources: Gaston Ouellet, age 57
Auditors: PricewaterhouseCoopers LLP

LOCATIONS

HQ: 1188 Sherbrooke St. West,
Montreal, Quebec H3A 3G2, Canada
Phone: 514-848-8000 **Fax:** 514-848-8115
US HQ: 6060 Parkland Blvd., Cleveland, OH 44124
US Phone: 440-423-6600 **US Fax:** 440-423-6667
Web site: http://www.alcan.com

Alcan Aluminium operates bauxite mines in Australia,
Brazil, Ghana, India, and Jamaica; alumina plants in
Australia, Brazil, Canada, India, Jamaica, and the UK;
and manufacturing plants or sales offices in more than
35 countries.

1999 Sales

	$ mil.	% of total
US	3,067	42
Europe	2,340	32
Asia/Pacific	877	12
Canada	620	8
South America	371	5
Other regions	49	1
Total	**7,324**	**100**

PRODUCTS/OPERATIONS

1999 Sales

	$ mil.	% of total
Global fabrication group	5,607	76
Primary metal group	1,689	23
Other	28	1
Total	**7,324**	**100**

Selected Products and Services

Fabrication Group
Castings
Extrusions (automobile components, doors, and
windows; extrusion ingots)
Flat-rolled products (foil and sheet)
Flexible packaging
Recycling
Wire and cable

Primary Metal Group
Alumina refining
Aluminum activities
Bauxite mining
Power generation

COMPETITORS

Alcoa	Industria	Rio Tinto Limited
Carso	Española Del	Rio Tinto plc
Commercial	Aluminio	Ryerson Tull
Metals	Kaiser Aluminum	SEPI
Corus Group	MAXXAM	Silgan
CVRD	Mitsui	SMI
Graenges	Nissho Iwai	Southwire
Hydro	Noranda	Trans-World
Aluminium	Ormet	Metals
Imsa	Pechiney	VAW Aluminium
	Quanex	

HISTORICAL FINANCIALS & EMPLOYEES

NYSE: AL FYE: December 31	Annual Growth	12/90	12/91	12/92	12/93	12/94	12/95	12/96	12/97	12/98	12/99
Sales ($ mil.)	(2.0%)	8,757	7,748	7,596	7,232	8,216	9,287	7,614	7,777	7,789	7,324
Net income ($ mil.)	(1.8%)	543	(36)	(112)	(104)	96	263	410	485	399	460
Income as % of sales	—	6.2%	—	—	—	1.2%	2.8%	5.4%	6.2%	5.1%	6.3%
Earnings per share ($)	(1.4%)	2.33	(0.25)	(0.60)	(0.54)	0.34	1.06	1.74	2.09	1.71	2.06
Stock price - FY high ($)	—	24.50	24.00	22.75	22.38	28.13	36.63	36.13	40.31	34.50	42.00
Stock price - FY low ($)	—	16.63	17.25	15.25	16.88	19.75	23.38	28.38	26.06	18.69	22.94
Stock price - FY close ($)	8.7%	19.50	20.00	17.63	20.75	25.38	31.13	33.63	27.63	27.06	41.38
P/E - high	—	11	—	—	—	83	35	21	20	20	20
P/E - low	—	7	—	—	—	58	22	16	13	11	11
Dividends per share ($)	(6.7%)	1.12	0.86	0.45	0.30	0.30	0.45	0.60	0.60	0.60	0.60
Book value per share ($)	1.1%	22.99	22.12	20.64	19.86	20.74	21.40	21.46	22.32	24.42	25.38
Employees	(4.4%)	54,100	50,200	46,500	43,900	43,900	39,000	34,000	33,000	36,000	36,000

STOCK PRICE HISTORY

HIGH/LOW/CLOSE

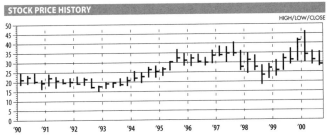

1999 FISCAL YEAR-END

Debt ratio: 15.4%
Return on equity: 8.6%
Cash ($ mil.): 315
Current ratio: 1.66
Long-term debt ($ mil.): 1,011
No. of shares (mil.): 218
Dividends
  Yield: 1.4%
  Payout: 29.1%
Market value ($ mil.): 9,034

ALCATEL

Alcatel is putting a French twist on high-tech communications. Paris-based Alcatel primarily makes telecommunications equipment for public networks, homes, and businesses. Its products include optical and wireless networking gear and underwater networking systems. The company also makes power and telecommunications cables. Alcatel counts itself at or near the top of many of the markets it serves. About 55% of sales are in Europe.

Chairman and CEO Serge Tchuruk has built Alcatel into a telecommunications superpower.

He has overseen an extensive restructuring that has included lightening its stakes in non-core businesses such as engineering, nuclear power, and defense electronics. Alcatel has also cut staff and plans to spin off its energy and telecom cable business to the public.

Alcatel's intent on advancing further into the fiercely competitive US market (about 20% of sales) is evidenced by acquisitions of complementary telecom companies that bolster its holdings of technologies including fiber-optic switching and digital subscriber line systems.

HISTORY

In 1898 Pierre Azaria combined his electric generating company with three others to form Compagnie Générale d'Électricité (CGE). As one of Europe's pioneer electric power and manufacturing companies, CGE expanded operations in France and abroad through acquisitions. After the French government nationalized electric utilities in 1946, CGE diversified into the production of telecommunications equipment, consumer appliances, and electronics.

In 1970 CGE bought Alcatel, a French communications pioneer founded in 1879 that had introduced digital switching exchanges. CGE combined its telecommunications division with Alcatel to form CIT Alcatel.

The Mitterrand government nationalized CGE in 1982. The next year the company traded its electronics units for Thomson's communications businesses, making CGE the world's fifth-largest telephone equipment maker. Later, CGE combined Alcatel with ITT's phone equipment operations to form Alcatel NV, a Brussels-based company that started off as the world's second-largest telecommunications enterprise, after AT&T.

In 1987 the government sold CGE to the public. Two years later CGE and UK-based The General Electric Company, plc, (GEC, now known as Marconi plc) combined their power systems and engineering businesses to create GEC Alsthom NV. The company adopted the Alcatel Alsthom name in 1991 (shortened to Alcatel in 1998).

Turnaround specialist Serge Tchuruk, the former head of French oil giant TOTAL, was chosen to lead the company in 1995.

Deregulation and intense competition in the European telecom market, along with massive writeoffs of bad investments dating back to the 1980s, led to a $5 billion loss in 1995, Alcatel's first loss and the largest to date by a French company. As a result Alcatel divested non-

strategic assets and cut its workforce by more than 12,500 employees. The company bounced back with a profit in 1996.

Following the recommendation of the French government, in 1998 Alcatel, Dassault Industries, and Aerospatiale (now Aerospatiale Matra) joined forces to buy part of the state's stake in defense electronics group Thomson-CSF. Intensifying its telecommunications focus, Alcatel sold its main engineering unit (Cegelec) to GEC Alsthom in 1998 and then spun off the venture as ALSTOM. That year Alcatel bought Packet Engines (Gigabit Ethernet products) and networking specialist DSC Communications to further push into the US market. When Alcatel's stock plummeted after slumping orders caused it to issue a profit warning later that year, DSC shareholders sued, alleging that Alcatel sat on the news.

In 1999 Alcatel acquired several US-based data network equipment makers, including Xylan and Assured Access, and formed a new unit to focus on networking software and services. To boost profit margins, Alcatel planned to cut about 10% of its workforce, primarily in the US, over the next two years. The company also won a contract to build Europe's largest and fastest data network.

In early 2000 Alcatel swapped all but 10% of its stake in nuclear power firm Framatome for an additional 10% of Thomson-CSF. This raised its stake in Thomson-CSF to 25%. The company also bought US-based Genesys Telecommunications (computer telephony software) and Canadian equipment maker Newbridge Networks for $7.1 billion. It later said it would spin off and take public its cable business by the end of 2000. Alcatel also sold 20% of its Optronics optical components unit to create the first European tracking stock.

Chairman and CEO: Serge Tchuruk
President and CFO: Jean-Pierre Halbron
COO; CEO Alcatel Americas: Krish Prabhu
President, Carrier Networking: Pearse Flynn
President, e-Business: Olivier Houssin
President, Optics: Christian Reinaudo
President, Europe, Middle East, Africa, and India: Julien De Wilde
President, Asia/Pacific: Ron Spithill
Chief Technology Officer: Martin De Prycker
Secretary General: Jacques Dunogué
President, Cables and Components: Gérard Houser
President, Telecom: Yvon Raak
President, Energy: Bruno Thomas
President, Mobile Communications: Gerard Dega
Auditors: Deloitte Touche Tohmatsu

LOCATIONS

HQ: 54, rue La Boétie, 75008 Paris, France
Phone: +33-1-40-76-10-10 **Fax:** +33-1-40-76-14-00
US HQ: 1000 Coit Rd., Plano, TX 75075
US Phone: 972-519-3000 **US Fax:** 972-519-4122
Web site: http://www.alcatel.com

Alcatel has operations in more than 130 countries.

1999 Sales by Origin

	$ mil.	% of total
Europe		
France	6,862	29
Germany	2,476	11
Other countries	6,967	30
North America	3,663	16
Asia	722	3
Other regions	2,545	11
Total	**23,235**	**100**

PRODUCTS/OPERATIONS

1999 Sales

	$ mil.	% of total
Networking	7,177	31
Internet & optics	5,647	24
Enterprise & consumer	3,746	16
Energy cables	3,607	16
Telecom components	2,901	12
Other	157	1
Total	**23,235**	**100**

Selected Products and Services
Asymmetric and very-high bit rate digital subscriber line
Broadband wireless products
Cable television systems
Cables and power accessories
Microwave systems
Optical fiber
Private branch exchange (PBX) systems
Routers and switches
Satellite platforms and stations

COMPETITORS

3Com	Hughes	Philips
Ascom Holding	Electronics	Electronics
AT&T Broadband	Hyundai	Pirelli S.p.A.
Atos Origin	Electronics	QUALCOMM
Cap Gemini	Koor	Sagem
Cisco Systems	Lucent	Samsung
Cookson Group	Marconi	Electronics
Corning	Matsushita	SANYO
Ericsson	Communication	Siemens
Fujikura	Motorola	Sony
Harris	NEC	Sumitomo
Corporation	Nokia	Electric
Hitachi	Nortel Networks	Industries
	Oki Electric	Toshiba

HISTORICAL FINANCIALS & EMPLOYEES

NYSE: ALA FYE: December 31	Annual Growth	12/90	12/91	12/92	12/93	12/94	12/95	12/96	12/97	12/98	12/99
Sales ($ mil.)	(2.1%)	28,246	30,815	29,270	26,456	31,400	32,709	31,269	30,854	24,906	23,235
Net income ($ mil.)	(4.7%)	1,007	1,190	1,277	1,195	678	(5,216)	526	774	2,741	650
Income as % of sales	—	3.6%	3.9%	4.4%	4.5%	2.2%	—	1.7%	2.5%	11.0%	2.8%
Earnings per share ($)	(13.7%)	—	—	1.93	1.68	0.98	(0.65)	0.70	0.97	3.08	0.69
Stock price - FY high ($)	—	—	—	27.13	29.50	30.75	22.13	19.13	28.50	47.13	46.06
Stock price - FY low ($)	—	—	—	22.63	21.63	15.38	15.38	14.25	15.50	15.94	20.38
Stock price - FY close ($)	8.9%	—	—	24.75	28.63	17.00	17.50	16.00	25.31	24.44	45.00
P/E - high	—	—	—	14	18	32	—	29	29	15	67
P/E - low	—	—	—	12	13	16	—	21	16	5	30
Dividends per share ($)	—	—	—	0.00	0.00	0.41	0.61	0.31	0.00	0.39	0.00
Book value per share ($)	(0.8%)	—	—	69.31	68.28	76.41	46.32	50.30	44.71	62.98	65.52
Employees	(6.2%)	205,500	213,100	203,000	196,500	203,000	191,830	190,600	189,500	118,000	115,712

STOCK PRICE HISTORY

HIGH/LOW/CLOSE

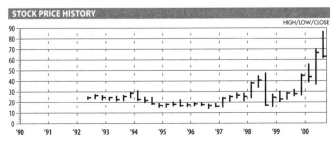

1999 FISCAL YEAR-END

Debt ratio: 22.9%
Return on equity: 5.5%
Cash ($ mil.): 2,953
Current ratio: 1.49
Long-term debt ($ mil.): 3,620
No. of shares (mil.): 186
Dividends
 Yield: —
 Payout: —
Market value ($ mil.): 8,353

ALITALIA - LINEE AEREE ITALIANE

OVERVIEW

Italy's former airline monopoly is en route to privatization. Based in Rome, Alitalia - Linee Aeree Italiane serves about 135 destinations in more than 65 countries. The airline, which operates from hubs in Rome and Milan, flies more than 160 aircraft and carries 25 million passengers each year. The Italian government still owns 53% of Alitalia but plans to sell its stake.

Alitalia has shed some of its baggage from its days as a state-owned enterprise. Labor squabbles have been soothed with an employee ownership plan, and its bottom line strengthened. As European competition grows, Alitalia has launched low-fare carrier Alitalia Team and regional Alitalia Express.

Other subsidiaries include SIGMA, which provides travel industry data processing products, and Italiatour, a tour promoter.

But one of Alitalia's major initiatives, a two-year partnership with Dutch airline KLM, has crashed and burned. KLM pulled out of the partnership, which had combined passenger and cargo operations of the two airlines under a single management, because of problems with operations at the new Malpensa airport near Milan and the Italian government's foot-dragging in selling off its stake. Alitalita has retained its code-sharing agreements with Continental and British Midland.

HISTORY

Alitalia got off the ground in 1946 as Alitalia Aerolinee Italiane Internazionali. The airline was 40%-owned by BEA (British European Airways, later part of British Airways) and 60%-owned by the Italian government. Alitalia was intended to be an international carrier; TWA and the Italian state set up Linee Aeree Italiane (LAI) for domestic flights.

Alitalia began flying in 1947 with a Turin-Rome-Catania route, and service to Africa and Brazil was launched from Rome in 1948. To better compete with other European carriers, Alitalia and LAI merged in 1957 and took the name Alitalia - Linee Aeree Italiane. The government bought the shares held by BEA and TWA and assigned Alitalia to IRI, the Italian state holding company. The new airline's fleet boasted 37 aircraft.

By 1960 Alitalia carried a million passengers and had introduced its first jets. By 1968 it had an all-jet fleet. The stylized "A" tailfin logo appeared a year later, and in 1970 Alitalia adopted use of the Boeing 747.

But Alitalia began losing money in the 1970s. Facing rising fuel prices, inflation, and labor strikes, it responded by cutting underused routes and buying fuel-efficient Boeing 727s.

In the early 1980s Alitalia diversified by creating Sigma (travel-related information systems) and Italiatour (tour operator). Diversification came, however, at the expense of the airline's expansion, and it began losing market share to rivals Air France and Lufthansa. In 1988 Alitalia brought in Carlo Verri from the private sector to deal with labor and structural problems. He secured labor contracts and developed aircraft financing, but his auspicious start ended with a fatal car crash in 1989. Alitalia limped through the early 1990s with

losses, aging equipment, and a reputation for poor service.

IRI hired former IBM executive Renato Riverso as chairman in 1994. With deregulation fast approaching, Alitalia penned code-sharing partnerships with Continental (1994) and Canadian Airlines (1995). In 1995 several labor strikes flared up amid talk of restructuring and cost-cutting measures. After receiving little government support, Riverso resigned in 1996. His short-lived reign laid a foundation: Labor tensions were eased with the promise of an employee-owned share in the company.

Europe's air transportation market was opened to competition in 1996 (after a long process that began in 1983). Alitalia began low-fare carrier Alitalia Team, signed on Italian regional airline Azzurra as a code-share partner the next year, and set up its own regional carrier, Alitalia Express. In 1997 it also achieved its first annual profit since 1988.

IRI reduced its stake in Alitalia to 53% in 1998, and employees got their 20% stake. Alitalia began an alliance with Dutch carrier KLM, and in 1999 Alitalia and KLM completed a "virtual merger" that unified their management structures for passenger and cargo joint ventures and allowed them to share profits. KLM ditched the partnership in 2000, however, and demanded Alitalia repay $91 million it had spent to upgrade an Italian airport. Alitalia protested KLM's termination of the alliance, and the dispute between the carriers wound up in arbitration proceedings.

IRI was liquidated in 2000, and the state holding company's stake in Alitalia was to be transferred to the Treasury Ministry.

OFFICERS

Chairman and President: Fausto Cereti
CEO: Domenico Cempella
Director Human Resources: Claudio Carli
Director Finance: Giovanni Lionetti
SVP and Area Manager for North America and Mexico:
Paolo Rubino
Auditors: Deloitte and Touche spa

LOCATIONS

HQ: Alitalia - Linee Aeree Italiane S.P.A.
Viale A. Marchetti 111, 00148 Rome, Italy
Phone: +39-06-6562-2151   **Fax:** +39-06-6562-4733
US HQ: 666 5th Ave., 6th Fl., New York, NY 10103
US Phone: 212-903-3300   **US Fax:** 212-903-3350
Web site: http://www.alitalia.it

Alitalia - Linee Aeree Italiane serves about 135
destinations in Africa, Asia, Australia, Europe, the
Middle East, and North America.

PRODUCTS/OPERATIONS

1999 Aircraft Fleet

	No.
McDonnell Douglas 80	89
Airbus A321	22
Boeing 767	12
Boeing 747	11
McDonnell Douglas 11	8
Aerospatiale ATR42	7
Aerospatiale ATR72	7
McDonnell Douglas 83	5
Airbus A320	2
DC9-51	2
Total	**165**

Selected Subsidiaries
Alitalia Express (regional airline)
Alitalia Team (low-fare airline)
Atitech (maintenance)
Eurofly (45%, domestic charter flights)
Italiatour (tour promotion)
Racom Teledata (information technology services)
SIGMA - Società Italiana Gestione Multi Accesso (92%,
data processing systems and automated ticketing
services)

Selected Code-Sharing Partnerships
Air Seychelles
Azzurra Air
Braathens
British Midland
Continental Airlines
Croatia Airlines
CSA-Czech
Cyprus
Finnair
LOT-Polish
Meridiana
Minerva

COMPETITORS

Aer Lingus	Ryanair
Air France	SAirGroup
AMR	SAS
British Airways	TWA
easyJet	UAL
Iberia	US Airways
Lufthansa	Virgin Atlantic Airways

HISTORICAL FINANCIALS & EMPLOYEES

Italian: AZA FYE: December 31	Annual Growth	12/90	12/91	12/92	12/93	12/94	12/95	12/96	12/97	12/98	12/99
Sales (€ mil.)	9.0%	—	—	2,777	3,447	3,700	4,061	4,036	4,432	4,620	5,068
Net income (€ mil.)	—	—	—	(9)	(178)	(149)	1	(629)	226	211	6
Income as % of sales	—	—	—	—	—	—	0.0%	—	5.1%	4.6%	0.1%
Earnings per share (€)	(85.7%)	—	—	—	—	—	—	—	0.15	0.14	0.00
Stock price - FY high (€)	—	—	—	—	—	—	—	—	1.55	4.87	3.62
Stock price - FY low (€)	—	—	—	—	—	—	—	—	0.57	1.29	2.16
Stock price - FY close (€)	29.5%	—	—	—	—	—	—	—	1.41	3.15	2.37
P/E - high	—	—	—	—	—	—	—	—	11	36	1,207
P/E - low	—	—	—	—	—	—	—	—	4	9	720
Dividends per share (€)	—	—	—	—	—	—	—	—	0.00	0.00	0.00
Book value per share (€)	77.1%	—	—	—	—	—	—	—	0.36	1.17	1.13
Employees	1.1%	—	—	18,928	20,152	18,676	17,982	16,507	15,740	19,600	20,497

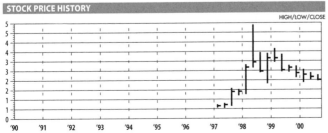

STOCK PRICE HISTORY
HIGH/LOW/CLOSE

1999 FISCAL YEAR-END
Debt ratio: 0.1%
Return on equity: 0.3%
Cash (€ mil.): 110
Current ratio: 1.16
Long-term debt (€ mil.): 305
No. of shares (mil.): 1,548
Dividends
  Yield: —
  Payout: —
Market value ($ mil.): 3,662

ALL NIPPON AIRWAYS CO., LTD.

OVERVIEW

All Nippon Airways (ANA) has Japan covered. Tokyo-based ANA is the country's #2 airline overall (after Japan Airlines), but it ranks as the #1 domestic carrier by serving 51% of the market. ANA operates a fleet of more than 140 jetliners (mostly Boeings) and flies to more than 50 Japanese cities and to 32 international destinations in 17 countries.

In addition to its passenger and cargo services, ANA is involved in a number of businesses that complement its airline operations, including ground support and aircraft maintenance and hotel operations. The company's ANA Hotels division owns hotels in Europe and the Asia/Pacific region, as well as in Japan.

ANA has been doubly challenged by Japan's lingering recession and the sweeping deregulation that has led to greater domestic and international competition. To reduce costs, the airline has resorted to cutting jobs, streamlining management, and closing some affiliated businesses. It has stepped up international flights, while shifting more domestic routes to its Air Nippon subsidiary.

Seeking strength in numbers, ANA has joined the global Star Alliance, which includes such ANA code-sharing partners as UAL's United Airlines, Lufthansa, and Brazil's VARIG. The airline is 7%-owned by Japan's Nagoya Railroad.

HISTORY

Two domestic Japanese air carriers that started in 1952 — Nippon Helicopter and Aeroplane Transport and Far East Airlines — consolidated operations in 1957 as All Nippon Airways (ANA).

Throughout the 1960s ANA developed a domestic route network linking Japan's largest cities — Tokyo, Osaka, Fukuoka, and Sapporo — and its leading provincial centers, including Nagoya, Nagasaki, Matsuyama, and Hakodate. During this period domestic traffic grew at an annual rate of 30% to 60%.

In 1970 the Japanese cabinet formulated routes for its major airlines, giving ANA scheduled domestic service and unscheduled international flights. That year Tokuji Wakasa became ANA's chairman and the company began a program of diversification that led to the establishment of ANA Trading, international charter service (starting with Hong Kong), and a hotel subsidiary. Air Nippon, a regional domestic airline, was started in 1974.

The company established Nippon Cargo Airlines, a charter service set up jointly with four steamship lines, in 1978. ANA carried 19.5 million passengers that year, but its growth slowed between 1978 and 1980. High jet fuel prices caused a $45.6 million loss in 1979, but ANA rebounded a year later. In 1982 ANA opened international charter service to Guam. The company founded ANA Sports in 1984 to manage the company soccer team.

Japan deregulated air routes in 1985, allowing ANA to offer scheduled international flights. The airline offered its first regular flight from Tokyo to Guam in 1986 and soon added service to Los Angeles and Washington, DC. Flights to China, Hong Kong, and Sydney began a year later.

Between 1988 and 1990 ANA added flights to Bangkok, London, Moscow, Saipan, Seoul, Stockholm, and Vienna. In 1988 ANA bought a minority stake in Austrian Airlines and set up the domestic computer reservation system (CRS). The company's international CRS, INFINI (a joint venture with CRS co-op ABACUS), went online in 1990.

ANA started World Air Network Charter (WAC) in 1991 to serve travelers from Japan's smaller cities. That year ANA opened its first European hotel (in Vienna), was listed on the London Stock Exchange, and opened a flight school in the US for its pilots.

In 1992 ANA premiered a hotel in Beijing. In 1995 the airline announced that it would increase its international traffic by more than 30%. As part of this strategy ANA and Air Canada began a code-sharing service in 1996 between Osaka and Vancouver, and a year later ANA became the first Japanese airline to operate a Boeing 777 on an international route (between Tokyo and Beijing).

As the Asian financial crisis sent Japanese airlines to the brink, a pilot strike in 1998 dashed ANA's hopes for a 15% pay cut. To cope, ANA formed alliances with UAL's United Airlines, Lufthansa, and Brazil's VARIG. ANA extended those partnerships in 1999 by joining the global Star Alliance. To shore up its financial strength, ANA reorganized domestic routes, dropping some unprofitable ones and shifting others to its Air Nippon unit; it also announced plans to launch low-cost air service for international routes in Asia. Competition intensified when Japan fully deregulated domestic fares in 2000, sparking a fare war.

President and CEO; Executive Director, Safety Promotion: Kichisaburo Nomura
SEVP Sales and Marketing: Yoji Ohashi
SEVP Associated Businesses Development, Safety Promotion, Operations, Control Center, Flight Operations, Engineering, and Maintenance: Yoshiyuki Nakamachi
SEVP Executive Office, General Affairs, Legal Affairs, Personnel, and Employee Relations: Isao Yagi
Managing Director Cargo & Mail Sales and Environmental Affairs: Masahiro Kinoshita
Managing Director Information Technology Management and B.P.R. Promotion: Wataru Kubo
Managing Director; General Manager Sales and Marketing, Osaka Sales Office: Yasuyuki Nishikawa
Managing Director; General Manager Sales and Marketing, Tokyo Sales Office: Motohiro Higashisono
Managing Director Corporate Planning, Public Relations, Government and Industrial Affairs, and Corporate Finance: Yasushi Morohashi
Managing Director Marketing Star Alliance Activities Promotion: Kazuhisa Shin
Managing Director Flight Operations: Manabu Ouchi
Managing Director In-Flight Services: Yuzuru Maki
Managing Director International and Regulatory Affairs, Purchasing and Facilities, and Airport Affairs: Hiromichi Toya
Senior Director Airport Operations and Services: Koichiro Ono
Senior Director; General Manager, Europe and Middle East (London Office): Koichi Nomura
Senior Director Engineering and Maintenance: Suguru Omae
Senior Director; General Manager The Americas (New York Office): Tadashi Ota
Auditors: Century Ota Showa & Co.

HQ: Zen Nippon Kuyu Kabushiki Kaisha,
3-5-10 Haneda Airport,
Ota-ku, Tokyo 144-0041, Japan
Phone: +81-3-5756-5665 **Fax:** +81-3-5756-5659
US HQ: 1251 Avenue of the Americas, 8th Fl.,
New York, NY 10020
US Phone: 212-840-3700 **US Fax:** 212-840-3704
Web site: http://www.ana.co.jp

All Nippon Airways flies to more than 50 cities in Japan, and serves 32 international destinations in 17 countries.

2000 Sales

	% of total
Domestic passenger	52
International passenger	13
International cargo	3
Domestic cargo	2
Other	30
Total	**100**

Accor	FlightSafety
Air France	Hyatt
AMR	JAL
British Airways	Japan Air System
Carlson	Kinki Nippon Railway
Cathay Pacific	KLM
Central Japan Railway	Northwest
China Airlines	Qantas
Continental Airlines	Singapore Airlines
Delta	TWA
East Japan Railway	Virgin Atlantic Airways
Evergreen Marine	

OTC: ALNPY FYE: March 31	Annual Growth	3/91	3/92	3/93	3/94	3/95	3/96	3/97	3/98	3/99	3/00
Sales ($ mil.)	8.0%	5,714	6,583	7,737	8,342	10,563	9,019	8,254	8,120	8,990	11,465
Net income ($ mil.)	—	82	55	(10)	(91)	(86)	(80)	35	(41)	(40)	(144)
Income as % of sales	—	1.4%	0.8%	—	—	—	—	0.4%	—	—	—
Earnings per share ($)	—	0.12	0.08	(0.01)	(0.13)	(0.12)	(0.11)	0.05	(0.03)	(0.03)	(0.10)
Stock price - FY high ($)	—	6.80	7.14	5.58	7.41	7.48	26.61	28.41	13.50	9.00	8.13
Stock price - FY low ($)	—	4.53	4.66	4.25	5.75	6.23	5.86	12.11	7.00	5.60	4.13
Stock price - FY close ($)	(0.1%)	5.86	4.66	5.41	6.08	6.81	25.98	12.50	10.25	6.33	5.81
P/E - high	—	57	89	—	—	—	—	568	—	—	—
P/E - low	—	38	58	—	—	—	—	242	—	—	—
Dividends per share ($)	—	0.07	0.08	0.07	0.06	0.07	0.06	0.05	0.00	0.00	0.00
Book value per share ($)	(11.9%)	2.01	2.03	2.23	2.30	2.43	1.77	1.62	1.26	0.65	0.64
Employees	7.4%	—	—	—	—	—	21,096	21,240	22,956	25,420	28,064

HIGH/LOW/CLOSE

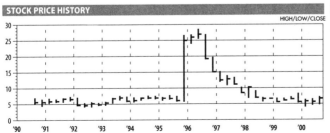

Debt ratio: 0.7%
Return on equity: —
Cash ($ mil.): 1,520
Current ratio: 0.89
Long-term debt ($ mil.): 800
No. of shares (mil.): 1,443
Dividends
  Yield: —
  Payout: —
Market value ($ mil.): 8,382

ALLIANZ AG

OVERVIEW

Munich, Germany-based Allianz lives up to its name: The world's #2 insurance company (AXA is #1) is a global alliance of some 100 subsidiaries, joint ventures, and affiliates.

Allianz offers a range of insurance products and services, including life, health, and property/casualty. Other businesses include risk consulting, loss-prevention services, and public investment funds. It also offers such services as residential mortgages and corporate financing. The company is making a major push into global asset management, focusing on fund management for private and institutional investors. It also plans to set up a global Internet portal.

Allianz is part of a web of interlocking German corporate ownership. It holds stakes in the country's top banks (Deutsche Bank, Bayerische Hypotheken und Vereinsbank, and Dresdner Bank), as well as 25% of the world's largest reinsurer, Munich Re (which has an equal stake in Allianz). The two are reducing those stakes to 20% each.

Ready to make the most of its global position, Allianz has adopted more transparent accounting and is looking to expand its operations through acquisitions in such key markets as Asia and the US, where it has listed its stock on the NYSE.

HISTORY

Carl Thieme founded Allianz in Germany in 1890. That year the company took part in the creation of the Calamity Association of Accident Insurance Companies, a consortium of German, Austrian, Swiss, and Russian firms, to insure international commerce.

By 1898 Thieme had established offices in the UK, Switzerland, and the Netherlands. His successor, Paul von der Nahmer, expanded Allianz into the Balkans, France, Italy, Scandinavia, and the US. After a hiatus during WWI, Allianz returned to foreign markets.

In WWII, Allianz insured Auschwitz, Dachau, and other death camps. After the German defeat, the victors seized Allianz's foreign holdings, except for a stake in Spain's Plus Ultra. In the 1950s Allianz repurchased confiscated holdings in Italian and Austrian companies.

Allianz saturated the German market and began a full-scale international drive in the late 1950s and 1960s. It became Europe's largest insurer through a series of acquisitions beginning in 1973. Allianz formed Los Angeles-based Allianz Insurance in 1977.

In 1981 Allianz launched a takeover (which turned hostile) of the UK's Eagle Star insurance company. After a 1983 bidding joust with Britain's B.A.T Industries (now part of Zurich Financial Services), Allianz withdrew.

The firm consoled itself by shopping. In 1984 it won control of Riunione Adriatica di Sicurta (RAS), Italy's second-largest insurance company. Two years later the firm bought Cornhill in the UK (on its third try). As the Iron Curtain crumbled, Allianz in 1989 acquired 49% of Hungaria Biztosito. Its *drang nach Osten* continued the next year after national reunification, when it gained control of Deutsche Versicherungs AG, East Germany's insurance

monopoly. Allianz that year became the first German insurer licensed in Japan; it also bought the US's Fireman's Fund Insurance.

Natural disasters led to large claims and set the company back in 1992, the first time in 20 years it lost money from its German operations. Allianz restructured operations that year; profits surged in 1993, mostly from international business.

Allianz expanded in Mexico in 1995, forming a life and health insurance joint venture with Grupo Financiero BanCrecer. The company set up an asset management arm in Hong Kong in 1996 with an eye to further Asian expansion, getting a license in China the next year. In 1997 after Holocaust survivors sued Allianz and other insurers for failing to pay on life policies after WWII, Allianz agreed to participate in a repayment fund.

In 1998 Allianz bought control of Assurances Générales de France; it was the white knight that prevented Assicurazioni Generali from taking the company. In 1999 Allianz said it would restructure some of its insurance operations, including spinning off its marine and aviation lines, to better compete in the multinational market. That year US subsidiary Allianz Life bought Life USA Holding. The next year Allianz bought 70% of PIMCO Advisors Holdings to strengthen its asset management operations.

In 2000 the company continued its push into Asia, buying a 12% stake in Hana Bank of South Korea and planning to boost its ownership of Malaysia British Assurance Life. It also agreed to buy asset manager Nicholas-Applegate.

Chairman: Henning Schulte-Noelle
Member Management Board (Reinsurance, Europe and ART): Detlev Bremkamp
Member Management Board and Director Personnel, and Property and Casualty Insurance, Germany; Chairman, Allianz Versicherungs: Reiner Hagemann
Member Management Board (North and South America): Herbert Hansmeyer
Member Management Board (Life and Health Insurance, Germany); Chairman, Allianz Lebensversicherungs: Gerhard Rupprecht
Member of Management Board and CFO: Paul Achleitner
Member of Management Board (Asia/Pacific, Central/Eastern Europe, Near East/Africa): Michael Diekmann
Chairman, President, and CEO, Allianz Insurance (US): Wolfgang Schlink
Auditors: KPMG Deutsche Treuhand-Gesellschaft

LOCATIONS

HQ: Königinstrasse 28, D-80802 Munich, Germany
Phone: +49-89-3-80-00   **Fax:** +49-89-34-99-41
US HQ: 3400 Riverside Dr., Ste. 300, Burbank, CA 91505
US Phone: 818-972-8000   **US Fax:** 818-972-8466
Web site: http://www.allianz.com

1999 Premiums

	% of total
Europe	
Germany	41
Other countries	42
North & South America	15
Africa & Asia	2
Total	**100**

PRODUCTS/OPERATIONS

1999 Assets

	% of total
Cash & equivalents	1
Real estate	4
Loans	4
Other investments	71
Receivables	8
Other assets	12
Total	**100**

Selected Holdings

Allianz Fire and Marine Insurance Japan Ltd.
Allianz Insurance Company (US)
Assurances Générales de France (51%)
Cornhill Insurance PLC (UK)
Deutsche Bank AG (5%)
Dresdner Bank AG (22%)
Fireman's Fund Insurance Company (US)
Munchener Ruckversicherungs-Gesellschaft AG (Munich Re, 25%)
Ost-West Allianz Insurance Company (Russia)

COMPETITORS

Aachener und	ING	State Farm
Munchener	MetLife	Sumitomo
AEGON	Mitsui Marine	Marine & Fire
AIG	& Fire	Tokio Marine
Allstate	Munich Re	and Fire
AXA	New York Life	Winterthur
CGNU plc	Nippon Life	Yasuda Fire &
Citigroup	Prudential	Marine
Credit Lyonnais	Prudential plc	Insurance
ERGO	Royal & Sun	Zurich Financial
Generali	Alliance	

HISTORICAL FINANCIALS & EMPLOYEES

NYSE: AZ FYE: December 31	Annual Growth	12/90	12/91	12/92	12/93	12/94	12/95	12/96	12/97	12/98	12/99
Assets ($ mil.)	16.4%	98,559	118,727	127,939	136,104	162,848	199,835	200,554	212,165	399,865	385,486
Net income ($ mil.)	19.6%	449	251	313	554	620	1,133	1,062	1,133	2,123	2,249
Income as % of assets	—	0.5%	0.2%	0.2%	0.4%	0.4%	0.6%	0.5%	0.5%	0.5%	0.6%
Employees	10.7%	45,483	61,158	74,263	69,859	67,785	69,236	65,836	73,290	105,676	113,584

NET INCOME HISTORY

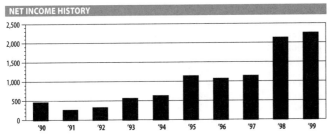

1999 FISCAL YEAR-END

Equity as % of assets: 10.7%
Return on assets: 0.6%
Return on equity: —
Long-term debt ($ mil.): —
Sales ($ mil.): 70,028

ALLIED DOMECQ PLC

OVERVIEW

Like a single girl with meddling relatives, Allied Domecq is under pressure to pair up. Bristol, England-based Allied Domecq is the world's second-largest spirits maker (behind Diageo), with a number of brands at or near the top of their respective categories, including Ballantine's, Beefeater, Courvoisier, Hiram Walker's, Kahlua, and Sauza. The distiller also distributes spirits and offers a variety of specialty spirits and wines such as brandy, cordials, liqueurs, and sherry.

The spirits industry has been consolidating since 1997, and plenty of suitable matches (via joint venture or acquisition) have been suggested for Allied Domecq. The company has been receptive to potential pairings; to make itself more attractive, it sold its UK pubs business. With that business gone, nearly 90% of the company's sales pour in from spirits and wines.

The rest of Allied Domecq's sales come from its quick-service restaurant franchises, including Dunkin' Donuts and Baskin-Robbins, which combined have more than 9,500 locations worldwide (65% in the US), as well as the Togo's Eateries sandwich chain, with 250 restaurants. Warren Buffett's Berkshire Hathaway owns about 3% of the company.

HISTORY

The "allied" in Allied Domecq dates back to the 1961 merger of three regional English breweries: Ind Coope, Tetley, and Ansell. The oldest of these was an Essex brewing facility created by Edward Ind to provide beer for an inn he bought in 1799. Ind's brewery merged with the Coope Brewery in 1845, and the resulting Ind Coope Brewery established a solid position in southern England's beer market.

Joshua Tetley entered the business in 1822 by purchasing a Leeds brewery with a following in northern England; however, central England was the realm of Joseph Ansell, a hops merchant who opened a brewery in 1881. Ansell Brewery ale became popular in Birmingham and the Midlands.

Tetley's 1960 merger with another brewery, Walker Cain, was followed the next year by the formation of Ind Coope Tetley Ansell Limited, which took the name Allied Breweries in 1963. Five years later the greatly fortified brewing operation purchased SVPW, a wine and spirits company also formed through a 1961 triple merger. In 1978 Allied bought its first food company, J. Lyons and Company, which owned the Baskin-Robbins ice-cream chain (founded in Glendale, California, in 1945) and several food brands. The company changed its name to Allied-Lyons three years later.

Allied-Lyons survived an unsuccessful takeover attempt by Elders IXL in 1985 and later battled Canada's Reichmann family over control of Hiram Walker. The firm walked away with Hiram Walker's liquor division. It bought Dunkin' Donuts in 1989 and Mister Donut the next year.

The 1990 acquisition of Whitbread's liquor business brought the company a long-sought-after premium white liquor brand, Beefeater gin. Allied-Lyons shifted its brewing business into an ill-fated brewing and wholesaling joint venture with Carlsberg, under the name Carlsberg-Tetley, two years later. (It coincided with a downturn in the brewing industry, and Allied-Lyons sold its 50% stake in 1996.) As part of its focus on core operations, Allied-Lyons paid more than $1 billion for the remaining 68% of Spanish distiller Pedro Domecq in 1994. The deal created the #2 distiller in the world, and the company changed its name to Allied Domecq.

In 1994 and 1995 the company sold nearly all its food operations, including its Tetley tea interests. In 1997 Allied Domecq acquired 200-strong California sandwich franchise chain Togo's Eateries and started a $100 million push to remodel 2,700 Baskin-Robbins to boost lagging sales.

Allied Domecq sold its Irish drinks unit, Cantrell & Cochrane, to investment firm BC Partners in 1999. Also in 1999 the company revealed that famed US investor Warren Buffett's Berkshire Hathaway had acquired a small Allied Domecq stake. Allied Domecq finance director Philip Bowman succeeded CEO Tony Hales that year. After a bidding war with Whitbread, in late 1999 pub operator Punch Taverns spent $4.4 billion for Allied Domecq's 3,600 pubs as well as its stake in First Quench Retailing.

In August 2000 Allied Domecq said it would bid for Seagram's spirits and wine business against chief rival Diageo and its bidding partner Pernod Ricard. Allied Domecq then obtained Seagram's rights to Captain Morgan Old Spiced rum from the Puerto Rican distiller, Destileria Serralles, in October 2000. In dispute, Seagram claims that the rights cannot be sold unless the auction of its brands *en masse* falls through.

Chairman: Sir Christopher Hogg, age 63
Chief Executive: Philip Bowman, age 46
Group Finance Director: Graham C. Hetherington, age 40
President and CEO, Allied Domecq Spirits, USA: Martin Jones
President, The Americas, Allied Domecq Spirits & Wine: George F. McCarthy, age 62
President, Europe, Allied Domecq Spirits & Wine: David Scotland, age 51
President, Customer Services and Planning: Richard G. Turner, age 50
Group Human Resources Director: Ian Jamieson
Auditors: KPMG Audit Plc

LOCATIONS

HQ: The Pavilions, Bridgewater Rd., Bedminster Down, Bristol BS13 8AR, United Kingdom
Phone: +44-117-978-5000   **Fax:** +44-117-978-5300
US HQ: 355 Riverside Ave., Westport, CT 06880
US Phone: 203-221-5400   **US Fax:** 203-221-5444
Web site: http://www.allieddomecq.co.uk

1999 Sales

	$ mil.	% of total
Europe		
UK	2,991	46
Other countries	1,327	20
US	1,324	20
Mexico	457	7
Canada	135	2
Other regions	343	5
Adjustments	(1,000)	—
Total	**5,577**	**100**

PRODUCTS/OPERATIONS

1999 Sales

	$ mil.	% of total
Spirits & wines	3,382	52
Discontinued		
UK retail	2,509	38
Cantrell & Cochrane	208	3
Restaurants	478	7
Adjustments	(1,000)	—
Total	**5,577**	**100**

Selected Products and Brands
Baskin-Robbins ice cream
Bourbon (Maker's Mark)
Brandy (Centenario, Don Pedro, Fundador, Presidente)
Canadian Whiskey (Canadian Club)
Dunkin' Donuts
Cognac (Courvoisier, VSOP, Imperial, Napoleon)
Gin (Beefeater, Crown Jewel, Oliphant, Wiser's)
Liqueurs (Frangelico, Kahlua, Tia Maria, Tuaca)
Sherry (Harveys Bristol Cream, La Ina)
Scotch (Ballantine's, Glendronach, Laphroaig, Teacher's)
Tequila (Sauza)
Togo's Eateries
Vodka (Borzoi, Grand Duke, Oliphant, Hiram Walker's)
Wine (Callaway, Clos du Bois, William Hill Winery)

COMPETITORS

Bacardi	Friendly Ice	LVMH
Ben & Jerry's	Cream	Pernod Ricard
Brown-Forman	Gallo	Remy Cointreau
Constellation	Guinness/UDV	Robert Mondavi
Brands	Heaven Hill	Seagram
CoolBrands	Distilleries	Sonic
Dairy Queen	Jose Cuervo	TCBY
Fortune Brands	Kendall-Jackson	Wendy's
Foster's Brewing	Krispy Kreme	Winchell's

HISTORICAL FINANCIALS & EMPLOYEES

OTC: ALDCY FYE: August 31	Annual Growth	8/90	8/91	8/92	8/93	8/94	8/95	8/96	8/97	8/98	8/99
Sales ($ mil.)	(3.7%)	7,808	7,665	7,937	7,899	8,178	13,834	8,402	7,186	7,237	5,577
Net income ($ mil.)	(16.0%)	631	545	654	389	480	636	66	646	460	132
Income as % of sales	—	8.1%	7.1%	8.2%	4.9%	5.9%	4.6%	0.8%	9.0%	6.4%	2.4%
Earnings per share ($)	(20.4%)	0.86	0.66	0.74	0.45	0.55	0.63	0.06	0.62	0.44	0.11
Stock price - FY high ($)	—	9.42	10.55	12.02	12.41	10.33	9.81	8.61	8.88	10.31	10.00
Stock price - FY low ($)	—	8.50	7.94	8.33	8.06	7.89	7.78	6.56	6.63	7.00	6.53
Stock price - FY close ($)	0.3%	8.86	8.92	10.47	8.78	8.05	7.78	7.17	7.63	8.75	9.07
P/E - high	—	11	16	16	28	19	16	144	14	23	91
P/E - low	—	10	12	11	18	14	12	109	11	16	59
Dividends per share ($)	(3.1%)	0.32	0.33	0.35	0.36	0.33	0.61	0.37	0.39	0.43	0.24
Book value per share ($)	(6.2%)	6.09	5.27	5.28	4.41	3.85	3.44	2.19	2.19	1.98	3.41
Employees	(9.1%)	—	—	—	—	—	—	54,000	50,871	49,709	40,495

STOCK PRICE HISTORY

HIGH/LOW/CLOSE

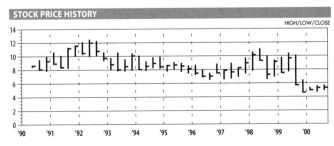

1999 FISCAL YEAR-END

Debt ratio: 25.5%
Return on equity: 3.7%
Cash ($ mil.): 378
Current ratio: 1.22
Long-term debt ($ mil.): 1,251
No. of shares (mil.): 1,068
Dividends
  Yield: 0.0%
  Payout: 2.2%
Market value ($ mil.): 9,688

ANDERSEN WORLDWIDE

OVERVIEW

Where's the rest of me? Out celebrating. Formerly THE accounting/consulting powerhouse, Andersen Worldwide has lost its 11-year battle to prevent the Andersen Consulting unit from leaving the fold — and taking its nearly 60% of firm sales with it.

Andersen Worldwide, still a Big Five stalwart, now consists of Arthur Andersen, no longer even the top dog accountant. The company offers traditional auditing services, internal audit and tax process oversight and outsourcing services, and the Andersen Legal Network, as well as Arthur Andersen's human resources, international trade, and risk consulting services (which competes with Andersen Consulting — a sore point between the parties).

There were cultural differences, too. The tight discipline that earned Arthur Andersen's professional staff the sobriquet "Arthur Androids" did not appeal to the consultants.

But the bottom line was the bottom line. As the audit business became subject to pricing pressure (in part because the Big Five accounting firms priced their audit services to attract consulting clients), the consultants flourished and finally tired of sharing their profits with the auditors who had formerly subsidized them.

An arbitrator for the International Chamber of Commerce awarded Andersen Worldwide $1 billion in compensation from Andersen Consulting (far less than the nearly $15 billion it hoped for) and awarded the accountants rights to the Andersen name. Andersen Consulting plans to name itself Accenture.

HISTORY

Arthur Andersen went to work in Price Waterhouse's Chicago office in 1907. In 1913 he and Clarence DeLany formed Andersen, DeLany & Company. The establishment of both the Federal Reserve System and the federal income tax that year increased the demand for accounting services. After DeLany's departure in 1918, the firm became Arthur Andersen & Co.

The company grew rapidly in the 1920s and began performing financial investigations — the basis for its consulting practice. When Samuel Insull's utility empire collapsed in 1932, Andersen was appointed the bankruptcy trustee. The firm contined to expand during the 1930s and 1940s.

Andersen dominated the firm until his death in 1947. His successor, Leonard Spacek, who headed the firm until 1963; continued to expand in the US and began its foreign expansion. The consulting business became a separate unit in 1954. It grew slowly; by 1979 it accounted for just over one-fifth of revenues. Nine years later, after a flood of corporate reorganizations, fees had risen to 40% of total sales.

The rise of the consultants and the accompanying power struggle resulted in the 1989 formation of Andersen Worldwide as an umbrella for both units. But it did not solve the issue of financial dominance and the formation of another consulting unit by Arthur Andersen in 1990 (to serve smaller companies) only increased tensions.

The consultancy in the 1990s built its information technology business through alliances for client service and implementation with major technology companies like Microsoft and Sun Microsystems. Its share of the business grew too, to more than half of sales.

During the same period the accountancy was hit by legal fallout from the failure of S&Ls whose books it had audited (it made a financial settlement with the US government in 1993) and by an evolving standard that held accountants increasingly liable for detecting fiscal misdeeds by its clients.

The rift between the audit and consulting sides widened in 1997 when CEO Lawrence Weinbach announced his retirement. When voting deadlocked, the board appointed accounting partner W. Robert Grafton as CEO. Soon thereafter, Andersen Consulting's partners voted to break away.

In 1998 a migration of workers between the units brought rumors that the split was at hand, but the dispute went into arbitration in 1999.

In 2000, both sides moved into venture funding and e-commerce; Arthur Andersen announced a deal with govWorks.com for a business-to-government e-commerce venture.

Andersen Worldwide lauded the arbitrator's decision to allow the units to go their separate ways, despite the disappointing termination award. However, shortly after the decision, Managing Partner James Wadia announced his resignation.

Arthur Andersen's growing network of attorneys faces legal restrictions on the business association between lawyers and nonlawyers. Its remaining consulting operations face growing pressure from the SEC's campaign against potential conflicts of interest arising from the provision of both consulting and auditing services to the same company.

Managing Partner and CEO: W. Robert Grafton
Interim Managing Partner Arthur Andersen:
Louis P. Salvatore
Managing Partner and CFO, Arthur Andersen:
Clement W. Eibl
Managing Partner, Office of the CEO, Arthur Andersen: Terry E. Hatchett
Managing Partner and General Counsel, Arthur Andersen: Daniel D. Beckel
Managing Partner, Assurance and Business Advisory, Arthur Andersen: Michael L. Bennett
Managing Partner, Global Business Consulting, and Acting Chief Information Officer, Arthur Andersen: Richard E.S. Boulton
Managing Partner, Global Corporate Finance, Arthur Andersen: Martin E. Thorp
Managing Partner, Global Risk Management, Arthur Andersen: Robert G. Kutsenda
Managing Partner, Global 1000, Arthur Andersen: James D. Edwards
Managing Partner, Human Resources and Partner Matters, Arthur Andersen: Jerome P. Montopoli
Managing Partner, Tax, Legal, and Business Advisory, Arthur Andersen: Alberto E. Terol
Managing Partner Worldwide, Communications and Integrated Marketing, Arthur Andersen: Matthew P. Gonring
Area Managing Partner, Europe, Middle East, India, and Africa, Arthur Andersen: Xavier de Sarrau
Area Managing Partner, Latin America, Arthur Andersen: José Luis Vázquez
Country Managing Partner, United States, Arthur Andersen: Steve M. Samek

HQ: 33 W. Monroe St., Chicago, IL 60603
Phone: 312-580-0033   **Fax:** 312-507-6748
Web site: http://www.arthurandersen.com

Andersen Worldwide operates in 83 countries.

1999 Sales

	$ mil.	% of total
Consulting	9,000	56
Accounting	7,300	44
Total	**16,300**	**100**

Services
Assurance
Assurance and Process Assessment Services (financial audit assurance and process assessment; internal audit, regulatory compliance, information used in strategic transactions)
Business Consulting
Corporate Finance (M&A advisory, strategic planning, capital markets assistance)
eBusiness (business transformation, strategy, implementation)
Human Resources Consulting (compensation, incentives, human resources management strategy, employee benefits)
Legal Services (Andersen Legal Network — M&A, labor, real estate, banking and finance, intellectual property, and information technology legal services)
Outsourcing (design, implementaion, and operation of finance and related support functions)
Risk Consulting (management of risks related to business process, technology, regulatory complaince, government contracting, fraud, and treasury and trading operations)
Tax Services (local, national, and international tax strategies for corporations and the wealthy)

American Management
Arthur D. Little
Bain & Company
BDO International
Booz-Allen
Boston Consulting
Deloitte Touche Tohmatsu
Ernst & Young
Grant Thornton International
KPMG
Marsh & McLennan
McKinsey & Company
Mynd
PricewaterhouseCoopers
Towers Perrin
WorldCom

Partnership FYE: August 31	Annual Growth	8/90	8/91	8/92	8/93	8/94	8/95	8/96	8/97	8/98	8/99
Sales ($ mil.)	16.4%	4,160	4,948	5,577	6,017	6,738	8,134	9,499	11,300	13,900	16,300
Employees	10.1%	56,801	59,797	62,134	66,478	72,722	82,121	91,572	104,933	123,791	135,000

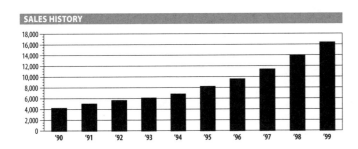

ANGLO AMERICAN PLC

OVERVIEW

Anglo American's name might be a little misleading — it's never been an American company. But when it comes to diamonds and gold, Anglo American delivers the real thing. The company owns stakes in the world's #1 gold (50%, Anglogold), platinum (50%, Anglo Platinum), and diamond (33%, De Beers) producers; it also is one of the largest independent coal miners. Anglo American also holds more than a 20% stake in South Africa's largest financial institution, FirstRand. Additional company interests include base metals, forest products, and industrial minerals.

Unable to send its money overseas during apartheid, Anglo American plc, formerly Anglo American Corporation of South Africa, bought a number of non-core, industrial assets in South Africa. It is now selling off its interests in those companies, particularly industrial operations. Meanwhile, Anglo plans to continue acquisitions of gold and forest products companies. The conglomerate has moved to the UK and has begun trading on the London Stock Exchange to reach international investors.

Descendants of the founding Oppenheimer family control Anglo American.

HISTORY

In 1905 the Oppenheimers, a German family with a major interest in the Premier Diamond Mining Company of South Africa, began buying some of the region's richest gold-bearing land. The family formed Anglo American Corporation of South Africa in 1917 to raise money from J. P. Morgan and other US investors. The name was chosen to disguise the company's German background during WWI.

Under Ernest Oppenheimer the company bought diamond fields in German Southwest Africa (now Namibia) in 1920, breaking the De Beers hegemony in diamond production. Oppenhiemer's 1928 negotiations with Hans Merensky, the person credited with the discovery of South Africa's "platinum arc," lead to Anglo American's interest in platinum.

The diamond monopoly resurfaced in 1929 when Anglo American won control of De Beers, formed by Cecil Rhodes in 1888 with the help of England's powerful Rothschild family.

Anglo American and De Beers had become the largest gold producers in South Africa by the 1950s. They were also major world producers of coal, uranium, and copper. In the 1960s and 1970s Anglo American expanded through mergers and cross holdings in industrial and financial companies. It set up Luxembourg-based Minorco to own holdings outside South Africa and help the company avoid sanctions placed on firms doing business in the apartheid country.

Minorco sold its interest in Consolidated Gold Fields in 1989, and in 1990 it bought Freeport-McMoRan Gold Company (US). In 1993 Minorco bought Anglo American's and De Beers' South American, European, and Australian operations as part of a swap that put all of Anglo American's non-African assets, except diamonds, in Minorco's hands. Some analysts claimed the company had moved the

assets to protect them from possible nationalization by the new, black-controlled South African government. The company spun off insurer African Life to a group of black investors in 1994.

Anglo American bought a stake in UK-based conglomerate Lonrho (now Lonmin) in 1996. In 1997 Anglo American made mining acquisitions in Zambia, Colombia, and Tanzania and began reorganizing its gold and diamond operations. In 1998 the company's First National and Southern Life financial units merged with Rand Merchant Bank's Momentum Life Assurers to form FirstRand, of which Anglo American owns 20%.

The company left its homeland for London in 1999, changed its name to Anglo American plc, and wrapped up the acquisitions of many of its minority interests including Amcoal, Amgold, Amic, and Minorco. Also, Anglo American upped its share in Anaconda Nickel (Australia) from 3% to 23%. Later in 1999 Anglo American agreed to take an 80% stake in the Nchanga and Konkola copper mines owned by Zambia Consolidated Copper Mines.

In 2000 the company bought UK building materials company Tarmac plc. Anglo American's De Beers agreed to pay $590 million for Anglovaal Mining's stake in De Beers' flagship Venetia diamond mine and $900 million for Royal Dutch Shell's Australian coal mining business. On the disposal side, the company agreed to sell its 68% stake in LTA for about $130 million. The company also agreed to sell its Tarmac America unit (construction materials) to Greece-based Titan Cement for $636 million. It also sold its 14% stake in Li & Fung, a Hong Kong trading company. Harry Oppenheimer died that year at the age of 92.

OFFICERS

Chairman and CEO: Julian Ogilvie Thompson, age 66
VC; Chairman, Anglo Platinum, Highveld Steel:
Leslie Boyd, age 63
VC; Deputy Chairman, FirstRand, South African Eagle Insurance: Michael W. King, age 63
Executive Director; Chairman, Anglo Coal, and Anglo Base Metals: J. W. Campbell, age 50
DirectorFinance: Anthony W. Lea, age 51
Executive Director; Chairman, Anglo Industries, Forest Products, Industrial Minerals: A. J. Trahar, age 50
Group Technical Director: T. C. A. Wadeson
VP, HR Planning and Development: Moira Phillips
Secretary: Nicholas Jordan
Auditors: Deloitte & Touche

LOCATIONS

HQ: 20 Carlton House Terrace,
London SW1Y 5AN, United Kingdom
Phone: +44-20-7698-8540 **Fax:** +44-20-7698-8555
Web site: http://www.angloamerican.co.uk

Anglo American plc has operations in Africa, Australia, Europe, and the Americas.

PRODUCTS/OPERATIONS

Selected Subsidiaries
Anglo Base Metals (copper, lead, and zinc)
Anglo Coal (coal mines)
Anglo Ferrous Metals (steel)
Anglo Forest Products (fiber, paper, and pulp)
Anglogold (50%, gold mines)
Anglo Industrial Minerals (cement, potash, and salt)
Ango Industries (aluminum, building materials, trading companies)
Anglo Platinum (50%, platinum mines)
De Beers (33%, diamonds)
FirstRand (20%, financial services)
South African Eagle Insurance (25%, financial services)

COMPETITORS

ASARCO	Newmont Mining
Barrick Gold	Noranda
BHP	Peñoles
Brascan	Phelps Dodge
Centromin	Placer Dome
CVRD	Rio Algom
Freeport-McMoRan	Rio Tinto Limited
Copper & Gold	Rio Tinto plc
Harmony Gold	Shell Transport
Homestake Mining	UM
Inco Limited	WMC Limited
Namibian Minerals	

HISTORICAL FINANCIALS & EMPLOYEES

Nasdaq (SC): AAUK FYE: December 31	Annual Growth	3/91	3/92	3/93	3/94	3/95	3/96	3/97	3/98	*12/98	12/99
Sales ($ mil.)	34.7%	795	829	629	1,367	1,577	2,633	3,207	10,269	6,907	11,578
Net income ($ mil.)	9.1%	710	765	584	641	761	1,101	1,607	1,169	789	1,552
Income as % of sales	—	89.3%	92.2%	92.9%	46.9%	48.3%	41.8%	50.1%	11.4%	11.4%	13.4%
Earnings per share ($)	6.0%	2.35	2.51	1.93	3.46	4.10	4.72	6.87	4.99	3.33	3.98
Stock price - FY high ($)	—	34.25	41.50	36.75	55.13	60.50	75.75	68.75	65.13	59.00	70.75
Stock price - FY low ($)	—	23.00	29.00	16.25	22.00	36.50	51.25	51.25	32.00	22.50	27.25
Stock price - FY close ($)	9.2%	29.38	34.00	24.50	40.50	54.25	64.38	61.25	45.88	28.00	65.13
P/E - high	—	15	17	19	16	15	16	10	13	18	18
P/E - low	—	10	12	8	6	9	11	7	6	7	7
Dividends per share ($)	3.0%	1.03	0.94	1.00	4.49	0.93	1.28	1.30	1.53	1.07	1.34
Book value per share ($)	5.7%	25.53	25.71	24.86	24.92	29.88	27.51	33.28	39.32	38.74	42.01
Employees	—	—	—	—	—	—	—	—	—	—	113,000

* Fiscal year change

STOCK PRICE HISTORY

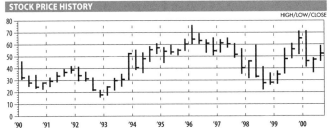

HIGH/LOW/CLOSE

1999 FISCAL YEAR-END

Debt ratio: 13.2%
Return on equity: 12.2%
Cash ($ mil.): 1,303
Current ratio: 1.97
Long-term debt ($ mil.): 2,456
No. of shares (mil.): 385
Dividends
  Yield: 2.1%
  Payout: 33.7%
Market value ($ mil.): 25,075

ASAHI SHIMBUN PUBLISHING

OVERVIEW

Asahi Shimbun (Rising Sun Newspaper) is *The New York Times* of Japan. An influential, international newspaper with 25 bureaus worldwide, it has a domestic circulation of 8.4 million for its morning edition and 4.3 million for its evening edition, which together give the company one of the highest circulations in the world. Privately owned, Tokyo-based Asahi Shimbun Publishing has about 20 printing plants throughout Japan and uses 3,900 delivery agents that employ 90,000 people. The company produces international satellite versions in Heerlen, the Netherlands, and in Hong Kong, London, Los Angeles, New York City, and Singapore, and it offers articles on two company Web sites as well as electronic signboards on bullet trains and city streets. It

also produces an English-language newspaper, *Asahi Evening News.*

Asahi Shimbun publishes some 400 books each year; titles include the *Sazae-san* comic book, *Sato Eisaku Nikki (Diaries of Eisaku Sato,* former prime minister), and *Kaido wo yuku (Walking the Highway)*. In addition, the company publishes 18 magazines, including *Shukan Asahi (Weekly Asahi,* news magazine) and *Yochien Mama (Kindergarten Mama)*.

Although the company's primary focus is on its publishing business, Asahi Shimbun is diversifying into event and seminar coordination and videocassette series production. It also has interests in a 4,500-member health club and the TV Asahi television network.

HISTORY

The co-founders of the *Asahi Shimbun* (first published in Osaka, Japan, in 1879) were Ryohei Murayama and Riichi Ueno, sons of wealthy merchants. Like other newspapers founded in the late 19th century, their paper attracted members of Japanese noble families who saw opposition journalism as a vehicle for expressing dissent (against the ruling Meiji government) without resorting to violence. Initially, the *Asahi Shimbun* was a four-page daily with a circulation of 1,000. By 1883 it was the most widely read newspaper in Japan. It expanded to Tokyo in 1888 and became the first Japanese newspaper publisher to have foreign correspondents in Europe and the US and the first to use rotary presses and cast its own type.

A critic of the government and the military, Asahi Shimbun Publishing defied the government censorship of newspaper coverage of the Rice Riots of 1918, caused when housewives plundered the warehouses of rice merchants who were speculating on rice prices. As a result, some of the newspaper's senior reporters were put in jail. The company successfully launched two weeklies, *Shukan Asahi* (1922) and *Asahi Graph* (1923). Its continued criticism of the armed forces led to a military boycott of *Asahi Shimbun,* culminating in an assault on its Tokyo office by army officers in 1936. Military censorship contributed to the newspaper's one-sided reporting during WWII.

The company launched its English-language newspaper, *Asahi Evening News,* and the English-language review, *Japan Quarterly,* in 1954. In 1959 Asahi Shimbun became the first publisher in the world to use facsimile and offset printing to publish daily newspapers.

In the late 1970s Asahi Shimbun was involved in major investigations and groundbreaking reports on collusion between government, big business, and the civil service, such as the Lockheed scandal involving under-the-table payments to Japanese politicians. In 1986 Asahi Shimbun introduced its first International Satellite Edition, transmitted via satellite.

Two Asahi Shimbun journalists were killed in 1987 by a shotgun-wielding intruder in the paper's Osaka bureau. Undeterred, in 1988 *Asahi Shimbun* broke the "Recruit Affair," another bribery scandal, which led to the resignation of then-Prime Minister Noboru Takeshita and other top politicians. This was followed in 1992 with an exclusive on the ¥500 million kickback to Japanese political kingmaker Shin Kanemaru in connection to scandals centering on parcel delivery service Tokyo Sagawa Kyubin. These scandals and their exposure that year touched off a nationwide political reform movement.

In 1995 Asahi Shimbun photographers got an exclusive when the publisher was the first to beam images of the Sakhalin (Russia) earthquake around the world. In 1996 the company teamed up with publishing software company Electronic Book Technologies to create a real-time news information service on the World Wide Web. The following year SOFTBANK and News Corp. sold their shares of TV Asahi to Asahi Shimbun to promote future cooperation of Japanese TV programming for SOFTBANK and News Corp.'s Japan Sky Broadcasting (JSkyB) satellite broadcasting network.

President: Shinichi Hakoshima, age 61
President, Ashai National Broadcasting Company:
  Michisada Hirose
Managing Director Administration, Personnel, and
  Environment: Shin-ichi Hakoshima
Managing Director Finance: Akio Ozaki

HQ: Asahi Shimbun Publishing Company
  5-3-2 Tsukiji, Chuo-ku, Tokyo 104-11, Japan
Phone: +81-3-3545-0131   **Fax:** +81-3-3545-8450
US HQ: 845 3rd Ave., 11th Fl., New York, NY 10022
US Phone: 212-317-3030   **US Fax:** 212-317-3039
Web site: http://www.asahi.com

Selected Books
Asahi Nenkan (almanac)
Asahi Shimbun News Photo Album
Chiezo (dictionary of current terminology)
Excerpts from Asahi Shimbun (articles)
Junior Asahi Nenkan (social studies)
Minryoku (database on regional economies)
Sato Eisaku Nikki (diary of former prime minister)
Sazae-san (comic book)

Selected Magazines
AERA (news)
Asahi Camera (photography)
Asahi Graph (photography)
Asahi Pasocon (personal computers)
Kagaku Asahi (science)
Shukan Asahi (news)
Yochien Mama (mothers of small children)

Selected Newspapers
Asahi Evening News
Asahi Shimbun

Other
Asahi Sports Club BIG-S Takenotsuka
Sponsorship of educational and cultural activities
TV (TV Asahi)

Associated Press
Dow Jones
Hachette Filipacchi Médias
International Herald Tribune
News Corp.
Nippon Television
Reuters
SOFTBANK
Tokyo Broadcasting System
United News & Media
Yomiuri Shimbun

Private FYE: March 31	Annual Growth	3/91	3/92	3/93	3/94	3/95	3/96	3/97	3/98	3/99	3/00
Sales ($ mil.)	(3.2%)	—	—	—	—	4,650	3,785	3,376	3,135	3,187	3,954
Employees	(0.7%)	—	—	—	—	7,832	7,698	7,580	7,543	7,470	7,543

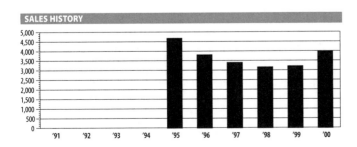

AVENTIS

And Aventis said: Let there be life sciences. Schiltigheim, France-based Aventis — the merged pharmaceutical operations of Rhône-Poulenc and Hoechst — is one of the world's largest drug companies. The predecessors sold or spun off their chemical operations before merging; Hoechst expects to take two years to complete the spinoffs, which include its Celanese chemical business. Rhône-Poulenc was also required by US and European trade regulators to divest its thrombin inhibitor drugs.

What's left? The new company is divided into pharmaceutical and agricultural units; its extensive product roster includes leading names Allegra (allergies), Taxotere (cancer), Lovenox (thrombosis), and Amaryl (diabetes). Aventis aims to used the combined heft of its predecessors' sales operations to make a bigger push into the lucrative US market.

Aventis is in the drug industry's new wave: Earlier mergers focused on bulking up, but new combinations emphasize a narrower approach. By divesting its industrial segments, Aventis hopes to be lean and mean in a world where drug development speed is more important than having a foothold (or even a top spot) in a noncore sector. Aventis may even spin off its agriculture business.

Aventis dates back to pharmacist Étienne Poulenc's purchase of a Parisian apothecary in 1858. The Établissements Poulenc Frères, established in Paris in 1900, developed such synthetic drugs as arsenobenzol, used to treat the previously incurable syphilis. Poulenc branched into vaccines and veterinary products after WWI.

Société Chimique des Usines du Rhône began producing dyes in Lyons in 1895. In 1919 it launched perfume business Rhodia. Faced with German competition in Europe, Usines du Rhône switched to making specialty chemicals, then merged with Poulenc in 1928.

Post-WWII drug and chemical company buys helped Rhône-Poulenc dominate the French chemical industry and rank third in Europe by 1970.

In the 1970s lower tariffs exposed Rhône-Poulenc to international competition. It failed to capitalize on the success of Thorazine when it licensed the US marketing rights to SmithKline. Rhône-Poulenc lost more than $500 million between 1980 and 1982, when it was nationalized by the Mitterrand government, which installed 39-year-old Loïk Le Floch-Prigent at the helm. He eliminated poorly performing units, cut the payroll, and returned Rhône-Poulenc to profitability.

In 1986 Jean-René Fourtou took over from Le Floch-Prigent. He sold 20 businesses and bought more than 30, including Union Carbide's agricultural chemical operations (1986) and Stauffer's industrial chemical business (1987).

In 1990 the French government transferred 35% of Roussel-Uclaf, France's #3 drugmaker, to Rhône-Poulenc, which that year merged its drug business with US pharmaceutical firm Rorer (a 90-year-old US company that had developed Maalox in the 1950s), to form Rhône-Poulenc Rorer (RPR).

Rhône-Poulenc was privatized in 1993 and expanded into biotechnology, buying 37% of Applied Immune Sciences. In 1994 the firm took over France's #2 OTC drug distributor. In 1996 the FDA cleared the company's Taxotere (derived from the yew tree) to treat advanced breast cancer.

In 1997 Rhône-Poulenc bought out the third of RPR it didn't own. Also that year RPR agreed to pay 20% of a $670 million industry settlement involving HIV-infected hemophiliacs, primarily in France. Costs related to the RPR deal led to a huge loss for 1997.

Rhône-Poulenc in 1998 sold its lawn-and-garden operations to US-based Scotts, paving the way for a merger of its drug, agrochemical, and veterinary medicine businesses with those of Germany's chemical giant-cum-drug maven Hoechst AG. Rhône-Poulenc became Aventis in 1999, absorbing Hoechst. The predecessors' US subsidiaries, Hoechst Marion Roussel and Rhône-Poulenc Rorer Pharmaceuticals, merged into Aventis Pharmaceuticals.

In 2000 the firm agreed to sell a French R&D unit to DuPont Pharmaceuticals. That year it requested approval of a chest-pain drug made from leech saliva. Aventis originally thumbed its nose at the hysteria over genetically modified (GM) products, suing Monsanto over rights to GM cotton. However, after an unapproved GM corn (StarLink) made its way into taco shells from Kraft Foods, Aventis decided to suspend StarLink seed sales. Also that year controversial "abortion pill" RU-486, made by Roussel Uclaf, was approved by the FDA. Aventis agreed to pay 22 US states in a vitamin price-fixing lawsuit settlement involving Roche Holdings and Takeda Chemical Industries.

OFFICERS

Chairman, Management Board: Jürgen Dormann, age 60
VC, Management Board: Jean-René Fourtou, age 61
Chairman of the Supervisory Board Aventis Pharma:
  Igor Landau, age 55
Chairman of the Supervisory Board Aventis
  CropScience: Horst Waesche, age 60
Group EVP and CFO: Patrick Langlois, age 54
Group EVP, Human Resources Officer: René Pénisson,
  age 58
Chairman of the Management Board, Aventis Pharma:
  Richard J. Markham, age 50
Chairman of the Management Board, Adventis
  CropScience: Alain Godard, age 54
Auditors: PricewaterhouseCoopers

LOCATIONS

HQ: Espace Européen de l'Enterprise,
  16 avenue de l'Europe,
  F-67300 Schiltigheim, France
Phone: +33-3-88-99-11-00   **Fax:** +33-3-88-99-11-01
US HQ: 500 Arcola Rd., Collegeville, PA 19426
US Phone: 610-454-8000   **US Fax:** 610-454-3573
Web site: http://www.aventis.com

PRODUCTS/OPERATIONS

1999 Sales

	% of total
Aventis Pharma	75
Aventis Agriculture	25
Total	**100**

Selected Products

Pharmaceuticals
Allegra/Telfast (allergies)
Amaryl (diabetes)
Arava (rheumatoid arthritis)
Campto (colorectal cancer)
Copaxone (multiple sclerosis)
Lovenox/Clexane (cardiovascular conditions)
Refludan (cardiovascular conditions)
Synercid (life-threatening infections)
Taxotere (breast and ovarian cancer)

Products in Development
Cariporide (cardiovascular uses)
Flavopiridol (cancer)
GA-EPO (anemia)
Hexavac (hexa-valent vaccine)
HMR 1098 (sudden cardiac death)
Inhaled insulin (diabetes type I and II)
Ketek (respiratory tract infections)
Meningo ACWY (meningitis vaccine)
P53 gene therapy (cancer)
Refludan (unstable angina pectoris)
Rilutek (Parkinson's disease)
RSV vaccine (respiratory tract infections)

COMPETITORS

Abbott Labs	Glaxo Wellcome
BASF	Merck
Baxter	Novartis
Bayer	Pfizer
Bristol-Myers Squibb	Pharmacia
Dow Chemical	Roche Holding
DuPont	SmithKline Beecham

HISTORICAL FINANCIALS & EMPLOYEES

NYSE: AVE FYE: December 31	Annual Growth	12/90	12/91	12/92	12/93	12/94	12/95	12/96	12/97	12/98	12/99
Sales ($ mil.)	(2.1%)	15,375	16,134	14,781	13,606	16,171	17,273	16,535	14,933	15,502	12,714
Net income ($ mil.)	—	215	236	274	162	359	435	528	(646)	921	(859)
Income as % of sales	—	1.4%	1.5%	1.9%	1.2%	2.2%	2.5%	3.2%	—	5.9%	—
Earnings per share ($)	—	—	—	—	—	—	—	—	(2.47)	2.02	(2.51)
Stock price - FY high ($)	—	—	—	—	—	—	—	—	47.00	58.63	68.56
Stock price - FY low ($)	—	—	—	—	—	—	—	—	29.63	35.81	43.38
Stock price - FY close ($)	13.5%	—	—	—	—	—	—	—	44.19	50.25	56.88
P/E - high	—	—	—	—	—	—	—	—	—	29	—
P/E - low	—	—	—	—	—	—	—	—	—	17	—
Dividends per share ($)	2.4%	—	—	—	—	—	—	—	0.61	0.00	0.64
Book value per share ($)	(15.8%)	—	—	—	—	—	—	—	19.52	24.41	13.84
Employees	1.1%	91,571	89,051	83,283	81,678	81,582	82,556	75,250	68,377	65,180	101,000

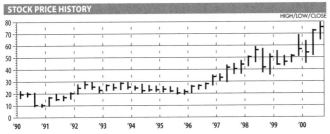

STOCK PRICE HISTORY
HIGH/LOW/CLOSE

1999 FISCAL YEAR-END

Debt ratio: 37.6%
Return on equity: —
Cash ($ mil.): 497
Current ratio: 0.83
Long-term debt ($ mil.): 6,496
No. of shares (mil.): 780
Dividends
  Yield: 1.1%
  Payout: —
Market value ($ mil.): 44,356

AXA

OVERVIEW

Ask an insurance question, get an AXA answer. Paris-based AXA, which started as a sleepy collection of mutual insurance companies, is today the world's #1 insurance company (ahead of Germany's Allianz) and a financial management powerhouse. AXA is the nucleus for more than 50 major subsidiaries. Mutuelles AXA (a group of eight mutuals) controls AXA through its approximately 25% stake.

In the US, AXA owns 58% (and plans to buy the rest) of AXA Financial (formerly The Equitable Companies), which owns 57% of investment manager Alliance Capital Management. AXA Financial also owns 70% of brokerage Donaldson, Lufkin & Jenrette, which Credit Suisse First Boston is buying. The company also has major subsidiaries in the UK (Sun Life & Provincial Holdings), Australia (National Mutual), and Belgium (Royale Belge). The companies offer life insurance, personal and commercial property/casualty insurance, reinsurance, financial services, and real estate investment services.

Rather than trying to run a cross-border organization, AXA instead builds businesses in each country, rebranding them under the AXA name. It is also establishing an Internet portal that it hopes will prevent the need for further acquisitions.

Retiring Chairman Claude Bébéar brought a North American style to the once-genteel practice of business in France. The company wielded its power in the bank takeover struggle that resulted in the formation of BNP Paribas.

HISTORY

AXA dates to the 1817 formation of regional fire insurer Compagnie d'Assurances Mutuelles contre l'incendie in Rouen, France (northwest of Paris). In 1881 France's first mutual life insurer was founded: Mutuelle Vie.

In 1946 these two operations and the younger Anciennes Mutuelles Accidents (founded 1922) were brought together by Sahut d'Izarn (general manager of Compagnie d'Assurances) as the Groupe Ancienne Mutuelle. Later members included Ancienne Mutuelle of Calvados (1946), Ancienne Mutuelle of Orleans (1950), Mutualité Générale (1953), and Participation (1954).

A long-term thinker, d'Izarn named not only his successor, Lucien Aubert, but also Aubert's successor: Claude Bébéar, a 23-year-old friend of d'Izarn's son. Never having held a job, Bébéar found the whole thing amusing and decided to try it.

Groupe Ancienne Mutuelle prospered during the 1960s, thanks to d'Izarn's disciplined management; but his technophobia kept the company from entering the computer age.

D'Izarn died in 1972. Aubert capitulated to worker demands during a series of strikes in the early 1970s; Bébéar ended a 1974 strike by threatening to use force against an employee sit-in, then ousted Aubert.

Bébéar spent the rest of the 1970s upgrading the firm's technology. During this period the company became known as Mutuelles Unies.

Bébéar then began building the firm through a series of spectacular acquisitions. In 1982 Mutuelles Unies gained control of crisis-ridden stock insurer Drouot. Two years later the company's name became AXA (which has no meaning and was chosen because it is pronounced the same in most Western languages). When another old-line insurer, Providence, went on the market, AXA went after it. Providence's management was entertaining another offer when AXA bought tiny, inactive Bayas Tudjus, which held the right to a seat on the Providence board. Bébéar capitalized on small stockholders' dissatisfaction to spark a bidding war and used a new issue of Drouot stock in 1986 to buy Providence — France's first hostile takeover.

AXA bought lackluster US firm Equitable (now AXA Financial) in 1991, infusing $1 billion into the firm in return for the right to own up to 50% of its stock upon demutualization in 1992. AXA moved into Asia with the purchase of Australia's National Mutual in 1995.

Bébéar consolidated the operations into a global organization. In 1996 AXA bought the ailing Union des Assurances de Paris, which had done poorly since its 1994 privatization. It bought the 52% of Belgian insurer Royale Belge SA it didn't already own, as well as Belgian savings bank Anhyp in 1998.

In 1999 Bébéar raised hackles when he supported the Société Générale-Paribas bank merger, then supported BNP's hostile takeover attempt of both (which garnered only Paribas). That year AXA bought Guardian Royal Exchange, then sold the life and pensions business to Dutch insurer AEGON; Bébéar announced his retirement in 1999. In 2000 AXA took control of Japan's Nippon Dantai Life Insurance. It also agreed to buy the 44% of Sun Life & Provincial Holdings and the 40% of AXA Financial that it didn't already own.

Chairman of the Management Board: Claude Bébéar,
age 65, $2,975,344 pay
Vice Chairman of the Management Board:
Henri de Castries, age 46, $1,581,742 pay
**Member of Management Board; Group Executive
President, Human Resources, Communication, and
Synergies:** Françoise Colloc'h, $1,116,361 pay
**Member of the Management Board; Group Executive
President, Finance, Control and Strategy:**
Gérard de La Martinière, $983,589 pay
**Member of the Management Board; CEO, AXA
Financial:** Edward Miller, $5,372,780 pay
**Member of the Management Board; Chairman and
CEO, Insurance Companies in France:** Claude Tendil,
$1,428,524 pay
Auditors: Befec-Price Waterhouse

HQ: 25, avenue Matignon, 75008 Paris, France
Phone: +33-1-40-75-57-00   **Fax:** +33-1-40-75-47-92
US HQ: 1290 Avenue of the Americas, 13th Fl.,
New York, NY 10104
US Phone: 212-554-1234   **US Fax:** 212-468-1272
Web site: http://www.axa.com

1999 Sales

	% of total
Europe	
France	29
UK	18
Germany	11
Belgium	4
US	21
Asia/Pacific	6
Other regions	11
Total	**100**

1999 Sales

	% of total
Life insurance	55
Property & casualty insurance	20
International insurance	6
Asset management	3
Other financial services	16
Total	**100**

Selected Subsidiaries
AXA Colonia Konzern (86%, Germany)
AXA Direct
AXA Equity & Law Plc (99%, UK)
AXA Financial (58%, US)
AXA France Assurance
AXA Insurance Investment Holding (Singapore)
AXA Life Insurance Co (Japan)
AXA UK
Finaxa Belgium (Belgium)
Gelderland (Germany)
Jour Finance
Lor Finance (99%)
Mofipar
National Mutual International (Australia)
Parcolvi (99%, Belgium)
Société Beaujon (99%)
Vinci Belgium (99%, Belgium)
Vinci BV (The Netherlands)

AEGON	Dai-ichi Mutual	New York Life
AGF	Fortis (NL)	Nippon
AIG	Merrill Lynch	LifePrudential
Allianz	MetLife	Sumitomo Life
CIGNA	Nationwide	The Hartford

NYSE: AXA FYE: December 31	Annual Growth	12/90	12/91	12/92	12/93	12/94	12/95	12/96	12/97	12/98	12/99
Assets ($ mil.)	33.7%	37,438	42,255	119,980	141,166	149,525	192,205	216,438	402,573	449,436	511,032
Net income ($ mil.)	13.4%	658	459	280	229	425	556	734	1,322	1,788	2,035
Income as % of assets	—	1.8%	1.1%	0.2%	0.2%	0.3%	0.3%	0.3%	0.3%	0.4%	0.4%
Earnings per share ($)	13.8%	—	—	—	—	—	—	1.96	2.03	2.48	2.89
Stock price - FY high ($)	—	—	—	—	—	—	—	32.00	39.88	72.50	76.81
Stock price - FY low ($)	—	—	—	—	—	—	—	25.75	29.25	40.94	56.44
Stock price - FY close ($)	31.1%	—	—	—	—	—	—	31.50	39.00	72.25	71.00
P/E - high	—	—	—	—	—	—	—	16	20	29	27
P/E - low	—	—	—	—	—	—	—	13	14	17	20
Dividends per share ($)	15.6%	—	—	—	—	—	—	0.65	0.75	0.99	1.01
Book value per share ($)	8.8%	—	—	—	—	—	—	17.93	30.99	22.57	23.11
Employees	25.4%	—	15,037	27,472	43,340	35,000	36,625	36,695	80,613	78,943	92,008

HIGH/LOW/CLOSE

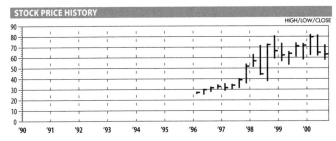

Equity as % of assets: 3.2%
Return on assets: 0.4%
Return on equity: 12.6%
Long-term debt ($ mil.): 8,189
No. of shares (mil.): 713
Dividends
  Yield: 0.0%
  Payout: 0.3%
Market value ($ mil.): 50,600
Sales ($ mil.): 82,956

AXEL SPRINGER VERLAG AG

OVERVIEW

With more than 65 subsidiaries under its umbrella, Axel Springer Verlag has sprung into nearly every aspect of the media industry. The Hamburg-based company is a German media giant, publishing 180 newspapers and magazines including *Bild,* the #1 German newspaper. The company churns out its publications from the five German printing plants it operates.

While newspapers and magazines bring in more than 70% of its revenue, Axel Springer is also active in book publishing, putting forth German editions of tomes by authors such as Mario Puzo, Wally Lamb, and Guido Knopp. The company has ownership interests in a string of publishing firms (Ansata, Bucher, Claasen, Cormoran, Econ, Integral) that stretches across Europe.

Its roots may be in print journalism, but Axel Springer is no stranger to electronic media. The company's broadcasting interests span seven radio stations, a handful of TV production companies, and 41% of German TV station SAT.1. Axel Springer has agreed to merge SAT.1 with German TV station operator Pro Sieben Media to form Germany's largest commercial TV group (Axel Springer will own 11% of the new company). Axel Springer's Internet holdings include stakes in Web search and navigation service WSI Webseek Infoservice, Internet bookseller Booxtra, and online editions of several of its print publications.

Axel Springer is intent on evolving into an international media firm. The company also has created venture capital unit AS Venture to boost its Internet holdings. The family of late founder Axel Springer owns just over 50% of the company; German media firm KirchGruppe owns 40%.

HISTORY

Hinrich Springer (whose newspaper publishing business had been closed by Nazi minister of propaganda Joseph Goebbels in 1941) and his son Axel founded the company as Axel Springer Verlag GmbH in Hamburg in 1946. That year they launched a magazine, *Nordwestdeutsche Hefte,* using transcripts of radio broadcasts. In 1948 Axel Springer unveiled *Hamburger Abendblatt,* and by 1950 it was Hamburg's best-selling newspaper. Two years later the company debuted the tabloid *Bild Zeitung,* later renamed *Bild.* The success of the paper helped fund his company's expansion in newspaper publishing.

The company bought the daily *Die Welt* in 1953 and *Berliner Morgenpost* in 1959. Axel Springer moved its headquarters to Berlin in 1966. Fiercely supportive of the reunification of Germany, Axel Springer positioned the company's headquarters immediately next to the Berlin Wall.

In the 1970s the company expanded into the regional newsletter and magazine market. Axel Springer's growing control over German media did not go unnoticed, however, and opposition to the company's power was demonstrated when its Hamburg office was bombed in 1972 (the company was the target of arson again in 1998). Springer considered selling the entire company, but opted for the sale of several individual publications instead.

The company continued its expansion by joining part of a German satellite consortium set up in 1983, and in 1985 it acquired stakes in cable TV and bought two Munich radio stations. Axel Springer died in 1985, the same year his company went public. In 1989 German media firm KirchGruppe began buying shares in Axel Springer Verlag.

In 1996 Axel Springer entered the Czech and Slovak newspaper markets with the purchase of a 49% stake in Dutch firm Ringier-Taurus. The company formed a joint venture in 1998 with Infoseek (now part of Walt Disney Internet Group) and other partners to launch a German-language Web search service. It also bought 95% of German book publisher ECON + LIST Verlagsgesellschaft. August Fischer, former chief executive of News Corp.'s News International, was appointed chairman and CEO that year. A 1998 bid to buy UK-based media firm Mirror Group proved unsuccessful.

In 1999 Axel Springer acquired stakes in Los Angeles-based TV production company GRB Entertainment, German TV and film production company ProFilm, and a 90% interest in Schwartzkopff TV-Productions. The following year the company agreed to merge its 41%-owned TV station SAT.1 with German TV station operator Pro Sieben Media to create Germany's largest commercial TV group (Axel Springer will own 11% of the new company). Also that year Axel Springer established AS Venture (a venture capital firm focusing on investments in Internet companies) and entered into a joint venture with DEAG Entertainment and Deutsche Lufthansa to form a Web-based marketplace for events, travel, and leisure.

OFFICERS

Chairman Supervisory Board: Bernhard Servatius
Chairman and CEO: August A. Fischer
VC: Mathias Döpfner, age 38
Director Finance: Falk Ettwein
Director Printing: Rudolf Knepper
Director Magazines: Christian Delbrück
Director Personnel: Otto Schroeder
Director Electronic Media: Ralf Kogeler
Auditors: PwC Deutsche Revision Aktiengesellschaft

LOCATIONS

HQ: Axel-Springer-Platz 1, D-20350 Hamburg, Germany
Phone: +49-04034724499   **Fax:** +49-04034725540
US HQ: 500 5th Ave., Ste. 2800, New York, NY 10110
US Phone: 212-972-1720   **US Fax:** 212-972-1724
Web site: http://www.asv.de/englisch/home-e.htm

Axel Springer Verlag has operations in Europe, Japan, and the US.

PRODUCTS/OPERATIONS

1999 Sales

	% of total
Newspapers	50
Magazines	23
Printing	21
Books	3
Electronic Media	3
Total	**100**

Selected Operations

Electronic media
AS ADAMO
AutoEuro (70%)
Booxtra (25%)
CompuTel
GRB Entertainment (US, 51%)
SAT.1 (41%)
Schwartzkopff TV (90%)
Seven radio stations
SPORT1 (26%)
WSI Webseek Infoservice (25%)

Magazines
Allegra
Auto Bild
Bild der Frau
Familie & Co
Funk UHR
Hammer
Hörzu
Journal für die Frau
Mädchen
Miss Beauty @nd More
Musikexpress/Sounds
Popcorn
Sport Bild
TVneu

Newspapers
AktienResearch
B.Z.
B.Z. am Sonntag
Berliner Morgenpost
Bild
Bild am Sonntag
Bildwoche
Computer Bild
Computer Bild Spiele
Die Welt
Euro am Sonntag
Finanzen
Hamburger Abendblatt
Welt am Sonntag

COMPETITORS

Bertelsmann
Capital Media
Deutsche Telekom
EM.TV
EMAP
Future Network
Hachette Filipacchi Médias
HarperCollins
IPC Media
Modern Times Group
News Corp.
Pearson
PrimaCom
Reed Elsevier
Schibsted
Simon & Schuster
Time Warner
Verlagsgruppe Georg von Holtzbrinck
VNU

HISTORICAL FINANCIALS & EMPLOYEES

German: SPR FYE: December 31	Annual Growth	12/90	12/91	12/92	12/93	12/94	12/95	12/96	12/97	12/98	12/99
Sales (€ mil.)	4.4%	1,807	1,882	1,779	1,964	2,025	2,114	2,260	2,351	2,460	2,664
Net income (€ mil.)	18.3%	33	6	29	37	61	73	84	108	141	151
Income as % of sales	—	1.8%	0.3%	1.6%	1.9%	3.0%	3.4%	3.7%	4.6%	5.7%	5.7%
Earnings per share (€)	18.3%	9.77	1.69	8.61	10.92	17.88	21.35	24.66	33.48	41.56	44.31
Stock price - FY high (€)	—	452.49	382.45	317.00	357.90	355.35	493.40	512.31	868.68	828.29	1,210.00
Stock price - FY low (€)	—	310.35	229.57	231.10	247.98	311.89	311.89	432.04	465.28	467.83	730.00
Stock price - FY close (€)	13.9%	368.13	241.84	302.68	324.67	318.53	493.40	467.83	618.66	715.81	1,185.00
P/E - high	—	46	226	37	33	20	23	21	26	20	27
P/E - low	—	32	136	27	23	17	15	18	14	11	16
Dividends per share (€)	9.9%	6.14	6.14	6.14	6.14	7.67	8.69	10.23	12.27	13.29	14.32
Book value per share (€)	9.9%	75.72	71.12	79.68	84.25	88.72	98.35	111.82	131.43	155.06	177.32
Employees	0.4%	12,112	12,620	12,663	12,187	13,331	12,646	12,346	12,195	13,331	12,504

STOCK PRICE HISTORY

HIGH/LOW/CLOSE

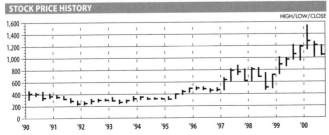

1999 FISCAL YEAR-END

Debt ratio: 5.9%
Return on equity: 26.7%
Cash (€ mil.): 114
Current ratio: 2.42
Long-term debt (€ mil.): 38
No. of shares (mil.): 3
Dividends
  Yield: 0.0%
  Payout: 0.3%
Market value ($ mil.): 4,048
Sales ($ mil.): 2,677

BACARDI LIMITED

OVERVIEW

Bacardi Limited seems to have found the right mix of spirits. The Pembroke, Bermuda-based company is the world's #3 wine and spirits group, after giants Diageo and Allied Domecq, selling its products in 170 countries. Among its most popular offerings are more than a dozen varieties of Bacardi, the world's #1 rum brand; Martini & Rossi vermouth; Dewar's Scotch whisky; and Bombay gin; as well as vodka, tequila, cognac, sparkling wine, and Hatuey beer.

Steeped in liquor lore, Bacardi claims the first Cuba Libre (rum and cola) was made with its product in 1898. Bottles feature Bacardi's trademark bat logo, said to have been inspired by bats (an omen of good luck) that lived in the first distillery. To round out its white liquor portfolio, the distiller is looking to buy a high-profile vodka or tequila. Some 500 descendants of founder Facundo Bacardi y Maso own the company.

HISTORY

Facundo Bacardi y Maso immigrated to Cuba from Spain in 1830. He started in the liquor business as a rum salesman for John Nunes, an Englishman who owned a small distillery in Santiago, Cuba. In 1862 Facundo, his brother Jose, and a French wine merchant bought Nunes' distillery and began producing a smoother rum from a formula created by Facundo after years of trial and error. The more mixable quality of Bacardi's rum proved to be a key to its success. In 1877 Facundo passed company leadership to his sons; the eldest, Emilio, took over running the company (and spent some of his spare time in jail for his anti-Spanish activities).

Bacardi Limited struggled during the 1890s as Cuba's economy foundered. The business was thrown into even greater turmoil when revolutionary leader Jose Marti began what would be the final fight for Cuban independence. One of Marti's biggest supporters was Emilio, who earned another stay in jail and then exile for his sympathies. After Cuba gained its independence in 1902, Bacardi grew rapidly, getting a further boost from Prohibition as Havana became "the unofficial US saloon." (Prohibition did, however, end a venture in the US.)

In the 1920s the company moved into brewing. It expanded its rum operations in the 1930s, opening a distillery in Mexico (1931) and another in Puerto Rico (1935). In 1944 it opened Bacardi Imports in the US and built up its overseas operations during the 1950s.

Amid all its success, Bacardi again became embroiled in Cuban politics during the late 1950s. Although some company leaders showed open opposition to Cuban leader Fulgencio Batista and support for Fidel Castro, others opposed Castro. As a result of the 1959 revolution, the Bacardi family was forced into exile, fleeing to the US and Europe. Castro seized Bacardi's assets in 1960. However, the expropriation was not a fatal blow since both the

Mexican and Puerto Rican operations had been outearning the Cuban operations since the 1940s. Bacardi continued to enjoy explosive growth during the 1960s and 1970s. In 1977 some family members sold about 12% of the Bacardi empire to Hiram Walker.

By 1980 Bacardi was the #1 liquor brand in the US, but a series of family squabbles and bad decisions threatened the company. Bacardi Capital, set up to manage the empire's money, lost $50 million in 1986 after some risky bond investments soured. That year the empire's leadership started to buy up shares in Bacardi companies, including those sold to Hiram Walker and the 10% of Bacardi Corporation that had been sold to the public in 1962. The companies spent more than $241 million to buy back their shares, even as a dissident faction of the family claimed the move was designed to conceal financial information.

In 1990 Bacardi introduced wine cooler-like Bacardi Breezers. In an effort to diversify and to increase its European markets, the company paid $1.4 billion in 1993 for a majority stake in Martini & Rossi. In 1996 family lawyer George Reid became president and CEO, the first non-family member to head the company.

Bacardi acquired the rights to the Havana Club trademark in 1997 from the Arechabala family, another clan exiled from Cuba. The move exacerbated a dispute in the US with France's Pernod Ricard, which had partnered with the Cuban government to sell spirits under the Havana Club name. Adding two more top-flight liquor brands to its roster, Bacardi bought the Dewar's Scotch whisky and Bombay gin brands from Diageo in 1998 for $1.9 billion.

In March 2000 Reid resigned and Ruben Rodriguez was appointed president and CEO. When Manuel Jorge Cutillas retired in July 2000, Rodriguez added chairman to his titles.

OFFICERS

Chairman, President, and CEO: Ruben Rodriguez
CFO: Ralph Morera
VP Public Relations: Jorge Rodriguez
Human Resources: Alana Rogers

LOCATIONS

HQ: 65 Pitts Bay Rd., Pembroke HM 08, Bermuda
Phone: 441-295-4345   **Fax:** 441-292-0562
Web site: http://www.bacardi.com

Bacardi Limited has production facilities in the Bahamas, Brazil, Canada, Martinique, Mexico, Panama, Puerto Rico, Spain, and Trinidad.

PRODUCTS/OPERATIONS

Selected Brands

Rum
Bacardi (8, 151, 1873 Solera, Anejo, Black, Carta Blanca, Exclusiv, Gold, Light, Limon, Select, Solera, Spice)
Castillo (Anejo, Gold, White)
Estelar Suave
Ron Bacardi Anejo

Other Spirits and Beverages
Alcohol-based aperitif (Pastis Casanis, Pastis Duval)
Amaretto (DiSaronno Amaretto)
Beer (Hatuey)
Brandy (Gran Reserva Especial, Vergel, Viejo Vergel)
Champagne (Charles Volner, Veuve Amiot)
Cognac (Exshaw, Gaston de la Grange, Otard)
Gin (Bombay, Bombay Sapphire, Bosford, Martini)
Liqueur (B&B, Benedictine, China Martini, Nassau Royale)
Low-alcohol beverage (Bacardi & Cola, Bacardi Breezer, Caribbean Classics, Martini Brand Jigger)
Scotch whisky (Dewar's, Glen Deveron, William Lawson's Finest Blend, William Lawson's Scottish Gold)
Sparkling wine (Grande Auguri, Martini & Rossi Asti Spumante, Montelera Riserva, Martini Brand Asti, Martini Brand Riesling)
Tequila (Camino Real)
Vodka (Eristoff, Martini, Natasha, Russian Prince)
Wine-based spirits (Martini & Rossi Bianco, Extra Dry, and Rosso; Martini Brand Bianco, Extra Dry, Rose, Rosso, and Vermouth; Noilly Prat; St. Raphael)

COMPETITORS

Allied Domecq	LVMH
Brown-Forman	Pernod Ricard
Constellation Brands	Remy Cointreau
Fortune Brands	Robert Mondavi
Gallo	Seagram
Heaven Hill Distilleries	Sebastiani Vineyards
Highland Distillers	Suntory
Jose Cuervo	

HISTORICAL FINANCIALS & EMPLOYEES

Private FYE: March 31	Annual Growth	3/91	3/92	3/93	3/94	3/95	3/96	3/97	3/98	3/99	3/00
Estimated sales ($ mil.)	8.0%	—	—	—	—	—	—	—	2,400	2,500	2,800
Employees	(1.6%)	—	—	—	—	—	—	—	6,200	6,200	6,000

SALES HISTORY

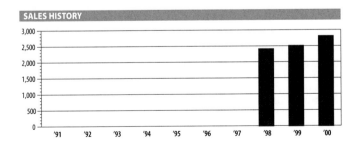

BAE SYSTEMS

OVERVIEW

BAE SYSTEMS is a lean, mean, fighting-machine . . . maker. The Farnborough, UK-based firm, formerly British Aerospace, is the world's #4 aerospace company, trailing only Boeing, Lockheed Martin, and EADS. Its defense unit makes the Harrier, Hawk, and Tornado fighter aircraft and it is working on the next-generation Eurofighter Typhoon. Other products include tactical missiles, air-defense systems, patrol aircraft, artillery locators, shipbuilding, communications and navigation systems.

The company's commercial aerospace unit makes Avro jet aircraft for regional markets.

BAE SYSTEMS also owns 20% of Airbus Industrie, the European commercial airliner consortium, of which the European Aeronautic Defence & Space Company (EADS) owns 80%.

BAE is continuing to concentrate on what it considers core activities. Through the company's association with Airbus, BAE's commercial aircraft segment will focus on providing products for planes with more than 100 seats. BAE will also begin using its airborne technology in its land and naval systems and is beefing up its defense electronics operations by buying units from Lockheed Martin.

HISTORY

Post-Wright brothers and pre-WWII, a host of aviation companies sprang up to serve the British Empire — too many to survive after the war when the empire contracted. Parliament took steps in 1960 to save the industry by merging companies to form larger, stronger entities — Hawker-Siddeley Aviation and British Aircraft Corporation (BAC).

Hawker-Siddeley, made up of aircraft and missiles divisions, was created by combining A.V. Roe, Gloster Aircraft, Hawker Aircraft, Armstrong Whitworth, and Folland Aircraft. It attained fame in the 1960s for developing the Harrier "jump jet."

BAC was formed from the merger of Bristol Aeroplane, English Electric, and Vicker-Armstrong. In 1962 it joined France's Aerospatiale to build the supersonic Concorde and became a partner in ventures to develop the Tornado and Jaguar fighters. The cost of these ventures, plus the commercial failure of the Concorde, was more than the company could bear. Realizing British aviation was again in trouble, the British government nationalized BAC and Hawker-Siddeley in 1976 and merged them in 1977 with Scottish Aviation to form British Aerospace (BAe).

BAe joined the Airbus consortium in 1979. A partial privatization of the company began in 1981 when the government sold 52% to the public (the remaining stake was sold in 1985). Also in 1981 BAe announced a joint venture with Comsat General and announced that it would be the prime contractor for L-SAT-1, the European Space Agency's telecommunications satellite.

In 1987 BAe bought Steinheil Optronik (optical equipment) and Ballast Nedam Groep (civil and marine engineering). In 1990 BAe bought 76% of Liverpool Airport (sold 1997) and formed Ballast Nedam Construction.

BAe began to restructure its troubled regional aircraft division in 1992 by laying off thousands of workers and closing a major plant. The company sold Ballast Nedam and its corporate jet business to Raytheon and won a $7.5 billion contract from Saudi Arabia for Tornado jets in 1993. BAe sold its satellite business in 1994.

Matra BAe Dynamics, the world's third-largest maker of tactical missiles, was formed in a 1996 merger between BAe and Lagardère subsidiary Matra Hachette. BAe's emphasis on large jetliners led to the 1998 breakup of Aero International, its two-year-old regional-aircraft joint venture with Aerospatiale (France, now Aerospatiale Matra) and Alenia (Italy). Shortly thereafter, BAe spent $454 million for a 35% stake in Swedish military jet maker Saab AB. Also in 1998 BAe bought Siemens' UK- and Australia-based defense electronics operations. In 1999 BAe bought the electronic systems defense unit of Marconi Electronic Systems (MES) for $12.7 billion (including US-based Tracor). The company immediately changed its name to BAE SYSTEMS to remove the British influence from its name.

In 2000 the UK government agreed to loan BAE about $836 million to support the Airbus A3XX superjumbo airliner project. The same year BAE agreed to form a business-to-business aerospace and defense Web site with Boeing, Lockheed Martin, and Raytheon. BAE also acquired Lockheed Martin's control-systems unit for about $510 million. The prime contractor for the UK's new Type 45 destroyer, BAE was named to build two of the first three Type 45s. Around the same time, the company agreed to spend about $1.67 billion for a group of Lockheed Martin's defense electronics businesses, including its Sanders airborne electronics unit.

Chairman: Richard Evans, age 57, $695,000 pay
CEO: John Weston, age 48, $575,000 pay
COO: Mike Turner, age 51, $432,000 pay
COO: Peter Gershon, age 53, $37,000 pay
CEO Australia: Peter Anstiss
Chief of Staff: Roger Hawksworth
Group Engineering Director: Dave Gardner
Group Finance Director: George Rose, age 47, $423,000 pay
Group Human Resources Director: Terry Morgan
Group Marketing Director: Charles Masefield, age 60, $35,000 pay
Auditors: KPMG Audit Plc

LOCATIONS

HQ: Warwick House, Farnborough Aerospace Center, Farnborough, Hampshire GU14 6YU, United Kingdom
Phone: +44-125-237-3232   **Fax:** +44-125-238-3000
US HQ: 15000 Conference Center Dr., Ste. 200, Chantilly, VA 20151
US Phone: 703-802-0080   **US Fax:** 703-227-1610
Web site: http://www.bae.co.uk

1999 Sales

	$ mil.	% of total
Europe		
UK	2,378	16
Other countries	4,077	28
Middle East	3,978	28
US & Canada	2,460	17
Australasia/Pacific	716	5
Far East	572	4
Central & South America	149	1
Africa	104	1
Total	**14,434**	**100**

PRODUCTS/OPERATIONS

1999 Sales

	$ mil.	% of total
Defense	9,435	62
Commercial aerospace	4,801	32
MES	736	5
Other	57	1
Adjustments	(595)	—
Total	**14,434**	**100**

Selected Products

Active missile decoy systems	Missile warheads
Air data systems	Navigation systems
Airbus A310 aircraft	Night vision goggles
Avro RJ 100 aircraft	Naval combat systems
Engine management systems	Offshore patrol vessels
Explosives and demolition charges	Satellite commmunications
Harrier aircraft	Tactical communications
Hawk aircraft	Tornado aircraft
Military flight controls	Torpedoes and depth charges
Missile actuation/control systems	Vanguard class ballistic submarines

COMPETITORS

A.B.Dick	Glock
Beretta	Honeywell International
Boeing	Lockheed Martin
Bombardier	Northrop Grumman
Colt's	SEPI
Cordant Technologies	Thomson-CSF
EADS	

HISTORICAL FINANCIALS & EMPLOYEES

OTC: BAESY FYE: December 31	Annual Growth	12/90	12/91	12/92	12/93	12/94	12/95	12/96	12/97	12/98	12/99
Sales ($ mil.)	(3.7%)	20,342	19,758	15,100	15,898	11,193	8,896	11,079	14,059	14,294	14,434
Net income ($ mil.)	(0.3%)	537	(284)	(1,341)	(316)	219	214	530	265	1,149	524
Income as % of sales	—	2.6%	—	—	—	2.0%	2.4%	4.8%	1.9%	8.0%	3.6%
Earnings per share ($)	—	—	—	—	—	—	—	—	—	—	1.00
Stock price - FY high ($)	—	—	—	—	—	—	—	—	—	—	29.00
Stock price - FY low ($)	—	—	—	—	—	—	—	—	—	—	26.23
Stock price - FY close ($)	—	—	—	—	—	—	—	—	—	—	27.00
P/E - high	—	—	—	—	—	—	—	—	—	—	29
P/E - low	—	—	—	—	—	—	—	—	—	—	26
Dividends per share ($)	—	—	—	—	—	—	—	—	—	—	0.52
Book value per share ($)	—	—	—	—	—	—	—	—	—	—	16.53
Employees	(4.7%)	129,100	115,700	103,800	88,800	47,900	45,400	47,000	43,400	47,900	83,400

STOCK PRICE HISTORY

HIGH/LOW/CLOSE

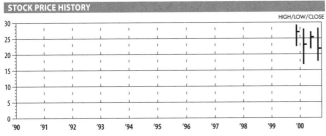

1999 FISCAL YEAR-END

Debt ratio: 0.2%
Return on equity: 6.8%
Cash ($ mil.): 1,312
Current ratio: 1.20
Long-term debt ($ mil.): 2,515
No. of shares (mil.): 729
Dividends
  Yield: 0.0%
  Payout: 0.5%
Market value ($ mil.): 19,670

BANCO SANTANDER CENTRAL

OVERVIEW

This bank isn't all BS — it has a little CH too. Banco Santander Central Hispano (BSCH) is Spain's #1 bank, as well as one of the largest in Europe and, with its presence in more than a dozen countries there, Latin America.

About 80% of the bank's sales come from its retail banking operations in Spain (where it has some 6,000 branches), other countries in Europe, and Latin America. Its Latin American holdings include Argentina's Banco Rio de la Plata, Chile's Banco de Santiago, and Mexico's

Grupo Financiero Serfin. In Europe, BSCH also has stakes in the Royal Bank of Scotland, Germany's Commerzbank, and France's Société Générale. Other services include asset management and global wholesale banking.

BSCH continues to weave its web of operations and holdings. While it seeks acquisitions in Latin America (it's already the top banking group in the region), it is adding revenue streams in Europe by creating new products with its partners.

HISTORY

Banco Santander Central Hispano (BSCH) was created by the merger of Banco Santander and Banco Central Hispanoamericano (BCH) in 1999.

In 1857 a group of Basque businessmen formed Banco Santander to finance Latin American trade. The emergence of Cantabria as a leading province after WWI helped the bank expand, first regionally, then nationally.

The Botín family has been closely identified with the bank for decades. Before his death in 1923, Emilio Botín served as a board member, then for a few years as chairman. The post was held by his son Emilio Botín Sanz de Sautuola from 1950 to 1986, when *his* son Emilio Botín Rios (known as Don Emilio) took over.

Spanish banks were spared the worst of the Great Depression (thanks to their isolation and the country's shunning the gold standard), but Spain's civil war was draining. In the early 1940s, Santander expanded into Madrid and other major Spanish cities and merged with a few rivals. In the 1950s and 1960s, as interest rates were controlled and mergers halted, banks competed by building branch networks and investing overseas, particularly in Latin America.

Tight economic controls were relaxed after Franco's death in the 1970s. Despite global recession, Santander continued to invest in Latin America through the mid-1980s, forming Bankinter with Bank of America (now part of a much larger Bank of America) in 1965.

In the late 1980s, Santander prepared to compete in a deregulated Spain and Europe, forming alliances with Royal Bank of Scotland, Kemper (now part of Zurich Financial Services), and Metropolitan Life Insurance. In 1989 the bank jump-started competition by introducing Spain's first high-interest account.

In the 1990s Santander focused on home. Spurned by Banco Hispano Americano, it acquired a 60% stake in the ailing Banco Español de Credito (Banesto); Banesto became wholly

owned in 1998. The bank took a hit when Latin America plunged into an economic crisis in 1998. With profit margins falling, the bank merged with BCH in 1999.

BCH was formed by the 1991 merger of Banco Central and Banco Hispano Americano (BHA). BHA was established in 1900 by investors in Latin America; Central was founded in 1919. The mixed banks offered both commercial and investment banking; they funded industrialization and investment in Latin America and became two of Spain's largest banks before the civil war.

After the war, BHA sold its Latin American assets when the currency dried up, while Central used mergers and acquisitions to expand across Spain. Isolated from WWII and the global economy by Franco, the two banks used their dual strategies to fund overseas investment and domestic branch growth.

After Franco's death, the banks faced increased competition at home and abroad. BHA struggled with the costs of its purchases in the 1980s. With major stakes in almost every industry, Central proved fairly immune to the roller-coaster economy. Central bought BHA in 1991 to remain competitive as Spain entered the European Economic Community in 1992.

Following the merger, BCH trimmed 20% of its branches, fired some 10,000 employees, and sold unprofitable holdings. Focused on Latin America, the bank took small stakes in small banks. Losing its edge, BCH merged with Santander in 1999.

In 2000 the company focused on expanding in Europe and Latin America. Among its European moves were its purchase of Portugal's Champalimaud financial group and an alliance with Société Générale to buy investment fund management firms, particularly in the US. In Latin America the bank bought Brazil's Banco Meridional and Grupo Financiero Serfin, Mexico's #3 bank.

Chairman: Emilio Botín-Sanz
Chairman of the Executive Committee:
José María Amusátegui de la Cierua
First Vice-Chairman and CEO:
Ángel Corcóstegui Guraya
Second Vice-Chairman: Jaime Botín-Sanz
Third Vice-Chairman: Matías Rodríguez Inciarte
Fourth Vice-Chairman: Santiago Foncillas Casáus
General Comptroller: José Tejón
Head of Human Resources: José Manuel Rostro
Auditors: Arthur Andersen

LOCATIONS

HQ: Banco Santander Central Hispano S.A.
Plaza de Canalejas,1, 28014 Madrid, Spain
Phone: +34-91-558-10-31   **Fax:** +34-91-552-66-70
Web site: http://www.bch.bsch.es

Banco Santander Central Hispano has operations in
almost 40 countries in Africa, Asia and the Pacific Rim,
Europe, and North and South America.

1999 Sales

	% of total
North & South America	51
Europe	
Spain	40
Other countries	9
Total	**100**

PRODUCTS/OPERATIONS

1999 Assets

	$ mil.	% of total
Cash & equivalents	6,270	2
Government securities	29,925	12
Bonds	25,792	10
Stocks	5,565	2
Net loans	128,360	50
Receivables	30,437	12
Other assets	31,876	12
Total	**258,225**	**100**

Selected Subsidiaries
Banco Central Hispano U.S.A.
Banco de Asunción, S.A. (98%, Paraguay)
Banco de Santa Cruz (92%, Bolivia)
Banco de Santiago (44%, Chile)
Banco Mexicano, S.A. (84%, Mexico)
Banco Santander Brazil (89%)
Banco Santander Colombia, S.A. (61%)
Banco Santander Peru
Banco Santander Uruguay
Banco Tornquist (Argentina)
CC-Bank (Germany)
Finconsumo (50%, Italy, finance)
Santander Investment Securities N. York (US)
Sistemas 4B, S.A. (71%, credit cards)

COMPETITORS

Banco Bilbao	Banco do Brasil	Chase Manhattan
Banco Comercial	Banco Ganadero	Deutsche Bank
Portugues	Banco Popular	Dresdner Bank
Banco de Galicia	Español	Espírito Santo
y Buenos Aires	Bank of America	HSBC Holdings
Banco de la	Bankinter	Itausa
Nacion	BBVA Banco	
Argentina	BHIF	

HISTORICAL FINANCIALS & EMPLOYEES

NYSE: STD FYE: December 31	Annual Growth	12/90	12/91	12/92	12/93	12/94	12/95	12/96	12/97	12/98	12/99
Assets ($ mil.)	18.5%	55,966	60,324	61,411	73,098	114,269	135,243	149,954	171,353	180,925	258,225
Net income ($ mil.)	11.7%	588	736	515	465	759	837	919	1,086	997	1,586
Income as % of assets	—	1.1%	1.2%	0.8%	0.6%	0.7%	0.6%	0.6%	0.6%	0.6%	0.6%
Earnings per share ($)	(0.3%)	0.44	0.55	0.39	0.35	0.28	0.33	0.36	0.57	0.54	0.43
Stock price - FY high ($)	—	4.58	4.65	4.12	4.46	4.33	4.15	5.31	8.38	13.32	11.95
Stock price - FY low ($)	—	2.83	3.23	2.75	3.12	2.83	2.71	3.64	4.97	5.96	7.66
Stock price - FY close ($)	12.6%	3.90	3.58	3.19	3.88	3.18	4.10	5.29	8.14	9.38	11.34
P/E - high	—	10	8	11	13	15	13	15	15	25	28
P/E - low	—	6	6	7	9	10	8	10	9	11	18
Dividends per share ($)	6.5%	0.13	0.14	0.15	0.12	0.05	0.12	0.16	0.20	0.22	0.23
Book value per share ($)	17.3%	1.09	1.43	1.39	1.53	2.40	2.80	2.44	2.30	4.11	4.59
Employees	29.1%	—	—	—	20,661	29,232	42,043	45,847	72,740	73,964	95,442

STOCK PRICE HISTORY

HIGH/LOW/CLOSE

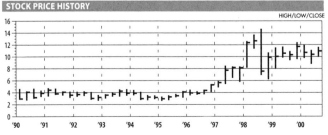

1999 FISCAL YEAR-END

Equity as % of assets: 6.5%
Return on assets: 0.7%
Return on equity: 13.0%
Long-term debt ($ mil.): —
No. of shares (mil.): 3,668
Dividends
  Yield: 0.0%
  Payout: 0.5%
Market value ($ mil.): 41,593
Sales ($ mil.): 24,332

BANK OF MONTREAL

OVERVIEW

Like the lyrics lilting from the lips of Quebecoise pop chanteuse Celine Dion, *that's* the way it is for Bank of Montreal (being #3, that is). Barred from achieving titanic growth through merger with #1 Royal Bank of Canada or #2 Canadian Imperial Bank of Commerce, Bank of Montreal has set its sights on steady, piecemeal expansion.

The bank's operations are Canada's oldest, consisting of more than 1,000 branches serving consumers, businesses large and small, and institutions at home and abroad. Its Nesbitt Burns subsidiary offers brokerage, investment banking, and merchant banking services. Based in Chicago, its Harris Bank has a large branch network there and offers corporate banking services throughout the Midwest. Bank of Montreal also owns 16% of Mexico's largest bank, BBVA Bancomer, and has operations in Asia and Europe.

After reorganizing along operational lines, the bank is focused on building its business lines through acquisitions and organic growth. Bank of Montreal is snapping up buys south of its border, but it may sell its stake in BBVA Bancomer, which is 30%-owned by Spain's Banco Bilbao Vizcaya Argentaria (BBVA).

HISTORY

Montreal was a key port for fur and agriculture trade by the early 1800s. To finance these activities, the Montreal Bank (Canada's first) opened in 1817. Chartered in 1822, the bank officially became Bank of Montreal. Its ties with the US were strong, and nearly 50% of its original capital came from Yanks.

When the fur trade shifted northward to Hudson Bay in the 1820s, the bank diversified. In 1832 Bank of Montreal financed Canada's first railroad, the Champlain & St. Lawrence. The bank also grew through acquisitions, including the Bank of Canada (1831) and the Bank of the People (1840). It opened a branch in New York in 1859.

Canada united in confederacy in 1867, and Bank of Montreal expanded west. During the 1860s, it became Canada's de facto central bank until the 1935 creation of the Bank of Canada. By 1914 Bank of Montreal was the nation's largest bank. It bought the British Bank of North America (1918), Merchants Bank of Canada (1922), and Molsons Bank (1925). During the Depression, however, its growth ground to a halt.

WWII pumped up Canada's economy and the company's finances. Bank of Montreal enjoyed even greater growth during the postwar boom. It began expanding internationally, particularly in Latin America. But the bank failed to capitalize on the growth of consumer and small-business lending during the 1960s and was the last major Canadian bank to issue a credit card (in 1972). In 1975 Bank of Montreal hired William Mullholland, a Morgan Stanley veteran, to run the company. Mullholland closed unprofitable branches and modernized operations.

The bank bought Chicago-based Harris Bankcorp in 1984. As Canada's banking industry deregulated, Bank of Montreal moved into investment banking, acquiring one of Canada's largest brokerages, Nesbitt Thomson, in 1987.

The Latin American debt crisis and the recession of the late 1980s and early 1990s hit Bank of Montreal hard. It tumbled into the red in 1989, partly because of loan defaults. The next year Matthew Barrett replaced Mullholland as chairman and began overhauling operations, focusing on consumer and middle-market business banking and on cutting costs.

By 1994 nonperforming assets were down, and Bank of Montreal began growing again. It bought brokerage Burns Fry and merged it with Nesbitt Thomson to form Nesbitt Burns, thus increasing its presence in merchant and investment banking and securities. It added to its Harris Bank network with the purchase of Suburban Bancorp. The next year Bank of Montreal expanded its private banking business for wealthy individuals; it also began targeting aboriginal Canadians.

Eyeing international growth, Bank of Montreal bought an interest in Mexico's Grupo Financiero Bancomer (now BBVA Bancomer) in 1996 and opened branches in Beijing (1996) and Dublin, Ireland (1997). It agreed in 1998 to merge with Royal Bank of Canada, but Canada's finance minister rejected the merger.

Barrett stepped down as CEO and chairman in 1999; the firm named F. Anthony Comper its new CEO. The bank realigned its operations to focus on retail and commercial banking, investment banking, and wealth management and cut some 2,450 jobs. Eyeing growth in the US, in 2000 Bank of Montreal agreed to buy Florida's Village Banc of Naples, as well as Seattle brokerage Freeman Welwood. Also that year subsidiary Harris Bank began offering wireless banking.

Chairman and CEO: F. Anthony Comper
VC, Corporate Services and Organizational Development: Gary S. Dibb
VC, Investment Banking Group; Chairman and CEO, Nesbitt Burns: R. Jeffrey Orr
VC, Office of Strategic Management: Keith O. Dorricott
VC, Personal and Commercial Client Group: Jeffrey S. Chisholm, age 51
VC, Personal and Commercial Client Group: Ronald G. Rogers, age 52
VC, Private Client Group; Deputy Chair, Nesbitt Burns: William A. Downe
VC: Brian J. Steck
President and COO, Private Client Group; Deputy Chair, Nesbitt Burns: Gilles G. Ouellette
EVP and CFO: Karen Maidment, age 42
EVP Human Resources: Harriet H. Stairs
Auditors: KPMG LLP; PricewaterhouseCoopers LLP

LOCATIONS

HQ: 119 St. Jacques, Montreal, Quebec H2Y 1L6, Canada
Phone: 514-877-7373   **Fax:** 514-877-7399
US HQ: 430 Park Ave., New York, NY 60603
US Phone: 212-758-6300   **US Fax:** 212-605-1677
Web site: http://www.bmo.com

Bank of Montreal operates in Asia, Europe, Latin America, and North America.

1999 Loans

	% of total
Canada	55
US	39
Other countries	6
Total	**100**

PRODUCTS/OPERATIONS

1999 Assets

	$ mil.	% of total
Cash & equivalents	16,337	10
Securities	29,413	19
Net loans	93,799	60
Other assets	17,200	11
Total	**156,749**	**100**

Selected Subsidiaries

Bank of Montreal Assessoria e Servicos Ltda. (Brazil)
Bank of Montreal Capital Corporation
Bank of Montreal Capital Markets (Holdings) Limited (UK)
  Bank of Montreal Europe Limited (UK)
BMO Nesbitt Burns International Ltd. (UK)
Bank of Montreal Holding Inc.
  Bank of Montreal Asia Limited (Singapore)
  Bank of Montreal Securities Canada Limited
Bank of Montreal Investor Services Limited
Bank of Montreal Ireland plc
Bank of Montreal Mortgage Corporation
Bankmont Financial Corp. (US)
  BMO Financial, Inc. (US)
  Harris Bankcorp, Inc. (US)
  Nesbitt Burns Securities Inc. (US)
BMO Ireland Finance Company
Cebra Inc.
The Trust Company of Bank of Montreal

COMPETITORS

Bank of America	Northern Trust
BANK ONE	Royal Bank of Canada
Canadian Imperial	Scotiabank
Citigroup	Standard Chartered
GE Capital	Toronto-Dominion Bank
Laurentian Bank	Wells Fargo

HISTORICAL FINANCIALS & EMPLOYEES

NYSE: BMO FYE: October 31	Annual Growth	10/90	10/91	10/92	10/93	10/94	10/95	10/96	10/97	10/98	10/99
Assets ($ mil.)	8.6%	74,816	87,912	87,977	88,490	102,153	113,435	126,949	147,586	144,216	156,749
Net income ($ mil.)	8.6%	447	530	516	537	610	737	873	927	875	939
Income as % of assets	—	0.6%	0.6%	0.6%	0.6%	0.6%	0.6%	0.7%	0.6%	0.6%	0.6%
Earnings per share ($)	7.8%	—	—	—	—	2.20	2.53	3.09	3.28	3.02	3.21
Stock price - FY high ($)	—	—	—	—	—	18.63	23.13	30.88	44.63	60.69	46.06
Stock price - FY low ($)	—	—	—	—	—	18.38	17.13	21.38	28.75	33.44	33.50
Stock price - FY close ($)	15.5%	—	—	—	—	18.50	22.25	30.38	43.13	40.88	38.06
P/E - high	—	—	—	—	—	8	9	10	13	20	14
P/E - low	—	—	—	—	—	8	7	7	9	11	10
Dividends per share ($)	—	—	—	—	—	0.00	0.94	1.04	1.50	1.76	1.85
Book value per share ($)	8.9%	—	—	—	—	18.21	19.92	21.81	24.18	25.99	27.95
Employees	(0.2%)	33,580	32,130	32,126	32,067	34,769	33,341	33,468	34,286	33,400	32,844

STOCK PRICE HISTORY

HIGH/LOW/CLOSE

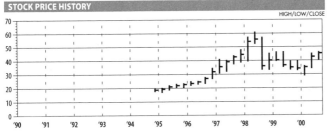

1999 FISCAL YEAR-END

Equity as % of assets: 4.8%
Return on assets: 0.6%
Return on equity: 15.7%
Long-term debt ($ mil.): 3,203
No. of shares (mil.): 267
Dividends
  Yield: 4.9%
  Payout: 57.6%
Market value ($ mil.): 10,163
Sales ($ mil.): 11,341

THE BANK OF TOKYO-MITSUBISHI

Japan's banking Goliath has taken a tumble during the Asian economic crisis and its home country's recession. The Bank of Tokyo-Mitsubishi (BTM) lost its place as the world's largest bank: It's now #5; Mizuho Holdings is #1. Its more than 300 offices in Japan and more than 400 overseas provide consumer and business banking, foreign exchange, investment management, leasing, lending, and securities services, as well as trust services through Nippon Trust Bank. BTM owns about 8% of Mitsubishi Group. Meiji Life Insurance owns about 6% of BTM.

Too proud to accept government handouts to cover bad debt, the firm is the only major Japanese bank which has paid back all the bailout money showered upon the entire sector in 1998. But BTM didn't let pride stop it from going overseas to help it along. The bank

has been selling its debts to foreign investors, particularly institutional money managers. BTM's drive to rid itself of its debt has incurred high losses but allowed it to slash its set-aside for bad debts.

Having lost its place atop the global banking industry, BTM was faced as well with the loss of its national crown as competitors merged. However, it hopes that it will secure its place atop Japan's banking peak with a planned union with Mitsubishi Trust and Nippon Trust; alliances with Tokio Marine and Fire Insurance and Meiji Mutual are being considered as well, to create a financial services giant.

In the meantime, the company is reorganizing operationally including retail banking, domestic institutional sales, global customer service, investment banking, asset management, and US operations.

Mitsubishi Bank emerged from the exchange office of the original Mitsubishi *zaibatsu* (industrial group) in 1885. It had evolved into a full-service bank by 1895 and became independent in 1919, though its primary customers were Mitsubishi group companies. The bank survived WWII, but a US fiat dismantled the *zaibatsu* after the war. Mitsubishi Bank reopened as Chiyoda Bank in 1948. After reopening offices in London and New York, the bank readopted the Mitsubishi name.

In the 1950s Mitsubishi Bank became the lead lender for the reconstituted Mitsubishi group (*keiretsu*). In the 1960s it followed its Mitsubishi partners overseas, helping finance Japan's growing international trade. In 1972 it acquired the Bank of California and began doing more business outside the group.

Japan's overinflated real estate market of the 1980s devastated many Japanese banks, including Nippon Trust Bank Ltd., of which Mitsubishi owned 5%. Japan's Ministry of Finance urged Mitsubishi to bail Nippon out; as a reward for raising its stake in Nippon to 69% and assuming a mountain of unrecoverable loans, the ministry allowed Mitsubishi to begin issuing debt before other Japanese banks.

In 1995 Mitsubishi Bank and Bank of Tokyo agreed to merge.

Bank of Tokyo (BOT) was established in 1880 as the Yokohama Specie Bank; the Iwasaki family, founders of the Mitsubishi group, served on its board. With links to the Imperial family, the bank was heavily influenced by government policy. With Japan isolated after the Sino-Japanese

War, its international operations suffered greatly even before WWII. Completely dismantled after WWII, the bank was re-established in 1946 as the Bank of Tokyo, a commercial city bank bereft of its foreign exchange business. During the 1950s the government re-established it as a foreign exchange specialist, but regulations limited its domestic business.

BOT evolved into an investment bank in the 1970s; its reputation as the leading foreign exchange bank brought in international clients and successful derivatives trading and overseas banking. By the time BOT and Mitsubishi Bank agreed to merge, BOT had 363 international offices (only 37 in Japan) with more foreign than Japanese employees.

The two banks merged in 1996 to form The Bank of Tokyo-Mitsubishi (BTM); Mitsubishi was the surviving entity. Their California banks merged to create Union Bank of California (UnionBanCal). The next year BTM reorganized its operations but had problems assimilating its disparate corporate cultures.

In 1998 BTM was fined for bribing ministry officials with entertainment gifts and posted a huge loss after writing off $8.4 billion in bad debt. Losses continued in 1999, and the bank responded by reorganizing operationally, cutting jobs and offices, and selling stock in UnionBanCal. BTM also announced several deals, including a partnership with Lehman Brothers for investment banking and the purchase of a stake in second-tier brokerage firm Kokusai Securities.

Chairman: Satoru Kishi, age 70
Deputy Chairman: Kenji Yoshizawa
President and Director of Finance: Shigemitsu Miki, age 65
Deputy President: Shin Nakahara
Senior Managing Director: Yasuyuki Hirai
Senior Managing Director: Tetsuo Shimura
Senior Managing Director: Hiroshi Watanabe
Senior Managing Director: Masamichi Yamada
Auditors: Deloitte Touche Tohmatsu

HQ: Tokyo Mitsubishi Ginko
(The Bank of Tokyo-Mitsubishi Ltd.)
7-1, Marunouchi 2-chome,
Chiyoda-ku, Tokyo 100-8388, Japan
Phone: +81-3-3240-1111   **Fax:** +81-3-3240-4197
US HQ: 1251 Avenue of the Americas,
New York, NY 10020
US Phone: 212-782-4000   **US Fax:** 212-782-6414
Web site: http://www.btm.co.jp

The Bank of Tokyo-Mitsubishi operates in Africa, Asia, Europe, North America, the Pacific Rim, and South America.

2000 Sales

	$ mil.	% of total
Japan	12,076	53
US	5,314	24
Asia & Pacific Rim	2,000	9
Europe	1,898	8
Other regions	1,376	6
Total	**22,664**	**100**

2000 Assets

	$ mil.	% of total
Cash & equivalents	60,612	9
Trading account	62,040	9
Securities	141,590	20
Net loans	388,067	56
Receivables	29,842	4
Other assets	17,417	2
Total	**699,568**	**100**

Selected Subsidiaries
Banco de Tokyo-Mitsubishi Brasil S/A
Bank of Tokyo-Mitsubishi (Australia) Ltd.
Bank of Tokyo-Mitsubishi (Canada)
BTM Lease (Deutschland) GmbH (Germany)
BTM Leasing & Finance, Inc. (US; leasing)
Nippon Trust Bank Limited
Sime Diamond Leasing (Singapore) Pte. Limited
Tokyo Mitsubishi Asset Management, Ltd.
Tokyo Trust Bank, Ltd.
Tokyo-Mitsubishi International (HK) Ltd. (Hong Kong)
Tokyo-Mitsubishi International plc (UK; capital markets and derivative products)
Tokyo-Mitsubishi Securities Co., Ltd.
UnionBanCal Corporation (US; bank holding company)

ABN AMRO	Dai-Ichi Kangyo	Royal Bank of
Bank of America	Deutsche Bank	Canada
Barclays	Dresdner Bank	Sakura Bank
Caisse Nationale	Fuji Bank	Sanwa Bank
de Crédit	HSBC Holdings	Shinsei Bank
Agricole	Industrial Bank	Société Générale
Chase Manhattan	of Japan	Sumitomo
Citigroup	J.P. Morgan	Tokai Bank
Credit Suisse	ORIX	UBS

NYSE: MBK FYE: March 31	Annual Growth	3/91	3/92	3/93	3/94	3/95	3/96	3/97	3/98	3/99	3/00
Assets ($ mil.)	7.0%	381,620	390,466	432,084	459,362	608,980	509,706	675,079	651,975	623,741	699,568
Net income ($ mil.)	(7.9%)	727	561	485	375	410	266	261	(5,811)	(2,895)	346
Income as % of assets	—	0.2%	0.1%	0.1%	0.1%	0.1%	0.1%	0.0%	—	—	0.0%
Earnings per share ($)	(17.7%)	0.23	0.18	0.15	0.11	0.13	0.09	0.06	(1.24)	(0.62)	0.04
Stock price - FY high ($)	—	18.33	21.66	21.66	27.85	26.42	24.04	24.00	20.69	14.69	17.06
Stock price - FY low ($)	—	10.83	15.35	10.00	20.59	19.75	18.45	14.00	11.88	5.94	11.44
Stock price - FY close ($)	(2.2%)	17.26	15.35	19.87	24.99	23.09	21.38	15.63	12.06	14.00	14.19
P/E - high	—	80	120	144	232	203	267	400	—	—	284
P/E - low	—	47	85	67	172	152	205	233	—	—	191
Dividends per share ($)	5.4%	0.05	0.05	0.06	0.07	0.07	0.00	0.08	0.04	0.00	0.08
Book value per share ($)	5.8%	4.01	4.34	5.09	5.68	8.05	8.02	6.17	4.41	4.75	6.66
Employees	(1.0%)	—	—	—	19,300	19,300	19,300	19,304	18,386	17,900	18,200

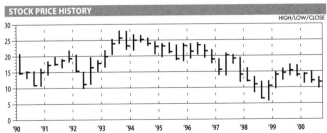

HIGH/LOW/CLOSE

Equity as % of assets: 4.4%
Return on assets: 0.1%
Return on equity: 1.4%
Long-term debt ($ mil.): 67,687
No. of shares (mil.): 4,675
Dividends
  Yield: 0.6%
  Payout: 200.0%
Market value ($ mil.): 66,345
Sales ($ mil.): 22,664

BARCLAYS PLC

OVERVIEW

The eagle has molted. London-based Barclays (whose logo is a regal eagle) is the #2 UK banking firm by assets behind HSBC Holdings. Barclays has neatened up its business into four areas: retail banking (savings, checking, credit cards, consumer loans, and private banking for wealthy clients), corporate banking, Barclays Global Investors, and Barclays Capital, which concentrates on fixed-income, foreign exchange, and derivatives activities, among others. Barclays also sells life insurance and manages pensions. The company has given up its effort to become a global securities industry powerhouse.

Barclays operates in about 60 countries worldwide. The company has bought fellow UK bank Woolwich to boost its mortgage lending operations and its Internet banking unit, which it is promoting heavily.

HISTORY

The eagle that is Barclays' symbol first spread its wings in 1736 when James Barclay united family goldsmithing and banking businesses. As other family members joined the London enterprise, it became known as Barclays, Bevan & Tritton (1782).

Banking first became regulated in the 19th century. To ward off takeovers, 20 banks combined with Barclays in 1896. The new firm, Barclay & Co., began preying on other banks. Within 20 years it bought 17, including the Colonial Bank, chartered in 1836 to serve the West Indies and British Guiana (now Guyana). Renamed Barclays Bank Ltd. in 1917, it weathered the Depression as the UK's #2 bank.

Barclays began expanding again after WWII, and by the late 1950s it had become the UK's top bank. It had a computer network by 1959, and in 1966 it introduced the Barclaycard in conjunction with Bank of America's BankAmericard (now Visa).

In 1968 the UK's Monopolies Commission barred Barclays' merger with two other big London banks, but had no objections to a two-way merger, so Barclays bought competitor Martins.

Barclays moved into the US consumer finance market in 1980 when it bought American Credit, 138 former Beneficial Finance offices, and Bankers Trust's branch network.

During the 1980s, London banks faced competition from invading overseas banks, local building societies, and other financial firms. Banking reform in 1984 led to formation of a holding company for Barclays Bank PLC.

To prepare for British financial deregulation in 1986, Barclays formed Barclays de Zoete Wedd (BZW) by merging its merchant bank with two other London financial firms. Faced with sagging profits, Barclays sold its California bank in 1988 and its US consumer finance business in 1989.

In 1990 Barclays bought private German bank Merck, Finck & Co. and Paris bank L'Européenne de Banque. The company countered 1992's bad-loan-induced losses by accelerating a cost-cutting program begun in 1989. To appease stockholders, chairman and CEO Andrew Buxton (a descendant of one of the bank's founding families) gave up his CEO title, hiring Martin Taylor (previously CEO of textile firm Courtaulds) for the post.

The company sold its Australian retail banking business in 1994, then began trimming other operations, including French corporate banking and US mortgage operations. However, it bought the Wells Fargo Nikko Investment Company to boost Pacific Rim operations.

Barclays' piecemeal sale of BZW signaled its failure to become a global investment banking powerhouse. In 1997 it sold BZW's European investment banking business to Credit Suisse First Boston, retaining the fixed-income and foreign exchange business. (Credit Suisse bought Barclays' Asian investment banking operations in 1998.)

Losses in Russia and a $250 million bailout of US hedge fund Long-Term Capital Management hit Barclays Capital in 1998. Taylor resigned that year in part because of his radical plans for the bank. Sir Peter Middleton stepped in as acting CEO; Barclays later tapped Canadian banker Matthew Barrett for the post. (Middleton also became chairman upon Buxton's retirement.)

Barclays in 1999 started a move toward online banking at the expense of traditional branches. The company announced free lifetime Internet access for new bank customers.

In 2000 the company launched a business-to-business Web site and invested in a small business portal venture with Internet service provider Freeserve. The bank ruffled feathers that year when it announced the closure of about 170 mostly rural UK branches. Also in 2000, the company agreed to sell its Dial auto leasing unit to ABN AMRO and bought Woolwich plc.

Chairman: Sir Peter Middleton, age 65, $951,000 pay
Group Chief Executive: Matthew W. Barrett, age 55, $308,000 pay
Chief Executive, Corporate Banking, Barclays PLC and Barclays Bank PLC: Chrisopher J. Lendrum, age 53, $294,000 pay
Chief Executive, Retail Financial Services, Barclays PLC and Barclays Bank PLC: John S. Varley, age 43, $356,000 pay
Finance Director, Barclays PLC and Barclays Bank PLC: David Allvey, age 54, $163,000 pay
Chairman, Barclays Global Investors: Patricia C. Dunn
Chief Executive, Barclays Capital: Robert E. Diamond Jr.
Managing Director, Markets and Solutions: David Roberts
Managing Director, Wealth Management, Retail Financial Services: Bob Hunter
Group Director of Strategic Planning and Corporate Development: Gary Dibb
Director, Group Credit Policy: Andrew Bruce
Director, Group Human Resources: Sally Bott
Director, Group Risk: Tim Shepheard-Walwyn
Director, Planning, Operations, and Technology: Graham Pimlott
Chief Information Officer: David Weymouth
Chief Accountant: Geoffrey Mitchell
Group Secretary and Group General Counsel: Howard Trust
Joint Secretary Barclays Bank PLC: Alison Dillon
Auditors: PricewaterhouseCoopers

HQ: 54 Lombard St.,
London EC3P 3AH, United Kingdom
Phone: +44-20-7699-5000   **Fax:** +44-20-7699-2460
US HQ: Barclays Capital, New York, NY 10038
US Phone: 212-412-4000   **US Fax:** 212-412-7300
Web site: http://www.barclays.co.uk

Barclays has more than 1,700 branches and offices in the UK and offices in about 60 other countries.

Selected Operations
Barclays Capital (fixed-income and foreign exchange)
Barclays Global Investors (institutional investment manager)
Barclays Private Banking (asset management services)
Retail Financial Services (worldwide retail operations)

Bank of New York	HSBC Holdings
Canadian Imperial	Industrial Bank of Japan
Chase Manhattan	J.P. Morgan
Citigroup	Lloyds TSB
Crédit Lyonnais	Royal Bank of Canada
Credit Suisse	Standard Chartered
Dai-Ichi Kangyo	UBS
Deutsche Bank	Vanguard Group
Halifax	

NYSE: BCS FYE: December 31	Annual Growth	12/90	12/91	12/92	12/93	12/94	12/95	12/96	12/97	12/98	12/99
Assets ($ mil.)	5.2%	260,332	258,193	225,839	245,609	254,161	262,187	318,528	387,583	364,250	411,695
Net income ($ mil.)	15.9%	755	452	(520)	463	1,845	2,118	2,807	1,866	2,222	2,842
Income as % of assets	—	0.3%	0.2%	—	0.2%	0.7%	0.8%	0.9%	0.5%	0.6%	0.7%
Earnings per share ($)	16.4%	1.91	1.14	(1.30)	1.15	4.53	4.71	7.14	4.89	5.87	7.48
Stock price - FY high ($)	—	30.75	36.00	30.50	39.00	40.00	50.25	70.00	115.63	130.88	130.00
Stock price - FY low ($)	—	22.00	24.00	20.13	22.50	30.00	36.00	42.00	63.75	58.38	85.00
Stock price - FY close ($)	16.9%	28.25	28.00	23.25	37.75	38.25	45.25	68.75	109.19	90.00	115.13
P/E - high	—	16	32	—	34	9	11	10	24	22	17
P/E - low	—	12	21	—	20	7	8	6	13	10	11
Dividends per share ($)	3.2%	1.68	1.64	2.00	0.81	1.59	1.81	3.33	3.17	3.67	2.24
Book value per share ($)	2.5%	29.49	26.85	34.05	19.37	23.76	26.75	24.90	25.18	26.31	36.67
Employees	(4.5%)	—	—	—	—	—	89,300	87,400	83,200	78,600	74,300

HIGH/LOW/CLOSE

Equity as % of assets: 3.3%
Return on assets: 0.7%
Return on equity: 21.2%
Long-term debt ($ mil.): 7,428
No. of shares (mil.): 374
Dividends
  Yield: 0.0%
  Payout: 0.3%
Market value ($ mil.): 43,036
Sales ($ mil.): 21,097

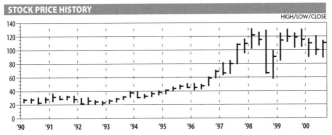

BASF AKTIENGESELLSCHAFT

The world is BASF's ester. Based in Ludwigshafen, Germany, BASF is Europe's largest chemical company. It has manufacturing facilities in about 40 countries and does business worldwide through five business segments: plastics and fibers (including polyolefins and polystyrene), colorants and finishing products (dyes, coatings), chemicals (plasticizers, solvents), oil and gas, and health and nutrition (pharmaceuticals, fertilizers). BASF uses what it calls Verbund strategy throughout its facilities — plants are both customers and suppliers of each other. The company continues to expand overseas, particularly in Asia, but Europe still accounts for nearly 60% of sales.

BASF has set its sights on expanding its North American operations with plans to invest in excess of $2 billion there by 2004. The company also intends to increase sales and production in the Asia/Pacific region.

HISTORY

Originally named Badische Anilin & Soda-Fabrik, BASF AG was founded in Mannheim, Germany, by jeweler Frederick Englehorn in 1861. Unable to find enough land for expansion in Mannheim, BASF moved to nearby Ludwigshafen in 1865. The company was a pioneer in coal tar dyes, and it developed a synthetic indigo in 1897. Its synthetic dyes rapidly replaced more expensive organic dyes.

BASF scientist Fritz Haber synthesized ammonia in 1909, giving BASF access to the market for nitrogenous fertilizer (1913). Haber received a Nobel Prize in 1919 but was later charged with war crimes for his work with poison gases. Managed by Carl Bosch, another Nobel Prize winner, BASF joined the I.G. Farben cartel with Bayer, Hoechst, and others in 1925 to create a German chemical colossus. Within the cartel BASF developed polystyrene, PVC, and magnetic tape. Part of the Nazi war machine, I.G. Farben made synthetic rubber and used labor from the Auschwitz concentration camp during WWII.

After the war I.G. Farben was dismantled. BASF regained its independence in 1952 and rebuilt its war-ravaged factories. Strong postwar domestic demand for basic chemicals aided its recovery, and in 1958 BASF launched a US joint venture with Dow Chemical (BASF bought out Dow's half in 1978). The company moved into petrochemicals and became a leading manufacturer of plastic and synthetic fiber.

In the US the company purchased Wyandotte Chemicals (1969), Chemetron (1979), and Inmont (1985), among others. In 1990 BASF became the first outsider to buy a major chemical company in post-communist East Germany when it purchased Synthesewerk Schwarzheide (SYS).

To expand its natural gas business in Europe, the company signed deals with Russia's Gazprom and France's Elf Aquitaine in 1991.

BASF bought Mobil's polystyrene-resin business and gained almost 10% of the US market.

BASF bought Imperial Chemical's polypropylene business in 1994 and became Europe's second-largest producer of the plastic. The next year the company paid $1.4 billion for the pharmaceutical arm of UK retailer Boots. In 1996 the SYS plant turned its first profit and the company sold its magnetic-tape business to the KOHAP Group of South Korea.

In 1997 BASF formed a joint venture with PetroFina (BASF Fina Petrochemicals) to build the world's largest olefin plant in Port Arthur, Texas. It also merged its European polypropylene operations with Hoechst's.

BASF made seven major acquisitions in 1998, including the complexing business of Ciba Specialty Chemicals. It also made six divestitures, which included its European buildings-paints operations to Akzo Nobel N.V.

In 1999 the US fined the company $225 million for its part in a worldwide vitamin price-fixing cartel; BASF also faced a class-action suit as a result of the scheme. That year the company moved into oil and gas exploration in Russia through a partnership with Russia's Gazprom. BASF also merged its textile operations into Bayer and Hoechst's DyStar joint venture, forming a $1 billion company that is one of the world's leading dye makers.

BASF completed its acquisition of Rohm & Haas' industrial coatings business and agreed to buy American Home Products' Cyanamid division (herbicides, fungicides, and pesticides) in 2000. That year BASF expanded its super-absorbents business by paying $656 million for US-based Amcol International's Chemdal International unit. The company also opened a new $16.8 million acrylic polymer plant in the Philippines, announced plans for a new vitamin pre-mix plant in Malaysia, and agreed to sell its Novolen polypropylene technology to ABB.

OFFICERS

Chairman, Board of Executive Directors:
Jürgen F. Strube
Deputy Chairman, Board of Executive Directors:
Max Dietrich Kley
Member of Board of Executive Directors; President, BASF Corporation: Peter Oakley
President, Antwerp Works: Antoon Dieusaert
President, BASF AG Site Engineering:
Werner Wüchner
President, Central Europe Division:
Dieter Thomaschewski
President, North America Coatings and Colorants:
Frank E. McKulka
President, Fiber Products Division: Wolfgang Hapke
President, Finance Division: Eckhard Müller
President, Human Resources Division:
Hans-Hermann Dehmel
President, Industrial Chemicals Division:
Rainer Strickler
President, Oil and Gas Division: Herbert Detharding
President, Planning and Controlling Division:
Elmar Frommer
President, Polyurethanes/PVC Division:
Jean-Pierre Dhanis
Auditors: Deloitte & Touche GmbH

LOCATIONS

HQ: Carl-Bosch St. 38, 67056 Ludwigshafen, Germany
Phone: +49-621-60-0   **Fax:** +49-621-60-42525
US HQ: 3000 Continental Dr. North,
Mount Olive, NJ 07828
US Phone: 973-426-2600   **US Fax:** 973-426-2610
Web site: http://www.basf.com

BASF AG makes products in about 40 countries and conducts business in more than 170.

1999 Sales

	% of total
Europe	58
North America	23
Asia/Pacific & Africa	13
South America	6
Total	**100**

PRODUCTS/OPERATIONS

1999 Sales

	$ mil.	% of total
Plastics & fibers	9,130	29
Colorants & finishing products	6,843	22
Health & nutrition	5,994	19
Chemicals	4,701	15
Oil & gas	3,265	10
Other	1,604	5
Total	**31,537**	**100**

COMPETITORS

Air Products	Eni	Mitsubishi
Akzo Nobel	Exxon Mobil	Chemical
American Home	FMC	Novartis
Ashland	Formosa Plastics	Pfizer
Bayer	Glaxo Wellcome	Phillips
BP	Henkel	Petroleum
Bristol-Myers	Hercules	PPG
Squibb	Hoffmann-La	Roche Holding
Degussa-Hüls	Roche	Royal
Dow Chemical	Honeywell	Dutch/Shell
DSM	International	Sony
DuPont	Huntsman	TOTAL FINA ELF
Eastman	LG Group	Union Carbide
Eli Lilly	Merck	

HISTORICAL FINANCIALS & EMPLOYEES

NYSE: BF FYE: December 31	Annual Growth	12/90	12/91	12/92	12/93	12/94	12/95	12/96	12/97	12/98	12/99
Sales ($ mil.)	0.1%	31,144	30,675	27,462	24,802	30,052	32,153	31,642	31,011	32,439	31,537
Net income ($ mil.)	5.9%	739	684	379	493	829	1,718	1,842	1,799	1,994	1,243
Income as % of sales	—	2.4%	2.2%	1.4%	2.0%	2.8%	5.3%	5.8%	5.8%	6.1%	3.9%
Earnings per share ($)	—	—	—	—	—	—	—	—	—	—	2.00
Stock price - FY high ($)	—	—	—	—	—	—	—	—	—	—	52.25
Stock price - FY low ($)	—	—	—	—	—	—	—	—	—	—	51.38
Stock price - FY close ($)	—	—	—	—	—	—	—	—	—	—	52.13
P/E - high	—	—	—	—	—	—	—	—	—	—	26
P/E - low	—	—	—	—	—	—	—	—	—	—	26
Dividends per share ($)	—	—	—	—	—	—	—	—	—	—	1.14
Book value per share ($)	—	—	—	—	—	—	—	—	—	—	22.89
Employees	(2.8%)	134,647	129,434	213,254	112,020	106,266	106,565	103,406	104,979	105,945	104,628

STOCK PRICE HISTORY

HIGH/LOW/CLOSE

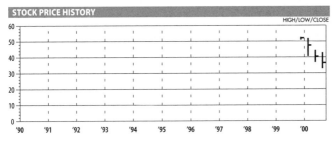

1999 FISCAL YEAR-END

Debt ratio: 8.4%
Return on equity: 8.4%
Cash ($ mil.): 995
Current ratio: 2.31
Long-term debt ($ mil.): 1,301
No. of shares (mil.): 621
Dividends
 Yield: 0.0%
 Payout: 0.6%
Market value ($ mil.): 32,372

BASS PLC

OVERVIEW

Bass is a big fish in the big pond of pubs, beverages, and hotels. The London-based company's Bass Leisure Retail division owns more than 2,500 pubs, restaurants, bowling alleys, and other leisure businesses in the UK. The company lures its pub patrons by brewing and distributing a variety of brand name beers such as Bass Ale, Caffrey's, and Carling (Bass Brewers is the UK's #2 brewer after Scottish & Newcastle). It makes soft drinks under the Britvic tag (through a 50%-owned subsidiary co-owned by Allied Domecq, Whitbread, and

Pepsi) and is the UK distributor of Pepsi and 7 UP. Bass Brewers distributes its products to about 80 countries.

The company's Bass Hotels & Resorts (BHR) is one of the world's largest hotel operators and franchisers with more than 2,800 Holiday Inn, Crowne Plaza, and Inter-Continental hotels in more than 90 countries. Bass is concentrating on its hotel operations (about 40% of earnings) and is selling its brewing division to Interbrew for about $3.5 billion.

HISTORY

Before 1777, William Bass merely delivered the beer. From then on, Bass brewed it as well, settling on the pure water of Burton-on-Trent, England, that allowed him to brew lighter ales than those in London. When Bass' grandson Michael took charge in 1827, the brewery had 10,000 barrels of beer on the wall. In 1876 Bass became the first company to gain trademark protection (for its red triangle) under the British Trademark Registration Act of 1875. By the time of Michael Bass' death in 1884, the 145-acre Bass brewery was the largest ale and bitter brewery in the world.

Most British brewers employed the tied-house system, in which breweries controlled and supplied beer to their own pubs, limiting distribution but assuring them a market for their beer. But Bass opted for the free-trade system, relying on expanded distribution through resellers to create growing demand for its brew. World War I and the temperance movement hurt all brewers as consumers turned to movies and other diversions instead of evenings at the local pub. The tied-house pubs responded by improving their facilities to lure teetotalers back, while Bass' sales suffered when the pubs serving its beer failed to follow suit.

Bass bought several breweries in the 1920s (including rival Worthington & Company in 1926). In 1961 Bass merged with Mitchells & Butler. Back on the rise, Bass joined forces with Charrington United (Carling Black Label lager and pubs) in 1967 to build a nationwide network of breweries and pubs. By 1970 Bass' British market share approached 25%. When growth slowed in the 1980s, Bass sold less-profitable pubs and diversified. The rapid growth of the company's Crest Hotel chain (started in 1969) encouraged Bass to make other hospitality acquisitions, including Horizon Travel (packaged holidays) in 1987. The next year Bass agreed to buy the

Memphis-based Holiday Inn chain from Holiday Corp. Holiday Inns had been founded by Kemmons Wilson as a family-oriented hotel chain in 1952. Wilson, who was credited with inventing motel franchising, made it one of the world's largest lodging chains. The Holiday Inn sale was completed in 1990 and Bass began a $1 billion renovation. After discovering many of the hotels didn't meet zoning laws, Bass sued Promus (acquired by Hilton Hotels in 1999), settling for $49 million in 1995.

Once active in the gaming business, Bass sold its Gala chain of bingo clubs, Maygay and Barcrest amusement machine businesses, and its chain of nearly 900 Coral betting shops in 1997. Bass refocused its efforts on its hotel business in 1998 when it paid Japan's Saison Group $3 billion for the Inter-Continental Hotels & Resorts chain. The company also opened its first of more than 40 planned Staybridge Suites, a Holiday Inn brand catering to extended-stay travelers.

In 1999 it announced plans to invest more than $700 million in its hotel operations and moved its Bass Hotels & Resorts headquarters from Atlanta to the main corporate headquarters in London. Bass also teamed with Punch Taverns to buy almost 3,600 pubs from Allied Domecq. (Bass helped Punch bankroll the deal and bought 550 of the pubs.) Bass bought 59 Southern Pacific Hotel Corp. hotels in the Asia/Pacific region from Hale International Ltd. in 2000.

In 2000, after more than two centuries of making beer, Bass agreed to sell its brewing operations to rival Interbrew for about $3.5 billion. As a result the company will have to search for a new name. Bass also bought Bristol Hotels & Resorts, a franchisor of about 110 hotels (including Bass' own Crowne Plaza and Holiday Inn) in the US and Canada.

Chairman and Chief Executive: Sir Ian Prosser, age 56
Deputy Chairman: Sir Michael S. Perry, age 65
Director, Finance; Chairman Britvic Soft Drinks:
Richard C. North, age 49
Chairman and CEO, Bass Hotels & Resorts:
Tom Oliver, age 58
CEO, Bass Brewers and Bass International Brewers:
Iain J. G. Napier, age 50
CEO, Bass Leisure Retail: Tim Clarke, age 42
Secretary and Director, Personnel: Spencer Wigley,
age 57
Manager, Harvester: Angela Warren
**Senior VP Development, EMEA, Bass Hotels &
Resorts:** Tom Huffsmith
External Communication Manager, Bass PLC:
Julia Lalla-Maharajh
Senior Brand Manager, Hooch: Helen Olle
Sales and Events Manager, Browns: David Harriott
Strategic Planning Manager, Bass PLC: John Butterfield
Brand Manager, It's A Scream: Susie Maley
Sales Support Representative, Bass Brewers:
Julie Evans
Team Coordinator, Britvic Soft Drinks: Chris Garwood
Director Group Communications: Pugh Phillips
Auditors: Ernst & Young

LOCATIONS

HQ: 20 N. Audley St.,
London W1Y 1WE, United Kingdom
Phone: +44-207-409-1919   **Fax:** +44-207-409-8503
Web site: http://www.bass.com

Bass PLC owns or operates more than 2,500 pubs and
restaurants in the UK and 2,800 hotels in more than 90
countries; additionally, it distributes its beverages to
about 80 countries.

PRODUCTS/OPERATIONS

Selected Brands

Bass Brewers	**Hotels**
Bass Ale	Crowne Plaza
Caffrey's	Holiday Inn Express
Carling	Holiday Inn
Grolsch	Inter-Continental
Hooper's Hooch	Staybridge Suites by
Worthington	Holiday Inn

Britvic Soft Drinks	**Pubs and Restaurants**
7 UP	All Bar One
J2O	Browns
Pepsi	Edwards
Robinsons	O'Neill's
Tango	Vintage Inns

COMPETITORS

Accor	Marriott International
Allied Domecq	Nomura Securities
Best Western	Punch Taverns Group
Carlsberg	Rank
De Vere Group	Scottish & Newcastle
Diageo	Starwood Hotels & Resorts
Enterprise Inns	Whitbread
Foster's Brewing	Wolverhampton &
Greene King	Dudley Breweries
Hilton	

HISTORICAL FINANCIALS & EMPLOYEES

NYSE: BAS FYE: September 30	Annual Growth	9/90	9/91	9/92	9/93	9/94	9/95	9/96	9/97	9/98	9/99
Sales ($ mil.)	(0.9%)	8,364	7,675	7,656	6,661	7,019	7,188	7,996	8,495	7,830	7,715
Net income ($ mil.)	(1.4%)	722	644	770	470	550	602	695	404	1,104	637
Income as % of sales	—	8.6%	8.4%	10.1%	7.1%	7.8%	8.4%	8.7%	4.8%	14.1%	8.3%
Earnings per share ($)	(2.9%)	1.03	0.81	0.71	0.55	0.63	0.64	0.79	0.91	1.33	0.79
Stock price - FY high ($)	—	10.31	10.69	11.63	10.06	9.25	11.00	13.19	14.66	20.06	17.00
Stock price - FY low ($)	—	7.13	7.25	8.00	6.75	7.00	7.75	10.00	11.75	10.50	10.63
Stock price - FY close ($)	4.4%	8.50	8.88	9.75	7.06	8.19	10.13	12.19	13.75	12.19	12.56
P/E - high	—	10	13	16	18	15	17	17	16	15	21
P/E - low	—	7	9	11	12	11	12	13	13	8	13
Dividends per share ($)	(7.6%)	1.10	0.36	0.38	0.31	0.33	0.40	0.40	0.17	0.40	0.54
Book value per share ($)	(8.7%)	15.53	7.38	6.88	5.88	6.51	6.67	6.93	6.87	5.50	6.84
Employees	(2.1%)	90,138	98,345	90,104	84,095	81,105	75,845	84,872	83,461	82,616	74,451

STOCK PRICE HISTORY HIGH/LOW/CLOSE

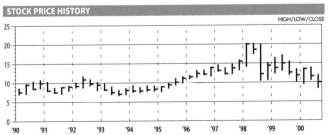

1999 FISCAL YEAR-END
Debt ratio: 38.8%
Return on equity: 13.0%
Cash ($ mil.): 300
Current ratio: 0.78
Long-term debt ($ mil.): 3,459
No. of shares (mil.): 798
Dividends
  Yield: 4.3%
  Payout: 68.4%
Market value ($ mil.): 10,022

BAYER AG

OVERVIEW

You could get a headache trying to name all of Bayer AG's products. The Leverkusen, Germany-based firm and creator of aspirin makes health care and agricultural products and polymers (plastics, synthetic rubber). Bayer is one of the world's biggest chemical companies (on par with the likes of BASF and DuPont). US subsidiary Bayer Corporation makes plastics, polymers, health care products, and agricultural chemicals.

Bayer spends nearly 12% of revenues on R&D, with much of that money going to fuel advances in its health care unit. The success of drugs such as Cibrobay and Avalox (used to treat infectious diseases) is prompting the company to expand its biotechnology research. Bayer's chemicals division has been hurt by poor prices, but its polymers segment has benefited from the acquisition of Lyondell Chemical's polyol business (raw materials for polyurethanes).

HISTORY

Friedrich Bayer founded Bayer in Germany in 1863 to make synthetic dyes. Research led to such discoveries as Antinonin (synthetic pesticide, 1892), aspirin (1897), and synthetic rubber (1915).

Under Carl Duisberg, Bayer allegedly made the first poison gas used by Germany in WWI. During the war the US seized Bayer's US operations and trademark rights and sold them to Sterling Drug.

In 1925 Bayer, BASF, Hoechst, and other German chemical concerns merged to form I.G. Farben Trust. Their photography businesses, combined as Agfa, also joined the trust. Between wars Bayer developed polyurethanes and the first sulfa drug (Prontosil, 1935).

During WWII the trust took over chemical plants of Nazi-occupied countries, used slave labor, and helped make Zyklon B gas used to kill people at Auschwitz. At war's end, Bayer lost its 50% of Winthrop Laboratories (US) and Bayer of Canada (to Sterling Drug). The 1945 Potsdam Agreement called for the breakup of I.G. Farben, and Bayer AG emerged in 1951 as an independent company with many of its original operations, including Agfa.

After rebuilding in West Germany, Bayer AG and Monsanto formed a joint venture (Mobay, 1954). Bayer AG later bought Monsanto's share (1967). In the 1960s the company offered more dyes, plastics, and polyurethanes, and added factories worldwide. Agfa merged with Gevaert (photography, Belgium) in 1964; Bayer AG retained 60%. Over the next decades, it acquired Miles Labs (Alka-Seltzer, US, 1978), the rest of Agfa-Gevaert (1981), Compugraphic (electronic imaging, US, 1989), and Nova's Polysar (rubber, Canada, 1990).

Bayer AG integrated its US holdings under the name Miles in 1992 (renamed Bayer Corporation in 1995). The next year it introduced its first genetically engineered product, Kogenate hemophilia treatment. It regained US rights to the Bayer brand and logo in 1994 by paying SmithKline Beecham $1 billion for the North American business of Sterling Winthrop.

Bayer AG formed a joint venture with Swiss rival Roche Holding in 1996 to market over-the-counter (OTC) Roche drugs in the US, becoming a leading US OTC marketer. After a 1997 US Department of Justice investigation into the citric-acid business, a US subsidiary of Bayer paid a $50 million fine for price-fixing. That year Bayer, Baxter International, Rhône-Poulenc Rorer, and Green Cross agreed to a $670 million settlement over blood products that infected thousands of hemophiliacs with HIV during the 1980s.

In 1998 Bayer sold the food-ingredients arm of its Haarmann & Reimer unit to Tate & Lyle. It also sold Agfa's photocopier business. Bayer bought US-based Chiron's diagnostics operations for $1.1 billion and formed a research alliance with Millennium Pharmaceuticals (giving Bayer AG a 14% stake in Millennium). It also planned to close factories and drop poor-selling drugs as it expanded its US and Asian health care businesses. Bayer spun off all but 26% of its photographic and electronic prepress business as Agfa-Gevaert (later reducing its stake to 10%).

In 1999 Holocaust survivors sued Bayer for its role in Nazi medical experiments. That year Bayer, Hoechst, and BASF merged their textile activities to form the world's largest dye-making company.

Bayer boosted its polyurethane business in 2000, paying $2.5 billion for US-based Lyondell Chemical's polyols unit. Bayer also formed a joint venture with Exelixis Pharmaceuticals to develop gene-based insecticides and announced it would develop an anti-impotence drug to rival Pfizer's Viagra. Late in the year Bayer acquired US polymer and specialty chemical company Sybron in a deal worth about $325 million.

Chairman, Supervisory Board: Hermann J. Strenger
Chairman of the Board of Management:
Manfred Schneider, age 61
Chairman of the Board Committee for Finance:
Werner Wenning, age 53
**Chairman of the Board Committee for Marketing and
Logistics:** Werner Spinner, age 51
**Chairman of the Board Committee for Research and
Development:** Pol Bamelis, age 61
**Chairman of the Board Committee for Technology and
Environment:** Udo Oels, age 56
**Member of the Board Committees for Marketing and
Logistics and for Human Resources:** Gottfried Zaby,
age 49
President and CEO, Bayer Corporation:
Helge H. Wehmeier

HQ: Werk Leverkusen, 51368 Leverkusen, Germany
Phone: +49-214-305-8992   **Fax:** +49-214-307-1985
US HQ: 100 Bayer Rd., Pittsburgh, PA 15205
US Phone: 412-777-2000   **US Fax:** 412-777-2034
Web site: http://www.bayer-ag.de

Bayer AG operates on six continents, primarily in
Europe, the Far East, and North America.

1999 Sales

	$ mil.	% of total
Europe	12,881	47
North America	7,777	28
Latin America	1,623	6
Asia, Africa & Australia	3,089	11
Discontinued operations	2,141	8
Total	**27,511**	**100**

1999 Sales

	$ mil.	% of total
Polymers	9,372	34
Health care	8,425	31
Chemicals	3,730	14
Agriculture	3,116	11
Adjustment	2,868	10
Total	**27,511**	**100**

Selected Operations and Products
Animal health products
Basic and fine chemicals
Crop-protection products
Consumer care products (over-the-counter drugs)
Diagnostics (laboratory products)
Dyes and pigments
Fibers and plastics
Flavors and fragrances
Petrochemicals (50%, EC Erdolchemie)
Pharmaceuticals
Specialty metals

Abbott Labs	Eni	Norsk Hydro
Akzo Nobel	Glaxo Wellcome	Novartis
American Home	Hercules	Perrigo
Products	Huntsman	Pfizer
ATOFINA	ICI Americas	Pharmacia
BASF	IFF	Roche Holding
Bristol-Myers	ITOCHU	Schering-Plough
Squibb	Johnson &	SmithKline
Dow Chemical	Johnson	Beecham
DuPont	Lyondell	Union Carbide
Eastman	Chemical	
Chemical	Merck	
Eli Lilly	3M	

OTC: BAYZY FYE: December 31	Annual Growth	12/90	12/91	12/92	12/93	12/94	12/95	12/96	12/97	12/98	12/99
Sales ($ mil.)	(0.1%)	27,818	27,895	25,410	23,585	28,022	31,006	31,533	30,580	32,931	27,511
Net income ($ mil.)	5.4%	1,257	1,200	935	763	1,271	1,665	1,768	1,635	1,894	2,012
Income as % of sales	—	4.5%	4.3%	3.7%	3.2%	4.5%	5.4%	5.6%	5.3%	5.8%	7.3%
Earnings per share ($)	4.0%	1.94	1.84	1.42	1.15	1.84	2.37	2.52	2.25	2.59	2.75
Stock price - FY high ($)	—	18.50	18.28	19.77	21.67	24.34	27.11	42.75	46.00	52.63	47.75
Stock price - FY low ($)	—	12.69	13.91	15.48	15.66	21.28	23.75	26.88	33.00	36.00	34.00
Stock price - FY close ($)	14.0%	14.52	18.27	16.61	20.66	23.41	26.44	40.63	36.88	41.75	47.25
P/E - high	—	10	10	14	19	13	11	17	20	20	17
P/E - low	—	7	8	11	14	12	10	11	15	14	12
Dividends per share ($)	4.7%	0.87	0.86	0.68	0.63	0.84	1.04	1.10	1.06	1.20	1.31
Book value per share ($)	2.7%	16.43	16.64	16.04	15.18	15.49	18.04	18.86	18.21	20.53	20.89
Employees	(3.8%)	171,100	164,200	156,400	153,866	148,248	142,900	142,200	144,600	145,100	120,400

HIGH/LOW/CLOSE

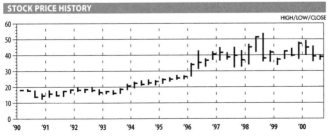

Debt ratio: 0.1%
Return on equity: 13.3%
Cash ($ mil.): 3,155
Current ratio: 2.21
Long-term debt ($ mil.): 2,370
No. of shares (mil.): 730
Dividends
  Yield: 0.0%
  Payout: 0.5%
Market value ($ mil.): 34,509

BAYERISCHE MOTOREN WERKE AG

OVERVIEW

A steel Beemer supports much of the frame of Europe's auto industry. Munich, Germany-based Bayerische Motoren Werke (BMW) makes sedans, coupes, wagons, and the new X5 SUV. BMW's other operations include a growing motorcycle line, and software firm softlab GmbH. The company has sold its stake in aircraft joint venture BMW Rolls-Royce, in exchange for a 10% stake in Rolls-Royce plc.

As the European auto industry moves toward consolidation, BMW has been the subject of merger talks. But the Quandts, a German family that controls almost half of BMW, have downplayed such speculation. In hopes of remaining independent, BMW has ditched its money-losing Rover operations. It sold the Land Rover SUV unit to Ford and its Rover Cars to Phoenix Consortium for $15.

HISTORY

BMW's logo speaks to the its origin: a propeller in blue and white, the colors of Bavaria. In 1913 Karl Rapp opened an aircraft engine design shop near Munich. He named it Bayerische Motoren Werke (BMW) in 1917. The end of WWI brought German aircraft production to a halt and BMW shifted to making railway brakes until the 1930s. Meanwhile, BMW debuted its first motorcycle in 1923, the R32. BMW began carmaking in 1928 by buying small-car company Fahrzeugwerke Eisenach.

In 1933 BMW launched a line of larger cars. BMW built aircraft engines for Hitler's Luftwaffe in the 1930s, and stopped all auto and motorcycle production in 1941. BMW chief Josef Popp resisted and was ousted. Under the Nazis, BMW operated in occupied countries and developed the world's first production jet engine and built rockets.

With its factories dismantled after WWII, BMW survived by making kitchen and garden equipment. In 1948 BMW introduced a one-cylinder motorcycle, and it sold well as cheap transportation in postwar Germany. BMW autos in the 1950s were too big and expensive and sold poorly. When motorcycle sales dropped, BMW escaped demise in the mid-1950s by launching the Isetta, a seven-foot, three-wheeled "bubble car."

Herbert Quandt saved BMW in 1959 by buying control for $1 million. Quandt's BMW focused on sports sedans and released the first of the "New Range" of BMWs in 1961. Success of the niche enabled BMW to buy automaker Hans Glas in 1966.

In the 1970s BMW's European exports soared, and the company set up a distribution subsidiary in the US. It produced larger cars that put the company on par with Mercedes-Benz.

Rapid export growth in the US, Asia, and Australia continued in the 1980s, but Japanese bikes and poor demand hurt motorcycle sales. The launch of BMW's luxury vehicles in 1986 heated up the BMW-Mercedes rivalry. BMW's US sales peaked that year and fell 45% by 1991.

However, in 1992 BMW outsold Mercedes in Europe for the first time and became the first European carmaker to operate a US plant since Volkswagen pulled out in 1988.

BMW teamed with the UK's Rolls-Royce aerospace firm in 1990 to make jet engines. One powered the Gulfstream V, now the executive jet of choice.

The company bought UK carmaker Rover from British Aerospace and Honda in 1994 and introduced a cheaper vehicle, the four-wheel-drive Discovery. It launched Highlander Land Rover in 1996 to meet a growing demand for 4X4 utility vehicles. In 1997 the company announced plans to make a Hog-like motorcycle to rival Harley-Davidson. BMW offered to buy the luxury Rolls-Royce auto unit (including the Bentley) from UK-based Vickers in 1998, but lost out when Volkswagen (VW) countered with a higher offer. BMW got the last laugh, however, when aircraft engine maker Rolls-Royce sold the Rolls brand name and logo to BMW for $66 million (VW gets to use the name until 2003). Also in 1998 BMW was hit by a class action lawsuit brought by Holocaust survivors seeking compensation for their work as slave laborers during WWII.

BMW announced 1,500 job cuts in mid-1998 at its money-losing Rover unit, then up to 2,500 more through attrition. As Rover's plants continued their downward trend in 1999, BMW's board forced out chairman Brend Pischetsrieder, who spearheaded the Rover acquisition in 1994. The UK later pledged to help pay for renovations at Rover's Longbridge plant to save about 14,000 jobs and prevent it from moving operations to Hungary.

In 2000 BMW agreed to sell its Land Rover SUV operations to Ford in a deal worth about $2.7 billion. The same year BMW handed over its Rover Cars operations and MG brand to the Phoenix Consortium, a UK-based group led by former Rover CEO John Towers, for a token sum of about $15.

Chairman, Supervisory Board: Volker Doppelfeld
Deputy Chairman, Supervisory Board; Chairman of the Works Council: Manfred Schoch
Chairman, Management Board: Joachim Milberg
Executive Director: Hagen Lüderitz
General Counsel: Dieter Löchelt
Chairman and CEO, BMW (US): Tom Purves
EVP Finance and CFO, BMW (US): Werner Adelberger
Manager Human Resources BMW (US): John Brunner
Auditors: KPMG Deutsche Treuhand-Gesellschaft

LOCATIONS

HQ: Petuelring 130, D-80788 Munich, Germany
Phone: +49-893-822-4272   **Fax:** +49-893-822-4418
US HQ: 300 Chestnut Ridge Rd.,
Woodcliff Lake, NJ 07675
US Phone: 201-307-4000   **US Fax:** 201-307-4095
Web site: http://www.bmw.com

1999 Sales

	€ mil.	% of total
Europe		
Germany	9,206	27
UK	4,826	14
Other countries	8,118	24
North America	8,098	23
Asia	2,534	7
Other regions	1,620	5
Total	**34,402**	**100**

PRODUCTS/OPERATIONS

1999 Sales

	€ mil.	% of total
BMW automobiles	19,673	57
Rover automobiles	7,427	22
Financial services	5,748	17
Motorcycles	767	2
Other	787	2
Total	**34,402**	**100**

Selected Products

Automobiles
3 Series (Compact, convertible, coupe, sedan, touring)
5 Series (Sedan, touring)
7 Series (Luxury sedan)
M Models (Coupe, roadster, sedan)
X5 (Sport utility vehicle)
Z3 (Coupe, roadster)
Z8 (Sports car)

Motorcycles
F Series (F 650, F 650 ST)
K Series (K 1200 LT, K 1200 RS)
R Series (R 850 GS, R 850 R, R 1100 R, R1100 RS, R 1100 RT, R 1100 S, R 1150 GS, R 1200)

COMPETITORS

DaimlerChrysler	Nissan
Fiat	Peugeot
Ford	Renault
General Motors	Saab Automobile
Harley-Davidson	Suzuki
Honda	Toyota
Kawasaki Heavy Industries	Volkswagen
Mazda	Yamaha
Mitsubishi	

HISTORICAL FINANCIALS & EMPLOYEES

Frankfurt: BMW FYE: December 31	Annual Growth	12/90	12/91	12/92	12/93	12/94	12/95	12/96	12/97	12/98	12/99
Sales (€ mil.)	10.6%	13,896	15,256	15,973	14,836	21,538	23,593	26,723	30,748	32,280	34,402
Net income (€ mil.)	7.2%	354	385	386	268	354	351	416	637	462	663
Income as % of sales	—	2.5%	2.5%	2.4%	1.8%	1.6%	1.5%	1.6%	2.1%	1.4%	1.9%
Earnings per share (€)	10.6%	—	—	—	—	0.61	0.61	0.68	1.04	0.79	1.01
Stock price - FY high (€)	—	—	—	—	—	14.69	13.25	17.16	24.41	39.13	32.00
Stock price - FY low (€)	—	—	—	—	—	11.42	10.52	11.72	16.13	17.80	23.04
Stock price - FY close (€)	20.4%	—	—	—	—	12.13	11.70	16.79	21.27	25.72	30.65
P/E - high	—	—	—	—	—	24	22	25	23	50	32
P/E - low	—	—	—	—	—	19	17	17	16	23	23
Dividends per share (€)	7.4%	—	—	—	—	0.28	0.27	0.29	0.39	0.39	0.40
Book value per share (€)	0.3%	—	—	—	—	6.23	6.39	7.06	7.93	9.63	6.32
Employees	5.9%	70,948	74,385	74,106	71,201	109,362	115,763	116,112	109,600	115,927	118,489

STOCK PRICE HISTORY

HIGH/LOW/CLOSE

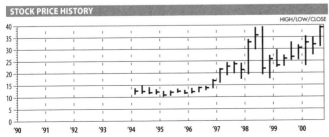

1999 FISCAL YEAR-END

Debt ratio: 0.3%
Return on equity: 12.8%
Cash (€ mil.): 2,055
Current ratio: 2.13
Long-term debt (€ mil.): 1,708
No. of shares (mil.): 622
Dividends
 Yield: 0.0%
 Payout: 0.4%
Market value ($ mil.): 19,071

BCE INC.

Telecom deregulation has been a wake-up call for BCE, and the Montreal-based company is transforming itself into a major global player. BCE is still Canada's largest telecom company: Its 80%-owned Bell Canada provides long-distance and local phone service to more than 8 million customers with some 12.6 million access lines, mainly in Ontario and Quebec. BCE also owns stakes in local phone companies across Canada, and its Bell Mobility unit serves 1.4 million cellular customers and nearly 500,000 PCS customers.

Bell Canada has heard the call of the Web as well. Its Bell Nexxia operates an Internet protocol network that stretches across Canada and serves businesses and service providers. The company is also plunking down $1.5 billion to upgrade its facilities for high-speed Internet access.

Reaching for the sky, BCE's Telesat owns 12 satellites and has 250 customers, and its TMI Communications provides mobile satellite services. Bell ExpressVu has some 500,000 direct-to-home satellite TV customers, and BCE's CTV subsidiary is a leading Canadian TV broadcaster.

The company has agreed to combine its broadcasting and Internet portal assets with Thomson's *The Globe and Mail* (Canada's leading newspaper), and the Globe Interactive Web site. BCE will own 70% of the new company.

Making a major move beyond the provinces, BCE's 74%-owned Bell Canada International (BCI) owns interests in telephony, wireless, and cable TV providers in Latin America and the Asia/Pacific region. And BCE is looking to become an even stronger international force with its purchase of Teleglobe, a carrier's carrier with a worldwide network.

HISTORY

Alexander Graham Bell experimented with the telephone in his native Canada before moving to the US in the mid-1870s. His father sold his Canadian patent rights to National Bell Telephone (now AT&T), which combined with Canada's Hamilton District Telegraph to form Bell Telephone Company of Canada. Known as Bell Canada, it received a charter in 1880 and settled in Montreal. By 1882 it had 40 exchanges. AT&T owned 48% of the company in 1890, but by 1925 Canadians owned 95% of Bell Canada. (AT&T severed all ties in 1975).

As telecommunications needs grew, the company began buying smaller exchanges (1954). It acquired a 90% stake in telecom equipment maker Northern Electric in 1957 and the rest in 1964. After Bell Canada reduced the stake in 1973, Northern became Northern Telecom in 1976 (now Nortel Networks). Bell Canada also invested in a satellite joint venture (Telesat, 1970) and formed Bell Canada International (BCI) to provide international telecom consulting (1976).

In 1983, responding to proposed legislation that would have calculated manufacturing profits in phone rate formulas, Bell created Bell Canada Enterprises (renamed BCE in 1988) as a holding company to separate unregulated businesses from phone carriers. BCE branched out with stakes in gas pipelines (1983) and real estate (1985) but dropped out of the ventures to focus on its core telecom business (1989). It began providing wireless phone service in 1985.

As deregulation rolled into Canada in the 1990s, Bell Canada had to maintain high long-distance rates to subsidize its regulated local service. In 1993 it bought stakes in cable operator Jones Intercable and the UK's Cable & Wireless (C&W).

BCE took a loss in 1997, writing down assets in preparation for full competition. Also that year it floated part of BCI, following contracts for cellular systems in Brazil and India. BCE began staging a comeback in 1998 when it sold its shares in Jones Intercable and C&W. It made new investments, including 100% of Telesat Canada, a part of fONOROLA's fiber network, and more than 40% of computer consulting firm CGI Group. Insider Jean Monty (who had steered Nortel's turnaround) became CEO.

Through an alliance with MCI WorldCom (now WorldCom), the company gained access to a global network in 1999. Also that year Ameritech (now part of SBC) bought a 20% stake in Bell Canada, which snapped up the 35% of its wireless subsidiary that it didn't already own and a 20% stake in Manitoba Telecom Services.

In 2000 Bell Canada spun off nearly all of its 40% Nortel stake to shareholders. That year it bought broadcaster CTV, and went on to buy global broadband services provider Teleglobe in a more than $7 billion stock deal. BCE also agreed to combine its broadcasting and Internet portal assets with Thomson's *The Globe and Mail* newspaper to form a new company.

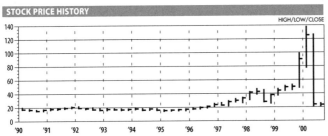

OFFICERS

Chairman, President, and CEO: Jean C. Monty,
$2,567,000 pay
Chief Corporate Officer: C. Wesley M. Scott,
$430,833 pay (prior to promotion)
Chief Human Resources and Administration Officer:
Georgina Wyman
CFO: William D. Anderson, $625,900 pay
Chief Legal Officer: Martine Turcotte
Chief Strategy Officer: Peter J. M. Nicholson,
$370,000 pay
VP Taxation: Barry W. Pickford
Corporate Secretary: Marc J. Ryan
Auditors: Deloitte & Touche LLP

LOCATIONS

HQ: 1000, rue de La Gauchetiere Ouest, Bureau 3700,
Montreal, Quebec H3B 4Y7, Canada
Phone: 514-870-8777   **Fax:** 514-786-3970
Web site: http://www.bce.ca

BCE mainly operates in Canada, but it also has interests
and operations in Brazil, Canada, Colombia, Mexico,
South Korea, Taiwan, the US, and Venezuela.

1999 Sales

	$ mil.	% of total
Canada	9,075	92
US	96	1
Other countries	654	7
Total	**9,825**	**100**

PRODUCTS/OPERATIONS

1999 Sales

	$ mil.	% of total
Local & access services	3,745	38
Long-distance & network services	2,704	28
Wireless services	1,268	13
Other	2,108	21
Total	**9,825**	**100**

Selected Subsidiaries

BCE Emergis (65%, e-commerce)
BCE Media
  Bell ExpressVu (direct-to-home satellite TV)
  Telesat Canada (satellite communications)
  TMI Communications (mobile satellite services)
Bell ActiMedia (directory publishing)
Bell Canada (80%, local and long-distance service)
Bell Canada International (BCI, 74%, telecom
  investments outside Canada)
Bell Mobility (wireless phone and paging)
Bell Nexxia (data services for businesses)
CTV (broadcast TV)
Teleglobe (international carrier services)

COMPETITORS

America Online	PageNet
AT&T Canada	Regional Cablesystems
BT	Rogers Communications
Call-Net Enterprises	RSL Communications
Cancom	Shaw Communications
Clearnet Communications	Sprint
Cogeco Cable	STAR Telecommunications
EDS	TELUS
IBM	Videotron
ICG Communications	WebLink Wireless
Microcell	WorldCom
Telecommunications	

HISTORICAL FINANCIALS & EMPLOYEES

NYSE: BCE FYE: December 31	Annual Growth	12/90	12/91	12/92	12/93	12/94	12/95	12/96	12/97	12/98	12/99
Sales ($ mil.)	(5.2%)	15,839	17,208	16,347	14,977	15,449	18,059	20,554	23,217	17,735	9,825
Net income ($ mil.)	16.0%	989	1,150	1,093	(496)	840	574	841	(1,074)	2,970	3,773
Income as % of sales	—	6.2%	6.7%	6.7%	—	5.4%	3.2%	4.1%	—	16.7%	38.4%
Earnings per share ($)	16.1%	1.51	1.74	1.66	(0.92)	1.25	0.82	1.24	(1.77)	4.57	5.77
Stock price - FY high ($)	—	20.00	21.31	21.63	19.00	19.38	17.50	25.38	34.00	46.63	98.31
Stock price - FY low ($)	—	15.13	16.69	16.06	16.00	15.81	14.50	17.19	22.00	25.63	37.31
Stock price - FY close ($)	20.3%	17.06	20.63	16.25	17.44	16.06	17.25	23.88	33.31	37.94	90.19
P/E - high	—	13	12	13	—	16	21	20	—	10	17
P/E - low	—	10	10	10	—	13	18	14	—	6	6
Dividends per share ($)	1.6%	1.08	1.12	1.09	1.03	0.99	0.99	1.00	1.36	1.36	1.25
Book value per share ($)	2.1%	15.98	16.68	15.85	13.39	13.08	13.19	13.74	10.79	13.77	19.21
Employees	(8.2%)	119,000	124,000	124,000	118,000	116,000	121,000	118,450	122,000	58,000	55,000

STOCK PRICE HISTORY

HIGH/LOW/CLOSE

1999 FISCAL YEAR-END

Debt ratio: 32.9%
Return on equity: 39.9%
Cash ($ mil.): 1,655
Current ratio: 0.99
Long-term debt ($ mil.): 6,069
No. of shares (mil.): 644
Dividends
  Yield: 1.4%
  Payout: 21.7%
Market value ($ mil.): 58,065

BENETTON GROUP S.P.A.

OVERVIEW

Benetton Group has worked up a literal and figurative sweat. Based in Treviso, Italy, the global, family-run enterprise sells United Colors of Benetton, Sisley, and other brand-name clothes, accessories, and sporting goods in more than 120 countries; Europe accounts for 70% of sales. Its products are sold in more than 7,000 franchised Benetton stores, in franchised and company-owned megastores, and in department and sporting goods stores. Benetton also licenses its name for items ranging from fragrances and fashion accessories to diapers and paint. Chairman Luciano

Benetton, his brother and deputy chairman and managing director Gilberto, and other family members own about 70% of Benetton through Edizione Holding.

The company's Playlife division sells outdoor gear — Prince tennis rackets, Nordica ski equipment, Rollerblade in-line skates, and Killer Loop snowboards.

Benetton's controversial ads, a mix of provocative images and political stances (bloody soldiers, a priest and a nun kissing), have won a following as well as critics — some franchise owners think the ads drive away customers.

HISTORY

Luciano Benetton began selling men's clothing while still in his teens in post-WWII Treviso, Italy. His younger, artistic sister, Giuliana, knitted colorful and striking sweaters for a small, local clientele. In 1955 the two pooled their skills. Giuliana sold Luciano's accordion and a younger brother's bicycle, raising enough money to purchase a knitting machine. Luciano then marketed her moderately priced sweaters.

Demand for their clothes grew, and the pair did so well that 10 years later they built a factory in Ponzano, near Treviso. Siblings Gilberto and bicycleless Carlo joined the business, and the first Benetton store opened in Belluno, in the Alps, in 1968. The Benetton Group opened a store in Paris the next year. By 1975 Benetton had 200 stores in Italy and had set up headquarters in a 17th-century villa. In 1979 the company opened five stores in the US.

Through the early to mid-1980s, the company averaged one store opening a day; Benetton was the first Western retailer to enter Eastern Europe. The company's controversial advertising program began in 1984 with ads depicting such provocative images as then-president Ronald Reagan with AIDS lesions.

When it went public in 1986, Benetton had almost 600 stores in the US. That year it established a factory in the US. In the late 1980s Edizione Holding, the family's investment firm, also bought a hotel chain and ski equipment maker Nordica.

Benetton began losing US market share in the late 1980s. The company misread American styles, wrongly assuming that sweaters selling well in Paris would do the same in New York City. Competition from The Gap and The Limited hurt also, and overexpansion brought complaints from franchisees that the stores were cannibalizing each other's sales. (In New

York City there were seven stores on Fifth Avenue alone.) In the early 1990s The Gap established stores in the already-mature European market, and Benetton began looking for new markets.

Edizione increased its investments in those years, acquiring 80% of Prince Manufacturing, a US maker of tennis equipment, and purchased a 50% interest in the TWR group, a racecar manufacturer. The company formed Benetton Legs in 1991 to produce and sell pantyhose in Europe.

In 1995 Benetton won its second lawsuit against German retailers who refused to pay for merchandise because they said sales had been hurt by the company's shock advertising. The next year it opened a United Colors of Benetton megastore on Fifth Avenue in New York City, the first to combine Edizione's clothing, sporting goods, and accessories under one roof.

Benetton bought Edizione's sports equipment and apparel collection, Benetton Sportsystem, and renamed the division to Playlife in 1998. Benetton began selling the sporting goods (such items as market-leading Rollerblade in-line skates and Nordica ski boots) through specialty sports stores and a new chain of Playlife megastores.

Trying to win back penny-pinching but stylish US consumers, Benetton in 1998 cut a deal to sell Benetton USA-brand clothing in Sears, Roebuck & Co. stores. In early 2000, however, Sears yanked the Italian goods from its store after customers complained about Benetton's anti-death penalty ad campaign. Soon after, Benetton and controversial ad man Oliviero Toscani parted ways. Benetton's ads are now produced by an ad agency Toscani founded.

Chairman: Luciano Benetton
Deputy Chairman and Joint Managing Director:
Gilberto Benetton
Joint Managing Director: Carlo Gilardi
CFO: Giancarlo Bottini
Accounting and Financial Control Officer:
Giovanni Zoppas
Credit and Supplier Accountant Officer:
Gianni Zampieri
Tax, Legal, and Corporate Affairs Officer:
Pierluigi Bortolussi
Marketing Director: Mauro Benetton
Press and Communications Director: Laura Pollini
Public Relations Manager: Paola Innocente
General Counsel and Temporary Personnel Manager:
Giovanni Tretti
Auditors: Deloitte & Touche

HQ: Villa Minelli, 31050 Ponzano Veneto, Treviso, Italy
Phone: +39-0422-519111   **Fax:** +39-0422-969501
Web site: http://www.benetton.com

Benetton Group sells its products in more than 120
countries.

1999 Sales

	% of total
Europe	72
North & South America	14
Other regions	14
Total	**100**

1999 Sales

	% of total
United Colors of Benetton	61
Sisley	14
Rollerblade	8
Nordica	5
Prince	5
Killer Loop	1
Playlife	1
Other	5
Total	**100**

Selected Brands
Casual wear
  Sisley (higher-fashion men's and women's clothing)
  United Colors of Benetton
Sports equipment and sportswear
  Killer Loop (snowboarding clothing and equipment)
  Nordica (ski boots)
  Prince (tennis rackets)
  Rollerblade (in-line skates)

Abercrombie & Fitch	Levi Strauss
adidas-Salomon	The Limited
Amer Group	Liz Claiborne
American Eagle Outfitters	Mossimo
AnnTaylor	Nautica Enterprises
Burton Snowboards	NIKE
Calvin Klein	Polo
Columbia Sportswear	Quiksilver
The Gap	Skis Rossignol
Head-Tyrolia-Mares	Spalding
J. Crew	Tommy Hilfiger
K2	Variflex

NYSE: BNG FYE: December 31	Annual Growth	12/90	12/91	12/92	12/93	12/94	12/95	12/96	12/97	12/98	12/99
Sales ($ mil.)	1.1%	1,805	2,008	1,704	1,602	1,717	1,866	1,890	2,055	2,318	1,996
Net income ($ mil.)	3.9%	118	144	125	121	130	139	162	164	177	168
Income as % of sales	—	6.6%	7.2%	7.3%	7.6%	7.5%	7.4%	8.6%	8.0%	7.6%	8.4%
Earnings per share ($)	4.8%	1.21	1.58	1.59	1.61	1.62	1.65	2.10	1.52	1.96	1.85
Stock price - FY high ($)	—	17.44	17.68	22.25	31.27	35.47	23.45	26.70	34.00	48.44	46.56
Stock price - FY low ($)	—	11.06	12.27	17.08	17.56	20.68	15.39	19.96	22.01	28.25	30.88
Stock price - FY close ($)	13.5%	14.55	17.56	18.40	30.54	22.49	22.25	23.93	32.63	39.75	45.44
P/E - high	—	14	11	14	19	22	14	13	22	25	25
P/E - low	—	9	8	11	11	13	9	10	14	14	17
Dividends per share ($)	15.0%	0.63	0.25	0.33	0.31	0.33	0.32	0.52	0.00	0.00	2.21
Book value per share ($)	8.1%	6.12	73.46	73.59	72.83	102.14	115.28	132.13	126.44	147.77	12.38
Employees	9.1%	3,000	3,600	5,800	5,900	6,300	6,018	5,973	7,421	7,235	6,585

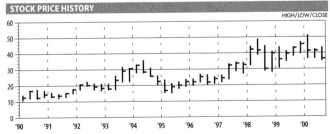

HIGH/LOW/CLOSE

Debt ratio: 29.7%
Return on equity: 13.6%
Cash ($ mil.): 224
Current ratio: 1.78
Long-term debt ($ mil.): 476
No. of shares (mil.): 91
Dividends
  Yield: 4.9%
  Payout: 119.5%
Market value ($ mil.): 4,125

BERTELSMANN AG

OVERVIEW

Pick up a book, listen to a CD, read a magazine, watch European TV, or surf the Internet, and it's likely you'll have a brush with Bertelsmann, one of the world's largest media conglomerates. While it still calls Gütersloh, Germany, home, Bertelsmann has extended its reach to span 600 companies in 53 countries.

The company's 1998 purchase of Random House positioned Bertelsmann as the world's largest English-language publisher. The company also operates several book clubs and owns 41% of online bookseller barnesandnoble.com.

Bertelsmann's music division, BMG Entertainment has more than 200 music labels (Arista Records, RCA Records). BMG has branched into the online music arena through GetMusic, its joint venture with Universal Music Group.

Gruner + Jahr (75% owned by Bertelsmann) publishes more than 80 magazines worldwide

(*Parents*) and nearly a dozen European newspapers. In 2000 Bertelsmann combined its broadcasting interests (50% of CLT-Ufa) with Pearson TV and Groupe Bruxelles Lambert's Audiofina into a new public company called RTL Group. RTL, of which Bertelsmann owns 37%, includes 22 television channels and 18 radio stations across 11 European countries.

Intent on capturing the attention of the Web-surfing public, Bertelsmann has stakes in a host of e-commerce and Internet services companies. It also owns Internet music retailer CDnow and has formed an alliance with online music service Napster.

In 1999 Reinhard Mohn, a descendant of founder Carl Bertelsmann, transferred his 90% voting control of Bertelsmann to an administrative company controlled by Bertelsmann executives and the Mohn family.

HISTORY

Carl Bertelsmann founded Bertelsmann in Gütersloh, Germany, in 1835. The company grew during the 19th century as a publisher of hymnals and religious materials.

For decades the company asserted that the Nazis shuttered its plants during WWII, because they were producing religious materials. However, in 2000 historians uncovered evidence indicating that the closures actually were undertaken in support of the war effort. The historians also determined that Bertelsmann published material for Hitler's army, and that then Bertelsmann head Heinrich Mohn (a descendant of Carl Bertelsmann) had been a sponsoring member of the SS. After WWII Mohn's son, Reinhard Mohn (who had been captured by the Allies and interned in a Kansas POW camp), set about to rebuild the company and resume publishing.

Bertelsmann boosted book sales by launching Germany book clubs during the 1950s. It branched into music in 1958 by launching music company Ariola. Bertelsmann later bought Germany's UFA (TV and film production, 1964) and an interest in publisher Gruner + Jahr. In the US, Bertelsmann bought 51% of Bantam Books in 1977 (and the rest in 1981) and Arista Records in 1979.

Bertelsmann increased its US presence in 1986 when it bought RCA Records and control of Doubleday Publishing. In 1993 Mohn transferred substantial voting shares in the company to the Bertelsmann Foundation.

The company teamed up with America Online in 1995 to form AOL Europe. In 1997 Bertelsmann broadcasting subsidiary UFA and Luxembourg-based broadcaster CLT formed CLT-Ufa, a joint venture to expand into the TV and radio market across Europe.

Bertelsmann's purchase of Random House in 1998 cemented its status in the publishing world. The company also took a 50% stake in online bookseller barnesandnoble.com (its stake was reduced to 41% when barnesandnoble.com went public the next year). Thomas Middelhoff became chairman and CEO in 1998.

In 1999 Bertelsmann acquired nearly 87% of scientific publisher Springer Verlag. That year Reinhard Mohn transferred his controlling stake in the company to Bertelsmann Verwaltungsgesellschaft, an administrative company controlled by Bertelsmann executives and the Mohn family.

In 2000 Bertelsmann agreed to sell its half-interest in AOL Europe to AOL, and spun off Lycos Europe, its joint venture with Lycos (it retained about 27%). Also in 2000 Bertelsmann bought online music retailer CDnow.

In late 2000 the company entered into an alliance with online music service Napster. Bertelsmann agreed to drop its lawsuit against Napster and allow the company to use its music catalogue. In return Napster will establish a membership service and give Bertelsmann the option of purchasing a stake in the company.

Chairman and CEO: Thomas Middelhoff, age 46
Deputy Chairman, Executive Board; Chairman,
Gruner + Jahr AG: Gerd Schulte-Hillen, age 59
CFO: Siegfried Luther, age 55
Chairman, BertelsmannSpringer: Jürgen Richter, age 58
Chairman, BMG Entertainment: Michael Dornemann,
age 55
Chairman and CEO, Random House, Inc.:
Peter W. Olson
Chairman and President, Bertelsmann Arvato AG:
Gunter Thielen, age 57
CEO, Bol.com: Heinz Wermelinger
CEO, Gruhner + Jahr: Daniel B. Brewster
CEO, RTL Group: Didier Bellens
President and CEO, Bertelsmann Book AG:
Frank Wössner, age 59
President and CEO, Bertelsmann Multimedia Group:
Klaus Eierhoff, age 46
President and CEO, BMG Entertainment:
Strauss Zelnick
Head of Ballantine Publishing Group: Gina Centrello,
age 39
Chief Creative Officer: Rolf Schmidt-Holtz
Human Resources: Gert Stuerzebecher
Auditors: KPMG Deutsche Treuhand-Gesellschaft

HQ: Carl-Bertelsmann-Strasse 270,
D-33311 Gütersloh, Germany
Phone: +49-52-41-80-0   **Fax:** +49-52-41-751-66
US HQ: 1540 Broadway, New York, NY 10036
US Phone: 212-930-4000   **US Fax:** 212-930-4955
Web site: http://www.bertelsmann.de

Bertelsmann has operations in 53 countries.

1999 Sales

	% of total
Europe	
Germany	28
Other countries	29
US	35
Other regions	8
Total	**100**

1999 Sales

	% of total
Books	31
BMG Entertainment	30
Gruner + Jahr	20
Arvato	14
Professional information	3
Multimedia	2
Total	**100**

Selected Book Publishers and Book Clubs
Bertelsmann Lexikothek
Der Club
Doubleday Direct (US)
Random House (US)

Selected Music Companies
Arista (US)
BMG Distribution (US)
CDnow (US)
RCA Records (US)

Selected Magazines and Newspapers
Family Circle (US)
McCall's (US)
Parents (US)
Stern

Selected Multimedia Companies
barnesandnoble.com (41%, UK)
Bertelsmann Broadband Group
GetMusic (joint venture with Universal Music Group)
Lycos Europe (joint venture with Terra Lycos)

Advance	Hearst	Time Warner
Publications	KirchGruppe	Universal Music
Amazon.com	Lagardère	Group
Axel Springer	McGraw-Hill	Verlagsgruppe
Columbia House	News Corp.	Georg von
Hachette	Pearson	Holtzbrinck
Filipacchi	PRIMEDIA	Viacom
Médias	Reed Elsevier	Virgin Group
Harcourt	Schibsted	VNU
General	Seagram	Walt Disney
Havas	Sony	Wolters Kluwer

Private FYE: June 30	Annual Growth	6/90	6/91	6/92	6/93	6/94	6/95	6/96	6/97	6/98	6/99
Sales ($ mil.)	6.2%	7,992	7,985	10,469	10,050	11,589	14,889	14,126	12,860	12,700	13,725
Net income ($ mil.)	5.1%	306	298	373	388	478	592	594	585	621	480
Income as % of sales	—	3.8%	3.7%	3.6%	3.9%	4.1%	4.0%	4.2%	4.5%	4.9%	3.5%
Employees	4.5%	43,509	45,110	48,781	50,437	51,767	57,397	57,996	57,173	57,807	64,937

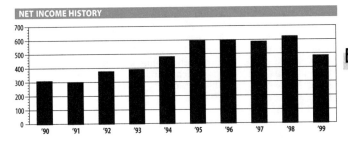

Bertelsmann

BHP LIMITED

OVERVIEW

BHP, known as the "Big Australian," is learning to be a nimble one as well in order to be more competitive. Formerly Broken Hill Proprietary, the Melbourne-based company operates scores of businesses in some 40 countries. It is among the world's top producers of raw steel, iron ore, copper, coal, and petroleum. BHP's petroleum unit, with proved reserves of 590 million barrels of oil and 4.8 trillion cu. ft. of gas, has offshore production operations in Australia, North America, and the UK.

BHP has been forced to change its ways as Australia's protective tariffs crumble, Asia's economy remains dormant, and the mining industry suffers from stagnant profits and slumping commodity prices. Under new leadership (US-born Paul Anderson), BHP has slashed top management from 80 to 40 and sold its power, engineering, insurance, and information technology businesses to concentrate on core operations.

HISTORY

In 1883 Charles Rasp, a boundary rider for the Mt. Gipps sheep station, believed valuable ore lay in the Broken Hill outcrop in New South Wales, Australia. He gathered a few young speculators, and The Broken Hill Proprietary Company (BHP) was incorporated in 1885. BHP immediately found a massive lode of silver, lead, and zinc. None of the founders knew how to run a mine, so they recruited US engineers William Patton and Herman Schlapp. From the beginning, labor and management clashed. The founding directors set up the head office in Melbourne, far from the mine, and gambled with gold sovereigns in the boardroom. But the miners worked in dangerous conditions. An 1892 labor strike was the first of BHP's bitter strikes.

In 1902 the new general manager, Guillaume Delprat, invented a flotation process that recovered valuable metals from iron ore waste. Delprat also foresaw a future in steel, although Australia had no steel industry. BHP commissioned the Newcastle steelworks in 1915 and soon became the country's largest steel producer. Essington Lewis took over from Delprat in 1921 and established BHP's tradition of internal promotion. BHP's 1935 purchase of Australian Iron and Steel, its only competitor, gave it a virtual steel monopoly, while high tariffs protected it from outside competition. Its exhausted Broken Hill mine was closed that year.

In the 1960s BHP got into oil when it partnered with Esso Standard, the Australian subsidiary of Standard Oil of New Jersey, for offshore exploration. In 1967 the partners found oil in the Bass Strait, which soon supplied 70% of Australia's petroleum. In the 1960s and 1970s, BHP began expanding its iron ore, manganese, and coal interests. Meanwhile, public opposition mounted to BHP's market power and labor practices, and in 1972 the government took steps to limit BHP's power, removing some subsidies and tax breaks.

The weak steel market of the 1970s and 1980s caused BHP to lay off almost a third of its steelworkers in 1983, but with government intervention, BHP radically improved its steel productivity. In 1984 BHP bought Utah International's mining assets from General Electric (including Chile's rich Escondida copper mine). In 1986 corporate raider Robert Holmes á Court took a run at BHP; BHP decided to become an international mining company to prevent further raids. Its acquisitions in the late 1980s included ERG Inc. and Monsanto Oil (combined into BHP Americas), Aquila Steel, and Pacific Refining in Hawaii.

The peace deal with Holmes á Court gave BHP about 37% of Foster's Brewing, but in 1992 BHP took a $700 million write-down after Foster's stock declined. BHP also bought Arizona-based Magma Copper in 1996, but plunging world copper prices forced a $420 million write-down.

With new worries over Asia's economic troubles, BHP soon was struggling. In 1997 BHP sold most of its stake in Foster's, and three senior executives resigned. In 1998 the company unloaded Pacific Refining, which was acquired by Tesoro Petroleum for about $275 million.

As BHP's woes continued, CEO John Prescott resigned; Paul Anderson was recruited from Duke Energy to succeed Prescott. In 1999 D. R. Argus took over as chairman, replacing Jeremy Ellis. In a restructuring move, the company sold its engineering, power, insurance and information techonology businesses in 1999 and 2000. BHP also announced plans to sell $2 billion worth of steel operations, which would cut that business in half. In 2000 the company shortened its official name to BHP Limited.

OFFICERS

Chairman: Don R. Argus, age 62
Managing Director and CEO: Paul M. Anderson, age 55, $7,093,239 pay
CFO: Chip W. Goodyear, $1,083,333 pay
VP and Chief Legal Counsel: John Fast
VP and Chief Information Officer: Cassandra Matthews
VP Corporate Finance: Anna Lou Fletcher
VP Market Risk Management: Rowen Bainbridge
VP Human Resources: Tom F.R. Brown
President, BHP Minerals: Ron J. McNeilly, age 57, $1,954,167 pay
President, BHP Petroleum: Philip S. Aiken, $1,224,833 pay
President, BHP Steel: Kirby C. Adams, $799,061 pay
President, BHP Coal Queensland: Rick Gazzard
Chief Strategic Officer: Brad A. Mills, $818,582 pay
Auditors: Arthur Andersen

LOCATIONS

HQ: BHP Tower, D Bourke Place, 600 Bourke St., 48th Fl., Melbourne, Victoria 3000, Australia
Phone: +61-3-9609-3333   **Fax:** +61-3-9609-3015
US HQ: BHP Tower, 1360 Post Oak Boulevard, Ste. 150, Houston, TX 77056
US Phone: 713-961-8500   **US Fax:** 713-961-8400
Web site: http://www.bhp.com.au

BHP has operations in some 40 countries.

2000 Sales

	% of total
Australia	62
North America	14
South America	8
Other countries	16
Total	**100**

PRODUCTS/OPERATIONS

2000 Sales

	% of total
Minerals	37
Steel	36
Petroleum	24
Services	3
Total	**100**

Business Divisions

Minerals	Refractory products
Coal	Sheet steel
Copper	Wire products
Diamonds	
Lead	**Petroleum**
Silver	Crude oil refining and
Zinc	marketing
	Gas production and
Steel	refining
Raw steel	Petroleum exploration
Pipes and tubes	

COMPETITORS

Anglo American	Koch
BP	Mitsubishi
Chevron	Nippon Steel
Codelco	PDVSA
Corus Group	Phelps Dodge
CVRD	Rio Tinto plc
Elf Aquitaine	Royal Dutch/Shell
Eni	Sumitomo
Exxon Mobil	Texaco
Freeport-McMoRan	TOTAL FINA ELF
Copper & Gold	Zambia Copper

HISTORICAL FINANCIALS & EMPLOYEES

NYSE: BHP FYE: June 30	Annual Growth	5/91	5/92	5/93	5/94	5/95	5/96	5/97	5/98	5/99	*6/00
Sales ($ mil.)	0.9%	11,878	10,933	10,938	12,201	13,270	15,271	15,983	13,264	12,553	12,841
Net income ($ mil.)	(1.2%)	1,083	390	820	947	873	835	313	(923)	(1,509)	971
Income as % of sales	—	9.1%	3.6%	7.5%	7.8%	6.6%	5.5%	2.0%	—	—	7.6%
Earnings per share ($)	(3.2%)	1.45	0.64	1.28	1.42	1.13	1.04	0.36	(1.09)	(1.73)	1.08
Stock price - FY high ($)	—	20.19	23.75	22.13	28.00	31.19	31.81	30.31	30.00	23.88	28.50
Stock price - FY low ($)	—	14.19	18.31	14.13	18.63	24.94	24.31	24.75	16.63	12.94	18.75
Stock price - FY close ($)	2.6%	18.81	21.94	19.94	26.88	25.50	30.19	28.88	17.19	20.75	23.75
P/E - high	—	14	37	17	20	28	31	84	—	—	26
P/E - low	—	10	29	11	13	22	23	69	—	—	17
Dividends per share ($)	0.9%	0.60	0.63	0.59	0.55	0.69	0.38	0.81	0.36	0.63	0.65
Book value per share ($)	(0.2%)	7.02	8.02	7.39	8.88	10.75	12.02	11.60	8.51	6.48	6.91
Employees	(4.3%)	52,000	51,000	47,000	48,000	49,000	60,000	61,000	55,000	50,000	35,000

* Fiscal year change

STOCK PRICE HISTORY

HIGH/LOW/CLOSE

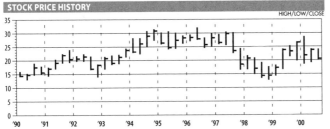

2000 FISCAL YEAR-END

Debt ratio: 36.2%
Return on equity: 16.4%
Cash ($ mil.): 408
Current ratio: 0.89
Long-term debt ($ mil.): 3,504
No. of shares (mil.): 894
Dividends
  Yield: 2.7%
  Payout: 60.2%
Market value ($ mil.): 21,242

BNP PARIBAS GROUP

Ménage a trois? Mais non! Paris-based Banque Nationale de Paris ruined the proposed coupling of Société Générale and Paribas by trying to take them both and create the world's first trillion-dollar bank. Société Générale's shareholders fought off the would-be Romeo, but Paribas succumbed, catapulting the newly merged BNP Paribas Group to #1 in France.

Paris-based BNP Paribas has more than 2,000 French offices and operations in about 85 other countries. It owns BancWest, a US West Coast bank company, and has a joint venture with Germany's Dresdner Bank. Retail banking and business banking each contribute more than one-third of the company's revenues. BNP Paribas also offers private banking, asset management, insurance, and specialized financial services.

At the behest of regulators, BNP Paribas divested its nearly one-third stake in Société Générale. It also must integrate the predecessor banks' operations in the face of hostility from Paribas shareholders and executives who did not support the takeover.

BNP Paribas Group's predecessor Banque Nationale de Paris (BNP) is the progeny of two state banks with parallel histories; each was set up to jump-start the economy after the revolution of 1848.

For a century, Paris-based Comptoir National d'Escompte de Paris (CNEP) apachedanced between private and public status, depending on government whim. It was the #3 bank in France from the late 19th century through the 1950s.

Banque National pour le Commerce et l'Industrie (BNCI) started in Alsace, a region that was part of Germany from the Franco-Prussian War until WWI. BNCI served as an economic bridge between Germany and France, which had to give the bank governmental resuscitation during the Depression. By the 1960s BNCI had passed CNEP in size.

French leader Charles de Gaulle expected banking to drive post-WWII reconstruction, and in 1945 CNEP and BNCI were nationalized. In 1966 France's finance minister merged them and they became BNP. That year the company started an association with Dresdner Bank of Germany, under which the two still operate joint ventures, primarily in Eastern Europe.

By 1993 privatization was again in vogue, and BNP was cut loose by the government. It expanded outside France to ameliorate the influences of the French economy and government. Even before it was privatized, BNP was involved in such politically charged actions as the bailout of OPEC money repository Banque Arabe and the extension of credit to Algeria's state oil company Sonatrach.

The privatized BNP looked overseas in the late 1990s. In 1997 alone, it won the right to operate in New Zealand, bought Laurentian Bank and Trust of the Bahamas, took control of its joint venture with Egypt's Banque du Caire, and opened a subsidiary in Brazil.

BNP bought failed Peregrine Investment's Chinese operations in 1998. That year the bank also expanded in Peru, opened an office in Algeria, opened a representative office in Uzbekistan, set up an investment banking subsidiary in India, and bought Australian stock brokerage operations from The Prudential Insurance Company of America.

After a decade of globe-trotting, BNP brought it on home in 1999 and set off a year of tumult in French banking. As France's other two large banks (Société Générale and Paribas) made plans to merge, BNP decided it would absorb both banks as a means to get a bigger chunk of the to-be-privatized Crédit Lyonnais and to protect France from Euro-megabank penetration by creating the globe's largest bank.

Executives at Société Générale (SG) had other ideas, forming a cartel called "Action Against the BNP Raid." Meanwhile, BNP tried to boost to controlling stakes its holdings in the two banks. (In Europe's cross-ownership tradition, the target banks also owned part of BNP.) France's central bank tried unsuccessfully to negotiate a deal (the government supported the triumvirate merger). A war of words was played out in the media, and finally shareholders had to vote on the proposals. In the end, BNP won control of Paribas, but not SG. As BNP prepared to integrate a reluctant Paribas into its operations, regulators ordered BNP to relinquish its stake in SG. The newly merged company was dubbed BNP Paribas Group.

In 2000 BNP Paribas and Avis Group launched a fleet-management joint venture. BNP also made plans to buy 150 shopping centers from French retailer Carrefour and to buy the 40% of merchant bank Cobepa that it does not already own. Also that year BNP and Dresdner Bank planned to end several Eastern European joint ventures.

Chairman and CEO: Michel Pébereau, age 58
President and COO: Baudouin Prot
Group EVP: Georges Chodron de Courcel
Group EVP: Vivien Lévy-Garboua
Advisor to the Chairman: Jacques Henri Wahl, age 68
Advisor to the Chairman: Christian Aubin
SEVP Domestic Network and General Manager, Human Resources: Bernard Lemée
SEVP Domestic Network: Alain Moynot
CFO: Philipe Bordenave
EVP International Trade Finance: Jacques Desponts
EVP Organization and Information Systems: Hervé Gouezel
EVP Structured Finance: Michel Konczaty
EVP Management Audit and Inspection: Marc Lavergne
EVP Products and Markets: Yves Martrenchar
EVP Equities: Chantal Mazzacurati
EVP Operational and Technical Support: Michel Passant
Chairman of the Management Board of Banexi: Pierre Mariani
EVP Large Corporations and Institutions: Ervin Rosenberg
EVP Risks (International Banking and Finance): Jean Thomazeau
Auditors: Arthur Andersen; Barbier Frinault & Autres; Befec-Price Waterhouse; Salustro Reydel

HQ: 16, boulevard des Italiens, 75009 Paris Cedex 09, France
Phone: +33-1-40-14-45-46   **Fax:** +33-1-40-14-75-46
US HQ: 499 Park Ave., New York, NY 10022
US Phone: 212-415-9600   **US Fax:** 212-415-9629
Web site: http://www.bnpgroup.com

BNP Paribas Group operates on six continents.

1999 Sales

	% of total
Corporate & investment banking	38
Retail banking	
Domestic	27
International	9
Specialized financial services	14
Private banking, asset management & insurance	12
Total	**100**

Selected Subsidiaries & Affiliates
BancWest (US retail banking)
Banque Directe (online banking)
BNP Lease
Cardif (insurance & asset management)
Cetelem (consumer loans)
Cobepa (merchant banking)
Cofica (vehicle lending & insurance)
Cortal (securities trading)
Credit Universel
Natio Assurances
Segece (commercial real estate development)
Sinvin (real estate)
UCB (mortgage lending)

ABN AMRO
Banco Bilbao
Banco Comercial Portugues
Banco Popular Español
Bank of America
Barclays
Caisse d'Epargne
Caisse Nationale de Credit Agricole
CCF
Chase Manhattan
Citigroup
Crédit Lyonnais
Dai-Ichi Kangyo
Deutsche Bank
Generale de Belgique
HSBC Holdings
Natexis
Société Générale
UBS
Wells Fargo

Euronext Paris: BNP FYE: December 31	Annual Growth	12/90	12/91	12/92	12/93	12/94	12/95	12/96	12/97	12/98	12/99
Assets (€ mil.)	14.6%	204,201	226,535	231,087	225,089	221,381	242,962	283,716	310,214	324,832	698,625
Net income (€ mil.)	22.1%	246	448	331	155	252	272	588	909	1,114	1,484
Income as % of assets	—	0.1%	0.2%	0.1%	0.1%	0.1%	0.1%	0.2%	0.3%	0.3%	0.2%
Earnings per share (€)	40.6%	—	—	—	1.01	1.36	1.42	2.85	4.31	5.16	7.80
Stock price - FY high (€)	—	—	—	—	45.58	44.14	40.35	34.36	53.36	87.35	93.45
Stock price - FY low (€)	—	—	—	—	41.64	34.61	27.82	26.15	29.85	40.11	66.25
Stock price - FY close (€)	13.1%	—	—	—	43.83	37.43	33.68	30.61	48.77	70.16	91.60
P/E - high	—	—	—	—	45	32	28	12	12	17	12
P/E - low	—	—	—	—	41	25	20	9	7	8	8
Dividends per share (€)	24.9%	—	—	—	0.46	0.49	0.55	0.82	1.07	1.50	1.75
Book value per share (€)	3.6%	—	—	—	41.08	41.00	40.96	43.09	46.85	50.32	50.72
Employees	5.5%	—	—	—	56,141	54,469	53,600	52,762	52,702	56,286	77,472

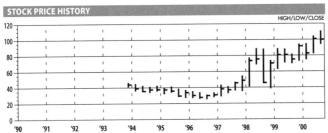

HIGH/LOW/CLOSE

Equity as % of assets: 3.3%
Return on assets: 0.3%
Return on equity: —
Long-term debt (€ mil.): 27,594
No. of shares (mil.): 450
Dividends
  Yield: 0.0%
  Payout: 0.2%
Market value ($ mil.): 40,993
Sales ($ mil.): 30,687

BOMBARDIER INC.

OVERVIEW

Bombardier moves people and things through water and air, across snow, and over hill and dale. The Montreal-based firm is the #3 civil aerospace company in the world, trailing Boeing and Airbus. The company also makes rail equipment, along with snowmobiles and other motorized consumer vehicles. Bombardier's business aircraft and regional air transport include the Canadair, de Havilland, and Learjet brands.

The company's consumer offerings include snowmobiles (Ski-Doo and Lynx), personal watercraft (Sea-Doo), and tracked utility and maintenance vehicles. Its rail products include monorails, locomotives, TGV high-speed-train equipment, and rapid-transit cars. The Bombardier Capital Group provides financing and leasing services.

Bombardier is pursuing international growth outside of North America and Western Europe. Intent on focusing on its core businesses, the company plans to sell its units that can't generate the revenues needed to meet its target of 30% growth earnings per share. The proceeds will help pay for its planned purchase of DaimlerChrysler's Adtranz rail systems unit. The Bombardier family owns more than 50% of the company.

HISTORY

Bombardier got its start in the 1920s when mechanic Joseph-Armand Bombardier began converting old cars into snowmobiles. He founded L'Auto-Neige Bombardier Limited in 1942 to make commercial snow vehicles. In 1959 Bombardier introduced the first personal snowmobile, the Ski-Doo.

At age 27, Laurent Beaudoin became the company's president in 1966. Bombardier went public in 1969. When the bottom dropped out of the snowmobile business due to the energy crisis in 1973, Beaudoin diversified, and in 1974 Bombardier won its first mass-transit contract to build Montreal subway cars. Expanding further into mass transportation, Bombardier merged with MLW-Worthington Limited, a builder of diesel engines and diesel-electric locomotives. In 1978 the company became Bombardier Inc.

During the 1980s Bombardier continued to diversify. It expanded into military vehicles and became the leading supplier to the North American rail transit industry. The company entered the European railcar market in 1986, the same year it bought Canadair, Canada's largest aerospace firm, from the government.

Founded in 1920 as the aircraft division of Canadian Vickers, Canadair became a separate company producing military and civilian aircraft in 1944. Acquired by Electric Boat (later General Dynamics) in 1947, it was nationalized by the Canadian government in 1976. In 1978 Canadair introduced its Challenger 600 business jet, which became a major seller.

Bombardier began development of a commuter aircraft, the Canadian Regional Jet (a 50-seat derivative of the Challenger), in 1989. That year it bought Short Brothers PLC, an Irish manufacturer of civil and military aircraft, defense systems, and aircraft components.

In 1990 the company bought US-based Learjet and its service centers, and two years later it acquired a stake in de Havilland, a regional aircraft maker, which it jointly owns with the Province of Ontario. In 1996 Amtrak selected an international consortium headed by Bombardier to produce high-speed trains, electric locomotives, and train-maintenance facilities. Also in 1996, the Global Express business jet made its first flight.

The company received its first orders for its latest model of the Canadair Regional Jet in 1997. In 1998 Bombardier doubled the size of its European operations by buying German railcar maker Deutsche Waggonbau. It also announced plans to launch a 90-seat regional jet — its largest so far. At the 43rd Paris airshow in 1999, Bombardier announced the launch of its all-new business jet — the eight-passenger Continental, which could be gracing the skies by 2002.

After deciding that its 50% stake in Shorts Missile Systems Ltd. (SMS) did not meet its strategic needs, Bombardier sold its stake to Thomson in 2000. Also that year, Bombardier landed a $817 million contract to supply Spanish carrier Air Nostrum with 44 planes. It also inked a $2 billion deal to make 94 regional jets for Delta Air Lines; the Delta order includes options for an additional 406 aircraft through 2010. Not long afterward, Bombardier agreed to buy DaimlerChrysler's Adtranz rail systems unit for about $750 million cash.

In 2000 two members of the company's flight test crew were fatally injured when the Challenger developmental aircraft they were testing crashed.

Chairman: Laurent Beaudoin, $1,000,000 pay
VC: J. R. Andre Bombardier
VC: Jean-Louis Fontaine, $661,500 pay
President and CEO: Robert E. Brown, $2,800,000 pay
EVP; Chairman Bombardier Capital: Yvan Allaire,
$1,444,200 pay
SVP: Carroll L'Italien
VP Acquisitions: Francois Thibault
VP and Treasurer: Francois Lemarchand
VP, Communications and Public Relations: Michel Lord
VP Finance: Louis Morin, $647,245 pay
VP, Legal Services and Assistant Secretary:
Daniel Desjardins
Auditors: Chartered Accountants

LOCATIONS

HQ: 800 Rene-Levesque Blvd. West,
Montreal, Quebec H3B 1Y8, Canada
Phone: 514-861-9481   **Fax:** 514-861-2740
US HQ: 1 Learjet Way, Wichita, KS 67209
US Phone: 316-946-2000   **US Fax:** 316-946-2163
Web site: http://www.bombardier.com

Bombardier has production facilities in Austria, Belgium,
Canada, China, the Czech Republic, Finland, France,
Germany, Mexico, Switzerland, the UK, and the US.

2000 Sales

	C$ mil.	% of total
The Americas	8,448	63
Europe	4,362	31
Asia	327	3
Australia	166	1
Other regions	316	2
Total	**13,619**	**100**

PRODUCTS/OPERATIONS

2000 Sales

	C$ mil.	% of total
Aerospace	8,126	59
Transportation equipment	3,446	25
Recreational products	1,473	11
Bombardier Capital	739	5
Adjustments	(165)	—
Total	**13,619**	**100**

Selected Products and Services

Aircraft and industrial equipment financing and leasing	Monorails
	Rapid-transit cars
	Real-estate development
Amphibious aircraft	Regional aircraft
Bombardier all-terrain vehicles	Single-level and bi-level railcars
Business aircraft	Sea-Doo watercraft
Dealer inventory financing	Small engines
Freight cars	Subway cars
Locomotives for passenger trains	Trams
	Turbotrains
Lynx and Ski-Doo snowmobiles	Utility vehicles

COMPETITORS

Airbus Industrie of North America	Fairchild Dornier	Polaris Industries
Arctic Cat	Fiat	Raytheon
BMW	Gulfstream	Siemens
Boeing	Aerospace	Suzuki
Brunswick	Lockheed Martin	Textron
DaimlerChrysler	Moog	Trinity
Embraer	Northrop	Industries
Executive Jet	Grumman	Yamaha
	Outboard Marine	

HISTORICAL FINANCIALS & EMPLOYEES

Toronto: BBDB FYE: January 31	Annual Growth	1/91	1/92	1/93	1/94	1/95	1/96	1/97	1/98	1/99	1/00
Sales (C$ mil.)	18.8%	2,892	3,059	4,448	4,769	5,943	7,123	7,976	8,509	11,500	13,619
Net income (C$ mil.)	24.5%	100	108	133	176	242	154	406	420	554	719
Income as % of sales	—	3.5%	3.5%	3.0%	3.7%	4.1%	2.2%	5.1%	4.9%	4.8%	5.3%
Earnings per share (C$)	21.3%	0.18	0.18	0.22	0.28	0.37	0.23	0.58	0.59	0.77	1.02
Stock price - FY high (C$)	—	2.58	4.32	3.42	5.47	6.32	10.07	12.55	17.00	23.75	32.25
Stock price - FY low (C$)	—	1.61	1.94	2.60	2.41	4.44	5.66	8.00	12.40	13.25	19.10
Stock price - FY close (C$)	35.3%	1.97	4.29	2.91	5.29	5.69	9.94	11.93	14.00	22.50	29.95
P/E - high	—	14	24	16	20	17	44	22	29	31	32
P/E - low	—	9	11	12	9	12	25	14	21	17	19
Dividends per share (C$)	17.9%	0.05	0.05	0.06	0.06	0.08	0.11	0.11	0.16	0.17	0.22
Book value per share (C$)	18.2%	1.16	1.42	1.68	2.18	2.56	2.71	3.28	4.26	5.11	5.24
Employees	7.4%	—	—	—	36,500	37,000	40,000	41,150	47,778	53,000	56,000

STOCK PRICE HISTORY

HIGH/LOW/CLOSE

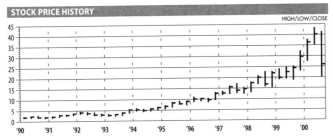

2000 FISCAL YEAR-END

Debt ratio: 0.6%
Return on equity: 20.2%
Cash (C$ mil.): 1,664
Current ratio: 1.42
Long-term debt (C$ mil.): 4,795
No. of shares (mil.): 689
Dividends
  Yield: 0.0%
  Payout: 0.2%
Market value ($ mil.): 20,630

BOUYGUES S.A.

OVERVIEW

Although Bouygues (pronounced "bweeg") has felt the squeeze of the global recession, its many diversified international holdings have kept the French company in the black. With headquarters outside Paris, Bouygues is one of Europe's largest industrial groups and operates more than 40 subsidiaries and affiliates in two main business sectors: construction and services. The group has operations in 80 countries.

Spun off from the main group, Bouygues Construction is a group of building and civil works firms. Its Colas subsidiary provides road construction and maintenance internationally; it also produces emulsions. Serving the oil and gas industry, its Bouygues Offshore builds oil platforms. Other construction subsidiaries include ETDE (power and data transmission networks construction) and Bouygues Immobilier (property management).

On the services side of the business, public utilities management firm Saur designs, constructs, and manages water and sewage services, and it provides solid waste management and cleansing services. In France Bouygues' telecom holdings include a 40% stake in Television Francaise-1 (TF1), the nation's oldest and leading TV channel; a 54% stake in #3 mobile phone operator Bouygues Telecom; and Infomobile, a radio paging company.

Chairman Martin Bouygues and his brother Olivier, sons of the company's founder, together own more than 16% of Bouygues through holding company SCDM.

HISTORY

With $1,700 in borrowed money, Francis Bouygues, son of a Paris engineer, started Entreprise Francis Bouygues in 1952 as an industrial works and construction firm in the Paris region of France. Within four years his firm had expanded into property development.

By the mid-1960s Bouygues had entered the civil engineering and public works sectors and developed regional construction units across France. In 1970 it was listed on the Paris stock exchange. Four years later the company established Bouygues Offshore to build oil platforms.

In 1978 the firm built Terminal 2 of Paris' Charles de Gaulle airport. Three years later it won the contract to construct the University of Riyadh in Saudi Arabia (then the world's largest building project at 3.2 million sq. ft.), which was completed in 1984. That year Bouygues acquired France's #3 water supply company, Saur, and power transmission and supply firm ETDE.

Expansion continued in 1986 with the purpose of the Screg Group, which included Colas, France's top highway contractor. The next year the company led a consortium to buy 50% of newly privatized network Television Francaise-1 (TF1), France's leading TV channel. Bouygues became the largest shareholder with a 25% stake (increased to 40% by 1999). In 1988 the company began building the Channel Tunnel (completed in 1994) and moved into ultramodern headquarters, dubbed Challenger, in Saint-Quentin-En-Yvelines, outside Paris.

After rumors of failing health, Francis Bouygues resigned as chairman in 1989. A year later he founded feature film production company Ciby 2000 (now part of TF1). His youngest son, Martin, took the helm, and the family patriarch, called France's "Emperor of Concrete," remained on the board until his death (1993).

Despite fears that the group would suffer without its founder's leadership, Bouygues continued to grow with the 1989 acquisition of a majority interest in Grands Moulins de Paris, France's largest flour milling firm (sold in 1998). In 1990 it purchased Swiss construction group Losinger.

The company entered the telecom industry in 1993 with a national paging network and added a mobile phone license a year later. In 1996 the group listed 40% of Bouygues Offshore's shares on the New York and Paris stock exchanges. Also that year it launched mobile phone operator Bouygues Telecom and entered a partnership with Telecom Italia.

By 1999 Bouygues Telecom had reached 2 million customers, and Bouygues bought back a 20% share held by the UK's Cable and Wireless to increase its stake to nearly 54%. That year Bouygues Offshore bought Norwegian engineering firm Kvaerner, and the group spun off its construction sector, creating Bouygues Construction.

After word circulated that Deutsch Telekom wanted to acquire the group's telecom unit, Bouygues became the target of takeover rumors. Francois Pinault, France's richest businessman, became Bouygues' largest non-family shareholder when he increased his stake to 15%. Then Pinault's biggest rival, Bernard Arnault, upped his stake to more than 10% of the group, fueling speculation of a battle over control of the board.

Chairman and CEO: Martin Bouygues, age 47
VC and COO: Michel Derbesse, age 64
Group Director, Economics and Finance:
Olivier Poupart-Lafarge, age 56
Group Director Human Resources: Michel Maitre
Group Director, Utilities; Chairman and CEO, Saur:
Olivier Bouygues, age 49
Group Director, Road; Chariman and CEO, Colas:
Alain Dupont, age 59
Group Director, Property; Chairman and CEO,
Bouygues Immobilier: Claude Durrande, age 62
Group Director, Telecommunications; Chairman and
CEO, BouyguesTelecom: Philippe Montagner, age 56
Group Director, Media; Chairman and CEO, TF1:
Patrick Le Lay, age 58
Auditors: Mazars & Guerard; SFA & Associes

LOCATIONS

HQ: 1, avenue Eugène Freyssinet,
78061 St. Quentin-en-Yvelines Cedex, France
Phone: +33-1-30-60-23-11   **Fax:** +33-1-30-60-48-61
Web site: http://www.bouygues.fr

1999 Sales

	% of total
Europe	
France	64
Western Europe	11
Eastern Europe	3
Africa	9
USA/Canada	6
Asia/Pacific	6
Middle East	1
Central & South America	—
Total	**100**

PRODUCTS/OPERATIONS

1999 Sales

	% of total
Construction	
Building & civil works	35
Roads	30
Property	6
Services	
Public utilities management	15
Television	11
Telecommunications	1
Other	2
Total	**100**

COMPETITORS

Autostrade	Groupe GTM
AWG	Halliburton
Azurix	HBG
Balfour Beatty	HOCHTIEF
Bechtel	Hyundai Engineering
Bilfinger + Berger	and Construction
Bovis Lend Lease	Montgomery Watson
Cegetel	Philipp Holzmann
Communication	RSL Communications
Telesystems International	Severn Trent
CSCEC	Skanska
Dragados	Suez Lyonnaise des Eaux
Eiffage	Technip
FCC	Telesystem International
Fluor	Wireless
France Telecom	Vivendi

HISTORICAL FINANCIALS & EMPLOYEES

Euronext Paris: EN FYE: December 31	Annual Growth	12/90	12/91	12/92	12/93	12/94	12/95	12/96	12/97	12/98	12/99
Sales (€ mil.)	12.3%	—	—	—	—	—	—	11,186	13,884	14,789	15,857
Net income (€ mil.)	(14.7%)	—	—	—	—	—	—	100	115	81	62
Income as % of sales	—	—	—	—	—	—	—	0.9%	0.8%	0.5%	0.4%
Earnings per share (€)	(21.6%)	—	—	—	—	—	—	0.42	0.45	0.31	0.20
Stock price - FY high (€)	—	—	—	—	—	—	—	8.95	11.01	19.15	67.50
Stock price - FY low (€)	—	—	—	—	—	—	—	6.88	7.29	10.28	17.53
Stock price - FY close (€)	98.4%	—	—	—	—	—	—	8.16	10.49	17.56	63.70
P/E - high	—	—	—	—	—	—	—	22	24	62	338
P/E - low	—	—	—	—	—	—	—	17	16	33	88
Dividends per share (€)	0.0%	—	—	—	—	—	—	0.26	0.26	0.26	0.26
Book value per share (€)	17.3%	—	—	—	—	—	—	4.45	4.90	4.92	7.19
Employees	2.0%	—	—	—	—	—	—	105,036	105,668	103,350	111,352

STOCK PRICE HISTORY

HIGH/LOW/CLOSE

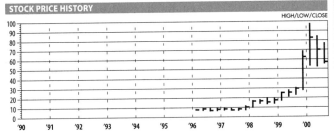

1999 FISCAL YEAR-END

Debt ratio: 52.9%
Return on equity: 3.6%
Cash (€ mil.): 521
Current ratio: 1.01
Long-term debt (€ mil.): 2,453
No. of shares (mil.): 303
Dividends
  Yield: 0.0%
  Payout: 1.3%
Market value ($ mil.): 19,379
Sales ($ mil.): 15,953

BP AMOCO P.L.C.

OVERVIEW

There's no ocean wide enough to keep two oil companies from a merger. London-based BP Amoco, formed from the 1998 merger of British Petroleum and US-based Amoco, is the world's #3 integrated oil company, after Exxon Mobil and Royal Dutch/Shell, and it has expanded again with the acquisition of Atlantic Richfield Company (ARCO).

The new BP has proved reserves of about 19.3 billion barrels of oil equivalent, including large Alaskan holdings that have helped make it the #1 US oil and gas producer. BP also has significant production activities in Canada, the Gulf of Mexico, the North Sea, and Indonesia. It is expanding its presence in China, where ARCO had operations, through investments in PetroChina and Sinopec.

BP owns 29,000 service stations worldwide, including more than 17,100 in the US. Also a top refiner (3.2 million barrels of oil per day capacity) and manufacturer of petrochemicals and specialty chemicals, BP has expanded with the acquisition of motor-oil maker Burmah Castrol.

The company is rolling out a new worldwide brand, BP, but will continue to use the Castrol, Amoco, and ARCO brands in some markets.

HISTORY

BP Amoco was born on two sides of the Atlantic. In the US, Amoco emerged from Standard Oil Trust, organized by John D. Rockefeller in 1882. In 1886 he bought Lima (Ohio) oil, a high-sulfur crude, anticipating the discovery of a sulfur-removing process. Such a process was, indeed, patented in 1887, and in 1889 Standard organized Standard Oil of Indiana, which later established such innovations as company-owned service stations and a research lab at the refinery.

Overseas, British Petroleum (BP) was a twinkle in the eye of English adventurer William D'Arcy, who began oil exploration of Persia in 1901. In 1908, bankrolled by Burmah Oil, D'Arcy's firm was the first to strike oil in the Middle East. D'Arcy and Burmah Oil formed Anglo-Persian Oil in 1909, and the British government took a 51% stake in 1914.

Back in the US, Standard was broken up into 33 independent oil firms in 1911. Standard Oil of Indiana kept its oil refining and US marketing operations. In 1925 it added a few Mexican and Venezuelan firms, including Pan American Petroleum and Transport, which held half of American Oil Co., known for Amoco antiknock gasoline. It began Amoco Chemicals in 1945.

Anglo-Persian took the BP name in 1954 and bought its own Standard Oil: After making a strike in Alaska in 1969, BP swapped Alaskan reserves for a 25% interest (later upped to 55%) in Standard Oil of Ohio (SOHIO). BP also struck North Sea oil in 1970. But falling oil and copper prices in the mid-1980s and a dry hole in the Beaufort Sea hurt earnings. Under Robert Horton, SOHIO sold off units. BP also bought livestock feed producer Purina Mills (1986, sold 1998) and the rest of SOHIO (1987).

Standard Oil of Indiana had its own problems, including being kicked out of Iran after the Islamic revolution, and causing a major oil spill off the French coast in 1978. The firm, which became Amoco in 1985, bought Canada's Dome Petroleum in 1988, making it the largest private owner of North American gas reserves, but the big purchase proved hard to swallow.

In 1992 Amoco hurled itself into overseas oil exploration. It was the first foreign oil company to explore the Chinese mainland. But by 1995 production was down. That year John Browne, often compared to Rockefeller, became BP's CEO. In 1996 BP and Mobil merged their European fuel and lubricants operations, and the British government sold its remaining stake in BP.

As oil prices tumbled, BP bought Amoco in a $52 billion deal in 1998 and formed BP Amoco. The new oil major agreed the next year to buy US-based Atlantic Richfield in a deal that closed in 2000. BP Amoco sold ARCO's Alaskan properties to Phillips for $7 billion to gain regulatory approval for the purchase. To cut costs as it integrated acquisitions, BP Amoco planned to sell $10 billion in assets by 2001, including its Canadian oil properties.

An asset the company didn't want to lose — its stake in Siberian oil fields — was nearly taken away in a controversial 1999 bankruptcy sale before BP Amoco and Russia's Tyumen Oil agreed to cooperate. In 2000 BP Amoco and Shell Oil sold their stakes in Altura Energy to Occidental Petroleum for $3.6 billion. Also that year BP Amoco bought motor-oil maker Burmah Castrol for $4.7 billion. It paid $1.5 billion for the 18% of former ARCO exploration and production unit Vastar Resources that it didn't already own.

The company adopted BP as its worldwide brand in 2000 and announced plans to change its name.

Chairman: Peter D. Sutherland, age 53
Deputy Chairman: Sir Ian Prosser, age 56
Group Chief Executive: Sir John Browne, age 51, $2,490,000 pay
Deputy Group Chief Executive: Rodney F. Chase, age 56, $1,491,000 pay
Chief Executive, Exploration and Production: Richard L. Olver, age 53, $1,183,000 pay
Chief Executive, Chemicals: Byron Grote
Chief Executive, Refining and Marketing: W. Doug Ford, age 56
CFO: John G. S. Buchanan, age 56, $1,330,000 pay
Executive Director, Policies and Technology: Chris S. Gibson-Smith, age 54, $1,169,000 pay
Director of Human Resources: Nick Starritt
Auditors: Ernst & Young

HQ: Britannic House, 1 Finsbury Circus, London EC2M 7BA, United Kingdom
Phone: +44-20-7496-4000   **Fax:** +44-20-7496-4630
US HQ: 200 E. Randolph Dr., Chicago, IL 60601
US Phone: 312-856-6111   **US Fax:** 212-451-8088
Web site: http://www.bp.com

1999 Sales

	$ mil.	% of total
US	38,786	41
Europe		
UK	30,223	32
Other countries	5,973	6
Other regions	19,365	21
Adjustments	(10,781)	—
Total	**83,566**	**100**

1999 Sales

	$ mil.	% of total
Refining & marketing	62,893	67
Exploration & production	21,649	23
Chemicals	9,392	10
Other businesses	198	—
Adjustments	(10,566)	—
Total	**83,566**	**100**

Selected Products and Services

Chemical intermediates	Oilfield development
Coal mining	Pipelines and
Feedstock	transportation
Gas processing and	Polymers
marketing	Solar power
Oil and gas exploration	Transportation and
Oil refining and marketing	shipping
Oil supply and trading	

Amerada Hess	Eni	PDVSA
Ashland	Enron	PEMEX
BASF	Exxon Mobil	PETROBRAS
Bayer	Hercules	Phillips
BG Group	Huntsman	Petroleum
BHP	ICI Americas	Royal
Canadian Pacific	Imperial Oil	Dutch/Shell
Cargill	Kerr-McGee	Sinclair Oil
Chevron	Koch	Sunoco
Coastal	Lyondell	Texaco
Conoco	Chemical	Tosco
Dow Chemical	Norsk Hydro	TOTAL FINA
DuPont	Occidental	ELF

NYSE: BP FYE: December 31	Annual Growth	12/90	12/91	12/92	12/93	12/94	12/95	12/96	12/97	12/98	12/99
Sales ($ mil.)	3.1%	63,765	60,970	50,357	51,709	51,827	56,000	76,602	71,783	68,304	83,566
Net income ($ mil.)	4.2%	3,235	776	(694)	910	2,468	1,740	4,370	4,080	3,260	4,686
Income as % of sales	—	5.1%	1.3%	—	1.8%	4.8%	3.1%	5.7%	5.7%	4.8%	5.6%
Earnings per share ($)	(0.9%)	1.56	0.44	(0.39)	0.51	1.36	0.94	2.34	2.13	1.02	1.44
Stock price - FY high ($)	—	21.56	19.38	16.59	16.34	21.31	25.97	35.94	46.50	48.66	62.63
Stock price - FY low ($)	—	14.91	15.47	10.28	10.53	14.59	18.91	23.63	32.44	36.50	40.19
Stock price - FY close ($)	13.3%	19.22	16.44	11.44	16.00	19.97	25.53	35.34	39.84	45.38	59.31
P/E - high	—	14	44	—	32	16	28	15	22	48	40
P/E - low	—	10	35	—	21	11	20	10	15	36	26
Dividends per share ($)	4.9%	0.90	1.04	0.91	0.42	0.44	0.68	0.66	0.00	0.00	1.38
Book value per share ($)	1.3%	11.87	5.54	4.18	3.97	4.72	4.93	5.82	6.07	12.95	13.33
Employees	(4.1%)	116,750	111,900	97,650	84,000	60,000	56,650	53,150	56,450	96,650	80,400

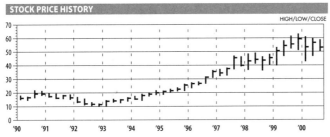

HIGH/LOW/CLOSE

Debt ratio: 18.2%
Return on equity: 11.4%
Cash ($ mil.): 1,331
Current ratio: 1.01
Long-term debt ($ mil.): 9,644
No. of shares (mil.): 3,247
Dividends
 Yield: 2.3%
 Payout: 95.8%
Market value ($ mil.): 192,600

BRIDGESTONE CORPORATION

OVERVIEW

Bridgestone's fortunes are in a skid due to tire recalls, but the Tokyo-based company is working hard to regain control. As one of the world's largest tire makers, Bridgestone supplies tires to such car giants as Ford and General Motors; tires account for about 80% of sales. The company also makes tires for heavy equipment (off-road mining vehicles) and aircraft. In addition to tires, Bridgestone makes a variety of products that include automotive belts and hoses, building materials, and golf and tennis balls.

Bridgestone's retail channels include its own outlets in the US and Japan and large retailers such as Montgomery Ward. It has manufacturing facilities in more than 20 countries worldwide, including 43 tire plants. To become king of the road, Bridgestone is boosting its operations in emerging markets such as China, India, and Russia. The company's main concern, however, is damage control relating to the recall of 6.5 million faulty tires by its Bridgestone/Firestone subsidiary.

HISTORY

In 1906 Shojiro Ishibashi and his brother Tokujiro assumed control of the family's clothing business. They focused on making *tabi,* traditional Japanese footwear, and in 1923 began working with rubber for soles. In 1931 Shojiro formed Bridgestone (Ishibashi means "stone bridge" in Japanese) to make tires, and during that decade the company began producing auto tires, airplane tires, and golf balls. Bridgestone followed the Japanese military to occupied territories, where it built plants. The company's headquarters moved to Tokyo in 1937.

Although Bridgestone lost all of its overseas factories in WWII, the Japanese plants escaped damage. The company began making bicycles in 1946 and signed a technical assistance pact with Goodyear five years later, enabling Bridgestone to import badly needed technology. In the 1950s and 1960s, Bridgestone started making nylon tires and radials and again set up facilities overseas, mostly elsewhere in Asia. The company benefited from the rapid growth in Japanese auto sales in the 1970s. Shojiro died at age 87 in 1976.

In 1983 Bridgestone bought a plant in LaVergne, Tennessee, from tire maker Firestone. Five years later Bridgestone topped Italian tire maker Pirelli's bid and bought the rest of Firestone for $2.6 billion, valuing the tire manufacturer at a lofty 26 times its earnings. Bridgestone/Firestone became Bridgestone's largest subsidiary. Harvey Firestone founded his tire business in 1900 and expanded with the auto industry in the US. In the 1920s he leased 1 million acres in Liberia for rubber plantations and established a chain of auto supply and service outlets. After WWII Firestone started making synthetic rubber and automotive components, expanded overseas, and acquired US tire producers Dayton Tire & Rubber and Seiberling.

At the time of Firestone's purchase, General Motors (GM) dropped it as a supplier. Bridgestone/Firestone compensated for this loss in volume by selling more tires through mass-market retailers. It began selling tires to GM's Saturn Corporation in 1990.

During the early 1990s Bridgestone bought Colonial Rubber Works, a US roofing material manufacturer, and America Off The Road Company, which makes tires for heavy equipment. To improve its distribution, in 1992 Bridgestone renamed its 1,550 North American MasterCare auto service centers "Tire Zone at Firestone" and took the unheard-of step of selling rival Michelin's tires. It expanded operations in Brazil, Indonesia, Mexico, Thailand, and the US the next year.

Bridgestone's US operations have been plagued with problems, such as disputes with the United Rubber Workers (URW) union. Tensions rose in 1995 when the company hired 2,300 permanent replacement workers during a plant strike. In 1996 Bridgestone set up a tire manufacturing joint venture with Tata Enterprises, India's leading conglomerate. Also that year, after URW members had become part of United Steelworkers of America, the two sides approved a new contract.

Expanding its markets, Bridgestone opened a retail outlet in Moscow in 1999 and acquired a radial tire plant in China from South Korea's Kumho Industrial Company in 2000. That year the company recalled millions of Firestone ATX, ATX II and Wilderness AT tires after dozens of incidents where the tires came apart at highway speeds. The affected tires have been used on light trucks and SUVs since 1990, many of them as original equipment on the Ford Explorer. Not long after the recall Bridgestone/Firestone chairman and CEO Masatoshi Ono retired and was replaced by John Lampe.

President, Chairman, and CEO: Yoichiro Kaizaki
EVP; Adviser to the President, International
  Operations and Director, Product Planning Division:
  Tadakazu Harada
EVP; Adviser to the President, Steel Cord
  Manufacturing and President, Bridgestone Cycle:
  Katsuyoshi Shibata
EVP; Chairman and CEO, Bridgestone/Firestone, Inc.:
  John Lampe
SVP Chemical and Industrial Products: Nobuhiro Koike
SVP Original Equipment Sales: Keisuke Suzuki
SVP Replacement Tire Sales: Akira Sonoda
SVP Tire Development: Shigeo Watanabe
Director Human Resources Division: Takeshi Hattori
Auditors: Asahi & Co.

HQ: 10-1, Kyobashi 1-chome,
  Chuo-ku, Tokyo 104-8340, Japan
Phone: +81-3-3567-0111   Fax: +81-3-3535-2553
US HQ: 50 Century Blvd., Nashville, TN 37214
US Phone: 615-872-5000   US Fax: 615-872-1599
Web site: http://www.bridgestone.co.jp

Bridgestone sells its products worldwide and has factories
in Africa, Asia, Australia, Europe, and the Americas.

1999 Sales

	% of total
The Americas	41
Japan	41
Europe	11
Other regions	7
Total	**100**

1999 Sales

	% of total
Tires	79
Other products	21
Total	**100**

Selected Products

Air springs	Hoses
Aircraft tires	Inflatable rubber dams
Belts	Marine barriers
Bicycles	Motorcycle tires
Building materials	Office equipment
Bus tires	components
Car tires	Tennis balls
Construction equipment	Tennis rackets
tires	Tennis shoes
Dampers	Thermal insulating
Fish breeding reservoirs	polyurethane foam
Golf balls	Truck tires
Golf clubs	Waterproofing materials

ARBED	K2
Armstrong Holdings	Michelin
Avon Rubber	3M
Brunswick	Newell Rubbermaid
Callaway Golf	Pacific Dunlop
Continental AG	Sime Darby
Cooper Tire & Rubber	Sumitomo
Goodyear	TBC
Huffy	Wingate Partners

OTC: BRDCY FYE: December 31	Annual Growth	12/90	12/91	12/92	12/93	12/94	12/95	12/96	12/97	12/98	12/99
Sales ($ mil.)	5.0%	13,143	14,122	13,977	14,297	16,018	16,294	16,923	16,624	19,689	20,403
Net income ($ mil.)	43.7%	33	60	227	254	320	523	608	300	921	868
Income as % of sales	—	0.3%	0.4%	1.6%	1.8%	2.0%	3.2%	3.6%	1.8%	4.7%	4.3%
Earnings per share ($)	10.8%	—	—	—	—	—	6.68	7.62	3.70	10.32	10.07
Stock price - FY high ($)	—	—	—	—	—	—	154.25	194.00	255.00	255.00	310.00
Stock price - FY low ($)	—	—	—	—	—	—	144.00	152.50	215.00	214.00	207.00
Stock price - FY close ($)	9.7%	—	—	—	—	—	154.00	190.50	227.00	219.00	223.00
P/E - high	—	—	—	—	—	—	23	25	69	25	31
P/E - low	—	—	—	—	—	—	22	20	58	21	21
Dividends per share ($)	4.2%	—	—	—	—	—	1.16	1.12	1.10	1.07	1.37
Book value per share ($)	4.3%	—	—	—	—	—	71.28	72.53	68.61	83.06	84.40
Employees	0.7%	95,276	83,081	85,835	87,332	89,711	89,418	92,458	96,204	97,767	101,489

HIGH/LOW/CLOSE

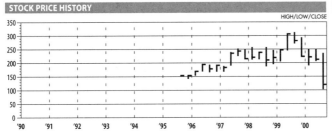

Debt ratio: 16.1%
Return on equity: 12.2%
Cash ($ mil.): 756
Current ratio: 1.32
Long-term debt ($ mil.): 1,392
No. of shares (mil.): 86
Dividends
  Yield: 0.0%
  Payout: 0.1%
Market value ($ mil.): 19,205

BRITISH AIRWAYS PLC

OVERVIEW

Never have so many flown so much on one cross-border carrier. Europe's largest airline, British Airways (BA) flies more than 365 aircraft (including subsidiaries' planes) and serves more than 230 destinations in some 90 countries. Based in Harmondsworth, UK, the carrier works out of major hubs in London — Heathrow and Gatwick.

BA has built a global network through partnerships. It owns 25% of Australia's Qantas Airways and 9% of Spain's Iberia. A proposed alliance between BA and AMR's American Airlines has been unable to get off the ground with regulators, but the two airlines have come together in the Oneworld global marketing alliance, along with Cathay Pacific Airways, Finnair, Iberia, and Qantas.

Even though it's still in the air, BA has had a rough year. It moved into the red for the first time since it was privatized, and CEO Bob Ayling was replaced by Rod Eddington. Looking to relieve intense competitive pressures, the carrier also attempted to merge with KLM, but the deal never took off. BA is looking to make money by putting its low-fare carrier Go up for sale.

HISTORY

British Airways has a jet trail winding back to 1916 and its biplane-flying ancestor, Aircraft Transport and Travel, which in 1919 launched the world's first daily international air service (between London and Paris). Concerned about subsidized foreign competition, British authorities in 1924 merged Aircraft Transport and Travel successor Daimler Airways with other fledgling British carriers — British Air Marine Navigation, Handley Page, and Instone Air Line — to form Imperial Airways.

Imperial pioneered routes from London to India (1929), Singapore (1933), and — in partnership with Qantas Empire Airways — Australia (1934). Competition on European routes emerged in the 1930s from upstart British Airways; in 1939 the government, troubled by the threat to Imperial, nationalized and merged the two airlines to form British Overseas Airways Corporation (BOAC).

After WWII, BOAC continued as the UK's international airline, but state-owned British European Airways (BEA) took over domestic and European routes. In 1972 the government combined the duo to form British Airways (BA).

BA and Air France jointly introduced supersonic passenger service in 1976 with the Concorde — a PR victory that contributed to years of losses. Colin Marshall became CEO in 1983 and reduced manpower and routes.

In 1987 the government sold BA to the public, and the airline bought chief UK rival British Caledonian. Hoping to become a globe-spanning carrier, in 1992 BA tried to gain a 44% stake in USAir (which became US Airways). American Airlines, United, and Delta strongly objected, demanding equal access to UK markets. BA settled for a 25% stake, the maximum foreign ownership allowed by US law, in 1993. It also bought 25% of Qantas.

That year BA settled a libel suit brought by UK competitor Virgin Atlantic Airways, which accused BA of waging a smear campaign against it. The settlement cost BA about $5 million, and Virgin Atlantic followed with a $1 billion antitrust suit in the US (dismissed in 1999). In 1994 BA paid out $4 million to settle yet another Virgin Atlantic suit, this one claiming BA had done sloppy maintenance on Virgin aircraft. BA also sold British Caledonian.

In 1996 Marshall turned over the CEO job to Bob Ayling, who had joined BA in 1985. BA and American Airlines agreed to coordinate prices and schedules and to share market data for their transatlantic routes. Though the deal met regulatory obstacles from the start, in 1997 BA sold its stake in US Airways. BA and American also took the lead in forming the Oneworld global alliance (which took effect in 1999).

The next year BA launched low-fare European carrier Go. In 1999 BA and American all but abandoned plans for their comprehensive transatlantic linkup after US regulators denied antitrust immunity. Meanwhile, as fuel prices rose and passenger numbers fell, BA announced it would cut unprofitable routes and use smaller planes.

Ayling resigned in 2000, and Marshall stepped in as temporary CEO before Rod Eddington, a veteran of Cathay Pacific and Ansett, was appointed. Also that year BA took a 9% stake in Iberia and sold its interest in France's Air Liberte.

BA grounded its Concordes in 2000, three weeks after the crash of an Air France Concorde outside Paris in which 113 people were killed. The airline also put its no-frills carrier Go up for sale that same year.

Chairman: Lord Colin Marshall of Knightsbridge, age 66
Deputy Chairman: Michael Angus, age 70
CEO: Roderick Eddington, age 50
CFO: Derek Stevens, age 61
Director Technical Operations: Colin Matthews, age 44
Director Investments and Joint Ventures:
  Roger Maynard, age 57
Director For People: Mervyn Walker, age 41
Director Customer Service and Operations: Mike Street
General Counsel: Robert Webb, age 51
Director Communications: Simon Walker, age 46
Director Strategy: David Spurlock, age 32
Director Marketing: Martin George
Director Sales: Dale Moss
Director Flight Operations: Mike Jeffrey
Auditors: Ernst & Young

LOCATIONS

HQ: Waterside, PO Box 365,
  Harmondsworth UB7 0GB, United Kingdom
Phone: +44-20-8562-4444   **Fax:** +44-20-8759-4314
US HQ: 75-20 Astoria Blvd., Jackson Heights, NY 11370
US Phone: 718-397-4967   **US Fax:** 718-397-4364
Web site: http://www.british-airways.com

British Airways serves more than 230 destinations in
some 90 countries.

2000 Sales

	% of total
Europe	38
The Americas	36
Africa, Middle East &	
Indian subcontinent	14
Far East & Australasia	12
Total	**100**

PRODUCTS/OPERATIONS

2000 Aircraft

	No.
Boeing 737	85
Boeing 747	72
Boeing 757	53
Turbo Props	34
Boeing 777	33
Boeing 767	27
Fokker	15
McDonnell Douglas	14
Airbus A320	10
Avro RJ100	8
Airbus A319	6
Concorde	6
Embraer RJ145	2
Total	**365**

Major Subsidiaries and Affiliates
British Airways Capital Ltd. (89%, airline finance)
British Airways Finance B.V. (airline finance,
  Netherlands)
British Airways Holidays Ltd. (package holidays)
Deutsche BA Luftfahrtgesellschaft mbH (German
  airline)
Go Fly Ltd.(low-fare airline)
Iberia Lineas Aereas de Espana SA (9%, Spain)
Qantas Airways Ltd. (25%, Australia)

COMPETITORS

Air France	SAS
All Nippon Airways	Singapore Airlines
Delta	Swire Pacific
JAL	UAL
KLM	US Airways
Lufthansa	Virgin Atlantic Airways
Northwest Airlines	

HISTORICAL FINANCIALS & EMPLOYEES

NYSE: BAB FYE: March 31	Annual Growth	3/91	3/92	3/93	3/94	3/95	3/96	3/97	3/98	3/99	3/00
Sales ($ mil.)	5.7%	8,632	9,069	8,421	9,360	11,634	11,843	13,705	14,447	14,367	14,245
Net income ($ mil.)	—	166	443	269	425	405	722	907	769	332	(33)
Income as % of sales	—	1.9%	4.9%	3.2%	4.5%	3.5%	6.1%	6.6%	5.3%	2.3%	—
Earnings per share ($)	—	2.34	5.38	3.37	4.10	3.97	6.75	8.32	7.02	3.09	(0.32)
Stock price - FY high ($)	—	39.38	48.63	57.50	74.13	68.50	83.00	107.38	125.13	114.75	88.50
Stock price - FY low ($)	—	24.50	25.75	37.38	41.50	54.88	63.50	77.50	83.88	52.13	42.25
Stock price - FY close ($)	6.6%	30.13	42.88	44.63	60.00	65.75	82.00	104.75	104.06	68.63	53.75
P/E - high		17	8	16	17	16	11	12	17	37	—
P/E - low		11	4	10	9	13	8	8	11	17	—
Dividends per share ($)	14.5%	1.86	1.76	2.09	1.80	1.88	1.75	2.73	2.20	0.00	6.28
Book value per share ($)	8.0%	23.22	38.27	24.76	28.44	35.45	39.63	48.80	53.44	50.38	46.36
Employees	2.0%	54,427	50,409	48,960	48,628	53,060	55,296	58,210	60,770	64,051	65,157

STOCK PRICE HISTORY

HIGH/LOW/CLOSE

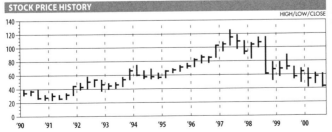

2000 FISCAL YEAR-END

Debt ratio: 67.4%
Return on equity: —
Cash ($ mil.): 164
Current ratio: 0.77
Long-term debt ($ mil.): 10,371
No. of shares (mil.): 108
Dividends
  Yield: 11.7%
  Payout: —
Market value ($ mil.): 5,813

BRITISH AMERICAN TOBACCO P.L.C.

OVERVIEW

Tobacco companies worldwide have been stocking up on smokes and British American Tobacco (BAT) has been leading the way. London-based BAT, the world's #2 cigarette company (behind Philip Morris), makes about 320 brands sold in 180 countries worldwide. Its top brands include Benson & Hedges, Kent, Kool, Lucky Strike, and Rothmans, as well as regional smokes such as GPC, made by US subsidiary Brown & Williamson.

Formerly known as B.A.T Industries, the company took its lead role in the late-1990s redistribution of global cigarette assets by spinning off its financial services business and buying Netherlands-based Rothmans International. In 2000 BAT packed in Imperial Tobacco, Canada's dominant tobacco company.

Along with its US rivals, BAT has reached settlements with all 50 states to avoid litigation regarding smoking-related illnesses. Individual suits continue, but no verdicts in which Brown & Williamson was ordered to pay damages have survived past appeal.

Companies controlled by South African billionaire Anton Rupert own about 25% of BAT.

HISTORY

After a year of vicious price-cutting between Imperial Tobacco (UK) and James Buchanan Duke's American Tobacco in the UK, Imperial counterattacked in the US. To end the cigarette price war in the UK, the firms created British American Tobacco (BAT) in 1902. The truce granted Imperial the British market, American the US market, and they jointly owned BAT in the rest of the world.

With Duke in control, BAT expanded into new markets. In China it was selling 25 billion cigarettes a year by 1920. When the Communist revolution ended BAT's operations in China, the company lost more than 25% of its sales (although China later re-emerged as a major export market for the company's cigarettes).

A 1911 US antitrust action forced American to sell its interest in BAT and opened the US market to the company. BAT purchased US cigarette manufacturer Brown & Williamson in 1927 and continued to grow through geographical expansion until the 1960s. In 1973 BAT and Imperial each regained control of its own brands in the UK and Continental Europe. Imperial sold the last of its stake in BAT in 1980.

Fearing that mounting public concern over smoking would limit the cigarette market, BAT acquired nontobacco businesses; it changed its name to B.A.T Industries in 1976. The acquisitions of retailers Saks (1973), Argos (UK, 1979), Marshall Field (1982), and others diversified the company's sales base. B.A.T then developed a taste for insurance firms, buying the UK's Eagle Star and Allied Dunbar, and the US's Farmers Group in the 1980s. Responding to a 1989 hostile takeover bid from Sir James Goldsmith, it sold its retail operations, retaining its tobacco and financial services.

In 1994 B.A.T acquired former American Tobacco for $1 billion. In 1997 the company acquired Cigarrera de Moderna (with 50% of Mexico's cigarette sales) and formed a joint venture with the Turkish tobacco state enterprise, Tekel. Brown & Williamson joined its US rivals in 1997 in reaching a tentative $368.5 billion settlement to end lawsuits brought by about 40 states, but within a year the deal collapsed.

B.A.T's tobacco operations were spun off in 1998 as British American Tobacco (BAT). The financial services operations were merged with Zurich Insurance to create two holding companies: Allied Zurich (UK) and Zurich Allied (Switzerland). With the changes, Martin Broughton became chairman of BAT. In late 1998 BAT and its rivals reached a settlement covering 46 states for about $206 billion. (Four states already had settled for $40 billion.)

The company in 1999 paid $8.2 billion to buy Dutch cigarette company Rothmans International (Rothmans, Dunhill) from Switzerland's Compagnie Financiere Richemont and South Africa's Rembrandt Group — both controlled by Anton Rupert. With the purchase, BAT received a controlling stake in Canada's Rothmans, Benson & Hedges (RBH). Also that year the US government filed a massive lawsuit against Big Tobacco to recover health care costs and profits allegedly derived from fraud.

In early 2000 BAT bought the 58% of Canada's Imasco it didn't already own. (Formerly called Imperial Tobacco Company of Canada, Imasco was created in 1908 with help from BAT.) As part of the deal, Imasco sold off its financial services and BAT received its Imperial Tobacco unit (which has no connection to the UK's Imperial Tobacco Group). Also that year BAT unloaded its share of RBH via public offering (rather than wait for a buyer).

Chairman: Martin F. Broughton, age 52, $1,335,171 pay
Deputy Chairman: Kenneth H. Clarke, age 59,
$100,000 pay
Managing Director: Ulrich G. V. Herter, age 58,
$940,620 pay
Deputy Managing Director: William P. Ryan, age 64,
$571,154 pay
Corporate and Regulatory Affairs Director:
Michael Prideaux, age 49
Finance Director: Keith S. Dunt, age 52, $603,550 pay
Human Resources Director: David Stevens, age 58
Legal Director: Neil Withington, age 43
Marketing Director: Jimmi Rembiszewski, age 49
Operations Director: John Jewell, age 50
Director, Smoking Tobacco and Cigars: Chris Bischoff
Regional Director Africa: Tony Jones, age 52
Regional Director America-Pacific: Nick Brookes
Regional Director Amesca: Dick Green, age 56
Regional Director Asia-Pacific: Tony Johnston, age 52
Regional Director Europe: Paul Adams, age 46
Regional Director Latin America:
Antonio Monteiro de Castro, age 54
Secretary: Philip Cook
Auditors: PricewaterhouseCoopers

Selected International Cigarette Brands
Barclay
Benson & Hedges
Capri
Carlton
Dunhill
John Player Gold Leaf
Kent
Kool
Lucky Strike
Misty
Pall Mall
Peter Stuyvesant
Player's
Rothmans
State Express 555
Viceroy
Winfield

Selected Other Products and Brands
Cigars (Dunhill, Mercator, Schimmelpenninck)
Fine cut tobaccos (Ajja, Belgam, Javaanse Jongens,
Samson, Schwarzer Krauser)
Pipe tobaccos (Captain Black, Clan, Dunhill, Erinmore)

HQ: Globe House, 4 Temple Place,
London WC2R 2PG, United Kingdom
Phone: +44-20-7845-1000   **Fax:** +44-20-7240-0555
US HQ: 200 Brown & Williamson Tower, 401 S. 4th St.,
Louisville, KY 40202
US Phone: 502-568-7000   **US Fax:** 502-568-7494
Web site: http://www.bat.com

British American Tobacco operates more than 95
factories in about 65 countries on six continents.

Altadis
Austria Tabak
China National Tobacco
Gallaher
Imperial Tobacco Group
Japan Tobacco
Lorillard Tobacco
Philip Morris
R.J. Reynolds Tobacco
Reemtsma
Swedish Match
Swisher International
Tiedemanns
Vector

AMEX: BTI FYE: December 31	Annual Growth	12/90	12/91	12/92	12/93	12/94	12/95	12/96	12/97	12/98	12/99
Sales ($ mil.)	60.7%	—	—	—	—	—	—	—	11,766	24,202	30,374
Net income ($ mil.)	2.7%	—	—	—	—	—	—	—	852	574	898
Income as % of sales	—	—	—	—	—	—	—	—	7.2%	2.4%	3.0%
Earnings per share ($)	19.2%	—	—	—	—	—	—	—	—	0.73	0.87
Stock price - FY high ($)	—	—	—	—	—	—	—	—	—	19.38	22.25
Stock price - FY low ($)	—	—	—	—	—	—	—	—	—	15.00	10.19
Stock price - FY close ($)	(41.4%)	—	—	—	—	—	—	—	—	17.50	10.25
P/E - high	—	—	—	—	—	—	—	—	—	26	27
P/E - low	—	—	—	—	—	—	—	—	—	20	12
Dividends per share ($)	—	—	—	—	—	—	—	—	—	0.00	1.05
Book value per share ($)	5,194.2%	—	—	—	—	—	—	—	—	0.14	7.16
Employees	(4.2%)	—	—	—	—	—	—	—	117,339	101,081	107,620

HIGH/LOW/CLOSE

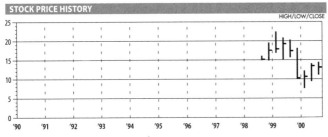

Debt ratio: 49.1%
Return on equity: 22.8%
Cash ($ mil.): 2,994
Current ratio: 1.55
Long-term debt ($ mil.): 7,502
No. of shares (mil.): 1,088
Dividends
  Yield: 10.2%
  Payout: 120.7%
Market value ($ mil.): 11,157

BBC

By no means a fragile senior citizen, the 77-year-old British Broadcasting Corporation (BBC) — fondly referred to by Brits as "Auntie" or "the Beeb" — is the dominant broadcaster in the UK. The London-based, government-backed company offers the UK two public TV channels (BBC ONE and BBC TWO), a 24-hour cable news channel (BBC NEWS 24), five national radio networks, and an online news service. BBC Worldwide, the BBC's commercial subsidiary, offers several international TV channels (BBC PRIME, BBC AMERICA). BBC Worldwide also is involved in several other commercial ventures. It has formed a new subsidiary for its Internet operations, including its freebeeb.net Internet access service business and the Beeb.com e-commerce site, and sold a 13.5% stake in the

unit (called beeb Ventures) to TH Lee Global Internet Ventures. The BBC World Service broadcasts radio programming in more than 40 languages and is the sole source of news in some parts of the world.

Established by royal charter, the BBC is governed by a 12-member board appointed by the Queen. It derives 95% of its funding from annual license fees paid by TV set owners in the UK. Its foundation in public service, however, leaves the BBC in an awkward position in the face of increasing competition. The BBC's growing involvement in commercial ventures has prompted public grumbling that it is straying from its public service role. Its proposals to increase license fees to fund a move into digital television and a plan to create a commercial film division, are also drawing fire.

Established as the British Broadcasting Company Limited in 1922, the BBC was founded by a group of radio manufacturers aiming to block any single manufacturer from grabbing a broadcasting monopoly. Under general manager John Reith, BBC radio programming grew to include news, cultural events, sports, and weather. A burgeoning social and cultural presence led to its re-establishment in 1927 under a new royal charter. The organization was renamed the British Broadcasting Corporation and the charter ensured it would remain outside the control of the British Parliament.

By 1935 BBC radio had reached about 95% of the British population. TV broadcasting debuted the next year, but the cost of TV sets limited audience numbers to about 20,000. Those who could afford a TV got to see the coronation of King George VI and Wimbledon. TV broadcasting would be short-lived, however: Beginning in 1939 and throughout WWII, the signal was blacked out when the transmitter proved a good aircraft direction finder.

Although TV screens went dark, BBC radio served a vital role during WWII. Its broadcasts to occupied territories and the airing of Prime Minister Winston Churchill's wartime speeches elevated the BBC's reputation as a news broadcaster. Following WWII, BBC TV transmission resumed in 1946. The 1953 broadcast of the coronation of Queen Elizabeth II helped launch the television age of the 1950s. In 1955 commercial broadcaster Independent Television Network became the BBC's first rival for viewers. The BBC introduced its second public TV

channel (BBC TWO) in 1964. By 1969 both BBC ONE and BBC TWO were broadcasting in color.

The corporate culture of the BBC during the 1970s and 1980s was dominated by financial upheaval. Budget cuts combined with growing competition prompted the formation of a committee to review the BBC's financing alternatives. Although the committee's 1986 report did not permit commercial advertising on the BBC, it did lead to more flexibility in funding.

Sir John Birt was appointed the BBC's director general in 1992, and the reorganization and cost-cutting program he instituted fueled the debate over the company's move toward commercialization. Through BBC Worldwide, the BBC inched away from its public service roots. In 1997 the BBC privatized its domestic TV and radio transmission business and launched its 24-hour cable news channel. UKTV (a commercial TV joint venture with Flextech) also went on the air that year. In 1998 the BBC began digital broadcasts. It teamed with Discovery Communications to launch BBC America, a US cable channel, and teamed with Scottish Power to provide free Internet access.

In 1999 Greg Dyke, who had been chief executive of Pearson Television, was named to succeed Birt, who left in January 2000. Shortly after Dyke took the reins, he announced a massive restructuring of the organization designed to cut costs (hundreds of jobs will be eliminated), foment more partnerships with private entities, and increase the amount of money spent on programming.

Chairman: Christopher Bland
VC: Gavyn Davies
Director General: Greg Dyke, age 53, $142,000 pay
(partial-year salary)
Director, Finance, Property, and Business Affairs:
John Smith, $201,000 pay
Director, News: Tony Hall, $223,000 pay
Director, Marketing and Communications:
Matthew Bannister, $214,000 pay
Acting Joint Director, Factual and Learning:
Michael Stevenson
Acting Joint Director, Factual and Learning:
Lorraine Heggessey
Director, Human Resources and Internal
Communications: Gareth Jones, $43,000 pay
(partial-year salary)
Director, Public Policy: Caroline Thompson
Director, Television: Mark Thompson
Director, Distribution and Technology: Philip Langsdale
Director of Drama, Entertainment, and Children:
Alan Yentob
Director, Radio: Jenny Abramsky
Director, Nations and Regions: Pat Loughrey
Director, Strategy: Caroline Fairbairn
Chief Executive, BBC Worldwide Limited:
Rupert Gavin, $294,000 pay
Chief Executive, BBC Resources: Margaret Salmon,
$212,000 pay
Director, New Media: Ashley Highfield
Director, BBC World Service: Mark Byford, $218,000 pay
Auditors: KPMG

HQ: British Broadcasting Corporation,
Broadcasting House, Portlands Place,
London W1A 1AA, United Kingdom
Phone: +44-20-7580-4468   **Fax:** +44-20-7765-1181
US HQ: 7475 Wisconsin Ave., Ste. 110,
Bethesda, MD 20814
US Phone: 301-347-2233   **US Fax:** 301-656-8591
Web site: http://www.bbc.co.uk

The British Broadcasting Corporation has operations in
England, Northern Ireland, Scotland, Wales, and the US;
its programming is seen in more than 180 countries.

Selected Television Channels
BBC America (US cable channel)
BBC CHOICE (digital channel)
BBC NEWS 24 (24-hour news programming)
BBC ONE (news and entertainment programming)
BBC ONLINE (Internet site)
BBC TWO (entertainment and educational programming)
BBC WORLD (international news programming)

Selected Radio Networks
Radio 1 (news and music programming)
Radio 2 (news and music programming)
Radio 3 (classical music programming)
Radio 4 (news, educational, and dramatic programming)
Radio 5 Live (talk radio programming)

Selected BBC Worldwide Publications
CD-ROMs
 French Experience
 Pingu
Magazines
 BBC Music
 Radio Times
 Teletubbies

Selected Affiliations
British Sky Broadcasting Group (UK digital TV)
Discovery Communications (US cable TV)
Microsoft (UK interactive TV)

Selected Subsidiaries
BBC Resources (broadcast facilities)
BBC Worldwide (global marketing unit)
beeb Ventures (86.5%, oversees Internet interests)

BSkyB
Capital Radio
Carlton Communications
Chrysalis Group
Cox Communications
Daily Mail and
 General Trust
Flextech
Future Network
Granada Compass

GWR Group
Liberty Media
 International
Pearson
SMG
Telewest
Time Warner
United News & Media
Yorkshire-Tyne Tees
 Television Holdings

Government-owned FYE: March 31	Annual Growth	3/91	3/92	3/93	3/94	3/95	3/96	3/97	3/98	3/99	3/00
Sales ($ mil.)	11.1%	—	—	—	—	2,826	2,776	3,825	4,159	4,593	4,780
Employees	5.6%	—	—	—	—	—	19,000	19,517	21,023	23,119	23,640

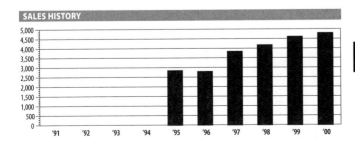

BRITISH SKY BROADCASTING

OVERVIEW

The sky's the limit for the UK's largest pay-TV provider, British Sky Broadcasting (BSkyB). Based in Isleworth, the company beams programming to 4.2 million subscribers in the UK and Ireland; it also has 4.4 million cable customers. Offering more than 100 channels, the firm covers everything from entertainment to news and sports. BSkyB is scoring big points as a major sports broadcaster with rights to the leading football (soccer) leagues in England and Scotland, and it's acquired minority stakes in several teams. It will expand its sport-related offerings with the acquisition of Web-site operator Sports Internet.

Facing intense competition from leading cable rivals, BSkyB is aggressively rolling out its digital service. The company was the first to offer digital satellite TV service in the UK, and it has been encouraging its customers to switch from analog to digital by giving away free digital set-top boxes. Its efforts have paid off as some 2.8 million of its 4.2 million direct-to-home (DTH) satellite customers use digital service.

Sky Global Networks, an affiliate of BSkyB chairman Rupert Murdoch's News Corp., owns 40% of BSkyB. French conglomerate Vivendi owns 24%.

HISTORY

Australian-born media czar Rupert Murdoch, after taking control of several British newspapers, moved into satellite TV service in the UK in 1989 when his News Corp. holding company started Sky Television. SkyTV used an Astra satellite to deliver four channels. By broadcasting SkyTV's programs via satellites owned by the Luxembourg-based Astra group, Murdoch avoided restrictions of the British Broadcasting Act, which prohibited owners of national newspapers from owning more than 20% of a TV company.

In 1990 a consortium of companies, including Chargeurs, Granada, and Pearson, set up rival satellite TV service British Satellite Broadcasting. The rivals faced a consumer market slow to adapt to new technology and a shrinking advertising base caused by an economic recession; both companies posted huge losses (SkyTV's weekly losses grew to more than $20 million in 1990). In the wake of such financial hemorrhaging, the firms merged that year and became British Sky Broadcasting (BSkyB), a slimmer operation with five channels.

In 1993 BSkyB teamed up with US media group Viacom to produce a Nickelodeon channel (children's programming) for the UK market. The firm allied with QVC to launch a British version of the home shopping channel. By year's end, more than 3 million UK homes were receiving BSkyB's programs.

BSkyB sold about 20% of itself to the public in 1994, dropping News Corp.'s stake from 50% to 40%. That year it reinforced its position as the top UK sports broadcaster by launching Sky Sports 2 and acquiring rights to such popular sports as boxing, cricket, rugby, and soccer. BSkyB teamed with rival BBC in 1995 to acquire more sports programming. It also

formed an alliance with international news agency Reuters in an effort to strengthen its Sky News Channel.

In 1996 BSkyB formed a joint venture with Scottish Television to launch Sky Scottish, a channel focusing on news and sports. In 1997 BSkyB began developing digital satellite TV and interactive services in the UK through British Interactive Broadcasting, a joint venture with British Telecommunications, HSBC Holdings, and Matsushita Electric Industrial. (The service, Sky Digital, was launched in 1998 and offers subscribers about 150 channels.)

Managing director Sam Chisholm and his deputy, David Chance, resigned in 1997, opening the door for Murdoch's 29-year-old daughter, Elisabeth, to take a greater role at BSkyB. (She left the company in 2000.) Mark Booth (formerly with Murdoch's Japanese Sky Broadcasting) became CEO. BSkyB launched its digital pay-per-view TV in the UK in 1997.

In 1999 the government blew the whistle on BSkyB's plan to buy UK soccer team Manchester United for $1 billion, saying it would have reduced competition in soccer broadcasting. (BSkyB retained its minority stake in the team.)

Fox/Liberty Networks CEO Tony Ball replaced Booth as CEO in 1999 after Booth was named to head a News Corp.-backed new media company. French conglomerate Vivendi bought Pathe's stake in BSkyB, along with those of Granada and Pearson, and Rupert Murdoch took over as chairman of BSkyB. In 2000, BSkyB paid $1 billion for a 24% stake (later reduced) in Germany's KirchPayTV.

News Corp. in 2000 spun off its satellite holdings, including BSkyB, to form a new company, Sky Global Networks.

OFFICERS

Chairman; Chairman, CEO, and Executive Director, News Corporation: Rupert Murdoch
Chief Executive: Tony Ball, $1,400,000 pay
COO: Richard Freudenstein, age 35
CFO: Martin Stewart, $550,000 pay
Director of New Media: John Swingewood
Head of Human Resources: Craig McCoy
Head of Sky News: Nick Pollard
Chief Executive skysportstore.com: Bob McCulloch
Company Secretary: David Gormley
Auditors: Arthur Andersen

LOCATIONS

HQ: British Sky Broadcasting Group,
6 Centaurs Business Park, Grant Way,
Isleworth, Middlesex TW7 5QD, United Kingdom
Phone: +44-20-7705-3000 **Fax:** +44-20-7705-3030
Web site: http://www.sky.com

British Sky Broadcasting provides cable and satellite TV services throughout the UK and Ireland.

PRODUCTS/OPERATIONS

2000 Sales

	% of total
Direct-to-home subscribers	64
Cable & DTT subscribers	17
Advertising	13
Other	6
Total	**100**

Selected Services
Sky Box Office (pay-per-view movies)
Sky Cinema (classic cinema programming)
Sky MovieMax (action, comedy, and adventure movies)
Sky News (five news channels)
Sky One (key general entertainment channel)
Sky Pictures (original film production)
Sky Productions (original non-film production)
Sky Premier (premium movie channel)
Sky Sports (five sports channels plus MUTV)

Selected Subsidiaries and Affiliates
Australian News Channel Pty Limited
(33%, 24-hour news)
British Sky Broadcasting Limited (satellite TV services)
Granada Sky Broadcasting Limited (80%, general entertainment channels)
KirchPayTV (23%, Germany)
The History Channel (UK) (50%, history programming)
Music Choice Europe Limited (49%, audio music channels)
MUTV (33%, Manchester United football channel)
National Geographic Channel UK (50%, natural history channel)
Nickelodeon UK (50%, children's satellite TV service)
OpenTV (80%, set-top box software)
QVC (UK) (20%, home shopping channel)
Sky Five Text Limited (50%, text service)

COMPETITORS

BBC	NTL
Bertelsmann	SMG
CANAL+	Telewest
Carlton Communications	Time Warner
Daily Mail and General Trust	United News & Media
Flextech	Yorkshire-Tyne Tees Television Holdings
Métropole Télévision	

HISTORICAL FINANCIALS & EMPLOYEES

NYSE: BSY FYE: June 30	Annual Growth	6/91	6/92	6/93	6/94	6/95	6/96	6/97	6/98	6/99	6/00
Sales ($ mil.)	36.6%	169	408	618	850	1,240	1,563	2,114	2,390	2,439	2,801
Net income ($ mil.)	—	(1,376)	(329)	(123)	143	218	362	480	415	(450)	(412)
Income as % of sales	—	—	—	—	16.9%	17.6%	23.2%	22.7%	17.4%	—	—
Earnings per share ($)	—	—	—	—	—	0.83	1.27	1.45	1.45	(1.56)	(1.42)
Stock price - FY high ($)	—	—	—	—	—	27.88	43.50	66.75	47.63	59.25	201.94
Stock price - FY low ($)	—	—	—	—	—	22.88	26.00	40.88	34.13	40.63	52.13
Stock price - FY close ($)	34.8%	—	—	—	—	26.13	40.63	44.69	42.63	56.13	116.13
P/E - high	—	—	—	—	—	34	34	40	33	—	—
P/E - low	—	—	—	—	—	28	20	24	24	—	—
Dividends per share ($)	—	—	—	—	—	0.00	0.53	0.68	0.72	0.34	0.00
Book value per share ($)	—	—	—	—	—	(4.28)	(3.29)	(2.45)	(1.74)	(3.43)	3.22
Employees	44.2%	—	575	1,025	2,403	3,054	4,025	4,580	4,634	8,271	10,730

STOCK PRICE HISTORY
HIGH/LOW/CLOSE

2000 FISCAL YEAR-END
Debt ratio: 68.6%
Return on equity: —
Cash ($ mil.): 426
Current ratio: 1.51
Long-term debt ($ mil.): 2,142
No. of shares (mil.): 304
Dividends
Yield: —
Payout: —
Market value ($ mil.): 35,340

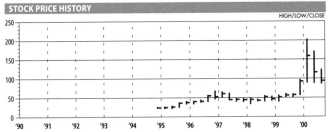

BRITISH TELECOMMUNICATIONS PLC

OVERVIEW

Once upon a time, the rivals of London-based British Telecommunications (BT) could have fit into one of the company's signature red phone booths. But competition is in full swing, and it's taking its toll on the UK's dominant phone company. Ordered to upgrade and open its domestic networks, BT is restructuring and increasingly looking abroad for opportunities.

BT still operates primarily in the UK, where it offers local and long-distance phone service with about 28 million access lines. But data now crowds out voice to make up most of BT's network traffic: The company's data services include Internet access and corporate leased lines. BT Cellnet is the #2 UK mobile phone operator (behind Vodafone), and BT is expanding its mobile Internet offerings.

In a major restructuring, BT plans to turn itself into a holding company. It intends to spin off its UK fixed-line network into a new company and create a separate retail fixed-line unit, to go along with its broadband ISP (Ignite) and its consumer ISP (BTopenworld). It is placing its domestic and international wireless businesses under the BT Wireless umbrella and spinning off its Yellow Pages businesses as Yell. The company plans to sell off minority stakes in BT Wireless and Yell.

The key to BT's global strategy is a venture with AT&T, called Concert, that combines most of the companies' international operations. BT also owns stakes in telecom and Internet companies throughout Europe, including France's Cegetel and Germany's VIAG Interkom.

HISTORY

In 1879 the British Post Office got the exclusive right to operate telegraph systems. When private firms tried to offer phone service, the government objected, arguing in court that its telegraph monopoly was imperiled. The courts agreed, and the Post Office was empowered to license private phone companies, collect a 10% royalty, and operate its own systems. The National Telephone Company, a private firm, emerged as the leading telephone outfit, competing with the Post Office. When National Telephone's license expired in 1911, the Post Office took over and became the monopoly phone company.

In 1936 the phone system introduced its familiar red public call offices (phone booths in US parlance). The kiosks were designed by Sir Giles Gilbert Scott for King George V's jubilee. Under a 1981 law, telecommunications were split from the Post Office and placed under the new British Telecommunications (BT). The government also allowed competitor Mercury Communications — a joint effort of Cable and Wireless (C&W), British Petroleum (BP), and Barclays Merchant Bank — to enter the marketplace. (C&W bought out BP and Barclays in 1984.) The Thatcher government soon called for the privatization of BT.

After the Telecommunications Act of 1984, BT went public in one of the largest UK stock offerings in history. The act set up an Office of Telecommunications (OFTEL) to regulate BT. The next year Cellnet, BT's joint venture with Securicor, launched its mobile phone network.

BT bought control of Canadian telephone equipment maker Mitel (1986) and 20% of US cellular firm McCaw Cellular (1989, sold to AT&T in 1994).

In 1990 the British government opened the UK to more phone competition. Challengers included cable companies offering phone service (many owned by US Baby Bells), cellular companies, and European carriers such as France Telecom. BT responded by improving its network and cutting about 100,000 jobs.

The government sold almost all its remaining shares in BT in 1993. The next year the company bought a 20% stake in MCI, the US's #2 long-distance carrier, and the two formed the Concert Communications Services joint venture to compete in the international arena.

In 1996 BT announced its plan to buy out MCI, but as losses mounted from MCI's expansion into the US local market, BT in 1997 lowered its bid and lost MCI to upstart WorldCom, which changed its name to MCI Worldcom, then back to WorldCom. In 1998 BT bought the remaining 25% stake in Concert. But BT found a new US partner in AT&T, and the two agreed in 1999 to merge most of their international operations (including Concert) in a global joint venture, called Concert.

Also in 1999 BT landed other deals overseas in continental Europe, Latin America (a 20% stake in ImpSat), Asia (with AT&T, a 30% stake in Japan Telecom), and the US, where it bought systems integration firm Control Data Systems and Yellow Book USA. At home BT bought out Securicor's stake in Cellnet (now BT Cellnet). In 2000 the UK government sold its remaining stake in the company, making BT's privatization complete.

Chairman, British Telecommunications and Concert:
Sir Iain Vallance, age 57, $708,000 pay
Deputy Chairman: Lord Marshall of Knightsbridge,
age 66, $75,000 pay
Chief Executive: Sir Peter Bonfield, age 55,
$1,225,000 pay
Group Finance Director: Philip Hampton
Group Managing Director BT UK: Bill Cockburn,
age 57, $740,000 pay
CEO, Ignite: Alfred Mockett
CEO, BTopenworld: Andy Green
CEO, BT Wireless: Peter Erskine
Chairman, Yellow Book USA: John Condron
CEO, BT Wholesale: Paul Reynolds
CEO, BT Retail: Pierre Danon, age 44
Group Personnel Manager: John Steele
Auditors: PricewaterhouseCoopers

HQ: BT Centre, 81 Newgate St.,
London EC1A 7AJ, United Kingdom
Phone: +44-20-7356-5000   **Fax:** +44-20-7356-5520
US HQ: 40 E. 52nd St., New York, NY 10022
US Phone: 212-418-7787   **US Fax:** 212-418-7788
Web site: http://www.bt.com

British Telecommunications operates primarily in the
UK, but it owns or has stakes in operations in about 50
other countries, including Argentina, Australia, Belgium,
Brazil, Canada, China, Colombia, Ecuador, France,
Germany, Hong Kong, India, Indonesia, Ireland, Italy,
Japan, Korea, Malaysia, Mexico, New Zealand, the
Netherlands, the Philippines, Singapore, South Africa,
Spain, Sweden, Switzerland, Thailand, Taiwan, the US,
and Venezuela.

2000 Sales

	$ mil.	% of total
Fixed network	9,414	32
Exchange line	5,618	19
Mobile communications	3,458	12
Private services	1,808	6
Customer-premises equipment supply	1,350	4
Yellow Pages & other directories	1,023	3
Other sales & services	4,004	13
Other operations	3,145	11
Total	**29,820**	**100**

Selected Subsidiaries and Affiliates
BT (Worldwide) Limited (international networks)
BT Cellnet (mobile phone operator)
BT North America Inc. (communications services and
products, US)
Concert (international telecom joint venture with AT&T)
Yellow Book USA (yellow pages publishing, US)

America Online	Deutsche	SITA
Andersen	Telekom	Telecom
Consulting	E.ON	Corporation of
BCE	Energis	New Zealand
Cable and	France Telecom	Telecom Italia
Wireless	Freeserve	Telefónica
COLT Telecom	Global One	Tesco
Computer	Infonet Services	Unisys
Sciences	NTL	Virgin Group
Demon Internet	One 2 One	Vodafone
	Orange	WorldCom

NYSE: BTY FYE: March 31	Annual Growth	3/91	3/92	3/93	3/94	3/95	3/96	3/97	3/98	3/99	3/00
Sales ($ mil.)	2.9%	23,000	23,153	20,035	20,307	22,521	22,048	24,486	26,145	27,322	29,820
Net income ($ mil.)	(1.2%)	3,637	3,548	1,846	2,624	2,806	3,031	3,405	2,852	4,807	3,274
Income as % of sales	—	15.8%	15.3%	9.2%	12.9%	12.5%	13.7%	13.9%	10.9%	17.6%	11.0%
Earnings per share ($)	(2.1%)	5.94	5.76	3.00	4.23	4.51	4.82	5.38	4.46	7.30	4.92
Stock price - FY high ($)	—	64.50	74.00	70.63	74.88	64.88	65.50	73.75	115.25	181.25	245.00
Stock price - FY low ($)	—	40.75	54.13	53.88	57.00	53.88	50.75	49.25	60.75	102.25	143.00
Stock price - FY close ($)	13.4%	60.88	54.75	66.75	57.50	63.25	56.63	70.00	109.38	164.19	188.13
P/E - high	—	11	13	24	18	14	14	14	26	24	45
P/E - low	—	7	9	18	13	12	11	9	14	14	26
Dividends per share ($)	3.2%	2.67	2.71	2.88	2.54	2.84	2.97	1.85	0.00	5.46	3.54
Book value per share ($)	2.8%	30.08	33.13	29.89	31.14	31.19	30.75	28.68	28.12	37.22	38.68
Employees	1.1%	—	—	—	—	—	130,700	127,500	129,200	124,700	136,800

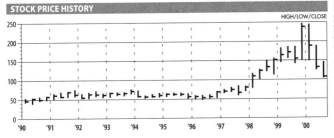

HIGH/LOW/CLOSE

Debt ratio: 25.3%
Return on equity: 13.3%
Cash ($ mil.): 403
Current ratio: 0.52
Long-term debt ($ mil.): 8,531
No. of shares (mil.): 651
Dividends
  Yield: 1.9%
  Payout: 72.0%
Market value ($ mil.): 122,416

BULL

OVERVIEW

Bull thinks the potential of the e-economy is no bull. Louveciennes, France-based Bull has moved beyond its roots in computer hardware to focus on information technology (IT) and e-commerce services such as systems integration, deployment, and outsourcing. Bull's products include network management and security software, smart cards and payment terminals, and computer hardware such as PCs, laptops, and servers. Bull's clients come primarily from the government, finance, telecommunications, and manufacturing markets. Clients in Western Europe account for more than 80% of sales.

Restructuring costs have gored Bull's earnings. The company is still seeing red despite improving sales in its service sectors, mainly because of charges related to layoffs and global services business development.

The French government, Japanese computer maker NEC, Motorola, and state-owned France Telecom each owns about 17% of Bull.

HISTORY

Bull is named for Norwegian engineer Fredrik Bull, who in 1921 invented a punch card machine. Georges Vieillard, a French bank employee, bought the patents for Bull's machine in 1931. Vieillard, who wanted to develop a better adding machine, persuaded the owners of a punch card supplier to finance his venture, and Compagnie des Machines Bull was incorporated in Paris in 1933.

The company started competing with IBM in 1935, after unveiling a tabulator capable of printing up to 150 lines a minute. Bull went on to confound its American rival by pioneering the use of germanium diodes (instead of electron tubes) in its first mainframe computer (1952). But the battle of one-upmanship was costly. Bull defaulted on a $4 million loan payment in 1964 and, faced with financial ruin, jumped at the chance when General Electric (US) offered to buy a 50% stake (later increased to 66%). The company (renamed Bull-GE) continued to lose money until 1969. It became Compagnie Honeywell Bull in 1970 when GE sold its computer businesses to Honeywell.

Meanwhile, in 1966 the French government had formed Compagnie Internationale pour l'Informatique (CII) to ensure the survival of the French computer industry. CII merged with Honeywell Bull in 1975 to form CII-Honeywell Bull (CII-HB). Initially Honeywell owned a 47% stake in the company, but in 1982 it accepted a gradual buyout offer from the French government. CII-HB then merged with three other French computer companies (Transac, Sems, and R2E) to form Groupe Bull in 1983.

In 1987 the company entered a US-based three-way mainframe computer partnership (Honeywell Bull) with Honeywell and NEC. Originally owning 42.5% of the venture, Bull upped its share to 72% and renamed it Bull HN Information Systems. In 1989 the company bought Zenith's ZDS, a leading US laptop and PC maker.

In 1991 the company acquired the rest of Bull HN. The next year the European Commission approved a state injection of $1.3 billion into debt-laden Bull. In 1993 the firm bought a 19.9% stake in Packard Bell, and teamed it with Zenith Data Systems to jointly develop desktop PCs.

Jean-Marie Descarpentries was named CEO in 1993 (the company's third CEO in as many years). He reduced Bull's Paris offices from 25 to five and reorganized the sprawling conglomerate. In 1995 Bull recorded a small profit, its first since 1988.

To improve Packard Bell's cash flow, in 1996 Bull and NEC provided a $650 million infusion — partly in cash and partly through Packard Bell's acquisition of Zenith. (As part of the deal, Bull got a minority interest in Packard Bell NEC.)

In 1997 Descarpentries stepped down as chairman. He was succeeded by former Lyonnaise des Eaux (now Suez Lyonnaise) executive Guy de Panafieu, who invested in the company's infrastructure (to the detriment of earnings) to expand its core strengths in servers, services, and new software technology. In 1998 the company shortened its name to Bull and bought NBS Technology's European smart card operations. Restructuring costs slashed 1998 earnings.

In 1999 Bull began providing services in Europe for Microsoft software. That year Packard Bell NEC's operations were folded into NEC, and the Packard Bell brand name was eliminated. Bull said it would take up to about a $230 million charge related to the closing.

Bull continued to tweak its bulky corporate structure in 2000, selling off several units, including its printer manufacturing operations. Bull formed subsidiary Evidian to boost its e-business security software line. It also acquired Arcanet, Italy's leading telecom applications company.

OFFICERS

Chairman and CEO: Guy de Panafieu
COO: Cyrille du Peloux
EVP Evidian: Henry Ancona
EVP Consulting and Systems Integration:
Werner Fuhrmann
EVP Finance and Administration: Gervais Pellissier
EVP Human Resources: Jacques Chevallier
EVP Infrastructure and Systems: Didier Breton
EVP Infrastructure and Systems: Hervé Mouren
EVP Marketing and Communications:
Catherine Dumesnil
EVP Outsourcing and Support Services: Noël Saille
EVP Sales: Alain Zeitoun
EVP Smart Cards and Terminals Division: David Lévy
EVP, Strategy, Technology, and Partnerships; General Manager, North and South America: Don Zereski
VP, Business Development, North American E-Business: Colin Scott
Auditors: Deloitte Touche Tohmatsu

LOCATIONS

HQ: 68, route de Versailles, 78430 Louveciennes, France
Phone: +33-1-39-66-60-60   **Fax:** +33-1-39-66-60-62
US HQ: 300 Concord Rd., Billerica, MA 01821
US Phone: 978-294-6000   **US Fax:** 978-294-3635
Web site: http://www.bull.com

Bull has offices in nearly 100 countries.

1999 Sales

	€ mil.	% of total
Western Europe	3,130	83
North America	263	7
Other regions	376	10
Total	**3,769**	**100**

PRODUCTS/OPERATIONS

1999 Sales

	€ mil.	% of total
Services		
Outsourcing & support services	1,129	30
Consulting & systems integration	894	24
Products		
Infrastructure & systems	1,513	40
Smart cards & terminals	180	5
BullSoft (software)	60	1
Adjustments	(7)	—
Total	**3,769**	**100**

Services	
Customer support	Servers (GCOS, Intel, UNIX)
Consulting	Storage products (EMC
Systems integration	and Epoch)
Products	Smart cards, terminals, and related equipment
Communications products (France Telecom, Motorola, 3COM)	Software (security, networking, and Web applications)
PCs (NEC)	

COMPETITORS

Amdahl	EDS	NCR
Andersen	Finsiel	NEC
Consulting	Fujitsu	Oki Electric
Apple Computer	Gateway	Samsung
Atos Origin	Gemplus	Sema Group
Cap Gemini	Getronics	SGI
Capita	Hewlett-Packard	Siemens
CMG	Hitachi	Software AG
Compaq	IBM	Sun
Computer	ICL	Microsystems
Associates	Intel	Toshiba
Dell Computer	Logica	Unisys

HISTORICAL FINANCIALS & EMPLOYEES

Euronext Paris: BUL FYE: December 31	Annual Growth	12/90	12/91	12/92	12/93	12/94	12/95	12/96	12/97	12/98	12/99
Sales (€ mil.)	(3.7%)	5,272	5,099	4,602	4,307	4,561	4,064	3,666	3,752	3,801	3,769
Net income (€ mil.)	—	(1,035)	(503)	(720)	(773)	(299)	47	57	92	3	(288)
Income as % of sales	—	—	—	—	—	—	1.1%	1.6%	2.5%	0.1%	—
Earnings per share (€)	—	—	—	—	—	—	0.48	0.43	0.59	0.02	(1.74)
Stock price - FY high (€)	—	—	—	—	—	—	12.44	10.73	11.09	16.31	10.34
Stock price - FY low (€)	—	—	—	—	—	—	1.84	4.13	4.80	4.80	4.87
Stock price - FY close (€)	16.0%	—	—	—	—	—	4.41	4.70	9.67	6.39	7.99
P/E - high	—	—	—	—	—	—	26	25	19	816	—
P/E - low	—	—	—	—	—	—	4	10	8	240	—
Dividends per share (€)	—	—	—	—	—	—	0.00	0.00	0.00	0.00	0.00
Book value per share (€)	(6.0%)	—	—	—	—	—	2.27	2.84	3.51	3.37	1.78
Employees	(9.4%)	44,476	39,878	35,175	31,735	27,902	24,000	21,700	21,267	20,646	18,358

STOCK PRICE HISTORY

HIGH/LOW/CLOSE

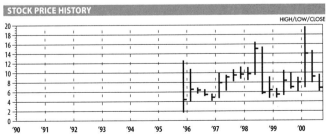

1999 FISCAL YEAR-END

Debt ratio: 33.5%
Return on equity: —
Cash (€ mil.): 154
Current ratio: 1.13
Long-term debt (€ mil.): 148
No. of shares (mil.): 165
Dividends
  Yield: —
  Payout: —
Market value ($ mil.): 1,328
Sales ($ mil.): 3,787

CABLE AND WIRELESS PLC

OVERVIEW

Telegraph cables and short-wave radio have given way to new-spun webs of optical fiber, but Cable and Wireless nonetheless promotes its name like never before. Guided by a new focus on the corporate data and Internet market, London-based Cable and Wireless (C&W) provides telecommunications services in 70 countries worldwide.

C&W, which has been re-branding far-flung subsidiaries with its famous name, remains a major provider of international voice and traditional telephone services in several countries. Its 53%-owned Cable & Wireless Optus is a leading competitor to Telstra in Australia.

The company's primary aim, however, is to be a leading worldwide player in the business IP (Internet protocol) market. A new business unit, Cable & Wireless Global, provides Internet access, data transport, LAN design and installation, and Web hosting — all supported by C&W's international connections and its major fiber-optic networks spanning Europe and the US. C&W has sharpened this IP focus through acquisitions and divestitures.

C&W has sold its stake in UK mobile phone operator One 2 One, its UK consumer telephony and cable TV businesses, and its majority stake in the former Cable & Wireless HKT, Hong Kong's dominant telecom. Meanwhile, C&W has been buying business ISPs throughout Europe, has accelerated the build-out of its European network, and has opened the first of its data centers for Web hosting.

HISTORY

British cable and telegraph veteran John Pender began Eastern Telegraph in 1872. When Pender died in 1896, Eastern and associated companies owned one of every three miles of telegraph cable on the planet.

As the new century began, telecommunications expanded to include the wireless radio communications promoted by inventor Guglielmo Marconi, head of the UK's Marconi Wireless Telegraph. After WWI, the industry grew in importance, and, partly to counter a threat from a new US company called ITT, UK companies, including Marconi Wireless and Eastern Telegraph, joined to form Cable and Wireless (C&W) in 1929.

C&W began providing telegraph and telephone services in the UK's far-flung colonies, from Hong Kong to the Philippines to the Cayman Islands. It was nationalized in 1947, and in the 1950s C&W began losing franchises in former colonies or had local governments strip it of its monopolies.

The Thatcher government returned C&W to private ownership in 1985. C&W began building a network of undersea fiber-optic cables and satellites to link the Caribbean, Hong Kong, Japan, the UK, and the US. To complete the task, C&W assembled the world's largest commercial fleet of cable ships.

C&W joined British Petroleum (BP) and Barclays Merchant Bank in 1982 to form Mercury Communications as a rival to giant British Telecom (BT). C&W bought out BP and Barclays in 1984. The next year Mercury won the right to interconnect with BT.

As the 1990s began, C&W was adrift. In 1993 C&W and U S WEST's cable unit (later MediaOne) launched a digital cellular service — One 2 One — in the UK, but overall C&W wasn't making much headway in Europe. In 1996 merger talks with BT to build the world's largest telecom company failed. Dick Brown, an American, was named C&W's CEO. Under Brown's direction C&W disposed of underperforming assets and created Cable & Wireless Communications (CWC) by combining Mercury with cable firms NYNEX CableComms, Bell Cablemedia, and Videotron.

When the UK handed over Hong Kong to China in 1997, C&W — in a bid to get access to the mainland market — sold a stake in Hong Kong Telecom to China Telecom. When MCI agreed to merge with WorldCom in 1998, C&W bought MCI's Internet business (later selling the US dial-up operation to Prodigy).

Hong Kong Telecom became Cable & Wireless HKT in 1999. Brown left that year and was succeeded by Graham Wallace, former boss of CWC. C&W won a bidding war with NTT for Japan's International Digital Communications. C&W sold its undersea-cable operations to Global Crossing and struck a deal to sell its UK consumer phone and cable TV business to rival NTL. It also sold One 2 One for about $11 billion to Deutsche Telekom.

More such activity continued in 2000. To build its European Internet presence, C&W agreed to spend $1 billion to buy eight business ISPs and expand its network. It formed the Cable & Wireless Global business unit to consolidate its worldwide Internet Protocol (IP) network operations. The company also completed the sale of Cable & Wireless HKT to Pacific Century CyberWorks.

OFFICERS

Chairman: Ralph Robbins, age 67
Deputy Chairman: Sir Winfried F. W. Bischoff, age 59
Chief Executive: Graham M. Wallace, age 51
Executive Director Finance: Robert E. Lerwill, age 48
Executive Director Corporate Development:
Stephen R. Pettit, age 49
CEO, Global Operations: Mike McTighe
CEO, Regional Businesses: Don Reed
President, Cable & Wireless USA: Alan Gibbs
Company Secretary: Ken Claydon
Director, Group Human Resources: Martin Hayton
Auditors: KPMG Audit Plc

LOCATIONS

HQ: 124 Theobalds Rd., London WC1X 8RX,
United Kingdom
Phone: +44-20-7315-4000   **Fax:** +44-20-7315-5000
US HQ: 8219 Leesburg Pike, Vienna, VA 22182
US Phone: 703-790-5300   **US Fax:** 703-848-0748
Web site: http://www.cwplc.com

Cable and Wireless has operations in about 70 countries, including Australia, the Caribbean region (including Antigua, the Cayman Islands, Jamaica, Panama, and Trinidad), Hong Kong, the UK, and the US.

2000 Sales

	$ mil.	% of total
UK	4,420	30
Hong Kong	3,590	24
Australia	2,629	18
Caribbean	1,546	11
North America	1,415	10
Other	1,061	7
Total	**14,661**	**100**

PRODUCTS/OPERATIONS

2000 Sales

	$ mil.	% of total
Business		
Voice	6,490	44
Data	2,432	17
IP	894	6
Consumer	4,431	30
Other	414	3
Total	**14,661**	**100**

Selected Subsidiaries and Affiliates
Cable and Wireless (WI) Ltd. (British Virgin Islands)
Cable & Wireless Global
Cable & Wireless Grenada (70%)
Cable & Wireless IDC (98%, Japan)
Cable & Wireless Optus Limited (53%, Australia)
Optus@Home (joint venture with Excite@Home)
Cable & Wireless USA
Eastern Telecommunications Philippines, Inc. (40%)
Telecommunications Services of Trinidad & Tobago Ltd.
(TSTT, 49%)

COMPETITORS

AT&T	France Telecom	Telecom Italia
BBC	Global Crossing	Teleglobe
BellSouth	Infonet Services	Telewest
BSkyB	NTL	Telstra
BT	PSINet	Verizon
Deutsche	SBC	WorldCom
Telekom	Communications	
Equant	Sprint	

HISTORICAL FINANCIALS & EMPLOYEES

NYSE: CWP FYE: March 31	Annual Growth	3/91	3/92	3/93	3/94	3/95	3/96	3/97	3/98	3/99	3/00
Sales ($ mil.)	13.9%	4,534	5,514	5,788	6,978	8,320	8,420	9,919	11,704	12,803	14,661
Net income ($ mil.)	41.0%	585	562	778	764	409	926	1,110	2,153	1,463	12,905
Income as % of sales	—	12.9%	10.2%	13.4%	10.9%	4.9%	11.0%	11.2%	18.4%	11.4%	88.0%
Earnings per share ($)	27.3%	0.82	0.79	1.08	1.05	0.56	1.57	1.49	2.86	1.82	7.21
Stock price - FY high ($)	—	15.69	16.81	16.81	25.13	22.50	25.25	25.50	38.63	49.88	75.25
Stock price - FY low ($)	—	10.81	12.38	13.38	16.00	16.50	19.00	18.25	22.50	25.75	32.00
Stock price - FY close ($)	17.2%	13.44	13.38	16.50	20.25	18.88	24.25	23.75	37.75	36.94	56.00
P/E - high	—	19	21	16	24	40	16	17	14	30	10
P/E - low	—	13	16	12	15	29	12	12	8	16	4
Dividends per share ($)	8.0%	0.34	0.37	0.38	0.36	0.42	0.49	0.61	0.00	0.20	0.68
Book value per share ($)	12.6%	5.47	5.70	6.31	6.68	7.40	6.72	6.74	6.82	9.70	15.86
Employees	8.5%	—	—	—	—	—	39,636	37,488	46,550	50,671	54,919

STOCK PRICE HISTORY

HIGH/LOW/CLOSE

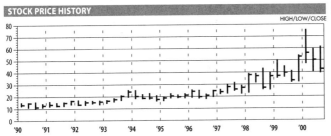

2000 FISCAL YEAR-END

Debt ratio: 40.4%
Return on equity: 127.4%
Cash ($ mil.): 7,948
Current ratio: 1.68
Long-term debt ($ mil.): 8,738
No. of shares (mil.): 813
Dividends
  Yield: 1.2%
  Payout: 9.4%
Market value ($ mil.): 45,551

CADBURY SCHWEPPES PLC

Did a Cadbury bar stain your shirt? Some Schweppes club soda will get it out. London-based Cadbury Schweppes is a leading confectioner worldwide and the world's #3 soft-drink producer. Its confections are the market leaders in the UK, with mainstay brands Cadbury, including the famous Créme Egg, and Trebor. Its US candy brands — which include Cadbury, Peter Paul, and York — are licensed to Hershey Foods. In other countries, the firm markets its powerful Cadbury brand with regional brands such as Bim Bim (Egypt), Poulain (France), and Wedel (Poland).

Through subsidiary Dr Pepper/Seven Up, Cadbury Schweppes has about 15% of the US market for soft drinks (well behind The Coca-Cola Company's 44% and PepsiCo's 31%). Its key beverage brands include Dr Pepper, 7 UP (US, Puerto Rico; PepsiCo owns 7 UP outside the US), and Schweppes; others include A&W Root Beer, Canada Dry, Clamato, Crush, Hawaiian Punch, and Mott's.

Cadbury Schweppes sold much of its beverage business in 160 countries to Coca-Cola and now operates mainly in Australia, North America, and Western Europe. Additionally, it bought Pepsi Cola Bottlers Australia, which increased Cadbury Schweppes' market share in Australia to 25%. The company also bought Snapple Beverage Group (maker of Snapple drinks and Royal Crown Cola, among others) from Triarc Companies. It also owns approximately 25% of the Camelot Group, which operates the UK's National Lottery.

Cadbury Schweppes is the product of a merger between two venerable British firms: Schweppes, the world's first soft-drink maker, and Cadbury, a candy confectionery. Schweppes began in 1783 in London, where Swiss national Jacob Schweppe first sold his artificial mineral water. The company introduced a lemonade in 1835 and tonic water (containing antimalarial quinine) and ginger ale in the 1870s. Beginning in the 1880s Schweppes expanded worldwide. In the 1960s it diversified into food products.

John Cadbury opened a coffee and tea shop in Birmingham, England, in 1824. He sold cocoa for drinking, which proved so popular that in 1831 he began making cocoa and was producing 15 varieties of chocolates by 1841. The Cadbury's Dairy Milk bar, launched in 1905, became Britain's best-selling candy bar. Cadbury had established dominant market positions across the British Empire by the early 1900s.

The companies merged in 1969. Under Dominic Cadbury (great-grandson of founder John), Cadbury Schweppes acquired Peter Paul (Mounds, Almond Joy) in 1978 while increasing beverage sales in Europe and Asia. In 1982 it acquired applesauce and juice maker Duffy-Mott.

Cadbury Schweppes' businesses seemed to thrive during the next few years, but by 1985 British candy demand slowed, and US candy distributors' stockpiling accounted for much of the perceived growth in sales. The firm was restructured the next year and sold its non-candy and non-beverage businesses. It then acquired Canada Dry, the rights to Sunkist soda, and 34% of Dr Pepper (reduced to 18% when Dr Pepper merged with Seven Up in 1988).

Fatigued by Mars' and Hershey Foods' US dominance, Cadbury Schweppes signed a licensing agreement with Hershey in 1988, ending its direct involvement in the US candy market. The company added the Orange Crush and Hires brands in 1989, and it acquired candy makers Trebor and Bassett and the non-cola soft-drink operations of Source Perrier in 1990.

The Camelot Group, a UK consortium that includes Cadbury Schweppes, was picked in 1994 to operate the UK's National Lottery. Cadbury Schweppes had built up a 25% stake in Dr Pepper/Seven Up by 1995, when it bought the remainder for $2.5 billion, making it the world's #3 soft-drink company. John Sunderland was appointed chief executive of Cadbury Schweppes in 1996.

As part of the company's plan to narrow its focus, in 1999 Cadbury Schweppes sold its beverage operations in more than 160 countries (excluding Australia, Continental Europe, and the US) to The Coca-Cola Company for $973 million. Also in 1999 Cadbury Schweppes bought the Hawaiian Punch brand from Procter & Gamble for $203 million.

In October 2000 the company acquired Snapple Beverage Group (including the Royal Crown Cola, Snapple, Mistic, and Stewart's brands) from Triarc Companies in a deal worth about $1.45 billion. Deciding to continue soft-drink operations in Australia, that month Cadbury Schweppes also bought Pepsi Cola Bottlers Australia (a joint venture between Lion Nathan and Pepsi Cola), giving it a 25% market share in that country. In November 2000 the company bought Chinese chewing gum-maker Wuxi-Leaf Confectionery.

Chairman: Derek Bonham, age 56
Group Chief Executive: John M. Sunderland,
$1,544,000 pay
COO: John F. Brock, $1,280,000 pay
(prior to promotion)
Group Finance Director: David J. Kappler,
$1,037,000 pay
President and CEO, Dr Pepper/Seven UP: Doug Tough
President, Mott's: Brad Irwin
Group Secretary and Chief Legal Officer:
Mike A. C. Clark
Chief Human Resources Officer: Robert J. Stack,
age 48, $733,000 pay
Chief Strategy Officer: Todd Stitzer, age 47
Investor Relations Director: Sally Jones
Managing Director Asia/Pacific: Gil Cassagne
Auditors: Arthur Andersen

HQ: 25 Berkeley Sq., London W1X 6HT,
United Kingdom
Phone: +44-20-7409-1313   **Fax:** +44-20-7830-5200
US HQ: 5301 Legacy Dr., Plano, TX 75024
US Phone: 972-637-7000   **US Fax:**
Web site: http://www.cadburyschweppes.com

1999 Sales & Operating Income

	Sales		Operating Income	
	$ mil.	% of total	$ mil.	% of total
Europe				
UK	1,598	23	197	17
Other countries	1,322	19	100	9
The Americas	2,695	39	624	55
Pacific Rim	878	13	155	14
Africa & other regions	457	6	57	5
Total	**6,950**	**100**	**1,133**	**100**

1999 Sales & Operating Income

	Sales		Operating Income	
	$ mil.	% of total	$ mil.	% of total
Confections	3,608	52	473	42
Beverages				
Continuing	3,234	47	634	56
Discontinued	108	1	26	2
Total	**6,950**	**100**	**1,133**	**100**

Selected Brand Names

Confections
Bim Bim (Egypt)
Cadbury
Cadbury's Dairy Milk
Peter Paul
Sharps (UK)
Trebor
York

Beverages
7 UP (US and Puerto Rico)
A&W Root Beer
Canada Dry

Crush
Dr Pepper (Australia,
    Canada, Europe, Mexico,
    US)
Hawaiian Punch
Mott's
Nehi
RC Cola
Schweppes
Snapple
Squirt
Sunkist (licensed)
Welch's (licensed, US)

Archibald Candy
Bass
Campbell Soup
Coca-Cola
Cott
CSM
Ferolito,
    Vultaggio
Herman Goelitz
    Candy

Hershey
Kraft Foods
    International
Lindt & Sprungli
Mars
National
    Beverage
National Grape
    Cooperative
Nestle

Ocean Spray
PepsiCo
Pernod Ricard
Russell Stover
See's Candies
Tootsie Roll
Virgin Group
Whitman

NYSE: CSG FYE: Saturday nearest Dec. 31	Annual Growth	12/90	12/91	12/92	12/93	12/94	12/95	12/96	12/97	12/98	12/99
Sales ($ mil.)	1.5%	6,072	6,043	5,108	5,511	6,306	7,417	8,759	6,893	6,814	6,950
Net income ($ mil.)	13.0%	346	380	296	360	422	480	591	1,143	589	1,037
Income as % of sales	—	5.7%	6.3%	5.8%	6.5%	6.7%	6.5%	6.7%	16.6%	8.6%	14.9%
Earnings per share ($)	8.4%	0.98	1.04	0.81	0.91	0.99	0.97	1.17	3.52	1.16	2.02
Stock price - FY high ($)	—	13.43	16.13	19.19	15.56	16.25	17.69	17.88	21.97	35.06	34.63
Stock price - FY low ($)	—	10.03	11.30	13.44	12.69	12.50	12.31	14.38	15.06	20.13	22.25
Stock price - FY close ($)	7.9%	12.25	16.06	13.69	15.00	13.50	16.63	17.06	20.69	34.56	24.19
P/E - high	—	14	16	24	17	16	18	15	6	30	17
P/E - low	—	10	11	17	14	13	13	12	4	17	11
Dividends per share ($)	4.6%	0.44	0.47	0.50	0.66	0.61	1.22	1.08	0.27	0.46	0.66
Book value per share ($)	6.1%	4.22	4.67	4.43	4.87	5.65	4.12	4.41	5.46	6.01	7.16
Employees	(4.5%)	—	—	—	—	—	42,911	41,320	38,656	37,425

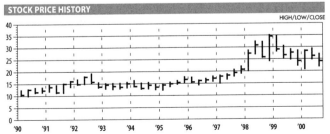

HIGH/LOW/CLOSE

Debt ratio: 12.2%
Return on equity: 31.1%
Cash ($ mil.): 244
Current ratio: 1.03
Long-term debt ($ mil.): 503
No. of shares (mil.): 505
Dividends
    Yield: 2.7%
    Payout: 32.7%
Market value ($ mil.): 12,222

CANADIAN IMPERIAL BANK

OVERVIEW

What's an empire to do when it starts to feel stodgy but certain growth avenues have been closed? Toronto-based Canadian Imperial Bank of Commerce (CIBC), Canada's #2 bank (Royal Bank of Canada is #1), has tried to grow through megamergers and diversification (both stopped short by the government) and now faces the prospect of good old-fashioned organic expansion.

CIBC operates in four segments: retail banking, small business banking, corporate and investment banking, and wealth management. Through its more than 1,200 branches, the bank offers deposit and loan products, credit

cards, and such investment services as brokerage, mutual funds, trust services, and investment management to its consumer and commercial clients. Its broker-dealer arm, CIBC World Markets, underwrites securities, advises on mergers and acquisitions, arranges corporate finance, and provides debt, equity, derivatives, and foreign exchange trading services.

As it continues to wait for significant financial reform to sweep overbanked Canada, CIBC has focused on its core banking operations. To build its customer base, the bank is targeting small businesses in Canada and retail banking customers in growing cities in the US.

HISTORY

In 1858 Bank of Canada was chartered; Toronto financier William McMaster bought the charter in 1866 when investors failed to raise enough money to open it and changed the name to Canadian Bank of Commerce.

Canadian Bank of Commerce opened in 1867, bought the Gore Bank of Hamilton (1870), and expanded within seven years to 24 branches in Ontario as well as Montreal and New York. Led by Edmund Walker, the bank spread west of the Great Lakes with the opening of a Winnipeg, Manitoba, branch in 1893 and joined the Gold Rush with branches in Dawson City, Yukon Territory, and Skagway, Alaska, in 1898.

As the new century began, the bank's purchases spanned the breadth of Canada, from the Bank of British Columbia (1901) to Halifax Banking (1903) and the Merchants Bank of Prince Edward Island (1906). More buys followed in the 1920s; the bank's assets peaked in 1929 and then plunged during the Depression. It recovered during WWII.

In 1961 Canadian Bank of Commerce merged with Imperial Bank of Canada to become Canadian Imperial Bank of Commerce. Imperial Bank was founded in 1875 by Henry Howland; it went west to Calgary and Edmonton and became known as "The Mining Bank." It bought Barclays Bank (Canada) in 1956.

As the energy and agriculture sectors declined in the early 1980s, two of CIBC's largest borrowers, Dome Petroleum and tractor maker Massey Ferguson, defaulted on their loans. Donald Fullerton became the bank's CEO in 1984 and slashed costs, increasing profits to record levels. Earnings were hit again in 1987 when Brazil, a big CIBC creditor, suspended payment on its foreign debts.

Deregulation opened investment banking to

CIBC, which in 1988 bought a majority share of Wood Gundy, one of Canada's largest investment dealers; CIBC also purchased Merrill Lynch Canada's retail brokerage business.

In 1992 CIBC added substantially to its loss reserves (resulting in an earnings drop of 98%) to cover real estate losses from developer Olympia & York and others. This launched more cost-cutting as the company reorganized by operating segments.

Deregulation allowed CIBC to begin selling insurance in 1993; the company built a collection of life, credit, personal property/casualty, and nonmedical health companies.

In 1996 the bank formed Intria, a processing and technical support subsidiary. The next year CIBC Wood Gundy became CIBC World Markets, and CIBC bought securities firm Oppenheimer & Co. and added its stock underwriting and brokerage abilities to CIBC World Markets.

In 1998, increasing foreign competition prompted CIBC and Toronto-Dominion to plan a merger (as did Royal Bank of Canada and Bank of Montreal); the government halted both plans citing Canada's already highly concentrated banking industry.

Spurned, the bank overhauled its operations to spark growth in the late 1990s. To cut costs it eliminated some 4,000 jobs and sold its more than $1 billion real estate portfolio. It teamed with Winn-Dixie (1999) and Safeway (2000) supermarket chains to operate electronic branches in the US and thus penetrate the lucrative US retail banking market; it also announced plans for a small-business banking subsidiary at home (2000). The firm scaled back its disappointing international operations and began selling its insurance units.

Chairman and CEO: John S. Hunkin
VC CIBC World Markets: David Kassie
VC Electronic Commerce, Technology, and Operations:
  David Marshall
VC Treasury and Balance Sheet Management:
  Wayne C. Fox
SEVP and Chief Administrative Officer: Ron Lalonde
SEVP Corporate Development; Chairman and CEO,
  CIBC World Markets Inc.: Richard E. Venn
SEVP Retail and Business Banking: Mike Pedersen
SEVP Risk Management: Gerry E. Beasley
SEVP Wealth Management: Gerry McCaughey
EVP and CFO: John C. Doran
EVP Human Resources: Joyce Phillips
EVP Legal and Compliance: Michael Capatides
Auditors: Arthur Andersen LLP;
  PricewaterhouseCoopers LLP

LOCATIONS

HQ: Canadian Imperial Bank of Commerce,
  Commerce Ct., Toronto, Ontario M5L 1A2, Canada
Phone: 416-980-2211   Fax: 416-980-5026
US HQ: 425 Lexington Ave., New York, NY 10017
US Phone: 212-856-4000   US Fax: 212-856-4178
Web site: http://www.cibc.com

Canadian Imperial Bank of Commerce has operations in
Asia, Europe, North America, and the Caribbean.

1999 Sales

	% of total
Canada	57
US	26
Caribbean	12
Other countries	5
Total	**100**

PRODUCTS/OPERATIONS

1999 Sales

	$ mil.	% of total
Loan interest	7,623	55
Other interest	2.168	16
Fees	1,881	14
Commissions	803	6
Trading account	397	3
Investment gains	393	3
Other income	419	3
Total	**13,684**	**100**

Selected Subsidiaries
CIBC Australia Holdings Limited
CIBC Finance Inc.
CIBC Insurance Management Company Limited
CIBC Mortgage Corporation
CIBC Securities Inc.
CIBC (Suisse) S.A. (Switzerland)
CIBC Trust Corporation
CIBC U.K. Holdings Limited
The Dominion Realty Company Limited

COMPETITORS

Bank of America	J.P. Morgan
Bank of Montreal	Lehman Brothers
Bank of New York	Merrill Lynch
Barclays	Morgan Stanley Dean
Bear Stearns	Witter
Chase Manhattan	National Bank of Canada
Citigroup	Paine Webber
Credit Suisse	Royal Bank of Canada
Dai-Ichi Kangyo	Salomon Smith Barney
Deutsche Bank	Holdings
Goldman Sachs	Scotiabank
HSBC Holdings	State Farm
Industrial Bank of Japan	Toronto-Dominion Bank

HISTORICAL FINANCIALS & EMPLOYEES

NYSE: BCM FYE: October 31	Annual Growth	10/90	10/91	10/92	10/93	10/94	10/95	10/96	10/97	10/98	10/99
Assets ($ mil.)	6.3%	97,787	107,769	106,678	106,988	111,608	133,336	148,688	168,996	182,339	170,150
Net income ($ mil.)	0.2%	687	715	10	553	658	755	1,020	1,101	684	699
Income as % of assets	—	0.7%	0.7%	0.0%	0.5%	0.6%	0.6%	0.7%	0.7%	0.4%	0.4%
Earnings per share ($)	3.4%	—	—	—	—	—	—	—	—	1.46	1.51
Stock price - FY high ($)	—	—	—	—	—	—	—	—	—	41.31	29.19
Stock price - FY low ($)	—	—	—	—	—	—	—	—	—	15.81	19.06
Stock price - FY close ($)	7.8%	—	—	—	—	—	—	—	—	19.94	21.50
P/E - high	—	—	—	—	—	—	—	—	—	28	19
P/E - low	—	—	—	—	—	—	—	—	—	11	13
Dividends per share ($)	(9.2%)	—	—	—	—	—	—	—	—	1.20	1.09
Book value per share ($)	7.6%	—	—	—	—	—	—	—	—	17.36	18.68
Employees	2.8%	35,811	34,593	42,773	41,511	40,807	39,329	41,606	42,446	47,171	46,000

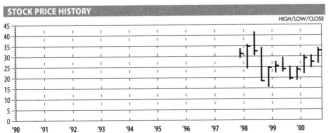

STOCK PRICE HISTORY
HIGH/LOW/CLOSE

1999 FISCAL YEAR-END
Equity as % of assets: 4.4%
Return on assets: 0.4%
Return on equity: 11.5%
Long-term debt ($ mil.): 3,055
No. of shares (mil.): 402
Dividends
  Yield: 5.1%
  Payout: 72.2%
Market value ($ mil.): 8,649
Sales ($ mil.): 13,684

CANAL+

OVERVIEW

Paris-based CANAL+ is the largest pay-television operator in Europe. With about 14 million subscribers (mostly in France, Italy, Poland, and Spain), CANAL+ primarily offers movies and sports, but also offers theme channels. The company is also one of Europe's leading digital TV programmers, with 4 million subscribers. CANAL+ also owns the majority of Paris Saint-Germain, one of France's top soccer clubs.

CANAL+'s government license requires it to invest 9% of its annual revenues in French film production. Through subsidiary Le Studio CANAL+ (which trades separately), the company is involved in the production of French films, and the company owns 35% of Expand, one of Europe's leading TV production companies.

Vivendi has agreed to buy the 51% of CANAL+ it doesn't already own for about $14 billion (it began acquiring a stake in 1983). The utility and media giant also is buying Seagram (owner of Universal Studios) and plans to combine all three firms into a new media giant called Vivendi Universal.

HISTORY

André Rousselet rejected the pay-TV concept in 1982 when he was head of Havas advertising agency. But soon after, he agreed that Havas should enter show business. Havas was under government control, so Rousselet went to his golfing partner, President François Mitterrand, for approval (Rousselet had been Mitterrand's chief of staff). To skirt the Socialist influence on early-1980s France, Rousselet used his political connections to the channel's advantage, easing its entry to the airwaves.

After CANAL+ signed on in 1984, it came to be called "Canal Minus" as subscriptions flattened out and the company lost money. Rousselet, who had left Havas to become chairman of the channel, kept CANAL+ out of bankruptcy by putting the fall 1985 season's slate of movies on in the spring — reasoning that there might not be a CANAL+ over which to air them later. Subscribers responded, and by the end of 1986, the company broke even.

Over the next five years, CANAL+ was a cash factory. It went public in France in 1987; in spite of a market crash, shares sold out. In 1988 the company's profits were higher than the three French networks combined, and it reduced its debt to zero. However, the firm made a bad investment that year when it joined with Compagnie Générale des Eaux to buy TVS (UK), whose US TV production unit, MTM Entertainment, was losing money and later lost its license as a franchisee for the ITV television network in the UK.

In 1990 CANAL+ acquired 5% (later upped to 17%) of independent US production company Carolco, investing in *Terminator 2*, and later co-producing *Basic Instinct*. Both became hits, but Carolco soon started losing money and later sought bankruptcy protection.

CANAL+ expanded more successfully into other countries, establishing channels as part owner with others in Belgium (1989), Spain (1990), Germany (1991), and North Africa (1991). Thematic channels came on line as well. CANAL+ bought 15% of MCM-Euromusique in 1992.

Rousselet resigned in 1994 over increasing government influence in the company's affairs. He was replaced by company president Pierre Lescure. That year CANAL+ signed a deal with Bertelsmann to collaborate on the future development of digital technology for pay TV.

In 1996 the company began offering Europe's first commercial satellite digital television service. It also greatly expanded its program library by buying Carolco Pictures' film library and acquiring UGC DA, with one of the largest program libraries in Europe.

CANAL+ bought Dutch media group Nethold in 1997 in a deal that gave it most of Europe's digital TV market outside Germany and the UK. It raised its stake in one of France's main cable operators, Compagnie Générale de Videocommunication, from 20% to about 77%. It also bowed out of Germany by selling its interest in German channel Premiere to KirchGruppe in exchange for a 45% stake in Italian channel Telepiu.

In 1998 CANAL+ agreed to provide editorial content in a new Internet venture with America Online and Bertelsmann. The following year it teamed with Vivendi to create VivendiNet, which will channel content to mobile phones, PCs, and TV in all languages. Vivendi also struck a related deal with phone company Vodafone AirTouch to launch Vizzavi, a multi-access interactive portal operating across Europe. V-Net will become part of Vizzavi.

In 2000 Vivendi agreed to buy the rest of the company for about $14 billion. Vivendi also is buying Canadian beverage and entertainment firm Seagram for $34 billion, and will combine all three firms into Vivendi Universal.

OFFICERS

Chairman and CEO: Pierre Lescure
Deputy Chairman and General Counsel:
Marc-André Feffer
COO: Denis Olivennes
SVP Finance: Richard Lenormand
EVP Commercial Operations, France and CANAL+
Group: Bruno Delecour
EVP Development and International Affairs:
Laurent Perpere
EVP Group Subsidiaries: Vincent Grimond
EVP Italian Operations: Michel Thoulouze
EVP Programming: Alain de Greef
CEO, CANALNUMEDIA; Co-CEO, VIVENDINET:
Alex Berger
SVP Human Resources: Phillipe Duranton
SVP Development and Strategic Planning:
Bernard Guillou
SVP Corporate and European Affairs:
Claudine Ripert-Landler
SVP Communications: Sylvie Ruggieri
Deputy EVP France: Bruno Thibadeau
Auditors: Barbier Frinault & Autres; Salustro Reydel

LOCATIONS

HQ: 85/89, Quai Andre-Citroen,
75711 Paris Cedex 15, France
Phone: +33-1-44-25-10-00   **Fax:** +33-1-44-25-12-34
US HQ: 301 N. Canon Dr., #207, Beverly Hills, CA 90210
US Phone: 310-247-0994   **US Fax:** 310-247-0998
Web site: http://www.cplus.fr

CANAL+ has subscribers in Africa, Belgium, France,
Italy, the Netherlands, Poland, Spain, and several
Scandinavian countries.

PRODUCTS/OPERATIONS

1999 Sales

	% of total
Subscriptions	79
Advertising & sponsorship	3
Other	18
Total	**100**

Selected Operations
CANAL+ Image (97%, management and distribution of
TV programming and movies)
CANAL+ Nederland (pay TV, The Netherlands)
CANAL+ Television (pay TV, Nordic countries)
CanalSatellite (70%, marketing of satellite-broadcast
theme channels)
Expand (35%, television production)
Le Studio CANAL+ (majority stake; motion picture
production)
NC Numericable (63%, cable TV)
TELE+ (99%, Pay TV, Italy)

Selected Theme Channels
Canal Jimmy (series)
Ciné Cinémas (movies)
Comédie! (comedy)
Demain! (jobs and training)
Game One (sports)
i-television (news)
MCM Euromusique (music)
Paris Première (entertainment and fashion)
Planète (documentaries)

COMPETITORS

Groupe AB	Liberty Media	TF1
Bertelsmann	Mediaset	Time Warner
DIRECTV	News Corp.	United Pan-
France Telecom	Pathé	Europe

HISTORICAL FINANCIALS & EMPLOYEES

OTC: CNPLY FYE: December 31	Annual Growth	12/90	12/91	12/92	12/93	12/94	12/95	12/96	12/97	12/98	12/99
Sales ($ mil.)	11.9%	1,202	1,347	1,436	1,465	1,793	2,069	2,240	2,268	2,888	3,307
Net income ($ mil.)	—	178	208	200	203	117	136	143	255	(33)	(338)
Income as % of sales	—	14.8%	15.4%	13.9%	13.9%	6.5%	6.6%	6.4%	11.3%	—	—
Earnings per share ($)	—	1.88	2.19	1.95	1.96	1.12	1.22	1.26	1.73	(0.20)	(2.68)
Stock price - FY high ($)	—	37.86	40.38	53.58	49.81	38.91	37.77	49.25	43.75	14.38	30.00
Stock price - FY low ($)	—	31.39	31.06	36.36	37.36	29.52	23.53	37.88	33.00	8.63	12.00
Stock price - FY close ($)	(1.2%)	32.27	39.38	39.77	37.80	32.03	37.53	49.08	34.00	13.59	28.96
P/E - high	—	20	18	27	25	35	31	39	25	—	—
P/E - low	—	17	14	19	19	26	19	30	19	—	—
Dividends per share ($)	1.3%	0.71	0.77	0.90	0.84	0.56	0.61	0.77	0.65	0.70	0.80
Book value per share ($)	8.6%	4.27	5.04	9.37	10.34	12.22	14.18	15.76	12.26	14.25	8.99
Employees	14.0%	1,429	1,550	1,697	2,031	2,084	2,219	2,402	3,000	3,816	4,635

STOCK PRICE HISTORY

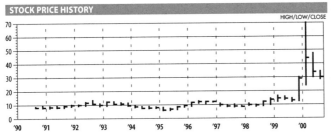

HIGH/LOW/CLOSE

1999 FISCAL YEAR-END

Debt ratio: 49.4%
Return on equity: —
Cash ($ mil.): 457
Current ratio: 0.89
Long-term debt ($ mil.): 1,106
No. of shares (mil.): 126
Dividends
  Yield: 0.0%
  Payout: —
Market value ($ mil.): 3,648

CANON INC.

OVERVIEW

Canon's doctrine is based on image. The Tokyo-based company is one of the world's largest makers of printers and other computer peripherals (37% of sales), copiers, and business systems. Its other popular offerings include camcorders, fax machines, scanners, cameras, and optical products for semiconductor manufacturing, broadcasting, and medical treatment.

Once known only for cameras, Canon has seen its photographic business drop to nearly 10% of sales as its office equipment operations prospered. Peripherals have shot past copiers as the largest sales group amid falling PC prices, which have opened up consumer spending on printers and scanners. Faced with strong competition and falling sales of business machines, the company continues to pursue digital, network-compatible, color, multimedia, and other new technologies in developing its products.

Canon adheres to the *kyosei* philosophy (living and working together for the common good), which stresses respect for local cultures and customs and more local control of subsidiaries. The company has not relied on Japanese revenues for decades — international business accounts for 70% of sales.

HISTORY

Takeshi Mitarai and a friend, Saburo Uchida, formed Seiki Kogaku Kenkyusho (Precision Optical Research Laboratory) in Tokyo in 1933 to make Japan's first 35mm camera. In 1935 the camera was introduced under the brand name Kwanon (the Buddhist goddess of mercy) — but later renamed Canon. In response to a pre-WWII military buildup, the company made X-ray machines for the Japanese.

In 1947 the company became Canon Camera Company as the brand name gained popularity. It opened its first overseas branch — in New York — in 1955. Canon diversified into business equipment by introducing the first 10-key electronic calculator (1964) and a plain-paper photocopier (1968) independent of Xerox's patented technology. Canon dropped "Camera Company" from its name in 1969. The company invented the "liquid dry" copying system, which uses plain paper and liquid developer, in 1972. It failed to produce new cameras and was surpassed by Minolta as Japan's top camera exporter. Sales were sluggish in the early 1970s, and in 1975 Canon suspended dividends for the first time since WWII.

At that time Canon's managing director, Ryuzaburo Kaku, convinced Mitarai that the company's problems stemmed from indecisive leadership and weak marketing. Kaku turned Canon around, unleashing the electronic AE-1 in a media blitz that in 1976 included the first-ever TV commercials for a 35mm camera. With automated features, the AE-1 appealed to the clumsiest photographers. Its success catapulted Canon past Minolta as the world's #1 camera maker.

In 1979 Canon introduced the first copier to use a dry developer. As the copier market matured in the early 1980s, Canon shifted to making other automated office equipment, including laser printers and fax machines.

Mitarai died in 1984. Minolta the next year again displaced Canon as the world's #1 camera maker, when it introduced a fully automated model. But Canon came back in 1987 with the electronic optical system (EOS) autofocus camera, which returned the company to preeminence in 1990. That year the company initiated an ink cartridge recycling program. Canon teamed up with IBM in 1992 to produce portable PCs. In 1993 Takeshi Mitarai's son Hajime, who had joined Canon in 1974, was named president and began expanding product development.

In 1995 Canon introduced the world's first color ferroelectric liquid crystal display, which could replace cathode-ray tubes in computer and TV screens as the industry standard. When Hajime died that year, cousin Fujio Mitarai, a 34-year Canon employee who served as the head of Canon U.S.A. in the 1980s, was named president and CEO (Kaku remained chairman). In 1996 the company made Canon Latin America a direct subsidiary of Canon U.S.A., with the *kyosei* idea that regionalized control would make the subsidiary more efficient.

Canon stopped making PCs in 1997. The next year the company announced its Hyper Photo System, which combines a scanner, PC server, and printer to produce photo prints, and expanded its copier remanufacturing operations. In 1999, after 16 years of production, Canon stopped making optical memory cards. That year Kaku resigned, and the company opened a research and development facility in the US.

In 2000 Canon and Toshiba began jointly developing technology for flat-panel displays.

President and CEO: Fujio Mitarai
Senior Managing Director; Chief of OEM Business:
Takashi Kitamura
Senior Managing Director; Chief of Technology and
Product Development; Group Executive, Technology
Management; Group Executive, Platform Technology
Development; Group Executive, Display
Development: Ichiro Endo
Senior Managing Director; Chief of H.R.M., General
Affairs, and Marketing; Group Executive, Human
Resources Management and Organization:
Yukio Yamashita
Managing Director; Group Executive, Finance and
Accounting: Yoshizo Tanaka
Managing Director; President Canon U.S.A.:
Kinya Uchida
Auditors: KPMG

LOCATIONS

HQ: 30-2, Shimomaruko 3-chome, Ohta-ku,
Tokyo 146-8501, Japan
Phone: +81-3-3758-2111   **Fax:** +81-3-5482-5135
US HQ: 1 Canon Plaza, Lake Success, NY 11042
US Phone: 516-488-6700   **US Fax:** 516-328-5069
Web site: http://www.canon.com

1999 Sales

	$ mil.	% of total
Americas	8,948	35
Japan	7,759	30
Europe	7,221	28
Other regions	1,780	7
Total	**25,708**	**100**

PRODUCTS/OPERATIONS

1999 Sales

	$ mil.	% of total
Business machines		
Computer peripherals	9,466	37
Copying machines	8,256	32
Business systems	3,493	14
Cameras	2,719	10
Optical & other products	1,774	7
Total	**25,708**	**100**

Selected Products

Printers	Lenses
Scanners	Broadcast equipment
Copiers	Medical equipment
Fax machines	Semiconductor production
Cameras and camcorders	equipment
Liquid crystal display	Binoculars
(LCD) video projectors	Calculators

COMPETITORS

Agfa	Leica Camera	Philips
Applied Materials	Lexmark	Electronics
Asahi Optical	International	Pitney Bowes
ASM	Matsushita	Polaroid
Lithography	Minolta	Ricoh
Casio Computer	NEC	SANYO
Eastman Kodak	Nikon	Seiko
Fuji Photo	Corporation	Seiko Epson
Fujitsu	Novellus	Sharp
Harris	Systems	Sony
Corporation	Océ	Toshiba
Hewlett-Packard	Oki Electric	Ultratech
Hitachi	Olivetti	Stepper
IBM	Olympus	Xerox
Konica		

HISTORICAL FINANCIALS & EMPLOYEES

NYSE: CAJ FYE: December 31	Annual Growth	12/90	12/91	12/92	12/93	12/94	12/95	12/96	12/97	12/98	12/99
Sales ($ mil.)	8.1%	12,725	14,976	15,338	16,452	19,410	21,026	22,054	21,239	24,364	25,708
Net income ($ mil.)	4.8%	452	418	288	189	312	534	812	914	945	689
Income as % of sales	—	3.6%	2.8%	1.9%	1.1%	1.6%	2.5%	3.7%	4.3%	3.9%	2.7%
Earnings per share ($)	3.3%	0.58	0.52	0.38	0.24	0.36	0.61	0.92	1.04	1.07	0.78
Stock price - FY high ($)	—	13.20	12.03	11.80	14.23	18.50	19.08	22.75	32.10	24.96	40.94
Stock price - FY low ($)	—	9.03	8.85	9.45	10.70	13.73	14.40	17.15	19.95	17.00	19.25
Stock price - FY close ($)	17.6%	9.40	11.38	11.00	13.75	17.00	18.28	22.00	23.35	21.50	40.56
P/E - high	—	23	23	31	59	51	31	25	30	23	52
P/E - low	—	16	17	25	45	38	24	19	19	16	24
Dividends per share ($)	8.0%	0.07	0.08	0.08	0.10	0.11	0.12	0.11	0.14	0.15	0.14
Book value per share ($)	30.7%	1.22	1.43	1.47	1.62	1.89	1.97	1.98	1.95	2.27	13.52
Employees	4.4%	54,381	62,700	64,512	64,535	67,672	72,280	75,628	78,767	79,799	79,800

STOCK PRICE HISTORY

HIGH/LOW/CLOSE

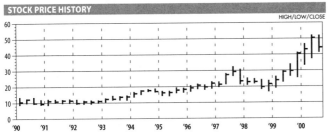

1999 FISCAL YEAR-END

Debt ratio: 12.1%
Return on equity: 6.4%
Cash ($ mil.): 4,710
Current ratio: 1.70
Long-term debt ($ mil.): 1,620
No. of shares (mil.): 872
Dividends
Yield: 0.3%
Payout: 17.9%
Market value ($ mil.): 35,350

CAP GEMINI ERNST & YOUNG

OVERVIEW

One of the bigger constellations in Europe's information technology (IT) services horizon is brightening its glow in US skies. Paris-based Cap Gemini Ernst & Young specializes in systems integration and software development services, which combine for about half of sales. The rest comes from management and IT consulting, outsourcing, and other computing support to global companies in the financial services, life sciences, telecommunications, manufacturing, and utilities markets. Cap Gemini is Europe's largest technology services firm but trails US-based IBM and EDS in that region in overall sales.

After a failed attempt to establish itself on US soil in the mid-1990s, the acquisition of Ernst & Young's consulting business finally gives Cap Gemini credibility in the largest IT services market on the globe. The $11 billion cash and stock deal, which brings onboard nearly 18,000 employees, extends the company's breadth of expertise.

In a rapid-fire succession of deals, Cap Gemini has also forged alliances with players such as Cisco, Sun Microsystems, and Oracle to boost its e-business expertise and shed its low-tech image as a legacy systems integrator.

Cap Gemini has long embraced training and teamwork. Its Cap Gemini University — located in a medieval chateau — educates employees on changes and trends in computing and helps them develop skills to work in any culture.

French holding company Cie. Générale d'Industrie et de Participations (CGIP) owns 20% of Cap Gemini; founder and chairman Serge Kampf owns 12%.

HISTORY

Serge Kampf founded software house Sogeti in 1967 at Grenoble, France, his hometown. He had an economics degree and had held a variety of jobs — from selling bakery ovens and computers to working for the French national telephone company. Frustrated as an executive with French computer company Groupe Bull, he resigned and started Sogeti.

Believing that the future of information technology (IT) would be in support rather than hardware, Kampf focused on providing computer services to companies outside Paris that were being overlooked by his larger competitors. He was immediately successful and three years later opened a Paris branch. In 1973 Kampf changed the focus of the company, abandoning the more specialized activities of data processing for general consulting, software, and technical assistance.

Cap Gemini Sogeti was created two years later by merging Sogeti with two French software service companies, C.A.P. (Computerized Applications Programming, started 1962) and Gemini (1969). At first it operated as a "body shop," a loose organization of freelance programmers offering temporary help to computer users. It set up a consulting team in the US in 1978 and around that time began a series of US acquisitions that led to the formation of Cap Gemini America (1981). Meanwhile the parent had become France's leading computer services firm.

The company acquired a 42% stake in French competitor Sesa in 1982; six years later it bought the rest as part of a new strategy to become a global operator with a range of ser-

vices. Cap Gemini Sogeti's 1990 purchase of Hoskyns Group, the UK's largest computer services company, was just one of a string of acquisitions aimed at fulfilling that goal (over a five-year period, it bought 22 European and American companies for a total of $1.1 billion). To raise money for his international expansion plans, Kampf sold 34% of the company to German carmaker Daimler-Benz (now DaimlerChrysler) in 1991.

The mid-1990s brought more than a dozen partnerships, including deals with French chemical conglomerate Rhône-Poulenc (1995, now Aventis) and British Steel (1996, now Corus Group). Also in 1996 the company launched its year 2000 date fixing software. It completed the reorganization creating holding company Cap Gemini and moved its corporate headquarters to Paris.

In 1997 Daimler-Benz sold its stake (then 24%) in Cap Gemini. The next year Cap Gemini bought the UK finance and commerce arm of AT&T. The company sold its UK training unit in 1999 to focus its UK operations on IT services. Expanding further into the US that year, the company bought telecommunications specialist Beechwood.

In 2000 Cap Gemini edified its US presence (and changed its name) with the $11 billion purchase of the consulting business of Ernst & Young. Vice chairman Geoff Unwin took over as CEO that year; Kampf remains chairman. The company also teamed with Cisco to form a networking design and consulting joint venture.

Chairman: Serge Kampf
VC and CEO: Geoff Unwin
COO: Paul Hermelin
Managing Director Capabilities: Pierre Hessler
Managing Director Sectors: Terrence Ozan
Group VP and CFO: Frédéric Lemoine
Group VP North America: Dale Wartluft
Group VP Offerings and Marketing: Mark Hauser
Director Global Staffing: Carolyn Nimmy
Manager US: Mike Meyer
Auditors: Ernst & Young

HQ: Place de l'Etoile, 11 rue de Tilsitt,
75017 Paris, France
Phone: +33-1-47-54-50-00   **Fax:** +33-1-42-27-32-11
US HQ: 1114 Avenue of the Americas, 29th Fl.,
New York, NY 10036
US Phone: 212-768-2066   **US Fax:** 212-768-9797
Web site: http://www.capgemini.com

Cap Gemini Ernst & Young has operations in Austria, Belgium, Denmark, Finland, France, Germany, Italy, Japan, Latvia, the Netherlands, Norway, Poland, Portugal, Singapore, South Africa, Spain, Sweden, Switzerland, the UK, and the US.

1999 Sales

	% of total
France	26
UK	22
Benelux countries	18
US	13
Scandinavia	11
Other countries	10
Total	**100**

1999 Sales

	% of total
Software development	27
Systems integration	24
Outsourcing	23
Management consulting	15
IT consulting	8
Other	3
Total	**100**

Selected Services
Electronic commerce
Euro conversion
Information technology consulting
Management consulting
Systems integration

AGENCY.COM
American Management
Andersen Consulting
Atos Origin
Bull
CIBER
CMG
Compaq
Computer Horizons
Computer Sciences
Deloitte Touche Tohmatsu
EDS
Finsiel
Getronics
Hewlett-Packard
IBM
ICL

Icon Medialab
iGATE
iXL Enterprises
Keane
Logica
marchFIRST
Organic
Perot Systems
PricewaterhouseCoopers
Razorfish
Renaissance Worldwide
Sapient
Sema Group
Siemens
Unisys

Euronext Paris: CAP FYE: December 31	Annual Growth	12/90	12/91	12/92	12/93	12/94	12/95	12/96	12/97	12/98	12/99
Sales (€ mil.)	13.3%	1,398	1,529	1,812	1,681	1,551	1,727	2,259	3,076	3,955	4,310
Net income (€ mil.)	12.1%	95	85	(11)	(65)	(14)	8	43	116	188	266
Income as % of sales	—	6.8%	5.6%	—	—	—	0.5%	1.9%	3.8%	4.8%	6.2%
Earnings per share (€)	2.7%	2.68	1.98	(0.25)	(1.47)	(0.30)	0.15	0.71	1.84	2.73	3.41
Stock price - FY high (€)	—	57.46	53.45	44.89	32.34	34.52	28.02	39.03	79.58	155.04	269.30
Stock price - FY low (€)	—	39.26	31.78	21.86	21.10	23.87	18.77	18.52	35.06	71.38	125.90
Stock price - FY close (€)	22.2%	41.53	38.67	24.04	25.46	25.46	21.04	38.25	72.99	136.75	252.00
P/E - high	—	21	27	—	—	—	187	55	43	57	79
P/E - low	—	15	16	—	—	—	125	26	19	26	37
Dividends per share (€)	4.7%	0.66	0.84	0.93	0.00	0.00	0.00	0.00	0.30	0.53	1.00
Book value per share (€)	3.2%	13.55	20.25	17.98	18.67	19.26	18.71	21.90	24.81	32.52	18.05
Employees	8.6%	18,919	16,892	21,374	20,559	19,823	22,079	25,950	31,094	34,606	39,626

HIGH/LOW/CLOSE

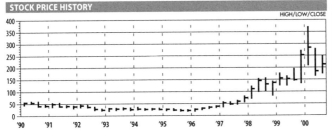

Debt ratio: 9.2%
Return on equity: 14.6%
Cash (€ mil.): 193
Current ratio: 1.54
Long-term debt (€ mil.): 143
No. of shares (mil.): 78
Dividends
  Yield: 0.0%
  Payout: 0.3%
Market value ($ mil.): 19,735
Sales ($ mil.): 4,330

CARLSBERG A/S

They drink it here; they drink it there; they drink this Danish beer everywhere. Based in Copenhagen, Carlsberg has breweries in 40 countries. The company's beers, sold primarily under the Carlsberg and Tuborg labels, have about 70% of Denmark's beer market. Yet, more than 85% of its beer is sold outside Denmark, in about 150 other countries. In addition, it maintains licensing agreements with such industry leaders as Canada's Labatt and Japan's Suntory.

Carlsberg's Coca-Cola Nordic Beverages subsidiary mixes up soft drinks for Scandinavia. Carlsberg also has a 40% interest in wine and spirits firm Vingaarden. Its beverages may occasionally cause consumers to lose focus, but the firm itself doesn't want to: It is selling its interests in noncore businesses, including housewares maker Royal Scandinavia and Copenhagen's Tivoli Gardens amusement park, in order to concentrate on beverages.

Carlsberg took over the brewing business of Norwegian conglomerate Orkla to produce a global brewer with dominant market share in Denmark, Norway, Sweden, Russia, and three Baltic states. The company has also agreed to buy the beverage operations of Swedish firm Feldschlösschen Hürlimann, a deal that will make Carlsberg the top beverage group in Switzerland.

The Carlsberg Foundation, a charitable organization that supports science and the humanities, owns 55% of Carlsberg (at least 51% ownership is required by charter).

Carlsberg stems from the amalgamation of two proud Danish brewing concerns. Captain J. C. Jacobsen founded the first of these in Copenhagen; his father had worked as a brewery hand before acquiring his own small brewery in 1826. Studious and technically minded, J. C. inherited the brewery in 1835. He opened the Carlsberg Brewery (named for his son Carl) in 1847 and exported his first beer (to the UK) in 1868. J. C. established the Carlsberg Foundation in 1876 to conduct scientific research and oversee brewery operations.

Carl, who conflicted with his father over brewery operations, opened a new facility (New Carlsberg) adjacent to his dad's in 1881. Both men bestowed gifts upon their city, such as a church, an art museum, a royal castle renovation, and Copenhagen Harbor's famous Little Mermaid statue. Father and son willed their breweries to the foundation, which united them in 1906.

Tuborgs Fabrikker was founded in 1873 by a group of Danish businessmen who wanted to establish a major industrial project (including a brewery, a glass factory, and a sulfuric acid works) on a piece of land around Tuborg Harbor. Philip Heyman headed the group and in 1880 spun off all operations but the brewery.

Carlsberg and Tuborg became Denmark's two leading brewers. After WWII, both launched intense marketing plans to carry their beers outside the country. Between 1958 and 1972 they tripled exports and established breweries in Europe and Asia. Both brewers' desire to grow internationally influenced their decision to merge, which they did in 1969 as United Breweries.

During the 1980s the firm diversified, forming Carlsberg Biotechnology in 1983 to extend its research to other areas. It strengthened its position in North America through licenses with Anheuser-Busch (1985) and John Labatt (1988). United Breweries reverted to the old Carlsberg name in 1987.

Carlsberg and Allied-Lyons (now Allied Domecq) combined their UK brewing, distribution, and wholesaling operations under the name Carlsberg-Tetley in 1992. The $876 million venture created the UK's third-largest brewer (behind Bass and Courage).

Bass acquired Allied's 50% of Carlsberg-Tetley in 1996 but sold its stake to Carlsberg in 1997 upon orders from antitrust regulators. Also in 1997 Carlsberg and Coca-Cola set up Coca-Cola Nordic Beverages to bottle and distribute soft drinks in Nordic countries. That year Poul Svanholm retired after 25 years as CEO; he was replaced by Flemming Lindelov, former president of Tulip (a meat company).

Labatt began marketing Carlsberg beers in the US in 1998 after Anheuser-Busch ended its distribution relationship. Carlsberg greatly boosted its 1998 sales by acquiring a 60% stake in Finnish brewer Sinebrychoff. In 1999 Carlsberg sold a 60% stake in Vingaarden to Finland's Oy Marli, which has an option to buy the other 40%. The brewer also announced that year it would sell its stakes in Royal Scandinavia and the Tivoli amusement park.

In 2000 Carlsberg took over the brewing business of Norwegian firm Orkla for $1.15 billion. Later that year the company inked a deal with Swedish firm Feldschlösschen Hürlimann to buy its beverage operations.

Chairman: Poul C. Matthiessen
Deputy Chairman: Erik B. Rasmussen
President and Group CEO: Flemming Lindelov
CFO: Joern P. Jensen, age 36
Group Managing Director, International: Michael C. Iuul
Group Managing Director, Nordic Region and Denmark Division: Nils Smedegaard Andersen, age 40
EVP Corporate Technology Organisation: Svend Erik Albrethsen
EVP Corporate Technology Organisation: Klaus Bock
SVP Denmark Division: Helge Ussing
Chief Executive UK Division: Ebbe Dinesen
Finance Director UK Division: Steve C. Bailey
Marketing and Managing Director, Take Home Sales, UK Division: Doug Clydesdale
Auditors: KPMG C. Jespersen; PricewaterhouseCoopers

HQ: 100 Ny Carlsberg Vej,
DK-1799 Copenhagen V, Denmark
Phone: +45-33-27-33-27   **Fax:** +45-33-27-47-11
Web site: http://www.carlsberg.com

Carlsberg operates about 100 subsidiaries, most of which are outside Denmark. Its beer is brewed in about 40 countries and sold in 150, while its soft drinks are made and sold in Denmark, Finland, Iceland, Norway, and Sweden.

1999 Sales By Country of Production

	% of total
Beverages	
Denmark	20
Other countries	70
Other	10
Total	**100**

Selected Affiliates and Subsidiaries
A/S Kjøbenhavns Sommer-Tivoli
  (43%, amusement park)
Beer Thai (1991) Co. Ltd. (8%)
Carlsberg Finans A/S
Carlsberg-Tetley PLC (UK)
Ceylon Brewery Ltd. (8%, Sri Lanka)
Coca-Cola Nordic Beverages A/S (51%)
Danish Malting Group A/S
Falcon Holding AB (Sweden)
Gorkha Brewery Limited (48% Nepal)
Hannen Brauerei GmbH (Germany)
Hue Brewery Ltd. (35%, Vietnam)
Israel Beer Breweries Ltd. (20%)
J.C. Bentzen A/S
Nuuk Imeq A/S (24%, Greenland)
OAO Vena (66%, Russia)
Ókocimskie Zaklady Piwowarskie S.A. (45%, Poland)
Oy Sinebrychoff Ab (Finland)
Panonska Pivovara d.o.o. (40%, Croatia)
Royal Scandinavia A/S (65%, housewares)
South-East Asia Brewery Ltd. (35%, Vietnam)
Southern Bottlers Limited (58%, Malawi)
Türk Tuborg Bira ve Malt Sanayii A.S. (2%, Turkey)
Unicer S.A.-Uniao Cervejeira S.A. (31%, Portugal)
Vingaarden A/S (40%, wines and spirits)

Anheuser-Busch	Grolsch	Scottish &
Asahi Breweries	Guinness/UDV	Newcastle
Bass Brewers	Heineken	South African
Brauerei BECK	Holsten-Brauerei	Breweries
Brown-Forman	Interbrew	Tsingtao
Corning	Kirin	Waterford
Foster's Brewing	Oneida	Wedgwood

Copenhagen: CARL-A.CO FYE: September 30	Annual Growth	9/90	9/91	9/92	9/93	9/94	9/95	9/96	9/97	9/98	9/99
Sales (DK mil.)	8.4%	15,141	14,462	14,957	15,595	16,919	17,072	17,965	19,378	29,321	31,285
Net income (DK mil.)	4.7%	768	802	854	910	802	1,003	1,063	1,242	1,641	1,164
Income as % of sales	—	5.1%	5.5%	5.7%	5.8%	4.7%	5.9%	5.9%	6.4%	5.6%	3.7%
Earnings per share (DK)	4.1%	12.73	13.29	13.36	14.24	12.54	15.69	16.63	19.43	25.68	18.21
Stock price - FY high (DK)	—	265.66	409.16	381.02	302.00	333.00	313.00	360.00	422.00	515.00	433.00
Stock price - FY low (DK)	—	213.22	240.46	255.00	238.00	240.00	242.00	269.60	334.00	325.00	252.00
Stock price - FY close (DK)	0.6%	242.39	374.26	255.00	295.00	263.00	310.00	355.00	368.00	370.00	255.00
P/E - high	—	21	31	29	21	27	20	22	22	20	24
P/E - low	—	17	18	19	17	19	15	16	17	13	14
Dividends per share (DK)	3.2%	3.00	3.00	3.00	3.00	3.00	3.00	3.40	3.60	4.00	4.00
Book value per share (DK)	3.7%	91.25	100.79	104.77	115.30	122.72	130.31	144.33	150.92	151.05	126.22
Employees	6.7%	12,192	11,494	13,777	17,762	17,481	17,563	18,519	18,081	20,589	21,906

HIGH/LOW/CLOSE

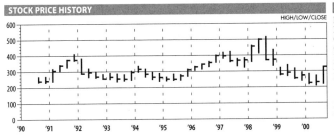

Debt ratio: 20.2%
Return on equity: 10.8%
Cash (DK mil.): 3,240
Current ratio: 1.32
Long-term debt (DK mil.): 2,997
No. of shares (mil.): 94
Dividends
  Yield: 0.0%
  Payout: 0.2%
Market value ($ mil.): 3,431
Sales ($ mil.): 4,483

CARREFOUR SA

OVERVIEW

Carrefour is in the express lane toward growth. Europe's #1 retailer, the Paris-based company is an originator of hypermarkets — huge department store and supermarket combinations that sell food, clothing, electronics, and household appliances, among other items, at discounted prices. Carrefour operates nearly 9,000 stores in 25-plus countries. In addition to Carrefour hypermarkets, its chains include Champion and Stoc supermarkets, Dia and Minipreco discount stores, Shopi and Codec convenience stores, and Picard Surgelés frozen food stores (which will be sold off). Its

Comptoirs Modernes supermarket chain operates in Brazil, France, and Spain.

Unable to build new stores in its homeland due to regulations protecting smaller stores, Carrefour relies on expansion through acquisitions. Most notable was its blockbuster merger with rival French retailer Promodès; the combined company is the world's #2 retailer, behind Wal-Mart Stores.

The company has other interests that range from automobile centers and insurance in France to Costco warehouse clubs in the UK to PETsMART pet supply superstores in the US.

HISTORY

Although its predecessor was actually a supermarket opened by Marcel Fournier and Louis Defforey in a Fournier's department store basement in Annecy, France, the first Carrefour supermarket was founded in 1963 at the intersection of five roads (Carrefour means "crossroads"). That year Carrefour opened a vast store, dubbed a hypermarket by the media, in Sainte-Genevieve-des-Bois, outside Paris.

The company opened outlets in France and moved into other countries, including Belgium (1969), Switzerland (1970 — the year it went public), Italy and the UK (1972), and Spain (1973). Carrefour stepped up international expansion during the mid-1970s after French legislation limited its growth within the country.

Carrefour imported its French-style hypermarkets to the US (Philadelphia) in 1988. Scant advertising, limited selection, and a union strike led Carrefour to close it US operations in 1993. Carrefour opened its first hypermarket in Taiwan in 1989. The next year it formed Carma, a 50-50 joint venture with Groupama, to sell insurance. Carrefour paid over $1 billion for two rival chains (the bankrupt Montlaur chain and Euromarche) in 1991.

Daniel Bernard replaced Michel Bon, the hard-charging expansion architect, in 1992 after a 50% drop in first-half profits. A year later Carrefour partnered with Mexican retailer Gigante to open a chain of hypermarkets in Mexico. (In 1998 Carrefour bought Gigante's share of the joint venture.) In 1996 the company bought a 41% stake in rival GMB (Cora hypermarket chain) and sold its 11% stake in US warehouse retailer Costco (it now owns 20% of Costco UK). The next year Carrefour allowed 16 hypermarkets owned by Guyenne et Gascogne, Coop Atlantique, and Chareton to operate under the Carrefour name. It opened

its first hypermarket in Poland (1997) and the Czech Republic (1998).

The company made its biggest acquisition to date in 1998 when it acquired French supermarket operator Comptoirs Modernes (with about 800 stores under the Stoc, Comod, Marche Plus banners). Carrefour also purchased 23 Lojas Americanas department stores in Brazil in late 1998.

In August 1999 Carrefour announced a deal even bigger than the one for Comptoirs Modernes — a $16.3 billion merger with fellow French grocer Promodès, which operated more than 6,000 hypermarkets, supermarkets, convenience stores, and discount stores in Europe. Paul-Auguste Halley and Leonor Duval Lemonnier founded Promodès in Normandy, France, in 1961. Initially a wholesale food distributor, Promodès opened its first supermarket in 1962. A cash-and-carry wholesale outlet followed in 1964, and a hypermarket opened in 1970. They branched into convenience stores (Shopi and 8 à Huit) during the 1970s.

In order to gain regulatory approval to acquire Promodès, Carrefour divested its 42% stake in the Cora chain and sold about 35 other stores. The acquisition of Promodès was completed in 2000.

In 2000, the company joined with retailer Sears and software maker Oracle, among others, to form Internet-based supply exchange GlobalNetXchange. In July 2000 Carrefour agreed to purchase Belgian retailer GB (about 500 stores) from holding company GIB for $624 million. In October 2000 Carrefour said it would form a joint venture with Swiss retailer Maus to run some 10 hypermarkets in Switzerland; Carrefour will own about 40%. Also that month the company announced it would sell its Picard Surgelés stores.

OFFICERS

Chairman and CEO: Daniel Bernard, age 53
CFO: Hervé Defforey, age 49
Chief Marketing and Merchandising Officer:
William Anderson
Secretary: Etienne Van Dyck
Managing Director, DIA International: Javier Campo
Director, Americas: Philippe Jarry, age 50
Director, Asia: René Brillet, age 58
Director, Europe: Joël Saveuse, age 46
Director, France: Léon Salto
Director, Organization and Systems: Bruce Johnson, age 48
Director, Supermarkets: Jean-Claude Plassart
Human Resources France: Dominique Brard
Auditors: Arthur Andersen; Barbier Frinault & Autres; KPMG Audit

LOCATIONS

HQ: 6, avenue Raymond Poincaré, 75116 Paris, France
Phone: +33-1-53-70-19-00   **Fax:** +33-1-53-70-86-16
Web site: http://www.carrefour.com

Carrefour has operations in Argentina, Belgium, Brazil, Chile, China, Colombia, the Czech Republic, France, Greece, Hong Kong, Indonesia, Italy, Malaysia, Mexico, Monaco, Poland, Portugal, Singapore, South Korea, Spain, Taiwan, Thailand, and Turkey.

1999 Sales

	% of total
Europe	
France	62
Other countries	16
Americas	15
Asia	7
Total	**100**

PRODUCTS/OPERATIONS

Selected Subsidiaries

Hypermarkets
Beijing Jiachuang Commercial (60%, China)
Brepa (Brazil)
Carrefour Argentina
Carrefour Mexico
Carrefour France
Carrefour Korea
Carrefour Polska (Poland)
Cencar (Thailand)
Euromarche
Promohypermarkt (94%, Germany)
Pryca (69%, Spain)
PT Cartisa Properti (70%, Indonesia)

Other Activities
Carfuel (petroleum products)
Costco UK (20%, warehouse club)
Immobiliere Carrefour (real estate)
Metro France (20%, warehouse club)
PETsMART Inc. (12%, pet supplies, US)
Picard Surgelés (79%, frozen foods)
Providange (51%, auto centers)
S2P (60%, consumer credit)

COMPETITORS

ALDI	METRO AG
Auchan	Pinault-Printemps-
Casino Guichard	Redoute
Dairy Farm International	Primisteres Reynoird
Holdings	Rallye
Delhaize	Rinascente
E.Leclerc	Royal Ahold
Galeries Lafayette	Tengelmann Group
Generale Supermercati	Tesco
Lidl & Schwarz Stiftung	Wal-Mart

HISTORICAL FINANCIALS & EMPLOYEES

Euronext Paris: CA FYE: December 31	Annual Growth	12/90	12/91	12/92	12/93	12/94	12/95	12/96	12/97	12/98	12/99
Sales (€ mil.)	13.9%	11,563	15,302	17,858	18,782	20,779	22,046	23,615	25,805	27,409	37,364
Net income (€ mil.)	15.5%	206	184	204	459	324	539	476	546	647	755
Income as % of sales	—	1.8%	1.2%	1.1%	2.4%	1.6%	2.4%	2.0%	2.1%	2.4%	2.0%
Earnings per share (€)	14.9%	0.90	0.80	0.88	1.99	1.40	2.32	2.06	2.37	2.66	3.14
Stock price - FY high (€)	—	16.06	20.02	23.91	37.07	39.20	51.15	87.58	113.60	111.29	193.20
Stock price - FY low (€)	—	12.70	13.14	16.97	19.03	28.97	34.28	50.59	69.87	71.35	92.40
Stock price - FY close (€)	33.2%	13.87	19.59	20.00	36.44	37.45	50.31	85.78	79.78	107.20	183.10
P/E - high	—	18	25	27	19	28	22	43	48	42	62
P/E - low	—	14	16	19	10	21	15	25	29	27	29
Dividends per share (€)	13.9%	0.28	0.28	0.30	0.36	0.44	0.54	0.66	0.76	0.82	0.90
Book value per share (€)	20.5%	4.92	5.82	6.67	7.97	8.02	19.39	16.08	19.56	19.83	26.32
Employees	15.9%	51,300	76,200	79,500	81,500	95,900	102,900	103,600	113,289	132,875	193,952

STOCK PRICE HISTORY

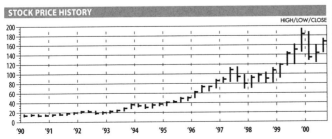

HIGH/LOW/CLOSE

1999 FISCAL YEAR-END
Debt ratio: 50.3%
Return on equity: 13.4%
Cash (€ mil.): 839
Current ratio: 0.91
Long-term debt (€ mil.): 6,733
No. of shares (mil.): 252
Dividends
  Yield: 0.0%
  Payout: 0.3%
Market value ($ mil.): 46,439
Sales ($ mil.): 37,542

CASINO GUICHARD-PERRACHON

OVERVIEW

The only chips you'll find at Casino Guichard-Perrachon are the edible kind. The Saint-Etienne, France-based company owns and operates about 2,000 hypermarkets and supermarkets, mostly in France, but also in Asia, Europe, and Latin America. About 70% of the company's sales come from its Geant hypermarkets (warehouse-style stores that sell groceries and other merchandise) and its supermarkets under the Casino, Franprix, and Leader Price banners. Casino also has more than 2,200 Petit Casino convenience stores, as well as Spar and Vival franchised convenience stores. France's Rallye SA owns more than 61% of the company's voting shares; the Guichard family owns about 9%.

Casino also owns about 57% of US-based retailer Smart & Final, which sells food and nonfood items in bulk and runs a food distribution business. The French retailer is growing rapidly in Poland and is spreading through Latin America and Asia by acquiring stakes in regional grocery companies.

Casino also operates restaurants (Casino Cafeteria), automobile service centers, food processing facilities, and wine-bottling plants.

HISTORY

Frenchman Geoffroy Guichard married Antonia Perrachon, the daughter of a grocer, in 1889 in Saint-Etienne, France. Three years later Geoffroy took over his father-in-law's general store, which was a converted "casino" or musical hall. In 1898 the company became Societe des Magasins du Casino. By 1900, when it became a joint stock company, Casino had 50 stores, and it opened its 100th store in 1904. That year the company introduced its first private-label product: canned sardines. In 1917 Guichard named his two sons, Mario and Jean, as managers.

By WWI there were about 215 branches, with more than 50 of those in Saint-Etienne. From 1919 to the early 1920s the company opened several factories to manufacture goods such as food, soap, and perfumes. In 1925 the elder Guichard retired, leaving the day-to-day operations of Casino to his two sons. (Geoffroy died in 1940.) WWII took a heavy toll on the company: About 70 Casino stores were leveled and another 450 were damaged.

Casino introduced its supermarket format in Grenoble in 1960. Seven years later it began opening cafeterias. Casino opened its first Geant hypermarket in Marseille in 1970 and formed Casino USA in 1976. Initially developed to run cafeterias, Casino USA bought an interest in the California-based Thriftimart volume retailer in 1983, renaming the company after Thriftimart's Smart & Final banner warehouse stores.

Two years later Casino acquired regional retailer CEDIS, adding 16 hypermarkets, 116 supermarkets, and 722 smaller stores in eastern France. In 1990 it acquired food retailer La Ruche Meridionale (18 hypermarkets and 112 supermarkets in southern France). Casino bought the food operations (nearly 300 hypermarkets and supermarkets) from Rallye SA in 1992, giving Rallye roughly 30% of the company. The company opened its first hypermarket in Warsaw, Poland, in 1996.

A year later Christian Couvreux was named president of the board of directors. That September rival Promodès made a roughly $4.5 billion hostile takeover bid for Casino. Guichard family members voted against the Promodès offer, instead backing a $3.9 billion friendly offer from Rallye. Casino also launched a massive counterattack — buying more than 600 Franprix and Leader Price supermarket stores from food manufacturer TLC Beatrice for $576 million, as well as acquiring a 21% stake in hypermarket chain Monoprix (which in turn bought Prisunic). Promodès withdrew its bid four months later.

Expanding internationally in 1998, Casino acquired a 75% stake in Libertad (Argentine supermarket chain), 50% of Uruguay's Disco group (food retailer), and opened its first hypermarket in Taichung, Taiwan.

In 1999 Casino boosted its presence in Latin America by purchasing a 25% stake in Exito, a leading grocer in Colombia and Venezuela, and by buying a 26% stake in Brazilian Companhia Brasileira de Distribuicao. The company then acquired 66% of Big C — the largest retailer in Thailand. Also in 1999 retailer Cora SA and Casino formed a joint venture purchasing company (called Opera) to buy food and nonfood goods for Casino and Cora stores. It also acquired 100 convenience stores (converted to the Petit Casino banner) in southwest France from retailer Guyenne et Gascogne.

In 2000 Casino agreed to buy a controlling stake in Uniwide, the Phillippines' largest food retailer. It also bought 51% of French online retailer Cdiscount.com, which sells CDs, videos, CD-ROMs, and DVDs.

Chairman, Management Board and CEO:
Christian Couvreux
Chairman, Supervisory Board: Antoine Guichard
VC, Supervisory Board: Yves Guichard
Managing Director, Management Board and CFO:
Pierre Bouchut
Director Corporate Communications: Philippe Bastien
Director of Human Resources: Thierry Bourgeron
Auditors: Bernard Roussel; Ernst & Young Audit

LOCATIONS

HQ: B.P. 306-24, rue de la Montat,
F-42008 Saint-Etienne Cedex 2, France
Phone: +33-4-77-45-31-31   **Fax:** +33-4-77-21-85-15
Web site: http://www.casino.fr

1999 Sales

	€ mil.	% of total
France	12,697	81
US	1,691	11
Argentina	439	3
Poland	374	3
Thailand	311	2
Uruguay	97	—
Taiwan	29	—
Total	**15,638**	**100**

PRODUCTS/OPERATIONS

Selected Operations
Big C (68%, Thailand)
Casino (supermarkets)
Casino Cafeteria
Casino USA (57% stake in Smart & Final)
Companhia Brasileira de Distribuicao (22%,
   Pao de Acucar supermarkets in Brazil)
Disco (50%, supermarkets in Uruguay)
Exito (25%, supermarkets in Columbia)
Franprix (70%, supermarkets)
Geant (hypermarkets)
Leader Price (70%, supermarkets)
Libertad (80%, hypermarkets in Argentina)
Monoprix (22%, supermarkets)
Opera (50%, joint purchasing venture with Cora SA)
Petit Casino (convenience stores)
Spar (franchised convenience stores)
Vival (franchised convenience stores)

COMPETITORS

ALDI
Auchan
Carrefour
E.Leclerc
Guyenne et Gascogne
ITM Entreprises
Primisteres Reynoird
Royal Ahold
Tesco
Wal-Mart

HISTORICAL FINANCIALS & EMPLOYEES

Euronext Paris: CO FYE: December 31	Annual Growth	12/90	12/91	12/92	12/93	12/94	12/95	12/96	12/97	12/98	12/99
Sales (€ mil.)	9.6%	6,841	6,466	9,389	9,606	9,528	9,777	10,190	11,609	14,155	15,638
Net income (€ mil.)	17.8%	60	81	67	69	75	97	128	170	216	262
Income as % of sales	—	0.9%	1.3%	0.7%	0.7%	0.8%	1.0%	1.3%	1.5%	1.5%	1.7%
Earnings per share (€)	19.2%	—	—	—	—	1.14	0.91	0.91	1.03	1.78	2.74
Stock price – FY high (€)	—	—	—	—	—	31.25	24.54	38.49	55.80	90.55	129.70
Stock price – FY low (€)	—	—	—	—	—	20.25	19.54	21.39	35.83	50.48	80.00
Stock price – FY close (€)	37.6%	—	—	—	—	23.02	21.66	36.83	51.07	88.73	113.70
P/E – high	—	—	—	—	—	27	27	42	54	51	47
P/E – low	—	—	—	—	—	18	21	24	35	28	29
Dividends per share (€)	10.8%	—	—	—	—	0.76	0.61	0.61	0.69	1.19	1.27
Book value per share (€)	9.3%	—	—	—	—	20.03	20.80	22.60	28.89	32.86	31.28
Employees	8.8%	—	—	46,084	45,326	52,045	52,482	54,856	58,626	73,468	83,086

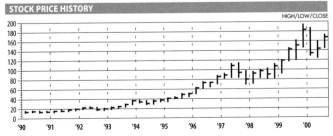

STOCK PRICE HISTORY
HIGH/LOW/CLOSE

1999 FISCAL YEAR-END

Debt ratio: 46.8%
Return on equity: 9.5%
Cash (€ mil.): 692
Current ratio: 0.76
Long-term debt (€ mil.): 2,710
No. of shares (mil.): 98
Dividends
  Yield: 0.0%
  Payout: 0.5%
Market value ($ mil.): 11,243
Sales ($ mil.): 15,713

CASIO COMPUTER CO., LTD.

CASIO COMPUTER, like the data its more well-known products showcase, marches on. Though the Tokyo-based company is Japan's #1 watchmaker, more than one-third of its sales come from calculators, office computers, and other data processing equipment. CASIO also manufactures visual and communications devices (pagers, LCD TVs, handheld PCs, answering machines), and laptop musical keyboards and other electronic components. The company keeps sales ticking along by regularly introducing newer, trendier versions of its products, from timepieces with built-in global positioning systems to palmtop computers for busy professionals.

Watches, however, remain CASIO's center-piece. They account for about 28% of the company's sales, bolstered by the strong marketing of shock-resistant and youth-oriented watch brands.

Among the first to develop handsets for Japan's PHS (Personal Handyphone System) wireless communications system, CASIO also pioneered the consumer marketing of low-end digital cameras and economical color printers. To beat the clock in the market for time saving products, CASIO is developing mobile electronic devices that run on Microsoft's Windows CE operating system.

The three younger brothers of late founder Tadao Kashio continue to run CASIO.

HISTORY

In 1942 Tadao Kashio started a Tokyo-based machine shop, Kashio Manufacturing. His brother, Toshio, later joined him. After reading about a 1946 computing contest in which an abacus bested an electric calculator, Toshio, an inventor, wrote a note to himself: "Abacus is human ability; calculator is technology." In 1950 he began developing a calculator. The other Kashio brothers — Yukio, a mechanical engineer, and Kazuo, who took over sales — joined the company in the 1950s.

The brothers incorporated in 1957 as CASIO, an anglicization of the family name. That year the company launched its first product, an electronic calculator featuring an innovative floating decimal point display; it was the first Japanese-built electronic calculator. CASIO took advantage of new transistor technology to create electronic calculators, and in 1965 it introduced the first electronic desktop calculator with memory. In 1970 the company began exporting to the US.

In the 1970s only CASIO and Sharp emerged as significant Japanese survivors of the fierce "calculator war." CASIO's strategy of putting lots of new functions on a proliferation of small models and selling them at rock-bottom prices worked not only with calculators but with digital watches as well. The company introduced its first digital watch in 1974 and went on to dominate the market.

CASIO expanded its product line into electronic music synthesizers (1980), pocket TVs (1983), and thin-card calculators (1983). Determined to break away from the production of delicate timepieces, CASIO introduced shock-resistant (G-Shock) digital watches in 1983. In the mid-1980s sales were hurt by a rising yen

and stiff price competition from developing Asian nations. The company responded by releasing sophisticated calculators for such specialized users as architects and insurance agents. To offset the effects of the yen's heightened value in the late 1980s, CASIO moved manufacturing to Taiwan, Hong Kong, South Korea, California, and Mexico. Kazuo Kashio was named president in 1988.

In 1990 CASIO established CASIO Electronic Devices to sell LCDs and chip-on-film components. In 1991 the company acquired a capital interest in Asahi, a producer of communications equipment and light electrical appliances. CASIO moved much of its production overseas in 1994, primarily to Thailand and Malaysia, after the high yen contributed to a nearly 28% drop in exports.

The company introduced its first digital camera in 1995. The next year CASIO launched its Cassiopeia handheld PC, and in 1997 it entered the US pager market.

In 1998 CASIO formed subsidiary CASIO Soft to develop Microsoft Windows CE-based software for handheld PCs and other mobile devices. It also introduced a palm-sized version of Cassiopeia, and a wristwatch (PC Cross) that exchanges information with a PC using infrared technology.

Two watches — the Pro Trek with global positioning system functions and the 5mm-thin Film Watch Pela — hit the market in 1999. A weakened yen that brought high overseas profits but poor Asian sales, plus an uncovered embezzlement of $30 million, helped cause a loss for fiscal 1999, CASIO's first annual drop into the red ink.

OFFICERS

Chairman: Toshio Kashio
President: Kazuo Kashio
EVP: Yukio Kashio
Senior Managing Director: Shigeki Maeno
Senior Managing Director: Shinichi Onoe
Managing Director: Masayuki Hakata
Managing Director: Osamu Shimizu
Managing Director: Yozo Suzuki
Auditors: Asahi & Co.

LOCATIONS

HQ: Casio Keisanki Kabushiki Kaisha
6-2, Hon-machi 1-chome, Shibuya-ku,
Tokyo 151-8543, Japan
Phone: +81-3-5334-4111   **Fax:** +81-3-5334-4921
US HQ: 570 Mount Pleasant Ave., Dover, NJ 07801
US Phone: 973-361-5400   **US Fax:** 973-361-3819
Web site: http://www.casio.co.jp

2000 Sales

	$ mil.	% of total
Asia	3,168	72
North America	512	13
Europe	209	5
Total	**3,889**	**100**

PRODUCTS/OPERATIONS

2000 Sales

	$ mil.	% of total
Data processing equipment	1,438	37
Electronic & other components	1,185	30
Electronic timepieces	801	21
Visual/communications equipment	465	12
Total	**3,889**	**100**

Selected Products

Audio equipment	LCDs, other components
Calculators	Office computers
Clocks	Pagers
Data collectors	Personal word processors
Digital cameras (QV series)	PHS (Personal Handyphone
Electronic cash registers	System) wireless
Electronic musical	telephone handsets
instruments	Telephone answering
Handheld PCs (Cassiopeia,	machines
Pocket Viewer)	Vision-related products
Handy terminals (bar code	(LCD TVs)
scanners)	Watches

COMPETITORS

Apple Computer	Matsushita	SANYO
Canon	Minolta	Seiko
Citizen Watch	Mitsubishi	Sharp
Compaq	Motorola	Siemens
Dell Computer	NCR	Sony
Eastman Kodak	NEC	Swatch
Fossil	Nikon	Texas
Fuji Photo	Oki Electric	Instruments
Fujitsu	Olympus	Thomson-CSF
Hewlett-Packard	Palm	Timex
Hitachi	Philips	Toshiba
Hyundai	Psion	Yamaha
IBM	Ricoh	Zebra
LG Group	Samsung	

HISTORICAL FINANCIALS & EMPLOYEES

OTC: CSIOY FYE: March 31	Annual Growth	3/91	3/92	3/93	3/94	3/95	3/96	3/97	3/98	3/99	3/00
Sales ($ mil.)	5.6%	2,384	2,885	3,758	3,735	4,641	3,841	3,709	3,773	3,788	3,889
Net income ($ mil.)	(1.3%)	65	79	61	52	58	6	30	88	(72)	58
Income as % of sales	—	2.7%	2.7%	1.6%	1.4%	1.3%	0.2%	0.8%	2.3%	—	1.5%
Earnings per share ($)	(1.7%)	2.44	2.96	2.29	1.93	2.11	0.23	1.08	3.17	(2.59)	2.10
Stock price – FY high ($)	—	110.13	111.22	99.22	129.16	138.58	104.38	106.08	99.00	95.50	108.00
Stock price – FY low ($)	—	67.31	79.27	68.50	86.22	103.91	82.66	69.92	66.25	64.50	58.00
Stock price – FY close ($)	2.1%	82.77	82.72	85.22	123.59	105.31	95.50	69.94	85.75	71.00	100.00
P/E – high	—	45	38	43	67	66	454	98	31	—	51
P/E – low	—	28	27	30	45	49	359	65	21	—	28
Dividends per share ($)	3.4%	0.89	0.94	1.09	1.22	1.50	1.17	1.01	0.94	1.05	1.20
Book value per share ($)	4.2%	40.61	45.14	53.27	60.83	73.28	58.11	51.45	50.05	64.35	58.93
Employees	1.9%	—	—	—	17,285	18,407	18,797	18,725	18,668	17,783	19,325

STOCK PRICE HISTORY

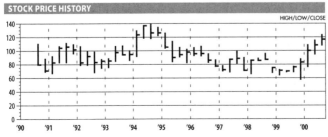

HIGH/LOW/CLOSE

2000 FISCAL YEAR-END

Debt ratio: 46.4%
Return on equity: 3.4%
Cash ($ mil.): 576
Current ratio: 1.71
Long-term debt ($ mil.): 1,386
No. of shares (mil.): 27
Dividends
  Yield: 0.0%
  Payout: 0.6%
Market value ($ mil.): 2,716

CLUB MÉDITERRANÉE S.A.

OVERVIEW

The images that probably enter your mind when someone mentions Club Med are precisely what Club Méditerranée — the company that introduced the one-price, food-and-fun resort village — is struggling to change. The Paris-based company is determined to revamp its 1970s "sea, sex, and sun" image into something more contemporary and less like a singles' scene. The company reports that some 65% of sales come from families.

Club Med has a global presence, with some 150 leisure operations in 40 countries, including 114 resort villages, 12 villas, a cruise ship operation, and a French tour operator. Nearly three-quarters of its visitors come from Europe; more than 1.5 million people visit Club Med resorts annually.

Club Med brought in Philippe Bourguignon, who performed corporate CPR on Euro Disney, to turn the tide. He returned Club Med to profitability in 1998 by refocusing on a single brand, renovating its villages, and positioning its Club Med resorts in the mid-market vacation range. He also has tried new concepts such as Club Med World recreational centers and licensing products under the Club Med name.

Exor, owned by the Agnelli family of Italy, owns 19% of Club Med.

HISTORY

Belgian diamond cutter Gérard Blitz dreamed up the Club Méditerranée concept as an escape from the post-WWII doldrums in Europe. In 1950 he convened a gathering of charter members on the island of Majorca, where the group slept in tents, cooked their own food, and had a great deal of fun. The Club Med philosophy was born — vacation villages in exotic locations, combining low prices and simple amenities with community spirit and entertainment.

Frenchman Gilbert Trigano, who provided the tents for that first gathering, came on board as the managing director of the company in 1954 and launched a major expansion drive. Polynesian-style huts replaced the tents at the newly opened location in Greece in 1954, and in 1956 the company set up its first ski resort in Leysin, Switzerland. Club Méditerranée was incorporated the following year.

The Rothschild Group was the company's main shareholder from 1961 until 1988, providing the capital for much of Club Méditerranée's expansion. The company went public in 1966.

Club Méditerranée expanded into the cruise line business during the late 1960s, but surly crews and the outbreak of the Arab-Israeli War in 1967 scuttled plans. In the late 1960s Club Méditerranée gained a foothold in the US, opening an office in New York and a hotel in Northern California. In the 1970s the company became one of the biggest leisure groups in France through a series of mergers and acquisitions. The 1970s and 1980s also saw the company hone its freewheeling, anything-goes image.

Club Med, Inc., was set up in New York in 1984 to handle the company's business in the Americas and Asia. Trigano relaunched the cruise line concept in 1990. Club Méditerranée's expansion came to a crashing halt in 1991 as the company suffered its first-ever loss. Political unrest in its prime tourist locations plagued operations, leading in 1993 to a major loss and Trigano's resignation (though he remained as a director). His son Serge took over as chairman that year and set about cutting costs. Lawsuits plagued the company in 1996 — one involving the fatal crash of a Club Med plane, the other involving a black-face minstrel show.

Board members looking to turn around losses created a new position for Serge Trigano in 1997 and replaced him as chairman with Philippe Bourguignon, who helped revive Euro Disney. To boost profits, the company sold its *Club Med 1* cruise ship, as well as other assets that were outside the scope of its core resort business. It also phased out its lower-priced Club Aquarius resorts as part of its efforts to refocus on a single brand. But Club Med suffered record losses in 1997, and Trigano and his father later resigned.

With its restructuring plan in full swing in 1998, Club Med made its way back into the black. The company began renovating its village resorts and consolidating and centralizing its administrative offices. Club Med also implemented a new advertising campaign in 1998 and announced plans to open new ski resorts in the US and Canada, as well as Club Med at Paris Bercy, a recreational center in Paris. In 1999 Club Med bought French travel company Jet Tours Holding. In 2000 the company branched into e-commerce through its creation of Internet subsidiary Club Med On Line. It also purchased its third US village in 2000 in Crested Butte, Colorado.

Chairman, Supervisory Board:
Tiberto Ruy Brandolini d'Adda
VC, Supervisory Board: Willy Stricker
Chairman, Executive Board and CEO:
Philippe Bourguignon, age 51
**Assistant Director General, Finance, Development, and
International Relations:** Henri Giscard d'Estaing
Marketing, Sales, and Transportation: Yves Martin
Operations: Serge Ravailhe
Human Resources: Laurent Amelineau
Development and Asset Management: Jacques Ehrmann
Quality and Environment: Franck Gueguen
Strategy and Special Projects: Maria Outters
Special Projects and Tour Operating: Laurent Therezien
Finance and Information Systems: Michel Wolfovski
Director Communications: Christian Mure
Strategy and Special Projects: Jérôme Maton
Marketing: Alain Pourcelot
Club Med Products-Worldwide: Jean-Michel Landau
Asian Operations: Maurice Benzaquen
Auditors: Cogerco-Flipo; Ernst & Young Audit

LOCATIONS

HQ: 11 rue de Cambrai, 75019 Paris Cedex 19, France
Phone: +33-1-53-35-35-53   **Fax:** +33-1-53-35-36-16
Web site: http://www.clubmed.com.

Selected Club Med Resort Locations

Australia	Malaysia
Bahamas	Maldives
Croatia	Mexico
Cuba	Montenegro
Dominican Republic	Morocco
Egypt	Portugal
France	Saint Lucia
French West Indies	Saint Martin
Greece	Senegal
Haiti	Spain
Indonesia	Switzerland
Israel	Thailand
Italy	Tunisia
Ivory Coast	Turkey
Japan	US

PRODUCTS/OPERATIONS

Selected Brands
Club Med
Club Med Business
Club Med Cruises
Club Med Voyages
Jet Tours

COMPETITORS

Accor	Preussag
American Classic Voyages	Rank
Carlson	Royal Caribbean Cruises
Carnival	Royal Olympic Cruises
ClubCorp	Sandals Resorts
Hilton	Starwood Hotels & Resorts
Hyatt	Worldwide
Marriott International	Sun International Hotels
P&O	Vail Resorts
P&O Princess Cruises	Walt Disney

HISTORICAL FINANCIALS & EMPLOYEES

OTC: CLMDY FYE: October 31	Annual Growth	10/90	10/91	10/92	10/93	10/94	10/95	10/96	10/97	10/98	10/99
Sales ($ mil.)	(0.4%)	1,612	1,376	1,578	1,378	1,704	1,734	1,562	1,423	1,534	1,560
Net income ($ mil.)	(6.8%)	78	(3)	31	(50)	18	35	(145)	(224)	31	41
Income as % of sales	—	4.8%	—	2.0%	—	1.1%	2.0%	—	—	2.0%	2.6%
Earnings per share ($)	(11.5%)	1.59	(0.06)	0.57	(0.91)	0.33	0.51	(2.12)	(3.20)	0.41	0.53
Stock price - FY high ($)	—	22.64	19.95	19.89	15.53	17.58	22.05	19.75	16.50	17.00	23.88
Stock price - FY low ($)	—	14.86	13.53	13.55	11.73	10.47	15.20	12.38	11.75	13.13	14.50
Stock price - FY close ($)	3.1%	17.47	14.83	14.17	11.73	17.05	15.66	12.38	15.38	15.25	23.00
P/E - high	—	14	—	35	—	53	43	—	—	41	45
P/E - low	—	9	—	24	—	32	30	—	—	32	27
Dividends per share ($)	—	0.39	0.35	0.23	0.23	0.00	0.00	0.00	0.00	0.00	0.00
Book value per share ($)	(5.7%)	—	11.76	12.62	10.52	11.24	13.30	10.43	5.96	17.11	7.35
Employees	0.0%	—	—	—	—	—	—	20,000	19,400	20,000	20,000

STOCK PRICE HISTORY

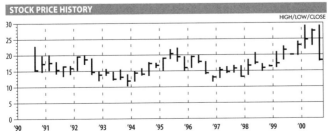

HIGH/LOW/CLOSE

1999 FISCAL YEAR-END

Debt ratio: 33.8%
Return on equity: 7.7%
Cash ($ mil.): 95
Current ratio: 0.42
Long-term debt ($ mil.): 288
No. of shares (mil.): 77
Dividends
  Yield: —
  Payout: —
Market value ($ mil.): 1,770

COLES MYER LTD.

OVERVIEW

Coles Myer is the top dingo of Australian retailers. As leader of the pack, the Tooronga, Victoria-based company operates more than 2,000 supermarket, discount, and specialty stores in Australia and New Zealand. Nearly 60% of sales come from food and liquor chains, including Coles and Bi-Lo supermarkets, the fast-food Red Rooster chain, and Liquorland.

Other businesses include department stores (Myer Grace Bros) and discount stores such as Fosseys (being converted to Target Country), Kmart, and Target. (Coles Myer holds the rights to use the Kmart and Target names in Australia and New Zealand.) It also runs Katies, which sells women's apparel, and five Local Hero hotels.

The company's focus of late has been concept stores, some of which are deeply stocked stores-within-stores. While some have taken off, including its office supply chain, Officeworks, others such as toy seller World 4 Kids and Myer Home (now closed) have struggled. Other Coles Myer test stores sell furniture and health and beauty items.

Former chairman Solomon Lew, a central figure in a long-running financial scandal at Coles Myer, owns about 5% of the company.

HISTORY

After studying US and UK chain-store retailing, including the five-and-dime stores of S. S. Kresge, George James Coles opened his first "3d, 6d, and 1/-" discount variety store in 1914 in a working-class neighborhood of Collingwood, Australia. Coles expanded to a larger store five years later. With the formation of G. J. Coles & Coy in 1921, Coles spent the 1920s and 1930s opening stores in other Australian cities. The company went public in 1927. Following WWII the firm embarked on a major acquisition binge. Coles & Coy bought Selfridges (Australasia — New South Wales, 1950), F&G Stores (Victoria, 1951), and Penneys (Queensland, 1956). The company expanded into food retailing in 1958 with the purchase of the 54-store John Connell Dickins chain. A year later it acquired Beilby's of South Australia and, in 1960, the Matthews Thompson group of 265 outlets in New South Wales.

Coles & Coy opened its first major discount store, Colmart, in 1968 and opened its first Kmart the following year through a joint venture with S. S. Kresge. In 1978 it bought out the renamed Kmart Corporation's interest in return for stock.

The company bought several liquor store chains in 1981, including Liquorland and Mac the Slasher (converted to the Liquorland banner). Coles & Coy began opening Super K food and general merchandise stores in 1982. Two years later it bought Katies, a women's apparel chain with 117 stores.

Coles & Coy became Coles Myer in 1986 when it merged with the Myer Emporium chain of Melbourne. Founded in 1900 by Sidney Myer, the company went public in 1925 and began opening Target stores in 1970. At the time of the merger, Myer was Australia's #3 retailer and largest department store chain, with 56 department stores, 68 Target stores, 122 Fosseys variety stores, 45 Country Road stores (spun off in 1987), and a number of Red Rooster fast-food outlets.

In 1987 Coles Myer entered discount food retailing with the acquisition of 25 Bi-Lo supermarkets. The next year it moved outside Australia when it opened a Kmart in New Zealand. In 1993 the company introduced World 4 Kids toy and recreation stores and a chain of office supply stores, Officeworks. That year Coles Myer repurchased the 21.5% stake owned by Kmart while continuing to use the Kmart name in Australia and New Zealand.

When finance director Philip Bowman was fired in 1995, he sued the company for wrongful dismissal. Bowman claimed he was investigating a 1990 transaction that cost the company $18 million while indirectly benefiting chairman Solomon Lew by the same amount. The "Yannon" deal resulted in Lew's ouster as chairman, though he stayed on the board of directors. Bowman's suit was settled for $1.1 million. In 1997 former chairman and CEO Brian Quinn was found guilty of conspiring to defraud Coles Myer of $3.5 million (used to pay for renovations to his Melbourne home) and sentenced to four years in prison.

In 1997 and 1998 Coles Myer tested more than a dozen concept stores, including Myer Megamart (furniture and electronics), Target Home (home furnishings), and Essentially Me (health and beauty items). The trend continued in 1999 with let's eat (a combination restaurant and grocery). It also began converting Fosseys stores to Target Country (smaller Target stores).

In March 2000 Coles Myer created an e-commerce unit, e.colesmyer, under which it consolidated all of its online businesses.

Chairman: Stanley D. M. Wallis, age 60
CEO and Managing Director: Dennis K. Eck, age 56, $4,141,903 pay
CFO: John P. Schmoll, age 50, $674,916 pay
Chief Administration Officer: Tim Hammon, age 45, $760,400 pay
Chief Information Officer; Managing Director e.colesmyer: Jon Wood, age 39
Managing Director, Bi-Lo: Gerry Masters, age 43
Managing Director, Myer Grace Bros: Terry McCartney, age 46, $679,358 pay
Managing Director, Apparel and Home: Gary Nye, age 47, $636,634 pay
Managing Director, General Merchandise: Geoff Sadler, age 51
Managing Director, Liquorland: Craig Watkins, age 47
Managing Director, Coles & Logistics: Alan Williams, age 52, $661,170 pay
General Manager of Human Resources: Peter Nelson
Secretary: Kevin Elkington
Auditors: PricewaterhouseCoopers

LOCATIONS

HQ: 800 Toorak Rd., Tooronga, Victoria 3146, Australia
Phone: +61-3-9829-3111   **Fax:** +61-3-9829-6787
Web site: http://www.colesmyer.com.au

Coles Myer operates more than 2,000 retail stores in Australia and New Zealand.

PRODUCTS/OPERATIONS

2000 Sales

	$ mil.	% of total
Food & liquor	8,251	57
General merchandise	2,204	15
Myer Grace Bros	2,129	15
Apparel & home	1,440	10
Other	391	3
Adjustments	(1)	—
Total	**14,414**	**100**

COMPETITORS

David Jones
Davids Limited
Franklins Holdings
Harris Scarfe Holdings
Harvey Norman Holdings
Woolworths

HISTORICAL FINANCIALS & EMPLOYEES

NYSE: CM FYE: Last Sunday in July	Annual Growth	7/91	7/92	7/93	7/94	7/95	7/96	7/97	7/98	7/99	7/00
Sales ($ mil.)	2.4%	11,635	11,295	10,463	11,782	12,396	14,583	14,298	12,499	14,614	14,414
Net income ($ mil.)	(4.1%)	254	276	284	314	293	217	290	215	255	174
Income as % of sales	—	2.2%	2.4%	2.7%	2.7%	2.4%	1.5%	2.0%	1.7%	1.7%	1.2%
Earnings per share ($)	(4.8%)	1.87	1.73	1.65	1.78	1.45	1.49	2.02	1.51	1.77	1.20
Stock price - FY high ($)	—	25.48	29.16	28.18	30.14	27.56	30.00	42.75	42.50	48.00	47.38
Stock price - FY low ($)	—	17.15	23.15	19.11	23.28	22.66	24.25	27.38	29.50	27.38	27.63
Stock price - FY close ($)	2.0%	25.24	25.11	25.97	24.01	25.00	27.75	40.75	29.50	46.50	30.19
P/E - high	—	14	17	17	17	18	20	21	28	27	39
P/E - low	—	9	13	12	13	15	16	14	20	15	23
Dividends per share ($)	5.4%	0.82	0.90	0.58	1.08	1.21	0.72	1.39	0.73	1.23	1.32
Book value per share ($)	(11.3%)	32.50	31.53	13.63	15.16	14.08	14.00	13.08	11.48	12.63	11.08
Employees	1.0%	143,182	132,543	136,195	135,365	143,281	152,744	148,000	148,346	151,284	157,000

STOCK PRICE HISTORY

HIGH/LOW/CLOSE

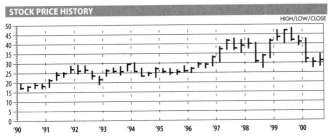

2000 FISCAL YEAR-END

Debt ratio: 42.2%
Return on equity: 10.1%
Cash ($ mil.): 153
Current ratio: 1.23
Long-term debt ($ mil.): 1,178
No. of shares (mil.): 146
Dividends
 Yield: 4.4%
 Payout: 110.0%
Market value ($ mil.): 4,394

COMINCO LTD.

Getting shafted is quite all right with Cominco, a Vancouver-based mining company. Cominco is the world's largest producer of zinc concentrate and is among the top five producers of zinc metal. The company's operations include smelting and refining, and it produces lead, copper, and molybdenum and germanium concentrates, in addition to copper, silver, and gold. More products include copper sulfate, copper arsenate, sulfuric acid, sulfur dioxide, and ammonium sulfate fertilizer. Zinc products account for almost 65% of Cominco's sales. Its mining, smelting, and refining operations are in Canada, Peru, and the US.

Higher metal prices have helped Cominco return to profitability, along with its own cost-cutting efforts and an increase in production. Teck Corporation, a Vancouver-based mining investment company, owns 45% of Cominco.

In 1906 The Consolidated Mining and Smelting Company of Canada (shortened to Cominco Ltd. in 1966) was formed as a subsidiary of the Canadian Pacific Railway by the consolidation of the St. Eugene, Centre Star, and War Eagle mining claims, staked in the early 1890s. At the time, a huge mining camp had sprung up, creating the town of Trail, the hub of several mining and refining operations. In 1909 Cominco bought the Sullivan Mine at Kimberley, British Columbia, which formed the basis for much of its zinc and lead sales.

The company built Canada's first copper refinery at Trail in 1915, and the following year it built, at the government's request, one of the first electrolytic zinc refineries to supply zinc for its brass needs in WWI. By 1919 Cominco had developed a differential flotation process that enabled the separation of lead, zinc, and iron minerals from ore into high-grade concentrates.

By the late 1920s the communities of Trail and Kimberley had expanded and environmental complaints about the smelting fumes and chemical by-products had increased. In 1931 Cominco responded by building an ammonium sulphate fertilizer plant as part of a sulfur-recovery process, siphoning off the sulfuric acids and other by-products of its mining operations. In 1938 the company bought Montana Phosphate Products (later Cominco American) as a source of phosphate rock for its fertilizer business.

WWII created a big demand for metal and fertilizer products (ammonium nitrates for explosives) during the 1940s. After the war Cominco began modernizing and got involved in the development of transportation, transmission lines, power plants, and additional production facilities throughout the region to support its operations.

In 1956 the company established Cominco Products, in Spokane, Washington, to warehouse fertilizers and liquid-fertilizer conversion facilities. In the late 1950s and early 1960s, as the electronics industry developed, Cominco built specialized plants for high-purity metals in Trail and Spokane.

Cominco Explorations (UK) Ltd. and Cominco Exploration Pty Ltd. were formed in 1965 for potential mining in the UK and Australia, respectively. Cominco Products merged with Cominco American in 1966 to bring together all its US mining, exploration, fertilizer, and high-purity-metal operations.

In the late 1970s Cominco started a $425 million modernization program at its facilities in Kimberley and Trail. In 1980 it bought the Bethlehem Copper Corporation. The company began construction of the Red Dog Mine in Alaska in 1989.

Cominco increased its global zinc operations during the 1990s. Cominco spun off its fertilizer operations as Cominco Fertilizers (later named Agrium) in 1993. It sold its remaining fertilizer interests to Agrium the next year. Heavy debt and dropping metal prices forced Cominco to divest its other noncore businesses in 1997.

In 1998 the firm initiated plans to construct a high-tech copper refinery in British Columbia. The refinery is expected to increase Cominco's share of the copper market. It also plans to increase its zinc output at Red Dog Mine. Cominco entered an option agreement with International Annax Ventures (Australia) in 1999 to explore for zinc in Indonesia.

Canadian mineral producer Aur Resources agreed in 2000 to buy Cominco's 76% stake in Compania Minera Quebrada Blanca, which operates the Quebrada Blanca copper mine in Chile. Expatriate Resources agreed to pay $13 million for Cominco's Kudz Ze Kayah zinc property in the Yukon Territory. Parent Teck Corporation bought an additional million shares of Cominco that year, boosting its stake to 45%.

Chairman; President and CEO, Teck: Norman B. Keevil
President and CEO: David A. Thompson, $1,126,400 pay
VP Business Development: Bryan Morris
VP Environment and Corporate Affairs:
Douglas H. Horswill
VP Exploration: Jon A. Collins
VP Finance and CFO: Glen B. Darou, $410,400 pay
VP Human Resources: James A. Utley
VP Marketing and Sales: Roger A. Brain, $342,000 pay
VP Metal Production: Roger H. Watson, $406,800 pay
VP Mines: Ronald M. Henningson, $347,000 pay
Treasurer: Michael K. Longinotti
General Counsel and Secretary: Gerard L. Manuel
Auditors: KPMG LLP

LOCATIONS

HQ: 500-200 Burrard St., Vancouver,
British Columbia V6C 3L7, Canada
Phone: 604-682-0611 **Fax:** 604-685-3019
US HQ: 15918 E. Euclid Ave., Spokane, WA 99216
US Phone: 509-747-6111 **US Fax:** 509-459-4400
Web site: http://www.cominco.com

Cominco operates mines, smelters, and refineries in
Canada, Peru, and the US. It maintains exploration
offices in Canada, Chile, Mexico, Namibia, Peru, Turkey,
and the US, and sales offices in Canada and Singapore.

1999 Sales

	% of total
North America	49
Asia	23
Europe	20
Latin America	7
Other regions	1
Total	**100**

PRODUCTS/OPERATIONS

1999 Sales

	% of total
Zinc	64
Copper	12
Gold & silver	7
Lead	6
Other	11
Total	**100**

Selected Products

Concentrates	Lead
Copper	Silver
Germanium	Zinc
Lead	
Molybdenum	**Other Products**
Zinc	Ammonium sulfate
	fertilizer
Refined Metals	Copper arsenate
Bismuth	Copper sulfate
Cadmium	Germanium dioxide
Copper	Sulfur
Gold	Sulfur dioxide
Indium	Sulfuric acid

COMPETITORS

ASARCO	Noranda
Freeport-McMoRan	Phelps Dodge
Copper & Gold	Rio Algom
Freeport-McMoRan	Rio Tinto plc
Sulphur	Southern Peru Copper
Inco Limited	Toho Zinc
Kennecott	WMC Limited
METALEUROP	Zambia Copper

HISTORICAL FINANCIALS & EMPLOYEES

AMEX: CLT FYE: December 31	Annual Growth	12/90	12/91	12/92	12/93	12/94	12/95	12/96	12/97	12/98	12/99
Sales ($ mil.)	(0.7%)	1,210	1,134	1,154	742	801	1,124	1,259	1,156	1,054	1,137
Net income ($ mil.)	9.8%	47	(36)	(24)	(86)	94	76	111	(52)	(15)	110
Income as % of sales	—	3.9%	—	—	—	11.8%	6.8%	8.8%	—	—	9.7%
Earnings per share ($)	10.6%	0.52	(0.48)	(0.33)	(1.10)	1.15	0.89	1.30	(0.61)	(0.17)	1.29
Stock price - FY high ($)	—	24.00	22.13	19.63	16.25	19.38	21.88	27.13	30.00	19.25	21.88
Stock price - FY low ($)	—	16.75	17.13	13.38	10.63	14.00	14.88	19.13	13.88	8.63	11.31
Stock price - FY close ($)	1.5%	18.50	18.63	13.75	15.00	17.75	20.63	25.00	15.44	11.50	21.13
P/E - high	—	46	—	—	—	17	25	21	—	—	17
P/E - low	—	32	—	—	—	12	17	15	—	—	9
Dividends per share ($)	(4.2%)	0.44	0.44	0.33	0.00	0.00	0.00	0.11	0.26	0.30	0.30
Book value per share ($)	(1.7%)	14.27	13.33	11.39	9.86	10.55	11.88	12.72	11.82	11.01	12.24
Employees	(4.7%)	7,910	7,588	6,826	6,738	6,738	6,738	5,822	5,776	4,142	5,127

STOCK PRICE HISTORY

HIGH/LOW/CLOSE

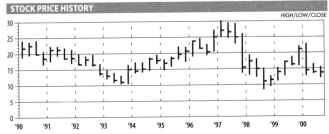

1999 FISCAL YEAR-END

Debt ratio: 28.7%
Return on equity: 12.2%
Cash ($ mil.): 99
Current ratio: 2.05
Long-term debt ($ mil.): 421
No. of shares (mil.): 86
Dividends
  Yield: 1.4%
  Payout: 23.3%
Market value ($ mil.): 1,807

COMPUTACENTER PLC

OVERVIEW

Computacenter can help with your computaneeds. The Hatfield, UK-based company, the UK's largest PC reseller, distributes both computer hardware and software to large corporations and government agencies. Computacenter also offers a variety of services (accounting for about 20% of sales) ranging from computer consultation and installation to network support and management. Clients include Railtrack Group, Royal & Sun Alliance Insurance Group, and British Petroleum.

CEO Michael Norris, who heartily subscribes to the motto, "Dinner at home is a lost sales opportunity," has maintained Computacenter's steady growth by expanding its geographic scope and the range of its services. The company, which sells its products in Belgium, France, Germany, and Luxembourg, has seen substantial growth in its operations outside the UK. Computacenter has also followed an industrywide trend by expanding its offerings beyond reselling. It founded electronic procurement software company Biomni, and offers Web-site hosting and monitoring through its iGroup division.

Co-founders Philip Hulme (chairman) and Peter Ogden (a nonexecutive director) own about 45% of the company.

HISTORY

Computacenter's story is nothing if not about timing. It began at the dawn of the PC revolution, and blossomed because the company's two founders were already awake. Computacenter was formed in 1981 by management consultant Philip Hulme and ex-Morgan Stanley executive Peter Ogden. The UK entrepreneurs, who met while seeking MBAs at Harvard University in the early 1970s, started their computer distribution business after perceiving a need among large corporations for computer systems more adaptable than the wall-sized, expensive mainframes then in vogue.

By 1983, thanks mainly to the birth of IBM's PC, Computacenter was generating sales of £1.5 million. The next year Computacenter created a sibling company called Computasoft to specialize in financial-sector applications. Computacenter by 1984 had a branch network of six locations. In 1989 it joined the International Computer Group, a joint venture formed that year to cater to international organizations with global service concerns.

In 1990 Investcorp, a development capital firm for a consortium of rich Arab investors, bought a 30% stake in Computacenter (In 1995 Investcorp sold its stake at a strong profit). The company continued to ride the corporate networked PC trend and in 1993 logged $526 million in sales and cemented its reputation as the UK's #1 desktop services firm.

Michael Norris, who began at Computacenter as a junior salesman in 1984, was named CEO in 1994. Using his background as one of the company's star sellers, Norris intensified Computacenter's organic growth. The company also re-engineered its maintenance business that year. Computacenter suffered a bit of infamy in 1994 after four people were murdered during a robbery on a yacht in the Caribbean. The yacht, named for the company, was owned by Odgen.

In 1995 Computacenter won the largest desktop contract in Europe, signing an agreement with British Telecommunications. That year the company bought French firm Networx SA and made it a majority-owned Computacenter subsidiary. The company in 1996 beefed up its technical acumen to include consulting and major networking support. Sales that year exceeded $1.3 billion.

Sales reached the $1.8 billion mark in 1997, and the company bought German firm BITService and revamped it into a German subsidiary. Computacenter went public in 1998 in the midst of a high-tech stock frenzy that made 30 of its employees millionaires overnight. The already wealthy Hulme and Ogden donated most of their money to individual charitable trusts.

Also in 1998, in a continuing effort to expand its services, Computacenter forged an alliance with Microsoft to supply planning and support services to Windows NT customers. That year the company founded its e-commerce division, iGroup, which develops Internet commerce strategies and provides Web-site monitoring and hosting services.

In 1999 Computacenter signed a three-year contract renewal with telecom giant British Telecommunications to provide systems maintenance and e-commerce implementation services. Later that year Computacenter launched a 50-50 joint venture with Computasoft. The new company, Biomni, develops business-to-business software for electronic trading networks. Computacenter announced in 2000 its plan to take Biomni public.

Chairman: Philip W. Hulme, age 51
CEO: Michael J. Norris, age 38
Director Finance: Tony Conophy, age 42
General Manager, iGroup: Richard Archer, age 40
Director IT: Gordon Channon, age 52
General Manager Technical Services: Mike Davies, age 39
General Manager Corporate Development and Marketing: Martin Hellawell, age 35
Managing Director Supply Chain Services: John Joslin, age 41
Managing Director Enterprise Sales: Chris New, age 41
Secretary: Alan Pottinger, age 42
Managing Director Human Resources: Craig Routledge, age 42
Auditors: Ernst & Young

LOCATIONS

HQ: Hatfield Ave., Hatfield,
Hertfordshire AL10 9TW, United Kingdom
Phone: +44-17-0763-1000   **Fax:** +44-17-0763-9966
Web site: http://www.computacenter.co.uk

Computacenter has operations in Belgium, France, Germany, and the UK.

1999 Sales

	% of total
UK	82
France & Belgium	13
Germany	4
Other countries	1
Total	**100**

PRODUCTS/OPERATIONS

Services
Configuration
Disaster recovery
E-commerce consulting
Management outsourcing
Procurement
Systems planning and implementation
Technical support
Training

COMPETITORS

Atos Origin
Bull
Cap Gemini
CMG
Compaq
Dell Computer
DiData
EDS
GE Capital
Getronics
IBM
ICL
Logica
Misys
Morse Holdings
Sema Group
Siemens
Unisys

HISTORICAL FINANCIALS & EMPLOYEES

London: CCC FYE: December 31	Annual Growth	12/90	12/91	12/92	12/93	12/94	12/95	12/96	12/97	12/98	12/99
Sales (£ mil.)	36.8%	—	—	—	—	—	503	805	1,134	1,586	1,761
Net income (£ mil.)	55.7%	—	—	—	—	—	9	27	31	39	53
Income as % of sales	—	—	—	—	—	—	1.8%	3.4%	2.7%	2.5%	3.0%
Earnings per share (p)	19.6%	—	—	—	—	—	—	—	—	23.50	28.10
Stock price - FY high (p)	—	—	—	—	—	—	—	—	—	830.00	1,143.00
Stock price - FY low (p)	—	—	—	—	—	—	—	—	—	355.00	375.00
Stock price - FY close (p)	131.3%	—	—	—	—	—	—	—	—	440.00	1,017.50
P/E - high	—	—	—	—	—	—	—	—	—	35	41
P/E - low	—	—	—	—	—	—	—	—	—	15	13
Dividends per share (p)	16.0%	—	—	—	—	—	—	—	—	2.50	2.90
Book value per share (p)	40.2%	—	—	—	—	—	—	—	—	66.40	93.10
Employees	35.6%	—	—	—	—	—	1,510	2,099	2,844	3,939	5,100

STOCK PRICE HISTORY

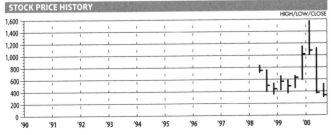

HIGH/LOW/CLOSE

1,600
1,400
1,200
1,000
800
600
400
200
0

'90 '91 '92 '93 '94 '95 '96 '97 '98 '99 '00

1999 FISCAL YEAR-END

Debt ratio: 19.1%
Return on equity: —
Cash (£ mil.): 64
Current ratio: 1.37
Long-term debt (£ mil.): 40
No. of shares (mil.): 181
Dividends
  Yield: 0.0%
  Payout: 0.1%
Market value ($ mil.): 297,675
Sales ($ mil.): 2,848

CORUS GROUP PLC

OVERVIEW

Keeping a stiff upper lip is mandatory for Corus Group (formerly British Steel), the UK's biggest steel company. London-based Corus makes and distributes steel products, including stainless steel, coated and uncoated strip products, tubular products, and wire rod, which are used in construction, carmaking, and mechanical engineering. The company also produces aluminum. Corus became a steel giant with its 1999 purchase of Dutch rival Koninklijke Hoogovens.

Corus has been battered by cheap imported steel from Asia and Eastern Europe and by the strength of the British pound in comparison to other currencies. The company has trimmed its workforce about 10% over two years. The low price of steel drove the company into its consolidation with Koninklijke Hoogovens; further expansion into European and US markets is in the works.

HISTORY

It took decades of aggressive government regulation of the UK steel industry to hammer out British Steel. The process began with price-control measures in the 1930s and in 1950 the Labour government followed up by nationalizing steel producers on the grounds that they represented an unduly powerful oligopoly. A Conservative government took over in 1951 and sold most of the nationalized firms, primarily to their former shareholders. In place of nationalization, an Iron Steel Board — with the power to set maximum steel prices and with the final say on large investments — was formed.

The presence of price controls and an ever-present chance of renationalization discouraged capital investment. Even so, technological innovations such as continuous casting and oxygen-based production enabled UK steelmakers to double production between 1945 and 1960. Meanwhile, competition from European producers stiffened, as did competition from a rebuilt Japan. To add to the UK steel industry's woes, demand began slacking off in the 1960s.

In 1964 the Labour Party, which was committed to renationalizing steel, returned to power. It passed the Iron and Steel Act of 1967, nationalizing about 90% of the UK's steelmaking capacity under a new holding company, British Steel Corporation (BSC). However, specialized, nonintegrated companies and rerolling companies remained freestanding, allowing them to benefit from price controls on BSC steel. BSC consisted of 14 crude steel companies' assets with a 475,000-ton annual capacity. The government compensated shareholders based on stock market values, paying much more than the companies were worth. To make matters worse, the companies' return on capital was a meager 3.7%.

BSC began consolidating its small, outdated facilities into larger works with advanced equipment. In the midst of a huge investment program, the mid-1970s energy crisis hit and steel demand fell; the company began closing its outdated mills. A 1980 strike cost BSC a large chunk of its market share and showed that steel requirements could be met through imports. That year the European Commission (EC) established production limits to reduce the steel glut. It also decided to regulate the amount of state aid steel producers could receive. By the end of 1980, BSC's workforce had been reduced to about 130,000 people — half its size when the companies were nationalized in 1967. During the 1980s BSC disposed of about $1 billion in noncore assets to focus on efficient steelmaking. State aid to European steel producers was largely prohibited in 1985 and the EC's quota system ended in 1988.

The British Steel Act of 1988 privatized BSC, and British Steel was born. The company recorded big profits in 1990, but then a recession hit and British Steel suffered two years of losses before returning to profitability in 1994. The next year the company announced plans to expand its operations in emerging markets such as Asia, Central Europe, and Latin America. In 1996 British Steel sold about 6,000 tons of rails to Latin America. The next year it built a steel plant in Alabama — its first outside the UK — and sold its British Steel Forgings unit, which made components for the aerospace and automobile industries.

In 1998 British Steel joined other steelmakers in asking the EC to investigate Asian steel dumping. Stiff competition and a strong domestic currency caused the company to suffer a loss for fiscal 1999. That year British Steel paid $2.4 billion for Dutch steelmaker Koninklijke Hoogovens (it owns 95% and is buying the rest). At the same time, British Steel became Corus, a name chosen because it has no significant meaning in any language.

Chairman: Brian Moffat, age 60, $769,461 pay
Deputy Chairman: Hendrikus de Ruiter
Co-Chief Executive: John M. Bryant, age 55, $461,122 pay
Co-Chief Executive: J. Fokko van Duyne
Executive Director Financial: John L. Rennocks, age 53, $378,109 pay
Executive Director Asia/Pacific: Anthony P. Pedder, age 49, $414,160 pay
Executive Director Eastern Europe: John B. McDowall, age 57, $433,907 pay
Executive Director North America: Harold Homer, age 58, $422,623 pay
Executive Director Technology: Jeff Edington, age 60, $378,095 pay
Director Personnel: Allen Johnston
Secretary: Richard Reeves
Auditors: PricewaterhouseCoopers LLP

LOCATIONS

HQ: 15 Marylebone Rd., London NW1 5JD, United Kingdom
Phone: +44-20-7314-5500
US HQ: 475 N. Martingale Rd., Ste. 400, Schaumburg, IL 60173
US Phone: 847-619-0400   **US Fax:** 847-619-0468
Web site: http://www.corusgroup.com

1999 Sales

	$ mil.	% of total
Europe		
UK	6,641	66
Other countries	2,215	22
North America	989	10
Other regions	243	2
Total	**10,088**	**100**

PRODUCTS/OPERATIONS

1999 Sales

	$ mil.	% of total
Stainless steel	1,959	19
Coated strip products	1,818	18
Sections & plates	1,523	15
Uncoated strip products	1,481	15
Distribution	1,402	14
Engineering steels	725	7
Tubular products	518	5
Wire rod	321	3
Carbon steel	164	2
Other	177	2
Total	**10,088**	**100**

Selected Products

Aluminum
Engineering steels
    Railway and foundry products (railway track)
    Section plates (heavy construction and shipbuilding)
    Strip products
    Tinplate
    Tubes and pipes
Stainless steel

COMPETITORS

Allegheny Technologies
ARBED
Bethlehem Steel
BÖHLER-UDDEHOLM
Carpenter Technology
Co-Steel
Cockerill Sambre
GS Industries
Kawasaki Steel
Kobe Steel
LTV
Nippon Steel
Nucor
Pohang Iron & Steel
Sumitomo Metal
    Industries
ThyssenKrupp
Usinor
USX-U.S. Steel

HISTORICAL FINANCIALS & EMPLOYEES

NYSE: CGA FYE: December 31*	Annual Growth	3/90	3/91	3/92	3/93	3/94	3/95	3/96	3/97	3/98	3/99
Sales ($ mil.)	2.0%	8,426	8,814	7,982	6,510	6,224	7,755	10,757	11,844	11,613	10,088
Net income ($ mil.)	—	930	338	(59)	(197)	103	759	1,186	508	378	(131)
Income as % of sales	—	11.0%	3.8%	—	—	1.6%	9.8%	11.0%	4.3%	3.3%	—
Earnings per share ($)	—	4.65	1.69	(0.35)	(0.98)	0.51	3.76	5.84	2.50	1.91	(0.66)
Stock price - FY high ($)	—	24.63	27.75	26.25	15.38	21.75	27.25	31.50	31.13	31.06	28.69
Stock price - FY low ($)	—	18.88	20.88	11.13	7.00	11.75	19.38	23.25	23.13	20.63	14.06
Stock price - FY close ($)	(1.7%)	23.63	24.75	11.88	13.38	20.38	26.25	29.50	26.63	24.25	20.19
P/E - high	—	5	16	—	—	43	7	5	12	16	—
P/E - low	—	4	12	—	—	23	5	4	9	11	—
Dividends per share ($)	2.2%	0.51	1.82	1.67	0.33	0.23	0.58	1.59	1.97	2.06	0.62
Book value per share ($)	(0.0%)	35.37	35.40	33.94	28.14	27.86	32.82	35.41	38.28	35.96	35.35
Employees	(2.5%)	—	—	—	—	—	—	50,100	52,900	50,000	46,500

*Beginning December 2000

STOCK PRICE HISTORY

HIGH/LOW/CLOSE

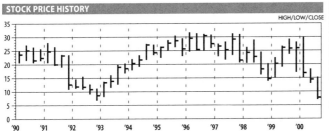

1999 FISCAL YEAR-END

Debt ratio: 0.0%
Return on equity: —
Cash ($ mil.): —
Current ratio: 0.00
Long-term debt ($ mil.): —
No. of shares (mil.): 198
Dividends
    Yield: 7.5%
    Payout: —
Market value ($ mil.): —

CREATIVE TECHNOLOGY LTD.

Creative Technology's products are a blast. The Singapore-based company generates nearly 40% of its sales from audio products, including the popular Sound Blaster brand of PC sound cards and the Nomad family of MP3 players. Creative also makes PC multimedia upgrade kits, graphics cards, digital videodiscs, digital PC cameras, and interactive computer animation software for the Internet (LAVA!). Its subsidiaries include PC speaker maker Cambridge Soundworks, data/fax modem maker Digicom Systems, and electronic musical instruments specialist Ensoniq. Business outside Singapore — mainly in the US and Ireland — accounts for 85% of sales.

A variety of alliances and partnerships boosted Creative to the top of the PC sound market. The company's customers include PC makers Dell, Hewlett-Packard, Gateway, IBM, and NEC. As its PC sound products leveled off and profits fell, Creative tuned its ear to the call of the Web.

The company's Internet initiative includes establishing e-commerce channels for consumers and businesses, developing Internet applications, providing venture funding and technology to budding Internet companies (it has invested in nearly 20), and rolling out a line of broadband communication devices. The company's venture fund has been used to grab chunks of Internet telephony provider Mediaring.com and online home entertainment seller hifi.com.

Co-founder and CEO Sim Wong Hoo owns about 30% of Creative.

With a $6,000 investment Sim Wong Hoo (chairman and CEO) and Ng Kai Wa (later joined by Chay Kwong Soon) founded Creative Technology in Singapore in 1981 to provide engineering services. The company began making Apple II clones for the Chinese market in 1984; two years later it started producing PC clones. From 1983 to 1988 most of Creative's revenues came from PCs. The company opened a US office in 1988.

With stiff competition in the PC market, Sim shifted Creative's focus to sound cards and other PC enhancements. The company introduced its first Sound Blaster audio card in 1989, and that soon became the industry standard. That year Creative launched PJS, an artificial intelligence-based Chinese operating system, and Views, a complementary word processor and desktop publisher with a more than 70,000-character alphabet. Also in 1989 Tandy ordered a large supply of Game Blasters — a sound card targeted at gamers — for its 8,000 Radio Shack stores, giving Creative a strong foothold in the US.

Creative established Avidtek, a majority-owned subsidiary, in Taiwan in 1991. That year the company launched the first of its market dominating upgrade kits, the Sound Blaster Multimedia Upgrade Kit, a software package bundled with a high-performance CD-ROM drive, the Sound Blaster Pro, and other software applications. The company went public in 1992. That year Creative set up a Beijing-based joint venture.

The growing popularity of multimedia was music to Creative's ears. More computers were being sold with sound cards and multimedia capabilities preinstalled, so the company signed deals to supply manufacturers, including Compaq and Dell. Creative also diversified. In 1993 it acquired ShareVision Technology (videoconferencing products) and E-mu Systems (digital sound production systems).

The company also tried its hand at communication products. In 1994 it acquired modem maker Digicom. The next year it released Phone Blaster, which combined voice mail, e-mail, and fax transmission functions. Also in 1995 Creative opened a factory in Malaysia and a distribution center in Ireland.

Cracks began to show in Creative's progress in 1995. The slowing of the sound board market caused a steep drop in profits and prompted the company to restructure and refocus on sound products. Ng resigned that year, and Chay left in 1996. Creative introduced Graphics Blaster add-on graphics accelerator cards and signed a deal for Samsung to build its CD-ROM drive products that year.

Opting to add new technology quickly through acquisitions, in 1997 Creative bought speaker maker Cambridge Soundworks; Ensoniq, maker of audio chips and electronic musical instruments; and the NetMedia Group of core logic chipset maker OPTi. In 1998 the company acquired Silicon Engineering, a maker of communications, multimedia, and storage integrated circuits. In 1999 Creative debuted the Nomad MP3 player, which plays digitally encoded music downloaded from PCs, and intensified plans to provide entertainment and e-commerce services and products.

Chairman and CEO: Sim Wong Hoo
VC, CFO, Treasurer, and Secretary: Ng Keh Long
President, Creative Labs, Inc. (US): Craig McHugh
Director Human Resources, Creative Labs, Inc. (US): Judith Martin
Senior Manager Public Relations: Theresa Pulido
Manager Investor Relations: Lisa Laymon
Manager Public Relations: Hector Martinez
Coordinator Product Reviews: Jared Peck
Coordinator Public Relations: Michelle Denny
Auditors: PricewaterhouseCoopers

LOCATIONS

HQ: 31 International Business Park, 609921, Singapore
Phone: +65-895-4000   **Fax:** +65-895-4999
US HQ: 1901 McCarthy Blvd., Milpitas, CA 95035
US Phone: 408-428-6600   **US Fax:** 408-428-6611
Web site: http://www.creative.com

Creative Technology has manufacturing plants in Malaysia and Singapore, and distribution centers in Ireland and the US.

2000 Sales

	$ mil.	% of total
US	599	45
Ireland	471	35
Singapore	203	15
Other countries	71	5
Total	**1,344**	**100**

PRODUCTS/OPERATIONS

2000 Sales

	% of total
Audio products	39
Multimedia upgrade kits	23
Graphic & video products	18
Speakers, communication & other products	20
Total	**100**

Selected Products
2-D/3-D graphic accelerator cards (the 3D Blaster line)
Broadband Internet access products
CDRewritable drives (Blaster CD-RW)
Desktop digital camera (Video Blaster WebCam)
Electronic musical instruments
Internet telephony
Live audio visual animation software (LAVA!)
Modems
Multimedia upgrade kits (sound card, drive, speakers, software)
PC digital videodiscs (Encore Dxr3)
Personal digital entertainment (Nomad MP3 players)
Portable digital PC camera (WebCam Freestyle)
Sound cards and chipsets (Sound Blaster)
Speakers (Cambridge Soundworks)

COMPETITORS

3Com	Intel	Polycom
3dfx	Matrox	SONICblue
3Dlabs	Electronic	Telex
ATI Technologies	Systems	Communications
Aureal	Microsoft	Trident
Bose	Motorola	Microsystems
Boston Acoustics	NeoMagic	VTEL
Cirrus Logic	NVIDIA	Yamaha
ESS Technology	PictureTel	

HISTORICAL FINANCIALS & EMPLOYEES

Nasdaq: CREAF FYE: June 30	Annual Growth	6/91	6/92	6/93	6/94	6/95	6/96	6/97	6/98	6/99	6/00
Sales ($ mil.)	55.8%	25	86	292	658	1,202	1,308	1,233	1,234	1,297	1,344
Net income ($ mil.)	38.8%	8	1	45	98	27	(38)	167	135	115	161
Income as % of sales	—	33.9%	0.7%	15.4%	14.9%	2.2%	—	13.5%	10.9%	8.9%	12.0%
Earnings per share ($)	19.0%	—	—	0.55	1.11	0.30	(0.43)	1.84	1.42	1.25	1.86
Stock price - FY high ($)	—	—	—	19.25	19.63	24.00	14.13	20.25	29.38	18.63	38.81
Stock price - FY low ($)	—	—	—	5.38	8.75	7.00	5.75	3.50	11.00	7.88	8.88
Stock price - FY close ($)	7.3%	—	—	14.63	17.25	9.38	6.00	17.00	12.38	13.44	23.88
P/E - high	—	—	—	35	17	80	—	11	20	15	20
P/E - low	—	—	—	10	8	23	—	2	7	6	5
Dividends per share ($)	—	—	—	0.00	0.00	0.00	0.00	0.00	0.00	0.50	0.25
Book value per share ($)	26.3%	—	—	1.89	3.09	3.45	3.04	5.88	6.70	6.67	9.69
Employees	34.1%	—	477	1,020	4,100	4,185	4,170	3,489	5,000	4,000	5,000

STOCK PRICE HISTORY
High/Low/Close

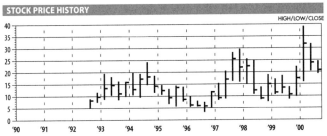

2000 FISCAL YEAR-END

Debt ratio: 3.4%
Return on equity: 24.0%
Cash ($ mil.): 286
Current ratio: 1.97
Long-term debt ($ mil.): 27
No. of shares (mil.): 80
Dividends
  Yield: 1.0%
  Payout: 13.4%
Market value ($ mil.): 1,918

CRÉDIT LYONNAIS

Even the lions of France's financial industry are being dragged into the scandals that have engulfed the *vieil* Crédit Lyonnais. Luckily for the *nouveau* Crédit Lyonnais, things are looking less bleak — possibly even rosy.

Crédit Lyonnais, privatized in 1999, appears to be rising above the seemingly never-ending problems that plagued it during the last half of the 1990s: Government bailouts, loans that went far beyond risky, domestic and foreign probes into fraud, and more. Even the loftiest of government and banking officials have been touched by the allegations and investigations.

The new-and-improved Crédit Lyonnais is 10%-owned by the government; 33% of the bank is controlled by an alliance that includes such investors as French bank Crédit Agricole (10%), German insurer Allianz (6%), and French insurer AXA (5%). The bank provides consumer, commercial, and investment banking; asset management; and securities trading services through about 1,900 branches in France and other offices around the world. Subsidiaries and affiliates also offer insurance.

HISTORY

Former lawyer, stockbroker, mine manager, and silk merchant Henri Germain founded Crédit Lyonnais in 1863 to provide business capital in booming Lyons, France. It expanded into Paris and Marseilles in 1865, and its focus shifted to Paris after Germain, a widower, married a Parisienne and took a seat in Parliament.

Its first foreign branch was in London, where the bank stashed assets to save them from the Franco-Prussian War of 1870-71 and ensuing civil unrest.

Germain died in 1905. The growing bank had branches as far away as Moscow by the advent of WWI, which sent France's economy into a tailspin from which it didn't recover until the 1920s. Crédit Lyonnais was hit hard by the Depression, but was the only French bank to continue paying dividends.

After WWII, Crédit Lyonnais was nationalized (along with most major French industrial companies). Continued expansion made it one of the world's 10 largest banks by the 1970s.

The 1960s and 1970s were marked by costly strikes, oil shocks, inflation, and bank president Jacques Chaine's assassination by an anarchist. Banking policy seesawed between socialist aims and capitalist ones.

Former Paribas head Jean-Yves Haberer took over in 1988. With enthusiasm rising for economic union, he began assembling a pan-European bank. The bank added branches and made what turned out to be risky deals relating to international ventures. When Europe's economy soured, so did many bank investments, including a 1990 loan to help shady Italian financier Giancarlo Paretti buy US filmmaker Metro-Goldwyn-Mayer (MGM). Defaults gave the bank a huge portfolio of distressed businesses.

Former insurance executive Jean Peyrelevade became chairman in 1993. He cut staff, streamlined operations, and sold assets (including 48% of the bank's interest in insurer Union des Assurances Fédérales). But his actions were too little, too late.

In 1994 Crédit Lyonnais' biggest shareholders — the French government and Thomson-CSF — gave the bank more than $850 million, followed by another infusion later that year. In 1995 the EU pledged $9.3 billion in support. (The bank vowed to get problem assets off the books — shunting them into a new French government-guaranteed entity — and to cut its global network by 35% and its European assets in half by the end of 1998.)

Crédit Lyonnais had to ask France for more money in 1996, the same year a suspicious fire gutted the bank's palatial Paris headquarters and destroyed thousands of company documents. The bank's woes were exacerbated the next year when internal auditors alleged Crédit Lyonnais officials had defrauded the bank of several billion francs through 1993. Nevertheless, by cutting costs and reducing operations, the bank turned a profit in 1997.

In 1998 the firm was snared in the Long-Term Capital Management hedge fund collapse, having made more than $30 million in personal loans to fund partners. Privatization efforts (including the sale of some foreign operations) were slowed by the debacle, but Crédit Lyonnais finally floated in 1999. Later that year US and California investigators looked for improprieties in the bank's takeover of a failed insurer, and the Japanese government rapped the bank's knuckles over another matter. Neither scandal, however, could compare to 2000's revelations that continuing investigations into Crédit Lyonnais' earlier problems were reaching into some of the highest government and central banking offices.

Chairman: Jean Peyrelevade, age 60
CEO: Dominique Ferrero
Member Executive Committee: Thierry Marraud
Member Executive Committee: Jean-Yves Durance
Member Executive Committee: Patrice Durand
Head of Human Resources Division: Philippe Wattier
Head of Information Technology: Aline Bec
Head of Business Planning and Analysis:
Jacques Sarrasin
**Head of Economic and Financial Research and
Strategy:** Jean-Paul Betbéze
Head of Group Financial Management Division:
Yves Perrier
Corporate Secretary and Head of Legal Affairs:
Jean-François Verny
Auditors: Befec-Price Waterhouse; Deloitte Touche
Tohmatsu; Mazars & Guérard

LOCATIONS

HQ: 19, boulevard des Italiens, 75002 Paris, France
Phone: +33-1-42-95-67-89   **Fax:** +33-1-42-95-94-37
US HQ: 1301 Avenue of the Americas,
New York, NY 10019
US Phone: 212-261-7000   **US Fax:** 212-459-3170
Web site: http://www.creditlyonnais.com

1999 Sales

	% of total
Europe	
France	71
Other countries	10
Americas	9
Asia	7
Africa/Middle East	3
Total	**100**

PRODUCTS/OPERATIONS

1999 Sales

	€ mil.	% of total
Interest income	10,656	75
Fee income	2,199	15
Trading income	1,206	8
Other	239	2
Total	**14,300**	**100**

Selected Operations
PT Bank CL Indonesia (80%)
Banque de l'Ile de France - BDEI
Cie de Gestion Foncière - Cogefo
CL Asset Securities Holding LLC
CL Capital Markets International
CL Développement Économique
CL Eurofactors Participations
CL Europe SA
CL Global Banking
CL Investissements Financiers Immobiliers (Clinfim)
CL Leasing Europe
CL Leasing Overseas
Crédit Lyonnais Asset Management
Interfimo (95%)
Lion Expansion
Slibail - Société Lyonnaise de crédit-bail

COMPETITORS

Allianz	Credit Suisse
Bank of America	Dai-Ichi Kangyo
Barclays	Deutsche Bank
BNP	HSBC Holdings
Caisse Nationale de Credit	Industrial Bank of Japan
Agricole	ING
CCF	J.P. Morgan
Chase Manhattan	Société Générale
Citigroup	UBS
Crédit Foncier de France	

HISTORICAL FINANCIALS & EMPLOYEES

Euronext Paris: CL FYE: December 31	Annual Growth	12/90	12/91	12/92	12/93	12/94	12/95	12/96	12/97	12/98	12/99
Assets (€ mil.)	(2.8%)	223,031	241,908	295,474	304,340	267,211	253,497	247,517	228,475	208,878	172,943
Net income (€ mil.)	(0.2%)	565	482	(282)	(1,052)	(1,845)	2	31	54	165	553
Income as % of assets	—	0.3%	0.2%	—	—	—	0.0%	0.0%	0.0%	0.1%	0.3%
Earnings per share (€)	(12.5%)	5.64	4.57	(2.49)	(7.67)	(11.89)	0.01	0.20	0.35	0.66	1.69
Stock price - FY high (€)	—	45.79	35.01	34.40	40.40	43.50	22.66	12.86	21.29	39.08	54.00
Stock price - FY low (€)	—	24.24	24.90	22.77	18.95	23.17	18.80	10.67	6.51	11.44	22.00
Stock price - FY close (€)	2.7%	35.57	28.51	25.31	23.68	38.87	22.46	11.94	15.90	32.17	45.40
P/E - high	—	8	8	—	—	—	2,266	64	61	59	32
P/E - low	—	4	5	—	—	—	1,880	53	19	17	13
Dividends per share (€)	(9.0%)	1.17	1.17	0.51	0.00	0.00	0.00	0.00	0.00	0.00	0.50
Book value per share (€)	(8.2%)	52.41	55.61	54.63	38.14	25.64	23.64	24.94	38.76	24.90	24.26
Employees	(5.7%)	68,486	70,567	71,446	71,351	68,464	59,018	56,748	50,789	46,400	40,550

STOCK PRICE HISTORY

HIGH/LOW/CLOSE

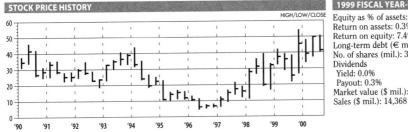

1999 FISCAL YEAR-END

Equity as % of assets: 4.6%
Return on assets: 0.3%
Return on equity: 7.4%
Long-term debt (€ mil.): 9,433
No. of shares (mil.): 327
Dividends
  Yield: 0.0%
  Payout: 0.3%
Market value ($ mil.): 14,898
Sales ($ mil.): 14,368

CREDIT SUISSE GROUP

Swiss banking's big cheese is playing second alphorn. Credit Suisse Group is the second-largest bank in its home country, after UBS. The Zurich-based firm provides consumer and business banking in its tiny home market through nearly 250 branches, but most of its business is in international banking.

It provides a range of services to wealthy individuals through its Credit Suisse Private Banking unit, with about 50 offices in Switzerland and 35 around the world. The prestigious Credit Suisse First Boston provides investment banking and institutional asset management services from some 55 offices worldwide,

carrying out Credit Suisse's esteemed corporate banking operations. Credit Suisse offers insurance through its Winterthur subsidiary, the heart of its retail bancassurance (banking and insurance) operations in Europe.

Eschewing European merger-mania, the company has expressed a desire to remain independent; it plans to grow internally, especially through expansion of its Internet banking and e-commerce businesses. It also expanded its Credit Suisse First Boston subsidiary with its purchase of US investment firm Donaldson, Lufkin & Jenrette.

In 1856, shortly after the creation of the Swiss federation, Alfred Escher opened Credit Suisse (CS) in Zurich. Primarily a venture capital firm, CS helped fund Swiss railroads and other industries. It later opened offices in Italy and helped establish the Swiss Bank Corporation.

CS shifted its focus to commercial banking in 1867 and sold most of its stock holdings. By 1871 it was Switzerland's largest bank, buoyed by the nation's swift industrialization. In 1895 CS helped create the predecessor of Swiss utility Electrowatt. Foreign activity grew in the 1920s. A run on banks in the Depression forced CS to sell assets at a loss and dip into reserves of unreported retained profits.

Trade declined in WWII, but neutrality left Switzerland's institutions intact and made it a major banking center, partly due to CS's role as a conduit for the Nazi's plundered gold. Foreign exchange and gold trading became important activities for CS after WWII. Mortgage and consumer credit acquisitions fueled domestic growth in the 1970s.

In 1978 the bank took a stake in US investment bank First Boston and, with it, formed London-based Credit Suisse-First Boston (CSFB). CS created holding company Credit Suisse First Boston (44% ownership) to own First Boston, CSFB, and Tokyo-based CS First Boston Pacific.

The stock market crash of 1987 led a damaged First Boston to merge with CSFB the next year. In 1990 CS (renamed CS Holding) injected $300 million into CSFB and shifted $470 million in bad loans from its books, becoming the first foreign owner of a major Wall Street investment bank.

In the early 1990s, CS Holding strengthened its insurance business with a Winterthur Insurance alliance. In 1993 and 1994 acquisi-

tions helped it gain share in its overbanked home market.

In 1996 CS Holding reorganized as Credit Suisse Group and grew internationally, including further merging the daredevil US investment banking operations into Credit Suisse's more staid and relationship-oriented corporate banking. It bought Winterthur (Switzerland's #2 insurer) in 1997, as well as Barclays' European investment banking business.

In 1996, Credit Suisse and other Swiss banks came under fire for refusing to relinquish assets from Jews' bank accounts from the Holocaust era and for gold trading with the Nazi regime. In 1997 the banks agreed to establish a humanitarian fund for Holocaust victims. A stream of lawsuits by American heirs and boycott threats from US states and cities led in 1998 to a tentative $1.25 billion settlement (unpopular in Switzerland); Credit Suisse is to pay one-third.

CS in 1998 moved to expand US money management operations by allying with New York-based Warburg Pincus Asset Management. By 1999 that joint venture — which was to give the investment firm access to CS's mutual fund distribution channels in Europe and Asia — had morphed into CS's planned $650 million purchase of Warburg Pincus Asset Management.

Japan revoked the license of the company's financial products unit for obstructing an investigation (the harshest penalty ever given to a foreign firm); it also accused CS of helping 60 others hide losses and cover up evidence.

In 2000 the company started a mortgage and home-buying Web site, announced that it would buy the Japanese securities operations of Schroders plc, and decided to allow searches of Holocaust-era accounts.

Chairman and CEO: Lukas Mühlemann
VC and Chief Risk Officer: Hans-Ulrich Doerig
VC: Peter Braebeck-Letmathe
CFO: Phillip K. Ryan
Chief of Staff and Acting Senior Executive Human Resources: Philip Hess
Corporate Secretary: Pierre Schreiber
General Counsel: David Frick
Head of Financial Services Management Division; CEO, Winterthur Group: Thomas Wellauer
Senior Executive Technology: Ahmad Abu El-Ata
Senior Executive Tax: Kurt Arnold
Senior Executive Accounting/Reporting: Peter Bachmann
Senior Executive Advisory: Alfred Gremli
Senior Executive Risk Management: Tobias Guldimann
Senior Executive Audit: Urs Hanni
Senior Executive Security: Jean-Pierre Huwyler
Senior Executive Investor Relations: Gerhard Beindorff
Senior Executive Public Affairs: Ulrich Pfister
Senior Executive Accounting Systems: Stefan Hilber
Senior Executive Group Communications: Karin Rhomberg
Chairman Japan: Yuji Suzuki
Auditors: KPMG Klynveld Peat Marwick Goerdeler SA

HQ: Paradeplatz 8, 8001 Zurich, Switzerland
Phone: +41-1-212-1616   **Fax:** +41-1-333-2587
US HQ: 11 Madison Ave., New York, NY 10010
US Phone: 212-325-2000   **US Fax:** 212-325-8249
Web site: http://www.credit-suisse.com

1999 Assets

	$ mil.	% of total
Cash & equivalents	1,974	—
Trading account	79,660	18
Net loans	169,589	37
Mortgage loans	54,399	12
Other investments	107,788	24
Other assets	40,836	9
Total	**454,246**	**100**

Primary Business Units & Subsidiaries
Credit Suisse (domestic banking)
Credit Suisse Asset Management
Credit Suisse First Boston
Credit Suisse Private Banking
Personal Financial Services Europe
Winterthur

ABN AMRO
Bank of Tokyo-Mitsubishi
Barclays
Bear Stearns
Citigroup
Credit Lyonnais
Dai-Ichi Kangyo
Deutsche Bank
Fuji Bank
Goldman Sachs
HSBC Holdings
J.P. Morgan
Merrill Lynch
Nomura Securities
Paine Webber
Salomon Smith Barney Holdings
Sumitomo
UBS

OTC: CSGKY FYE: December 31	Annual Growth	12/90	12/91	12/92	12/93	12/94	12/95	12/96	12/97	12/98	12/99
Assets ($ mil.)	11.6%	169,096	161,944	169,917	232,774	299,032	357,553	390,722	471,709	474,396	454,246
Net income ($ mil.)	44.8%	117	720	701	1,148	1,017	1,214	(1,930)	272	2,231	3,269
Income as % of assets	—	0.1%	0.4%	0.4%	0.5%	0.3%	0.3%	—	0.1%	0.5%	0.7%
Earnings per share ($)	7.4%	—	—	—	1.95	1.45	1.62	(2.53)	0.26	2.09	2.99
Stock price - FY high ($)	—	—	—	—	25.88	25.94	25.73	27.25	42.00	64.38	50.50
Stock price - FY low ($)	—	—	—	—	17.25	18.63	19.27	20.92	23.33	26.25	38.00
Stock price - FY close ($)	12.2%	—	—	—	24.81	20.38	25.69	25.50	39.00	38.75	49.43
P/E - high	—	—	—	—	13	18	16	—	162	31	17
P/E - low	—	—	—	—	9	13	12	—	90	13	13
Dividends per share ($)	10.5%	—	—	—	0.60	0.69	0.87	0.75	0.86	0.91	1.09
Book value per share ($)	4.4%	—	—	—	15.22	18.00	18.94	14.97	16.48	19.02	19.76
Employees	4.2%	44,153	44,323	51,787	56,804	53,243	33,527	34,821	62,242	62,300	63,963

HIGH/LOW/CLOSE

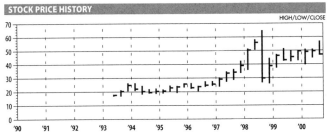

Equity as % of assets: 4.8%
Return on assets: 0.7%
Return on equity: 15.6%
Long-term debt ($ mil.): 32,426
No. of shares (mil.): 1,089
Dividends
  Yield: 0.0%
  Payout: 0.4%
Market value ($ mil.): 53,821
Sales ($ mil.): 47,287

DAEWOO GROUP

OVERVIEW

South Korea's economic crisis has brought a day of reckoning for the Daewoo Group, one of the nation's five largest *chaebol* (family-run conglomerates). The Seoul-based group's companies are engaged in a range of manufacturing and service activities, including trading (through flagship Daewoo Corporation), energy, automotive components, electronics and media, machinery, and textiles. The government has ordered the *chaebol* to restructure to reduce debt and swap businesses among themselves so that each *chaebol* ends up in only a few business sectors.

Former chairman Kim Woo-Choong had resisted the government's restructuring directives, but Daewoo's massive debt left him little choice. Daewoo has agreed to a restructuring plan in which it will sell or spin off its construction, electronics, and shipbuilding units and much of its telecommunications business. It is also selling car maker DAEWOO MOTOR, Korea's #2 car company behind Hyundai.

HISTORY

The Korean character for "risk" combines the characters for "crisis" and "chance," both of which have figured prominently in former chairman Kim Woo-Choong's high-rolling career. In 1967 Kim and To Dae Do put their names together with $18,000 (much of it borrowed) to create Daewoo, a textile exporting company. Kim soon bought out To and used low-cost South Korean labor to turn Daewoo into a profitable clothing maker, garnering Sears, J. C. Penney, and Montgomery Ward as accounts. As Korea's economy took off, Daewoo entered construction.

In 1976 dictator Park Chung Hee asked Kim to take over a government-owned plant that hadn't earned a profit in 37 years. Kim did, lived on-site for nine months, and Daewoo Heavy Industries was born.

At the same time, most Korean construction firms were following the flow of oil money to the Middle East. To avoid competition, Kim sought riskier construction contracts and landed $2 billion worth in Libya. Payment up front eliminated political and economic risks. In the late 1970s Daewoo came to the rescue again, taking on the government's 50% share of faltering GM Korea, thus creating DAEWOO MOTOR.

During the 1980s Kim inked a string of big export deals in which low-cost goods were exchanged for technology. Daewoo companies became involved in projects with Caterpillar, Northern Telecom (now Nortel Networks), Boeing, Lockheed, and General Dynamics, among others. As part of a deal with General Motors, Daewoo began making the Pontiac LeMans in 1986 (the companies ended their liaison in 1992).

Daewoo entered electronics in the mid-1980s by purchasing a foundering custom chip maker, and acquired Leading Edge, a bankrupt PC marketer, in 1989. That year a government bailout kept the group from collapsing under the shipbuilding company's losses.

Kim, a national presidential contender in 1992, was among the Korean industrial and political leaders caught up in a bribery scandal in the mid-1990s. He received a two-year suspended sentence.

Daewoo merged its shipbuilding and heavy industry units in 1994. Two years later Daewoo was prepared to acquire a stake in Thomas SA, a French consumer and defense electronics company, when the French government suspended the sale. In 1997 Saudi billionaire Prince al-Waleed bin Talal made a $50.5 million investment in Daewoo, convertible into a 5.9% ownership interest.

Early in 1998 Daewoo bought a 53.5% stake in the automotive unit of troubled Ssangyong, even as Korea's other *chaebol* retreated from their expansion plans amid the Asian financial crisis. DAEWOO MOTOR made its US debut that year, introducing three models.

As its debt mounted in 1999, Daewoo was forced to work with creditors and the government to restructure its operations. The group allowed creditors to take over profitable brokerage firm Daewoo Securities, and it agreed to sell or spin off its construction and shipbuilding businesses and much of its telecommunications unit. It also put its automotive manufacturing company up for sale. Taking responsibility for the group's troubles, Kim resigned that year, taking a dozen top Daewoo executives with him. He and his family later left the country, and they have been reported to be living in Germany.

In 2000 Ford bid $6.9 billion to win the exclusive right to negotiate to buy DAEWOO MOTOR. Later that year, however, Ford withdrew from talks with Daewoo's creditors.

President: Suh Hyung-Suk
President: Chang Byung-Ju
Executive Director Finance and Administration (CFO), Daewoo Corporation: Kim Seong-Sik
Manager Automotive Components: K. R. Min
Manager Chemical: Y. K. Kim
Manager Commodity: K. W. Nam
Manager Machinery and Plant: K. H. Kim
Manager Non-Ferrous Metal: I. S. Chun
Manager Steel and Metal: D. G. Oh
Manager Textile: K. R. Kim
Human Resources, Daewoo Corporation: M. H. Chae
Auditors: KPMG San Tong Corp.

LOCATIONS

HQ: 541 Namdaemunno 5 Ga, Chung-gu,
CPO Box 2810, Seoul, South Korea
Phone: +82-2-759-2114   **Fax:** +82-2-753-9489
US HQ: 85 Challenger Rd., Ridgefield Park, NJ 07660
US Phone: 201-229-4500   **US Fax:** 201-440-2244
Web site: http://www.daewoo.com

Daewoo sells its products worldwide.

PRODUCTS/OPERATIONS

Major Divisions
Automotive Components
Chemicals
Commodities
Energy
Machinery
Media and Electronics
Metals
Non-ferrous Metals
Textiles

COMPETITORS

DaimlerChrysler
Ford
General Motors
Hitachi
Honda
Hyundai
Kia Motors
LG Group
Marubeni
Mitsubishi
Mitsui
NEC
Nissan
Samsung
Siemens
Sony
Sumitomo
Toshiba
Toyota
Volkswagen

DAI NIPPON PRINTING CO., LTD.

OVERVIEW

Dai Nippon Printing (DNP) is doing its part to raise Japan's GNP. The Tokyo-based company is the world's second-largest commercial printer (after Quebecor World), covering commercial, specialty, and book and magazine printing, as well as packaging. It produces advertising materials, books, magazines, and catalogs at 33 plants in Japan and seven overseas. Other products include decorative wood materials, photomasks (used in making semiconductors), lead frames, and fax machine ribbons. DNP also owns a majority stake in Hokkaido Coca-Cola Bottling (which generates 6% of sales).

Book and magazine and commercial printing accounts for 53% of the company's sales; decorative materials and packaging, 25%; and the rest comes from electronic components and information media supplies.

DNP is implementing strategies to counter the effects of the Asian economic crisis and to respond to changing global needs. The company is positioning itself as a complete provider of information communications, offering clients marketing and promotional support, as well as cross-media services. It also is emphasizing its environmentally friendly products and has reorganized its production systems and undertaken a number of cost-cutting measures.

HISTORY

In 1876 Shueisha, the predecessor to Dai Nippon Printing (DNP), was established in central Tokyo. As the only modern printing firm in Japan, it was well-positioned to attract the business of the emerging newspaper and book industries. The company originally used a movable-type hand printer, but became the first private industry to use steam power in Japan when it updated its presses in 1884.

Following Japanese victories over China and Russia at the turn of the century, Japan embarked on a period of military and economic expansion. This was matched by a growing demand for printing. In 1927 Japan published 20,000 book titles and 40 million magazines. The country's first four-color gravure printing system was inaugurated the following year. In 1935 Shueisha changed its name to Dai Nippon Printing following its merger with Nisshin Printing.

The 1930s and 1940s were lean times for printers; Japan's repressive military government suppressed publishers and banned books. WWII devastated the publishing industry, along with the rest of the Japanese economy, but the publishing industry recovered soon after the end of the war. DNP was assisted in its recovery by government contracts; in 1946 it was designated by the Ministry of Finance to print ¥100 notes. In 1949 the company entered the securities printing business, and in 1951 it expanded into packaging and decorative interiors production. DNP re-emerged in 1958 as Japan's largest printing firm.

In 1963 DNP followed Toppan in setting up an office in Hong Kong. Both Hong Kong and Singapore had become havens for Shanghai printing entrepreneurs who had emigrated in the face of the Communist takeover of China in 1949. These cities became centers for low-cost, high-quality color printing for British and American book publishers. In 1973 DNP overtook R. R. Donnelley as the world's largest printer. The next year the company set up a subsidiary in the US, DNP (America), Inc.

DNP moved into the information processing business in the 1980s, developing a credit card-sized calculator in 1985, a digital color printer system in 1986, and a Japanese-language word processor in 1987. The company launched Hi-Vision Static Pictures in 1989 to market a process that converted data into a form used by high-definition TV. In 1990 DNP bought a controlling stake in Tien Wah Press, the #1 printer in Singapore.

The next year DNP completed the first construction stage of its Okayama plant, dedicated to information media supplies (mainly transfer ribbons for color printers). The second stage, specializing in interior decorative materials, was completed in 1993.

In 1994 the company launched its Let's Go to an Amusement Park! virtual reality software system. Two years later DNP produced an integrated circuit card for about a tenth of current costs, giving it a major competitive edge in the magnetic card market.

The company announced in 1997 it would create a satellite cable channel for DIRECTV called Book TV, which it hopes will give the printing and publishing industries a boost. The following year DNP joined 10 other Japanese companies in developing Nippon Fantasy World, a $225 million theme park set to open in Tokyo by 2003.

In 1999 the company began selling CD-ROMs online through subsidiary TransArt.

Chairman, President, and CEO: Yoshitoshi Kitajima
Senior Managing Director: Ryozo Kitami
Senior Managing Director: Ken-ichi Nakamura
Senior Managing Director: Jitsuo Okauchi
Senior Managing Director: Michiji Sato
Senior Managing Director: Taira Takahashi
Senior Managing Director: Koichi Takanami
Managing Director and CFO: Masayoshi Yamada
Managing Director: Kosuke Hirabayashi
Managing Director: Shigeru Kanda
Managing Director: Mitsusuke Sato
Managing Director: Minoru Suzuki
Managing Director: Satoshi Saruwatari
Managing Director: Kuniaki Kamei
Managing Director: Mitsuhiko Hakii
Human Resources DNP America: Naomi Reis
Auditors: Meiji Audit Corporation

LOCATIONS

HQ: Dai Nippon Insatsu Kabushiki Kaisha
1-1, Ichigaya Kagacho 1-chome, Shinjuku-ku,
Tokyo 162-8001, Japan
Phone: +81-3-5225-8220   **Fax:** +81-3-5225-8239
US HQ: 335 Madison Ave., 3rd Fl., New York, NY 10017
US Phone: 212-503-1060   **US Fax:** 212-286-1501
Web site: http://www.dnp.co.jp

Dai Nippon Printing has plants in Denmark, Hong Kong,
Indonesia, Japan, Malaysia, Singapore, and the US.

PRODUCTS/OPERATIONS

Selected Products and Services

Electronic Components & Information Media Supplies
Battery electrodes
Color filters
Lead frames
Photomasks
Ribbons (printers, fax machines)
Shadowmasks

Information Media
Bank notes
Books
Business forms
Calendars
Catalogs
Direct mail
Magazines
Plastic cards
Posters
Promotional publications

Lifestyle Products
Decorative materials
Packaging

COMPETITORS

DuPont Photomasks	Photronics
International Imaging	Quad/Graphics
Materials	Quebecor World
Japan Times	R. R. Donnelley
Kodansha	Scitex
Nihon Keizai Shimbun	Toppan Printing

HISTORICAL FINANCIALS & EMPLOYEES

OTC: DNPCY FYE: March 31	Annual Growth	3/91	3/92	3/93	3/94	3/95	3/96	3/97	3/98	3/99	3/00
Sales ($ mil.)	4.3%	8,321	9,359	10,376	11,149	13,782	11,611	10,583	10,044	10,659	12,139
Net income ($ mil.)	2.1%	306	331	366	397	568	494	454	425	256	368
Income as % of sales	—	3.7%	3.5%	3.5%	3.6%	4.1%	4.3%	4.3%	4.2%	2.4%	3.0%
Earnings per share ($)	(7.6%)	—	—	—	—	—	6.58	6.02	5.60	3.31	4.80
Stock price - FY high ($)	—	—	—	—	—	—	183.00	198.00	240.00	172.00	195.75
Stock price - FY low ($)	—	—	—	—	—	—	149.34	153.00	158.50	125.00	146.00
Stock price - FY close ($)	(2.9%)	—	—	—	—	—	183.00	169.00	165.00	149.00	163.00
P/E - high	—	—	—	—	—	—	28	33	43	52	41
P/E - low	—	—	—	—	—	—	23	25	28	38	30
Dividends per share ($)	3.4%	—	—	—	—	—	1.49	1.48	1.35	1.51	1.70
Book value per share ($)	3.5%	—	—	—	—	—	100.01	91.82	90.30	99.34	114.98
Employees	4.0%	—	—	—	—	—	—	—	—	34,000	35,347

STOCK PRICE HISTORY

HIGH/LOW/CLOSE

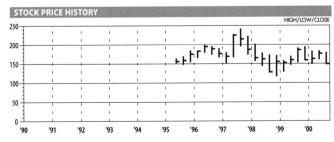

2000 FISCAL YEAR-END

Debt ratio: 5.3%
Return on equity: 4.5%
Cash ($ mil.): 1,767
Current ratio: 1.60
Long-term debt ($ mil.): 484
No. of shares (mil.): 76
Dividends
  Yield: 0.0%
  Payout: 0.4%
Market value ($ mil.): 12,380

THE DAIEI, INC.

OVERVIEW

Born during an earlier economic crisis, The Daiei is now struggling to survive its current economic woes. The Kobe, Japan-based company is one of that country's largest retailers and, while it is best known for its majority ownership in more than 7,200 Lawson convenience stores (#2 in Japan, after 7-Eleven), it also includes about 85 subsidiaries engaged in a variety of retail, restaurant, hotel, and real estate businesses.

Daiei retail outlets include supermarkets, discount stores, department stores, general merchandise stores, and specialty shops. Its stores carry numerous private-label products ranging from clothing to household items to food items. The weakened Japanese economy has triggered Daiei to close stores, restructure management, and sell off chunks of its real estate assets. It has also sold shares of Lawson to affiliated companies and outside investors to reduce debt.

HISTORY

The Daiei founder, Isao Nakauchi, narrowly escaped death and the law before launching his first Daiei corner drugstore. As a Japanese soldier serving in the Philippines in WWII, he came under heavy fire but survived. He later thanked sloppy American engineering (the bombs that fell near him did not explode) for his survival. After the war he and his brother made a fortune selling penicillin above the legal price; his brother was arrested for his part in the dealings.

Nakauchi launched his Housewives' Store Daiei in Osaka in 1957 at the depth of the post-Korean War depression. The low prices of a discount drugstore appealed to hard-pressed consumers, and the success of the first store prompted Nakauchi to open others in the Osaka area. He also took advantage of the depression at the wholesale level, buying up surplus goods from cash-strapped manufacturers.

In 1958 the company opened in Sannomiya and introduced the concept of the discount store chain to Japan. Over the next three decades, Daiei diversified its offerings while staying focused on its "for the customers" philosophy, i.e., very low prices.

The company expanded into Tokyo in 1964 with the purchase of Ittoku and opened its first suburban store in 1968 near Osaka. By 1972 Daiei was not only a nationwide chain, it was also Japan's #1 supermarket operator (with 75 stores) and #2 retailer. In 1974 the company overtook Mitsukoshi to become Japan's top retailer. A year later Daiei opened its first convenience store, Lawson.

Showing an increasing interest in sourcing from international businesses, Daiei teamed up with J. C. Penney (1976) and Marks and Spencer (1978) for retailing and Wendy's and Victoria Station (both in 1979) for restaurants. The retailer entered the US market with the 1980 purchase of Holiday Mart, a three-store discount chain in Hawaii, where it also set up its first purchasing office; over the next 14 years, it established purchasing offices in 12 countries.

Daiei entered the hotel business in 1988 by winning the contract for a $2.2 billion recreation center in Fukuoka. In 1992 the company opened the first American-style membership warehouse in Japan (Kobe), Kou's Wholesale Membership Club. That year Daiei acquired 42% of major retailer Chujitsuya. The company launched private-label products in 1994, unnerving market brand leaders by undercutting their prices. Also that year Daiei merged with retail affiliates Chujitsuya, Uneed Daiei, and Dainaha, establishing Japan's first nationwide network of stores.

When Japan lifted a 50-year ban on holding companies in 1997, Daiei was the first to take advantage of the relaxed laws, forming K.K. Daiei Holding Corporation to oversee its non-retail businesses. Daiei was hit hard in 1997 and 1998 as Japan's consumer spending slowed just as many of its stores were undergoing renovation. In response, in 1998 it began selling real estate assets, restructuring operations, and closing unprofitable stores. It also sold part of its stake in Lawson to affiliated companies.

In 1999 Tasdasu Toba became president, replacing founder Nakauchi, who remained chairman of Daiei. In early 2000 trading company Mitsubishi agreed to purchase a 20% stake in convenience store chain Lawson (Daiei and subsidiaries would retain about 75% of the company); Daiei said it planned to take Lawson public to reduce debt. Daiei later closed four of its poorly performing restaurant chains, including Victoria Station and Sbarro Japan.

Amid allegations of an insider trading scandal, Toba resigned as president and Nakauchi resigned as chairman and CEO in October 2000. Later that month Hiroshige Sasaki, a former managing director, became acting president. Sasaki will be replaced by Kunio Takagi as the head of Daiei in May 2001.

President Designate: Kunio Takagi
Acting President, EVP, Vice Chief Executive Operating Director, Deputy General Director in charge of Retail Business, and Divisional Manager Hard Line Merchandising Business Division: Hiroshige Sasaki
EVP, Vice Chief Executive Operating Director, General Director in charge of Retail Business, and Divisional Manager Office of Retail Business Planning & Support: Kazuo Kawa
Senior Managing Director, Senior Executive Operating Director, and Divisional Manager Office of General Affairs Planning: Tadashi Inoue
Managing Director, Senior Executive Operating Director, and Divisional Manager Office of Store Development and Planning: Kiyoshi Oyamada
Managing Director, Executive Operating Director, and Divisional Manager Food Line Merchandising Business Division: Hidehito Nishiyama
Managing Director, Executive Operating Director, and Divisional Manager Staff in charge of Three Years Revitalization Planning: Toshio Hasumi
President, Daiei Holding: Jun Nakauchi
President, Lawson: Kenji Fujiwara
Auditors: Deloitte Touche Tohmatsu

LOCATIONS

HQ: 4-1-1, Minatojima Nakamachi, Chuo-ku, Kobe 650-0046, Japan
Phone: +81-78-302-5001   Fax: +81-78-302-5572
US HQ: 801 Kaheka St., Honolulu, HI 96814
US Phone: 808-973-6600   US Fax: 808-941-6457
Web site: http://www.daiei.co.jp

The Daiei operates retail locations throughout Japan and maintains purchasing offices in China, Europe, the Philippines, and the US.

PRODUCTS/OPERATIONS

Selected Operations
Big Boy (family restaurants)
Daiei (general merchandise)
D-Mart (discount stores)
Fukuoka Daiei Hawks (professional baseball team)
Gourmet City (supermarkets)
Hyper Mart (discount superstore)
Kou's Wholesale Membership Clubs (warehouse stores)
Lawson (convenience stores)
Sea Hawk Hotel & Resort
Topos (discount outlets)

COMPETITORS

Daimaru
Isetan Company
Ito-Yokado
JUSCO
Keiyo Company
Kojima
Marui
Matsuzakaya Co.
Mitsukoshi
Mycal Corporation
Seiyu
Takashimaya
Tokyu Department Store Co.
Uny

HISTORICAL FINANCIALS & EMPLOYEES

Nasdaq (SC): DAIEY FYE: Last day in February	Annual Growth	2/91	2/92	2/93	2/94	2/95	2/96	2/97	2/98	2/99	2/00
Sales ($ mil.)	4.7%	17,177	19,365	21,269	25,395	33,344	30,120	26,069	25,085	25,436	25,883
Net income ($ mil.)	—	72	78	61	52	(524)	48	(99)	10	(238)	(200)
Income as % of sales	—	0.4%	0.4%	0.3%	0.2%	—	0.2%	—	0.0%	—	—
Earnings per share ($)	—	0.37	0.39	0.30	0.20	(1.52)	0.14	(0.28)	0.03	(0.98)	(0.56)
Stock price - FY high ($)	—	34.00	23.13	16.50	30.50	37.75	26.25	28.75	15.88	7.88	10.88
Stock price - FY low ($)	—	15.38	14.63	9.75	15.75	20.00	19.50	12.75	6.50	4.38	5.69
Stock price - FY close ($)	(11.3%)	21.38	14.75	14.50	30.50	20.00	24.25	13.75	7.75	6.38	7.25
P/E - high	—	92	59	55	153	—	188	—	588	—	—
P/E - low	—	42	38	33	79	—	139	—	241	—	—
Dividends per share ($)	—	0.25	0.26	0.28	0.32	0.34	0.31	0.22	0.13	0.08	0.00
Book value per share ($)	(13.3%)	5.32	5.54	6.06	4.52	4.74	4.08	3.10	3.28	2.46	1.47
Employees	(2.3%)	17,000	16,800	19,000	19,000	19,000	18,687	16,686	16,929	16,600	13,776

STOCK PRICE HISTORY

HIGH/LOW/CLOSE

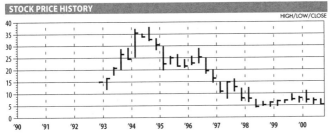

2000 FISCAL YEAR-END

Debt ratio: 82.7%
Return on equity: —
Cash ($ mil.): 1,824
Current ratio: 0.38
Long-term debt ($ mil.): 2,497
No. of shares (mil.): 357
Dividends
  Yield: —
  Payout: —
Market value ($ mil.): 2,587

THE DAI-ICHI KANGYO BANK

Now everybody knows the troubles The Dai-Ichi Kangyo Bank (DKB) has seen. Japan's third-largest bank (Bank of Tokyo-Mitsubishi is #1 and Sumitomo Bank #2), scandal-fraught DKB is merging with Industrial Bank of Japan and Fuji Bank in hopes that three wrongs will create a right. The union of the three debt-ridden banks, which created Mizuho Holdings, the world's largest bank by assets, will not be fully completed until 2002. The banks' operations are gradually being merged into Mizuho Holdings and the bank operates as a subsidiary of the holding company. The trio has also announced plans to cut a mere 6,000 jobs and 150 branches over five years.

Dai-Ichi Kangyo Bank offers a range of consumer, business, corporate, and international banking services. These services include deposits and loans, bond underwriting, mergers and acquisitions, asset management, and investment management.

To better compete in Japan's deregulating financial services industry, DKB reorganized operationally: Unit "companies" now oversee customer and consumer banking; corporate banking; international banking; and market and trading. Two more units oversee the bank's internal operations. In hopes of responding more quickly to clients' needs, the company has given the units relative autonomy for marketing and creating products and services. DKB has also joined with such firms as J.P. Morgan to extend its asset management and investment services.

Dai-Ichi Kokuritsu Bank, the first bank organized under the Japanese National Bank Act of 1872, was founded in 1873. The public company became the focus of a minor *zaibatsu*, a group of about 100 cross-owned companies.

After WWII, many of the *zaibatsu* reformed as *keiretsu*, although the Dai-Ichi group was less structured than most. The Japanese government in 1971 sponsored a merger between Dai-Ichi and Nippon Kangyo Bank (founded 1897), creating the nation's largest bank. The merger created a strict balance of power between Dai-Ichi and Kangyo executives, institutionalizing a culture clash between the two banks that slowed growth, particularly overseas. In 1978 the bank formed the influential Sankinkai (third Friday) council, whose members included leaders from 47 major Japanese firms.

Japan enjoyed an unprecedented boom in the 1980s. The country's commercial institutions began a nationwide building boom and a worldwide business and real estate shopping spree, frequently overpaying. DKB became, for a time, the world's largest bank (by assets) in 1984. By the end of the decade real estate and stock prices were wildly inflated. In the early 1990s the bubble burst, leaving DKB (and other banks) holding bad loans and devalued assets. As economic activity slowed, loan loss reserves increased, paring profits. DKB tried to offset reduced lending business with increased consumer business, but Japanese families were seized by a crisis of confidence.

Nonperforming loans continued to rise in the mid-1990s despite the creation of a government agency, the Cooperative Credit Purchasing Company, to buy up the bad assets (usually at a loss to the banks). The company also began selling off its portfolio of nonperforming US loans.

In response to domestic troubles, DKB began targeting foreign markets, establishing offices in Indonesia and China and enhancing its presence elsewhere to attract new local business rather than the foreign business of Japanese customers. Anticipating Japan's Big Bang program of financial reforms, in 1996 Dai-Ichi disposed of a package of poorly performing assets and suffered its first-ever loss the following year.

Bank president Katsuhiko Kondo and chairman Tadashi Okuda resigned in 1997 as a result of a payoff scandal linking the company to racketeers. The scandal eventually led to the conviction of six DKB executives; former chairman Kuniji Miyazaki, who had been questioned by prosecutors, hanged himself. Also in 1997 the bank's US-based lease and aircraft financing subsidiary The CIT Group went public; Dai-Ichi Kangyo continued to hold 78% of the company's stock.

In 1998 DKB bought Kankaku Securities to offer investment services to the retail market and formed a joint venture with J.P. Morgan to offer trust funds through DKB's domestic branches. In an effort to pick up the pieces and to raise reserve capital, the bank sold a big chunk of its holdings in The CIT Group, retaining 44% ownership in it. As losses continued in 1999, DKB agreed to merge with Industrial Bank of Japan and Fuji Bank to form the world's largest bank; the banks came together under the umbrella of Mizuho Holdings in 2000.

President and CEO: Katsuyuki Sugita
Deputy President: Toshikuni Nishinohara
**Deputy President; President Customer & Consumer
 Banking:** Tadashi Kudo
Deputy President: Nobuhiro Mori
**Senior Managing Director; President International
 Banking Corporation:** Takatsugu Murai
**Senior Managing Director; President Corporate
 Banking Company:** Masato Tsutsui
Senior Managing Director: Akira Miyagawa
**Senior Managing Director Customer & Consumer
 Banking:** Shigeki Hosaka
Senior Managing Director: Kuniya Sakai
Managing Director: Michio Shishido
Managing Director: Takayasu Tanaka
Managing Director: Osamu Abe
Managing Director: Yoshiro Aoki
Managing Director: Kenji Minani
Managing Director: Tadao Noda
Managing Director: Yasuo Tsunemi
Managing Director: Ken Aoki
Managing Director: Masami Yamashita
Managing Director: Yutaka Matsunami
Auditors: Century Audit Corporation

LOCATIONS

HQ: Dai-Ichi Kangyo Ginko
 The Dai-Ichi Kangyo Bank, Limited
 1-5, Uchisaiwaicho 1-chome,
 Chiyoda-ku, Tokyo 100-0011, Japan
Phone: +81-3-3596-1111   **Fax:** +81-3-3596-2179
US HQ: 1 World Trade Center, Ste. 4911,
 New York, NY 10048
US Phone: 212-466-5200   **US Fax:** 212-524-0579
Web site: http://www.dkb.co.jp/english

Dai-Ichi Kangyo Bank operates in some 30 countries.

2000 Sales

	% of total
Asia	85
Other	7
The Americas	5
Europe	3
Total	**100**

PRODUCTS/OPERATIONS

2000 Sales

	% of total
Interest income	80
Fees & commissions	11
Trading income	2
Other income	7
Total	**100**

Selected Subsidiaries
Aseambankers Malaysia Berhad (5%)
P.T. Bank Dai-Ichi Kangyo Indonesia (85%)
Chekiang First Bank Ltd. (Hong Kong)
The CIT Group, Inc. (44%, US)
Dai-Ichi Kangyo Australia Limited
Dai-Ichi Kangyo Bank (Canada)
Dai-Ichi Kangyo Bank (Deutschland) AG (Germany)
Dai-Ichi Kangyo Bank of California
P.T. Dai-Ichi Kangyo Panin Leasing (52%, Indonesia)
Dai-Ichi Kangyo Trust Company of New York
DKB Asia Limited (Hong Kong)
DKB Data Services (USA) Inc.
DKB Financial Products, Inc. (US)
DKB Futures (Singapore) Pte Ltd.
DKB International Public Limited Company (UK)
DKB Investment Management International Limited
 (44%, UK)
The Islamic Bank of Brunei Berhad (14%)
The Yellow River International Leasing Co., Ltd.
 (5%, China)

COMPETITORS

ABN AMRO	J.P. Morgan
Bank of America	Nikko Securities
Bank of Tokyo-Mitsubishi	Nippon Credit Bank
Chase Manhattan	Nomura Securities
Citigroup	Sakura Bank
Commerzbank AG	Sanwa Bank
Deutsche Bank	Shinsei Bank
Fuji Bank	Sumitomo
HSBC Holdings	Tokai Bank
Industrial Bank of Japan	UBS

HISTORICAL FINANCIALS & EMPLOYEES

Subsidiary FYE: March 31	Annual Growth	3/91	3/92	3/93	3/94	3/95	3/96	3/97	3/98	3/99	3/00
Assets ($ mil.)	0.8%	458,964	475,831	490,084	533,533	625,086	514,479	453,614	433,103	460,838	492,842
Net income ($ mil.)	0.3%	652	629	405	113	324	734	(1,429)	(541)	(3,738)	671
Income as % of assets	—	0.1%	0.1%	0.1%	0.0%	0.1%	0.1%	—	—	—	0.1%
Employees	(2.0%)	18,640	18,703	18,849	19,189	19,061	18,069	17,425	16,965	17,100	15,540

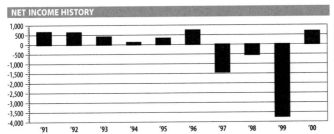

NET INCOME HISTORY

2000 FISCAL YEAR-END
Equity as % of assets: 4.7%
Return on assets: 0.1%
Return on equity: —
Long-term debt ($ mil.): 18,785
Sales ($ mil.): 19,065

DAIMLERCHRYSLER AG

OVERVIEW

The German aristocrat sweeps the American working-class girl off her feet, and they drive off into the sunset. Bad romance novel? No, it was the largest industrial marriage in history: Daimler-Benz's $37 billion acquisition of Chrysler created Stuttgart, Germany-based DaimlerChrysler, the world's third-largest carmaker in sales (behind GM and Ford) and #5 in cars sold. Chrysler enjoyed great success with its minivans and had been trying to duplicate the feat with sport utility vehicles (SUVs), and conservative Daimler-Benz made Mercedes-Benz luxury cruisers, SUVs, commercial vehicles, and aerospace products.

Before the merger Chrysler — whose brands included Chrysler, Dodge, Eagle, Jeep, and Plymouth — depended primarily on its North American sales, and Daimler-Benz was typecast as a maker of luxury cars and trucks. (Its Freightliner unit is the US's #1 heavy truck maker.) The merger expands Chrysler's international reach and brings its broad-market expertise to help Daimler expand its product line, particularly in Europe where the company is aiming at the small car market.

The company is looking to expand car manufacturing in South America and to increase its presence in the Pacific Rim through mergers and acquisitions. It has taken a 9% stake in Hyundai Motor (South Korea) and a 34% stake in Mitsubishi Motors (Japan).

Major stockholders of DaimlerChrysler include Deutsche Bank (12%) and the government of Kuwait (7%).

HISTORY

Former Buick president and General Motors VP Walter Chrysler was hired to get Maxwell Motor Car Company out of receivership in 1920. He became president in 1923, introduced the Chrysler automobile in 1924, and renamed the company after himself in 1925. Three years later the company acquired Dodge and introduced the low-priced Plymouth and the more luxurious DeSoto. Chrysler retired in 1935.

By 1950 Chrysler had slipped to third place. The company misjudged customer demands in the 1960s by introducing small cars before their time and in the 1970s by maintaining large car production.

Facing bankruptcy, Chrysler negotiated $1.5 billion in loan guarantees from the US government and brought in former Ford president Lee Iacocca as CEO in 1978. By 1983 it had repaid its loans, seven years ahead of schedule. The company introduced the first minivan in 1984. Iacocca was replaced by GM's head of European operations, Robert Eaton, in 1992.

Hurt by Ford's Model T and WWI, two German motor companies, Daimler and Benz, merged in 1926. Daimler-Benz bought Auto Union (Audi) in 1958 (sold to Volkswagen in 1966). The company's Mercedes cars gained notoriety and sales expanded worldwide in the 1970s. Daimler-Benz diversified in the 1980s, buying aerospace, heavy truck (Freightliner), and consumer and industrial electrical companies. Although diversification continued, sales slowed and in 1993 the company began cutting jobs.

Losses at its aerospace unit forced Daimler-Benz into the red in 1995. Also that year the company and ABB Asea Brown Boveri formed joint venture Adtranz, the #1 train maker in the world, and Jürgen Shrempp became chairman.

In 1998 Daimler-Benz acquired Chrysler and introduced a subcompact car, the smart, in Europe. In 1999 DaimlerChrysler rolled both companies' financial services units into DaimlerChrysler Interservices (DEBIS) and acquired the remaining shares of Adtranz.

North American influence in the company began to fade in 2000 with the exit of US management, including co-chairman Robert Eaton. Prior to his retirement Eaton announced DaimlerChrysler's goal to become the world's #1 carmaker through partnerships or acquisitions; executives confirmed that the company was in talks with Honda, Fiat, and Peugeot Citroën.

In 2000 the company agreed to pay $1.9 billion for a 34% stake in Mitsubishi Motors. The same year it took a 9% stake in South Korea-based Hyundai Motor and the two bid jointly on DAEWOO MOTORS (also based in South Korea), but Ford was named exclusive bidder (though it later withdrew its bid). Bouncing back from disappointment, DaimlerChrysler agreed to buy Canada-based truck maker Western Star Holdings for $456 million and paid about $473 million for the 79% of Detroit Diesel (heavy-duty truck engines) that it didn't already own. The company also agreed to sell its rail systems unit, Adtranz, to Bombardier for $725 million in cash.

In less buoying news, DaimlerChrysler announced that it was recalling 1.4 million minivans due to reports of fuel seal leaks near the engine.

OFFICERS

Chairman Supervisory Board: Hilmar Kopper
VC Supervisory Board: Erich Klemm
Chairman Management Board: Jürgen E. Schrempp
Passenger Cars Mercedes-Benz and smart:
Jürgen Hubbert, age 61
President and CEO, DaimlerChrysler Corp.:
James P. Holden, age 49
Commercial Vehicles: Dieter Zetsche, age 46
Product Strategy, Design and Passenger Car Operations, Chrysler, Plymouth, Jeep, and Dodge:
Thomas C. Gale, age 56
Aerospace and Industrial Non-Automotive:
Manfred Bischoff, age 57
Services: Klaus Mangold, age 56
Finance and Controlling: Manfred Gentz, age 58
Corporate Development and IT Management, Industrial Holdings: Eckhard Cordes, age 49
Global Procurement and Supply: Gary C. Valade, age 57
Research and Technology: Klaus-Dieter Vöhringer, age 59
Human Resources and Labor Relations Director:
Günther Fleig, age 51
Auditors: KPMG Deutsche Treuhand-Gesellschaft

LOCATIONS

HQ: Epplestrasse 225, 70546 Stuttgart, Germany
Phone: +49-711-17-170   **Fax:** +49-711-17-94075
US HQ: 1000 Chrysler Dr., Auburn Hills, MI 48326
US Phone: 248-512-2950   **US Fax:** 248-512-2912
Web site: http://www.daimlerchrysler.com

DaimlerChrysler has operations in Austria, Argentina, Brazil, Canada, France, Germany, Hungary, Indonesia, Mexico, South Africa, Spain, Sweden, Turkey, the UK, and the US.

PRODUCTS/OPERATIONS

1999 Sales

	% of total
Passenger cars	
Chrysler, Plymouth, Jeep & Dodge	41
Mercedes-Benz & smart	24
Commercial vehicles	17
Services	8
Aerospace	6
Other	4
Total	**100**

Selected Car Makes

Chrysler	**Jeep**
Cirrus	Grand Cherokee
Concorde	Jamboree
PT Cruiser	
Sebring	**Mercedes-Benz**
Town & Country	**Plymouth** (discontinued
Dodge	after 2001 model year)
Caravan	Breeze
Neon	Grand Voyager
Ram	Neon
Stratus	Voyager
Viper	**smart** (compact cars)

COMPETITORS

Alstom	Isuzu	Renault
BMW	MAN	Saab Automobile
Boeing	Mazda	Siemens
Fiat	Mitsubishi	Suzuki
Ford	Navistar	Toyota
General Motors	Nissan	Volkswagen
Honda	PACCAR	Volvo
Hyundai	Peugeot	

HISTORICAL FINANCIALS & EMPLOYEES

NYSE: DCX FYE: December 31	Annual Growth	12/90	12/91	12/92	12/93	12/94	12/95	12/96	12/97	12/98	12/99
Sales ($ mil.)	(2.3%)	—	—	—	—	—	—	—	—	154,615	151,035
Net income ($ mil.)	2.3%	—	—	—	—	—	—	—	—	5,656	5,785
Income as % of sales	—	—	—	—	—	—	—	—	—	3.7%	3.8%
Earnings per share ($)	(0.3%)	—	—	—	—	—	—	—	—	5.75	5.73
Stock price - FY high ($)	—	—	—	—	—	—	—	—	—	99.06	108.63
Stock price - FY low ($)	—	—	—	—	—	—	—	—	—	74.50	65.31
Stock price - FY close ($)	(18.8%)	—	—	—	—	—	—	—	—	96.06	78.00
P/E - high	—	—	—	—	—	—	—	—	—	16	21
P/E - low	—	—	—	—	—	—	—	—	—	12	13
Dividends per share ($)	—	—	—	—	—	—	—	—	—	0.00	2.50
Book value per share ($)	1.8%	—	—	—	—	—	—	—	—	35.57	36.19
Employees	5.8%	—	—	—	—	—	—	—	—	441,500	466,938

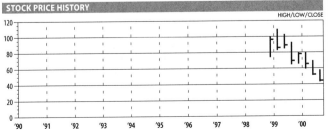

STOCK PRICE HISTORY HIGH/LOW/CLOSE

1999 FISCAL YEAR-END
Debt ratio: 43.5%
Return on equity: 16.1%
Cash ($ mil.): 9,163
Current ratio: 0.93
Long-term debt ($ mil.): 27,962
No. of shares (mil.): 1,003
Dividends
  Yield: 3.2%
  Payout: 43.6%
Market value ($ mil.): 78,254

DANKA BUSINESS SYSTEMS PLC

The story of Danka Business Systems is currently printed in red ink. Headquartered in London (but with its main operations in St. Petersburg, Florida), Danka is a distributor of photocopiers, network printers, and other automated office equipment, parts, and supplies (from Canon, Ricoh, and others). Supplies, rentals, and services such as technical support, document management outsourcing, and training account for two-thirds of sales.

Danka has incurred massive restructuring debts as a result of efforts to trim operational fat and keep pace with top copier seller Xerox, which moved early into the digital market. Amidst continuing losses, two Danka CEOs resigned in the last two years. The most recent was Larry Switzer, promoted into the position as part of a 1998 turnaround effort.

Equity firm Cypress Group owns 22% of the company.

HISTORY

Daniel Doyle saw an opportunity in 1977 to enlarge his prospects by selling Japanese copiers. Doyle and a partner, Frank McPeak, started Danka that year by relocating in the hot-growth Tampa region and buying local office equipment specialist Gulf Coast Business Machines. The company was named from letters in the partners' first names.

In its first 10 years revenues grew at a compounded annual rate of more than 50%. Prosperity resulted from owner Doyle's aggressive, larger-than-life grit. He sold rabbits at age 10, and grew up reading books on becoming rich. As a 26-year-old sales manager at Litton Industries in 1967, Doyle made his copier quota for the year in one day when he chartered a helicopter to fly area executives to a downtown Cleveland hotel for a sales pitch.

Danka continued developing relationships with the copier dealers who sold Japanese models from Canon, Ricoh, and others. In 1986 McPeak retired and Doyle, searching for ways to boost expansion, sold Danka to a UK firm for tax purposes. The new corporate parent, Danka Business Systems PLC, began trading on the London Stock Exchange in 1986.

By 1988 the company had 28 sales and service offices around the US. That year it added fax machines to its product line. In 1992 Danka started trading American Depositary Receipts (ADRs) on the Nasdaq so US investors could more easily buy shares. It raised $86 million in a 1994 ADR offering.

Between 1993 and 1996, driven by Doyle's sales zeal, Danka bought more than 100 copier dealers in an acquisition tear, including Saint Group (1994), which sharpened its image in Europe, and two Australian companies (1996). Strong sales of copier supplies and service contracts pushed revenues over $1 billion for the first time in 1996.

The intense pace culminated in a financial paper jam when Danka bought Eastman Kodak's money-losing copier business and its document management outsourcing operations in 1996. The $588 million purchase doubled Danka's size and gave it instant global credibility in large corporations. But efforts to transmute Kodak's buttoned-down sales atmosphere into Danka's no-holds-barred brand of doing business caused fights over pay and perks. Many Kodak representatives quit; the two sales forces at one point competed with each other, and clients complained about receiving house calls from two ends of the same company. This failure to integrate the teams left sales and shares lowered.

The company reduced its workforce by some 1,200 employees through layoffs and attrition during 1997. That December, after Doyle announced that sales would be off for the quarter, Danka lost $1 billion of its $1.76 billion market value in a day. Shareholders began filing lawsuits accusing Danka of securities fraud (all were dismissed in 2000).

The company cut another 5% of its workforce in 1998, shuffled management, and drastically trimmed operations. Doyle chose Brian Merriman, a veteran respected for turning around Toshiba's office equipment unit, to lead operations. Later that year Doyle and chairman Mark Vaughn-Lee resigned under pressure. CFO Larry Switzer, a former executive with Fruit of the Loom, was named CEO.

In 1999, in the shadow of heavy losses for the fiscal year, Danka restructured, selling its fax business, Omnifax, to rival Xerox and terminating 1,400 more jobs. Also that year Danka established distribution deals with Canon and Kodak, and received an investment from Cypress Group giving that company 22% of Danka's voting power. Switzer resigned in 2000, amidst company warnings of earnings shortfalls; director Michael Gifford was named interim CEO.

Chairman: David W. Kendall, age 65
Interim CEO: Michael Gifford
President and COO: Brian L. Merriman, age 63,
$1,599,000 pay
EVP and CFO: F. Mark Wolfinger, age 45,
$1,107,000 pay
SVP Marketing: John Heagney
SVP Human Resources, North America: Rick Davis
Auditors: KPMG Audit Plc

LOCATIONS

HQ: Masters House, 107 Hammersmith Rd.,
London W14 0QH, United Kingdom
Phone: +44-20-7603-1515   **Fax:** +44-20-7603-8448
US HQ: 11201 Danka Circle North,
St. Petersburg, FL 33716
US Phone: 727-576-6003
Web site: http://www.danka.com

Danka Business Systems has offices in Australia,
Austria, Belgium, Brazil, Canada, Chile, Colombia,
Denmark, France, Germany, Italy, Mexico, the
Netherlands, New Zealand, Norway, Panama, the
Philippines, Puerto Rico, Spain, Sweden, Switzerland,
the UK, the US, and Venezuela.

2000 Sales

	$ mil.	% of total
US	1,385	55
Europe		
UK	228	9
Netherlands	161	7
Germany	153	6
Other countries	332	13
Other regions	237	10
Total	**2,496**	**100**

PRODUCTS/OPERATIONS

2000 Sales

	$ mil.	% of total
Service, supplies & rentals	1,645	66
Retail equipment	734	30
Wholesale	117	4
Total	**2,496**	**100**

Services
Document management outsourcing
Leasing
Maintenance
Supply contracts
Support
Training

Distributed Products
Color printers
Digital copiers
High-volume copiers
Software
Toner, developer, and other supplies
Workgroup copiers and printers

Distributed Brands
Canon
Heidelberger Druckmaschinen
Ricoh
Toshiba

COMPETITORS

A.B.Dick	Lanier	Océ
Daisytek	Worldwide	Office Depot
Global Imaging	Lexmark	Olivetti
Systems	International	Pitney Bowes
Hewlett-Packard	Minolta	Seiko Epson
IKON	Nashua	Sharp
	Nu-kote Holding	Xerox

HISTORICAL FINANCIALS & EMPLOYEES

Nasdaq (SC): DANKY FYE: March 31	Annual Growth	3/91	3/92	3/93	3/94	3/95	3/96	3/97	3/98	3/99	3/00
Sales ($ mil.)	37.1%	—	200	337	789	802	1,240	2,101	3,349	2,897	2,496
Net income ($ mil.)	(6.5%)	—	18	21	39	39	45	42	52	(295)	10
Income as % of sales	—	—	8.8%	6.3%	5.0%	4.9%	3.6%	2.0%	1.6%	—	0.4%
Earnings per share ($)	(21.0%)	—	—	0.52	0.59	0.80	0.88	0.72	0.90	(5.18)	0.10
Stock price - FY high ($)	—	—	—	10.25	23.25	28.13	44.50	51.88	51.31	23.75	14.13
Stock price - FY low ($)	—	—	—	4.44	9.19	17.13	22.50	22.25	12.38	1.75	4.25
Stock price - FY close ($)	(6.8%)	—	—	10.00	19.63	26.25	42.25	31.44	18.38	5.00	6.13
P/E - high	—	—	—	20	38	34	49	70	56	—	141
P/E - low	—	—	—	9	15	21	25	30	13	—	43
Dividends per share ($)	—	—	—	0.03	0.08	0.10	0.12	0.19	0.24	0.13	0.00
Book value per share ($)	23.0%	—	—	1.54	5.38	4.31	8.07	8.21	8.44	3.00	6.56
Employees	27.2%	—	2,480	2,660	5,350	7,080	10,500	21,800	20,000	18,000	17,000

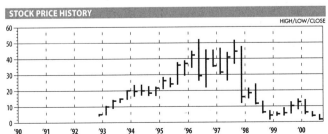

STOCK PRICE HISTORY — HIGH/LOW/CLOSE

2000 FISCAL YEAR-END
Debt ratio: 65.0%
Return on equity: 5.9%
Cash ($ mil.): 65
Current ratio: 1.87
Long-term debt ($ mil.): 715
No. of shares (mil.): 59
Dividends
  Yield: —
  Payout: —
Market value ($ mil.): 359

GROUPE DANONE

OVERVIEW

You say Danone, I say Dannon; let's call the whole thing one of the largest food producers in the world. The Paris-based company, known as Groupe Danone throughout most of the world (but Dannon in the US) is the world leader in dairy products. Its dairy division (desserts, cheese, and yogurt) accounts for 45% of sales and includes the Danone and Galbani brands. Danone is also #1 globally in sweet biscuits (including major European brand LU) and #2 in bottled water (Evian, Volvic), behind Nestlé. It owns almost 45% of glassmaker BSN Emballage.

In addition to its major brands, Danone has dozens of regional brands, including Amoy Asian-style snacks in Europe, Jacob's biscuits in the UK, and HP and Lea & Perrins sauces in the UK and US, respectively.

Danone has found that increasing sales by billions of dollars in acquisitions doesn't mean a similar gain in profits. Hence, it has divested a sack full of grocery product businesses, thrown out its European beer operations, and sold control of its glass-packaging unit to focus on core products. Danone is expanding in Asia, South America, and Eastern Europe.

Company founder Antoine Riboud is honorary chairman; his son Franck runs the firm. Italy's Agnelli family owns almost 5% .

HISTORY

In 1965 Antoine Riboud replaced his uncle as chairman of family-run Souchon-Neuvesel, a Lyons, France-based maker of glass bottles. Antoine quickly made a mark in this field — he merged the firm with Boussois, a major French flat-glass manufacturer, creating BSN in 1966.

Antoine enlarged BSN's glass business and filled the company's bottles by acquiring well-established beverage and food concerns. In 1970 BSN purchased Brasseries Kronenbourg (France's largest brewer), Société Europeenne de Brasseries (another French brewer), and Evian (mineral water, France). The 1972 acquisition of Glaverbel (Belgium) gave BSN 50% of Europe's flat-glass market. The next year BSN merged with France's Gervais Danone (yogurt, cheese, Panzani pasta; founded in 1919 and named after founder Isaac Carasso's son Daniel).

Increasing energy costs depressed flat-glass earnings, so BSN began divesting those businesses. In the late 1970s it acquired interests in brewers in Belgium, Spain, and Italy.

BSN bought Dannon, the leading US yogurt maker (co-founded by Daniel Carasso, who had continued making Danone yogurt in France until WWII), in 1982. It established a strong presence in the Italian pasta market by buying stakes in Ponte (1985) and Agnesi (1986). BSN also purchased Generale Biscuit, the world's #3 biscuit maker (1986), and RJR Nabisco's European cookie and snack-food business (1989).

In a series of acquisitions starting in 1986, BSN took over Italy and Spain's largest mineral water companies and several European pasta makers and other food companies. Adopting the name of its leading international brand, BSN became Groupe Danone in 1994.

Antoine's son, Franck, succeeded him as chairman in 1996. Better known as a windsurfing champion than for the 15 years he'd spent at Danone, Franck surprised many with a restructuring that focused the company on three core businesses: dairy, beverages (specifically water and beer), and biscuits.

By 1997 Danone had begun shedding grocery products, and the trend continued throughout the next two years. The company simultaneously stepped up acquisitions of dairy, beer, biscuit, and water companies in developing markets. The company's 1998 purchase of AquaPenn Spring Water for $112 million doubled its US water-bottling production capacity. Danone in 1999 completed a merger and subsequent sale of part of its BSN Emballage glass-packaging unit to UK buyout firm CVC Capital Partners for $1.23 billion.

Thirsty for the #2 spot in US bottled water sales, Danone gulped down McKesson Water (the #3 bottled water firm in the US after Nestlé and Suntory) for $1.1 billion in February 2000. In April 2000 Danone's joint venture Finalrealm (which includes several European equity firms), with Burlington Biscuits (Nabisco and Hicks, Muse, Tate & Furst), acquired 87% of leading UK biscuit maker United Biscuits. Danone bought Naya (bottled water, Canada) in June 2000. The following month, Danone sold its brewing operations (#2 in Europe) in Belgium, France, and Italy to Scottish & Newcastle for more than $2.6 billion; it is holding on to its Chinese beer interests.

In 2000 Danone (through a joint venture with AmBev) agreed to acquire about 57% of Uruguay's leading mineral water producer and #2 brewer, Compania Salus. It also entered into an alliance with China's largest dairy, Shanghai Bright.

Chairman and CEO: Franck Riboud, age 44
VC and COO: Jacques Vincent, age 54
SEVP: Christian Laubie, age 61
EVP Finance: Emmanuel Faber
EVP: Philippe Jaeckin, age 61
EVP Dairy Products Worldwide: Jan Bennink
EVP International Strategy: Georges Casala
EVP Biscuits Worldwide: Jean-Louis Gourbin
EVP Asia/Pacific: Simon Israel
EVP Water Worldwide: Pedro Medina
SVP Human Resources: Jean-René Buisson
Auditors: Befec-Price Waterhouse; Mazars & Guerard

HQ: 7, rue de Téhéran, 75008 Paris, France
Phone: +33-1-44-35-20-20   **Fax:** +33-1-42-25-67-16
US HQ: 120 White Plains Rd., Tarrytown, NY 10591
US Phone: 914-366-9700   **US Fax:** 914-366-2805
Web site: http://www.danonegroup.com

Danone Groupe's products are made at almost 150
plants worldwide and sold in 120 countries on six
continents.

1999 Sales

	$ mil.	% of total
Europe		
France	5,009	35
Other countries	5,131	36
Other regions	3,996	29
Adjustments	(721)	—
Total	**13,415**	**100**

1999 Sales

	$ mil.	% of total
Fresh dairy	6,036	45
Beverages	3,598	26
Biscuits	2,848	21
Other foods	532	4
Containers	505	4
Adjustments	(104)	—
Total	**13,415**	**100**

Selected Grocery Products
Amoy (Asian foods)
Blédina
Danone
Fali
HP (sauces)
Lea & Perrins (sauces)

Biscuits Gardeil	Kraft Foods
China Resources	Land O'Lakes
Enterprise	Lion Nathan
Coca-Cola	Nabisco Holdings
ConAgra Foods	Nestlé
Dairy Crest	Owens-Illinois
Dairy Farmers of America	PepsiCo
Diageo	Saint-Gobain
Ezaki Glico	Suntory
General Mills	Unilever
Heinz	Vivendi
Hillsdown Holdings	

NYSE: DA FYE: December 31	Annual Growth	12/90	12/91	12/92	12/93	12/94	12/95	12/96	12/97	12/98	12/99
Sales ($ mil.)	2.9%	10,372	12,718	12,815	11,841	14,394	16,185	16,041	14,687	15,154	13,415
Net income ($ mil.)	3.0%	529	595	623	578	661	435	646	608	701	688
Income as % of sales	—	5.1%	4.7%	4.9%	4.9%	4.6%	2.7%	4.0%	4.1%	4.6%	5.1%
Earnings per share ($)	7.0%	—	—	—	—	—	—	—	0.83	0.96	0.95
Stock price - FY high ($)	—	—	—	—	—	—	—	—	18.75	30.69	29.50
Stock price - FY low ($)	—	—	—	—	—	—	—	—	15.41	16.94	21.50
Stock price - FY close ($)	14.1%	—	—	—	—	—	—	—	17.88	28.13	23.28
P/E - high	—	—	—	—	—	—	—	—	22	31	30
P/E - low	—	—	—	—	—	—	—	—	18	17	22
Dividends per share ($)	—	—	—	—	—	—	—	—	0.00	0.00	0.00
Book value per share ($)	(2.7%)	—	—	—	—	—	—	—	9.70	10.32	9.18
Employees	5.9%	45,254	59,158	58,063	56,419	68,181	73,823	81,579	80,631	78,945	75,965

HIGH/LOW/CLOSE

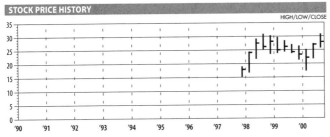

Debt ratio: 36.3%
Return on equity: 9.9%
Cash ($ mil.): 468
Current ratio: 1.12
Long-term debt ($ mil.): 3,539
No. of shares (mil.): 676
Dividends
  Yield: —
  Payout: —
Market value ($ mil.): 15,729

DELHAIZE "LE LION" S.A.

OVERVIEW

There's no lying around for Delhaize "Le Lion" — the Brussels-based supermarket chain has nearly 2,200 stores on three continents, although US operations account for more than half of the stores and 70% of the company's sales. Delhaize America's 1,400-plus stores operate along the East Coast, mostly as Food Lion, although the subsidiary also operates Cub Foods, Hannaford, Kash n' Karry, Save-A-Lot, Save 'n Pack, and Shop 'n Save stores, and the online grocery store HomeRuns.com.

Delhaize has about 550 stores in Belgium and Luxembourg under the AD Delhaize, Delhaize, Delhaize 2, Delhaize City, Di, Superettes, and Tom & Co. names. The company also has interests in supermarkets in the Czech Republic (Delvita, Sama), France (Stoc Supermarché, Marché Plus), Greece (Alfa-Beta), Indonesia (Super Indo), Romania (Mega Image), Singapore (Shop N Save), Slovakia (Delvita), and Thailand (Food Lion Thailand).

The company has been making acquisitions and opening new stores worldwide.

HISTORY

Two brothers and a brother-in-law — all teachers — founded Delhaize in 1867 in Charleroi, Belgium. Jules Delhaize was a professor of commercial sciences, and he wanted to try out his ideas about food retailing, such as creating a network of stores and a centralized warehouse and charging set prices for items. He enlisted the aid of his brother Edouard and his brother-in-law Jules Vieujant. The trio picked the symbol that has become synonymous with the company — the lion, because it represented strength and it was the emblem of their native country. A third brother, Adolphe, later started his own food retailing operation, also with multiple branches. (His operations were merged into Delhaize in 1950.)

The company moved to Brussels in 1871. In the early 1880s the company moved closer to a rail line for better transportation services, opened a large warehouse and other operations, and began setting up factories to produce its own brand-name foods and beverages.

Although it still had stores only in Belgium (more than 500 by 1914), the company had an international presence because of its appearance at exhibitions such as the St. Louis World's Fair in 1904. After WWI the company began investigating possibilities for international trade by sending a delegation to the US and Canada.

At the beginning of WWII, Delhaize had 744 branches and 1,500 affiliated shops, including several in the Belgian Congo. At war's end, Delhaize started closing some of its factories, although it kept a few.

Taking a page from the American supermarkets it had been studying, Delhaize in 1957 opened Europe's first full self-serve supermarket, complete with pre-packaged meat, frozen foods, and fresh produce, and the look of American stores — bright colors, checkout stands, and fluorescent lighting.

Delhaize went public in 1962 as S.A. Delhaize Frères et Cie "Le Lion."

In 1972 Jacques LeClercq, the great-grandson of Jules Delhaize, persuaded the Delhaize board that future opportunities for growth lay in the US. Two years later, as "padlock laws" were being enacted to halt the spread of hypermarkets in Belgium and similar restrictions were occurring in other European countries, the company bought 32% of Food Town, an American chain with 19 stores. (Delhaize bought a controlling interest in Food Town in 1976.) A few years later Delhaize bought Food Giant in Atlanta and began expanding beyond the supermarket in Belgium, setting up the Di body care shops and, in 1981, the AD (Delhaize Affiliates) chain to offer wholesale and management advice services.

Food Town became Food Lion in 1983. Two years later Delhaize opened a new chain, Cub Food, in Atlanta. In 1989 it set up Caddy-Home, a home-delivery service, and Tom & Co., stores selling pet foods and supplies.

International expansion was the byword for the 1990s. Delhaize set up Delvita in 1991 in the Czech Republic. Further acquisitions included controlling interests in Alfa-Beta Vassilopoulos (Greece, 1992) and the PG chain (France, 1994), the Kash n' Karry chain (US, 1996), and interests in supermarket chains in Thailand and Indonesia (1997). In 1999 the company acquired 49% of Shop N Save (Singapore), 50 Interkontakt stores (Europe), and 28 Farmer Jack stores (US).

Expansion continued in 2000 with further acquisitions in Thailand and Romania and the mid-year US acquisition of Hannaford Bros. Soon after, Delhaize announced plans to acquire all of Delhaize America and integrate the US operations.

Chairman: Gui de Vaucleroy
CEO; Chairman, Delhaize America:
  Pierre-Olivier Beckers
CFO Group: Jean-Claude Coppieters 't Wallant
**Officer Financial Planning, Control and Development
  Group:** Dominique Raquez
Chairman, Alfa-Beta: Raphael Moissis
**President and CEO, Delhaize America; President and
  CEO, Food Lion:** R. William McCanless
**VC, Delhaize America; President and CEO, Hannaford
  Bros.:** Hugh G. Farrington, age 55, $723,097 pay
President and CEO, Super Discount Markets:
  Preston Slayden
President, Kash n' Karry: Bruce Dawson
General Manager Asia: Denis Knoops
**General Manager Belgium and Grand Duchy of
  Luxembourg and Delhaize Belgium:** Renaud Cogels
General Manager Delvita: Jiri Poulicek
General Manager Europe (Outside Benelux):
  Denis Ricklin
General Manager Food Lion Thailand:
  Wiwat Avasiriphongs
General Manager P.G.: Francois Rainaut
Executive Director Shop N Save: Michael Gian
Executive Director Super Indo: Sugiyanto Wibawa
**Secretary and Director of Human Resources
  Development Group:** Pierre Dumont
Auditors: Deloitte & Touche

1999 Stores

	No.
US	
Food Lion & Kash n' Karry	1,276
Cub Foods & Save-A-Lot	20
Hannaford & Shop 'n Save	108
Belgium & Luxembourg	
AD Delhaize & Superette	251
Di	116
Supermarché Delhaize "Le Lion"	115
Tom & Co.	57
Delhaize 2	14
Czech Republic	
Delvita & Sama	99
France	
Stoc Supermarché & Marché Plus	50
Greece	
Alfa-Beta	48
Singapore	
Shop N Save	25
Indonesia	
Super Indo	14
Slovakia	
Delvita	14
Thailand	
Food Lion	13
Total	**2,220**

HQ: rue Osseghem 53, Molenbeek-St.-Jean,
  B-1080 Brussels, Belgium
Phone: +32-2-412-21-11   **Fax:** +32-2-412-21-94
US HQ: 2110 Executive Dr., Salisbury, NC 28147
US Phone: 704-633-8250   **US Fax:** 704-636-5024
Web site: http://delhaize-le-lion.be

ALDI	Laurus	Shaw's
Carréfour	Lidl & Schwarz	Tengelmann
Casino Guichard	METRO AG	Tesco
Etn Fr. Colruyt	Publix	Wal-Mart
Kroger	Royal Ahold	Winn-Dixie

Euronext Brussels: DEL FYE: December 31	Annual Growth	12/90	12/91	12/92	12/93	12/94	12/95	12/96	12/97	12/98	12/99
Sales (€ mil.)	9.0%	6,598	7,680	8,098	9,072	9,440	9,134	10,222	12,608	12,912	14,310
Net income (€ mil.)	6.9%	93	108	158	25	100	93	108	122	149	170
Income as % of sales	—	1.4%	1.4%	2.0%	0.3%	1.1%	1.0%	1.1%	1.0%	1.2%	1.2%
Earnings per share (€)	16.1%	—	—	—	—	—	—	2.09	2.36	2.87	3.27
Stock price - FY high (€)	—	—	—	—	—	—	—	47.10	52.06	84.28	91.70
Stock price - FY low (€)	—	—	—	—	—	—	—	29.95	35.20	46.60	64.90
Stock price - FY close (€)	17.0%	—	—	—	—	—	—	46.73	46.60	75.36	74.80
P/E - high	—	—	—	—	—	—	—	23	22	29	28
P/E - low	—	—	—	—	—	—	—	14	15	16	20
Dividends per share (€)	11.5%	—	—	—	—	—	—	0.67	0.74	0.84	0.93
Book value per share (€)	15.5%	—	—	—	—	—	—	13.55	16.23	17.59	20.87
Employees	8.6%	—	—	—	—	—	89,702	94,360	107,320	118,942	124,933

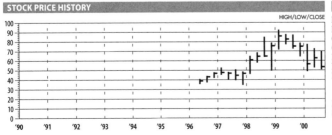

HIGH/LOW/CLOSE

Debt ratio: 50.4%
Return on equity: 17.0%
Cash (€ mil.): 282
Current ratio: 1.09
Long-term debt (€ mil.): 1,104
No. of shares (mil.): 52
Dividends
  Yield: 0.0%
  Payout: 0.3%
Market value ($ mil.): 3,910
Sales ($ mil.): 14,379

DELOITTE TOUCHE TOHMATSU

OVERVIEW

This company isn't "deloitted" by the changes in the accounting/consulting industry. New York-based Deloitte Touche Tohmatsu (DTT, which operates as Deloitte & Touche LLC in the US) is swimming against the tide that is breaking up the combined operations built up during the 1980s and 1990s.

Operating in more than 130 countries, DTT has pursued a strategy of using accountants and consultants in concert to provide seamless service in auditing, accounting, strategic planning, information technology, financial management, and productivity. This makes DTT extra vulnerable to the drive by the SEC to force audit firms to divest their consultants because of a perceived conflict of interest between getting and retaining consulting clients and offering impartial fiscal assurance.

HISTORY

In 1845 William Deloitte opened an accounting office in London. At first he solicited business from bankrupts. The growth of joint stock companies and the development of stock markets in the mid-19th century created a need for standardized financial reporting and fueled the rise of auditing. Deloitte moved into the new field. The Great Western Railway appointed him as its independent auditor (the first anywhere) in 1849.

In 1890 John Griffiths, who became a partner in 1869, opened the company's first US office in New York City. Four decades later, branches had opened throughout the US. In 1952 the firm partnered with Haskins & Sells, which operated 34 US offices.

Deloitte aimed to be "the Cadillac, not the Ford" of accounting. The firm, which became Deloitte Haskins & Sells in 1978, began shedding its conservatism as competition heated up; it was the first of the Big Eight firms, for example, to use aggressive ads. In 1984 Deloitte Haskins & Sells tried to merge with Price Waterhouse. The deal was dropped after Price Waterhouse's UK partners objected.

The Big Eight accounting firms became the Big Six in 1989 when Ernst & Whinney merged with Arthur Young to become Ernst & Young. Also that year Deloitte Haskins & Sells joined the flamboyant Touche Ross (founded, 1899) to become Deloitte & Touche. Touche Ross's Japanese affiliate's name, Ross Tohmatsu (founded 1968) rounded out the current name. The merger was engineered by Deloitte's Michael Cook and Touche's Edward Kangas, in part to unite the former firm's US and European strengths with the latter's Asian presence. Cook continued to oversee US operations with Kangas presiding over international operations. Many affiliates, particularly in the UK, rejected the merger and defected to competing firms.

As auditors were increasingly held accountable for the financial results of their clients, legal action soared. In the 1990s Deloitte was sued because of its actions relating to Drexel Burnham Lambert junk-bond king Michael Milken, the failure of several savings and loans, and clients' bankruptcies.

Nevertheless, in 1995 the SEC chose Michael Sutton, the firm's national director of auditing and accounting practice, as its chief accountant. That year DTT formed Deloitte & Touche Consulting to consolidate its US and UK consulting operations; its Asian consulting operations were later added to the group to facilitate regional expansion.

In 1996 the firm formed a corporate fraud unit (with special emphasis on the Internet) and bought PHH Fantus, the leading corporate relocation consulting company. The next year Deloitte and Thurston Group (a Chicago-based merchant bank) teamed up to form NetDox, a system for delivering legal, financial, and insurance documents via the Internet. In 1997 amid a new round of mergers in the industry, rumors swirled that a merger of DTT and Ernst & Young had been scrapped because the firms could not agree on relative ownership of the two firms' partners. DTT disavowed plans to merge and launched an ad campaign directly targeted against its rivals.

In 1998 the firm's overseas expansion was hit by the Asian economic crisis, but the silver lining of the situation was a rise in restructuring and workout consulting. In 1999 the firm sold its accounting staffing service unit (Re:sources Connection) to its managers and Evercore Partners, citing possible conflicts of interest with its core audit business. Also that year Kangas stepped down as CEO and was succeeded by James Copeland, and Deloitte Consulting decided to sell its computer programming subsidiary to CGI Group.

In 2000 the company's Deloitte Consulting announced it would start a business-to-business e-commerce venture with Chase Manhattan.

Chairman: Piet Hoogendoorn
CEO: James E. Copeland Jr.
COO: J. Thomas Presby
CFO: William A. Fowler
Chairman and CEO, Deloitte & Touche USA:
Douglas M. McCracken, age 50
Chief Executive and Senior Partner, Deloitte & Touche (UK): John P. Connolly
National Director U. S. International Operations:
Tom Schiro
Director Communications: David Read
Director Finance: Gerald W. Richards
Director Human Resources: Martyn Fisher
National Director, Human Capital and Actuary Practice, Deloitte & Touche LLP: Ainar D. Aijala Jr.
National Director, Human Resources, Deloitte & Touche LLP: James H. Wall
National Director, Marketing, Communications, and Public Relations, Deloitte & Touche LLP:
Gary Gerard
National Director, Operations, Deloitte & Touche LLP:
William H. Stanton
Counsel: Joseph J. Lambert
General Counsel Deloitte & Touche LLP:
Philip R. Rotner

LOCATIONS

HQ: 1633 Broadway, New York, NY 10019
Phone: 212-492-4000 **Fax:** 212-492-4111
Web site: http://www.deloitte.com

Deloitte Touche Tohmatsu operates through about 700 offices in more than 130 countries.

PRODUCTS/OPERATIONS

Selected Services
Accounting and auditing
Information technology consulting
Management consulting
Mergers and acquisitions consulting
Tax advice and planning

Selected Representative Clients
Allstate
DaimlerChrysler
General Motors
Merrill Lynch
MetLife
Microsoft
Mitsubishi
Nortel Networks
Procter & Gamble
Sears

Selected Affiliates
Akintola Williams & Co. (Cameroon)
Braxton Associates
C. C. Chokshi & Co. (India)
D&T Corporate Finance Europe Ltd. (UK)
Deloitte & Touche Central Europe (Czech Republic)
Deloitte & Touche Consulting Group/ICS
Hans Tuanakotta & Mustofa (Indonesia)
The IDOM Group
Nautilus Indemnity Holdings Ltd. (Bermuda)
Shawki & Co. (Egypt)
Tohmatsu & Co. (Japan)

COMPETITORS

Andersen Worldwide	H&R Block
Arthur D. Little	KPMG
BDO International	Marsh & McLennan
Booz-Allen	McKinsey & Company
Boston Consulting	PricewaterhouseCoopers
EDS	Towers Perrin
Ernst & Young	Watson Wyatt
Grant Thornton	

HISTORICAL FINANCIALS & EMPLOYEES

Partnership FYE: August 31	Annual Growth	8/90	8/91	8/92	8/93	8/94	8/95	8/96	8/97	8/98	8/99
Sales ($ mil.)	10.8%	4,200	4,500	4,800	5,000	5,200	5,950	6,500	7,400	9,000	10,600
Employees	4.7%	59,700	56,000	56,000	56,000	56,600	59,000	63,440	65,000	82,000	90,000

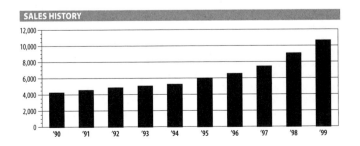

SALES HISTORY

DENTSU INC.

OVERVIEW

Unlike Godzilla, Dentsu is one monster that doesn't leave Japan in ruins. The Tokyo-based company is the top advertising conglomerate in Japan and ranks among the largest in the world. With domestic clients including Sony, Kirin Brewery, and Fuji, Dentsu controls more than 20% of Japan's advertising market and more than 50% of prime-time television ads. Its also has a network of international agencies, including affiliates in a dozen Asian countries operated through its joint venture with US-based Young & Rubicam.

Like other international ad giants, Dentsu provides a growing number of corporate services beyond creative advertising, including public relations and corporate communications, event planning and management, and market research. The company also is active in content development, with units involved in movie and television production, as well as software development for CD-ROMs and Web sites. In addition, Dentsu is a growing force in sports marketing, partnering with the NHL to promote hockey in Japan. (It also promoted the 1998 Nagano Winter Olympic Games.)

While Dentsu has outdistanced its closest domestic rival, Hakuhodo (with about 12% market share), the company is coming under fire from conglomerates WPP Group and Omnicom, which have both taken equity in Japanese agencies. Dentsu has also lagged behind its rivals in adapting to new technologies such as the Internet. To meet these challenges, Dentsu is preparing to list its shares as a publicly traded company; it is planning to do so in 2001. News services Kyodo News and Jiji Press together own about 40% of Dentsu.

HISTORY

Seeing a need for a Japanese wire service, Sino-Japanese war correspondent Hoshiro Mitsunaga founded Telegraphic Service Co. in 1901. Mitsunaga let newspapers pay their wire service bills with advertising space, which his advertising agency, Japan Advertising (also founded in 1901) resold. In 1907 he merged the two companies as Nihon Denpo-Tsushin Sha (Japan Telegraphic Communication Company). Known as Dentsu for short (the name was officially changed in 1955), the company gained Japanese rights to the United Press wire in 1908 and began extracting even more favorable advertising rates from its clients.

With its mix of content and advertising, Dentsu became a leading Japanese communications business. But in 1936 Japan's government consolidated all news services into its propaganda machine, Domei, taking half of Dentsu's stock. During WWII, all of Japan's advertising agencies were combined into 12 entities. Following the war, US occupation forces dismantled Domei, and its 50% holding in Dentsu stock was transferred to two new press agencies, Kyodo and Jiji.

Hideo Yoshida, who became president of Dentsu in 1947, began the task of rebuilding the company, currying favor by employing the sons of politicians and business leaders. He also helped build the television industry in Japan by investing in start-up broadcasters. Their gratitude translated into preferential treatment for Dentsu, leading to its decades-long domination of Japanese TV advertising.

By 1973 Dentsu had become the world's largest advertising agency, but the company's growth stalled with the slowing Japanese economy. Slow to expand overseas (it formed a joint venture with Young & Rubicam in 1981), foreign billings accounted for just 7% of revenues in 1986. The next year Saatchi & Saatchi passed Dentsu as the world's #1 advertising group. Young & Rubicam/Dentsu later joined with Havas' Eurocom to form HDM Worldwide (named after Havas, Dentsu, and Y&R's Marsteller).

Dentsu rebounded with Japan's economic boom in the late 1980s, but the company continued to struggle abroad. Eurocom pulled out of HDM Worldwide in 1990, and the newly named Dentsu, Young & Rubicam Partnerships reorganized to focus on North America, Asia, and Australia. Dentsu joined with Collett Dickenson Pearce to maintain its presence in Europe after HDM's demise. Restructuring in 1996 created several new units, including one to focus on the Olympics, and in 1997 the company set up the Interactive Solution Center to focus on digital media.

In 1998 the company agreed to buy UK ad agency Harari Page and announced plans for its own public offering. In 2000 Dentsu took a 20% stake in Bcom3 Group (formerly BDM), the new advertising holding company formed by the merger of The Leo Group and MacManus Group. It also formed a Japanese Internet services joint venture with US consulting company marchFIRST (DENTSUmarchFIRST). Each company contributed $30 million to the venture.

OFFICERS

President: Yutaka Narita
EVP: Tateo Mataki
EVP: Yasutoshi Kimura
EVP: Sunao Horiuchi
Senior Managing Director: Ayao Morita
Senior Managing Director: Fumio Oshima
Managing Director: Kazuo Miyakawa
Managing Director: Hideaki Furukawa
Managing Director: Hitoshi Hanatsuka
Managing Director (HR): Ko Matsumoto
Managing Director: Tetsu Nakamura
Managing Director: Tatsuyoshi Takashima
Executive Director: Masatoshi Murakami
Executive Director: Ichiro Saita
Senior Executive Officer: Kenjiro Abe
Senior Executive Officer: Takehiko Kimura
Senior Executive Officer: Teizo Tsutsumi
Senior Executive Officer: Isao Maruyama
Senior Executive Officer: Tsoyoshi Takeuchi
Senior Executive Officer: Masahiro Akashi
Auditors: KPMG

LOCATIONS

HQ: 1-11-10,Tsukiji, Chuo-ku, Tokyo 104-8426, Japan
Phone: +81-3-5551-5111   **Fax:** +81-3-5551-2013
US HQ: 488 Madison Ave., 23rd Fl., New York, NY 10022
US Phone: 212-829-5120   **US Fax:** 212-829-0009
Web site: http://www.dentsu.co.jp

PRODUCTS/OPERATIONS

Selected Operations and Clients

Operations
Domestic Group Companies
  cyber communications (Internet advertising)
  DENTSUmarchFIRST (Internet services, joint venture
    with marchFIRST)
  Dentsu Music Publishing (copyright licensing)
  Dentsu Research (market research)
  Dentsu Tec (sales promotion, events and exhibitions)
  Dentsu, Sudler & Hennessy (advertising)
  Dentsu Wunderman Cato Johnson (direct marketing)
  Dentsu Young & Rubicam (51%, advertising)
Overseas Network
  Bcom3 Group (20%, advertising, US)
  Colby Effler & Partners (advertising, US)
  DCA Advertising (US)
  DCC Communications (advertising, Canada)
  Dentsu Europe (advertising, UK)
  Dentsu USA (advertising)
  JSM + Communications (advertising, US)
  The Lord Group (50%, US advertising)
  Renegade Marketing Group (advertising, US)

Clients

Asahi Chemical	Kirin Brewery
Industry Co.	Matsushita Electric
Bell Atlantic	Industrial
Canon	McDonald's
Central Japan Railway	Panasonic
Citibank	SEGA Corporation
East Japan Railway	Siemens
Fuji Photo Film	Sony
Hitachi	Suntory
Honda	Suzuki
Kao Corporation	Toyota

COMPETITORS

Asatsu-DK	Interpublic Group
Bcom3	Omnicom
Cordiant Communications	Publicis
Group	Tokyu Corporation
Grey Global	True North
Hakuhodo	WPP Group
Havas Advertising	

HISTORICAL FINANCIALS & EMPLOYEES

Private FYE: March 31	Annual Growth	3/91	3/92	3/93	3/94	3/95	3/96	3/97	3/98	3/99	3/00
Sales ($ mil.)	30.1%	1,423	1,481	1,385	1,622	2,026	12,441	11,962	11,787	12,870	15,163
Net income ($ mil.)	3.8%	140	134	55	24	72	129	110	68	37	196
Income as % of sales	—	9.8%	9.0%	4.0%	1.5%	3.6%	1.0%	0.9%	0.6%	0.3%	1.3%
Employees	(0.4%)	6,000	5,811	5,834	5,972	5,910	5,820	5,679	5,683	5,806	—

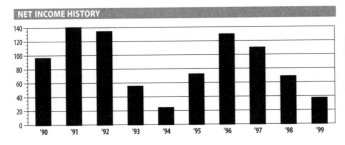

NET INCOME HISTORY

DEUTSCHE BANK AG

OVERVIEW

Germany no longer gets top billing.
Deutsche Bank, Europe's most influential financial institution, took its place at the top of the financial arena's credits when it became the world's #1 bank with its 1999 purchase of New York-based Bankers Trust. The next year, however, it was outdone by Mizuho Holdings (formed by the merger of Fuji Bank, Dai-Ichi Kangyo Bank, and Industrial Bank of Japan) and had to take second billing under the new #1 bank.

Deutsche Bank offers retail services primarily in Germany, but its investment banking and asset management units operate worldwide. The bank continues to seek to pair its troubled retail operations with those of another bank. It is also looking to build its investment banking operations to compete with Goldman Sachs, Merrill Lynch, and other key players.

However, a failed merger with Dresdner Bank has marred Deutsche Bank's reputation, making future purchases more difficult. Despite that failure, the bank plans to step into the online brokerage arena by purchasing the 84% of National Discount Brokers Group that it doesn't already own.

Deutsche Bank and insurer Allianz are the core of a tangled web of cross-ownership among German corporations. Deutsche is seeking to unravel the situation: It is gradually selling big chunks of Allianz.

HISTORY

Georg von Siemens opened Deutsche Bank in Berlin in 1870. Three years later the firm opened an office in London and was soon buying other German banks. In the late 1800s Deutsche Bank helped finance Germany's electrification (carried out by Siemens AG) and railroad construction in the US and the Ottoman Empire. Von Siemens ran the bank until his death in 1901.

The bank survived post-WWI financial chaos by merging with Disconto-Gesellschaft and later helped finance the Nazi war machine. Many nations wouldn't trade in the reichsmark, so it conducted foreign trade in gold, much of it stolen from Holocaust victims. After the war, the Allies split the company into 10 banks; it became extinct in Soviet-controlled East Germany.

The bank was reassembled in 1957 and primarily engaged in commercial banking, often taking direct interests in its customers. It added retail services in the 1960s. In 1975, to prevent the Shah of Iran from gaining a stake in Daimler-Benz (now DaimlerChrysler), the bank bought 29% of that company.

The firm opened an investment banking office in the US in 1971 and a branch office in 1978. In the 1980s it expanded geographically, buying Bank of America's Italian subsidiary (1986) and UK merchant bank Morgan Grenfell (1989); it also moved into insurance, creating life insurer DB Leben (1989).

Terrorists killed chairman Alfred Herrhausen, a symbol of German big business, in 1989. After German reunification in 1990, successor Hilmar Kopper oversaw the bank's re-establishment in eastern Germany.

In 1994 Deutsche Bank bought most of ITT's commercial finance unit. The company began growing its global investment banking operations in 1995 under its Morgan Grenfell subsidiary, but corporate culture clashes and slow progress in investment banking prompted a restructuring in 1998.

In 1997 Deutsche Bank moved into the US mutual fund market and bought the pension fund operations of the Australian state of New South Wales. Deutsche Bank's global aspirations were set back in 1998 when losses on investments in Russia trimmed its bottom line. Still trying to put WWII behind it, the bank accepted responsibility for its wartime dealing in gold seized from Jews but has rejected compensation for victims forced by the Nazis to labor in companies in which it holds stakes.

In 1999 the bank acquired Bankers Trust Corporation. Despite a decision to divest its industrial portfolio, in 1999 the company bought Tele Columbus, the #2 cable network in Germany, and Piaggio, the Italian maker of the famed Vespa motor scooter. The company also bought Ciba Specialty Chemicals' performance polymers division. On the banking front, it bought Chase Manhattan's Dutch auction business and sought a foothold in Japan through alliances with Nippon Life Insurance and Sakura Bank.

In 2000 the company agreed to merge with Dresdner Bank (after which they would spin off their retail banking businesses), but the merger collapsed, in part over the fate of investment banking subsidiary Dresdner Kleinwort Benson. That year Deutsche Bank formed DB Venture Partners, entering the European venture capital fray. It also began pushing its online retail banking operations.

Chairman Supervisory Board: Hilmar Kopper
Chairman Management Board: Rolf E. Breuer
Managing Director, Controlling, Taxes, and Audit:
Clemens Börsig
Managing Director, Group Division Corporates and Real Estate: Carl L. von Boehm-Bezing
Managing Director, Group Division Global Corporates and Institutions: Josef Ackermann
Managing Director, Group Division Global Corporates and Institutions: Ronaldo H. Schmitz
Managing Director, Group Division Global Technology and Services: Hermann-Josef Lamberti
Managing Director, Group Division Retail and Private Banking and Human Resources:
Tessen von Heydebreck
Managing Director, Treasury and Market Risk Management: Thomas Fischer
Auditors: KPMG Deutsche Treuhand-Gesellschaft

LOCATIONS

HQ: Taunusanlage 12, 60262 Frankfurt, Germany
Phone: +49-69-910-91000 **Fax:** +49-69-910-34227
US HQ: 31 W. 52nd St., New York, NY 10101
US Phone: 212-469-8000 **US Fax:** 212-469-3210
Web site: http://www.deutsche-bank.de

1999 Sales

	% of total
Europe	
Germany	45
Other countries	22
North America	24
Asia/Pacific/Africa	8
South America	1
Total	**100**

PRODUCTS/OPERATIONS

1999 Assets

	$ mil.	% of total
Cash & equivalents	21,984	3
Trading account	234,118	28
Private placements	116,007	14
Net loans	346,175	41
Investments	70,543	8
Other assets	55,069	6
Total	**843,896**	**100**

COMPETITORS

ABN AMRO	HSBC Holdings
BANK ONE	HypoVereinsbank
Bankgesellschaft Berlin	Industrial Bank of Japan
Barclays	Intuit
BNP	J.P. Morgan
BSCH	KfW
Charles Schwab	Lehman Brothers
Chase Manhattan	Merrill Lynch
Citigroup	Morgan Stanley Dean
Commerzbank AG	Witter
ConSors Discount-Broker	National Australia Bank
Crédit Lyonnais	Rabobank Group
Credit Suisse	Salomon Smith Barney
DG BANK	Holdings
Dresdner Bank	Société Générale
E*TRADE	Toronto-Dominion Bank
E-Loan	UBS
Goldman Sachs	

HISTORICAL FINANCIALS & EMPLOYEES

OTC: DTBKY FYE: December 31	Annual Growth	12/90	12/91	12/92	12/93	12/94	12/95	12/96	12/97	12/98	12/99
Assets ($ mil.)	13.6%	267,335	295,461	307,618	320,145	382,468	501,923	574,823	579,843	735,325	843,896
Net income ($ mil.)	15.9%	685	910	1,107	1,247	1,107	1,474	1,439	567	2,026	2,583
Income as % of assets	—	0.3%	0.3%	0.4%	0.4%	0.3%	0.3%	0.3%	0.1%	0.3%	0.3%
Earnings per share ($)	11.8%	1.57	1.97	2.41	2.65	2.29	2.89	2.76	1.07	3.80	4.27
Stock price - FY high ($)	—	50.72	45.03	47.53	52.73	50.80	51.09	51.88	75.50	87.38	86.00
Stock price - FY low ($)	—	36.23	33.00	39.78	38.55	41.94	44.22	45.13	45.25	47.50	49.00
Stock price - FY close ($)	8.7%	39.75	44.17	40.09	50.39	46.45	47.48	46.25	70.13	57.75	84.00
P/E - high	—	32	23	20	20	22	18	19	71	23	20
P/E - low	—	23	17	17	15	18	15	16	42	13	11
Dividends per share ($)	2.3%	0.94	0.92	0.93	0.95	1.06	1.25	1.17	1.00	1.32	1.15
Book value per share ($)	5.4%	23.58	25.39	24.86	24.96	21.62	39.13	38.51	33.58	38.84	37.86
Employees	3.5%	68,552	71,400	74,256	73,176	73,450	74,119	74,356	76,141	95,847	93,232

STOCK PRICE HISTORY

HIGH/LOW/CLOSE

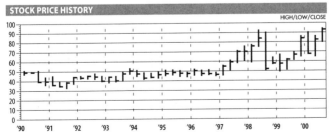

1999 FISCAL YEAR-END

Equity as % of assets: 2.8%
Return on assets: 0.3%
Return on equity: 11.8%
Long-term debt ($ mil.): 99,507
No. of shares (mil.): 614
Dividends
  Yield: 0.0%
  Payout: 0.3%
Market value ($ mil.): 51,605
Sales ($ mil.): 51,358

DEUTSCHE TELEKOM AG

OVERVIEW

Deutsche Telekom is leading the charge as Europe's former state-owned telecommunications monopolies confront competition. The Bonn-based company, still 58%-owned by the German government, is Europe's largest telecom company and one of the biggest in the world, behind NTT and AT&T.

In Germany, Deutsche Telekom has more than 48 million access lines as the dominant fixed-line operator. It also provides businesses with data services such as leased lines and frame relay service, and it sells telecom equipment and publishes phone directories. The company's ISP, T-Online, is the largest in Europe, with about 6 million customers. Through its nine regional cable-TV operations, in which it is selling majority stakes, Deutsche Telekom is Germany's #1 cable provider.

Deutsche Telekom's T-D1 wireless network is #2 in Germany (behind Vodafone's D2 network), with about 13 million subscribers. Counting customers from its stakes in other European mobile phone operators (including One 2 One in the UK), the company's T-Mobile International unit serves more than 22 million customers overall. Deutsche Telekom plans to move into the US mobile phone market with the acquisition of VoiceStream Wireless.

With competition flourishing in Germany, Deutsche Telekom is working hard to lose its bureaucratic image and reposition itself as a slimmer, customer-friendly organization by eliminating jobs, reducing rates, and offering discount plans. The company has sold a minority stake in T-Online to the public and plans to do the same with T-Mobile.

HISTORY

Deutsche Telekom was formed by the 1989 separation of West Germany's telecommunications services from the nation's postal system. Dating back to the 15th century (when the Thurn und Taxis private postal system was created for German principalities), the service covered Austria, France, the Netherlands, and most of Germany by the 1850s. After the 1866 Austro-Prussian War, it became part of the North German Postal Confederation. When the German Empire was formed in 1871, the postal operation became the Deutsche Reichspost (later the Bundespost). Shortly thereafter, the newly invented telephone was introduced in Germany.

Post-WWI inflation shook the Bundespost, and the government allowed it to try new organizational structures. A 1924 law allowed the state-run service to operate as a quasi-commercial company.

Hitler came to power in 1933, and the postal service became an instrument of Nazi surveillance. After WWII occupation forces began rebuilding Germany's badly damaged infrastructure. In 1947 the American-British zone returned postal authority to Germans, and in 1949 the USSR established the state of East Germany.

Only by the 1960s did West Germany's postal and phone services meet modern standards. Privatization of the Bundespost became a political cause when many complained about the monopoly's cost and inefficiency. Efforts to privatize the agency (named Deutsche Telekom in 1989) intensified with the 1990 German reunification. Faced with updating the antiquated

phone system of the former East Germany, political opposition to taking Deutsche Telekom public faded.

The company began operating T-D1, its mobile phone network, in 1992, and the next year it launched T-Online, now Germany's largest online service provider. In 1996 Deutsche Telekom finally went public and raised more than $13 billion in Europe's largest IPO. It also launched Global One with France Telecom and Sprint; as part of the partnership, Deutsche Telekom took a 10% stake in Sprint.

In 1998 European Union (EU) member countries opened their phone markets to competition, and Deutsche Telekom's long-distance market share quickly eroded. Under EU pressure, in 1999 Deutsche Telekom said it would sell its cable network, which it divided into nine regional units.

Deutsche Telekom's plan to merge with Telecom Italia in 1999 blew up in its face: Olivetti butted in and took over Telecom Italia, while an angry France Telecom filed a lawsuit claiming that Deutsche Telekom's merger plan had violated their agreements. (The case was settled in 2000.)

Undaunted, Deutsche Telekom forged ahead with its international expansion plans, buying French fixed-line carrier SIRIS and UK wireless provider One 2 One. In 2000 the company sold its stake in Global One to France Telecom.

Later in 2000 Deutsche Telekom agreed to pay $5.3 billion for a controlling stake in DaimlerChrysler's Debis Systemhaus information technology services unit. It also launched an IPO of its Internet subsidiary, T-Online.

OFFICERS

Chairman Supervisory Board: Hans-Dietrich Winkhaus
VC Supervisory Board: Rudiger Schulze
Chairman, Board of Management; Group Strategy, Communication, Auditing and Organization, Government Regulations, Competition Policy, and Regulatory Affairs: Ron Sommer
Finance and Controlling: Karl-Gerhard Eick
Human Resources and Legal Affairs: Heinz Klinkhammer
International Division: Jeffrey A. Hedberg
Networks, Purchasing, Environmental Protection, Carrier Services and Broadcasting and Broadband Cable: Gerd Tenzer
Product Marketing: Detlev Buchal, age 55
Sales and Service: Josef Brauner
Technology and Services: Hagen Hultzsch, age 59
Auditors: PwC Deutsche Revision

LOCATIONS

HQ: Friedrich-Ebert-Allee 140, 53113 Bonn, Germany
Phone: +49-228-181-0 **Fax:** +49-228-181-8872
Web site: http://www.dtag.de

Deutsche Telekom operates primarily in Europe. It also has operations in North America and Latin America.

PRODUCTS/OPERATIONS

1999 Sales

	% of total
Network communications	48
Mobile communications	12
International	8
Carrier services	8
Data communications	8
Broadcasting and broadband cable	5
Terminal equipment	3
Other	8
Total	**100**

Selected Subsidiaries and Affiliates
DeTeCSM GmbH (computer services)
DeTe Immobilien
DeTeKabelService
DeTe Medien (directories)
DeTeSystem
Magyar Tavkozlesi Rt. (60%, telecom services, Hungary)
SIRIS S.A.S. (fixed-line telecom services, France)
T-Data
T-Mobile International AG (wireless telecom services)
T-Online International AG

COMPETITORS

America Online	France Telecom	NTT
AT&T	Hungarian	Siemens
Belgacom	Telephone	Swisscom
BT	and Cable	Tele Danmark
Cable and	IBM	Telecom Italia
Wireless	KPN	Telefónica
COLT Telecom	Lagardère	Telia
Debitel	Metromedia	Vodafone
EDS	MobilCom	WorldCom

HISTORICAL FINANCIALS & EMPLOYEES

NYSE: DT FYE: December 31	Annual Growth	12/90	12/91	12/92	12/93	12/94	12/95	12/96	12/97	12/98	12/99
Sales ($ mil.)	3.1%	27,114	31,049	33,282	33,927	41,184	45,997	40,917	37,559	41,868	35,796
Net income ($ mil.)	4.7%	838	(82)	(1)	1,199	2,320	3,667	1,140	1,837	2,630	1,265
Income as % of sales	—	3.1%	—	—	3.5%	5.6%	8.0%	2.8%	4.9%	6.3%	3.5%
Earnings per share ($)	(7.3%)	—	—	—	—	—	—	0.54	0.67	0.96	0.43
Stock price - FY high ($)	—	—	—	—	—	—	—	22.25	25.00	33.63	71.94
Stock price - FY low ($)	—	—	—	—	—	—	—	20.13	16.13	17.00	35.88
Stock price - FY close ($)	51.6%	—	—	—	—	—	—	20.38	18.63	32.75	71.00
P/E - high	—	—	—	—	—	—	—	41	37	35	167
P/E - low	—	—	—	—	—	—	—	37	24	18	83
Dividends per share ($)	—	—	—	—	—	—	—	0.00	0.35	0.67	0.65
Book value per share ($)	2.5%	—	—	—	—	—	—	10.74	9.46	10.38	11.56
Employees	(2.4%)	212,205	209,000	231,000	232,964	229,474	213,467	201,060	191,000	186,000	170,000

STOCK PRICE HISTORY
HIGH/LOW/CLOSE

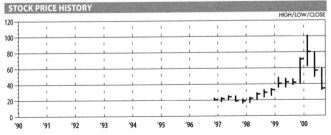

1999 FISCAL YEAR-END
Debt ratio: 49.1%
Return on equity: 4.0%
Cash ($ mil.): 1,183
Current ratio: 0.81
Long-term debt ($ mil.): 33,721
No. of shares (mil.): 3,030
Dividends
 Yield: 0.9%
 Payout: 151.2%
Market value ($ mil.): 215,102

DIAGEO PLC

OVERVIEW

Diageo's holiday parties must be the talk of the town. The London-based enterprise, formed by the 1997 merger of alcoholic beverage giant Guinness with food and spirits company Grand Metropolitan, is the world's largest producer of alcoholic drinks. Its Guinness/UDV division, with labels such as Guinness Stout, Harp Lager, Johnnie Walker Scotch, Tanqueray gin, and Smirnoff vodka, stocks bars and shelves in 200 countries around the globe. It will add several brands, including Crown Royal whiskey, with its planned purchase of Seagram's drinks business.

Diageo also owns Guinness World Records (which produces the famous *Guinness Book of World Records*); 45% of tequila maker José Cuervo; and 34% of Moët Hennessy, the wine and spirits unit of French luxury goods maker LVMH Moët Hennessy Louis Vuitton. LVMH, in turn, owns about 3% of Diageo.

In order to focus on spirits, wine, and beer as well as shed less profitable operations, Diageo has agreed to sell its Pillsbury unit (whose food brands include Green Giant, Häagen-Dazs, and Old El Paso) to General Mills for $10.5 billion; the divestiture will give the company a 33% stake in General Mills.

Diageo also has indicated its planned public offering of Burger King (the #2 burger chain, after McDonald's) is an initial step toward eventually selling the chain.

HISTORY

Diageo — from the Latin word for "day" and the Greek word for "world" — was born from Guinness and GrandMet's 1997 merger to fight flat liquor sales and spirited competitors.

Guinness began business in 1759 with the lease of a small brewery in Dublin, Ireland, where Arthur Guinness made ales and porters (by 1799 he had begun specializing in porters). Managed by the third generation of Guinnesses, the company went public as a London-based firm in 1886.

In the 1950s managing director Hugh Beaver was credited with conceiving the *Guinness Book of World Records*. During the 1970s Guinness bought more than 200 companies, with disappointing results. Guinness refocused on brewing and distilling operations in the late 1980s by selling noncore businesses and acquiring firms such as Schenley (Dewar's). In 1988 and 1989 it bought 24% of LVMH Moët Hennessy Louis Vuitton (later exchanged for 34% of LVMH's wine and spirits business). More acquisitions followed in the 1990s, capped by Guinness' 1997 announcement of its $19 billion merger with Grand Metropolitan.

GrandMet was established by Maxwell Joseph, who dropped out of school in 1926 to work for a real estate agency in London. In 1931 he set off on his own and began acquiring properties for resale, but WWII and a weak British economy slowed his progress. Joseph's first hotel purchase was a bomb-damaged wreck in London in 1946. He bought progressively larger and more prestigious hotels, and by 1961 GrandMet had gone public.

Diversification began in 1970 with the purchases of catering firms, restaurants, and betting shops. In the early 1970s, in what was the largest British takeover up to that time,

GrandMet bought brewer Truman Hanburg, followed by Watney Mann, which owned International Distillers & Vintners, makers of Bailey's, Bombay Gin, and J&B Scotch.

GrandMet looked overseas through the 1970s, taking over the Liggett Group, a US cigarette maker (sold in 1986) whose Paddington unit was the US distributor of J&B Scotch. In 1981 the company bought Intercontinental Hotels from Pan Am (sold 1988) and began a restructuring around its food and drink segments in 1982. In 1987 it bought Heublein (Smirnoff, Lancers, José Cuervo). Two years later it bought The Pillsbury Company (Burger King, Häagen-Dazs, and Green Giant) in a hostile takeover. Pillsbury was founded in 1869 in Minneapolis as a flour miller; it acquired the Burger King chain in 1967.

When Diageo was created, the companies and brands were divided among four divisions: The Pillsbury Company, Burger King, Guinness, and United Distillers & Vintners. In January 2000, Diageo sold its 88% stake in Spanish brewer Cruzcampo to Heineken.

In September 2000, COO Paul Walsh, a former Pillsbury CEO, took over as CEO of both Diageo and its newly combined alcoholic beverage division, Guinness/UDV. Under investor pressure to focus on its liquor and beer businesses, Diageo announced plans to eventually spin off Burger King to the public. The company already has agreed to sell its Pillsbury unit to cereal giant General Mills.

In December Diageo, along with fellow wine and spirits producer Pernod Ricard, agreed to pay $8.15 billion for Seagram's drinks business which holds several brands, including Crown Royal and VO Canadian whiskies, Captain Morgan rum, and Sterling Vineyards.

Chairman: Lord Blyth, age 60
CEO; CEO Guinness/UDV: Paul S. Walsh, age 44, $987,000 pay (prior to promotion)
Group Finance Director: Nicholas C. Rose, age 42, $7,000 pay (partial-year salary)
CEO United Distillers & Vintners: John M. J. Keenan, age 63, $851,000 pay
CEO Pillsbury: John N. Lilly, age 44
CEO Burger King: Dennis N. Malamatinas, age 44, $748,000 pay
CEO Guinness: Colin A. Storm, age 60, $456,000 pay
Group Investor Relations Director: Catherine James
Group Human Resources Director: Gareth Williams
Company Secretary: Roger H. Myddelton, age 57
Auditors: KPMG Audit Plc

LOCATIONS

HQ: 8 Henrietta Place, London W1M 9AG, United Kingdom
Phone: +44-207-927-5200   **Fax:** +44-207-927-4600
US HQ: 200 S. 6th St., Minneapolis, MN 55402
US Phone: 612-330-4966   **US Fax:** 612-330-5200
Web site: http://www.diageo.com

Diageo has operations in more than 50 countries and sells its products in more than 200.

2000 Sales

	$ mil.	% of total
North America	8,550	48
Europe	6,340	35
Asia/Pacific	1,343	7
Latin America	1,057	6
Other regions	708	4
Total	**17,998**	**100**

PRODUCTS/OPERATIONS

2000 Sales

	$ mil.	% of total
Spirits & wine	7,537	42
Packaged food	5,780	32
Beer	3,254	18
Fast food	1,427	8
Total	**17,998**	**100**

Selected Affiliates, Properties, and Subsidiaries
Burger King Corporation (US)
Gleneagles Hotels PLC (golf resort, Scotland)
Guinness/UDV
José Cuervo SA (45%, Mexico)
Moët Hennessy (34%, France)
The Pillsbury Company (US)
    Ice Cream Partners USA (joint venture with Nestlé USA)

COMPETITORS

Allied Domecq	Dreyer's	Nabisco
Anheuser-Busch	Earthgrains	Holdings
Bacardi	Fortune Brands	Nestlé
Bass Brewers	Foster's Brewing	Pernod Ricard
Ben & Jerry's	Gallo	Remy Cointreau
Brown-Forman	General Mills	Rich Products
Campbell Soup	Heineken	Sara Lee
Chiquita Brands	Interbrew	Scottish &
CKE Restaurants	International	Newcastle
ConAgra Foods	Multifoods	Seagram
Constellation	Kellogg	Subway
Brands	Kraft Foods	TRICON
Danone	Mars	Unilever
Dean Foods	McDonald's	Wendy's
Del Monte	Molson	

HISTORICAL FINANCIALS & EMPLOYEES

NYSE: DGE FYE: June 30	Annual Growth	6/91	6/92	6/93	6/94	6/95	6/96	6/97	6/98	6/99	6/00
Sales ($ mil.)	11.5%	6,776	7,608	6,590	6,890	7,339	7,253	8,107	29,497	18,278	17,998
Net income ($ mil.)	4.0%	1,044	1,175	792	640	1,003	922	1,174	2,230	619	1,480
Income as % of sales	—	15.4%	15.4%	12.0%	9.3%	13.7%	12.7%	14.5%	7.6%	3.4%	8.2%
Earnings per share ($)	(13.0%)	—	—	—	—	—	—	—	2.30	0.69	1.74
Stock price - FY high ($)	—	—	—	—	—	—	—	—	51.13	51.75	44.56
Stock price - FY low ($)	—	—	—	—	—	—	—	—	35.94	33.00	24.38
Stock price - FY close ($)	(13.9%)	—	—	—	—	—	—	—	48.00	43.00	35.56
P/E - high	—	—	—	—	—	—	—	—	22	74	20
P/E - low	—	—	—	—	—	—	—	—	16	47	11
Dividends per share ($)	(48.8%)	—	—	—	—	—	—	—	5.45	1.30	1.43
Book value per share ($)	(1.4%)	—	—	—	—	—	—	—	8.59	21.53	8.35
Employees	18.2%	18,873	24,788	24,032	23,264	23,774	21,533	20,555	77,029	72,000	72,474

STOCK PRICE HISTORY

HIGH/LOW/CLOSE

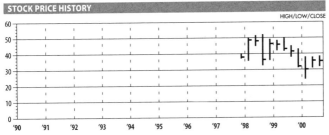

2000 FISCAL YEAR-END

Debt ratio: 44.1%
Return on equity: 11.6%
Cash ($ mil.): 1,612
Current ratio: 0.99
Long-term debt ($ mil.): 5,635
No. of shares (mil.): 856
Dividends
    Yield: 4.0%
    Payout: 82.2%
Market value ($ mil.): 30,422

AB ELECTROLUX

OVERVIEW

Unlike nature, AB Electrolux adores vacuums — and other appliances, too. The Stockholm-based company is the world's leading producer of vacuum cleaners, including brands Eureka (US) and Electrolux (outside of the US and Canada). The company is also the world's top maker of major appliances, including refrigerators, freezers, ovens, washing machines, and dishwashers, under the AEG, Electrolux, and Frigidaire brands, among others.

In addition to household appliances (which account for nearly 75% of sales), Electrolux makes food and beverage machines for the food service industry, commercial laundry equipment, and outdoor items such as Husqvarna chainsaws and Weed Eater lawn trimmers.

The company is buying the Electrolux name in North America from long-unaffiliated Electrolux LLC. Through Investor AB — which also has stakes in Saab and other multinational companies — the Wallenberg family controls 21% of Electrolux's voting power.

HISTORY

Swedish salesman Axel Wenner-Gren saw an American-made vacuum cleaner in a Vienna, Austria, store window in 1910 and envisioned selling the cleaners door-to-door, a technique he had learned in the US. Two years later he worked with fledgling Swedish vacuum cleaner makers AB Lux and Elektromekaniska to improve their existing designs. The two companies merged to form AB Electrolux in 1919. When the board of the new company balked at Wenner-Gren's suggestion to mass-produce vacuum cleaners, he guaranteed Electrolux's sales through his own sales company.

In the 1920s the company used the "Every home — an Electrolux home" slogan as Wenner-Gren drove his sales force on and launched new sales companies in Europe and North and South America. Company lore has him paying a sales call on the Vatican, in competition with four other vacuum cleaner salesmen. After the others had swept their preassigned portions of the carpet, Wenner-Gren pushed his Electrolux over the area cleaned by the competition, dumped out a large pile of dust, and won the order. He scored another publicity coup by securing the blessing of Pope Pius XI to vacuum the Vatican, gratis, for a year. By the end of the 1920s, Electrolux had purchased most of Wenner-Gren's sales companies (excluding Electrolux US) and had gambled on refrigerator technology and won. By buying vacuum cleaner maker Volta (Sweden, 1934), it gained retail distribution.

Despite the loss of Eastern European subsidiaries during WWII, the company did well until the 1960s, when it backed an unpopular refrigeration technology. Swedish electrical equipment giant ASEA, controlled by Marcus Wallenberg, bought a large stake in Electrolux in 1964, and in 1967 he installed Hans Werthen as chairman. Werthen slashed overhead and sold the company's minority stake in Electrolux

US to Consolidated Foods. (The US Electrolux business was taken private in 1987.)

Since 1970 Electrolux has bought more than 300 companies (many of them troubled appliance makers), updated their plants, and gained global component manufacturing efficiencies. Acquisitions included National Union Electric (Eureka vacuum cleaners, US, 1974), Tappan (appliances, US, 1979), Zanussi (appliances, industrial products; Italy; 1984), White Consolidated Industries (appliances, industrial products; US; 1986), and Lehel (refrigerators, Hungary, 1991). By 1996 the company had acquired a 41% interest in Refrigeração Paraná, Brazil's #2 manufacturer of appliances. (Electrolux owned it all by 1998.)

To better focus on its "white goods" (washers, refrigerators, etc.), in 1996 Electrolux began selling noncore businesses. In 1997, under new CEO Michael "Mike the Knife" Treschow, the company launched a restructuring plan involving the closing of about 25 plants and the elimination of more than 12,000 jobs, mostly in Europe. The plan worked: Electrolux's profits more than quadrupled in 1998. Also that year the company formed a joint venture in India with Voltas Limited, forming that country's largest refrigerator manufacturer.

Electrolux acquired the European operations of chainsaw maker McCulloch, North America, in 1999. To strengthen its Asian presence, Electrolux teamed up with Toshiba for future collaboration on household appliances. Also that year the company said it would sell its vending machine unit and professional refrigeration business. In May 2000 the company agreed to buy the Electrolux brand name in North America from long-unaffiliated US company Electrolux LLC (which will remain independent.)

Chairman: Rune Andersson
Deputy Chairman: Jacob Wallenberg
President and CEO: Michael Treschow
Head of Business Sector Floor-care Products and Small Appliances: Hans Straberg
Head of Business Sector Professional Indoor Products: Detlef Munchow
Head of Business Sector White Goods and Outdoor Products, North America: Robert E. Cook
Head of Business Sectors Professional Outdoor Products and Consumer Outdoor Products, Outside North America: Bengt Andersson
Head of Business Sectors White Goods Europe and New Markets: Wolfgang Konig
Head of Group Staff Communication and Public Affairs: Lars-Goran Johansson
Head of Group Staff Controlling, Accounting, Taxes, Auditing, IT: Johan Bygge
Head of Group Staff Legal: Cecilia Vieweg
Head of Group Staff Organizational Development and Management Resources: Lilian Fossum
Head of Group Staff Treasury: Matts P. Ekman
Auditors: KPMG

LOCATIONS

HQ: S:t Goransgatan 143,
SE-105 45 Stockholm, Sweden
Phone: +46-8-738-60-00   **Fax:** +46-8-656-44-78
Web site: http://www.electrolux.com

1999 Sales

	$ mil.	% of total
Europe	7,040	50
North America	5,592	40
Other regions	1,391	10
Total	**14,023**	**100**

PRODUCTS/OPERATIONS

1999 Sales

	$ mil.	% of total
Household appliances	10,203	73
Outdoor products	2,501	18
Professional appliances	1,286	9
Other	33	—
Total	**14,023**	**100**

Selected Household Appliance Brands

AEG	Kelvinator	Tornado
Allwyn	Maxclean	Volta
Corbero	McCulloch	Voss
Dito Sama	Menalux	Wascomat
Dometic	Molteni	Washex
Electrolux	Partner	Weed Eater
Elektro-Helios	Rex	VOE
Eureka	Rosenlew	White-
Frigidaire	Samus	Westinghouse
Husqvarna	Tappan	Zanker
Jonsered	Therma	Zanussi
Juno	Tricity Bendix	Zoppas

COMPETITORS

Black & Decker	Hitachi
Bosch-Siemens Hausgerate	Hussmann International
Brasmotor	Maytag
Deere	Merloni Elettrodomestici
enodis	Middleby
GE Appliances	Moulinex
Glynwed International	Toro
Goodman Holding	Vorwerk
	Whirlpool

HISTORICAL FINANCIALS & EMPLOYEES

Nasdaq: ELUX FYE: December 31	Annual Growth	12/90	12/91	12/92	12/93	12/94	12/95	12/96	12/97	12/98	12/99
Sales ($ mil.)	(0.5%)	14,632	14,280	11,366	12,015	14,527	17,312	15,983	14,295	14,503	14,023
Net income ($ mil.)	15.7%	132	68	26	70	650	411	269	45	491	490
Income as % of sales	—	0.9%	0.5%	0.2%	0.6%	4.5%	2.4%	1.7%	0.3%	3.4%	3.5%
Earnings per share ($)	15.7%	0.72	0.40	0.14	0.38	4.15	1.14	1.47	0.24	2.68	2.67
Stock price - FY high ($)	—	20.50	18.95	19.55	14.95	22.45	21.45	24.75	36.35	41.20	51.69
Stock price - FY low ($)	—	6.80	10.95	10.25	10.60	13.75	15.50	15.70	22.35	21.75	30.75
Stock price - FY close ($)	17.9%	11.40	15.70	13.45	13.60	20.35	16.55	23.10	27.60	34.88	50.25
P/E - high	—	28	47	140	39	5	19	17	151	15	19
P/E - low	—	9	27	73	28	3	14	11	93	8	12
Dividends per share ($)	—	0.00	0.00	0.75	0.28	0.28	0.55	0.70	0.00	0.00	0.72
Book value per share ($)	0.3%	16.06	31.11	25.89	22.09	30.07	34.79	35.60	28.42	16.50	16.52
Employees	(5.2%)	150,900	134,200	119,200	109,400	114,100	112,300	112,140	105,950	99,322	92,926

STOCK PRICE HISTORY

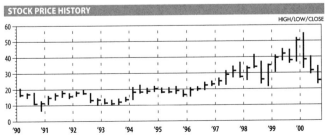

HIGH/LOW/CLOSE

1999 FISCAL YEAR-END

Debt ratio: 39.3%
Return on equity: 16.2%
Cash ($ mil.): 1,210
Current ratio: 1.87
Long-term debt ($ mil.): 1,960
No. of shares (mil.): 183
Dividends
  Yield: 1.4%
  Payout: 27.0%
Market value ($ mil.): 9,200

ELF AQUITAINE

There's nothing elfin about this company. Paris-based Elf Aquitaine, a subsidiary of France's TOTAL FINA ELF, explores for oil and gas in about 30 countries and has proved reserves of 4.2 billion barrels of oil equivalent. Elf produces in more than a dozen countries, but the bulk of its production comes from the North Sea and West Africa's Gulf of Guinea. The company has five refineries in Europe and sells gas through more than 5,200 service stations in Europe and West Africa.

TOTAL FINA bought Elf in 2000 in order to compete more effectively in the consolidating oil and gas industry, but it also gained a big presence in chemicals. Elf's former Elf Atochem subsidiary, which became ATOFINA when combined with the former TOTAL FINA's chemical operations, produced petrochemicals, chlorochemicals, fertilizers, and other basic chemicals. The Elf acquisition also gave TOTAL FINA a stake in drugmaker Sanofi-Synthelabo.

HISTORY

Just before WWII, the French government formed Régie Autonome des Pétroles (RAP) to exploit natural gas reserves discovered in Saint Marcet in the Aquitaine region of southwestern France. During the war the Vichy government created Société Nationale des Pétroles d'Aquitaine (SNPA), a public company that was majority-owned by the state, with a mandate to find oil. After the war President Charles de Gaulle set up the Bureau de Recherches de Pétrole (BRP) as a holding company for RAP and the government's stake in SNPA.

SNPA struck a large gas field at Lacq (1951), and BRP, through subsidiaries, discovered oil and gas in Algeria (1956), Gabon (1956), and the Congo (1957). In 1965 RAP and BRP were consolidated under Entreprise de Recherches et d'Activites Petrolieres (ERAP), which also oversaw the government's SNPA stake. The company began adding refining facilities, and in 1967 ERAP consolidated seven trademarks under the name Elf (which has no meaning in French). SNPA invested in petrochemicals with the formation of ATO, Aquitaine Total Organico (1969).

Elf-ERAP's Algerian fields were nationalized in 1971, but it recouped the loss through discoveries in the North Sea. At the dawn of the energy crisis, SNPA diversified into pharmaceuticals by forming Sanofi in 1973. In 1976 Elf-ERAP and SNPA merged into Société Nationale Elf Aquitaine, of which the French government initially owned 70%. The merged company continued its international expansion. In 1979 it spun off Sanofi but retained majority ownership.

Atochem was built from France's fractured chemical industry in 1983 and placed under Elf Aquitaine. It bought US-based chemical maker Pennwalt and Dow Chemical's Racon unit in 1989 and three years later combined its acrylic plastic business with the Plexiglas operations of the US's Rohm and Haas's to form AtoHaas.

Former government functionary Philippe Jaffre took over as chairman in 1993 and was entrusted with preparing Elf for privatization. He replaced Loik LeFloche-Pringent, who was indicted in 1996 for misconduct relating to his management of Elf. Jaffre had to clean up after a small team of Elf executives who bilked the company of some $250 million between 1989 and 1993. Elf is said to have paid million-dollar kickbacks to a government official through his mistress, a lobbyist for the oil company.

Jaffre slashed costs, sold noncore operations, and laid off thousands, sparking labor demonstrations. In 1994 the company was privatized through a public offering, but the French government retained a 13% stake in the firm. In 1996 Elf bought US-based Findley Adhesives and British company Laporte's adhesives and sealants businesses to solidify its position in specialty chemicals. That year the government sold its remaining shares in the company.

In 1998 Elf bought out Rohm and Haas' 5% stake in AtoHaas to form Atoglas, which makes acrylic sheets and resins. The next year Sanofi sold its beauty division before completing a merger with drug company Synthelabo, a unit of L'Oréal, to form Sanofi-Synthelabo. Also in 1999 Elf lost out to Norsk Hydro and Statoil in a bid to gain control of Norway's Saga Petroleum.

After a protracted takeover tussle, Elf in 1999 agreed to be bought by French rival TOTAL FINA in a $48.7 billion deal. As the companies worked to close the deal, TOTAL veteran Pierre Vaillaud replaced Jaffre as Elf's chairman and CEO. Vaillaud in turn was replaced by TOTAL FINA CEO Thierry Desmarest in 2000. That year TOTAL FINA bought 95% of Elf and became TOTAL FINA ELF. The new company gained control of the remainder of Elf later in 2000.

Chairman and CEO, Elf Aquitaine and TOTAL FINA
ELF; Chairman, TOTAL: Thierry Desmarest, age 54
EVP, Finance; EVP and President, Strategy and Risk
Management, TOTAL FINA ELF: Bruno Weymuller
EVP Chemicals: Jacques Puéchal
EVP, Exploration and Production; EVP and President,
Exploration and Production, TOTAL FINA ELF:
Jean-Luc Vermeulen
EVP, Refining, Marketing, and Trading; VC, EVP and
President, Trading, Gas and Power, TOTAL FINA
ELF: Bernard de Combret
SVP, France; Secretary General, TOTAL FINA ELF:
Yves Edern
SVP, Germany; Marketing, France, TOTAL FINA ELF:
André Tricoire
SVP, Human Resources and Communications;
Executive Career Management, TOTAL FINA ELF:
Michel Bonnet
SVP, Research, Technology, and Environment:
Pierre Castillon
SVP Spain and Business Development: Antoine Jonglez
SVP and Chief Adminstrative Officer; Legal Affairs and
Agreements, TOTAL FINA ELF: Nicholas David
SVP Elf Atochem: René Deleuze
SVP, Elf Atochem; Fine Chemicals, Engineering
Plastics, Hutchinson, TOTAL FINA ELF: Jean-
Bernard Lartigue
SVP, Elf Atochem; Industrial Specialties and
Performance Polymers, TOTAL FINA ELF:
Michel Perratzi
SVP, Africa, Elf Exploration-Production; Americas,
TOTAL FINA ELF: Jean-François Gavalda
SVP, Europe and United States, Elf Exploration-
Production; Northen Europe, TOTAL FINA ELF:
Yves-Louis Darricarrére
SVP, Middle East, CIS, and Latin America, Elf
Exploration-Production: Joël Bouchaud
SVP, Natural Gas, Elf Exploration-Production:
Michel Romieu
SVP, Technology, Elf Exploration-Production:
Giles Rappeneau
Chairman, Elf Atochem; EVP and SEVP, Chemicals,
TOTAL FINA ELF: François Périer
Auditors: Ernst & Young; Cailliau Dedouit et Associés

HQ: 2 place de la Coupole,
    92400 Courbevoie La Défense 6, France
Phone: +33-1-47-44-45-46   Fax: +33-1-47-44-73-66
US HQ: 444 Madison Ave., 20th Fl., New York, NY 10022
US Phone: 212-922-3000   US Fax: 212-922-3001

Elf Aquitaine operates in Africa, Asia, Australia, Europe,
the Middle East, and North and South America.

1999 Sales

	% of total
France	28
Other European countries	38
North America	7
Other	27
Total	**100**

1999 Sales

	% of total
Downstream	66
Chemicals	24
Upstream	6
Pharmaceuticals	4
Total	**100**

BP
Chevron
Conoco
Eni
Exxon Mobil
Norsk Hydro
Occidental
PDVSA
PEMEX
PETROBRAS
Phillips Petroleum
Royal Dutch/Shell
Sinopec Group
Texaco
Unocal

Subsidiary FYE: December 31	Annual Growth	12/90	12/91	12/92	12/93	12/94	12/95	12/96	12/97	12/98	12/99
Sales ($ mil.)	0.4%	34,475	38,740	36,310	35,483	38,897	42,470	44,812	42,250	37,865	35,797
Net income ($ mil.)	0.0%	2,087	1,891	1,118	181	(1,019)	1,027	1,343	931	634	2,088
Income as % of sales	—	6.1%	4.9%	3.1%	0.5%	—	2.4%	3.0%	2.2%	1.7%	5.8%
Employees	(4.9%)	90,000	86,900	87,900	94,300	89,500	85,500	85,400	83,700	84,350	57,400

Debt ratio: 21.3%
Return on equity: 13.5%
Cash ($ mil.): 1,693
Current ratio: 0.98
Long-term debt ($ mil.): 4,482

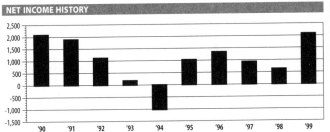

EMI GROUP PLC

OVERVIEW

Pumpkins and Ice and everything Spice, that's what EMI is made of. London-based EMI, which abandoned a merger with Time Warner's Warner Music Group to appease European regulators examining the merger of Time Warner and AOL, markets albums by such artists as Garth Brooks, TLC, Smashing Pumpkins, Ice Cube, the Backstreet Boys, and the Spice Girls on a cache of well-known labels, including Capitol Records, Virgin, Priority, and its eponymous imprint. Preparing itself for the growing Internet economy, the company also offers more than 100 albums for digital downloading on the Internet. In 2000 the firm sold its one-third stake of on-line music seller musicmaker.com.

Although EMI is the world's #3 music company (behind Seagram's Universal Music Group and Sony Music Entertainment), it is struggling in the US. The company ranks last among the Big 5 label groups in the US market (the world's largest), with a market share that has fallen below 10%. EMI is also the world's largest music publisher with rights to more than a million songs, including classics (*New York, New York; Over the Rainbow*), as well as current hits by Matchbox 20 and Puff Daddy. In addition to its music business, the company owns 43% of HMV Media Group, a joint venture with Advent International that operates HMV music stores and the struggling Waterstone's bookstore chain.

HISTORY

Electric & Musical Industries (EMI) was established in 1931 as a successor to a 19th-century gramophone producer. It gradually expanded operations to produce everything from radar systems during WWII to the first television system for the BBC. In 1955 the company bought Los Angeles-based Capitol Records, which was founded in 1942 and featured artists such as Frank Sinatra and Nat "King" Cole. EMI became a major force in the entertainment industry over the next decades, topping off a string of buys with the purchase of Associated British Picture Corporation in 1969.

EMI suffered through the 1970s with money-losing films and the PR sting of signing the outrageous punk group The Sex Pistols in 1976 (the company canceled its contract with the band in 1978). In 1979 the struggling firm was bought by appliance and electronics giant Thorn Electrical Industries (founded by Jules Thorn as the Electrical Lamp Service Company in 1928) for $356 million. Renamed THORN EMI in 1980, the conglomerate continued to suffer losses and lacked strategic focus. Colin Southgate, named CEO in 1985, streamlined THORN EMI's operations to four business sectors (music, technology, rental and retail, and lighting). The company acquired 50% of Chrysalis Records in 1989, and the next year it added Filmtrax music publishing (UK). Also in 1990 the company's HMV stores unit opened its first US superstore in New York City.

In 1992 the company acquired Virgin Records, whose artists included Mick Jagger and Phil Collins, for $960 million. The purchase boosted EMI's US market share and made it one of the world's top music companies. THORN EMI sold its lighting division the next year, and in 1995 it bought UK bookstore business Dillons (later merged with and re-branded Waterstone's).

In 1996 EMI and Thorn split into separately traded companies to maximize the value of its disparate assets; however, share prices plunged when profits failed to materialize. The next year EMI paid $132 million for 50% of Berry Gordy's Jobete companies and its 15,000-song Motown catalog. The Spice Girls, five women brought together by a newspaper ad, became one of Virgin's biggest moneymakers that year.

To focus more on music and less on retail, EMI transferred its HMV and Dillons chains to HMV Media Group, a joint venture with Advent International, in 1998. That year EMI Music head James Fifield resigned with a healthy buyout package after Southgate scotched a succession plan that would have made Fifield CEO. The following year Eric Nicoli, former CEO of food company United Biscuit, was tapped as Southgate's replacement.

Seeking a bigger presence on the Internet, the company bought an equity stake in music Web site musicmaker.com in 1999 (which it sold in 2000). Also in 1999 it paid Windswept Pacific $200 million for the rights to some 40,000 songs, including such standards as *Louie Louie* and *Why Do Fools Fall in Love?* The following year the company began offering Internet downloads of more than 100 albums and agreed to merge its music operations into a joint venture with Time Warner's Warner Music Group (the deal was later scrapped in an attempt to please European regulators examining the merger of Time Warner and AOL).

Chairman and CEO: Eric L. Nicoli, age 49
CEO, EMI Music Publishing Worldwide:
  Martin Bandier, age 58
CEO, EMI Recorded Music: Ken Berry, age 48
**Group Finance Director; EVP and CFO, EMI Recorded
  Music:** Tony Bates, age 44
Secretary and Group General Counsel: Charles Ashcroft
**VC, Virgin Music Group Worldwide and Virgin Records
  America:** Nancy Berry
EVP EMI Recorded Music: Stephen Barraclough
EVP and CFO, EMI Music Publishing: Roger Faxon
SVP New Media, EMI Recorded Music: Jay Samit
SVP Human Resources, EMI Recorded Music:
  Jane Sullivan
Auditors: Ernst & Young

HQ: 4 Tenterden St., Hanover Sq.,
  London W1A 2AY, United Kingdom
Phone: +44-20-7355-4848   **Fax:** +44-20-7495-1307
US HQ: 2751 Centerville Rd., Ste. 205,
  Wilmington, DE 19808
US Phone: 302-994-4100   **US Fax:** 302-994-4299
Web site: http://www.emigroup.com

2000 Sales

	$ mil.	% of total
Europe		
UK	484	13
Other countries	1,154	30
North America	1,157	30
Asia/Pacific	710	19
Other regions	294	8
Total	**3,799**	**100**

2000 Sales

	$ mil.	% of total
Recorded music	3,236	85
Music publishing	563	15
Total	**3,799**	**100**

Selected Labels	Selected Artists
Blue Note	Backstreet Boys
Capitol Records	Beatles
Capitol Nashville	Garth Brooks
Caroline Records	Ice Cube
Chrysalis	Janet Jackson
EMI Classics	Lenny Kravitz
Frank Sinatra	Pink Floyd
Narada	Radiohead
Parlophone	Smashing Pumpkins
Priority	Spice Girls
Virgin Records America	

BMG Entertainment
Chrysalis Group
Death Row
KOCH International
Sony Music Entertainment
Time Warner
Universal Music Group
Viacom
Virgin Group
Walt Disney

OTC: EMIPY FYE: March 31	Annual Growth	3/91	3/92	3/93	3/94	3/95	3/96	3/97	3/98	3/99	3/00
Sales ($ mil.)	(8.3%)	—	—	—	6,369	7,309	7,720	6,530	5,535	3,811	3,799
Net income ($ mil.)	(1.1%)	—	—	—	299	173	343	254	382	234	281
Income as % of sales	—	—	—	—	4.7%	2.4%	4.4%	3.9%	6.9%	6.1%	7.4%
Earnings per share ($)	3.0%	—	—	—	—	—	—	0.59	0.94	0.60	0.64
Stock price - FY high ($)	—	—	—	—	—	—	—	27.31	23.19	20.50	26.25
Stock price - FY low ($)	—	—	—	—	—	—	—	19.72	14.13	10.38	13.00
Stock price - FY close ($)	0.2%	—	—	—	—	—	—	20.56	17.00	14.13	20.68
P/E - high	—	—	—	—	—	—	—	47	25	34	41
P/E - low	—	—	—	—	—	—	—	34	15	17	20
Dividends per share ($)	1.3%	—	—	—	—	—	—	0.49	0.54	0.52	0.51
Book value per share ($)	91.5%	—	—	—	—	—	—	0.42	(2.28)	(2.76)	2.94
Employees	(1.2%)	—	—	—	—	—	—	—	10,452	10,292	10,208

HIGH/LOW/CLOSE

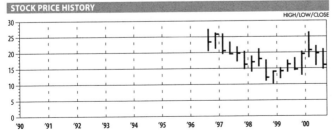

Debt ratio: 34.4%
Return on equity: 800.8%
Cash ($ mil.): 424
Current ratio: 0.61
Long-term debt ($ mil.): 606
No. of shares (mil.): 394
Dividends
  Yield: 0.0%
  Payout: 0.8%
Market value ($ mil.): 8,152

ENEL S.P.A.

Arrivederci monopolio! Rome-based Enel has given up its monopoly status and is racing into the deregulating power marketplace. With a generating capacity of 57,000 MW (almost 75% of Italy's total), the utility serves 29 million customers. CEO Francesco Tato has prepared Enel for competition by unbundling electricity operations and trimming staff by 25,000 employees. Passed in 1999, Italy's Bersani Decree made it official: Enel has been ordered to divest 15,000 MW of its capacity, transfer the national grid to an independent operator, and turn over its municipal distribution networks to local governments.

Large power users (30% of the market) are now able to choose their own supplier; all users will have customer choice by 2002. Enel is also facing a 17% rate cut to be phased in over three years. The Italian government, which has floated about 30% of the utility, plans to reduce its ownership below 50%.

Enel isn't just sipping cappuccino while competitors rush in: The company is moving to become a multi-utility. Its majority-owned WIND Telecomunicazioni provides fixed-line and wireless telecom services to more than 6 million customers. Enel plans to combine Wind with Infostrada, Italy's #2 fixed-line operator (6.1 million customers), which it is buying from Vodafone. Enel has acquired Colombo Gas, a gas distributor with 75,000 customers in northern Italy, and three water operations in the southern region. Internationally, Enel is building power plants in Albania and Argentina.

HISTORY

Italy's energy consumption doubled in the 1950s as the country experienced a period of rapid industrialization and urbanization. A tight-knit oligopoly controlled the electric power industry and included Edison, SADE, La Centale, SME, and Finelettrica. The economic boom pushed into the 1960s, and the Italian government created Enel (Ente Nazionale per l'Energia Elettrica) in 1962 to nationalize the power industry. In 1963 Enel began gradually buying some 1,250 electric utilities. About 160 municipal utilities and the larger independents, such as Edison, were left out of the takeover.

The company spent the late 1960s and early 1970s connecting Italy's unwieldy transmission network and building new power plants, including the La Spezia thermoelectric plant (600 MW). Construction costs, coupled with the high prices Enel was required to pay for its takeover targets, caused the utility to become steeped in debt. The Arab oil embargoes of the early 1970s made matters worse, and the Italian government helped Enel with an endowment in 1973.

The energy crisis also prompted Enel to build its first nuclear power plant, Caorso, which came on line in 1980. However, nuclear power was short-lived in Italy: After the 1986 Chernobyl accident, a national referendum forced Enel to deactivate its nukes in 1987. The firm also stepped up its development of renewable energy sources in the 1980s.

Meanwhile, Enel opened its Centro Nazionale de Controllo (CNC) in Rome in 1985 to supervise Italy's power grid. The next year the company turned its first profit.

To begin disassembling Enel's monopoly, the Italian government in 1992 opened the power generation market to outside producers and converted Enel into a joint stock company (with the state holding all of the shares). Following the European Union's 1997 directive to deregulate Europe's power industry, Enel unbundled its utility activities. Italy's Bersani Decree (passed in 1999) outlined the restructuring process: Enel was ordered to divest 15,000 MW of its generating capacity; a state-controlled operator was set up to oversee Italy's grid; and large users were allowed to choose their own suppliers.

In response, Enel began to diversify in 1998. It started WIND Telecomunicazioni, a joint venture with France Telecom and Deutsche Telekom. (Deutsche Telekom sold its stake to the other partners in 2000.) WIND began offering fixed-line and mobile telecom services to corporations in 1998 and extended the services to residential users the next year. Enel also began building water infrastructure to serve local distributors and purchased three water operations in southern Italy.

Also in 1999 the government floated 30% of Enel in one of the world's largest IPOs at the time. The next year the company bought Colombo Gas, a northern Italian gas distributor with about 75,000 customers. It also announced a joint venture with US-based Internet Capital Group to develop business-to-business e-commerce services targeting European utilities, and it agreed to buy fixed-line telephone company Infostrada. Overseas, Enel made plans to build power plants in Albania and Argentina.

OFFICERS

Chairman: Chicco Testa
CEO: Francesco Tato
Auditing: Antonio Cardani
Company Secretary and Legal Affairs: Claudio Sartorelli
Finance, Planning, Control, and Administration (CFO):
  Fulvio Conti
Human Resources: Angelo Delfino
Institutional Relations: Massimo Romano
Media Relations and External Communications:
  Stefano Lucchini
Real Estate and Logistics (SEI): Francesco Massa
Relations with Regulatory Authority: Giuseppe Carta
Strategic Planning: Mario Barozzi
Image and Communications: Mario Dal Co
CEO, Enel Distribuzione: Roberto Iodice
CEO, Enel Produzione: Antonino Craparotta
CEO, Enel Trade: Roberto Formigoni
CEO, Erga: Paolo Pietrogrande
CEO, Terna: Sergio Mobili
CEO, WIND: Tommaso Pompei
CEO, FTL: Lorenzo Bronzi
CEO, Elettrogen: Vincenzo Cannatelli
Auditors: Ernst & Young S.p.A.

LOCATIONS

HQ: Viale Regina Margherita, 137, 00198 Rome, Italy
Phone: +39-06-8509-1   **Fax:** +39-06-8585-7097
Web site: http://www.enel.it

Enel provides utility services in Italy and is building
power plants in Albania and Argentina.

PRODUCTS/OPERATIONS

1999 Energy Mix

	% of total
Thermal	70
Hydroelectric	29
Other	1
Total	**100**

Selected Subsidiaries
CESI SpA Centro Elettrotecnico Sperimentale Italiano
  (65%, research)
CISE Tecnologie Innovative Srl (research)
CONPHOEBUS Scrl (research)
CONSORZIO SICILTECH (99%, business development)
ELETTROAMBIENTE SpA (waste-to-energy operations)
Enel Produzione SpA (electricity)
ISMES SpA (research)
Sei SpA (real estate)
SOCIETA IMMOBILIARE DALMAZIA TRIESTE SpA
  (real estate)
So.l.e. SpA (public lighting equipment and service)
WIND Telecomunicazioni SpA (57%)

COMPETITORS

ABB	Hidrocantabrico
ACEA	Iberdrola
AEM	Infostrada
Autostrade	International Power
E.ON	RWE
EDF	Sondel
Edison	Telecom Italia
Edison International	Tractebel
Endesa (Spain)	TXU Europe
Enron	Unión Fenosa

HISTORICAL FINANCIALS & EMPLOYEES

NYSE: EN FYE: December 31	Annual Growth	12/90	12/91	12/92	12/93	12/94	12/95	12/96	12/97	12/98	12/99
Sales ($ mil.)	(3.8%)	44,277	44,634	33,737	31,343	31,277	35,915	37,973	34,323	33,177	31,225
Net income ($ mil.)	5.4%	1,799	883	(640)	141	2,006	2,732	2,930	2,893	2,725	2,877
Income as % of sales	—	4.1%	2.0%	—	0.5%	6.4%	7.6%	7.7%	8.4%	8.2%	9.2%
Earnings per share ($)	1.3%	—	—	—	—	—	3.41	3.66	3.62	3.41	3.59
Stock price - FY high ($)	—	—	—	—	—	—	34.75	53.50	63.94	74.50	69.75
Stock price - FY low ($)	—	—	—	—	—	—	30.50	34.25	47.88	50.38	52.25
Stock price - FY close ($)	12.6%	—	—	—	—	—	34.25	51.63	57.06	67.75	55.13
P/E - high	—	—	—	—	—	—	10	15	18	22	19
P/E - low	—	—	—	—	—	—	9	9	13	15	15
Dividends per share ($)	—	—	—	—	—	—	0.00	1.36	1.42	1.57	1.59
Book value per share ($)	6.2%	—	—	—	—	—	18.18	20.85	20.97	23.64	23.16
Employees	(6.4%)	130,745	131,248	124,032	106,391	100,000	86,422	83,424	75,729	78,906	72,023

STOCK PRICE HISTORY

HIGH/LOW/CLOSE

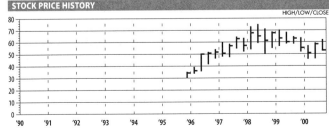

1999 FISCAL YEAR-END

Debt ratio: 20.6%
Return on equity: 15.4%
Cash ($ mil.): 1,220
Current ratio: 1.12
Long-term debt ($ mil.): 4,821
No. of shares (mil.): 800
Dividends
  Yield: 2.9%
  Payout: 44.3%
Market value ($ mil.): 44,105

ENI S.P.A.

OVERVIEW

Integrated energy entity Eni is Italy's enterprising international answer to Edison, Enron, Exxon Mobil, and Elf. One of Italy's largest companies, Rome-based Eni operates natural gas networks, electric power plants, refineries, service stations, and engineering concerns. As one of the world's leading oil and gas operators, Eni has proved reserves of more than 5.5 billion barrels of oil equivalent, most of it in Italy and North and West Africa. The company's oil and gas holdings and exploration and production efforts extend into more than 30 countries on five continents.

Subsidiary Snam is engaged in natural gas supply, transmission, and distribution worldwide, and AgipPetroli operates Eni's oil refining and distribution business. Other subsidiaries include EniChem, a petrochemicals manufacturer; Snamprogetti, a refinery and chemical plant engineering and construction group; and Saipem, an oil field services company.

Eni has been expanding outside its traditional bases of Africa and Italy, with ventures in more than 70 other countries in the Americas, the Asia/Pacific region, Europe, and the Middle East. It is gaining assets in the North Sea and Gulf of Mexico with its acquisition of British-Borneo Oil & Gas. Under CEO Vittorio Mincato, and in response to Italy's energy liberalization movement, Eni is increasing its natural gas holdings and adding electricity generating power units. The Italian government owns 36% of the company.

HISTORY

Although the Italian parliament formed Ente Nazionale Idrocarburi (National Hydrocarbon Agency) in 1953, Enrico Mattei is the true father of Eni. In 1945 Mattei, a partisan leader during WWII, was appointed northern commissioner of Agip, a state-owned petroleum company founded in 1926 by Mussolini, and ordered to liquidate the company. Mattei, instead, ordered the exploration of the Po Valley, where workers found methane gas deposits in 1946.

When Eni was created in 1953, Mattei was named president. His job was to find energy resources for an oil-poor country. He initiated a series of joint ventures with several Middle Eastern and African nations, offering better deals than his large oil company rivals, which he dubbed the Seven Sisters.

Mattei didn't stick to energy: By the time he died in a mysterious plane crash in 1962, Eni had acquired machinery manufacturer Pignone, finance company Sofid, Milan newspaper *Il Giorno*, and textile company Lane Rossi. Eni grew during the 1960s, partly because of a deal made for Soviet crude in 1958 and a joint venture with Esso in 1963. It also expanded its chemical activities.

By the early 1970s losses in Eni's chemical and textile operations, the oil crisis, and the Italian government's dumping of unprofitable companies on Eni hurt its bottom line. Former finance minister Franco Reviglio took over in 1983 and began cutting inefficient operations.

EniChem merged with Montedison, Italy's largest private chemical company, in 1988, but clashes between the public agency and the private company made Montedison sell back its stake in 1990. Eni became a joint stock company in 1992, but the government retained a majority stake.

Franco Bernabe took over Eni following a 1993 bribery scandal and began cutting noncore businesses. The Italian government began selling Eni stock in 1995. In 1996 Eni signed on to develop Libyan gas resources and build a pipeline to Italy. A year later the company merged its Agipa exploration and production subsidiary into its main operations. Eni also took a 35% stake in Italian telecom company Albacom.

The government cut its stake in Eni from 51% to 38% in 1998. That year Vittorio Mincato, a company veteran, succeeded Bernabe as CEO. In 1999 Eni and Russia's RAO Gazprom, the world's largest natural gas production firm, agreed to build a controversial $3 billion natural gas pipeline stretching from Russia to Turkey. Eni agreed to invest $5.5 billion to develop oil and gas reserves in Libya; it also sold interests in Saipem and Nuovo Pignone, as well as some of its Italian service stations.

Chairman Renato Ruggiero resigned in 1999, amid disagreements with CEO Mincato, after only four months on the job. The Italian government, which began liberalizing the country's natural gas industry in 2000, appointed Gian Maria Gros-Pietro as Ruggiero's replacement. In 2000 Eni paid about $910 million for a 33% stake in Galp, a Portugese oil and gas company that also has natural gas utility operations. Also that year Eni agreed to acquire British-Borneo Oil & Gas in a $1.2 billion deal.

Chairman: Gian Maria Gros-Pietro
Managing Director and CEO: Vittorio Mincato
Executive Officer for Finance: Marco Mangiagalli
Executive Officer for Administration: Roberto Jaquinto
Executive Officer for Institutional Relations:
Alberto Meomartini
Executive Officer for Legal Affairs: Carlo Grande
Executive Officer for Planning and Development:
Alfredo Moroni
Executive Officer for Personnel and Organization:
Renato Roffi
Chairman and Managing Director, Eni International
Holding: Angelo Ferrari
Chairman, EniChem: Fabrizio d'Adda
Chairman, Snam: Salvatore Russo
Chairman, Snamprogetti: Luigi Patron
Chairman, AgipPetroli: Gilberto Callera
Auditors: Arthur Andersen S.p.A.

LOCATIONS

HQ: Piazzale Enrico Mattei 1, 00144 Rome, Italy
Phone: +39-06-59-821   **Fax:** +39-06-59-822-141
US HQ: 666 5th Ave., New York, NY 10103
US Phone: 212-887-0328   **US Fax:** 212-246-0009
Web site: http://www.eni.it/english/home.html

1999 Sales

	% of total
Europe	
Italy	61
Other EU	12
Other countries	6
The Americas	10
Asia	6
Africa	5
Total	**100**

PRODUCTS/OPERATIONS

1999 Sales

	% of total
Refining & marketing	44
Natural gas	31
Petrochemicals	12
Oil field services & engineering	9
Exploration & production	4
Total	**100**

Major Group Companies and Divisions
Agip SpA (exploration and production)
AgipPetroli SpA (oil refining and distribution)
EniChem SpA (petrochemicals)
Saipem SpA (oil field services)
Snam SpA (natural gas supply, transmission, and
distribution)
Snamprogetti SpA (contracting and engineering)

COMPETITORS

Amerada Hess	Koch
Anonima Petroli Italiana	Lyondell Chemical
Ashland	Norsk Hydro
BASF AG	Occidental
Bayer AG	PDVSA
BG Group	PEMEX
BP	PETROBRAS
Chevron	Phillips Petroleum
Coastal	Royal Dutch/Shell
Conoco	Sunoco
Dow Chemical	Texaco
DuPont	TOTAL FINA ELF
E.ON	Union Carbide
Enron	Unocal
ERG S.p.A.	USX-Marathon
Exxon Mobil	

HISTORICAL FINANCIALS & EMPLOYEES

NYSE: E FYE: December 31	Annual Growth	12/90	12/91	12/92	12/93	12/94	12/95	12/96	12/97	12/98	12/99
Sales ($ mil.)	(3.8%)	44,277	44,634	33,737	31,343	31,277	35,915	37,973	34,323	33,177	31,225
Net income ($ mil.)	5.4%	1,799	883	(640)	141	2,006	2,732	2,930	2,893	2,725	2,877
Income as % of sales	—	4.1%	2.0%	—	0.5%	6.4%	7.6%	7.7%	8.4%	8.2%	9.2%
Earnings per share ($)	1.3%	—	—	—	—	—	3.41	3.66	3.62	3.41	3.59
Stock price - FY high ($)	—	—	—	—	—	—	34.75	53.50	63.94	74.50	69.75
Stock price - FY low ($)	—	—	—	—	—	—	30.50	34.25	47.88	50.38	52.25
Stock price - FY close ($)	12.6%	—	—	—	—	—	34.25	51.63	57.06	67.75	55.13
P/E - high	—	—	—	—	—	—	10	15	18	22	19
P/E - low	—	—	—	—	—	—	9	9	13	15	15
Dividends per share ($)	—	—	—	—	—	—	0.00	1.36	1.42	1.57	1.59
Book value per share ($)	6.2%	—	—	—	—	—	18.18	20.85	20.97	23.64	23.16
Employees	(6.4%)	130,745	131,248	124,032	106,391	100,000	86,422	83,424	75,729	78,906	72,023

STOCK PRICE HISTORY

HIGH/LOW/CLOSE

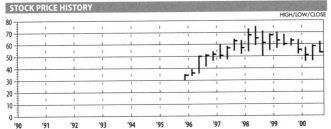

1999 FISCAL YEAR-END

Debt ratio: 20.6%
Return on equity: 15.4%
Cash ($ mil.): 1,220
Current ratio: 1.12
Long-term debt ($ mil.): 4,821
No. of shares (mil.): 800
Dividends
  Yield: 2.9%
  Payout: 44.3%
Market value ($ mil.): 44,105

E.ON AG

OVERVIEW

It's too early to tell whether E.ON is a company for the ages — it was only formed in 2000, from the merger of Germany's VEBA and VIAG conglomerates. E.ON, which is based in Düsseldorf, has operations in chemicals, distribution/logistics, electricity, oil and gas, real estate, and telecommunications. However, the company plans to concentrate on the energy and specialty chemicals sectors.

E.ON has brought together two of Germany's largest electric utilities, VEBA's PreussenElektra and VIAG's Bayernwerk, as E.ON Energie. E.ON Energie is Germany's largest power company, outstripping RWE, and one of the largest in Europe. E.ON also has stakes in electricity companies elsewhere in Europe, including Scandinavia and the Netherlands.

The company's other energy-related business is integrated oil company VEBA Oel, which has proved reserves of 654 million barrels of oil equivalent. VEBA Oel's Aral service station chain is Germany's largest.

Degussa-Hüls, the former VEBA's chemicals subsidiary, makes basic, specialty, and performance chemicals. It is being combined with the former VIAG chemicals business, SKW Trostberg; the new company will be known as Degussa.

Other E.ON units include VIAG Telecom and real estate developer Viterra. VIAG Telecom owns a 45% stake in German fixed-line and wireless carrier VIAG Interkom, which partner BT is buying. E.ON plans to sell off other holdings, which include metals distributor Klöckner and a majority stake in logistics provider Stinnes. It has sold its semiconductor and electronics distribution businesses. To gain regulatory approval to form E.ON, VEBA and VIAG agreed to sell their stakes in electric utilities BEWAG and VEAG and coal producer LAUBAG.

HISTORY

VEBA (originally Vereinigte Elektrizitats-und Bergwerks AG) was formed in 1929 in Berlin to consolidate Germany's state-owned electricity and mining interests. These operations included PreussenElektra, an electric utility formed by the German government in 1927; Hibernia, a coal mining firm founded in 1873; and Preussag, a mining and smelting company founded in 1923.

In the 1930s VEBA produced synthetic gasoline (essential to the German war machine) from coal at its Hibernia plant. In 1938 the company and chemical cartel I. G. Farben set up Chemische Werke Hüls to make synthetic rubber. After WWII, VEBA's assets in western Germany were transferred to the government, and several executives were arrested. Preussag was spun off in 1959.

In 1965 the government spun off VEBA to the public. That year the company entered trading and transportation by buying Stinnes (founded in the 1890s), one of West Germany's largest industrial companies. In 1969 VEBA transferred its coal mining interests to Ruhrkohle and a few years later moved into oil exploration and development with its DEMINEX subsidiary. The company shortened its name to VEBA in 1970.

Baron Rudolf von Bennigsen-Foerder, a proponent of "capitalism with a human face," became chairman in 1971 and allowed benefits and subsidiaries to proliferate.

The West German government sold its remaining stake in VEBA in 1987. In a changed regulatory environment, large investors were able to accumulate big portions of stock, and their dissatisfaction with the company's lackluster results made it a takeover target. In response, new chairman Ulrich Hartmann began cutting noncore businesses and reducing staff.

In 1990 VEBA began accumulating mobile communications, corporate networking, and cable TV companies. It allied with the UK's Cable and Wireless (C&W) in 1995 to develop a European mobile phone business, but in 1997 C&W sold its interest to VEBA (as part of the deal, VEBA gained a 10% stake in C&W, which it sold in 1999). In anticipation of the 1998 deregulation of the German telecom market, VEBA and RWE merged their German telecom businesses in 1997.

VEBA acquired a 36% stake in Degussa, a specialty chemicals company, in 1997; two years later Degussa merged with Hüls to form a separately traded chemical company called Degussa-Hüls, in which VEBA took a 62% stake. VEBA sold a 30% stake in Stinnes to the public in 1999 and made plans to list more shares. The company's telecom venture sold its fixed-line telephone business, its cable TV unit, and its stake in mobile phone operator E-Plus.

These moves, however, were just the prelude to a bigger deal: a $14 billion merger agreement between VEBA and fellow German conglomerate VIAG. The partners announced plans to dump noncore businesses and beef up their energy and chemicals holdings. VEBA and VIAG completed their merger in 2000, and the combined company adopted the name E.ON.

Co-Chairman of the Board of Management and
  Co-CEO: Ulrich Hartmann, age 61
Co-Chairman of the Board of Management and
  Co-CEO: Wilhelm Simson, age 61
Member of the Board of Management: Hans M. Gaul,
  age 58
Member of the Board of Management; Chairman of the
  Supervisory Board, Stinnes: Manfred Krüper, age 58
Member of the Board of Management:
  Erhard Schipporeit, age 51
Human Resources: Corrina Wimmer
Auditors: PwC Deutsche Revision

LOCATIONS

HQ: Bennigsenplatz 1, D-40474 Düsseldorf, Germany
Phone: +49-211-4579-1   Fax: +49-211-4579-501
US HQ: 605 3rd Ave., New York, NY 10158
US Phone: 212-922-2700   US Fax: 212-922-2798
Web site: http://www.eon.com

PRODUCTS/OPERATIONS

Selected Subsidiaries and Affiliates
Degussa-Hüls AG (62%, chemicals)
E.ON Energie (electric utility)
Klöckner & Co AG (metals distribution)
MEMC Electronic Materials, Inc.
  (72%, silicon wafers, US)
Schmalbach-Lubeca (60%, packaging)
SKW Trostberg (chemicals)
Stinnes AG (65%, logistics)
VAW Aluminum
VEBA Oel AG (oil and gas exploration, production,
  refining, and marketing)
VIAG Telecom
Viterra (real estate)

COMPETITORS

AGIV	Exxon Mobil
Akzo Nobel	France Telecom
BASF AG	ICI
Bayer AG	Lufthansa
BP	mg technologies
Deutsche Post	Royal Dutch/Shell
Deutsche Telekom	RWE
Dow Chemical	TOTAL FINA ELF
DuPont	Vodafone
EDF	WorldCom
Enel	

HISTORICAL FINANCIALS & EMPLOYEES

NYSE: EON FYE: December 31	Annual Growth	12/90	12/91	12/92	12/93	12/94	12/95	12/96	12/97	12/98	12/99
Sales ($ mil.)	4.3%	36,467	39,148	40,352	38,160	46,010	50,335	47,989	46,212	50,200	53,392
Net income ($ mil.)	13.8%	844	856	749	692	982	1,470	1,582	1,570	1,404	2,693
Income as % of sales	—	—	2.3%	2.2%	1.9%	1.8%	2.1%	2.9%	3.3%	3.4%	2.8%	5.0%
Earnings per share ($)	38.7%	—	—	—	—	—	—	—	3.12	2.80	6.00
Stock price - FY high ($)	—	—	—	—	—	—	—	—	69.00	72.63	66.31
Stock price - FY low ($)	—	—	—	—	—	—	—	—	51.13	47.25	41.50
Stock price - FY close ($)	(14.8%)	—	—	—	—	—	—	—	69.00	59.88	50.06
P/E - high	—	—	—	—	—	—	—	—	22	26	11
P/E - low	—	—	—	—	—	—	—	—	16	17	7
Dividends per share ($)	—	—	—	—	—	—	—	—	0.00	0.00	0.00
Book value per share ($)	7.7%	—	—	—	—	—	—	—	24.89	27.46	28.87
Employees	2.3%	106,877	116,979	129,802	128,348	126,875	125,158	123,727	126,734	132,337	131,602

STOCK PRICE HISTORY

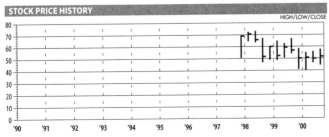

HIGH/LOW/CLOSE

1999 FISCAL YEAR-END

Debt ratio: 16.8%
Return on equity: 19.0%
Cash ($ mil.): 1,580
Current ratio: 1.79
Long-term debt ($ mil.): 2,924
No. of shares (mil.): 503
Dividends
  Yield: —
  Payout: —
Market value ($ mil.): 25,170

ERICSSON

OVERVIEW

Ericsson is no red-headed stepchild, although Nokia beats it like one in mobile phone sales. Stockholm-based Ericsson trails its Finnish rival and Motorola in handset sales, but it is the world leader in the less visible wireless infrastructure market. Ericsson's core products for telecommunications providers account for 70% of sales. The company also makes enterprise networking and communications systems, modems, components, cable, and military electronics, including radar and communications systems.

President Kurt Hellström (called "the cowboy" because of his affinity for Harley-Davidsons) is pulling Ericsson out of a slump left behind by former CEO Sven-Christner Nilsson, who left in mid-1999. Profits had fallen after the company was slow to market with new handset models and fixed-line business dropped. Hellström responded by cutting costs, trimming the company's bloated workforce, and pushing new phone models to market.

Hellström has set a long-term goal of overtaking Motorola for the #2 position in handset sales, but the company is now focusing on combining its strengths in mobile communications and networking to lead the pack as third-generation wireless technologies emerge, particularly Bluetooth (which Ericsson founded). Ericsson is also putting particular emphasis on mobile commerce software and services, both internally and through partnerships with companies such as Visa and Microsoft.

HISTORY

Lars Magnus Ericsson opened a telegraph repair shop in Stockholm in 1876, the same year Alexander Graham Bell applied for a US patent on the telephone. Within two years Ericsson was making telephones. His firm grew rapidly, supplying equipment first to Swedish phone companies and later to other European companies. In 1885 Ericsson crafted a combination receiver-speaker in one handset.

In 1911, Ericsson and SAT, the Stockholm telephone company, merged under the Ericsson banner. The company adopted its present name in 1926. In 1930 international financier Ivar "The Match King" Kreuger, owner of the Swedish Match Company, won control of Ericsson. His triumph was short-lived; Krueger committed suicide in 1932 and one of his creditors, Sosthenes Behn's ITT, took over.

ITT in 1960 sold its interest in Ericsson to the top Swedish industrialist family, the Wallenbergs. In 1975 Ericsson introduced its computer-controlled exchange, called AXE. Buoyed by AXE's success, the company unveiled the "office of the future" in the early 1980s, diversifying into computers and office furniture. Ericsson's timing was off: The demand for office automation never materialized and profits plunged. Electrolux chairman Hans Werthen was recruited to split his time between the two companies and rescue Ericsson. The company shed its computer business (to Nokia, 1988) and refocused on telephone equipment. It dusted off its aging AXE system for the burgeoning cellular market and quickly won key contracts.

The company and aircraft maker Saab merged their military aviation electronics operations as Ericsson Saab Avionics in 1996 (dissolved in 1998). In 1998 manager Sven-Christer Nilsson was appointed CEO; he announced reorganization plans, including 14,000 layoffs.

After Ericsson fought bitterly with rival QUALCOMM over wireless standards and patents, the companies settled in 1999, signing a cross-licensing deal and agreeing to push for the standardization of third-generation technology based on QUALCOMM's code-division multiple access technology. As a part of the deal, Ericsson also purchased QUALCOMM's infrastructure business. To expand its Internet offerings, Ericsson purchased Internet router maker Torrent Networking Technologies and Internet telephony company Touchwave. Later that year the company formed a unit to develop mobile e-commerce software and services. It also teamed up with software giant Microsoft to develop Internet applications for wireless devices.

By mid-1999, Nilsson was pushed out for moving too slowly on restructuring plans and was replaced as CEO by chairman Lars Ramqvist, who put many of the duties on president Kurt Hellström. Hellström immediately set out to simplify the company's managerial and accounting structure, and continue to trim its workforce and slow-growth businesses.

The next year, the company continued to reshape by divesting noncore businesses (including its private radio systems, power supply, and equipment shelter operations). Ericsson also agreed with Nokia and Motorola to develop a standard for secure wireless transactions.

Chairman and CEO: Lars Ramqvist
Deputy Chairman: Tom Hedelius
Deputy Chairman: Marcus Wallenberg
President: Kurt Hellström
EVP and CFO: Sten Fornell
EVP Asia/Pacific: Kjell Sörme
EVP Consumer Products: Jan Wäreby
EVP Corporate Office Sweden: Johan Siberg
EVP Enterprise Solutions: Haijo Pietersma
EVP Latin America: Bengt Forssberg
EVP Network Operators and Service Providers:
Mats Dahlin
EVP North America: Per-Arne Sandstrom
EVP Western Europe: Ragnar Bäck
SVP Corporate Legal Affairs: Carl Olof Blomqvist
SVP Human Resources and Organization: Britt Reigo
SVP Marketing and Strategic Business Development:
Torbjörn Nilsson
Auditors: PricewaterhouseCoopers

LOCATIONS

HQ: Telefonaktiebolaget LM Ericsson,
Telefonvägen 30, SE-126 25 Stockholm, Sweden
Phone: +46-8-719-0000   **Fax:** +46-8-719-1976
US HQ: 100 Park Ave., 27th Fl., New York, NY 10017
US Phone: 212-685-4030   **US Fax:** 212-213-0159
Web site: http://www.ericsson.com

1999 Sales

	$ mil.	% of total
Europe, Middle East & Africa	13,501	53
Asia/Pacific	5,267	21
Latin America	3,543	14
North America	2,956	12
Total	**25,267**	**100**

PRODUCTS/OPERATIONS

1999 Sales

	$ mil.	% of total
Network operators	17,584	65
Consumer products	5,443	20
Enterprise solutions	2,029	8
Other	1,971	7
Adjustments	(1,760)	—
Total	**25,267**	**100**

Selected Products and Services

Cables	Remote-access servers
Cellular phones	Routers and switches
Consulting	Small and medium-sized
Cordless phones	telephone systems
Integration	Training
LAN/WAN servers	Two-way radios
Microwave links	Wireless LAN devices
Modems	Wireless local-loop/radio
Network design	local-loop systems
Radar systems	

COMPETITORS

3Com	Hitachi	Philips
ADC Telecom	Lucent	Electronics
Alcatel	Marconi	QUALCOMM
Andrew	Communications	Racal Electronics
Corporation	Matsushita	Sagem
Ascom Holding	Mitsubishi	Samsung
AT&T	Electric	Electronics
Cabletron	Motorola	Scientific-Atlanta
CIENA	NEC	Siemens
Cisco Systems	Nokia	Spirent
Fujitsu	Nortel Networks	Tellabs
Harris	Oki Electric	Toshiba
Corporation		

HISTORICAL FINANCIALS & EMPLOYEES

Nasdaq: ERICY FYE: December 31	Annual Growth	12/90	12/91	12/92	12/93	12/94	12/95	12/96	12/97	12/98	12/99
Sales ($ mil.)	13.2%	8,289	8,275	6,644	7,622	11,342	14,902	18,291	21,219	22,760	25,267
Net income ($ mil.)	9.8%	612	160	68	340	531	813	1,033	1,511	1,609	1,423
Income as % of sales	—	7.4%	1.9%	1.0%	4.5%	4.7%	5.5%	5.6%	7.1%	7.1%	5.6%
Earnings per share ($)	8.0%	0.08	0.02	0.01	0.05	0.09	0.11	0.13	0.22	0.21	0.16
Stock price - FY high ($)	—	1.49	1.25	0.85	1.88	1.99	3.28	3.97	6.33	8.50	16.81
Stock price - FY low ($)	—	0.81	0.48	0.56	0.73	1.25	1.68	2.17	3.58	3.75	5.13
Stock price - FY close ($)	36.3%	1.01	0.60	0.83	1.26	1.72	2.44	3.77	4.66	5.98	16.42
P/E - high	—	19	42	85	38	22	30	31	29	40	105
P/E - low	—	10	16	56	15	14	15	17	16	18	32
Dividends per share ($)	—	0.01	0.02	0.02	0.00	0.03	0.02	0.03	0.00	0.00	0.04
Book value per share ($)	16.2%	0.43	0.44	0.35	0.37	0.45	0.67	0.76	0.85	1.00	1.66
Employees	4.4%	70,238	71,247	66,232	69,597	76,144	84,513	93,949	100,774	103,667	103,290

STOCK PRICE HISTORY

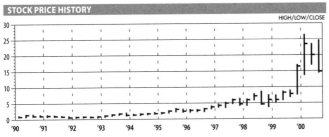

HIGH/LOW/CLOSE

1998 FISCAL YEAR-END

Debt ratio: 53.4%
Return on equity: 17.5%
Cash ($ mil.): 1,825
Current ratio: 1.81
Long-term debt ($ mil.): 2,861
No. of shares (mil.): 7,805
Dividends
Yield: 0.4%
Payout: 33.3%
Market value ($ mil.): 128,158

ERIDANIA BÉGHIN-SAY

OVERVIEW

Sugar and spice and everything nice — that's what Eridania Béghin-Say is made of. Paris-based Eridania Béghin-Say cooks up comestibles that fuel the body, including olive oil (#1 worldwide), sugars, herbs, and spices. The business is organized into five core production groups: oilseed processing (CanAmera Food and Central Soya); starch and derivatives (Cerestar); sugar and derivatives (Ceresucre); food oils, herbs, and spices (Cereol); and animal nutrition (Provimi). In addition to its namesake brands, it also makes products under the Carapelli, Koipe, and Lesieur labels. Eridania Béghin-Say concocts ingredients used mainly by the food industry but also in the animal feed, chemical/pharmaceutical,

cosmetic, fuels, and paper industries. These ingredients include ethanol fuel, fermentation alcohol, and lecithin.

Eridania Béghin-Say continues to recover from the Asian, Brazilian, and Russian financial crises and weak commodities markets such as sugar, which is at an all-time low. The company is reorganizing and streamlining operations, while divesting some non-core operations. It is aggressively marketing its Carapelli olive oil in the US through a joint venture with Hormel.

Italy's industrial giant Montedison owns about 51% of Eridania Béghin-Say; fellow Italian conglomerate Compart owns 35% of Montedison and is buying the rest.

HISTORY

Sugar makers and sellers Etablissements Say and F. Béghin were founded in France in 1812 and 1821, respectively. They merged in 1973 to form Béghin-Say, a leader in France's sugars market.

Eridania, another sugar maker, was founded in 1899 in Italy, becoming a leader in its home market. In 1978 diversified holding company Ferruzzi acquired 53% of Eridania for a song from an indebted friend, Attilio Monti. Ferruzzi, a secretive Italian family firm, already owned 10% of Eridania.

In 1980 Ferruzzi was caught trying to gain control of Béghin-Say through a Luxembourg investment vehicle and by investing in European Sugar, which owned 24% of Béghin-Say. The French interceded in the takeover, ironing out a settlement in 1981 in which Ferruzzi agreed that it would own no more than 50% of Béghin-Say and management would remain French. (Ferruzzi had acquired 50% of Béghin-Say by 1986.)

Besides its sugar operations, Béghin-Say owned France's leading maker of sanitary paper, Kayersberg. (It sold 50% of Kayersberg to James River in 1987 and 50% to Montedison in 1989.) Under Ferruzzi's wing, Béghin-Say and Eridania began buying other food processing firms. In 1987 they each bought 50% of Corn Products International's European starch and derivatives business and renamed the company Cerestar. The next year Béghin-Say bought Italiana Olli e Risi and the oils and fats operations of Lesieur (including its Koipe unit).

Ferruzzi in 1991 purchased enough shares of Béghin-Say to boost its total to 60%. However, Ferruzzi was heavily indebted to several Italian banks and was forced to reorganize to survive.

It moved Eridania's industrial assets into an enlarged Béghin-Say in 1992 and renamed the company Eridania Béghin-Say. The remaining Eridania shell was renamed Finanziaria Agroindustriale and merged into Montedison, which took a 52% stake in Eridania Béghin-Say. Meanwhile, Ferruzzi almost went belly-up, emerging with the name Compart in 1996. Other acquisitions in the early 1990s included Groupe Ducros (spices and baking products) and Continental Grain (Italy).

Stefano Meloni became chairman and CEO of Eridania Béghin-Say in 1994. Taking advantage of an upsurge in the olive oil market, the company launched its Carapelli olive oil in the US in 1995 after introducing it in Northern Europe. Also that year it sold 88% of American Maize's Swisher International Tobacco unit and acquired American Maize Products. (American Maize was merged into the Cerestar subsidiary.) In 1998 Eridania Béghin-Say entered Eastern Europe with several industrial investments.

A health and nutrition division was established in 1999 to create functional foods, including a cholesterol-lowering soy protein. Later that year Eridania Béghin-Say sold the majority of its seed business to Novartis. The company formed Carapelli USA, a joint venture with Hormel, in early 2000 to aggressively market the Carapelli olive oil line (Italy's top olive oil) in the US. In June 2000 Eridania Béghin-Say agreed to sell its spice and herbs business (Ducros) to seasonings giant McCormick & Company for about $400 million.

Chairman and CEO: Stefano Meloni
VC: Enrico Bondi
CFO: Angela Triulzi, age 54
Chairman, Central Soya, Cerestar USA, and Eridania Béghin-Say America: Carl Hausmann
Chairman, Cereol: Aldo Marsegaglia
Chairman, Cerestar: Silvio Kluzer
Chairman, Provimi: Wim Troost
CEO, Ceresucre: Jérôme de Pelleport
Corporate Secretary: Jean-Marie Pillois
Director of Planning, Strategy, and Management Accounting: Adrian Steed
Auditors: Deloitte Touche Tohmatsu

HQ: 14, blvd. du Général Leclerc, F 92572 Neuilly-sur-Seine Cedex, France
Phone: +33-1-41-43-11-50   **Fax:** +33-1-41-43-11-51
US HQ: 1946 W. Cook Rd., Fort Wayne, IN 46818
US Phone: 219-425-5100   **US Fax:** 219-425-5330

Eridania Béghin-Say has subsidiaries in Asia, Europe, North America, South Africa, and South America.

1999 Sales

	€ mil.	% of total
Europe		
France	1,900	21
Other EU countries	3,997	44
Non-EU countries	891	10
North America	1,675	18
Other regions	547	6
Adjustments	87	1
Total	**9,097**	**100**

1999 Sales

	€ mil.	% of total
Oilseed Processing & Marketing	3,571	39
Sugar & Derivatives	1,941	22
Starch & Derivatives	1,568	17
Olive Oil, Herbs & Spices	981	11
Animal Nutrition	942	10
Sundry	94	1
Total	**9,097**	**100**

Selected Products

Baking and dessert ingredients	Olive oil
	Peanut and soybean oil
Caramel	Rice
Citric acid	Seed oil (crude, refined)
Dextroses	Starches
Herbs and spices	Sunflower seed oil
Industrial sugars	Syrups (fructose, glucose)
Maize	Table-top sugars
Mustards and seasonings	Vinegars

ADM	Bunge	Honen
Ag Processing	International	Imperial Sugar
Agribrands	Cargill	Nisshin Oil Mills
International,	Cenex Harvest	NOF
Inc.	States	NutraSweet
Ajinomoto	Ceval	PPB Group
American Crystal	Corn Products	Riceland Foods
Sugar	International	Südzucker AG
Associated	CSM	Tate & Lyle
British Foods	CSR Limited	U.S. Sugar
Bestfoods	Goodman Fielder	Worms & Cie
	Goya	

Euronext Paris: BG FYE: December 31	Annual Growth	12/90	12/91	12/92	12/93	12/94	12/95	12/96	12/97	12/98	12/99
Sales (€ mil.)	5.2%	5,743	6,236	7,583	7,761	7,742	7,745	8,381	9,703	10,004	9,097
Net income (€ mil.)	(6.2%)	165	115	195	205	184	233	253	290	283	93
Income as % of sales	—	2.9%	1.8%	2.6%	2.6%	2.4%	3.0%	3.0%	3.0%	2.8%	1.0%
Earnings per share (€)	(20.4%)	—	—	—	—	—	8.95	9.74	11.17	11.50	3.60
Stock price - FY high (€)	—	—	—	—	—	—	128.97	138.88	152.45	211.90	153.80
Stock price - FY low (€)	—	—	—	—	—	—	103.06	104.28	112.05	129.73	97.00
Stock price - FY close (€)	(4.4%)	—	—	—	—	—	128.06	127.29	143.45	147.42	106.80
P/E - high	—	—	—	—	—	—	14	14	14	18	43
P/E - low	—	—	—	—	—	—	12	11	10	11	27
Dividends per share (€)	1.3%	—	—	—	—	—	5.03	5.03	5.34	5.34	5.30
Book value per share (€)	3.5%	—	—	—	—	—	113.21	119.18	124.97	132.71	129.92
Employees	(3.2%)	—	—	25,036	24,198	22,298	20,790	21,195	20,653	21,693	20,000

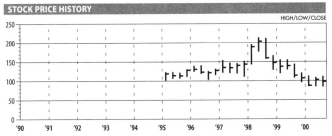

Debt ratio: 43.2%
Return on equity: 2.3%
Cash (€ mil.): 214
Current ratio: 2.52
Long-term debt (€ mil.): 2,562
No. of shares (mil.): 26
Dividends
  Yield: 0.0%
  Payout: 1.5%
Market value ($ mil.): 2,784
Sales ($ mil.): 9,140

ERNST & YOUNG INTERNATIONAL

OVERVIEW

Accounting may actually be the *second* oldest profession, and Ernst & Young is one of the oldest practitioners. The New York-based concern, one of the Big Five accounting firms, has more than 660 offices in about 130 countries.

The company's audit and accounting business provides internal audit and accounting advice and oversight. The firm has one of the world's largest tax practices, particularly serving the needs of multinational clients that have to comply with multiple local tax laws.

After spending most of the 1980s and 1990s building their consulting businesses, The Big Five have all moved toward spinning off or otherwise shedding these operations, partly from internal pressures and partly because of the percieved conflict of interest in performing audits for clients who may also be large consulting customers. Ernst & Young was the first to split off its consultancy, selling it to French consultancy Cap Gemini Group.

Ernst & Young is now following the industry trend in adding legal affiliates to provide more comprehensive professional services. Among its initiatives in this area is the formation of law-firm McKee, Nelson, Ernst & Young.

HISTORY

The 1494 Luca Pacioli's *Summa di Arithmetica* — the first text on double-entry bookkeeping — was published in Venice. But it was almost 500 years before accounting became a profession.

In 1849 Frederick Whinney joined the UK firm of Harding & Pullein, formed after R. P. Harding's hatmaking business ended up in court. Whinney's ledgers were so clear that he was advised to take up accounting, which was a growth field as stock companies proliferated.

Whinney became a name partner in 1859 and his sons followed him into the business. The firm became Whinney, Smith & Whinney (WS&W) in 1894.

After WWII, WS&W formed an alliance with Ernst & Ernst (founded in Cleveland in 1903 by brothers Alwin and Theodore Ernst). The alliance provided that each firm would operate on the other's behalf within their respective countries.

Whinney merged with Brown, Fleming & Murray in 1965 to become Whinney Murray. In 1979 Whinney Murray, another UK firm, Turquands Barton Mayhew, and Ernst & Ernst merged to form Ernst & Whinney. But Ernst & Whinney wasn't done merging. Ten years later, when it was the fourth-largest accounting firm, it merged with #5 Arthur Young, which had been founded by Scotsman Arthur Young in 1895 in Kansas City. Long known as "old reliable," Arthur Young fell on hard times in the 1980s because its audit relationships with failed S&Ls led to expensive litigation (which led to a $400 million settlement in 1992).

Thus, the new firm of Ernst & Young faced a rocky start. In 1990, it fended off rumors of collapse. The next year it slashed payroll, even thinning its partner roster.

Exhausted by the S&L wars, in 1994 the firm replaced its pugnacious general counsel, Carl Riggio, with the more cost-conscious Kathryn Oberly.

In the mid-1990s Ernst & Young concentrated on consulting, particularly in software applications. It also grew through acquisitions. In 1996 the firm bought Houston-based Wright Killen & Co., a petroleum and petrochemicals consulting firm, to form Ernst & Young Wright Killen. It also entered new alliances that year with Washington-based ISD/Shaw, which provided banking industry consulting, and India's Tata Consulting, among others.

In 1997 Ernst & Young was sued for a record $4 billion for its alleged failure to effectively handle the 1993 restructuring of the defunct Merry-Go-Round Enterprises retail chain (it settled the suit for $185 million in 1999). On the heels of a merger deal between Coopers & Lybrand and Price Waterhouse, Ernst & Young agreed in 1997 to merge with KPMG International. But E&Y called off the negotiations in 1998, citing the uncertain regulatory process they faced.

In 1999 Ernst & Young launched a worldwide media blitz aimed at raising awareness of the firm's full range of services, which that year included the company's new technology incubator. That year the firm reached a settlement in lawsuits regarding accounting errors at Informix and Cendant and sold its UK and Southern African trust and fiduciary businesses to Royal Bank of Canada.

In 2000 the firm became the first of the Big Five firms to sell its consultancy—to French company Cap Gemini Group for about $11 billion. That year the company agreed to buy Washington Counsel, a lobbying firm. It also started a venture to provide online financial advice with E*TRADE and spun off Intellinex L.L.C., its online corporate training division.

Chairman: Philip A. Laskawy
Senior VC: William L. Kimsey
VC Assurance and Advisory Services: John F. Ferraro
VC Consulting Services: Antonio Schneider
VC Finance, Technology, and Administration:
Hilton Dean
VC Global Accounts: David A. Reed
VC Human Resources: Lewis A. Ting
VC Intrastructure: John G. Peetz Jr.
VC Regional Integration and Entrepreneurial Growth
Companies: Jean-Charles Raufast
VC Regional Integration and Planning:
Richard N. Findlater
VC Tax and Legal Services: Andrew B. Jones
Executive Partner: Paul J. Ostling
National Director, SALT Practice and Procedure:
Prentiss Willson Jr.
General Counsel: Kathryn A. Oberly

LOCATIONS

HQ: 787 7th Ave., New York, NY 10019
Phone: 212-773-3000   **Fax:** 212-773-6350
Web site: http://www.eyi.com

Ernst & Young has more than 660 offices in over 130 countries.

PRODUCTS/OPERATIONS

Selected Services

Consulting
"Build" Services (business transformation, supply chain management, and package-enabled reengineering)
"Operate" Services (deploying and managing information technology operations and financial and human resources administration)
"Think" Services (planning, research, business modeling, and technology architecture development)

Corporate Finance
Business valuation
Financial analysis
Financing
Integration
Mergers and acquisitions

Tax Services
Corporate reorganizations
Customs duties
Foreign-exchange transactions
International financing
Mergers and acquisitions
Value-added taxes

Selected Clients

American Express	Marubeni
BankAmerica	McDonald's
Coca-Cola	Mobil
Eli Lilly	Time Warner
Hanson	US Postal Service
Hoover's, Inc.	USF&G
Knight Ridder	Wal-Mart
Lockheed Martin	

COMPETITORS

American Management	Grant Thornton
Andersen Worldwide	International
Arthur D. Little	IBM
Bain & Company	KPMG
BDO International	Marsh & McLennan
Booz-Allen	McKinsey & Company
Boston Consulting	Mynd
Computer Sciences	Perot Systems
Deloitte Touche Tohmatsu	PricewaterhouseCoopers
EDS	Towers Perrin

HISTORICAL FINANCIALS & EMPLOYEES

Partnership FYE: September 30	Annual Growth	9/90	9/91	9/92	9/93	9/94	9/95	9/96	9/97	9/98	9/99
Sales ($ mil.)	10.7%	5,006	5,406	5,701	5,839	6,020	6,867	7,800	9,100	10,900	12,510
Employees	5.3%	61,591	61,173	58,900	58,377	61,287	68,452	72,000	79,750	85,000	97,800

SALES HISTORY

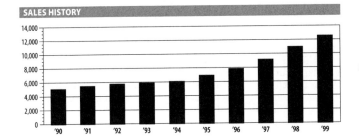

ESPÍRITO SANTO FINANCIAL GROUP

OVERVIEW

The Espírito's willing to do what it takes to stay strong in a unifying European economy. Luxembourg-based Espírito Santo Financial Group (ESFG) controls an empire whose pillars are Banco Espírito Santo e Comercial de Lisboa, and Companhia de Seguros Tranquilidade, Portugal's largest insurer. Entities associated with the founding Espírito Santo family are the company's major shareholders.

ESFG's other holdings include stockbroker Espírito Santo Dealer (formerly ESER), investment bank Banco Espírito Santo de Investimento, and Banco Internacional de Crédito, which concentrates on mortgage lending and private banking. About 400 Espírito Santo banking branches provide consumer and business banking services, and sell the lion's share of Tranquilidade's insurance, pension, and investment products. Although ESFG focuses on Portugal, it operates in Europe, and North and South America.

ESFG has benefited from Portugal's position in the EU (the country has been a major recipient of financial aid) and from the privatization of the country's formerly state-controlled economy.

HISTORY

The Espírito Santo financial empire traces its roots to a bank founded by José Maria de Espírito Santo Silva in Lisbon in 1884. After WWI, Portugal underwent a major banking expansion, and in 1920 the Espírito Santo family established Banco Espírito Santo, which grew rapidly thanks to postwar expansion and speculation.

After José Maria's oldest son, José, fled the bank and the country in scandal, his brother, Ricardo, led the massive growth of both the bank and the family's fortune. During the 1930s, the Espírito Santos acquired a major interest in insurance company Tranquilidade, and in 1937 Banco Espírito Santo merged with Banco Comercial de Lisboa (founded 1875) to create Banco Espírito Santo e Comercial de Lisboa.

The family's fortunes were aided by dictator Antonio de Oliveira Salazar, who came to power in 1933. During WWII, Salazar declared Portugal neutral, and the country became a sanctuary for many of Europe's elite, who brought the Espírito Santos business and contacts.

The Espírito Santo empire was fostered by Salazar's postwar protectionist policies. Banco Espírito Santo became one of Portugal's largest banks and Tranquilidade one of its largest insurance companies. The family also acquired large coffee, sugar, and palm-oil plantations in Portugal's colonies Angola and Mozambique. At their peak, the Espírito Santo holdings were valued at $4 billion.

But the family's fortunes turned with political upheaval in Portugal during the 1970s. In 1974 the military overthrew Salazar's successor, Marcelo Caetano. A year later the leftist government nationalized Portugal's major corporations, including Banco Espírito Santo and Tranquilidade.

The family fled to London and pooled their savings to create a new company in Luxembourg, Espírito Santo Financial Holding (ESFH). In the late 1970s they got a banking license in Brazil and later set up a fund management company in Switzerland and banks in Miami and Paris. The family's name attracted business and investors.

The Portuguese government in 1986 reprivatized financial services organizations. That year ESFH and France's Crédit Agricole opened Banco Internacional de Crédito in Portugal. After raising money on the Eurobond market, ESFH bought back control of Tranquilidade in 1990. A year later the company and a group of investors, including Crédit Agricole, reacquired control of Banco Espírito Santo.

In 1993 ESFH reduced its interest in Banco Internacional de Crédito to 47% (it regained 100% control in 1997). Since then the company has concentrated on Portugal. In the early 1990s recession rocked the economy — and the company. But in the mid-1990s, despite poor commercial demand, consumer-related services rebounded.

ESFH expanded its commercial banking network in 1995 and 1996. In 1997 the company and Brazil's Monteiro Aranha bought more than 60% of that country's Banco Boavista. The company also dropped "Holding" in favor of "Group," and the next year ESFG, in a vote of confidence in Brazil, moved to raise its holdings in Banco Boavista.

In 1999, amid a flurry of speculation about Spanish/Portuguese banking mergers, the company agreed to buy a majority interest in Spanish brokerage Benito y Monjardin.

In 2000 ESFG bought the majority stake of French credit institution Via Banque from BNP Paribas.

Chairman: Ricardo Espírito Santo Silva Salgado
VC: José Manuel P. Espírito Santo Silva
Director: Manuel Villas-Boas
SVP: Mário A. F. Cardoso
SVP: Erich Dahler
SVP: Jean-Luc Schneider
Secretary: Teresa de Souza
Auditors: PricewaterhouseCoopers

LOCATIONS

HQ: Espírito Santo Financial Group S.A.,
33, Queen Street, London EC4R 1ES,
United Kingdom
Phone: +44-171-332-4350   **Fax:** +44-171-332-4355
US HQ: 320 Park Avenue, 29th Fl., New York, NY 10022
US Phone: 212-702-3410   **US Fax:** 212-750-3888
Web site: http://www.esfg.com

Espirito Santo Financial Group has operations in Brazil, the Cayman Islands, France, Luxembourg, Portugal, Spain, Switzerland, the UK, and the US.

1999 Sales

	% of total
Portugal	92
Spain	2
Switzerland	1
Other countries	5
Total	**100**

PRODUCTS/OPERATIONS

Selected Subsidiaries
Banco Boavista-InterAtlantico (BBIA, Brazil)
Banco Espírito Santo de Investimento SA (Portugal)
Banco Espírito Santo do Oriente SARL
(BES-ORIENTE, Macao)
Banco Espírito Santo e Comercial de Lisboa SA
(BES, Portugal)
Banco Internacional de Credito SA (BIC, Portugal)
Cia. de Seguros Tranquilidade SA (insurance, Portugal)
Compagnie Financiere Espírito Santo SA (asset
management, Switzerland)
Espírito Santo Activos Financeiros SGPS SA
(holding company, Portugal)
Espírito Santo Bank Ltd. (US)
Espírito Santo Dealer

COMPETITORS

Banco Bilbao
Banco Comercial Portugues
Banco de Comercio e Industria
Banco Portugues do Atlantico
BNP
BSCH
Caisse Nationale de Credit Agricole
Chase Manhattan
Chemical
Citigroup
Credit Suisse
Deutsche Bank
Itausa
J.P. Morgan
Merrill Lynch
Société Générale
UBS

HISTORICAL FINANCIALS & EMPLOYEES

NYSE: ESF FYE: December 31	Annual Growth	12/90	12/91	12/92	12/93	12/94	12/95	12/96	12/97	12/98	12/99
Assets ($ mil.)	34.6%	2,267	2,971	14,794	13,451	15,633	21,827	24,838	25,646	33,169	32,821
Net income ($ mil.)	15.5%	23	19	38	42	25	30	39	51	71	84
Income as % of assets	—	1.0%	0.6%	0.3%	0.3%	0.1%	0.1%	0.2%	0.2%	0.2%	0.3%
Earnings per share ($)	17.4%	—	—	—	—	—	0.98	1.25	1.57	1.53	1.86
Stock price - FY high ($)	—	—	—	—	—	—	14.13	13.63	22.50	27.44	20.13
Stock price - FY low ($)	—	—	—	—	—	—	8.50	10.63	12.75	12.50	14.31
Stock price - FY close ($)	7.3%	—	—	—	—	—	11.88	13.25	20.31	19.56	15.75
P/E - high	—	—	—	—	—	—	14	11	14	17	11
P/E - low	—	—	—	—	—	—	9	9	8	8	8
Dividends per share ($)	(11.9%)	—	—	—	—	—	1.08	0.55	0.00	0.00	0.65
Book value per share ($)	(7.3%)	—	—	—	—	—	12.58	12.22	8.73	10.59	9.28
Employees	0.3%	—	—	8,895	8,215	8,411	8,489	8,408	9,047	—	—

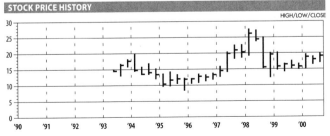

STOCK PRICE HISTORY HIGH/LOW/CLOSE

1999 FISCAL YEAR-END
Equity as % of assets: 1.4%
Return on assets: 0.3%
Return on equity: 17.7%
Long-term debt ($ mil.): 3,770
No. of shares (mil.): 48
Dividends
  Yield: 4.1%
  Payout: 34.9%
Market value ($ mil.): 755
Sales ($ mil.): 3,187

FIAT S.P.A.

Italian governments come and go, but Fiat has been around for a century. Based in Turin, Italy, Fiat's range of interests includes cars, commercial vehicles, tractors, and construction equipment. Its auto lines include compacts and sedans such as the Fiat Seicento and its well-known Alfa Romeo, Ferrari, Lancia, and Maserati sports cars. Fiat's commercial vehicle operations are run mainly through its Iveco subsidiary. Fiat also operates CNH Global, its agriculture and construction equipment division and a leading maker of tractors and backhoes. Other Fiat operations include insurance, railway systems, aviation, and publishing systems.

Overcapacity in the auto market has led to

sharp profit declines for Fiat. To gain the economies of scale it needs to remain competitive, Fiat has agreed to trade a 20% stake in its car unit to GM for a 5.1% stake in the world's #1 carmaker. The deal will help protect Fiat's market position in South America and allow GM to take advantage of Fiat's access to Eastern Europe. It would also make Fiat one of GM's largest shareholders. Under the agreement, Fiat Auto has the option to sell 80% to GM later, should Fiat choose to do so. To beef up its other operations, Fiat launched bids to buy the outstanding minority stakes in its Toro Assicurazioni (insurance) and Magnetti Marelli (automotive components) units. The founding Agnelli family owns about 30% of Fiat.

HISTORY

Ex-cavalry officer Giovanni Agnelli founded Fabbrica Italiana di Automobili Torino (Fiat) in 1899. Between 1903 and 1918 the automaker expanded into trucks, rail cars, aviation, and tractors. Protected by tariffs, Fiat became Italy's dominant auto company.

WWII boosted Fiat's fortunes, but bombs damaged many of its plants. With US support, Fiat rebuilt and survived by exporting and by building plants abroad. As growth in Italy resumed, Fiat began making steel and construction equipment.

After the European Community forced Italy to lower tariffs in 1961, Fiat lost market share, although foreign sales helped offset its woes. Giovanni Agnelli II (the founder's grandson) became chairman in 1966. Fiat then bought high-end Italian carmakers Lancia and Ferrari in 1969.

The company formed Fiat Auto S.p.A. in 1979, bringing together the Fiat, Lancia, Autobianchi, Abarth, and Ferrari lines. The next year Cesare Romiti became managing director and cut 23,000 jobs and broke union influence at Fiat. The company closed its unprofitable US car operations in 1983. Fiat and British Ford combined their truck operations in 1986, and Fiat also bought Alfa Romeo that year.

In 1989 Fiat purchased 49% of luxury carmaker Maserati (it bought the rest in 1993). Fiat and Ford merged their farm and construction equipment divisions in 1991 to form Fiat subsidiary New Holland (renamed CNH Global in 1999). After posting its biggest loss in 1993, Fiat restructured.

Slow car sales in Italy prompted Fiat to temporarily lay off about 74,000 workers in 1996, and chairman Agnelli stepped down. In 1997

Agnelli's successor, Romiti, and financial director Paolo Mattioli were convicted of falsifying records and illegally financing political parties. They were barred from employment at Fiat.

Paolo Fresco, former vice chairman of General Electric, replaced Romiti as head of Fiat in 1998. Challenged with slumping car sales in Italy and South America, the company sold its chemicals and telecom businesses. Car-price wars in Europe contributed to a stark downward shift in 1998 profits.

Deals abounded in 1999. Fiat's New Holland subsidiary bought agricultural and construction equipment maker Case Corporation for around $4.3 billion and changed its name to CNH Global. Also, Fiat began making light commercial trucks in China with Yuejin Motor. Fiat's truck-making division agreed in 1999 to buy vehicle-leasing company Fraikin for $596 million.

Other deals in 1999 included Fiat's Comau robotics unit's purchase of a 51% stake in France-based Renault Automation; the two began a bus-making joint venture and combined their foundry operations under Fiat subsidiary Teksid. Also, Fiat bought Progressive Tool & Industries (automated welding equipment, US) for $350 million.

To expand its auto business outside Europe, Fiat agreed in 2000 to trade a 20% stake in its car unit for a 5.1% stake in GM. Fiat also launched bids to buy the outstanding minor stakes in its Toro Assicurazioni (insurance) and Magnetti Marelli (automotive components) units. The same year Alstom agreed to buy a 51% stake in Fiat's rail unit (Fiat Ferrovia) and GM and Fiat engaged in talks to buy South Korea's DAEWOO MOTOR.

Honorary Chairman: Giovanni Agnelli
Chairman: Paolo Fresco
CEO: Paolo Cantarella
CFO: Damien Clermont
Chief Administration Officer: Carlo Gatto
EVP: Francesco Paolo Mattioli
EVP: Paolo Monferino
SVP External Relations and Communication:
Paolo Annibaldi
SVP Human Resources: Pier Luigi Fattori
Co-Chairman, CNH Global NV: Umberto Quadrino
Chairman and CEO, CNH Global NV: Jean Pierre Rosso
Chairman and CEO, Ferrari SpA:
Luca C. di Montezemolo
President and CEO, Fiat U.S.A., Inc.: Danieoe Rulli
CEO, Fiat Auto SpA: Roberto Testore
CEO, Iveco NV: Giancarlo Boschetti
Secretary: Franzo Grande Stevens
Auditors: Price Waterhouse S.p.A.

HQ: 250 Via Nizza, 10136 Turin, Italy
Phone: +39-011-686-1111   **Fax:** +39-011-686-3798
US HQ: 375 Park Ave., Ste. 2073, New York, NY 10152
US Phone: 212-355-2600   **US Fax:** 212-308-2968
Web site: http://www.fiat.com/eng/default.htm

Fiat operates 249 plants located primarily in Brazil, France, Germany, Poland, Spain, the UK, the US.

1999 Sales

	$ bil.	% of total
Europe	38.7	79
North America	3.9	8
South America	3.7	8
Other regions	2.4	5
Total	**48.7**	**100**

1999 Sales

	% of total
Automobiles	47
Commercial vehicles	14
Automotive-related	14
Agricultural & construction equipment	10
Insurance	4
Other	11
Total	**100**

Selected Brand Names

Automobiles	Agricultural and Construction Equipment
Alfa Romeo	Case
Ferrari	Case IH
Fiat	New Holland
Lancia-Autobianchi	O&K
Maserati	Steyr

Commercial Vehicles
Iveco (buses, diesel
engines, trucks)

AGCO	Hyundai	PACCAR
AUDI	Ingersoll-Rand	Peugeot
BMW	Isuzu	Porsche
Caterpillar	JLG Industries	Renault
DaimlerChrysler	Kia Motors	Saab Automobile
Deere	Mazda	Suzuki
FMC	Mitsubishi	Toyota
Ford	Navistar	Volkswagen
Halliburton	Nissan	Volvo
Honda	Oshkosh Truck	

NYSE: FIA FYE: December 31	Annual Growth	12/90	12/91	12/92	12/93	12/94	12/95	12/96	12/97	12/98	12/99
Sales ($ mil.)	(0.4%)	50,627	49,229	40,555	33,325	43,046	51,382	50,993	53,480	56,535	48,741
Net income ($ mil.)	(14.3%)	1,427	971	373	(1,040)	623	1,355	1,561	1,368	728	356
Income as % of sales	—	2.8%	2.0%	0.9%	—	1.4%	2.6%	3.1%	2.6%	1.3%	0.7%
Earnings per share ($)	—	—	—	—	(2.42)	1.16	0.50	4.24	4.24	1.31	0.62
Stock price - FY high ($)	—	—	—	—	44.31	41.81	38.41	33.63	37.50	49.00	41.75
Stock price - FY low ($)	—	—	—	—	18.41	22.27	27.04	23.63	24.77	24.25	27.00
Stock price - FY close ($)	(4.1%)	—	—	—	23.63	33.63	28.63	27.95	29.50	35.25	30.13
P/E - high	—	—	—	—	—	36	77	8	9	37	67
P/E - low	—	—	—	—	—	19	54	6	6	19	44
Dividends per share ($)	(39.6%)	—	—	—	13.18	0.00	0.18	0.58	0.60	0.00	0.64
Book value per share ($)	6.3%	—	—	—	4.88	5.00	5.54	9.19	7.88	8.29	7.06
Employees	(3.5%)	303,238	287,957	270,876	260,951	248,200	237,426	237,865	239,457	234,454	220,000

Debt ratio: 65.9%
Return on equity: 2.5%
Cash ($ mil.): 1,919
Current ratio: 4.01
Long-term debt ($ mil.): 25,003
No. of shares (mil.): 367
Dividends
  Yield: 2.1%
  Payout: 103.2%
Market value ($ mil.): 11,070

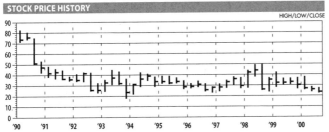

HIGH/LOW/CLOSE

FLETCHER CHALLENGE LIMITED

OVERVIEW

Fletcher Christian could identify with this predicament: Fletcher Challenge is sailing its bounty of companies into an uncertain future. Auckland-based Fletcher Challenge, New Zealand's largest business enterprise, is actually three separately traded companies, which concentrate on building materials, oil and gas, and timber, respectively. However, the group is in the midst of a restructuring, in which oil and gas unit Fletcher Challenge Energy will be sold and the other business units will emerge as independent companies.

The #1 building materials maker in New Zealand, Fletcher Challenge Building makes steel, concrete, plasterboard, and wood fiber products. Fletcher Challenge Energy is an integrated oil and gas company with fields in Canada, Brunei, and New Zealand. Fletcher

Challenge Forests has timber assets in New Zealand, Chile, and Argentina and is moving into biotechnology. The company has sold its former Fletcher Challenge Paper unit.

One of the group's strengths has been its vertical integration — for example, Fletcher Challenge Forests helps supply Fletcher Challenge Building with the raw materials it needs. This has helped the group weather the storms of cyclical downturns in the commodity markets, and, more recently, the roiling of the Asian currency markets (which has depressed consumer demand).

To help in the group's restructuring, Fletcher Challenge is forming a new company, Rubicon, which will wind up with the forest unit's biotechnology assets and other noncore operations.

HISTORY

Fletcher Challenge was created by the coming together of three New Zealand companies — Challenge Corporation, Fletcher Holdings, and Tasman Pulp and Paper — in 1981.

Challenge was a Dunedin-based livestock partnership founded in 1861 by John Wright and Robert Robertson. Christened Wright Stephenson & Co. in 1868, the firm expanded throughout New Zealand and opened its first overseas office, in London, in 1906. Wright Stephenson diversified into fertilizers (1920), breeding stock (1922), automobiles (1927), electrical appliances (1937), land development (1945), and bicycle and lawn mower manufacturing (1962). Under the chairmanship of Ronald Trotter, the firm merged with NMA Company of New Zealand (a livestock broker founded in 1864) to form Challenge Corporation in 1972.

Fletcher was founded in Dunedin as a construction company in 1909 by Scottish immigrant James Fletcher; the company became Fletcher Construction Company in 1919. Through the 1930s the company bought several suppliers, such as marble quarries and brickworks, and in 1939 started producing wood-based building materials. It was reorganized as Fletcher Holdings in 1940.

Tasman Pulp and Paper, partly owned by Fletcher and the New Zealand government, was formed in 1952. The government sold its stake in 1979. Fletcher wound up with 56% of Tasman, Challenge with 28%. The marriage of these three companies in 1981 created Fletcher Challenge, an entity that generated 8% of New Zealand's total GNP.

With Trotter as CEO and Hugh Fletcher (James Fletcher's grandson) as COO, Fletcher Challenge moved into the Canadian paper business, buying the Canadian forest products operations of Crown Zellerbach (renamed Crown Forest Industries) in 1983 and control of British Columbia Forest Products in 1987. The company bought Petrocorp (oil and gas, 1988) and Rural Bank (financial services, 1989) from the New Zealand government. Fletcher Challenge acquired UK Paper in 1990 and 90% of Cape Horn Methanol in Chile a year later.

Pulling back from a decade of expansion, the company paid down debt by unloading some noncore assets, including Crown Packaging (part of Crown Forest) in 1992. It sold one-third of Natural Gas Corp., New Zealand's main gas distributor, to the public.

Fletcher Challenge restructured its four divisions as publicly traded companies in 1996. A weak global paper market hurt Fletcher Challenge's revenues in 1997, and the company sold its US-based Blandin Paper.

In 1999 the company decided to focus on building and forests: It announced plans to spin off Fletcher Challenge Energy and to sell Fletcher Challenge Paper to Fletcher Challenge Canada. Minority shareholders of Fletcher Challenge Canada voted down the deal, however, and in 2000 Norway's Norske Skog bought Fletcher Challenge Paper. Later that year Fletcher Challenge agreed to sell Fletcher Challenge Energy to Apache and Shell and announced plans to separate its remaining business units into independent companies.

Chairman: Roderick Deane
CEO: Michael J. Andrews
Chief Executive, Fletcher Challenge Building:
Terry N. McFadgen
Chief Executive, Fletcher Challenge Energy: Greig Gailey
Chief Executive, Concrete and Infrastructure Group:
John Illingsworth
Chief Executive, Fletcher Construction; Commercial Director, Fletcher Challenge Building: Mark Binns
Chief Executive, Fletcher Challenge Forests: Ian Boyd
Chief Executive, Living Solutions: Neil Gunn
Chief Executive, Steel, Merchants, and International, Fletcher Challenge Building: Ken Howard
COO, Fletcher Challenge Energy: Lloyd Taylor
CFO, Fletcher Challenge Energy: Paul Chrystall
Director, Performance Improvement and Planning, Fletcher Challenge Building: Bill Roest
General Manager, Fletcher Challenge Energy Brunei: Chris Newton
General Manager, Fletcher Challenge Energy New Zealand: Rick Webber
Group Treasurer and Commercial Director: John McDonald
Group Taxation Manager and Corporate Secretary: Martin C. Farrell
Auditors: PricewaterhouseCoopers

HQ: Fletcher Challenge House, 810 Great South Rd., Penrose, Auckland, New Zealand
Phone: +64-9-525-9000   **Fax:** +64-9-525-9023
Web site: http://www.fcl.co.nz

2000 Sales

	$ mil.	% of total
Pacific Rim		
New Zealand	2,024	55
Australia	349	9
Other countries	97	3
North America	992	27
South America	189	5
Asia	51	1
Total	**3,702**	**100**

Fletcher Challenge Building
Aggregates, cement, and concrete products
Building products merchandising
Construction
Gypsum plasterboard
Steel and steel products

Fletcher Challenge Energy
Oil and gas exploration, development, production, and marketing
Power generation

Fletcher Challenge Forests
Log and lumber marketing

Abitibi-Consolidated
Alberta Energy
Amcor
AssiDoman
Boise Cascade
Bowater
BP
Canfor
Consolidated Papers
Crown Vantage
Devon Energy
Dominion Resources
Domtar
Exxon Mobil
Georgia-Pacific Group
Imperial Oil
International Paper
Johns Manville
Kimberly-Clark
Mead
Murphy Oil
Norske Skog
Petro-Canada
Royal Dutch/Shell
Smurfit-Stone Container
UPM-Kymmene
USG
Westvaco
Weyerhaeuser
Willamette

Holding company FYE: June 30	Annual Growth	6/91	6/92	6/93	6/94	6/95	6/96	6/97	6/98	6/99	6/00
Sales ($ mil.)	(6.7%)	6,915	5,463	5,093	4,827	5,684	6,258	5,882	3,767	4,115	3,702
Net income ($ mil.)	(6.3%)	320	(86)	205	311	311	335	113	100	54	179
Income as % of sales	—	4.6%	—	4.0%	8.3%	5.5%	5.4%	1.9%	2.7%	1.3%	4.8%
Employees	(9.7%)	35,000	31,000	24,000	22,000	22,000	23,000	21,000	20,000	16,000	14,000

Debt ratio: 33.0%
Return on equity: —
Cash ($ mil.): 493
Current ratio: 1.74
Long-term debt ($ mil.): 2,178

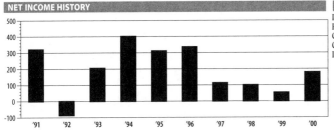

FORMOSA PLASTICS CORPORATION

OVERVIEW

Formosa Plastics is foremost in its industry. The Taipei, Taiwan-based company is one of the world's largest producers of polyvinyl chloride (PVC) and a leader in that country's petrochemical industry. A member of industrial giant Formosa Plastics Group (FPG), Formosa Plastics makes acrylic fiber and yarn, polyethylene, caustic soda chlorine, calcium carbonate, and acrylic acid. Formosa Plastics subsidiaries include Formosa Plastics Corporation, U.S.A. (natural gas drilling; chemical and petrochemical production) and Everex Systems (servers, workstations, PCs). Joint ventures include Formosa Komatsu Silicon Corp. (with Komatsu

Electronic Metals Co.), a maker of silicon wafers, and Formosa Asahi Spandex Co. with Asahi Chemical Industry Co.

The Taiwanese government fears the country's industry may become too dependant on doing business in China and regulates the issue closely. Despite this fact, Formosa Plastics, along with FPG's other units, have developed a thermal plant in China's Fujian province. The company is planning further Chinese investment, including a PVC plant. Founder and chairman Yung-ching Wang is one of Taiwan's wealthiest industrialists.

HISTORY

In 1932 Yung-ching Wang borrowed $200 from his father, a Taiwanese tea merchant, to buy a rice mill near the town of Jiayi. The mill was destroyed by Allied bombs in 1944, but Wang went on to make a fortune in timber and founded Formosa Plastics, a small polyvinyl chloride (PVC) plant, in 1954. He bought the technology from the Japanese, later joking that he didn't even know then what the "P" in PVC stood for.

At first Wang had trouble finding buyers for his PVC resins. In 1958 he set up his own resin processor, Nan Ya Plastics, and later formed Formosa Chemicals & Fibre to make rayon backing for PVC leather (1965). For the next 15 years, the company grew into the Formosa Plastics Group (FPG), an exclusively Taiwanese enterprise.

Between 1980 and 1988 Wang bought 14 US PVC manufacturers, including Imperial Chemical's vinyl chloride monomer plant (1981), Stauffer Chemical's PVC plant (1981), and Manville Corporation's PVC businesses (1983). He started building a Texas PVC plant in 1981 and cut construction costs up to 40% by importing equipment from Taiwan. When the PVC market became saturated in the mid-1980s, Wang diversified, building plants to make semiconductor chemicals.

Wang bought several Texas-based oil and gas properties in 1988, including 218 producing wells, a gas-processing plant, and a pipeline firm. Faced with stricter pollution controls in Taiwan, Wang began building an ethylene plant in Point Comfort, Texas, in 1988.

In 1992 Wang wanted to build an ethylene complex in mainland China, where there were no pollution controls. Taiwan balked at the proposal, suggesting that FPG build at home. Attempting to circumvent a Taiwanese law

against direct investment in the mainland, Wang sought Chinese approval through subsidiary Formosa Plastics Corporation, U.S.A. In 1993 Chinese authorities rejected a plan that would require them to finance up to two-thirds of a $7 billion petrochemical complex.

Formosa Plastics bought bankrupt US computer maker Everex Systems in 1993. Meanwhile, the group's focus again turned to mainland China when Nan Ya Plastics made plans in 1994 to build three plants along China's Long River.

The 1995 death of Wang's mother (at age 108) set off a power struggle between family factions. The company won licenses in 1996 to build power plants, which would make FPG Taiwan's first private-sector power supplier and end a 50-year government utility monopoly. That year, in defiance of Taiwan's policy of limiting investment in China, FPG announced it would build a power plant there. Pressure from the Taiwanese government put the project on hold in 1997.

FPG upped its investment in a new Taiwanese petrochemical complex in 1998. It formed ventures with Asahi Chemical to make spandex fiber, and with France's Renault to make hybrid (gasoline/electric) cars. Also that year the group admitted to combining mercury-laden waste with cement and sneaking the toxic mixture to Cambodia disguised as 3,000 tons of cement block. FPG apologized after villagers living near the dump became ill.

Undaunted by a history of animosity between the two countries, Formosa Plastics and FPG's other flagship companies in 1999 invested a 60% stake in the production of power plants in the Chinese province of Fujian. The following year, the company announced plans to build a PVC plant in China as well.

Chairman: Yung-ching Wang
President: C. T. Lee
CFO: W. H. Hung
President, Formosa Plastics Corporation, U.S.A.:
Susan Wang
VP Human Resources (U.S.): Roger Toth

LOCATIONS

HQ: 201 Tun Hwa North Rd., Taipei, Taiwan
Phone: +886-22-712-2211   **Fax:** +886-22-712-9211
US HQ: 9 Peach Tree Hill Rd., Livingston, NJ 07039
US Phone: 201-992-2090   **US Fax:** 201-716-7456
Web site: http://www.fpc.com.tw/enfpc/suba1-1.htm

PRODUCTS/OPERATIONS

Selected Products and Activities
Acrylic acid
Acrylic ester
Acrylic fiber and yarn
Calcium carbonate
Carbon fiber
Caustic soda chlorine
Natural gas drilling, processing, and transmission
Petrochemical production
Plastic products
Polyvinyl chloride (PVC)
Polypropylene

Selected Affiliates and Subsidiaries
Everex Systems Incorporated
Formosa Heavy Industries Corp.
Formosa Petrochemical Corp.
Formosa Plastics Corporation, USA
Yungchia Chemical Industries Corp.

COMPETITORS

BASF AG	ICI
Bayer AG	Jilin Chemical
Borden Chemicals	LG Group
BP	Lyondell Chemical
Dow Chemical	Norsk Hydro
DuPont	Occidental
Eastman Chemical	Phillips Petroleum
Elf Aquitaine	PVC Container
Hercules	PW Eagle
Huntsman	Shanghai Petrochemical
IBM	Union Carbide
ICC Industries	Yizheng Chemical

HISTORICAL FINANCIALS & EMPLOYEES

Taiwan: 1301 FYE: December 31	Annual Growth	12/89	12/90	12/91	12/92	12/93	12/94	12/95	12/96	12/97	12/98
Sales (NT$ mil.)	4.0%	30,426	29,578	31,704	30,911	27,165	40,037	43,741	43,913	47,907	43,376
Net income (NT$ mil.)	7.6%	3,181	3,627	3,222	3,860	3,877	5,500	5,426	6,103	5,047	6,144
Income as % of sales	—	10.5%	12.3%	10.2%	12.5%	14.3%	13.7%	12.4%	13.9%	10.5%	14.2%
Earnings per share (NT$)	7.9%	1.07	1.16	0.99	1.25	1.07	1.79	1.80	2.06	1.80	2.13
Stock price - FY high (NT$)	—	56.75	62.30	37.84	37.84	43.51	52.95	43.60	56.54	62.77	63.60
Stock price - FY low (NT$)	—	36.82	22.85	23.46	24.18	23.82	34.79	28.67	25.89	42.11	34.20
Stock price - FY close (NT$)	1.3%	41.61	30.03	32.36	24.72	43.51	42.79	30.83	52.23	55.70	46.64
P/E - high	—	53	54	51	30	41	30	24	27	35	30
P/E - low	—	34	20	24	19	22	19	16	13	23	16
Dividends per share (NT$)	7.0%	0.38	0.47	0.53	0.52	0.51	0.68	0.75	0.68	0.72	0.70
Book value per share (NT$)	14.2%	—	7.42	8.83	9.73	10.60	12.04	13.37	13.30	15.69	21.51
Employees	(2.0%)	5,145	4,650	4,767	—	3,345	3,449	3,585	3,891	4,109	4,274

STOCK PRICE HISTORY

HIGH/LOW/CLOSE

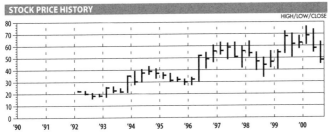

1998 FISCAL YEAR-END

Debt ratio: 24.3%
Return on equity: 11.7%
Cash (NT$ mil.): 461
Current ratio: 0.93
Long-term debt (NT$ mil.):
19,599
No. of shares (mil.): 2,831
Dividends
  Yield: 0.0%
  Payout: 0.3%
Market value ($ mil.): 4,207
Sales ($ mil.): 1,382

FOSTER'S BREWING GROUP LIMITED

OVERVIEW

Sure, Foster's Brewing Group can boast that "Foster's is Australian for beer," but can it boast that the brand means "beer" anywhere else? Almost 90% of the Southbank, Australia, company's sales come from down under, where its beers, including Foster's, Victoria Bitter, and Carlton Lager, have more than 55% of the market share. Its Mildara Blass division is tops in Australian wine and makes premium wines such as Wolf Blass, Yellowglen, and Rothbury Estate while operating a growing business in mail-order wine clubs. Foster's also bought California winery Beringer Wine Estates in October 2000.

In the US, the company sells Foster's through its Foster's USA unit, in which it owns almost 50%; Miller Brewing owns the rest. To expand distribution channels for beer and wine, Foster's operates Australian Leisure and Hospitality, which includes about 90 liquor shops and about 150 hotels in Australia. It also owns The Continental Spirits Company, which makes some spirits brands and distributes Seagram's brands in Australia and New Zealand. The company has been expanding its wine marketing businesses: In addition to owning wine club Cellarmaster Wines, Mildara Blass bought Windsor Vineyards (a direct marketer of wine in the US) and one-fourth of Wine Planet (online retailer).

HISTORY

Upon finding that Australia's only beers were English-styled ales served at room temperature, American emigrants W. M. and R. R. Foster built a lager brewery near Melbourne in 1888 and gave customers ice to chill their Foster's Lager. The brothers began exporting in 1901 when Australians left to serve in the Boer War in South Africa. Carlton and United Breweries Proprietary (CUB) was formed in 1907 when the brothers merged their operations with five other breweries, including Victoria and Carlton. Several of the company names, including Foster's, were kept as beer brands.

Over the years CUB acquired stakes in trading company Elder Smith Goldsbrough Mort and Henry Jones (IXL), a diversified food company owned by John Elliott. Faced with a takeover, in 1981 Elder Smith was merged into Henry Jones, forming Elders IXL. CUB became that firm's largest stockholder, with 49%, in 1983. When CUB became a takeover target that year, Elders came to its rescue by acquiring more than half of that brewery, instantly making Elders one of Australia's largest companies; Elders bought the rest of CUB in 1984.

Elders expanded internationally with it purchases of UK's Courage Breweries (1986) and Canada's Carling O'Keefe Breweries (1987). In 1989 Carling O'Keefe and Molson formed a joint venture, Molson Breweries. To fight possible takeover attempts, that year Harlin Holdings (led by Elliott) offered to buy a 17% stake of Elders from two companies, but regulators forced the firm to extend its offer to all shareholders. As a result, Harlin ended up with more than 55% of Elders. The deal saddled Elders with debt, and in 1990 the company began selling its non-brewing assets. Also that year Elliott resigned as chairman and CEO,

and Elders changed its name to Foster's Brewing Group.

Foster's purchased the brewing interests of Grand Metropolitan (now Diageo) in 1991; the deal created the Inntrepreneur joint venture, a UK pub operator (sold to Japan's Nomura Securities in 1997). Elliott's investment firm went bankrupt in 1992 and Australian conglomerate Broken Hill Proprietary (BHP), which also owned 19% of Elders, assumed control of its shares. (BHP sold its stake in 1997.) Also in 1992 Molson Breweries chief Ted Kunkel became CEO. He wrote off over $2 billion in non-brewing assets that were still on the books and sold 10% of the brewer's interest in Molson.

In 1996 Foster's entered the wine business, buying Mildara Blass and Rothbury Wines. Foster's bought wine clubs Bourse du Vin International (the Netherlands) and 51% of Germany's Heinrich Maximilian Pallhuber (later acquiring the rest) in 1998.

Also in 1998 Foster's sold its Canadian brewing interests — 50% of Molson Breweries and 25% of Coors Canada — to The Molson Companies (but retained a 25% interest in Molson USA). In July 1998 Foster's acquired the Austotel Trust hotel chain from Brierley Investments, making it the largest operator of hotels in Australia.

Subsidiary Mildara Blass acquired the US direct wine marketer Windsor Vineyards and a 25% interest in online wine retailer Wine Planet in early 2000. In October 2000 Foster's bought Beringer Wine Estates, a leading California winery, for about $1.2 billion. Foster's later increased its ownership in Molson USA, after Molson exited the venture, to 49.9%; the distributor was renamed Foster's USA.

Chairman: Frank J. Swan, age 58
President and CEO: Edward T. Kunkel, $2,067,180 pay
Deputy CEO: Nuno D'Aquino, $1,049,092 pay
(prior to promotion)
SVP and CFO; SVP and CFO, Total Service:
Trevor O'Hoy, $632,731 pay (prior to promotion)
SVP Commercial Affairs and Secretary: Peter A. Bobeff,
$966,734 pay
**SVP and Managing Director, Foster's International
Beer Business:** Richard W. Scully
SVP Corporate Affairs: Graeme Willersdorf
Managing Director, Mildara Blass Wines: Terry Davis
Managing Director, Carlton and United Breweries:
James King, $806,695 pay (prior to promotion)
Managing Director, Lensworth: John O'Grady,
$1,005,761 pay
Group Director, Personnel: Rick H. Beker
Auditors: PricewaterhouseCoopers

HQ: 77 Southbank Blvd., Southbank,
Victoria 3006, Australia
Phone: +61-3-9633-2000   **Fax:** +61-3-9633-2002
US HQ: 11921 Freedom Dr., Ste. 550, Reston, VA 20190
US Phone: 703-904-4321   **US Fax:** 703-904-4336
Web site: http://www.fosters.com.au

2000 Sales

	$ mil.	% of total
Australia & Pacific	1,787	88
Europe	117	6
The Americas	82	4
Asia	49	2
Total	**2,035**	**100**

2000 Sales

	$ mil.	% of total
Beer	918	45
Leisure	522	26
Wine	425	21
Property & investments	85	4
Other	85	4
Total	**2,035**	**100**

Selected Products and Brands

Beer	Wines
Carlton	Andrew Garrett
Crown Lager	Beringer
Foster's	Chateau Sourverain
Matilda Bay	Flanagan's Ridge
Melbourne Bitter	Rothbury Estate
Powers	Stags' Leap
Redback	Wolf Blass
Victoria Bitter	Yellowglen

Accor	Diageo	Peerless
Adolph Coors	FEMSA	Importers
Allied Domecq	Gallo	S&P
Anheuser-Busch	Gambrinus	San Miguel
Asahi Breweries	Geerlings	Scottish &
Asia Pacific	& Wade	Newcastle
Breweries	Heineken	Starwood Hotels
Bass	Interbrew	& Resorts
Boston Beer	Kirin	Worldwide
Brauerei BECK	Lion Nathan	Terlato Wine
Carlsberg	Marriott	Tsingtao
Danone	International	

OTC: FBRWY FYE: June 30	Annual Growth	6/91	6/92	6/93	6/94	6/95	6/96	6/97	6/98	6/99	6/00
Sales ($ mil.)	(9.4%)	4,968	4,748	4,174	3,052	3,106	1,853	1,979	3,086	2,068	2,035
Net income ($ mil.)	—	(33)	(710)	207	205	204	231	189	277	244	269
Income as % of sales	—	—	—	4.9%	6.7%	6.6%	12.5%	9.5%	9.0%	11.8%	13.2%
Earnings per share ($)	10.6%	—	—	—	—	0.09	0.12	0.10	0.16	0.14	0.15
Stock price - FY high ($)	—	—	—	—	—	1.67	1.90	2.12	2.45	3.16	4.88
Stock price - FY low ($)	—	—	—	—	—	1.40	1.40	1.50	1.26	2.00	2.56
Stock price - FY close ($)	16.3%	—	—	—	—	1.53	1.50	1.90	2.40	2.80	3.25
P/E - high	—	—	—	—	—	19	16	21	15	23	33
P/E - low	—	—	—	—	—	16	12	15	8	14	17
Dividends per share ($)	4.4%	—	—	—	—	0.07	0.09	0.08	0.07	0.09	0.09
Book value per share ($)	(2.8%)	—	—	—	—	0.94	1.18	1.11	0.91	1.04	0.81
Employees	(1.6%)	16,300	14,900	10,083	—	14,024	10,436	10,379	8,207	12,718	14,094

HIGH/LOW/CLOSE

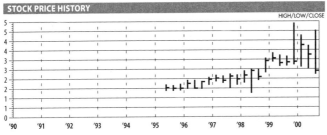

Debt ratio: 40.0%
Return on equity: 16.2%
Cash ($ mil.): 306
Current ratio: 1.34
Long-term debt ($ mil.): 925
No. of shares (mil.): 1,708
Dividends
Yield: 0.0%
Payout: 0.6%
Market value ($ mil.): 5,550

FRANCE TELECOM

Adieu, monopole; bonjour, competition.
Paris-based France Telecom provides local, long-distance, and international calling services, as well as wireless phone service and data transmission. The former monopoly has 34 million fixed-line telephone subscribers and about 11 million wireless subscribers (through its Itineris unit) in France, and its majority-owned Wanadoo is a leading French ISP.

Moving beyond its home territory, France Telecom has taken stakes in several European mobile networks. In its biggest international expansion, the company has acquired Orange, the UK's #3 mobile phone company. It plans to combine Orange with Itineris and the rest of its mobile phone operations to form a European wireless powerhouse that will rival Vodafone. France Telecom has announced plans to sell a 15% stake in the new wireless company to the public. In addition, France Telecom operates Global One, which provides international data and voice services to more than 30,000 business customers.

Though mandated by law to be France Telecom's majority owner, the French government has reduced its stake to 54%.

Shortly before he abdicated, King Louis Philippe laid the groundwork for France's state-owned telegraphic service. Established in 1851, the operation became part of the French Post Office in the 1870s, about the time Alexander Graham Bell invented the telephone. The French government licensed three private companies to provide telegraph service, and during the 1880s they merged into the Société Générale de Téléphones (SGT). In 1883 the country's first exchange was initiated in Rheims. Four years later an international circuit was installed connecting Paris and Brussels. The government nationalized SGT in 1889.

By the turn of the century France had more than 60,000 phone lines, and in 1924 a standardized telephone was introduced. Long-distance service improved with underground cabling, and phone exchanges in Paris and other leading cities became automated during the 1930s.

WWII proved a major setback to the French government's telephone operations, Direction Générale des Télécommunications (DGT), because a large part of its equipment was destroyed or damaged. For the next two decades France lagged behind other nations in telephony infrastructure development. An exception to this technological stagnation was Centre National d'Etudes des Télécommunications (CNET), the research laboratory formed in 1944 that eventually became France Telecom's research arm.

In 1962 DGT was a key player in the first intercontinental television broadcast, between the US and France, via a Telstar satellite. The company began to catch up with its peers when it developed a digital phone system in the mid-1970s. In 1974 CNET was instrumental in the launch of France's first experimental communications satellite. In another technological advance, DGT began replacing its paper directories with the innovative Minitel online terminals in 1980.

The French government created France Telecom in 1988. In 1993 France Telecom and Deutsche Telekom teamed up to form the Global One international telecommunications venture, and Sprint joined the next year. Global One was formally launched in 1996. Also that year France Telecom began providing Internet access.

In 1997 the government sold about 20% of France Telecom to the public. With Europe's state telephone monopolies ending in 1998, France Telecom reorganized and brought prices in line with those of its competitors.

Tightening their alliance, Deutsche Telekom and France Telecom in 1998 announced plans to construct a fiber-optic network linking 16 European countries. But the alliance came apart the next year when France Telecom sued Deutsche Telekom over the German company's plan (since abandoned) to merge with Telecom Italia. The lawsuit was settled in 2000.

In 2000 France Telecom paid $4.3 billion to Deutsche Telekom and Sprint to take full ownership of Global One, and it agreed to pay $3.6 billion for a 29% stake in Germany's MobilCom. Later in 2000 France Telecom snatched up UK mobile phone operator Orange in a $37.5 billion cash and stock deal after Vodafone was forced to divest the company before merging with Mannesmann. The Orange acquisition reduced the French government's stake in France Telecom to 54%. France Telecom also invested $4.5 billion in UK cable operator NTL, sold its stake in Mexican telecom giant Telmex, and agreed to sell its 49.9% stake in Noos, the joint venture with Suez Lyonnaise that is France's #1 cable TV operator.

OFFICERS

Chairman and CEO: Michel Bon, age 57
SEVP Public Affairs: Gérard Moine, age 51
SEVP Corporate Communications:
Marie-Claude Peyrache, age 48
EVP Finance and Human Resources:
Jean-Louis Vinciguerra, age 54
EVP Large Business; COO, Business Services Division:
Jacques Champeaux, age 51
EVP Mass Market, Product and Services Division;
COO, Consumer Services Division: Jean-
François Pontal, age 54
EVP Development; COO, Corporate Technology and
Development Division: Jean-Jacques Damlamian
EVP Network; COO, Network Services Division:
Jean-Yves Gouiffés, age 50
Corporate Secretary: Jacques Burillon, age 57
Auditors: Ernst & Young Audit; Salustro Reydel

LOCATIONS

HQ: 6, Place d'Alleray, 75505 Paris Cedex 15, France
Phone: +33-1-44-44-22-22   **Fax:** +33-1-44-44-95-95
US HQ: 1270 Avenue of the Americas, 28th Fl.,
New York, NY 10020
US Phone: 212-332-2100   **US Fax:** 212-245-8605
Web site: http://www.francetelecom.fr

France Telecom has investments and operations in more
than 75 countries worldwide.

1999 Sales

	% of total
France	87
International	13
Total	**100**

PRODUCTS/OPERATIONS

1999 Sales

	% of total
Fixed-line telephony	58
Mobile telecommunications	17
Leased lines & data transmission	9
Information services	6
Equipment sales & rentals	5
Broadcasting & cable TV services	4
Other	1
Total	**100**

Selected Services

Calling cards	Local telephone service
Data transmission	Long-distance
Directories	Mobile phone service
Equipment sales and	(digital, GSM-900)
rentals	Pay phones
International calling	Radio and television
Internet access (Wanadoo)	broadcasting
Leased lines	Radiopaging

COMPETITORS

America Online	Debitel	Sprint
AT&T	Deutsche	Swiss Telecom
Belgacom	Telekom	Swisscom
Bertelsmann	Global Crossing	Tele Danmark
Bouygues	Global	Telecom Italia
BT	TeleSystems	Telefónica
Cable and	KPN	Telenor
Wireless	Mannesmann AG	Telia
CANAL+	Olivetti	United
Carrier1	Portugal	Pan-Europe
International	Telecom	Vodafone
Cegetel	RSL	WorldCom
COLT Telecom	Communications	

HISTORICAL FINANCIALS & EMPLOYEES

NYSE: FTE FYE: December 31	Annual Growth	12/90	12/91	12/92	12/93	12/94	12/95	12/96	12/97	12/98	12/99
Sales ($ mil.)	3.4%	20,287	22,285	22,183	21,449	26,716	30,112	29,144	26,039	28,938	27,424
Net income ($ mil.)	11.1%	1,079	394	598	811	1,857	1,873	406	2,469	2,700	2,788
Income as % of sales	—	5.3%	1.8%	2.7%	3.8%	7.0%	6.2%	1.4%	9.5%	9.3%	10.2%
Earnings per share ($)	4.2%	—	—	—	—	—	—	—	2.47	2.69	2.68
Stock price - FY high ($)	—	—	—	—	—	—	—	—	38.13	83.00	134.50
Stock price - FY low ($)	—	—	—	—	—	—	—	—	32.63	35.44	67.00
Stock price - FY close ($)	92.6%	—	—	—	—	—	—	—	36.00	78.94	133.50
P/E - high	—	—	—	—	—	—	—	—	15	31	49
P/E - low	—	—	—	—	—	—	—	—	13	13	25
Dividends per share ($)	—	—	—	—	—	—	—	—	0.00	1.10	0.88
Book value per share ($)	9.2%	—	—	—	—	—	—	—	15.57	19.47	18.58
Employees	2.0%	—	—	—	154,548	167,882	167,660	165,200	159,335	165,000	174,262

STOCK PRICE HISTORY

HIGH/LOW/CLOSE

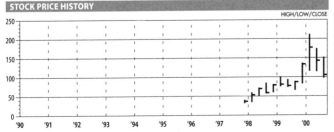

1999 FISCAL YEAR-END

Debt ratio: 39.3%
Return on equity: 14.3%
Cash ($ mil.): 2,441
Current ratio: 0.78
Long-term debt ($ mil.): 12,319
No. of shares (mil.): 1,025
Dividends
  Yield: 0.7%
  Payout: 32.8%
Market value ($ mil.): 136,786

FUJI PHOTO FILM CO., LTD.

OVERVIEW

Fuji Photo Film Co. enjoys accentuating the negatives. As Japan's #1 photographic film and paper producer, Tokyo-based Fuji sells about 70% of all photographic film on its home turf; internationally, it has hammered away at rival Eastman Kodak's lead, and the two are now virtually tied. Fuji also offers photo-developing equipment and conventional and digital cameras. Additionally, the company makes videocassettes, motion picture film, and batteries. Fuji's information systems unit (X-ray imaging products, floppy disks, CD-ROMs, industrial chemicals) accounts for about 40% of sales.

The company has zoomed in on Kodak in the US by using heavy promotions and price cuts on film and cameras.

HISTORY

Mokichi Morita, president of Japan's leading celluloid maker (Dainippon Celluloid Company, founded 1919), decided to start making motion picture film in the early 1930s. Movies were becoming popular in Japan, but there was no domestic film supplier. Working with a grant from the government, Dainippon Celluloid established Fuji Photo Film Co., an independent company, in 1934 in Minami Ashigara Village, near Mount Fuji.

At first the company had trouble gaining acceptance in Japan as a quality film producer but, with the help of German emulsion specialist Dr. Emill Mauerhoff, overcame its product deficiencies, producing black-and-white photographic film (1936) and the first Japanese-made color film (1948). In the meantime Fuji added 35mm photographic film, 16mm motion picture film, and X-ray film to its product line. By the early 1940s the company was operating four factories and a research laboratory in Japan. Its first overseas office, opened in Brazil in 1955, was followed by offices in the US (1958) and Europe (1964).

Fuji continued to expand its product line, adding magnetic tape in 1960. Two years later it formed Fuji Xerox, a Japanese joint venture, to sell copiers with Rank Xerox (UK, now known as Xerox Limited). It operated as a private-label film supplier in the US and did not market its products under its own brand name until 1972.

International marketing VP Minoru Ohnishi became Fuji's youngest president in 1980 at age 55. To decrease dependence on Japanese film sales, he built sales in the US — agreeing to sponsor the 1984 Los Angeles Olympics, after Eastman Kodak refused to, was key — and pumped money into the production of videotapes, floppy disks, and medical diagnostic equipment. Fuji introduced Fujicolor Quicksnap, the world's first 35mm disposable camera, in 1986. It began establishing US manufacturing operations in South Carolina two years later.

The company created FUJIFILM Microdevices, a Japanese subsidiary, to produce image-processing semiconductors in 1990.

New consumer product offerings the next year included the Fujix Digital Still Camera System, which stores images electronically and allows computer-image processing and transmission. In 1992 Fuji scientists completed a crude artificial "eye" that could be a forerunner of more efficient eyes for robots. The following year it launched the Pictrostat instant print system, which produces color prints in one minute from photos, slides, and objects.

Fuji was forced to temporarily raise US prices in 1994 after Kodak accused it of illegally dumping its photographic paper exported to the US. But Fuji skirted the problem in 1995 by making the paper at its South Carolina plant. That year Kodak asked for economic sanctions against Fuji and the Japanese government, saying that the government encouraged Fuji to use exclusive contracts to control photographic film distribution, thus keeping Kodak from selling film in many stores. (The case was rejected by the World Trade Organization in 1997.)

The firm unveiled the Advanced Photo System (co-developed with four other companies, including Kodak) in 1996, combining conventional photography with digital-image processing and printing technology. Also that year Fuji bought six off-site wholesale photofinishing plants from Wal-Mart (the largest US provider of photofinishing services) and won contracts to provide supplies to all of Wal-Mart's in-store one-hour photo labs.

In 1997 it chopped film prices in the US and began manufacturing film in South Carolina. In 1999 Fuji introduced a high-quality image sensor for digital cameras (Super CCD) and Instax, an instant picture camera. Fuji and Sony launched HiFD, a floppy disk with 140 times the storage capacity of traditional disks, in early 2000. Fuji later announced plans to develop more efficient, low-cost ink jet printers through an alliance with Xerox and Sharp Corp. In May 2000 Shigetaka Komori replaced Masayuki Muneyuki as president.

Chairman and CEO: Minoru Ohnishi
VC: Masayuki Muneyuki
President: Shigetaka Komori
EVP: Mitsutaka Sofue
EVP: Tasuku Imai
EVP: Yasuo Tanaka
SVP: Nobuo Wakuya
SVP: Kotaro Aso
SVP: Nobuyuki Hayashi
SVP: Jun Hayashi
SVP: Takashi Matsushima
SVP: Akikazu Mikawa
VP Human Resources, Fuji Photo Film U.S.A.:
Joseph Convery
Treasurer, Fuji Photo Film U.S.A.: Noboru Tanaka
Auditors: Ernst & Young

LOCATIONS

HQ: Fuji Shashin Film Kabushiki Kaisha,
26-30, Nishiazabu 2-chome, Minato-ku,
Tokyo 106-8620, Japan
Phone: +81-3-3406-2111   **Fax:** +81-3-3406-2173
US HQ: 555 Taxter Rd., Elmsford, NY 10523
US Phone: 914-789-8100   **US Fax:** 914-789-8295
Web site: http://www.fujifilm.co.jp

Fuji Photo Film Co. has operations in Asia, Australia,
Europe, and North and South America.

2000 Sales

	$ mil.	% of total
Japan	6,561	48
Other countries	7,097	52
Total	**13,658**	**100**

PRODUCTS/OPERATIONS

2000 Sales

	$ mil.	% of total
Information systems	5,709	42
Imaging systems	4,582	34
Photofinishing systems	3,357	24
Total	**13,658**	**100**

Selected Products

Information Systems
Data storage media
Graphic systems
Industrial materials and equipment
Medical imaging products
Office automation systems

Imaging Systems
Electronic imaging systems
Motion picture films
Optical products
Photographic films

Photofinishing Systems
Instant color print systems
Photographic papers, equipment, and chemicals
Processing and printing service

COMPETITORS

Agfa	Nikon Corporation
Canon	Olympus
Eastman Kodak	Philips Electronics
Hewlett-Packard	Polaroid
Imation	Ricoh
Konica	Sharp
Lanier Worldwide	Sony
Matsushita	Toshiba
Minolta	Xerox

HISTORICAL FINANCIALS & EMPLOYEES

Nasdaq (SC): FUJIY FYE: March 31	Annual Growth	10/91	10/92	10/93	10/94	*3/95	3/96	3/97	3/98	3/99	3/00
Sales ($ mil.)	5.4%	8,543	9,162	10,157	11,009	5,403	10,119	10,098	10,440	11,883	13,658
Net income ($ mil.)	1.5%	725	607	569	658	315	680	688	673	591	827
Income as % of sales	—	8.5%	6.6%	5.6%	6.0%	5.8%	6.7%	6.8%	6.4%	5.0%	6.1%
Earnings per share ($)	0.9%	1.49	1.18	1.09	1.28	0.59	1.23	1.34	1.31	1.15	1.61
Stock price - FY high ($)	—	28.06	23.88	26.31	25.25	23.94	30.31	34.38	43.50	44.00	47.50
Stock price - FY low ($)	—	22.25	19.00	18.94	19.38	19.38	22.25	28.45	32.75	31.50	30.63
Stock price - FY close ($)	7.2%	23.63	20.75	23.19	23.81	23.38	28.88	32.75	36.75	37.38	44.00
P/E - high	—	20	20	24	20	41	25	26	33	38	30
P/E - low	—	14	16	17	15	33	18	21	25	27	19
Dividends per share ($)	11.7%	0.07	0.10	0.12	0.14	0.07	0.07	0.25	0.09	0.08	0.19
Book value per share ($)	17.1%	6.86	8.32	10.02	11.59	13.25	11.35	21.08	21.06	23.33	28.45
Employees	6.0%	21,946	24,868	25,074	26,555	27,565	29,903	33,154	36,580	37,551	37,151

* Fiscal year change

STOCK PRICE HISTORY

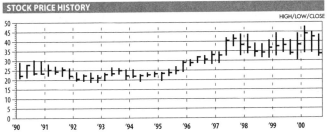

2000 FISCAL YEAR-END

Debt ratio: 1.4%
Return on equity: 6.2%
Cash ($ mil.): 6,399
Current ratio: 2.82
Long-term debt ($ mil.): 204
No. of shares (mil.): 515
Dividends
  Yield: 0.4%
  Payout: 11.8%
Market value ($ mil.): 22,644

FUJITSU LIMITED

OVERVIEW

Like a hot basketball shooter, Fujitsu's trying to hit nothing but net — Internet, that is. Tokyo-based Fujitsu Limited comprises roughly 500 companies with operations in more than 100 countries. Computers and information technology account for more than two-thirds of sales. The company is one of Japan's top two PC makers, wrestling with NEC for #1, and a leading maker of servers, software, storage devices, and peripherals such as printers and scanners. Fujitsu's information technology (IT) services include systems installation and management. The company also makes communications systems, consumer electronics, semiconductors, and electronic components. Important subsidiaries include US server maker Amdahl and ICL, a leading UK-based IT services firm.

Fujitsu thinks it can achieve truly monstrous growth by recreating itself as an Internet services company. It acquired Japan's largest Internet service provider (ISP), Nifty Serve, and merged it with another ISP, InfoWeb. In addition to its Internet services blitz (Fujitsu's business strategy is "Everything on the Internet"), the company has targeted flash memory and system-on-a-chip circuits as growth areas.

Fujitsu continues to partner with top tech firms for growth in other areas. Fujitsu and Germany's Siemens have combined most of their European computer operations (Fujitsu-Siemens Computers). Other alliances include a company formed with Hitachi to commercialize plasma display panels for televisions (Fujitsu Hitachi Plasma Display) and a joint venture with AMD that manufactures flash memory for devices such as cell phones and digital cameras (Fujitsu AMD Semiconductor).

HISTORY

Siemens and Furukawa Electric created Fuji Electric in 1923 to produce electrical equipment. Fuji spun off Fujitsu, its communications division, in 1935. Originally a maker of telephone equipment, Fujitsu produced antiaircraft weapons during WWII. After the war it became one of four major suppliers to state-owned monopoly Nippon Telegraph and Telephone (NTT) and continued to benefit from Japan's rapid economic recovery in the 1950s and 1960s.

With encouragement from Japan's Ministry of International Trade and Industry (MITI), Fujitsu developed the country's first commercial computer in 1954. MITI erected trade barriers to protect Japan's new computer industry and in the early 1960s sponsored the production of mainframe computers, directing Fujitsu to develop the central processing unit. The company expanded into semiconductor production and factory automation in the late 1960s. Its factory automation business was spun off as Fujitsu Fanuc in 1972.

Fujitsu gained badly needed technology when it bought 30% of IBM-plug-compatible manufacturer Amdahl in 1972. By 1979 Fujitsu had passed IBM to become Japan's #1 computer manufacturer. In Europe, Fujitsu entered into computer marketing ventures with Siemens (1978) and ICL (1981). In the US it teamed with TRW to sell point-of-sale systems (1980), assuming full control of the operation in 1983. Fujitsu released its first supercomputer in 1982.

Fujitsu bought 80% of UK mainframe maker ICL (from STC) in 1990 for $1.3 billion. In 1993 it formed a joint venture with Advanced Micro Devices to make flash memory products.

The company doubled its share of Japan's PC market in 1995 to more than 18% and the next year expanded its PC business globally. In 1997 Fujitsu paid about $878 million for the 58% of Amdahl it didn't already own. The next year it bought the 10% of ICL it didn't own. Fujitsu's 1998 earnings suffered from a slump in the semiconductor market, Amdahl-related expenses, and a weak Asian economy.

Also in 1998 Naoyuki Akikusa, son of a former NTT president, became head of Fujitsu. He began trimming some operations while ramping up the company's Internet activities. Fujitsu in 1999 became full owner of online services provider Nifty Serve, making it Japan's largest Internet service provider. Also that year Siemens and Fujitsu combined their European computer operations in a 50-50 joint venture (Fujitsu Siemens Computers) as one part of a larger global alliance. A restructuring of Fujitsu's semiconductor operations caused losses for 1999.

Akikusa's reorganization continued in 2000. Fujitsu overhauled its server business (subsidiary Amdahl ceased production of IBM-compatible mainframes) and accelerated production of flash memory.

Chairman: Tadashi Sekizawa
President and CEO: Naoyuki Akikusa
SEVP Management and Administration:
Keizo Fukagawa
EVP Computer Business; President, Personal Systems:
Tadayasu Sugita
EVP; President, Electronic Devices: Kazunari Shirai
EVP International Sales and Marketing; President,
International Computer Business and Corporate
Branding: Kazuto Kojima
EVP Finance, Accounting and Corporate Planning:
Takashi Takaya
Administration, Personnel, and Employee Relations:
Takahiko Okada
Auditors: Century Ota Showa & Co.

HQ: 6-1, Marunouchi 1-chome, Chiyoda-ku,
Tokyo 100-8211, Japan
Phone: +81-3-3216-3211   **Fax:** +81-3-3216-9365
US HQ: 3055 Orchard Dr., San Jose, CA 95134
US Phone: 408-432-1300   **US Fax:** 408-432-1318
Web site: http://www.fujitsu.co.jp

Fujitsu Limited has about 500 subsidiaries and affiliate
companies in more than 100 countries.

2000 Sales

	$ mil.	% of total
Asia & Oceania		
Japan	31,631	64
Other countries	3,504	7
Europe	7,727	16
Americas	6,492	13
Africa & Middle East	222	—
Total	**49,576**	**100**

2000 Sales

	$ mil.	% of total
Software & services	18,636	38
Information processing	15,144	30
Telecommunications	7,287	15
Electronic devices	5,360	11
Financing	1,067	2
Other operations	2,082	4
Total	**49,576**	**100**

Alcatel	Micron Technology
AMD	Mitsubishi
Apple Computer	Motorola
Atmel	National Semiconductor
Bull	NEC
Canon	Nortel Networks
Cisco Systems	Oki Electric
Compaq	Philips Electronics
Dell Computer	Samsung
EDS	SANYO
Gateway	Seagate
Hewlett-Packard	SGI
Hitachi	Sharp
Hyundai	Siemens
IBM	SOFTBANK
Intel	Sony
LG Group	STMicroelectronics
LSI Logic	Sun Microsystems
Lucent	Toshiba
Matsushita	Unisys

OTC: FJTSY FYE: March 31	Annual Growth	3/91	3/92	3/93	3/94	3/95	3/96	3/97	3/98	3/99	3/00
Sales ($ mil.)	9.9%	21,134	25,879	30,143	30,553	37,640	35,075	36,378	37,464	43,988	49,576
Net income ($ mil.)	(4.1%)	588	92	(284)	(367)	520	588	373	42	(114)	403
Income as % of sales	—	2.8%	0.4%	—	—	1.4%	1.7%	1.0%	0.1%	—	0.8%
Earnings per share ($)	(5.3%)	1.63	0.23	(0.78)	(1.01)	1.40	1.63	1.01	1.01	(0.31)	1.00
Stock price - FY high ($)	—	51.00	44.89	28.34	51.02	57.66	63.34	52.50	75.50	79.50	230.00
Stock price - FY low ($)	—	34.98	24.17	20.14	28.00	42.86	44.42	43.50	45.75	42.00	77.50
Stock price - FY close ($)	15.6%	42.08	25.56	27.38	49.63	50.05	46.19	52.00	53.00	79.50	155.00
P/E - high	—	31	195	—	—	41	39	52	686	—	230
P/E - low	—	21	105	—	—	31	27	43	416	—	78
Dividends per share ($)	1.9%	0.38	0.38	0.35	0.39	0.56	0.47	0.40	0.38	0.42	0.45
Book value per share ($)	3.5%	22.75	24.16	26.44	32.06	34.02	29.84	26.26	23.91	25.95	31.03
Employees	2.9%	145,872	155,779	161,974	163,990	164,364	164,800	167,000	180,000	188,000	188,053

HIGH/LOW/CLOSE

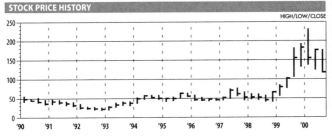

Debt ratio: 19.7%
Return on equity: 3.7%
Cash ($ mil.): 2,983
Current ratio: 1.25
Long-term debt ($ mil.): 10,975
No. of shares (mil.): 393
Dividends
  Yield: 0.0%
  Payout: 0.5%
Market value ($ mil.): 60,851

GALLAHER GROUP PLC

OVERVIEW

It no longer bears the Royal seal of approval, but Weybridge, UK-based Gallaher Group is still the top UK cigarette maker. Its cigarettes include four of the top six UK brands: premium-priced Benson and Hedges (formerly the Royals' official brand) and Silk Cut, mid-priced Berkeley, and low-priced Mayfair. Although 93% of its sales come from cigarettes, Gallaher also controls half of the UK cigar market with #1 brand Hamlet, and it makes hand-rolling and pipe tobacco.

Gallaher was spun off in 1997 from Fortune Brands, the result of a flurry of tobacco-related lawsuits in the US. Although unlikely to breed multimillion-dollar jury verdicts, Europe presents its own problems: Gallaher and other firms are fighting the European Union's ban on tobacco advertising (scheduled to start in 2001). Gallaher is focusing on building brand identification in current markets and seeking new international markets for its products. The company became the leading tobacco company in Russia with its August 2000 purchase of Vector Group's Ligget-Ducat.

HISTORY

Tom Gallaher started his business making and selling pipe tobacco in Londonderry, Ireland, in 1857. By 1873 he had moved his business to Belfast. By 1888 Gallaher was making cigarettes (which had become popular) and flake tobacco. That year Gallaher opened its first London office. The firm was incorporated as Gallaher Limited in 1896. In 1908 it bought Ireland's entire tobacco crop. Gallaher died in 1927.

In 1955 Gallaher bought the UK and Ireland units of cigarette firm Benson and Hedges. Richard Benson and William Hedges launched their firm in England in 1873; they pioneered selling tobacco in sealed tins for freshness. In 1877 Queen Victoria endorsed Benson and Hedges with her Royal Warrant. As more women began smoking in the early 1900s, Benson and Hedges made specialized cigarettes for them, including some with floral designs.

Gallaher bought J. Wix and Sons (Kensitas cigarettes) from American Tobacco in 1962 for a Gallaher stake. American Tobacco had increased its stake to 67% by 1968; it renamed itself American Brands in 1970 as it added nontobacco products.

Diversifying in the 1970s, Gallaher bought Dollond & Aitchison Group (optical services/products, 1970), created retail franchise Marshell Group (tobacco and confectionery concessions, 1971), and bought TM Group (Vendepac and other cigarette and snack vending machines, 1973) and Forbuoys (tobacco, sweets, and newspapers stores; 1973). In 1974 it expanded to Italy through Dollond & Aitchison. American Brands controlled 100% of Gallaher by 1975.

The company continued its acquisitions in the 1980s, including NSS Newsagents in 1986 (550 stores, combined with the 450-store Forbuoys subsidiary). By 1987 Gallaher was the #1 UK tobacco manufacturer. In 1990 the firm acquired Scotland's Whyte & Mackay Distillers.

During the early 1990s Gallaher expanded to France, Spain, and Greece. In 1993 it cut 15% of its workforce, blaming cigarette taxes for lower sales. Gallaher had become Ireland's #1 tobacco firm by 1994.

When parent American Brands sold US subsidiary American Tobacco to British American Tobacco Industries (B.A.T) in 1994, Gallaher sold B.A.T its Silk Cut rights outside Europe in exchange for a manufacturing deal. To focus on tobacco and distilling, Gallaher sold Dollond & Aitchison that year and the next year sold its other noncore units (including Forbuoys and TM Group). It also closed several plants during this period.

Twelve people sued Gallaher and rival Imperial Tobacco in 1996, alleging the firms continued using tar in cigarettes after discovering its link to cancer. (The lawsuit achieved group-action status but was later abandoned because the statute of limitations had expired.)

As US tobacco-related litigation skyrocketed, in 1997 American Brands renamed itself Fortune Brands and spun off Gallaher Group, which floated on the London Stock Exchange in May — the first time a UK firm de-merged from a US parent. In 1998 it began exporting to China.

In 1999 Gallaher bought the UK tobacco business of RJR Nabisco (the Dorchester and Dickens & Grant brands and distribution of Camel and More). In a sign of tobacco's fall from favor, the Royal Palace withdrew Queen Victoria's 122-year-old endorsement of Benson and Hedges.

Gallaher entered 2000 with new CEO Nigel Northridge. In August 2000 the company bought Russian cigarette maker and distributor Liggett-Ducat from Vector Group for about $400 million.

OFFICERS

Chairman: Peter Wilson, age 58, $754,000 pay
(prior to title change)
Deputy Chairman: Sir Graham J. Hearne, age 62,
$65,000 pay
CEO: Nigel Northridge, age 44, $447,000 pay
(prior to promotion)
Business Development Director: Nigel Simon, age 44,
$345,000 pay (prior to promotion)
Finance Director: Mark Rolfe
Managing Director, Continental Europe Division:
Yann Tardif
Managing Director, UK Division: Barry Jenner
Operations Director (HR): William Curry, age 52,
$287,000 pay
Secretary: Nigel Bulpitt
Corporate Affairs Manager: Jeff Jeffery
Media and Parliamentary Affairs Manager: Mark Phillips
Head of Corporate Affairs: Ian Birks
Head of Investor Relations: Claire Jenkins
Head of Manufacturing: Nigel Dunlop
Group Legal Adviser: Christopher Fielden, age 57,
$374,000 pay
Auditors: PricewaterhouseCoopers

LOCATIONS

HQ: Members Hill, Brooklands Rd., Weybridge,
Surrey KT13 0QU, United Kingdom
Phone: +44-1932-859-777 **Fax:** +44-1932-832-792
Web site: http://www.gallaher-group.com

Gallaher Group sells tobacco products in Asia,
Continental Europe, Ireland, Kazakhstan, Russia, and
the UK and through remote mobile operators (which
succeed duty free shops in the European Union). It
manufactures products in Kazakhstan and the UK.

1999 Sales & Operating Profit

	Sales $ mil.	Sales % of total	Operating Profit $ mil.	Operating Profit % of total
UK	6,293	90	562	83
Other countries	724	10	118	17
Adjustment	—	—	(6)	—
Total	**7,017**	**100**	**674**	**100**

PRODUCTS/OPERATIONS

Selected Products and Brands

Cigarettes
Distribution — UK (Camel, More)
Low-priced (Dickens & Grant, Dorchester, Mayfair,
Sovereign)
Mid-priced (Berkeley Superkings, Prima, Novost, LD)
Premium (Benson and Hedges, Silk Cut)
Regional — Far East (Sobranie, Sobranie Pinks and Mints)

Other
Cigars (Hamlet, Sobranie Cuban Collection)
Hand-rolling tobacco (Amber Leaf, Old Holborn)
Pipe tobacco (Condor)

COMPETITORS

Altadis	Lorillard Tobacco
Austria Tabak	Philip Morris International
British American Tobacco	Swedish Match
China National Tobacco	Taiwan Tobacco & Wine
Imperial Tobacco Group	Tchibo Holding
Japan Tobacco	Vector

HISTORICAL FINANCIALS & EMPLOYEES

NYSE: GLH FYE: December 31	Annual Growth	12/90	12/91	12/92	12/93	12/94	12/95	12/96	12/97	12/98	12/99
Sales ($ mil.)	(1.7%)	—	—	—	—	—	—	—	7,264	7,061	7,017
Net income ($ mil.)	(0.8%)	—	—	—	—	—	—	—	396	361	390
Income as % of sales	—	—	—	—	—	—	—	—	5.5%	5.1%	5.6%
Earnings per share ($)	0.2%	—	—	—	—	—	—	—	2.31	2.09	2.32
Stock price - FY high ($)	—	—	—	—	—	—	—	—	24.00	31.25	29.50
Stock price - FY low ($)	—	—	—	—	—	—	—	—	16.00	19.50	14.19
Stock price - FY close ($)	(15.0%)	—	—	—	—	—	—	—	21.31	27.19	15.38
P/E - high	—	—	—	—	—	—	—	—	10	15	13
P/E - low	—	—	—	—	—	—	—	—	7	9	6
Dividends per share ($)	39.1%	—	—	—	—	—	—	—	0.77	0.79	1.49
Book value per share ($)	—	—	—	—	—	—	—	—	(5.10)	(4.83)	(4.80)
Employees	—	—	—	—	—	—	—	—	—	—	—

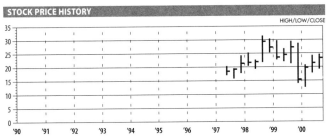

STOCK PRICE HISTORY HIGH/LOW/CLOSE

1999 FISCAL YEAR-END

Debt ratio: 100.0%
Return on equity: —
Cash ($ mil.): 48
Current ratio: 1.14
Long-term debt ($ mil.): 1,334
No. of shares (mil.): 166
Dividends
Yield: 9.7%
Payout: 64.2%
Market value ($ mil.): 2,546

OAO GAZPROM

Gazprom, which evolved from the former natural gas ministry of the Soviet Union, is now Russia's largest company — as well as the world's largest gas producer. The Moscow-based titan, which still enjoys its monopoly status in Russia, is involved in most phases of the gas industry, including gas exploration, processing, transportation, and marketing.

Operating Russia's extensive gas pipeline system, Gazprom delivers natural gas to the Commonwealth of Independent States and Baltic states, which constituted the states of the former USSR. Gazprom also exports gas to some 25 countries in Europe and expects to boost exports by 20% after completing two huge gas pipelines, Blue Stream and Yamal-Europe. It produces 93% of Russia's natural gas and controls one-fourth of the world's gas reserves.

Exports to Europe are critical to the company, burdened by debt because of the insolvency of Russian consumers and hordes of nonpaying customers. Gazprom also holds strategic partnerships with Western energy companies, including Germany's Ruhrgas, which owns almost 4% of the company's shares. Other partners include Eni of Italy, Royal Dutch/Shell, and Finland's Fortum.

Among Gazprom's holdings are its own telecommunications network and interests in Russian financial institutions and a polypropylene plant. In a controversial deal, Gazprom is trying to take over Russia's leading independent media group, Media-MOST, which owed the gas giant huge sums of money. The Russian government owns 38% of Gazprom.

HISTORY

Following the breakup of the Soviet Union in the early 1990s, one of the first priorities of the Russian government was to move some state monopolies toward a free-market economics system. A presidential decree in 1992 moved the company toward privatization by calling for the formation of a Russian joint-stock company to explore for and produce gas, gas condensates, and oil; provide for gas processing; operate gas wells; and build gas pipelines and storage facilities. By 1993 the government had converted its natural gas monopoly, Gazprom, into a joint-stock company.

The new Gazprom was 15%-owned by Gazprom workers and 28% by people living in Russia's gas-producing regions. The state retained a 40% share. The company inherited all of the export contracts to Western and Central Europe of the Commonwealth of Independent States.

Thanks to the power of Viktor Chernomyrdin (Gazprom's former Soviet boss and gas industry minister, who became Russia's prime minister in 1992), the company was able to enjoy large tax breaks and maintain its role as a monopoly — even as other industries were being more deeply privatized. However, the privatization of Gazprom was later attacked as being manipulated to profit the company's top management, including Chernomyrdin. Top managers were rumored to have received from 1% to 5% each of shares — holdings potentially worth $1.2 billion to $10 billion each.

Needing to raise cash, in 1996 Gazprom offered 1% of its stock to foreigners, the first sale of stock to foreign investors. In 1997 Gazprom and Royal Dutch/Shell formally became partners. That year Gazprom began building its Blue Stream pipeline across the Black Sea to Turkey. Italian group Eni helped back the project and became a joint partner by 1999.

In 1998 Gazprom acquired a stake in Promostroibank, Russia's fourth-largest financial institution. German energy powerhouse Ruhrgas acquired a 3% stake in Gazprom in 1998, which it increased to nearly 4% in 1999. Also in 1999 Gazprom started building its Yamal-Europe pipeline, which was to stretch to Germany for exports to Europe.

The next year an attempt by Gazprom to muscle into Hungary's chemicals sector by offering cheaper raw materials was blocked by Hungary's TVK and Borsodchem and their allies. Also in 2000 Gazprom became embroiled in a politically controversial issue when it called for the country's leading private media holding group, Media-MOST, to sell the gas giant its shares in order to settle millions of dollars of debt. Because Media-MOST held NTV television, a major critic of Russian president Vladimir Putin, the deal was alleged to have been directed by the Kremlin. A government probe into the deal was later ordered.

The alignment of Gazprom's board changed in 2000 after the annual shareholder meeting. For the first time in Gazprom's history, company managers did not have a majority of seats. A new chairman, Dimitri Medvyedev, second in command to Putin, was elected to replace Chernomyrdin.

Chairman: Dmitri Medvyedev, age 34
Deputy Chairman and Chairman, Management Committee: Rem Ivanovich Vyakhirev, age 66
First Deputy Chairman, Management Committee: Vyacheslav Vasilevich Sheremet, age 59
Deputy Chairman, Management Committee: Nikolay Nikiforovich Guslisty, age 67
Deputy Chairman, Management Committee: Aleksandr Alekseevich Pushkin, age 48
Deputy Chairman, Management Committee: Valerii Vladimirovich Remizov, age 52
Deputy Chairman, Management Committee: Pyotr Ivanovich Rodionov, age 49
Chief Accountant and Deputy Chairman, Management Committee: Irina N. Bogatyreva
Deputy Chairman, Management Committee: Segey K. Dubinin
Auditors: ZAO PricewaterhouseCooopers

LOCATIONS

HQ: 16 Nametkina, 117884 Moscow B-420, Russia
Phone: +7-095-719-3001   **Fax:** +7-095-719-8333
Web site: http://www.gazprom.ru

OAO Gazprom operates Russia's extensive gas pipeline system and delivers natural gas to 25 countries in Western and Eastern Europe, the Commonwealth of Independent States, and the Baltic states.

PRODUCTS/OPERATIONS

Selected Subsidiaries
Gazexport
Gazflot
Gazprom Finance B.V
Gazpromavia
Gazpromokhrana
Gazpromrazvitiye
Informgaz
IRTsGazprom
Kubangazprom
Lentransgaz
Mostransgaz
Nadymgazprom
Novourengoy GCC
Permtransgaz
Servicegazprom
Szhizhenny gas
Tattransgaz
Tomsktransgaz
TyumenNIIGiprogaz
Tyumentransgaz
Ulyanovskgazservice
Volgotransgaz

COMPETITORS

BP
Gasunie
LUKOIL
Sibneft
Sidanco Oil
Statoil Energy
Tatneft
Yukos

HISTORICAL FINANCIALS & EMPLOYEES

Russian FYE: December 31	Annual Growth	12/90	12/91	12/92	12/93	12/94	12/95	12/96	12/97	12/98	12/99
Sales ($ mil.)	(13.1%)	—	—	—	—	24,444	13,110	20,780	23,300	6,732	12,113
Net income ($ mil.)	—	—	—	—	—	1,782	3,217	1,682	6,509	1,105	(2,883)
Income as % of sales	—	—	—	—	—	7.3%	24.5%	8.1%	27.9%	16.4%	—
Employees	(4.1%)	—	—	—	—	367,000	375,000	398,600	362,200	278,400	298,000

Due to hyperinflation, this company is reported in US$.

1999 FISCAL YEAR-END
Debt ratio: 22.3%
Return on equity: —
Cash ($ mil.): 467
Current ratio: 0.98
Long-term debt ($ mil.): 8,487

NET INCOME HISTORY

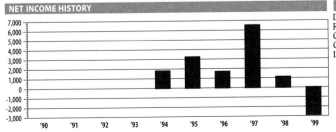

GEORGE WESTON LIMITED

George Weston Limited serves milk, cookies . . . and fish. The Toronto-based company is organized into two divisions: Loblaw Companies Limited and Weston Food Processing. More than 80% of the company's sales come from 63%-owned Loblaw, the #1 supermarket operator in Canada, with such chains as Loblaws, Provigo, and Dominion. Loblaw is also Canada's largest wholesale food distributor, supplying its own stores, franchised stores, and independent grocers. Its Weston Food business is heavily focused on the fresh and frozen baking industry in Canada and the US (including Interbake

Foods in the US), but it also runs dairy operations in Ontario and has operations that can sardines and farm salmon.

Already a strong food retailer in most Canadian provinces, Loblaw has stepped up its efforts in the lucrative Quebec market by acquiring food retailer Provigo, its largest purchase to date. Meanwhile, Weston Food has sold noncore operations, including its forest products business, and it plans to expand its bakery and biscuit operations through acquisitions.

Chairman Galen Weston controls more than 60% of George Weston.

A baker's apprentice, George Weston began delivering bread in Toronto with a single horse in 1882. He added the Model Bakery in 1896 and began making cookies and biscuits in 1908.

Upon George's death in 1924, his son Garfield took control of the company and took it public as George Weston Limited in 1928. Having popularized the premium English biscuit in Canada, Garfield acquired bakeries in the UK to make cheap biscuits (uncommon at the time). He grouped the bakeries as a separate public company called Allied Bakeries in 1935 (it later became Associated British Foods and is still controlled by the Weston family).

Expansion-minded Garfield led the company into the US with the purchase of Associated Biscuit in 1939. By the late 1930s George Weston was making cakes, breads, and almost 500 kinds of candy and biscuits.

During the 1940s the company made a number of acquisitions, including papermaker E.B. Eddy (1943), Southern Biscuit (1944), Western Grocers (1944, its first distribution company), Dietrich's Bakeries (1946), and William Neilson (1948, chocolate and dairy products).

In 1953 it acquired a controlling interest in Loblaw Groceterias, Canada's largest grocery chain. George Weston continued its acquisitions during the 1950s and 1960s, adding grocer National Tea and diversifying into packaging (Somerville Industries, 1957) and fisheries (British Columbia Packers, 1962; Conners Bros., 1967).

By 1970, when Garfield's son Galen became president, the company's holdings were in disarray. Galen brought in new managers, consolidated the food distribution and sales operations under Loblaw Companies Limited, and cut back on National Tea (which shrank from over 900

stores in 1972 to 82 in 1993). When Garfield died in 1978, Galen became chairman.

Ever since Galen, a polo-playing chum of Prince Charles, was the target of a failed kidnapping attempt by the Irish Republican Army in 1983, the family has kept a low public profile.

George Weston became the #1 chocolate maker in Canada with its purchase of Cadbury Schweppes' Canadian assets in 1987. The 1980s concluded with a five-year price war in St. Louis among its National Tea stores, Kroger, and a local grocer. This ultimately proved fruitless, as National was dismembered between Schnuck Markets and Schwegmann Giant Super Markets in 1995, ending Loblaw's US retail presence. As part of its divestiture of underachieving subsidiaries, the company sold its Neilson confectionery business back to Cadbury Schweppes in 1996 and sold its chocolate products company in 1998.

In early 1998 Loblaw set its sights on Quebec, Canada, buying Montreal-based Provigo; it also added the 80-store Agora Foods franchise supermarket unit in eastern Canada from Oshawa Group. Later George Weston acquired Oshawa Foods' Fieldfresh Farms dairy business. Also that year the company's US-based Maplehurst Bakeries purchased the frozen-bagel business of Quaker Oats, and its Stroehmann Bakeries added Pennsylvania-based Maier's Bakery. In mid-1998 George Weston sold its E.B. Eddy paper business to papermaker Domtar (giving it a 20% stake in Domtar).

The firm sold its British Columbia Packers fisheries unit in 1999 to the US's International Home Foods. In late 1999 George Weston agreed to buy Australian meat processor Don Smallgoods from Bunge International.

Chairman: W. Galen Weston, age 59, $2,400,000 pay
President (CEO); President, Loblaw: Richard J. Currie, age 62, $2,450,000 pay
CFO: Donald G. Reid, age 50, $794,266 pay
SVP Labour Relations: Roy R. Conliffe, age 49
SVP, Secretary and General Counsel: Stewart E. Green, age 55
SVP Finance: Richard P. Mavrinac, age 47
VP Legal Counsel: Michael N. Kimber, age 44
President, Weston Foods Canadian Operations: Ralph A. Robinson, age 51, $763,750 pay
President, Weston Foods US Operations: Gary J. Prince, age 48, $745,833 pay
President and CEO, Connors Bros.: Terrence McDonnell, age 62
Director of Human Resources: Sue Mackintosh
Auditors: KPMG LLP

LOCATIONS

HQ: 22 St. Clair Ave. East, Suite 1901,
Toronto, Ontario M4T 2S7, Canada
Phone: 416-922-2500   **Fax:** 416-922-7791
US HQ: 2821 Emerywood Pkwy., Ste. 210,
Richmond, VA 23294
US Phone: 804-755-7107   **US Fax:** 804-755-7173
Web site: http://www.weston.ca

George Weston Limited's Loblaw Companies Limited operates in Canada, and its Weston Foods divisions operate in Canada and the US.

1999 Sales

	C$ mil.	% of total
Canada	19,482	93
US	1,369	7
Total	**20,851**	**100**

PRODUCTS/OPERATIONS

1999 Sales

	C$ mil.	% of total
Food distribution	18,783	88
Food processing	2,578	12
Adjustments	(510)	—
Total	**20,851**	**100**

Selected Loblaw Banners

Dominion	Provigo
Fortino's Supermarkets	SuperValu
IGA	valu-mart
Loblaws	Zehrs Food Plus
Lucky Dollar	Zehrs Markets
no frills	

Selected Weston Foods Operations
Connors Bros. Ltd. (sardine and herring canning and salmon aquaculture)
Heritage Salmon (salmon aquaculture, US)
Interbake Foods Inc. (cookies and crackers, US)
Maplehurst Bakeries Inc. (frozen bakery products, US)
Neilson Dairy (milk processor, Canada)
Ready Bake Foods Inc. (frozen bakery products)
Stroehmann Bakeries LC (fresh-baked goods, US)
Weston Bakeries Ltd. (fresh-baked goods)

COMPETITORS

Campbell Soup	IGA
Canada Safeway	Interstate Bakeries
Earthgrains	Metro
Empire Company	Nabisco Holdings
Flowers Industries	Pillsbury
Goodman Fielder	Unilever

HISTORICAL FINANCIALS & EMPLOYEES

Toronto: WN FYE: December 31	Annual Growth	12/90	12/91	12/92	12/93	12/94	12/95	12/96	12/97	12/98	12/99
Sales (C$ mil.)	7.5%	10,856	10,770	11,599	11,931	13,002	12,966	12,709	13,921	14,726	20,851
Net income (C$ mil.)	12.2%	125	92	48	57	117	190	239	244	773	351
Income as % of sales	—	1.2%	0.9%	0.4%	0.5%	0.9%	1.5%	1.9%	1.8%	5.2%	1.7%
Earnings per share (C$)	13.7%	0.84	0.60	0.28	0.40	0.83	1.34	1.73	1.82	5.82	2.67
Stock price - FY high (C$)	—	14.58	15.50	13.33	15.17	14.67	16.75	22.28	41.17	60.00	65.75
Stock price - FY low (C$)	—	12.25	11.83	11.00	11.33	11.67	13.67	15.25	22.17	37.33	46.90
Stock price - FY close (C$)	16.6%	13.92	12.25	12.33	12.33	14.08	16.75	22.28	40.67	58.50	55.25
P/E - high	—	17	26	48	38	18	13	13	23	10	25
P/E - low	—	15	20	39	28	14	10	9	12	6	18
Dividends per share (C$)	8.5%	0.23	0.23	0.23	0.23	0.23	0.24	0.29	0.32	0.40	0.48
Book value per share (C$)	10.0%	8.45	8.75	9.03	9.14	9.92	11.00	11.87	13.16	18.14	19.98
Employees	7.1%	64,200	63,700	62,600	69,600	77,100	76,650	81,030	87,330	124,000	119,100

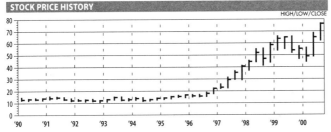

STOCK PRICE HISTORY
HIGH/LOW/CLOSE

1999 FISCAL YEAR-END
Debt ratio: 49.7%
Return on equity: 14.0%
Cash (C$ mil.): 699
Current ratio: 0.96
Long-term debt (C$ mil.): 2,584
No. of shares (mil.): 131
Dividends
  Yield: 0.0%
  Payout: 0.2%
Market value ($ mil.): 7,241

GLAXO WELLCOME PLC

OVERVIEW

Glaxo Wellcome and SmithKline Beecham have battled for the title of Britain's drug czar, but the Greenford, UK-based company and its rival will be one of the kings of the drugmaking world after their planned merger.

Glaxo produces medicines for respiratory ailments (about 30% of sales), gastrointestinal disorders, and cancer, as well as anesthetics, antibiotics, and antivirals. Patent expiration has generics claiming market share for its top sellers, herpes drug Zovirax and heartburn treatment Zantac; but Zantac still accounts for 8% of the company's sales. Other treatments include Combivir for AIDS, Ventolin for bronchial

asthma and bronchitis, Epivir HBV for hepatitis B, and Zofran for cancer treatment-induced nausea. North America accounts for about 45% of sales. Research foundation The Wellcome Trust owns about 5% of the company.

The company sees its merger with SmithKline (the new firm will be dubbed Glaxo SmithKline) as an opportunity to expand its market share, threatened as patent expirations for its more popular products leave it vulnerable to competition with generics. The two pharmas hope their combined drug pipelines will produce future winners to increase sales.

HISTORY

Englishman Joseph Nathan started an import-export business in New Zealand in 1873. He obtained the rights to a process for drying milk and began producing powdered milk in New Zealand, selling it as a baby food under the Glaxo name.

Nathan's son Alec, dispatched to London to oversee baby food sales in Britain, increased Glaxo's name recognition by publishing the *Glaxo Baby Book,* a guide to child care. After WWI, the company began distribution in India and South America.

In the 1920s Glaxo launched vitamin D-fortified formulations. It entered the pharmaceutical business with its 1927 introduction of Ostelin, a liquid vitamin D concentrate, and continued to grow globally in the 1930s, introducing Ostermilk (vitamin-fortified milk).

Glaxo began making penicillin and anesthetics during WWII; it went public in 1947. A steep drop in antibiotic prices in the mid-1950s led Glaxo to diversify; it bought veterinary, medical instrument, and drug distribution firms.

In the 1970s the British Monopolies Commission quashed both a hostile takeover attempt by Beecham and a proposed merger with retailer and drugmaker Boots. Glaxo launched US operations in 1978.

In the 1980s Glaxo shed nondrug operations to concentrate on pharmaceuticals. A 1981 marketing blitz launched antiulcer drug Zantac (to vie with SmithKline Beecham's Tagamet) in the US, where Glaxo's sales had been small. The company boosted outreach by contracting to use Hoffmann-La Roche's sales staff. The Zantac sales assault gave Glaxo leadership in US antiulcer drug sales.

Under CEO (now chairman) Sir Richard Sykes, Glaxo in 1995 made a surprise bid for UK rival Wellcome. Founded in 1880 by Americans

Silas Burroughs and Henry Wellcome to sell McKesson-Robbins' products outside the US, Burroughs Wellcome and Co. began making its own products two years later. It performed poorly until it increased funding for research and development in the 1950s. By the 1990s the company, which fostered Nobel Prize-winning researchers, led the world in antiviral medicines. Its primary drug products were Zovirax (launched 1981) and Retrovir (1987).

Though an earlier bid by Glaxo had been rejected, Sykes won the takeover by getting backing from Wellcome Trust, Wellcome's largest shareholder.

In 1997 the company formed a new genetics division, buying Spectra Biomedical and its gene variation technology. The FDA that year approved antidepressant Zyban to help smokers quit, and the company pulled diabetes drug Romozin (Rezulin in the US) from the UK market over concerns that it caused liver damage.

Glaxo in 1998 ended its joint venture with Warner-Lambert (begun in 1993), selling its former partner the Canadian and US marketing rights to acid blocker Zantac 75.

In 1999 Glaxo trimmed its product line, selling the US rights to several anesthesia products, including Ultiva. The firm also announced some 3,400 jobs (half from the UK) would be cut. Also that year Glaxo threatened to leave the UK after the National Health Service (NHS) opted not to cover antiflu inhalant Relenza, claiming the drug is not cost-effective; the NHS began to relax its position in 2000. Its antibiotic Raxar was withdrawn after seven people died after taking it.

The FDA in 2000 approved Glaxo's Lotronex for irritable bowel syndrome, but several hospitalizations linked to the drug prompted the FDA to request it be within from the American market. The company complied.

OFFICERS

Chairman: Sir Richard Sykes, age 57, $1,183,000 pay
Deputy Chairman: Roger Hurn, age 61, $60,000 pay
Chief Executive, Business Operations, Manufacturing, and Human Resources: Robert Ingram, age 57, $861,000 pay
Executive Director, Science and Technology: James E. Niedel, age 55, $568,000 pay
Executive Director, Finance and Investor Relations: John Coombe, age 54, $537,000 pay
Executive Director Legal Services, Intellectual Property, Corporate Policy, Public Affairs, and Business Development: Jeremy Strachan, age 55, $498,000 pay
Executive Director, Asia/Pacific, Latin America, Africa, and the Middle East: James Cochrane, age 55, $482,000 pay
Director Group, Medical, Regulatory, and Product Strategy: James Palmer, age 46
Director, North America: George Morrow, age 48
Director, Worldwide Human Resources: Tony Mehew
Director, Worldwide Manufacturing and Product Supply: Tim Tyson, age 47
Auditors: PricewaterhouseCoopers

LOCATIONS

HQ: Glaxo Wellcome House, Berkeley Ave., Greenford, Middlesex UB6 0NN, United Kingdom
Phone: +44-020-8966-8000   **Fax:** +44-020-8966-8330
US HQ: 499 Park Ave., New York, NY 10022
US Phone: 212-308-5186   **US Fax:** 212-308-5263
Web site: http://www.glaxowellcome.co.uk

Glaxo Wellcome has operations in Africa, Asia and the Pacific Rim, Europe, North America, and South America. Its products are sold in more than 150 countries around the world.

1999 Sales

	% of total
US	42
Europe	34
Asia/Pacific	14
Other	10
Total	**100**

PRODUCTS/OPERATIONS

1999 Sales

	% of total
Respiratory	29
Antivirals	19
Central nervous system disorders	16
Bacterial infections	10
Gastrointestinal	8
Oncology	6
Dermatologicals	3
Cardiovascular	3
Anesthesia	1
Other products	5
Total	**100**

COMPETITORS

Abbott Labs	Genentech
American Home Products	Hoffmann-La Roche
Amgen	Johnson & Johnson
AstraZeneca	Merck
Aventis	Mylan Labs
Barr Labs	Novartis
Bayer AG	Novo Nordisk A/S
Bristol-Myers Squibb	Pfizer
Chiron	Sanofi-Synthélabo
Dura Pharmaceuticals	Schering-Plough
Eli Lilly	SmithKline Beecham

HISTORICAL FINANCIALS & EMPLOYEES

NYSE: GLX FYE: December 31	Annual Growth	6/91	6/92	6/93	6/94	6/95	*12/95	12/96	12/97	12/98	12/99
Sales ($ mil.)	10.7%	5,517	7,797	7,353	8,730	10,320	15,850	14,284	13,181	13,248	13,718
Net income ($ mil.)	7.9%	1,481	1,966	1,800	2,011	1,655	3,691	3,420	3,056	3,047	2,926
Income as % of sales	—	26.8%	25.2%	24.5%	23.0%	16.0%	23.3%	23.9%	23.2%	23.0%	21.3%
Earnings per share ($)	5.6%	0.99	1.31	1.19	1.32	1.05	0.23	1.94	1.72	1.70	1.61
Stock price - FY high ($)	—	22.13	35.25	30.25	22.00	22.00	25.50	28.38	34.38	48.50	69.69	76.19
Stock price - FY low ($)	—	12.94	20.19	16.25	14.75	16.63	18.75	22.25	29.88	47.13	48.06
Stock price - FY close ($)	11.9%	20.25	25.38	16.88	16.63	24.38	28.13	31.75	47.88	69.50	55.88
P/E - high	—	22	27	25	17	24	123	18	28	41	47
P/E - low	—	13	15	14	11	16	82	11	17	28	30
Dividends per share ($)	11.1%	0.50	1.03	0.62	0.75	0.94	0.00	0.98	0.00	0.00	1.29
Book value per share ($)	(2.4%)	3.47	4.52	4.47	5.11	0.41	1.21	1.18	1.70	2.47	2.79
Employees	4.3%	—	—	—	—	—	65,702	53,808	53,068	54,350	60,726

* Fiscal year change

STOCK PRICE HISTORY

HIGH/LOW/CLOSE

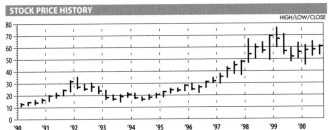

1999 FISCAL YEAR-END

Debt ratio: 28.6%
Return on equity: 61.2%
Cash ($ mil.): 351
Current ratio: 1.16
Long-term debt ($ mil.): 2,036
No. of shares (mil.): 1,820
Dividends
  Yield: 2.3%
  Payout: 80.1%
Market value ($ mil.): 101,724

GRANADA COMPASS PLC

Granada Compass (formerly Granada Group) didn't invent the TV dinner, but it does bring together dining and television programming. London-based Granada Compass is a hospitality, media, and catering conglomerate. Forte Hotels, Granada Compass' hospitality operations, includes some 500 hotels throughout the UK and in Europe. Its Heritage, Le Meridien, and Posthouse brands offer premium lodging, while its 175 unit Travelodge chain provides a budget-minded alternative. Along the UK's roadways, Granada Compass operates some 40 roadside service areas offering travelers fuel, retail stores, food, and lodging. Granada Compass also has interests in TV and VCR rental shops through a joint venture with Thorn UK.

The company's 2000 acquisition of Compass Group expanded its services in the restaurant and catering business. Granada Compass provides meals and hospitality in about 70 countries at airports, hospitals, schools, and military bases through a number of operating companies like Eurest, Bateman, Chartwells, and Canteen. It operates several licensed franchises of Burger King, Pizza Hut, and Sbarro, as well as some 4,500 company-owned eateries like Upper Crust, Ritazza, and StopGap.

Granada Media's high-profile broadcasting operations include four franchises in Britain's Independent Television Network. Yorkshire TV, Tyne Tees, and Granada operate in the north and northeast of England, while Granada Media's London Weekend Television (LWT) broadcasts in the London area, a territory it shares with rival Carlton Communications. Its stations reach nearly 50% of the viewing audience. Carlton and Granada Media also share ownership of ONdigital, the UK's start-up terrestrial digital broadcaster. Granada Sky Broadcasting, 50%-owned with British Sky Broadcasting, offers pay channels like Granada Breeze and Granada Men & Motors.

HISTORY

Granada Compass traces its roots to the Edmonton Empire, a north-London theater built by Alexander Bernstein in 1906. After Bernstein died in 1922, his sons Cecil and Sidney set up a chain of movie theaters during the 1920s and incorporated their business as Granada Theatres Ltd. in 1934. Granada went public the next year. Between 1936 and 1938, it opened a cinema every three months.

In 1955 Granada was granted a TV broadcasting license for the north of England. Changing its name to Granada Group Ltd. in 1957, the company began diversifying in the late 1950s. Granada first got into the TV rental business and later started Granada Motorway Services. By 1967 Granada was operating more than 200 TV rental showrooms nationwide and later expanded into North America. Sidney Bernstein resigned in 1979, and his nephew Alex took over as chairman.

During the 1980s, the company's TV production arm gained international acclaim with shows like *Brideshead Revisited* (1981) and *The Jewel in the Crown* (1984). In 1986 it fended off a hostile bid from rival leisure company The Rank Organisation (now The Rank Group). By the end of the 1980s, Granada had disposed of its theater operations and invested in startup British Satellite Broadcasting (later British Sky Broadcasting) in 1990. Overextended and facing a recession, Granada sold its bingo businesses in 1991.

That year chief executive Derek Lewis resigned, and Irish-born Gerry Robinson took over. The former chief of catering giant Compass Group, Robinson fired nearly all of the senior management during his first year. Under his acquisitive management, Granada bought the Sutcliffe Group, a major catering firm, from cruise operators P & O for $500 million in 1993 and the next year acquired London Weekend Television for $150 million.

Robinson replaced Bernstein as chairman in 1996, and Granada TV head Charles Allen was appointed as chief executive. Buying Forte for $6.1 billion that year added hotel operations and Little Chefs restaurants. The next year the company bought the 73% of Yorkshire Tyne Tees Television it did not already own in a deal valued at about $1.1 billion. In 1998 Granada's digital TV joint venture ONdigitial (with Carlton Communications) began broadcasting.

In 1999 the company disposed of its stake in BSkyB and acquired fish and chips chain Harry Ramsden's. A proposed merger between rivals Carlton and United News & Media that year threatened Granada's dominance in UK television. In 2000 Granada proposed its own merger with either company, temporarily derailing the deal. (It was all moot anyway when Carlton and United canceled their deal after it raised too many competition concerns.) Later that year, the company agreed to purchase hospitality firm Compass Group, and spun off its media business as Granada Media. (Granada Compass retained about 83% of the new TV company.)

Chairman: Gerry Robinson, age 51, $1,020,000 pay
Chief Executive; Chairman, Granada Media, GMTV, LWT, YTTV, Forte Hotels, Granada Restaurants and Services and Granada Technology: Charles Allen, age 42, $820,000 pay
Finance Director: Henry Staunton, age 51, $405,000 pay
Commmercial Director; Chairman, Granada Pension Scheme: Graham Parrott, age 50, $285,000 pay
Human Resources Director: Stephanie Monk, age 56, $257,000 pay
Auditors: KPMG Audit Plc

LOCATIONS

HQ: Stornoway House, 13 Cleveland Row, London SW1A 1GG, United Kingdom
Phone: +44-20-7451-3000   **Fax:** +44-20-7451-3002
Web site: http://www.granada.co.uk

1999 Sales

	£ mil.	% of total
Europe		
UK	3,732	91
Other countries	307	7
Other regions	63	2
Total	**4,102**	**100**

PRODUCTS/OPERATIONS

1999 Sales

	£ mil.	% of total
Restaurants	1,754	43
Media	998	24
Hotels	970	24
Technology	359	9
Other	21	—
Total	**4,102**	**100**

Granada Media (83%)
Broadcasting
Pay TV
Programming
Interactive

Selected Catering Operations
Bateman (health care services)
Canteen Corporation (corrections services and vending)
Chartwells (education food services)
Eurest (workplace food service contracts)
Letheby & Christopher (sporting and leisure events)
Medirest (health care services)
Restaurant Associates (sporting and leisure events)
Roux Fine Dining (executive hospitality)

Selected Hospitality Operations
Roadside Travel
  Granada Motorway Services
  Harry Ramsden's
  Little Chef
  Travelodge
Granada Food Services
  Sutcliffe Catering

Selected Hotel Chains
Le Meridien
Posthouse
Heritage

COMPETITORS

Accor
Bass
BBC
BSkyB
Carlton
  Communications
De Vere Group
Dixons Group

Flextech
Greene King
Hilton Group
HTV Group
Hyatt
NTL
Rank
Sodexho

Starwood Hotels
  & Resorts
Worldwide
Telewest
Thistle Hotels
United News &
  Media
Whitbread

HISTORICAL FINANCIALS & EMPLOYEES

London: GCP FYE: September 30	Annual Growth	9/90	9/91	9/92	9/93	9/94	9/95	9/96	9/97	9/98	9/99
Sales (£ mil.)	12.8%	1,392	1,392	1,340	1,615	2,098	2,301	3,817	4,091	4,031	4,102
Net income (£ mil.)	32.9%	67	10	77	126	192	253	294	472	557	866
Income as % of sales	—	4.8%	0.7%	5.7%	7.8%	9.2%	11.0%	7.7%	11.5%	13.8%	21.1%
Earnings per share (p)	17.1%	11.00	6.00	7.50	7.50	16.00	20.50	18.50	26.80	29.45	45.40
Stock price - FY high (p)	—	175.50	106.00	146.50	225.00	300.00	342.00	448.00	490.50	608.50	762.00
Stock price - FY low (p)	—	64.00	61.00	76.00	116.50	220.00	237.50	309.50	367.75	345.50	335.00
Stock price - FY close (p)	25.5%	67.50	83.50	131.00	225.00	254.50	317.50	428.25	438.00	375.50	520.50
P/E - high	—	16	18	20	30	19	17	24	18	21	17
P/E - low	—	6	10	10	16	14	12	17	14	12	7
Dividends per share (p)	5.4%	6.00	3.50	4.00	4.50	5.00	4.00	6.50	7.25	8.35	9.60
Book value per share (p)	4.3%	85.00	85.00	65.00	50.00	45.00	50.00	60.00	69.64	88.75	124.01
Employees	13.5%	25,257	22,562	18,385	28,025	42,878	39,085	66,850	70,538	72,293	78,871

STOCK PRICE HISTORY

HIGH/LOW/CLOSE

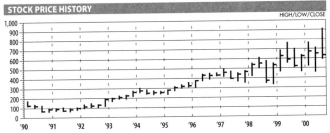

1999 FISCAL YEAR-END

Debt ratio: 45.7%
Return on equity: 44.6%
Cash (£ mil.): 323
Current ratio: 0.75
Long-term debt (£ mil.): 1,928
No. of shares (mil.): 1,847
Dividends
  Yield: 0.0%
  Payout: 0.2%
Market value ($ mil.): 1,583,440
Sales ($ mil.): 6,755

GUCCI GROUP N.V.

OVERVIEW

For a while it looked like Gucci Group was going to hell in a black patent leather handbag. Sales were as skimpy as chiffon, and imprudent licensing had sheared away its control of the Gucci brand. But the Amsterdam-based Italian fashion house has been stunningly reclad by president and CEO Domenico De Sole, an Italian educated at Harvard Law School, and creative director Tom Ford, a Texan whose designs have consistently received industry raves.

Gucci is known for products sporting the company's famous interlocking-G logo, including handbags and other leather goods (about 40% of sales), shoes, ties, scarves, watches, jewelry, eyewear, and perfume. It also designs women's and men's ready-to-wear clothing. Company-owned and franchised Gucci stores operate worldwide; about 40% of Gucci's sales come from Asia. The company almost doubled its size with the 1999 purchase of Sanofi Beaute, which included most of French fashion house Yves Saint Laurent.

At least as intriguing as Gucci's fortunes has been the question of its control. Retailer and catalog company Pinault-Printemps-Redoute owns 42% of Gucci, while luxury rival LVMH owns at least 20%.

HISTORY

Guccio Gucci began his leather goods business in Florence, Italy, in 1923, later fabricating a pedigree that said the family had been saddlemakers to Florence's aristocrats. In 1935 Gucci Group's leather supply was cut off when the League of Nations sanctioned Italy after Mussolini's invasion of Ethiopia. Gucci turned to making canvas bags trimmed with Italian leather.

By the 1950s such luminaries as Grace Kelly, Elizabeth Taylor, and Queen Elizabeth patronized Gucci shops. The first American Gucci shop opened in New York in 1953. With Guccio's death that year, the company's reins passed to son Aldo, who turned the Gucci name into a global fashion brand. Through licensing, Aldo put his family's name on thousands of items. In 1974 the company launched its men's and women's ready-to-wear lines.

By the mid-1980s Gucci was struggling. Family tensions had arisen when Aldo's son Paolo set out to sell products under the Paolo Gucci name; he was allegedly beaten at a Gucci board meeting. In 1983 Aldo's brother Rodolfo died, leaving his 50% stake in Gucci to son Maurizio, setting up a feud worthy of Italian opera. Paolo charged his father with tax evasion, and Aldo was forced out in 1984 and later sentenced to prison. Aldo and son Roberto accused Maurizio of forgery, but his one-year jail sentence on fraud charges was overturned.

The Aldo faction sold its half of Gucci in 1987 to Bahrain-based Investcorp, which had backed the buyout of Tiffany & Co. a few years earlier.

Maurizio took Gucci's helm in 1989. To give Gucci goods more cache, he reined in the rampant licensing of the Gucci name — it had appeared on everything from key chains to scotch — and reduced the number of outlets selling Gucci items. As a result, cash flow dwindled, and amid a global recession, Gucci lost money.

In 1993 Investcorp bought out Maurizio, the last remaining Gucci involved in the company. (Maurizio was murdered in 1995; his ex-wife and four others were convicted in the slaying.)

Investcorp named Gucci America chief Domenico De Sole president in 1994. De Sole turned Gucci around with the help of Tom Ford, a Gucci designer since 1990. Investcorp took Gucci public in 1995 and sold the rest of its stake in 1996.

Italian fashion house Prada revealed in 1998 that it had acquired a 9.5% stake in Gucci. Prada sold its stake to LVMH in early 1999 as the French luxury goods kingpin quickly accumulated Gucci shares. Gucci issued millions of new shares in order to dilute LVMH's stake from 34% to 26%. LVMH promptly sued to block the move but was unsuccessful.

Another player got involved in March 1999: Pinault-Printemps-Redoute. With Gucci's approval, the French retailer and catalog firm paid $2.9 billion for more than 40% of the company. (Gucci again issued new shares, diluting LVMH's stake.)

Mais non, said LVMH, which immediately made an offer to buy all of Gucci. Gucci rejected LVMH's $8.25 billion bid, and LVMH continued to challenge the Pinault-Printemps-Redoute deal in court. Gucci bought Sanofi Beaute for about $960 million in late 1999. The deal included Yves Saint Laurent's (YSL) non-couture business and such fragrances as Oscar de la Renta. Days later the company purchased 70% of Italian shoemaker Calzaturificio Sergio Rossi.

In 2000 Gucci upped the ante in its rivalry with LVMH when it said it would buy Swiss luxury firm Boucheron (jewelry, watches, and fragrances) for $144.8 million.

Chairman, President, and CEO: Domenico De Sole
EVP and CFO: Robert Singer
EVP, Director of Strategy and Acquisitions:
James McArthur
VP: Massimo Macchi
President, Gucci America: Patricia Malone
President, Gucci Division: Brian Blake
President, YSL Beaute: Chantal Roos
Group Controller: Riccardo Galardi
Creative Director: Tom Ford
Director, Corporate Communications: Tomaso Galli
Director, E-Business: Richard Swanson
Director, Human Resources: Renato Ricci
Director, Investor Relations and Corporate
Development: Cedric Magnelia
General Counsel: Allan Tuttle
Auditors: PricewaterhouseCoopers N.V.

LOCATIONS

HQ: Rembrandt Tower, 1 Amstelplein,
1096 HA Amsterdam, The Netherlands
Phone: +31-20-462-1700   **Fax:** +31-20-465-3569
US HQ: 50 Hartz Way, Secaucus, NJ 07094
US Phone: 201-867-8800   **US Fax:** 201-392-2679
Web site: http://www.gucci.com

Gucci Group's major markets are Asia (especially Japan), Europe, and the US.

PRODUCTS/OPERATIONS

Major Products
Eyewear
Gifts
Jewelry
Leather goods
Perfume
Ready-to-wear apparel
Scarves
Shoes
Ties
Watches

COMPETITORS

AnnTaylor	Jil Sander
Armani	Jones Apparel
Bally	Kenneth Cole
Calvin Klein	Liz Claiborne
Chanel	LVMH
Christian Dior	Phillips-Van Heusen
Donna Karan	Polo
Escada	Prada
Etienne Aigner	Rolex
Gianni Versace	Tiffany
Hermès	Tommy Hilfiger
Hugo Boss	Yves Saint-Laurent Groupe

HISTORICAL FINANCIALS & EMPLOYEES

NYSE: GUC FYE: January 31	Annual Growth	1/91	1/92	1/93	1/94	1/95	1/96	1/97	1/98	1/99	1/00
Sales ($ mil.)	35.1%	—	—	—	203	264	500	881	975	1,043	1,236
Net income ($ mil.)	—	—	—	—	(22)	18	83	168	176	195	330
Income as % of sales	—	—	—	—	—	6.8%	16.6%	19.1%	18.0%	18.7%	26.7%
Earnings per share ($)	20.0%	—	—	—	—	—	1.68	2.76	2.86	3.28	3.48
Stock price - FY high ($)	—	—	—	—	—	—	42.00	80.50	77.88	75.25	121.50
Stock price - FY low ($)	—	—	—	—	—	—	25.63	39.38	28.75	31.50	61.00
Stock price - FY close ($)	27.3%	—	—	—	—	—	40.63	69.75	39.81	68.81	106.81
P/E - high	—	—	—	—	—	—	0	0	27	23	34
P/E - low	—	—	—	—	—	—	0	0	10	9	17
Dividends per share ($)	—	—	—	—	—	—	0.00	0.30	0.30	0.40	0.40
Book value per share ($)	89.8%	—	—	—	—	—	2.98	5.48	7.52	9.86	38.71
Employees	14.7%	—	—	—	1,157	1,176	1,504	1,954	2,000	—	

STOCK PRICE HISTORY

High/Low/Close

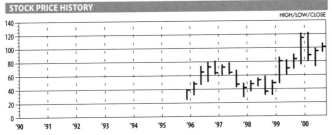

2000 FISCAL YEAR-END

Debt ratio: 3.6%
Return on equity: 14.9%
Cash ($ mil.): 2,948
Current ratio: 3.53
Long-term debt ($ mil.): 143
No. of shares (mil.): 100
Dividends
  Yield: 0.4%
  Payout: 11.5%
Market value ($ mil.): 10,654

HANSON PLC

Breaking rocks in the hot sun is no punishment for Hanson. The London-based company is what's left of the Hanson Group — once a huge industrial conglomerate before it broke off into four separate yet publicly traded enterprises involving tobacco, coal, chemicals, and timber.

The "new" Hanson produces building materials. Its Hanson Building Materials America unit operates building-materials businesses in the US and Canada. Its Hanson Quarry Products Europe is a leading UK producer of aggregates and concrete products, and operates landfills and a marine aggregates dredging business. Hanson Pacific has quarries and aggregate plants in Malaysia, the Philippines, and Singapore. Hanson Bricks Europe is a leading UK brickmaker.

Hanson has bought a dozen businesses in North America to take advantage of the fragmented building-materials industry in the US. The company is also growing in Australia with the purchase of ready-mix concrete, aggregates and cement company Pioneer International.

HISTORY

In the 1950s and 1960s James Hanson and Gordon White were British *bon vivants*. Hanson was once engaged to Audrey Hepburn, and White dated Joan Collins. However, they later became better known as sharp businessmen.

Through the Wiles Group, a fertilizer business they took over in 1964, Hanson and White sought poorly managed companies in mature industries at low prices. Within 10 years Hanson and White had collected 24 such businesses with sales in excess of $120 million.

Perceiving an antibusiness attitude in the UK, White formed a New York subsidiary, Hanson Industries, in 1973. He made his first American purchase in 1974, buying Seacoast (animal feed). Other purchases in hot dogs, shoes, and batteries followed, including conglomerate US Industries in 1984. That year the company acquired leading UK brick maker London Brick.

In bitterly fought hostile takeovers in 1986, Hanson acquired SCM (Smith-Corona office equipment, Glidden Paints, Durkee's Famous Foods, SCM Chemicals) and Imperial Group (cigarettes, beer, food, hotels, restaurants). It acquired US cement maker Kaiser Cement in 1987. The company changed its name to Hanson PLC that year.

Hanson acquired Peabody (coal) in 1990 and Beazer PLC, a UK construction firm with extensive US holdings, a year later. During 1992 the company sold a number of assets; the next year it bought Quantum Chemicals (propane distribution) for $3.4 billion. Hanson took Beazer Homes (home building materials, US) public in 1994, retaining 30%.

In 1995 the company spun off some of its US operations as U.S. Industries and sold its 62% stake in Suburban Propane, a major US propane distributor. It also reorganized Beazer's US operations as Cornerstone Construction & Materials. Timber business

Willamette bought 1.1 million acres of Hanson timberland in the US for $1.6 billion. Hanson also merged its Butterley Brick and London Brick into one company, Hanson Brick. Also in 1995 founder White died.

The Hanson conglomerate in 1996 began to split up its operations, creating four separate public companies focused on chemicals (Millennium Chemicals), tobacco (Imperial Tobacco), energy (Energy Group PLC), and building materials and equipment (Hanson PLC). In 1997 Cornerstone Construction & Materials acquired Concrete Pipe and Products. James Hanson retired that year.

Joining the consolidation of the US building-materials sector, Hanson bought six US firms in 1998 — HG Fenton (aggregates and ready-mix concrete), Becker Minerals (aggregates), Condux (concrete pipe), Gifford-Hill American (aggregates), and Nelson & Sloan (aggregates and ready-mix concrete). Also that year the company paid $155 million to settle environmental liabilities inherited when it purchased Koppers Company in 1991.

In 1999 Hanson sold Grove Worldwide — a world-leading maker of cranes and materials-handling equipment — to Robert Bass' investment firm, Keystone, and also sold its 24% stake in Westralian Sands Ltd. (titanium and zircon, Australia). Hanson bought the North American brick business of Canada-based Jannock for $258 million and launched a $2.5 billion bid for Australia's Pioneer International (completed in 2000). Late in 1999 Hanson further bolstered its US aggregates operations by purchasing San Francisco (Jones Sand) and North Carolina (Brewer Sand) sand businesses.

The company's acquisitions in 2000 included US concrete pipe and products makers Joelson Taylor, Cincinnati Concrete Pipe, and Milan Concrete Products.

Chairman: Christopher Collins, age 60
Chief Executive: Andrew J. H. Dougal, age 48,
$450,000 pay
Finance Director: Jonathan Nicholls, age 42,
$337,000 pay
Legal Director: Graham Dransfield, age 48, $405,000 pay
Chief Executive, Hanson Australia: Mike Ogden
Chief Executive, Hanson Building Materials America:
Alan Murray, age 46, $556,000 pay
Chief Executive, Hanson Bricks Europe:
Richard Manning
Chief Executive, Hanson Pacific: Hugh Winokur
Chief Executive, Hanson Quarry Products Europe:
Simon Vivian, age 42, $216,000 pay
Secretary: Paul Tunnacliffe
Financial Controller: Ian Peters
Auditors: Ernst & Young

LOCATIONS

HQ: 1 Grosvenor Place,
London SW1X 7JH, United Kingdom
Phone: +44-20-7245-1245   **Fax:** +44-20-7235-3455
US HQ: Monmouth Shores Corporate Park,
Neptune, NJ 07753
US Phone: 732-919-9777   **US Fax:** 732-919-1149
Web site: http://www.hansonplc.com

Hanson has manufacturing plants in Australia, Canada, Europe, Malaysia, the Philippines, and Singapore.

1999 Sales

	$ mil.	% of total
North America	1,736	56
UK	1,171	38
Other countries	196	6
Total	**3,103**	**100**

PRODUCTS/OPERATIONS

1999 Sales

	$ mil.	% of total
Hanson Building Materials	1,736	56
Hanson Quarry Products	977	32
Hanson Bricks Europe	335	11
Other operations	55	1
Total	**3,103**	**100**

Operating Businesses

Hanson Building Materials America
Hanson Aggregates
Hanson Bricks America
Hanson Pipe & Products

Hanson Quarry Products Europe
Hanson Aggregates
Hanson Concrete Products
Hanson Waste Management and Recycling

Hanson Bricks Europe
Hanson Brick UK
Hanson Baksteen Nederland
Hanson Desimpel
Hanson Klinker Deutschland

COMPETITORS

BayWa
Blue Circle Industries
Heidelberger Zement
Lafarge SA
Martin Marietta Materials
Readymix
Tarmac
Vulcan Materials

HISTORICAL FINANCIALS & EMPLOYEES

NYSE: HAN FYE: December 31	Annual Growth	12/90	12/91	12/92	12/93	12/94	12/95	12/96	12/97	12/98	12/99
Sales ($ mil.)	(15.0%)	13,412	13,467	15,638	14,467	17,655	17,673	3,995	4,993	3,029	3,103
Net income ($ mil.)	(12.9%)	1,875	1,937	1,936	1,098	1,679	1,604	496	1,286	589	540
Income as % of sales	—	14.0%	14.4%	12.4%	7.6%	9.5%	9.1%	12.4%	25.8%	19.4%	17.4%
Earnings per share ($)	(35.5%)	—	—	—	—	—	—	—	9.88	4.51	4.11
Stock price - FY high ($)	—	—	—	—	—	—	—	—	27.00	41.88	50.94
Stock price - FY low ($)	—	—	—	—	—	—	—	—	22.00	20.81	31.88
Stock price - FY close ($)	32.4%	—	—	—	—	—	—	—	23.00	39.00	40.31
P/E - high	—	—	—	—	—	—	—	—	6	14	16
P/E - low	—	—	—	—	—	—	—	—	5	7	10
Dividends per share ($)	—	—	—	—	—	—	—	—	0.00	0.42	2.59
Book value per share ($)	43.5%	—	—	—	—	—	—	—	11.11	19.60	22.89
Employees	(15.9%)	80,000	70,000	75,000	80,000	74,000	75,000	76,000	80,000	16,000	16,800

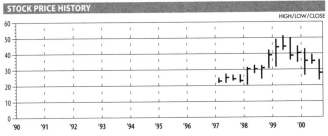

STOCK PRICE HISTORY
HIGH/LOW/CLOSE

1999 FISCAL YEAR-END

Debt ratio: 35.3%
Return on equity: 19.5%
Cash ($ mil.): 2,095
Current ratio: 1.59
Long-term debt ($ mil.): 1,625
No. of shares (mil.): 130
Dividends
  Yield: 6.4%
  Payout: 63.0%
Market value ($ mil.): 5,256

HEINEKEN N.V.

OVERVIEW

"Think global, drink local" could be the motto for Heineken. Based in Amsterdam, Heineken is the world's #2 brewer (after Anheuser-Busch). It sells its beverages in more countries than any other — 170 — thanks in part to its slew of regional and national breweries. Bubbling up is its eponymous malt, the top beer in Europe (where the company rings up about 70% of its sales). Heineken is the #2 imported beer in the US (behind Corona from Grupo Modelo, which tapped the #1 spot after nearly 65 years of Heineken dominance). In addition to Heineken, its international brands are Amstel (#2 in Europe, after Heineken) and Murphy's Irish Stout. The company also distributes soft drinks (Pepsi) in addition to other nonalcoholic beverages in the Netherlands.

Heineken has solidified its European base by buying breweries in central Europe, Italy, and Spain. The company plans to grow steadily in new markets such as Asia and South America; political unrest has impeded its growth in Africa.

The founding Heineken family owns 50% of Heineken Holding, which, in turn, owns 50% of Heineken.

HISTORY

Every Sunday morning Gerard Heineken's mother was appalled by crowds of drunken Dutchmen who had consumed too much gin the night before. Heineken, who wanted his mother's financial backing, insisted that drunkenness would decrease if people drank beer instead of gin and pointed out that there were no good beers in Holland. His strategy worked. In 1863 Heineken's mother put up the money to buy De Hooiberg (The Haystack), a 271-year-old brewery in Amsterdam.

Gerard proved his aptitude for brewing and within 10 years had established a brewery in Rotterdam. He named his brewery Heineken in 1873 and launched the company's lucrative foreign trade by exporting beer first to France three years later. (By the 1950s half the beer brewed by the company was for export.) The company perfected the yeast strain (Heineken A-yeast) in 1886 that it still uses in its beer today.

In 1917 Gerard's son Dr. Henri Pierre Heineken inherited the firm and decided to expand operations to the US, making a voyage to that country himself. While at sea, Henri Pierre met Leo van Munching, a ship's bartender who displayed a remarkable knowledge of beer. Recognizing van Munching's talent, Henri Pierre hired him as Heineken's US importer. Prohibition killed the US operations, although the company entered new markets elsewhere; after repeal, Heineken was the first foreign beer to reenter the US market.

After WWII, Henri Pierre sent his son, Alfred, to learn the business under van Munching, who had created a national distribution system in the US. Alfred succeeded his father in 1953 and stepped down in 1989.

Heineken bought the Amstel Brewery in Holland (founded 1870) in 1968. Two years later it became a producer of stout through the acquisition of James J. Murphy in Cork, Ireland.

Facing a consolidation of the European market, Heineken launched a campaign in the 1980s to expand its European beer operations, purchasing breweries in France, Greece, Ireland, Italy, and Spain.

In 1991 Heineken bought the van Munching US import business and a majority interest in Hungarian brewer Komaromi Sorgyar, its first Eastern European investment. Two years later Karel Vuursteen was appointed chairman.

The firm cut over 1,300 jobs in 1993 and then overcame its first-ever labor dispute in 1994. The company also sold its spirits and wine operations that year. In 1995 Heineken began a major spending spree, acquiring Interbrew Italia and 66% of Zlaty Bazant, the largest Slovakian brewery and maltworks. (It acquired the rest in 1999.) The company bought Birra Moretti, Italy's third-largest brewery, in 1996. It also purchased interests in two African breweries.

To boost its sales in Poland, in 1998 Heineken raised its stake in brewer Zaklady Piwowarskie W. Zywcu (Zywiec) to 75%, bought a minority stake in Brewpole, and merged the companies to create the #1 Polish brewer. Tragedy struck its Rwandan beer subsidiary in 1998 when Hutu rebels massacred more than 30 employees on a bus on their way to work.

Also in 1998 Heineken bought about 25% of Pivara Skopje, the largest brewery in the former Yugoslav republic of Macedonia, through its Brewinvest joint venture. In 1999 the brewer bought about 18% of Israel's leading brewer, Tempo (Goldstar and Maccabee beers).

In January 2000 Heineken bought Diageo's 88% stake in Spanish brewer Cruzcampo and later upped its ownership to almost 99%. Cruzcampo was merged with Heineken's Spanish brewer El Aguila in June to create Heineken España.

Chairman, Supervisory Board: Robert Hazelhoff
Chairman, Executive Board: Karel Vuursteen
VC, Executive Board: Anthony Ruys
Member, Executive Board: S. W. W. Lubsen
President and CEO, Heineken USA:
  Frank Van der Minne
Auditors: KPMG Accountants N.V.

LOCATIONS

HQ: Tweede Weteringplantsoen 21,
  1017 ZD Amsterdam, The Netherlands
Phone: +31-20-523-92-39   **Fax:** +31-20-626-35-03
US HQ: 50 Main St., White Plains, NY 10606
US Phone: 914-681-4100   **US Fax:** 914-681-4110
Web site: http://www.heinekencorp.nl

Heineken has more than 110 breweries in more than 50
countries and sells its products in over 170 countries.

1999 Sales

	$ mil.	% of total
Europe		
The Netherlands	1,068	15
Other countries	4,046	56
Western Hemisphere	899	13
Asia/Pacific	735	10
Africa	312	4
Adjustments	122	2
Total	**7,182**	**100**

PRODUCTS/OPERATIONS

Selected Beer Brands

33 Export	Maccabee
Aguila	Moretti
Amstel	Murphy's
Buckler	Piton
Cruzcampo	Primus
Dreher	Quilmes
EB	Star
Fischer	Tiger
Goldstar	Vos
Guinness (licensed)	Warka
Heineken	Wieckse Witte
Ichnusa	Zagorka
Kaiser	Zywiec

COMPETITORS

Adolph Coors	Gambrinus
Allied Domecq	Grolsch
Ambev	Grupo Modelo
Anheuser-Busch	Guinness/UDV
Asahi Breweries	Interbrew
Bass Brewers	Kirin
Bavaria S.A.	Lion Nathan
Boston Beer	Miller Brewing
Brauerei BECK	Molson
Carlsberg	San Miguel
Cervecerias Unidas	Scottish & Newcastle
Constellation Brands	South African Breweries
FEMSA	Taiwan Tobacco & Wine
Foster's Brewing	Whitbread

HISTORICAL FINANCIALS & EMPLOYEES

OTC: HINKY FYE: December 31	Annual Growth	12/90	12/91	12/92	12/93	12/94	12/95	12/96	12/97	12/98	12/99
Sales ($ mil.)	4.4%	4,861	5,078	4,918	4,647	5,751	6,492	7,052	6,668	7,361	7,182
Net income ($ mil.)	10.2%	217	239	255	267	382	413	379	376	522	519
Income as % of sales	—	4.5%	4.7%	5.2%	5.7%	6.6%	6.4%	5.4%	5.6%	7.1%	7.2%
Earnings per share ($)	10.2%	0.69	0.76	0.81	0.85	1.11	1.32	1.21	1.37	1.66	1.66
Stock price - FY high ($)	—	8.35	9.37	13.96	14.65	19.29	29.19	37.36	29.92	60.75	68.00
Stock price - FY low ($)	—	5.63	7.39	9.07	10.11	13.79	18.88	27.36	24.00	27.76	43.50
Stock price - FY close ($)	21.7%	8.26	9.37	12.14	14.53	19.29	28.41	28.32	27.76	60.00	48.50
P/E - high	—	12	12	17	17	17	22	31	22	37	41
P/E - low	—	8	10	11	12	12	14	23	18	17	26
Dividends per share ($)	7.4%	0.21	0.21	0.25	0.23	0.26	0.35	0.32	0.32	0.37	0.40
Book value per share ($)	5.0%	5.94	6.26	6.40	6.51	8.00	9.39	8.33	8.03	8.60	9.18
Employees	2.7%	28,908	27,502	25,320	23,997	26,197	27,379	31,682	32,421	33,511	36,733

STOCK PRICE HISTORY

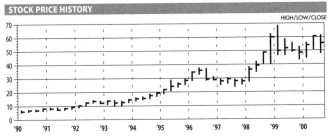

HIGH/LOW/CLOSE

1999 FISCAL YEAR-END

Debt ratio: 14.6%
Return on equity: 18.6%
Cash ($ mil.): 1,171
Current ratio: 1.40
Long-term debt ($ mil.): 492
No. of shares (mil.): 314
Dividends
  Yield: 0.0%
  Payout: 0.2%
Market value ($ mil.): 15,209

HENKEL KGAA

OVERVIEW

Henkel is cleaning up by sticking with a winning formula: combining cleaning products, adhesives, and cosmetics into a multibillion-dollar business. Based in Düsseldorf, Henkel is one of Germany's largest chemical companies. Operating about 340 companies in more than 70 countries, Henkel is the global leader in the production of oleochemicals, adhesives, and surface technologies and is also one of Europe's major producers of detergents, fabric softeners, and household cleaning products. The founding Henkel family still controls the company.

Henkel plans to spin off its chemicals-making subsidiary under the name Cognis, or partner it with another chemical company in a joint venture. As part of its strategy of focusing on detergents and household cleaner, the company has also agreed to sell its plant care operations (Substral).

HISTORY

In 1876 Fritz Henkel, a chemical plant worker, started Henkel & Cie in Aachen to make a universal detergent. Henkel moved the company to Düsseldorf in 1878 and launched Henkel's Bleaching Soda, one of Germany's first brand-name products. In the 1880s the company began making water glass, an ingredient of its detergent, which differs from soap in the way it emulsifies dirt. Henkel debuted Persil, a detergent that eliminated the need for rubbing or bleaching clothes, in 1907. Persil became a leading detergent in Germany.

Henkel set up an Austrian subsidiary in 1913. In response to a postwar adhesives shortage, the company started making glue for its own packaging and soon became Europe's leading glue maker. Henkel began making cleansers with newly developed phosphates in the late 1920s.

When Fritz died in 1930, Henkel stock was divided among his three children. In the 1930s the company sponsored a whaling fleet that provided fats for its products, and by 1939 the firm had 16 plants in Europe.

During WWII Henkel lost most of its foreign plants and made unbranded soap in Germany. After the war the company retooled its plants, branched out into personal care products, and competed with Unilever, Procter & Gamble, and Colgate-Palmolive for control of the German detergent market. (By 1968 Henkel dominated, with a nearly 50% share.)

In 1960 Henkel bought its first US company, Standard Chemicals (renamed Henkel Corp. in 1971). Konrad Henkel, who took over in 1961, modernized the company's image by making changes in management structure and marketing techniques. Henkel patented a substitute for environmentally harmful phosphates, acquired 15% of Clorox in 1974, and bought General Mills' chemical business in 1977.

Henkel, owned at the time by 66 family members, went public with nonvoting shares in 1985. It bought US companies Nopco (specialty chemicals) and Parker Chemical (metal surface pretreatment) in 1987 and Emery, the #1 US oleochemicals maker, in 1989.

Henkel reorganized its product lines in 1991 by selling several noncore businesses. It built plants in the growing US and Asian markets and trimmed facilities in Germany, where high pay and benefit levels made production less profitable. That year Henkel formed a partnership with Ecolab (of which it owned 24%); acquired interests in Hungary, Poland, Russia, and Slovenia; and introduced Persil in Spain and Portugal. In 1994 Henkel expanded into China and bought 25% of a Brazilian detergent maker. These acquisitions left the company bloated, leading it to close plants and cut jobs.

The company continued its expansion in 1995 when it acquired Hans Schwarzkopf GmbH; the purchase made Henkel the #1 hair-coloring manufacturer in Germany. The company bought Novamax Technologies, a US-based maker of metal-surface treatments, in 1996. The next year Henkel paid $1.3 billion for US adhesive giant Loctite, its biggest purchase to date. In 1998 it bought Ohio-based adhesives maker Manco. Henkel pushed into the US toiletries market in 1998 by paying $93 million for DEP and creating a new subsidiary, Schwarzkopf & DEP Inc.

In 1999 Henkel created a new chemicals unit, Cognis, to focus primarily on palm kernel- and coconut oil-based products. To strengthen Cognis, Henkel bought Laboratoires Serobiologiques, a French producer of ingredients for the cosmetic and food industries, and divested specialty paper chemicals operations. Henkel also formed a joint venture with soap maker Dial (Dial/Henkel LLC); the joint venture later bought the Custom Cleaner home dry cleaning business from Creative Products Resource.

Henkel picked up Yamahatsu Sangyo, a Japanese maker of hair colorants, in 2000.

Chairman: Albrecht Woeste
VC and Chairman of the Works Council:
  Winfried Zander
President and CEO: Hans-Dietrich Winkhaus
Deputy Chief Executive Officer: Ulrich Lehner
EVP Adhesives: Guido De Keersmaecker, age 57
EVP Cosmetics and Toiletries: Uwe Specht, age 56
EVP Detergents and Household Cleaners:
  Klaus Morwind, age 56
EVP Finance and Logistics: Jochen Krautter, age 57
EVP Industrial and Institutional Hygiene, Surface
  Technologies, and Human Resources: Roland Schulz
President and CEO, Henkel Corporation (US):
  Robert Lurcott
Auditors: KPMG Deutsche Treuhand-Gesellschaft

HQ: Henkelstr. 67, D-40191 Düsseldorf, Germany
Phone: +49-211-797-3533   **Fax:** +49-211-798-4040
US HQ: 2200 Renaissance Blvd., Ste. 200,
  Gulph Mills, PA 19406
US Phone: 610-270-8100   **US Fax:** 610-270-8165
Web site: http://www.henkel.com/intl

1999 Sales

	$ mil.	% of total
Europe		
Germany	3,063	27
Other countries	4,933	43
North America	1,901	17
Asia & Australia	930	8
Latin America	448	4
Africa	141	1
Total	**11,416**	**100**

1999 Sales

	$ mil.	% of total
Chemical products	2,618	23
Detergents & household cleaners	2,586	22
Adhesives	2,513	22
Cosmetics & toiletries	1,823	16
Industrial & institutional hygiene & surface technologies	1,777	16
Other	99	1
Total	**11,416**	**100**

Selected Products

Bath and shower products	Industrial and packaging adhesives
Bath and toilet cleansers	
Consumer and craftsmen adhesives	Inorganic products
	Oleochemicals
Dental care and oral hygiene products	Organic specialty chemicals
Hair salon products	Perfumes and fragrances
Household cleansers	

3M	Crompton	L'Oréal USA
Akzo Nobel	Degussa-Huls	MacAndrews
Alusuisse Lonza	Dial	& Forbes
American Home Products	Dow Chemical	PPG
	DuPont	Procter
ATOFINA	Estée Lauder	& Gamble
Avon	H.B. Fuller	Rohm and Haas
BASF AG	Hercules	S.C. Johnson
Bayer AG	ICI Americas	Shiseido
Beiersdorf	Illinois Tool	Unilever
BFGoodrich	Works	
Colgate-Palmolive	Koor	
	L'Oréal	

OTC: HENKY FYE: December 31	Annual Growth	12/90	12/91	12/92	12/93	12/94	12/95	12/96	12/97	12/98	12/99
Sales ($ mil.)	4.0%	8,027	8,490	8,698	7,975	9,080	9,875	10,575	11,155	12,802	11,416
Net income ($ mil.)	3.9%	287	291	248	221	299	339	334	348	436	406
Income as % of sales	—	3.6%	3.4%	2.9%	2.8%	3.3%	3.4%	3.2%	3.1%	3.4%	3.6%
Earnings per share ($)	(8.8%)	—	—	—	—	—	—	—	2.97	3.75	2.47
Stock price - FY high ($)	—	—	—	—	—	—	—	—	58.00	91.00	88.00
Stock price - FY low ($)	—	—	—	—	—	—	—	—	48.00	52.63	55.00
Stock price - FY close ($)	(0.8%)	—	—	—	—	—	—	—	56.63	80.50	55.75
P/E - high	—	—	—	—	—	—	—	—	20	24	36
P/E - low	—	—	—	—	—	—	—	—	16	14	22
Dividends per share ($)	7.7%	—	—	—	—	—	—	—	0.75	0.93	0.87
Book value per share ($)	7.3%	—	—	—	—	—	—	—	19.33	20.66	22.27
Employees	4.3%	38,803	41,475	42,244	40,480	40,590	41,664	46,665	53,753	56,291	56,600

HIGH/LOW/CLOSE

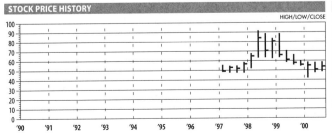

Debt ratio: 15.4%
Return on equity: 12.9%
Cash ($ mil.): 142
Current ratio: —
Long-term debt ($ mil.): 590
No. of shares (mil.): 146
Dividends
  Yield: 0.0%
  Payout: 0.4%
Market value ($ mil.): 8,139

HILTON GROUP PLC

OVERVIEW

Hilton Group (formerly Ladbroke) knows how to cover its bets, as well as its beds. The Watford, UK-based gambling and hotel company is the UK's #1 operator of betting shops (more than 2,000), offering live, online, and telephone betting on a variety of events including cricket, soccer, football, rugby, greyhound racing, and golf. In addition, Hilton Group offers offtrack and telephone betting, casinos, bingo, and slot machine arcades in Belgium, Latin America, the Middle East, the UK, and the US, although it is selling its non-European gambling operations.

Hilton Group's other major business line is, naturally, hotels: It holds the exclusive rights to the Hilton Hotel name outside the US. The company's Hilton International unit, which operates more than 220 hotels in more than 50 countries, accounts for about one-fourth of the group's revenues. (The company adopted the Hilton name in 1999 in an effort to strengthen its ties with the US hotelier.) It is expanding, opening about a dozen hotels a year largely in Europe.

HISTORY

The Hilton Group has its origins in the late 1800s in the village of Ladbroke in central England, where a local racehorse trainer and his friend set up a partnership as commission agents to take bets on horse races. Although betting was illegal, it was allowed on an unofficial basis, and by 1900 the partnership had established itself in London's plush West End.

Ladbroke and Co. was sold to a business group, Beaver Holdings, in 1956. Cyril Stein, who would lead the company for more than three decades, joined the consortium in 1956 and was soon appointed managing director. He became chairman in 1966.

The group kept a fairly low profile until the legalization of offtrack betting gave the company impetus to expand. By the time Ladbroke Group went public in 1967, it had 109 offtrack betting shops in operation. By 1971 there were 660 licensed "Ladbrokes" betting shops around Britain.

Stein steered the company on a diversification course during the 1970s and 1980s. In 1972 it acquired the London & Leeds Development Corporation, a real estate company with projects in Amsterdam, Brussels, Paris, and the eastern US. It also established four real estate companies in the UK.

Ladbroke ventured into the hotel business with the purchase of three British hotels in 1973. In the late 1970s the company suffered a major setback when its casino ventures in London were closed down and it was taken to court. Found guilty of violating government gaming laws, the firm abandoned the casino business in 1979.

In 1984 the company bought the Belgian Le Tierce betting shop chain. It broke into the US market in 1985 with the acquisition of the Detroit Race Course.

Ladbroke beat out competitors to buy the

91-hotel Hilton International chain from Allegis Corporation for more than $1 billion in 1987. This purchase made Ladbroke one of the world's top hotel operators.

The company expanded its gaming operations with the 1989 purchase of the Vernons football (soccer) pools concern, one of only two such operators in the UK market.

Ladbroke re-entered the casino business in 1994, paying $75 million for three London casinos. Also that year Stein retired as chairman. Though Ladbroke's property and retail division suffered in the 1990s, the hotel chain expanded. By 1995 there were 160 hotels in operation. The company opened its first bingo hall, in Buenos Aires, Argentina, in 1995, and opened three in São Paulo, Brazil.

In 1997 Ladbroke entered into a sales and marketing alliance with Hilton Hotels (the owner of the US Hilton hotel chain). Formed to promote the Hilton brand throughout the world, the alliance also prompted the merger of the two companies' sales offices.

In 1998 Ladbroke acquired Coral betting shops (the UK's third-largest string of betting shops) from leisure group Bass plc. However, the company sold the chain for about $655 million (to a venture capital company backed by Morgan Grenfell Private Equity, a subsidiary of Deutsche Bank) after UK legislators ruled the deal would lessen competition in the betting industry. Ladbroke expanded its US presence by buying Colorado Gaming and Entertainment. In 1999 the company bought hotelier Stakis, owner of 54 hotels and 22 casinos in the UK and Ireland, as well as 68 LivingWell health clubs, for $2 billion in stocks and cash, and then changed its name to Hilton Group. The following year David Michels, CEO of Hilton International and former CEO of Stakis, replaced Paul George as CEO of the Hilton Group.

Chairman: John B. H. Jackson, age 70
Chief Executive: David Michels, age 53, $320,000 pay
(prior to promotion)
Director, Group Finance: Brian G. Wallace, age 46,
$332,000 pay
SVP Human Resources: Brian Taker
Chief Executive, Ladbrokes Betting Worldwide: Chris Bell
President, Hilton International: Anthony Harris
President, Hilton, The Americas: Howard Friedman
President, Hilton, Europe, Africa, and Middle East:
Jurgen Fischer
President, Hilton, Asia/Pacific: Koos Klein
Managing Director, Ladbroke Casinos: Ian Payne
Managing Director, International Gaming and Betting:
Alan Ross
Auditors: Ernst & Young

HQ: Maple Ct., Central Park, Reeds Crescent, Watford,
Hertfordshire WD1 1HZ, United Kingdom
Phone: +44-20-7856-8000   **Fax:** +44-20-7856-8001
Web site: http://www.hiltongroup.com

Hilton Group has hotels in 50 countries and gaming
operations in Belgium, Latin America, the Middle East,
the UK, and the US.

1999 Sales

	% of total
Europe	
UK	57
Other countries	17
The Americas	23
Asia & Australia	2
Other regions	1
Total	**100**

1999 Sales

	% of total
Betting & gaming	73
Hotels	27
Total	**100**

Major Subsidiaries and Related Companies
Hilton International Co. (hotels, US)
Hilton International Hotels (UK)
Inter-National Hotel Services
Ladbroke Argentina (Argentina)
Ladbroke Casinos
Ladbroke Gaming (US)
Ladbroke Hotels
Ladbroke Racing Corporation (US)
Ladbrokes International (Gibraltar)
Ladbrokes Limited
LivingWell Health & Leisure
Satellite Information Services (Holdings) (23%)
Stakis (hotels, UK)
Tierce Ladbroke (betting, Belgium)
Vernons Pools (betting)

Accor
Bass Hotels & Resorts
Camelot Group
Carlson
Coral Eurobet
Four Seasons Hotels
Granada Compass
Hyatt
Loews
Marriott International
Millennium & Copthorne
Hotels
Nomura Securities
Rank
Ritz Carlton
Stanley Leisure
Starwood Hotels & Resorts
Worldwide
Thistle Hotels
William Hill
Wyndham International
Zetters

OTC: HLTGY FYE: December 31	Annual Growth	12/90	12/91	12/92	12/93	12/94	12/95	12/96	12/97	12/98	12/99
Sales ($ mil.)	(0.6%)	7,336	7,082	6,294	5,285	5,794	5,679	6,456	6,278	7,769	6,954
Net income ($ mil.)	(9.9%)	398	288	(63)	22	(476)	93	35	248	354	155
Income as % of sales	—	5.4%	4.1%	—	0.4%	—	1.6%	0.5%	4.0%	4.6%	2.2%
Earnings per share ($)	—	—	—	—	—	—	—	—	—	—	0.11
Stock price - FY high ($)	—	—	—	—	—	—	—	—	—	—	8.75
Stock price - FY low ($)	—	—	—	—	—	—	—	—	—	—	5.88
Stock price - FY close ($)	—	—	—	—	—	—	—	—	—	—	6.25
P/E - high	—	—	—	—	—	—	—	—	—	—	81
P/E - low	—	—	—	—	—	—	—	—	—	—	54
Dividends per share ($)	—	—	—	—	—	—	—	—	—	—	0.13
Book value per share ($)	—	—	—	—	—	—	—	—	—	—	2.60
Employees	(8.6%)	—	—	—	—	—	—	70,000	71,000	46,702	53,483

HIGH/LOW/CLOSE

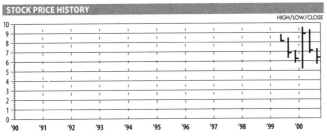

Debt ratio: 33.0%
Return on equity: 4.9%
Cash ($ mil.): 173
Current ratio: 0.53
Long-term debt ($ mil.): 1,927
No. of shares (mil.): 1,500
Dividends
  Yield: 0.0%
  Payout: 1.2%
Market value ($ mil.): 9,373

HITACHI, LTD.

OVERVIEW

Hitachi equals hi-tech, right? True, but it's a low-tech company, too. The Tokyo-based conglomerate makes both state-of-the-art electronics and heavy machinery. It is one of the world's leading manufacturers of powerful, corporate transaction-oriented mainframes (#2 behind IBM), as well as semiconductors, PCs, workstations, and various other information system and telecommunications technologies.

Hitachi also makes elevators and escalators, industrial robots and control systems, and power plant equipment. Low-tech products include ceramic materials, metals, wire, and cable. Hitachi's consumer goods range from audio and video equipment to refrigerators and washing machines; the company also has operations in financial services, property management, and transportation.

A member of Fuji Bank's Fuyo *keiretsu* (a collection of affiliated companies with no official status as a group), Hitachi is restructuring in light of a sales slump in semiconductor, LCD, and industrial markets. The company is banking on a major emphasis on Internet-related and information technology businesses to restore its prosperity.

HISTORY

Namihei Odaira, an employee of Kuhara Mining in the Japanese coastal city of Hitachi, wanted to prove that Japan did not have to depend on foreigners for technology. In 1910 he began building electric motors in Kuhara's engineering and repair shop. Japanese power companies were forced to buy Odaira's generators when WWI made imports scarce. Impressed, they reordered, and in 1920 Hitachi (meaning "rising sun") became an independent company.

During the 1920s acquisitions and growth turned Hitachi into a major manufacturer of electrical equipment and machinery. In the 1930s and 1940s, Hitachi developed vacuum tubes and lightbulbs and produced radar and sonar for the Japanese war effort. Postwar occupation forces removed Odaira and closed 19 Hitachi plants. Reeling from the plant closures, war damage, and labor strife, Hitachi was saved from bankruptcy by US military contracts during the Korean War.

In the 1950s Hitachi became a supplier to NTT, the state-owned telecommunications monopoly. Japan's economic recovery led to strong demand for the company's communications and electrical equipment. Hitachi began mass-producing home appliances, radios, TVs, and transistors. The group spun off Hitachi Metals and Hitachi Cable in 1956 and Hitachi Chemical in 1963.

With the help of NTT, the Ministry of International Trade and Industry, and technology licensed from RCA, Hitachi produced its first computer in 1965. During that decade Hitachi built factories in Southeast Asia and started manufacturing integrated circuits.

Hitachi launched an IBM-compatible computer in 1974. The company sold its computers in the US through Itel until 1979, when Itel was bought by National Semiconductor, and afterward through National Semiconductor's NAS (National Advanced Systems) unit. In 1982 FBI agents caught Hitachi staff buying documents allegedly containing IBM software secrets. Settlement of a civil lawsuit required Hitachi to make payments for IBM for eight years as compensation for the use of IBM's software.

When in the late 1980s the rising Japanese yen hurt exports, Hitachi focused on its domestic market and invested heavily in factory automation. But a recession at home caused earnings to fall. In 1988 the company and Texas Instruments joined in the costly development and production of 16-megabyte DRAM semiconductor chips. In 1989 Hitachi bought 80% of NAS, giving it direct control of its US distribution.

Despite its rivalry with IBM, in 1991 Hitachi began to resell IBM notebook PCs under its own name in Japan. In a major move to combat sluggish consumer electronics sales, in 1994 Hitachi merged with its marketing subsidiary, Hitachi Sales Corp. Hitachi used joint ventures to beef up its international presence, including a 1995 agreement with India's Tata Group.

Tokyo police in 1997 began investigating Hitachi, charging that the company and others had paid off a corporate racketeer. A slump that year in microchip prices, coupled with the Asian economic turmoil that resulted in reduced consumer product sales, led to Hitachi's falling revenues and profits in 1998. Etsuhiko Shoyama took over as president in 1999, replacing Tsutomu Kanai, who became chairman. Hitachi posted the worst loss in its history that year, prompting the firm to combine some subsidiaries, announce layoffs, and emphasize the development of Internet businesses and other information technology units.

Chairman: Tsutomu Kanai
VC: Hiroshi Kuwahara
President: Etsuhiko Shoyama
EVP and Chief Financial Officer: Yoshiki Yagi
EVP: Shigemichi Matsuka
EVP Corporate Export Regulation Division:
Yoshiro Kuwata
EVP: Yuushi Samuro
EVP Power Business Supervisory and Quality
Assurance Division: Takashi Kawamura
SVP and General Manager Secretary's Office:
Kazuo Kumagai
SVP; President and CEO, Semiconductor and
Integrated Circuits: Tadashi Ishibashi
SVP Finance: Kaichi Murata
SVP; President and CEO, Power and Industrial
Systems: Katsukuni Hisano
SVP; President and CEO, Information and
Telecommunication Systems: Toshihiko Odaka
SVP Human Resources Development Department:
Kotaro Muneoka
Auditors: KPMG

LOCATIONS

HQ: Hitachi Seisakusho Kabushiki Kaisha,
6, Kanda-Surugadai 4-chome, Chiyoda-ku,
Tokyo 101-8010, Japan
Phone: +81-3-3258-1111   **Fax:** +81-3-3258-2375
US HQ: 50 Prospect Ave., Tarrytown, NY 10591
US Phone: 914-332-5800   **US Fax:** 914-332-5555
Web site: http://www.hitachi.co.jp

Hitachi operates more than 1,000 subsidiaries and
associated companies worldwide; it has corporate offices
in the Asia/Pacific region, Europe, and North America.

PRODUCTS/OPERATIONS

2000 Sales

	% of total
Information systems & electronics	31
Power & industrial systems	24
Services & other	22
Materials	14
Consumer products	9
Total	**100**

Selected Products

Information Systems and Electronics	Compressors
Computers and peripherals	Control equipment
Liquid crystal displays	Elevators and escalators
Medical electronics	HVAC equipment
Picture tubes	Industrial robots
Semiconductors	Power plants
Software	
Telephone exchanges	**Services and Other**
Test equipment	Financial services
	General trading
Power and Industrial Systems	Printing
	Property management
Auto equipment	Transportation

COMPETITORS

Alstom	Matsushita	SGI
Amdahl	McDermott	Siemens
Bull	Micron	Sony
Compaq	Technology	Texas
Ericsson	Mitsubishi	Instruments
Fluor	Motorola	Toshiba
Fujitsu	NEC	United
Hewlett-Packard	Nippon Steel	Technologies
IBM	Nortel Networks	Whirlpool
Intel	Samsung	

HISTORICAL FINANCIALS & EMPLOYEES

NYSE: HIT FYE: March 31	Annual Growth	3/91	3/92	3/93	3/94	3/95	3/96	3/97	3/98	3/99	3/00
Sales ($ mil.)	3.7%	55,025	58,388	67,863	72,174	87,713	75,771	68,735	63,764	65,929	76,163
Net income ($ mil.)	(22.8%)	1,637	960	696	637	1,316	1,322	712	26	(2,800)	160
Income as % of sales	—	3.0%	1.6%	1.0%	0.9%	1.5%	1.7%	1.0%	0.0%	—	0.2%
Earnings per share ($)	(22.6%)	4.69	2.78	2.04	1.88	3.80	3.74	2.06	0.10	(8.40)	0.47
Stock price - FY high ($)	—	108.38	92.75	73.38	92.50	110.88	114.13	107.88	117.50	77.00	164.50
Stock price - FY low ($)	—	76.75	56.25	55.50	67.00	82.88	93.50	86.00	67.50	40.19	67.00
Stock price - FY close ($)	3.7%	87.75	58.75	73.38	88.88	101.63	97.63	87.88	73.50	72.75	121.88
P/E - high	—	23	33	36	49	29	31	52	1,175	—	350
P/E - low	—	16	20	27	36	22	25	42	675	—	143
Dividends per share ($)	(2.4%)	0.71	0.70	0.75	0.86	0.94	0.54	0.43	0.00	0.00	0.57
Book value per share ($)	3.2%	61.07	66.97	80.81	87.94	106.60	89.65	79.34	73.55	71.03	81.29
Employees	1.0%	309,757	324,929	331,505	330,637	331,673	331,852	330,152	331,494	328,351	337,911

STOCK PRICE HISTORY

HIGH/LOW/CLOSE

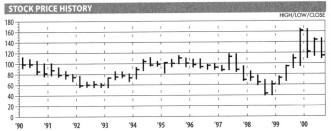

2000 FISCAL YEAR-END

Debt ratio: 34.0%
Return on equity: 0.6%
Cash ($ mil.): 12,806
Current ratio: 1.51
Long-term debt ($ mil.): 13,989
No. of shares (mil.): 334
Dividends
  Yield: 0.0%
  Payout: 1.2%
Market value ($ mil.): 40,681

HOLLINGER INC.

What's led by Black and read all over? Hollinger. Controlled by newspaper baron Conrad Black, the Toronto-based company publishes newspapers, magazines, and other publications in Canada, Israel, the UK, and the US, primarily through Hollinger International (of which it owns about 41%, giving it about 75% of the voting power). Worldwide, Black's newspaper empire is behind only News Corp. and Gannett in terms of circulation. The company is also moving to the Web, having acquired stakes in topjobs.net (recruitment), TheTrip.com (travel), and www.StockHouse.com (financial information).

Its Chicago Group publishes the *Chicago Sun-Times* and about 80 other papers. Its Community Newspaper Group publishes about 100 (mostly small) community newspapers in 17 US states and the *The Jerusalem Post,* an Israeli English-language daily.

The main publication of the company's UK-based newspaper group, The Telegraph Group, is *The Daily Telegraph,* the largest non-tabloid daily in the UK. The group's other operations include the *Electronic Telegraph* news Web site, and *The Spectator* magazine.

Hollinger publishes the *National Post, Ottawa Citizen,* and *The Gazette* (Montreal), among other leading daily newspapers. It also owns 85% of Hollinger Canadian Newspapers, which publishes newspapers, shoppers, trade magazines, and other specialty publications through the operations of Southam and Sterling Newspapers. Hollinger has agreed to sell a number of assets, including 13 of its larger daily newspapers and a 50% stake in the *National Post,* to CanWest Global Communications for $3.5 billion. The company is selling hundreds of its newspapers so it can focus on its more lucrative papers and Internet operations.

A born entrepreneur, Conrad Black bought his first share of stock (in General Motors) at age eight. Some of his early childhood deals weren't quite so constructive: He was expelled from a private school at age 14 for selling exams and was kicked out of one law school after spending all his time playing the stock market.

Black entered publishing in 1969 when he and Peter White founded Sterling Newspapers and bought the *Sherbrooke Record.* The two added to their flagship with a group of small daily papers in British Columbia, Quebec, and Prince Edward Island. In 1975 Black bought his father's 22% of the Ravelston Corporation, which owned Argus, a company formed in 1945 by E. P. Taylor to invest in breweries, malting and bottling operations, and a chemical business. Black took control of the company in the late 1970s by obtaining a loan through Sterling.

After assuming the leadership of Argus (through Ravelston), Black sold off chunks of the business to refine the company's holdings to key businesses. The company adopted the Hollinger name (left over from Argus's early investment in Hollinger Consolidated Gold Mines) in 1985 and gained control of struggling newspaper *The Daily Telegraph* (London), which it turned around by cutting staff and modernizing. In 1989 the firm purchased Jerusalem Post Publications.

Hollinger continued to acquire and restore struggling companies in the 1990s. It bought a stake in Southam in 1992 and acquired the

Sun-Times Company, publisher of the *Chicago Sun-Times,* in 1994.

Hollinger purchased two daily and 12 non-daily papers in 1995 from Armadale, a closely held Canadian firm. Hollinger also bought 19 paid-circulation papers (12 dailies and seven weeklies) and several free publications from Canadian publisher Thomson Corporation. That year it sold its interests in the Telegraph Group, Southam, and John Fairfax (an Australian publisher) to subsidiary Hollinger International.

In 1996 Hollinger International assumed full control of the Telegraph Group, increased its stake in Southam to about 51%, and formed Hollinger Digital to coordinate new media businesses, especially on the Web. It sold most of its John Fairfax holdings to New Zealand-based Brierley Investments. In 1997 Hollinger International made an unsuccessful bid to buy the rest of Southam. It sold a stack of community newspapers to Leonard Green & Partners in 1998. Also that year, Southam launched Canada's *National Post,* its first national newspaper.

In 1999 Hollinger International finally bought all of Southam. Also that year Hollinger combined the smaller publications of Southam, Sterling Newspapers, and UniMedia into Hollinger Canadian Newspapers (in which it holds an 85% stake). In 2000 the company decided to sell off more than 300 of its Canadian and American community newspapers and trade magazines in order to concentrate on its larger papers.

Chairman and CEO, Hollinger Inc., Hollinger International, Hollinger Canadian Publishing Holdings, Southam: Conrad M. Black, $466,967 pay
Deputy Chairman, President and COO: F. David Radler
VC; Deputy Chairman and CEO, Telegraph Group: Daniel W. Colson, $245,280 pay
EVP and CFO: Jack A. Boultbee
VP and Secretary: Charles G. Cowan
VP Editorial: Barbara A. Black
VP and General Counsel: Peter Y. Atkinson
Chairman, Hollinger Digital Inc: Richard N. Perle
President and CEO, UniMedia Inc: Marc Bourgault
Publisher and Chief Executive, The Spectator (1828) Limited: Kimberly A. Fortier
Managing Director, Telegraph Group Limited: Jeremy W. Deedes
Publisher Jerusalem Post: Tom Rose
Treasurer: Larry O. Spencer
Controller: Frederick A. Creasey
Auditors: KPMG LLP

LOCATIONS

HQ: 10 Toronto St., Toronto, Ontario M5C 2B7, Canada
Phone: 416-363-8721   **Fax:** 416-364-2088
US HQ: 401 N. Wabash Ave., Chicago, IL 60611
US Phone: 312-321-2299   **US Fax:** 312-321-0629

Hollinger publishes newpapers in Canada, Israel, the US, and the UK.

1999 Sales

	C$ mil.	% of total
Canada	1,648	51
UK	868	27
US	725	22
Total	**3,241**	**100**

PRODUCTS/OPERATIONS

Selected Newspapers
Calgary Herald (Canada)
Chicago Sun-Times
The Daily Telegraph (London)
Edmonton Journal (Canada)
The Gazette (Montreal)
The Jerusalem Post
National Post (Canada)
Ottawa Citizen (Canada)
Post-Tribune (Gary, IN)
The Vancouver Sun

Selected Subsidiaries
Hollinger International (75% voting power; newspapers; Canada, Israel, UK, US)
Chicago Group (the *Chicago Sun-Times* newspaper and other US newspapers)
Community Group (smaller newspapers in the US, *Jerusalem Post* in Israel)
Hollinger Canadian Newspapers, L.P. (85%; newspapers, magazines, specialty titles)
Southam (newspapers and magazines)
Sterling Newspapers Group (newspapers)
Telegraph Group (*The Daily Telegraph* and other UK papers)

COMPETITORS

Central Newspapers	Independent News	Thomson Corporation
Copley Press	Knight Ridder	Torstar
Daily Mail and General Trust	Lee Enterprises	Tribune
Dow Jones	MediaNews	Trinity Mirror
E. W. Scripps	Modern Times Group	Washington Post
Gannett	New York Times	
Hearst	News Corp.	

HISTORICAL FINANCIALS & EMPLOYEES

Toronto: HLGC FYE: December 31	Annual Growth	12/90	12/91	12/92	12/93	12/94	12/95	12/96	12/97	12/98	12/99
Sales (C$ mil.)	16.6%	811	807	903	856	1,271	1,513	1,879	3,117	3,319	3,241
Net income (C$ mil.)	18.3%	34	31	74	25	118	17	46	171	111	155
Income as % of sales	—	4.2%	3.9%	8.2%	3.0%	9.3%	1.1%	2.5%	5.5%	3.4%	4.8%
Earnings per share (C$)	38.3%	0.24	0.30	1.14	0.31	1.96	0.03	0.58	2.94	3.35	4.43
Stock price - FY high (C$)	—	14.00	13.00	13.50	14.38	17.50	13.25	14.05	13.85	19.35	22.40
Stock price - FY low (C$)	—	10.00	9.88	9.75	8.50	12.13	9.38	9.75	10.50	11.80	12.00
Stock price - FY close (C$)	1.9%	11.38	11.63	10.63	13.75	12.63	10.13	12.90	12.00	16.00	13.50
P/E - high	—	58	43	12	46	9	442	24	5	6	5
P/E - low	—	42	33	9	27	6	313	17	4	4	3
Dividends per share (C$)	(1.7%)	0.70	0.40	0.70	0.40	0.50	0.60	0.60	3.10	0.60	0.60
Book value per share (C$)	16.9%	0.91	0.84	1.07	1.24	0.84	0.64	0.80	(2.77)	(2.04)	3.73
Employees	—	—	—	—	—	—	—	—	—	—	3,100

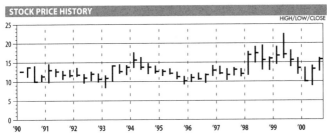

STOCK PRICE HISTORY — HIGH/LOW/CLOSE

1999 FISCAL YEAR-END
Debt ratio: 94.5%
Return on equity: 431.7%
Cash (C$ mil.): 74
Current ratio: 0.59
Long-term debt (C$ mil.): 2,394
No. of shares (mil.): 37
Dividends
  Yield: 0.0%
  Payout: 0.1%
Market value ($ mil.): 346
Sales ($ mil.): 2,232

HONDA MOTOR CO., LTD.

Big Three? *Hai!* — or, if you prefer English — Yes! Honda, Japan's #2 automaker (behind Toyota and just ahead of Nissan), makes car models that include the Accord, the Acura, the economical Civic, and the sporty Prelude, as well as its gasoline-electric hybrid — the Insight. Honda is also the world's #1 motorcycle maker, with models from scooters to highway cruisers. Its power products division manufactures lawn mowers, snowblowers, outboard motors, and portable generators.

While the rest of the automotive industry seems to be in the grips of acquisition/merger fever, Honda, the world leader in the manufacture of internal combustion engines (about 11 million per year), has stated publicly that it wants to remain on its own. The company's nearly 120 factories in 33 countries give it the global reach and technological strength it needs to compete against the automotive giants. Honda plans to leverage its engine prowess through supply agreements with the likes of GM and through increased demand for gas-electric hybrids and the development of fuel cell-powered vehicles.

HISTORY

Soichiro Honda (Japan's counterpart to Henry Ford) spent six years as an apprentice at Tokyo service station Art Shokai before opening his own branch of the repair shop in Hamamatsu in 1928. He also raced cars and in 1931 received a patent for metal spokes that replaced wood in wheels.

Honda started a piston ring company in 1937. During WWII the company produced metal propellers for Japanese bombers. When bombs and an earthquake destroyed most of his factory, Honda sold it to Toyota in 1945.

In 1946 Honda began motorizing bicycles with war-surplus engines. When this proved popular, Honda began making engines. The company was renamed Honda Motor Co. in 1948 and began producing motorcycles. In 1949 Soichiro Honda hired Takeo Fujisawa to manage the company so Honda could focus on engineering. Honda's innovative overhead valve design made its early 1950s Dream model a runaway success. In 1952 the smaller Cub, sold through bicycle dealers, accounted for 70% of Japan's motorcycle production.

Funded by a 1954 public offering and Mitsubishi Bank, Honda expanded capacity and began exporting. American Honda Motor Company was formed in Los Angeles in 1959, accompanied by the slogan, "You meet the nicest people on a Honda," in a campaign crafted to counter the stereotypical biker image. Honda added overseas factories in the 1960s and began producing lightweight trucks, sports cars, and minicars.

Honda introduced the Civic in 1972 to tap into the US car market. Four years later it introduced the Accord, which featured an innovative frame adaptable for many models. In 1982 Accord production started at Honda's Ohio plant, which made exports for Japan.

Ex-Honda engineer Nobuhiko Kawamoto was named president in 1990, a year before Soichiro Honda died. Kawamoto cut costs and continued to expand the company internationally. In 1992 Honda established the first joint venture to manufacture motorcycles in China. That year the Big Three US automakers (GM, Ford, and Chrysler), clamoring for trade sanctions against Japanese carmakers, threw Honda out of the US carmakers trade association.

In 1997 Honda bought Peugeot's plant in Guangzhou, China, and announced plans to boost US vehicle production by building an all terrain vehicle (ATV) production plant in South Carolina. American Honda agreed in 1998 to pay $330 million to settle a class-action lawsuit filed by 1,800 dealers who accused Honda of delivering popular models only to dealers who paid bribes (18 executives from American Honda were convicted). The same year Hiroyuki Yoshino, an engineer with US management experience, succeeded Kawamoto as CEO.

Honda's joint venture in China began turning out Accords in 1999. The company planned to cut back production in Japan while, once again, increasing capacity in the US, partly through a minivan and SUV factory to be built in Alabama. Also, Honda and GM agreed to a deal in which Honda will supply low-emission V6 engines and automatic transmissions to GM, while Isuzu, a GM affiliate, will supply Honda with diesel engines. True to Honda's go-it-alone style, the deal has no equity component.

In 2000 Honda announced that its super low-emission engine (as called for by US regulators) would make its mass-market debut in 2001, apparently well ahead of competitor versions. Also Honda recalled 500,000 cars in Japan due to problems with audio systems and engine oil seals.

Chairman and Representative Director:
Yoshihide Munekuni
President and Representative Director:
Hiroyuki Yoshino
EVP and Representative Director; COO, Regional Operations; President, Honda North America, Inc.; President, American Honda Motor Co., Inc.:
Koichi Amemiya
Senior Managing and Representative Director:
Masaki Iwai
Senior Managing and Representative Director:
Katsuro Suzuki
Senior Managing and Representative Director:
Takeo Fukui
Senior Managing and Representative Director:
Michiyoshi Hagino
Auditors: Century Ota Showa & Co.

LOCATIONS

HQ: Honda Giken Kogyo Kabushiki Kaisha,
1-1, 2-chome, Minami-Aoyama, Minato-ku,
Tokyo 107-8556, Japan
Phone: +81-3-3423-1111   **Fax:** +81-3-5412-1515
US HQ: 540 Madison Ave., 32nd Fl., New York, NY 10022
US Phone: 212-355-9191   **US Fax:** 212-813-0260
Web site: http://www.honda.co.jp/english

2000 Sales

	$ mil.	% of total
Japan	32,484	44
North America	31,385	42
Europe	6,392	9
Other regions	4,133	5
Adjustments	(16,939)	—
Total	**57,455**	**100**

PRODUCTS/OPERATIONS

2000 Sales

	$ mil.	% of total
Automobiles	46,736	81
Motorcycles	6,773	12
Financial services	1,363	2
Other	2,721	5
Adjustments	(138)	—
Total	**57,455**	**100**

Selected Cars and Trucks
Accord
Acura
Civic
Insight (gasoline-electric hybrid)
Passport (SUV)
Prelude

Helix (scooter)
Nighthawk 750
Valkyrie

Selected Power Products
Commercial mowers
Engines
Lawn mowers
Marine motors
Portable generators
Pumps
Snowblowers

Selected Motorcycles
FourTrax (ATV)
Gold Wing

COMPETITORS

Black & Decker
BMW
Briggs & Stratton
Brunswick
Caterpillar
Daewoo
DaimlerChrysler
Deere
Fiat
Ford
General Motors

Harley-Davidson
Hyundai
Isuzu
Kawasaki Heavy Industries
Kia Motors
Mazda
Mitsubishi
Nissan
Outboard Marine
Peugeot
Renault

Saab Automobile
Suzuki
Textron
Toro
Toyota
Triumph Motorcycles
Volkswagen
Volvo
Yamaha

HISTORICAL FINANCIALS & EMPLOYEES

NYSE: HMC FYE: March 31	Annual Growth	3/91	3/92	3/93	3/94	3/95	3/96	3/97	3/98	3/99	3/00
Sales ($ mil.)	7.3%	30,592	33,084	35,981	37,673	45,821	39,984	42,654	45,418	51,688	57,455
Net income ($ mil.)	18.4%	543	489	334	231	711	666	1,782	1,973	2,530	2,472
Income as % of sales	—	1.8%	1.5%	0.9%	0.6%	1.6%	1.7%	4.2%	4.3%	4.9%	4.3%
Earnings per share ($)	18.5%	1.10	1.00	0.68	0.47	1.46	1.36	3.66	4.05	5.20	5.08
Stock price - FY high ($)	—	24.13	25.50	25.50	34.00	37.75	46.25	65.13	76.56	92.75	94.00
Stock price - FY low ($)	—	17.38	18.50	17.75	23.00	29.88	27.50	42.00	57.00	51.31	65.00
Stock price - FY close ($)	16.1%	21.13	22.88	25.50	32.38	32.88	43.00	58.50	71.00	89.13	81.25
P/E - high	—	22	26	38	72	26	34	18	19	18	19
P/E - low	—	16	19	26	49	20	20	11	14	10	13
Dividends per share ($)	8.4%	0.17	0.18	0.19	0.22	0.24	0.13	0.11	0.00	0.00	0.35
Book value per share ($)	9.9%	15.91	17.08	18.56	19.38	24.13	22.09	22.97	24.98	30.03	37.33
Employees	3.1%	85,500	90,500	90,900	91,300	92,800	96,800	91,300	109,400	112,200	112,400

STOCK PRICE HISTORY

HIGH/LOW/CLOSE

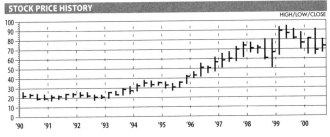

2000 FISCAL YEAR-END

Debt ratio: 22.9%
Return on equity: 15.1%
Cash ($ mil.): 4,056
Current ratio: 1.12
Long-term debt ($ mil.): 5,413
No. of shares (mil.): 487
Dividends
  Yield: 0.4%
  Payout: 6.9%
Market value ($ mil.): 39,586

HOPEWELL HOLDINGS LIMITED

Sir Gordon Wu believes in faith, Hopewell, and charity. The chairman of Hong Kong-based Hopewell Holdings, who has pledged $100 million to his alma mater, Princeton University, made his fortune through real estate and heavy construction. Hopewell's activities include property investment and management, hotel operations and management (including the Kowloon Panda hotel), and infrastructure development. The company's properties are mainly concentrated in Hong Kong, and its infrastructure projects (toll roads and bridges) are primarily in China's fast-growing Guangdong province.

Asian economic instability coupled with a few missteps in the region have cost the company dearly. Hopewell had to halt construction on a 1,320-MW power plant in Indonesia after it was 80% complete. In addition, the Thai government canceled an elevated road and train project in Bangkok after several delays, changes, and rising costs because of currency devaluation. (The Thai government is in negotiations with Hopewell to resolve the situation.) Still recovering from the fiscal nightmares, Hopewell is looking for a strong performance from its Chinese infrastructure projects to get back on track.

HISTORY

Sir Gordon Wu's Hopewell Holdings empire grew from humble beginnings. His father started out as a Hong Kong taxi owner and driver and helped finance Gordon's first-class education — he received an engineering degree from Princeton University.

On his return to Hong Kong in 1962, Wu took a job in the government's land department. He later left to help his father develop a property business. When his father retired in 1969, custom forbade Wu Sr. from handing the company over to Gordon, the seventh of nine children. Instead, he liquidated the company and guaranteed a $2.5 million loan to his son to start a property company of his own.

By 1972 Wu's company was large enough to be listed on the Hong Kong Stock Exchange as Hopewell Holdings Limited. But his American-style "can-do" approach gained him some enemies in Hong Kong. He took on the local government after it had banned him from building a towering headquarters in central Hong Kong and won. The result was the 66-floor Hopewell Centre.

While visiting nearby Guangzhou in China to promote a hotel project in the early 1980s, Wu spotted opportunity in the region's frequent power outages. Realizing that the province would boom in the 1980s and 1990s, Wu dropped the hotel idea and persuaded China to let him build a power plant. By 1987 the 700-megawatt plant was on line. Other major Chinese infrastructure projects followed, including contracts for two more power stations in Guangdong province and a contract to build China's first modern highway, a six-lane toll road linking the cities of Guangzhou and Hong Kong. Wu attributed his outstanding success in negotiating with the Chinese authorities to 11 years of lobbying and consuming

gallons of *mao tai* (a very potent liquor served at formal dinners in China).

In 1990 Wu gained a contract for a mass transit system in Bangkok. But almost immediately the project was delayed by political unrest in Thailand, and then by bureaucratic red tape.

Hopewell spun off 40% of its power subsidiary, Consolidated Electric Power Asia (CEPA), in 1993. The sale helped fund other projects, including the Guangdong toll road and a power plant in the Philippines. But the Philippines project ran into problems in 1995: Although the plant was completed, the local electric utility refused to take the power, resulting in litigation and even less cash flow. That year Wu set the company up for another fall when he pledged $100 million to Princeton. (The Asian economic crisis allowed him to give only a third of the amount by 1999.)

By late 1995 Hopewell was hemorrhaging money. After failing to raise funds by spinning off several transport projects as a public company in 1996, Hopewell sold CEPA to US utility Southern Company.

The Asian financial contagion of 1997 and 1998 didn't help matters. In 1998 the elevated train project in Bangkok was halted by the Thai government, and Hopewell lost its $153 million stake in Peregrine Investment Holdings when the Hong Kong-based firm collapsed. Hopewell also stopped work on a major Indonesian power plant that it was building in a venture. The firm fell into the red in 1998.

That year, however, the company gained a contract to help build a toll road in southern China and in 1999 won another contract for a toll road in the Philippines. By the end of 1999 it had regained profitability, although it lost its listing on the Hong Kong index.

Honorary Chairman: James M. H. Wu
Chairman and Managing Director: Gordon Y. S. Wu
Deputy Managing Director: Eddie P. C. Ho
Executive Director; Managing Director, Mega Hotels Management Limited: Joachim Burger
Executive Director: Henry H. M. Lee
Executive Director; Director, Hopewell (Thailand) Limited: David Y. Lui
Executive Director; Director, Hopewell (Thailand) Limited: Colin H. Weir
Finance Director: Robert V. J. Nien
General Manager, Delta Roads Limited: Alan C. H. Chan
Director, Delta Roads Limited: Li Jia Huang
Director, Hopewell Engineering and Construction Limited: Tony H. Y. Leung
Director, Hopewell Engineering and Construction Limited: Leo K. K. Leung
Group Finance Controller: Godfrey C. T. Hui
Deputy Financial Controller: Ricky W. K. Leung
Project Controller: A. Wing Louie
Assistant to Managing Director: Cheng Hui Jia
Director of Human Resources: Simatha Yung
Auditors: Deloitte Touche Tohmatsu

LOCATIONS

HQ: Hopewell Centre, 64th Fl.,
183 Queen's Rd. East, Hong Kong
Phone: +852-2528-4975   **Fax:** +852-2865-6276
Web site: http://irasia.com/listco/hk/hopewell

Hopewell Holdings operates primarily in Asia, including China, Hong Kong, Indonesia, the Philippines, and Thailand.

PRODUCTS/OPERATIONS

Selected Holdings and Projects
Bangkok Elevated Road and Train System (BERTS, Thailand)
Guangzhou-Shenzhen-Zhuhai Super Highway (six-lane toll road, China)
Hopewell Centre (office building, Hong Kong)
Kowloon Panda (hotel, Hong Kong)
Tanjung Jati-B (80%, power station, Indonesia)

COMPETITORS

ABB
AES
Alstom
Bechtel
Fluor
Foster Wheeler
GE
Hutchison Whampoa
Jardine Matheson
Marriott International
McDermott
Peter Kiewit Sons'
Siemens
Sime Darby
Swire Pacific

HISTORICAL FINANCIALS & EMPLOYEES

OTC: HOWWY FYE: June 30	Annual Growth	6/89	6/90	6/91	6/92	6/93	6/94	6/95	6/96	6/97	6/98
Sales ($ mil.)	3.5%	140	138	127	210	373	298	281	306	368	191
Net income ($ mil.)	—	66	80	93	210	262	315	271	99	(219)	(363)
Income as % of sales	—	47.3%	58.4%	73.2%	100.0%	70.2%	105.8%	96.5%	32.5%	—	—
Earnings per share ($)	—	—	—	—	—	—	—	0.31	0.11	(0.25)	(0.41)
Stock price - FY high ($)	—	—	—	—	—	—	—	4.38	5.36	4.16	3.18
Stock price - FY low ($)	—	—	—	—	—	—	—	2.94	2.05	2.34	0.50
Stock price - FY close ($)	(50.8%)	—	—	—	—	—	—	4.20	2.66	3.06	0.50
P/E - high	—	—	—	—	—	—	—	14	47	—	—
P/E - low	—	—	—	—	—	—	—	9	18	—	—
Dividends per share ($)	(67.5%)	—	—	—	—	—	—	0.29	0.13	0.13	0.01
Book value per share ($)	(20.2%)	—	—	—	—	—	—	4.64	4.35	3.23	2.36
Employees	(12.5%)	—	—	—	—	7,783	7,983	6,288	7,095	5,318	4,000

STOCK PRICE HISTORY
HIGH/LOW/CLOSE

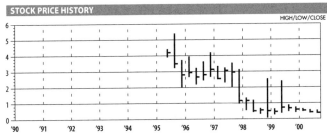

1998 FISCAL YEAR-END
Debt ratio: 39.1%
Return on equity: —
Cash ($ mil.): 45
Current ratio: 0.63
Long-term debt ($ mil.): 1,328
No. of shares (mil.): 876
Dividends
  Yield: 0.0%
  Payout: —
Market value ($ mil.): 438

HSBC HOLDINGS PLC

OVERVIEW

HSBC Holdings is facing a strange new world with a stiff upper lip. London-based HSBC, the UK's #1 banking company, is the parent of Hongkong and Shanghai Bank, a leading bank in Hong Kong with a strong presence in China. It also owns HSBC Bank plc, New York-based HSBC Bank USA (formerly Marine Midland Bank), and 62% of Hong Kong's Hang Seng Bank. The Hong Kong Monetary Authority owns 13% of the company.

HSBC's banking and financial services subsidiaries extend into Central and South America and the Pacific Rim. (It has more than 5,000 offices in 80 countries.) Services include banking, asset management, investment banking, finance, securities trading, and insurance.

The conservative bank rode out the Asian crisis well-protected by its position in the more developed Asian economies such as Hong Kong. HSBC is hoping that its move into mainland China and its purchase of the late Edmond Safra's US investment banking businesses will jolt growth. The company is also fueling its expansion into continental Europe with its acquisition of Crédit Commercial de France. The company is rebranding its operations under the HSBC name for global recognition.

HISTORY

Scotsman Thomas Sutherland and other businessmen in 1865 opened the doors to Hongkong & Shanghai Bank, financing and promoting British imperial trade in opium, silk, and tea in East Asia. It soon established a London office and created an international branch network emphasizing China and East Asia. It claims to have been the first bank in Thailand (1888).

War repeatedly disrupted, but never demolished, the bank's operations. During WWII the headquarters were temporarily moved to London. The bank's chief prewar manager, Sir Vandeleur Grayborn, died in a Japanese POW camp. After the Communists took power in China in 1949, the bank gradually withdrew; by 1955 only its Shanghai office remained (it was later closed). The bank played a key role in Hong Kong's postwar growth by financing industrialists who fled there from China.

In the late 1950s Hongkong & Shanghai Bank's acquisitions included the British Bank of the Middle East (founded in 1889, this business evolved into the Saudi British Bank) and Mercantile Bank (with offices in India and Southeast Asia). In 1965 the company bought 62% of Hang Seng, Hong Kong's #2 bank. It also added new subsidiaries, including Wayfoong (mortgage and small-business finance, 1960) and Wardley (investment banking, Hong Kong, 1972).

In the late 1970s and into the 1980s, China began opening to foreign business. The bank added operations in North America to capitalize on business between China and the US and Canada (much of which was transacted through Hong Kong because China lacked financial infrastructure until the late 1980s). Acquisitions included Marine Midland Bank (US, 1980), Hongkong Bank of Canada (1981), 51% of treasury securities dealer Carroll McEntee & McGinley (US, 1983), most of the assets and liabilities of the Bank of British Columbia (1986), and Lloyds Bank Canada (1990).

Following the 1984 agreement to return Hong Kong to China, Hongkong and Shanghai Bank began beefing up in the UK, buying London securities dealer James Capel & Co. (1986) and the UK's #3 bank, Midland plc (1992). In 1993 the company formed London-based HSBC Holdings and divested assets, most notably its interest in Hong Kong-based Cathay Pacific Airways.

The company then began expanding in Asia again, particularly in Malaysia, where its Hongkong Bank Malaysia Berhad became the country's first locally incorporated foreign bank. HSBC returned to China with offices in Beijing and Guangzhou.

Latin American banks acquired in 1997 were among the non-Asian operations that cushioned HSBC from the worst of 1998's economic crises. Nonetheless, The Hong Kong Monetary Authority took a stake in the bank to shore up the stock exchange and foil short-sellers.

In 1999 China's government made HSBC a loan for mainland expansion. That year the company was foiled in its attempt to buy South Korea's government-owned Seoulbank, but did buy the late Edmond Safra's Republic New York and Safra Republic Holdings (it negotiated a $450 million discount on the $10 billion deal after a Japanese probe of Republic's securities division caused delays).

In 2000 the company unveiled several online initiatives, including Internet ventures with Cheung Kong (Holdings) and Merrill Lynch. HSBC bought Crédit Commercial de France and agreed to buy a controlling stake in Bangkok Metropolitan Bank.

Group Chairman and Executive Director; Chairman, HSBC Bank plc, HSBC USA Inc., HSBC Bank USA, and HSBC Bank Middle East: John R. H. Bond, age 58, $524,000 pay
Deputy Chairman: Baroness Lydia Dunn, age 59
Deputy Chairman: Peter Walters, age 68
Group Chief Executive: Keith R. Whitson, age 56, $412,000 pay
CEO, HSBC Bank plc; Chairman, HSBC Asset Finance Limited: William R. P. Dalton, age 56, $400,000 pay
Executive Director; Chairman and Executive Director, The Hongkong and Shanghai Banking Corporation: David Eldon, age 54, $397,000 pay
Group Finance Director: Douglas J. Flint, age 44, $361,000 pay
Auditors: KPMG Audit Plc

HQ: 10 Lower Thames St., London EC3R 6AE, United Kingdom
Phone: +44-020-7260-0500   **Fax:** +44-020-7260-0501
US HQ: 1 HSBC Center, Buffalo, NY 14203
US Phone: 716-841-2424   **US Fax:** 716-841-5391
Web site: http://www.hsbc.com

HSBC Holdings operates in 80 countries.

1999 Banking Income

	% of total
Asia/Pacific	
Hong Kong	28
Other countries	11
Europe	39
North America	14
Latin America	8
Total	**100**

1999 Assets

	$ mil.	% of total
Cash & equivalents	6,183	1
Treasury & agency securities	23,227	4
Foreign government securities	9,911	2
Bonds	110,135	19
Stocks	4,481	1
Net loans	353,861	62
Receivables	5,829	1
Other	55,512	10
Total	**569,139**	**100**

Selected Subsidiaries & Affiliates
British Arab Commercial Bank Limited
Egyptian British Bank S.A.E.
Hang Seng Bank Limited (Hong Kong)
The Hongkong and Shanghai Banking Corporation Limited (Hong Kong)
HSBC Bank Argentina S.A.
HSBC Bank Australia Limited
HSBC Bank Malaysia Berhad
HSBC Bank Middle East (Channel Islands)
HSBC Bank USA
The Saudi British Bank (Saudi Arabia)
Wells Fargo HSBC Trade Bank, N.A. (joint venture, US)

Bank of America	Deutsche Bank
Bank of China	Hutchison Whampoa
Barclays	Industrial Bank of Japan
Canadian Imperial	J.P. Morgan
Chase Manhattan	Lloyds TSB
Citigroup	Royal Bank of Canada
Credit Lyonnais	Standard Chartered
Credit Suisse First Boston	UBS
Dai-Ichi Kangyo	

NYSE: HBC FYE: December 31	Annual Growth	12/90	12/91	12/92	12/93	12/94	12/95	12/96	12/97	12/98	12/99
Assets ($ mil.)	11.0%	—	—	—	304,439	315,325	351,466	401,904	472,431	483,128	569,139
Net income ($ mil.)	12.5%	—	—	—	2,668	3,212	3,815	5,287	5,534	4,318	5,408
Income as % of assets	—	—	—	—	0.9%	1.0%	1.1%	1.3%	1.2%	0.9%	1.0%
Earnings per share ($)	—	—	—	—	—	—	—	—	—	—	3.25
Stock price - FY high ($)	—	—	—	—	—	—	—	—	—	—	71.50
Stock price - FY low ($)	—	—	—	—	—	—	—	—	—	—	53.13
Stock price - FY close ($)	—	—	—	—	—	—	—	—	—	—	71.38
P/E - high	—	—	—	—	—	—	—	—	—	—	22
P/E - low	—	—	—	—	—	—	—	—	—	—	16
Dividends per share ($)	—	—	—	—	—	—	—	—	—	—	0.57
Book value per share ($)	—	—	—	—	—	—	—	—	—	—	19.75
Employees	7.7%	—	—	—	—	—	109,093	109,298	132,969	145,000	146,897

HIGH/LOW/CLOSE

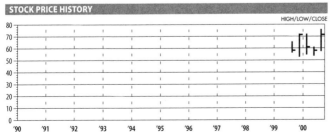

Equity as % of assets: 5.9%
Return on assets: 1.0%
Return on equity: 17.8%
Long-term debt ($ mil.): 13,166
No. of shares (mil.): 1,692
Dividends
  Yield: 0.8%
  Payout: 17.5%
Market value ($ mil.): 120,748
Sales ($ mil.): 38,789

HUDSON'S BAY COMPANY

OVERVIEW

Here's a company that's traveled a fur piece from its 17th-century roots. Toronto-based Hudson's Bay Company (HBC) is not only Canada's leading department store retailer, with about 40% of the market there, but also its oldest corporation. Its department and discount store chains stretch from Newfoundland to British Columbia. Zellers, which accounts for about 60% of company sales, is Canada's #2 chain of discount department stores (trailing Wal-Mart), with more than 300 outlets. HBC's 100 or so Bay traditional department stores focus on more upscale fashion merchandise and home furnishings. HBC also operates

Fields, a chain of over 100 small clothing stores in Western Canada, and Best Value, a chain of about 30 discount stores.

The company faces increasing pressure from discounters and specialty stores. As a countermeasure, HBC bought the 112 stores of Kmart Canada in 1998 and has been renovating and enlarging its Zellers stores to make them more upscale (like Target). Some Zellers stores have been converted to its no-frills Best Value format. HBC also has been diversifying into specialty formats such as Home Outfitters (bedding and linen) and Hudson's Bay Company Outfitters (outdoor wear).

HISTORY

In 1668 the British ketch *Nonsuch* reached the bay named for explorer Henry Hudson. The ship returned to Britain the following year laden with furs, attracting the attention of King Charles II, who in 1670 granted a royal trading charter to a party of 18 men. Hudson's Bay Company (HBC) built a series of fortifications and engaged in a seesaw battle with French warships for control of the bay that continued until 1713, when the Treaty of Utrecht placed the bay officially in British hands. From the company's base at York Factory, company explorers began to penetrate Canada's vast interior. In 1774 Samuel Hearne established the firm's first inland post on the Saskatchewan River.

During the late 18th century, the Montreal-based North West Company, a rival fur-trading concern, threatened HBC's dominance. After a period of violent clashes between the competing traders, the two competitors merged under the Hudson's Bay Company name in 1821, giving the company control over 173 posts throughout 3 million square miles of wilderness. It transferred possession of company-chartered land to the Canadian government in 1869.

By the turn of the century, HBC had transformed many posts into stores to serve growing Canadian cities. In 1929 the company formed Hudson's Bay Oil and Gas. It acquired the Henry Morgan department store chain in 1960 and five years later changed its store name to Bay. HBC finally moved its headquarters from London to Winnipeg in 1970 (and later to Toronto).

The company expanded its department store holdings in the late 1970s by purchasing Zellers, Fields, and Simpsons. Newspaper magnate Kenneth Thomson bought 75% of HBC in 1979 (the last of the family's interest was sold

in 1997). Mired in debt during the 1980s from its prolific acquisitions, the company sold its oil and gas operations, its large fur houses (under pressure from animal-rights activists), and 179 of its original stores in the far north.

During a steep recession in 1990, the company spun off its Markborough real estate subsidiary to shareholders and purchased the Towers Bonimart chain of discount department stores. It later integrated Towers stores into its Zellers chain and converted six of its Simpsons high-fashion stores into the Bay stores, selling the rest to Sears for $37 million.

HBC in 1995 opened the first of its Zellers Plus larger stores with expanded merchandise (almost twice as large as its average format) to compete with Wal-Mart. Profits dropped almost 80% that year because of a Wal-Mart price war and depressed Christmas sales. In 1997 Bill Fields, former head of Blockbuster Entertainment, succeeded CEO George Kosich. Fields liquidated old inventory at Zellers, writing off more than $100 million. (The move, along with restructuring, created a loss for fiscal 1998.)

In 1998 the company bought Kmart Canada (112 discount stores) for $168 million. HBC then set about converting about 60 former Kmarts into Zellers stores; about 40 weaker stores were closed, and about a dozen were converted to specialty stores. Fields, who had touted the growth potential of the Kmart stores, resigned suddenly in early 1999 and was replaced as president and CEO by George Heller, head of the Zellers chain.

Governor: L. Yves Fortier
President and CEO: George J. Heller, $2,078,538 pay
EVP and CFO: Gary J. Lukassen
EVP; President and COO, The Bay: Marc Chouinard,
$815,000 pay
EVP; President and COO, Zellers: Thomas Haig,
$750,000 pay
EVP and Chief Information Officer: David F. Poirier,
$1,425,000 pay
EVP Logistics, Distribution, and Transportation:
Peter A. Kenyon
SVP Human Resources: David J. Crisp
SVP Real Estate and Development: Donald C. Rogers
SVP Shared Services: William J. Luciano
VP, Secretary and General Counsel: James A. Ingram
Auditors: KPMG LLP

LOCATIONS

HQ: 401 Bay St., Ste. 500, Toronto,
Ontario M5H 2Y4, Canada
Phone: 416-861-6112   **Fax:** 416-861-4720
Web site: http://www.hbc.com

2000 Stores

	The Bay	Zellers
Ontario	36	139
Quebec	19	61
British Columbia	19	41
Alberta	16	30
Manitoba	3	9
Nova Scotia	3	15
Saskatchewan	3	12
New Brunswick	—	12
Newfoundland	—	7
Prince Edward Island	—	2
Total	**99**	**328**

PRODUCTS/OPERATIONS

2000 Sales & Operating Income

	Sales		Operating Income	
	C$ mil.	% of total	C$ mil.	% of total
Zellers	4,598	60	150	37
Bay	2,594	35	128	32
Financial services	309	4	124	31
Other	104	1	(6)	—
Adjustments	(309)	—	(124)	—
Total	**7,296**	**100**	**272**	**100**

Stores
Bay (department stores)
Best Value (discount stores)
Fields (small-town clothing stores)
Home Outfitters (household furnishings)
Hudson Bay Company Outfitters (outdoor gear)
Zellers (discount stores)

COMPETITORS

Canadian Tire
Chateau Stores of Canada
Costco Wholesale
Dylex
The Gap
Gendis
Home Depot
North West Company
Reitmans
Sears Canada
Spiegel
Toys "R" Us
Wal-Mart

HISTORICAL FINANCIALS & EMPLOYEES

Toronto: HBC FYE: January 31	Annual Growth	1/91	1/92	1/93	1/94	1/95	1/96	1/97	1/98	1/99	1/00
Sales (C$ mil.)	4.4%	4,970	5,032	5,152	5,442	5,829	5,985	6,007	6,447	7,075	7,296
Net income (C$ mil.)	0.7%	90	78	117	148	151	35	36	(90)	40	96
Income as % of sales	—	1.8%	1.6%	2.3%	2.7%	2.6%	0.6%	0.6%	—	0.6%	1.3%
Earnings per share (C$)	(5.8%)	2.01	1.61	2.32	2.72	2.66	0.59	0.61	(1.47)	0.55	1.17
Stock price - FY high (C$)	—	34.00	37.00	32.25	41.13	32.63	28.75	25.10	38.00	34.30	23.85
Stock price - FY low (C$)	—	15.75	23.88	25.50	29.25	22.88	17.13	16.00	23.80	15.60	13.80
Stock price - FY close (C$)	(5.2%)	24.00	29.25	29.38	32.38	23.75	17.50	23.85	25.75	15.70	14.80
P/E - high	—	17	23	14	15	12	49	41	—	62	20
P/E - low	—	8	15	11	11	9	29	26	—	28	12
Dividends per share (C$)	(8.5%)	0.80	0.80	0.80	0.80	0.92	0.92	0.72	0.72	0.72	0.36
Book value per share (C$)	3.0%	23.53	24.43	25.92	28.56	30.76	30.24	29.92	27.54	27.58	30.62
Employees	2.7%	55,000	56,500	56,400	62,200	63,700	60,900	60,000	61,500	65,000	70,000

STOCK PRICE HISTORY
HIGH/LOW/CLOSE

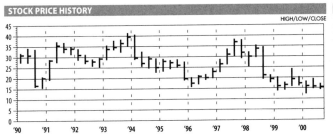

2000 FISCAL YEAR-END
Debt ratio: 23.6%
Return on equity: 4.4%
Cash (C$ mil.): 8
Current ratio: 2.06
Long-term debt (C$ mil.): 700
No. of shares (mil.): 74
Dividends
  Yield: 0.0%
  Payout: 0.3%
Market value ($ mil.): 1,095

HUTCHISON WHAMPOA LIMITED

Hutchison Whampoa has a hand in just about everything in Hong Kong. The company, one of Hong Kong's oldest *hongs* (trading companies), has extensive holdings in ports and shipping, food processing and distribution, retailing, manufacturing, and telecommunications (including fixed-line, mobile phone, and paging services). The group owns hotels, a sizable portfolio of Hong Kong properties, and additional real estate in the Bahamas, China, Japan, and the UK. Hutchison Whampoa also has interests in energy and financial services.

The firm is well placed to benefit from Hong Kong's reversion to Chinese sovereignty, thanks to the connections of its rags-to-riches chairman, Li Ka-shing, who has spent years building business relationships inside China. Li's Cheung Kong (Holdings) Limited owns 49.9% of Hutchison Whampoa. In turn, Hutchison Whampoa owns about 85% of Cheung Kong Infrastructure, which has interests in Asian

transportation, energy, and construction material businesses.

One of the firm's oldest and most lucrative segments is shipping. In addition to owning a controlling interest in Hongkong International Terminals, which handles traffic passing through Hong Kong's container port (the world's second busiest, behind Singapore), Hutchison Whampoa has large investments in terminal operations in southern China. It owns 40% of Shanghai Container Terminals and has other facilities throughout the Pearl River delta. The company also owns three key ports on Britain's East Coast: Thamesport, Harwich International, and Felixstowe, the UK's largest container port.

With an eye to the future, the firm is investing heavily in telecom projects in Hong Kong and buying stakes in communications and technology companies in Asia and Europe.

Hongkong and Whampoa Dock was the first registered company in Hong Kong. The enterprise was founded in 1861 when it bought dry docks in Whampoa (near Canton, China) after the kidnapping and disappearance of the docks' owner, John Couper, during the Second Opium War (1856-60). It bought docks in Hong Kong in 1865.

Founded in 1880 by John Hutchison, Hutchison International became a major Hong Kong consumer goods importer and wholesaler. It took control of Hongkong and Whampoa Dock and in A. S. Watson (drugstores, supermarkets, soft drinks) during an acquisition spree in the 1960s. The purchases entailed a complex web of deals that fell apart in the mid-1970s. To save Hutchison International, the Hongkong & Shanghai Bank took a large stake in the company and brought in Australian turnaround specialist Bill Wyllie. Wyllie slashed expenses, sold 103 companies in 1976, and bought the rest of Hongkong and Whampoa Dock in 1977. The company became Hutchison Whampoa that year.

In a surprise move, in 1979 Hongkong & Shanghai Bank sold its 23% stake in Hutchison to Cheung Kong Holdings: Cheung Kong founder Li Ka-shing, who began his career at age 14 by selling plastic flowers, became the first Chinese to control a British-style *hong*. Wyllie left in 1981.

In the 1980s Hutchison redeveloped its older dockyard sites, which had become prime real

estate. The company's International Terminals unit grew with Hong Kong's container traffic into the world's largest privately owned container terminal operator. In the 1980s the firm diversified into energy (buying stakes in utility Hongkong Electric and Canada-based Husky Oil) and precious metals and mining. It also moved into telecommunications, buying Australian paging and UK mobile telephone units in 1989.

The following year the *hong* launched the AsiaSat I satellite in a venture with Cable & Wireless (C&W) and China International Trust & Investment. More acquisitions followed, including European mobile phone businesses and telecom equipment makers. In 1996 the firm reorganized its Hong Kong telecom operations into Hutchison Telecommunications and launched its European wireless operations as a new public company, Orange.

In 1999 the company and C&W sold their stakes in AsiaSat. It also traded its stake in Orange to Mannesmann, acquiring 10% of the German conglomerate, which itself was acquired by Vodafone Air Touch in 2000. Also in 1999 Hutchison Whampoa and Global Crossing formed a $1.2 billion telecom joint venture to build a fiber-optic network in China.

The next year Hutchison Whampoa, Dutch phone company KPN, and Japanese mobile phone giant NTT DoCoMo formed an alliance to bid on next-generation mobile phone licenses in Europe.

OFFICERS

Chairman: Li Ka-shing, age 71
Deputy Chairman: Victor T. K. Li, age 35
Group Managing Director: Canning K. N. Fok, age 48
Deputy Group Managing Director:
Susan M. F. Chow Woo, age 46
Group Finance Director: Frank J. Sixt, age 48
Executive Director: Kam Hing Lam, age 53
Executive Director: Dominic K. M. Lai
Executive Director: George C. Magnus, age 64
Company Secretary: Edith Shih
General Manager Human Resources: Mary Tung
Auditors: PricewaterhouseCoopers

LOCATIONS

HQ: Hutchison House, 22nd Floor,
10 Harcourt Road, Hong Kong
Phone: +852-2128-1188   **Fax:** +852-2128-1705
Web site: http://www.hutchison-whampoa.com

Hutchison Whampoa operates in Hong Kong and
mainland China. It has other, diversified holdings in a
number of countires, including Australia, the Bahamas,
Canada, Germany, Ghana, India, Indonesia, Israel, Japan,
Macao, Myanmar, Panama, Singapore, Sri Lanka,
Switzerland, Taiwan, Thailand, the UK, and the US.

1999 Sales

	% of total
Hong Kong	70
Asia	11
North America	8
Mainland China	6
Europe	5
Total	**100**

PRODUCTS/OPERATIONS

1999 Sales

	% of total
Retail, manufacturing & other services	39
Property development & holdings	19
Ports & related services	19
Telecommunications	13
Energy, infrastructure, finance & investment	10
Total	**100**

Selected Subsidiaries and Affiliates
A. S. Watson & Co., Limited (foods and retail holding
company)
Hongkong and Whampoa Dock Co., Limited
Hongkong Electric Holdings Limited (30%, utility)
Hongkong International Terminals Limited (89%)
Hongkong United Dockyards Limited (50%)
Husky Energy (Canada)
Hutchison Properties Limited
Hutchison Telecommunications Limited
Port of Felixstowe Limited (90%, UK)
Procter & Gamble-Hutchison Limited (20%, consumer
products)
Shanghai Container Terminals Limited (40%, China)
tom.com limited (40%, Internet portal)

COMPETITORS

AT&T	Nextel
BT	SBC Communications
Cable and Wireless	SkyTel Communications
China Mobile (Hong Kong)	Sprint PCS
Deutsche Telekom	Swire Pacific
France Telecom	Verizon
Hopewell Holdings	Wharf Holdings
Jardine Matheson	

HISTORICAL FINANCIALS & EMPLOYEES

OTC: HUWHY FYE: December 31	Annual Growth	12/90	12/91	12/92	12/93	12/94	12/95	12/96	12/97	12/98	12/99
Sales ($ mil.)	14.9%	2,048	2,469	2,716	3,205	3,899	4,530	4,740	5,755	6,633	7,135
Net income ($ mil.)	47.7%	451	428	394	816	1,037	1,237	1,554	1,635	1,124	15,102
Income as % of sales	—	22.0%	17.3%	14.5%	25.5%	26.6%	27.3%	32.8%	28.4%	16.9%	211.7%
Earnings per share ($)	43.8%	0.74	0.70	0.62	1.16	1.43	1.71	2.15	2.07	1.45	19.50
Stock price - FY high ($)	—	8.50	10.58	12.91	25.56	27.17	30.31	40.38	53.00	36.25	66.70
Stock price - FY low ($)	—	4.94	7.63	8.95	9.59	18.17	16.19	28.75	29.25	18.00	30.50
Stock price - FY close ($)	27.1%	7.69	9.38	9.75	24.91	20.22	30.03	39.25	31.10	34.75	66.70
P/E - high	—	11	15	21	22	19	18	19	26	25	3
P/E - low	—	7	11	14	8	13	9	13	14	12	2
Dividends per share ($)	10.7%	0.42	0.44	0.36	0.44	0.60	0.76	0.97	1.02	0.83	1.05
Book value per share ($)	25.8%	5.19	5.85	6.91	8.81	10.21	10.52	11.52	14.44	14.05	40.84
Employees	10.9%	13,000	15,000	17,700	22,500	26,855	29,137	27,733	31,271	32,000	33,000

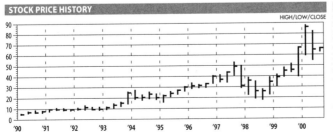

STOCK PRICE HISTORY HIGH/LOW/CLOSE

1999 FISCAL YEAR-END
Debt ratio: 24.7%
Return on equity: 71.0%
Cash ($ mil.): 5,173
Current ratio: 1.34
Long-term debt ($ mil.): 10,380
No. of shares (mil.): 775
Dividends
 Yield: 0.0%
 Payout: 0.1%
Market value ($ mil.): 51,703

HYUNDAI GROUP

OVERVIEW

Hyundai Group is so vertically integrated that it hurts the neck. Seoul-based Hyundai (which in the US is pronounced to rhyme with "Sunday") is one of South Korea's five largest *chaebol* (family-run industrial groups). Core business areas are auto manufacturing and services, electronics (Hyundai is one of the world's leading makers of dynamic random access memory, or DRAM), home and industrial construction, financial services, and shipbuilding. The group is also engaged in trade, shipping, petrochemical production and oil refining, and machinery, metals, and aircraft manufacturing.

Still untangling itself from Asia's economic crisis of the late 1990s, Hyundai is selling unprofitable companies and scaling back on domestic investments. The *chaebol* have been ordered by the government to combine overlapping businesses. Hyundai has announced plans to spin off two profitable units: Hyundai Automotive (including Hyundai Motor and Kia Motors) and Hyundai Heavy Industries.

Hyundai is controlled by the family of founder Chung Ju-Yung, although regulators are pushing to weaken the family's role.

HISTORY

Eager to get off the farm, 18-year-old Chung Ju-Yung stole his father's cow and sold it to pay his way to Seoul. After WWII Chung went into business repairing trucks for US armed forces in South Korea. In 1947 Chung started Hyundai Engineering and Construction, the first Korean contractor to win overseas construction projects, and Hyundai Motor was formed in 1967 to assemble Fords.

Chung was a gambler. When Hyundai (the name means "the present time") won a $1 billion contract in the 1970s to build a port in Jubail, Saudi Arabia, Chung saved money by using Korean parts and not insuring the shipments, risking ruin. The gamble paid off, and Hyundai became a major player in Middle East construction.

In the 1970s Chung was supported by the militarist Park government, and his Hyundai enterprises multiplied. He began building the world's largest shipyard (Hyundai Heavy Industries) in 1973, despite having no experience in shipbuilding. Chung succeeded thanks to government backing, near-monopoly conditions, and an extremely hardworking Korean labor force. With help from 15%-owner Mitsubishi Motors, Hyundai Motor built the first Korean car, the Pony, in 1975. Chung created Hyundai Corp., the group's international trading arm, the next year.

Never deterred by any lack of experience, Hyundai Group formed Hyundai Electronics Industries in 1983 to produce semiconductors and microcomputer equipment. It spent heavily on electronics, but without success.

Its low labor costs led Hyundai to start an export drive in the 1980s. It began shipping the Pony to Canada in 1984 and became #4 in auto sales there the next year. In the US the group introduced Blue Chip-brand PCs in 1986 and — in the most-successful launch of an imported car in US history — the inexpensive Excel subcompact.

Then things fell apart. When the military government relinquished power, workers, no longer strictly controlled, began a rash of strikes that continued well into the mid-1990s. Wage increases led to the export of jobs. Car exports fell as South Korea's currency rose and as quality problems with Hyundai cars increased.

Hyundai suffered political backlash after Chung's failed 1992 presidential campaign (he ran on an antigovernment platform). Besides denying Hyundai loans, the government refused the group permission to list some subsidiaries in the OTC market and subjected it to retaliatory audits. An abject apology by Chung in 1993 improved the situation.

In 1995 Hyundai acquired AT&T's electronics business, Symbios (originally part of NCR), and the next year bought Maxtor, a US maker of disk drives. But by 1998 the economy had worsened. To raise cash, Hyundai sold Symbios and spun off about 52% of Maxtor to the public. But Hyundai's auto business wasn't cut back: After a monthlong strike Hyundai Motor backed off plans to cut some 2,600 auto workers, and it joined with other group members to buy a 51% stake in ailing competitor Kia Motors. That year Hyundai — one of several *chaebol* fined for illegally funneling money to weak subsidiaries — was slapped with a $28 million fine.

In 1999 Hyundai bought control of LG Group's semiconductor operations (now Hyundai MicroElectronics) and made plans to consolidate the unit with its own electronics business. As Hyundai and its creditors negotiated the group's restructuring in 2000, Chung stepped down as honorary chairman. Feuding among members of the Chung family complicated reorganization efforts.

President and Representative Director, Hyundai Corporation: Chung Chai-Kwan
Director, Accounting, Hyundai Corporation: Kim Yeon-Seon
Chairman, President, and CEO, Hyundai Electronic Industries: Park Chong Sup
Chairman and CEO, Hyundai Motor and Kia Motors: Chung Mong Koo
Chairman, Hyundai Heavy Industries: Kim Hyung Byuk
President and CEO, Hyundai Engineering and Construction: Kim Yoon-kyu
President and CEO, Hyundai Heavy Industries: Cho Choong Hooy
Human Resources, Hyundai Corporation: Kim Minju
Investor Relations, Hyundai Corporation: Lee Sunkyung
Auditors: Young Wha Accounting Corporation

HQ: 140-2, Kye-dong, Chongro-ku, Seoul 110-793, South Korea
Phone: +82-2-746-1114   **Fax:** +82-2-741-2341
Web site: http://www.hyundai.net

Hyundai Group does business in 180 countries.

Selected Business Divisions and Group Affiliates

Automobiles
Hyundai Motor Co.
Hyundai Precision & Industry Co., Ltd.
Kia Motors Corp.

Construction
Hyundai Engineering & Construction Co., Ltd.
Korea Industrial Development Co., Ltd.

Electronics
Hyundai Autonet Co., Ltd.
Hyundai Electronics Industries Co., Ltd.
Hyundai Elevator Co., Ltd.
Hyundai MicroElectronics)

Finance and Services
Hyundai Asan Corp.
Hyundai Corp.
Hyundai Finance Corp.
Hyundai Investment Trust Management Co., Ltd.
Hyundai Logistics Co., Ltd.
Hyundai Merchant Marine Co., Ltd.
Hyundai Research Institute
Hyundai Securities Co., Ltd.
Hyundai Unicorns Baseball Club

Heavy Industries
Hyundai Heavy Industries Co., Ltd.
Hyundai Mipo Dockyard Co., Ltd.
Hyundai Petrochemical Co., Ltd.
Hyundai Pipe Co., Ltd.
Inchon Iron and Steel Co., Ltd.

Bechtel	IBM	Samsung
Compaq	Isuzu	Schneider
Daewoo	ITOCHU	Siemens
Deere	LG Group	SK Group
Fiat	Marubeni	Tenneco
Ford	Mitsubishi	Automotive
Fujitsu	Motorola	Texas
General Motors	National	Instruments
Hitachi	Semiconductor	Toyota
Honda	NEC	

IKEA INTERNATIONAL A/S

OVERVIEW

If you're looking for fussy furniture in neutral tones, IKEA is not the place for you. Based in Humlebaek, Denmark, IKEA International is one of the world's leading furniture retailers, with about 160 franchised stores in about 30 countries and an international mail-order business. Known for its use of bold colors and creative product names (a Ticka alarm clock, a Ringo stool), the company sells furniture and other household items, including dinnerware, pillows, lighting, and rugs. IKEA's stores feature restaurants serving Swedish cuisine.

The company built its reputation by designing inexpensive furniture in sleek Scandinavian styles. To cut transportation costs and reduce damage to merchandise, IKEA ships its products unassembled (Europeans call it "flat-pack"); customers assemble the goods at home. IKEA designs its products and contracts out much of the manufacturing to 2,150 suppliers in some 55 countries.

IKEA is owned by Netherlands-based Stichting Ingka, a charitable foundation whose honorary chairman is IKEA founder Ingvar Kamprad. The frugal, hands-on leader has made headlines with revelations that he had Nazi sympathies and is an alcoholic.

HISTORY

At the age of 17, Ingvar Kamprad formed his own company in Sweden in 1943, peddling fish, vegetable seeds, and magazines by bicycle. He called the company IKEA, an acronym for his name and the village in which he grew up (Elmtaryd, Agunnaryd). Four years later he added the newly invented ballpoint pen to his product assortment and started a mail-order catalog.

In 1950 Kamprad added furniture and housewares to his mail-order products, and in 1953 he bought a furniture factory and opened a small showroom. The showroom was a hit with price-conscious Swedes and was replaced by the first official IKEA store in 1958. The first store outside Sweden was established in 1963 in Norway. Two years later the company opened its flagship store in Stockholm, a 150,000-sq.-ft. marvel whose round design was inspired by the Guggenheim Museum in New York. The store featured a nursery, a restaurant, a bank, and parking spaces for 1,000 cars. By 1969 two more stores were opened in Sweden and another in Denmark.

A fire badly damaged the Stockholm store in 1973, but the subsequent fire sale pulled in more shoppers than the store's grand opening. That year IKEA expanded beyond Scandinavia, opening stores in Switzerland and Germany. In 1976 it opened its first store outside Europe, in Canada, and during the late 1970s and early 1980s, it entered Australia, the Canary Islands, Hong Kong, Iceland, Kuwait, Saudi Arabia, and Singapore. To avoid questions of succession after his death, Kamprad in 1980 transferred ownership of the company to a charitable foundation. IKEA opened its first US store, in Philadelphia, in 1985. Anders Moberg was named president of IKEA in 1986. By 1991 there were seven outlets in the US and 95 total in 23 countries. IKEA began its push into Eastern Europe two years later, but at the same time struggled with economic downturns in its major markets, Germany and Scandinavia.

A company TV advertising campaign in 1994 included one spot featuring a gay couple, with no apparent fallout. But Kamprad's reluctant announcement that he had associated with pro-Nazi groups in the 1940s and 1950s brought a torrent of bad press. The revelation prompted IKEA to reconsider opening a store in Israel, believing the Israeli government would not sanction the investment. Instead, Jewish groups claimed the company was deliberately avoiding the country. IKEA agreed in 1995 to open an Israeli store and was finally granted a license for a franchise to Blue Square - Israel Ltd. in 1997.

That year IKEA announced plans to build about 20 plants over five years in the Baltics, Bulgaria, and Romania, a move designed to reduce its dependence on contract manufacturers and nearly double its own manufacturing capacity. Also in 1997 it began offering prefab housing in Sweden with construction firm Skanska.

IKEA opened its largest store (400,000 sq. ft.) outside Europe in Chicago in 1998 and announced plans to open more stores in Russia, China, and Eastern Europe. Also that year Kamprad acknowledged that he has been dependent on alcohol for much of his adult life. In 1999 Anders Dahlvig was named group president, replacing Moberg, who left to take a position with retailer Home Depot. In March 2000 the company opened its first store in Moscow, with plans for more Russian locations.

Honarary Chairman: Ingvar Kamprad
Group President: Anders Dahlvig
CFO: Hans Gydell
President, IKEA North America: Jan Kjellman
CFO, IKEA North America: Donald Ball
Manager, Human Resources: Karl Lonn
Manager, Human Resources, North America:
  Pernille Spiers-Lopez

LOCATIONS

HQ: Ny Strandvej 21, DK-3053 Humlebaek, Denmark
Phone: +45-49-15-50-00   **Fax:** +45-49-15-50-01
US HQ: 496 W. Germantown Pike,
  Plymouth Meeting, PA 19462
US Phone: 610-834-0180
Web site: http://www.ikea.com

1999 Sales

	% of total
Europe	
Germany	24
The UK	12
France	8
Sweden	8
Other	31
North America	
The US	10
Other	4
Asia	3
Total	**100**

PRODUCTS/OPERATIONS

Selected Products

Armchairs	Instruments for children
Bath accessories	Kitchen organizers
Bath suites	Kitchen units
Bean bags	Leather sofas
Bed linens	Lighting
Beds and bedroom suites	Mattresses
Bookcases	Mirrors
Boxes	Office chairs and suites
CD storage	Posters
Ceiling lamps	Rugs
Children's furniture	Sofas and sofa beds
Clocks	Spotlights
Coffee tables	Stools
Cookware	Table lamps
Cord management	Toy storage
Desk accessories	TV cabinets and stands
Dining tables and chairs	Utility storage
Dinnerware	Video storage
Entertainment units	Wall shelves and systems
Floor lamps	Wardrobe units
Frames	Window treatments

COMPETITORS

Bombay Company
Euromarket Designs
Great Universal Stores
Heilig-Meyers
Horten
Hulsta-Werke Huls
John Lewis Partnership
METRO AG
MFI Furniture
Otto Versand
Pier 1 Imports
Pinault-Printemps-Redoute
Skandinavisk Holding
Williams-Sonoma

HISTORICAL FINANCIALS & EMPLOYEES

Private FYE: August 31	Annual Growth	8/90	8/91	8/92	8/93	8/94	8/95	8/96	8/97	8/98	8/99
Sales ($ mil.)	10.0%	3,415	3,777	4,721	4,294	4,809	5,487	6,149	5,885	7,026	8,075
Employees	13.2%	—	—	—	—	26,600	26,600	33,400	36,400	36,400	49,400

SALES HISTORY

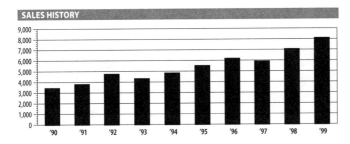

IMPERIAL CHEMICAL INDUSTRIES

OVERVIEW

Selling many of its commodities operations, London-based Imperial Chemical Industries (ICI) has moved from the madding crowd of commodity chemical production to focus on specialty products and paints. Its specialty products group consists of National Starch (industrial adhesives, starch), Quest (fragrance, food ingredients, flavors), and Industrial Specialties (oleochemicals, surfactants, catalysts, silica products). Its paint offerings include the Alba, Dulux, and Glidden brands. Specialty products and paints account for 67%

of sales. ICI's industrial chemicals segment makes petrochemicals and caustic soda, chlorine, sulfuric acid, and refrigerants.

ICI began transforming itself from being a bulk chemicals company, vulnerable to cyclical pricing, when it bought Uniliver's specialty chemicals business. It gained market share in specialty starches, industrial adhesives, fragrances, and flavors. To remedy heavy debt associated with the purchase, ICI has disposed of more than 50 companies.

HISTORY

Imperial Chemical Industries (ICI) began in 1926 when four British chemical companies (Nobel Industries; Brunner, Mond and Company; United Alkali; and British Dyestuffs) merged to compete with German cartel I. G. Farben. The most-famed ICI predecessor, Nobel Industries, was created as the British arm of Alfred Nobel's explosives empire. Nobel mixed nitroglycerin with porous clay to make dynamite. In 1886 he created the London-based Nobel Dynamite Trust to embrace British and German interests. After Nobel's death in 1896, the empire unraveled, and WWI severed the German and UK components of the Nobel firm. The British arm became Nobel Industries (1920).

In 1929 ICI and American chemical company DuPont signed a patents-and-process agreement to share research information. Around the same time it focused on research and between 1933 and 1935 created some 87 new products, including polyethylene.

After WWII the cartel club began to disband. The US government won antitrust sanctions against the DuPont-ICI alliance in 1952, and ICI faced new competition from the sundered components of I. G. Farben (Bayer, BASF, Hoechst). ICI added foreign operations in the 1960s, but fortunes declined, and in 1980 it posted losses and cut its dividend for the first time.

The company recruited turnaround artist John Harvey-Jones in 1982. He cut layers of decision making, reorganized along product lines, and added non-UK directors to the board. ICI also shifted production from bulk chemicals such as soda and chlorine to high-margin specialty chemicals such as pharmaceuticals and pesticides.

Harvey-Jones bought 100 companies between 1982 and his retirement in 1987. ICI expanded in the US market by purchasing

Beatrice's chemical operations (1985) and Glidden paints (1986).

ICI sold its nylon business to DuPont in 1992 and spun off its pharmaceutical and agricultural operations as Zeneca (now AstraZeneca) in 1993. It opened its first plant in China (1994), a paint factory, and named 30-year Unilever veteran Charles Miller Smith its new CEO in 1995.

In 1997 ICI bought Unilever's specialty chemicals unit in a deal worth about $8 billion. The same year it picked up Canada-based St. Clair Paint & Wallpaper. ICI then sold its polyester resin and intermediates operations (1997) and film business (1998) to Dupont for around $2 billion. In 1998 ICI paid $560 million for specialty chemicals maker Acheson Industries. ICI's attempts to reduce debt from the Unilever purchase stumbled when W. R. Grace & Co. terminated its deal to buy ICI's Crosfield silicas and catalysts business and DuPont and NL Industries backed out of the $1 billion purchase of ICI's titanium dioxide business.

Still saddled with debt, ICI sold a rash of companies in 1999: its utilities and services division to Enron for about $500 million; its polyurethanes and titanium-dioxide businesses and some petrochemicals businesses to US-based Huntsman for about $2.8 billion; its industrial coatings and auto refinish businesses in the Americas and Europe, and Germany-based coatings business to PPG Industries for $684 million; and its acrylics division (raw materials such as methylacrylates and value-added products such as Lucite and Perspex) to Belgium-based Ineos Acrylics for $833 million. That year ICI announced it would trim jobs.

Continuing to divest in 2000 ICI sold paint distribution network Master Distribution to Lafarge SA; it also agreed to sell its 30% stake in Huntsman ICI Holdings to joint venture partner Huntsman for $365 million.

OFFICERS

Chairman: Charles Miller Smith, age 60, $730,000 pay
VC: Rob J. Margetts, age 53, $615,000 pay
CEO: Brendan R. O'Neill, age 51, $777,000 pay
CFO: Alan G. Spall, age 55, $546,000 pay
EVP Coatings; Chairman and CEO, ICI Paints:
John D. G. McAdam, age 51, $373,000 pay
EVP Industrial Specialties: Richard N. Stillwell, age 50
EVP Strategy and Group Control: Rona A. Fairhead, age 38
Chairman and CEO, Quest International:
Paul Drechsler, age 43, $346,000 pay
Chairman, ICI Americas, Inc.: J. R. Danzeisen
General Counsel: Michael H. C. Herlihy, age 46
Auditors: KPMG Audit Plc

LOCATIONS

HQ: Imperial Chemical Industries PLC,
Imperial Chemical House, Millbank,
London SW1P 3JF, United Kingdom
Phone: +44-20-7834-4444   **Fax:** +44-20-7834-2042
US HQ: 10 Finderne Avenue, Bridgewater, NJ 08807
US Phone: 908-203-2800   **US Fax:** 908-685-6956
Web site: http://www.ici.com

1999 Sales

	$ mil.	% of total
Europe		
UK	3,262	28
Other countries	1,997	17
The Americas		
US	3,385	29
Other countries	1,023	9
Asia/Pacific	1,841	16
Other regions	108	1
Total	**11,616**	**100**

PRODUCTS/OPERATIONS

1999 Sales

	% of total
Specialty products & paints	67
Industrial chemicals	18
Discontinued operations	15
Total	**100**

Selected Products

Adhesives and sealants
Automotive refinish
Decorative paints
Flavor, fragrance, and food-ingredient products
Food products
Industrial starches
Lubricants
Packaging coatings
Petrochemicals
Surfactants
Specialty synthetic polymers

COMPETITORS

Air Products
 and Chemicals
Akzo Nobel
BASF AG
Bayer AG
Dow Chemical
DuPont
E.ON
Eastman Chemical
Elf Aquitaine
Engelhard
Ferro
Formosa Plastics
H.B. Fuller

Hercules
Huntsman
Lyondell Chemical
mg technologies
Millennium Chemicals
Mitsubishi Chemical
Occidental
Phillips Petroleum
PPG
Rohm and Haas
Royal Dutch/Shell
Sherwin-Williams
TOTAL FINA ELF
Union Carbide

HISTORICAL FINANCIALS & EMPLOYEES

NYSE: ICI FYE: December 31	Annual Growth	12/90	12/91	12/92	12/93	12/94	12/95	12/96	12/97	12/98	12/99
Sales ($ mil.)	(8.1%)	24,909	23,361	18,218	15,730	14,381	15,927	18,016	14,395	15,093	11,616
Net income ($ mil.)	(6.6%)	755	1,014	(861)	204	294	830	471	428	320	407
Income as % of sales	—	3.0%	4.3%	—	1.3%	2.0%	5.2%	2.6%	3.0%	2.1%	3.5%
Earnings per share ($)	12.1%	—	—	—	1.14	1.63	4.58	3.33	2.35	1.77	2.26
Stock price - FY high ($)	—	—	—	—	47.75	54.50	53.00	60.00	71.38	80.50	52.63
Stock price - FY low ($)	—	—	—	—	38.00	44.00	43.50	45.88	45.00	30.38	31.00
Stock price - FY close ($)	(1.7%)	—	—	—	47.25	46.50	46.75	52.00	64.94	34.94	42.56
P/E - high	—	—	—	—	42	33	11	18	9	26	19
P/E - low	—	—	—	—	33	27	9	14	6	10	11
Dividends per share ($)	(4.8%)	—	—	—	2.94	1.77	2.06	2.18	2.42	2.10	2.19
Book value per share ($)	(36.5%)	—	—	—	33.15	32.30	33.59	34.08	1.33	1.36	2.16
Employees	(9.6%)	132,100	123,600	114,000	67,000	67,500	64,800	64,000	69,500	58,700	53,500

STOCK PRICE HISTORY

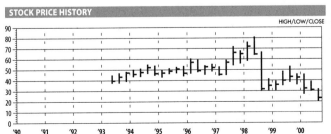

1999 FISCAL YEAR-END

Debt ratio: 90.2%
Return on equity: 126.9%
Cash ($ mil.): 436
Current ratio: 1.23
Long-term debt ($ mil.): 3,639
No. of shares (mil.): 182
Dividends
 Yield: 5.1%
 Payout: 96.9%
Market value ($ mil.): 7,746

IMPERIAL OIL LIMITED

OVERVIEW

By any empirical measurement, Imperial Oil is Canada's largest integrated oil company. The Toronto-based company, which is 70%-owned by Exxon Mobil, is the leading Canada-based producer, refiner, and marketer of petroleum products; one of Canada's largest natural gas producers; and a major supplier of petrochemicals. It owns one-quarter of the world's largest oil sands joint venture, Syncrude, which produces heavy crude oil and light synthetic oils. The company has proved reserves of 1.7 billion barrels of oil and natural gas liquids and 1.7 trillion cu. ft. of natural gas. Imperial sells gasoline to motorists at 2,500 Esso service stations; it

markets other petroleum products, such as heating oil and diesel fuel under the Esso name and other brands throughout Canada.

Most of Imperial's production comes from fields in Alberta and the Northwest Territories. At Cold Lake, Alberta, the company uses steam to recover very heavy crude and related products from oil sands deposits.

Imperial has reduced employment and closed service stations to stay competitive; it is also selling noncore assets and underperforming units (including refineries). Management is seeking to boost production from its plentiful oil sands holdings at Cold Lake.

HISTORY

London, Ontario, boomed from the discovery of oil in the 1860s and 1870s, but when the market for Canadian kerosene became saturated in 1880, 16 refiners banded together to form the Imperial Oil Company.

The company refined sulfurous Canadian oil, nicknamed "skunk oil" for its powerful smell. Imperial faced tough competition from America's Standard Oil, which marketed kerosene made from lighter, less-odorous Pennsylvania crude. Guided by American expatriate Jacob Englehart, Imperial built a better refinery and hired a chemist to develop a process to clean sulfur from the crude.

By the mid-1890s Imperial had expanded from coast to Canadian coast. Cash-starved from its expansion, the company turned to old nemesis Standard Oil, which bought controlling interest in Imperial in 1898. That interest is today held by Exxon Mobil.

After the turn of the century, Imperial began producing gasoline to serve the new automobiles. The horseless carriages were spooking the workhorses at the warehouse where fuel was sold, so an Imperial manager in Vancouver opened the first Canadian service station in 1907. The company marketed its gas under the Esso banner borrowed from Standard Oil.

An Imperial crew discovered oil in 1920 at Norman Wells in the remote Northwest Territories. In 1924 a subsidiary sparked a new boom with a gas well discovery in the Turner Valley area northeast of Edmonton. But soon Imperial's luck ran as dry as the holes it was drilling; it came away empty from the next 133 consecutive wells. That string ended in 1947 when it struck oil in Alberta at the Leduc No. 1. To get the oil to market, Imperial invested in the Interprovincial Pipe Line from Alberta to Superior, Wisconsin.

During the 1970s oil crisis, Imperial continued to search for oil in northern Canada. It found crude on land near the Beaufort Sea (1970) and in its icy waters (1972). The company formed its Esso Resources Canadian Ltd. subsidiary in 1978 to oversee natural resources production.

In 1989 Texaco, still reeling from a court battle with Pennzoil, sold Texaco Canada to Imperial. To diminish debt and comply with regulators, Imperial agreed to sell some of Texaco Canada's refining and marketing assets in Atlantic Canada, its interests in Interhome Energy, and oil and gas properties in western Canada.

Imperial reorganized in 1992, centralizing several units, and in 1993 closed its refinery at Port Moody, British Columbia. It sold most of its fertilizer business in 1994; disposed of 339 unprofitable gas stations in 1995; and the next year closed down Canada's northernmost oil refinery at Norman Wells.

In 1997 Imperial announced an ambitious program to expand Syncrude's oil sands bitumen upgrading plant. In 1998 Exxon agreed to buy Mobil, which had substantial Canadian oil assets. In 1999 Canada pre-approved the potential merger of Imperial Oil and Mobil Canada. Later that year Exxon completed its purchase of Mobil to form Exxon Mobil.

In the face of public pressure for cleaner gasoline (Imperial had been implicated by government tests as Canada's "dirtiest" oil producer), CEO Bob Peterson told shareholders in 2000 that he did not agree with the theory of global warming.

Chairman, President, and CEO: Robert B. Peterson,
age 62, $1,165,833 pay
SVP Finance and Administration and Controller:
Patrick T. Mulva, age 48, $337,917 pay
SVP Products and Chemicals Division: Brian J. Fischer,
age 53, $482,083 pay
SVP Resources Division: K.C. Williams, age 50,
$443,500 pay
VP and General Counsel: Ronald C. Walker, age 58,
$360,333 pay
VP and Treasurer: John F. Kyle
VP Human Resources: R.F. Lipsett
Corporate Secretary: John Zych
Auditors: PricewaterhouseCoopers LLP

LOCATIONS

HQ: 111 St. Clair Ave. W., Toronto,
Ontario M5W 1K3, Canada
Phone: 800-567-3776
Web site: http://www.imperialoil.ca

Imperial Oil's exploration and development are conducted
primarily in Alberta and the Northwest Territories. It
owns two refineries in Ontario, and one each in Alberta
and Nova Scotia. It also operates petrochemical and
plastics plants in Ontario and Nova Scotia.

PRODUCTS/OPERATIONS

1999 Sales

	% of total
Petroleum products	80
Natural resources	13
Chemicals	7
Total	**100**

Selected Products and Operations

Petroleum	Chemicals
Marketing	Benzene
Refining	Ethylene
Supply	Plasticizer intermediates
Transportation	Resins
	Solvents

Natural Resources
Exploration and
development
Land holdings
Petroleum and natural gas
production

COMPETITORS

Abraxas Petroleum	Occidental
Alberta Energy	PDVSA
Anderson Exploration	PEMEX
Ashland	Petro-Canada
BHP	PETROBRAS
BP	Phillips Petroleum
Canadian Natural	Pioneer Natural Resources
Canadian Pacific	Royal Dutch/Shell
Chevron	Suncor
Coastal	Sunoco
Conoco	Talisman Energy
Devon Energy	Texaco
Dominion Resources	TOTAL FINA ELF
DuPont	TrizecHahn
Elf Aquitaine	Ultramar Diamond
Eni	Shamrock
Koch	Unocal
Lyondell Chemical	USX-Marathon
Murphy Oil	

HISTORICAL FINANCIALS & EMPLOYEES

AMEX: IMO FYE: December 31	Annual Growth	12/90	12/91	12/92	12/93	12/94	12/95	12/96	12/97	12/98	12/99
Sales ($ mil.)	(5.0%)	11,226	7,944	7,041	6,725	7,781	6,810	7,577	7,463	5,815	7,091
Net income ($ mil.)	(2.2%)	493	140	153	211	310	377	574	593	358	402
Income as % of sales	—	4.4%	1.8%	2.2%	3.1%	4.0%	5.5%	7.6%	7.9%	6.2%	5.7%
Earnings per share ($)	2.6%	0.74	0.24	0.26	0.36	0.62	0.65	1.09	1.28	0.81	0.93
Stock price - FY high ($)	—	19.86	17.57	13.28	12.99	11.99	12.99	15.78	21.73	21.35	24.44
Stock price - FY low ($)	—	15.28	11.20	10.32	10.41	9.66	10.66	11.61	14.49	13.38	14.50
Stock price - FY close ($)	2.8%	16.86	11.57	10.57	11.28	10.99	12.03	15.65	21.29	16.06	21.63
P/E - high	—	27	73	51	36	19	20	14	17	26	26
P/E - low	—	21	47	40	29	16	16	11	11	17	16
Dividends per share ($)	4.0%	0.52	0.52	0.50	0.47	1.16	0.43	0.36	0.69	0.55	0.74
Book value per share ($)	(6.4%)	12.94	10.09	8.97	8.52	8.89	7.44	6.98	6.89	6.26	7.11
Employees	(8.6%)	14,702	11,936	10,152	9,470	8,252	7,800	7,480	7,100	6,700	6,550

STOCK PRICE HISTORY

HIGH/LOW/CLOSE

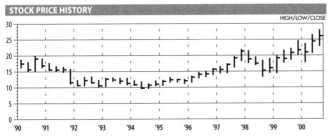

1999 FISCAL YEAR-END

Debt ratio: 21.8%
Return on equity: 13.9%
Cash ($ mil.): 425
Current ratio: 1.07
Long-term debt ($ mil.): 856
No. of shares (mil.): 431
Dividends
  Yield: 3.4%
  Payout: 79.6%
Market value ($ mil.): 9,333

IMPERIAL TOBACCO GROUP PLC

Imperial Tobacco Group wants to go up in smoke. The Bristol, UK-based company is the #2 UK cigarette firm (behind Gallaher Group). It makes and sells cigarettes such as premium brands Embassy and Regal, mid-priced Superkings and JPS (John Player Special), and low-priced Lambert & Butler. It also makes the world's #1 roll-your-own tobacco (Drum) and top UK brand Golden Virginia, as well as cigars, cigarette paper, and pipe tobacco. Imperial Tobacco sells products around the world although the UK rings up more than half of its sales.

Like rivals British American Tobacco and Gallaher, Imperial was spun off from a conglomerate eager to distance itself from increasingly problematic tobacco operations (it was part of Hanson until that group's 1996 four-way demerger). Like its fellow cigarette makers, Imperial is facing the European Union's ban on tobacco advertising scheduled to begin in 2001. Meanwhile, the company is expanding to new markets such as Africa and Asia. It has also expanded by acquiring several brands, including Peter Stuyvesant, in Australia and New Zealand.

HISTORY

Imperial Tobacco Group was formed in 1901 to fight American Tobacco's invasion of the UK. American Tobacco had become the dominant US tobacco company partly by using a large cash reserve to undercut competitors. When it bought UK tobacco and cigarette factory Ogden's that year, 13 UK tobacco firms responded by registering as The Imperial Tobacco Company. The firms (including Wills, Lambert & Butler, and John Player & Sons) continued to make and sell their products separately.

As expected, American Tobacco cut prices, and Imperial fought back, acquiring the Salmon & Cluckstein tobacco shop chain and offering bonuses to retailers that sold its products. When Imperial threatened US expansion in 1902, American Tobacco surrendered: It gave Ogden's to Imperial and halted its Ireland and Great Britain business in exchange for Imperial's pledge to stay out of the US (except for buying tobacco leaf). The two formed the British American Tobacco Company (BAT) to sell both firms' cigarettes overseas. But when American Tobacco split into four companies in 1911 and sold its BAT interest, the agreement was modified to let Imperial sell some of its brands in the US.

By the 1950s Imperial controlled more than 80% of the UK tobacco market, but its share decreased during the 1960s due partly to competition from Gallaher Group (Benson & Hedges). Imperial diversified, buying companies such as Golden Wonder Crisps snack food (1961) and the Courage & Barclay brewery (1972). In 1973 BAT and Imperial agreed that each firm would control its own brands in the UK and Continental Europe. Imperial sold the last of its stake in BAT in 1980. It bought US hotel and restaurant chain Howard Johnson in 1980 but sold it to Marriott Hotels in 1985.

Conglomerate Hanson Trust paid $4.3 billion for Imperial in a 1986 hostile takeover, ending a four-month battle between Hanson and food group United Biscuits. Hanson reduced Imperial's tobacco brands from more than 100 to five brand families (a move that decreased its UK market share to 33% by 1990). It also sold Imperial's drinks unit, including Courage and John Smith beer, to Elders IXL (now Foster's Brewing). Between 1986 and 1993 Hanson cut Imperial's tobacco operations from five factories and 7,500 employees to three factories and 2,600 employees; it also sold Imperial's restaurant and food operations.

As UK cigarette consumption dropped, Imperial began expanding overseas in 1994. By 1996 exports has risen to 15% of sales. That year Hanson, aiming to improve its falling share price, split its operations into four companies. Gareth Davis became CEO of Imperial. Also that year 12 people sued Imperial and rival Gallaher Group, alleging the firms continued using tar in cigarettes after knowing of its links to cancer (the lawsuit achieved group-action status but was later abandoned as the statute of limitations had expired).

Facing further declining UK cigarette sales and a government tax hike, Imperial bought the world's #1 cigarette paper brand, Rizla (1997), and Sara Lee's cut-tobacco unit, Douwe Egberts Van Nelle (1998), which it renamed Van Nelle Tabak. That acquisition added Drum hand-rolling tobacco and Amphora pipe tobacco to Imperial's brands. In 1999 the company added a bevy of Australian and New Zealand brands (Horizon, Brandon, Flagship, Peter Stuyvesant) from BAT, which unloaded the brands as part of its purchase of Rothmans International.

Chairman: Derek Bonham, age 56
VC: Anthony Alexander, age 61
Chief Executive: Gareth Davis, age 49
Secretary: Richard Hannaford, age 53
Finance Director: Robert Dyrbus, age 47
Corporate Affairs Director: Clive Inston, age 53
Human Resources Director: George E. C. Lankester
Business Development Director: Stuart Painter, age 63
**Group Finance Manager, Corporate Development and
  Investor Relations:** Allison Cooper
Auditors: PricewaterhouseCoopers LLP

LOCATIONS

HQ: PO Box 244, Upton Road, Southville,
  Bristol BS99 7UJ, United Kingdom
Phone: +44-117-963-6636   **Fax:** +44-117-966-7405
Web site: http://www.imperial-tobacco.com

1999 Sales

	% of total
UK	58
Other countries	42
Total	**100**

PRODUCTS/OPERATIONS

Selected Products and Brands

Cigarettes
Low-priced (Horizon, John Brandon, Lambert & Butler,
  Richmond)
Mid-priced (Escort, John Player, JPS/John Player
  Special, Peter Jackson, Superkings)
Premium (Embassy, Peter Stuyvesant, Regal)

Other
Cigarette Paper (Rizla Green, Rizla Red, Tally-Ho)
Cigars (Carl Upmann, Castella, Classic, Henri
  Wintermans, King Edward Coronets, Panama)
Pipe Tobacco (Amphora, St Bruno Ready Rubbéd)
Roll Your Own Tobacco (Blend 11, Brandaris, Champion,
  Dr Pat, Drum, Drum Milde, Five Star, Flagship,
  Golden Virginia, Greys, Horizon, Log Cabin, Pocket
  Edition, Roverstone, Rotterdam Shag, Stockman, Van
  Nelle, Virginia Gold)

COMPETITORS

Altadis
Austria Tabak
British American Tobacco
Gallaher
General Cigar
Japan Tobacco
Philip Morris International
Reemtsma
Skandinavisk Tobakskompagni
Swedish Match
Swisher International
Tiedemanns
UST

HISTORICAL FINANCIALS & EMPLOYEES

NYSE: ITY FYE: Saturday nearest Sept. 30	Annual Growth	9/90	9/91	9/92	9/93	9/94	9/95	9/96	9/97	9/98	9/99
Sales ($ mil.)	(30.8%)	—	—	—	—	—	—	5,969	6,257	1,611	1,979
Net income ($ mil.)	(4.5%)	—	—	—	—	—	—	542	342	392	473
Income as % of sales	—	—	—	—	—	—	—	9.1%	5.5%	24.4%	23.9%
Earnings per share ($)	—	—	—	—	—	—	—	—	—	—	1.82
Stock price - FY high ($)	—	—	—	—	—	—	—	—	—	—	24.88
Stock price - FY low ($)	—	—	—	—	—	—	—	—	—	—	18.13
Stock price - FY close ($)	—	—	—	—	—	—	—	—	—	—	23.50
P/E - high	—	—	—	—	—	—	—	—	—	—	14
P/E - low	—	—	—	—	—	—	—	—	—	—	10
Dividends per share ($)	—	—	—	—	—	—	—	—	—	—	1.08
Book value per share ($)	—	—	—	—	—	—	—	—	—	—	(9.33)
Employees	19.7%	—	—	—	—	—	—	2,800	3,296	3,630	4,800

STOCK PRICE HISTORY

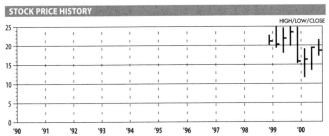

1999 FISCAL YEAR-END

Debt ratio: 100.0%
Return on equity: —
Cash ($ mil.): 336
Current ratio: 0.69
Long-term debt ($ mil.): 2,205
No. of shares (mil.): 260
Dividends
  Yield: 4.6%
  Payout: 59.3%
Market value ($ mil.): 6,120

INCO LIMITED

OVERVIEW

Inco turns nickel into gold. The Toronto-based company is the world's #1 producer of nickel, used primarily for manufacturing stainless steel. Inco also mines and processes cobalt, copper, gold, silver, and platinum. Inco also manufactures nickel battery materials and nickel foams, flakes, and powders for use in catalysts, electronics, and paints. Its primary mining and processing operations are in Canada, China, Indonesia, Japan, New Caledonia, South Korea, Taiwan, and the UK.

Digging its way in a challenging nickel market, the company continues to reduce base costs, develop new low-cost orebodies, and increase its value-added nickel products business. The company has expanded its processing facilities at PT International Nickel Indonesia, commissioned a nickel processing plant in Wales, and created Inco Special Products to increase production of value-added nickel products.

HISTORY

In 1883 a Canadian Pacific Railway blacksmith discovered copper and nickel deposits in the Sudbury Basin. Two companies — the Orford Nickel and Copper Company and the Canadian Copper Company — tried to exploit the ore but couldn't separate the copper from the nickel. Nickel was all but worthless at the time. In 1890 Orford, led by Robert Thompson, patented a process to separate the two metals just as the US Navy was beginning to use a nickel-steel alloy for armaments.

Enter financier J. P. Morgan, architect of U.S. Steel. With Morgan's help Orford and Canadian Copper combined with five smaller companies in 1902 to form New Jersey-based International Nickel Company. In 1916 the company formed a Canadian subsidiary, International Nickel Company of Canada.

Sales plummeted after WWI, and in a 1928 restructuring the Canadian subsidiary became the parent company. In 1929 International Nickel bought Mond Nickel, a British metals refiner. With the Mond deal, International Nickel controlled the world's nickel output, and in the 1950s it accounted for 85% of noncommunist production.

Oil crises and inflation decreased demand for metals and battered International Nickel in the 1970s and early 1980s. In 1974 the company bought ESB Ray-O-Vac, the world's largest maker of batteries. Two years later the company shortened its name to Inco Limited. The battery operations were sold in the early 1980s.

Inco suffered from lack of demand for its metals until 1986. Then-CEO Donald Phillips cut employees and boosted productivity at Inco's mines and refineries. When demand for stainless steel began its upswing in the late 1980s and prices rose, Inco's results went from dismal to delightful. Sales more than doubled from 1987 to 1989.

Metal prices declined again in the early 1990s in response to a North American recession and the entry of former Iron Curtain countries into the metals markets. In response, Inco cut costs and nickel production to try and cut the worldwide surplus. The company also reorganized. In 1991 it merged its gold interests with Consolidated TVX Mining (in 1993 it sold its 62% interest in TVX). These actions could not stave off a loss in 1992.

As the US economy recovered and new Asian markets developed, demand rose again. Exploration activities revved up with new ore discoveries in 1994 and 1995, but demand exceeded the supply of processed ore. In 1995 Inco bought a 25% share of the copper, cobalt, and nickel rights to rich deposits at Voisey's Bay in Newfoundland and Labrador; the following year it bought the remaining rights along with their holder, mining company Diamond Fields (the total cost was $3.2 billion).

Along with the Voisey's Bay purchase, Inco decided to unload some of its nonmining businesses. The company spun off Doncasters (aircraft components) in 1997. About 4,700 miners went on strike that year, cutting the company's nickel production by more than half.

As rising worldwide nickel production drove prices down in 1998, the company reduced its workforce by more than 1,400. It also sold Inco Alloys International to Special Metals for $365 million and used $310 million of that to reduce debt.

In 1999 Inco entered into joint ventures with Dowa Mining of Japan to search for deposits of copper, zinc, silver, and gold in Indonesia and Turkey. The company shut down its Manitoba nickel production facility that year after being unable to reach a contract agreement with labor. Inco also created Inco Special Products and commissioned a $14 million nickel processing plant in Wales to increase its sales of value-added nickel products.

Chairman and CEO: Michael D. Sopko, $605,000 pay
President: Scott M. Hand, $514,000 pay
EVP and CFO: Anthony E. Munday, $242,000 pay
EVP, General Counsel, and Secretary: Stuart F. Feiner, $302,000 pay
EVP Marketing: Peter J. Goudie
EVP Operations: Peter C. Jones, $299,500 pay
VP Environmental and Health Science: Bruce R. Conard
VP Exploration: Robert A. Horn
VP Human Resources: Lorne M. Ames
President and CEO, P.T. International Nickel Indonesia: Rumengan Musu
President and Director General, Goro Nickel S.A.: Peter G. Garritsen
President and Representative Director, Inco Limited, Japan: Shozo Kawaguchi
President, Inco Asia Limited and Inco Pacific Sales Limited: C.M. Shih
President, Inco United States: Richard L. Guido
President, International Nickel: David J. Anderson
Auditors: PricewaterhouseCoopers LLP

HQ: 145 King St. West, Ste. 1500,
Toronto, Ontario M5H 4B7, Canada
Phone: 416-361-7511 **Fax:** 416-361-7781
US HQ: Park 80 West-Plaza Two, Saddlebrook, NJ 07662
US Phone: 201-226-2000 **US Fax:** 212-368-4870
Web site: http://www.incoltd.com

Inco Limited's core subsidiaries operate mines and facilities in Canada, China, Indonesia, Japan, New Caledonia (in the southwest Pacific), South Korea, Taiwan, and the UK. The company also operates in France, Guatemala, and the US.

1999 Nickel Sales

	% of total
US	24
Asia	
Japan	21
Other countries	35
Europe	15
Other regions	5
Total	**100**

1999 Sales

	$ mil.	% of total
Primary nickel	1,658	79
Copper	196	9
Precious metals	152	7
Cobalt	48	2
Other	59	3
Total	**2,113**	**100**

Selected Products

Cobalt	Primary nickel
Copper	Rhodium
Palladium	Silver
Platinum	

Anglo American	Freeport-	Placer Dome
Barrick Gold	McMoRan	Rio Algom
BHP	Copper & Gold	Rio Tinto plc
Carso	Grupo Mexico	Southern Peru
Codelco	Newmont	Copper
CVRD	Mining	Trelleborg
Eramet	Noranda	WMC Limited
Falconbridge	Norilsk Nickel	Zambia Copper
	Phelps Dodge	

NYSE: N FYE: December 31	Annual Growth	12/90	12/91	12/92	12/93	12/94	12/95	12/96	12/97	12/98	12/99
Sales ($ mil.)	(4.2%)	3,108	2,999	2,559	2,131	2,484	3,471	3,105	2,367	1,766	2,113
Net income ($ mil.)	(30.4%)	441	83	(18)	28	22	227	179	75	(76)	17
Income as % of sales	—	14.2%	2.8%	—	1.3%	0.9%	6.5%	5.8%	3.2%	—	0.8%
Earnings per share ($)	—	4.18	0.74	(0.21)	0.08	0.03	1.82	1.09	0.25	(0.63)	(0.05)
Stock price - FY high ($)	—	31.88	38.00	34.38	27.75	31.25	38.00	36.75	37.63	20.69	23.69
Stock price - FY low ($)	—	22.13	23.88	19.13	17.38	21.38	23.50	28.75	17.00	8.25	10.38
Stock price - FY close ($)	(0.9%)	25.38	30.50	22.38	26.88	28.63	33.25	31.88	17.00	10.44	23.50
P/E - high	—	8	51	—	347	1,042	21	31	151	—	—
P/E - low	—	5	32	—	217	713	13	25	68	—	—
Dividends per share ($)	—	1.00	1.00	0.85	0.40	0.40	0.40	0.40	0.40	0.10	0.00
Book value per share ($)	5.0%	16.44	16.32	15.29	15.11	15.56	16.95	22.59	22.40	21.71	25.50
Employees	(6.9%)	19,387	18,369	17,724	16,087	15,709	15,818	16,308	14,278	11,007	10,198

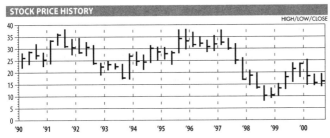

HIGH/LOW/CLOSE

Debt ratio: 20.0%
Return on equity: 0.5%
Cash ($ mil.): 38
Current ratio: 1.56
Long-term debt ($ mil.): 1,154
No. of shares (mil.): 182
Dividends
  Yield: —
  Payout: —
Market value ($ mil.): 4,267

INDUSTRIAL BANK OF JAPAN

OVERVIEW

Forget the Big Bang, the Industrial Bank of Japan (IBJ) is joining the Big Bank. Trying to get its house in order for Japan's Big Bang of financial deregulation (set to be complete in 2001), Tokyo-based IBJ joined with Fuji Bank and Dai-Ichi Kangyo Bank, forming the world's largest bank, Mizuho Holdings. IBJ is a subsidiary of Mizuho Holdings until the merger is fully completed in 2002.

IBJ is the largest of Japan's long-term credit banks (leading Shinsei Bank and Nippon Credit Bank) and offers wholesale loans and financial services to big corporations and institutional investors. In anticipation of deregulation, the firm is moving into investment advisory and asset management services, including mergers and acquisitions, investment banking, and trust services.

IBJ was still recovering from the collapse of Japan's overheated real estate market when another financial crisis in Asia reared its head. The multiple whammies have led IBJ to improve its risk-management processes, increase its capital reserves, and speed up efforts to ditch the bank's mountain of bad debt.

HISTORY

After Japan met the West in the 19th century, the Meiji Restoration undertook a national effort to modernize (1868). Prince Masayoshi Matsukata, the Meiji finance minister, shaped the country's new banking system. His plan included specialized, government-controlled banks designed to provide long-term financing for commerce.

Industrial Bank of Japan began operating in 1902. It lent money to the fledgling industries arising from the Meiji reforms. Almost immediately IBJ had to finance Japan's first war against a European power, Russia (with the help of US investment house Lehman-Kuhn Loeb, a predecessor of today's Lehman Brothers).

IBJ grew along with Japanese industry. It helped fund pre-WWII Japanese incursions into China; it also helped finance the military during the war. When defeat grew imminent, the government in 1944 ordered IBJ and three other banks to grant 2,000 key companies unlimited credit.

US occupiers "demilitarized" IBJ by forcing it to write down ¥7.5 billion in war-related loans. The US spared the bank after the Japanese government convinced the US that IBJ was essential to the national recovery. However, its direct links with the government were severed. With the economy still tottering, in 1952 Japan reorganized its banking system, reestablishing its industrial combines (formerly known as *zaibatsu*, now *keiretsu*) around individual city banks (to handle daily banking) and forming the long-term credit banks. IBJ prospered during Japan's resurgence in the 1950s and 1960s. The company helped create Nippon Steel in the 1960s.

In 1971 the bank began opening overseas branches to serve the foreign operations of its clients. IBJ fell prey in the 1980s to reduced loan demand. Part of this was due to the slowdown in activity after the oil shocks of the 1970s, but there was also a shift in the structure of finance as clients began raising money directly through corporate bonds.

IBJ began diversifying. It started issuing Eurobonds, and in 1985 it bought New York-based merchant bank J. Henry Schroder Bank & Trust. It also bought Aubrey G. Lanston & Co., a primary dealer in US Treasuries (1986), and formed The Bridgeford Group (US, 1990) to focus on mergers and acquisitions.

At the same time, demand for real estate loans was growing amid a binge of real estate speculation and development in Japan, and IBJ found plenty of business lending to *jusen* (mortgage companies). In 1992 the market collapsed, taking Japan's economy and much of its banking system with it. IBJ's earnings began declining from their all-time high in 1991 to a loss in 1996, when the company bit the bullet and wrote down 37% of its bad loans.

A collapse in Asian markets in 1997 and a bribery scandal that claimed one of IBJ's managing directors in 1998 further burdened the bank. Looking to move into new markets and battle declines in both banking and brokering, IBJ and brokerage Nomura Securities agreed in 1998 to form two joint ventures, aiding IBJ's shift from wholesale to investment banking.

In 1999 IBJ was one of 15 major banks to benefit from the government's ¥7.5 trillion bank-reform fund, intended to help heal the banks' loan wounds. Other reforms included allowing banks to deal independently in insurance and securities. IBJ that year agreed to a three-way merger with Fuji and Dai-Ichi Kangyo. In 2000 the banks combined under Mizuho Holdings, the world's largest bank, offering a sorely needed way for the banks to deflate swollen operations and employment rolls.

OFFICERS

Chairman: Yoh Kurosawa
President and CEO: Masao Nishimura, age 67
Deputy President: Yoshiyuki Fujisawa
Deputy President: Yozo Okumoto
Managing Director: Tsutomu Abe
Managing Director: Yuji Igarashi
Managing Director: Kisaburo Ikeda
Managing Director (CFO): Mitsunori Kanesaka
Managing Director: Shinji Kubo
Managing Director; Managing Director and General Manager, Grand Cayman Branch, Nassau Branch, and New York Branch: Shoji Noguchi
Managing Director: Toshiaki Ohuchi
Managing Director: Takashi Okamoto
Managing Director: Hiroshi Saito
Managing Director: Hiroshi Suzuki
Managing Director: Takao Suzuki
Managing Director: Yuji Suzuki
Managing Director: Yuji Watanabe
Managing Director: Masatake Yashiro
Managing Director: Masayuki Yasuoka
Managing Director, Personnel Department: Ikuo Kaminishi
Auditors: Chuo Audit Corporation

LOCATIONS

HQ: Nippon Kogyo Ginko
(Industrial Bank of Japan, Limited),
3-3, Marunouchi 1-chome, Chiyoda-ku,
Tokyo 100-8210, Japan
Phone: +81-3-3214-1111   **Fax:** +81-3-3201-7643
US HQ: 1251 Avenue of the Americas,
New York, NY 10020
US Phone: 212-282-3000   **US Fax:** 212-282-4250
Web site: http://www.ibjbank.co.jp/English

Industrial Bank of Japan has 26 branches in Japan and 18 overseas offices, as well as numerous foreign subsidiary and affiliate offices.

PRODUCTS/OPERATIONS

2000 Assets

	$ mil.	% of total
Cash & equivalents	6,186	2
Investment securities	71,851	18
Loans & bills discounted	215,906	54
Customers' liabilities for acceptances & guarantees	10,050	2
Trading assets	37,211	9
Other	61,293	15
Total	**402,497**	**100**

Selected Subsidiaries and Affiliates

PT. Bank IBJ Indonesia
Banque IBJ (France) S.A.
The Bridgeford Group (US)
IBJ Asia Securities Ltd.
IBJ Asset Management International Ltd.
IBJ Australia Bank Ltd.
IBJ Investment Trust Management Co., Ltd.
IBJ Nomura Financial Products plc
IBJ NW Asset Management Co., Ltd.
IBJ Securities Co., Ltd.
IBJ Trust and Banking Co., Ltd.
IBJ Whitehall Bank & Trust Co.
IBJ-BA Consulting Investitionsberatung GmbH
IBJ-DL Financial Technology Co., Ltd.
The Industrial Bank of Japan Trust Co.
Kogin Investment, Ltd.
Nomura IBJ Global Investment Advisors, Inc.
Nomura-IBJ Investment Services Co., Ltd.
Shinko Securities Co., Ltd.

COMPETITORS

Asahi Bank
Bank of Tokyo-Mitsubishi
Chase Manhattan
Citigroup
Credit Lyonnais
Credit Suisse
Dai-Ichi Kangyo
Daiwa
Deutsche Bank
Fuji Bank
HSBC Holdings
Mitsubishi Trust and Banking
Nippon Credit Bank
Nomura Securities
Norinchukin Bank
Sakura Bank
Sanwa Bank
Shinsei Bank
Sumitomo Bank
Tokai Bank

HISTORICAL FINANCIALS & EMPLOYEES

Subsidiary FYE: March 31	Annual Growth	3/91	3/92	3/93	3/94	3/95	3/96	3/97	3/98	3/99	3/00
Assets ($ mil.)	2.6%	320,501	331,939	365,589	410,840	468,290	375,184	374,643	369,954	387,595	402,497
Net income ($ mil.)	—	469	442	356	213	343	(593)	103	(1,523)	(1,522)	670
Income as % of assets	—	0.1%	0.1%	0.1%	0.1%	0.1%	—	0.0%	—	—	0.2%
Employees	3.8%	5,293	5,151	5,300	5,466	5,400	5,433	5,175	4,971	4,800	7,394

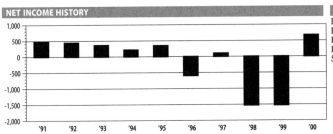

NET INCOME HISTORY

2000 FISCAL YEAR-END
Equity as % of assets: 3.8%
Return on assets: —
Return on equity: —
Long-term debt ($ mil.): 183,461
Sales ($ mil.): 28,431

ING GROEP N.V.

OVERVIEW

Together ING stands — a decreasingly rare hybrid of banking, insurance, and financial services. One of the top five global financial services companies (along with Citigroup and AXA), Amsterdam-based ING Groep offers life, health, and disability products; personal insurance lines (auto and fire coverage); commercial property/casualty insurance; and reinsurance. ING's banking lines range from humble post office deposit accounts (the Postbanks) in the Netherlands to consumer and corporate banking throughout Europe. Other lines are corporate finance, securities, and investment and asset management services (through its ING banking network and Barings subsidiaries) and auto, airplane, and other equipment leasing.

The company has recovered from investment banking arm ING Barings' spectacular crash and burn after the double whammies of the Nick Leeson trading scandal and the Asian and Russian economic crises. The unit, newly overhauled, has reduced its exposure in emerging markets and now focuses on serving mid-sized European businesses involved in such industries as media and telecommunications.

Other interests include investments in the German and French banking industries with ownership stakes in Allgemeine Deutsche Direktbank, Crédit Commercial de France, and BHF-BANK (ING plans to buy the 58% it doesn't own). The company is increasing its global holdings through acquisitions and has a license to do business in China.

HISTORY

ING Groep's roots go back to 1845 when its earliest predecessor, the Netherlands Insurance Co., was founded. The firm began expanding geographically; in 1903 it added life insurance. In 1963 it merged with the century old Nationale Life Insurance Bank to form Nationale-Nederland (NN). Over the next three decades, the company grew primarily through acquisitions in Europe, North America, and Australia. In 1986 NN became the first European life insurance company to be licensed in Japan.

Another predecessor, the Rijkspostspaarbank (State Savings Bank), was founded in 1881 to provide Dutch citizens with simple post office savings accounts. In 1918 the Postcheque-en Girondienst (giro) system was established to allow people to use vouchers drawn on their savings accounts to pay bills. This system became the main method of settling accounts (instead of bank checking accounts, which became standard in the US).

Rijkspostspaarbank and Postcheque merged in 1986 to become Postbank. Postbank merged in 1989 with the Nederlandse Middenstandsbank (founded 1927) to become NMB Postbank. The vast amounts of cash tied up in the post office savings and giro systems fueled NMB's business.

In 1991, as the Europe economic union became a reality, and barriers between banking and insurance began to fall, NN merged with NMB Postbank to form Internationale Nederland Groep (ING). ING began cutting costs, shedding redundant offices and unprofitable operations in both its segments. In the US, where insurance and banking were legally divided, the company "debanked" itself in order to keep its more lucrative insurance

operations (but retained the right to provide banking services to those operations).

In the 1990s ING sought to increase its investment banking and finance operations. In 1995 it took over UK-based Barings Bank (personal banker to the Queen of England) after Nicholas Leeson, a trader in Barings' Singapore office, lost huge sums of money in derivatives trading. The acquisition gave the firm a higher profile but cost more than anticipated and left it embroiled in lingering legal actions.

In 1996 ING bought Poland's Bank Slaski (the company first entered Poland in 1994). The next year it expanded its securities business by acquiring investment bank Furman Selz, doubled its US life insurance operations by purchasing Equitable of Iowa, and listed on the NYSE. In 1998 ING's acquisition strategy again involved Europe and North America: It bought Belgium's Banque Bruxelles Lambert and Canadian life insurer Guardian Insurance Co. (from Guardian Royal Exchange now part of Sun Life and Provincial).

In 1999 ING turned eastward, kicking off asset management operations in India and buying a minority stake in Korea's HC&B (formerly Housing & Commercial Bank). In 2000 the company bulked up its North American operations with the purchase of 40% of Savia SA, a Mexican insurance concern. It also bought US firm ReliaStar Financial in a $6 billion deal and made plans to purchase Charterhouse Securities from Crédit Commercial de France.

Chairman of the Executive Board:
Godfried van der Lugt, age 59
VC of the Executive Board: E. Kist, age 55
Member Executive Board and CFO: Cees Maas, age 52
**Member Executive Board; Chairman, ING Asset
  Management:** Alexander Rinnooy Kan, age 50
Member Executive Board; Chairman, ING Europe:
Michel Tilmant, age 47
Member Executive Board; Chairman, ING Europe:
Hessel Lindenbergh, age 56
**Member Executive Board; Chairman, ING Americas
  and ING Asia/Pacific:** Fred Hubbell, age 48
**General Manager, Human Resources and Management
  Development:** Phillip de Koneng Gans
Auditors: Ernst & Young

HQ: Strawinskylaan 2631,
1000 ZZ Amsterdam, The Netherlands
Phone: +31-20-541-54-11   **Fax:** +31-20-541-54-44
US HQ: 5780 Powers Ferry Rd., Atlanta, GA 30327
US Phone: 770-980-3300   **US Fax:** 770-980-3301
Web site: http://www.inggroup.com

1999 Sales

	$ mil.	% of total
Europe		
The Netherlands	23,637	40
Other countries	8,982	15
North America	19,193	32
Australia	4,407	8
Asia	2,261	4
South America	734	1
Other regions	198	—
Adjustments	(241)	—
Total	**59,171**	**100**

1999 Assets

	$ mil.	% of total
Cash & equivalents	5,024	1
Bonds	126,208	25
Stocks	29,634	6
Net loans	203,655	41
Other investments	41,765	9
Other assets	91,063	18
Total	**497,349**	**100**

Selected Companies
ING Bank N.V.
ING Barings Holdings Ltd.
ING Capital Markets (Hong Kong) Ltd.
ING Life Insurance Company Ltd. Japan
ING North America Insurance Corporation
ING Verzekeringen N.V.
  ReliaStar Financial Corp.
Mercantile Mutual Holdings Limited
The Halifax Insurance Company

ABN AMRO	Credit Lyonnais	Lehman
AEGON	Credit Suisse	Brothers
AGF	Deutsche Bank	Lloyd's of
AIG	Fortis (NL)	London
Allianz	GeneralCologne	Merrill Lynch
Allstate	Re	MetLife
AXA	Generali	Prudential
Barclays	Goldman Sachs	Prudential plc
Bear Stearns	HSBC Holdings	Swiss Life
Chubb	HypoVereinsbank	UBS
CIGNA	Legal & General	Union des
Citigroup	Group	Assurances
CNP Assurances		Fédérales

NYSE: ING FYE: December 31	Annual Growth	12/90	12/91	12/92	12/93	12/94	12/95	12/96	12/97	12/98	12/99
Assets ($ mil.)	13.2%	163,182	173,909	177,392	174,034	203,913	246,356	279,985	306,232	460,563	497,349
Net income ($ mil.)	21.0%	895	919	1,006	1,042	1,327	1,647	1,922	2,026	3,113	4,967
Income as % of assets	—	0.5%	0.5%	0.6%	0.6%	0.7%	0.7%	0.7%	0.7%	0.7%	1.0%
Earnings per share ($)	40.2%	—	—	—	—	—	—	—	2.59	3.25	5.09
Stock price - FY high ($)	—	—	—	—	—	—	—	—	53.00	76.75	70.00
Stock price - FY low ($)	—	—	—	—	—	—	—	—	38.88	36.06	47.44
Stock price - FY close ($)	0.1%	—	—	—	—	—	—	—	42.31	62.19	61.00
P/E - high	—	—	—	—	—	—	—	—	20	23	14
P/E - low	—	—	—	—	—	—	—	—	15	11	9
Dividends per share ($)	—	—	—	—	—	—	—	—	0.00	0.64	2.34
Book value per share ($)	(79.4%)	—	—	—	—	—	—	—	24.64	32.82	36.59
Employees	9.8%	—	—	—	—	49,030	51,176	52,144	58,106	64,162	82,750	86,040

HIGH/LOW/CLOSE

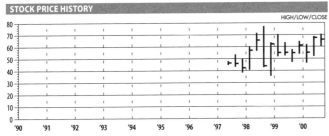

Equity as % of assets: 7.1%
Return on assets: 1.0%
Return on equity: 14.4%
Long-term debt ($ mil.): 85,984
No. of shares (mil.): 967
Dividends
  Yield: 3.8%
  Payout: 46.0%
Market value ($ mil.): 58,985
Sales ($ mil.): 59,171

INTERBREW S.A.

OVERVIEW

Budweiser may call itself the King of Beers, but Interbrew has a genuine baron in charge. Leuven, Belgium-based Interbrew is one of the world's largest brewers. The company has about 120 brands of lagers, premium beers, and specialty brews, which it sells in more than 100 countries. Among them are its flagship beer, Stella Artois, Bass Ale (#1 imported ale in the US), and Carling (#1 lager in the UK), as well as popular brews Hoegaarden, Labatt Blue, Leffe, and Rolling Rock. Interbrew owns Canada's Labatt Brewing, 30% of Mexican brewer FEMSA Cerveza (Dos Equis, Tecaté), and 70% of Labatt U.S.A. (FEMSA Cerveza owns the remaining 30% of Labatt U.S.A.) Labatt U.S.A. imports Interbrew's Canadian and Mexican beers.

Flat demand in its core market of Belgium spurred Interbrew to expand internationally; now Belgium only rings up 10% of the brewer's sales. The company added Whitbread PLC's brewing business and Bass Brewers (a division of Bass PLC) in 2000; the two purchases give Interbrew about one third of the UK beer market. Interbrew has also been focusing on untapped markets such as South Korea, where it controls about half of the market share, and Russia, where it has joined forces with Sun Brewery to form the #2 Russian brewer.

Interbrew operates about 20 Belgian Beer Cafe theme pubs globally. Interbrew owns the Toronto Blue Jays but is selling the baseball team to cable firm Rogers Communications. It is also selling the Blue Jays' ballpark, the SkyDome. Members of the founding Artois and Piedboeuf families control the company, which went public on the Brussels exchange in 2000.

HISTORY

Monks at the Leffe Abbey in Belgium were brewing beer as early as 1240, and surviving records from 1366 mention Belgium's Den Horen brewery. Belgian master brewer Sebastien Artois (best known for his Stella Artois lager) took over Den Horen in 1717. In 1853 the Piedboeuf family founded a brewery at Liege and established the Jupiler lager. Albert Van Damme assumed management of that brewery in 1920.

Over the years, the Artois and Piedboeuf families took over or established operations both in and outside Belgium. Direct descendants (the clans de Spoelberch, Van Damme, and de Mevius) of the two families were still managing the companies in 1987 when they decided the key to survival in the fragmented European beer market was to merge.

Artois-Piedboeuf-Interbrew acquired the Hoegaarden brewery in Belgium in 1989. The company changed its name to Interbrew three years later, acquired another Belgian brewery (Belle-Vue), and bought stakes in breweries in Bulgaria, Croatia, and Hungary. In 1995 Dommelsche Bierbrouwerij bought Allied Breweries Nederland, an Allied Domecq subsidiary, and Interbrew acquired the Oranjeboom breweries in the Netherlands.

The company purchased John Labatt Ltd. for $2 billion in 1995. Labatt, named for an Irish farmer who bought a stake in a London, Ontario, brewery in 1847, went public in 1940. The brewer diversified into food in the mid-1960s, and in 1980 it began brewing Budweiser for Anheuser-Busch in Canada. Labatt bought Latrobe Brewing (Rolling Rock beer, US) in 1987 and 22% of Mexico's FEMSA Cerveza in 1994 (increased to 30% in 1998). Labatt also owned the Toronto Argonauts football team, 90% of the Toronto Blue Jays, and various broadcast properties.

Interbrew sold many noncore assets, including Lehigh Valley Dairies (US) and John Labatt Retail (pubs, UK), in 1996. Also that year the company established joint ventures in the Dominican Republic and the US (to import Mexican beers through FEMSA).

In 1998 Interbrew paid $250 million for 50% of the Doosan Group's Oriental Brewery, South Korea's second-largest brewer, and bought a majority stake in Russian brewer Rosar. The next year Interbrew combined its Russian operations in 1999 with Sun Brewing, forming #2 Russian brewer Sun-Interbrew. It then bought Korea's Jinro-Coors Brewery for about $378 million. Also in 1999, Labatt U.S.A. took over the US license to brew and sell Lowenbrau from Miller Brewing and Hugo Powell was named CEO.

Interbrew bought Britain's third-largest brewer, Whitbread Beer Company, in May 2000 for $590 million. Having gained a foothold in the UK market, the company then bought Bass Brewers from Bass PLC in August 2000 for more than $3 billion. In September, Ted Rogers of Rogers Communications (Canada's leading cable company) agreed to buy 80% of the Toronto Blue Jays from Interbrew. In December 2000, Interbrew went public, offering about 20% of the company in Belgium's largest-ever IPO (the money was to be used to pay for its recent as well as future acquisitions).

Chairman: Baron Paul De Keersmaeker
CEO: Hugo Powell
EVP and CFO: Luc Missorten
EVP Controlling and Planning: Jo Van Biesbroeck
EVP Legal and Corporate Affairs: Patrice J. Thys
**EVP Marketing and International Business
Development:** Paul N. Cooke
EVP Strategy and Business Development:
Stefan Descheemaeker
EVP Technical Americas: Larry Macauley
EVP (Acting) Technical Europe-Asia: Ludo Degelin
EVP Asia: Andre Weckx
EVP Central Europe: Jaak De Witte
EVP Eastern Europe: Michel Naquet-Radiguet
**EVP North America; President, Labatt Brewing
Company:** Fred Jaques
EVP Western Europe: Ignace Van Doorselaere
Director of Human Resources: Peter Van Lindt
Auditors: Klynveld Peat Marwick Goerdeler

LOCATIONS

HQ: Vaartstraat 94, B-3000 Leuven, Belgium
Phone: +32-16-24-71-11   **Fax:** +32-16-24-74-07
US HQ: 101 Merrit 7, Norwalk, CT 06856
US Phone: 203-750-6600   **US Fax:** 203-750-6699
Web site: http://www.interbrew.com

Interbrew has operations in Belgium, Bulgaria, Canada,
China, Croatia, France, Hungary, Montenegro, the
Netherlands, Romania, Russia, South Korea, Ukraine,
the UK, and the US. It has interests in or licensing
agreements with brewers in Australia, the Dominican
Republic, Italy, Luxembourg, Mexico, and Sweden, and
offices in Singapore. Interbrew sells its beer in more
than 100 countries.

PRODUCTS/OPERATIONS

Selected Brands and Countries of Operation
International (Bass Ale, Belle-Vue, Carling, Hoegaarden,
  Jupiler, Labatt, Leffe, Rolling Rock, Samuel Adams
  outside US, Stella Artois)
Belgium (Julius, Hougaerdse Das, Piedboeuf, Safir,
  Vieux Temps)
Bulgaria (Astika, Kamenitza)
Canada (Alexander Keith's, Kokanee; licensed —
  Budweiser, Carlsberg, Guinness)
China (Best Ice, Jinling Dry, Yali Dry)
Croatia (Bozicno, Ozujsko Pivo, Tomislav Pivo)
Dominican Republic (Soberana)
France (La Bécasse)
Hungary (Borsodi Sor)
Mexico (Bohemia, Dos Equis, Sol, Tecaté)
Montenegro (Nik Gold, Niksico Pivo)
The Netherlands (Dommelsch, Hertog Jan, Oranjeboom)
Romania (Bergenbier, Hopfen Konig)
Russia (Klinskoye, Sibirskaya Korona, Tolstyak)
South Korea (Cafri, OB Lager)
UK (Boddingtons, Caffrey's, Murphy's, Wadworth 6X,
  Worthington Bitter)
Ukraine (Chernigivski Pivo, Gubernator, Taller Pils)
US (Lowenbrau — licensed)
Uniline Brewery D.O.O. (51%, Bosnia-Herzegovina)
Whitbread Beer Company (UK)
Zagrebacka Pivovara DD (72%, Croatia)

COMPETITORS

Adolph Coors	CBR Brewing	Redhook Ale
Anheuser-Busch	Constellation	San Miguel
Asahi Breweries	Brands	Sapporo
Asia Pacific	Foster's Brewing	Breweries
Breweries	Gambrinus	Scottish &
BBAG	Grolsch	Newcastle
Binding-Brauerei	Grupo Modelo	South African
Blaue Quellen	Guinness/UDV	Breweries
Mineral	Heineken	Suntory
Boston Beer	Holsten-Brauerei	Swire Pacific
Brau und	Kirin	Tsingtao
Brunnen	Lion Nathan	Yanjing
Brauerei BECK	Miller Brewing	
Carlsberg	Molson	

HISTORICAL FINANCIALS & EMPLOYEES

Euronext Brussels: INTB FYE: December 31	Annual Growth	9/90	9/91	9/92	9/93	9/94	*12/95	12/96	12/97	12/98	12/99
Sales ($ mil.)	14.3%	—	1,556	2,029	1,629	1,526	2,757	3,016	2,886	4,200	4,532
Net income ($ mil.)	18.2%	—	61	45	47	84	117	127	144	222	232
Income as % of sales	—	—	3.9%	2.2%	2.9%	5.5%	4.3%	4.2%	5.0%	5.3%	5.1%
Employees	12.0%	—	9,810	10,948	9,778	8,143	13,237	13,735	13,835	16,727	24,348

* Fiscal year change

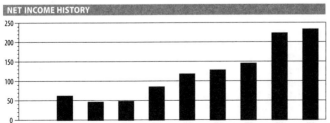

NET INCOME HISTORY

1999 FISCAL YEAR-END
Debt ratio: 49.6%
Return on equity: —
Cash ($ mil.): 309
Current ratio: 1.21
Long-term debt ($ mil.): 1,967

INVENSYS PLC

London-based Invensys is known the world over for its turn-ons. The company — created from Siebe's 1999 purchase of BTR, a UK-based industrial manufacturer with some $13 billion in annual sales, is one of the world's largest makers of controls and industrial automation equipment. The company is forming a new unit — Invensys Software and Systems — around the operations of struggling Dutch enterprise resource planning software maker Baan Company.

Most of Invensys' sales have come from the valves and meters that control everything from the temperature on portable heaters to the operations of entire factories. It also makes computer-based industrial automation equipment, semiconductor surge protection devices, safety shutdown systems, and air compressors, among other products. Most of its sales are to manufacturers in North America and Europe.

Prior to the BTR purchase, Siebe made a habit of buying smaller companies to build its market presence. Despite its huge operation, the company is not well known, because few of its products carry the Siebe label. The acquisition of BTR added expertise in automotive components, power drives, process control, and specialist engineering equipment.

To stay profitable through a period of heavy acquisition, CEO Allen Yurko is restructuring Invensys to divest noncore businesses, consolidate operations, and cut jobs.

Immigrant Austrian artillery officer Augustus Siebe started Siebe in London in 1819. A life-long inventor, Siebe's creations included the world's first diving suit, breechloading rifles, carbon arc lamps, and early ice-making machines.

From the 1890s to the early 1970s, Siebe made its name as a marine engineering firm and breathing apparatus maker, developing products such as submarine escape and diving equipment for the Royal Navy and other clients. General Dynamics veteran Barrie Stephens took over management of the struggling Siebe in 1963. The business-savvy Stephens cut costs, restructured, terminated half the workforce, and in the late 1960s started making acquisitions.

With its 1972 purchase of European safety equipment specialist James North & Sons, Siebe began transforming from a marine-based engineer to a controls and engineering company. It expanded into continental Europe, and then in 1982 moved into North America with the purchase of garage equipment business Tecalemit.

Also included in that buy were two healthy electronic controls businesses, which Stephens tried but failed to sell. When Siebe acquired compressed air company CompAir in 1985, it also got three pneumatic controls companies in the bargain. Without trying, the company had established a controls presence, which was strengthened further in 1986 when Siebe bought US appliance controls firm Robertshaw. The acquisitions in the next year of US concerns Ranco and Barber-Colman added automotive, industrial, and commercial building controls.

In 1990 Siebe hit the jackpot with the $650 million purchase of Foxboro, which had developed a UNIX-based system capable of controlling entire oil refineries and automobile plants. With the Foxboro purchase, Siebe's control business began seriously challenging Honeywell. In 1994 American Allen Yurko, who had joined Siebe as a VP in 1989, was named CEO.

Since 1995 the company has bought more than a dozen firms, including food and drinks industry equipment maker AVP (1997), and factory application software company Wonderware, temperature controls maker Eurotherm, and industrial power supply maker Electronic Measurement (all in 1998). To offset costs associated with its acquisitions, Siebe also started restructuring in 1998. That year Stephens retired, and the company sold off its North Safety Products Business (personal safety and life support products) to Norcross Safety Products.

In early 1999 Siebe acquired engineering rival BTR plc in a $6 billion deal that nearly tripled Siebe's size; the combined company changed its name to BTR Siebe and later to Invensys. That year the company sold more than a dozen businesses, including its automotive and aerospace operations. It agreed to sell 90% of its Paper Technology Group to investment firm Apax Partners in a deal valued at about $800 million. Invensys' 1999 acquisitions included Best Power, a maker of uninterruptible power supplies, purchased from industrial products maker SPX for around $240 million.

In early 2000 Invensys formed a pact with Microsoft to develop standards for connecting home appliances to the Internet. Later that year the company gained control of Netherlands-based Baan Company, a near-bankrupt maker of software that allows manufacturers to manage their internal operations, in a $709 million deal.

Chairman: Colin Marshall, $250,000 pay
CEO: Allen M. Yurko, age 49, $1,205,629 pay
COO: Jim F. Mueller, age 54, $353,973 pay
CFO: Kathleen A. O'Donovan, age 43, $620,400 pay
SVP and Chief Legal Officer: James Bays
SVP and Director of Corporate Communications:
Victoria Scarth
SVP and Director of Corporate Strategy and Development: John Saunders
SVP and Director of Human Resources:
Regina Hitchery
CEO Controls Division: Rod Powell
CEO Industrial Drive Systems Division: Rick Armbrust
CEO Intelligent Automation Division: Bruce Henderson
Auditors: Ernst & Young

HQ: Carlisle Place, London SW1P 1BX, United Kingdom
Phone: +44-20-7834-3848   **Fax:** +44-20-7834-3879
US HQ: 33 Commercial St., Foxboro, MA 02035
US Phone: 508-543-8750   **US Fax:** 508-549-6750
Web site: http://www.invensys.com

Invensys has division headquarters in Massachusetts, North Carolina, Virginia, and Wisconsin, and operations worldwide.

2000 Sales

	% of total
North America	47
Europe	
UK	9
Other countries	26
Asia/Pacific	12
Other regions	6
Total	**100**

2000 Sales

	% of total
Controls	30
Intelligent automation	29
Power systems	19
Industrial drive systems	16
Disposal group	6
Total	**100**

Principal Divisions

Controls	**Power Systems**
Appliance Controls	Energy Storage
Climate Controls	Energy Systems
Intelligent Building Systems	Power Conversion
Meters	Secure Power
Motors	**Industrial Drive Systems**
Sensors	Air Systems
Intelligent Automation	Airport Baggage Automation
APV	Industrial Drives
Field Measurement and Control	Industrial Motors
Flow Controls	Power Transmission
Foxboro Worldwide	**Disposal Group**
Rail Systems	Automotive
Safety Systems	Environmental
Wonderware	Paper Technology

ABB	Schlumberger
Emerson	Siemens
GE Industrial Products and Systems	SPX
Honeywell International	Texas Instruments
Rockwell International	Tomkins
	Vicor

OTC: IVNSY FYE: First Saturday in April	Annual Growth	3/91	3/92	3/93	3/94	3/95	3/96	3/97	3/98	3/99	3/00
Sales ($ mil.)	(14.0%)	—	—	—	—	—	—	—	19,496	15,185	14,426
Net income ($ mil.)	—	—	—	—	—	—	—	—	1,753	(169)	(380)
Income as % of sales	—	—	—	—	—	—	—	—	9.0%	—	—
Earnings per share ($)	—	—	—	—	—	—	—	—	—	(0.09)	(0.20)
Stock price - FY high ($)	—	—	—	—	—	—	—	—	—	9.75	11.88
Stock price - FY low ($)	—	—	—	—	—	—	—	—	—	7.38	7.44
Stock price - FY close ($)	0.0%	—	—	—	—	—	—	—	—	8.88	8.88
P/E - high	—	—	—	—	—	—	—	—	—	—	—
P/E - low	—	—	—	—	—	—	—	—	—	—	—
Dividends per share ($)	23.0%	—	—	—	—	—	—	—	—	0.20	0.25
Book value per share ($)	(42.7%)	—	—	—	—	—	—	—	—	2.00	1.15
Employees	(11.5%)	—	—	—	—	—	—	—	155,409	130,626	121,683

HIGH/LOW/CLOSE

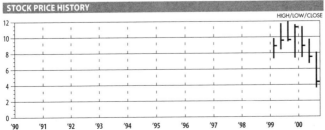

Debt ratio: 36.3%
Return on equity: —
Cash ($ mil.): 923
Current ratio: 0.94
Long-term debt ($ mil.): 1,143
No. of shares (mil.): 1,749
Dividends
 Yield: 0.0%
 Payout: —
Market value ($ mil.): 15,531

ISPAT INTERNATIONAL N.V.

OVERVIEW

Ispat is literally steel — in Sanskrit, that is. Based in the Netherlands but essentially run from London, Ispat International has stretched its acquisitive global arms to become one of the world's leading steelmakers. The company uses an electric arc minimill process to make flat (sheet, slab) and long (bars, pipes, structural, wire rod) steel products. The company has its own fleet of ships to deliver goods worldwide. Ispat saves money in its steel production by using a cheaper processed iron ore called direct-reduced iron instead of steel scrap.

The company is part of founder and CEO Lakshmi Mittal's LNM Group, which also makes steel in Indonesia (Ispat Indo) and Kazakhstan (Ispat Karmet). Ispat operates through subsidiaries in Canada, the Caribbean, Germany, Ireland, and Mexico, With its much heralded purchase of Inland Steel Industries' steelmaking operations (renamed Ispat Inland), it also has entered the US. Indian entrepreneur Mittal (fittingly pronounced "metal") has long marked the US steelmaking market as a target for infiltration. The company has a history of snatching up steel mills on the cheap and turning them around to become profitable.

In light of economic weakness in Asia — which has depressed earnings — Ispat has reduced costs at existing operations. The company has continued to buy steel mills and expand production. It is also part of a joint venture with Commerce One to link metals buyers and sellers online.

HISTORY

Ispat International is the product of decades of steelmaking by India's Mittal family. In 1967 patriarch Mohan Mittal unsuccessfully tried to open a steel mill in Egypt. He and his four younger brothers then set up a steel company in India, but squabbles pushed Mohan to chart his own course, eventually giving rise to the Ispat empire. Mohan's son Lakshmi began working part-time at the family steel mill while in school; he started full-time at 21, after graduating in 1971.

Mohan set up an operation in Indonesia in 1975 (Ispat Indo) and put Lakshmi in charge. The next year, fueled by ambitions and held back by government regulations in India, Lakshmi formed Ispat International in Jakarta, Indonesia, to focus on expansion through acquisitions. He spent the next decade strengthening the Indonesian operations and perfecting the minimill process by using direct-reduced iron (DRI).

Ispat took advantage of the recessionary late 1980s and early 1990s by making a string of acquisitions. In 1988 it took over the management of Trinidad and Tobago's state steel companies (bought in 1994; renamed Caribbean Ispat).

In 1992 Ispat bought Mexico's third-largest (albeit bankrupt) steel and DRI producer. Two years later the aggressively growing Ispat acquired Canada's Sidbec-Dosco steelmaker. Also that year Lakshmi took exclusive control of international operations, leaving his brothers Pramod and Vinod to control the Indian divisions.

The mid-1990s brought more acquisitions, with Ispat buying Germany's Hamburger Stahlwerks and a mill in Kazakhstan in 1995. The next year Ispat purchased Ireland's only steelmaker, Irish Steel. Lakshmi moved to London in 1996, where he purchased a home on Bishops Avenue, or "millionaire's row." (King Fahd of Saudi Arabia is a neighbor).

In 1997 Ispat bought the long-product (wire rod) division of Germany's Thyssen AG (renamed Ispat Stahlwerk Ruhrort and Ispat Walzdraht Hochfeld). Ispat also completed a $776 million IPO — the steel industry's biggest, outside of privatizations.

Ispat International moved inland in 1998, purchasing Chicago-based Inland Steel and renaming it Ispat Inland. With this purchase Ispat also picked up the steel-finishing operations of I/N Tek (60% Inland-owned joint venture with Nippon Steel) and I/N Kote (50% Inland-owned joint venture with NSC).

In 1999 Ispat formed a joint venture with Mexican steelmaker Grupo Imsa to make flat-rolled steel to sell throughout North and South America, with the exception of Brazil. It also paid $96 million for France-based Usinor's Unimetal, Trefileurope, and Société Metallurgique de Revigny subsidiaries, which specialize in carbon long products. That year the company's Ispat Inland subsidiary became the target of a US federal criminal grand jury investigation and a related civil lawsuit for allegedly defrauding the Lousiana Highway Department. The next year Ispat responded to a downturn in the steel industry by starting a Web-based joint venture with Commerce One to connect buyers and sellers in the worldwide metals market. It also offered to buy VSZ, Slovakia's #1 steelworks, for about $480 million.

Chairman and CEO: Lakshmi N. Mittal
President and COO: Johannes Sittard
CFO: Bhikam C. Agarwal
President and CEO, Ispat Europe S.A.:
Malay Mukherjee
President and CEO, Ispat North America:
Robert J. Darnall
President and CEO, Ispat Sidbec:
Richard Jean-Pierre LeBlanc
President and COO, Ispat Inland: Dale E. Wiersbe
Managing Director Ispat Hamburger Stahlwerke:
Gerhard Renz
Managing Director Ispat Mexicana:
Manavathu Raman-Pillai Rajappan Nair
Auditors: Deloitte & Touche

LOCATIONS

HQ: Rotterdam Bldg., Aert van Nesstraat 45,
3012 CA Rotterdam, The Netherlands
Phone: +31-10-2829465   **Fax:** +31-10-2829468
US HQ: 30 W. Monroe St., Chicago, IL 60603
US Phone: 312-899-3959   **US Fax:** 312-899-3921
Web site: http://www.ispat.com

Based in the Netherlands and run from its London
headquarters, Ispat International has steelmaking
operations in Canada, France, Germany, Ireland,
Mexico, Trinidad and Tobago, and the US.

1999 Sales

	% of total
US & Canada	65
Europe	20
Other regions	15
Total	**100**

PRODUCTS/OPERATIONS

1999 Sales

	% of total
Flat products	60
Long products	40
Total	**100**

Selected Products

Direct reduced iron (DRI)
Flat steel
Long steel
Bars, Pipes, Structural
Wire (products and rod)

Selected Subsidiaries

Consorcio Minero Benito Juarez Peña Colorada SA de
CV (50%; mining and pelitizing; Mexico)
Empire Iron Mining Partnership (40%, taconite pellets)
I/N Tek (60%, cold rolling)
I/N Kote (50%, galvanizing)
Irish Ispat Limited (Ireland)
Ispat Hamburger Stahlwerke GmbH (Germany)
Ispat Inland Inc.
Ispat Mexicana, SA de CV (Mexico)
Ispat Sidbec Inc. (Canada)
Sorevco (50%, galvanizing plant, Canada)

COMPETITORS

Acme Metals	Corus Group	Oregon Steel
AK Steel Holding	Dofasco	Mills
Corporation	Geneva Steel	Rouge Industries
Algoma Steel	Highveld Steel	Stelco
Bethlehem Steel	& Vanadium	ThyssenKrupp
Birmingham	LTV	USX
Steel	National Steel	USX-U.S. Steel
Chaparral Steel	Nippon Steel	Vallourec
Co-Steel	Nucor	Weirton Steel

HISTORICAL FINANCIALS & EMPLOYEES

NYSE: IST FYE: December 31	Annual Growth	12/90	12/91	12/92	12/93	12/94	12/95	12/96	12/97	12/98	12/99
Sales ($ mil.)	46.7%	—	—	320	396	735	1,828	1,774	2,190	3,492	4,680
Net income ($ mil.)	(13.2%)	—	—	229	280	246	556	613	289	237	85
Income as % of sales	—	—	—	71.6%	70.7%	33.5%	30.4%	34.6%	13.2%	6.8%	1.8%
Earnings per share ($)	(46.3%)	—	—	—	—	—	—	—	2.46	1.93	0.71
Stock price - FY high ($)	—	—	—	—	—	—	—	—	30.00	30.25	16.13
Stock price - FY low ($)	—	—	—	—	—	—	—	—	17.75	4.75	6.88
Stock price - FY close ($)	(13.6%)	—	—	—	—	—	—	—	21.63	7.75	16.13
P/E - high	—	—	—	—	—	—	—	—	12	16	23
P/E - low	—	—	—	—	—	—	—	—	7	2	10
Dividends per share ($)	—	—	—	—	—	—	—	—	0.00	0.15	0.15
Book value per share ($)	(46.4%)	—	—	—	—	—	—	—	23.39	6.31	6.72
Employees	29.4%	—	—	—	—	—	5,358	5,839	7,550	15,000	15,000

STOCK PRICE HISTORY

HIGH/LOW/CLOSE

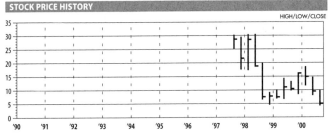

1999 FISCAL YEAR-END

Debt ratio: 71.9%
Return on equity: 10.3%
Cash ($ mil.): 170
Current ratio: 1.50
Long-term debt ($ mil.): 2,184
No. of shares (mil.): 127
Dividends
  Yield: 0.9%
  Payout: 21.1%
Market value ($ mil.): 2,049

ISUZU MOTORS LIMITED

A real trooper, Isuzu Motors keeps on truckin' to grab its share of the popular sport utility vehicle (SUV) market. Besides producing SUVs such as the Trooper, Amigo, and Rodeo, Tokyo-based Isuzu makes passenger cars and microbuses. Isuzu is one of the world's top makers of medium- and heavy-duty trucks, as well as diesel engines. It also makes Hombre pickups and Oasis minivans.

Isuzu has the pedal to the metal toward becoming the world's leading manufacturer of diesel engines and large commercial vehicles. The company plans to turn out 1.8 million diesel engines by 2005. With the number of automakers that can efficiently build both gas and diesel engines diminishing, Isuzu is betting that most manufacturers will turn to outside suppliers for their diesel requirements. Isuzu, which is using joint ventures to increase its manufacturing capacity, also has access to General Motors' deep pockets: The US behemoth owns 49% of Isuzu.

After collaborating on car and truck production for 21 years, Tokyo Ishikawajima Shipbuilding and Engineering and Tokyo Gas and Electric Industrial formed Tokyo Motors, Inc., in 1937. The partners began by producing the A truck (1918) and the A9 car (1922) under licenses from Wolseley (UK). A lengthy study of diesel technology resulted in the introduction of the company's first air-cooled diesel motor in 1937.

Tokyo Motors made its first truck under the Isuzu nameplate in 1938. It spun off Hino Heavy Industries in 1942. By 1943 the company was selling trucks powered by its own diesel engines, mostly to the Japanese military.

By 1948 the company was Japan's premier maker of diesel engines. The company renamed itself Isuzu (Japanese for "50 bells") in 1949. With generous public- and private-sector financing and truck orders from the US Army during the Korean War, Isuzu survived and refined its engine- and truck-making prowess. A pact with the Rootes Group (UK) enabled Isuzu to enter automaking. Beginning in 1953, Isuzu built Rootes' Hillman Minx in Japan. The company attempted to marry diesels with autos in 1961, but a few years later discontinued the noisy auto.

Despite its strong reputation as a truck builder, Isuzu suffered financially, and by the late 1960s its bankers were shopping the company around to more stable competitors. General Motors, after witnessing rapid Japanese progress in US and Asian auto markets, bought about 34% of Isuzu in 1971. During the 1970s Isuzu launched the popular Gemini car and gained rapid entry to the US through GM, exporting such vehicles as the Chevy Luv truck and the Buick Opel.

As exports to GM waned, Isuzu set up its own dealer network in the US in 1981. That year GM CEO Roger Smith told stunned Isuzu chairman T. Okamoto that Isuzu lacked the global scale GM sought. Smith asked Okamoto for help in buying a piece of Honda. After Honda declined and GM settled for 5% of Suzuki, Isuzu extended its GM ties, building the Geo Storm and establishing joint production facilities in the UK and Australia.

Despite a high-profile advertising campaign featuring pathological liar Joe Isuzu, the company suffered in the 1980s in its efforts to gain any kind of significant share of the US passenger car market. Post-1985 yen appreciation hurt exports. Subaru-Isuzu Automotive, a joint venture with Fuji Heavy Industries, initiated production of Rodeos in Lafayette, Indiana, in 1989.

After Isuzu lost nearly $500 million in 1991 and continued to lose money the next year, it called on GM for help. GM responded by sending Donald Sullivan, a strategic business planning expert, to become Isuzu's #2 operations executive.

Isuzu signed a joint venture with Jiangxi Automobile Factory and ITOCHU in 1993 to build light-duty trucks in China. In 1996 Isuzu weathered a public relations storm when *Consumer Reports* magazine claimed that the top-selling Trooper sport utility vehicle was prone to tip over at relatively low speeds. Isuzu dismissed the report as unscientific, and the National Highway Traffic Safety Administration sided with the automaker. In 1997 Izuzu sued the magazine for defamation. That year it agreed to develop GM's diesel engines and began building a plant in Poland to supply engines to GM's German subsidiary Opel AG.

In 1998 GM and Isuzu announced a joint venture to make diesel engines in the US. Later that year Isuzu announced restructuring plans that included cutting 4,000 jobs and reducing the number of its domestic marketing subsidiaries. In 1999 the plant in Poland opened, and GM boosted its stake in Isuzu to 49%. Late in the year Isuzu agreed to form a ● joint venture with Toyota to manufacture buses.

OFFICERS

Chairman and Representative Director: Kazuhira Seki
President and Representative Director: Takeshi Inoh
Managing Director: Shigeo Saigusa
Managing Director: Robin A. Toussaint
Managing Director: Yoshinori Ida
Managing Director: Kichiro Tsubaki
Managing Director: Yu Shiga
Managing Director: Tohru Kajiyama
Executive Director: Katsutoshi Ichimasa
Executive Director: Tadaomi Takayama
Executive Director: Masao Takahara
Executive Director: Goro Miyazaki
Executive Director: Hidetsugu Usui
Executive Director: Masami Awata
Executive Director: Tsutomu Matsubayashi
Executive Director: Yoshio Kagawa
Executive Director: Itaru Takayanagi
Executive Director: Hiromasa Tsutsui
Auditors: Century Audit Corporation

LOCATIONS

HQ: Isuzu Jidosha Kabushiki Kaisha,
26-1, Minami-oi 6-chome, Shinagawa-ku,
Tokyo 140-8722, Japan
Phone: +81-3-5471-1141   **Fax:** +81-3-5471-1043
US HQ: 13340 183rd St., Cerritos, CA 90702
US Phone: 562-229-5000   **US Fax:** 562-229-5463
Web site: http://www.isuzu.co.jp

2000 Sales

	$ mil.	% of total
Japan	10,737	64
North America	5,074	31
Other regions	815	5
Adjustments	(2,432)	—
Total	**14,194**	**100**

PRODUCTS/OPERATIONS

2000 Sales

	$ mil.	% of total
Automotive	13,567	95
Finance	899	5
Other	195	—
Adjustments	(467)	—
Total	**14,194**	**100**

Selected Vehicles and Brands

Light-Duty Vehicles
ELF light-duty trucks
Journey microbus
Mu 4-wheel-drive RVs
Wizard 4-wheel-drive RVs

Heavy- and Medium-Duty Vehicles
GIGA heavy-duty trucks
Hombre 4-wheel-drive trucks
Spirit 4X4 trucks

Passenger Cars
ASKA luxury sedan
Gemini compact family sedan

Sport Utility Vehicles
Amigo
Oasis
Rodeo
Trooper
VehiCROSS

COMPETITORS

BMW
Caterpillar
Cummins Engine
DaimlerChrysler
Fiat
Ford
General Motors
Honda
Hyundai
Kubota
Mazda
Mitsubishi
Navistar
Nissan
Oshkosh Truck
PACCAR
Penske
Peugeot
Renault
Scania
Suzuki
Toyota
Volkswagen
Volvo

HISTORICAL FINANCIALS & EMPLOYEES

OTC: ISUZF FYE: March 31	Annual Growth	3/91	3/92	3/93	3/94	3/95	3/96	3/97	3/98	3/99	3/00
Sales ($ mil.)	3.0%	10,832	11,887	13,595	15,546	8,763	15,681	15,536	13,524	13,593	14,194
Net income ($ mil.)	—	(440)	(218)	(37)	29	75	350	77	45	52	(982)
Income as % of sales	—	—	—	—	0.2%	0.9%	2.2%	0.5%	0.3%	0.4%	—
Earnings per share ($)	—	(4.27)	(2.11)	(0.36)	0.28	0.73	3.39	0.75	0.44	0.49	(7.80)
Stock price - FY high ($)	—	65.77	42.11	39.30	49.39	55.06	59.19	57.50	39.50	20.50	34.37
Stock price - FY low ($)	—	33.36	20.22	17.34	24.27	41.47	35.39	36.75	14.75	14.00	19.75
Stock price - FY close ($)	(5.9%)	39.97	20.30	39.05	45.05	47.09	57.94	40.00	20.00	20.50	23.20
P/E - high	—	—	—	—	176	75	17	77	90	42	—
P/E - low	—	—	—	—	87	57	10	49	34	29	—
Dividends per share ($)	—	0.00	0.00	0.00	0.00	0.00	0.00	0.44	0.37	0.00	0.00
Book value per share ($)	7.2%	6.75	5.16	5.36	6.64	8.43	10.54	9.45	9.30	12.25	12.63
Employees	(0.5%)	13,600	13,299	13,084	13,500	13,500	14,317	13,877	13,520	15,300	12,963

STOCK PRICE HISTORY

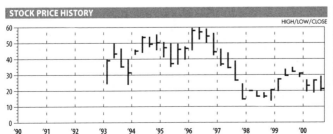

HIGH/LOW/CLOSE

2000 FISCAL YEAR-END

Debt ratio: 72.4%
Return on equity: —
Cash ($ mil.): 941
Current ratio: 8.75
Long-term debt ($ mil.): 4,188
No. of shares (mil.): 126
Dividends
 Yield: —
 Payout: —
Market value ($ mil.): 2,931

ITOCHU CORPORATION

OVERVIEW

Like baseball's Sammy Sosa, *sogo shosha* (general trading company) ITOCHU is a big hitter. The Tokyo-based company is Japan's #3 *sogo shosha* behind Mitsui and Mitsubishi. It operates in seven business groups: aerospace, electronics, and multimedia; energy and chemicals; finance, realty, insurance, and logistics services; food, forest products, and general merchandise; metals and minerals; and automobile and industrial machinery; and textiles.

These divisions scarcely reflect the company's scope and geographic diversity —

more than 1,000 subsidiaries and affiliates in over 80 countries. ITOCHU's interests range from Italian textile mills to Australian gold mines, and from Japanese convenience stores to Chinese breweries.

The weakness of the Japanese economy has forced the company to scale back in many areas. Divesting unprofitable operations, the company is focusing on expected moneymakers — multimedia, consumer and retail, financial services, and natural resource development. It is also investing in US-based technology companies.

HISTORY

When Chubei Itoh organized his own wholesale linen business, C. Itoh & Co. in 1858, he was only 18. The youthful entrepreneur actually founded two trading companies because his retail operations became another leading *sogo shosha,* Marubeni. As Japan opened to foreign trade in the 1860s, the firm prospered and was one of Osaka's largest textile wholesalers by the 1870s. C. Itoh established a trade office in San Francisco in 1889.

By 1919 C. Itoh had trading offices in New York, Calcutta, Manila, and four cities in China. When an earthquake disrupted the operations of its Tokyo-based competitors in 1923, the company won new business. Although it was not one of the *zaibatsu* (industrial groups) that flourished in Japan during the period between the world wars, C. Itoh benefited from the general increase in trade.

In 1941 C. Itoh was merged with two other trading companies, Marubeni and Kishimoto, into a new company, Sanko Kabushiki Kaisha. Marubeni and C. Itoh were separated in 1949. C. Itoh supplied UN troops with provisions during the Korean War; profits were used to diversify into petroleum, machinery, aircraft, and automobiles.

After the oil crisis of 1973 demonstrated Japan's vulnerability to oil import disruptions, C. Itoh actively participated in the development of petroleum production technology. To prevent the failure of Japan's 10th-largest trading company, Ataka, the Japanese government arranged a merger in 1977, making C. Itoh the third-largest *sogo shosha.*

The company established Japan Communications Satellite (JCSAT) with Mitsui and Hughes Communications in 1985. JCSAT launched its first two satellites in 1989 and 1990. The following year C. Itoh and Toshiba joined Time Warner in a limited partnership, Time Warner Entertainment Company, to

produce and distribute movies and television programs and to operate cable TV systems in the US. C. Itoh, Time Warner, and Toshiba formed another joint venture to distribute Warner Bros. films and develop amusements parks in Japan.

C. Itoh changed its name to ITOCHU, a transliteration of its Japanese name, in 1992. After sales dropped the next year, ITOCHU began selling poorly performing subsidiaries, reducing its investment portfolio by more than one-third.

In 1996 the company formed an alliance with US oil company Atlantic Richfield to buy Coastal Corp.'s western US coal operations, and it took a stake in a massive project led by Amoco and British Petroleum (which merged in 1998 to form BP Amoco) to develop oil and gas deposits in the Caspian Sea. That year PerfecTV! (a joint venture with Sumitomo and other Japanese companies) began satellite broadcasting. Also in 1996 ITOCHU bought stakes in the Asia Broadcasting and Communications Network, a satellite communications company, and in Dicomed, a US maker of digital cameras.

In 1997 ITOCHU reorganized its six business groups into eight, adding multimedia to one segment and creating a finance and insurance unit. Later that year, as Asian financial markets crumpled, it wrote off nearly $2 billion in non-performing assets, leading to a loss for the year. To help cover its losses, the company sold 40% of its stake in Time Warner in 1998 on the US open market for about $420 million; in 1999 the company sold its remaining stake for $373 million. ITOCHU also sold low-performing real estate investments and laid plans to divest about one-third of its subsidiaries.

In 2000 ITOCHU and Marubeni teamed up with US-based online steel trader MetalSite LP to offer an e-commerce system for Japanese steel products.

Chairman: Minoru Murofushi
President and CEO: Uichiro Niwa
**VC; Chairman and CEO, ITOCHU International;
Chairman, ITOCHU Europe:** Jay W. Chai
EVP; President Food: Hiroshi Sumie
VC: Masahisa Naitoh
**Senior Managing Director; President, Chemicals,
Forest Products, and General Merchandise:**
Junichi Taniyama
Senior Managing Director; President Textile:
Makoto Kato
Senior Managing Director and CFO: Sumitaka Fujita
**Senior Managing Director, Human Resources and
Affiliates Administration:** Yushin Okazaki
Auditors: KPMG

LOCATIONS

HQ: Itochu Shoji Kabushiki Kaisha,
5-1, Kita-Aoyama 2-chome, Minato-ku,
Tokyo 107-8077, Japan
Phone: +81-3-3497-2121   **Fax:** +81-3-3497-4141
US HQ: 22-24th Fl., Bank of America Tower,
335 Madison Ave., New York, NY 10017
US Phone: 212-818-8000   **US Fax:** 212-818-8361
Web site: http://www.itochu.co.jp

2000 Sales

	$ mil.	% of total
Asia		
Japan	93,558	82
Other countries	10,383	9
North America	6,161	5
Europe	2,459	2
Other regions	1,847	2
Total	**114,408**	**100**

PRODUCTS/OPERATIONS

2000 Sales

	% of total
Food, forest products & general merchandise	28
Energy & chemicals	23
Plant, automobile & industrial machinery	17
Metals & ores	9
Textiles	9
Aerospace, electronics & multimedia	7
Finance, realty, insurance & logistics	6
Other	1
Total	**100**

COMPETITORS

ADM	Mitsui
AT&T	Nestlé
Cable and Wireless	Nippon Steel
Daewoo	Nippon Television
DaimlerChrysler	NTT
Dow Chemical	Philip Morris
Exxon Mobil	Samsung
Fluor	SEPI
George Weston	Sharp
Hutchison Whampoa	Sprint
Hyundai	Sumitomo
Klöckner	Tokyo Broadcasting
LG Group	System
Lockheed Martin	TOMEN
Marubeni	TOTAL FINA ELF
Matsushita	Unilever
MAXXAM	WorldCom
Mitsubishi	

HISTORICAL FINANCIALS & EMPLOYEES

OTC: ITOCY FYE: March 31	Annual Growth	3/91	3/92	3/93	3/94	3/95	3/96	3/97	3/98	3/99	3/00
Sales ($ mil.)	(3.1%)	151,519	155,059	167,808	162,944	192,615	152,233	123,325	116,815	116,704	114,408
Net income ($ mil.)	—	224	91	33	(137)	94	86	101	(714)	(286)	(832)
Income as % of sales	—	0.1%	0.1%	0.0%	—	0.0%	0.1%	0.1%	—	—	—
Earnings per share ($)	—	1.57	0.62	0.24	(0.96)	0.66	0.77	0.71	(5.01)	(2.00)	(5.83)
Stock price - FY high ($)	—	61.66	57.38	40.84	67.75	78.86	71.98	76.50	55.00	25.25	57.00
Stock price - FY low ($)	—	40.67	35.38	27.30	41.95	54.80	55.30	43.25	18.38	17.25	23.50
Stock price - FY close ($)	0.1%	52.63	36.16	40.61	67.63	61.33	70.22	48.50	21.75	17.63	53.33
P/E - high	—	39	93	170	—	119	93	108	—	—	—
P/E - low	—	26	57	114	—	83	72	61	—	—	—
Dividends per share ($)	—	0.43	0.45	0.52	0.58	0.69	0.56	0.52	0.45	0.00	0.00
Book value per share ($)	(3.9%)	26.51	27.94	30.83	31.77	36.18	29.89	29.84	24.07	20.22	18.59
Employees	(3.2%)	7,108	7,149	7,449	7,434	7,345	7,182	6,999	6,675	5,775	5,306

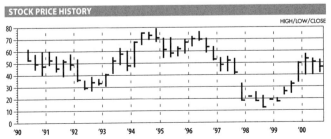

STOCK PRICE HISTORY
HIGH/LOW/CLOSE

2000 FISCAL YEAR-END

Debt ratio: 90.1%
Return on equity: —
Cash ($ mil.): 2,489
Current ratio: 1.14
Long-term debt ($ mil.): 24,258
No. of shares (mil.): 143
Dividends
  Yield: —
  Payout: —
Market value ($ mil.): 7,602

ITO-YOKADO CO., LTD.

OVERVIEW

It's not a sci-fi movie, but it sure sounds like one: A giant mother ship controlling thousands of small units linked via satellite, infesting the landscape, and ready to sell you — Big Gulps! Tokyo-based Ito-Yokado Co., one of Japan's largest retailers, franchises about 8,200 7-Eleven convenience stores in Japan (through its 51%-owned Seven-Eleven Japan Co.). Its 72%-owned US 7-Eleven, Inc., subsidiary licenses the 7-Eleven name throughout the world and operates 5,700 outlets in North America.

In Japan Ito-Yokado also runs more than 400 other retail stores (superstores, supermar-

kets, discounters, and clothing stores), about 500 Denny's restaurants, and more than 300 Famil restaurants. It holds the Japanese franchises for Robinson's department stores and Oshman's sporting goods stores. The company also operates a few superstores in China through a joint venture, several food manufacturing facilities, and a publishing company.

Ito-Yokado is also expanding its private-label clothing line, IY Basics (IYB), hoping the brand will reach 50% of its total apparel sales. The company's Seven-Eleven Japan unit has been investing in online retailers selling books and cars.

HISTORY

After fighting in WWII, 21-year-old Masatoshi Ito joined his mother and brother in running a small family clothing shop (founded 1913) in Tokyo that grew into a department store. Ito took over the store when his brother died in 1956. Two years later the company was incorporated as Kabushiki Kaisha Yokado.

Ito visited the US in 1961, meeting with officials of National Cash Register (who wanted to sell cash registers to Japanese retailers who were still using abacuses) and retailers such as Sears and Safeway. Confident that US-style self-service retailing could work in Japan, Ito opened two hypermarkets (food, clothing, and household products) in Tokyo. By 1965, the year he changed the operation's name to Ito-Yokado Co., he had opened six more stores.

Famil, a chain of family-style restaurants, was launched in 1972, as were several Denny's restaurant franchises in Japan. Ito returned to the US that year to meet with Dallas-based Southland, owner of the 7-Eleven convenience store chain, and in 1974 he opened Japan's first 7-Eleven. The 7-Elevens quickly stole much of the market from the family-owned shops that dominated Japanese retailing. (The 7-Elevens were small enough to avoid triggering Japan's Large-Scale Retail Store Law, a law designed to protect small family stores by establishing rigid controls over store sizes and hours.) Ito co-opted his fallen competitors by recruiting them to become 7-Eleven franchisees. In 1975 Ito-Yokado established its YorkMart subsidiary to open supermarkets in areas that could not support its hypermarkets.

In the 1980s Ito acquired Japanese rights to Robinson's department stores (from the May Company) and Oshman's sporting goods

stores. The company bought 58 7-Elevens in Hawaii in 1989 and the next year acquired 70% of the bankrupt Southland for $430 million. Ito-Yokado closed hundreds of unprofitable US 7-Eleven stores and began remodeling and improving merchandise quality in the rest.

Ito, along with several other heads of major corporations, was found in 1992 to have paid protection money to local mobsters, known as *sokaiya*, to prevent disruption of the company's annual meeting. Ito resigned, remaining a director and honorary chairman, and was replaced by Toshifumi Suzuki, who had overseen the development of point-of-sale technology at the Japanese 7-Elevens.

Earnings remained flat as sales rose slowly in the early 1990s, reflecting consumer uncertainty. In 1996 Ito-Yokado signed a joint venture agreement to develop superstores in China. Able to maintain its own supply channels rather than use Chinese vendors, the company opened its first store in Sichuan (1997), followed by a second superstore in Beijing (1998). With the Asian markets weak, and after years of cutting the store count in the US, Southland began expanding again in 1997.

Southland changed its name to 7-Eleven, Inc., in 1999. Seven-Eleven Japan Co. joined with SOFTBANK and two other companies in 1999 to form an online bookselling joint venture, e-Shopping! Books. In late 1999 Ito-Yokado applied for a banking license in Japan to establish an Internet bank that would be accessible through Web kiosks in its retail locations.

Honorary Chairman: Masatoshi Ito
President and CEO: Toshifumi Suzuki
EVP: Hyozo Morita
EVP: Nobutake Sato
Senior Managing Director: Akihiko Hanawa
Senior Managing Director: Yasuhisa Ito
Senior Managing Director: Isao Kobayashi
Managing Director: Toshie Henmi
Managing Director: Akira Hinosawa
Managing Director: Sakae Isaka
Managing Director: Atsushi Kamei
Managing Director and CFO: Akira Miyauchi
Managing Director: Sakue Mizukoshi
Managing Director: Noritoshi Murata
Managing Director: Shinichiro Sugi
Auditors: ChuoAoyama Audit Corporation

LOCATIONS

HQ: 1-4, Shibakoen 4-chome, Minato-ku,
Tokyo 105-8571, Japan
Phone: +81-3-3459-2111 **Fax:** +81-3-3459-6873
US HQ: 1 Union Sq., Ste. 2828, Seattle, WA 98101
US Phone: 206-667-8973 **US Fax:** 206-667-8971
Web site: http://www.itoyokado.iyg.co.jp

2000 Sales

	% of total
Japan	70
North America	30
Total	**100**

PRODUCTS/OPERATIONS

2000 Sales

	% of total
Superstores	56
Convenience stores	40
Restaurants	4
Total	**100**

Principal Retail and Restaurant Operations

Superstores and Other Retail Operations
Daikuma discount stores
Ito-Yokado superstores
Mary Ann womenswear boutiques
Oshman's sporting goods stores (Japan)
Robinson's department stores (Japan)
Steps menswear shops
York Benimaru supermarkets
YorkMart supermarkets

Convenience Stores
7-Eleven, Inc. (72%, US)
Seven-Eleven Japan Co., Ltd. (51%)

Restaurants
Denny's Japan
Famil

COMPETITORS

Carréfour	Marui	Tosco
Casey's General	Matsuzakaya Co.	Ultramar
Stores	Mycal	Diamond
Daiei	Corporation	Shamrock
Daimaru	Seiyu	Uny
FamilyMart	Takashimaya	Wal-Mart
Isetan Company	Tokyu	
JUSCO	Department	
Kojima	Store Co.	

HISTORICAL FINANCIALS & EMPLOYEES

Nasdaq: IYCOY FYE: Last day in February	Annual Growth	2/91	2/92	2/93	2/94	2/95	2/96	2/97	2/98	2/99	2/00
Sales ($ mil.)	8.8%	13,768	22,585	25,871	27,735	29,771	27,543	24,949	24,642	27,225	29,308
Net income ($ mil.)	(2.0%)	521	568	552	565	737	730	614	555	555	433
Income as % of sales	—	3.8%	2.5%	2.1%	2.0%	2.5%	2.7%	2.5%	2.3%	2.0%	1.5%
Earnings per share ($)	(3.3%)	—	1.39	1.35	0.34	0.45	1.79	1.50	1.36	1.36	1.06
Stock price - FY high ($)	—	—	37.31	34.94	57.00	57.88	66.31	61.88	61.88	69.50	119.38
Stock price - FY low ($)	—	—	27.75	27.00	29.50	42.75	44.25	41.75	42.50	40.50	54.00
Stock price - FY close ($)	7.7%	—	32.69	29.69	57.00	45.25	56.38	44.13	54.25	59.25	59.06
P/E - high	—	—	27	26	168	129	37	41	46	51	109
P/E - low	—	—	20	20	87	95	25	28	31	30	49
Dividends per share ($)	5.9%	—	0.19	0.22	0.27	0.31	0.18	0.27	0.28	0.27	0.30
Book value per share ($)	30.1%	—	2.72	3.33	3.99	4.80	4.80	4.47	4.45	19.72	22.24
Employees	15.8%	31,110	32,076	33,077	33,629	34,597	36,932	38,149	39,245	113,921	116,636

STOCK PRICE HISTORY

HIGH/LOW/CLOSE

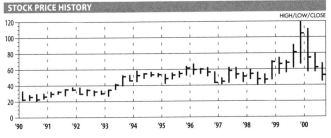

2000 FISCAL YEAR-END

Debt ratio: 24.1%
Return on equity: 5.0%
Cash ($ mil.): 4,515
Current ratio: 1.56
Long-term debt ($ mil.): 2,879
No. of shares (mil.): 408
Dividends
  Yield: 0.5%
  Payout: 28.3%
Market value ($ mil.): 24,103

J SAINSBURY PLC

OVERVIEW

For well over a century J Sainsbury has been helping its customers bring home the bacon. Lately, the London-based company has been helping them put it in the bank, too. The UK's second-largest food retailer (it lost its #1 title to Tesco), J Sainsbury operates five retail chains in the UK and the US, as well as a bank in the UK.

Stiff competition from price-chopping rivals Tesco and Wal-Mart-owned ASDA Group has made the wheels wobble a bit at Sainsbury's Supermarkets, which account for about 70% of the company's sales. Most of its 400-plus UK

supermarkets — which get about 40% of their sales from private-label products — are undergoing a five-year refurbishment program. Sainsbury also operates about a dozen Savacentre large-sized supermarkets in the UK, nearly 300 Homebase home and garden supply superstores in the UK, and about 170 Shaw's Supermarkets and Star Markets in New England. Sainsbury's Bank is a joint venture with the Bank of Scotland.

The Sainsbury family owns about 35% of the company.

HISTORY

Newlyweds John James and Mary Ann Sainsbury established a small dairy shop in their London home in 1869. Customers flocked to the clean and efficient store, a far cry from most cluttered and dirty London shops. They opened a second store in 1876. By 1914, 115 stores had been opened, and the couple's sons had entered the business.

During WWI the company's stores established grocery departments to meet demand for preserved products, such as meat and jams, which were sold under the Sainsbury's label.

Mary Ann died in 1927 and John James the next year. Son John Benjamin, wholly devoted to the family business, took charge. (He is reported to have said on his deathbed, "Keep the stores well lit.") In the 1930s, he engineered the company's first acquisition, the Thoroughgood stores. Sales dropped by 50% during WWII, and some shops were destroyed by German bombing. Under third-generation leader Alan John Sainsbury, the company opened its first self-service store in 1950. The 75,000-sq.-ft. store opened in 1955 in Lewisham was considered to be the largest supermarket in Europe.

J Sainsbury went public in 1973 and through the early 1970s increased nonfood merchandise sales. It established a joint venture with British Home Stores in 1975, forming the Savacentre hypermarkets (the company bought out its partner in 1989).

Sainsbury partnered with Grand Bazaar Innovation Bon Marche, of Belgium, in 1979 to establish Homebase, a high-end, do-it-yourself chain (it bought the remaining 25% in 1996).

By 1983 most of Sainsbury's 229 stores were clustered in the south of England. A mature market and stiff competition forced the company to look elsewhere — both overseas and close to home. It began buying out US-based Shaw's Supermarkets in New England and in 1984 opened its first Scottish hypermarket. By

1987 the grocer owned 100% of Shaw's, which had 60 stores in Massachusetts, Maine, and New Hampshire.

In 1991 Sainsbury came under competitive pressure from Tesco and the Argyll Group (later renamed Safeway PLC), which also began building superstores. It responded with an expansion drive of its own, including opening its first Scottish supermarket (in Glasgow) the next year.

The company introduced its own version of classic cola in 1994 in packaging similar to Coca-Cola's but stopped after Coca-Cola threatened a lawsuit. Also that year it purchased a $325 million stake in Maryland-based Giant Food and opened its first store in France (at Calais). Sainsbury bought home improvement retailer Texas Homecare from UK leisure concern Ladbroke in 1995 and integrated it into its Homebase unit.

Royal Ahold bought Giant Food, including Sainsbury's 20% stake, in 1998. David Sainsbury — a great-grandson of the founders — retired as chairman in 1998 to pursue politics, marking the first time a Sainsbury has not headed up the company in its more-than-a-century history.

As part of a cost-cutting effort, in 1999 Sainsbury announced plans for 2,200 job cuts, more than half in management. It then announced plans to open 200 convenience stores, called Sainsbury's Local, over three years. In June 1999 Sainsbury bought the 53-store Star Markets chain of Massachusetts for $476 million, merging it into its Shaw's operations. In March 2000 Sir Peter Davis took over as CEO of Sainsbury's Supermarkets, replacing David Bremner. In summer 2000 the retailer announced it was considering strategic alternatives for its Homebase chain, including a possible sale, alliance, or joint venture.

Chairman: George Bull, age 63
Group Chief Executive; Chairman and Managing Director, Sainsbury's Supermarkets; Chairman, Homebase: Peter Davis, age 58
President: Lord Sainsbury of Preston Candover
Group Finance Director: Roger Matthews, age 57
Group Human Resources and Information Systems Director: John E. Adshead, age 55
Group Property and Environmental Affairs Director; Property Director, Sainsbury's Supermarkets: Ian Coull, age 49
CEO Shaw's Supermarkets: Ross McLaren
Managing Director Homebase: Kate Swann
Retail Director Sainsbury's Supermarkets: Robin Whitbread, age 49
Auditors: PricewaterhouseCoopers

LOCATIONS

HQ: Stamford House, Stamford St., London SE1 9LL, United Kingdom
Phone: +44-20-7695-6000 **Fax:** +44-20-7695-7610
US HQ: 750 W. Center St., West Bridgewater, MA 02379
US Phone: 508-313-4000 **US Fax:** 508-313-3112
Web site: http://www.j-sainsbury.co.uk

J Sainsbury operates more than 800 stores in the UK and the US and a bank in the UK.

2000 Sales

	% of total
UK	88
US	12
Total	**100**

PRODUCTS/OPERATIONS

2000 Sales

	% of total
Sainsbury's Supermarkets	70
Shaw's/Star Markets	18
Homebase	7
Savacentre	5
Total	**100**

Other Operations
Egyptian Distribution Group SAE (25%, food retailing, Egypt)
Hampden Group plc (29%, do-it-yourself retailing, UK and Ireland)
Hedge End Park Limited (50%, real estate, UK)

COMPETITORS

Boots Company
Budgens
Castorama
CVS
DeMoulas Super Markets
Hannaford Bros.
John Lewis Partnership
Kingfisher
Marks & Spencer
Meyer International
RMC Group
Safeway plc
Somerfield
Stop & Shop
Tesco
Wal-Mart
Wm Morrison Supermarkets

HISTORICAL FINANCIALS & EMPLOYEES

OTC: JSNSY FYE: First Saturday in March	Annual Growth	2/91	2/92	2/93	2/94	2/95	2/96	2/97	2/98	2/99	2/00
Sales ($ mil.)	6.3%	14,946	15,285	13,807	15,721	17,988	20,651	21,815	23,877	26,291	25,983
Net income ($ mil.)	(2.2%)	679	770	717	211	849	747	656	802	957	557
Income as % of sales	—	4.5%	5.0%	5.2%	1.3%	4.7%	3.6%	3.0%	3.4%	3.6%	2.1%
Earnings per share ($)	(8.0%)	—	—	—	—	—	1.62	1.42	1.69	1.99	1.16
Stock price - FY high ($)	—	—	—	—	—	—	31.25	26.88	33.88	40.38	29.00
Stock price - FY low ($)	—	—	—	—	—	—	22.50	20.13	19.25	23.63	16.50
Stock price - FY close ($)	(8.2%)	—	—	—	—	—	23.25	20.50	29.63	23.88	16.50
P/E - high	—	—	—	—	—	—	19	19	20	20	25
P/E - low	—	—	—	—	—	—	14	14	11	12	14
Dividends per share ($)	5.4%	—	—	—	—	—	0.74	0.75	0.92	0.92	0.91
Book value per share ($)	7.8%	—	—	—	—	—	11.77	11.97	14.37	15.64	15.90
Employees	4.2%	—	—	—	—	—	160,435	165,992	175,551	178,000	189,227

STOCK PRICE HISTORY

HIGH/LOW/CLOSE

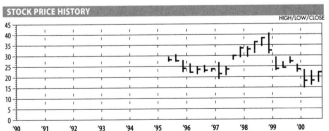

2000 FISCAL YEAR-END

Debt ratio: 16.7%
Return on equity: 7.4%
Cash ($ mil.): 851
Current ratio: 0.76
Long-term debt ($ mil.): 1,535
No. of shares (mil.): 481
Dividends
 Yield: 0.1%
 Payout: 0.8%
Market value ($ mil.): 7,939

JAPAN AIRLINES COMPANY, LTD.

OVERVIEW

Japan Airlines (JAL) has finally flown back into the black after several years of consecutive losses, but the future remains hazy. The #1 airline in Asia (ahead of All Nippon Airways), Tokyo-based JAL flies more than 31 million passengers each year to some 75 destinations in 29 countries — primarily in the Asia/Pacific region — with a fleet of more than 135 Boeing airliners. JAL also owns the international chain of Nikko hotels, offers tour packages, hauls air cargo, and provides aircraft maintenance and ground support services.

Japan's chronic recession and Asia's economic crisis have taken their toll on JAL, causing passenger and cargo traffic to decline. At the same time, competition has been growing, with the deregulation wave making its way to Japan's shores. Struggling to defend its operations and cut costs, JAL has trimmed its workforce, added new aircraft, and launched JAL Express, a low-fare domestic carrier.

JAL's code-sharing partners include American Airlines, Canadian Air, Cathay Pacific, and Swissair; the carrier is also being courted by the global Oneworld alliance led by American and British Airways.

HISTORY

After WWII, Japan was not allowed to form its own airline until the end of US occupation in 1951. That year a group of bankers led by Seijiro Yanagito founded Japanese Air Lines (JAL). JAL was essentially a revival of the pre-war Nihon Koku Kabushiki Kaisha (Japan Air Transport Company), the national airline created by the Japanese government in 1928 and dissolved by the Allies in 1945. Since the Allied Peace Treaty forbade the airline to use Japanese flight crews, it leased both pilots and equipment from Northwest. In 1953 the airline was reorganized as Japan Airlines, with the government and the public owning equal shares.

Under Yanagito, who ran the airline until 1961, JAL expanded quickly, opening a transpacific route from Tokyo to San Francisco in 1954 and extending regional service to Hong Kong in 1955, Bangkok in 1956, and Singapore in 1958. A polar route from Tokyo to London and Paris gave the airline a foothold in Europe in 1961. Service to Moscow began in 1967, and that year JAL formed Southwest Airlines (now Japan TransOcean Air) to serve the islands of Japan.

In 1974 JAL suspended flights to Taipei, the mainstay of Chinese nationalists, in favor of new service to Beijing and Shanghai. Japan Asia Airways, a new subsidiary, resumed flights to Taipei the next year.

JAL ran into problems in the early 1980s: In 1982 a mentally unstable pilot crashed a plane into Tokyo Bay, killing 24; and in 1985 a JAL 747 crashed into a mountainside, killing all but four of the 524 on board. The worst single-plane accident in history, the disaster led to the resignation of most of JAL's top executives.

Facing a strong US currency in 1985, JAL signed an 11-year, $3 billion aircraft contract with Boeing, set at a fixed exchange rate of 184 yen per dollar. But the contract would haunt the airline in the 1990s, denying JAL the benefit of a weakened dollar that would fall below ¥100.

The government sold its stake in JAL to the public in 1987. With air transport no longer nationalized, overseas routes were opened to the company's longtime domestic rival, All Nippon Airways (ANA).

In 1992 JAL reported its first loss ($100 million) since privatization, the result of high labor costs and the expansion of its fleet and facilities. With Japan sliding into recession, the company announced a five-year, $4.8 billion belt-tightening program.

Falling short of those cost-cutting goals, in 1993 JAL announced it would close half its North American offices, suspend recruitment, and freeze salaries. It also signed an agreement with ANA to share some aircraft maintenance costs. Traffic increased in 1994, but JAL was forced to cut prices to meet lower competing fares. The opening of Osaka's new airport boosted the carrier's overseas traffic but increased competition by allowing more international flights into Japan.

In 1995 JAL hooked up with American Airlines to connect computer reservation systems and act as agents for each other's cargo businesses. But JAL's losses continued, and chairman Susumu Yamaji and president Akira Kondo resigned in 1998. That year the airline announced job cuts, restructured routes, and launched low-cost domestic carrier JAL Express.

JAL finally posted a profit again in 1999. It also added Alitalia and Iberia Airlines as code-sharing partners, and it reduced its stake in delivery giant DHL from 26% to 6%. JAL came under renewed pressure in 2000, when government deregulation of domestic fares sparked a price war.

OFFICERS

President; Chairman, Flight Safety Board, Restructuring Committee, CS Promotion Committee, Business Activities Reappraisal Committee: Isao Kaneko
EVP; Chairman, Flight Safety Committee; Chief Officer, Operations and Engineering Group; SVP, Flight Operations Division; SVP, Flight Safety Board: Yasushi Yuasa
EVP; Chief Officer, Industrial Relations; SVP, Corporate Planning and Information Systems: Zenta Yokoyama
SVP Passenger Sales; President Passenger Sales: Toshiki Okazaki
SVP Corporate Affairs, Public Relations, Executive Office, and Strategic Research; SVP, Associated Business: Toshiyuki Shinmachi
SVP Human Resources, Personnel and Organization Administration and Industrial Relations; SVP and General Manager, Medical Services; SVP and Deputy General Manager, Associated Business: Hidekazu Nishizuka
Executive Officer and CEO, The Americas: Kazunari Yashiro
Auditors: Showa Ota & Co.

LOCATIONS

HQ: Nippon Koku Kabushiki Kaisha, 4-11 Higashi-shinagawa 2-chome, Shinagawa-ku, Tokyo 140-8637, Japan
Phone: +81-3-5460-3191   **Fax:** +81-3-5460-5929
US HQ: 655 5th Ave., New York, NY 10022
US Phone: 212-310-1454   **US Fax:** 212-310-1230
Web site: http://www.jal.co.jp

PRODUCTS/OPERATIONS

2000 Sales

	$ mil.	% of total
Passenger	8,683	58
Cargo	1,698	11
Other	4,699	31
Total	**15,080**	**100**

Selected Subsidiaries
Airport Ground Service Co., Ltd. (96%)
AXESS International Network Inc. (75%, computer reservation system)
JAL Express Co., Ltd. (domestic regional carrier)
JAL Hotels Co., Ltd. (89%, hotel management)
JAL Trading Inc. (70%, wholesale and retail sales, insurance agency)
JALPAK Co., Ltd. (77%, package tours)
JALways Co., Ltd. (82%, charter services)
Japan Asia Airways Co., Ltd. (90%, regional services)
Japan TransOcean Air Co., Ltd. (51%, air transport)

COMPETITORS

Accor	Hyatt
Air Canada	Japan Air System
Air France	Kinki Nippon Railway
All Nippon Airways	KLM
British Airways	Korean Air
Carlson	Lufthansa
Central Japan Railway	Northwest Airlines
China Airlines	Singapore Airlines
China Eastern Airlines	Skymark
Continental Airlines	Thai Airways
Delta	TWA
East Japan Railway	UAL
Evergreen Marine	Virgin Atlantic Airways
Garuda	West Japan Railway

HISTORICAL FINANCIALS & EMPLOYEES

Nasdaq (SC): JAPNY FYE: March 31	Annual Growth	3/91	3/92	3/93	3/94	3/95	3/96	3/97	3/98	3/99	3/00
Sales ($ mil.)	7.6%	7,794	8,202	11,178	9,581	15,578	13,670	12,638	11,982	13,051	15,080
Net income ($ mil.)	7.3%	99	(100)	(417)	(247)	(169)	(86)	(117)	(477)	223	186
Income as % of sales	—	1.3%	—	—	—	—	—	—	—	1.7%	1.2
Earnings per share ($)	14.9%	0.06	(0.06)	(0.23)	(0.14)	(0.09)	(0.04)	(0.13)	(0.54)	0.25	0.21
Stock price - FY high ($)	—	26.43	18.88	11.63	16.00	15.63	14.75	16.88	9.63	6.88	8.56
Stock price - FY low ($)	—	13.88	10.75	8.63	10.38	11.75	11.63	7.75	5.13	4.38	4.25
Stock price - FY close ($)	(11.6%)	17.25	11.38	11.00	12.38	14.00	14.63	7.88	6.69	6.19	5.69
P/E - high	—	441	—	—	—	—	—	—	—	28	41
P/E - low	—	231	—	—	—	—	—	—	—	18	20
Dividends per share ($)	—	0.05	0.05	0.06	0.00	0.00	0.00	0.00	0.00	0.00	0.04
Book value per share ($)	(3.7%)	3.55	3.36	3.32	3.56	3.63	2.85	2.24	1.58	2.03	2.52
Employees	(1.5%)	21,156	21,451	21,991	21,396	21,396	20,030	19,046	17,863	16,325	18,535

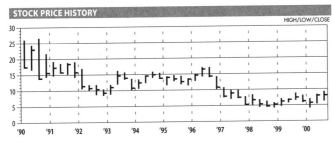

STOCK PRICE HISTORY HIGH/LOW/CLOSE

2000 FISCAL YEAR-END
Debt ratio: 80.5%
Return on equity: 9.2
Cash ($ mil.): 1,317
Current ratio: 1.03
Long-term debt ($ mil.): 9,253
No. of shares (mil.): 889
Dividends
  Yield: 0.7%
  Payout: 19.0%
Market value ($ mil.): 5,081

JAPAN TOBACCO INC.

OVERVIEW

Not all the smoke in Japan comes from pollution. Tokyo-based Japan Tobacco is the world's third-largest tobacco company, after Philip Morris and British American Tobacco. It controls more than 75% of Japan's cigarette market with nine of Japan's top 10 brands, including flagship Mild Seven (the world's #2 cigarette), Caster, and Seven Stars. Japan Tobacco also produces Marlboros (#1 in the world) for Philip Morris in Japan. The company exports its products to Asia, Europe, and the US, and it owns UK-based Manchester Tobacco.

Under heavy attack by western tobacco companies in Japan, Japan Tobacco expanded its foreign operations by purchasing RJR Nabisco's international tobacco unit (now JT International), which makes and sells Camel, Salem, and Winston brands outside the US. Most of its sales come from cigarettes and other tobacco items.

Japan Tobacco also has operations in agribusiness, engineering, food and beverages, pharmaceuticals, and real estate. The firm operates Burger King restaurants in Japan and owns Japan Beverage (vending machines, formerly Unimat Corporation). Japan Tobacco's food division (formerly Pillsbury Japan) makes processed foods, and its beverage unit produces teas and soft drinks.

The Japanese Finance Ministry owns two-thirds of the company, which has an exclusive right to produce tobacco in Japan.

HISTORY

In 1898, roughly 325 years after tobacco was introduced in Japan, the nation's Ministry of Finance formed a bureau to monopolize the production of the crop. The purpose of the monopoly was to fund military and industrial expansion. In 1905 the bureau also became responsible for a salt monopoly.

During WWII, Japan's tobacco leaf import supply from North and South America grew scarce and led to cigarette rationing. In 1949 the government began operating the tobacco production bureau as a business: the Japan Tobacco and Salt Public Corporation.

The company launched Hope, the first Japanese-made filter cigarette, in 1957, and it became the world's top seller a decade later. As the number of Japanese smokers increased, Japan Tobacco and Salt began making cigarette papers and filters. In 1972 it began printing mild packaging "warnings": "Be careful not to smoke excessively for your health."

Japan Tobacco and Salt began selling Marlboro cigarettes licensed from Philip Morris in 1973. In 1974 it launched its "Smokin' Clean" ad campaign featuring smokers enjoying the outdoors. The Mild Seven brand (its current best-seller) went on sale in 1977; it became the world's #1 cigarette in 1981 but dropped to #2 (behind Marlboro) in 1993.

When its tobacco monopoly ended in 1985, the government established the firm as Japan Tobacco (a government-owned joint stock company). As competition from foreign imports increased, it expanded into other areas. It formed Japan Tobacco International (cigarette exports mainly to the US and Southeast Asia) in 1985, moved into agribusiness and real estate operations that year, and created JT Pharmaceutical

Co. in 1986. In 1987 cigarette import tariffs ended, and importers lowered prices to match the company's; its sales and market share declined. During the late 1980s it introduced HALF TIME beverages and its first low-tar cigarettes (Mild Seven Lights is now the world's #1 light cigarette).

In 1992 Japan Tobacco bought its first overseas production facility, Manchester Tobacco. Former Ministry of Finance official Masaru Mizuno became CEO that year — and soon took up smoking. Also in 1992 Japan Tobacco and Agouron Pharmaceuticals agreed to jointly develop immune system drugs. The government sold about 20% of the firm's stock to the public in 1994 and 13% in 1996. The firm began operating Burger King restaurants in Japan in 1996. The Salt Monopoly Law was rescinded in 1997, so salt operations and assets were transferred to the newly created Salt Industry Center of Japan. Japan Tobacco bought Pillsbury Japan in 1998.

Japan Tobacco in 1999 paid $8 billion for R.J. Reynolds International, the international tobacco unit of RJR Nabisco. The company then renamed the unit, which has operations in 70 countries worldwide, JT International. It also bought the food products division of Asahi Chemical and Torii Pharmaceutical from Asahi Breweries. Also in 1999 Japan Tobacco came out against a proposed Health and Welfare Ministry plan to cut Japanese cigarette consumption in half by 2010; it would be bad for the tobacco industry, the company explained.

In February 2000 slow sales prompted Japan Tobacco to announce it would reduce its workforce by 6,100 positions by 2005 — 4,100 domestic jobs within five years and 2,000 international jobs within three years.

Chairman: Masaru Mizuno
President and CEO: Katsuhiko Honda
SEVP: Shunpei Nishikata
SEVP: Hideo Tada
SEVP: Masami Tsuboshima
Executive Director Biological/Pharmacological Research Laboratories: Tsumoru Miyamoto
Executive Director, Corporate Scientific and Regulatory Affairs: Yoshihiko Ohkawa
Executive Director Domestic Leaf Tobacco General Division: Mutsumi Makinoda
Executive Director Finance: Akira Watanabe
Executive Director, General Administration, Legal Affairs, Corporate Communications, Corporate Citizenship, Advertising, and Internal Audit: Minoru Umeno
Executive Director Planning: Takao Seki
Executive Director Tobacco Headquarters: Kazuei Obata
Managing Director, Personnel and Labor Relations: Yasuo Takayama
Managing Director Pharmaceutical Division: Takashi Kato
Managing Director, Product and Tobacco: Hideshi Fujishiro
Auditors: Deloitte Touche Tohmatsu

HQ: Nihon Tabako Sangyo,
2-1, Toranomon 2-chome, Minato-ku,
Tokyo 105-8422, Japan
Phone: +81-3-3582-3111   **Fax:** +81-3-5572-1441
US HQ: 375 Park Ave. Ste. 1307, New York, NY 10152
US Phone: 212-319-8990   **US Fax:** 212-319-8993
Web site: http://www.jtnet.ad.jp

2000 Sales

	% of total
Tobacco	92
Food	4
Pharmaceuticals	2
Other	2
Totals	**100**

Selected Cigarette Brands
Cabin and Cabin Mild
Camel (outside of the US)
Caster and Caster Mild
Frontier
Hope (10)
Marlboro Light Menthol (licensed, Philip Morris)
Mild Seven (regular, Lights, Super Lights)
Salem (outside of the US)
Seven Stars
Winston (outside of the US)

Ajinomoto	Kraft Foods International
Altadis	Mitsubishi Chemical
Asahi Breweries	Nisshin Flour Milling
Austria Tabak	Philip Morris International
British American Tobacco	Reemtsma
China National Tobacco	Suntory
Gallaher	Unilever
Imperial Tobacco Group	Vector

Tokyo: 2914 FYE: March 31	Annual Growth	3/91	3/92	3/93	3/94	3/95	3/96	3/97	3/98	3/99	3/00
Sales (¥ bil.)	21.0%	—	—	—	—	1,684	1,728	1,807	1,733	3,876	4,371
Net income (¥ bil.)	(6.1%)	—	—	—	—	69	67	80	58	74	50
Income as % of sales	—	—	—	—	—	4.1%	3.9%	4.4%	3.3%	1.9%	1.2%
Earnings per share (¥)	(6.1%)	—	—	—	—	34,728	33,974	40,098	29,010	37,317	25,396
Stock - FY high (¥ thou.)	—	—	—	—	—	1,220	1,020	1,020	1,040	1,310	1,540
Stock - FY low (¥ thou.)	—	—	—	—	—	766	710	748	782	870	686
Stock - FY close (¥ thou.)	(1.9%)	—	—	—	—	811	990	820	996	115	735
P/E - high	—	—	—	—	—	35	30	25	36	35	61
P/E - low	—	—	—	—	—	22	21	19	27	23	27
Dividends per share (¥)	0.0%	—	—	—	—	7,000	7,000	7,000	7,000	7,000	7,000
Book value per share (¥)	5.2%	—	—	—	—	593,110	616,090	648,773	669,861	723,551	763,291
Employees	(2.0%)	—	—	—	—	23,208	22,625	22,160	20,384	20,509	21,000

HIGH/LOW/CLOSE

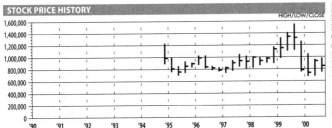

Debt ratio: 26.9%
Return on equity: 3.4%
Cash (¥ mil.): 353,955
Current ratio: 1.98
Long-term debt (¥ mil.): 560,668
No. of shares (mil.): 2
Dividends
  Yield: 0.0%
  Payout: 0.3%
Market value ($ mil.): 13,924
Sales ($ mil.): 41,431

JARDINE MATHESON HOLDINGS

OVERVIEW

If it hadn't been for Jardine Matheson, Hong Kong might not have had to revert to Chinese sovereignty, because it might never have been ceded to the British at all. The role of the *hong* (diversified trading company) in the instigation of the 19th-century Opium Wars that forced the cession of the colony remains a sore point in Jardine's relationship with China.

The traditional basis of Hong Kong-based Jardine Matheson's wealth is Hong Kong real estate (especially that of the central district). Other interests include banking and financial services; insurance; supermarkets (Dairy Farm), and restaurants; shipping; hotels (Mandarin Oriental); and construction. The company has diversified geographically, but Asia/Pacific is where the money is — some 74% of its revenues come from that region.

Despite the Opium Wars legacy and, more recently, Jardine's advocacy of democratic reforms in Hong Kong, the Chinese government allows Jardine to participate in projects on the mainland.

Members of the Keswick family, who are descendants of co-founder William Jardine, control the company through an elaborate structure of cross-shareholdings.

HISTORY

Scotsmen William Jardine and James Matheson met in Bombay in 1820. In 1832 they founded Jardine, Matheson in Canton, the only Chinese city then open to foreigners. The company started shipping tea from China to Europe and smuggling opium from India to China. In 1839 Chinese authorities tried to stop the drug trade, seizing 20,000 chests of opium, 7,000 of them Jardine's. Jardine persuaded Britain to send gunboats to China, precipitating the First Opium War. China lost the war and ceded Hong Kong to Britain in 1842.

Jardine moved to Hong Kong and resumed trading opium. The Second Opium War (1856-60) resulted in the opening of 11 more ports and the legalization of opium imports. Jardine flourished and later branched into the more legitimate fields of brewing, textiles, banking, insurance, and sugar. It formed Hongkong Land (HKL), a real estate company; introduced steamships to China; and built the country's first railroad line. The company earned the sobriquet "the Princely Hong" because of its high-society officers with free-spending habits.

The Sino-Japanese War and WWII shut the company down. In 1945, with China gripped by civil war, Jardine reopened in Hong Kong. Attempts to re-establish operations in China ended in 1954 after the Communist takeover. The company went public in 1961.

By 1980 the costs that had been incurred in an acquisition program begun in the 1970s made Jardine a takeover target. *Taipan* (big boss) David Newbigging defended the company by erecting a bulwark of crossholdings of it and HKL stock. The resulting debt pushed Jardine to the brink of bankruptcy, forcing it to sell assets.

Simon Keswick succeeded Newbigging in 1984 and reorganized the company, making investments in Mercedes-Benz distributorships and fast-food franchises that helped turn Jardine around. As the UK and China negotiated the transfer of Hong Kong to Chinese control, Keswick moved Jardine's legal home to Bermuda. Jardine continued to be plagued by takeover attempts, however, particularly by Li Ka-shing, who was assisted by China's investment organization, CITIC. In a 1986 anti-takeover transaction, the company created Jardine Strategic Holdings to hold interests in HKL and its spinoffs. When the Chinese army put down student demonstrations in Beijing two years later, Keswick called the Chinese government "a thuggish, oppressive regime."

To increase its holdings outside of Hong Kong, Jardine bought 26% of Trafalgar House in 1993 but sold its stake in the troubled British conglomerate in 1996, which contributed to lower profits. Jardine delisted five of its companies from the Hong Kong stock exchange in 1994. Continuing to expand geographically, the company acquired 20% of India's Tata Industries and bought London's Hyde Park Hotel in 1996.

Hong Kong was returned to China in 1997, and in a display of public fence-mending, Chinese Vice Premier Zhu Rongji welcomed Jardine's participation in mainland ventures. But Jardine's stormy relationship with China continued even as Jardine's profits dropped during the Asian economic crisis. In 1999 China closed down Jardine's Beijing and Guangzhou brokerage offices (and banned the two chief China officers from the business for life), claiming that Jardine was engaging in unauthorized activities.

In 2000 the Keswicks turned back an attempt by a US-based group of stockholders to seize control of the company.

Chairman: Henry Keswick
Managing Director, Jardine Matheson Holdings, Dairyfarm, Hongkong Land, Jardine Strategic, and Mandarin Oriental; Chairman, Jardine Matheson Ltd.: Percy Weatherall
Group Audit Controller: Keith Stephenson
Group Finance Director: Norman Lyle
Group Financial Controller: P. M. Kam
Group General Counsel: James Watkins
Group Head Human Resources: Ritchie Bent
Group Legal Manager: Simon Tuxen
Group Secretary, General Manager Corporate Services, and Director Group Corporate Affairs: Neil McNamara
Group Tax Manager: Betty Chan
Head Human Resources: Martin Barrow
Auditors: PricewaterhouseCoopers

LOCATIONS

HQ: Jardine Matheson Holdings Limited,
48th Fl., Jardine House, GPO Box 70, Hong Kong
Phone: +852-2843-8388   **Fax:** +852-2845-9005
Web site: http://www.jardines.com

1999 Sales

	$ mil.	% of total
Asia/Pacific		
Australia & New Zealand	3,584	34
Hong Kong & China	3,185	30
Southeast Asia	620	6
Northeast Asia	461	4
Europe		
UK	1,754	16
Other countries	609	6
North America	462	4
Total	**10,675**	**100**

PRODUCTS/OPERATIONS

1999 Sales

	$ mil.	% of total
Dairy Farm	5,918	55
Jardine International Motors	2,807	26
Jardine Pacific	1,706	16
Mandarin Oriental	179	2
Other	65	1
Total	**10,675**	**100**

Selected Subsidiaries and Affiliates
Cycle & Carriage Ltd. (25%, motor and property group, Singapore)
Dairy Farm International Holdings Ltd., (55%, supermarkets, restaurants)
Jardine International Motor Holdings Ltd., (auto distribution)
Jardine Lloyd Thompson (33%, insurance and brokerage, UK)
Jardine Pacific Holdings Ltd. (auto dealerships, engineering and construction, property, restaurants, shipping and financial services, trading and distribution)
Jardine Strategic Holdings Ltd. (62%, holding)
Mandarin Oriental International Ltd. (59%, hotels)
Matheson & Co., Ltd. (holding and management, UK)

COMPETITORS

Accor	Hutchison	McDonald's
Cheung Kong	Whampoa	Mitsubishi
Holdings	Hyatt	Samsung
China Resources	Hyundai	Seiyu
Enterprise	ITOCHU	Sime Darby
Daiei	Kumagai Gumi	Swire Pacific
Hopewell	Marriott	
Holdings	International	
HSBC Holdings	Marubeni	

HISTORICAL FINANCIALS & EMPLOYEES

OTC: JARLY FYE: December 31	Annual Growth	12/90	12/91	12/92	12/93	12/94	12/95	12/96	12/97	12/98	12/99
Sales ($ mil.)	6.6%	5,992	7,190	7,900	8,425	9,558	10,636	11,605	11,522	11,230	10,675
Net income ($ mil.)	(0.9%)	226	359	348	424	453	420	536	476	117	207
Income as % of sales	—	3.8%	5.0%	4.4%	5.0%	4.7%	3.9%	4.6%	4.1%	1.0%	1.9%
Earnings per share ($)	(4.9%)	—	0.51	0.57	0.67	0.77	0.72	0.52	0.56	0.09	0.34
Stock price - FY high ($)	—	—	5.00	8.47	10.47	10.55	9.19	8.50	8.35	5.50	5.50
Stock price - FY low ($)	—	—	3.88	5.00	5.41	6.13	5.30	5.45	4.18	1.38	2.38
Stock price - FY close ($)	(3.9%)	—	5.00	5.52	10.41	7.13	6.84	6.50	5.10	2.29	3.63
P/E - high	—	—	10	15	16	14	13	16	15	65	16
P/E - low	—	—	8	9	8	8	7	10	7	16	7
Dividends per share ($)	5.7%	—	0.16	0.19	0.22	0.25	0.25	0.25	0.25	0.22	0.25
Book value per share ($)	23.3%	—	1.25	1.42	1.90	2.75	4.50	5.55	9.32	6.43	6.68
Employees	2.5%	120,000	120,000	200,000	200,000	220,000	200,000	200,000	175,000	160,000	150,000

STOCK PRICE HISTORY

HIGH/LOW/CLOSE

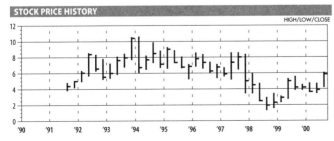

1999 FISCAL YEAR-END

Debt ratio: 22.6%
Return on equity: 4.0%
Cash ($ mil.): 1,601
Current ratio: 1.22
Long-term debt ($ mil.): 1,554
No. of shares (mil.): 797
Dividends
 Yield: 0.1%
 Payout: 0.7%
Market value ($ mil.): 2,894

KAO CORPORATION

OVERVIEW

Striking a sudsy pose, Kao aims to be a model of good hygiene. Tokyo-based Kao (pronounced "cow") is Japan's largest maker of personal care products and laundry and cleaning products. Its top brands include Attack (Japan's #1 laundry detergent), Family Pure dishwashing detergent, Laurier sanitary napkins, Success shampoo, Sofina cosmetics, Bioré skin care products, and Super Merries disposable diapers. Kao also makes cooking oils and fatty chemicals (mainly surfactants) for its own and industrial uses. It also makes printer and copier toner products as well as plastics used in products such as sneaker soles.

Although popular in Japan, Kao is still striving to attain the international scope of rivals like Procter & Gamble (P&G) and Unilever. Subsidiaries Goldwell and Guhl Ikebana make hair care products in Europe, and its Andrew Jergens subsidiary makes skin care products in North America. To bring new products to market, Kao invests heavily in research and development. (Its R&D division is three times that of P&G.) The company also plans to make over-the-counter products through a joint venture with Swiss pharmaceuticals firm Novartis.

Many of its products may be slippery, but Kao bigwigs try not to be. Kao stands apart from the traditionally stuffy Japanese management style with a nonhierarchical structure that encourages debate among employees.

HISTORY

Tomiro Nagase founded the Kao Soap Company in 1887; shortly afterward, he began selling bars under the motto, "A Clean Nation Prospers." Kao's longtime rivalry with Procter & Gamble (P&G) was foreshadowed when it adopted a moon trademark in 1890 strikingly similar to the one chosen by P&G eight years earlier.

Kao moved into detergents in the 1940s. In the 1960s the company struck upon an idea that would vertically integrate it and set it apart from other consumer products manufacturers: It set up a network of wholesale distributors ("hansha") who only sell Kao products. The hansha system improved distribution time and cut costs by eliminating middlemen.

Yoshio Maruta, one of several chemical engineers to run Kao, took over as president in 1971. Maruta presented himself as more Buddhist scholar than corporate honcho; during his 19 years at the top, he gave the company a wider vision through his emphasis on creativity and his insistence on an active learning environment. To encourage sharing of ideas, the company used open conference rooms for meetings and anyone interested could attend and participate in any meeting.

Under Maruta, Kao launched a string of successful products in new areas in the 1980s. In 1982 the company introduced its Sofina cosmetics line, emphasizing the line's scientifc basis in a break from traditional beauty products marketing. The next year its Super Merries diapers (with a new design that reduced diaper rash) trounced P&G's Pampers in Japan. Its popular Attack laundry detergent (the first concentrated laundry soap) led the market within six months of its 1987 debut.

Seeking a way to enter the US market, Kao bought the Andrew Jergens skin care company — based in Cincinnati, as is P&G — in 1988. (It also purchased a chemical company to supply the materials to make Jergens' products.) P&G and Unilever braced themselves for the new competition, but Kao didn't deliver, releasing products like fizzy bath tablets that didn't sell well in a nation of shower-takers. In 1989 it bought a 75% interest in Goldwell, a German maker of hair care and beauty products sold through hair stylists. (By 1994 Kao owned all of Goldwell.)

In the mid-1980s Kao built a name for itself in the floppy disk market and became the top producer of 3 1/2-in. floppy disks in North America by 1990. However, competition crowded the field and drove the price of disks down. In 1997 the company stopped production of floppy disks in the US.

Chemical engineer Takuya Goto took over as president that year. As Japanese consumers tightened their purse strings, Kao looked to other Asian markets and the US for potential consumers and found a willing audience in the US for its Bioré face strips. In 1998 Kao purchased Bausch & Lomb's skin care business, gaining the Curel and Soft Sense lotion brands. The company then sold its information technology operations in Canada, Germany, Ireland, and the US to Zomax Optical Media.

Late in 1998 Kao established a joint venture with Novartis to make baby foods and over-the-counter drugs such as stomach medicines; the companies plan to begin launching products sometime in 2000.

OFFICERS

Chairman: Fumikatsu Tokiwa
President: Takuya Goto
EVP: Kazuya Inbe
EVP: Shotaro Watanabe
Senior Managing Director: Michinori Mochizuki
Senior Managing Director: Sumiaki Sasaki
Managing Director: Masanori Sakata
Managing Director: Kunihiko Hachiya
Managing Director: Kinji Miwa
Managing Director: Toshio Hoshino
Auditors: Deloitte Touche Tohmatsu

LOCATIONS

HQ: 14-10 Nihonbashi Kayabacho, 1-chome, Chuo-ku, Tokyo 103-8210, Japan
Phone: +81-3-3660-7111   **Fax:** +81-3-3660-7103
Web site: http://www.kao.co.jp

Kao sells its products primarily in Asia but also in Africa, Australia, Europe, and North America.

2000 Sales

	% of total
Japan	77
Other countries	23
Total	**100**

PRODUCTS/OPERATIONS

2000 Sales

	% of total
Household	83
Chemical	17
Total	**100**

Selected Products

Fatty chemicals and edible oils (fatty acids, fatty alcohols, fatty amines, glycerine)

Hygiene and bath products (sanitary napkins, disposable diapers, bath additives)

Laundry and cleaning products (laundry detergents, laundry finishers, kitchen and other household detergents, fabric softeners)

Personal care products and cosmetics (soap, body cleansers, shampoos, conditioners, hair care products, cosmetics and skin care products, toothpastes, toothbrushes)

Specialty chemicals (asphalt emulsifiers, concrete additives, de-inking agents, toner and toner binders, water treatment chemicals)

Selected Brand Names

Bioré (skin care)
BuB Shower (shower gel)
Curel (lotion)
Emal (laundry detergent)
Jergens (skin care)
Laurier (sanitary napkins)
Lavenus (hair care)
LC2 (hair care)
More Excellent (dishwashing detergent)
Relief Pants (adult incontinence product)
Sofina (cosmetics)
Soft Sense (lotion)
Success (shampoo)
Super Merries (disposable diapers)

COMPETITORS

Alticor	Kanebo	Procter &
Colgate-	Kimberly-Clark	Gamble
Palmolive	Lion Corporation	Shiseido
Johnson &	Nisshin Oil Mills	Unicharm
Johnson	Pfizer	Unilever

HISTORICAL FINANCIALS & EMPLOYEES

OTC: KAOCY FYE: March 31	Annual Growth	3/91	3/92	3/93	3/94	3/95	3/96	3/97	3/98	3/99	3/00
Sales ($ mil.)	4.8%	—	5,491	6,714	7,532	9,205	7,791	7,281	6,818	7,711	7,979
Net income ($ mil.)	15.9%	—	151	178	216	274	229	231	184	290	491
Income as % of sales	—	—	2.7%	2.6%	2.9%	3.0%	2.9%	3.2%	2.7%	3.8%	6.2%
Earnings per share ($)	15.5%	—	—	—	—	—	4.21	3.77	2.46	4.69	7.50
Stock price - FY high ($)	—	—	—	—	—	—	132.00	136.50	151.00	226.00	307.00
Stock price - FY low ($)	—	—	—	—	—	—	112.00	99.00	105.00	129.50	218.00
Stock price - FY close ($)	25.3%	—	—	—	—	—	124.00	109.00	130.00	218.00	306.00
P/E - high	—	—	—	—	—	—	31	36	61	48	41
P/E - low	—	—	—	—	—	—	27	26	43	28	29
Dividends per share ($)	12.5%	—	—	—	—	—	1.19	1.23	1.11	1.34	1.90
Book value per share ($)	4.7%	—	—	—	—	—	60.11	57.93	52.27	61.53	72.12
Employees	(0.3%)	—	—	7,147	7,177	7,161	7,106	6,994	6,875	6,900	7,000

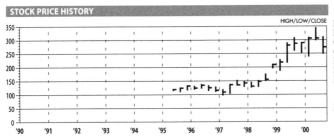

STOCK PRICE HISTORY
HIGH/LOW/CLOSE

2000 FISCAL YEAR-END
Debt ratio: 11.0%
Return on equity: 11.9%
Cash ($ mil.): 198
Current ratio: 1.61
Long-term debt ($ mil.): 555
No. of shares (mil.): 62
Dividends
  Yield: 0.0%
  Payout: 0.3%
Market value ($ mil.): 18,985

KARSTADT QUELLE AG

Karstadt Quelle is a shopping paradise born of the retail consolidation trend sweeping Europe. The Essen, Germany-based company has three principal business segments: retail, mail order, and services (primarily travel-related). One of Europe's largest retailers, Karstadt Quelle is best known for operating about 210 Karstadt and Hertie department stores throughout Germany. It also has nearly 200 other outlets under the names Runners Point (athletic clothing and shoes), Wehmeyer (apparel), and World of Music, among others. Karstadt Quelle is also a leader in mail-order (Quelle and Neckermann) and

travel services (C&N Touristic, a joint venture with Lufthansa).

Quelle has been an Internet pioneer and was first online in 1995; since its 1999 merger with Karstadt, Karstadt Quelle has launched one of Europe's largest online shopping sites, My-World, which features more than one million products. The site also offers online news reports and chat rooms.

The company is pressing for a relaxation of Germany's strict store-hours laws, which curtail shopping during weekends and evenings. Schickedanz-Holding, owned by the Riedel and Herl families, now owns 48% of Karstadt Quelle.

In 1881 Rudolph Karstadt opened a store in Mecklenburg, Germany, selling candy, apparel, and fabric. His store was one of Germany's first department stores; it offered separate departments for merchandise and offered low, fixed prices and cash-only sales. In 1885 Theodor Althoff took control of his mother's haberdashery, wool, and linen shop in Westfalen, Germany. He adopted the same business model as Karstadt.

Rudolph Karstadt AG was founded in 1920 and soon merged with Althoff's business. Six years later Karstadt founded EPA Einheitspreis, an American-style discount store. The company grew rapidly, reaching 89 outlets in 1929. But overexpansion and a worldwide depression hurt Karstadt, and it found itself in financial trouble by 1931. With the help of a bank consortium, the company restructured that year.

Karstadt operated 67 stores in 1939, but by the end of WWII, only 45 remained in West Germany and most were heavily damaged. (The company lost the remainder to East Germany and the Iron Curtain.) Postwar economic reform and reconstruction boosted personal incomes; as a result, Karstadt's sales rose too. In 1948 the retailer was accepted into "Interkontinentale Warenhausgruppe" (the "Intercontinental Department Store Group").

In 1971 Karstadt and mail-order firm Quelle founded travel firm TransEuropa-Reisen, which became became KS-Touristik-Beteiligungs in 1972. (Karstadt sold its share in 1976.) In 1976 Karstadt became a major shareholder in Germany's third-largest mail-order company, Neckermann Versand, which was restructured into a public limited company. The next year Karstadt upped its stake to 51% of Neckermann Versand, and it controlled virtually all of the

company by 1984. (Neckermann Versand travel subsidiary NUR Neckermann+Reisen became NUR Touristik in 1982.) Karstadt also founded Runners Point in 1984.

The company in 1988 opened a distribution center in Unna, Germany, which allowed the centralized supply of outlets with "batch goods" (goods that are available for reorder for a longer period). When the wall came down, bringing trade barriers with it, Karstadt established cooperation agreements with 10 Centrum and four Magnet department stores in the former East Germany. The same sort of agreement was set up with GUM department store in Moscow in 1992.

In 1993 Karstadt opened Optic Point Warenhandelsgesellschaft and acquired Hertie Waren- und Kaufhaus in 1994, making it by far Germany's largest department store group, surpassing Kaufhof. In 1995 the company extended its travel empire with the acquisition of 51% of business travel chain Euro Lloyd Reiseburo from Lufthansa, a move which gave it 208 travel agencies and a 6% share of the German travel market. Euro Lloyd went online the next year.

In 1997 retail group Schickedanz bought 20% of Karstadt when two banks decided to sell their shares. A year later Karstadt formed travel group C&N Touristik with Lufthansa (regulations forced the companies to sell Euro Lloyd, which was picked up by Swiss-based Kuoni). Karstadt also transferred its NUR Touristik operations to C&N Touristik (adversely affecting 1998 sales).

In 1999 the company purchased mail-order company Quelle from Schickedanz-Holding. The new company, Karstadt Quelle, is one of Europe's largest retailers.

Chairman Supervisory Board: Hans Meinhardt
Chairman and CEO: Wolfgang Urban
Deputy Chairman: Wolfgang Pokriefke
Director of Finance: Norbert Nelles
Director of HR: Andreas Hartisch
Auditors: BDO Deutsche Warentreuhand AG

LOCATIONS

HQ: Theodor-Althoff-Strasse 7, 45133 Essen, Germany
Phone: +49-20-17271   **Fax:** +49-20-1727-5216
Web site: http://www.karstadtquelle.com

Karstadt Quelle has operations in Austria, Belgium, Eastern Europe, France, Germany, the Netherlands, and Scandinavia.

1999 Sales

	% of total
Germany	91
EU countries	8
Other countries	1
Total	**100**

PRODUCTS/OPERATIONS

1999 Sales

	% of total
Retail stores	50
Mail order	48
Other	2
Total	**100**

Selected Operations

Mail Order
Neckermann
Quelle

Retail
Karstadt (department stores)
Runners Point (athletic apparel and shoes)
Schaulandt (electronics)
Schurmann (electronics)
Wehmeyer (apparel)
WOM World of Music (95%)

Services
C&N Touristic (50%; tourism)
INTELLIUM Systems & Services (group IT)
Le Buffet Catering
Profectis (technical customer service)

COMPETITORS

AVA AG
Edeka Zentrale
Massa
METRO AG
Otto Versand
Preussag
Wal-Mart

HISTORICAL FINANCIALS & EMPLOYEES

German: KAR FYE: December 31	Annual Growth	12/90	12/91	12/92	12/93	12/94	12/95	12/96	12/97	12/98	12/99
Sales (€ mil.)	7.6%	7,686	8,757	9,458	9,568	12,364	12,318	12,295	12,161	9,327	14,843
Net income (€ mil.)	(5.0%)	116	131	115	116	21	56	30	84	102	73
Income as % of sales	—	1.5%	1.5%	1.2%	1.2%	0.2%	0.5%	0.2%	0.7%	1.1%	0.5%
Earnings per share (€)	63.9%	—	—	—	—	—	—	0.36	1.00	1.21	1.59
Stock price - FY high (€)	—	—	—	—	—	—	—	31.90	37.12	50.87	48.70
Stock price - FY low (€)	—	—	—	—	—	—	—	25.10	24.49	28.73	30.55
Stock price - FY close (€)	15.6%	—	—	—	—	—	—	26.18	31.80	44.58	40.40
P/E - high	—	—	—	—	—	—	—	89	37	42	31
P/E - low	—	—	—	—	—	—	—	70	24	24	19
Dividends per share (€)	6.7%	—	—	—	—	—	—	0.51	0.51	0.56	0.62
Book value per share (€)	(0.6%)	—	—	—	—	—	—	14.73	15.14	15.43	14.45
Employees	5.9%	—	—	—	75,951	108,286	105,129	99,991	94,463	89,399	107,422

STOCK PRICE HISTORY

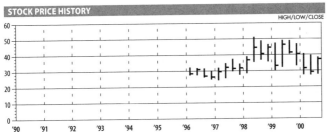

HIGH/LOW/CLOSE

1999 FISCAL YEAR-END

Debt ratio: 25.7%
Return on equity: 4.5%
Cash (€ mil.): 217
Current ratio: 1.71
Long-term debt (€ mil.): 586
No. of shares (mil.): 118
Dividends
  Yield: 0.0%
  Payout: 0.4%
Market value ($ mil.): 4,772
Sales ($ mil.): 14,914

KINGFISHER PLC

OVERVIEW

There are plenty of fish shopping in the sea, and Kingfisher is angling for them. The London-based group runs several large retail chains with a total of more than 2,700 stores. Among them are Superdrug, the UK's #2 drugstore chain (behind Boots The Chemist) with about 700 stores, and Woolworths, a general merchandise chain of some 800 stores. Kingfisher also operates three electronics chains: Darty, France's leading electrical retailer with more than 160 stores; Comet, with more than 260 stores in the UK; and BUT, with about 235 stores (mostly franchised) in France. About 40% of sales come from outside of the UK, mainly in France, and the company has merged its B&Q chain with France's Castorama, creating Europe's #1 do-it-yourself chain of some 500 stores. (Kingfisher has a 55% stake in the new group.) Kingfisher also operates music and video distribution and retail businesses (Entertainment UK and MVC, respectively), and it owns 45% of Libertysurf (a free Internet access service in France that controls Web portal Nomade.fr).

Kingfisher is shifting focus to its home improvement and electronics operations; it plans to spin off its Woolworths and Superdrug businesses.

HISTORY

The beginning of Kingfisher is directly tied to the former US Woolworth chain (now Venator Group). With the success of F.W. Woolworth general merchandise stores in the US, founder Frank Woolworth expanded overseas, first to Canada, then in 1909 to Liverpool, England. By 1914 Woolworth's UK subsidiaries had 31 stores, including one in Dublin, Ireland.

Growing quickly, the company went public in 1931, with its US parent retaining a 53% stake. The company spent most of the postwar years rebuilding bombed stores and had 762 stores by 1950, roughly the same number it had at the start of the war. Expansion resumed in the 1950s, and in 1958 Woolworth opened its 1,000th store. (It peaked with 1,141 stores in the late 1960s.)

In 1967 the company opened its first Woolco Department Store, modeled after the US Woolco stores of its parent. However, other retailers had cut into sales, and by 1968 it lost its place as Britain's leading retailer to Marks and Spencer. To compensate, Woolworth began closing unprofitable stores while remodeling others to speed up service. In 1973 it opened Shoppers World, a catalog showroom. By the late 1970s the company had recovered, and in 1980 it made its first takeover, buying B&Q, a chain of 40 do-it-yourself stores.

An investment group acquired Woolworth in 1982 using the vehicle Paternoster Stores. (The US parent sold its stake in Woolworth.) Nearly two decades of diversification followed. The company, renamed Woolworth Holdings, closed unprofitable Woolworth stores and sold its Shoppers World stores in 1983 and its Ireland Woolworth stores in 1984. It also acquired Comet, a UK home electronics chain, and continued to expand B&Q.

Two years later all of its F.W. Woolworth stores were renamed Woolworths, and food and clothing lines were abandoned. Also in 1986 the company sold its Woolco stores and bought record and tape distributor Record Merchandisers (later renamed Entertainment UK). The next year Woolworth Holdings acquired Superdrug, a chain of 297 discount drugstores. Adding to its Superdrug chain, in 1988 the company acquired and integrated two UK pharmacy chains: 110-store Tip Top Drugstores and 145-store Share Drug.

To reflect its growing diversity of businesses, the company was renamed Kingfisher in 1989. Expanding further into electronics, in 1993 Kingfisher acquired Darty, with 130 stores. Also that year the firm founded retailer Music and Video Club (MVC).

With several chains struggling, a boardroom shake-up in 1995 resulted in Geoffrey Mulcahy stepping down as chairman (he became CEO); John Banham stepped into the chair position the following year. In 1998 Kingfisher increased its presence in France by taking control of electronics chain BUT. It also merged its B&Q chain with the do-it-yourself stores of France's Castorama in 1998 and gained a 55% stake in the new group, which is still traded separately under the Castorama name.

Following the lead of rival Dixons, in 1999 Kingfisher launched its own free Internet access service in France called Libertysurf (in conjunction with luxury mogul Bernard Arnault). Soon thereafter, Libertysurf acquired 70% of Objectif Net and its Web site, Nomade.fr. Kingfisher's planned purchase of food retailer ASDA Group collapsed in June 1999 after being outbid by Wal-Mart Stores.

In September 2000 Kingfisher announced plans to split the company, shifting focus to its do-it-yourself and electronics operations.

Chairman: John Banham, age 59, $200,000 pay
CEO: Geoffrey Mulcahy, age 58, $1,261,000 pay
Group Finance Director: Phillip Rowley, age 47, $476,000 pay
CEO e-Kingfisher: Ian Cheshire
CEO Castorama Dubois Investissements: Jean-Hugues Loyez, age 51, $472,000 pay
Head of Corporate Center Human Resources: Lee Golding
Secretary: Helen Jones
Director of Investor Relations: Andrew Mills
Auditors: PricewaterhouseCoopers

LOCATIONS

HQ: North West House, 119 Marylebone Rd., London NW1 5PX, United Kingdom
Phone: +44-20-7724-7749   **Fax:** +44-20-7724-0355
Web site: http://www.kingfisher.co.uk

Kingfisher operates stores mostly in the UK, but also in Austria, Belgium, Brazil, Canada, France, Germany, Italy, Luxembourg, the Netherlands, Poland, Singapore, and Taiwan.

PRODUCTS/OPERATIONS

2000 Sales

	$ mil.	% of total
DIY	7,334	42
Electrical	5,163	29
General merchandise	4,965	28
Other	167	1
Total	**17,629**	**100**

Operations
Castorama-Dubois Investissements (55%, do-it-yourself stores)
  B&Q (UK)
  Brico-Depot (France)
  Castorama (France)
  Dubois Materiaux (France)
  NOMI (Poland)
  Reno-Depot (Canada)
Electrical
  BCC (Holland)
  BUT (98%, France)
  Comet (UK)
  Darty (France)
  Electric City (Singapore)
  New Vanden Borre (Belgium)
  Promarkt (Austria, Germany, and Luxembourg)
General Merchandise
  MVC (UK, music and video)
  Superdrug (UK, drugstores)
  Woolworths (UK, general merchandise)

Other Operations
Chartwell Land (UK, retail property developers)
Entertainment UK (music and video wholesaler)
Libertysurf (45%, France, Internet access provider)

COMPETITORS

Alliance UniChem	InterTAN
ASDA Group	J Sainsbury
Auchan	Marks & Spencer
Body Shop	METRO AG
Boots Company	Pinault-Printemps-
Carréfour	Redoute
Casino Guichard	Tengelmann Group
Dixons Group	Tesco
Great Universal Stores	Thorn
House of Fraser	Virgin Group

HISTORICAL FINANCIALS & EMPLOYEES

OTC: KNGFY FYE: January 31	Annual Growth	1/91	1/92	1/93	1/94	1/95	1/96	1/97	1/98	1/99	1/00
Sales ($ mil.)	22.0%	—	—	—	—	—	7,958	9,310	10,458	12,282	17,629
Net income ($ mil.)	18.2%	—	—	—	—	—	347	445	631	720	677
Income as % of sales	—	—	—	—	—	—	4.4%	4.8%	6.0%	5.9%	3.8%
Earnings per share ($)	16.9%	—	—	—	—	—	0.52	0.66	0.93	1.04	0.97
Stock price - FY high ($)	—	—	—	—	—	—	8.75	11.19	15.59	23.00	36.75
Stock price - FY low ($)	—	—	—	—	—	—	6.38	7.75	10.50	14.00	15.25
Stock price - FY close ($)	17.4%	—	—	—	—	—	8.08	10.75	15.50	20.75	15.34
P/E - high	—	—	—	—	—	—	17	17	17	22	38
P/E - low	—	—	—	—	—	—	12	12	11	13	16
Dividends per share ($)	18.3%	—	—	—	—	—	0.24	0.30	0.38	0.43	0.47
Book value per share ($)	25.9%	—	—	—	—	—	2.90	3.41	4.27	6.34	7.28
Employees	11.9%	—	—	—	—	—	75,501	77,254	83,364	78,133	118,416

STOCK PRICE HISTORY

HIGH/LOW/CLOSE

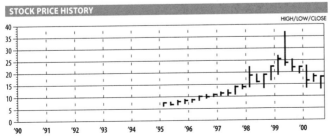

2000 FISCAL YEAR-END

Debt ratio: 14.0%
Return on equity: 14.6%
Cash ($ mil.): 253
Current ratio: 0.94
Long-term debt ($ mil.): 809
No. of shares (mil.): 684
Dividends
  Yield: 0.0%
  Payout: 0.5%
Market value ($ mil.): 10,495

KIRIN BREWERY COMPANY, LIMITED

OVERVIEW

A mythical eastern unicorn called a *kirin* — a symbol of good fortune — brands the Kirin beer bottle. But Tokyo-based Kirin Brewery Company, one of Japan's — and the world's — largest brewers, may need more than luck in its battle with archrival Asahi Breweries. Kirin (part of the Mitsubishi *keiretsu,* or association of companies) makes three of Japan's most popular beers: Kirin Lager (trailing Asahi's Super Dry, Japan's #1 beer), Ichiban Shibori (Kirin Ichiban in North America), and Kirin Tanrei, the happo-shu (low malt) market leader. It also sells beer in Europe.

Kirin owns 45% of Lion Nathan, through whom it is expanding beer operations in China. In reciprocal deals with Anheuser-Busch,

Kirin brews Budweiser beer in Japan while Anheuser-Busch makes Kirin in the US.

Beer is what keeps it buzzing, but Kirin has a variety of other operations. Kirin Beverage offers canned teas and coffees, soft drinks, and Tropicana fruit juices. Through a venture with beverage giant Seagram, it sells Chivas Regal whiskey, Martell cognac, and other wines and liquors.

To lessen its reliance on beer, Kirin has a number of other businesses, including flower growing and food processing. Its pharmaceuticals unit has developed two popular blood treatments. Other businesses include several restaurant chains around the world, including Shakey's Pizza Parlor (Japan).

HISTORY

American William Copeland went to Yokohama, Japan, in 1864 and five years later established the Spring Valley Brewery, the first in Japan, to provide beer for foreign nationals. Lacking funds to continue the brewery, Copeland closed it in 1884. The next year a group of foreign and Japanese businessmen reopened it as Japan Brewery. The business created the Kirin label in 1888 and was soon profitable.

The operation was run primarily by Americans and Europeans at first, but by 1907 Japanese workers had filled the ranks and adopted the Kirin Brewery Company name. Sales plummeted during WWII when the government limited brewing output. After the war, the US occupation forces inadvertently assisted Kirin when they split Dai Nippon Brewery (Kirin's main competitor) into two companies (Asahi and Sapporo Breweries) while leaving Kirin intact. The company pressed its advantage and became Japan's leading brewer during the 1950s.

Kirin made rapid technological advances in the 1960s (the decade when beer passed sake as Japan's favorite drink), developing superior strains of malting barley and finding new ways to control fermentation. During the 1970s it introduced several soft drinks, and it branched into hard liquor in 1972 through a joint venture with Seagram (Kirin-Seagram).

The firm bought several Coca-Cola bottling operations in New England and Japan in the 1980s. Kirin also entered the pharmaceuticals business, in part through a joint venture with US-based Amgen. In 1988 the brewer launched its Kirin Wine Club line and signed an agreement with Molson Companies to produce Kirin

beer for the North American market. In 1989 Kirin bought Napa Valley's Raymond Vineyards.

In 1991 Kirin formed a partnership to market Tropicana drinks in Japan. It also entered an alliance with Sankyo (Japan's #2 drug company) in 1991 to market Kirin's medication for anemia, which it had developed with Amgen. Chairman Hideyo Motoyama resigned in 1993 after four company executives were arrested for allegedly paying about $300,000 to a group of racketeers who had threatened to disrupt Kirin's annual meeting. Also in 1993 it agreed with Anheuser-Busch to distribute Budweiser in Japan. (It became a licensed brewer of Anheuser-Busch in 1999.) Joint venture Kirin-Amgen won the rights to make thrombopoietin (TPO), a blood platelet growth stimulator developed by Danish drug company Novo Nordisk, in 1995.

Yasuhiro Satoh became president of Kirin in 1996. The brewer moved into China that year through an agreement with China Resources (Shenyang) Snowflake Brewery (China's second-largest brewer). To brew its beers in the US, the company formed Kirin Brewery of America, also in 1996.

In response to losing market share to Asahi, Kirin closed two plants and cut its workforce in 1998 and introduced Tanrei, a cheaper, low-malt beer that quickly captured half its market. Building on its presence in China, Kirin bought 45% of brewer Lion Nathan (based in Australia and New Zealand) for $742.5 million that year. Kirin added a new beer to its shelves in 1999 with Lager Special Light.

President: Yasuhiro Satoh
EVP: Kanoh Nakamura
Senior Managing Director: Yoshio Enomoto
Senior Managing Director: Koichiro Aramaki
Senior Managing Director: Yoshiyuki Morioka
Managing Director: Masao Mawatari
Managing Director: Kunpei Kitamura
Managing Director: Naomichi Asano
Managing Director: Hideo Chida
Managing Director: Takeshi Ichimasa
Managing Director: Kouhei Fukami
Managing Director: Yoshikazu Arai
President, Kirin Brewery of America: Satoru Shimura
VP Administration and Management, Kirin Brewery of America: Junpei Watanabe
Head Accountant (CFO) Kirin Brewery of America: Keiji Iijima
Assistant Accountant Kirin Brewery of America: Kay Yoshida
Auditors: Asahi & Co.

HQ: 10-1 Shinkawa 2-chome, Chuo-ku,
Tokyo 104-8288, Japan
Phone: +81-3-5540-3411   **Fax:** +81-3-5540-3547
US HQ: 2400 Broadway, Ste. 240,
Santa Monica, CA 90404
US Phone: 310-829-2400   **US Fax:** 310-829-0424
Web site: http://www.kirin.co.jp

Kirin Brewery Company operates 12 breweries in Japan.
The company has subsidiaries and affiliates in Asia,
Australia, Europe, and the US.

1999 Sales

	$ mil.	% of total
Beer	8,488	95
Pharmaceutical products	327	4
Other	45	1
Total	**8,860**	**100**

Selected Products and Brands
Agribio (Kirin carnation, mum, and petunia; kalanchoe)
Beer (Ichiban Shibori, Kirin Lager, Lager Special Light)
Liquors and wines (Absolut, Boston Club, Chivas Regal,
  Martell, Myers', Perrier-Jouet, Robert Brown)
Pharmaceuticals (ESPO glycoprotein, GRAN white-blood
  cell stimulant)
Restaurants and food (Giraffe, Kirin City, Koiwai Pure
  Butter, Makiba Milk, Shakey's Pizza Parlor)
Soft drinks (Cadi, Fire, Issen, Jive Coffee, Kirin Lemon,
  Kiriri, Naturals, Supli, Tropicana 100% Juice)
Yeast-related (Brewer's yeast, GBF, Kirin Chloerlla 5.5,
  mushroom-growing medium, RNA, yeast extract)

Adolph Coors	Gallo	Sapporo
Allied Domecq	Heineken	Breweries
Anheuser-Busch	Interbrew	Snow Brand Milk
Asahi Breweries	ITOCHU	Products
Asia Pacific	LVMH	South African
Breweries	Mercian	Breweries
Bass Brewers	Miller Brewing	Suntory
Carlsberg	Nippon Beet	Swire Pacific
Chugai	Sugar	Taiwan Tobacco
Danone	Novartis	& Wine
Diageo	Pepsi Bottling	Takara Shuzo
Dole	Red Bull	TRICON
FEMSA	S&P	Tsingtao
Foster's Brewing	San Miguel	Yanjing

Nasdaq: KNBWY FYE: December 31	Annual Growth	12/90	12/91	12/92	12/93	12/94	12/95	12/96	12/97	12/98	12/99
Sales ($ mil.)	5.3%	5,557	12,260	12,846	14,111	17,054	15,865	13,750	6,649	7,735	8,860
Net income ($ mil.)	0.5%	311	345	383	385	524	389	296	195	234	325
Income as % of sales	—	5.6%	2.8%	3.0%	2.7%	3.1%	2.5%	2.2%	2.9%	3.0%	3.7%
Earnings per share ($)	26.3%	0.39	3.07	3.61	3.60	4.98	3.70	2.80	1.90	2.20	3.20
Stock price - FY high ($)	—	133.28	121.25	111.00	134.50	127.75	123.50	134.25	108.25	126.88	136.50
Stock price - FY low ($)	—	83.30	90.63	0.00	91.75	100.00	97.50	97.00	69.00	68.00	95.19
Stock price - FY close ($)	0.4%	104.25	105.00	91.25	103.00	112.25	119.50	98.50	73.38	123.75	107.75
P/E - high	—	56	39	31	37	26	33	48	57	58	43
P/E - low	—	35	30	0	25	20	26	35	36	31	30
Dividends per share ($)	10.7%	0.39	0.54	0.61	0.72	0.80	1.29	0.90	0.49	0.46	0.97
Book value per share ($)	6.6%	38.88	43.05	47.31	55.54	66.10	66.59	60.90	55.13	61.84	69.00
Employees	(1.0%)	7,686	7,856	8,086	8,242	8,242	8,391	8,380	8,128	8,400	7,030

HIGH/LOW/CLOSE

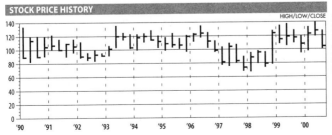

Debt ratio: 3.6%
Return on equity: —
Cash ($ mil.): 597
Current ratio: 1.26
Long-term debt ($ mil.): 263
No. of shares (mil.): 103
Dividends
  Yield: 0.9%
  Payout: 30.3%
Market value ($ mil.): 11,071

KLM ROYAL DUTCH AIRLINES

OVERVIEW

KLM Royal Dutch Airlines is learning about divorce, Italian style. The Amstelveen, Netherlands-based airline flies to some 300 destinations in nearly 90 countries with its fleet of 120 aircraft and its regional subsidiary, cityhopper. KLM had married its passenger and cargo operations with those of Italian carrier Alitalia to form a new European giant. But KLM has pulled out of the arrangement, citing uncertainty over Alitalia's ability to use an uncrowded Milan-area airport for a hub and the Italian government's slowness is selling off its 53% stake in the airline.

The breakup doesn't leave the Dutch airline flying solo, however. KLM and its code-sharing partner Northwest are forming the Wings global marketing alliance. KLM has also signed a marketing agreement with Continental and hopes to sweet-talk the US airline into joining Wings.

The world's oldest international airline has launched a low-fare European carrier called buzz, and it has stakes in smaller airlines, including Martinair and Kenya Airways. KLM also has interests in computer reservation systems and catering operations. The Dutch government owns 14% of KLM.

HISTORY

Flight lieutenant Albert Plesman founded Koninklijke Luchtvaart Maatschappij voor Nederland en Kolonien (Royal Airline Company for the Netherlands and Colonies) in The Hague in 1919. Queen Wilhelmina granted the honorary title of *koninklijke* (or royal), and Dutch businessmen financed the venture. Early passengers — who flew in an open cockpit with the pilot — were issued leather jackets, goggles, gloves, and parachutes.

Under Plesman's leadership KLM established service between Amsterdam and London, Copenhagen, Brussels, and Paris in the early 1920s. The airline initiated the longest air route in the world, from Amsterdam to Indonesia, in 1928 and extended its European network in the years before WWII. Hitler's occupation of Holland shut down KLM's European operations in 1940; the Germans imprisoned Plesman from 1940 to 1942, bombing or confiscating two-thirds of KLM's planes.

After the war Plesman quickly re-established commercial service, using 47 US military surplus airplanes, and in 1946 KLM became the first continental European airline to offer scheduled service from Europe to the US. Plesman died in 1953, and KLM began trading on the NYSE in 1957.

KLM formed KLM Helikopters to serve offshore drilling platforms in the North Sea in 1965 (49% of the unit, renamed KLM ERA Helicopters, was sold in 1991). In 1966, to provide commuter flights within the Netherlands, the airline established NLM Dutch Airlines, renaming it cityhopper in 1976. It addressed overcapacity problems in the 1970s by converting the rear portions of its 747s to cargo space.

In 1988 KLM bought 40% of Dutch charter airline Transavia (increased to 80% in 1991) and began looking for partners to help it compete in key markets. It bought 10% of Covia Partnership, owner and operator of United Airlines' Apollo computer reservation system (1988), and invested in Wings Holdings, a company formed to buy Northwest Airlines (1989). In 1991 KLM bought 35% of Air Littoral, a French regional airline, and 40% of ALM Antillean Airlines.

Airline deregulation in Europe spawned numerous efforts to develop strategic relationships. A deal giving KLM and British Airways 20% each of Belgium's national airline, Sabena, fell apart in 1990, and KLM-British Airways merger talks collapsed in early 1992.

American Airlines and British Airways invited KLM in 1996 to join a proposed alliance, which would combine transatlantic flights and marketing. However, the plan would have required KLM to sell its Northwest stake. That year KLM executed a buyback of about 13% of KLM stock from the Dutch government; it also took a 25% stake in Kenya Airways.

In 1998 KLM sold back its 19% stake in Northwest Airlines for about $1.1 billion, while forming a strategic partnership with the carrier. The deal resolved a feud stemming from KLM's attempt to increase its Northwest stake to 25%.

Meanwhile, in 1997 KLM and Italian carrier Alitalia announced a partnership that would later evolve into the integration of their fleets. Two years later the two airlines launched the KLM-Alitalia Passenger Venture. Although remaining an independent company, KLM contributed its fleet and personnel to the operation, as did Alitalia.

In 2000 KLM's low-fare European service, buzz, began service from its hub at London's Stansted airport. Also that year KLM terminated its passenger and cargo joint operations with Alitalia. The company discussed a potential merger with British Airways, but negotiations were called off in 2000.

Chairman: Conrad J. Oort
VC: Floris A. Maljers
President and CEO: Leo M. van Wijk
Managing Director and CFO: Rob J. N. Abrahamsen
Managing Director and COO: Peter F. Hartman
Managing Director and Chief Human Resources Officer: Cees van Woudenberg
General Secretary: Hans E. Kuiperi
Auditors: KPMG Accountants N.V.

LOCATIONS

HQ: Koninklijke Luchtvaart Maatschappij N.V.
Amsterdamseweg 55,
1182GP Amstelveen, The Netherlands
Phone: +31-20-649-9123   **Fax:** +31-20-648-8069
Web site: http://www.klm.nl

2000 Sales

	$ mil.	% of total
Europe	2,436	40
North America	1,157	19
Asia/Pacific	1,045	17
Central & South America	438	7
Middle East/South Asia	373	6
Africa	349	6
Charters	220	5
Total	**6,018**	**100**

PRODUCTS/OPERATIONS

2000 Sales

	$ mil.	% of total
Passengers	4,362	72
Cargo	903	15
Other	753	13
Total	**6,018**	**100**

Selected Subsidiaries and Affiliates
Braathens ASA (30%, regional airline, Norway)
buzz (European low-fare airline, UK)
Galileo International Inc. (10%, computerized reservation system)
Kenya Airways Ltd. (26%)
KLM Catering Services Schiphol bv
KLM cityhopper bv (European regional airline)
KLM uk Holdings Ltd.
Martinair Holland nv (50%, International cargo and passenger carrier)
Polygon Insurance Company Ltd. (31%)
Transavia Airlines bv (80%, charters and scheduled holiday service)

COMPETITORS

Air Canada	Iberia
Air France	Lufthansa
Airborne Freight	SAirGroup
All Nippon Airways	SAS
AMR	Singapore Airlines
Austrian Airlines	Tower Air
BAX Global	TWA
British Airways	UAL
CNF	UPS
Delta	US Airways
DHL	Virgin Atlantic Airways
FedEx	Virgin Group
Finnair	

HISTORICAL FINANCIALS & EMPLOYEES

NYSE: KLM FYE: March 31	Annual Growth	3/91	3/92	3/93	3/94	3/95	3/96	3/97	3/98	3/99	3/00
Sales ($ mil.)	6.5%	3,426	4,290	4,549	4,619	5,969	5,769	5,516	5,666	5,718	6,018
Net income ($ mil.)	—	(330)	68	(311)	55	305	330	126	1,059	223	322
Income as % of sales	—	—	1.6%	—	1.2%	5.1%	5.7%	2.3%	18.7%	3.9%	5.4%
Earnings per share ($)	—	(8.32)	1.57	(7.85)	0.72	4.40	4.72	2.13	5.19	4.79	6.85
Stock price - FY high ($)	—	25.99	32.66	30.16	36.32	43.32	52.32	49.65	58.49	66.23	45.49
Stock price - FY low ($)	—	14.66	17.50	16.66	18.00	31.33	39.32	31.33	37.66	30.66	17.06
Stock price - FY close ($)	1.3%	18.66	25.66	20.66	32.99	39.82	46.32	38.16	54.15	36.99	21.00
P/E - high	—	—	21	—	50	10	11	23	11	14	7
P/E - low	—	—	11	—	25	7	8	15	7	6	7
Dividends per share ($)	(2.1%)	1.15	0.00	0.69	0.00	0.00	1.27	1.32	0.07	0.00	0.95
Book value per share ($)	1.4%	36.24	37.57	30.32	29.78	38.27	39.35	33.01	46.47	50.45	41.23
Employees	1.5%	26,385	25,977	26,650	24,610	29,047	25,003	26,385	26,811	28,374	30,159

STOCK PRICE HISTORY

HIGH/LOW/CLOSE

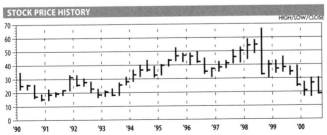

2000 FISCAL YEAR-END

Debt ratio: 64.8%
Return on equity: 0.1%
Cash ($ mil.): 638
Current ratio: 1.10
Long-term debt ($ mil.): 3,548
No. of shares (mil.): 47
Dividends
  Yield: 4.5%
  Payout: 13.9%
Market value ($ mil.): 983

KOMATSU LTD.

OVERVIEW

Like a sumo wrestler, Komatsu can throw a lot of weight around. The diversified Tokyo-based company is the world's #2 construction equipment maker, behind Caterpillar. For building or mining, Komatsu makes everything from bulldozers and wheel loaders to dump trucks and debris crushers.

Komatsu ("little pine tree" in Japanese) also makes industrial machinery such as laser cutting machines and sheet-metal presses. The electronics division produces liquid crystal display manufacturing equipment, and silicon wafers. The civil engineering and construction

unit makes prefabricated structures and offers contracting, real estate sales, and leasing services. Other products include generators, diesel engines, and computer software.

In response to weak demand for construction equipment in Japan, Komatsu is consolidating, reducing inventory, and closing three plants to cut costs. The company recorded its first loss in fiscal 1999, although sales were buoyed by strong demand for construction equipment in the US and Europe. With Asia slowly recovering, Komatsu has struck deals to make heavy equipment in India and Russia.

HISTORY

Komatsu's roots are in the Takeuchi Mining Company, founded in Japan in 1894. The company grew during WWI, and in 1917 it created an in-house ironworks, to make machine tools and mining equipment, which was separated in 1921 to create Komatsu Manufacturing. The firm grew into one of Japan's major makers of machine tools and pumps by consistently adding new products to its line. Komatsu introduced its first metal press in 1924 and in 1931 made Japan's first crawler-type farm tractor. Four years later Komatsu began making high-grade casting and specialty steel materials.

During WWII Komatsu made munitions and bulldozers for the Japanese Navy; in 1947 it offered a bulldozer based on the model it had built for the navy. It began making construction machinery and industrial vehicles as Japan rebuilt its infrastructure. In 1948 the company began building diesel engines.

Komatsu continued to expand during the 1950s. It produced motor graders in 1952, which became its first construction equipment export (to Argentina) in 1955. The next year the company made snow vehicles for the Japanese Antarctic Expedition Team.

During the 1960s the firm entered joint ventures with US manufacturers, including Cummins Engine (1961), Bucyrus Erie (1963), and International Harvester (1965). Komatsu established its first overseas subsidiary, Komatsu Europe in 1967 and introduced the world's first radio-controlled bulldozer.

The company changed its name to Komatsu Limited in 1970. It continued to expand internationally establishing subsidiaries in the US, Brazil, and Germany (1970), Singapore (1971), and Panama (1972). Komatsu began making bulldozers in Mexico in 1976 and opened an Australian subsidiary two years later.

During the early 1980s the firm pushed further into the US market, going head-to-head with Caterpillar and adopting the slogan *Maru C,* meaning "encircle the cat." A strong dollar helped Komatsu undercut Caterpillar's prices by as much as 30%. In 1986 the company opened its first US factory in Chattanooga, Tennessee. In 1988 it merged American construction equipment manufacturing operations with those of Dresser Industries, creating Komatsu Dresser.

Komatsu partnered with semiconductor giant Applied Materials in 1993 and entered the LAN market the next year with a print server and two types of hubs.

Dresser pulled out of money-losing Komatsu Dresser in 1994. Komatsu expanded its construction equipment operations outside Japan in the mid-1990s, when it formed a joint venture in Vietnam and opened plants in China. Komatsu joined with German conglomerate Mannesmann in 1996 to make giant hydraulic excavators for the mining industry.

In 1997 Komatsu set up a joint venture with India's Larsen & Toubro to make hydraulic excavators. A semiconductor industry downturn prompted Komatsu to close some of its American silicon wafer operations in 1998. However, international expansion continued with mass-production of cast parts in China and the reopening of its heavy machinery plant in Thailand. Hammered by low demand for construction equipment in Japan (down nearly 80% over three years) Komatsu recorded its first loss in fiscal 1999 and closed plants. The company sold to Applied Materials its 50% stake in their joint venture for $87 million in cash. In 2000 company president Satoru Anzaki hired former GM manager Keith Sheldon to overhaul the company's ailing global finances. The move is considered a bold one as the hiring of foreign managers is rare in Japanese business culture.

Chairman: Tetsuya Katada
President: Satoru Anzaki
EVP, Corporate Administration, External Corporate Affairs, and Industrial Machinery: Toshitaka Hagiwara
EVP, Corporate Planning, Corporate Communications, and Electronics: Masahiro Sakane
Executive Managing Director, IT and Development: Norimichi Kitagawa
Executive Managing Director, Research, Environment, and Safety Management: Koji Ogaki
Global Financial Officer: Keith Sheldon, age 53
Senior Executive Officer; President, Engines and Hydraulics Business Division: Kunihiko Komiyama
Senior Executive Officer; President, Japanese Marketing Division: Hisashi Wada
Senior Executive Officer, Accounting, Finance, and Internal Audit: Masaru Fukase
Auditors: Arthur Andersen

LOCATIONS

HQ: 2-3-6 Akasaka, Minato-ku, Tokyo 107-8414, Japan
Phone: +81-3-5561-2687   **Fax:** +81-3-3582-8332
US HQ: 440 N. Fairway Dr., Vernon Hills, IL 60061
US Phone: 847-970-4100   **US Fax:** 847-970-4187
Web site: http://www.komatsu.com

2000 Sales

	$ mil.	% of total
Asia/Pacific		
Japan	5,377	53
Other countries	967	9
The Americas	2,355	23
Europe	1,200	12
Middle East & Africa	350	3
Total	**10,249**	**100**

PRODUCTS/OPERATIONS

2000 Sales

	$ mil.	% of total
Construction & mining equipment	6,927	68
Electronics	877	9
Civil engineering & construction services	764	7
Industrial machinery	300	3
Other	1,381	13
Total	**10,249**	**100**

Selected Products and Services

Ammunition	Industrial gases
Armored vehicles	LCD manufacturing
Bulldozers	equipment
Civil engineering	Logistics
contracting	Machine tools
Construction robots	Real estate sales and
Diesel engines	leasing
Excimer lasers	Silicon wafers
Finance	Steel processing
Forklift trucks	machinery
Hydraulic equipment	Tunnel-boring machines

COMPETITORS

Bechtel	Hitachi	Mitsubishi
Caterpillar	Honeywell	Mitsui
CNH Global	International	Navistar
Cymer	Hyundai	Peter Kiewit
Daewoo	Ingersoll-Rand	Sons'
Deere	Isuzu	Shimizu
Ford	Kubota	Sumitomo
Harnischfeger	McDermott	Volvo

HISTORICAL FINANCIALS & EMPLOYEES

OTC: KMTUY FYE: March 31	Annual Growth	3/91	3/92	3/93	3/94	3/95	3/96	3/97	3/98	3/99	3/00
Sales ($ mil.)	4.3%	7,033	6,920	7,572	8,232	10,617	9,317	8,877	8,297	8,913	10,249
Net income ($ mil.)	(5.8%)	222	82	26	13	118	133	147	145	(104)	130
Income as % of sales	—	3.2%	1.2%	0.3%	0.2%	1.1%	1.4%	1.7%	1.7%	—	1.3%
Earnings per share ($)	(5.5%)	0.89	0.33	0.11	0.05	0.47	0.53	0.59	0.59	(0.43)	0.54
Stock price - FY high ($)	—	36.78	28.39	25.26	36.68	39.12	35.92	40.00	33.00	23.25	27.50
Stock price - FY low ($)	—	25.81	16.72	16.64	25.58	25.83	26.96	26.20	15.50	16.25	17.00
Stock price - FY close ($)	(3.3%)	25.81	19.85	25.26	35.03	28.93	35.69	27.50	19.00	20.50	19.00
P/E - high	—	41	86	230	734	83	68	68	56	—	51
P/E - low	—	29	51	151	512	55	51	44	26	—	32
Dividends per share ($)	1.7%	0.20	0.20	0.30	0.31	0.37	0.37	0.30	0.26	0.24	0.23
Book value per share ($)	3.1%	14.90	15.71	18.07	20.02	26.85	22.83	18.15	17.03	18.34	19.66
Employees	1.9%	24,000	26,300	26,313	28,446	28,040	27,917	27,007	26,871	31,785	28,522

STOCK PRICE HISTORY

HIGH/LOW/CLOSE

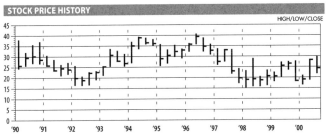

2000 FISCAL YEAR-END

Debt ratio: 33.3%
Return on equity: 2.8%
Cash ($ mil.): 781
Current ratio: 1.49
Long-term debt ($ mil.): 2,381
No. of shares (mil.): 242
Dividends
  Yield: 0.0%
  Payout: 0.4%
Market value ($ mil.): 4,602

KOOR INDUSTRIES LTD.

OVERVIEW

Koor Industries hopes to grow in its core industries. Based in Tel Aviv, Koor is Israel's largest holding company, with operating subsidiaries in agrochemicals, defense electronics, telecommunications, tourism, and real estate.

A new era for the company began in 1998 when Jonathan Kolber, then CEO of Claridge Israel, succeeded legendary Israeli industrialist Benjamin Gaon as Koor's CEO. Claridge Israel, a unit of Canadian billionaire Charles Bronfman's investment firm, owns 35% of Koor.

Kolber wants Koor to concentrate on its holdings in export-based telecom companies (ECI Telecom, Telrad Networks, Nortel Networks Israel) and defense electronics businesses (Elisra-Tadiran Group). Following its acquisition of Tadiran Telecom, Koor's ECI Telecom unit is looking for opportunities in the North American telecom equipment market. Koor has disposed of some 30 noncore assets, including its 50% stake in Mashav, Israel's cement monopoly. The group plans to divest its 60% stake in agrochemicals group Makhteshim-Agan Industries.

HISTORY

Koor Industries is an offshoot of Solel Boneh, a construction company formed in 1924 in British Palestine by the Histadrut Labour Federation. Solel Boneh founded Koor in 1944 to build factories to provide employment for Jewish refugees arriving during WWII.

An Arab attack quickly followed Israel's creation in 1948. Israel prevailed, but the threat of future conflicts spurred development of its defense industry. In 1952 Koor teamed with a Finnish firm to create Soltam, an Israeli artillery manufacturer. The previous year, it had diversified into telecommunications equipment with Telrad.

Koor continued to expand and diversify through joint ventures, creating a steel company in 1954 and Alliance Tire & Rubber in 1955 (it bought full control of Alliance in 1983). Koor and the Israeli government founded Tadiran (defense electronics, 1962), and Koor acquired chemical maker Makhteshim (1963) and food processor Hamashbir Lata (1970). The Sinai campaign (1956), Six-Day War (1967), and Yom Kippur War (1973) continued to spur Israeli defense spending. However, with Histadrut's emphasis on socialist aims, Koor never became very profitable. Successful subsidiaries were offset by money-losers.

The company was hurt in the 1980s by a government program that cut subsidies and lowered trade barriers. Inflation damaged Koor's global competitiveness. With the help of junk bond guru Michael Milken, Koor raised $105 million in a 1986 debt issue. That year, however, Koor posted its first loss in 20 years, and losses widened in 1987. Benjamin Gaon became CEO in 1988 and began restructuring the heavily indebted company, which by then had about 130 units. He kept closing plants, but the company incurred a loss in 1988 and a record $369 million deficit in 1989. Gaon negotiated a new arrangement with creditors in 1991.

By 1992 Gaon's cost cutting had begun to pay off, and the company returned to profitability. Histadrut sold out in 1995, severing a link to Koor's socialist past. That year the company raised nearly $120 million in an international IPO, and Northern Telecom (now Nortel Networks) acquired 20% of Telrad (sold back to Koor in 2000).

Koor continued divesting assets to focus on its core businesses. ITT Sheraton International took a 50% stake in Koor Tourism in a 1996 alliance to manage hotels in Israel, and Henkel bought 50% of Koor's detergent operations. Discontinued operations included Beep-A-Call (wireless paging, 1995), Gamda Trade (food retail, 1996), and TAMI (food industry, 1997).

In 1995 Gaon sowed the seeds for his departure by selling a controlling stake in Koor to the Shamrock Group, a Disney family investment firm. Disagreements with Gaon over Koor's strategy led Shamrock to sell its stake in 1997 to Claridge Israel, an investment fund controlled by Canadian billionaire Charles Bronfman. Jonathan Kolber, then CEO of Claridge Israel, replaced Gaon in 1998.

Kolber made plans to increase exports and focus on Koor's telecom equipment, defense electronics, and agrochemicals segments, while scaling back in construction materials. In 1998 Koor bought a stake in Israel's ECI Telecom, which merged with Tadiran Telecom in 1999. Koor also dumped several noncore assets (including cable TV, energy, and software services units), raising more than $360 million. It then sold its 50% stake in cement group Mashav.

In 2000 Koor and Nortel Networks launched Nortel Networks Israel to deliver high-performance Internet products to carrier and enterprise customers.

OFFICERS

Chairman: Charles Bronfman, age 69
VC and CEO; Chairman, ECI Telecom: Jonathan Kolber, age 38
President; Chairman, Makhteshim-Aqan, Tadiran, Elisra, Koor Properties and Koor Trade: Danny Biran, age 57
EVP and CFO: Yuval Yanai
SVP and Manager, Koor's Venture Capital: Yiftach Atir
VP Mergers and Acquisitions: Gil B. Leidner, age 49
VP (HR): Aron Zuker, age 54
Senior Analyst and Director Investor Relations: Einat Wilf
General Counsel and Corporate Secretary: Shlomo Heller, age 56
Auditors: Somekh Chaikin

LOCATIONS

HQ: Platinum House, 21 Ha'arba'ah St., Tel Aviv 64739, Israel
Phone: +972-3-623-8333 **Fax:** +972-3-623-8334
Web site: http://www.koor.co.il

PRODUCTS/OPERATIONS

1999 Sales

	$ mil.	% of total
Telecommunications equipment		
ECI Telecom	1,115	42
Telrad	466	17
Agrochemicals		
Makhteshim-Agan Industries	853	32
Defense electronics	229	9
Adjustments	(92)	—
Total	**2,571**	**100**

Selected Subsidiaries and Affiliates

Telecommunications Equipment
ECI Telecom Ltd. (33%)
Nortel Networks Israel (28%)
Telrad Networks

Agrochemicals
Makhteshim-Agan Industries Ltd. (60%)

Defense Electronics
BVR Systems (28%)
The Elisra Tadiran Group

Other
Knafaim-Arkia Holdings (28%, flight and tourism operator)
Koor Properties
Koor Trade
Sheraton-Moriah Israel (55%, hotels)

COMPETITORS

Alcatel	NEC
Ampal-American Israel	Oryx Technology
Andrew Corporation	Pharmacia
Clal Industries	Philips Electronics
DuPont	QUALCOMM
Elron	Raytheon
Ericsson	Rockwell International
GE	Siemens
Harris Corporation	The Israel Corporation
Hughes Electronics	Toshiba
Lucent	

HISTORICAL FINANCIALS & EMPLOYEES

NYSE: KOR FYE: December 31	Annual Growth	12/90	12/91	12/92	12/93	12/94	12/95	12/96	12/97	12/98	12/99
Sales ($ mil.)	0.4%	2,485	2,354	2,218	2,360	2,804	3,256	3,525	3,565	3,034	2,571
Net income ($ mil.)	—	(48)	89	136	126	129	156	181	138	11	132
Income as % of sales	—	—	3.8%	6.1%	5.4%	4.6%	4.8%	5.1%	3.9%	0.4%	5.1%
Earnings per share ($)	(5.6%)	—	—	—	—	—	2.09	2.27	1.74	0.15	1.66
Stock price - FY high ($)	—	—	—	—	—	—	20.88	21.50	23.75	26.56	25.38
Stock price - FY low ($)	—	—	—	—	—	—	16.63	15.00	16.88	12.50	16.00
Stock price - FY close ($)	(0.3%)	—	—	—	—	—	20.25	17.13	21.94	17.44	20.00
P/E - high	—	—	—	—	—	—	9	9	13	177	15
P/E - low	—	—	—	—	—	—	7	6	9	83	10
Dividends per share ($)	—	—	—	—	—	—	0.00	0.24	0.00	0.62	0.42
Book value per share ($)	4.2%	—	—	—	—	—	11.40	13.96	14.65	12.30	13.42
Employees	(2.5%)	18,450	16,000	16,337	17,184	20,700	20,600	21,000	21,500	15,035	—

STOCK PRICE HISTORY

HIGH/LOW/CLOSE

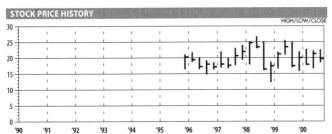

1999 FISCAL YEAR-END

Debt ratio: 48.1%
Return on equity: 13.1%
Cash ($ mil.): 349
Current ratio: 1.13
Long-term debt ($ mil.): 980
No. of shares (mil.): 79
Dividends
  Yield: 2.1%
  Payout: 25.3%
Market value ($ mil.): 1,573

KPMG INTERNATIONAL

OVERVIEW

KPMG is fighting for dominance in the field of accounting and is willing, not only to tie one hand behind its back, but to cut one of them off entirely. The Amstelveen, Netherlands-based Big Five firm (PricewaterhouseCoopers is #1) has split its consulting operations from audit offerings and is going to take them public.

Traditionally a confederation of accounting firms based in more than 150 nations, in recent years KPMG has more closely linked its more than 800 offices and organized them geographically as KPMG Americas (North and South America and Australasia), and KPMG Europe (Europe, Africa, Asia, and the Middle East). KPMG is the only one of the Big Five whose practice is larger outside the US.

KPMG's consulting operation is the most Internet savvy of the accounting/consulting firms and the plan to split the divisions arose largely to facilitate a $1 billion investment in its online-related services by Cisco Systems (worth 20% of the consulting business; an investment in an accounting firm by a nonaccounting company is taboo). There are also perceived conflicts of interest in providing both audit and consulting services, as well as issues regarding the company's newest field of endeavor, offering legal services through affiliated law firms.

HISTORY

Peat Marwick was founded in 1911, when William Peat, a London accountant, met James Marwick during an Atlantic crossing. Marwick and Roger Mitchell had formed Marwick, Mitchell & Company in New York in 1897. Peat and Marwick agreed to ally their firms temporarily, and in 1925 they merged as Peat, Marwick, Mitchell, & Copartners.

In 1947 William Black became senior partner, a position he held until 1965. He guided the firm's 1950 merger with Barrow, Wade, Guthrie, one of the US's oldest firms, and built its consulting practice. Peat Marwick restructured its international practice as PMM&Co. (International) in 1972 (in 1978 renamed Peat Marwick International).

The next year several European accounting firms led by Klynveld Kraayenhoff (the Netherlands) and Deutsche Treuhand (Germany) began forming an international accounting federation. Needing an American member, the European firms encouraged the merger of two American firms founded around the turn of the century, Main Lafrentz and Hurdman Cranstoun. Main Hurdman & Cranstoun joined the Europeans to form Klynveld Main Goerdeler (KMG), named after two of the member firms and the chairman of Deutsche Treuhand, Reinhard Goerdeler. Other members were C. Jespersen (Denmark), Thorne Riddel (Canada), Thomson McLintok (UK), and Fides Revision (Switzerland).

Peat Marwick merged with KMG in 1987 to form Klynveld Peat Marwick Goerdeler (KPMG). KPMG lost 10% of its business as competing clients departed. Professional staff departures followed in 1990 when, as part of a consolidation, the firm trimmed its partnership rolls.

In the 1990s the Big Six all faced lawsuits arising from an evolving standard holding auditors responsible for the substance, rather than merely the form of clients' accounts. KPMG was hit by suits stemming from its audits of defunct S&Ls and litigation relating to the bankruptcy of Orange County, California (settled for $75 million in 1998).

Nevertheless KPMG kept growing, expanding its consulting division with the acquisition of banking consultancy Barefoot, Marrinan & Associates in 1996.

In 1997, after Price Waterhouse and Coopers & Lybrand announced their merger, KPMG and Ernst & Young announced one of their own. But they called it quits the next year, fearing that regulatory approval of the deal would be too onerous.

The creation of PricewaterhouseCoopers (PwC) and increasing competition in the consulting sides of all of the Big Five brought a realignment of loyalties in their national practices. KPMG Consulting's Belgian group moved to PwC and its French group went to Computer Sciences Corporation. Andersen Worldwide nearly wooed away KPMG's Canadian consulting group, but the plan was foiled by the ever-sullen Andersen Consulting group and by KPMG's promises of more money. It was against this background that the deal with Cisco Systems took place. In addition to the cash infusion, Cisco agreed to let KPMG provide installation and system management (neither of which Cisco provides) to Cisco's customers.

In 2000 KPMG announced its IPO plans for the consulting group, but continued to rail against the SEC's calls for the severing of relationships between consulting and auditing organizations.

Chairman; Chairman and CEO, KPMG LLP:
Stephen G. Butler
CEO: Paul C. Reilly
CFO: Joseph E. Heintz
Regional Executive Partner Americas: Lou Miramontes
Regional Executive Partner Asia/Pacific: John Sim
Regional Executive Partner, Europe, Middle East, and Africa: Colin Holland
International Managing Partner Assurance:
Hans de Munnik
International Managing Partner Consulting:
Jim McGuire
International Managing Partner Financial Advisory Services: Gary Colter
International Managing Partner, Infrastructure and Resources: Don Christiansen
International Managing Partner Markets:
Alistair Johnston
International Managing Partner, Tax and Legal:
Hartwich Lübmann
Deputy Chairman KPMG LLP: Robert W. Alspaugh
VC, Consulting, KPMG LLP: Randolph C. Blazer
Chief Marketing Officer KPMG LLP:
Timothy R. Pearson
National Industry Director, Banking Practice, KPMG LLP: Robert F. Arning
General Counsel KPMG LLP: Claudia L. Taft
Partner, Human Resources, KPMG LLP:
Timothy P. Flynn

LOCATIONS

HQ: Burgemeester Rijnderslaan 20,
1185 MC Amstelveen, The Netherlands
Phone: +31-20-656-6700   **Fax:** +31-20-656-6777
US HQ: 345 Park Ave., New York, NY 10154
US Phone: 212-758-9700   **US Fax:** 212-758-9819
Web site: http://www.kpmg.com

KMPG has operations in over 800 cities in more than 150 countries.

PRODUCTS/OPERATIONS

Selected Areas of Industry Expertise
Banking and finance
Building and construction
Energy and natural resources
Government
Health care and life sciences
Industrial products
Information, communications, and entertainment
Insurance
Retail and consumer products
Transportation

Representative Clients
Aetna U.S. Healthcare
Apple Computer
AT&T Broadband & Internet Services
Bankers Trust
City of New York
Motorola
NBC
Oxford Health Plans
PepsiCo
Pfizer
PhyCor
Smithsonian Institution
Tenet
Wells Fargo

COMPETITORS

Andersen Worldwide	H&R Block
Aon	Hewitt Associates
Arthur D. Little	IBM
Bain & Company	Marsh & McLennan
BDO International	McKinsey & Company
Booz-Allen	Perot Systems
Boston Consulting	PricewaterhouseCoopers
Deloitte Touche Tohmatsu	Towers Perrin
EDS	Watson Wyatt
Ernst & Young	

HISTORICAL FINANCIALS & EMPLOYEES

Partnership FYE: September 30	Annual Growth	9/90	9/91	9/92	9/93	9/94	9/95	9/96	9/97	9/98	9/99
Sales ($ mil.)	9.6%	5,368	6,011	6,150	6,000	6,600	7,500	8,100	9,200	10,600	12,200
Employees	3.1%	77,300	75,000	73,488	76,200	76,200	72,000	77,000	83,500	85,300	102,000

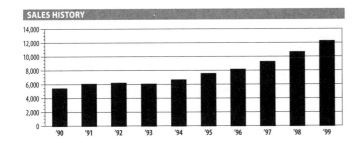

SALES HISTORY

KUBOTA CORPORATION

OVERVIEW

Kubota's an old hand when it comes to turning Japanese soil. The Osaka-based company is Japan's top maker of tractors and farm equipment, as well as iron ductile pipe used in water-supply systems. Kubota also makes industrial castings (ductile tunnel segments), PVC pipe, fire-resistant siding, cement roofing, and other building materials, waste recycling plants, and agricultural and industrial engines. It also builds water- and sewage-treatment plants.

Kubota's industrial machinery sales — primarily for vending machines — have increased sharply but not enough to overcome sluggish demand for engines and construction machinery resulting from a slow housing market in Asia.

For years Kubota has worked to meet a demand for large-scale farm equipment, although those efforts have given way to an emphasis on smaller, less-expensive rice transplanters and combine harvesters. The company is expanding operations in the US and in other parts of Asia.

HISTORY

The son of a poor farmer and coppersmith, Gonshiro Oode left home in 1885 at age 14 and moved to Osaka to find work. He began as an apprentice at the Kuro Casting Shop, where he learned about metal casting. He saved his money and in 1890 opened Oode Casting.

Oode's new shop grew rapidly, thanks to the industrialization of the Japanese economy and the expansion of the iron and steel industries. One of Oode's customers, Toshiro Kubota, took a liking to the hard-working young man, and in 1897 Kubota adopted him. Oode changed his name to Kubota and changed the name of his company to Kubota Iron Works.

Kubota made a number of technological breakthroughs in the early 1900s, including a new method of producing cast-iron pipe developed in 1900. The company became the first to make the pipe in Japan and continued to grow as the country modernized its infrastructure.

Kubota began making steam engines, machine tools, and agricultural engines in 1917 and also began exporting products to countries in Southeast Asia. In 1930 the company restructured and incorporated. It continued to add product lines, including agricultural and industrial motors.

Although WWII brought massive destruction to Japan, the peacetime that followed created plenty of work for Kubota's farm equipment and pipe operations as the country rebuilt. By 1960 the company was Japan's largest maker of farm equipment, ductile iron pipe, and cement roofing materials. That year Kubota introduced the first small agricultural tractor in Japan.

Over the next three decades, Kubota expanded its products and its geographic reach. The company grew overseas during the 1960s and 1970s by creating subsidiaries in Taiwan (1961), the US (1972), Iran (1973), France (1974), and Thailand (1977). It also made a major push into the US high-tech industry during the 1980s with the 44% purchase of supercomputer graphics company Ardent (1985). Two years later Kubota bought disk company Akashic Memories, and in 1989 it formed a joint venture with disk drive maker Maxtor to build optical storage products.

While loading up on high-tech operations, Kubota also expanded its lower-tech core businesses in the US. The company opened its first US manufacturing plant in 1989 in Gainesville, Georgia, to make front-end loader attachments, and in 1990 it bought a 5% interest in Cummins Engine.

The next year Kubota took over the operations of Stardent Computers, which had struggled since being formed in a 1989 merger of Ardent and Stellar Computer. However, the company was unable to revive its graphic workstation business and in 1994 dissolved its California-based Kubota Graphics subsidiary.

Continuing its tradition of commercializing innovative products, in 1995 Kubota introduced roofing materials with TV antennae built in. It also formed subsidiary Kubota Biotech to develop and sell biotechnological products such as biological insecticides. In 1996 Kubota launched a rice-cultivation machine for use in large fields.

The next year Kubota gave its unprofitable computer hard disk business the boot with the sale of Akashic Memories and the management buyout of subsidiary Maxoptix, a maker of computer memory storage drives. To broaden its customer base and escape expensive import customs duties, Kubota established a joint venture in 1998 to make farm equipment in China. It also refocused manufacturing efforts away from its troubled homeland and made plans to start new operations in Indonesia and the US.

Chairman and Representative Director:
Osamu Okamoto
President and Representative Director:
Yoshikuni Dobashi
**Executive Managing Director and Representative
Director:** Takeshi Oka
Executive Managing Director: Mitsuo Iwanaga
Executive Managing Director: Tomomi Soh
Executive Managing Director: Mikio Kinoshita
Auditors: Deloitte Touche Tohmatsu

LOCATIONS

HQ: 2-47 Shikitsuhigashi 1-chome, Naniwa-ku,
Osaka 556-8601, Japan
Phone: +81-6-6648-2111 **Fax:** +81-6-6648-3862
US HQ: 320 Park Ave., 23rd Fl., New York, NY 10022
US Phone: 212-355-2440 **US Fax:** 212-355-2124
Web site: http://www.kubota.co.jp

2000 Sales

	$ mil.	% of total
Japan	8,806	85
North America	1,045	10
Other regions	453	5
Adjustments	(990)	—
Total	**9,314**	**100**

PRODUCTS/OPERATIONS

2000 Sales

	$ mil.	% of total
Industrial products & engineering	4,772	51
Engines & machinery	3,528	37
Building materials & housing	1,121	12
Adjustments	(107)	—
Total	**9,314**	**100**

Selected Products

**Industrial Products
and Engineering**
Environmental
control plants
Ceramic membrane
filtration systems
Crushing machines
Landfill leachate
treatment plants
Melting furnaces
Sewage-treatment plants
Submerged-membrane
filters
Super-fire systems
Pipe and fluid
systems engineering
Cast-iron pipes
Earthquake-proof
water-storage tanks
Fountains
Perma pipe
Pumps
Steel pipe
Valves
Water-quality
monitoring systems
Water-supply
information systems

**Internal Combustion
Engines and Machinery**
Construction equipment
Excavators
Farm equipment
and engines
Air-cooled
gasoline engines
Combines
Generators
Oil and air-cooled
diesel engines
Radio-controlled
lawn mowers
Rice transplanters
Tractors
Water-cooled
diesel engines

**Building Materials
and Housing**
Bath systems
Cement siding
Household wastewater-
treatment systems
(septic tanks)
Outer wall cladding
Roofing tiles

COMPETITORS

AGCO	Fiat	Mitsubishi
Caterpillar	Hyundai	Nippon Steel
CNH Global	Isuzu	NKK
Daewoo	Kawasaki Steel	Sekisui House
Deere	Komatsu	Sumitomo
Ebara	Lafarge SA	

HISTORICAL FINANCIALS & EMPLOYEES

NYSE: KUB FYE: March 31	Annual Growth	3/91	3/92	3/93	3/94	3/95	3/96	3/97	3/98	3/99	3/00
Sales ($ mil.)	4.3%	6,350	6,849	8,468	9,510	11,393	10,110	9,206	7,799	8,072	9,314
Net income ($ mil.)	13.0%	51	32	50	80	226	243	233	165	125	155
Income as % of sales	—	0.8%	0.5%	0.6%	0.8%	2.0%	2.4%	2.5%	2.1%	1.5%	1.7%
Earnings per share ($)	12.3%	0.73	0.45	0.71	1.13	3.11	3.13	3.05	2.17	1.68	2.08
Stock price - FY high ($)	—	145.75	120.00	92.00	135.00	160.00	142.00	142.00	102.00	60.00	86.50
Stock price - FY low ($)	—	91.00	0.00	0.00	102.50	128.00	122.00	86.25	44.75	34.75	49.25
Stock price - FY close ($)	(5.4%)	114.88	86.00	90.50	125.00	128.00	129.00	91.00	55.25	51.25	69.50
P/E - high	—	200	267	131	119	49	42	43	44	34	39
P/E - low	—	125	0	0	91	39	36	26	19	20	22
Dividends per share ($)	2.7%	0.78	0.73	0.82	0.94	1.02	0.51	0.48	0.00	0.42	0.99
Book value per share ($)	7.2%	32.12	33.78	39.95	42.81	51.23	44.06	40.59	37.69	49.77	60.18
Employees	(0.7%)	15,490	15,756	15,908	16,046	16,046	21,000	18,500	15,586	15,156	14,594

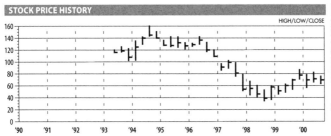

STOCK PRICE HISTORY HIGH/LOW/CLOSE

2000 FISCAL YEAR-END
Debt ratio: 34.2%
Return on equity: 4.0%
Cash ($ mil.): 742
Current ratio: 1.47
Long-term debt ($ mil.): 2,201
No. of shares (mil.): 70
Dividends
Yield: 1.4%
Payout: 47.6%
Market value ($ mil.): 4,899

KYOCERA CORPORATION

OVERVIEW

Kyocera Corporation is heeding the call — Kyocera, phone home. The Kyoto, Japan-based company, long known for its ceramic semiconductor packaging, has dialed in to the cellular phone market as well. The company is a major producer of semiconductor casing and electronic components, such as capacitors, connectors, and resistors. Its ceramic division generates almost 65% of sales and makes products that can be found in such diverse items as gas turbine engines, mechanical components, knives, and artificial hip joints.

Semiconductor manufacturers are turning to cost-effective, lightweight plastic casings, a trend that has forced Kyocera to devote more resources toward developing plastic laminate manufacturing technology. At the same time, Kyocera is finding new uses for its ceramic products and has diversified beyond its traditional package market to manufacture solar cells, cartridge-free printers, cameras, camcorders, and multimedia products such as videoconferencing systems. Japan accounts for more than 50% of Kyocera's sales.

Kyocera has made efforts to diversify further by expanding its telecommunications operations and entering the health food market. It is also acquiring failed copier maker Kyocera Mita (formerly Mita Industrial).

HISTORY

Born to a poor Japanese family in 1932, Kazuo Inamori never quite fit the mold. He went to work for Shofu Industries (ceramic insulators) in the mid-1950s, only to quit three years later after an argument with supervisors. He started Kyoto Ceramic with seven colleagues in 1959, a time when leaving an established company to start a new one was nearly unheard of in Japan; the eight men took a blood oath of loyalty to seal their commitment to the new firm. Their first product was a ceramic insulator for cathode-ray tubes. In the late 1960s the company developed the ceramic package for integrated circuits (ICs) that has made it a world-class supplier.

Kyoto Ceramic started manufacturing in the US in 1971. A few years later the company began to diversify its interests when it ventured into artificial gemstones (Crescent Vert, 1977) and dental implants (New Medical, 1978). In 1979 Inamori bought control of failing Cybernet Electronics (Japanese citizens-band radio maker), using it to move Kyoto Ceramic into the production of copiers and stereos; he also formed Kyocera Feldmuhle (industrial ceramics and cutting tools, US) with West German partner Feldmuhle.

The company merged five subsidiaries in 1982, forming Kyocera Corporation. The 1983 acquisition of Yashica moved it into the production of cameras and other optical equipment. That year Kyocera ran into trouble. At the time Nippon Telegraph and Telephone (NTT) was the only legal supplier of phones in Japan, and when Kyocera started marketing cordless phones without the required approval, the government forced it to recall the phones.

The government abolished NTT's monopoly in 1984, and Kyocera joined 24 other companies to form Daini-Denden ("second phone company") — now DDI. That year Inamori established the Inamori Foundation, which awards annual prizes for achievement in advanced technology, basic sciences, and creative arts.

In 1988 Inamori set up Kyocera regional offices in Asia, Europe, and the US. The company bought Elco (electronic connectors, US) in 1989 and AVX (now 70%, multilayer ceramic capacitors, US) in 1990.

In order to diversify further, Kyocera entered into a series of alliances in the 1990s that included partnerships with Canon to produce video and electronic optical equipment, with Carl Zeiss (Germany) to make cameras and lenses, and with Cirrus Logic to make integrated chips for a cordless phone project.

The company's Guangdong-based optical instrument joint venture began making cameras and lenses for the Chinese market in 1996. The next year Inamori went into partial retirement with plans to become a Zen Buddhist monk. In 1998 the company took over failed copier maker Mita Industrial, which had been a major buyer of Kyocera's electronic components.

In 1999 Kyocera acquired Golden Genesis (solar electric systems, US) and changed the company's name to Kyocera Solar, Inc. In the same year Kyocera's product line grew even more diverse as it entered the health food market and began selling mushroom products in Japan. Late in 1999, Kyocera agreed to purchase the wireless phone business of QUALCOMM.

Early in 2000 the company's acquisition of failed copier maker Mita Industrial (which changed its name to Kyocera Mita Corporation) was approved. The deal included the forgiveness (by Mita's creditors) of most of Mita's debt and a cash infusion in Kyocera Mita by Kyocera.

Chairman Emeritus: Kazuo Inamori
Chairman and Representative Director: Kensuke Itoh
President and Representative Director:
Yasuo Nishiguchi
EVP and Representative Director: Noboru Nakamura
EVP and Representative Director: Michihisa Yamamoto
EVP and Representative Director: Masahiro Umemura
Senior Managing Director and Representative Director:
Yasuo Akashi
Senior Managing Director and Representative Director (HR): Atsushi Mori
Senior Managing Director and Representative Director:
Benedict P. Rosen
Director and CFO: Hideki Ishida
Auditors: PricewaterhouseCoopers

LOCATIONS

HQ: 6 Takeda Tobadono-cho, Fushimi-ku,
Kyoto 612-8501, Japan
Phone: +81-75-604-3500　**Fax:** +81-75-604-3501
US HQ: 8611 Balboa Ave., San Diego, CA 92123
US Phone: 858-576-2600　**US Fax:** 858-492-1456
Web site: http://www.kyocera.co.jp

Kyocera has 50 operations in 20 countries throughout the Americas, Asia, Europe, and the Middle East.

2000 Sales

	$ mil.	% of total
Asia		
Japan	3,831	50
Other countries	1,426	18
US	1,260	16
Europe	1,037	13
Other regions	225	3
Total	**7,779**	**100**

PRODUCTS/OPERATIONS

2000 Sales

	$ mil.	% of total
Ceramic and related products	5,210	67
Electronic equipment	2,144	27
Optical instruments	374	5
Finance and other	109	1
Adjustments	(58)	—
Total	**7,779**	**100**

Selected Products and Services

Cameras and camcorders	Hotel operations
Consumer-related parts	Leasing
Credit finance	Office renting
Electronic components	Semiconductor parts
Fine ceramic parts	Telecommunications
Information equipment	equipment

COMPETITORS

Asahi Glass	Minolta	Ricoh
Canon	Mitsubishi	Saint-Gobain
Eastman Kodak	Motorola	Samsung
Ericsson	NEC	SANYO
Fuji Photo	NGK Insulators	Seiko
Graphic	Nokia	Sharp
Packaging	NTT	Showa Denko
Hitachi	Oki Electric	Sony
IBM	Philips	Sumitomo Metal
Johnson Matthey	Electronics	Industries
LG Group	Pioneer	Toshiba
Lucent	Pitney Bowes	Xerox
Matsushita	Polaroid	

HISTORICAL FINANCIALS & EMPLOYEES

NYSE: KYO FYE: March 31	Annual Growth	3/91	3/92	3/93	3/94	3/95	3/96	3/97	3/98	3/99	3/00
Sales ($ mil.)	10.1%	3,280	3,416	3,758	4,177	5,760	6,048	5,764	5,454	6,007	7,779
Net income ($ mil.)	8.8%	229	204	209	359	500	771	368	354	239	489
Income as % of sales	—	7.0%	6.0%	5.5%	8.6%	8.7%	12.8%	6.4%	6.5%	4.0%	6.3%
Earnings per share ($)	8.7%	1.22	1.09	1.12	1.92	2.66	4.10	1.96	1.86	1.26	2.58
Stock price – FY high ($)	—	63.00	50.50	42.63	67.38	77.13	92.00	77.50	85.50	59.00	280.94
Stock price – FY low ($)	—	40.63	29.75	25.50	40.50	60.50	63.25	53.50	43.31	39.81	50.75
Stock price – FY close ($)	15.2%	46.50	32.50	40.56	62.50	72.75	67.25	56.88	53.63	52.63	166.00
P/E – high	—	52	46	38	35	29	22	40	46	47	109
P/E – low	—	33	27	23	21	23	15	27	23	32	20
Dividends per share ($)	7.1%	0.27	0.32	0.39	0.39	0.43	0.24	0.27	0.45	0.22	0.50
Book value per share ($)	17.7%	9.46	10.32	11.99	14.15	17.87	16.68	15.31	15.21	34.26	41.00
Employees	(0.2%)	14,031	14,473	10,682	13,470	13,300	13,162	13,270	13,594	13,759	13,746

STOCK PRICE HISTORY

HIGH/LOW/CLOSE

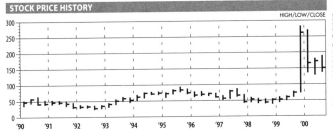

2000 FISCAL YEAR-END

Debt ratio: 2.6%
Return on equity: 6.8%
Cash ($ mil.): 1,737
Current ratio: 2.17
Long-term debt ($ mil.): 205
No. of shares (mil.): 189
Dividends
　Yield: 0.3%
　Payout: 19.4%
Market value ($ mil.): 31,386

LAGARDÈRE SCA

OVERVIEW

Lagardère combines media and aerospace into a moneymaking conglomerate. Through its Hachette Filipacchi Médias subsidiary, Paris-based Lagardère publishes more than 200 magazines in 33 countries. Titles include *Elle, Paris Match, Premiere,* and *Car & Driver*. The company also publishes French regional newspapers and books (including textbooks, travel guides, and literature). In addition, Lagardère owns one of Europe's leading print media distribution firms (Hachette Distribution Services) and is expanding its interests in digital media on the Internet, radio, and TV.

Lagardère's non-media holdings include an 11%-stake in European Aeronautic Defence and Space Company (EADS), the world's #3 aerospace and defense firm (behind Boeing and Lockheed). It also manufactures automobiles through its Matra Automobile subsidiary. Lagardère founder, general partner (the company is a publicly traded limited partnership), and CEO Jean-Luc Lagardère and his brother Arnaud control the company through ARCO and Lagardère Capital et Management.

HISTORY

Lagardère's flagship publishing business, Hachette, traces its origins back to 1826, when schoolteacher Louis Hachette bought a small bookstore and publishing business in Paris. He published his first periodical, a teacher's journal, in 1827 and began buying rights to primary school texts in 1831. Business took off when France enacted a law in 1833 calling for free primary schooling. Librairie Hachette received an enormous order from the Ministry of Public Education, including orders for 500,000 alphabet primers.

An 1851 visit to British bookseller WH Smith in London convinced Hachette that rail passengers would buy books from stores in stations. The next year he began signing contracts with French railroads and soon had a virtual monopoly. Hachette started the Bibliothèque de Chemins de Fer (Railway Library) series of books and travel guides in 1853. Two years later it began publishing entertainment magazine *Le Journal pour Tous*. Louis Hachette died in 1864.

Around the turn of the century, Hachette bought France's leading newspaper distributors, and it acquired major French printing and binding companies in 1920. Hachette launched fashion magazine *Elle* in 1945, and the company acquired control of French publishers Grasset, Fayard, and Stock in the 1950s. Hachette diversified in the 1970s with poor results.

Jean-Luc Lagardère, who had gained control of aerospace and defense firm Matra at the age of 35 in 1963, gained control of Hachette in 1980. He launched international spinoffs of its magazines, including a successful US *Elle* in 1985 in partnership with media maven Rupert Murdoch.

In the late 1980s Hachette bought an interest in the #2 French radio station, Europe 1;

helped start another, Europe 2; purchased the second-largest magazine distributor in the US, Curtis Circulation; and bought Salvat, a Spanish encyclopedia publisher. Hachette spent over $1.1 billion on Grolier (encyclopedias) and US publisher Diamandis Communications in 1988 and bought out Murdoch's share of *Elle*.

The company purchased 25% of a money-losing French TV network, La Cinq, in 1990. The station collapsed a year later, causing Hachette to write off $643 million. To cover the huge debt, Lagardère merged Matra with Hachette in 1993 and united the disparate companies under the holding company that bears his name. Lagardère bankrolled John F. Kennedy Jr.'s political magazine *George* in 1995 (JFK Jr. died in a plane crash in 1999 and *George* folded in 2001).

With French industry decreasing its reliance on defense business, Lagardère merged its Matra defense business with France's state-owned aerospace firm, Aerospatiale, in 1999 forming one of Europe's largest aerospace companies (Lagardère held 33% of the new entity). Not long after, the new Aerospatiale Matra agreed to merge with Germany's DaimlerChrysler Aerospace and Construcciones Aeronauticas of Spain to form European Aeronautic Defence and Space Company.

The deal, completed the following year, created the world's third-largest aerospace company (Lagardère retained about 11% of the new firm). Also in 2000 the company sold publishing firm Grolier to Scholastic Corp. for about $400 million and bought the rest of Hachette Filipacchi Médias from its minority shareholders. The same year Jean-Luc Lagardère escaped a 1988 fraud charge when a judge ruled that the time limit for prosecution had expired (Paris prosecutors are appealing).

General Partner and CEO: Jean-Luc Lagardère
General Partner and Co-CEO: Philippe Camus
General Partner and Co-CEO: Arnaud Lagardère
EVP Human Relations and Communications:
Thierry Funck-Brentano
SVP and CFO: Dominique D'Hinnin
Chairman and CEO, Matra BAe Dynamics:
Fabrice Bregier
Chairman and CEO, Matra Automobile:
Philippe Guedon
CEO Hachette Filipacchi Médias:
Gerald de Roquemaurel
**Managing Director Strategic Coordination, High
Technology Sector:** Jean-Louis Gergorin
**Managing Director International Operations, High
Technology Sector:** Jean-Paul Gut
**Secretary and General Counsel; Chairman, Lagardère
Sociétés:** Pierre Leroy
Auditors: Barbier Frinault & Autres; Mazars & Guerard

LOCATIONS

HQ: 4 rue de Presbourg, 75016 Paris Cedex 16, France
Phone: +33-1-40-69-1600   **Fax:** +33-1-40-69-2131
US HQ: 1633 Broadway, 45th Fl., New York, NY 10019
US Phone: 212-767-6753   **US Fax:** 212-767-5635
Web site: http://www.lagardere.fr

1999 Sales

	€ mil.	% of total
France	4,455	36
Europe	4,171	34
North America	2,539	21
Asia	568	5
Middle East	300	2
Other	252	2
Total	**12,285**	**100**

PRODUCTS/OPERATIONS

1999 Sales

	% of total
Media & multimedia	56
High technology	35
Automobile & transit	9
Total	**100**

Selected Operations

European Aeronautic Defence and
Space Company (11%)
Lagardère Medias
Digital Media
Radio
Television
Hachette Filipacchi Médias
Hachette Distribution Services (3,300 newsstands)
Hachette Filipacchi Magazines
Car & Driver
Elle
Entrevue
George
Paris Match
Premiere
Hachette Livre (literature, textbooks, travel guides)
Matra Automobile

COMPETITORS

Advance	Havas	PRIMEDIA
Publications	Hearst	Raytheon
BAE SYSTEMS	Lockheed Martin	Reader's Digest
Bertelsmann	Meredith	Siemens
Boeing	News Corp.	Time Warner
Bombardier	Northrop	Viacom
Encyclopaedia	Grumman	Walt Disney
Britannica	Pearson	

HISTORICAL FINANCIALS & EMPLOYEES

Euronext Paris: MMB FYE: December 31	Annual Growth	12/90	12/91	12/92	12/93	12/94	12/95	12/96	12/97	12/98	12/99
Sales (€ mil.)	5.3%	—	8,097	8,400	8,229	8,083	8,016	8,598	10,047	10,692	12,285
Net income (€ mil.)	—	—	(68)	15	24	94	96	158	210	280	341
Income as % of sales	—	—	—	0.2%	0.3%	1.2%	1.2%	1.8%	2.1%	2.6%	2.8%
Earnings per share (€)	25.8%	—	—	—	0.70	0.82	0.84	1.33	1.72	2.26	2.78
Stock price – FY high (€)	—	—	—	—	23.16	25.57	19.44	28.36	30.79	44.94	54.00
Stock price – FY low (€)	—	—	—	—	12.78	16.51	12.59	13.72	21.07	22.09	28.00
Stock price – FY close (€)	15.5%	—	—	—	22.71	18.90	13.72	21.71	30.34	36.21	54.00
P/E – high	—	—	—	—	33	31	23	21	18	20	19
P/E – low	—	—	—	—	18	20	15	10	12	10	10
Dividends per share (€)	15.5%	—	—	—	—	0.38	0.43	0.46	0.56	0.67	0.78
Book value per share (€)	12.4%	—	—	—	9.39	9.62	9.45	11.63	15.50	16.23	18.95
Employees	7.1%	—	28,460	44,394	41,394	40,326	43,622	47,172	46,230	49,961	49,285

STOCK PRICE HISTORY

HIGH/LOW/CLOSE

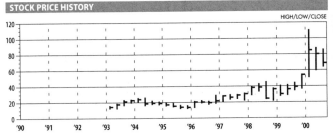

1999 FISCAL YEAR-END

Debt ratio: 35.5%
Return on equity: 16.0%
Cash (€ mil.): 681
Current ratio: 1.75
Long-term debt (€ mil.): 1,276
No. of shares (mil.): 123
Dividends
 Yield: 0.0%
 Payout: 0.3%
Market value ($ mil.): 6,650
Sales ($ mil.): 12,343

LAIDLAW INC.

OVERVIEW

Neither waste disposal nor medical services shall distract Laidlaw from its focus on transportation. The Burlington, Ontario-based company is North America's largest school bus operator and the leading intercity passenger carrier. Through its Education Services division, Laidlaw's school buses transport 2.3 million students daily, and its Transit and Tour Services division provides daily city transportation through about 225 contracts in the US and Canada. This unit also owns and operates intercity carrier Greyhound Lines. The US's largest passenger bus company, Greyhound serves more than 3,700 destinations in the US and Canada; it also provides services in Mexico.

Laidlaw's American Medical Response unit provides ambulance and nonemergency transportation to 5 million people in 36 US states. The firm's health care division also provides emergency room management for 300 hospitals through its EmCare operation. Formerly a leader in the solid waste market, Laidlaw holds a 44% stake in environmental services company Safety-Kleen, which is undergoing an investigation of its accounting practices. Laidlaw has announced plans to sell the Safety-Kleen stake, along with its ambulance and emergency room management operations, in order to concentrate on its bus operations.

HISTORY

North America's largest school bus and ambulance company didn't start out that way; it had to gobble up many a company first. In 1959 Michael DeGroote acquired Laidlaw Transport, a regional trucking firm in Hagersville, Ontario, for $300,000 from founder Robert Laidlaw. Over the next decade the Belgian-born DeGroote established Laidlaw as a grand acquisitor, making dozens of purchases.

Not long after Laidlaw went public in 1969, acquisitions had positioned the company as a competitor in several industries, including solid waste services (1969), the school bus industry (1972), public transit systems (1985), and hazardous and chemical waste management (1986).

Waste management operations cleaned up for Laidlaw in the 1970s and 1980s, spurring the company's rapid growth; but by the late 1980s that business was starting to decay. DeGroote disposed of his stake in Laidlaw, selling it to Canadian Pacific in 1988. He stayed on to direct the company's continuing acquisitions of small Canadian and US firms. From 1988 to 1991, Laidlaw bought 78 waste service firms and 30 passenger service businesses. DeGroote retired as chairman and CEO in 1991.

In 1993 James Bullock, who was CEO of a Canadian commercial real estate firm, was brought in to revive Laidlaw. That year Laidlaw began providing private ambulance services through its purchase of San Diego-based MedTrans.

Bullock began selling Laidlaw's noncore businesses in 1994 and sold its trash-hauling service and its stake in UK-based water and solid waste management firm Attwoods in 1995. The company used the proceeds to buy U.S. Pollution Control Industries (USPCI), Union Pacific Railway's waste management

business. USPCI was combined with Laidlaw's hazardous waste management services to create one of the largest hazardous waste firms in North America. Laidlaw kept 67% of the new firm, called Laidlaw Environmental Services.

Laidlaw also bought Mayflower Group's school bus and public transit operations in 1995, as well as CareLine, the US's #3 health care transportation firm. In 1996 Laidlaw sold its 24% interest in ADT, a security alarm and car auction firm, and acquired the school bus operations of Scott's Hospitality, which gave Laidlaw 30% of the Canadian school bus market and 25% of the US market.

Laidlaw sold Laidlaw Waste Management in 1996 and spun off its environmental services unit the following year, after a reverse acquisition by Rollins Environmental Services. Refocused on transportation and health care services, the company bought American Medical Response, the US's largest privately owned ambulance service. The purchase doubled the size of Laidlaw's ambulance operations, which were renamed American Medical Response. Other 1997 acquisitions included Vancom, the US's largest privately owned school bus operator. Laidlaw also bought EmCare, the US's top private operator of emergency rooms, and added Spectrum Emergency Care.

In 1998 Laidlaw Environmental Services was renamed Safety-Kleen after its acquisition of that company, and Laidlaw reduced its stake in the unit. In 1999 Laidlaw bought Greyhound Lines in a $650 million deal. The company also announced plans to sell its health care businesses and its stake in Safety-Kleen to focus on bus operations. Later that year COO John Grainger replaced Bullock as president and CEO.

Chairman: Peter N. T. Widdrington
President and CEO: John R. Grainger
SVP and CFO: Leslie W. Haworth
SVP, General Counsel, and Secretary: Ivan R. Cairns
CEO EmCare: Leonard M. Riggs Jr.
President, Laidlaw Transit Education Services:
  Robert E. Hach
VP and Controller: Wayne R. Bishop
VP Risk Management: Jeffrey Cassell
VP Human Resources: William S. Schilling
VP Communications: Thomas A. G. Watson
Auditors: PricewaterhouseCoopers LLP

HQ: 3221 N. Service Rd., PO Box 5028,
  Burlington, Ontario L7R 3Y8, Canada
Phone: 905-336-1800   **Fax:** 905-336-3976
Web site: http://www.laidlaw.com

Laidlaw operates throughout the US and Canada.
Through subsidiary Greyhound Lines, Laidlaw also
serves parts of Mexico.

1999 Sales

	$ mil.	% of total
Education services	1,335	59
Transit & tour services	928	41
Total	**2,263**	**100**

Major Operations
Education services (school buses)
Transit and tour services (city buses)
  Greyhound Lines (intercity and cross-country
    bus services)
Emergency healthcare services
  American Medical Response (emergency medical
    services and ambulance transportation)
  EmCare (emergency department management)

AMR
Amtrak
Atlantic Express Transportation
Coach USA
Continental Airlines
Delta
FirstGroup
Hertz
MTA
National Express Group
Ryder
Southwest Airlines
UAL

NYSE: LDW FYE: August 31	Annual Growth	8/90	8/91	8/92	8/93	8/94	8/95	8/96	8/97	8/98	8/99
Sales ($ mil.)	3.0%	1,738	1,882	1,926	1,993	2,128	2,517	2,296	3,031	3,690	2,263
Net income ($ mil.)	—	248	(344)	139	(292)	91	133	162	611	346	(1,119)
Income as % of sales	—	14.3%	—	7.2%	—	4.3%	5.3%	7.0%	20.1%	9.4%	—
Earnings per share ($)	—	—	—	—	—	—	—	—	1.92	1.05	(3.39)
Stock price - FY high ($)	—	—	—	—	—	—	—	—	16.50	16.63	10.75
Stock price - FY low ($)	—	—	—	—	—	—	—	—	14.38	8.63	5.69
Stock price - FY close ($)	(34.6%)	—	—	—	—	—	—	—	14.63	8.96	6.25
P/E - high	—	—	—	—	—	—	—	—	9	16	—
P/E - low	—	—	—	—	—	—	—	—	7	8	—
Dividends per share ($)	128.0%	—	—	—	—	—	—	—	0.05	0.26	0.26
Book value per share ($)	(17.4%)	—	—	—	—	—	—	—	8.50	9.36	5.79
Employees	10.1%	29,995	26,800	35,500	37,000	40,000	50,850	65,925	79,500	80,000	71,400

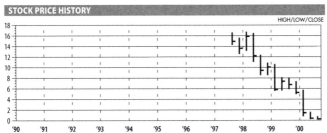

HIGH/LOW/CLOSE

Debt ratio: 61.9%
Return on equity: —
Cash ($ mil.): 58
Current ratio: 1.16
Long-term debt ($ mil.): 3,113
No. of shares (mil.): 330
Dividends
  Yield: 4.2%
  Payout: —
Market value ($ mil.): 2,064

LEGO COMPANY

OVERVIEW

The LEGO Company has always claimed to make kids smarter, but now they're making LEGOs smarter than kids. The company, based in Billund, Denmark, makes plastic LEGO toys, which have evolved from simple building blocks into themed playsets. (The company has made more than 200 billion pieces since 1949.) Its Mindstorms kits use high-tech sensors, voice-recognition technology, and PCs to allow children to create and program robots and other toys; other high-tech products include CD-ROM games. LEGO Media produces video games, software, books, and the like for children. The word LEGO is derived from the Danish words for "play well."

LEGO sells its products in 130 countries; the US is its single largest market, accounting for one-third of the company's sales. The company also operates LEGO Imagination Center stores (at Walt Disney World and the Mall of America) and LEGOLAND theme parks (Denmark, the UK, and California), which feature LEGO sculptures, rides, and exhibits. The company licenses the LEGO name for a variety of children's products, including clothing and watches; it also operates LEGO retail outlets in the US and Europe.

LEGO is owned by Kjeld Kirk Kristiansen, grandson of the company's founder, and his family.

HISTORY

Ole Kirk Christiansen opened a carpentry shop in 1916 in Denmark and began making carved wooden toys in 1932. Two years later Ole held a contest among his employees to name the company, from which came LEGO. A fire destroyed the LEGO factory in 1942, but the company quickly resumed manufacturing.

The availability of quality plastic following WWII prompted the company to add plastic toys to its line. The predecessor to the common LEGO block was invented in 1949; called Automatic Binding Bricks, they fit on top of each other but did not snap together.

After hearing criticism that no company made a comprehensive toy system, in 1954 Ole's son Godtfred assembled a list of 10 product criteria for LEGO's toys, including that they have lots of compatible components. After reviewing its lines, the company decided that the Automatic Binding Bricks had the most potential. After the launch of the first LEGO playset in 1955, the firm introduced the "stud and tube" snap-together LEGO building block in 1958. LEGOs were soon one of the most popular toys in Europe. When a second fire in 1960 destroyed its warehouse facility for wooden toys, the company ceased production of wooden toys in favor of plastics.

Luggage-maker Samsonite began manufacturing and distributing LEGOs in the US in 1961 under license. LEGO's first LEGOLAND park, built from 42 million LEGO blocks, opened in Billund, Denmark, in 1968. The following year the company introduced the DUPLO line of large-sized LEGOs for preschoolers. By 1973, after relatively lackluster US sales, Samsonite opted not to renew its license, and The LEGO Company set up a sales and production facility in Connecticut. A massive television advertising campaign followed, and US sales increased tenfold by 1975.

Aiming for the preteen market, the company introduced the more-complex LEGO Technic model sets in 1977 and the popular LEGOLAND Space playset two years later. However, LEGO hit a bump when its patent for the LEGO brick expired in 1981. A slew of knockoffs flooded the market, but none more competitive than Tyco Toys' Super Blocks, which were actually interchangeable with LEGOs.

The first LEGO Imagination Center opened in Minneapolis in 1992, and the second followed in Walt Disney World five years later. In 1993 the company began licensing its name for apparel. Two years later Godtfred died; his son, Kjeld, who changed the spelling of Christiansen to Kristiansen, succeeded him.

In the 1990s growth of the video game industry far outpaced the growth of the construction toys market, and LEGO suffered. With profits shrinking, in 1998 the company reversed its tradition of avoiding commercial tie-ins, snapping together an agreement to produce building kits and figures based on the popular *Star Wars* movies and Disney's Winnie the Pooh.

However, those events came too late to prevent LEGO from suffering its first loss since the 1930s. The company began cutting up to 10% of its workers in 1999. Also in 1999 it opened its third LEGOLAND in Carlsbad, California. To reach more girls, LEGO introduced its Scala products, dolls, and Lego-like furniture and accessories in mid-1999.

LEGO bought smart toys developer Zowie Intertainment in 2000, marking the first time the company purchased another toy maker. The company also announced that a fourth LEGOLAND theme park would open in 2003.

Chairman: Mads Ovlisen
President and CEO: Kjeld Kirk Kristiansen
EVP and COO: Poul Plougmann
EVP Asia/Pacific: Poul Ernst Rasmussen
EVP Global Business Support: Stig Toftgaard
EVP Global Markets: Peter Eio
EVP Global Supply Chain: Jens Bornstein
EVP New Business Development:
Torben Ballegaard Sorensen
Director of Human Resources: Anja Egeberg

LOCATIONS

HQ: LEGO Center, DK-7190 Billund, Denmark
Phone: +45-79-50-60-70   **Fax:** +45-75-35-33-60
US HQ: 555 Taylor Rd., Enfield, CT 06083
US Phone: 860-749-2291   **US Fax:** 860-763-6680
Web site: http://www.lego.com

The LEGO Company consists of about 50 different
companies in more than 30 countries; its products are
sold in some 130 countries.

Selected Countries of Operation

Australia	The Netherlands
Austria	New Zealand
Brazil	Norway
Canada	Poland
China	Portugal
Czech Republic	Singapore
Denmark	South Africa
Finland	South Korea
France	Spain
Germany	Sweden
Hungary	Switzerland
Italy	UK
Japan	US
Mexico	

PRODUCTS/OPERATIONS

Selected Products
LEGO DUPLO toys
  Animals
  Basic sets
  Dump trucks
  Fire trucks
  School buses
  Winnie the Pooh
LEGO Mindstorms toys
LEGO Primo toys
  Baby toys
  Motion toys
  Stack-N-Learn sets
LEGO Scala toys
LEGO System toys
  Aquazone
  Freestyle sets
  Insectoids
  Star Wars
  Value buckets
LEGO Technic
  Cyberslam
  Slizer Throwbots

Other Operations
LEGO Imagination Center (retail stores)
LEGO lifestyle products (licensing agreements for
  children's clothes, watches, bed linens, puzzles)
LEGO media products (books, music, software, videos)
LEGOLAND Parks (theme parks)

COMPETITORS

Bandai
DSI Toys
Hasbro
Mattel
Toymax International
Walt Disney
Zindart

HISTORICAL FINANCIALS & EMPLOYEES

Private FYE: December 31	Annual Growth	12/90	12/91	12/92	12/93	12/94	12/95	12/96	12/97	12/98	12/99
Sales ($ mil.)	3.2%	—	—	—	—	1,016	1,230	1,267	1,115	1,200	1,190
Employees	(3.6%)	—	—	—	—	—	9,660	9,450	9,867	8,670	8,350

SALES HISTORY

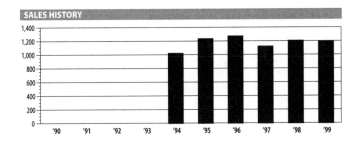

LG GROUP

LG Group used to be Lucky, but Asia's economic woes have brought hard times to this South Korean *chaebol* (family-run industrial group), one of the country's top five. Formerly Lucky Goldstar, the Seoul-based group consists of 42 affiliated companies that operate through more than 300 offices in more than 120 countries.

Its primary operations include chemicals and energy (LG Chemical, Korea's largest chemical company, and LG Petrochemical); electronics and telecommunications (LG Electronics and Dacom, leaders in Korea's consumer electronics and long-distance services, respectively). The company also provides financial services (LG Investment & Securities and LG Investment Trust Management) and trading and services (LG International and LG Engineering & Construction).

Luck has little to do with the *chaebol*'s future. Korea's government has ordered the country's *chaebol* to streamline their operations and let member companies stand or fall on their own.

During WWII Koo In-Hwoi made tooth powder for Koreans to use in place of salt, then the common dentifrice. Koo founded the Lucky Chemical Company in 1947 to make facial creams and, later, detergent, shampoo, and Lucky Toothpaste. The enterprise soon became Korea's only plastics maker. Koo established a trading company in 1953.

Emulating Japanese exporters, Koo formed Goldstar Company in 1958 to make fans. The company became the first company in Korea to make radios (1959), refrigerators (1965), TVs (1966), elevators and escalators (1968), and washing machines and air conditioners (1969). In 1967 Lucky collaborated with Caltex to build the Honam Oil Refinery, the first privately owned refinery in Korea. Both Lucky and Goldstar benefited from the *chaebol*'s cozy relationship with President Park Chung Hee's government (1962-79) and used plentiful loans from Korean banks to diversify into everything from energy and semiconductors to insurance. Lucky began petrochemical production in 1977 and later built the world's largest single-unit petrochemical plant in Saudi Arabia (1986).

During the 1970s and 1980s, Goldstar expanded rapidly as it took advantage of cheap Korean labor to export private-label electronics items to its large retail customers abroad. In the late 1970s the group began investing heavily in semiconductor production, in part to fulfill its own chip requirements. Goldstar companies teamed with more technically accomplished partners, including AT&T, NEC, Hitachi, and Siemens, and set out to capture office-automation and higher-end consumer electronics markets with Goldstar-brand goods.

In 1983 the *chaebol* became Lucky Goldstar. Although electronics sales grew rapidly, Lucky Goldstar's inefficient organizational structure slowed progress, and in 1984 archrival Samsung finally outdid it. In the late 1980s Lucky Goldstar suffered from rising wage rates, labor unrest, and Korean currency appreciation. In 1989 the group created Goldstar Electron (LG Semicon Co.) and in 1990 business rebounded. Lucky Goldstar acquired 5% of US television set maker Zenith in 1991.

In 1994 Lucky Goldstar signed an agreement with the government of the Sakha region in Russia to develop the Elga, the world's largest coal field. Lucky Goldstar became the LG Group in 1995, marking its new thrust: globalization. That year it acquired a controlling interest in troubled Zenith, by then the last TV manufacturer in the US.

The Asian contagion hit in 1997. LG Group announced that it would pull out of 90 business areas, but in 1998 it was one of several *chaebol* caught funneling money to ailing subsidiaries (the *chaebol* were collectively fined $93 million). LG Group members went abroad in 1998 looking for new partners: Among other deals, LG Chemicals allied with top drugmakers such as SmithKline Beecham, Warner-Lambert (now Pfizer), and Merck; and British Telecommunications bought a nearly 25% stake in LG Telecom.

Under government pressure to consolidate scattered businesses with those of other *chaebol*, LG Group in 1999 agreed to sell LG Semicon. After lengthy negotiations, the Hyundai Group took control of the unit, which became Hyundai MicroElectronics. Electronics giant Philips paid $1.6 billion for a 50% stake in LG Electronics' LCD unit. Meanwhile, LG Group acquired control of Dacom, one of South Korea's top long-distance carriers and a leading ISP. In 2000 Dacom opened a high-speed Internet line linking Hong Kong, Japan and Australia.

Chairman: Koo Bon-Moo, age 55
EVP: Chang Soo Kim
EVP: Hwan Duck Yu
EVP: Kun Hi Yu
EVP Advanced Technology: Kyu Chang Park
EVP Overseas Business Development: Yong Ak Ro
EVP Research and Development: In Ku Kang
EVP Strategy and Resource Management: John Koo
Senior Managing Director: Seong Dong Kim
Senior Managing Director: Kwang Ho Cho
Auditors: Samil Accounting Corporation

LOCATIONS

HQ: LG Twin Towers, 20 Yoido-dong, Youngdungpo-gu,
    Seoul 150-721, South Korea
Phone: +82-2-3773-1114   **Fax:** +82-2-3773-2200
US HQ: 1000 Sylvan Ave., Englewood Cliffs, NJ 07632
US Phone: 201-816-2000   **US Fax:** 201-816-0604
Web site: http://www.lg.co.kr

LG Group's companies operate in more than
120 countries.

PRODUCTS/OPERATIONS

Selected Subsidiaries and Affiliates

Chemicals and Energy
LG Chemical Ltd.
LG Energy Corp.
LG MMA Corp. (joint venture, organic chemicals)
LG Petrochemical Co., Ltd.
LG Power Co., Ltd.
LG-Caltex Oil Corp. (joint venture)
LG Siltron Inc. (silicon wafers)
LG-Caltex Gas Co., Ltd. (joint venture)
LG-Caltex Oil Corp. (joint venture)

Electronics and Telecommunications
LG Electronics Inc.
LG Industrial Systems Co., Ltd.
LG Micron Ltd.
LG Philips LCD Co. Ltd
LG TeleCom Ltd.
Zenith Electronics Corp.

Finance
LG Capital Services Corp.
LG Futures Co., Ltd.
LG Investment & Securities Co., Ltd.
LG Investment Trust Management Co., Ltd.

Service (Trading)
LG Department Store Co., Ltd.
LG Engineering & Construction Co., Ltd.
LG Home Shopping Inc.
LG International Corp. (general trading)
LG Mart Co., Ltd. (specialty markets)

COMPETITORS

Akzo Nobel	Hyundai	Samsung
AMD	IBM	SANYO
BASF AG	ITOCHU	Sharp
Bayer AG	Marubeni	SK Group
Compaq	Matsushita	Sony
Daewoo	Mitsubishi	Ssangyong
Dow Chemical	Mitsui	Sumitomo
DuPont	Motorola	Texas
Formosa Plastics	NEC	Instruments
Fujitsu	Nokia	Toshiba
GE	Nortel Networks	Union Carbide
Hewlett-Packard	Philips	
Hitachi	Electronics	

HISTORICAL FINANCIALS & EMPLOYEES

| Group
FYE: December 31 | Annual
Growth | 12/90 | 12/91 | 12/92 | 12/93 | 12/94 | 12/95 | 12/96 | 12/97 | 12/98 | 12/99 |
|---|---|---|---|---|---|---|---|---|---|---|---|
| Sales ($ mil.) | 7.1% | — | — | — | — | 38,967 | 64,263 | 70,015 | 46,707 | — | 55,000 |
| Employees | (0.4%) | — | — | — | — | — | — | 130,000 | 126,000 | 126,000 | 100,000 |

SALES HISTORY

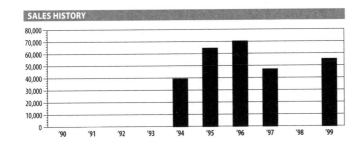

LLOYD'S OF LONDON

OVERVIEW

After a lot of R&R (reconstruction and renewal), Lloyd's of London is back at work as the world's leading insurance exchange. Not an insurance company, it regulates syndicates of wealthy individuals (called Names) and corporate underwriters that transact insurance business worth billions in premiums each year. Lloyd's is a top conduit for aviation and marine insurance as well as specialty insurance (such as policies covering art and jewelry or protecting against acts of terrorism).

Despite its overhaul, Lloyd's traditional focus on specialty lines has hampered its ability to compete against global firms offering more comprehensive service. Encouraged by Lloyd's to consolidate, some syndicates, infused with capital from corporate-owned managing agencies that enables them to completely underwrite a contract, are turning into full-service insurance companies. Corporate underwriters — ACE Limited and Berkshire Hathaway's GeneralCologne Re, for example — now account for most of Lloyd's capital backing, where Names once dominated.

Lloyd's is catching up to its rivals, particularly bargain-rate insurers who entered the offshore markets in the early 1990s. Catastrophic losses in recent years have forced them to raise their prices, making Lloyd's competitive again. But Lloyd's remains deeply in debt and is taking major cost-cutting steps — such as outsourcing operations ranging from data processing and catering to facilities management.

HISTORY

In 1688 Edward Lloyd opened Lloyd's Coffee House near London's docks. Maritime insurance brokers and underwriters met at Lloyd's, which offered a comfortable venue for exchanging shipping information. The loose association of brokers began publishing shipping newspaper *Lloyd's List* in 1734 (sold 1996).

The coffeehouse attracted people who used insurance as a cover for gambling — members who "insured" the gender of the transvestite Chevalier d'Eon, began Lloyd's tradition of specialty insurance.

In 1871 Parliament enacted the Lloyd's Act, which formed Lloyd's Corporation to oversee the activities of the underwriting syndicates (made up of Names with unlimited personal liability). In the 1880s the market began covering nonmarine risks. By 1900 Lloyd's members wrote 50% of the world's nonlife insurance.

Prompt claims payment after the 1906 San Francisco earthquake boosted the market's image in the US. After WWI, Lloyd's members began writing automotive, credit, and aviation insurance.

In 1981 and 1982 a syndicate managed by Richard Outhwaite wrote contracts on the future liabilities of old insurance contracts with claims (many with environmental exposure) still pending. That decade Lloyd's also attracted new Names: the merely well-off — highly paid people without great wealth — who pledged assets often overvalued in the 1980s boom. Exercising little oversight, Lloyd's let syndicates close their books on pending claims by reinsuring them repeatedly through new syndicates financed by neophyte Names.

The boom's end coincided with a rise in US environmental claims covered by insurance contracts such as those written by Outhwaite. When Names with reduced net worth balked at paying claims, Lloyd's faced disaster. From 1991 to 1994, the number of syndicates fell by half and premium rates increased. In 1993, with billions in claims and many Names refusing to pay or suing their syndicates for not disclosing the risks, Lloyd's imposed new underwriting and reporting rules, took control of most syndicates' back-office functions, and brought in capital by finally admitting corporate members (mostly foreign insurers).

Lloyd's reached a multibillion-pound settlement with most of its Names in 1996. It also required its active investors to help finance a new insurance company, Equitas, to cover old liabilities (billions in claims are still outstanding). In 1997 Lloyd's sought to increase the number of broker members. The next year, amid regulatory disagreements with Singapore's government and a faltering Asian economy, it called off plans to open an exchange branch there. In 1999 Lloyd's began cutting its operating costs. It also began bolstering its Central Fund with insurance rather than cash (providers include Swiss Re and The Chubb Corporation) and admitted pharmaceuticals powerhouse SmithKline Beecham's captive insurer into its marketplace.

As litigation dragged on in 2000 over whether a recalcitrant group of Names owed Lloyd's more than £50 million for claims, the corporation continued to trim costs by selling property.

Chairman: Max Taylor, age 52
Deputy Chairman: Saxon Riley, age 61
Chairman Lloyd's Regulatory Board: John Young
CEO: Nicholas E. T. Prettejohn, age 40
President, Lloyd's America: Wendy Baker
Development Director: Andrew Duguid
Finance Director, Lloyd's of London and Lloyd's America: Bob Hewes
Human Resources Director: Geoff Morgan
Legal Services Director: Sean McGovern
Managing Director Lloyd's America: Julian James
Marketing and Communications Director: Caroline Wagstaff
Regulatory Division Director: David Gittings
Head of Taxation: David Clissitt
Auditors: Ernst & Young

LOCATIONS

HQ: 1 Lime St., London EC3M 7HA, United Kingdom
Phone: +44-20-7327-1000   **Fax:** +44-20-7327-5599
US HQ: 590 5th Avenue, New York, NY 10036
US Phone: 212-382-4060   **US Fax:** 212-382-4070
Web site: http://www.lloyds.com

Lloyd's of London's syndicates operate in more than 100 countries.

PRODUCTS/OPERATIONS

1999 Sales

	% of total
Direct market charges	54
Subscriptions & application fees	21
Equitas-related fees	15
Other	10
Total	**100**

Selected Subsidiaries
Additional Securities Ltd. (overseas insurance reserves)
Centrewrite Ltd. (insurance)
Equitas Holdings Ltd. (reinsurance)
Lioncover Insurance Co. Ltd.
Lloyd's America, Inc. (liaison with US producers)

COMPETITORS

AGF
AIG
Allianz
Aon
AXA
CGNU plc
Chubb
Citigroup
Fortis (NL)
GeneralCologne Re
ING
Markel
Marsh & McLennan
Munich Re
Swiss Re
Tokio Marine and Fire
Zurich Financial Services

HISTORICAL FINANCIALS & EMPLOYEES

Insurance society FYE: December 31	Annual Growth	12/90	12/91	12/92	12/93	12/94	12/95	12/96	12/97	12/98	12/99
Assets ($ mil.)	(29.2%)	—	—	—	—	—	—	—	658	483	330
Net income ($ mil.)	47.2%	—	—	—	—	—	—	—	57	40	124
Income as % of assets	—	—	—	—	—	—	—	—	8.7%	8.3%	37.7%
Employees	(10.3%)	—	—	—	—	—	—	—	—	1,833	1,645

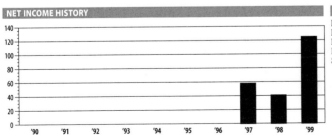

NET INCOME HISTORY

1999 FISCAL YEAR-END
Equity as % of assets: 0.0%
Return on assets: 30.6%
Return on equity: —
Long-term debt ($ mil.): 177
Sales ($ mil.): 266

LOGITECH INTERNATIONAL S.A.

OVERVIEW

Logitech enjoys being pushed around. Romanel-sur-Morges, Switzerland-based Logitech International is the world's #1 maker of computer mice and a major producer of other input devices such as touch pads, keyboards, trackballs, joysticks, and digital video cameras. The company, which was the #1 US seller of PC cameras, has seen its market share eroded by chip giant Intel (a newcomer to this market) despite steady growth in its camera sales. It sells its products directly to leading manufacturers (most of the world's largest PC makers are customers) as well as through distributors and retailers worldwide. To avoid high labor and overhead costs, Logitech performs its high-volume manufacturing in China.

Logitech's growth strategy includes enhancing functionality — especially Internet-related features — for its PC devices and expanding its product line beyond the PC platform. It continues to roll out new products like the WingMan Force Feedback Mouse, which lets video game players feel things like the recoil from weapons, and lets less violent users "feel" the difference between dragging a 1 GB and a 1 KB file across the desktop.

Co-founder and chairman Daniel Borel owns 10% of Logitech.

HISTORY

Italian Pierluigi Zappacosta and Swiss Daniel Borel met while studying computer engineering at Stanford University in the 1970s. The two wanted to bring the entrepreneurial spirit of California's Silicon Valley to Europe and start a high-tech company. At the time, though, there was little venture capital in Europe, and no European bank would lend them enough money.

In 1981 Zappacosta and Borel obtained the rights to sell a Swiss-designed mouse in the US and, with Swiss backers, started Logitech in California and Switzerland. The co-founders originally intended Logitech to be a software company in the mold of Microsoft, but this vision changed quickly as the importance of the mouse and other peripherals became apparent. The company improved its manufacturing process and soon developed a cordless mouse.

Hewlett-Packard was Logitech's first big client, quickly followed by others including Olivetti and AT&T. Logitech made its first foray into the US retail market in 1986, with limited success. Since its brand was not recognized and the company had a small advertising budget, it bypassed the regular retail route and offered its mouse at a discount through specialty computer magazines. Consumers, and later dealers and distributors, took notice; Logitech was soon supplying mice to Apple. With a new Taiwan manufacturing plant on line and increased capacity, it reached an agreement in 1988 to supply IBM. That year Logitech went public.

In 1991 Logitech formed a joint venture in China that involved funding from China National Aerotechnology Import and Export Corporation and the International Resources Technology Association of Hong Kong. That year the company also purchased 51% of Gazelle Graphics Systems, developer of single-board digitizers and cordless digitizing pens (Gazelle had developed the first trackball for Apple's PowerBook laptops). Logitech purchased the rest of Gazelle in 1993.

Logitech announced a new design for its stationary desktop mouse for Macintosh (TrackMan) in 1993. The next year Logitech eliminated 500 jobs. At that time Zappacosta announced that the company would shift its focus from mice to input devices such as cameras and scanners.

With stiff competition and pricing pressures eroding profits, Logitech struggled through 1995, closing factories and consolidating plants. After taking a $20 million restructuring charge, Logitech returned to profitability in 1996.

Logitech sold its scanner business in late 1997 to Storm Technology (which later went bankrupt). In 1998 Guerrino De Luca, a former executive at Apple Computer and Claris, joined the company as president and CEO, replacing Borel, who remains chairman. (Zappacosta stepped down as VC; he chairs fingerprint recognition systems maker DigitalPersona.) That year also saw Logitech buy the digital camera business of Connectix.

In 1999, the 30th anniversary of the mouse's invention, Logitech sold its 200 millionth digital rodent. Also that year it spun off SpotLife, which allows users to share video content through its Web site. In 2000 Logitech announced an agreement with Compaq to bundle its QuickCam cameras with Compaq Presario PCs, and one with Motorola to develop cordless PC peripherals based on the Bluetooth wireless protocol.

Chairman: Daniel V. Borel, age 50
President and CEO: Guerrino De Luca, age 47
SVP; General Manager Control Devices Division: Wolfgang Hausen, age 57
SVP Finance and CFO: Kristen Onken, age 50
SVP, Operations; General Manager, Far East: Erh-Hsun Chang, age 51
SVP Worldwide Sales and Marketing: Gregory Chambers, age 40
VP; General Manager Interactive Gaming: Ted M. Hoff
VP Video Business: Junien Labrousse
VP Worldwide Human Resources: Roberta Linsky
VP Worldwide Supply Chain: Steven Perotin
Auditors: PricewaterhouseCoopers SA

LOCATIONS

HQ: Moulin du Choc D, CH-1122 Romanel-sur-Morges, Switzerland
Phone: +41-21-863-51-11   **Fax:** +41-21-863-53-11
US HQ: 6505 Kaiser Dr., Fremont, CA 94555
US Phone: 510-795-8500   **US Fax:** 510-792-8901
Web site: http://www.logitech.com

Logitech International has operations in China, the Netherlands, Switzerland, Taiwan, and the US.

2000 Sales

	$ mil.	% of total
Europe	260	42
North America	253	41
Far East	103	17
Total	**616**	**100**

PRODUCTS/OPERATIONS

Selected Products
Cameras (QuickCam line)
Game controllers (Thunderpad line)
 Joysticks and wheels (WingMan line)
Keyboards (Cordless, iTouch, and NewTouch lines)
Mice (Cordless, MouseMan, Pilot, and Wheel lines)
Speakers (SoundMan line)
Trackballs (Marble and TrackMan lines)

COMPETITORS

Acer
Alps Electric
Apple Computer
Cherry
Creative Technology
Eastman Kodak
Fortune Brands
IBM
Intel
Interlink Electronics
Key Tronic
Labtec
Microsoft
Mitsumi Electric
Philips Electronics
Recoton
Sharp

HISTORICAL FINANCIALS & EMPLOYEES

Nasdaq: LOGIY FYE: March 31	Annual Growth	3/91	3/92	3/93	3/94	3/95	3/96	3/97	3/98	3/99	3/00
Sales ($ mil.)	16.0%	162	237	293	326	303	355	414	390	448	616
Net income ($ mil.)	9.7%	13	15	6	19	(17)	8	21	16	7	30
Income as % of sales	—	8.0%	6.3%	2.0%	5.8%	—	2.3%	5.1%	4.0%	1.6%	4.9%
Earnings per share ($)	4.8%	—	—	—	—	—	—	0.60	0.39	0.18	0.69
Stock price - FY high ($)	—	—	—	—	—	—	—	8.38	9.50	7.88	38.00
Stock price - FY low ($)	—	—	—	—	—	—	—	8.00	6.69	4.06	6.13
Stock price - FY close ($)	59.1%	—	—	—	—	—	—	8.13	7.94	6.44	32.75
P/E - high	—	—	—	—	—	—	—	14	23	41	50
P/E - low	—	—	—	—	—	—	—	13	16	21	8
Dividends per share ($)	—	—	—	—	—	—	—	0.00	0.00	0.00	0.00
Book value per share ($)	12.1%	—	—	—	—	—	—	3.07	3.27	3.49	4.32
Employees	12.8%	1,470	2,399	2,402	2,489	2,112	2,322	2,995	2,669	4,170	4,350

STOCK PRICE HISTORY

HIGH/LOW/CLOSE

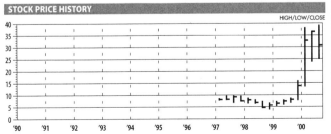

2000 FISCAL YEAR-END

Debt ratio: 1.6%
Return on equity: 18.8%
Cash ($ mil.): 49
Current ratio: 1.77
Long-term debt ($ mil.): 3
No. of shares (mil.): 42
Dividends
 Yield: —
 Payout: —
Market value ($ mil.): 1,363

LONMIN PLC

OVERVIEW

Lonmin, formerly Lonrho, no longer worships solely at the foot of the golden calf — platinum is more precious these days. The company, Africa's third-largest producer of platinum, has decided to concentrate completely on its platinum operations. Its assets include interests in Western Platinum and Eastern Platinum, gold mines in Zimbabwe, and more than 30% of Ghana-based Ashanti Goldfields. Lonmin operates primarily by owning beneficial interests in the mining operations of other companies.

In 2000 the company sold off its coal mining operations and its hotel and insurance businesses. By focusing on platinum, Lonmin is hoping to boost its production of the precious metal from 630,000 ounces to more than 800,000 ounces per year.

HISTORY

Founded in 1909 as the London & Rhodesian Mining & Land Company to acquire mining rights in Zambia and Zimbabwe, the company later expanded into real estate, ranching, and agriculture. Fifty years later, its sales still were only $11 million. In 1961 Roland "Tiny" Rowland traded his Rhodesian assets for a 48% interest in the company and managing directorship.

Rowland then bought the Beira oil pipeline (running from southern Rhodesia to Mozambique) in 1961. He changed the company's name to Lonrho in 1963 and shut down the pipeline in 1965 when economic sanctions were imposed against Rhodesia after white settlers declared independence. Rowland also bought a major interest in the Ashanti gold fields of Ghana in 1968.

In 1973 a group of directors tried to oust Rowland, claiming he had bribed African leaders and violated Rhodesian sanctions. A British inquiry cleared him but found that he had made questionable payments.

Lonrho bought Volkswagen and Audi distributors in the UK in 1975, Princess Hotels in 1979, and the *Observer* newspaper in 1981 (sold 1993). His attempt to buy retailer House of Fraser (owner of Harrod's) was frustrated by the British Mergers and Monopolies Commission in 1985.

Back in Africa, where Tanzania had nationalized Lonrho's operations in 1978, Rowland continued his politically incorrect dealings through the 1980s. He helped the Marxist government of Mozambique manage its agricultural resources and increased Lonrho's South African holdings despite sanctions against the government's policy of apartheid.

Weakened by debt and low commodity prices, Lonrho began shedding assets in the late 1980s. In 1992 Rowland sold a third of the Metropole Hotel chain to Libya and accepted a loan from Colonel Muammar al-Qaddafi. Lonrho's stock plummeted, attracting the attention of German financier Dieter Bock, who bought about 18% of the company that year.

Bock and Rowland were co-CEOs for about a year until Bock won control of the board. Rowland was forced out of management in 1994. Rowland, angered by Bock's plan to dismember the company, sold his 6% of the firm in 1995 but remained a frequent critic of its new management. In 1996 EU regulators rejected Bock's plan to spin off Lonrho's mining operations.

Bock resigned as CEO in 1996 and sold his 18% interest in Lonrho to South African titan Anglo American. Bock was replaced as CEO by Nicholas Morrell, a former executive with the *Observer*. Lonrho sold its Metropole Hotel chain to Stakis (UK) for $533 million that year and sold its Lonrho Sugar operations in 1997. Anglo sold its 26% stake in Lonrho to JCI in 1997. The next year the deal was restructured so that Anglo kept a 7% stake in Lonrho. Also in 1997 Sir John Craven was named chairman of the company.

In 1998 Lonrho bought Tavistock (a JCI coal operation). Also that year the company spun off its Lonrho Africa division, wrote off its Hondo Oil & Gas interest in Columbia, and sold its Princess Hotels chain to Canadian Pacific for about $540 million.

The company changed its name to Lonmin in 1999 and made a failed attempt to increase its interests in the Ashanti gold mines. Having decided to focus on platinum production that year, Lonmin sold its Duiker and Tweefontein coal operations for $209 million to Switzerland-based commodity house Glencore International in 2000.

Also in 2000 Lonmin sold its insurance broking interests in the UK to Sterling Insurance Group Limited, and it sold its hotel and casino interests in the Bahamas to Driftwood Freeport Limited, a Florida-based holding company.

Chairman: Sir John A. Craven, age 59, $120,000 pay
Deputy Chairman: Peter J. Harper, age 64, $50,000 pay
Chief Executive: Nicholas J. Morrell, age 52,
$450,000 pay
Director; Chief Executive Ashanti Goldfields:
Sam E. Jonah, age 50
Finance Director: John N. Robinson, age 45,
$100,000 pay (partial-year salary)
Chief Executive Mining Zimbabwe: Mike Marriott
President, Bahamas Hotels: John Price
Managing Director Duiker Mining: Hugh Stoyell, age 55
Managing Director F.E. Wright: Ray Antell
Managing Director Platinum Division:
G. Edward Haslam, age 55
COO - Mining South Africa: Terence A. Wilkinson
Group Secretary (HR): Michael J. Pearce
Group Financial Controller: A. Bradshaw
Group Technical Director: Chris Davies
Auditors: KPMG Audit Plc

LOCATIONS

HQ: 4 Grosvenor Place, London SW1X 7YL,
United Kingdom
Phone: +44-20-7201-6000   **Fax:** +44-20-7201-6100
Web site: http://www.lonmin.com

Lonmin conducts its mining activities in Ghana, South
Africa, and Zimbabwe.

1999 Sales

	$ mil.	% of total
Africa		
South Africa	722	81
Zimbabwe & Ghana	54	6
North & South America	110	12
Europe	10	1
Total	**896**	**100**

PRODUCTS/OPERATIONS

1999 Sales

	$ mil.	% of total
Platinum	404	45
Gold	54	6
Discontinued operations	438	49
Total	**896**	**100**

Selected Operations

Mining and Refining
Ashanti Goldfields Company (33%, Ghana)
Duiker Mining Ltd. (68%, South Africa, coal)
Eastern Platinum Ltd. (73%, South Africa)
Independence Gold Mining (Pvt.) Ltd. (Zimbabwe)
Western Platinum Ltd. (73%, South Africa)

COMPETITORS

Anglo American	Kinross Gold
Anglogold	Phelps Dodge
Barrick Gold	Placer Dome
De Beers	Rio Tinto plc

HISTORICAL FINANCIALS & EMPLOYEES

OTC: LOMNY FYE: September 30	Annual Growth	9/90	9/91	9/92	9/93	9/94	9/95	9/96	9/97	9/98	9/99
Sales ($ mil.)	(23.5%)	10,042	8,287	6,979	4,039	3,098	3,267	3,192	3,226	1,706	896
Net income ($ mil.)	(5.9%)	225	58	75	168	80	122	145	229	66	130
Income as % of sales	—	2.2%	0.7%	1.1%	4.1%	2.6%	3.7%	4.6%	7.1%	3.9%	14.5%
Earnings per share ($)	108.1%	—	—	—	—	—	—	—	—	0.37	0.77
Stock price - FY high ($)	—	—	—	—	—	—	—	—	—	5.50	10.50
Stock price - FY low ($)	—	—	—	—	—	—	—	—	—	3.38	4.63
Stock price - FY close ($)	105.5%	—	—	—	—	—	—	—	—	5.05	10.38
P/E - high	—	—	—	—	—	—	—	—	—	15	14
P/E - low	—	—	—	—	—	—	—	—	—	9	6
Dividends per share ($)	0.3%	—	—	—	—	—	—	—	—	0.29	0.29
Book value per share ($)	11.7%	—	—	—	—	—	—	—	—	5.54	6.19
Employees	(12.7%)	108,759	113,094	106,309	99,309	127,450	121,012	94,881	73,779	55,382	32,027

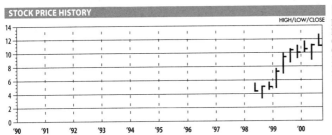

STOCK PRICE HISTORY HIGH/LOW/CLOSE

1999 FISCAL YEAR-END
Debt ratio: 15.0%
Return on equity: 14.0%
Cash ($ mil.): 110
Current ratio: 1.16
Long-term debt ($ mil.): 175
No. of shares (mil.): 160
Dividends
  Yield: 0.0%
  Payout: 0.4%
Market value ($ mil.): 1,657

L'ORÉAL SA

OVERVIEW

Beauty may only be skin deep, but fortunately for L'Oréal — the world's #1 cosmetics company — there's a lot of epidermis out there. Clichy, France-based L'Oréal makes makeup, perfume, and hair and skin care products for women as well as men. Its cosmetics generally fall under four divisions: Professional (salon hair care), Consumer (hair and skin care, makeup), Luxury (beauty products, fragrances), and Active Cosmetics (dermo-cosmetic products). Almost 90% of the company's sales come from ten brands: Biotherm, Laboratoires Garnier, Lancôme, L'Oréal, Maybelline, Redken, Helena Rubinstein, Vichy, and perfumes Giorgio Armani and Ralph Lauren.

Other subsidiaries include Galderma (dermatology products), a joint venture with Nestlé, and Sanofi-Synthélabo, a French pharmaceuticals group in which L'Oréal has a 19.5% stake. L'Oréal's Paris headquarters houses a large research department that employs more than 2,100 scientists and files for about 400 patents a year.

Liliane Bettencourt is L'Oréal's primary stockholder. She and her family own 51% of Gesparal, the holding company that owns 54% of L'Oréal. (Nestlé owns the remaining shares of Gesparal.)

HISTORY

Parisian Eugène Schueller, a chemist by trade, invented the first synthetic hair dye in 1907. Schueller quickly found a market for his products with local hairdressers and in 1909 established L'Oréal to pursue his growing hair products operation. The company's name came from its first hair color, Auréole (French for "aura of light").

L'Oréal expanded to include shampoos and soaps, all under the watchful direction of the energetic Schueller, who was known to taste hair creams to ensure that they were made up of the exact chemical composition that he required. In the 1920s the company began advertising on the radio (before its French competitors).

Demand for L'Oréal's products intensified after WWII. In 1953 the company formed licensee Cosmair to distribute its hair products to US beauty salons, and Cosmair soon offered L'Oréal's makeup and perfume as well. When Schueller died in 1957, control of L'Oréal passed to right-hand man François Dalle. Dalle carried L'Oréal's hair care products into the consumer market and overseas and sold its soap units in 1961. The next year it launched Elnett, a popular hairspray.

The company went public in 1963; Schueller's daughter, Liliane Bettencourt, retained a majority interest. Diversification came in 1965 with the acquisition of upscale French cosmetics maker Lancôme. A string of cosmetics acquisitions followed. L'Oréal entered the pharmaceuticals business in 1973 by purchasing Synthélabo. Bettencourt traded nearly half of her L'Oréal stock for a 3% stake in Swiss food producer Nestlé in 1974. L'Oréal purchased a minority stake in the publisher of French fashion magazine *Marie Claire* three years later.

During the 1980s L'Oréal vaulted from relative obscurity to become the world's #1 cosmetics company, largely through acquisitions. These included Warner Communications' cosmetics operations (Ralph Lauren and Gloria Vanderbilt brands, 1984), Helena Rubinstein (US beauty products, 1988), Laboratoires Pharmaeutiques Goupil (1988), and made its first major investment in Lanvin (1989). Englishman Lindsay Owen-Jones became CEO in 1988.

In 1989 L'Oréal stopped testing cosmetics on animals. Chairman Jacques Correze died in 1991 during another investigation into his Nazi war activities. (He had served five years in prison.) In 1994 the company purchased control of Cosmair from Nestlé and Bettencourt. It acquired two generic drug companies in 1995: Lichtenstein Pharmazeutica in Germany and Irex in France. That year L'Oréal became the #2 US cosmetics maker (behind Procter & Gamble, maker of Cover Girl and Max Factor) by buying #3 Maybelline for $508 million.

L'Oréal added subsidiaries in Japan and China (1996) and in Romania and Slovenia (1997). It also acquired sun protection brand Ombrelle (#2 in Canada) in 1997 and ethnic hair care products maker Soft Sheen Products in 1998. Also in 1998 L'Oréal's 57%-owned Synthélabo subsidiary merged with Elf Aquitaine's pharmaceuticals unit, Sanofi. L'Oréal retained a 19.5% stake in the newly formed pharmaceuticals group, Sanofi-Synthélabo.

L'Oréal began an acquisitive spring 2000, agreeing to acquire Carson (an ethnic beauty products maker); family-owned, prestige cosmetics company Kiehl's Since 1851; and salon products maker Matrix Essentials (from Bristol-Myers Squibb).

Chairman and CEO: Lindsay Owen-Jones
VC: Jean-Pierre Meyers
VP Administration and Finance: Michel Somnolet
VP Consumer Products Division: Patrick Rabain
VP Corporate Communications and Public Relations:
Jean-Pierre Valériola
VP Human Resources: François Vachey
VP Luxury Products Division: Gilles Weil
VP Production and Technology: Marcel Lafforgue
VP Professional Products Division:
Alain Leprince-Ringuet
VP Research and Development: Jean-François Grollier
President and CEO, Cosmair (US): Guy Peyrelongue
Auditors: Patrice de Maistre and Pierre Coll

HQ: 41, rue Martre, 92117 Clichy, France
Phone: +33-1-47-56-70-00   **Fax:** +33-1-47-56-80-02
US HQ: 575 5th Ave., New York, NY 10017
US Phone: 212-818-1500   **US Fax:** 212-984-4999
Web site: http://www.loreal.com

L'Oréal sells its products across the world, including the
Americas, Asia, and Europe.

1999 Sales

	$ mil.	% of total
Western Europe	5,995	55
North America	2,972	28
Other regions	1,837	17
Total	**10,804**	**100**

1999 Sales

	% of total
Consumer products	56
Perfumes & beauty	26
Salon	11
Active cosmetics	5
Other cosmetics	2
Total	**100**

Selected Brands

Biotherm	Lancôme
Giorgio Armani (fragrances only)	Lanvin (ready-to-wear fashion)
Gemey	L'Oréal
Guy Laroche (fragrances only)	Maybelline
	Plénitude
Helena Rubinstein	Ralph Lauren (fragrances only)
Inne	
Kérastase	Redken
La Roche-Posay	Vichy

Alberto-Culver	Mary Kay
Alticor	Merle Norman
Avon	Novartis
BeautiControl Cosmetics	Nu Skin
Body Shop	Perrigo
Chanel	Procter & Gamble
Clarins	Puig Beauty & Fashion
Estée Lauder	Revlon
Hoffmann-La Roche	Shiseido
Intimate Brands	Unilever
Johnson & Johnson	Wella
LVMH	Yves Saint-Laurent Groupe

OTC: LORLY FYE: December 31	Annual Growth	12/90	12/91	12/92	12/93	12/94	12/95	12/96	12/97	12/98	12/99
Sales ($ mil.)	6.8%	5,953	6,438	6,796	6,783	8,923	10,872	11,627	11,537	13,428	10,804
Net income ($ mil.)	9.2%	358	415	416	437	585	641	674	665	839	791
Income as % of sales	—	6.0%	6.4%	6.1%	6.4%	6.6%	5.9%	5.8%	5.8%	6.3%	7.3%
Earnings per share ($)	8.9%	0.11	0.14	0.14	0.15	0.19	0.22	0.21	0.21	0.25	0.25
Stock price - FY high ($)	—	1.87	2.63	3.80	4.22	4.26	5.02	7.46	8.70	14.25	16.25
Stock price - FY low ($)	—	1.52	1.63	2.37	3.21	3.53	3.63	4.91	6.50	7.15	12.00
Stock price - FY close ($)	28.4%	1.68	2.63	3.51	4.02	3.71	4.87	7.42	7.60	14.10	15.97
P/E - high	—	16	19	26	28	22	22	35	42	57	66
P/E - low	—	13	12	16	21	19	16	23	31	29	49
Dividends per share ($)	10.8%	0.03	0.03	0.04	0.04	0.05	0.05	0.05	0.05	0.06	0.07
Book value per share ($)	9.5%	0.74	0.85	0.87	0.92	1.34	1.56	1.66	1.62	1.88	1.67
Employees	4.1%	29,286	29,877	31,908	32,261	38,972	39,929	43,158	47,242	49,665	42,164

HIGH/LOW/CLOSE

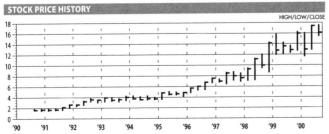

Debt ratio: 8.5%
Return on equity: 13.2%
Cash ($ mil.): 470
Current ratio: 1.14
Long-term debt ($ mil.): 528
No. of shares (mil.): 3,380
Dividends
  Yield: 0.0%
  Payout: 0.3%
Market value ($ mil.): 53,983

DEUTSCHE LUFTHANSA AG

OVERVIEW

Deutsche Lufthansa is in a dogfight with British Airways (BA) and other carriers in the European skies. Operating out of hubs in Frankfurt and Munich, the Cologne, Germany-based firm is Europe's #2 passenger airline (behind BA) and the world's #2 air cargo carrier behind FedEx. Counting code-sharing connections, the airline serves about 340 destinations in more than 90 countries.

Subsidiaries provide a range of transportation services, including catering, maintenance, and travel insurance services. Lufthansa also runs about 1,600 travel agency centers and owns a stake in Amadeus, one of the world's largest computerized airline reservation systems. In the cargo game, Lufthansa has combined its stake in delivery firm DHL with Deutsche Post's interest in the company; the new venture owns 50%

of DHL. Lufthansa is also making investments in Internet startups related to air freight and logistics, including its purchase of a 10% stake in Global Freight Exchange.

European airline deregulation, rising fuel prices, and air traffic constraints have applied pressure to Lufthansa's bottom line, but the carrier has still managed to turn a profit. It's even expanding its catering, ground services, and information technology operations.

The company is also riding high on the wings of the Star Alliance, the global marketing and code-sharing alliance that includes such major carriers as UAL's United, Air Canada, and All Nippon Airways. Member airlines share revenues on some routes, operate joint ticketing offices, and offer joint frequent-flier programs.

HISTORY

The Weimar government created Deutsche Luft Hansa (DLH) in 1926 by merging two private German airlines, Deutscher Aero Lloyd (founded in 1919) and Junkers Luftverkehr (established in 1921 by aircraft manufacturer Junkers Flugzeugwerke). DLH built what would become Europe's most comprehensive air route network by 1931. It served the USSR through Deruluft (formed 1921; dissolved 1941), an airline jointly owned by DLH and the Soviet government. In 1930 DLH and the Chinese government formed Eurasia Aviation Corporation to develop air transport in China.

DLH established the world's first transatlantic airmail service from Berlin to Buenos Aires in 1934 and went on to develop air transport throughout South America. The outbreak of WWII ended operations in Europe, and the Chinese government seized Eurasia Aviation in 1941. Klaus Bonhoeffer, head of DLH's legal department, led an unsuccessful coup against the Nazi leadership and was executed in 1945. Soon afterward all DLH operations ceased.

In 1954 the Allies allowed the recapitalization of Deutsche Lufthansa. The airline started with domestic routes, returned to London and Paris (1955), and then re-entered South America (1956). In 1958 it made its first non-stop flight between Germany and New York and initiated service to Tokyo and Cairo. Meanwhile, it started a charter airline with several partners in 1955. Lufthansa bought out its partners in 1959 and renamed the unit Condor two years later.

The carrier resumed service behind the Iron Curtain in 1966 with flights to Prague.

The stable West German economy helped Lufthansa maintain profitability through most of the 1970s.

The reunification of Germany in 1990 ended Allied control over Berlin airspace, allowing Lufthansa, which had bought Pan Am's Berlin routes, to fly there under its own colors for the first time since the end of WWII. The company began seeking international partners in 1991, but that year European air travel suffered its first-ever slowdown, forcing Lufthansa into the red for the first time since 1973.

The company restructured in 1994 into new business units: Lufthansa Technik, Lufthansa Cargo, and Lufthansa Systems. In 1995 it began to face increased domestic competition from Deutsche BA, a British Airways affiliate.

In 1997 the Star Alliance was formed, and Lufthansa signed a pact with Singapore Airlines. That year the German government sold its remaining 38% stake in Lufthansa. In 1998 Lufthansa and All Nippon Airways formed a code-sharing alliance, and Condor was combined with Karstadt's tour company NUR Touristik to form C&N Touristik.

In a plan to gain more access to London's Heathrow Airport, Lufthansa took a 20% stake in British Midland, which was admitted into the Star Alliance in 2000 along with Mexicana Airlines. That year Lufthansa Cargo and Deutsche Post created two joint ventures: Aerologic (management of the duo's joint 50% stake in DHL) and e-logic (e-commerce activities).

Chairman Supervisory Board: Klaus G. Schlede
Deputy Chairman Supervisory Board: Herbert Mai
Chairman: Jürgen Weber
CFO: Karl-Ludwig Kley
Chairman Condor Flugdienst: Dieter Heinen
Chairman Lufthansa Cargo: Jean-Peter Jansen
Chairman Lufthansa Technik: Wolfgang Mayrhuber
Chairman LSG Lufthansa Service Holding:
  Helmut Woelki
Chairman and Managing Director, Lufthansa Systems:
  Peter Franke
President and COO, Lufthansa German Airlines:
  Karl-Friedrich Rausch
Chief Executive Human Resources: Stefan Lauer
Auditors: PwC Deutsche Revision

LOCATIONS

HQ: Von-Gablenz-Strasse 2-6,
  D-50679 Cologne 21, Germany
Phone: +49-221-826-2444 **Fax:** +49-221-826-2286
US HQ: 1640 Hempstead Tpke., East Meadow, NY 11554
US Phone: 516-296-9200 **US Fax:** 516-296-9297
Web site: http://www.lufthansa.com

Deutsche Lufthansa serves about 340 destinations in
more than 90 countries.

1999 Destinations

	No.
Europe	
Germany	23
Other countries	123
America	124
Asia/Pacific	38
Africa & Middle East	32
Total	**340**

PRODUCTS/OPERATIONS

1999 Sales

	% of total
Lufthansa Passenger Airline	63
Lufthansa Cargo	16
Lufthansa Technik	7
Lufthansa CityLine	7
LSG Lufthansa Service	4
Other	3
Total	**100**

Selected Operations
C&N Touristic AG (50%, leisure travel services)
Delvag Luftfahrt-Versicherungs-AG (insurance)
Global Freight Exchange Ltd. (10%, online marketplace
  for air freight)
GlobeGround GmbH (airport ground services)
LSG Lufthansa Service Holding AG (LSG Sky Chefs,
  catering)
Lufthansa Cargo AG (cargo services)
Lufthansa CityLine GmbH (passenger airline)
Lufthansa Technik AG (technical services)

COMPETITORS

Accor	Cuisine	Northwest
Aer Lingus	Solutions	Airlines
Air France	Danzas	Otto Versand
Air Inter	Delta	Preussag
Airborne Freight	Deutsche Bahn	Qantas
AMR	DHL	Sabre
BAX Global	FedEx	SAirGroup
Braathens SAFE	Finnair	Swire Pacific
British Airways	Fritz	Travel Industry
Carlson	Iberia	Services
CNF	JAL	US Airways
Continental	KLM	Virgin Atlantic
Airlines	Liberty Travel	Airways

HISTORICAL FINANCIALS & EMPLOYEES

OTC: DLAKY FYE: December 31	Annual Growth	12/90	12/91	12/92	12/93	12/94	12/95	12/96	12/97	12/98	12/99
Sales ($ mil.)	3.2%	9,651	10,593	10,633	10,198	12,156	13,841	13,534	12,870	13,592	12,855
Net income ($ mil.)	63.9%	7	(287)	(243)	(58)	189	1,020	359	464	858	633
Income as % of sales	—	0.1%	—	—	—	1.6%	7.4%	2.7%	3.6%	6.3%	4.9%
Employees	1.6%	57,567	61,791	49,292	46,818	58,044	57,586	57,999	58,250	54,867	66,207

STOCK PRICE HISTORY

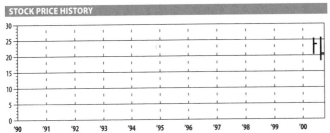

1999 FISCAL YEAR-END

Debt ratio: 38.4%
Return on equity: 16.7%
Cash ($ mil.): 226
Current ratio: 1.93
Long-term debt ($ mil.): 2,311

OAO LUKOIL

OVERVIEW

Many Russians look to LUKOIL for their oil and gas needs. LUKOIL, based in Moscow, is Russia's leading integrated oil company, producing 24% of the nation's crude oil. The company's proved reserves of 13.5 billion barrels of oil and 3.9 trillion cu. ft. of gas, primarily in western Siberia, exceed those controlled by Royal Dutch/Shell (10 billion barrels). The company is Russia's #2 company behind natural gas monopoly Gazprom.

LUKOIL is trying to transform itself from a top-heavy, bureaucratic enterprise into a decentralized, entrepreneurial company with hopes of competing in free markets. It has consolidated its large subsidiaries into two branches: one for exploration and production, the other for refining and marketing.

The company operates three refineries in Russia, one in the Ukraine, and one in Bulgaria. It also runs 1,100 gas stations, both in Russia as well as in the Baltic States and Central and Eastern Europe. Overall, LUKOIL has operations in 40 regions within Russia and 25 countries. It explores for oil and gas in Azerbaijan, Egypt, Iraq, Kazakhstan, and other areas in the Middle East and central Asia. Some 30% of its reserves are located outside of Russia.

With an appetite for expansion, the company is upping its production with refinery acquisitions, and is investing heavily in new oil patches, such as the Caspian Sea. And LUKOIL is moving into the US with its agreement to purchase Getty Petroleum Marketing.

Executives and employees own about 20% of LUKOIL. The Russian government owns 15%.

HISTORY

LUKOIL was the result of three major state-owned oil and gas exploration companies — Langepasneftegaz, Uraineftegaz, and Kogalymneftegaz — that had activities in Siberia and traced their origins to the discovery of oil in western Siberia in 1964. More than 25 years later, after the Soviet Union broke up, the oil and gas sector was one of the first industries marked for privatization.

In 1992 the Russian government called for Langepasneftegaz, Uraineftegaz, and Kogalymneftegaz to merge. LUKOIL was created in 1993 to hold the oil production enterprises. (The LUK of LUKOIL comes from the initials of the three companies.) Former Russian president Boris Yeltsin appointed Siberian oil veteran Vagit Alekperov as the firm's first president. The Russian government also formed several other large integrated oil companies, including Yukos, Surgutneftegaz, Sidanco, and Sibneft.

The holding company created LUKOIL Financial Company in 1994, which managed the oil products sector. LUKOIL went public on the fledgling Russian Trading System in 1994, and LUKOIL Financial was integrated into LUKOIL the next year.

During 1995 LUKOIL absorbed nine other enterprises, including oil exploration firms Astrakhanneft, Kaliningradmorneftegaz, and Permneft. That year it became the first Russian oil company to set up an exploration and production trading arm. In 1996 LUKOIL acquired a 41% stake in *Izvestia,* Russia's major independent newspaper.

Chevron and LUKOIL, with seven other oil and gas companies and three governments, agreed in 1996 to build a 1,500-kilometer pipeline to link the Kazakhstan oil fields to world markets.

In 1997 LUKOIL became the first Russian corporation to sell bonds to international investors, and the government announced plans to sell 15% of its stake in the firm. That year LUKOIL's 50%-owned Nexus Fuels unit opened its first gas stations located in the parking lots of US grocery stores (the partnership dissolved and Nexus went bankrupt in 2000).

LUKOIL began a partnership with DuPont's Conoco in 1998 to develop oil and natural gas reserves in Russia's northern territories. LUKOIL also acquired 51% of Romania's Petrorel refinery. In 1999 it acquired control of refineries in Bulgaria and Ukraine and a petrochemical firm in Saratov. It also acquired oil company KomiTEK in one of Russia's largest mergers.

The government sold a 9% stake in LUKOIL to a Cyprus-based unit, Reforma Investments, held in part by LUKOIL's "boss of bosses," Vagit Alekperov (gained at the bargain price of $200 million). Critics cited the sale as Yeltsin's bid to gain Alekperov's political support.

The company announced the first major oil find in the Russian part of the Caspian Sea in 2000, and formed a joint venture (Caspian Oil Company) with fellow Russian energy giants Yukos and Gazprom to exploit Caspian resources. Also that year, LUKOIL announced its intent to buy Getty Petroleum Marketing, a firm with more than 1,300 gas stations on the East Coast of the US.

Chairman: Valery Graifer, age 70
President: Vagit Y. Alekperov, age 49
First VP Downstream: Ralif R. Safin, age 46
First VP Upstream: Ravil U. Maganov, age 46
First VP Economics and Finance: Sergei P. Kukura, age 47
VP Finances and Investments: Alexander K. Matytsin, age 39
VP Administration, Social Development, and Human Resources: Anatoly A. Barkov, age 52
VP Economics and Planning: Anantoly G. Kozyrev
VP; General Director LUKOIL Trading House: Alexander S. Smirnov, age 52
VP Oil and Gas Production: Vitaly F. Lesnitchi, age 61
VP Petroleum Product Marketing and Sales: Vagit S. Sharifov, age 55
VP Oil Refining: Vladislav P. Bazhenov, age 62
Chief Accounting Officer: Lubov Khoba
Auditors: KPMG

HQ: 11 Sretenski Blvd., 101000 Moscow, Russia
Phone: +7-095-927-4444   **Fax:** +7-095-928-9841
Web site: http://www.lukoil.com

LUKOIL explores for oil and gas in a number of Central Asian and Middle Eastern countries, including Azerbaijan, Egypt, Iraq, Kazakhstan, and Russia.

1999 Sales

	% of total
Russia	
European region	50
West Siberia	11
Other countries	39
Total	**100**

1999 Sales

	% of total
Refining, supplies, marketing & transportation	75
Exploration & production	22
Petrochemicals & other activities	3
Total	**100**

Selected Subsidiaries

Refining, Supplies, Marketing, and Transportation
OAO LUKOIL Ukhtaneftepererabotka (refining)
OOO LUKOIL Kirovnefteprodukt (marketing)
OOO LUKOIL Permnefteorgsintez (refining)
OOO LUKOIL Permnefteprodukt (marketing)
OOO LUKOIL Volgogradnefteprodukt (marketing)

Exploration and Production
OAO KomiTEK
OOO LUKOIL Western Siberia
ZAO LUKOIL Perm

Other
LUKOIL International GmbH
OAO LUKOIL Arktik Tanker (shipping)
ZAO LUKOIL Neftekhim (petrochemicals)

Ashland	PEMEX	Surgutneftegaz
BP	PETROBRAS	Tatneft
Chevron	Phillips	Texaco
Elf Aquitaine	Petroleum	TOTAL FINA
Exxon Mobil	Rosneft	ELF
Imperial Oil	Royal	Tyumen Oil
Norsk Hydro	Dutch/Shell	Union Carbide
Occidental	Sibneft	Unocal
PDVSA	Sidanco Oil	Yukos

OTC: LUKOY FYE: December 31	Annual Growth	12/90	12/91	12/92	12/93	12/94	12/95	12/96	12/97	12/98	12/99
Sales ($ mil.)	10.6%	—	—	—	5,341	5,002	6,711	8,200	9,003	3,960	9,757
Net income ($ mil.)	(10.4%)	—	—	—	2,165	1,040	546	716	303	6	1,120
Income as % of sales	—	—	—	—	40.5%	20.8%	8.1%	8.7%	3.4%	0.1%	11.5%
Earnings per share ($)	16.2%	—	—	—	—	—	—	3.87	1.62	0.03	6.07
Stock price - FY high ($)	—	—	—	—	—	—	—	49.75	118.00	93.13	55.00
Stock price - FY low ($)	—	—	—	—	—	—	—	16.00	46.75	8.75	13.75
Stock price - FY close ($)	2.0%	—	—	—	—	—	—	47.12	91.50	15.75	50.00
P/E - high	—	—	—	—	—	—	—	13	73	2,739	9
P/E - low	—	—	—	—	—	—	—	4	29	257	2
Dividends per share ($)	6.2%	—	—	—	—	—	—	0.36	0.20	0.05	0.43
Book value per share ($)	36.2%	—	—	—	—	—	—	5.91	4.83	12.53	14.92
Employees	5.5%	—	—	—	86,900	82,900	119,824	94,236	107,000	90,000	120,000

HIGH/LOW/CLOSE

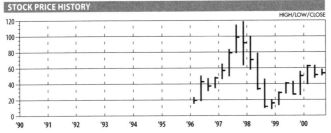

Debt ratio: 46.2%
Return on equity: 46.2%
Cash ($ mil.): 362
Current ratio: 1.33
Long-term debt ($ mil.): 2,360
No. of shares (mil.): 185
Dividends
  Yield: 0.0%
  Payout: 0.1%
Market value ($ mil.): 9,229

LVMH

OVERVIEW

Frenchman Bernard Arnault is a skilled pianist, but he is most adept at playing in luxury goods. Through several investment groups and companies (including Christian Dior), the aggressive businessman owns 47% of Paris-based LVMH Moët Hennessy Louis Vuitton, one of the world's largest luxury goods conglomerates. Arnault makes no secret of his desire to increase LVMH's holdings.

LVMH's armoire includes fashion houses (Christian Lacroix, Givenchy, and Kenzo), perfumes by the same chic names, luxury watches (Ebel, TAG Heuer), and leather goods (Louis Vuitton, Loewe). Arnault's Christian Dior makes the Dior fashion line separately from LVMH. The LVMH liquor cabinet contains only the best: Moët & Chandon, Dom Pérignon, and Hennessy (#1 cognac worldwide), among other wines and spirits.

The company has been focusing on controlling as much of its distribution as possible. In addition to selling online, it now has more than 1,000 retail outlets, including 260-plus Vuitton stores, DFS Group duty-free shops (61%-owned), Le Bon Marché, and hundreds of designer boutiques. Its Sephora self-serve cosmetics and fragrance chain boasts more than 300 stores.

HISTORY

Woodworker Louis Vuitton started his Paris career packing dresses for French Empress Eugenie. He later designed new types of luggage, and in 1854 he opened a store to sell his designs. In 1896 Vuiton introduced the LV monogram fabric that the company still uses. By 1900 Louis Vuitton had stores in the US and England, and by WWI Louis' son, Georges, had the world's largest retail store for travel goods.

Henry Racamier, a former steel executive who had married into the Vuitton family, took charge in 1977, repositioning the company's goods from esoteric status symbols to designer must-haves. Sales soared from $20 million to nearly $2.5 billion within a decade. Concerned about being a takeover target, Racamier merged Louis Vuitton in 1987 with Moët Hennessy (which made wines, spirits, and fragrances) and adopted the name LVMH Moët Hennessy Louis Vuitton.

Moët Hennessy had been formed through the 1971 merger of Moët et Chandon (the world's #1 champagne maker) and the Hennessy Cognac company (founded by Irish mercenary Richard Hennessy in 1765). Moët Hennessy acquired rights to Christian Dior fragrances in 1971.

Almost immediately Racamier and chairman Alain Chevalier disagreed about running LVMH. Racamier tried to reverse the merger and sought support in 1987 from outside investor Bernard Arnault (who already controlled the Dior fashion operations), inviting him to increase his interest in the company. Arnault gained control of 43% of LVMH and became chairman in 1989. Chevalier stepped down, but Racamier fought for control for another 18 months and then set up Orcofi, a partner of cosmetics rival L'Oréal.

LVMH bought the Givenchy Couture Group in 1988 and increased its fashion holdings with the 1993 purchases of Christian Lacroix and Kenzo couture and ready-to-wear operations (both from another Arnault company, Bon Marché).

In 1996 LVMH bought Celine fashions from Bon Marché, as well as the renowned Château d'Yquem winery and DFS Group (duty-free stores). Next LVMH bought France's #1 and #2 perfume chains, Sephora (1997) and Marie-Jeanne Godard (1998), giving it 20% of the French perfumery market. In 1998 LVMH integrated prestigious Paris department store Le Bon Marché, which was controlled by Arnault.

LVMH swiftly accumulated a 34% stake in Italian luxury goods maker Gucci in early 1999 and announced it wanted to buy all of it. But in a battle worthy of Italian opera, fellow French conglomerate Pinault-Printemps-Redoute thwarted LVMH by purchasing 42% of Gucci, which reduced LVMH's stake to 20%.

Through its newly formed LV Capital unit, in 1999 LVMH began acquiring stakes in a host of companies involved in everything from cosmetics to luxury shirts. One of the more unusual moves included a joint venture with fashion company Prada to buy 51% of design house Fendi. Also in 1999 LVMH added the Ebel, Chaumet, and TAG Heuer brands to its new watch division.

In early 2000 LVMH increased its distribution network by buying Miami Cruiseline Services, which operates duty-free shops on cruise ships. It also acquired L'Etude Tajan, France's #1 auction house (to go with its 1999 purchase of leading international auctioneer Phillips), as well as 67% of Italian fashion house Emilio Pucci. In late 2000 the company purchased 35% of Micromania, a French video game retailer with 100 stores.

OFFICERS

Chairman and CEO: Bernard Arnault
VC: Antoine Bernheim
Adviser to the Chairman and CEO: Pierre Gode
Executive Committee, Development and Acquisitions: Nicholas Bazire
Executive Committee, Fashion and Leather Goods: Yves Carcelle
Executive Committee Finance: Patrick Houel
Executive Committee Fragrances & Cosmetics: Patrick Choel
Executive Committee Human Resources: Concetta Lanciaux
Executive Committee Watches & Jewelry: Christian Viros
Executive Committee Wine & Spirits: Philippe Pascal
Chairman and CEO, Celine: Thierry Andretta, age 41
Auditors: Cogerco-Flipo; Ernst & Young Audit

LOCATIONS

HQ: LVMH Moët Hennessy Louis Vuitton SA,
30 avenue Hoche, 75008 Paris, France
Phone: +33-1-44-13-22-22   **Fax:** +33-1-44-13-21-19
US HQ: 19 E. 57th St., New York, NY 10022
US Phone: 212-931-2700   **US Fax:** 212-931-2730
Web site: http://www.lvmh.com

1999 Sales

	% of total
Europe	
France	41
Other countries	12
Asia	
Japan	11
Other countries	15
US	17
Other regions	4
Total	**100**

PRODUCTS/OPERATIONS

1999 Sales

	% of total
Fashion & leather goods	27
Selective retailing	25
Fragrances & cosmetics	20
Champagne & wines	18
Cognac & spirits	8
Other	2
Total	**100**

Selected Brands and Operations

Chandon Estates (wine)
Dom Pérignon (champagne)
Ebel (watches and jewelry)
Fendi (fashion, 51% in joint venture with Prada)
Givenchy (fashion)
Hennessy (cognac)
Le Bon Marché (retailer)
Louis Vuitton (leather goods)
Miami Cruiseline Services (duty-free shops)
Micromania (35%, video games)
Moët & Chandon (champagne)
Parfums Christian Dior
Parfums Givenchy
Sephora (online retailer)
TAG Heuer (watches and jewelry)

COMPETITORS

Allied Domecq	Hermès	Seagram
Brown-Forman	L'Oréal	Shiseido
Calvin Klein	Polo	Tiffany
Chanel	Prada	Yves Saint-
Estée Lauder	Puig Beauty &	Laurent Groupe
Gianni Versace	Fashion	
Gucci	Remy Cointreau	

HISTORICAL FINANCIALS & EMPLOYEES

Nasdaq: LVMHY FYE: December 31	Annual Growth	12/90	12/91	12/92	12/93	12/94	12/95	12/96	12/97	12/98	12/99
Sales ($ mil.)	9.2%	3,896	4,254	3,921	4,031	5,238	6,071	6,007	7,974	8,126	8,589
Net income ($ mil.)	0.5%	663	721	544	605	1,203	825	711	752	313	696
Income as % of sales	—	17.0%	17.0%	13.9%	15.0%	23.0%	13.6%	11.8%	9.4%	3.9%	8.1%
Earnings per share ($)	(2.5%)	0.39	0.39	0.29	0.33	0.22	0.38	0.33	0.37	0.14	0.31
Stock price - FY high ($)	—	7.69	6.44	6.76	6.16	6.75	8.38	11.25	11.43	9.35	18.30
Stock price - FY low ($)	—	4.76	4.86	5.06	4.50	5.01	5.95	8.18	6.03	5.10	8.25
Stock price - FY close ($)	14.9%	5.21	6.40	5.26	5.11	6.30	8.38	11.20	6.63	8.15	18.20
P/E - high	—	19	16	23	19	31	22	34	31	67	59
P/E - low	—	12	12	17	14	23	16	25	16	36	27
Dividends per share ($)	7.1%	0.07	0.07	0.08	0.07	0.08	0.10	0.14	0.10	0.15	0.13
Book value per share ($)	4.2%	1.91	1.96	1.89	2.01	2.61	2.90	3.06	3.06	3.33	2.75
Employees	11.6%	14,272	14,650	15,501	14,874	15,826	15,686	15,426	32,300	33,000	38,282

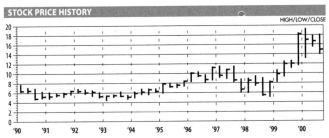

STOCK PRICE HISTORY
HIGH/LOW/CLOSE

1999 FISCAL YEAR-END

Debt ratio: 34.2%
Return on equity: 9.8%
Cash ($ mil.): 548
Current ratio: 0.92
Long-term debt ($ mil.): 3,508
No. of shares (mil.): 2,449
Dividends
 Yield: 0.7%
 Payout: 41.9%
Market value ($ mil.): 44,571

MAN AKTIENGESELLSCHAFT

This company really is da MAN when it comes to making commercial buses and trucks, ships, printing presses, engines, and mining equipment. Munich-based MAN Aktiengesellschaft is the holding company for the MAN Group, one of Europe's largest capital goods producers. Europe accounts for about two-thirds of MAN's sales, and the company is near the top of the heap in most of the markets in which it competes.

MAN Nutzfahrzeuge, the group's commercial vehicles business, accounts for about 35% of sales. Its primary activity is production of commercial trucks (6 to 50 tons) and buses. Other operations include manufacturing engines for vehicles, boats, and power plants, and fleet management. Ferrostaal is the group's next largest company. Its diverse industrial services include facility engineering and management, the construction of steel structures, and steel and metal trading.

MAN is also a leading maker of printing machines. Its MAN Roland Druckmaschinen segment manufactures printing machines such as web-fed offset presses for newspapers and books and sheet-fed offset presses for business printing and packaging. Another major company, MAN B&W Diesel is a world-leading maker of diesel engines for marine propulsion and power plants.

The MAN Group's industrial equipment and facilities segment includes seven main companies. These produce compressors and turbines for processing and power generation, aerospace components and lightweight bridges, automatic transmissions, and industrial gear units. The companies also make mining and materials-handling equipment and plant construction equipment. Other products include specialty boats (dredgers); salt-operated reactors (for the chemical industry); calendar rolls for paper machines; and plastics, steel, and nonferrous metal-processing equipment.

The MAN Group has been selling peripheral operations while boosting its core businesses through acquisitions. MAN's primary business, commercial vehicles, is in the midst of an industrywide consolidation in Europe. The MAN Group's MAN Nutzfahrzeuge (commercial vehicles) is considered a target, but MAN wants to maintain control of the division and has shown interest in buying other vehicle manufacturers. About two-thirds of MAN's executive pay is based on rate-of-return performance measures.

Carl August Reichenbach and Carl Buz leased an engineering plant in Augsburg, Germany, in 1844 and created MAN Aktiengesellschaft. Reichenbach, whose uncle had invented the flatbed printing press, began producing printing presses in 1845. On the same premises, Buz began manufacturing steam engines and industrial drive systems, and he soon added rotary printing presses, water turbines, pumps, and diesel engines. In 1898 the company took the name MAN (Maschinenfabrik Augsburg-Nurnberg) after merging with a German engineering company of the same name.

Another German heavy-industry company, Gutehoffnungshutte Aktienverein AG (GHH, with roots stretching to 1758), bought a majority interest in MAN in 1921. Through acquisitions and internal growth MAN emerged from the world wars as one of Germany's major heavy-industry companies, with added interests in commercial vehicles, shipbuilding, and plant construction. By 1955 MAN's commercial vehicles were a major division that would later grow to dominate the company's sales; MAN moved the division's headquarters to Munich that year.

During the 1970s an overseas recession caused the sales of some operations to slump, although MAN's commercial vehicles and printing-equipment businesses held steady. When economic hardship reached Europe in the 1980s, MAN sought markets outside its home region, especially targeting Asia, the Middle East, and the US. Late in the decade the company dropped its less-profitable products (lifts, pumps, heavy cranes) and began licensing more of its technology and subcontracting out more work. MAN moved its corporate headquarters to Munich in 1985 and merged with GHH in 1986.

After a fast start in the 1990s, Europe's economy again faltered and it began to take a toll on the company's sales. MAN's profits slumped in fiscal 1994. It laid off about 10% of its workforce between 1993 and 1995. As the economy recovered, so did MAN, so that by fiscal 1998, its stagnant profits had rebounded. Amid a consolidation trend among vehicle manufacturers, MAN acquired Polish truck maker Star in 1999. Rumors surfaced that year concerning MAN's interest in acquiring Daewoo's truck operations, as well as those of Fiat and Renault.

In 2000 MAN agreed to acquire Alstom's diesel engine business, maker of Mirrlees Blackstone, Paxman, and Ruston brand engines.

OFFICERS

Chairman of the Supervisory Board: Klaus Goette
Deputy Chairman of the Supervisory Board:
Gerlinde Strauss-Wieczorek
Deputy Chairman of the Supervisory Board:
Henning Schulte-Noelle
Chairman of the Executive Board: Rudolf Rupprecht
Member of the Executive Board; Chairman Ferrostaal:
Klaus von Menges
Member of the Executive Board; Chairman MAN B&W Diesel: Hans-Juergen Schulte
Member of the Executive Board; Chairman MAN Nutzfahrzeuge: Klaus Schubert
Member of the Executive Board Controlling:
Philipp J. Zahn
Member of the Executive Board Finances:
Ferdinand Graf Von Ballestrem
Auditors: BDO Deutsche Warentreuhand AG

LOCATIONS

HQ: Ungererstrasse 69, D-80805 Munich, Germany
Phone: +49-89-3-60-98-0   **Fax:** +49-89-3-60-98-2-50
Web site: http://www.ag.man.de

2000 Sales

	€ mil.	% of total
Europe		
Germany	4,418	30
Other countries	5,481	37
The Americas	2,169	15
Asia & Australia	1,693	12
Africa	820	6
Total	**14,581**	**100**

PRODUCTS/OPERATIONS

2000 Sales

	€ mil.	% of total
Commercial vehicles	5,712	39
Industrial services	2,474	17
Industrial systems & facilities	1,785	12
Printing machines	1,066	7
Diesel engines	3,415	24
Other	129	1
Total	**14,581**	**100**

Selected Products and Services
Buses and coaches
Diesel engines for marine propulsion and power plants
Engines for vehicles, boats, and power generation
Equipment for plant construction and shipbuilding
Exhaust gas turbochargers
Facility construction and contracting
Industrial compressors and turbines
Industrial gear units
Materials-handling equipment
Mining equipment
Offset printing presses
Plant and rolling-mill equipment
Plastics-processing equipment
Power generation compressors and turbines
Pressing and forging equipment
Space transport propulsion components and systems
Steel structure assembly
Transport logistics and fleet management
Trucks (6 to 50 tons gross weight)

COMPETITORS

Alstom	Fiat	Renault
Cummins	Goss Holdings	Scania
Engine	Navistar	USX
DaimlerChrysler	PACCAR	Volvo

HISTORICAL FINANCIALS & EMPLOYEES

German: MAN FYE: June 30	Annual Growth	6/91	6/92	6/93	6/94	6/95	6/96	6/97	6/98	6/99	6/00
Sales (€ mil.)	4.6%	9,730	9,802	9,608	9,277	9,511	10,364	10,918	12,677	13,256	14,581
Net income (€ mil.)	8.0%	195	209	113	77	131	155	164	292	371	389
Income as % of sales	—	2.0%	2.1%	1.2%	0.8%	1.4%	1.5%	1.5%	2.3%	2.8%	2.7%
Earnings per share (€)	32.3%	—	—	—	0.47	1.16	1.33	1.22	1.99	2.23	2.52
Stock price - FY high (€)	—	—	—	—	24.03	23.29	22.93	28.17	38.04	41.11	39.95
Stock price - FY low (€)	—	—	—	—	19.58	16.51	18.05	17.77	23.83	20.60	28.00
Stock price - FY close (€)	8.3%	—	—	—	20.12	18.18	19.51	27.76	35.89	33.00	32.50
P/E - high	—	—	—	—	51	20	17	23	19	18	16
P/E - low	—	—	—	—	42	14	14	15	12	9	11
Dividends per share (€)	18.6%	—	—	—	0.36	0.49	0.61	0.72	0.82	0.92	1.00
Book value per share (€)	7.1%	—	—	—	11.40	11.80	12.30	12.60	14.00	15.43	17.20
Employees	2.5%	—	—	62,720	58,527	56,503	57,826	62,564	64,054	66,838	74,324

STOCK PRICE HISTORY

HIGH/LOW/CLOSE

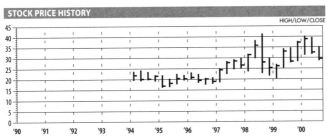

2000 FISCAL YEAR-END

Debt ratio: 2.3%
Return on equity: 14.0%
Cash (€ mil.): 457
Current ratio: 2.03
Long-term debt (€ mil.): 68
No. of shares (mil.): 110
Dividends
  Yield: 0.0%
  Payout: 0.4%
Market value ($ mil.): 3,412
Sales ($ mil.): 13,881

MANNESMANN AG

Bells are ringing for Mannesmann. The Dusseldorf, Germany-based group, which made its fortune in steel tubes and auto parts, is now hearkening to the call of telecommunications. Its telecom operations have proved to be an irresistible lure for Vodafone, the world's #1 mobile phone company by subscribers, and Mannesmann — after putting up fierce resistance — has been acquired. Vodafone owns 99% of the company.

What did Vodafone get? For starters, Mannesmann's D2 mobile phone network, which has surpassed Deutsche Telekom to become #1 in Germany, with more than 13 million subscribers. A Mannesmann-led consortium controls Mannesmann Arcor,

a fixed-line telecom venture that is #2 in Germany (behind Deutsche Telekom).

Mannesmann also provides Internet access in Germany through the Arcor, o.tel.o, and germany.net brands. Vodafone also was attracted to Mannesmann's telecom investments in Italy: #2 mobile phone operator Omnitel and fixed-line carrier Infostrada.

Even before Vodafone offered to buy the company, Mannesmann had announced plans to separate its telecom and industrial operations. Its automotive units (VDO and Sachs) and engineering divisions (Rexroth, Dematic, and Demag Krauss-Maffei) have been brought together as Atecs Mannesmann, which a Siemens-Robert Bosch joint venture has agreed to buy.

HISTORY

Reinhard and Max Mannesmann were working at their father's file factory in Germany when they devised a rolling process to make seamless steel tubes in 1885. The brothers started several tube mills and by 1890 had perfected the process of manufacturing tubes using a solid ingot. That year, with financing from the Siemens family, the Mannesmanns merged the mills into Deutsch-Osterreichische Mannesmannrohren-Werke. The brothers retired in 1893 and sold their stock in 1900.

Backed by Deutsche Bank, the firm moved into Austria, Italy, Silesia, and the UK, and it formed its first trading company in Buenos Aires in 1908. Dependence on suppliers led Mannesmann to vertically integrate, buying mines and raw steel factories in the 1920s. WWI and WWII cost the company its foreign assets twice since most of its plants were destroyed. The Allies divided Mannesmann into three separate businesses, but the units recovered and reunited in 1955.

Increased oil demand boosted the pipe business in the 1950s and 1960s. Faced with state-subsidized competition in world steel markets, Mannesmann restructured and exited its German mining operations. It bought 50% of G. L. Rexroth, which became a leader in hydraulics, in 1968 (and the rest in 1975). It also bought Demag (machinery, 1972), Fichtel & Sachs (clutches and suspensions, 1987), and Krauss-Maffei (plastics, 1990).

The firm set up Mannesmann Mobilfunk (mobile phones) in 1989. Cheap steel from Eastern Europe and the Soviet market's collapse caused a steep decline in orders. In response, the company focused on telecommunications. A 1994 news story alleging that the firm's

chairman Werner Dieter had committed fraud led to his resignation that year. Dieter agreed in 1996 to pay a massive fine to avoid a trial.

State-owned railway Deutsche Bahn chose Mannesmann in 1996 to lead a consortium to develop the telecom network of its DBKOM unit. The next year Mannesmann took a 25% stake in OliMan, a venture with Olivetti that owned part of Italy's wireless carrier Omnitel. It also took a 15% stake in #2 French carrier Cegetel and in 1998 bought nearly 75% of Austrian carrier tele.ring.

In 1999 the company joined with Vodafone AirTouch to buy Cellular Communications International, which held a stake in Omnitel. To help Olivetti finance its takeover of Telecom Italia, Mannesmann bought Olivetti's Infostrada and Omnitel stakes. Mannesmann also acquired UK mobile phone operator Orange.

Mannesmann's move into the UK angered Vodafone AirTouch (now Vodafone), which then launched a hostile bid to buy the company. After fighting to remain independent, Mannesmann was acquired in 2000 in a $180 billion stock deal. As a condition of the takeover, Vodafone had to find a buyer for Orange, and France Telecom was only too happy to step forward.

Also that year Mannesmann brought its automotive and engineering operations together under the Atecs Mannesmann umbrella. The company proposed to sell shares in Atecs Mannesmann to the public, but it agreed instead to sell the unit to a Siemens-Robert Bosch joint venture for $9.2 billion. It also agreed to sell its tubes business to Salzgitter.

Chairman of the Supervisory Board: Chris Gent
Chairman of the Executive Board: Julian Horn-Smith
Deputy Chairman of the Executive Board:
  Thomas Geitner
Member of the Executive Board: Albert Weismüller
Auditors: KPMG Deutsche Treuhand-Gesellschaft

HQ: Postfach 10 36 41, D-40027 Dusseldorf, Germany
Phone: +49-211-820-0   **Fax:** +49-211-820-18-46
US HQ: 450 Park Ave., New York, NY 10022
US Phone: 212-826-0040   **US Fax:** 212-826-0074
Web site: http://www.mannesmann.com

1999 Sales

	% of total
Europe	
Germany	46
Other EU	29
Other countries	3
North America	14
Latin America	3
Asia	
China	1
Other countries	2
Africa	1
Australia and other regions	1
Total	**100**

1999 Sales

	% of total
Engineering and automotive	53
Telecommunications	39
Tubes and other	8
Total	**100**

Selected Operations
Brueninghaus Hydromatik GmbH (engineering)
DMV Stainless BV (tubes, 33%, The Netherlands)
Fichtel & Sachs Industries, Inc. (automotive, US)
Krauss-Maffei AG (engineering)
Mannesmann Arcor AG & Co. (telecommunications)
Mannesmann Eurokom GmbH (telecommunications)
Mannesmann Mobilfunk (telecommunications, D2)
Mannesmann Pipe & Steel Corporation (US)
Mannesmann Pressfitting GmbH
Mannesmann Sachs AG (automotive)
Mannesmann Rexroth Corporation (engineering, US)
Uchida Hydraulics Co. Ltd. (51%, Japan)
VDO Control Systems, Inc. (automotive, US)

ABB	Marubeni
Bechtel	Nippon Steel
BorgWarner	Olivetti
BT	One 2 One
Debitel	Robert Bosch
Deutsche Telekom	RWE
E.ON	Siemens
Eaton	Telecom Italia
Fluor	ThyssenKrupp
France Telecom	TIM
Honeywell International	USX-U.S. Steel
LTV	Vodafone

OTC: MNNSY FYE: December 31	Annual Growth	12/90	12/91	12/92	12/93	12/94	12/95	12/96	12/97	12/98	12/99
Sales ($ mil.)	4.3%	15,994	15,997	17,282	16,083	19,617	22,322	22,500	21,736	19,784	23,377
Net income ($ mil.)	5.4%	310	193	39	(295)	219	488	391	339	654	499
Income as % of sales	—	1.9%	1.2%	0.2%	—	1.1%	2.2%	1.7%	1.6%	3.3%	2.1%
Earnings per share ($)	7.1%	1.00	0.79	0.37	(0.52)	0.97	1.46	1.43	1.45	2.23	1.85
Stock price - FY high ($)	—	23.74	19.81	19.95	24.71	29.63	34.06	43.20	51.80	117.00	246.00
Stock price - FY low ($)	—	14.54	12.71	12.78	14.32	24.18	25.31	32.40	36.80	52.80	124.00
Stock price - FY close ($)	34.0%	17.48	16.16	14.59	23.61	27.23	31.91	42.80	51.80	116.00	244.00
P/E - high	—	24	25	54	—	31	23	30	36	52	133
P/E - low	—	15	16	35	—	25	17	23	25	24	67
Dividends per share ($)	0.2%	0.60	0.59	0.37	0.29	0.39	0.56	0.58	0.56	0.71	0.61
Book value per share ($)	17.1%	11.69	11.78	10.67	9.78	12.46	13.82	13.60	13.27	16.93	48.25
Employees	0.6%	123,997	124,315	128,018	127,963	124,914	122,684	119,709	120,859	116,247	130,860

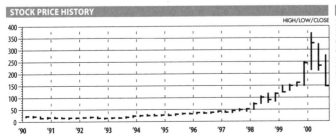

HIGH/LOW/CLOSE

Debt ratio: 37.1%
Return on equity: 3.3%
Cash ($ mil.): 951
Current ratio: 2.48
Long-term debt ($ mil.): 14,087
No. of shares (mil.): 494
Dividends
  Yield: 0.0%
  Payout: 0.3%
Market value ($ mil.): 120,567

MARCONI PLC

OVERVIEW

The identity crisis for The General Electric Company (GEC) has finally come to an end. Often confused with the US's General Electric, London-based GEC has changed its name to Marconi plc. The name change is the finishing touch on the company's transformation from defense industry conglomerate to its new role as an information technology company.

Marconi's business mix includes sprawling operations in industrial electronics and communications, with products ranging from telecommunications equipment to appliances. It also produces medical imaging equipment, petroleum retail equipment, and weighing systems.

Marconi has beefed up its data communications presence in the US with the purchases of RELTEC (access technology) and FORE Systems (broadband switching). It has sold its defense electronics business to British Aerospace (now BAE SYSTEMS) and is exiting an appliance joint venture it shares with the other General Electric. The big change at Marconi is the brainchild of CEO George Simpson, who intends to make his company more like the US's GE.

HISTORY

Hugo Hirst and Gustav Byng started an electrical equipment wholesale business in London in 1886. By 1889 The General Electric Company (GEC) was making bells, switches, and telephones. Soon GEC produced light bulbs (1893) and commercial electric motors (1896). A pioneer in factory electrification, GEC expanded to Europe, India, and South Africa by the time it went public in 1900.

GEC formed Peel-Connor Telephone Works in 1910. Work on television receivers began in 1935, and GEC eventually branched into nuclear power, computers, and semiconductors. In 1961 it merged with Radio & Allied Industries, founded by Michael Sobell. Sobell had brought his son-in-law Arnold Weinstock into his firm in the 1950s.

Weinstock joined GEC as managing director in 1963. He initiated its hostile takeover of Associated Electrical Industries in 1967 and merged GEC with English Electric, owner of radio and electronics pioneer Marconi Company, in 1968. In the US, GEC purchased RCA's medical diagnostic equipment maker Picker International Holdings in 1981 (now Marconi Medical Systems).

GEC and telecommunications firm Plessey formed GEC Plessey Telecommunications in 1988. GEC formed a joint venture with the US's GE in 1989, linking their appliance, medical equipment, and electrical products distribution businesses (General Domestic Appliances). GEC's joint venture with Siemens won British government approval to buy Plessey in 1989. GEC and Siemens later divided Plessey's businesses. (GEC sold its portion in 1998.) GEC also entered a joint venture with Alcatel Alsthom (now Alcatel) of France, combining their power generation, rail transport, and electrical distribution businesses. The company bought the defense operations of British electronics

company Ferranti International in 1990. In 1994 GEC ignited a fierce bidding war with British Aerospace over nuclear sub maker VSEL. GEC won the bid in 1995.

George Simpson, former head of British aerospace firm Lucas Industries, replaced Weinstock as GEC's managing director in 1996. That year the company acquired Hazeltine Corp., a US aircraft parts maker, and agreed to buy 50% of Italy's MAC-Alenia Communications. In 1997 GEC and Italy's Finmeccanica agreed to a limited combination of their defense businesses.

With a new focus on electronics, GEC bought Tracor, a Texas-based defense electronics and information technology company, in 1998 and spun off joint venture GEC ALSTHOM (now Alstom). In a $1.17 billion deal with Germany's Siemens, GEC agreed to exchange its 50% stake in Siemens GEC Communications for Siemens' 40% stake in GPT Holdings. The deal expanded GEC's telephone network switch business.

In 1999 GEC sold its defense electronics business (Marconi Electronic Systems) to British Aerospace for $12.7 billion (the deal gave GEC a 37% stake in British Aerospace, which changed its name to BAE SYSTEMS). It also continued buying telecom companies, paying $2.1 billion for US-based RELTEC, a leading maker of communications systems and components, and more than $4 billion for FORE Systems, a maker of Internet switching equipment. Late in 1999 GEC changed its name to Marconi.

In 2000 the company bought the telecommunications equipment business of Germany-based Bosch. It also agreed to Albany Partnership (wireless network development and maintenance services) for about $108 million, and Mariposa Technology (devices to build voice, video and data networks) for about $268 million.

Chairman: Roger Hurn, age 61, $250,000 pay
Chief Executive: George Simpson, age 57,
$1,007,000 pay
CEO, Marconi Systems and Marconi Capital:
M. J. Donovan, age 47, $131,000 pay
(partial-year salary)
Finance Director: John C. Mayo, age 44, $775,000 pay
Personnel Director: Robert I. Meakin, age 50,
$426,000 pay
CEO Marconi Communications Networks:
M. W. J. Parton, age 45, $181,000 pay
(partial-year salary)
Strategic Planning Director: J. R. Fryer
General Counsel: Jeffrey Gordon
CEO Marconi Communication Services: Neil Sutcliffe
Chairman Marconi Mobile Communications:
Sandro Gualano
Chief Marketing Officer: Jeffrey Brooks
Chief Technology Officer: J. Neil Viljoen
Secretary: Norman C. Porter, age 53
Auditors: Deloitte & Touche

HQ: 1 Bruton St., London W1X 8AQ, United Kingdom
Phone: +44-20-7493-8484   **Fax:** +44-20-7493-1974
Web site: http://www.marconi.com

2000 Sales

	$ mil.	% of total
Europe		
UK	3,181	35
Other countries	1,388	15
The Americas	3,988	44
Africa, Asia & Australasia	578	6
Total	**9,135**	**100**

2000 Sales

	$ mil.	% of total
Communication networks	4,046	44
Systems	2,606	29
Communication services	866	9
Mobile communications	471	5
Capital	1,135	13
Adjustments	11	—
Total	**9,135**	**100**

Selected Business Areas and Operations
Avery Berkel (weighing equipment)
Comstar (telecommunications, 50%, Russia)
EASAMS (database development, EDI & networking)
EEV (RF/microwave and specialist imaging components)
Fibreway (fiber-optic networking)
GDA (appliances)
Gilbarco (petroleum retailing equipment and systems)
Marconi Communications (cables; civil, military &
mobile communications; project management)
Marconi Medical Systems (medical imaging)
Videojet (ink jet printers)

ABB	Philips Electronics
BCE	Samsung
Daewoo	SANYO
Electrolux AB	Schneider
Harris Corporation	Sharp
Hitachi	Siemens
Honeywell International	Sony
Mitsubishi	Spirent
Motorola	

Nasdaq: MONI FYE: March 31	Annual Growth	3/91	3/92	3/93	3/94	3/95	3/96	3/97	3/98	3/99	3/00
Sales ($ mil.)	(7.4%)	18,300	17,605	14,214	14,333	16,164	16,782	18,252	18,566	12,299	9,135
Net income ($ mil.)	(1.7%)	969	939	810	798	883	951	668	1,132	1,700	834
Income as % of sales	—	5.3%	5.3%	5.7%	5.6%	5.5%	5.7%	3.7%	6.1%	13.8%	9.1%
Earnings per share ($)	—	—	—	—	—	—	—	—	—	—	0.54
Stock price - FY high ($)	—	—	—	—	—	—	—	—	—	—	33.92
Stock price - FY low ($)	—	—	—	—	—	—	—	—	—	—	22.95
Stock price - FY close ($)	—	—	—	—	—	—	—	—	—	—	23.45
P/E - high	—	—	—	—	—	—	—	—	—	—	63
P/E - low	—	—	—	—	—	—	—	—	—	—	43
Dividends per share ($)	—	—	—	—	—	—	—	—	—	—	0.17
Book value per share ($)	—	—	—	—	—	—	—	—	—	—	5.45
Employees	(8.6%)	118,529	104,995	93,228	86,121	82,251	82,967	79,846	71,963	84,000	53,000

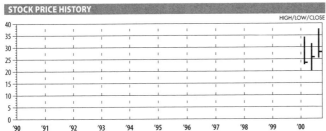

HIGH/LOW/CLOSE

Debt ratio: 16.8%
Return on equity: 9.7%
Cash ($ mil.): 869
Current ratio: 0.95
Long-term debt ($ mil.): 1,499
No. of shares (mil.): 1,362
Dividends
  Yield: 0.0%
  Payout: 0.3%
Market value ($ mil.): 31,939

MARKS AND SPENCER P.L.C.

Penny-pinching shoppers refer to it as "marked up and expensive." In Cockney rhyming slang, its moniker is "Marks and Sparks." By any name, London-based Marks and Spencer is a global retailer of clothing, food, and household goods with about 700 company-owned and franchised stores in more than 30 countries.

Its flagship Marks & Spencer chain (M&S), the UK's largest clothing retailer, has nearly 300 stores in the UK alone. Marks and Spencer also operates more than 220 Brooks Brothers clothing stores in the US and Asia and 25 Kings Super Markets in New Jersey.

The company's famous private label, the "very British" St Michael brand, is found on items ranging from tweed jackets to marmalade. M&S gets about 40% of its sales from prepared foods, such as its popular (and high-margin) ready-to-go meals. M&S also offers credit cards, life insurance, and pension funds.

Marks and Spencer has been criticized for short-sighted expansion efforts in the rest of Europe and being slow to modernize. The company has responded by reorganizing stores and operations, turning to cheaper suppliers outside the UK, and developing Autograph, a line of inexpensive designer clothing.

Fleeing anti-Semitic persecution in Russian Poland, 19-year-old Michael Marks immigrated to England in 1882. Eventually settling in Leeds, Marks eked out a meager existence as a traveling peddler until he opened a small stall at the town market in 1884. Because he spoke little English, Marks laid out all of his merchandise and hung a sign that read "Don't Ask the Price, It's a Penny," unaware at the time that self-service and self-selection would eventually become the retailing standard. His methods were so successful that he had penny bazaars in five cities by 1890.

Finding himself unable to run the growing operation single-handedly, Marks established an equal partnership with Englishman Tom Spencer, a cashier for a local distributor, forming Marks and Spencer in 1894. By the turn of the century, the company had 36 branches. Following the deaths of Spencer (1905) and Marks (1907), management of the company did not return to family hands until 1916, when Marks' son Simon became chairman.

Marks and Spencer broke with time-honored British retailing tradition in 1924 by eliminating wholesalers and establishing direct links with manufacturers. In 1926 the firm went public, and two years later it launched its now famous St Michael brand. The company quickly turned its attention to pruning unprofitable departments to concentrate on goods that had a rapid turnover. In 1931 the Marks & Spencer stores (M&S) introduced a food department that sold produce and canned goods.

The company sustained severe losses during WWII, when approximately half of its stores were damaged by bombing. Marks and Spencer rebuilt, and in 1964 Simon's brother-in-law Israel Sieff became chairman. The company expanded to North America a decade later by buy-

ing three Canadian chains: Peoples (general merchandise, sold 1992), D'Allaird's (women's clothing, sold 1996), and Walker's (clothing shops, converted to M&S). It opened its first store in Paris in 1975.

Derek Rayner replaced Sieff as chairman in 1984, becoming the first chairman hired from outside the Marks family since 1916. Under Rayner, Marks and Spencer moved into financial services by launching a charge card in 1985. The company expanded internationally, purchasing Kings Super Markets (US) and Brooks Brothers (upscale clothing stores) in 1988. Rayner retired in 1991, and CEO Richard Greenbury became chairman. The company's international expansion continued in the 1990s with new stores in Hong Kong, Hungary, Spain, and Turkey.

In 1996 Marks and Spencer added its first M&S store in Germany. The next year it paid Littlewoods $323 million for 19 UK stores, which it converted to M&S.

Greenbury, facing criticism that the company was too slow to expand and embrace new ideas, in 1999 was succeeded as CEO by handpicked heir Peter Salsbury. That year, continued poor sales led Marks and Spencer to cut 700 jobs, close its 38 M&S stores in Canada, and part ways with its clothing supplier of 30 years, William Baird. The company then began looking for a buyer for Kings Super Markets.

In early 2000 Marks and Spencer dodged a takeover attempt by investor Philip Green and later announced plans to expand Brooks Brothers throughout Europe. In April 2000 the company decided to hold on to Kings Super Markets, citing the chain's success and the devaluation of US food retailers. In another M&S shake-up, Chairman Luc Vandevelde took over as CEO in September, when Salsbury resigned.

Chairman and CEO: Luc Vandevelde, age 49
Group Finance Director: Robert Colvill, age 59
**Executive Director Marketing, M&S Direct, and
E-Commerce:** Alan McWalter, age 46
Director Personnel: Graham Oakley
Auditors: PricewaterhouseCoopers

LOCATIONS

HQ: Michael House, Baker St.,
London W1A 1DN, United Kingdom
Phone: +44-20-7935-4422   **Fax:** +44-20-7487-2679
Web site: http://www.marks-and-spencer.com

1999 Sales

	% of total
Europe	
UK	
Retailing	79
Financial services	5
Other countries	7
The Americas	8
Far East	1
Total	**100**

PRODUCTS/OPERATIONS

1999 Sales

	% of total
Retailing	96
Financial activities	4
Total	**100**

Operations

Brooks Brothers (clothing stores in the US and Asia)
Financial services (credit cards, personal loans, pension
products, life insurance)
Kings Super Markets (supermarkets in New Jersey)
Marks & Spencer (clothing and food stores in the UK,
Continental Europe, and Asia)

COMPETITORS

A&P	Kingfisher
Allders	Littlewoods Organisation
Arcadia	Liz Claiborne
ASDA Group	May
Benetton	Men's Wearhouse
Carréfour	New Look
Debenhams	NEXT plc
Federated	Nordstrom
Grand Union	Pathmark
Great Universal Stores	Safeway plc
Harrods	Somerfield
House of Fraser	Storehouse
Hudson's Bay	Syms
J Sainsbury	Target
J. C. Penney	Tengelmann Group
Jelmoli	Tesco
John Lewis Partnership	The Gap
Jos. A. Bank	

HISTORICAL FINANCIALS & EMPLOYEES

OTC: MASPY FYE: March 31	Annual Growth	3/91	3/92	3/93	3/94	3/95	3/96	3/97	3/98	3/99	3/00
Sales ($ mil.)	2.9%	10,112	10,118	9,012	9,707	10,955	11,012	12,840	13,787	13,265	13,087
Net income ($ mil.)	(5.4%)	681	639	750	858	1,011	997	1,236	1,386	600	413
Income as % of sales	—	6.7%	6.3%	8.3%	8.8%	9.2%	9.0%	9.6%	10.1%	4.5%	3.2%
Earnings per share ($)	(7.9%)	1.51	1.41	1.64	1.86	2.18	2.13	2.62	2.92	1.25	0.72
Stock price - FY high ($)	—	29.47	34.09	38.36	41.22	41.55	42.63	52.36	65.00	60.50	43.00
Stock price - FY low ($)	—	22.16	23.13	27.52	29.16	34.52	38.28	41.21	47.75	35.50	22.00
Stock price - FY close ($)	(0.3%)	24.66	30.36	30.52	36.30	40.75	38.47	47.89	60.50	39.75	23.97
P/E - high	—	20	24	23	22	19	20	20	22	48	60
P/E - low	—	15	16	17	16	16	18	16	16	28	31
Dividends per share ($)	0.3%	0.70	0.74	0.74	0.74	0.82	1.00	1.04	1.60	1.43	0.72
Book value per share ($)	6.5%	9.35	10.21	9.72	10.68	12.94	14.71	16.03	17.77	16.51	16.43
Employees	4.5%	—	—	—	—	63,331	65,498	68,208	71,297	75,492	—

STOCK PRICE HISTORY

HIGH/LOW/CLOSE

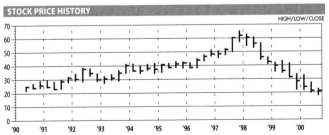

2000 FISCAL YEAR-END

Debt ratio: 14.0%
Return on equity: 5.2%
Cash ($ mil.): 1,098
Current ratio: 1.72
Long-term debt ($ mil.): 1,284
No. of shares (mil.): 478
Dividends
  Yield: 0.0%
  Payout: 1.0%
Market value ($ mil.): 11,468

MARUBENI CORPORATION

OVERVIEW

If love is a many-splendored thing, then trade is a Marubeni thing. One of Japan's largest *sogo shosha* (general trading companies), the Tokyo-based conglomerate is involved in practically every aspect of turning raw materials into consumer products. Marubeni trades in everything from fashion to forklifts and from chickens to country clubs. The firm has hundreds of affiliated companies in 80 countries, but it has been particularly active in Asia, where its diversity has enabled it to develop local industries and to help build utility and industrial infrastructures such as telephone systems, power plants, and water systems.

Marubeni has 20 business divisions in eight groups: agri-marine products; chemicals; construction, forest products, and general merchandise; natural gas exploration and petroleum sales; metal processing and market-ing; textile and apparel manufacturing and sales; and two machinery groups. One machinery group's operations include power plant construction, cable broadcast, telecommunications and Internet services, heavy machinery and agricultural equipment manufacturing, and car sales. The other machinery group is engaged in plant construction, shipping, industrial and medical equipment manufacturing, and aircraft leasing and sales.

The company has championed international expansion since the mid-1990s, but Japan's credit crunch and the Asian economic crisis have hurt Marubeni's production and processing operations across Southeast Asia. Although Marubeni has not given up on its key markets in China and across Asia, it also is exploring business opportunities in Central and South America, Central Europe, and South Africa.

HISTORY

Marubeni's origins are closely linked to those of another leading Japanese trading company. ITOCHU founder Chubei Itoh set up Marubeni Shoten K. K. in 1858 as an outlet in Osaka for his textile trading business (originally C. Itoh & Co.). The symbol for the store was a circle (*maru*) drawn around the Japanese word for red (*beni*). As C. Itoh's global operations expanded, the Marubeni store served as headquarters.

Marubeni was split off from C. Itoh in 1921 to trade textiles, although it soon expanded its operations to include industrial and consumer goods. To mobilize for World War II, the Japanese government reunited Marubeni and C. Itoh in 1941, merging them with another trading company, Kishimoto, into a new entity, Sanko Kabushiki Kaisha. In 1944 Sanko, Daido Boeki, and Kureha Spinning were ordered to consolidate into a larger entity to be called the Daiken Co., but the war ended before all operations were fully integrated.

Spun off from Daiken in 1949, Marubeni began trading internationally. It opened a New York office in 1951 and diversified into food, metals, and machinery. During the Korean War, Marubeni benefited from the UN's use of Japan as a supply base.

In 1955 Marubeni merged with Iida & Company and changed its name to Marubeni-Iida. It received a government concession to supply silicon steel and iron sheets critical to the growing Japanese auto and appliance industries. The company expanded into engineering — building factories, aircraft, and a nuclear reactor for the Japan Atomic Energy Research Institute — and into petrochemicals, fertilizers, and rubber products.

Marubeni-Iida was behind the Fuyo *keiretsu* formed in the early 1960s. Fuyo (another word for Mt. Fuji) is a powerful assemblage of some 150 companies, including Canon, Hitachi, and Nissan, that form joint ventures and develop think tanks.

In 1972 the firm became Marubeni Corp., and a year later it bought Nanyo Bussan, another trading company. In 1973 Marubeni's image was tarnished by allegations that it had hoarded rice for sale on the Japanese black market.

In the 1990s Marubeni won several major construction contracts: Among them Marubeni formed a venture in 1998 with John Laing and Turkey's Alarko Alsim to rebuild three airports in Uzbekistan.

Marubeni had begun offering Internet access in 1995, and two years later it launched an Internet-based long-distance telephone service. In 1999 the trading house formed two ventures with US firm Global Crossing, one to start operating Pacific Crossing One (the Japan-US cable) and another to lay a cable network in Japan.

That year Marubeni tied up with fellow trading company ITOCHU to integrate their steel processing subsidiaries in China to try to keep their Chinese businesses afloat. In 2000 ITOCHU and Marubeni formed an online steel trading joint venture with US-based e-commerce company MetalSite.

Chairman: Iwao Toriumi
President and CEO: Tohru Tsuji
EVP Business Solutions Department and Chief Information Officer: Masaru Mizuno
EVP Iron and Steel Division and Agri-Marine Products Division: Katsuo Koh
SVP Plant and Shipping Division, Transportation and Industrial Machinery Division: Tetsuo Nishizaka
SVP Textile Division, Development and Construction Division: Masao Matsui
VP; President and CEO, Marubeni America; Chairman, Marubeni Canada and Mexico: Yoshiya Toyoda
VP Presidents Office, Human Resources Department, Corporate Planning and Coordination Department, Forest Products and General Merchandise Division: Nobuo Katsumata
Auditors: Ernst & Young

HQ: 4-2, Ohtemachi 1-chome, Chiyoda-ku, Tokyo 100-8088, Japan
Phone: +81-3-3282-2111   **Fax:** +81-3-3282-7456
US HQ: 450 Lexington Ave., New York, NY 10017
US Phone: 212-450-0100   **US Fax:** 212-450-0700
Web site: http://www.marubeni.co.jp

2000 Sales

	% of total
Asia/Pacific	
Japan	72
Other countries	8
North America	10
Europe	3
Other regions	7
Total	**100**

Selected Products

Agricultural equipment
Apparel
Aviation
Cereals, oilseeds, and feed and food materials
Chlor alkali
Communications
Development and construction
Electric power and nuclear-related businesses
Electronics
Fabric
Fine chemicals
Foodstuffs and beverages
General merchandise
Heavy equipment
Housing materials
Industrial equipment
Inorganic chemicals and natural resources

Medical equipment
Multimedia
Nonferrous metals
Nuclear fuel
Petrochemicals and organic chemicals
Petroleum
Plants and related equipment
Plastics
Power generation
Pulp and paper
Railway and transportation
Raw materials
Ready-made goods
Rubber and rubber products
Shipping
Steel and steel products
Thermal coal
Vehicles
Yarn

Bechtel
Caterpillar
Daewoo
Deere
Hyundai
ITOCHU
Jardine Matheson

LG Group
Mannesmann AG
Mitsubishi
Mitsui
Navistar
Nichimen
Nippon Steel
Nissho Iwai

PACCAR
Rio Tinto plc
Rolls-Royce
Samsung
Sime Darby
Sumitomo
ThyssenKrupp
TOMEN

OTC: MARUY FYE: March 31	Annual Growth	3/91	3/92	3/93	3/94	3/95	3/96	3/97	3/98	3/99	3/00
Sales ($ mil.)	(3.9%)	138,466	140,366	134,553	129,867	148,688	126,246	112,848	102,506	100,413	96,438
Net income ($ mil.)	(24.5%)	243	85	10	53	120	141	162	129	(988)	19
Income as % of sales	—	0.2%	0.1%	0.0%	0.0%	0.1%	0.1%	0.1%	0.1%	—	0.0%
Earnings per share ($)	(24.4%)	1.62	0.57	0.06	0.36	0.80	0.94	1.09	0.87	(6.62)	0.13
Stock price - FY high ($)	—	57.58	50.19	40.16	51.23	58.28	58.72	59.84	46.50	20.75	43.00
Stock price - FY low ($)	—	38.36	32.86	24.45	37.95	44.66	47.19	28.00	17.00	13.00	18.00
Stock price - FY close ($)	(3.0%)	49.86	33.83	39.13	46.89	51.03	56.08	28.00	17.00	18.99	37.73
P/E - high	—	36	88	669	142	73	62	55	53	—	331
P/E - low	—	24	58	408	105	56	50	26	20	—	138
Dividends per share ($)	—	0.43	0.45	0.52	0.58	0.69	0.56	0.52	0.44	0.25	0.00
Book value per share ($)	(1.3%)	23.12	23.92	26.38	33.97	37.17	36.59	29.41	25.17	19.89	20.48
Employees	(1.8%)	9,935	9,949	10,000	10,006	9,911	9,533	9,282	9,041	8,618	—

HIGH/LOW/CLOSE

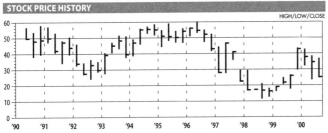

Debt ratio: 87.6%
Return on equity: 0.6%
Cash ($ mil.): 3,824
Current ratio: 1.14
Long-term debt ($ mil.): 21,698
No. of shares (mil.): 149
Dividends
  Yield: —
  Payout: —
Market value ($ mil.): 5,637

MATSUSHITA ELECTRIC INDUSTRIAL

OVERVIEW

The man with roots in a pine tree planted seeds that grew a global forest. Osaka-based Matsushita Electric Industrial (its founder's name means "lucky man under the pine tree") is the #1 consumer electronics maker in the world, ahead of Sony. Matsushita is the nucleus for a group of more than 220 overseas affiliates in about 45 countries. The group makes products sold around the world under the National, Panasonic, Quasar, JVC, Victor, and Technics brands.

Matsushita's top revenue generator is consumer products, which include TVs, VCRs, microwaves, cameras, and DVD players (it introduced the first DVD player in 1997). The company also makes industrial products (PCs, copiers, fax machines, cellular telephones, and industrial equipment) and components (batteries, compressors, semiconductors). Matsushita is expanding its multimedia and digital network-related businesses (including satellite and mobile communications systems). It plans to introduce the first DVD-audio players.

The company wrote the book on long-range planning: In 1932 founder Konosuke Matsushita created a 250-year business plan.

HISTORY

Grade school dropout Konosuke Matsushita took $50 in 1918 and went into business making electric plugs (with his brother-in-law, Toshio Iue, founder of SANYO). His mission, to help people by making high-quality, low-priced conveniences while providing his employees with good working conditions, earned him the sobriquet "god of business management." Matsushita Electric Industrial grew by developing inexpensive lamps, batteries, radios, and motors in the 1920s and 1930s.

During WWII the Japanese government ordered the firm to build wood-laminate products for the military. Postwar occupation forces prevented Matsushita from working at his firm for four years. Thanks to unions' efforts, he rejoined his namesake company shortly before it entered a joint venture with Dutch manufacturer Philips in 1952. The following year Matsushita moved into consumer goods, making televisions, refrigerators, and washing machines, and later expanding into high-performance audio products. Matsushita bought a majority stake in Victor Company of Japan (JVC, originally established by RCA Victor) in 1954. Its 1959 New York subsidiary opening began Matsushita's drive overseas.

Sold under the National, Panasonic, and Technics names, the firm's products were usually not cutting edge but were attractively priced. Under Masaharu Matsushita, the founder's son-in-law who became president in 1961, the company became Japan's largest home appliance maker, introducing air conditioners, microwave ovens, stereo components, and VCRs in the 1960s and 1970s. JVC developed the VHS format for VCRs, which beat out Sony's Betamax format.

Matsushita built much of its sales growth on new industrial and commercial customers in the 1980s. The company expanded its semiconductor, office and factory automation, auto electronics, audiovisual, housing, and air-conditioning product offerings that decade. Konosuke died in 1989.

The next year Matsushita joined the Japanese stampede for US acquisitions, buying Universal Studios owner MCA. In 1993 Yoichi Morishita was named president and the company acquired Philips' stake in the two firms' joint venture. Two years later, when cultural incompatibility depressed MCA's performance, Matsushita sold 80% of the company (now Universal) to liquor mogul Seagram, resulting in a fiscal 1996 loss.

Declining sales forced the firm to rethink its strategy; it began a multiyear restructuring, including a buildup in parts of Asia with cheaper labor and job cuts. In 1997 Matsushita consolidated most of its business units into basic categories: consumer products, industrial products, and components. Also in 1997 the downside of Matsushita's move into emerging Asian markets became apparent as many Southeast Asian countries suffered currency crises.

In fiscal years 1998 and 1999 the company's income dropped, partly due to a slow domestic economy. A lagging market led Matsushita to close its North American semiconductor operations in late 1998. Also that year the company bought a stake in Mobile Broadcasting (a digital satellite broadcasting venture of nine companies) and introduced digital TVs.

Matsushita in 1999 bought a 9% stake in Symbian, a venture created by the makers of 85% of the world's mobile phones (including Motorola and Nokia). Symbian intends to make its Epoc operating system the standard for mobile computing.

Honorary Chairman: Masaharu Matsushita
Chairman: Yoichi Morishita
VC: Masayuki Matsushita
President: Kunio Nakamura
EVP: Atsushi Murayama
EVP: Kazuhiko Sugiyama
Senior Corporate Auditor: Motoi Matsuda
Senior Managing Director: Osamu Tanaka
Senior Managing Director: Kazuo Toda
Managing Director: Sukeichi Miki
Managing Director: Kazuhiro Mori
Managing Director: Yukio Shohtoku
Auditors: KPMG

LOCATIONS

HQ: Matsushita Denki Sangyo Kabushiki Kaisha
(Matsushita Electric Industrial Co., Ltd.)
1006, Oaza Kadoma, Kadoma-shi,
Osaka 571-8501, Japan
Phone: +81-6-6908-1121   **Fax:** +81-6-6908-2351
US HQ: 375 Park Ave., Ste. 3608, New York, NY 10152
US Phone: 212-371-5447
Web site: http://www.mei.co.jp

Matsushita Electric Industrial operates more than 220 companies in over 45 countries.

2000 Sales

	% of total
Asia	
Japan	51
Other countries	18
North & South America	19
Europe	12
Total	**100**

PRODUCTS/OPERATIONS

2000 Sales

	% of total
Consumer products	
Video & audio equipment	23
Home appliances & household equipment	18
Industrial products	
Information & communications equipment	28
Industrial equipment	10
Components	21
Total	**100**

Selected Products

Air conditioners	Fax machines
Bicycles	Medical equipment
Cameras	Microwaves
Car navigation equipment	Refrigerators
CD players	Semiconductors
Cellular phones	Stereo equipment
Computers	TVs and VCRs
DVD players	Vending machines
Factory automation equipment	Washing machines

COMPETITORS

3M	NEC
Bose	Oki Electric
Compaq	Philips Electronics
Daewoo	Pioneer
Electrolux AB	Samsung
Fujitsu	SANYO
Hitachi	Sharp
IBM	Sony
Intel	Texas Instruments
LG Electronics	THOMSON multimedia
Maytag	Toshiba
Motorola	Whirlpool

HISTORICAL FINANCIALS & EMPLOYEES

NYSE: MC FYE: March 31	Annual Growth	3/91	3/92	3/93	3/94	3/95	3/96	3/97	3/98	3/99	3/00
Sales ($ mil.)	4.7%	46,934	56,120	60,826	64,307	78,069	64,102	61,903	59,259	63,668	71,118
Net income ($ mil.)	(6.9%)	1,841	1,001	331	238	1,017	(537)	1,112	703	113	971
Income as % of sales	—	3.9%	1.8%	0.5%	0.4%	1.3%	—	1.8%	1.2%	0.2%	1.4%
Earnings per share ($)	(6.6%)	8.33	4.57	1.60	1.14	4.74	(2.53)	4.90	3.12	0.54	4.52
Stock price - FY high ($)	—	149.88	131.00	110.00	176.00	188.00	172.50	188.00	211.00	195.00	303.00
Stock price - FY low ($)	—	114.00	93.50	83.00	108.00	131.50	140.00	142.88	135.13	128.00	173.50
Stock price - FY close ($)	10.4%	124.00	96.75	108.75	164.00	158.00	165.00	156.25	159.94	193.38	303.00
P/E - high	—	18	29	69	154	38	—	36	63	361	64
P/E - low	—	14	20	52	95	26	—	27	41	237	37
Dividends per share ($)	8.1%	0.60	0.87	0.85	0.98	1.15	0.58	0.50	0.00	0.46	1.21
Book value per share ($)	3.8%	116.69	125.70	141.13	152.37	174.40	152.80	141.17	134.04	142.77	163.79
Employees	—	—	—	—	—	—	—	—	—	282,000	290,448

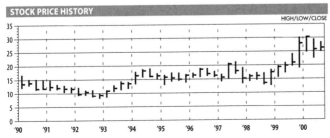

STOCK PRICE HISTORY   HIGH/LOW/CLOSE

2000 FISCAL YEAR-END
Debt ratio: 15.7%
Return on equity: 3.1%
Cash ($ mil.): 10,876
Current ratio: 1.73
Long-term debt ($ mil.): 6,273
No. of shares (mil.): 206
Dividends
  Yield: 0.4%
  Payout: 26.8%
Market value ($ mil.): 62,492

MAZDA MOTOR CORPORATION

OVERVIEW

Japan's #5 carmaker, Mazda Motor is hoping Ford can help tow it to a higher ranking. After years of losses and trailing competitors Toyota, Honda, Nissan, and Mitsubishi, the Hiroshima-based company is finally making money off its sedans (Millenia, 626), minivans (MPV), sports cars (Miata, RX-7), and pickup trucks (B-Series).

Mazda's recovery could be credited to Ford. After raising its stake in Mazda to a controlling 33% in 1996, Ford installed its own

management and sought to improve cash flow and reduce debt by closing sales outlets and selling hundreds of millions of dollars worth of holdings in other companies. Ford also consolidated businesses in the US, cut jobs, and tightened control over subsidiaries' operations and budgets.

The changes seem to have paid off. Mazda hopes to keep its momentum going by building a single brand image for Mazda models and by sharing platforms and technology with Ford.

HISTORY

Ingiro Matsuda founded cork producer Toyo Cork Kogyo in Hiroshima in 1920. The company changed its name to Toyo Kogyo in 1927 and began making machine tools. Impressed by Ford trucks used in 1923 earthquake-relief efforts, Matsuda had the company make a three-wheel motorcycle/truck hybrid in 1931.

The second Sino-Japanese War forced Toyo Kogyo to make rifles and cut back on its truck production. Although the company built a prototype passenger car in 1940, the outbreak of WWII refocused it on weapons. The August 1945 bombing of Hiroshima killed more than 400 Toyo Kogyo workers, but the company persevered, producing 10 trucks that December. By 1949 it was turning out 800 per month.

The company launched the first Mazda, a two-seat minicar, in 1960. The next year Toyo Kogyo licensed Audi's new rotary engine technology. After releasing a string of models, the company became Japan's #3 automaker in 1964. Toyo Kogyo introduced the first Mazda powered by a rotary engine, Cosmo/110S, in 1967, followed by the Familia in 1968.

The company grew rapidly and began exporting to the US in 1970. However, recession, high gas prices, and concern over the inefficiency of rotary engines halted growth in the mid-1970s. Sumitomo Bank bailed out Toyo Kogyo. The company shifted emphasis back to piston engines but managed to launch the rotary engine RX-7 in 1978.

Ford's need for small-car expertise and Sumitomo's desire for a large partner for its client led to Ford's purchase of 25% of Toyo Kogyo in 1979. The company's early 1980s GLC/323 and 626 models were sold as Fords in Asia, Latin America, and the Middle East.

Toyo Kogyo changed its name to Mazda Motor Corporation in 1984. ("Mazda" is loosely derived from Matsuda's name, but the carmaker has never discouraged an association with the Zoroastrian god of light, Ahura

Mazda.) The company opened a US plant in 1985, but a strong yen, expensive increases in production capacity, and a growing number of models led to increased overhead, soaring debt, and shrinking margins. By 1988 Mazda had begun to focus on sporty niche cars; it launched the hot-selling Miata in 1989.

The company faced more problems with the early 1990s' recession. In 1992 Mazda introduced a new 626 model. That year Mazda also sold half its interest in its Flat Rock, Michigan, plant to Ford. As the yen, development costs, and prices for its cars in the US all rose, sales in the US fell. In 1993 Mazda reorganized subsidiary Mazda of America by cutting staff.

Ford sank $481 million into Mazda in 1996, increasing its stake to 33%. That year the Ford-appointed former EVP of Mazda, Henry Wallace, became Mazda's president, making history as the first non-Japanese to head a major Japanese corporation. In 1997 Wallace resigned to become CFO of Ford's European operations, and former Ford executive James Miller replaced him. That year Mazda consolidated four US operations into Mazda North American Operations.

Restructuring continued in 1998 as Mazda consolidated some European operations and closed a plant in Thailand. In 1999 Mazda sold its credit division to Ford and its Naldec auto parts unit to Ford's Visteon unit. It announced plans to sell its stake in South Korean carmaker Kia Motors. Later in the year, another American, Ford's Mark Fields, took over as president.

In 2000 Mazda recalled 30,000 MPV minivans (year 2000) to fix a powertrain control module and asked owners of all year 2000 MPVs to bring in their vehicles for front-bumper reinforcement. Mazda also announced plans to close about 40% of its North American dealership outlets over the next three years.

OFFICERS

Representative Director and Chairman:
Kazuhide Watanabe
President: Mark Fields
CFO: Robert Shanks
General Manager, Personnel and Human Development:
Masaki Kand
Auditors: Asahi & Co.

LOCATIONS

HQ: Matsuda Jidosha Kogyo
3-1, Shinchi, Fuchu-cho, Aki-gun,
Hiroshima 730-91, Japan
Phone: +81-82-282-1111   **Fax:** +81-82-287-5190
US HQ: 7755 Irvine Center Dr., Irvine, CA 92623
US Phone: 949-727-1990   **US Fax:** 949-727-6101
Web site: http://www.mazda.co.jp

Mazda Motor Corporation has 18 main production
plants, including two Japanese facilities and locations in
Colombia, Ecuador, India, Iran, Pakistan, South Africa,
Taiwan, Thailand, the US, and Zimbabwe. Its sales and
service network includes about 1,800 sales outlets in
Japan and nearly 5,000 in other countries.

2000 Sales

	% of total
Japan	67
North America	22
Europe	8
Other regions	3
Adjustments	—
Total	**100**

PRODUCTS/OPERATIONS

Selected Models
626 (sedan)
Bongo (van)
B-Series (pickup)
Demio (compact wagon)
Familia (compact wagon)
Miata (sports car)
Millenia (sedan)
MPV (van)
Protegé (compact sedan)
RX-7 (sports car)

Selected Subsidiaries and Affiliates
AutoAlliance International, Inc. (US)
Autozam Inc.
Malox Co., Ltd.
Mazda Australia Pty. Ltd.
Mazda Motor Logistics Europe NV (Belgium)
Mazda Motor of America, Inc. (US)
Toyo Advanced Technologies Co., Ltd.

COMPETITORS

BMW	Kia Motors
Daewoo	Mitsubishi
DaimlerChrysler	Nissan
Fiat	Peugeot
Ford	Renault
Fuji Heavy Industries	Saab Automobile
General Motors	Suzuki
Honda	Toyota
Hyundai	Volkswagen
Isuzu	

HISTORICAL FINANCIALS & EMPLOYEES

Tokyo: 7261 FYE: March 31	Annual Growth	3/91	3/92	3/93	3/94	3/95	3/96	3/97	3/98	3/99	3/00
Sales (¥ mil.)	(2.5%)	2,714,352	2,722,469	2,593,447	2,188,200	2,204,129	1,842,891	1,894,200	2,041,428	2,057,097	2,161,572
Net income (¥ mil.)	(0.2%)	26,651	9,314	128	(48,993)	(41,156)	(11,879)	(17,548)	(6,802)	38,707	26,155
Income as % of sales	—	1.0%	0.3%	0.0%	—	—	—	—	—	1.9%	1.2%
Earnings per share (¥)	(1.6%)	24.77	8.65	1.18	(45.53)	(38.18)	(11.01)	(14.62)	(5.56)	31.66	21.39
Stock price - FY high (¥)	—	972	634	521	625	648	489	560	475	531	745
Stock price - FY low (¥)	—	530	445	385	310	392	292	295	205	311	290
Stock price - FY close (¥)	(6.2%)	621	452	485	470	410	430	336	342	460	350
P/E - high	—	39	73	442	—	—	—	—	—	17	35
P/E - low	—	21	51	326	—	—	—	—	—	10	14
Dividends per share (¥)	(13.7%)	7.50	7.50	6.00	0.00	0.00	0.00	0.00	0.00	4.00	2.00
Book value per share (¥)	(6.9%)	383.86	389.42	3.42	3.35	3.59	2.79	2.37	288.35	309.13	200.99
Employees	(4.7%)	36,349	37,052	34,167	33,118	27,321	26,072	24,891	31,665	24,076	23,549

STOCK PRICE HISTORY

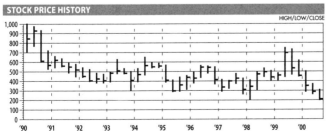

HIGH/LOW/CLOSE

2000 FISCAL YEAR-END
Debt ratio: 55.8%
Return on equity: 8.4%
Cash (¥ mil.): 233,593
Current ratio: 0.79
Long-term debt (¥ mil.): 310,205
No. of shares (mil.): 1,222
Dividends
  Yield: 0.0%
  Payout: 0.1%
Market value ($ mil.): 4,057
Sales ($ mil.): 20,495

METRO AG

OVERVIEW

After unhitching several unprofitable businesses, the streamlined "uber"-retailer METRO AG continues to add new stops throughout Europe. The Dusseldorf, Germany-based company is one of the world's leading retailers, operating some 2,100 wholesale stores, hypermarkets, supermarkets, department stores, and specialty stores in more than 20 countries in Europe, as well as in China, Turkey, and Morocco. METRO AG reaps about 40% of its sales outside Germany.

The company's METRO and Makro wholesale outlets sell food and other grocery and non-grocery items to businesses and institutional customers. Its more than 800 hypermarkets (Real) and supermarkets (Extra), located primarily in Germany, complete its food retailing operations. METRO AG also runs department stores (Galeria Kaufhof), consumer electronics chains (Media Markt, Saturn), and home improvement centers (Praktiker).

METRO AG has a minority stake (49%) in the Divaco group, a holding firm created to handle noncore businesses formerly run by METRO AG. METRO AG's other enterprises include advertising services, insurance services, and restaurant and catering companies.

METRO Holding AG, a Swiss company owned by METRO founder Otto Beisheim, Franz Haniel & Cie, and the Schmidt-Ruthenbeck family, owns about 60% of METRO AG.

HISTORY

METRO SB-Grossmarkte was founded by Otto Beisheim in the German town of Mulheim in 1964. A wholesale business serving commercial customers, it operated under the name METRO Cash & Carry. Three years later Beisheim received backing from the owners of Franz Haniel & Cie (an industrial company which was founded in 1756) and members of the Schmidt-Ruthenbeck family (also in wholesaling). This allowed METRO to expand rapidly in Germany and, in 1968, into the Netherlands under the name Makro Cash & Carry via a partnership with Steenkolen Handelsvereeniging (SHV). During the 1970s the company expanded its wholesaling operations within Europe and moved into retailing.

METRO's foray into retailing was aided during the next decade by the acquisition of department store chain Kaufhof AG. By the 1980s the rise of specialty stores had many department stores on the defensive, and Kaufhof's owners sold it to METRO and its investment partner, Union Bank of Switzerland.

As METRO's ownership interest in Kaufhof rose above 50%, the chain began converting some of its stores from department stores into fashion and sporting goods sellers. Kaufhof began acquiring a stake in computer manufacturer and retailer Vobis in 1989. In 1993 METRO, now operating as METRO Holding AG, acquired a majority interest in supermarket company Asko Deutsche Kaufhaus, which owned the Praktiker building materials chain. The reclusive Beisheim retired from active management the next year.

To cut costs and prepare for expansion into Asia, in 1996 METRO Holding merged its German retail holdings — Kaufhof; Asko;

another grocery operation, Deutsche SB Kauf; and its German cash-and-carry operations — into one holding company, METRO AG.

In 1998 METRO AG made several acquisitions and divestitures to focus on its core businesses. The company bought the 196-store Makro self-service wholesale chain from Dutch-based SHV for $2.7 billion. A month later METRO AG added to its German food operations by acquiring the 94-store German Allkauf hypermarket chain and then by purchasing the 20-store Kriegbaum chain.

Later that year METRO AG transferred its interests in noncore businesses, including office supply stores, footwear stores, discount stores, computer operations (including Vobis), and 25 unprofitable Kaufhof department stores to its Divaco (formerly Divag) unit. Divaco sold 165 German Tip discount stores in late 1998 to German retailer Tengelmann Group for about $375 million.

Hans-Joachim Korber became METRO AG's CEO in 1999. In early 2000 the company transferred 290 hypermarkets and department stores in Germany, Greece, Hungary, Luxembourg, and Turkey to a joint venture company (51% owned by Westdeutsche Landesbank) in an effort to raise cash for the expansion and remodeling of its core wholesale outlets. Expanding on the Internet, METRO AG acquired control of German e-commerce business Primus Online from another METRO Holding subsidiary.

The group announced in August that it will open food stores in Russia by 2002. Slovakia and Vietnam are also on METRO AG's expansion list, with store openings scheduled in late 2000 and 2001.

OFFICERS

Chairman Supervisory Board: Jan van Haeften
VC Supervisory Board: Klaus Bruns
CEO: Hans-Joachim Korber
Executive Board Member, Coach, Cash & Carry Business Unit: Theo de Raad
Executive Board Member, E-Commerce, IT, Logistics, Real Estate; Coach, Nonfood Specialty Business Unit: Zygmunt Meirdorf
Executive Board Member, Law, Personnel, Human Resources Development, Taxes, Associations: Wolf-Dietrich Loose
Executive Board Member, Purchasing/Import, Advertising; Coach, Food Retail Business Unit: Joachim Suhr
Auditors: Fasselt-Mette & Partner GmbH

LOCATIONS

HQ: Ivo-Beucker-Strasse 43, 40237 Dusseldorf, Germany
Phone: +49-211-6886-0   **Fax:** +49-211-6886-3759
Web site: http://195.227.51.132

METRO AG operates approximately 2,100 stores in more than 20 countries, primarily in Europe, but also in China, Morocco, and Turkey.

PRODUCTS/OPERATIONS

1999 Sales

	% of total
Cash & carry	45
Food retail	25
Nonfood specialty	20
Department stores	9
Other	1
Total	**100**

Retail Operations

Cash and Carry
Makro
METRO

Food Retail
Extra
Real

Nonfood Specialty Stores
Media Markt (consumer electronics)
Praktiker (home improvement)
Saturn (consumer electronics)

Department Store
Galeria Kaufhof

Other Operations

Dinea-Gastronomie (restaurants/catering)
Divaco (investment group)
METRO MGE Einkauf (purchasing)
METRO MGI Informatik (IT services)
METRO Real Estate Management (construction services)
METRO Werbegesellschaft (advertising)
Primus Online (Internet retailer)

COMPETITORS

ALDI
Carréfour
Edeka Zentrale
Karstadt
Lidl & Schwarz Stiftung
Rewe-Zentral
Royal Ahold
Tengelmann Group
Vendex
Wal-Mart

HISTORICAL FINANCIALS & EMPLOYEES

German: MEO FYE: December 31	Annual Growth	12/90	12/91	12/92	12/93	12/94	12/95	12/96	12/97	12/98	12/99
Sales (€ mil.)	15.9%	—	—	—	—	—	—	28,138	29,062	46,887	43,805
Net income (€ mil.)	21.0%	—	—	—	—	—	—	206	250	335	365
Income as % of sales	—	—	—	—	—	—	—	0.7%	0.9%	0.7%	0.8%
Earnings per share (€)	5.3%	—	—	—	—	—	—	3.80	4.01	4.45	4.44
Stock price - FY high (€)	—	—	—	—	—	—	—	30.46	49.50	68.00	77.05
Stock price - FY low (€)	—	—	—	—	—	—	—	25.67	24.35	31.33	47.60
Stock price - FY close (€)	26.4%	—	—	—	—	—	—	26.42	31.33	66.98	53.40
P/E - high	—	—	—	—	—	—	—	8	12	15	17
P/E - low	—	—	—	—	—	—	—	7	6	7	11
Dividends per share (€)	6.3%	—	—	—	—	—	—	0.85	1.02	1.02	1.02
Book value per share (€)	3.5%	—	—	—	—	—	—	11.34	11.50	13.60	12.56
Employees	20.1%	—	—	—	—	—	—	130,019	134,019	181,300	225,265

STOCK PRICE HISTORY
HIGH/LOW/CLOSE

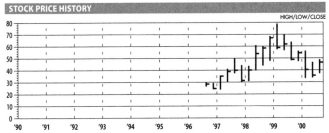

1999 FISCAL YEAR-END

Debt ratio: 35.3%
Return on equity: 9.2%
Cash (€ mil.): 1,162
Current ratio: 1.08
Long-term debt (€ mil.): 2,081
No. of shares (mil.): 304
Dividends
  Yield: 0.0%
  Payout: 0.2%
Market value ($ mil.): 16,300
Sales ($ mil.): 44,014

MICHELIN

OVERVIEW

The Michelin Man produces more than 800,000 tires a day — pity the Michelin Woman. Clermont-Ferrand, France-based Compagnie Générale des Établissements Michelin is the world's #2 tire maker, behind Goodyear and slightly ahead of Bridgestone. Chief among its 32,000 products are tires — for cars, trucks, motorcycles, planes, and agricultural vehicles. Michelin also makes wheels, inner tubes, and steel cables used in radial tires, as well as road maps, travel guides, and navigation CD-ROMs.

In response to the 6.5 million tires recalled by Bridgestone/Firestone, Michelin is stepping up production in the US to meet demand. The company is also revamping its operations in Asia. Michelin is spending $215 million to expand capacity in Thailand and build a plant in India. It also has plans for a joint venture in China with Shanghai Tyre & Rubber. Edouard Michelin, youngest son of patriarch François Michelin and the fourth generation of Michelins in the business, has been tapped to lead the company. Edouard and his father, along with partner René Zingraff, control the company.

HISTORY

After toying with making rubber balls, Edouard Daubree and Aristide Barbier formed a partnership in Clermont-Ferrand, France, in 1863 and entered the rubber business in earnest. Both men soon died, but Barbier in-law André Michelin, a successful businessman, took over the company in 1886. André recruited his brother, Edouard, a Parisian artist, to run the company, and in 1889 it was renamed Compagnie Générale des Établissements Michelin.

That year Edouard found that air-filled tires made bicycling more comfortable. But pneumatic tires were experimental and, because they were glued to the rims, required hours to change. In 1891 Edouard made a detachable bicycle tire that took only 15 minutes to change.

The Michelins promoted their tires by persuading cyclists to use them in long-distance races where punctures were likely. They demonstrated the applicability of such tires for cars in an auto race in 1895. In 1898 André commented that a stack of tires would look like a man if it had arms, a notion that led to the creation of Bibendum, the Michelin Man. André launched the *Michelin Guide* for auto tourists in 1900.

Expansion followed as Michelin opened a London office (1905) and began production in Italy (1906) and the US (in New Jersey) in 1908. Innovations included detachable rims and spare tires (1906), tubeless tires (1930), treads (1934), and modern low-profile tires (1937). During the Depression Michelin closed its US plant and accepted a stake in Citroën, later converted into a minority stake in Peugeot, in lieu of payment for tires.

Michelin patented radial tires in 1946. Expansion was largely confined to Europe in the 1950s but, thanks to radials, increased worldwide in the 1960s. Sears began selling Michelin radials in 1966. Radials took hold during the 1970s, and Michelin returned to manufacturing in the US, opening a plant in South Carolina in 1975.

Expanding aggressively (Michelin opened or bought a plant every nine months from 1960 to 1990), the company went into the red when economic conditions dipped in the early 1980s and in 1990 and 1991. The $1.5 billion purchase of Uniroyal Goodrich in 1990 contributed to the latter losses but improved Michelin's position in the US, the world's largest auto market.

In response to the losses, Michelin attacked its bloated infrastructure and reinvented itself along nine product lines (according to tire/vehicle type plus travel, suspension, and primary product manufacturing). It also consolidated facilities and cut about 30,000 jobs. The company continued to focus on R&D, bringing out new high-performance tires such as its "green" tire designed to help cars save fuel.

Michelin bought a majority interest in a Polish tire maker in 1995, and the next year it bought 90% of Taurus, a Hungarian firm that produces most of that country's rubber. Michelin joined German competitor Continental in 1996 to make private-label tires for independent distributors. The next year Michelin introduced for the automotive aftermarket a run-flat tire capable of traveling 50 miles after a puncture. The company acquired Icollantas, a Colombian tire group with two factories in Bogota and Cali, in 1998.

After leading the company for more than 40 years, patriarch François Michelin stepped down in 1999, leaving Edouard, his youngest son, in charge. Almost immediately, Edouard announced a restructuring that would cut 7,500 jobs in Europe, including almost 2,000 in France.

Managing Partner and General Partner:
Edouard Michelin, age 36
Managing Partner and General Partner:
François Michelin, age 73
Managing Partner and General Partner: René Zingraff
Finance Director: Eric Bourdais de Charbonniere
Personnel Director: Thierry Coudurier
Auditors: Dominique Paul; Stephane Marie

LOCATIONS

HQ: Compagnie Générale des Établissements Michelin,
12, cours Sablon, 63000 Clermont-Ferrand, France
Phone: +33-4-73-98-59-00   **Fax:** +33-4-73-98-59-04
US HQ: 1 Parkway South, Greenville, SC 29615
US Phone: 864-458-5000   **US Fax:** 864-458-6359
Web site: http://www.michelin.com

Michelin has more than 80 manufacturing facilities in
19 countries; six rubber plantations in Brazil and
Nigeria; and offices in more than 170 countries.

PRODUCTS/OPERATIONS

Selected Products and Services
Agricultural tires
Aircraft tires
Components (rubber and elastomers,
reinforcement material)
Earthmover tires
Passenger car and light-truck tires
Suspension systems (wheels, antivibration equipment,
assemblages)
Tourism services
Truck tires
Two-wheel tires

Selected Brands

BF Goodrich	Siamtyre
Kleber	Taurus
Kormorant	Tyre Master
Michelin	Uniroyal
Pneu Laurent	Wolber
Riken	

Selected Subsidiaries
Compagnie Financière Michelin (93%, Switzerland)
Manufacture Française des Pneumatiques Michelin (96%)
Michelin Aircraft Tire Corporation (93%, US)
Michelin Americas Research & Development
Corporation (93%, US)
Michelin Asia (Hong-Kong) Ltd. (93%)
Michelin Ceská republika sro (93%, Czech Republic)
Michelin Corporation (93%, US)
Michelin Investment Holding Company Limited (93%,
Bermuda)
Michelin Korea Co., Ltd. (93%)
Michelin North America, Inc. (93%, US)
Norsk Michelin Gummi A/S (93%, Norway)
Société d'Exportation Michelin
Société Michelin de Transformation des Gravanches (96%)
Spika SA
Taurus Rubber Company Ltd (93%, Hungary)
Transityre France SA (93%)

COMPETITORS

Bandag	Sime Darby
Bridgestone	Sumitomo
Continental AG	Toyo Tire & Rubber
Cooper Tire & Rubber	Vredestein
Goodyear	Yokohama Rubber

HISTORICAL FINANCIALS & EMPLOYEES

Euronext Paris: ML FYE: December 31	Annual Growth	12/90	12/91	12/92	12/93	12/94	12/95	12/96	12/97	12/98	12/99
Sales (€ mil.)	4.6%	9,564	10,313	10,191	9,650	10,248	10,078	10,861	11,075	13,102	14,395
Net income (€ mil.)	—	(733)	(107)	12	(559)	197	426	441	592	574	182
Income as % of sales	—	—	—	0.1%	—	1.9%	4.2%	4.1%	5.3%	4.4%	1.3%
Earnings per share (€)	—	(6.86)	(1.07)	0.15	(5.18)	1.83	3.72	3.69	4.32	3.89	1.15
Stock price - FY high (€)		26.98	21.40	33.69	32.32	41.77	35.51	42.99	61.44	62.34	49.49
Stock price - FY low (€)		8.84	9.60	18.90	19.97	28.51	28.20	29.32	41.89	28.51	30.30
Stock price - FY close (€)	16.9%	9.60	18.60	27.75	32.01	29.58	29.77	42.70	46.19	34.07	39.00
P/E - high		—	—	225	—	23	10	12	14	16	43
P/E - low		—	—	126	—	16	8	8	10	7	26
Dividends per share (€)	7.5%	0.37	0.00	0.23	0.00	0.34	0.42	0.50	0.50	0.64	0.71
Book value per share (€)	8.1%	15.85	16.01	15.85	10.37	12.35	15.75	20.46	29.05	30.72	31.87
Employees	(0.8%)	140,826	135,610	125,000	124,575	117,776	115,000	119,780	123,254	127,241	130,434

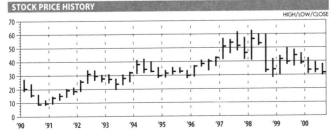

STOCK PRICE HISTORY HIGH/LOW/CLOSE

1999 FISCAL YEAR-END
Debt ratio: 22.6%
Return on equity: 4.3%
Cash (€ mil.): 695
Current ratio: 1.41
Long-term debt (€ mil.): 1,252
No. of shares (mil.): 135
Dividends
Yield: 0.0%
Payout: 0.6%
Market value ($ mil.): 5,279
Sales ($ mil.): 14,464

MINOLTA CO., LTD.

OVERVIEW

Minolta doesn't just get the picture, it also clicks as a manufacturer of office equipment. Though still a leading camera maker, the Osaka-based company gets nearly three-fourths of its sales from copiers, fax machines, scanners, and printers. Other products include binoculars, light and color meters, oximeters (for measuring blood oxygen), and microfilm devices. Minolta is also starry-eyed over its planetarium projectors.

The company is sharpening its focus on digital imaging products, from cameras and 3-D digitizer workstations, to advanced optical devices for image capture and display (including printers and projectors) and for semiconductor manufacturing. Its new Minolta Software Laboratory develops networking systems for office products.

Minolta continues to support its established line of high-end Advanced Photo System (APS) cameras, even though APS (a more versatile alternative to 35mm that Minolta developed in an alliance with other major camera and film companies) has failed to catch on with consumers outside Japan.

HISTORY

Kazuo Tashima, aided by German trader Wilhelm Heilemann and optical engineer Wilhelm Neumann, founded the Japan-Germany Camera Company (Nichi-Doku Shashinki Shoten) in Osaka in 1928 to make optical equipment. The company introduced the Nifcalette bellows camera in 1929. Heilemann and Neumann left in 1931.

In 1933 Tashima coined the name Minolta for his expanding line of cameras. Similar in sound to the Japanese expression for ripening rice fields (*minoru-ta*), Minolta is also an English acronym for Machinery and Instruments Optical by Tashima.

Tashima introduced the Minolta Vest, the camera that made Minolta a household word in Japan, in 1934. The company renamed itself Chiyoda Optics and Fine Engineering (Chiyoda Kogaku Seiko) and released the first Japanese twin-lens camera in 1937. During WWII it produced equipment such as binoculars and range finders for the Japanese military. Although Minolta's facilities were destroyed by Allied bombs in 1945, the company benefited from US postwar recovery loans.

Minolta expanded to the US and Europe in the 1950s, and increased its presence in Southeast Asia during the 1960s. It diversified into office equipment, producing its first copier, the Copymaster, in 1960. After astronaut John Glenn used a Minolta camera to take pictures from orbit in 1962, Tashima changed the firm's name to Minolta Camera Company.

Minolta overtook Nikon and Canon as the US's leading single-lens reflex (SLR) camera seller in 1973. The following year production of the successful EG 101 copier began. By 1975 exports made up about 80% of sales.

Minolta suffered in the late 1970s when Canon's automated AE-1 camera outsold Minolta's SR-T 101. It was not until 1985 that Minolta regained its leadership in the SLR market, by introducing the fully automated MAXXUM 7000.

In 1982 Tashima, who had directed Minolta for over 50 years, stepped into the chairmanship, and his son, Hideo, replaced him as president. (Kazuo died in 1985; Hideo became chairman in 1993.)

Minolta pegged escalating R&D expenses and price competition for its 1991 loss. Despite a reorganization and cost-cutting program, Minolta's losses grew in 1992. The company cut back on hiring and advertising, sold some real estate assets, and cut directors' salaries by 10%.

In 1994, to reflect its broader product line, the company changed its name to Minolta Co., Ltd. That year it stopped making video cameras for the Japanese market after sales fell sharply.

After rigorous restructuring efforts that included workforce cuts, Minolta returned to profitability in 1996. That year Minolta, Canon, Eastman Kodak, Fuji Photo, and Nikon debuted the Advanced Photo System, designed to replace the 35mm photography standard. In 1997 Minolta entered into a joint venture with chip maker LSI Logic to produce a lower-cost digital camera. Celebrating its 70th year, Minolta in 1998 introduced MIMS Plus, which can store and retrieve scanned images, documents, spreadsheets, e-mail, faxes, and microfilm. Despite increased sales, Minolta suffered lower earnings that year, thanks to the Asian financial crisis.

In 1999 Minolta acquired a 71% stake in US-based color printer maker QMS. That year Yoshikatsu Ota became the company's president. A 35-year Minolta employee, he had most recently headed the company's Image Information Products operations.

Chairman Emeritus: Sam Kusumoto
President: Yoshikatsu Ota
Senior Executive Director: Yoshihiko Higashiyama
Senior Executive Director: Norio Tashima
Executive Director: Norikatsu Shimizu
Executive Director: Masayoshi Inoue
President and CEO Minolta USA: Hiroshi Fujii
Manager Corporate Communications: Kanjii Wada
Auditors: Century Ota Showa & Co.

HQ: 3-13, Azuchi-machi 2-chome,
Chuo-ku, Osaka 541-8556, Japan
Phone: +81-6-6271-2251   **Fax:** +81-6-6266-1010
US HQ: 101 Williams Dr., Ramsey, NJ 07446
US Phone: 201-825-4000   **US Fax:** 201-825-7605
Web site: http://www.minolta.com

Minolta has manufacturing facilities in Brazil, China,
France, Hong Kong, Japan, Malaysia, and the US. The
company's products are marketed worldwide.

2000 Sales

	% of total
Japan	48
North America	21
Europe	20
Other regions	11
Total	**100**

2000 Sales

	% of total
Image information products	76
Optical products	22
Other	2
Total	**100**

Selected Products

Binoculars	Micrographics products
Book scanners	Optical system
Cameras	components
Colorimeters (color	Photocopiers
analyzers)	Photographic meters
Digital photography	Planetarium projection
Heart rate	equipment
monitor/oximeters	Printers
Light meters	Radiometric instruments

A.B.Dick	Global Imaging	Océ
Acer	Systems	Oki Electric
Agfa	Harris	Olivetti
Asahi Optical	Corporation	Olympus
Bell & Howell	Hewlett-Packard	Pitney Bowes
Canon	Konica	Polaroid
Casio Computer	Kyocera	Ricoh
Danka	Lanier	Scitex
Eastman Kodak	Worldwide	Seiko Epson
Evans &	Leica Camera	Sharp
Sutherland	Matsushita-	Sony
Excel	Kotobuki	Toshiba
Technology	Meade	Vivitar
Fuji Photo	Nikon	X-Rite
	Corporation	Xerox

Tokyo: 7753 FYE: March 31	Annual Growth	3/91	3/92	3/93	3/94	3/95	3/96	3/97	3/98	3/99	3/00
Sales (¥ mil.)	3.0%	370,503	356,129	348,398	321,080	333,656	365,751	448,074	490,258	506,075	482,767
Net income (¥ mil.)	—	(2,151)	(36,074)	(10,289)	(4,815)	(890)	4,245	10,290	16,428	9,002	3,144
Income as % of sales	—	—	—	—	—	—	1.2%	2.3%	3.4%	1.8%	0.7%
Earnings per share (¥)	—	(7.72)	(129.24)	(38.86)	(17.25)	(3.19)	15.20	36.85	58.83	32.13	11.22
Stock price - FY high (¥)	—	1,050	799	419	533	593	653	797	805	959	711
Stock price - FY low (¥)	—	535	400	289	331	380	300	601	526	481	360
Stock price - FY close (¥)	(6.4%)	746	416	362	465	425	591	739	795	618	412
P/E - high	—	—	—	—	—	—	43	22	14	30	63
P/E - low	—	—	—	—	—	—	20	16	9	15	32
Dividends per share (¥)	(3.8%)	8.50	4.25	0.00	0.00	0.00	2.50	5.50	6.00	7.00	6.00
Book value per share (¥)	(2.9%)	391.00	252.00	212.00	196.00	196.00	210.00	239.00	291.00	300.11	298.97
Employees	(3.4%)	6,608	6,741	6,826	5,701	5,450	4,821	4,658	4,600	4,760	4,841

HIGH/LOW/CLOSE

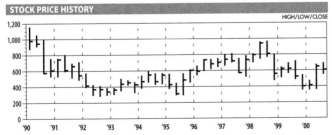

Debt ratio: 40.9%
Return on equity: 3.7%
Cash (¥ mil.): 23,726
Current ratio: 1.06
Long-term debt (¥ mil.): 57,910
No. of shares (mil.): 280
Dividends
  Yield: 0.0%
  Payout: 0.5%
Market value ($ mil.): 1,095
Sales ($ mil.): 4,758

MITSUBISHI GROUP

If you can eat it, wear it, watch it, listen to it, or drive it, the Mitsubishi Group makes it — and gathers the raw materials and produces the machines that get it made. Trailing Mitsui Group, Tokyo-based Mitsubishi Group is one of Japan's top *keiretsu*, a collection of affiliates with interlocking ownership but no official status as a group.

In Japanese *mitsubishi* means "three diamonds" — and a trinity of companies is the mother lode of Mitsubishi Group's more than 40 member firms. Of the three, Mitsubishi Heavy Industries makes heavy machinery; Mitsubishi Corporation, the chief trading company, merchant bank, and consulting firm, provides organizational oversight; and The Bank of Tokyo-Mitsubishi helps finance the group's activities.

Member companies also include Mitsubishi Electric, which makes everything from satellite technology to home electronics, auto unit Mitsubishi Motors (in which DaimlerChrysler is buying a controlling stake), and camera maker Nikon. Other members make steel and power plants, computers, metals, chemicals, food, and clothing.

The companies have been pinched by the Asian financial crisis: The Bank of Tokyo-Mitsubishi has been forced to take a government handout, and Mitsubishi Motors has struggled as car sales have fallen. The Mitsubishi Corporation is restructuring, cutting personnel costs as it focuses on food, information systems and services, infrastructure project development in emerging economies, and its energy and metals resources.

HISTORY

Yataro Iwasaki's close ties to the Japanese government (along with subsidies and monopoly rights) ensured the success of his shipping and trading company, Mitsubishi. Founded in 1870, Mitsubishi diversified into mining (1873), banking (1885), and shipbuilding (1887); it began to withdraw from shipping in the 1880s. During the next decade it invested in Japanese railroads and property.

In 1918 the Mitsubishi *zaibatsu* (conglomerate) spun off its central management arm, Mitsubishi Trading. By WWII the group was a huge amalgam of divisions and public companies. During the war it made warplanes (including the Zero fighter), ships, explosives, and beer.

The *zaibatsu* were dissolved by US occupation forces, and Mitsubishi was split into 139 entities. After the occupation, the Japanese government encouraged many of the former business groups to reunite (chiefly to provide capital for growth) around the old *zaibatsu* banks. In 1954 Mitsubishi Trading became the leader of the Mitsubishi Group and established Mitsubishi International (US), which became a leading exporter of US goods.

The 1964 merger of three Mitsubishi companies created Mitsubishi Heavy Industries, a top Japanese maker of ships, aircraft, plants, and heavy machinery. Mitsubishi Kasei, separated from Asahi Glass and Mitsubishi Rayon by a US fiat, became Japan's #1 chemical concern. Mitsubishi Electric emerged as one of the country's top electrical equipment and electronics makers. In 1971 Chrysler invested in Mitsubishi Motors and the company began making cars for the US automaker (the relationship was

ended in 1995). Also in 1971 Mitsubishi Trading was renamed Mitsubishi Corp.

Through the 1980s Japan seemed economically invincible. Then its "bubble economy" burst. The group fell behind in electronics and autos in the US, consumer demand dried up at home, and Mitsubishi Bank was left with a heavy burden of bad loans. Group members, which traditionally provided materials, supplies, and sales outlets for each other, began loosening *keiretsu* ties during Japan's recession of the 1990s.

Mitsubishi Bank merged with Bank of Tokyo in 1996 to form the biggest bank in the world, The Bank of Tokyo-Mitsubishi (BTM). In 1997 several Mitsubishi companies admitted paying off a corporate racketeer, setting off a wave of executive resignations.

In 1998, faced with deregulation, BTM agreed to team up with three other Mitsubishi financial units to form an investment trust company to defend against foreign rivals. Its efforts were to little avail. By 1999 BTM had tumbled from the top spot and was unable to keep the money freely flowing to fellow Mitsubishi members.

Hit hard by the Asian economic crisis, all the struggling Mitsubishi companies had to look outside of the *keiretsu* for help. In 1999 Mitsubishi Motors found a foreign partner, Volvo, for its truck making operations. Mitsubishi Oil merged with an outsider, Nippon Oil, to form Nippon Mitsubishi Oil. The following year DaimlerChrysler agreed to buy a controlling stake in Mitsubishi Motors for $2.1 billion.

Chairman, Mitsubishi Corporation: Minoru Makihara
President, CEO, and Chief Information Officer,
Mitsubishi Corporation: Mikio Sasaki
EVP and CFO, Mitsubishi Corporation: Koji Furukawa
EVP, Mitsubishi Corporation: Hiroshi Kawamura
EVP, Mitsubishi Corporation; President, Mitsubishi
International: Hironori Aihara
EVP, Mitsubishi Corporation; Group CEO, Metals:
Takeshi Sakurai
EVP, Mitsubishi Corporation; Group CEO, Machinery:
Naohisa Tonomura
Managing Director, Mitsubishi Corporation; Group
CEO, Chemicals: Yasuo Sone
Managing Director, Mitsubishi Corporation; Resident
Managing Director, China; President, Mitsubishi
Corporation (China) Investment: Yuzo Shinkai
Managing Director, Mitsubishi Corporation; Group
CEO, New Business Initiative: Yorihiko Kojima
Managing Director, Mitsubishi Corporation; Group
CEO, Living Essentials: Kanji Yamaguchi
Managing Director Mitsubishi Corporation; Chairman
and Managing Director, Mitsubishi Corporation
International; General Manager, Mitsubishi
Corporation European: Hiroshi Nemichi
Managing Director, Mitsubishi Corporation; Group
CEO, Fuels: Yukio Masuda
Managing Director, Mitsubishi Corporation; Group EVP
Metals; COO, Metals and Products Division:
Norio Okada
Managing Director, Mitsubishi Corporation; Group EVP
New Business Initiative: Susumu Kani
Managing Director, Mitsubishi Corporation; Group EVP
Living Essentials: Masaharu Goto
Managing Director, Mitsubishi Corporation; Group
CEO, IT and Electronics Business:
Takeshi Hashimoto
Auditors: Deloitte Touche Tohmatsu

HQ: Mitsubishi Corporation,
6-3, Marunouchi 2-chome,
Chiyoda-ku, Tokyo 100-8086, Japan
Phone: +81-3-3210-2121   Fax: +81-3-3210-8935
US HQ: 520 Madison Ave., New York, NY 10022
US Phone: 212-605-2000   US Fax: 212-605-2597
Web site: http://www.mitsubishi.or.jp

2000 Mitsubishi Corp. Sales

	% of total
Living essentials	28
Machinery	20
Fuels	19
Metals	18
Chemicals	10
Information systems & services	5
Total	**100**

Agilent Technologies	Levi Strauss
Bayer AG	LG Group
Bechtel	Marubeni
Bridgestone	Michelin
Daewoo	Mitsui
DaimlerChrysler	Nippon Steel
Dow Chemical	Nissan
DuPont	Samsung
Ford	Sime Darby
General Motors	Sumitomo
Honda	TOMEN
Hyundai	Toyota
Ito-Yokado	Yamaha
ITOCHU	

OTC: MSBHY* FYE: March 31	Annual Growth	3/91	3/92	3/93	3/94	3/95	3/96	3/97	3/98	3/99	3/00
Sales ($ mil.)	(1.1%)	140,303	136,335	140,158	142,996	171,829	144,438	127,566	118,928	115,024	127,309
Net income ($ mil.)	(6.5%)	464	397	249	179	251	312	359	358	262	253
Income as % of sales	—	0.3%	0.3%	0.2%	0.1%	0.1%	0.2%	0.3%	0.3%	0.2%	0.2%
Earnings per share ($)	(5.2%)	—	—	—	—	—	0.40	0.46	0.53	0.33	0.32
Stock price - FY high ($)	—	—	—	—	—	—	26.38	28.00	25.50	16.25	18.15
Stock price - FY low ($)	—	—	—	—	—	—	21.25	16.25	12.38	9.13	11.75
Stock price - FY close ($)	(8.9%)	—	—	—	—	—	26.38	18.00	16.13	13.25	18.15
P/E - high	—	—	—	—	—	—	66	61	48	49	56
P/E - low	—	—	—	—	—	—	53	35	23	28	36
Dividends per share ($)	0.7%	—	—	—	—	—	0.15	0.13	0.13	0.12	0.15
Book value per share ($)	(5.9%)	—	—	—	—	—	14.32	11.81	10.14	11.82	11.22
Employees	1.1%	—	—	—	10,297	13,929	9,241	12,613	8,401	11,650	10,993

* Information is for Mitsubishi Corporation only.

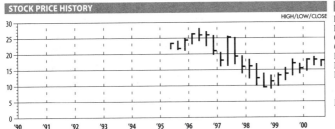

HIGH/LOW/CLOSE

Debt ratio: 75.5%
Return on equity: 3.0%
Cash ($ mil.): 4,516
Current ratio: 1.04
Long-term debt ($ mil.): 27,130
No. of shares (mil.): 784
Dividends
  Yield: 0.0%
  Payout: 0.5%
Market value ($ mil.): 14,222

MITSUI GROUP

Founded centuries ago by a samurai, Mitsui is still battling to make money. The Tokyo-based Mitsui Group is one of Japan's largest *keiretsu* (business groups connected through cross-ownership). Mitsui Group businesses include financial services (Sakura Bank, as well as Mitsui Marine & Fire Insurance and Mitsui Mutual Life Insurance), construction and real estate (Mitsui Construction, Mitsui Fudosan), and transportation and logistics (Mitsui O.S.K. Lines, Mitsui-Soko). Other members include Mitsui Engineering & Shipbuilding, Mitsui Mining & Smelting, Mitsui Mining Company, and the Mitsukoshi department store chain.

At the heart of the group is Mitsui & Co., the world's largest *sogo shosha* (general trading firm). Mitsui & Co. has more than 900 subsidiaries and associated companies with operations in chemicals, electronics, energy, food, iron and steel, machinery, nonferrous metals, and textiles. Mitsui & Co. is forging alliances to create new business. It has partnered with Royal Dutch/Shell Group and others in oil and gas development, America Online in Japanese Internet services, and NEC in making digital switching equipment.

While its size somewhat sheltered Mitsui from the Asian economic crisis, the group has experienced a decline in the trade of bulk items such as machinery and petroleum. In addition, its Sakura Bank, after being forced to ask Mitsui Group companies for capital, has announced plans for a merger with its rival Sumitomo Bank by 2002.

HISTORY

In the 17th century, unemployed samurai (warrior nobleman) Sokubei Mitsui opened a sake and soy sauce brewery at the urging of his wife, Shuho. After parental encouragement, their youngest son, Hachirobei, went to Edo (now Tokyo) and opened a dry goods store in 1673. Breaking with Japanese retailing tradition, the store offered merchandise at fixed prices on a cash-and-carry basis.

Hachirobei in 1683 opened a currency exchange that evolved into Mitsui Bank. The bank became the Osaka government's official money changer in 1691 and was the first to offer money orders in Japan. Before his death in 1694, Hachirobei drafted a unique succession plan to hand down control of the company to every related family, not just the eldest son's side.

The shogun's government called upon Mitsui in the mid-1800s to help finance its war against rebels. The family hired Rizaemon Minomura, an outsider with influence in the government, to protect the company from increasing demands for money. Mitsui became the bank of the Meiji government after Minomura astutely switched support to the winning rebels. Government industrialization pushed Mitsui into textiles, paper goods, and machinery. Minomura emphasized foreign trade and banking, creating Mitsui Bussan (now Mitsui & Co.) and Mitsui Bank in 1876. In the late 1800s Mitsui Bussan profited from a Japanese military buildup and formed a shipping line to take on Mitsubishi's monopoly. The Mitsui family withdrew from Mitsui Bussan management in 1936, following attacks by right-wing terrorists who opposed its democratic leanings.

Mitsui prospered during the 1930s as Japan's military prepared for war. After the defeat, occupation forces disbanded Japan's *zaibatsu* industrial groups, slicing Mitsui into more than 200 separate entities. By 1950 more than two dozen leaders of the former Mitsui companies began gathering the Mitsui Group back together. Trading firm Mitsui & Co. was established in 1959. The oil crises of the 1970s stalled the oil-dependent Japanese economy, prompting Mitsui companies to expand operations overseas and move into industries such as technology and aluminum.

The mammoth Sakura Bank was formed in 1990 with the merger of Mitsui Bank and Taiyo Kobe Bank. Other major ventures were to follow: In 1992 Mitsui & Co. joined with Marathon and Royal Dutch/Shell and others to search for oil and gas off Russia's Sakhalin Island; and Mitsui & Co. and other Japanese traders were enlisted by Oman in 1993 for a $9 billion liquefied natural gas transport venture. As cable TV emerged in Japan, Mitsui & Co. teamed up the next year with National Media Corp. to launch a home-shopping network.

In anticipation of deregulation in Japan's financial markets, four Mitsui Group firms' pension funds — Sakura Bank, Mitsui Marine & Fire Insurance, Mitsui Mutual Life Insurance, and Mitsui Trust and Banking — were linked in 1998. The next year Sakura Bank set aside old loyalties and announced a merger with Sumitomo Bank, the Sumitomo Group's main bank, by 2002. The group's Mitsui Trust and Banking also decided to merge with Chuo Trust and Banking in 2000.

OFFICERS

Chairman, Mitsui & Co.: Shigeji Ueshima
President and CEO, Mitsui & Co.: Shinjiro Shimizu
EVP and CFO, Mitsui & Co.: Toshikatsu Fukuma
General Manager, Personnel, Mitsui & Co.:
Yasunori Yakote
Auditors: Deloitte Touche Tohmatsu

LOCATIONS

HQ: 2-1, Ohtemachi 1-chome,
Chiyoda-ku, Tokyo 100-0004, Japan
Phone: +81-3-3285-1111   **Fax:** +81-3-3285-9819
US HQ: 200 Park Ave., 36th Fl., New York, NY 10166
US Phone: 212-878-4000   **US Fax:** 212-878-4800
Web site: http://www.mitsui.co.jp

Mitsui Group companies have operations worldwide.
Mitsui & Co. has offices in 93 countries.

PRODUCTS/OPERATIONS

2000 Sales (Mitsui & Co.)

	% of total
Machinery	20
Energy	19
Nonferrous metals	15
Chemicals	14
Iron & steel	11
Foods	9
General merchandise	6
Property & service business	3
Textiles	3
Total	**100**

Selected Mitsui Group Companies
Mitsui & Co.
Mitsui Construction Co.
Mitsui Engineering & Shipbuilding Co., Ltd.
Mitsui Fudosan Co., Ltd. (real estate)
Mitsui Marine & Fire Insurance
Mitsui Mining & Smelting Co., Ltd.
Mitsui Mining Company Ltd.
Mitsui Mutual Life Insurance Co.
Mitsui O.S.K. Lines, Ltd. (shipping and logistics)
Mitsui-Soko Co. Ltd. (transportation logistics)
Mitsukoshi Ltd. (department stores)

COMPETITORS

Daewoo
GE
Hyundai
ITOCHU
Kanematsu
Kawasaki Heavy Industries
Komatsu
LG Group
Marubeni
Mitsubishi
Nichimen
Nippon Steel
Nissho Iwai
Obayashi
Samsung
Sime Darby
Sumitomo
TOMEN

HISTORICAL FINANCIALS & EMPLOYEES

Nasdaq: MITSY* FYE: March 31	Annual Growth	3/91	3/92	3/93	3/94	3/95	3/96	3/97	3/98	3/99	3/00
Sales ($ mil.)	(1.9%)	148,264	134,163	133,903	134,984	167,367	139,511	131,878	131,626	117,373	125,116
Net income ($ mil.)	1.9%	292	203	153	149	303	283	293	248	250	346
Income as % of sales	—	0.2%	0.2%	0.1%	0.1%	0.2%	0.2%	0.2%	0.2%	0.2%	0.3%
Earnings per share ($)	5.7%	2.52	2.52	1.92	1.49	3.64	3.33	4.16	3.13	2.95	4.14
Stock price - FY high ($)	—	141.50	134.00	112.50	157.25	177.25	181.00	191.50	194.00	132.13	164.75
Stock price - FY low ($)	—	89.75	90.00	79.00	112.50	142.00	148.00	139.50	99.00	77.00	122.38
Stock price - FY close ($)	3.9%	117.00	96.50	109.00	144.50	153.13	181.00	146.00	125.75	132.13	164.50
P/E - high	—	56	53	59	106	49	54	46	62	45	40
P/E - low	—	36	36	41	76	39	44	34	32	26	30
Dividends per share ($)	6.2%	0.84	0.84	0.96	1.09	1.19	1.19	1.49	1.40	1.34	1.44
Book value per share ($)	3.8%	57.12	60.57	67.35	72.71	89.79	75.49	73.41	72.19	76.57	80.23
Employees	(0.9%)	—	11,528	8,929	8,670	8,341	7,974	7,783	7,538	10,957	10,702

*Information is for Mitsui & Co. Ltd. only.

STOCK PRICE HISTORY

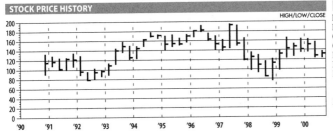

HIGH/LOW/CLOSE

2000 FISCAL YEAR-END

Debt ratio: 79.0%
Return on equity: 5.7%
Cash ($ mil.): 7,108
Current ratio: 1.25
Long-term debt ($ mil.): 23,910
No. of shares (mil.): 79
Dividends
  Yield: 0.0%
  Payout: 0.3%
Market value ($ mil.): 13,028

MOLSON INC.

OVERVIEW

Molson (formerly The Molson Companies) is into ice hockey and ice beer. The Montreal-based company's Molson Canada unit makes some of Canada's most popular brews, including Molson Canadian, Molson Export, and an all-star lineup of ice beers. In addition, nearly 20% of Molson's Canadian beer sales come from brewing non-Molson brands, including Foster's and Coors (Molson exports Foster's to the US). The company is in a heated shoot-out with Interbrew's Labatt for Canadian market share; both have about 45%.

The company regained control of its brewing operations by purchasing back the 50% stake owned by Foster's Brewing. The brewer sold its 130-store Beaver Lumber chain and its 25%

interest in Home Depot Canada to concentrate on suds, changing its name to Molson in 1999.

Molson owns the most successful team in the history of the National Hockey League, the Montreal Canadiens (winners of 24 Stanley Cup championships), and the Canadiens' home arena, Molson Centre. The company has put both the team and the arena on the selling block in an effort to further focus on it brewing operations. Molson is closing one brewery and cutting 10% of its workforce to cut costs. The Molson family controls more than 50% of the company's voting shares. Chairman Eric Molson, great-great-great-grandson of the founder, has about 33% of the votes.

HISTORY

John Molson founded what would become North America's oldest brewery in Montreal in 1786. The Molson Companies did a healthy business, thanks in large part to the lack of competition in the frontier city. In 1797 Molson added a lumberyard, and in 1809 he launched the *Accommodation,* Canada's first steamboat, to make runs between Montreal and Quebec City. Beer production grew, and the company continued to modernize.

Brewing sales stalled during the second half of the 1800s, and in 1897 Fred and Herbert, the fourth generation of Molsons to run the brewery, began to revitalize the company. The pair modernized the company's facilities, adding electric lighting, refrigeration, and pasteurization equipment. By 1900 sales had increased by 40%.

When a temperance movement swept through Canada during the 1910s, Molson and its fellow Quebec-based brewers started an anti-prohibition campaign. Quebec's citizens voted overwhelmingly against prohibition. Molson got a boost from Americans who came to drink in Montreal during the US Prohibition.

Sales took off again following WWII, and by 1950 the company was making 1.5 million bottles of beer a day. Molson opened a brewery in Toronto in 1955 and acquired Sick's Brewery (five breweries in Canada and two in the US, 1958), Fort Garry Brewery (Winnipeg, 1959), and Newfoundland Brewery (1962).

As part of a diversification program, in 1971 Molson acquired several home improvement retailers, including Aikenhead Hardware (converted to Home Depot stores in 1994) and Beaver Lumber. Molson made its first major US acquisition, chemical products maker Diversey,

in 1978. That year it also bought the Montreal Canadiens hockey team, which commenced playing in 1917.

In 1988 Molson merged its brewing operations with Carling O'Keefe Breweries (a subsidiary of Australian brewer Elders IXL, now called Foster's Brewing). Each company took a 50% stake in the venture, called Molson Breweries; their respective stakes were reduced to 40% as Miller Brewing bought 20% in 1993.

Now committed to brewing, Molson sold its Reno-Depot home improvement stores to Castorama in 1997. Molson and Foster's also bought back and split Miller Brewing's 20% stake in Molson Breweries that year. In 1998 Molson bought back Foster's stake — Molson is now the only large Canadian-owned brewer — and its 25% interest in Coors Canada. (Its stake is now about 50%.) Also in 1998 Molson sold its 25% interest in Home Depot Canada to The Home Depot.

Its Molson Breweries unit was renamed Molson Canada in 1999. Also that year the company sold its 130 Beaver Lumber outlets and dropped "The" and "Companies" from its name to reflect its focus on beer; it also put its stake in the Canadiens hockey team as well as Molson Centre arena up for sale. In May of 2000 Daniel J. O'Neill was appointed president and CEO of the corporation.

Molson bought back its brands in the US from Molson USA (renamed Foster's USA) in October 2000. Later that month it formed a joint venture with Adolph Coors to distribute its brands in the US and to develop the light beer segment in Canada. In November Molson purchased the Bavaria beer brand from the #3 global brewer, AmBev, for $213 million.

Chairman: Eric H. Molson
President and CEO: Daniel J. O'Neill
EVP and CFO: Robert Coallier
EVP; President, Club de Hockey Canadien and Molson Centre: Pierre Boivin
SVP Taxation: J. M. DeYoung
SVP International Brewing Strategy: P. L. Kelley
SVP, Chief Legal Officer, and Secretary: M. Giguère
SVP Human Resources: J.M. Grossett
VP and Controller: A.A. de Saldanha
VP Corporate Affairs: J.P. Macdonald
VP and Treasurer: K.J. Lahti
President, Ontario and Atlantic Region, Molson Canada: D. Perkins
President, Quebec Region, Molson Canada: R.H. Doin
President, Western Region, Molson Canada: B.A. Shier
SVP Quality Brewing, Molson Canada: P.M. Ferland
SVP and General Counsel, Molson Canada: F.A. Hausman
SVP Marketing, Molson Canada: Michael S. Downey
SVP Operations, Molson Canada: E.A. Liedtke
VP Marketing, Molson Canada: Andrew Barrett
Auditors: PricewaterhouseCoopers LLP

Selected Brands

Molson

Black Ice	Grand North
Brador	Ice
Canadian (regular,	Light
Ice, Light)	Red Jack
Cream Ale	Special Dry
Diamond	Spring Bock
Dry	Stock Ale
Exel	Ultra
Export and Export Ale	XXX
Golden	

Major Group Operations

Brewing
Coors Canada (50%, brewing and distribution)
Molson Canada

Sports and Entertainment
Molson Centre (21,400-seat arena)
Molstar Sports & Entertainment (produces NHL games for Canadian television)
Montreal Canadiens (NHL team)

HQ: 1555 Notre Dame St. East, Montréal, Quebec H2L 2R5, Canada
Phone: 514-521-1786   **Fax:** 514-598-6969
US HQ: 1606 Washington Plaza, Reston, VA 20190
US Phone: 703-709-6600   **US Fax:** 703-437-8620
Web site: http://www.molson.com

Molson operates breweries in Barrie and Toronto, Ontario; Edmonton, Alberta; Montreal; Regina, Saskatchewan; St. John's, Newfoundland; and Vancouver.

Adolph Coors	Genesee
Anchor Brewing	Guinness/UDV
Anheuser-Busch	Heineken
Bass Brewers	Interbrew
Big Rock Brewery	Kirin
Boston Beer	Miller Brewing
Boston Bruins	Ottawa Senators
Buffalo Sabres	Pyramid Breweries
Constellation Brands	S&P
Gambrinus	Sleeman Breweries

Toronto: MOL.A FYE: March 31	Annual Growth	3/91	3/92	3/93	3/94	3/95	3/96	3/97	3/98	3/99	3/00
Sales (C$ mil.)	(3.2%)	2,531	2,904	3,086	2,967	2,886	1,443	1,482	1,552	1,584	1,896
Net income (C$ mil.)	—	(39)	126	165	126	87	(306)	34	111	170	(44)
Income as % of sales	—	—	4.3%	5.3%	4.2%	3.0%	—	2.3%	7.2%	10.7%	—
Earnings per share (C$)	—	(0.72)	2.25	2.76	2.13	1.49	(5.27)	0.57	1.89	2.88	(0.74)
Stock price - FY high (C$)	—	29.08	35.25	36.00	28.88	22.63	25.13	25.10	27.75	28.25	28.00
Stock price - FY low (C$)	—	18.75	27.50	25.38	22.13	17.75	19.88	19.70	22.00	20.25	19.75
Stock price - FY close (C$)	(3.4%)	28.83	34.75	25.50	24.88	20.00	24.25	23.25	24.40	21.50	21.10
P/E - high	—	—	16	13	14	15	—	44	15	10	—
P/E - low	—	—	12	9	10	12	—	35	12	7	—
Dividends per share (C$)	0.8%	0.67	0.72	0.72	0.72	0.72	0.72	0.72	0.72	0.72	0.72
Book value per share (C$)	2.1%	14.41	16.32	19.75	22.28	23.88	15.59	15.48	16.60	18.78	17.32
Employees	(13.9%)	13,800	15,800	16,400	14,700	18,870	5,100	5,100	4,500	4,100	3,600

HIGH/LOW/CLOSE

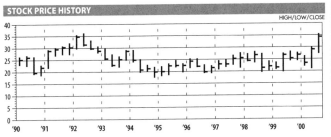

Debt ratio: 53.1%
Return on equity: —
Cash (C$ mil.): 70
Current ratio: 0.76
Long-term debt (C$ mil.): 1,162
No. of shares (mil.): 59
Dividends
  Yield: 0.0%
  Payout: —
Market value ($ mil.): 859
Sales ($ mil.): 1,304

MOORE CORPORATION LIMITED

OVERVIEW

How long will Moore's traditional customers call its name? One of the world's largest printers of paper business forms, the Toronto-based company is expanding and refolding operations to confront a computerized future where paper may become passe — or at least less prevalent. Moore produces and markets electronic and paper business forms, labels and label systems, print management equipment, bar-code systems, and data management systems, all with a focus toward finding a niche in the digital age. It also provides direct marketing fulfillment services, statement printing, and database software. Moore markets primarily in North America to government agencies and a variety of industries, including health care, finance, manufacturing, and telecommunications. The US accounts for three-quarters of sales.

A decrease in demand for paper products has prompted Moore to invest in electronic systems and services. The company has restructured three times in the 1990s; the latest involved the sale of its European and Australasian businesses to refocus on the North American market.

Toronto-based Trimark Investment Management owns about 20% of Moore.

HISTORY

UK-born printer Samuel Moore met sales-clerk John Carter in Toronto in 1879. Carter had an idea to bind together multiple sets of receipts with a single sheet of carbon paper between, rescuing salespeople from fumbling with separate sets of forms. Moore bought the idea, hired Carter, patented the product, and in 1882 formed Grip Printing and Publishing Company to produce the Paragon Black Leaf Counter Check Book.

As the forms business grew, Moore bought Kidder Press (1899), maker of the printing presses he used, and created box and form maker F.N. Burt (1909). In 1925 Moore's organization began selling inexpensive, single-use carbon paper to be bound into sets of business forms, eliminating handling entirely. The product proved popular and led to the development of snap-apart forms. The US government's use of carbon copies resulted in their acceptance as legal documents in business, boosting sales. In 1929 Moore began consolidating his namesake business.

By WWII all modern organizations were hooked on forms. They had become so important that US Army paper-pushers sent a transport plane on an emergency mission during the war to pick up Moore forms. Moore died in 1948.

Following WWII, the company grew globally. It formed Toppan Moore (Japan), a joint venture with Toppan Printing (sold in 1997). In what now seems like historical irony, increased computer use accelerated demand for Moore's forms.

In the 1970s and 1980s, Moore entered direct marketing, image processing, and database management but failed in its efforts to diversify into US computer supply retailing (MicroAge stores).

With declining sales and a $78 million loss in 1993, the company restructured, cutting 3,000 jobs and closing several plants. Moore began buying companies that would give it entry into new technology markets: Computer Resources Trust (1993, Australia's largest business forms company), Logidec Canada (1993, electronic publishing and printing), and an 18% stake — now 12% — in JetForm (1994, software and electronic forms).

Moore repeated its overhauls in 1994, closing nine plants and cutting more than 1,900 jobs. Late that year the company and Electronic Data Systems (EDS) entered a pair of 10-year concurrent contracts, worth $1 billion, whereby EDS will revamp Moore's internal information systems while Moore takes charge of all of EDS's business forms and commercial printing needs.

The company acquired On-Line Software, which develops real estate software, and formed a partnership with Xerox in 1996 to provide printing services to industries such as banking and insurance. The following year Moore purchased Peak Technologies, a distributor of barcode systems.

Ed Tyler became CEO in 1998. Reacting to stiff competition from new technology and hobbled by outdated manufacturing facilities, the company restructured again that year; it closed 10 plants and divested itself of its European forms and labels business and operations in Australia, New Zealand, and China. The restructuring contributed to a $548 million loss in 1998. Moore also launched a suite of software for document management that year.

In 1999 Moore entered into a joint venture to provide printing and design services to Argentina's postal department and purchased a 40% stake in Quality Color Press, a print management firm based in Edmonton, Alberta.

Chairman: Thomas E. Kierans, age 59
President and CEO: W. Ed Tyler, age 47, $2,238,150 pay
EVP: Thomas J. McKiernan, age 61, $888,208 pay
SVP and CFO: Michael S. Rousseau, age 41, $421,886 pay
SVP Business Development: James B. Currie, age 51
VP and General Counsel: Robert Z. Slaughter, age 45
VP Human Resources and Corporate Commmunications: Charles F. Canfield, age 50
VP; President, Logistics and Operations, Moore North America: Patrick T. Brong, age 55
VP; President Sales and Marketing, Moore North America: Siegfried E. Buck, age 50, $485,994 pay
VP; President, Peak Technologies: James D. Wyner, age 56, $475,183 pay
Auditors: PricewaterhouseCoopers LLP

LOCATIONS

HQ: 1 First Canadian Place,
Toronto, Ontario M5X 1G5, Canada
Phone: 416-364-2600   **Fax:** 416-364-1667
US HQ: 1200 Lakeside Dr., Bannockburn, IL 60015
US Phone: 847-607-6000   **US Fax:** 847-607-7735
Web site: http://www.moore.com

Moore has operations in Argentina, Belgium, Brazil, Canada, Chile, Costa Rica, El Salvador, France, Guatemala, Mexico, the UK, the US, and Venezuela.

1999 Sales

	$ mil.	% of total
North America		
US	1,831	76
Canada	219	9
Other regions	375	15
Total	**2,425**	**100**

PRODUCTS/OPERATIONS

1999 Sales

	% of total
Forms, labels & related products	69
Direct marketing programs & software	31
Total	**100**

Selected Products and Services
Bar coding
Commercial printing
Custom business forms and equipment
Facilities management
Integrated forms, labels, and electronic media
Labels
On-demand and data-based publishing
Pressure seal mailers and mailing services
Print management outsourcing

Selected Subsidiaries
Colleagues Group (UK's largest direct marketing services firm)
Peak Technologies (automatic data capture and transmission, warehouse management system)
Phoenix Group (database marketing)

COMPETITORS

American Banknote
Avery Dennison
Bell & Howell
Corporate Express
Deluxe
Equifax
infoUSA
John Harland
Merrill
NCR
New England Business Service
Pitney Bowes
Precept Business Services
R. R. Donnelley
Standard Register
Wallace Computer
Workflow Management
Xerox

HISTORICAL FINANCIALS & EMPLOYEES

NYSE: MCL FYE: December 31	Annual Growth	12/90	12/91	12/92	12/93	12/94	12/95	12/96	12/97	12/98	12/99
Sales ($ mil.)	(1.5%)	2,770	2,492	2,433	2,329	2,401	2,602	2,518	2,631	2,718	2,425
Net income ($ mil.)	(2.9%)	121	88	(2)	(78)	121	268	150	55	(548)	93
Income as % of sales	—	4.4%	3.5%	—	—	5.1%	10.3%	6.0%	2.1%	—	3.8%
Earnings per share ($)	(2.1%)	1.27	0.91	(0.02)	(0.78)	1.22	2.68	1.50	0.59	(6.19)	1.05
Stock price - FY high ($)	—	30.25	28.50	22.13	21.25	20.88	23.50	22.25	22.88	17.69	12.38
Stock price - FY low ($)	—	21.63	19.00	13.25	15.00	16.25	17.50	16.63	13.50	9.44	5.81
Stock price - FY close ($)	(13.7%)	22.75	21.25	17.13	19.13	18.88	18.75	20.50	15.13	11.00	6.06
P/E - high	—	24	31	—	—	17	9	15	39	—	12
P/E - low	—	17	21	—	—	13	7	11	23	—	6
Dividends per share ($)	(15.7%)	0.93	0.94	0.94	0.94	0.94	0.94	0.94	0.94	0.57	0.20
Book value per share ($)	(8.0%)	16.05	16.21	14.83	13.19	13.71	14.90	15.49	12.72	6.90	7.60
Employees	(5.0%)	25,021	23,556	23,124	22,014	19,890	18,771	18,849	20,084	17,135	15,812

STOCK PRICE HISTORY

HIGH/LOW/CLOSE

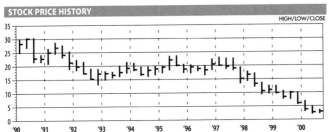

1999 FISCAL YEAR-END

Debt ratio: 23.1%
Return on equity: 14.4%
Cash ($ mil.): 38
Current ratio: 1.21
Long-term debt ($ mil.): 202
No. of shares (mil.): 88
Dividends
  Yield: 3.3%
  Payout: 19.0%
Market value ($ mil.): 536

NATIONAL AUSTRALIA BANK

OVERVIEW

This Aussie bank has *auss*-ome reach. National Australia Bank (NAB) is in not only Australia but also New Zealand, several Asian countries, Ireland, the UK, and the US. More than half of its sales are made outside Australia.

At home, the Melbourne-based bank offers retail banking (deposits, credit cards, mortgages, and other loans) and such business banking services as loans, leases, foreign exchange, and trade finance. Subsidiaries offer asset management, trustee services for retail and corporate clients, and other services.

Abroad, NAB owns regional banks Northern Bank (Northern Ireland), Yorkshire Bank (England), Clydesdale Bank (Scotland), National Irish Bank (Ireland), and Michigan National (US). Closer to home are its Bank of New Zealand and National Australia Bank Asia (based in Hong Kong), which primarily offers trade financing and foreign exchange. Other foreign operations include National Australia Life (UK life insurance and investment) and US mortgage firm HomeSide International.

Australia's #1 bank has diversified to defend against potential economic downturns that could zap individual units. Since the government has banned consolidation among Australia's top four banks (NAB; Westpac Banking; Australia and New Zealand Banking Group; and Commonwealth Bank of Australia), NAB takes advantage of market deregulation and consolidation abroad.

HISTORY

Formed in 1858 in Melbourne, National Bank of Australasia (NBA) just missed the peak of the Victoria gold rush. The bank expanded across the territory and was one of the first to lend to farmers and ranchers using land deeds as security. In the late 1870s, drought imperiled Victoria. Seeking greener pastures, NBA entered New South Wales in 1885, then headed into Western Australia. Economic instability continued; in 1893 the bank experienced its first panic and was shuttered for eight weeks. NBA reopened only to close a quarter of its branches between 1893 and 1896.

During the Australian commonwealth's early years, Western Australia was the bank's salvation as the economies in Victoria and South Australia stagnated. NBA helped fund Australia's WWI efforts through public loans. A postwar consolidation wave in banking swept up NBA, which made acquisitions in 1918 and 1922.

Overdue farm and ranch loans weakened the bank during the Depression. As WWII raged, the Commonwealth Bank (established in 1912) took greater control of Australia's banks. With competition among banks primarily limited to branch growth, NBA acquired Queensland National Bank in 1948 and Ballarat Banking Co., a traditional farm and ranch lender, in 1955. The bank diversified into consumer finance through acquisition. In the 1960s Australia experienced an economic boom as immigration and industrialization grew. The boom went bust in the 1970s as the world sunk into recession. Still under the Commonwealth Bank's tight control, the banks watched business that had once been theirs lost to building societies, merchant banks, and credit unions.

The 1980s brought banking deregulation. To vie with foreign banks entering Australia, NBA in 1981 merged with Commercial Banking Co. of Sydney and became the National Commercial Banking Corp. of Australia in 1982. (It took its present name in 1984.) Throughout the 1980s the bank diversified and moved into the US and Japan. It invested in property and made loans to foreign countries. All too quickly, though, property values sank and countries defaulted on loans.

To fight recession, NAB looked abroad for opportunities. In 1987 it bought Clydesdale Bank, Northern Bank, and National Irish Bank from Midland Bank Group (now part of HSBC Holdings). Three years later, NAB bought Yorkshire Bank, then turned the four banks around by linking them and tightening loan operations. In 1992 it bought the troubled Bank of New Zealand, again tightening loan operations. Three years later NAB claimed Michigan National in the US.

With the mid-1990s' economic recovery, NAB bought County NatWest Australia Investment Management in 1997 (which it said in 2000 it would sell). The next year it bought HomeSide to try to adapt the US mortgage firm's efficient operations for all its banks.

NAB in 2000 bought Lend Lease's MLC fund management group. It also announced plans to launch a separate stock for its European businesses, fueling speculation it might be on the prowl to buy a large UK bank. Australia's government that year accused NAB of credit card transaction price-fixing; the bank faces a possible fine of nearly $6 million.

Chairman: Mark R. Rayner, age 61
VC: David K. Macfarlane, age 69
Managing Director and CEO: Francis J. Cicutto
CFO: Robert M.C. Prowse
Executive General Manger, Business and Personal Financial Services: Glenn L.L. Barnes
Executive General Manager, Group Human Resources: Peter A. McKinnon
Executive General Manager, Group Risk Management: Robert B. Miller
Executive General Manager, Products and Services: Ross E. Pinney
CEO, Michigan National Corporation: Doug Ebert
Chairman and CEO, HomeSide International: Joe K. Pickett, age 54
Auditors: KPMG

LOCATIONS

HQ: National Australia Bank Limited,
500 Bourke St., GPO Box 84A,
Melbourne, Victoria 3000, Australia
Phone: +61-3-8641-3500   **Fax:** +61-3-8641-4916
US HQ: 200 Park Ave., 34th Fl., New York, NY 10166
US Phone: 212-916-9500   **US Fax:** 212-983-1969
Web site: http://www.national.com.au

1999 Sales

	% of total
Australia	47
UK	25
US	14
New Zealand	9
Asian countries	3
Ireland	2
Total	**100**

PRODUCTS/OPERATIONS

1999 Sales

	% of total
Loan interest	62
Other interest	15
Loan fees	6
Money transfer fees	5
Fees & commissions	5
Other income	7
Total	**100**

Selected Subsidiaries
National Americas Holdings Limited
Michigan National Corporation
National Americas Investment, Inc.
HomeSide International, Inc.
National Australia Finance (Asia) Limited
National Australia Group Europe Limited
Clydesdale Bank PLC (Group)
National Australia Group (NZ) Limited
Bank of New Zealand
National Australia Life Company Limited
National Australia Merchant Bank (Singapore) Limited
National Irish Holdings Limited
Northern Bank Limited
Yorkshire Bank PLC

COMPETITORS

Abbey National	HSBC Holdings
Allied Irish Banks	Lloyds TSB
ANZ	Mitsubishi Trust
Bank of Ireland	and Banking
Bank of Scotland	Northern Rock plc
Barclays	Royal Bank of Scotland
Commonwealth Bank	Westpac
of Australia	

HISTORICAL FINANCIALS & EMPLOYEES

NYSE: NAB FYE: September 30	Annual Growth	9/90	9/91	9/92	9/93	9/94	9/95	9/96	9/97	9/98	9/99
Assets ($ mil.)	8.7%	78,193	73,877	73,279	75,592	93,153	108,028	137,665	146,428	149,266	165,813
Net income ($ mil.)	12.8%	624	576	481	728	1,264	1,446	1,666	1,610	1,194	1,841
Income as % of assets	—	0.8%	0.8%	0.7%	1.0%	1.4%	1.3%	1.2%	1.1%	0.8%	1.1%
Earnings per share ($)	6.5%	3.36	2.94	1.94	2.82	4.71	5.18	5.69	5.50	4.09	5.93
Stock price - FY high ($)	—	27.63	28.75	31.63	39.13	46.63	46.63	53.00	81.25	80.00	97.75
Stock price - FY low ($)	—	22.75	19.50	25.63	23.50	37.13	37.25	41.38	52.50	59.06	56.88
Stock price - FY close ($)	13.3%	24.00	28.63	25.88	38.50	38.25	44.38	52.88	77.13	59.94	73.81
P/E - high	—	8	10	16	14	10	9	9	15	19	16
P/E - low	—	7	7	13	8	8	7	7	10	14	9
Dividends per share ($)	6.3%	1.99	1.97	1.67	0.82	2.18	2.93	3.27	3.43	3.15	3.44
Book value per share ($)	4.9%	26.58	25.17	22.49	21.54	26.53	29.16	33.48	30.78	31.44	40.72
Employees	4.3%	—	—	38,377	43,053	43,053	52,567	47,178	46,392	46,300	51,566

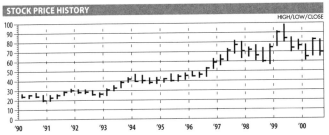

STOCK PRICE HISTORY   HIGH/LOW/CLOSE

1999 FISCAL YEAR-END
Equity as % of assets: 7.3%
Return on assets: 1.2%
Return on equity: 17.2%
Long-term debt ($ mil.): 7,266
No. of shares (mil.): 297
Dividends
Yield: 4.7%
Payout: 58.0%
Market value ($ mil.): 21,908
Sales ($ mil.): 12,810

NEC CORPORATION

OVERVIEW

NEC has quite a memory. The hundred year-old Tokyo-based company is in a constant tussle with Fujitsu to be Japan's leading PC maker. It is also the #2 worldwide supplier of computer chips, behind Intel, and a top maker of telecommunications products. Computers (from specialized fingerprint identification systems to supercomputers) and industrial electronic systems account for about 45% of sales. Other products include cellular phones, network routers, satellites, and other communication systems and equipment; and DRAM memory, plasma display panels, integrated circuits, and other electronic devices.

After two years of streamlining that included the elimination of its money-losing Packard Bell brand, NEC is looking to expand. The company is positioning itself as an online application hardware, software, and service force. True to its 20-year vision of "C&C" (the convergence of computers and communications), NEC has formed Internet-centric subsidiaries. NEC is also positioning its nearly 3 million-member-strong Internet provider, Biglobe, as an education and entertainment portal site.

NEC also hopes to dominate the mobile networking. It plans to spend more than $5 billion on acquisitions and some $9 billion in capital improvements over the next three years in an effort to lead the broadband market.

HISTORY

A group of Japanese investors, led by Kunihiko Iwadare, formed Nippon Electric Company (NEC) in a joint venture with Western Electric (US) in 1899 to import telephone equipment. NEC soon became a maker and a major supplier to Japan's Communications Ministry. Western Electric sold its stake in NEC in 1925. The company became affiliated with the Sumitomo *keiretsu* (industrial group) in the 1930s and went public in 1949.

After Nippon Telegraph and Telephone (NTT) was formed in 1952, NEC became one of its four leading suppliers. The post-WWII need to repair Japan's telephone systems and the country's continuing economic recovery resulted in strong demand from NTT for NEC's products. In the 1950s and 1960s NTT business represented over 50% of sales, even though NEC had expanded overseas, diversified into home appliances, and formed a computer alliance with Honeywell (US).

In the 1970s Honeywell's lagging position in computers hurt NEC; the company recovered through in-house development efforts and a mainframe venture with Toshiba. In 1977 CEO Koji Kobayashi articulated his revolutionary vision of NEC's future as an integrator of computers and communications through semiconductor technology.

NEC invested heavily in R&D and expansion, becoming the world's largest semiconductor maker in 1985. Despite its proprietary operating system, NEC garnered over 50% of the Japanese computer market in the 1980s. NEC entered into a mainframe computer partnership with Honeywell and France's Groupe Bull in 1987.

By the early 1990s NEC had lost its status as the world's largest semiconductor maker to Intel. NEC bought 20% of US computer maker Packard Bell in 1995. The following year NEC merged most of its PC business outside Japan with that company, creating Packard Bell NEC. Also in 1996 NEC created US subsidiary Holon Net Corp. to make hardware and software for Internet and intranet markets.

NEC took control of Packard Bell NEC in 1998, upping its stake to 53%. A sluggish Japanese economy and slumping memory prices contributed to NEC's drop in income for fiscal 1998. A defense contract scandal involving overbilling and improper hiring by an NEC unit forced the resignation of chairman Tadahiro Sekimoto and, later, president Hisashi Kaneko.

New president Koji Nishigaki, the first at NEC without an engineering background, led a sweeping reorganization to cut 10% of the company's workforce — 15,000 employees — over three years. He revamped NEC operations around Internet application hardware, software, and services. In 1998 NEC formed a rare pact with a Japanese rival, allying with Hitachi to consolidate memory chip operations. The restructuring of Packard Bell NEC (NEC by then owned 88%) helped cause a $1.3 billion loss for fiscal 1999, NEC's worst-ever drop. NEC folded up its Packard Bell NEC division later that year, imposing layoffs of about 80% of its staff, divesting it from the US retail market, and excising the historic Packard Bell brand name.

In 2000 NEC announced plans to spin off its software division. It also said it would expand wafer production and build plants for making memory, LSI, and liquid crystal display (LCD) driver chips to meet a growing demand caused by increasing sales of portable digital devices.

By mid-2000 the company launched an aggressive spending program in a move to lead the broadband mobile networking market.

Chairman: Hajime Sasaki
President: Koji Nishigaki
SEVP: Masato Chiba
SEVP; President, NEC Networks: Mineo Sugiyama
EVP: Eiichi Yoshikawa
EVP: Shigeo Matsumoto
EVP; President, NEC Electron Devices: Kanji Sugihara
EVP; President, NEC Solutions: Akinobu Kanasugi
SVP: Yoshio Omori
SVP: Kazuhiko Kanou
SVP: Yukihiko Baba
SVP: Iwao Shinohara
SVP: Kaoru Tosaka
SVP: Tatsuo Ishiguro
SVP: Norio Saito
SVP: Kaoru Yano
Auditors: PricewaterhouseCoopers

2000 Sales

	$ mil.	% of total
Hardware	22,045	40
Networks	14,833	27
Semiconductors	10,901	20
Other	7,028	13
Adjustments	(6,346)	—
Total	**48,461**	**100**

Selected Products

Auto electronics	Mobile communications
Broadcast equipment	PCs
Defense electronics	Semiconductor
Fiber-optic systems	manufacturing
Mainframe computers	equipment
Microwave	Semiconductors
communications	Satellite communications

HQ: Nippon Denki Kabushiki Kaisha
   7-1, Shiba 5-chome,
   Minato-ku, Tokyo 108-8001, Japan
Phone: +81-3-3454-1111   **Fax:** +81-3-3798-1510
Web site: http://www.nec-global.com

In Japan, NEC operates a network of 88 subsidiaries, 61 plants, and about 450 sales offices. Outside Japan, the company operates 175 subsidiaries and affiliates, and 64 plants, in 21 countries.

2000 Sales

	$ mil.	% of total
Japan	36,368	75
North America	5,065	10
Other regions	7,028	15
Total	**48,461**	**100**

3Com	IBM	Robert Bosch
Acer	Intel	Samsung
Alcatel	LSI Logic	SANYO
AMD	Lucent	Scientific-Atlanta
Apple Computer	Marconi	SGI
Atmel	Matsushita	Siemens
Cisco Systems	Micron	Sony
Compaq	Technology	STMicro-
Dell Computer	Motorola	electronics
eMachines	National	Sun
Ericsson	Semiconductor	Microsystems
Fujitsu	Nokia	Texas
Gateway	Nortel Networks	Instruments
Hewlett-Packard	Philips	Toshiba
Hitachi	Electronics	Unisys

Nasdaq: NIPNY FYE: March 31	Annual Growth	3/91	3/92	3/93	3/94	3/95	3/96	3/97	3/98	3/99	3/00
Sales ($ mil.)	7.0%	26,306	28,428	30,605	35,096	43,326	41,376	39,907	36,851	40,334	48,461
Net income ($ mil.)	(13.9%)	387	115	(393)	65	406	721	739	311	(1,339)	101
Income as % of sales	—	1.5%	0.4%	—	0.2%	0.9%	1.7%	1.9%	0.8%	—	0.2%
Earnings per share ($)	(14.4%)	1.22	0.37	(1.02)	0.25	1.32	2.11	2.09	0.91	(4.18)	0.30
Stock price - FY high ($)	—	71.50	59.50	39.88	54.75	64.75	75.25	65.00	74.00	60.50	149.50
Stock price - FY low ($)	—	45.75	34.13	24.50	34.25	45.13	51.00	49.88	48.63	31.00	52.13
Stock price - FY close ($)	11.6%	55.13	36.25	39.63	51.63	52.50	58.25	56.63	50.75	59.63	148.44
P/E - high	—	63	165	—	211	49	36	31	76	—	498
P/E - low	—	40	95	—	132	34	24	24	50	—	174
Dividends per share ($)	(1.2%)	0.30	0.32	0.34	0.39	0.42	0.25	0.23	0.00	0.23	0.27
Book value per share ($)	3.9%	20.61	21.49	22.79	24.89	29.48	26.56	25.84	25.19	23.19	29.11
Employees	3.1%	117,994	128,320	140,969	143,320	147,994	152,719	151,966	152,450	157,800	154,787

HIGH/LOW/CLOSE

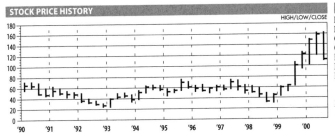

Debt ratio: 57.6%
Return on equity: 1.2%
Cash ($ mil.): 3,631
Current ratio: 1.10
Long-term debt ($ mil.): 12,875
No. of shares (mil.): 326
Dividends
   Yield: 0.2%
   Payout: 90.0%
Market value ($ mil.): 48,356

NESTLÉ S.A.

OVERVIEW

A cup of instant coffee, a chunk of chocolate — Nestlé knows it's the simple things that drive a global business. The world's #1 food company, Nestlé dominates in several food arenas. The Vevey, Switzerland-based company makes the world's #1 coffee (Nescafé) as well as spring water, milk products, cereals, ice cream, pasta, pet food, and chocolate and confections. Its global brands include Nestlé, Nescafé, Nestea, Buitoni, Maggi, and Friskies. The company also makes eye care products and owns a large, indirect stake in cosmetics giant L'Oréal.

Notable joint ventures include Cereal Partners Worldwide, with General Mills outside the US, and Ice Cream Partners USA, with Pillsbury's Häagen-Dazs.

Nestlé has long been an international company. Many of its brands are unique to particular countries, with products tailored to local tastes. Nestlé focuses on dominating international markets over the long term and has been patient for living standards to improve in developing nations. For the future, the company sees itself expanding into more specialty nutritional foods, and someday bringing more of L'Oréal under its roof.

HISTORY

Henri Nestlé purchased a factory in Vevey, Switzerland, in 1843 that made products ranging from nut oils to rum. In 1867 he developed a powder made from cow's milk and wheat flour as a substitute for mother's milk. Demand for the infant cereal outpaced his factory's capacity. He gave his company a nest logo, since his name meant "little nest." One year earlier two Americans, Charles and George Page, had founded the Anglo-Swiss Condensed Milk Company in Cham, Switzerland, using Gail Borden's milk-canning technology.

In 1875 Nestlé sold his eponymous company, then doing business in 16 countries. When Anglo-Swiss launched a milk-based infant food in 1878, Nestlé's new owners responded by introducing a condensed-milk product. In 1905, a year after Nestlé began selling chocolate, the companies ended their rivalry by merging under the Nestlé name.

Hampered by limited milk supplies during WWI, the company expanded into regions less affected by the war, such as the US. In 1929 it acquired Cailler, the first company to mass-produce chocolate bars, and Swiss General, inventor of milk chocolate.

An investment in a Brazilian condensed-milk factory during the 1920s paid an unexpected dividend when Brazilian coffee growers suggested the company develop a water-soluble "coffee cube." Released in 1938, Nescafé instant coffee quickly became popular. Other new products included Nestlé's Crunch bar (1938), Quik drink mix (1948), and Taster's Choice instant coffee (1966).

Nestlé expanded during the 1970s with acquisitions such as Beringer Brothers wines (sold in 1995), Stouffer's, and Libby's. Moving beyond foods in 1974, Nestlé acquired a 49% stake in Gesparal, a holding company that controls the French cosmetics company L'Oréal. It acquired pharmaceutical firm Alcon Laboratories three years later.

Helmut Maucher was named chairman and CEO in 1981. He began beefing up Nestlé's global presence and moving some decision-making power from headquarters to the provinces. Boycotters had long accused Nestlé of harming children in developing countries through the unethical promotion of infant formula, and Maucher ended the boycott by meeting with the critics and setting up a commission to police adherence to World Health Organization guidelines.

Nestlé gained significant leverage in the US when it bought Carnation in 1985 for $3 billion. Maucher doubled the company's chocolate business in 1988 with the $4 billion purchase of UK chocolate maker Rowntree (Kit Kat). Also in the 1980s Nestlé acquired Buitoni pastas.

The company expanded in the 1990s with the purchases of Butterfinger and Baby Ruth candies, Source Perrier water, Alpo pet food, and Ortega Mexican foods. Company veteran Peter Brabeck-Letmathe succeeded Maucher as CEO in 1997. He cleaned out Nestlé's pantry by selling noncore businesses (Contadina tomato products, Libby's canned meat products) but restocked with San Pellegrino (mineral water) and Dalgety's Spillers (pet food) in 1998.

By 1999 the company started rolling out its Nestlé Pure Life bottled water, marketing it toward the developing world. It continued cleaning house in 1999 by selling its Findus brand (fish, vegetables) and all its non-instant US coffee brands. Also that year Nestlé merged its US novelty ice-cream unit with operations of Pillsbury's Häagen-Dazs to form Ice Cream Partners USA. In 2000 Nestlé purchased snack maker PowerBar.

Chairman: Rainer E. Gut
VC: Fritz Gerber
CEO: Peter Brabeck-Letmathe
General Manager, Asia, Oceania, Africa, Middle East: Michael W. O. Garret
General Manager, Europe: Robert Raeber
General Manager, Finance, Control, Legal, Tax, Information Systems & Logistics, Purchasing, Export: Mario A. Corti
General Manager, Pharmaceutical and Cosmetic Products; Liaison with L'Oréal, Human Resources, Corporate Affairs: Francisco Castaner
General Manager, Strategic Business Units, Mineral Water, Marketing: Philippe Veron
General Manager, Technical, Production, Environment, Research & Development: Rupert Gasser
General Manager, United States of America, Canada, Latin America: Carlos E. Represas
Auditors: KPMG Klynveld Peat Marwick Goerdeler SA

PRODUCTS/OPERATIONS

1999 Sales & Profits

	Sales % of total	Profits % of total
Beverages	28	39
Milk products, nutrition & ice cream	26	22
Chocolate & confectionery	14	9
Pharmaceuticals	5	11
Prepared dishes, cooking aids & other	27	19
Total	**100**	**100**

Selected Subsidiaries, Joint Ventures, and Affiliates
Alcon Laboratories (ophthalmology products)
Cereal Partners Worldwide (with General Mills)
Coca-Cola Nestlé Refreshments, USA
Galderma (dermatology products, with L'Oréal)
Gesparal (49%, holding company for L'Oréal)
Ice Cream Partners USA (with Pillsbury)

LOCATIONS

HQ: Avenue Nestlé 55, CH-1800 Vevey, Vaud, Switzerland
Phone: +41-21-924-21-11   **Fax:** +41-21-924-28-13
US HQ: 800 N. Brand Blvd., Glendale, CA 91203
US Phone: 818-549-6000   **US Fax:** 818-549-6952
Web site: http://www.nestle.com

1999 Sales

	% of total
Food	
Europe	36
The Americas	30
Africa, Asia & Oceania	18
Other	16
Total	**100**

COMPETITORS

Abbott Labs	Lindt & Sprungli
Allergan	Mars
Barilla	Nabisco Holdings
Bausch & Lomb	Novartis
Bestfoods	Parmalat Finanziaria
Cadbury Schweppes	PepsiCo
Campbell Soup	Procter & Gamble
Colgate-Palmolive	Ralston Purina
ConAgra Foods	Revlon
Danone	Sara Lee
Heinz	Suntory
Hershey	Tchibo Holding
Kellogg	Unilever
Kraft Foods	

HISTORICAL FINANCIALS & EMPLOYEES

OTC: NSRGY FYE: December 31	Annual Growth	12/90	12/91	12/92	12/93	12/94	12/95	12/96	12/97	12/98	12/99
Sales ($ mil.)	2.9%	36,311	37,081	37,138	38,620	43,479	48,934	45,091	47,883	52,168	46,924
Net income ($ mil.)	5.9%	1,779	1,814	1,839	1,940	2,484	2,528	2,535	2,740	3,120	2,969
Income as % of sales	—	4.9%	4.9%	5.0%	5.0%	5.7%	5.2%	5.6%	5.7%	6.0%	6.3%
Earnings per share ($)	5.3%	2.39	2.44	2.46	2.57	3.20	3.22	3.22	3.48	3.97	3.80
Stock price - FY high ($)	—	31.47	31.84	40.89	44.50	47.83	55.84	60.00	76.00	110.00	113.50
Stock price - FY low ($)	—	26.00	25.83	30.53	33.58	38.00	45.48	51.63	51.50	74.25	71.38
Stock price - FY close ($)	14.3%	27.52	31.84	39.72	44.13	47.00	55.39	53.75	75.13	107.50	91.75
P/E - high	—	13	13	17	17	15	17	19	22	28	30
P/E - low	—	11	11	12	13	12	14	16	15	19	19
Dividends per share ($)	6.3%	0.78	0.78	0.79	0.84	1.01	1.15	1.12	1.20	1.38	1.35
Book value per share ($)	4.1%	14.13	15.17	12.71	13.94	16.66	19.31	20.26	20.69	21.27	20.22
Employees	1.7%	199,021	201,139	218,005	209,755	212,687	220,172	221,144	225,808	231,881	230,929

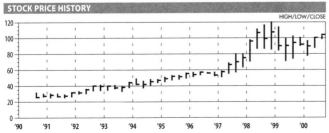

STOCK PRICE HISTORY   HIGH/LOW/CLOSE

1999 FISCAL YEAR-END
Debt ratio: 34.5%
Return on equity: 18.2%
Cash ($ mil.): 2,088
Current ratio: 1.22
Long-term debt ($ mil.): 3,083
No. of shares (mil.): 760
Dividends
  Yield: 0.0%
  Payout: 0.4%
Market value ($ mil.): 69,730

THE NEWS CORPORATION LIMITED

OVERVIEW

Cowabunga! Egad! No-brow Bart Simpson and the highbrow *Times* of London have the same parent — The News Corporation. Based in Sydney, chairman and CEO Rupert Murdoch's planetary media empire spans newspapers, books, magazines, movies, music, and TV, plus an airline and a sheep farm. News Corp. and Bertelsmann are in a virtual tie for the #4 position among media conglomerates behind Time Warner, Viacom, and Walt Disney.

Fox Entertainment Group (83%-owned by News Corp.) owns Twentieth Century Fox (movie and TV production and a large programming library), Fox Broadcasting (Fox TV network, which has 200 US affiliates), Fox Cable Networks, and 22 owned-and-operated US TV stations. (News Corp.'s agreement to buy Chris-Craft, which owns 10 TV stations, will give the firm one of the country's largest collection of TV stations.) Fox Entertainment Group also

owns the Los Angeles Dodgers and has options to buy minority interests in the Los Angeles Lakers and Kings.

News Corp.'s print holdings include the *New York Post,* four major UK newspapers, and scores of Australian papers as well as magazines. It also prints newspaper advertising inserts, and subsidiary HarperCollins publishes general-interest and religious books.

Murdoch in early 2000 announced a major restructuring at News Corp. that will place all of its satellite holdings into a new company, Sky Global Networks, which it is spinning off.

The controversial Murdoch and his family own about 30% of the company. Children Lachlan, Elisabeth, and James are all executives at News Corp. companies. Liberty Media owns an 8% stake in the company, which it plans to increase through a transfer of stock in GemStar-TV Guide.

HISTORY

In 1952 Rupert Murdoch inherited two Adelaide, Australia, newspapers from his father. After launching the *Australian,* the country's first national daily, in 1964, Murdoch moved into the UK market. He bought tabloid *News of the World,* a London Sunday paper, in 1968, and London's *Sun* the next year. In 1973 Murdoch hit the US, buying the *San Antonio Express-News* and founding the *Star* tabloid. He followed this up in 1976 by buying the *New York Post.* Murdoch formed News Corporation in Australia in 1979.

Murdoch bought the London *Times* and 40% of Collins Publishers, a London book publisher, in 1981. In 1983 Murdoch bought 13 US travel, hotel, and aviation trade magazines from Ziff-Davis, as well as film studio Twentieth Century Fox in 1985. In 1986 Murdoch, by then a US citizen, bought six Metromedia stations and launched Fox Broadcasting, the first new US TV network since 1948.

Print was not forgotten, however, and in the late 1980s News Corp. went on a buying spree, picking up US book publisher Harper & Row and the *New York Post,* as well as Triangle Publications (*TV Guide* and other magazines). It also bought textbook publisher Scott, Foresman and the rest of Collins Publishers.

In 1996 Murdoch launched the Fox News Channel, an all-news cable channel. In 1997 News Corp. bought direct marketer Heritage Media for about $1.3 billion, selling Heritage's TV and radio operations to Sinclair Broadcast Group. Murdoch also pulled off a cable pro-

gramming coup when News Corp.'s Fox Kids joint venture bought Pat Robertson's International Family Entertainment for $1.9 billion.

In 1998 the company bought the Los Angeles Dodgers and stakes in the new Los Angeles-area Staples Center sports arena. In 1998 News Corp. sold about 19% of Fox Entertainment in one of America's largest IPOs, raising $2.7 billion. Also that year News Corp. sold *TV Guide* to Tele-Communications Inc.'s (now AT&T Broadband & Internet) United Video Satellite Group (now Gemstar-TV Guide International) for $800 million in cash and a 21.5% interest in Gemstar-TV Guide International.

Also in 1998 News Corp.'s HarperCollins division bought Hearst Corp.'s book publishing operations (William Morrow, Avon Books). The company also bought the 50% of Fox/Liberty Networks (now Fox Sports Networks) it didn't own from Liberty Media and transferred ownership to Fox Entertainment. The deal gave Liberty an 8% stake in News Corp. The company was also finally able to break into the coveted German pay-TV market through BSkyB's agreement to buy 24% of KirchGruppe's Kirch PayTV (completed in 2000).

In 2000 News Corp. was able to possibly force out one of its Fox Broadcasting competitors by agreeing to buy TV station owner Chris-Craft. Most of Chris-Craft's stations are UPN affiliates. News Corp. will likely change those stations into FOX affiliates, which will probably force UPN to fold its operations.

OFFICERS

Chairman and CEO, News Corp. and Fox Entertainment: K. Rupert Murdoch, age 67
President and Co-COO; Chairman and CEO, News America; President and COO, Fox Entertainment: Peter Chernin, age 47
Co-COO, News Corp. and Fox Entertainment; EVP, News America; Chairman and CEO, Fox Television: Chase Carey, age 45
Deputy COO; Chairman and CEO, News Limited: Lachlan Murdoch, age 29
SEVP and CFO, News Corp. and News America: David F. DeVoe, age 51
SEVP and Group General Counsel; EVP, News America; SEVP and General Counsel, Fox Entertainment: Arthur M. Siskind, age 60
EVP; President, News America Digital Publishing; Chairman and CEO, STAR TV: James Murdoch, age 27
EVP Human Resources: Bill A. O'Neill
EVP Marketing: Roger Fishman
Chairman and CEO, Fox Television Stations: Mitchell Stern
President and CEO, Fox Cable Networks: Jeff Shell, age 34
Auditors: Arthur Andersen

LOCATIONS

HQ: 2 Holt St., Sydney 2010, Australia
Phone: +61-2-9288-3000   **Fax:** +61-2-9288-3292
US HQ: 1211 Avenue of the Americas, New York, NY 10036
US Phone: 212-852-7000   **US Fax:** 212-852-7145
Web site: http://www.newscorp.com

News Corp. operates in Asia, Australia, Europe, North America, and South America.

1999 Sales

	% of total
US	74
UK	16
Australia/Asia	10
Total	**100**

PRODUCTS/OPERATIONS

1999 Sales

	% of total
Filmed entertainment	33
Television	28
Newspapers	19
Magazines & inserts	10
Book publishing	6
Other operations	4
Total	**100**

COMPETITORS

Advance Publications	Pearson
Bertelsmann	Reed Elsevier
CANAL+	Sony
Cox Enterprises	Thomson Corporation
Hachette Filipacchi Médias	Time Warner
Hollinger	United News & Media
Liberty Media	Universal Studios
McGraw-Hill	Valassis Communications
NBC	Viacom
New York Times	Walt Disney

HISTORICAL FINANCIALS & EMPLOYEES

NYSE: NWS FYE: June 30	Annual Growth	6/90	6/91	6/92	6/93	6/94	6/95	6/96	6/97	6/98	6/99
Sales ($ mil.)	8.3%	6,948	6,551	7,626	7,124	8,468	8,641	10,285	10,727	11,716	14,271
Net income ($ mil.)	13.8%	224	(183)	375	576	973	969	802	546	1,086	714
Income as % of sales	—	3.2%	—	4.9%	8.1%	11.5%	11.2%	7.8%	5.1%	9.3%	5.0%
Earnings per share ($)	3.1%	0.54	(0.76)	0.70	0.94	1.02	1.84	0.49	1.12	0.77	0.71
Stock price - FY high ($)	—	9.03	7.08	11.53	14.90	21.06	23.25	25.13	23.63	33.25	36.81
Stock price - FY low ($)	—	4.75	1.79	3.75	10.41	13.24	14.38	18.50	17.25	17.00	20.19
Stock price - FY close ($)	21.6%	6.08	3.62	10.45	13.28	16.07	22.63	23.50	19.25	32.13	35.31
P/E - high	—	17	—	16	14	23	13	41	21	39	52
P/E - low	—	9	—	5	10	14	8	30	15	20	28
Dividends per share ($)	3.8%	0.05	0.03	0.07	0.05	0.05	0.07	0.04	0.09	0.04	0.07
Book value per share ($)	(16.6%)	98.12	21.33	81.56	17.28	20.63	22.24	26.15	33.99	18.95	19.12
Employees	3.0%	38,400	30,700	27,250	24,700	25,845	26,600	27,250	26,500	28,220	50,000

STOCK PRICE HISTORY

HIGH/LOW/CLOSE

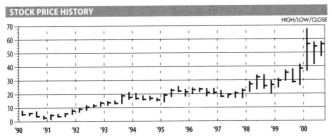

1999 FISCAL YEAR-END

Debt ratio: 37.3%
Return on equity: 4.0%
Cash ($ mil.): 4,912
Current ratio: 1.82
Long-term debt ($ mil.): 8,418
No. of shares (mil.): 942
Dividends
    Yield: 0.1%
    Payout: 6.8%
Market value ($ mil.): 33,276

NIKON CORPORATION

OVERVIEW

Paul Simon may still have a Nikon camera and love to take a photograph, but Nikon has aimed its lenses at a higher-margin market. The Tokyo-based company is one of the world's leading producers of the steppers used to etch circuitry onto semiconductor wafers. (ASM Lithography's proposed acquisition of Silicon Valley Group challenges this leading position.) Steppers and related equipment account for 60% of sales.

The range of Nikon's products offer a snapshot of the optical world. Its cameras have caught images from every manned space flight since Apollo 13. Its microscopes are used in schools and cell biology research laboratories,

and its eye examination equipment and prescription glasses and sunglasses are fixtures in opticians' offices worldwide. Other products include binoculars, electronic imaging equipment, inspection and measuring equipment, and surveying instruments.

The company, part of the huge Mitsubishi keiretsu, a group of businesses linked by cross-ownership, has adjusted operations in the wake of sluggish stepper sales in an effort to become more nimble. Nikon is reorganizing into seven more-autonomous divisions, an arrangement under which the parent corporation serves as a holding company.

HISTORY

Lensmaker Nippon Kogaku KK formed in 1917 with the merger of three large Japanese optical glassmakers. A year later it started optics production and research. The results gelled in 1921 when Nippon Kogaku started selling binoculars; the company introduced its first microscope four years later.

In 1932 the company adopted the brand name Nikkor for its lenses, which were attached to other manufacturers' cameras. By WWII the company had diversified into cameras, microscopes, binoculars, surveying equipment, measuring instruments, and eyeglass lenses. During this time the Japanese government bought nearly all of the company's products. Nippon Kogaku began using the Nikon brand name on its cameras in 1946.

In the early 1950s the company established US subsidiary Nikon Inc. Its first commercially available pocket camera was also introduced, but few of Nikon's cameras made it out of Japan. The world would not begin to appreciate the quality of Nikon's products until photojournalists began using them in the Korean War.

Continuing a European expansion in the 1960s, the company opened subsidiaries in Switzerland (1961) and the Netherlands (1968). The company, in conjunction with undersea explorer Jacques Cousteau and a partner, introduced an underwater camera system in 1963. The 1970s were years of development: The company introduced high-precision coordinate measuring instruments (1971) and sunglasses (1972), among other products. During the late 1970s Canon passed Minolta and Nikon as the world's top seller of cameras, setting off a battle that has seesawed ever since.

In 1980 the company developed its first stepper system for the fledgling semiconductor

industry. Nikon's US subsidiary merged with its US distributor, Ehrenreich Photo-Optical Industries, a year later. By 1984 Nikon controlled 53% of the Japanese stepper market. Nippon Kogaku changed its name in 1988 to Nikon Corporation.

The company further broadened its borders in the early 1990s, opening subsidiaries in South Korea (1990), Thailand (1990), Hungary (1991), Italy (1993), and Singapore (1995). When demand for chips dropped in the early 1990s, so did Nikon's sales: The company lost money in fiscal 1993 and fiscal 1994. It restructured its unprofitable camera division, cutting 33% of its staff to save cash. In 1995 Nikon developed a digital still camera in a joint partnership with Fuji Photo Film.

In 1996 Nikon Research Corporation of America was established to improve the company's technology. The subsidiary was meant to compete against Nikon's long-established research and development arm. With 60% of sales coming from steppers, that year the company shifted production homeward, moving the production of cameras and other lower-margin equipment overseas.

In 1997 Shoichiro Yoshida, a Nikon designer since the 1950s who became a proponent of the company's stepper business, was named president, replacing Shigeo Ono, who became chairman. A slumping Asian market and declining prices for chips caused demand for steppers to fall and left the company with slack earnings for fiscal 1998 and 1999. Rebounds in the markets for digital cameras and semiconductor equipment led Nikon back into the black in 2000.

Chairman: Shigeo Ono
President: Shoichiro Yoshida
EVP Technology: Tadao Tsuruta
EVP Finance, Administration, and Marketing: Kenji Enya
Managing Director, Business Administration: Yuji Obana
President, Precision Equipment: Teruo Shimamura
President, Imaging: Michio Kariya
President, Nikon-Essilor: Yoishi Nishida
President, Instruments: Takashi Tamori
Manager, Human Resources, Nikon Inc. (US):
Heidi Heyden
Auditors: Deloitte Touche Tohmatsu

HQ: Fuji Bldg., 2-3 Marunouchi 3-chome,
Chiyoda-ku, Tokyo 100-8331, Japan
Phone: +81-3-3214-5311 **Fax:** +81-3-3201-5856
US HQ: 1300 Walt Whitman Rd., Melville, NY 11747
US Phone: 631-547-4200 **US Fax:** 631-547-0299
Web site: http://www.nikon.com

Nikon has subsidiaries in Canada, China, the Czech
Republic, France, Germany, Hong Kong, Hungary, Italy,
the Netherlands, Singapore, South Korea, Sweden,
Switzerland, Taiwan, Thailand, the UK, and the US.

2000 Sales

	% of total
Asia	
Japan	33
Other countries	26
North America	26
Europe	14
Other regions	1
Total	**100**

2000 Sales

	% of total
Industrial instruments	60
Consumer products	40
Total	**100**

Products

Industrial Instruments
Industrial and other microscopes
Integrated circuit manufacturing equipment
Liquid crystal display manufacturing equipment
Measuring instruments
Medical imaging systems
Ophthalmic instruments
Optical disk stampers
Surveying instruments

Consumer
Binoculars and other specialized optical instruments
Cameras and lenses
Digital cameras
Eyeglasses
Glass art
Scanners

Asahi Optical
ASM Lithography
Canon
Eastman Kodak
Fuji Photo

Minolta
Olympus
Silicon Valley Group
Ultratech Stepper

Tokyo: 7731 FYE: March 31	Annual Growth	3/91	3/92	3/93	3/94	3/95	3/96	3/97	3/98	3/99	3/00
Sales (¥ mil.)	4.0%	—	272,370	231,924	246,165	288,485	332,799	379,089	372,145	305,764	371,801
Net income (¥ mil.)	4.7%	—	5,377	(8,813)	(4,357)	1,535	18,581	19,936	8,318	(18,232)	7,770
Income as % of sales	—	—	2.0%	—	—	0.5%	5.6%	5.3%	2.2%	—	2.1%
Earnings per share (¥)	4.7%	—	14.54	(23.82)	(11.78)	4.15	50.23	53.89	22.49	(49.28)	21.01
Stock price - FY high (¥)	—	—	1,440	871	1,100	1,140	2,660	1,920	2,660	1,682	4,370
Stock price - FY low (¥)	—	—	670	510	650	697	650	1,150	1,120	785	1,445
Stock price - FY close (¥)	24.4%	—	689	850	1,000	701	1,188	1,640	1,230	1,440	3,940
P/E - high	—	—	99	—	—	275	53	36	118	—	208
P/E - low	—	—	46	—	—	168	13	21	50	—	69
Dividends per share (¥)	(7.1%)	—	9.00	7.00	5.00	5.00	6.50	8.00	8.00	3.00	5.00
Book value per share (¥)	0.8%	—	422.00	385.26	367.12	358.22	401.88	448.16	462.64	435.23	450.11
Employees	(1.4%)	—	—	7,351	7,264	7,164	7,034	6,955	6,907	6,739	6,675

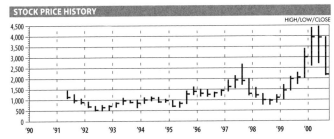

HIGH/LOW/CLOSE

Debt ratio: 54.2%
Return on equity: —
Cash (¥ mil.): 32,574
Current ratio: 1.39
Long-term debt (¥ mil.): 95,728
No. of shares (mil.): 370
Dividends
Yield: 0.0%
Payout: 0.2%
Market value ($ mil.): 13,805
Sales ($ mil.): 3,522

NINTENDO CO., LTD.

OVERVIEW

Like a video game action hero, Nintendo Co. is ready to fight. Headquartered in Kyoto, Japan, the video game company is in a battle for the video game console market (those used with TVs) with heavyweight Sony — and its #1 game console, PlayStation — while keeping an eye on #3 SEGA. Although Nintendo's N64 game console ranks second, its Game Boy handheld console dominates the handheld game market.

The company is the leading maker of game software, including hits *Pokémon* and *The Legend of Zelda: Ocarina of Time*. It has licensing agreements with other software makers, including Electronic Arts, to make games as well as with other companies to make trading cards and toys based on its characters.

Nintendo (which, loosely translated, means "leave luck to heaven") ruled the golden age of the video game industry, but more powerful machines introduced by Sony, a relative newcomer to video games, and SEGA have pared down its kingdom. (SEGA and Sony have 128-bit machines on the market.) Nintendo still uses the pricier cartridge technology format for performance's sake instead of moving to CD-ROMs (and the ability to offer more games) as its rivals have, but it plans to release the DVD-based Dolphin system in 2000.

President Hiroshi Yamauchi, great-grandson of the company's founder, owns 11% of Nintendo.

HISTORY

Nintendo Co. was founded in 1889 as the Marufuku Company to make and sell *hanafuda,* Japanese game cards. In 1907 the company began producing Western playing cards. It became the Nintendo Playing Card Company in 1951 and began making theme cards under a licensing agreement with Disney in 1959. During the 1950s and 1960s, Hiroshi Yamauchi took the company public and diversified into new areas (including a "love hotel"). The company took its current name in 1963.

Nintendo began making toys at the start of the 1970s and entered the budding field of video games toward the end of the decade by licensing Magnavox's Pong technology. Then it moved into arcade games. Nintendo established its US subsidiary, Nintendo of America, in 1980; its first hit was *Donkey Kong* ("silly monkey") and its next was *Super Mario Bros.* (named after Nintendo of America's warehouse landlord).

The company released Famicom, a technologically advanced home video game system, in Japan in 1983. With its high-quality sound and graphics, Famicom was a smash success, selling 15.2 million consoles and more than 183 million game cartridges in Japan alone. Meanwhile, in 1983 and 1984, the US home game market crashed, sending pioneer Atari up in flames. Nintendo persevered, successfully launching Famicom in the US in 1986 as the Nintendo Entertainment System (NES).

To prevent a barrage of independently produced, low-quality software (which had been a factor in Atari's demise), Nintendo established stringent licensing policies for its software developers. Licensees were required to have approval of every game design, buy the blank cartridges from the company, agree not to make the game for any of Nintendo's competitors, and pay Nintendo royalties for the honor of developing a game.

As the market became increasingly saturated, Nintendo sought new products, releasing Game Boy in 1989 and the Super Family Computer game system (Super NES in the US) in 1991. In a quest for new games, the company broke with tradition in 1994 by making design alliances with companies like Silicon Graphics and began giving other designers more favorable deals. After creating a 32-bit product in 1995, Nintendo launched the much-touted N64 game system in 1996. It also teamed with Microsoft and Nomura Research Institute on a satellite-delivered Internet system for Japan.

In 1998 Nintendo released Pokémon, which involves trading and training virtual monsters, in the US (it had been popular in Japan since 1996). The company also launched the video game *The Legend of Zelda: Ocarina of Time*, which sold 2.5 million units in about six weeks. New technologies for Game Boy in 1998 included the use of color graphics and a portable camera and printer.

Nintendo announced in 1999 that its next-generation game system, Dolphin (due out by the end of 2000), would use IBM's PowerPC microprocessor and DVD players made by consumer electronics giant Matsushita.

In early 2000 the company bought a 3% stake in convenience store operator Lawson in hopes of using its online operations to sell video games. Nintendo also teamed with advertising agency Dentsu to form ND Cube, a joint company that will develop game software for mobile phones and portable machines.

President: Hiroshi Yamauchi
EVP: Atsushi Asada
Managing Director: Akio Tsuji
Managing Director: Yoshihiro Mori
General Manager of Administration:
   Masaharu Matsumoto
Corporate Advisor: Yasuhiro Onishi
Director of Finance, Nintendo of America:
   Shirley Hornstein
Auditors: ChuoAoyama Audit Corporation

LOCATIONS

HQ: 60 Kamitakamatsu-cho, Fukuine,
   Higashiyama-ku, Kyoto 605-8660, Japan
Phone: +81-75-541-6111   **Fax:** +81-75-531-7996
US HQ: 4820 150th Ave. Northeast,
   Redmond, WA 98052
US Phone: 425-882-2040   **US Fax:** 425-882-3585
Web site: http://www.nintendo.co.jp

Nintendo Co. has offices and plants in Japan and major
subsidiaries in Australia, Canada, France, Germany, the
Netherlands, Spain, and the US.

PRODUCTS/OPERATIONS

Game Consoles
Game Boy
N64
Super Nintendo Entertainment System (Super NES)

Selected Games
Banjo-Kazooie
Diddy Kong Racing
Donkey Kong
GoldenEye 007
Ken Griffey Jr.'s Slugfest
Pokémon
Star Wars Episode I Racer
Super Mario series
Yoshi series
Zelda series

COMPETITORS

Electronic Arts
Hasbro
Havas
Midway Games
SEGA
SNK
Sony

HISTORICAL FINANCIALS & EMPLOYEES

OTC: NTDOY FYE: March 31	Annual Growth	3/91	3/92	3/93	3/94	3/95	3/96	3/97	3/98	3/99	3/00
Sales ($ mil.)	4.8%	3,463	4,405	5,681	4,726	4,803	3,302	3,378	4,015	4,806	5,279
Net income ($ mil.)	0.9%	489	655	771	512	481	558	529	629	720	531
Income as % of sales	—	14.1%	14.9%	13.6%	10.8%	10.0%	16.9%	15.7%	15.7%	15.0%	10.1%
Earnings per share ($)	1.0%	0.43	0.58	0.68	0.45	0.41	0.50	0.47	0.55	0.64	0.47
Stock price - FY high ($)	—	18.89	15.67	11.01	12.25	9.13	10.30	9.15	13.50	12.75	28.00
Stock price - FY low ($)	—	10.83	8.95	8.20	7.14	6.33	6.50	6.56	8.63	9.75	10.50
Stock price - FY close ($)	4.2%	15.13	9.11	10.63	8.14	7.64	8.00	8.97	10.63	10.63	21.99
P/E - high	—	44	27	16	27	22	21	19	25	20	60
P/E - low	—	25	15	12	16	15	13	14	16	15	22
Dividends per share ($)	18.7%	0.03	0.06	0.08	0.09	0.10	0.12	0.10	0.11	0.13	0.14
Book value per share ($)	12.9%	2.12	2.18	3.11	3.81	4.74	4.22	4.02	4.20	5.19	6.33
Employees	4.5%	777	825	943	568	927	952	980	1,002	1,100	1,150

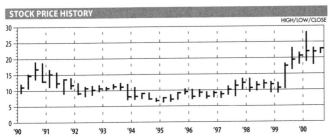

STOCK PRICE HISTORY
HIGH/LOW/CLOSE

2000 FISCAL YEAR-END
Debt ratio: 0.0%
Return on equity: 8.1%
Cash ($ mil.): 5,631
Current ratio: 4.79
Long-term debt ($ mil.): 0
No. of shares (mil.): 1,133
Dividends
   Yield: 0.0%
   Payout: 0.3%
Market value ($ mil.): 24,922

NIPPON LIFE INSURANCE COMPANY

OVERVIEW

There's foreign competition "nippon" at this company's heels. Osaka-based Nippon Life Insurance Company, the world's #3 insurer, leads the Japanese market. A door-to-door sales corps composed mostly of women peddles its plain-vanilla products, including individual and group life and annuity products. Deregulation has allowed the company to move into such areas as corporate and residential lending. Other activities include real estate development and management and a variety of educational and philanthropic projects. The majority of the company's overseas activities focus on providing coverage to Japanese companies and citizens abroad.

As the Japanese economy struggles to recover, Nippon Life has grappled with declining individual sales as consumers continue to cut back on expenditures. To attract customers, the company continues to broaden its sales channels, adding Internet and telephone sales and allowing customers to access loans directly through ATMs.

With deregulation in the financial services industry boosting competition, the company is expanding its offerings to include long-term health coverage, a 401(k)-like pension plan, and other such retirement investment products. Nippon Life is also partnering with such firms as Mitsubishi Trust and Banking Corp, Deutsche Bank, and Sakura Bank to offer investment trusts, personal lending, and other services.

HISTORY

Nippon Life, known as Nissay, was a product of the modernization that began after US Commodore Perry forced Japan to open its ports to foreigners in 1854. Industry and trade were Japan's first focus, but financial infrastructure soon followed. The country's first insurer (Meiji Mutual) opened in 1881. In 1889 Osaka banker Sukesaburo Hirose founded Nippon Life as a stock company. It grew and opened branches in Tokyo (1890) and Kyushu (1895).

In the 20th century, the company developed a direct sales force and began lending directly to businesses. Lending remained the backbone of its asset strategy through most of the century. The insurance market in Japan grew quickly until the late 1920s but had already slowed by the eve of the Depression.

After WWII, the company reorganized as a mutual and began mobilizing an army of women to build its sales of installment-premium, basic life policies. In 1962 the company began automating its systems and established operations in the US (1972) and London (1981).

As interest rates rose in the wake of the oil price hikes of the 1970s, the company began offering term life and annuities and slowly moved to diversify its assets from mostly government bonds (whose yields declined as rates rose) to stocks. This movement accelerated in the 1980s as the businesses that traditionally borrowed from Nippon Life turned directly to capital markets to raise money through debt issues. Seeking to replace its shrinking lending business, the company began investing in US real estate and businesses whose values rose in the mid-1980s. The company reached its zenith in 1987; it owned about 3% of total stocks on the Tokyo Exchange, held more real estate than Mitsubishi's real estate units, and had bought 13% of US brokerage Shearson Lehman from American Express.

By the end of the year, thanks to the US stock market crash, the value of the Shearson investment had fallen 40%. But the company felt confident enough of its importance as the world's largest insurance company (by assets) to crow its intentions to strong-arm Japan's Ministry of Finance into letting it diversify into trust and securities operations.

Then its bubble burst. In 1989 real estate crashed, and the stock market lost more than half its value. Japan's economy failed to improve, and Nippon Life was left struggling with nonperforming loans and assets whose value had declined. The company suffered further from policy cancellations and from the Ministry of Finance's focus on buoying banks (in 1997 the ministry asked Nippon Life to convert its subordinated debt from Nippon Credit Bank to stock). That year Nippon Life formed an alliance with Marsh & McLennan's Putnam Investments subsidiary to help manage its assets; the relationship deepened in 1998 when they began developing investment trust products. The company also formed an asset management joint venture with Deutsche Bank. The next year Nippon Life faced a shareholder lawsuit over its involvement in the collapse of Nippon Credit Bank; the company claims the Ministry of Finance tricked it into bailing out the bank even though it was beyond rescue.

Chairman: Josei Itoh
Executive VC: Kanji Kobayashi
President: Ikuo Uno
EVP and CFO: Tsuyoshi Nahara
Senior Managing Director: Hirokuni Imai
Senior Managing Director: Mitsuhiro Ishibashi
Senior Managing Director: Wataru Taguchi
Senior Managing Director: Yahuhiro Nakayama
Managing Director: Yoshikazu Yoshikawa
Managing Director: Shingo Okada
Managing Director: Kiyoshi Kitai
Managing Director: Kunie Okamoto
Managing Director: Eitaro Waki
Managing Director: Hideichiro Kobayashi
Managing Director: Ryoichi Uozaki
Managing Director: Hideo Achira
Managing Director: Kazumi Izumi
Managing Director: Hachiro Taneko
Managing Director: Takao Arai
Auditors: ChouAoyama Audit Corporation

HQ: Nippon Seimei Hoken Kabushiki Kaisha,
5-12, Imabashi 3-chome,
Chuo-ku, Osaka 541-8501, Japan
Phone: +81-6-6209-5525   **Fax:** +81-3-5510-7340
US HQ: 450 Lexington Ave., Ste. 3200,
New York, NY 10017
US Phone: 212-682-3000   **US Fax:** 212-682-3002
Web site: http://www.nissay.co.jp

2000 Sales

	% of total
Premiums	67
Investment income	28
Other	5
Total	**100**

Selected Subsidiaries
LMC Co., Ltd. (finance)
Nippon Life Insurance Company of America
Nippon Life Insurance Company of the Philippines, Inc.
Nissay Capital Co., Ltd. (venture capital)
Nissay Card Service Co., Ltd.
(credit card-related services)
Nissay Computer Co. Ltd. (data processing and
software development)
Nissay Credit Guarantee Co., Ltd.
Nissay General Insurance Company, Limited
Nissay Leasing Co., Ltd.
(leasing and mortgage-backed securities)
NISSEI LEASING HONG KONG LIMITED (finance)
NISSEI LEASING INTERNATIONAL, INC. (finance)
NLI Properties, Inc. (overseas real estate investment)
Seiko Building Management Co., Ltd.
(building management)
SEIWA REAL ESTATE CO., LTD.
Taisei Building Management Co., Ltd.
Yaesu Building Maintenance Co., Ltd.

Allianz
Asahi Mutual Life
AXA
AXA Nichidan
  Life Insurance
Chiyoda Mutual Life
Dai-ichi Mutual Life
Daido Life Insurance
ING

Kyoei Life Insurance
Meiji Life Insurance
Mitsui Mutual Life
Sumitomo Life
Taiyo Mutual Life
Toho Mutual
  Life Insurance
Tokio Marine and Fire
Yasuda Mutual Life

Mutual company FYE: March 31	Annual Growth	3/91	3/92	3/93	3/94	3/95	3/96	3/97	3/98	3/99	3/00
Assets ($ mil.)	5.7%	—	—	279,032	337,898	423,815	363,895	323,424	317,199	360,772	411,477
Net income ($ mil.)	(0.7%)	—	—	3,776	2,949	3,078	3,023	2,547	1,954	888	3,594
Income as % of assets		—	—	1.4%	0.9%	0.7%	0.8%	0.8%	0.6%	0.2%	0.9%
Employees	(11.5%)	—	—	—	—	—	—	86,695	75,851	—	60,000

Equity as % of assets: 2.5%
Return on assets: 0.9%
Return on equity: —
Long-term debt ($ mil.): —
Sales ($ mil.): 82,860

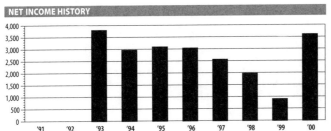

NIPPON STEEL CORPORATION

OVERVIEW

Nippon Steel, Japan's largest steel company, has braced itself against downturns in the cyclical steel market by diversifying into other areas, including electronics and communication products — a plan that has worked about as well as Japan's effort to conquer Asia during World War II. Second to only South Korea's POSCO in steel production, the Tokyo-based company's operations include steelmaking and steel fabrication (63% of sales); engineering and construction; chemicals, nonferrous metals, and ceramics; engineering and construction; electronics and information/communications; transportation; and energy, finance, and insurance services.

The Asian financial crisis — and especially the worst Japanese recession since the end of World War II — has dampened demand for most of the company's products and services, with the exception of titanium shipments. Steel products in particular have suffered from the weakened local economy and US-imposed, anti-dumping duties on Japanese steel. Although only about 30% of Nippon Steel's sales come from outside Japan, the US market has become increasingly important under current economic conditions. The Japanese recession has also forced the company to sell its domestic memory-chip operations to South Korea's United Microelectronics. To improve its per-share net profit, the company has sold treasury stocks from its capital reserves. Nippon Steel has also negotiated a strategic alliance with rival POSCO.

HISTORY

As Japan prepared for war, the government in 1934 merged Yawata Works, its largest steel producer, and other Japanese steelmakers into one giant company — Japan Iron & Steel. During postwar occupation, Japan Iron & Steel was ordered to dissolve. Yawata Iron & Steel and Fuji Iron & Steel emerged from the dissolution, and with Western assistance, the Japanese steel industry recovered from the war years. In the late 1960s Fuji Steel bought Tokai Iron & Steel (1967), and Yawata Steel took over Yawata Steel Tube Company (1968).

Yawata and Fuji merged in 1970 and became Nippon Steel, the world's largest steelmaker. In the 1970s the Japanese steel industry was criticized in the US; American competitors complained that Japan was "dumping" low-cost exports. Meanwhile, Nippon Steel aggressively courted China.

The company diversified in the mid-1980s to wean itself from dependence on steel. It created a New Materials unit in 1984 and retrained "redundant" steelworkers to make silicon wafers, and formed an Electronics Division in 1986. Nippon Steel began joint ventures with IBM Japan (small computers and software), Hitachi (office workstations), and C. Itoh (information systems for small and midsized companies) in 1988 as increased steel demand for construction and cars in Japan's "bubble economy" took the company to new heights.

In an atmosphere of economic optimism, the company spent more than four times the expected expense to build an amusement park capable of competing with Tokyo Disneyland. The company plowed ahead, spending more than ¥15 billion on the park. Space World amusement park opened on the island of Kyushu in 1990. The company's bubble burst that year.

In response, Nippon Steel cut costs and intensified its diversification efforts by targeting electronics, information and telecommunications, new materials, and chemicals markets. Seeking to remake its steel operations, the company began a drastic, phased restructuring in 1993 that included a step most Japanese companies try to avoid — cutting personnel.

Upgrading its steel operations, Nippon Steel and partner Mitsubishi in 1996 introduced the world's first mass-production method for making hot-rolled steel sheet directly from smelted stainless steel.

The company began operation of a Chinese steelmaking joint venture, Guangzhou Pacific Tinplate, in 1997. The next year its Singapore-based joint venture with Hitachi, Ltd. began mass-producing computer memory-chips in hopes of stemming semiconductor losses. But falling prices that year convinced Nippon Steel to get out of the memory-chip business, and in 1999 it sold its semiconductor subsidiary to South Korea's United Microelectronics.

Also in 1999 the US imposed anti-dumping duties on the company's steel products, and 500 former American POWs used as slave labor during World War II filed a class-action suit against the company seeking billions of dollars in damages. In 2000 Nippon Steel agreed to form a strategic alliance with South Korea-based Pohang Iron and Steel (POSCO), the world's #1 steel maker. The deal calls for the exploration of joint ventures, shared research, and joint procurement, as well as increased equity stakes in each other (at 2%-3%).

Chairman and Representative Director: Takashi Imai
President and Representative Director: Akira Chihaya
EVP and Representative Director (HR): Makoto Kihara
EVP and Representative Director: Iwao Koyama
EVP and Representative Director: Akio Mimura
EVP and Representative Director: Mutsumi Ohji
EVP and Representative Director: Tetsuo Seki
EVP and Representative Director: Ryoji Terakado
Managing Director: Hiroshi Suetsugu
Managing Director: Tetsuro Ohashi
Managing Director: Okitsugu Mantani
Managing Director: Tsuneyoshi Nishi
Managing Director: Shingo Satoh
Managing Director: Toshihiko Ono
Managing Director: Shiro Mochizuki
Managing Director: Hiroki Sasaki
Managing Director: Jyujiro Yagi
Auditors: ChuoAoyama Audit Corporation

LOCATIONS

HQ: Shin Nippon Seitetsu Kabushiki Kaisha,
6-3, Otemachi 2-chome,
Chiyoda-ku, Tokyo 100-8071, Japan
Phone: +81-3-3242-4111   **Fax:** +81-3-3275-5607
US HQ: 10 E. 50th St., 29th Fl., New York, NY 10022
US Phone: 212-486-7150   **US Fax:** 212-593-3049
Web site: http://www.nsc.co.jp

Nippon Steel has operations in the Americas, Asia,
Australia, and Europe.

2000 Sales

	% of total
Japan	80
Other countries	20
Total	**100**

PRODUCTS/OPERATIONS

2000 Sales

	% of total
Steelmaking & steel fabrication	63
Engineering & construction	15
Chemicals, nonferrous metals & ceramics	14
Urban development	6
Electronics, information/ communications & LSIs	5
Other businesses	9
Total	**100**

Selected Products and Services

Aluminum products	Pipes and tubes
Building construction	Plant and machinery
Ceramic coated products	Plates and sheets
Civil engineering	Real estate
Coal chemicals	Rental of buildings
Cokes	Silicon wafers
Communications services	Slag products
Computers and equipment	Specialty sheets
Data processing	Systems development and
Fabricated and processed	integration
steels	Titanium products
Marine construction	

COMPETITORS

Bechtel	Kobe Steel	Pohang Iron &
Bethlehem Steel	LTV	Steel
Corus Group	Mannesmann AG	Preussag
Fluor	Marubeni	Samsung
Hitachi	Mitsubishi	Sumitomo
Hyundai	Mitsui	ThyssenKrupp
Ito-Yokado	News Corp.	USX-U.S. Steel
Kawasaki Steel		

HISTORICAL FINANCIALS & EMPLOYEES

Tokyo: 5401 FYE: March 31	Annual Growth	3/91	3/92	3/93	3/94	3/95	3/96	3/97	3/98	3/99	3/00
Sales (¥ bil.)	(2.0%)	3,209	3,230	2,951	2,749	2,881	2,955	3,061	3,077	2,759	2,681
Net income (¥ bil.)	(20.9%)	91	78	2	(54)	(4)	55	3	6	11	11
Income as % of sales	—	2.8%	2.4%	0.1%	—	—	1.9%	0.1%	0.2%	0.4%	0.4%
Earnings per share (¥)	(20.5%)	13.00	11.00	0.00	(7.85)	(0.57)	7.91	0.50	0.86	1.68	1.64
Stock price - FY high (¥)	—	651	495	344	420	403	375	388	392	272	314
Stock price - FY low (¥)	—	371	295	229	295	293	275	283	146	177	215
Stock price - FY close (¥)	(7.1%)	475	313	335	322	335	368	340	214	243	245
P/E - high	—	50	45	—	—	—	47	776	456	162	191
P/E - low	—	29	27	—	—	—	35	566	170	105	131
Dividends per share (¥)	(14.3%)	6.00	6.00	6.00	6.00	2.50	2.50	2.50	2.50	1.50	1.50
Book value per share (¥)	(1.7%)	152.00	158.00	152.00	141.00	126.00	140.00	137.89	135.40	136.49	130.60
Employees	6.1%	—	—	—	—	—	—	—	35,500	35,000	40,000

STOCK PRICE HISTORY

HIGH/LOW/CLOSE

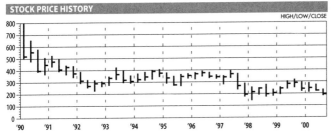

2000 FISCAL YEAR-END

Debt ratio: 64.2%
Return on equity: —
Cash (¥ mil.): 165,846
Current ratio: 0.85
Long-term debt (¥ mil.): 510,000
No. of shares (mil.): 6,807
Dividends
  Yield: 0.0%
  Payout: 0.9%
Market value ($ mil.): 15,797
Sales ($ mil.): 25,395

NIPPON TELEGRAPH AND TELEPHONE

OVERVIEW

Born in the era before deregulation roamed the earth, Tokyo-based Nippon Telegraph and Telephone (NTT) has grown into a telecommunications company of Jurassic proportions — the world's largest. NTT's local phone companies are virtual monopolies, its long-distance and mobile phone units dominate their markets, and NTT is also a leading ISP. The company additionally offers leased lines, telecom equipment, and data systems and services.

The Japanese government (which owns 53% of NTT) has restructured the giant into two regional phone companies, NTT East and NTT West, and a long-distance provider, NTT Communications. NTT had already spun off its successful cellular unit, NTT Mobile Communications Network (called DoCoMo), keeping a 67% stake.

Other changes have been wrought by the market. Criticized for continuing to promote last-generation ISDN as the key to high-speed Internet access, NTT has begun to test higher-speed digital subscriber line (DSL) service.

NTT has planted a massive foot in international markets by investing in local players. Holdings include Hong Kong's HKNet (49%) and Philippine Long Distance Telephone (15%). NTT has also agreed to buy a 49% stake in Australia-based Davnet's telecommunications unit. In the US, NTT owns Web-hosting company Verio and a 10% stake in fixed wireless carrier Teligent.

HISTORY

In 1889 the Japanese Ministry of Communications began telephone service, operated as a monopoly after 1900. In 1952 the ministry formed Nippon Telegraph and Telephone Public Corporation (NTT). Regulated by the Ministry of Posts and Telecommunications, NTT was charged with the task of rebuilding Japan's war-ravaged phone system. Another company, Kokusai Denshin Denwa (now KDD), was created in 1953 to handle international phone service.

Japanese authorities cast NTT in the image of AT&T but prohibited it from manufacturing to encourage competition among equipment suppliers. Nonethelesss, NTT bought most equipment from favored Japanese vendors. By the late 1970s NTT was a large bureaucracy, perceived as inefficient and corrupt. NTT's president quipped that the only equipment the firm would buy overseas was telephone poles and mops, but in 1981 NTT was forced to allow US companies to bid. The phone firm spent heavily in the 1980s, installing a nationwide fiber-optic network and high-speed ISDN lines.

In 1985 Japan privatized NTT as a precursor to deregulation. At its IPO NTT became the world's most valuable public company. NTT International was established to provide overseas telecom engineering, and NTT Data Communications Systems, Japan's largest systems integrator, was formed in 1988.

As Japan's stock market bubble burst in 1990, NTT chose AT&T, Motorola, and Ericsson to develop a digital mobile phone system. The next year formed NTT Mobile Communications Network, aka DoCoMo, as its mobile carrier. Following the deregulation of Japan's cellular market, NTT launched its Personal Handyphone Service (PHS) in 1995.

The Japanese government unveiled a plan to break up NTT in 1996, a year before the World Trade Organization spearheaded a historic agreement to open international telecom markets. Meanwhile, the government forced NTT to allow rivals to connect to its new, all-digital systems. Overseas, NTT bought a 12.5% stake in Teligent, a US local carrier, its first significant investment in the US.

In 1998 tiny Tokyo Telecommunications Net (a Tokyo Electric Power affiliate) offered discount phone rates, spurring NTT to do the same. NTT spun off DoCoMo in the world's largest IPO at the time.

The company lost its 1999 bidding war with the UK's Cable and Wireless for International Digital Communications. Also that year NTT split into three carriers, two near-monopoly regional local phone providers — NTT East and NTT West — and a long-distance and international carrier called NTT Communications. Unlike AT&T's breakup in 1984, this split featured a holding company — the new NTT — which owns the three carriers. The company announced plans to cut 21,000 jobs over three years at NTT West and NTT East.

NTT meanwhile pressed forward with international investments, taking a 49% stake in HKNet of Hong Kong, and agreeing to buy 49% of Davnet Telecommunications, a subsidiary of Australia's Davnet Ltd. In 2000 NTT paid $5 billion for the 90% of US Web-hosting company Verio that it didn't already own.

Chairman: Shigeo Sawada
President: Jun-ichiro Miyazu
SEVP Business Strategy: Yusuke Tachibana
SEVP Business Strategy: Norio Wada
SEVP: Haruki Matsuno
SVP: Kanji Koide
SVP Intellectual Property: Shigehiko Suzuki
SVP New Business, Information Sharing, and Network Development: Hiromi Wasai
SVP Legal Affairs: Toyohiko Takabe
SVP; Chairman Nippon Steel: Takashi Imai
President, NTT East: Hidekazu Inoue
President, NTT West: Kazuo Asada
President, NTT Communications: Masanobu Suzuki
President, NTT DoCoMo: Keiji Tachikawa
President, NTT DATA: Toshiharu Aoki
President and CEO, NTT America: Akihiko Okada
Auditors: PricewaterhouseCoopers

HQ: Nippon Denshin Denwa Kabushiki Kaisha,
(Nippon Telegraph and Telephone Corporation)
3-1, Otemachi 2-chome, Chiyoda-ku,
Tokyo 100-8116, Japan
Phone: +81-3-5205-5111   **Fax:** +81-3-5205-5589
US HQ: 101 Park Ave., 41st Fl., New York, NY 10178
US Phone: 212-661-0810   **US Fax:** 212-661-1078
Web site: http://www.ntt.co.jp

Nippon Telegraph and Telephone operates principally in Japan. The company also operates or has investments in operations throughout the Pacific Rim — including in Australia, Hong Kong, Indonesia, Malaysia, the Philippines, Singapore, Sri Lanka, and Thailand — and in the US.

2000 Sales

	$ mil.	% of total
Wireline services	53,917	55
Wireless services	35,118	36
Data communication	6,054	6
Other	2,867	3
Total	**97,956**	**100**

Selected Services

Conventional leased circuits	ISDN
	Local phone
Digital data-exchange	Long-distance
Digital mobile phone	Pocket pager
High-speed digital circuits	Systems development
Fax network	Telegram
Frame relay access	

Selected Subsidiaries
NTT Communications Corporation
NTT Data Corporation (54%)
NTT Mobile Communications Network (DoCoMo, 67%)
Verio

AT&T	Internet	SOFTBANK
BT	Initiative Japan	Sony
Cable and	Japan Telecom	Sumitomo
Wireless	KDDI	Telstra
Equant	Marubeni	Tokyo Electric
Fujitsu	Microsoft	Tokyo Telecom
Global One	NEC	Toyota
Infonet Services	PSINet	WorldCom

Tokyo: 9432 FYE: March 31	Annual Growth	3/91	3/92	3/93	3/94	3/95	3/96	3/97	3/98	3/99	3/00
Sales ($ mil.)	9.2%	44,467	48,134	56,616	56,536	69,569	74,610	71,262	71,591	80,411	97,956
Net income ($ mil.)	4.8%	1,856	1,663	1,332	403	960	2,582	2,031	1,625	4,582	2,821
Income as % of sales	—	4.2%	3.5%	2.4%	0.7%	1.4%	3.5%	2.9%	2.3%	5.7%	2.9%
Earnings per share ($)	4.3%	—	—	—	—	0.72	1.01	0.64	0.51	1.44	0.89
Stock price - FY high ($)	—	—	—	—	—	46.31	46.31	40.25	52.50	51.00	92.50
Stock price - FY low ($)	—	—	—	—	—	35.28	36.00	33.75	34.38	31.00	46.88
Stock price - FY close ($)	14.6%	—	—	—	—	39.94	37.00	35.88	42.31	48.75	78.81
P/E - high	—	—	—	—	—	64	46	63	103	35	104
P/E - low	—	—	—	—	—	49	36	53	67	22	53
Dividends per share ($)	—	—	—	—	—	0.00	0.11	0.04	0.00	0.09	0.39
Book value per share ($)	(0.1%)	—	—	—	—	18.01	15.40	13.56	13.01	15.35	17.92
Employees	(1.8%)	264,908	257,663	242,303	248,000	235,000	231,000	230,000	226,000	224,000	224,000

HIGH/LOW/CLOSE

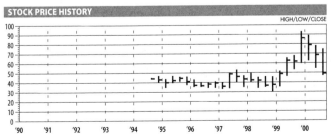

Debt ratio: 43.3%
Return on equity: 5.3%
Cash ($ mil.): 10,899
Current ratio: 0.96
Long-term debt ($ mil.): 43,385
No. of shares (mil.): 3,167
Dividends
  Yield: 0.5%
  Payout: 43.8%
Market value ($ mil.): 249,591

NISSAN MOTOR CO., LTD.

OVERVIEW

Nissan Motor Co. is happy to listen to Renault's backseat driving. After selling a 37% stake to France's Renault, Nissan — Japan's #3 automaker behind Toyota and Honda — is beginning to make a comeback after years of crippling losses. Based in Tokyo, Nissan offers a wide range of models, including its Altima, Infiniti, and Sentra cars, as well as its Frontier pickups and Xterra and Pathfinder SUVs.

Nissan's president and former Renault executive Carlos Ghosn — nicknamed "Le Cost-Killer" — has implemented measures to help navigate the company into financial recovery. After closing inefficient factories, reducing its workforce, curbing purchasing costs, and sharing operations with Renault, Nissan is enjoying its best financial results in 10 years.

HISTORY

In 1911 US-trained Hashimoto Masujiro established Tokyo-based Kwaishinsha Motor Car Works to repair, import, and make cars. Kwaishinsha made its first car, sporting its DAT ("fast rabbit" in Japanese) logo, in 1913. Renamed DAT Motors in 1925 and suffering from a strong domestic preference for American cars, the company consolidated with ailing Jitsuyo Motors in 1926. DAT introduced the son of DAT in 1931 — the Datsun minicar ("son" means "damage or loss" in Japanese, hence the spelling change).

Tobata Casting (cast iron and auto parts) bought Datsun's production facilities in 1933. Tobata's Yoshisuke Aikawa believed there was a niche for small cars, and the car operations were spun off as Nissan Motors that year.

During WWII the Japanese government limited Nissan's production to trucks and airplane engines; Nissan survived postwar occupation, in part, due to business with the US Army. The company went public in 1951 and signed a licensing agreement the next year with Austin Motor (UK), which put it back in the car business. A 40% import tax allowed Nissan to compete in Japan even though it had higher costs than those of foreign carmakers.

Nissan entered the US market in 1958, using the Datsun name; it established Nissan Motor Corporation in Los Angeles in 1960. Exports rose as factory automation resulted in higher quality and lower costs. In the 1970s Nissan expanded exports of fuel-efficient cars such as the Datsun B210.

The company's name change in the US from Datsun to Nissan during the 1980s confused customers and took six years to complete. In 1986 Nissan became the first major Japanese carmaker to build its products in Europe. It launched its high-end Infiniti line in the US in 1989.

Nissan and Japanese telecom firm DDI Corporation set up cellular telephone operations in 1992. Japan's recession resulted in a $450 million loss the next year. The company cut costs in 1993 and sold $200 million in real-estate holdings in 1994.

Seat-belt problems prompted the 1996 recall of more than a million vehicles, and Nissan suffered its fourth straight year of losses, posting an $834 million loss for 1996. Fiscal 1997 brought profits for Nissan in part the result of cost-cutting moves, sales to countries with currencies stronger than the yen, and the launching of new models. Also that year Nissan made plans to shift manufacturing of its Sentra models from the US to Mexico. In 1998 Nissan received a $827 million loan from the government-owned Japan Development Bank to restructure its debt.

Suffering under an estimated $30 billion in debt in 1999, Nissan invited major carmakers to buy into the company. Renault took a 37% stake and a 15% stake (later increased to 23%) in affiliate Nissan Diesel Motor for $5.4 billion. The stake gave Renault veto power and enabled it to install its chief cost-cutter, Carlos Ghosn, as chief operating officer. Ghosn announced plans to slash the number of suppliers, close five plants, and cut its workforce by 14% by 2002. Meanwhile, Nissan sold its interests in nine mobile-phone companies and its powder metallurgy business.

In 2000 Nissan sold its stake in Fuji Heavy Industries and announced that it was selling its aerospace business. The same year Ghosn became president of Nissan (in addition to being COO); Nissan's former president Yoshikazu Hanawa remained as CEO and chairman. Nissan also announced that it was developing a full-sized truck for the US market and that it and Renault were combining their European sales and marketing operations. Late in the year Nissan agreed to sell its 38% stake in seat maker Ikeda Bussan for about $100 million and its 17% stake in Yorozu Corp. (auto parts, Japan) for about $38 million. Later still, the company announced plans to build a $930 million manufacturing plant in the US.

Chairman and CEO: Yoshikazu Hanawa
VC and EVP, External and Government Affairs Department: Kanemitsu Anraku
President and COO: Carlos Ghosn
EVP and CFO: Thierry Moulonguet
EVP Domestic Marketing and Sales Group, Parts Division: Hiroshi Moriyama
EVP Manufacturing and Engineering Group, Powertrain Operations Group, and Industrial Machinery Division: Hisayoshi Kojima
EVP Overseas Operations Group, North America and European Operations: Norio Matsumura
EVP Planning Group, Corporate Planning Department, Program Management Office, Product Strategy and Planning Division, and Design Division: Patrick Pelata
EVP Purchasing Group: Itaru Koeda
Auditors: Century Ota Showa & Co.

LOCATIONS

HQ: Nissan Jidosha Kabushiki Kaisha,
17-1, Ginza 6-chome, Chuo-ku,
Tokyo 104-8023, Japan
Phone: +81-3-5543-5523   **Fax:** +81-3-3546-2669
US HQ: 18501 S. Figueroa St., Gardenia, CA 90248
US Phone: 310-771-5631   **US Fax:** 310-516-7967
Web site: http://global.nissan.co.jp

2000 Sales

	$ mil.	% of total
Japan	24,782	44
North America	20,922	37
Europe	8,273	15
Other regions	2,410	4
Total	**56,387**	**100**

PRODUCTS/OPERATIONS

Selected Models

Infiniti
G20
I30
Q45
QX4

Nissan
Altima (Americas)
Bluebird (Asia)
Cedric (Asia)
Cefiro (Asia)
Cima (Asia)
Cube (Asia)
Elgrand (Asia)
Fairlady Z (Asia)
Frontier (North America)
Gloria (Asia)
Laurel (Asia)
Lucino (Mexico)
March (Asia)
Maxima (Americas)

Micra (Europe)
Pathfinder (Americas)
Presage (Asia)
Presia (Asia)
President (Asia)
Primera (Asia, Europe)
Pulsar (Asia)
Quest (Americas)
Sentra (Americas)
Serena (Europe)
Skyline (Asia)
Stagea (Asia)
Sunny (Asia)
Terrano II (Europe)
Tino (Asia)
Tsubame (Mexico)
Tsuru (Mexico)
Urvan (Mexico)
Vanette Cargo (Europe)
Wingroad (Asia)
Xterra (North America)

COMPETITORS

BMW
Brunswick
Cordant
  Technologies
Daewoo
DaimlerChrysler
Deere
Fiat
Ford
Fuji Heavy
  Industries

GE
General Motors
Honda
Hyundai
Isuzu
Kia Motors
Lockheed Martin
Mazda
Mitsubishi
NACCO
  Industries

Outboard Marine
Peugeot
Saab Automobile
Suzuki
Toyota
Volkswagen
Volvo
Yamaha

HISTORICAL FINANCIALS & EMPLOYEES

Nasdaq (SC): NSANY FYE: March 31	Annual Growth	3/91	3/92	3/93	3/94	3/95	3/96	3/97	3/98	3/99	3/00
Sales ($ mil.)	3.2%	42,425	48,284	53,948	56,319	67,402	56,973	53,701	49,732	54,380	56,387
Net income ($ mil.)	—	347	762	(487)	(844)	(1,918)	(834)	627	(106)	(229)	(6,456)
Income as % of sales	—	0.8%	1.6%	—	—	—	—	1.2%	—	—	—
Earnings per share ($)	—	—	—	—	(0.34)	(0.76)	(0.66)	0.25	(0.08)	(0.18)	(3.40)
Stock price - FY high ($)	—	—	—	—	17.50	18.00	16.25	18.38	15.75	8.13	13.38
Stock price - FY low ($)	—	—	—	—	11.88	13.00	11.25	10.63	7.38	4.50	6.66
Stock price - FY close ($)	(10.7%)	—	—	—	16.00	14.75	15.38	11.88	7.94	7.50	8.13
P/E - high	—	—	—	—	—	—	—	74	—	—	—
P/E - low	—	—	—	—	—	—	—	43	—	—	—
Dividends per share ($)	—	—	—	—	0.11	0.12	0.12	0.11	0.00	0.00	0.00
Book value per share ($)	(15.4%)	—	—	—	12.21	13.14	10.19	8.70	7.73	8.25	4.47
Employees	0.3%	138,326	143,916	143,754	143,310	145,582	139,856	135,331	137,201	143,681	141,526

STOCK PRICE HISTORY

HIGH/LOW/CLOSE

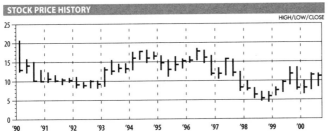

2000 FISCAL YEAR-END

Debt ratio: 64.0%
Return on equity: —
Cash ($ mil.): 4,629
Current ratio: 0.95
Long-term debt ($ mil.): 15,619
No. of shares (mil.): 1,963
Dividends
  Yield: —
  Payout: —
Market value ($ mil.): 15,960

NISSHO IWAI CORPORATION

OVERVIEW

Trading in all kinds of places is Nissho Iwai's calling. The Tokyo-based *sogo shosha* (general trading company) is one of the world's largest trading enterprises, with more than 600 affiliated companies in nearly 80 countries around the world. The company is engaged in a wide range of activities, from infrastructure construction (highways, airports, and harbors) to importing consumer goods (NIKE shoes and Philip Morris cigarettes).

In addition to constructing power plants and manufacturing chemicals, Nissho Iwai produces lumber for the housing industry, builds condominiums in Asia and the US, and operates a precious metals brokerage. Other activities include automobile export and distribution, shipbuilding, aircraft sales, and metals. The company has also moved into the information world and has stakes in satellite systems, cable TV operators, and telecom infrastructure projects in Latin America and China.

Rough economic conditions in Japan and the disastrous performance of Nissho Iwai's NI Finance unit (which ran up major losses from futures trading) have prompted the company to cut jobs, sell assets, and reorganize its operations. It has dissolved the NI Finance unit and sold its stakes in ISP Nifty and delivery firm DHL Worldwide Express. With a new president and headquarters, Nissho Iwai is restructuring into nine major divisions.

HISTORY

The Nissho and Iwai companies got their acts together as Nissho Iwai in 1968, but each company dates back to the middle of the 19th century. In 1863, Bunsuke Iwai opened a shop in Osaka to sell imported goods such as glass, oil products, silk, and wine. The Meiji government, which came to power in 1868, encouraged modernization and industrialization, a climate in which Iwai's business flourished. In 1877 Iwajiro Suzuki established a similar trading concern, Suzuki & Co., that eventually became Nissho.

After cotton spinning machines were introduced in Japan in the 1890s, both Iwai and Suzuki imported cotton. Iwai began to trade directly with British trader William Duff & Son (an innovation in Japan, where the middleman, or *shokan,* played the paramount role in international trade). Iwai became the primary agent for Yawata Steel Works in 1901 and was incorporated in 1912. Meanwhile, Suzuki, solely engaged in the import trade, emerged as one of the top sugar brokers in the world and established an office in London.

To protect itself from foreign competition, Iwai established a number of companies to produce goods in Japan, including Nippon Steel Plate (1914) and Tokuyama Soda (1918). Stagnation after WWI forced Suzuki to restructure. In 1928 the company sold many of its assets to trading giant Mitsui and reorganized the rest under a new name, Nissho Co.

Both Iwai and Nissho subsequently grew as they helped fuel Japan's military expansion in Asia in the 1930s. But Japan's defeat in WWII devastated the companies. When the occupation forces broke up Mitsui and other larger trading conglomerates, both companies took advantage of the situation to move into new business areas. In 1949 Nissho established Nissho Chemical Industry, Nissho Fuel, and Nijko Shoji (a trading concern). It also opened its US operations, Nissho American Corp., in 1952.

Poor management by the Iwai family led the company into financial trouble in the 1960s and prompted the Japanese government to instruct the profitable Nissho to merge with Iwai in 1968.

In 1979 Nissho Iwai was accused of funneling kickbacks from US aircraft makers to Japanese politicians. The scandal led to arrests, the resignation of the company's chairman, and the suicide of another executive. Nissho Iwai exited the aircraft marketing business in 1980.

Despite Japan's recession in the 1990s, Nissho Iwai managed to make some significant investments. In 1991 the company teamed up with the Russian government to develop a Siberian oil refinery. A year later Nissho acquired a stake in courier DHL International, and in 1995 it set up a unit to process steel plates in Vietnam.

However, in the late 1990s rough economic conditions caught up with the firm. It dissolved its NI Finance unit (domestic financing) in 1998 after its disastrous performance. The *sogo sosha* also began a major restructuring effort to get back on track.

In 1999 Nissho Iwai sold its headquarters, its 5% stake in DHL International, and its stake in a Japanese ISP, Nifty. CEO Masatake Kusamichi resigned, taking the blame for a loss that exceeded $800 million. He was replaced by Shiro Yasutake, who took charge of the firm's restructuring (it plans to shed 200 companies by 2002).

OFFICERS

President and CEO: Shiro Yasutake
VP Plant and Project, Industrial Systems and Automotive, Aerospace, Marine and Rolling Stock, Energy: Takayuki Mabuchi
Senior Managing Director, Corporate Planning, Strategy Promotion, Personnel, General Affairs, and Public Relations: Kosaku Nakatani
VP General Accounting, Finance, Financial Markets and Business, and Project Finance: Masanobu Kondo
Senior Managing Director, Chemicals, Housing Materials and General Merchandise, Consumer Products, Construction and Urban Development: Tomoyoshi Kondo
Senior Managing Director, Internal Auditing, Risk Management, ALM, Legal, and Credit: Susumu Tsuchida
Senior Managing Director, Investor Relations IT Promotion, International Planning and Co-ordination, and Group Planning and Co-ordination: Tokuichi Yamaguchi
Senior Managing Executive Officer, The Americas; President, Nissho Iwai American and Nissho Iwai Canada: Hidetoshi Nishimura
Auditors: Asahi & Co.

LOCATIONS

HQ: 4-5, Akasaka 2-chome, Minato-ku,
Tokyo 107-0052, Japan
Phone: +81-3-3588-2111   **Fax:** +81-3-3588-4136
US HQ: 1211 Avenue of the Americas,
New York, NY 10036
US Phone: 212-704-6500   **US Fax:** 212-704-6543
Web site: http://www.nisshoiwai.co.jp

Nissho Iwai operates in nearly 80 countries, mainly in Asia, Latin America, North America, and Europe.

PRODUCTS/OPERATIONS

Selected Operations
Aerospace
Automotive
Chemicals
Construction and urban development
Energy
Ferrous materials and coal
Foods
Housing materials and general merchandise
Industrial systems
Information businesses
Infrastructure projects
Logistics and insurance
Marine and transportation systems
Nonferrous metals
Precious metals
Steel products
Textiles
Wire rod and specialty steel

COMPETITORS

ITOCHU	Nichimen
Kanematsu	Sumitomo
Marubeni	TOMEN
Mitsubishi	Toyota Tsusho
Mitsui	

HISTORICAL FINANCIALS & EMPLOYEES

Tokyo: 8063 FYE: March 31	Annual Growth	3/91	3/92	3/93	3/94	3/95	3/96	3/97	3/98	3/99	3/00
Sales (¥ bil.)	(5.4%)	—	11,319	10,636	10,301	10,020	9,448	8,889	10,053	8,659	7,281
Net income (¥ bil.)	0.3%	—	10	3	11	5	(25)	15	3	(99)	10
Income as % of sales	—	—	0.1%	0.0%	0.1%	0.0%	—	0.2%	0.0%	—	0.1%
Earnings per share (¥)	(0.5%)	—	12.15	4.14	13.69	6.68	(31.94)	18.38	3.47	(112.69)	11.69
Stock price - FY high (¥)	—	—	719	490	523	559	592	633	525	335	156
Stock price - FY low (¥)	—	—	450	328	359	411	329	370	204	69	68
Stock price - FY close (¥)	(16.7%)	—	469	452	430	449	546	409	365	104	109
P/E - high	—	—	59	118	38	84	—	34	151	—	13
P/E - low	—	—	37	79	26	62	—	20	59	—	6
Dividends per share (¥)	—	—	5.00	5.00	5.00	5.00	5.00	5.00	5.00	0.00	0.00
Book value per share (¥)	(5.6%)	—	—	311.57	334.13	338.34	305.37	340.03	337.60	220.40	208.75
Employees	(18.9%)	—	—	—	—	—	—	—	—	18,158	14,718

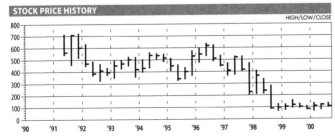

STOCK PRICE HISTORY   HIGH/LOW/CLOSE

2000 FISCAL YEAR-END
Debt ratio: 92.7%
Return on equity: —
Cash (¥ mil.): 298,779
Current ratio: 1.00
Long-term debt (¥ mil.):
1,182,109
No. of shares (mil.): 874
Dividends
  Yield: —
  Payout: —
Market value ($ mil.): 902
Sales ($ mil.): 68,968

NOKIA CORPORATION

OVERVIEW

Nokia has made mobile Internet the key to its success. Already the world's #1 mobile phone maker (ahead of Motorola and Ericsson), the Espoo, Finland-based company is headed by CEO Jorma Ollila, who has become a telecom poster child by saying he wants to "bring the Internet to everybody's pocket."

Although mobile phones account for two-thirds of sales, Nokia is increasingly emphasizing its infrastructure business as it develops technology for third-generation wireless networks. It already sells phones and servers for wireless application protocol, a watered-down version of the Internet for the small screens of mobile devices. Nokia, a founding member of the Bluetooth Special Interest Group, is emphasizing home and business communications through products like wireless networks and its interactive television set-top boxes.

But it's the third-generation wireless networks that hold the key for Nokia. Although the company was leaps and bounds ahead of its rivals with digital phones and dominated the European global system for mobile communications market, it lagged badly in the US market, where many big carriers had adopted QUALCOMM's code-division multiple access standard. Nokia is covering all the bases for the third generation by offering systems to ramp up all existing protocols, but it plans to work with Motorola for the standardization of the 1Xtreme technology, setting the stage for a battle with QUALCOMM's High Data Rate method.

HISTORY

Nokia got its start in 1865 when engineer Fredrik Idestam established a mill to manufacture pulp and paper on the Nokia River in Finland. Although Nokia flourished within Finland, the company was not well known to the rest of the world until it attempted to become a regional conglomerate in the early 1960s. French computer firm Machines Bull selected Nokia as its Finnish agent in 1962, and Nokia began researching radio transmission technology. In 1967, with the encouragement of Finland's government, Nokia merged with Finnish Rubber Works (a maker of tires and rubber footwear, formed in 1898) and Finnish Cable Works (a cable and electronics manufacturer formed in 1912) to form Nokia Corporation.

The oil crisis of 1973 created severe inflation and a large trade deficit for Finland. Nokia reassessed its heavy reliance on Soviet trade and shifted its focus to consumer and business electronics. Nokia's basic industries — paper, chemicals, electricity, and machinery — were modernized and expanded into robotics, fiber optics, and high-grade tissues.

The company acquired a 51% interest in the state-owned Finnish telecom company in 1981 and named it Telenokia. The next year Nokia designed and installed (in Finland) the first European digital telephone system. Also in 1982 Nokia acquired interests in Salora, Scandinavia's largest maker of color televisions, and Luxor, the Swedish state-owned electronics and computer firm.

Nokia acquired control of Sahkoliikkeiden, Finland's largest electrical wholesaler, in 1986. It created the largest IT group in Scandinavia, Nokia Data, by purchasing Ericsson Group's Data Division in 1988. Sales soared, but profits plunged because of stiff price competition in consumer electronics.

To raise cash, the company sold Nokia Data to IT services company ICL in 1991 and bought UK mobile phone maker Technophone, which had been #2 in Europe, after Nokia. Under the leadership of Jorma Ollila (appointed CEO in 1992 and chairman in 1999), Nokia intensified its focus on telecommunications and divested noncore units power (1994), televisions, and tire and cable machinery (1995).

It also began selling digital phones at the end of 1993. The company expected to sell 400,000; it shipped 20 million, and rode the phones' success to a billion-dollar profit in 1995.

Nokia sold more than 40 million mobile phones in 1998 and became the world's #1 mobile phone company. Extending its push into Internet capability, Nokia that year bought several small companies that develop e-commerce and telephony technologies. In 1999 Nokia penned deals to put its wireless application protocol (WAP) software into Hewlett-Packard's and IBM's network servers; it also unveiled several WAP-enabled phones that can access the Internet. Nokia widened its lead as the world's top seller of mobile phones, and made several acquisitions to strengthen its IP networks business.

In 2000 Nokia acquired secure transaction software maker Network Alchemy. Later that year it began pushing for the standardization of Motorola's 1Xtreme technology for third-generation wireless networks.

Chairman and CEO: Jorma Ollila, age 49
VC: Paul J. Collins
President; President, Nokia Communications Products: Pekka Ala-Pietilä, age 43
President, Nokia Mobile Phones: Matti Alahuhta, age 47
President, Nokia Networks: Sari Baldauf, age 44
EVP and CFO: Olli-Pekka Kallasvuo, age 46
EVP; Chief Technology Officer, Nokia Mobile Phones: Yrjö Neuvo, age 56
EVP; General Manager, Customer Operations, Nokia Networks: Mikko Heikkonen, age 50
EVP Corporate Relations and Trade Policy: Veli Sundbäck, age 53
EVP Europe & Africa, Nokia Mobile Phones: Anssi Vanjoki, age 43
SVP; President, Americas: Kari-Pekka Wilska
SVP Corporate Marketing: Martin Sandelin
SVP Human Resources: Hallstein Moerk
Auditors: KPMG; PricewaterhouseCoopers

HQ: Keilalahdentie 4, FIN-00045 Espoo, Finland
Phone: +358-9-180-71   **Fax:** +358-9-652-409
US HQ: 6000 Connection Dr., Irving, TX 75039
US Phone: 972-894-5000   **US Fax:** 972-894-5050
Web site: http://www.nokia.com

Nokia sells its products in more than 130 countries.

1999 Sales

	$ mil.	% of total
Europe	10,712	54
Americas	4,954	25
Asia/Pacific	4,288	21
Total	**19,954**	**100**

1999 Sales

	$ mil.	% of total
Nokia Mobile Phones	13,289	66
Nokia Networks	5,722	29
Other	943	5
Total	**19,954**	**100**

Selected Products and Services
Analog mobile cellular phones
Digital mobile cellular phones
Digital television set-top boxes
Handheld telephone/personal organizers
Multimedia displays
Phone accessories (batteries, cases, chargers)
Services to Internet service providers
Systems and infrastructure for analog and digital wireless networks and fixed-access networks
Technology for broadband and Internet protocol networking products

Alcatel	Oki Electric
Cisco Systems	Philips Electronics
Ericsson	Phone.com
Fujitsu	Pioneer
GE	QUALCOMM
Harris Corporation	Robert Bosch
Kyocera	Sagem
Lucent	Samsung
Marconi	SANYO
Matsushita Communication	Siemens
Mitsubishi Electric	Sony
Motorola	Sumitomo
NEC	Tellabs
Nortel Networks	Toshiba

NYSE: NOK FYE: December 31	Annual Growth	12/90	12/91	12/92	12/93	12/94	12/95	12/96	12/97	12/98	12/99
Sales ($ mil.)	14.1%	6,093	3,732	3,451	4,079	6,368	8,400	8,446	9,702	15,553	19,954
Net income ($ mil.)	44.5%	95	(146)	(78)	132	632	509	701	1,154	2,043	2,601
Income as % of sales	—	1.6%	—	—	3.2%	9.9%	6.1%	8.3%	11.9%	13.1%	13.0%
Earnings per share ($)	46.3%	—	—	—	—	—	0.12	0.16	0.26	0.46	0.55
Stock price - FY high ($)	—	—	—	—	—	—	4.88	3.70	6.40	15.68	49.00
Stock price - FY low ($)	—	—	—	—	—	—	1.95	1.95	3.45	4.16	15.58
Stock price - FY close ($)	110.3%	—	—	—	—	—	2.44	3.60	4.34	15.05	47.77
P/E - high	—	—	—	—	—	—	54	23	25	36	86
P/E - low	—	—	—	—	—	—	22	12	13	10	27
Dividends per share ($)	—	—	—	—	—	—	0.00	0.04	0.00	0.00	0.12
Book value per share ($)	24.9%	—	—	—	—	—	0.66	0.71	0.83	1.23	1.60
Employees	3.6%	37,336	29,167	26,700	25,800	28,600	31,948	31,723	36,647	44,543	51,177

HIGH/LOW/CLOSE

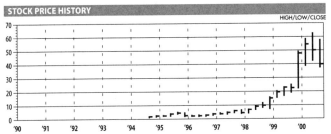

Debt ratio: 3.5%
Return on equity: 38.8%
Cash ($ mil.): 1,032
Current ratio: 1.69
Long-term debt ($ mil.): 271
No. of shares (mil.): 4,653
Dividends
  Yield: 0.3%
  Payout: 21.8%
Market value ($ mil.): 222,259

THE NOMURA SECURITIES CO., LTD.

OVERVIEW

This company can't take "nomura" this.

Tokyo-based Nomura Securities has been rocked by recession in Asia and economic meltdown in Russia — after being stung by bribery and racketeering scandals at home. As a result, Nomura's trading business has plummeted and it has lost clients at a time when US securities firms are entering the formerly protected Japanese market. The firm is still Japan's #1 securities house, however, and offers a wide variety of retail and institutional brokerage, corporate and governmental underwriting, asset management, and mergers and acquisitions services.

Nomura's problems are compounded by huge losses stemming from high-risk investments by US-based Nomura Holdings. Nomura has responded by reorganizing operations, downsizing foreign business, and centralizing management to focus on domestic retail services. In addition, deregulation of Japanese financial markets has allowed banks to underwrite c orporate bonds and soon gain access to equities markets. Nomura is reacting by forming alliances with banks to sell mutual funds. Although it is reducing direct overseas operations, the company maintains a presence in a few key finance areas and through joint ventures with the Industrial Bank of Japan in the UK (derivatives sales) and Japan (pension plan consulting) and investments in Czech breweries and UK pub properties.

HISTORY

Tokushichi Nomura started a currency exchange, Nomura Shoten, in Osaka in 1872 and began trading stock. The business was taken over by his son Tokushichi II, who in 1910 formed Nomura's first syndicate to underwrite part of a government bond issue. Nomura established the Osaka Nomura Bank in 1918. The bond department became independent in 1925 and was named Nomura Securities. The company opened a New York office in 1927, entering stock brokerage in 1938.

The firm rebuilt and expanded retail operations after WWII. It encouraged stock market investing by promoting "million ryo savings chests," small boxes in which people saved cash (ryo was an old form of currency); when savings reached 5,000 yen, savers could buy into investment trusts. The company distributed more than a million chests in 10 years.

Nomura followed clients overseas, helping underwrite a US issue of Sony stock in 1961 and opening a London office in 1962. It became Japan's leading securities firm after a 1965 stock market crash left rival Yamaichi Securities nearly bankrupt. The company grew rapidly in the 1970s, ushering investment capital in and out of Japan and competing with banks by issuing corporate debt securities.

As the Japanese economy soared in the 1980s, the firm opened Nomura Bank International in London in 1986 and bought 20% of US mergers and acquisitions advisor Wasserstein Perella in 1988.

Then the Japanese economic bubble burst. Nomura's stock toppled 70% from its 1987 peak and underwriting plummeted. In 1991 and 1992, amid revelations that Nomura and other brokerages had reimbursed favored clients'

trading losses, the company was accused of manipulating stock in companies owned by Japanese racketeers. Nomura's chairman and president — both named Tabuchi — resigned, admitting no wrongdoing. (In 1995 the two Tabuchis returned.)

Junichi Ujiie became president after 1997's payoff scandal and restructured operations to prepare for Japan's financial deregulation. Nomura invested in pub chain Inntrepreneur PLC and William Hill, a UK betting chain, in 1997. It also created an entertainment lending unit to lend against future royalties or syndication fees, and spun off a minority stake in its high-risk US real estate business, which ceased lending altogether the next year.

In 1998 Nomura was dealt a double blow when Asian economies collapsed and Russia defaulted on its debts; incurring substantial losses, the firm refocused on its domestic market and reduced overseas operations.

In 1999 Nomura bailed out its ailing property subsidiary Nomura Finance, crippled by the ever-sinking Japanese real estate market. Also that year Nomura invested heavily in UK real estate and gained 40% of the Czech beer market through a joint venture with South African Breweries.

The next year the company agreed to buy Hyder P.L.C., a water and power company in Wales. Also in 2000 the company decided to sell its assets in packindo parlors and "love" hotels, which are Japanese cultural traditions, but whose reputations are less than sparkling. Also, Britain's Securities and Futures Authority issued a reprimand and fined the company that year in response to attempts by Nomura traders to rig the Australian stock market in 1996.

President and CEO: Junichi Ujiie, age 54
EVP: Toshiaki Ito, age 51
EVP: Nobuyuki Koga
Executive Managing Director: Toshio Ando
Executive Managing Director: Hiroshi Toda
Executive Managing Director: Kazutoshi Inano
Managing Director: Kamezo Nakai
Managing Director, Global Investment Banking and Investment Banking Products Division: Hiromi Yamaji, age 45
Managing Director, European Division; President, Nomura International: Takumi Shibata, age 47
Managing Director, Global Risk Management Division, Finance & Risk Analysis (CFO), and Investor Relations Department: Kenichi Watanabe, age 47
Managing Director, Compliance Division, Business Conduct Advisory Department, and Ethics & Discipline Department: Takashi Fujita, age 51
Managing Director: Takashi Tsutsui
Managing Director: Hiroshi Inoue
Managing Director: Takashi Yanagiya
Director, Investment Banking Products Division: Yoshifumi Kawabata, age 47
Director, Corporate Development and Finance Department: Shogo Sakaguchi, age 47
Director, Planning Division and Corporate Communications: Masanori Itatani, age 46
Director, Marketing Divisions: Manabu Matsumoto, age 50
Director and Head of Americas Division; President, Nomura Securities International (US): Atsushi Yoshikawa, age 46
Head of Financial Research Center; General Manager, Investment Strategy Department of Financial Research Center: Kenichi Fukuhara, age 49
Auditors: Price Waterhouse

HQ: Nomura Shoken Kabushiki Kaisha,
1-9-1, Nihonbashi, Chuo ku, Tokyo 103-8011, Japan
Phone: +81-3-3211-1811   **Fax:** +81-3-3278-0420
US HQ: 2 World Financial Center, Bldg. B,
New York, NY 10281
US Phone: 212-667-9300   **US Fax:** 212-667-1058
Web site: http://www.nomura.co.jp

Nomura Securities has 123 branch offices in Japan and operates in 27 other countries.

2000 Sales

	$ mil.	% of total
Interest & dividends	3,319	30
Commissions	3,199	29
Underwriting & distribution	1,534	14
Other	3,027	27
Total	**11,079**	**100**

Bank of America	Goldman Sachs
Barclays	HSBC Holdings
Bear Stearns	Industrial Bank of Japan
Canadian Imperial	J.P. Morgan
Charles Schwab	Lehman Brothers
Citigroup	Merrill Lynch
Credit Lyonnais	Nikko Securities
Credit Suisse First Boston	Paine Webber
Dai-Ichi Kangyo	Prudential
Daiwa	Royal Bank of Canada
Deutsche Bank	UBS
GE	

OTC: NRSCY FYE: March 31	Annual Growth	3/91	3/92	3/93	3/94	3/95	3/96	3/97	3/98	3/99	3/00
Sales ($ mil.)	4.7%	7,343	4,937	5,085	6,611	6,235	8,083	7,906	7,582	5,525	11,079
Net income ($ mil.)	4.9%	925	154	(125)	482	(510)	764	(736)	323	(3,920)	1,417
Income as % of sales	—	12.6%	3.1%	—	7.3%	—	9.5%	—	4.3%	—	12.8%
Earnings per share ($)	4.8%	4.72	0.91	(0.71)	2.92	(2.10)	3.86	(3.75)	2.92	(19.96)	7.19
Stock price - FY high ($)	—	167.86	164.50	168.72	228.61	248.91	228.86	223.00	147.00	128.00	314.25
Stock price - FY low ($)	—	110.02	84.19	85.47	152.11	164.22	172.52	111.00	89.50	65.00	96.50
Stock price - FY close ($)	8.6%	149.27	91.00	163.52	209.23	187.50	220.02	120.00	116.50	104.00	314.25
P/E - high	—	36	181	—	78	—	59	—	50	—	44
P/E - low	—	23	93	—	52	—	45	—	31	—	13
Dividends per share ($)	2.9%	1.13	1.31	0.97	1.16	0.93	1.03	0.87	1.50	0.84	1.46
Book value per share ($)	(1.2%)	74.24	84.71	90.51	107.61	83.34	82.91	60.85	68.81	55.70	66.72
Employees	2.9%	12,000	12,800	12,200	10,948	10,440	10,306	9,938	9,888	12,900	15,581

HIGH/LOW/CLOSE

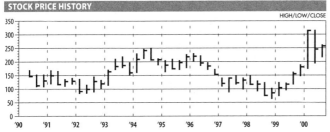

Debt ratio: —
Return on equity: 11.8%
Cash ($ mil.): —
Current ratio: —
Long-term debt ($ mil.): 28,369
No. of shares (mil.): 196
Dividends
  Yield: 0.0%
  Payout: 0.2%
Market value ($ mil.): 61,686

NORSK HYDRO ASA

OVERVIEW

Norsk Hydro is not a bottler of Norwegian spring water: It is Norway's largest publicly traded industrial company. The Oslo-based company is shedding noncore operations and focusing on three core areas: oil and energy, fertilizer and chemicals, and light metals. Hydro Norsk explores for and produces oil and gas — chiefly on the Norwegian continental shelf but also off the coasts of Angola, Canada, and other deepwater areas. Its proved reserves total more than 2 billion barrels of oil equivalent, and its 1999 takeover of rival Saga Petroleum has significantly boosted its energy production. To focus on deepwater plays, it has agreed to sell Saga UK, which has North Sea assets, to Conoco.

The company also has refining operations and markets its products through its own network of more than 700 stations in Sweden and through a joint venture with Texaco (nearly 950 stations in Norway, Denmark, and the Baltics). The company's lagging Hydro Agri unit, producing fertilizers and industrial chemicals and petrochemicals, accounts for about 35% of sales. It is also a leading European supplier of PVC pipe. Hydro Light Metals is the world's #3 aluminum company (behind Alcoa and Alcan). Through its Pronova unit, the company develops Omega 3 fatty acids and other products.

The government of Norway owns 44% of Norsk Hydro.

HISTORY

Norwegian entrepreneurs Sam Eyde and Kristian Birkeland began Norsk Hydro-Elektrisk Kvaelstofaktieselskap (Norwegian Hydro-Electric Nitrogen Corp.) in 1905. The company used electricity generated from waterfalls to extract nitrogen from the air to produce fertilizer.

After WWII the Norwegian government seized German holdings in Norsk Hydro and took a 48% stake in the company. It grew to be the largest chemical firm in Scandinavia. In 1965, when Norway granted licenses for offshore petroleum exploration, the company formed partnerships with foreign companies, including Phillips Petroleum, which spurred the North Sea boom in 1969 when it struck oil in the giant Ekofisk field, and Elf Aquitaine, which oversaw the Frigg discovery in 1971. The Norwegian state increased its share of Norsk Hydro to 51% in 1972.

The company also branched out with hydroelectric-powered aluminum processing at its Karmoy Works (1967) and with a fishfarming subsidiary, Mowi (1969). During much of the 1970s, it focused on oil and gas development, which added to the treasury and helped finance growth, often through acquisitions.

Norsk Hydro pushed into the European fertilizer market by buying Dutch company NSM in 1979; during the 1980s it acquired interests in fertilizer operations in France, Sweden, and the UK. In petrochemicals it expanded by buying two British PVC makers. Norsk Hydro-controlled Hydro Aluminum merged with ASV, another Norwegian aluminum company in 1986, and the company consolidated its aluminum holdings two years later.

Hydro served as operator in the Oseberg field, which began production in 1988 and grew

rapidly to become a major source of oil and gas. In 1990 it bought 330 Danish gasoline stations from UNO-X; in 1992 it purchased Mobil Oil's Norwegian marketing and distribution system. Two years later Norsk Hydro merged its oil and marketing operations in Norway and Denmark with Texaco's.

A weak world economy and increased competition limited its revenues in 1992 and 1993. The company countered slumping sales by selling noncore subsidiaries, including pharmaceutical unit Hydro Pharma (1992) and chocolate maker Freia Marabou (1993).

Norsk Hydro expanded further during the early 1990s, acquiring fertilizer plants in Germany, the UK, and the US, as well as W. R. Grace's ammonia plants in Trinidad and Tobago. The firm acquired Fisons' NPK fertilizer business in 1994. The company agreed to an asset swap with Petro-Canada in 1996, becoming a partner in oil and gas fields off the east coast of Canada.

The Norwegian government's stake in Norsk Hydro was reduced from 51% to 44% in 1999 when the company and state-owned Statoil made a deal to take over Saga Petroleum, Norway's leading independent oil producer, to keep it out of foreign hands.

In light of major losses in 1999 by Hydro Agri, the company said in early 2000 that it would close several European nitrogen fertilizer operations. However, it made plans to modernize and expand its Hydro Aluminum Sunndal facility, which would make it the largest aluminum plant in Europe. The company also agreed to sell Saga UK (its North Sea assets) to Conoco and its fish-farming unit to Dutch company Nutreco.

Chairman: Einar Kloster
President and CEO: Egil Myklebust
EVP: Thor Håkstad, age 54
EVP and CFO: Leiv L. Nergaard, age 55
EVP Agri: Thorleif Enger
EVP Light Metals: Eivind Reiten, age 47
EVP Oil and Energy: Tore Torvund
SVP Corporate Communications: Henrik Andenaes
SVP Health, Environment, and Safety: Raymond Pallen
SVP Human Resources: Alexandra Bech
SVP Infomation Systems and Chief Information Officer: Bjørn Vold, age 51
SVP Pronova and Corporate Finance and Control: Kjell Ramberg
SVP and General Counsel: Odd I. Biller
Auditors: Deloitte & Touche AS

HQ: Bygdoy alle 2, N-0240 Oslo N-0240, Norway
Phone: +47-22-43-21-00   **Fax:** +47-22-43-27-25
US HQ: 100 N. Tampa St., Ste. 3350, Tampa, FL 33602
US Phone: 813-222-3880   **US Fax:** 813-222-5741
Web site: http://www.hydro.com

1999 Sales

	% of total
Europe	
EU	63
Norway	10
Other Europe	5
US	10
Asia	5
Canada & other Americas	4
Africa	2
Australia & New Zealand	1
Total	**100**

1999 Sales

	% of total
Hydro Agri	36
Hydro Light Metals	29
Hydro Oil & Energy	23
Other	12
Total	**100**

Selected Operations

A/S Korn-og Foderstof Kompagniet (animal and fish feed, feedstuff; Denmark)
Aluminum extrusion
Aluminum metal products
Biomedical
Energy
Exploration and production
Gas and chemicals
Industrial insurance
Plant nutrition
Refining and marketing

Alcan	DuPont	PEMEX
Alcoa	E.ON	PETROBRAS
BASF AG	Eni	Phillips
Bayer AG	Exxon Mobil	Petroleum
BayWa	Farmland	Repsol YPF
BHP	Industries	Royal
BP	Formosa Plastics	Dutch/Shell
Cargill	ICI	SEPI
Cebeco-	IMC Global	Sinopec Group
Handelsraad	Kemira Oy	Statoil
Chevron	Mitsui	TOTAL FINA
Coastal	Occidental	ELF
ConAgra Foods	PDVSA	VEBA Oel
Devon Energy	Pechiney	

NYSE: NHY FYE: December 31	Annual Growth	12/90	12/91	12/92	12/93	12/94	12/95	12/96	12/97	12/98	12/99
Sales ($ mil.)	2.4%	10,365	9,987	8,373	8,293	10,554	12,606	13,167	13,069	12,827	12,804
Net income ($ mil.)	(1.6%)	493	(81)	254	399	597	1,128	963	707	494	427
Income as % of sales	—	4.8%	—	3.0%	4.8%	5.7%	8.9%	7.3%	5.4%	3.9%	3.3%
Earnings per share ($)	(3.6%)	2.40	(0.39)	1.24	1.94	2.74	4.91	4.21	3.08	2.16	1.73
Stock price - FY high ($)	—	41.75	32.75	28.25	30.38	41.00	46.38	53.63	61.25	51.75	46.63
Stock price - FY low ($)	—	24.25	20.00	19.38	21.75	28.38	35.00	40.50	45.63	30.56	32.75
Stock price - FY close ($)	3.7%	30.75	23.25	22.00	28.00	39.13	41.88	53.63	51.00	34.19	42.75
P/E - high	—	17	—	23	16	15	9	13	20	24	27
P/E - low	—	10	—	16	11	11	7	10	15	14	19
Dividends per share ($)	15.0%	0.53	0.54	0.47	0.37	0.42	0.68	0.79	0.98	0.00	1.86
Book value per share ($)	5.8%	17.05	15.16	14.16	14.72	19.93	25.64	24.72	27.12	27.74	28.42
Employees	1.5%	33,042	34,957	34,000	32,500	32,400	28,305	35,400	38,000	40,000	37,900

HIGH/LOW/CLOSE

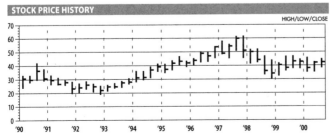

Debt ratio: 41.5%
Return on equity: 6.2%
Cash ($ mil.): 929
Current ratio: 1.59
Long-term debt ($ mil.): 5,279
No. of shares (mil.): 262
Dividends
 Yield: 4.4%
 Payout: 107.5%
Market value ($ mil.): 11,188

NORTEL NETWORKS CORPORATION

OVERVIEW

Nortel Networks has seen the future of telecommunications, and it's all optical. The #2 maker of telecom equipment (after Lucent), the Brampton, Ontario-based company is a leader in fiber-optic systems for high-capacity networks, and is looking to be the benefactor of carriers' bandwidth addiction. Nortel (formerly Northern Telecom) provides communications infrastructure equipment and services for packet-, Internet protocol-, and circuit-based networks, as well as wireless voice, data, and broadband systems. It also offers network management, e-business, and customer relationship management software.

Nortel has solidified its position as a top equipment maker through acquisitions, most notably in data networking (where it hopes to challenge Cisco) and fiber optics. CEO John Roth has used Nortel's 1998 $7 billion buy of Bay Networks to transform the company from a staid seller of simple telephone systems to a cutting-edge manufacturer of Internet gear.

Roth has shelled out billions in acquisition dollars to gain and protect Nortel's market dominance in the booming fiber-optic market. (The company says 75% of North American Internet traffic travels through its equipment.) Nortel is cutting costs by outsourcing noncore operations and shedding employees and plants. It also plans to offer shares of its fiber-optic components business to the public.

HISTORY

Nortel Networks traces its lineage to 1880, when Bell Telephone Company of Canada was established in Montreal four years after the invention of the telephone. In 1882 the Northern Electric and Manufacturing Company was founded to produce Bell Canada's mechanical equipment. Northern Electric pooled its resources with electrical wire maker Imperial Wire & Cable to form the Northern Electric Company in 1914.

During the 1930s the company created an electronics division and purchased a majority interest in Amalgamated Electric (1932). In the mid-1950s, the US Department of Justice forced majority shareholder Western Electric to sell its interest in Northern Electric, and Bell Canada purchased most of the shares. Northern Electric Laboratories was formed in 1958 to push research and development (it was spun off in 1971).

During the 1960s Northern Electric began supplying switching gear overseas. It remained wholly owned by Bell Canada until 1973, when that company began selling off stock. In 1976 Northern Electric was renamed Northern Telecom and became the first equipment company to introduce a digital switch. When AT&T approved use of the switch in its equipment in 1981, Nortel's growth took off.

Paul Stern became CEO in 1989 as Nortel thrived on its digital switch sales. The former IBM executive focused on cutting costs in lieu of technical advancement, and customer dissatisfaction built as the company failed to develop the software in its switching systems. Directors forced Stern out and replaced him with Jean Monty as CEO in 1992, just before the company suffered a loss of nearly $900 million for 1993.

Monty acted quickly, calming customers, revamping the software, and selling underused divisions and factories. In 1996 the company acquired data networking maker Micom Communications; the next year COO John Roth succeeded Monty.

Nortel boosted its networking expertise through such acquisitions as Bay Networks in 1998. The latter deal, worth $6.7 billion, led to a loss that year and prompted the 1999 name change to Nortel Networks. That year, Nortel acquired Shasta Networks, a maker of network management products for ISPs. It also continued to beef up its business offerings by acquiring computer-telephone integrator Periphonics, which it would later combine with 2000 acquisition Clarify (customer relationship management software) to offer high-margin business software and services.

Nortel increased its purchasing pace in 2000 to boost its fiber optics holdings. The company bought optical equipment startups Qtera, CoreTek, and Xros. It also purchased Architel Systems, a maker of service activation software for telecom providers. Later that year Nortel said it would sell and outsource some semiconductor operations to French chipmaker STMicroelectronics. The company also outsourced its information services to Computer Sciences Corporation.

Also in 2000 Bell Canada parent BCE distributed to its shareholders most of its 40% stake in Nortel. Later that year Nortel acquired Web switch maker Alteon WebSystems for $7.8 billion and Internet access equipment maker Sonoma Systems for over $500 million. The company also announced plans to take its fiber-optic components business public in mid-2001.

Chairman: Frank Charles Carlucci, age 69
VC, President, and CEO: John A. Roth, age 57,
$5,012,500 pay
COO: Clarence J. Chandran, age 51, $1,773,894 pay
(prior to promotion)
Chief Marketing Officer: Charles Childers
EVP; President, Enterprise Solutions:
F. William Conner, age 40
SVP and CFO: Frank A. Dunn, age 46
SVP and Chief Technology Officer: William R. Hawe
SVP and General Counsel: Nicholas J. DeRoma, age 53
**SVP; President, Service Provider Solutions, The
Americas:** Gary R. Donahee, age 53, $1,081,739 pay
SVP Human Resources: Margaret G. Kerr, age 54
**SVP, Information Systems and Chief Information
Officer:** Richard C. Ricks, age 40
Auditors: Deloitte & Touche LLP

HQ: 8200 Dixie Rd., Ste. 100, Brampton,
Ontario L6T 5P6, Canada
Phone: 905-863-0000   **Fax:** 905-863-8408
US HQ: 2221 Lakeside Blvd., Richardson, TX 75082
US Phone: 615-684-1000   **US Fax:**
Web site: http://www.nortelnetworks.com

Nortel Networks has operations in Australia, Brazil,
Canada, China, Ecuador, France, India, Ireland,
Malaysia, Mexico, the UK, and the US.

1999 Sales

	$ mil.	% of total
US	12,758	57
Canada	1,434	6
Other countries	8,025	37
Total	**22,217**	**100**

1999 Sales

	$ mil.	% of total
Service providers & carriers	16,761	75
Enterprise	5,376	25
Other	80	—
Total	**22,217**	**100**

Selected Products
Broadband wireless equipment
Digital coaxial cable equipment (through a joint venture
with ANTEC)
Digital switching equipment
Internet and data networking
Internet protocol, asynchronous transfer mode switches
Multiplexing equipment
Network and service management software
Optical networking equipment
Remote-access switches and network gateways
Ultralong-reach optical networking equipment
Wireless infrastructure equipment

3Com	Harris	ONI Systems
ADC Telecom	Corporation	PeopleSoft
Alcatel	Inter-Tel	QUALCOMM
Ascom Holding	InterVoice-Brite	Redback
BT	Juniper	Networks
Cabletron	Networks	Remedy
CIENA	Lucent	Scientific-Atlanta
Cisco Systems	Marconi	Siebel Systems
Corvis	Communications	Siemens
Deutsche	Motorola	Sycamore
Telekom	NEC	Networks
Ericsson	Nokia	Tellabs
Fujitsu	Oki Electric	

NYSE: NT FYE: December 31	Annual Growth	12/90	12/91	12/92	12/93	12/94	12/95	12/96	12/97	12/98	12/99
Sales ($ mil.)	14.1%	6,769	8,183	8,409	8,148	8,874	10,672	12,847	15,449	17,575	22,217
Net income ($ mil.)	—	460	515	548	(878)	408	473	623	829	(537)	(170)
Income as % of sales	—	6.8%	6.3%	6.5%	—	4.6%	4.4%	4.8%	5.4%	—	—
Earnings per share ($)	—	0.23	0.26	0.27	(0.45)	0.20	0.23	0.30	0.39	(0.25)	(0.08)
Stock price - FY high ($)	—	3.70	5.78	6.16	5.75	4.72	5.53	8.45	14.23	17.31	55.00
Stock price - FY low ($)	—	2.77	3.28	3.81	2.67	3.25	3.94	5.09	7.56	6.70	12.53
Stock price - FY close ($)	34.4%	3.53	5.63	5.38	3.86	4.17	5.38	7.73	11.09	12.50	50.50
P/E - high	—	16	22	23	—	24	24	28	36	—	—
P/E - low	—	12	13	14	—	16	17	17	19	—	—
Dividends per share ($)	8.0%	0.04	0.04	0.05	0.05	0.05	0.06	0.07	0.08	0.08	0.08
Book value per share ($)	11.0%	1.78	1.99	2.07	1.54	1.69	1.90	2.35	2.61	4.36	4.54
Employees	5.1%	49,039	57,059	57,955	60,293	57,054	63,715	68,000	73,000	75,052	76,700

HIGH/LOW/CLOSE

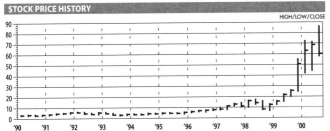

Debt ratio: 11.5%
Return on equity: —
Cash ($ mil.): 2,257
Current ratio: 1.68
Long-term debt ($ mil.): 1,624
No. of shares (mil.): 2,754
Dividends
Yield: 0.2%
Payout: —
Market value ($ mil.): 139,093

NOVARTIS AG

OVERVIEW

Can old drug dog Novartis learn new arts? One of the world's top five drug companies (Merck is #1), Basel, Switzerland-based Novartis (whose name is Latin for "new arts") has three business units: health care, agribusiness, and consumer health. Health care accounts for about 55% of sales and includes prescription and generic drugs and ophthalmic medications and products. The consumer health unit includes OTC, medical nutrition, and functional nutrition products. Its agribusiness division makes crop herbicides, insecticides, and fungicides; pet and farm animal medicines; and seeds. To focus on its less-controversial health care units, the firm has gotten rid of its agribusiness operations through a merger/ spinoff deal.

With drug sales slipping, particularly in the all-important US market, the company is hustling to get new drugs on the market. Perhaps taxed by the controversy surrounding genetically modified crops, the firm is eyeing "functional" foods (nutrient-fortified) and has caused a stir (this one positive) with a leukemia treatment that is still in trials. Novartis is said to be looking for a merger partner to improve its market position in the US.

HISTORY

Johann Geigy began selling spices and natural dyes in Basel, Switzerland, in 1758. A century later the Geigy family began producing synthetic dyes.

About that time Alexander Clavel entered the synthetic dye trade, forming the Gesellschaft fur Chemische Industrie Basel (Ciba). Ciba was Switzerland's #1 chemical firm at century's end.

After WWI, Ciba, Geigy, and Sandoz (a Basel synthetic dye maker founded in 1886) formed the Basel AG cartel to compete with German rival I.G. Farben. Basel AG used its profits to diversify into pharmaceuticals and other chemicals and to gain a foothold in the US.

Basel AG in 1929 merged with German and, later, French and British counterparts. WWII shattered the so-called Quadrapartite Cartel in 1939, leaving only Basel AG intact. Geigy scientist Paul Muller won a Nobel Prize in 1948 for inventing DDT. Basel AG voluntarily dissolved itself back into its component parts in 1951.

Ciba, Geigy, and Sandoz continued to diversify. Finding new markets in agricultural chemicals, Geigy had passed Ciba in sales by 1967. That year Sandoz bought the Wander group of companies (dietetic products). Ciba and Geigy merged in 1970 and began a series of US acquisitions, including Funk Seeds in 1974. Sandoz bought Minneapolis-based Northrup, King & Co. (1976) and Dutch seed company Zaadunie (1980).

Ciba-Geigy and US biotech company Chiron started a joint venture in 1986 to produce and market genetically engineered vaccines (Ciba-Geigy acquired 50% of Chiron in 1994). Sandoz also bought shares in US biotech companies, including Genetic Therapy and SyStemix in 1991. It bought Gerber (founded 1927) in 1994.

Ciba-Geigy and Sandoz formed Novartis in 1996. To win approval for the merger, Sandoz (whose Daniel Vasella became CEO of the new company) sold its corn herbicide and US animal health businesses.

Novartis spun off its specialty chemicals unit in 1997. The company agreed to a settlement worth up to $700 million in consumer rebates after a class-action suit claimed that CIBA Vision had unlawfully limited contact lens sales through discount stores to inflate prices.

In 1998 the company combined its East and West Coast gene therapy operations. It merged its OTC health and nutrition businesses into a new consumer health division, then in 1999 sold several units, including cracker maker Wasa, to focus the new division's operations.

In early 1999 chairman Alex Krauer, who had overseen the formation of Novartis, announced he would step down, leaving the post to Vasella. With fear of genetically modified foods growing, subsidiary Gerber said it would stop making baby food with such ingredients in 1999. That year the company announced plans to combine its agribusiness unit with AstraZeneca's and spin them off into a new company, Syngenta.

In 2000 Novartis planned to launch Altus Food, a joint venture with Quaker Oats to develop "functional" foods that promise added nutrition; but that year it announced that it had ended the use of genetically modified food ingredients. To boost its market share, CIBA Vision bought colored contact lens maker Wesley Jessen VisionCare. Also that year the Federal Trade Commission ordered the company to change its advertising and packaging for Doan's Pills to correct alleged deceptive advertising. In addition, the company completed its merger and spin off of its agribusiness unit.

Chairman, President, and CEO: Daniel Vasella
VC and Lead Director: Helmut Sihler
VC: Hans-Jorg Rudloff
Executive Director and CFO: Raymund Breu
Executive Director and International Coordination, Legal and Taxes: Urs Bärlocher
Executive Director, Novartis Switzerland and Group Technology: Hans Kindler
Executive Director, Human Resources: Norman Walker
Executive Director; CEO, Healthcare and Pharmaceuticals; Sector Head, Pharmaceuticals: A.N. Karabelas
Executive Director and COO, Pharmaceuticals: Thomas Ebeling
Executive Director; CEO, Consumer Health; Sector Head, Consumer Health: Al Piergallini
Executive Director; CEO, Agribusiness; Sector Head, Seeds: Heinz Imhof
Auditors: PricewaterhouseCoopers AG

LOCATIONS

HQ: Lichtstrasse 35, CH-4002 Basel, Switzerland
Phone: +41-61-324-1111   **Fax:** +41-61-324-8001
US HQ: 608 5th Ave., New York, NY 10020
US Phone: 212-307-1122   **US Fax:** 908-522-6897
Web site: http://www.novartis.com

1999 Sales

	% of total
Americas	47
Europe	36
Asia, Africa & Australia	17
Total	**100**

PRODUCTS/OPERATIONS

1999 Sales

	% of total
Health care	58
Agribusiness	22
Consumer health	20
Total	**100**

Operations
Animal products
Consumer products
Crop protection
Eye care
Nutrition products
Pharmaceuticals
Seeds

COMPETITORS

Abbott Labs	GNC
Allergan	Johnson & Johnson
Altana	Merck
American Home Products	Milnot Company
AstraZeneca	Nestlé
Aventis	Novo Nordisk A/S
Bausch & Lomb	Perrigo
Bristol-Myers Squibb	Pfizer
Cargill	Pharmacia
ConAgra Foods	Roche Holding
Dow Chemical	Sanofi-Synthélabo
DuPont	Savia
Eli Lilly	Schering
Essilor International	Schering-Plough
G.D. Searle	SmithKline Beecham
Genentech	Solvay
Glaxo Wellcome	

HISTORICAL FINANCIALS & EMPLOYEES

NYSE: NVS FYE: December 31	Annual Growth	12/90	12/91	12/92	12/93	12/94	12/95	12/96	12/97	12/98	12/99
Sales ($ mil.)	8.6%	9,684	9,874	9,824	10,144	12,128	31,138	27,009	21,329	23,051	20,404
Net income ($ mil.)	20.9%	757	818	1,019	1,146	1,325	3,652	1,717	3,565	4,409	4,185
Income as % of sales	—	7.8%	8.3%	10.4%	11.3%	10.9%	11.7%	6.4%	16.7%	19.1%	20.5%
Employees	5.0%	52,640	53,400	53,360	52,500	60,304	133,959	116,178	87,000	82,449	81,854

STOCK PRICE HISTORY

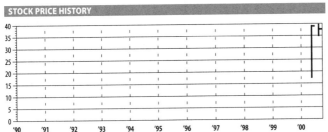

1999 FISCAL YEAR-END

Debt ratio: 21.0%
Return on equity: 18.2%
Cash ($ mil.): 3,947
Current ratio: 1.99
Long-term debt ($ mil.): 1,536

NOVO NORDISK A/S

OVERVIEW

Novo Nordisk is sweet on insulin. You would be, too, if you were the world's largest producer of the hormone.

About 80% of the Bagsvaerd, Denmark-based company's sales come from health products (primarily diabetes-related). In addition to insulin, Novo Nordisk produces injection and monitoring systems for diabetes care, as well as oral diabetes treatment NovoNorm (Prandin in the US). Other core areas include women's hormone-replacement products (treating menopause) and human growth hormones. The company also makes hemophilia treatment NovoSeven.

Novo Nordisk is also one of the world's largest makers of industrial enzymes, those little proteins that accelerate chemical reactions.

Novo Nordisk's enzymes are used for everything from helping breads stay fresh to giving new jeans that worn look, and the company continues to develop new enzymes and new applications.

The Novo Nordisk Foundation, which supports scientific and social causes, owns about 25% of the company.

Novo Nordisk plans to split its enzyme and health care operations into separate companies to give them more freedom to form partnerships, structure capital, and accomplish other tasks for growth, which are inhibited by the company's size. The firm is also planning to spin off its US-based biotech subsidiary ZymoGenetics.

HISTORY

Novo Nordisk was formed by the 1989 merger of Danish insulin producers Novo and Nordisk.

Soon after Canadian researchers extracted insulin from pancreas of cattle, Danish researcher August Krogh (1920 Nobel Prize winner in physiology) and physician Marie Krogh, his wife, teamed up with H. C. Hagedorn, also a physician, to found Nordisk Insulinlaboratorium. One of their lab workers was an inventor named Harald Pedersen, and in 1923 Nordisk hired Pedersen's brother, Thorvald, to analyze chemicals. The relationship was unsuccessful, however, and the brothers left the company.

The Pedersens decided to produce insulin themselves and set up operations in their basement in 1924. Harald also designed a syringe that patients could use for their own insulin injections. Within a decade their firm, Novo Terapeutisk Laboratorium, was selling its product in 40 countries.

Meanwhile, Nordisk introduced a slow-acting insulin in 1936. NPH insulin, launched in the US in 1950, soon became the leading longer-acting insulin. Nordisk later became a major maker of human growth hormone.

During WWII Novo produced its first enzyme, trypsin, used to soften leather. It began producing penicillin in 1947 and during the 1950s developed Heparin, a trypsin-based drug used to treat blood clots. The company unveiled more industrial enzymes in the 1960s.

In 1981 Novo began selling its insulin in the US through a joint venture with E. R. Squibb (now part of Bristol-Myers Squibb). The next year Novo was the first to produce human insulin (actually a modified form of pig insulin), and in 1983 Nordisk introduced the Nordisk

Infuser, a pump that constantly released small quantities of insulin. Two years later Novo debuted the NovoPen, a refillable injector that looked like a fountain pen.

By 1989 Novo was the world's #2 insulin maker (and the world's largest maker of industrial enzymes) when it merged with #3, Nordisk. By combining their research and market share, they were better able to complete globally with then #1 Eli Lilly. After the merger, Novo Nordisk introduced the NovoLet, the world's first prefilled, disposable insulin syringe.

The new firm, Novo Nordisk, introduced drugs for depression (Seroxat, 1992), epilepsy (Gabitril, 1995), and hemophilia (NovoSeven, 1995). In 1995 it entered a marketing alliance with Johnson & Johnson subsidiary LifeScan, the world's #1 maker of blood glucose monitors, and it began working with Rhône-Poulenc Rorer on estrogen replacement therapies.

Eli Lilly raised a new challenge in 1996 with the FDA approval of Humalog (the US's first new insulin product in 14 years), which is absorbed faster, giving users more flexibility in their injection schedule; Novo Nordisk's own fast-acting insulin product, NovoLog, received FDA approval four years later.

A 1998 marketing pact with Schering-Plough signaled Novo Nordisk's desire to boost sales of its diabetes drugs in the US, where Eli Lilly has historically dominated. In 1999 Novo Nordisk said it would split its health care and enzymes businesses to free them to seek more dynamic growth opportunities; the split is scheduled for late 2000 or early 2001.

Chairman: Vagn Andersen
VC: Palle Marcus
President and CEO: Mads Øvlisen
Deputy CEO Corporate Finance and Legal:
Kurt Anker Nielsen
Corporate EVP Corporate Strategy: Bruce Carter
Corporate EVP Corporate Staffs: Henrik Gürtler
Corporate EVP Enzyme Business: Steen Riisgaard
Corporate EVP Health Care: Lars Rebien Sørensen
Corporate VP Corporate Finance: Jesper Brandgaard
Corporate VP Enzyme Business Operations:
Peder H. Nielsen
Corporate VP Enzyme Development and Applications:
Per Falholt
Corporate VP Enzyme Research: Soren Carlsen
Corporate VP Health Care International Operations:
Lars A. Jorgensen
Auditors: PricewaterhouseCoopers

HQ: Novo Allé, 2880 Bagsvaerd, Denmark
Phone: +45-44-44-88-88   **Fax:** +45-44-49-05-55
US HQ: 405 Lexington Ave., Ste. 6400,
New York, NY 10017
US Phone: 212-867-0123   **US Fax:** 212-867-0298
Web site: http://www.novo.dk

Novo Nordisk has operations in nearly 70 countries.

1999 Sales

	% of total
Europe	48
North America	18
Japan	18
Other	16
Total	**100**

1999 Sales

	% of total
Diabetes	56
Other health care	22
Enzymes	22
Total	**100**

Selected Products

Health Care	Enzyme Applications
GlucaGen (gastrointestinal contrast agent)	Alcohol
	Animal feed
Norditropin (recombinant human growth hormone)	Baking
	Brewing
	Dairy
Novolin (insulin)	Detergent
NovoNorm/Prandin (oral diabetic treatment)	Fats and oils
	Leather
NovoPen (durable injection system)	Paper and pulp
	Personal care
NovoSeven (hemophilia treatment)	Protein
	Starch
Vagifem (hormone therapy)	Textile
	Wine and juice

Abbott Labs	Becton	Merck
Akzo Nobel	Dickinson	MiniMed
American Home	Bristol-Myers	Novartis
Products	Squibb	Pfizer
Amylin	Eli Lilly	Roche Holding
Pharmaceuticals	Genencor	Sankyo Co
Aventis	International	SmithKline
Baxter	Gist-Brocades	Beecham
Bayer AG	Glaxo Wellcome	TOTAL FINA
	Kikkoman	ELF

NYSE: NVO FYE: December 31	Annual Growth	12/90	12/91	12/92	12/93	12/94	12/95	12/96	12/97	12/98	12/99
Sales ($ mil.)	7.8%	1,443	1,662	1,701	1,935	2,223	2,474	2,502	2,481	2,812	2,833
Net income ($ mil.)	10.3%	135	157	203	211	235	282	303	324	378	326
Income as % of sales	—	9.3%	9.5%	11.9%	10.9%	10.6%	11.4%	12.1%	13.1%	13.4%	11.5%
Earnings per share ($)	8.8%	1.07	1.36	1.36	1.40	1.57	1.88	2.02	2.16	2.55	2.28
Stock price - FY high ($)	—	16.13	23.53	24.19	24.75	27.63	34.50	47.38	73.00	84.88	70.13
Stock price - FY low ($)	—	11.00	14.25	20.00	19.50	21.88	22.25	31.50	43.63	53.88	47.50
Stock price - FY close ($)	17.1%	15.59	22.38	22.19	24.75	23.75	34.25	46.75	72.13	66.50	64.63
P/E - high	—	16	17	18	18	18	18	23	34	33	31
P/E - low	—	11	10	15	14	14	12	16	20	21	21
Dividends per share ($)	17.1%	0.13	0.13	0.14	0.14	0.13	0.18	0.18	0.00	0.00	0.54
Book value per share ($)	7.0%	9.63	10.74	11.22	11.73	14.40	17.33	17.92	17.63	19.46	17.69
Employees	6.3%	8,742	9,627	10,733	11,648	12,847	12,997	13,395	14,175	14,857	15,184

HIGH/LOW/CLOSE

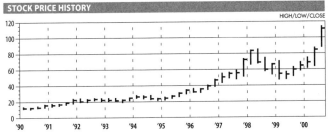

Debt ratio: 16.7%
Return on equity: 12.2%
Cash ($ mil.): 267
Current ratio: 2.43
Long-term debt ($ mil.): 505
No. of shares (mil.): 142
Dividends
Yield: 0.8%
Payout: 23.7%
Market value ($ mil.): 9,168

NTT DOCOMO

A decade of economic stagnation? Not for DoCoMo. Tokyo-based NTT Mobile Communications Network, better known as NTT DoCoMo, has watched a tsunami of demand for mobile phones sweep across Japan.

Spun off from Nippon Telegraph and Telephone (NTT), DoCoMo (meaning "anywhere") is the country's #1 wireless phone provider. Its 27.1 million subscribers translate to more than 50% of the Japanese market; worldwide, only Vodafone has more mobile phone subscribers. DoCoMo also offers paging, maritime and in-flight telephone service, and sells handsets and pagers. The company has scored big with the rollout of the popular i-mode service (about 12 million subscribers), which provides Internet access from mobile phones. DoCoMo is buying a stake in AOL Japan in a deal that will expand the company's i-mode content offerings.

An investment in the mobile phone unit of Dutch telecom provider KPN will establish DoCoMo's presence in Europe, and DoCoMo and KPN have joined Hutchison Whampoa in an alliance to bid on next-generation mobile phone licenses in European countries.

NTT has kept a 67% stake in DoCoMo.

NTT Mobile Communications Network began life in the nest of NTT. Formed in 1952 by the Japanese Ministry of Communications to rebuild Japan's war-ravaged phone system, NTT enjoyed a monopoly on fixed-line local and long-distance phone services until the 1990s.

NTT first went into mobile communications with a maritime telephone service in 1959, and in 1968 the company began offering paging services. Other services followed: car phone service (1979), in-flight telephone service (1986), and mobile telephone service (1987).

In 1991 NTT established a subsidiary to adopt these wireless segments: It launched operations in 1992 as NTT Mobile Communications Network under the leadership of NTT executive Kouji Ohboshi. The firm quickly took on the DoCoMo nickname. The year's end saw slightly more than a million analog mobile phone users in Japan — a market DoCoMo shared with upstart telecom companies DDI and IDO (a Toyota affiliate). Paging service was more popular, and DoCoMo won more than 3 million customers.

In 1993 DoCoMo launched digital mobile phone service based on a scheme called PDC (Personal Digital Cellular) — a system incompatible with the digital standards that would take root in Europe and the US. Experts predicted digital phones would help boost the number of Japanese mobile phone subscribers to perhaps 10 million, at the most, by 2000. Time would quickly prove them wrong.

Liberalization of the cellular phone market in 1994 triggered unexpected growth: Customers who previously had to lease mobile phones from the network operators could now buy them at retail stores. Further competition emerged in 1995 with the launch of personal handyphone services, or PHS (parent company NTT was among the companies providing PHS), but DoCoMo's subscriber count passed 3.5 million mobile phone users — about half the market.

The company launched a satellite-based mobile phone system in 1996 to serve customers beyond the range of cell sites, reaching ships and mountainous regions.

Financial crises rocked the Pacific Rim in 1997, and Japan's Fair Trade Commission rocked NTT by ordering it to cut its 95%-ownership of DoCoMo. Customers continued to flock to mobile phones despite economic turmoil, and DoCoMo passed the 15 million subscriber mark. In 1998 DoCoMo gave hope to Japan's low-flying market when it left the nest: Its mammoth IPO raised more than $18 billion. NTT's stake in DoCoMo was reduced to 67%.

Meanwhile, DDI had become the first Japanese carrier to launch a digital mobile phone network based on CDMA (code division multiple access). Though DoCoMo still used PDC, it renewed its efforts to help develop and standardize a next-generation, wideband version of CDMA.

In 1999 DoCoMo took over NTT's unprofitable PHS unit and rolled out a high-speed data service over the PHS network. It also launched its i-mode service, which gave customers limited Internet access on a specialized handset. To promote such new data services, DoCoMo agreed to launch a joint venture in Japan with Microsoft. DoCoMo still held more than half of Japan's wireless market, but Japan's CDMA carriers (DDI and IDO) and other competitors were stealing DoCoMo's share of new subscribers.

DoCoMo made its first move into Europe in 2000 — the company agreed to pay $4.5 billion for a 15% stake in the mobile phone unit of Dutch telecom provider KPN. Later that same year the company made a move into the US market when it agreed to pay $9.7 billion for a 16% stake in AT&T Wireless.

Chairman: Kouji Ohboshi
President and CEO: Keiji Tachikawa
SEVP: Norioki Morinaga
SEVP: Ryuji Murase
SEVP: Yoshinori Uda
EVP; SVP, NTT East: Nobuharu Ono
EVP: Shiro Tsuda
EVP: Toyotaro Kato
EVP: Shuichi Shindo
EVP: Masao Nakamura
EVP: Hideki Nomura
EVP: Itsuki Tomioka
SVP; Executive Manager Gateway Business:
Kei-ichi Enoki
SVP Marketing: Noboru Inoue
SVP: Eisuke Sugiyama
SVP: Kazushige Sakoh
SVP: Kota Kinoshita
SVP: Ken-ichi Aoki
SVP: Kimio Tani
SVP: Hideaki Nakashima
Auditors: Asahi & Co.

LOCATIONS

HQ: NTT Mobile Communications Network, Inc.,
11-1 Nagatacho-2-chome, Chiyoda-ku,
Tokyo 100-6150, Japan
Phone: +81-3-5156-1111   **Fax:** +81-3-5156-0271
US HQ: 101 Park Ave., 41st Fl., New York, NY 10178
US Phone: 212-808-2296   **US Fax:** 212-661-1078
Web site: http://www.nttdocomo.com

NTT Mobile Communications Network provides communications throughout Japan and in waters up to 200 nautical miles off Japan's coast.

PRODUCTS/OPERATIONS

2000 Sales

	% of total
Mobile phone services	96
Equipment sales	3
Paging service	1
Total	**100**

Selected Services

Cellular Services
10 Yen-Mail (cellular e-mail service)
i-mode (Internet access on cellular phones)
Information Dial (information service)
Mobile Q (information service)
World Call (direct international calling)

Paging Services
02-DO (payment option in which sending parties pay paging costs)
Group Message (message broadcasting to multiple pagers)
Info-Next (e-mail via pager)

COMPETITORS

AT&T	NEC
BT	Nokia
Ericsson	QUALCOMM
Japan Telecom	Siemens
KDDI	Toyota
Motorola	Vodafone

HISTORICAL FINANCIALS & EMPLOYEES

Tokyo: 9437 FYE: March 31	Annual Growth	3/91	3/92	3/93	3/94	3/95	3/96	3/97	3/98	3/99	3/00
Sales (¥ bil.)	35.7%	—	—	—	—	806	1,237	1,962	2,626	3,118	3,718
Net income (¥ bil.)	72.6%	—	—	—	—	16	21	29	120	204	252
Income as % of sales	—	—	—	—	—	2.0%	1.7%	1.5%	4.6%	6.6%	6.8%
Earnings per share (¥)	11.4%	—	—	—	—	—	—	—	—	23,645	26,330
Stock price - FY high (¥)	—	—	—	—	—	—	—	—	—	1,296,000	4,570,000
Stock price - FY low (¥)	—	—	—	—	—	—	—	—	—	810,000	1,162,000
Stock price - FY close (¥)	259.8%	—	—	—	—	—	—	—	—	1,170,000	4,210,000
P/E - high	—	—	—	—	—	—	—	—	—	55	174
P/E - low	—	—	—	—	—	—	—	—	—	34	44
Dividends per share (¥)	0.0%	—	—	—	—	—	—	—	—	1,000	1,000
Book value per share (¥)	11.5%	—	—	—	—	—	—	—	—	181,210	202,123
Employees	11.2%	—	—	—	—	5,945	6,323	6,901	7,557	9,342	10,098

STOCK PRICE HISTORY

HIGH/LOW/CLOSE

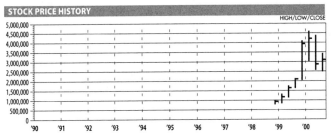

2000 FISCAL YEAR-END

Debt ratio: 40.2%
Return on equity: 13.7%
Cash (¥ mil.): 481,003
Current ratio: 1.20
Long-term debt (¥ mil.): 587,755
No. of shares (mil.): 10
Dividends
  Yield: 0.0%
  Payout: 0.0%
Market value ($ mil.): 381,175
Sales ($ mil.) 35,218

OBAYASHI CORPORATION

OVERVIEW

OBAYASHI's buildings shake, rattle, and roll. The Tokyo-based company, one of Japan's leading general contractors, is a pioneer in the development of earthquake-resistant building techniques.

The company provides services for every phase of construction, acting as architect, consultant, engineer, and systems designer for buildings and large-scale civil engineering projects worldwide. Its Technical Research Institute has developed an earthquake damage prediction system (Quake Mapper), as well as automated construction systems and innovative excavation equipment.

The company also sells real estate; sells and leases construction equipment and materials; provides building maintenance and security services; offers information processing services; manages hotels, restaurants, and other facilities; and offers insurance and financial services.

OBAYASHI's projects include Stadium Australia, the main venue for the Sydney 2000 Olympic Games. The company also built the spiraling bobsled and luge runs used during the 1998 Winter Olympics in Nagano; the underground Osaka Municipal Central Gymnasium, camouflaged by a tree-covered park; the Ted Williams tunnel in Boston; and completed restoration of port facilities in Kobe, Japan, damaged by a 1995 earthquake.

Shaken by the Asian economic crisis, OBAYASHI has reduced subcontracting fees and personnel expenses to counter the severe downturn in Japan's construction industry.

HISTORY

With the first wave of Japanese modernization in 1892 Yoshigoro Ohbayashi opened a small construction operation in Osaka. He joined with partner Kamezo Shirasugi in 1898 to lay the foundations for the OBAYASHI CORPORATION. Its first big contract came in 1901, for the construction of buildings for Osaka's Fifth National Industry Fair.

During the Russo-Japanese War, the young corporation built 100 barracks in three weeks, a feat that helped it win a contract to build Tokyo Station (completed in 1914). OBAYASHI executives were invited to the US by the Fluor Company in the early 1920s to study advanced construction techniques. After a 1923 earthquake and firestorm leveled much of Tokyo, OBAYASHI applied the technology it learned to build quake-resistant, fireproof buildings.

Like many Japanese companies, OBAYASHI is quiet about its history in the years leading up to WWII and the rebuilding that followed. However, the Korean War increased demand for company projects such as the Tokyo Station annex, the Japan Broadcasting Corporation building, and the first of 50 major dam projects.

In the 1960s OBAYASHI became the first Japanese construction company to build an internal research and development facility. Its Technical Research Institute developed the OWS-Soletanche Diaphragm Wall Construction Method, which it used on the New Osaka building in 1961 and has adapted to many other buildings since. In 1965 the company began its first major civil engineering project overseas, doing its part in a 32-year-long excavation in Singapore that reclaimed 2.6% of that country's land mass from the sea. Also that year OBAYASHI completed the first high-rise in Japan, Yokohama's 21-story Hotel Empire.

Expo '70 in Osaka showcased OBAYASHI's air-membrane dome and roof lift-up method. During the 1970s the company played key roles in Japan's massive highway building project. In 1979 it was the first Japanese construction company to be awarded a public works contract in the US.

OBAYASHI completed thousands of projects during the 1980s. These ranged from helping build the Tsukuba Expo '85 (which showcased Japan's scientific and technical achievements), to the restoration of the Katsura Rikyu Detached Palace, considered a national treasure.

In 1994 two former OBAYASHI executives were found guilty of giving a 10 million yen (about $100,000) bribe to the mayor of Sendai two years earlier. The company was one of several major construction companies involved in the scandal.

In the 1990s OBAYASHI "mole" machines chewed through the earth to create the Tokyo Bay Aqualine tunnel. In 1996 the company developed anti-earthquake construction methods for structures built on soft ground (almost a fifth of buildings in Tokyo).

OBAYASHI was hard hit in 1998 and 1999 as financial crises created turmoil in Japan's construction industry. The company responded by reducing its workforce by about 5%, taking advantage of economies of scale in materials purchasing, and working with subcontractors to cut costs.

Chairman and CEO: Yoshiro Obayashi
VC: Takeo Ohbayashi
VC: Takao Tsumuro
President: Shinji Mukasa
EVP: Toshiteru Arakawa
EVP: Masatoshi Inoue
EVP: Ryuji Kudo
EVP: Kenichi Yamashita
Senior Managing Director: Chiaki Goto
Senior Managing Director: Katsuaki Horikita
Senior Managing Director: Hidenobu Ikeda
Senior Managing Director: Wakao Oba
Senior Managing Director: Yoshihisa Obayashi
Auditors: Showa Ota & Co.

LOCATIONS

HQ: Obayashi Gumi Kabushiki Kaisha,
Shinagawa Intercity Tower B, 2-15-2, Konan,
Minato-ku, Tokyo 108-8502, Japan
Phone: +11-3-5769-1054   **Fax:** +11-3-5769-1923
US HQ: 592 5th Ave., 7th Fl., New York, NY 10036
US Phone: 212-930-1020   **US Fax:** 212-704-9880
Web site: http://www.obayashi.co.jp

OBAYASHI has operations in Australia, China, France,
Germany, India, Indonesia, Japan, Malaysia, Singapore,
Taiwan, Thailand, the Netherlands, the Philippines, the
UK, the US, and Vietnam.

PRODUCTS/OPERATIONS

2000 Sales

	% of total
Construction/civil engineering	94
Real estate and other	6
Total	**100**

Selected Subsidiaries
Citadel Corporation (construction, US)
E.W. Howell Co., Inc. (construction, US)
Hakusei Real Estate, Ltd.
Hakuto Real Estate, Ltd.
James E. Roberts-Obayashi Corporation (50%, housing
projects, US)
Miyagi Green Co., Ltd.
Obayashi Construction (Malaysia) Sdn. Bhd.
Obayashi Hawaii Corporation (residential and resort
development, US)
Obayashi Kawanishi Development, Ltd.
Obayashi Philippines Corporation (40%, construction)
Obayashi Projektbau GmbH (construction, Germany)
Obayashi Real Estate Corporation
OC America Construction, Inc. (US)
OC Finance Corporation
OC Real Estate Management, LLC (US)
P.T. Jaya Obayashi (49%, construction, Indonesia)
Taiwan Obayashi Corporation (construction)
Thai Obayashi Corporation Limited (49%, construction,
Thailand)

COMPETITORS

ABB	Kumagai Gumi
Bechtel	Mitsui
CSCEC	Parsons
Fluor	Shimizu
Hazama	Taisei
Hyundai	TOA
ITOCHU	Washington Group
Kajima	

HISTORICAL FINANCIALS & EMPLOYEES

Tokyo: FYE: March 31	Annual Growth	3/91	3/92	3/93	3/94	3/95	3/96	3/97	3/98	3/99	3/00
Sales (¥ bil.)	(3.8%)	—	1,539	1,539	1,653	1,422	1,244	1,541	1,487	1,380	1,132
Net income (¥ bil.)	(16.0%)	—	23	21	10	7	12	13	12	9	6
Income as % of sales	—	—	1.5%	1.4%	0.6%	0.5%	1.0%	0.8%	0.8%	0.6%	0.5%
Earnings per share (¥)	(16.2%)	—	31.35	28.19	13.45	9.82	16.12	18.28	15.73	11.93	7.66
Stock price - FY high (¥)	—	—	1,260	680	773	854	934	1,050	793	699	720
Stock price - FY low (¥)	—	—	670	428	536	620	601	638	345	403	298
Stock price - FY close (¥)	(7.2%)	—	680	595	670	644	918	726	655	660	375
P/E - high	—	—	40	24	57	87	58	57	50	59	94
P/E - low	—	—	21	15	40	63	37	35	22	34	39
Dividends per share (¥)	4.8%	—	5.50	8.00	8.00	8.00	8.00	8.00	8.00	8.00	8.00
Book value per share (¥)	2.3%	—	—	376.44	381.42	387.05	394.78	404.67	411.98	415.57	442.09
Employees	(1.1%)	—	—	12,157	12,418	12,415	12,146	11,856	12,184	11,584	11,261

STOCK PRICE HISTORY

HIGH/LOW/CLOSE

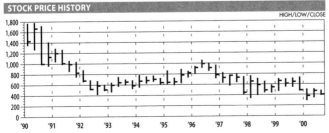

2000 FISCAL YEAR-END

Debt ratio: 64.1%
Return on equity: 0.0%
Cash (¥ mil.): 97,198
Current ratio: 0.97
Long-term debt (¥ mil.): 260,609
No. of shares (mil.): 745
Dividends
  Yield: 0.0%
  Payout: 1.0%
Market value ($ mil.): 2,647
Sales ($ mil.): 10,723

OKI ELECTRIC INDUSTRY COMPANY

OVERVIEW

Oki Electric Industry is okay with the rapid pace of technological change. About half of the Tokyo-based company's sales come from information systems, including computer, networking, underwater imaging, and telemetry products. Oki, which was formed in 1881 to make telephones, still gets 27% of its sales from telecommunications systems. The company also makes an array of electrical components, ranging from motorcycle ignition parts to integrated circuits.

Struggling to find its place in the ultrahot, high-tech global economy, Oki is refining the focus of its core segments. Its information systems unit will continue to concentrate on such products as e-commerce systems, automated teller machines, and intelligent transport systems for managing traffic. However, Oki's telecom focus has shifted to Internet protocol networking, and its components segment will concentrate on logic devices and large-scale integrated circuits rather than on the commodity memory chips (DRAMs) that have have long been a burden on the company's bottom line. New developments include computer telephony systems and iris recognition products for the financial and access control industries.

Oki has been slow to prune its operations (for example, company officials noted in 1992 that Oki would be hard-pressed to make money in semiconductors). As a result, sales have been stagnant in the 1990s and the company's stock has been anything but okay.

HISTORY

Engineer Kibataro Oki founded Meikosha in Tokyo in 1881 to produce telephones (only five years after they were invented). Meikosha was soon producing telegraphs, bells, and medical equipment. Its main factory adopted the name Oki Electric Plant in 1889, and the marketing division began operating under the name Oki & Company in 1896.

In 1907, a year after the founder's death, the Oki groups were united as a limited partnership. Divided again in 1912, they were recombined in 1917 as Oki Electric Co. Oki continued to expand its product line to include automatic switching equipment (1926) and electric clocks (1929).

The manufacturer produced communications equipment for the Japanese military during WWII, but after the war it started working on the teleprinter and added consumer goods such as portable stoves. The company adopted its present name, Oki Electric Industry Company, in 1949.

Oki entered the semiconductor and computer industries in the 1950s, joining Fujitsu, Hitachi, Mitsubishi, Nippon Electric Co., and Toshiba as one of Japan's Big Six electronics makers by 1960. It then began developing overseas businesses, particularly in Latin America, where it built communications networks in Honduras (1962) and Bolivia (1966) and radio networks in Brazil (1971).

In 1970 Oki formed a computer software unit. The company was a major telecommunications equipment supplier for the Japanese government until the mid-1970s, when the government increased its purchases from other companies. The result was a $7 million loss for Oki in 1978. Former Nippon Telegraph and Telephone executive Masao Miyake took over as president, initiating a dramatic reorganization into 15 business units.

Oki started building PCs in 1981. It consolidated its US operations as Oki America in 1984. A new financial crisis followed in the mid-1980s when the bottom fell out of the semiconductor market — Oki's earnings plummeted into the red in 1986. However, by the end of the decade Oki had become a major provider of automated teller machines (ATMs) and bank computer systems, and growth in the Japanese financial industry sparked a ninefold increase in Oki's sales in 1989.

In 1994 Oki established subsidiary Oki Data Corp., to handle printer and fax machine operations. In 1996 it developed a device that enables standard phones to route calls over the Internet and local-area networks; that product was introduced in 1998 as the BS1200 Internet Voice Gateway.

Plunging memory prices and higher taxes stymied Oki's recovery in fiscal 1998, so the company halted mass random-access memory (RAM) production and closed an assembly and testing facility. Oki shifted its semiconductor focus to large-scale integrated circuits and placed more emphasis on its information systems segment, which had seen increasing sales.

Further battered by the weak Asian economy, Oki restructured in 1999. That year the company bought Toshiba's ATM operations. It also launched an access control system that uses a person's iris for identification.

Chairman: Shiko Sawamura
President and CEO: Katsumasa Shinozuka
SEVP: Hajime Maeda
EVP; Chairman, Network System Company: Yasuo Sakaki
SVP and Chief Information Officer: Hiroshi Konishi
SVP and Chief Technology Officer: Kazunori Hata
SVP; President, Silicon Solutions Company:
  Masayoshi Ino
SVP; President, System Solutions Company:
  Yutaka Maeda
SVP; President, Network System Company:
  Yoshikatsu Shiraishi
SVP; General Manager Strategic Marketing:
  Takahisa Inagawa
Auditors: Century Ota Showa + Co.

LOCATIONS

HQ: Oki Denki Kogyo Kabushiki Kaisha,
  (Oki Electric Industry Company, Limited)
  7-12, Toranomon 1-chome, Minato-ku,
  Tokyo 105-8460, Japan
Phone: +81-3-3501-3111   **Fax:** +81-3-3581-5522
US HQ: 785 N. Mary Ave., Sunnyvale, CA 94085
US Phone: 408-720-1900   **US Fax:** 408-720-1918
Web site: http://www.oki.co.jp

Oki Electric Industry has operations in more than 20
countries and sells its products worldwide. The
company's overseas offices are in Beijing, London,
Shanghai, Singapore, and Sydney.

2000 Sales

	% of total
Japan	79
North America	11
Other regions	10
Total	**100**

PRODUCTS/OPERATIONS

2000 Sales

	% of total
Information systems	48
Telecommunications systems	25
Electronics	24
Other products	3
Total	**100**

Selected Products
Application-specific integrated circuits
Computer and networking products
Electronic automatic transmission controllers
Electronic fuel injection units
Memories
Microprocessors
Optoelectronic devices
Switching
Telecommunications terminals
Telemetry and telecontrol systems
Transmission systems
Underwater acoustic systems
Vehicle information and communication systems

COMPETITORS

Alcatel	ITOCHU	Nortel Networks
Bull	Lexmark	Philips
Canon	International	Electronics
Casio Computer	LSI Logic	Pioneer
Compaq	Lucent	Ricoh
Dell Computer	Matsushita	Samsung
Diebold	Minolta	SANYO
Ericsson	Mitsubishi	Sharp
Fujitsu	Motorola	Siemens
Hewlett-Packard	NCR	Sony
Hitachi	NEC	Tektronix
IBM	Nokia	Toshiba

HISTORICAL FINANCIALS & EMPLOYEES

Tokyo: 6703 FYE: March 31	Annual Growth	3/91	3/92	3/93	3/94	3/95	3/96	3/97	3/98	3/99	3/00
Sales (¥ mil.)	0.1%	660,923	681,283	639,620	651,511	656,989	748,331	732,225	764,596	673,170	669,776
Net income (¥ mil.)	(21.3%)	9,865	(488)	(32,935)	(17,500)	32,268	24,672	3,232	(8,074)	(47,421)	1,146
Income as % of sales	—	1.5%	—	—	—	4.9%	3.3%	0.4%	—	—	0.2%
Earnings per share (¥)	(21.5%)	16.50	(0.79)	(53.80)	(28.50)	52.70	40.30	5.28	(13.18)	(77.46)	1.87
Stock price - FY high (¥)	—	1,100	785	495	680	833	1,010	863	655	479	819
Stock price - FY low (¥)	—	582	428	290	380	508	411	501	200	210	410
Stock price - FY close (¥)	(0.8%)	750	450	460	575	580	822	591	310	468	696
P/E - high	—	67	—	—	—	16	25	163	—	—	438
P/E - low	—	35	—	—	—	10	10	95	—	—	219
Dividends per share (¥)	—	7.00	0.00	0.00	0.00	0.00	0.00	7.00	7.00	0.00	0.00
Book value per share (¥)	(3.4%)	317.00	234.78	255.03	246.17	314.94	355.65	352.27	331.16	230.78	232.87
Employees	2.6%	20,278	21,593	23,463	22,585	23,568	21,718	21,355	23,968	23,425	25,444

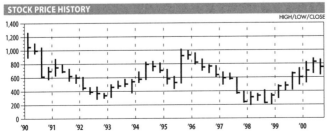

STOCK PRICE HISTORY
HIGH/LOW/CLOSE

2000 FISCAL YEAR-END
Debt ratio: 74.6%
Return on equity: 0.8%
Cash (¥ mil.): 66,776
Current ratio: 1.47
Long-term debt (¥ mil.): 255,669
No. of shares (mil.): 612
Dividends
  Yield: —
  Payout: —
Market value ($ mil.): 4,036
Sales ($ mil.): 6,344

OLIVETTI S.P.A.

OVERVIEW

Once typecast by its typewriters, Olivetti is redefining itself. The Ivrea, Italy-based holding company moved into the forefront of Italy's telecom industry with its 1999 hostile takeover of Telecom Italia, the former monopoly that is still the nation's top provider of fixed-line and mobile telecommunications. Through funding vehicle Tecnost, Olivetti controls 55% of Telecom Italia; after its planned merger with Tecnost, Olivetti will directly own the 55% stake.

Subsidiaries continue to offer Olivetti office and document management products (Olivetti Lexikon) and information technology systems (Tecnost Sistemi). Olivetti is also expanding its Internet and business network services and developing its call center services.

Luxembourg-based holding company Bell, led by Olivetti CEO Roberto Colaninno and Italian businessman Emilio Gnutti, owns about 30% of Olivetti.

HISTORY

Inspired by a trip to the US, Camillo Olivetti founded Olivetti in 1908 to produce the first Italian-made typewriter (introduced in 1911). After diversifying into office furniture, teleprinters, and adding machines, the company went public in 1932.

Camillo's son Adriano led Olivetti into computers, and in 1959 the company developed Italy's first mainframe. That year Olivetti bought control of ailing US typewriter maker Underwood, which later became Olivetti Corporation of America (OCA).

Following Adriano's death, the Olivetti family relinquished direct management of the firm, and in 1964 a consortium of bankers bought Olivetti. The firm, slow to switch from mechanical to electric office equipment in the 1960s, saw earnings stagnate.

Former Fiat executive Carlo De Benedetti bought 14% of the firm in 1978 (increased to 20% in 1988) and became CEO. De Benedetti slashed debt while increasing spending on research and development. Olivetti introduced its first electronic typewriter in 1978.

OCA suffered through more than a decade of losses, and in 1982 De Benedetti sold it to Dallas-based ATM maker Docutel for a 46% stake in that company. In 1985 Olivetti bought the rest of Docutel and used it to establish a new US unit, Olivetti USA.

The company unveiled its first PC in 1982, a year after IBM rolled out its first desktop machine. AT&T bought a 25% stake in Olivetti the next year, and Toshiba bought 20% of Olivetti's Japanese operations in 1985. De Benedetti hoped AT&T and Toshiba would boost Olivetti's global market share, but competition from lower-priced PCs hurt the company.

In Europe Olivetti expanded further, buying 80% of the UK's Acorn Computers Group (1985); Volkswagen's ailing office-products maker, Triumph-Adler (1986); and bank automation firms Bunker Ramo (1986) and I.S.C. Systems (1989). However, world demand for minicomputers had softened by the late 1980s, and in 1991 Olivetti posted its first loss in 13 years.

De Benedetti was convicted in 1992 of bankruptcy fraud in the scandal surrounding the 1982 collapse of Banco Ambrosiano. (His conviction was thrown out in 1998.) In 1995 Olivetti formed fixed-line operator Infostrada to rival Telecom Italia and its 36%-owned Omnitel Pronto venture (formed in 1989) began offering mobile phone service. De Benedetti, pressured to resign in 1996, chose Francesco Caio as his successor. But Caio clashed with De Benedetti and quit after 70 days. Roberto Colannino, another executive close to the former CEO, replaced him. That year Olivetti sold part of its stake in Omnitel Pronto: Mannesmann and Bell Atlantic each bought 5.8%.

In 1997 venture capitalists bought Olivetti's PC business. That year Olivetti and Mannesmann formed OliMan as a telecom holding company for Omnitel Pronto and Infostrada; the German firm got a 25% stake. Wang Laboratories (now Wang Global) bought Olivetti's Olsy computer services business in 1998 in a multimillion-dollar deal that gave Olivetti an almost 19% stake in Wang (later reduced to about 16%). Mannesmann upped its ownership in OliMan to 49% in 1999, and OliMan expanded its stake in Omnitel.

Olivetti paid $33 billion in a successful hostile takeover of larger rival Telecom Italia in 1999. To help raise cash, it sold its stakes in Omnitel Pronto and Infostrada to Mannesmann (later acquired by Vodafone) and agreed to sell its 80%-owned Ricerca subsidiary to Getronics. Plans to transfer Telecom Italia's 60% stake in Telecom Italia Mobile to Tecnost, Olivetti's acquisition vehicle, in exchange for Tecnost stock were abandoned after shareholders voiced disapproval. The next year Olivetti agreed to buy the 26% of Tecnost it doesn't already own and merge the two companies.

Chairman, Olivetti and Tecnost; Honorary Chairman, Telecom Italia: Antonio Tesone
CEO, Olivetti, Tecnost, and Telecom Italia; Chairman, Telecom Italia Mobile: Roberto Colaninno, age 56
General Manager; CEO, Olivetti Lexikon: Corrado Ariaudo
Administration and Financial Statements: Mario Ferrero
Communications: Mauro Giusto
Company Relations: Giorgio Arona
Control, Asset, and Risk Management: Roberto Vescovo
Corporate Finance: Luciano La Noce
Investor Relations: Carla Vidra
Legal Department: Loris Bisone
Licensing: Carlo Casuccio
Personnel: Dario Longo
Union Relations and Social Affairs: Angelo Landriani
Auditors: Coopers & Lybrand S.p.A.

HQ: Via Jervis 77, 10015 Ivrea, Torino, Italy
Phone: +39-0125-52-00   **Fax:** +39-0125-52-2524
US HQ: 765 US Hwy. 202, Bridgewater, NJ 08807
US Phone: 908-526-8200   **US Fax:** 908-526-8405
Web site: http://www.olivetti.it

The Olivetti group of subsidiaries and affiliates has operations in Argentina, Austria, Belgium, Bolivia, Brazil, Canada, Chile, China, Colombia, Costa Rica, Cuba, Czech Republic, Ecuador, France, Germany, Greece, Hong Kong, Hungary, India, Ireland, Israel, Italy, Japan, Kenya, Luxembourg, Mexico, the Netherlands, Nigeria, Panama, Peru, Poland, Portugal, Puerto Rico, Romania, Russia, San Marino, Serbia, South Africa, Spain, Sweden, Switzerland, Turkey, the UK, Ukraine, the US, Venezuela, and Yugoslavia.

1999 Sales

	% of total
Telecommunications services	96
Office & document management products	3
Other	1
Total	**100**

Selected Subsidiaries
Lottomatica S.p.A. (18%, betting and gaming systems)
O.I.S. S.p.A. (information technology products and services)
Olivetti Lexikon S.p.A. (office and document management products)
Olivetti Multiservices S.p.A. (Oms, real estate and related services)
Tecnost S.p.A. (73%, holding company)
 Telecom Italia S.p.A. (55%, telecommunications services)
 Tecnost Sistemi S.p.A. (specialized information technology systems)
 Telemedia Applicazioni S.p.A. (TeleAp, call center development)
Webegg S.p.A. (50%, business Internet and network consulting)

Alcatel	Italgas
Autostrade	Nokia
Belgacom	Océ
BT	Omnitel
Canon	Pitney Bowes
Deutsche Telekom	Ricoh
Enel	Verizon
Ericsson	Vodafone
France Telecom	WorldCom
Infostrada	

OTC: OLVTY FYE: December 31	Annual Growth	12/90	12/91	12/92	12/93	12/94	12/95	12/96	12/97	12/98	12/99
Sales ($ mil.)	15.9%	8,019	7,501	5,430	5,028	5,568	6,208	5,492	3,753	4,345	30,157
Net income ($ mil.)	65.6%	53	(401)	(440)	(271)	(417)	(1,008)	(603)	9	150	4,973
Income as % of sales	—	0.7%	—	—	—	—	—	—	0.2%	3.5%	16.5%
Earnings per share ($)	—	—	—	—	—	—	(0.74)	(0.23)	0.00	0.04	1.20
Stock price - FY high ($)	—	—	—	—	—	—	1.84	1.36	0.78	3.63	4.10
Stock price - FY low ($)	—	—	—	—	—	—	1.00	0.42	0.32	0.73	1.85
Stock price - FY close ($)	24.0%	—	—	—	—	—	1.22	0.50	0.55	3.43	2.88
P/E - high	—	—	—	—	—	—	—	—	293	104	3
P/E - low	—	—	—	—	—	—	—	—	120	21	2
Dividends per share ($)	—	—	—	—	—	—	0.00	0.00	0.00	0.00	0.19
Book value per share ($)	74.6%	—	—	—	—	—	0.60	0.40	0.41	0.81	5.54
Employees	10.2%	53,679	46,484	40,401	35,171	33,867	30,120	26,277	22,659	17,000	129,073

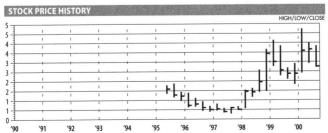

HIGH/LOW/CLOSE

Debt ratio: 42.5%
Return on equity: 35.0%
Cash ($ mil.): 1,170
Current ratio: 0.85
Long-term debt ($ mil.): 19,325
No. of shares (mil.): 4,721
Dividends
 Yield: 0.1%
 Payout: 0.2%
Market value ($ mil.): 13,598

OTTO VERSAND GMBH & CO.

OVERVIEW

Santa Claus' mailbags ain't got nothing on Otto's. Hamburg, Germany-based Otto Versand, the world's largest mail-order firm, sells merchandise in about 20 countries through nearly 60 subsidiaries. Customers order through print and CD-ROM catalogs and the Internet. Otto Versand publishes more than 600 different catalogs each year. The firm's products range from clothing, furniture, and household items (such as lamps and appliances) to high-tech equipment and sporting goods. Customers in Germany can get same-day delivery of many items.

Otto Versand has grown through acquisitions, entering non-mail-order businesses such as travel and computer sales. It controls Actebis Holding, a major computer distributor in Europe, and owns a majority stake in US-based Crate & Barrel, which sells housewares through catalogs and retail stores. The firm does about 90% of its business in Europe, Japan, and the US.

Chairman Michael Otto's family owns the majority of the firm. Separately, the Otto family controls US catalog retailer Spiegel.

HISTORY

East German refugee Werner Otto founded Otto Versand (German for "dispatch") in Hamburg, West Germany, in 1949. It distributed its first catalog in 1950; 300 hand-bound copies offered only shoes, but in 28 styles. Instead of being required to pay upon delivery, customers received bills with their orders; this was new for mail orders. By 1956 the firm employed 500 people; by 1958 the catalog had expanded to 200 pages, offering low-cost women's fashions and other products to 200,000 potential customers.

In 1963 Otto Versand began taking phone orders. Its catalog grew to 800 pages and 1 million copies by 1967. The following year it published the Post Shop Magazine, its first special-interest catalog, which targeted fashion-conscious youth. In 1969 Otto Versand formed Hanseatic Bank to offer customers monthly payment plans; three years later it formed the Hermes Express Package delivery service.

The firm began a shopping spree in the 1970s by investing in mail-order companies 3 Suisses International (France, 1974), Heinrich Heine (luxury clothes and household goods, West Germany, 1974) and Hanau (West Germany, 1979).

Werner's son Michael succeeded him as chairman in 1981, and in 1982 he led the acquisition of low-cost women's apparel firm Spiegel. Michael immediately revamped Spiegel into an upmarket retailer. The ownership of Spiegel was restructured in 1984, but the Otto family remained in control of the US company.

Throughout the 1980s the firm continued investing in European companies (entering the UK in 1986 and Austria in 1988) and began Otto-Sumisho in Japan (a joint venture, 1986). Its combined catalog circulation reached 200 million in 1987.

Otto Versand launched 24-hour delivery service in 1990; that year it expanded to the Polish market by forming joint venture Otto-Epoka. In 1991 it began 24-hour phone sales and acquired a majority stake in Grattan (the UK's fourth-largest mail-order firm). Acquisitions continued during the early and mid-1990s, including Margareta (Hungary), Postalmarket (Italy's largest mail-order firm), and Otto-Burlingtons (Germany-India joint venture).

Broadening its business areas, Otto Versand acquired a majority stake in Reiseland's 60 travel agencies in 1993 and bought two UK collection agencies in 1994. In 1994 it became Germany's first mail-order firm to offer an interactive CD-ROM catalog.

Four years later the firm bought a majority stake in US housewares retailer Crate & Barrel and bought the part of German computer wholesaler Actebis Holding it didn't already own. It then formed Zara Deutschland, a joint venture in Germany (with Spain's Inditex, distributor of adults' and kids' apparel under the Zara label), to sell clothing in a new chain of outlets, thus increasing its retail business. Otto Versand added to its travel business (about 140 locations) in 1998 with the purchase of 25 offices from American Express Germany. It closed Postalmarket that year because of problems with the Italian postal service.

Otto Versand made another big mail-order purchase in 1999 when it bought the Freemans catalog business (nearly $900 million in 1998 sales) from the UK's Sears PLC. The deal nearly doubled the company's UK mail-order market share, from 8% to 15%. In late 1999 the firm formed a joint venture with Harrods to sell fancy English goods online.

In early 2000 Otto Versand set up a joint venture with America Online and Deutsche Bank 24 to offer online banking, Internet service, and PCs.

Chairman and CEO: Michael Otto
CFO: Michael E. Cruesemann
Auditors: KPMG Deutsche Treuhand-Gesellschaft

HQ: Wandsbeker Strasse 3-7, 22172 Hamburg, Germany
Phone: +49-40-64-61-0   **Fax:** +49-40-64-61-85-71
Web site: http://www.otto.de

1999 Sales

	% of total
Germany	51
Other countries	49
Total	**100**

1999 Sales

	% of total
Mail order	41
Wholesale	23
Specialty mail order	21
In-store retail	12
Other	3
Total	**100**

Selected Subsidiaries
3 Suisses France
Actebis Holding
Crate & Barrel (majority stake)
Grattan
Handelgesellshaft Heinrich Heine GmbH
Hanseatic Bank GmbH
Otto-Sumisho (51%)
Reiseland GmbH (75%)

Bed Bath & Beyond
Blair
DAMARK International
Direct Marketing
Federated
Great Universal Stores
Hammacher Schlemmer & Co.
Hanover Direct
J. C. Penney
Karstadt
L.L. Bean
Lands' End
Lechters
Lillian Vernon
Linens 'n Things
Littlewoods Organisation
METRO AG
Pier 1 Imports
Pinault-Printemps-Redoute
Schickedanz
Vendex
Williams-Sonoma

Private FYE: Last day in February	Annual Growth	2/90	2/91	2/92	2/93	2/94	2/95	2/96	2/97	2/98	2/99
Sales ($ mil.)	10.5%	—	—	—	—	11,300	13,176	16,876	12,439	13,364	18,625
Employees	12.2%	—	—	—	—	—	39,817	41,221	46,500	41,476	63,000

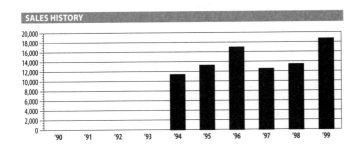

PACIFIC DUNLOP LIMITED

OVERVIEW

How diversified is Pacific Dunlop? Start with balloons, batteries, bedding, bras, car tires, and condoms — and that's just two letters of the alphabet. The Melbourne-based firm has more than 150 manufacturing plants to support its global operations.

One of Australia's largest companies, Pacific Dunlop has five major businesses: Ansell, one of the world's top makers of industrial and medical gloves and condoms and other latex products; GNB Technologies, a maker of auto and industrial batteries; Pacific Brands, which makes bedding, clothing, foam, footwear, and sporting goods; Pacific Distribution, a distributor of auto parts and electrical products through its 650 retail outlets in Australia and New Zealand; and South Pacific Tyres, a manufacturer (Dunlop and Goodyear, among others) that also operates 700 tire stores in Australia and New Zealand.

Pacific Dunlop's roster of brand-names include Berlei, Bonds, Dunlop, Goodyear, Marshall, and Sleepmaker.

As part of a restructuring to rebuild the strength of its portfolio, the company has divested itself of such noncore businesses as its lawsuit-scarred pacemaker components division and most of its food operations. A plan to sell its underperforming GNB Technologies batteries unit stalled, however.

HISTORY

Pacific Dunlop's history begins with a veterinarian, a tricycle, and a bumpy road. In 1887 John Boyd Dunlop, a veterinarian in Belfast, Northern Ireland, gave his son a tricycle for his birthday. When his son complained about the jolting ride on rough country roads, Dunlop came up with an air-filled tire. Dunlop sold the rights to his tire to a pair of businessmen who founded the Pneumatic Tyre Company in 1889. By 1892 it had expanded into continental Europe and North America, and the next year it created a branch office of Dunlop UK to make bike tires in Australia.

The company went public in 1899 as Dunlop Pneumatic Tyre Company of Australia. In 1903 it moved into a new, growing market: automobile tires. The company, which was incorporated as Dunlop Rubber Company of Australia in 1920, merged with Sydney-based Perdriau Rubber Company in 1929.

Dunlop concentrated on rubber-based products until the 1960s, when it began to diversify by adding clothing, textiles, and footwear. In 1969 it acquired glove maker Ansell Rubber. During the 1970s Dunlop expanded outside Australia.

By 1980 the company had acquired its archrival, tire maker Olympic Consolidated Industries. Founded in 1922, Olympic began producing auto tires in 1934. The acquisition also netted Olympic's cable business.

Led by John Gough, Dunlop continued to expand during the 1980s. In 1985 it acquired the North American operations of UK-based battery maker Chloride. Dunlop entered its South Pacific Tyres joint venture with Goodyear in 1986 to sell tires in Australia and New Zealand. That year it changed its name to Pacific Dunlop Limited.

In 1987 Pacific Dunlop expanded its battery operations when it bought a stake in GNB Holdings, maker of Champion batteries. It moved into the healthcare business in 1988 with the acquisition of Nucleus (now Cochlear) and its US pacemaker unit Telectronics, a group of high-technology medical product makers.

Food was added to the company's business mix with the 1991 acquisition of Australia's Petersville Sleigh. The purchase of meat products maker Plumrose in 1993 expanded those operations.

Telectronics recalled three models of pacemaker parts in 1994 after failures led to the deaths of several patients, and a year later the FDA suspended US manufacturing of the parts. That year Pacific Dunlop took losses related to the Telectronics problems totaling $241.5 million. It also began disposing of business lines, selling most of its food operations, part of its industrial products unit, and a footwear company. The firm spun off its Cochlear hearing device business in 1995 and sold Telectronics in 1996, the year Rod Chadwick became managing director. Gough retired as chairman in 1997 in the midst of another pacemaker lawsuit filed against the company.

Faced with harsh competition in the nonenergized US battery market, Pacific Dunlop agreed in 1998 to unload its GNB operations to metal recycler Quexco for a cut-rate $783 million, but the deal fell apart the next year. The company did manage to unload its cable business in 1999, however.

That year, to pump its profits, Pacific Dunlop made plans to float a 20% share of Ansell (to become Ansell Healthcare) in the US. The company also agreed to buy the medical glove unit of Johnson & Johnson for $98 million.

Chairman: John T. Ralph
CEO and Managing Director: Rod Chadwick
Executive General Manager Finance: Philip Gay
Executive General Manager Human Resources:
Mary Keely
Executive General Manager Manufacturing: John Eady
Executive General Manager Strategic Direction:
Ian Veal
Chief Information Officer: Russell Hulstrom
Secretary: John Rennie
President and CEO, GNB Technologies: Tom Minner
CEO, South Pacific Tyres: Robert McEniry
Managing Director, Ansell Healthcare: Harry Boon
Managing Director, Pacific Brands: Paul Moore
Managing Director, Pacific Distribution: Jo Farnik
Auditors: KPMG

1999 Sales

	% of total
Automotive & electrical distribution	26
Industrial & automotive batteries	24
Consumer goods	21
Protective & healthcare products	20
Tires	9
Total	**100**

Divisions
Pacific Distribution (automotive and electrical
distribution)
GNB Technologies (industrial and automotive batteries)
Pacific Brands (consumer goods)
Ansell (protective and healthcare products)
South Pacific Tyres (tires)

HQ: Level 3, 678 Victoria St., Richmond,
Victoria 3121, Australia
Phone: +61-3-9270-7270   **Fax:** +61-3-9270-7300
US HQ: 6121 Lakeside Dr., Ste. 200, Reno, NV 89511
US Phone: 775-824-4600   **US Fax:** 775-824-4626
Web site: http://www.pacdun.com

Pacific Dunlop has operations in Australia, China, India,
Indonesia, Malaysia, Mexico, New Zealand, the
Philippines, Sri Lanka, Thailand, the UK, and the US.

1999 Sales

	% of total
Australia	54
The Americas	30
Asia/New Zealand	10
Europe	6
Total	**100**

Alcatel	Johnson Controls
Allegiance	Michelin
Bandag	Rawlings
Bridgestone	Russell Corporation
C&D Technologies	Safeskin
Carter-Wallace	Sime Darby
Continental AG	Spalding
Cooper Tire & Rubber	SSL International
Exide	Tomkins
Federal-Mogul	Toyo Tire & Rubber
Fortune Brands	Unternehmensgruppe
Fruit of the Loom	Freudenberg
Hutchinson	VF

Nasdaq: PDLPY FYE: June 30	Annual Growth	6/90	6/91	6/92	6/93	6/94	6/95	6/96	6/97	6/98	6/99
Sales ($ mil.)	0.1%	4,002	3,845	4,421	6,305	5,077	6,033	5,538	4,311	3,700	4,037
Net income ($ mil.)	(13.9%)	268	150	141	260	221	67	(104)	133	15	69
Income as % of sales	—	6.7%	3.9%	3.2%	4.1%	4.4%	1.1%	—	3.1%	0.4%	1.7%
Earnings per share ($)	(18.8%)	1.76	0.84	0.58	1.03	0.84	0.26	(0.41)	0.51	0.06	0.27
Stock price - FY high ($)	—	15.45	16.02	16.59	14.20	17.00	13.75	10.25	11.63	11.63	7.75
Stock price - FY low ($)	—	12.04	11.93	13.64	10.68	11.59	7.88	8.25	7.63	5.63	5.63
Stock price - FY close ($)	(9.8%)	14.54	14.32	13.98	11.82	12.50	8.63	9.13	11.63	6.38	5.75
P/E - high	—	9	19	24	14	20	53	—	23	26	15
P/E - low	—	7	14	20	10	14	30	—	15	13	11
Dividends per share ($)	(4.8%)	0.53	0.59	1.11	0.51	0.51	0.62	0.66	0.42	0.41	0.34
Book value per share ($)	(2.1%)	4.90	4.99	6.02	8.38	6.33	5.72	5.29	5.18	3.95	4.05
Employees	(0.7%)	41,013	40,504	48,252	47,071	49,449	48,234	40,671	38,148	37,619	38,438

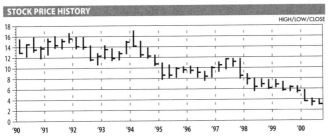

Debt ratio: 32.7%
Return on equity: 6.7%
Cash ($ mil.): 704
Current ratio: 1.19
Long-term debt ($ mil.): 513
No. of shares (mil.): 261
Dividends
  Yield: 5.9%
  Payout: 125.9%
Market value ($ mil.): 1,500

PEARSON PLC

Lucrative financial times mean a lot of read ink for Pearson. The London-based media giant is fast becoming a leading provider of financial information and business news with such titles as *The Financial Times* and *The Economist* (50%-owned) and its 60% stake in US-based Data Broadcasting Corporation (which owns 32% of MarketWatch.com). The company's Pearson Education unit (more than 50% of sales) is the world's top educational publisher through its imprints Scott Foresman, Addison Wesley Longman, and Prentice Hall. Pearson also publishes trade books through its Penguin Group (Penguin, Putnam, Viking).

In addition to printed works, the company is making significant Internet investments, including its *Financial Times* Web site (FT.com) and online educational services. Pearson is also active on the telly through its 22% interest in RTL Group. (RTL Group is the result of the 2000 merger of Pearson's TV assets with Bertelsmann and Audiofina's CLT-Ufa.) RTL owns 22 television channels and 18 radio stations across 11 European countries. It also produces programs such as *Baywatch* and *The Price is Right.*

Under CEO Marjorie Scardino, a native Texan, Pearson has shed many of its non-media assets, which once included Madame Tussaud's wax museums, and is moving to strengthen its printed content brands. In 2000 it launched a German version of *The Financial Times* with Bertelsmann's Gruner + Jahr, and bought children's book publisher Dorling Kindersley (now part of Penguin Group). Spain's Telefónica owns about 5% of the company.

HISTORY

In 1844 Samuel Pearson became a partner in a small Yorkshire building firm. When he retired in 1879 his grandson Weetman took over, moving the company to London in 1884. The business enjoyed extraordinary success — building the first tunnel under New York's Hudson River and constructing the drainage system in Mexico City. By the 1890s the company (incorporated as S. Pearson & Son in 1897) was the world's #1 contractor.

In the 1920s the company bought newspapers, a stake in Lazard Brothers, and engaged in oil exploration. Weetman died in 1927, and so did the construction business. His heirs then bought into several unrelated businesses. Pearson bought control of *The Financial Times* newspaper in 1957, a deal that also brought it 50% of *The Economist* (*The Financial Times* had acquired half of *The Economist* in 1928). The company later added stakes in vintner Chateau Latour (1963, sold 1988) and publisher Longman (1968). The firm went public in 1969.

During the 1970s Pearson bought Penguin Books (1971) and Madame Tussaud's (1978). In 1989 it added Addison-Wesley (educational publisher, US) and Les Echos (financial newspaper publisher, France) to the mix. The next year, Frank Barlow was appointed CEO and charged with bringing some focus to the group's diverse operations.

Concentrating on media interests, the company bought Thames Television in 1993 and Grundy Worldwide (game shows and soap operas) in 1995. It acquired HarperCollins Educational Publishing from News Corp. in 1996, as well as US publisher Putnam Berkley from MCA, gaining such authors as Tom Clancy and Amy Tan. Marjorie Scardino, a Texan who had been CEO of The Economist Group since 1992, replaced Barlow in 1997, becoming the first woman to lead a major UK company. She rounded out Pearson's TV holdings with the purchase of All American Communications that year for $373 million.

In 1998 Pearson bought the reference and educational publishing divisions of Simon & Schuster from Viacom for $4.6 billion. (Plans to sell the reference division to investment firm Hicks, Muse, Tate, & Furst fell through, however.) Also that year, it sold Tussaud's amusement business for about $550 million. In 1999 Pearson let go of its 50% interest in London investment bank Lazard Brothers.

As part of a long-term plan to build *The Financial Times* brand online, Pearson bought 60% of Data Broadcasting Corporation in 2000, and began to cross-promote the FT.com Web site with MarketWatch.com (which is 32%-owned by Data Broadcasting) as part of a $35 million marketing campaign. Pearson also purchased troubled UK publisher Dorling Kindersley for nearly $500 million. It plans to combine the firm with its Penguin unit.

Later in 2000, Pearson combined its TV operations with CLT-Ufa, co-owned by German media company Bertelsmann and Audiofina, into a new publicly traded broadcasting firm called RTL Group. Pearson owns 22% of RTL. In addition, Pearson purchased educational test processing firm National Computer Systems (now NCS Pearson).

Chairman: Dennis Stevenson, age 54, $268,000 pay
CEO: Marjorie M. Scardino, age 53, $930,000 pay
Group Finance Director: John Makinson, age 45,
$620,000 pay
Director for People; Chairman, Financial Times Group:
David Bell, age 53, $540,000 pay
Chairman and CEO, Pearson Education:
Peter Jovanovich
President, Penguin Group: David Wan
**CEO, Financial Times Group; Chairman, Data
Broadcasting Corp:** Stephen Hill
VP Human Resources: Randall Keller
Auditors: PricewaterhouseCoopers

LOCATIONS

HQ: 3 Burlington Gardens,
London W1X 1LE, United Kingdom
Phone: +44-20-7411-2000   **Fax:** +44-20-7411-2390
US HQ: 1330 Avenue of the Americas,
New York, NY 10019
US Phone: 212-641-2400   **US Fax:** 212-641-2500
Web site: http://www.pearson.com

1999 Sales

	$ mil.	% of total
North America	3,218	60
UK	879	16
Europe	837	16
Asia/Pacific	323	6
Other regions	129	2
Total	**5,386**	**100**

PRODUCTS/OPERATIONS

1999 Sales

	$ mil.	% of total
Pearson Education	2,788	52
FT Group	1,111	20
Penguin Group	913	17
Pearson Television	574	11
Total	**5,386**	**100**

Selected Operations

Pearson Education
Elementary education
FT Management (business
  education and
  management
  development)
Higher education
Macmillan Computer
  Publishing
NCS Pearson (educational
  test processing)
Secondary education

Financial Times Group
*Business Day & Financial
  Mail* (50%; South Africa)
Data Broadcasting Corp.
  (60%; US)
The Economist Group
  (50%)
The Financial Times
FT.com (financial news)

FTSE International
  (market indices, with
  London Stock Exchange)
Les Echos (France)
Recoletos (Spain)

Penguin Group
Allen Lane
Dorling Kindersley
Dutton
Frederick Warne
G.P. Putnam's Sons
Hamish Hamilton
Ladybird
Michael Joseph
North American Library
Penguin
Plume
Puffin
Riverhead Books
Twentieth Century Classics
Viking

COMPETITORS

1MAGE
Bell & Howell
Compass Learning
Daily Mail and
  General Trust
Dow Jones
Educational Testing
  Service
Harcourt General
HarperCollins
Havas
Houghton Mifflin
John Harland
John Wiley
Knowledge Universe
Learning Tree
McGraw-Hill
Moody's
New Horizons Worldwide

New York Times
News Corp.
PLATO Learning
Prometric
Random House
Reed Elsevier
Reuters
Scan-Optics
Simon & Schuster
Sylvan Learning
Thomson Corporation
Time
Touchstone Applied
  Science
United News & Media
Verlagsgruppe Georg
  von Holtzbrinck
Washington Post
Wolters Kluwer

HISTORICAL FINANCIALS & EMPLOYEES

NYSE: PSO FYE: December 31	Annual Growth	12/90	12/91	12/92	12/93	12/94	12/95	12/96	12/97	12/98	12/99
Sales ($ mil.)	11.5%	2,017	2,017	1,730	1,950	2,425	2,836	3,714	3,783	3,973	5,386
Net income ($ mil.)	12.1%	170	251	159	219	349	404	409	63	625	475
Income as % of sales	—	8.4%	12.4%	9.2%	11.2%	14.4%	14.3%	11.0%	1.7%	15.7%	8.8%
Employees	(4.2%)	29,410	28,492	27,966	15,514	17,215	19,422	17,383	18,306	18,400	20,000

STOCK PRICE HISTORY

1999 FISCAL YEAR-END

Debt ratio: 63.4%
Return on equity: —
Cash ($ mil.): 465
Current ratio: 1.45
Long-term debt ($ mil.): 3,694

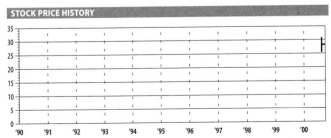

PECHINEY S.A.

OVERVIEW

Pechiney thrives on being a lightweight. The Paris-based company makes aluminum sheet and specialty products, aluminum extrusions, and metal and plastic packaging. In addition to being a leading European maker of primary aluminum and flat-rolled aluminum products, Pechiney also makes laminated tubes, aerosol cans, and plastic packaging for cosmetics and perfumes. Europe accounts for most of Pechiney's sales; the US accounts for 35%.

Plans to merge with Alcan Aluminium (Canada) and Alusuisse Lonza (Algroup, Switzerland) fell through when Alcan balked at EU demands that it sell some European factories (Alcan has since acquired Algroup). Undaunted, Pechiney agreed to acquire JPS Packaging. In the meantime, Pechiney has divested all but 45% of can maker American National Can and plans to sell the rest.

HISTORY

Pechiney traces its roots to Henri Merle, a young chemical engineer, who in 1855 founded Compagnie de Produits Chimiques d'Alais et de la Camargue. Located in Salindres, France, the company's single plant produced caustic soda, salt, pyrites, and limestone. The firm began producing aluminum in 1860, using a chemical process which was developed by Henri Sainte-Claire Deville.

In 1874 the man who would give the company its name, A. R. Pechiney, joined the firm. By 1877 Pechiney managed the firm, and trading and financial circles referred to the company as Pechiney.

While the company held a 30-year monopoly on producing aluminum, in 1886 Paul Héroult developed a more efficient electrolytic process, which he offered to the company. Pechiney declined the offer, and Héroult sold his process to Société Electrométallurgique Française (Froges). By 1889 Froges had forced Pechiney out of the aluminum business.

In 1897 Pechiney bought a company that used the Héroult process and began producing aluminum again. Adrien Badin succeeded A. R. Pechiney in 1914 and expanded the company into Norway and the US. Emile Boyoud and Louis Marlio took control in 1917 after Badin died. The company continued to expand during World War I to become one of France's largest aluminum producers.

Pechiney survived World War I because its plants resided in the south of France, an area which was largely untouched by the war. In 1921 the company merged with Froges to form the Compagnie des Produits Chimiques et Electrométallurgiques d'Alais, Froges et Camargue.

In the mid-1930s Jacques Level took the helm of the company, but died five years later. Marlio succeeded Level in 1939. The company survived WWII just has it had WWI. After the war, René Piaton took charge and had to contend with a power shortage that cut aluminum production in half. By 1947 production had recovered. In 1950 the company formally changed its name to Pechiney.

For the next three decades Pechiney worked toward two goals — finding new sources of energy and raw materials and integrating its nonferrous metals operations. The company expanded internationally, and in 1962 it bought US-based aluminum producer Howe Sound, later split into Howmet Aluminum and Howmet Turbine Components.

Pechiney merged with chemical company Ugine-Kuhlman in 1971. Pechiney Ugine Kuhlman survived the merger only to be battered by downturns in the steel and chemical sectors that led to huge losses. The French government, under socialist Pierre Mauroy, nationalized the company in 1982. The government restructured the company, shedding its special steels and chemical operations. A year later, the much smaller company reverted back to its Pechiney name and its basic product — aluminum. During the 1980s Pechiney began to expand again, opening plants in Australia and Canada. In 1986 it bought American National Can (ANC).

Jean-Pierre Rodier, a proponent of US-style management, became Pechiney's CEO in 1994, and the next year the French government privatized the firm. Pechiney spun off American National Can in 1999, but retained a 45% stake in the company.

Pechiney announced plans to merge with Alcan Aluminium of Canada and Switzerland-based Alusuisse Lonza Group (Algroup) in 2000. In mid-March the merger between Alcan and Algroup was approved by the European Commission, but Pechiney had to withdraw from the deal due to antitrust concerns. Pechiney gave up when Alcan balked at selling its 50% stake in German aluminum plant (Norf) to satisfy EU regulators. Later in the year Alcan acquired Algroup and Pechiney agreed to acquire US-based JPS Packaging.

Chairman and CEO: Jean-Pierre Rodier
COO Aluminum Sector: Philippe Varin, age 46
COO Ferroalloys: Jacques Gani
COO Packaging Sector: Christel Bories, age 35
SVP Finance: Jean-Dominique Sénard, age 46
SVP Human Resources: Gilles-Pierre Lévy, age 51
SVP International Trade: Bruno Poux-Guillaume
Auditors: PricewaterhouseCoopers

LOCATIONS

HQ: 7, place du Chancelier Adenauer,
   75116 Paris, France
Phone: +33-1-56-28-25-77   **Fax:** +33-1-56-28-33-38
US HQ: 8770 W. Bryn Mawr Ave., Chicago, IL 60631
US Phone: 773-399-8000   **US Fax:** 773-399-8090
Web site: http://www.pechiney.com

Pechiney has operations in more than 60 countries.

1999 Sales

	$ mil.	% of total
France	3,903	40
US	3,403	35
Other countries	2,429	25
Total	**9,735**	**100**

PRODUCTS/OPERATIONS

1999 Sales

	$ mil.	% of total
Aluminum		
Aluminum metal	1,968	20
Aluminum conversion	1,606	16
Packaging		
Food, health care & beauty	1,839	19
Beverage cans	1,327	14
International trade	2,648	27
Ferroalloys & other	347	4
Total	**9,735**	**100**

Selected Operations
Almet France (international trade)
Aluminium de Grece (60%, Greece)
Brandeis Brokers Limited (international trade, UK)
Cebal Italiana SA (84%)
Cebal Printal Oy (Finland)
Cebal Zhongshan Co. Ltd. (60%, China)
Invensil (ferroalloys, 77%)
Kenpack, Inc. (US)
Pechiney Aluminium Presswerk GmbH (Germany)
Pechiney Becancour Inc. (US)
Pechiney Cast Plate, Inc. (US)
Pechiney Consolidated Australia PTY Ltd.
Pechiney Trading Company SA (international trade,
  Switzerland)
Silicon Smelters (ferroalloys, 77%, South Africa)

COMPETITORS

Alcan	Crown Cork & Seal
Alcoa	Kaiser Aluminum
Caradon	Norsk Hydro
Consolidated Container	Ormet

HISTORICAL FINANCIALS & EMPLOYEES

NYSE: PY FYE: December 31	Annual Growth	12/90	12/91	12/92	12/93	12/94	12/95	12/96	12/97	12/98	12/99
Sales ($ mil.)	(2.7%)	—	—	11,826	10,644	11,066	14,161	12,576	11,755	11,754	9,735
Net income ($ mil.)	32.4%	—	—	37	(166)	(596)	299	(574)	301	365	262
Income as % of sales	—	—	—	0.3%	—	—	2.1%	—	2.6%	3.1%	2.7%
Earnings per share ($)	(12.4%)	—	—	—	—	—	2.70	(3.73)	1.90	2.23	1.59
Stock price - FY high ($)	—	—	—	—	—	—	17.88	24.25	26.13	25.25	36.44
Stock price - FY low ($)	—	—	—	—	—	—	16.75	17.13	16.50	14.13	15.69
Stock price - FY close ($)	21.1%	—	—	—	—	—	16.88	19.63	19.50	16.13	36.31
P/E - high	—	—	—	—	—	—	22	—	14	11	23
P/E - low	—	—	—	—	—	—	21	—	9	6	10
Dividends per share ($)	—	—	—	—	—	—	0.00	0.24	0.00	0.28	0.43
Book value per share ($)	(9.7%)	—	—	—	—	—	28.16	16.81	16.63	18.53	18.74
Employees	(10.2%)	—	—	63,287	59,212	37,474	37,214	35,612	33,960	33,200	29,840

HIGH/LOW/CLOSE

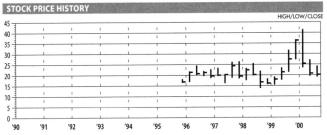

Debt ratio: 23.4%
Return on equity: 8.8%
Cash ($ mil.): 449
Current ratio: 1.29
Long-term debt ($ mil.): 911
No. of shares (mil.): 159
Dividends
  Yield: 1.2%
  Payout: 27.0%
Market value ($ mil.): 5,773

PENINSULAR AND ORIENTAL

OVERVIEW

The Peninsular and Oriental Steam Navigation Company (P&O) is looking for the light at the end of the Chunnel. The London-based company, northwestern Europe's largest passenger ferry operator, has seen its cross-Channel ferry business suffer since the Euro-tunnel linking England and France opened. This decline, coupled with the end of duty-free sales of tobacco and alcohol aboard ferries in 1999, prompted P&O to cut costs by merging its short sea route operation across the English Channel with Sweden's Stena Line.

Still, P&O has other resources to fall back on. Subsidiary Princess Cruises is the world's #3 cruise company behind Carnival and Royal Caribbean. Princess has enhanced its global cruise business by acquiring European cruise line Aida. However, in a major strategic shift, P&O has announced plans to spin off its cruise line business as P&O Princess Cruises to focus on its ports, ferries, and logistics operations.

Ranking among the world's leading port operators, P&O runs 27 terminals in 18 countries and has interests in 30 other ports. The company also carries cargo. Its P&O Nedlloyd Container Line, P&O's 50/50 joint venture with Dutch company Royal Nedlloyd, is one of the largest container shipping lines in the world. P&O also owns bulk shipper Associated Bulk Carriers.

HISTORY

In 1815 Scotsman Arthur Anderson joined the London office of shipbroker Brodie Willcox. They formed a partnership in 1822 and built a business based on trade between Britain and the Iberian Peninsula. Their ships ran guns and transported troops for the royalists during the Portuguese and Spanish civil wars of the 1830s.

The two men teamed up with Irish shipowner Richard Bourne in 1835 to establish the Peninsular Steam Navigation Company, which offered regular trading service between London and ports in Spain, Portugal, and Gibraltar. Two years later Bourne won a contract to carry mail by sea between England and Spanish and Portuguese ports. The company extended its mail routes to the Mediterranean, and in 1840 a contract for monthly mail deliveries to Alexandria, Egypt, allowed it to raise money to incorporate as a limited liability company, the Peninsular and Oriental Steam Navigation Company.

The firm began offering cruises in the 1840s and continued to add mail routes, including Suez/Calcutta (1843), Hong Kong (1845), and Sydney (1852). P&O's mail and passenger steamships provided vital logistical support to the expansion of the British Empire.

Between 1914 and 1946 P&O acquired several other shipping firms, including the British India Steam Navigation Company and the New Zealand Shipping Company. The company operated nearly 500 ships in the 1920s.

During WWII, P&O lost 182 ships that were drafted as troop carriers and cargo vessels. After the war, as aircraft took away its passenger and mail income, P&O added cruise ships and various forms of cargo ships, from containers to tankers.

By the 1970s P&O was involved in nearly every kind of merchant shipping. In 1974 it further diversified with the purchase of Britain's #4 construction company (at that time), Bovis Construction. Jeffrey Sterling joined P&O as chairman in 1983.

Two years later the firm acquired its chairman's Sterling Guarantee Trust, which owned US commercial properties and London's Earls Court and Olympia exhibition halls. In the late 1980s and early 1990s, chairman Sterling kept the company on a course of expansion: P&O bought Sitmar Cruises in 1988, formed P&O Asia in 1992, and acquired interests in Chinese container terminals.

But P&O had hit the business doldrums. To put some wind in its sails, P&O and rival Nedlloyd Groep merged their container shipping lines into P&O Nedlloyd Container Line in 1996 and spun off faltering Bovis Homes (residential construction) the next year. In 1998 it combined its ferries with those of Stena Line in order to compete against the Eurotunnel. P&O's *Grand Princess*, the biggest cruise ship in the world at the time, also came into service that year.

In 1999 P&O sold Bovis Construction to real estate group Lend Lease; it also sold Earls Court and Olympia. The next year the company announced plans to spin off its cruise line business to focus on its ferries, ports, and logistics units. It planed to add privately held Festival to its cruise line offerings before the spinoff, but a slump in the price of P&O's stock forced the company to call off the $400 million acquisition. Also in 2000 P&O pulled the IPO of bulk shipping unit Associated Bulk Carriers, citing poor market conditions.

OFFICERS

Chairman: Lord Sterling of Plaistow, age 65
Managing Director: Sir Bruce MacPhail, age 60
Chairman and Managing Director, P&O Australia; Chairman, P&O Ports and P&O Cold Logisitics: Richard J. Hein, age 64
Chairman and Managing Director, P&O Ferries; Chairman, P&O Trans European Holdings: G. D. S. Dunlop, age 57
Chairman, P&O Properties, P&O Shopping Centres, and P&O Developments: T. J. R. Harding, age 59
Director Cruise Division; President, Princess Cruises: Peter G. Ratcliffe, age 52
Finance Director: Nick L. Luff, age 33
Auditors: KPMG Audit Plc

LOCATIONS

HQ: The Pennisular and Oriental Steam Navigation Company, 79 Pall Mall, London SW1Y 5EJ, United Kingdom
Phone: +44-20-7930-4343   **Fax:** +44-20-7930-8572
US HQ: 10100 Santa Monica Blvd., Los Angeles, CA 90067
US Phone: 310-553-1770   **US Fax:** 310-277-6175
Web site: http://www.p-and-o.com

1999 Sales

	% of total
Europe	
UK & Ireland	34
Other countries	18
US & Canada	37
Australia, Far East & Pacific	9
Other regions	2
Total	**100**

PRODUCTS/OPERATIONS

1999 Sales

	% of total
Ports, ferries & logistics	50
Cruises	36
Property	14
Cargo shipping	—
Total	**100**

Selected Subsidiaries and Affiliates

Boston Wharf Company (property investment and development, US)
P&O North Sea Ferries Ltd.
P&O Polar Australia Pty. Ltd. (Antarctican research and resupply services)
P&O Scottish Ferries Ltd.
P&O Holidays Ltd. (passenger cruises)
P&O Developments Ltd. (property development)
P&O Properties Inc. (holding company, US)
P&O Nedlloyd Ltd. (50%, international transport)
Pacific Cold Storage Inc. (US)
Shekou Container Terminals Ltd. (25%, China)
Swan Hellenic Ltd. (passenger cruises)

COMPETITORS

A.P. Moller	Evergreen	Orient Overseas
Accor	Marine	International
Airtours	Hanjin Shipping	Royal Caribbean
Alfred McAlpine	Hapag Lloyd	Cruises
APL	Hutchison	Sea Containers
Carnival	Whampoa	Sodexho
COSCO	Mitsui O.S.K.	Marriott
Crowley	Lines	Services
Maritime	Neptune Orient	Stolt-Nielsen
CSX	Nippon Yusen	Vard
Eurotunnel	KK	

HISTORICAL FINANCIALS & EMPLOYEES

OTC: POSRY FYE: December 31	Annual Growth	12/90	12/91	12/92	12/93	12/94	12/95	12/96	12/97	12/98	12/99
Sales ($ mil.)	0.2%	9,719	9,161	8,350	8,490	9,372	10,182	12,154	9,735	9,813	9,926
Net income ($ mil.)	7.3%	345	326	290	595	374	366	430	548	452	650
Income as % of sales	—	3.6%	3.6%	3.5%	7.0%	4.0%	3.6%	3.5%	5.6%	4.6%	6.6%
Earnings per share ($)	3.0%	1.47	1.29	0.98	2.02	1.20	1.17	1.37	1.75	1.38	1.92
Stock price - FY high ($)	—	23.55	23.64	19.97	20.58	21.83	20.22	20.88	24.75	31.25	34.13
Stock price - FY low ($)	—	17.39	14.36	11.25	15.58	18.36	14.14	14.66	19.57	18.13	20.00
Stock price - FY close ($)	5.3%	20.69	15.97	15.27	19.11	19.08	14.77	19.59	23.09	24.25	33.00
P/E - high	—	16	18	20	10	18	17	15	14	23	18
P/E - low	—	12	11	11	8	15	12	11	11	13	10
Dividends per share ($)	(1.2%)	1.18	1.14	0.92	0.90	0.95	0.95	1.05	1.00	1.04	1.06
Book value per share ($)	1.0%	14.90	14.18	12.14	13.27	13.77	13.62	14.57	14.85	14.53	16.26
Employees	(1.8%)	—	—	71,133	51,755	61,467	66,924	71,205	69,533	68,333	62,674

STOCK PRICE HISTORY

HIGH/LOW/CLOSE

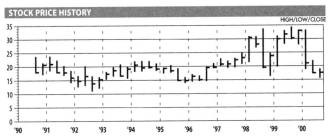

1999 FISCAL YEAR-END

Debt ratio: 26.8%
Return on equity: 12.3%
Cash ($ mil.): 179
Current ratio: 1.24
Long-term debt ($ mil.): 2,050
No. of shares (mil.): 344
Dividends
  Yield: 0.0%
  Payout: 0.6%
Market value ($ mil.): 11,354

PETRÓLEO BRASILEIRO S.A.

OVERVIEW

They've got an awful lot of coffee in Brazil and an awful lot of oil and gas — state-controlled PETRÓLEO BRASILEIRO (PETROBRAS) exploits the latter. The Rio de Janeiro-based company, Brazil's #1 industrial firm, is engaged in exploration for oil and gas; in production, refining, purchasing, transportation of oil and gas products; and production of petrochemicals. It has proved reserves of 10.1 billion barrels of oil equivalent.

Subsidiary Petrobras Distribuidora, which operates 7,200 gas stations, is Brazil's leading retailer of petroleum products, with a 34% market share. Petrobras Internacional, also known as Braspetro, conducts international exploration in Angola, Libya, Nigeria, the UK, the US, and Latin America.

Although most of PETROBRAS' wells are onshore, the bulk of its production comes from offshore; the otherwise slow-footed government-owned company is recognized as a leader in offshore drilling technology and deepwater wells. To boost its natural gas operations, PETROBRAS is investing $2 billion to build a pipeline from gas fields in Bolivia to Brazil. The company also plans to triple production outside Brazil to 300,000 barrels per day by 2005.

HISTORY

"O petróleo e nosso!"
"The oil is ours!" proclaimed the Brazilian nationalists' slogan in 1953, and President Getulio Vargas approved a bill creating a state-run monopoly on petroleum discovery, development, refining, and transport.

The same year PETRÓLEO BRASILEIRO (PETROBRAS) was created, a team led by American geologist Walter Link reported that the prospects of finding petroleum in Brazil were slim. The report outraged Brazilian nationalists, who saw it as a ploy for foreign exploitation. PETROBRAS proved it could find oil, but Brazil continued to import crude oil and petroleum products. By 1973 the company produced about 10% of the nation's needs.

When oil prices soared during the Arab embargo, the government, instead of encouraging exploration for domestic oil, pushed PETROBRAS into a program to promote alcohol fuels. The company was forced to raise gasoline prices to make the more costly gasohol attractive to consumers. During the 1979 oil crunch the price of gasohol was fixed at 65% of gasoline. But during the oil glut of the mid-1980s, PETROBRAS' cost of making gasohol was twice what it cost to buy gasoline — in other words, PETROBRAS lost money.

PETROBRAS soon began overseas exploration. In 1980 it found an oil field in Iraq, an important trading partner during the 1980s. The company also drilled in Angola and, through a 1987 agreement with Texaco, in the Gulf of Mexico.

In the mid-1980s PETROBRAS began production in the deepwater Campos basin off the Rio de Janeiro state coast. Discoveries there in 1988, in the Marlim and Albacora fields, more than tripled its oil reserves. It plunged deep into the thick Amazon jungle in 1986 to explore for oil, and by 1990 Amazon wells were making a significant contribution to total production. That year, to ease dependence on imports, PETROBRAS launched a five-year, $16.9 billion plan to boost crude oil production. It also began selling its mining and trading assets.

Before the invasion of Kuwait, Brazil relied heavily on Iraq, trading weapons for oil. After the invasion spawned increases in crude prices, PETROBRAS raised pump prices but, yielding to the government's anti-inflation program, still did not raise them enough to cover costs. It lost $13 million a day.

In 1993 the company sold 26% of Petrobras Distribuidora to the public and privatized several of its petrochemical and fertilizer subsidiaries. A 1994 presidential order, bent on stabilizing Brazil's 40%-per-month inflation, cut the prices of oil products. In 1995 the government loosened its grip on the oil and gas industry and allowed foreign companies to enter the Brazilian market. Subsequently, PETROBRAS teamed up with a Japanese consortium to build Brazil's largest oil refinery.

In 1997 PETROBRAS appealed a $4 billion judgment from a 1992 shareholder lawsuit; the suit alleged PETROBRAS had undervalued shares during the privatization of the loss-making Petroquisa affiliate. (The appeal was granted in 1999.)

As part of an effort to boost oil production, PETROBRAS also began to raise money abroad in 1999. The next year PETROBRAS and Spanish oil giant Repsol YPF agreed to swap oil and gas assets in Argentina and Brazil in a deal worth more than $1 billion.

Chairman: Rodolpho Torrinho Neto
President: Henri P. Reichstul, age 51
Finance Director: Ronnie Vaz Moreira
Corporate Affairs Director: Carlo A. de Aguiar Teixeira, age 57
Downstream Director: Albano de Souza Gonçalves, age 55
Engineering Director: Antonio L. Silva de Menezes, age 54
Upstream Director: José Coutinho Barbosa, age 59
Petrochemical, Thermoelectrical and Asset Management Director: Delcídio do Amaral Gomez, age 45
Corporate Communication: Ricardo Bastos Vieira
Corporate Exploration and Production:
Carlos A. Pereira de Oliveira
Environment, Quality and Industrial Safety:
José C. Rodriguea Moreira
Finance: Almir Guilherme Barbassa
Financial Planning: Gustavo Tardin Barbosa
Auditors: PricewaterhouseCoopers

HQ: PETRÓLEO BRASILEIRO S.A. - PETROBRAS,
Avenida República de Chile 65,
20035-900 Rio de Janeiro, Brazil
Phone: +55-21-534-4477   **Fax:** +55-21-534-3247
US HQ: 133 Avenue of the Americas, 16th Fl.,
New York, NY 10019
US Phone: 212-974-0777   **US Fax:** 212-974-1169
Web site: http://www.petrobras.com.br

PETRÓLEO BRASILEIRO S.A. - PETROBRAS explores for oil and gas in Brazil, as well as in Angola, Argentina, Bolivia, Colombia, Cuba, Ecuador, Equatorial Guinea, Libya, Nigeria, Peru, Trinidad and Tobago, the UK, and the US.

Selected Subsidiaries
Petrobras Distribuidora SA (BR; distribution and marketing of petroleum products, fuel alcohol, and natural gas)
Petrobras Gás SA (Gaspetro, management of the Brazil-Bolivia pipeline and other natural gas assets)
Petrobras Internacional SA (Braspetro; overseas exploration and production, marketing, and services)
Petrobras Química SA (Petroquisa, petrochemicals)
Petrobras Transporte SA (Transpetro, oil and gas transportation and storage)

Ashland	Lyondell Chemical
BHP	Norsk Hydro
BP	Occidental
Chevron	PDVSA
Coastal	PEMEX
Conoco	Phillips Petroleum
Devon Energy	Royal Dutch/Shell
Eni	Sunoco
Exxon Mobil	Texaco
Imperial Oil	TOTAL FINA ELF
Kerr-McGee	Unocal
Koch	USX-Marathon

NYSE: PBR FYE: December 31	Annual Growth	12/90	12/91	12/92	12/93	12/94	12/95	12/96	12/97	12/98	12/99
Sales ($ mil.)	(2.4%)	20,448	16,996	18,095	20,244	19,931	15,178	17,493	17,432	14,909	16,376
Net income ($ mil.)	7.4%	511	(236)	5	687	1,645	580	644	1,354	1,149	972
Income as % of sales	—	2.5%	—	0.0%	3.4%	8.3%	3.8%	3.7%	7.8%	7.7%	5.9%
Employees	(4.7%)	55,569	53,857	56,209	56,900	50,295	46,226	43,468	41,200	38,225	35,891

Debt ratio: 33.0%
Return on equity: 7.0%
Cash ($ mil.): 270
Current ratio: 0.81
Long-term debt ($ mil.): 4,781

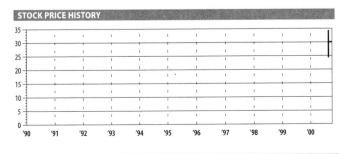

	'90	'91	'92	'93	'94	'95	'96	'97	'98	'99	'00

PETRÓLEOS DE VENEZUELA S.A.

OVERVIEW

Venezuela floats on a sea of oil, and state-owned Petróleos de Venezuela S.A. rules the waves. Known as PDVSA (pronounced pay-day-VAY-suh), the Caracas-based company is one of the largest integrated oil companies in the world. It boasts proved reserves of 76.9 billion barrels of oil — the most outside the Middle East — and 146.8 trillion cu. ft. of natural gas. PDVSA is one of the top exporters of oil to the US.

Although the company's exploration and production activities take place in Venezuela, PDVSA refines, markets, and transports petroleum products in Belgium, Germany, Sweden, the Caribbean, the UK, and the US, as well as

at home. Its Tulsa-based CITGO Petroleum subsidiary operates 14,000 gas stations in the US. PDVSA also has operations in coal and petrochemicals. Its BITOR subsidiary mines Venezuela's extensive bitumen reserves, turning the tarlike ooze into Orimulsion, a patented fuel marketed as an alternative to coal for electric generating plants.

In a move that requires foreign investment, PDVSA is expanding its production of petrochemicals, gas, and Orimulsion. However, investors will step carefully: While Venezuelan President Hugo Chavez says PDVSA is open to investors, he has been tightening state control over the oil company's operations.

HISTORY

On invitation from dictator Juan Vicente Gomez, Royal Dutch/Shell looked for oil in Venezuela just before WWI. After the war US companies plunged in. Standard Oil of Indiana (later BP Amoco) began Creole Petroleum in 1920 to explore in Venezuela, selling the company in 1928 to Standard of New Jersey (later Exxon Mobil).

When the Venezuelan government threatened to nationalize its oil industry in 1938, the foreign oil companies agreed to pay more taxes and royalties. But in 1945 Venezuela set a pattern for the rest of the world's oil-rich nations when it decreed it was a 50% partner in all oil operations. Venezuela was pivotal to OPEC's creation in 1960, and the next year the government created the Venezuelan Petroleum Corporation (CVP). CVP was granted the nation's unassigned petroleum reserves. By the early 1970s CVP produced about 2% of the nation's oil.

President Carlos Andres Perez nationalized oil holdings in 1975, paying only $1 billion for foreign-owned oil assets and creating Petróleos de Venezuela S.A. (PDVSA) to hold the properties. Venezuela formed stand-alone PDVSA subsidiaries: Shell operations became Maraven, Creole became Lagoven, and smaller companies combined into Corpoven. (All units were merged into PDVSA in 1998.)

Free of debt and buoyed by high crude prices in the late 1970s and early 1980s, PDVSA formed ventures (Ruhr Oel) with Germany's VEBA Oel and Sweden's Nynas Petroleum. In the US, it bought 50% of CITGO, the former refining and marketing arm of Cities Service Co., from Southland in 1986 (and the rest in 1990). PDVSA also bought a 50% stake in a Unocal refinery in 1989 to create joint venture UNO-VEN.

After the 1991 Gulf War, Venezuela increased its own production despite OPEC oil quotas. The next year PDVSA opened some marginal fields to foreign investment for the first time since the industry's 1975 nationalization.

Venezuelan President Rafael Caldera named Luis Giusti president of the company in 1994, and the next year Venezuela's oil industry was opened to foreign investment. In 1996 PDVSA began building a $1.5 billion plastics plant with Mobil. PDVSA and Unocal finally ended UNO-VEN the next year when UNO-VEN CEO David Tippeconnic took over as head of CITGO.

The rush for Venezuelan oil rights was on by 1997; one week's worth of bidding brought in $2 billion from top international oil companies. Meanwhile, PDVSA searched for facilities to refine the heavy crude, striking deals with Phillips in 1997 and Amerada Hess in 1998.

PDVSA's profits took a hit in 1998 when oil prices fell to record lows. Concerns arose about the firm's direction that year after populist Hugo Chavez was elected as Venezuela's president. Chavez and his allies sought to retain state control over PDVSA's resources and to keep a closer check on foreign partners.

In 1999 PDVSA, suffering from a devastated domestic economy, decided to expand its downstream operations globally. As part of that plan, it formed a Houston-based crude and products marketing firm, PDVSA Trading.

Tightening his control of the company, in 2000 Chavez appointed army generals to head up both PDVSA (General Guaicaipuro Lameda) and CITGO (General Oswaldo Contreras Maza). The appointments followed a management shake-up and an oil workers' strike.

Chairman and CEO: Gen. Guaicaipuro Lameda
VC: Aires Barreto
VC: Oswaldo Contreras Maza
VC: Carlos Jorda
VC; President, Pequiven: Eduardo Praselj
VC; President, PDVSA Gas: Domingo Marsicobetre
Executive Director Finance: Cesar Jimenez
Executive Director Human Resources: Luis Davila
Executive Director Planning: Jorge Kamkoff
Executive Director Refinement, Provision, and Commerce: Karl Mazeica
Secretary: Luis E. Duque Corredor
Auditors: Espineira, Sheldon y Asociados

HQ: Edificio Petroleos de Venezuela, Torre Este, Avenida Libertador, La Campiña, Apdo. 169, Caracas 1010-A, Venezuela
Phone: +58-2-708-4111   **Fax:** +58-2-708-4661
US HQ: 750 Lexington Ave., 59th St., 10th Fl., New York, NY 10022
US Phone: 212-339-7331   **US Fax:** 212-339-7727
Web site: http://www.pdv.com

Petróleos de Venezuela has exploration and production operations in Venezuela and conducts refining and marketing there and in Belgium, the Caribbean, Germany, Sweden, the UK, and the US.

Selected Subsidiaries and Affiliates

PDVSA Exploration and Production
Bitumenes Orinoco, SA (BITOR, bitumen and Orimulsion)
Carbozulia, SA (coal)
CVP
PDVSA Exploration
PDVSA Orinoco Belt
PDVSA Production

PDVSA Manufacturing and Marketing
Deltaven
Intevep, SA (research and support)
PDV Marina
PDVSA Gas
PDVSA Refining

Other
CIED
CITGO Petroleum Corp. (refining, marketing, and petrochemicals; US)
Palmaven, SA (agricultural assistance and conservation projects)
PDVSA Services
PDVSA Trading (crude oil and products marketing; US)
Pequiven, SA (petrochemicals)
SOFIP

Ashland	Norsk Hydro
BHP	Occidental
BP	PEMEX
Chevron	PETROBRAS
Coastal	Phillips Petroleum
Conoco	Royal Dutch/Shell
Devon Energy	Saudi Aramco
Eni	Sunoco
Exxon Mobil	Texaco
Imperial Oil	Tosco
Kerr-McGee	TOTAL FINA ELF
Koch	Ultramar Diamond
LASMO	Shamrock
Lyondell Chemical	USX-Marathon
NIOC	

Government-owned FYE: December 31	Annual Growth	12/90	12/91	12/92	12/93	12/94	12/95	12/96	12/97	12/98	12/99
Sales ($ mil.)	4.0%	22,997	22,273	21,426	21,275	22,157	26,041	33,855	34,801	25,526	32,648
Net income ($ mil.)	9.0%	1,300	441	338	1,089	2,074	3,614	4,382	4,505	663	2,818
Income as % of sales	—	5.7%	2.0%	1.6%	5.1%	9.4%	13.9%	12.9%	12.9%	2.6%	8.6%
Employees	(0.2%)	51,883	50,137	50,506	52,218	53,600	53,500	53,200	51,677	50,821	51,000

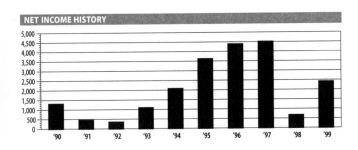

NET INCOME HISTORY

PETRÓLEOS MEXICANOS

OVERVIEW

Petróleos Mexicanos (PEMEX) takes oil from underground with one hand and puts cash in the coffers of Mexico's treasury with the other. A state-owned integrated oil company, Mexico City-based PEMEX accounts for 33% of the government's revenues, and 7% of the country's export earnings. PEMEX engages in oil and gas exploration and production, refining, and petrochemical production, and subsidiary P.M.I. Comercio Internacional manages international

trading operations. Mexico boasts massive oil and gas resources, with proved oil reserves of 28.4 billion barrels of oil equivalent.

Long recognized as the tangible expression of Mexican nationalism, PEMEX has faced popular opposition in its bid to follow other Latin American state oil companies and privatize some operations. PEMEX is, however, working to become more responsive to market conditions and expand its international scope.

HISTORY

Histories of precolonial Mexico recount the nation's first oil business: Natives along the Tampico coast gathered asphalt from naturally occurring deposits and traded with the Aztecs.

As the 20th century began, Americans Edward Doheny and Charles Canfield struck oil near Tampico. Their success was eclipsed in 1910 by a nearby well drilled by British engineer Weetman Pearson, leader of the firm that became Pearson PLC.

President Porfirio Díaz had welcomed foreign ownership of Mexican resources, but revolution ousted Díaz, and the 1917 Constitution proclaimed that natural resources belonged to the nation. Without enforcing legislation, however, foreign oil companies continued business as usual until a 1925 act limited their concessions. During a bitter labor dispute in 1938, President Lázaro Cárdenas expropriated foreign oil holdings — the first nationalization of oil holdings by a non-Communist state. Subsequent legislation created Petróleos Mexicanos (PEMEX).

Without foreign capital and expertise, the new state-owned company struggled, and Mexico had to import petroleum in the early 1970s. But for many Mexicans, PEMEX remained a symbol of national identity and economic independence. That faith was rewarded in 1972 when a major oil discovery made PEMEX one of the world's top oil producers again. Ample domestic oil supplies and high world prices during the Iranian upheaval in the late 1970s fueled a boom and a government borrowing spree in Mexico. Between 1982 and 1985 PEMEX contributed more than 50% of government revenues.

When oil prices collapsed in 1985, Mexico cut investment in exploration, and production dropped. To decrease its reliance on oil, Mexico began lowering trade barriers and encouraging manufacturing, even allowing some foreign ownership of petrochemical processing.

Elected in 1988, President Carlos Salinas de Gortari began to reform PEMEX. Labor's grip

on the company was loosened in 1989 when PEMEX's union leader was arrested and jailed after a gun battle. In 1992, after a PEMEX pipeline explosion killed more than 200 people in Guadalajara, four of its executives and several local officials were sent to prison, amid public cries for company reform.

President Ernesto Zedillo appointed Adrian Lajous Vargas head of PEMEX in 1994. Under the professorial Lajous, PEMEX began to adopt modern business practices (such as trimming its bloated payroll), look for more reserves, and improve its refining capability. Lajous tried to sell some petrochemical assets in 1995, but had to modify the scheme the next year after massive public protests by the country's nationalists. Still, PEMEX began selling off natural gas production, distribution, and storage networks to private companies.

Though oil prices were dropping, in 1998 Mexico finally upped PEMEX's investment budget and PEMEX dramatically increased exploration and production. In spite of 2000's looming national election (elections traditionally had caused bureaucrats to keep a low profile to protect their jobs), Lajous again fanned the flames of the opposition: In 1998 he signed a major deal to sell Mexican crude to Exxon's Texas refinery, and then in 1999 a four-year-old PEMEX/Shell joint venture announced that it would expand its US refinery.

In 1999 Lajous resigned and was replaced Rogelio Montemayor, a former governor. In 2000 Vicente Fox was elected as Mexico's new president, the country's first non-Institutional Revolutionary Party (PRI) leader in seven decades. He announced plans to replace PEMEX's politician-staffed board with professionals, and modernize the company, but he has ruled out privatizing PEMEX as politically unfeasible.

General Director: Rogelio Montemayor
General Director Exploration and Production:
José A. Ceballos Soberanis
General Director Gas and Basic Petrochemicals:
Marco Ramírez Silva
General Director Refining: Jaime M. Willars Andrade
Director Corporate Administration:
Manuel Gómezperalta Damirón
Director Corporate Finance: Juan M. Romero Ortega
General Director, Mexican Institute of Petroleum:
Gustavo Chapela Castañares
General Director, P.M.I. International Commercial:
Eduardo Martínez del Río Petricioli
Director Corporate Industrial Safety Systems:
Rafael Fernández de la Garza
General Controller: Gerardo Rueda Rábago
Manager Human Resources: Fernando Olimon
Coordinator Corporate Planning: Raul A. Livas Elizondo
Auditors: Coopers & Lybrand;
Despacho Roberto Casas Alatriste

HQ: Marina Nacional 329, Colonia Huasteca,
11311 México, D.F., Mexico
Phone: +52-5-531-6061   **Fax:** +52-5-531-6321
Web site: http://www.pemex.com

PEMEX Exploración y Producción (petroleum and
natural gas exploration and production)
PEMEX Gas y Petroquímica Básica (natural gas, liquids
from natural gas, and ethane processing)
PEMEX Petroquímica (petrochemical production)
PEMEX Refinación (refining and marketing)
P.M.I. Comercio Internacional (international trading)

Ashland
BHP
BP
Chevron
Coastal
Conoco
Devon Energy
Eni
Exxon Mobil
Imperial Oil
Koch
Norsk Hydro
Occidental
PDVSA
PETROBRAS
Phillips Petroleum
Royal Dutch/Shell
Sunoco
Texaco
TOTAL FINA ELF
Unocal
USX-Marathon

Government-owned FYE: December 31	Annual Growth	12/90	12/91	12/92	12/93	12/94	12/95	12/96	12/97	12/98	12/99
Sales ($ mil.)	2.6%	19,330	19,165	21,344	26,686	17,870	20,584	29,403	28,566	20,891	24,400
Employees	(2.6%)	167,952	166,896	125,000	106,951	119,928	119,928	120,945	121,220	131,433	132,000

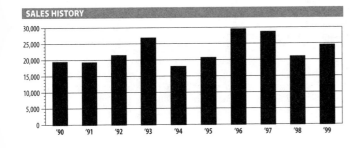

PSA PEUGEOT CITROËN S.A.

OVERVIEW

Euro Disney, Jerry Lewis-mania, the Eiffel Tower, and Puegeots — who could ask for anything more? Paris-based PSA Peugeot Citroën makes cars and light-utility vehicles under the Peugeot and Citroën marques. Ranked #2 in European sales (behind Volkswagen), Peugeot also claims the #2 spot in auto brand sales in its home country (behind arch-rival Renault). Peugeot makes engines and car parts (Peugeot Citroën Moteurs, 53%-owned Faurecia), industrial machinery (PCI), and also operates transport and financing subsidiaries. Smaller divisions make motorbikes, scooters, and light-armored vehicles.

In an era of automotive industry consolidation, Peugeot prefers partnerships over mergers. To compete and stay solo, the company focuses on efficiently rolling out new models and technologies and keeping down expenses through alliances with low-cost car component makers. Peugeot is also broadening its markets beyond Europe, which accounts for about 95% of sales.

The Peugeot family controls about 37% of Peugeot.

HISTORY

In 1810 brothers Frédéric and Jean-Pierre Peugeot made a foundry out of the family textile mill in the Alsace region of France and invented the cold-roll process for producing spring steel. Bicycle production began in 1885 at the behest of avid cyclist Armand Peugeot, Jean-Pierre's grandson.

Armand turned to automobiles and built Peugeot's first car, a steam-powered three-wheeler, in 1889. A gas-fueled Peugeot tied for first place in the 1894 Paris-Rouen Trials, the earliest auto race on record. That year the budding carmaker built the first station wagon, followed in 1905 by the first compact, the 600-pound "Le Bebe."

Peugeot built factories in France, including one in Sochaux (1912) that remains the company's main plant. It made the first diesel passenger car in 1922. The 1929 introduction of the reliable 201 model was followed by innovations such as synchromesh gears in 1936. The company suffered heavy damage in WWII, but quickly bounced back and began expanding overseas after the war.

In 1954 CEO Roland Peugeot rebuffed a board proposal calling for global expansion that would place the company in competition with US automakers. By 1976 the French government had persuaded Peugeot to merge with Citroën.

André Citroën founded his company in 1915, and in 1919 it became the first in Europe to mass-produce cars. Citroën hit the skids during the Depression and in 1934 handed Michelin a large block of stock in lieu of payment for tires. Citroën never fully recovered, though by 1976 the company's line ranged from the 2CV minicar (discontinued 1990) to limousines.

In 1978 Peugeot bought Chrysler's aging European plants and withering nameplates, including Simca (France) and Rootes (UK).

Peugeot changed the nameplates to Talbot but sales continued to slide. It lost nearly $1.2 billion from 1980 to 1984.

Jacques Calvet took over as CEO in 1984. He cut 30,000 jobs and spent heavily on modernization. Aided by the strong launch of the 205 superminicar, Peugeot returned to profitability in 1985, and by 1989 had halved its production break-even point. In the 1980s Peugeot inked production deals with Renault (industrial vehicles, motors, gearboxes) and Fiat (light trucks) and introduced a reasonably priced electric van in 1990.

Peugeot withdrew from the US in 1991 after five years of declining sales. A year later Renault and Peugeot developed electric cars and set up servicing centers throughout France. Citing an economic slump in 1993, Peugeot suffered its first loss ($239 million) since 1985. A French government incentive to replace cars over 10 years old boosted 1994 sales.

Peugeot and rival Renault together introduced a V6 engine in 1996. Jean-Martin Folz replaced Calvet as chairman and CEO in 1997; restructuring charges contributed to company losses that year. In 1998 the company began building Peugeots and Citroëns in the same plants and created its Faurecia unit when its ECIA subsidiary merged with car parts maker Bertrand Faure. In an effort to capitalize on the growing South American car market, the company purchased more than 80% of Argentina's Sevel, and built a plant in Brazil. In 1999 the company sold its flight systems supplier, SAMM, to TRW's Lucas Aerospace unit.

With demand for its cars falling steeply in South America due to the region's continuing economic crisis, Peugeot restructured its Brazil operations in 2000 and formed a new subsidiary, Citroën do Brasil.

OFFICERS

Honorary Chairman, Supervisory Board:
Roland Peugeot
Chairman, Supervisory Board: Pierre Peugeot
VC, Supervisory Board: Jean Boillot
Chairman, Managing Board and Executive Committee:
Jean-Martin Folz
**Member of Executive Committee; Director Citroën
Marque:** Claude Satinet
**Member of Executive Committee; Director Employee
Relations and Human Resources:** Jean-Luc Vergne
**Member of Executive Committee; Director Finance,
Control, and Performance:** Yann Delabrière
**Member of Executive Committee; Director Innovation
and Quality:** Robert Peugeot
**Member of Executive Committee; Director
Manufacturing and Components:** Roland Vardanega
**Member of Executive Committee; Director Peugeot
Marque:** Frédéric Saint-Geours
**Member of Executive Committee; Director Technical
Affairs, Purchasing:** Jean-Louis Silvant
Director Corporate Communications: Liliane Lacourt
Director Group Product Planning: Luc Epron
Director Legal Affairs: Jean-Claude Hanus
Director Public Relations: Xavier Fels
DIrector Strategy: Jean-Marc Nicolle
Director Technical Development: Jean-Louis Grégoire
Auditors: Coopers & Lybrand Audit; Costantin Associes

LOCATIONS

HQ: 75, avenue de la Grande-Armée,
75116 Paris, France
Phone: +33-1-40-66-55-11   **Fax:** +33-1-40-66-54-14
US HQ: 150 Clove Rd., Little Falls, NJ 07424
US Phone: 973-812-4444   **US Fax:** 973-812-2280
Web site: http://www.psa-peugeot-citroen.com

1999 Sales

	$ mil.	% of total
Europe		
France	13,445	36
UK	5,260	14
Spain	5,094	13
Germany	3,535	9
Italy	2,495	7
Other EU	4,259	11
Other countries	1,525	4
Americas	1,239	3
Other regions	1,136	3
Total	**37,988**	**100**

PRODUCTS/OPERATIONS

1999 Sales

	$ mil.	% of total
Automobile division	32,752	86
Automotive equipment	2,997	8
Finance companies	1,071	3
Transportation	659	2
Other	509	1
Total	**37,988**	**100**

COMPETITORS

BMW	Honda	Renco
Bridgestone	Hyundai	Saab Automobile
Caterpillar	Isuzu	Suzuki
Daewoo	Kia Motors	Toyota
DaimlerChrysler	Mazda	Volkswagen
Fiat	Mitsubishi	Yamaha
Ford	Nissan	
General Motors	Renault	

HISTORICAL FINANCIALS & EMPLOYEES

OTC: PEUGY FYE: December 31	Annual Growth	12/90	12/91	12/92	12/93	12/94	12/95	12/96	12/97	12/98	12/99
Sales ($ mil.)	2.2%	31,368	30,832	28,117	24,562	31,140	33,459	33,269	31,177	39,425	37,988
Net income ($ mil.)	(9.6%)	1,815	1,064	610	(239)	581	347	141	(462)	566	732
Income as % of sales	—	5.8%	3.5%	2.2%	—	1.9%	1.0%	0.4%	—	1.4%	1.9%
Earnings per share ($)	(9.6%)	9.07	5.34	3.03	(1.18)	2.81	1.73	0.72	(2.09)	2.91	3.64
Stock price - FY high ($)	—	29.92	22.89	29.58	27.48	38.97	38.55	39.38	34.38	54.70	57.00
Stock price - FY low ($)	—	17.69	15.58	18.22	18.22	25.77	33.27	25.75	22.88	30.00	30.50
Stock price - FY close ($)	12.8%	19.31	22.89	21.38	26.69	34.28	33.02	28.13	31.13	38.63	57.00
P/E - high	—	3	4	10	—	14	22	55	—	19	16
P/E - low	—	2	3	6	—	9	19	36	—	10	8
Dividends per share ($)	13.7%	0.78	0.63	0.45	0.00	0.28	0.31	0.24	0.37	0.88	2.47
Book value per share ($)	0.3%	46.27	49.81	48.07	42.64	52.00	57.08	54.77	46.02	49.53	47.59
Employees	0.5%	159,100	156,800	150,800	143,900	139,800	139,900	139,100	140,200	156,500	165,800

STOCK PRICE HISTORY

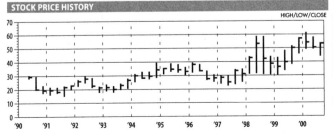

HIGH/LOW/CLOSE

1999 FISCAL YEAR-END

Debt ratio: 36.1%
Return on equity: 7.7%
Cash ($ mil.): 3,365
Current ratio: 0.95
Long-term debt ($ mil.): 5,107
No. of shares (mil.): 190
Dividends
  Yield: 0.0%
  Payout: 0.7%
Market value ($ mil.): 10,808

KONINKLIJKE PHILIPS ELECTRONICS

Koninklijke ("Royal") Philips Electronics wants consumers to tune in to its new look. The world's third-largest consumer electronics firm (behind Matsushita and Sony), Philips makes TVs, VCRs, CD and DVD players, and it counts Philips, Norelco, Marantz, and Magnavox among its brands. The Amsterdam-based company is also the world's #1 maker of lightbulbs, electric shavers, and picture tubes.

Other business includes small appliances, PC monitors, semiconductors, and medical systems. The company also owns a 27% stake in Taiwan Semiconductor Manufacturing.

In the last decade Philips has cut out deadweight — eliminating jobs and selling struggling businesses — to remain competitive. (In the process, chairman Cor Boonstra has acquired the *Godfather*-esque nickname "Corleone.") Boonstra isn't done yet; Philips plans to close one-third of its plants by 2002.

Gerard Philips (later joined by his brother Anton) founded Philips & Co. in the Dutch city of Eindhoven in 1891. Surviving an industry shakeout, Philips prospered as a result of Gerard's engineering and Anton's foreign sales efforts. The company had become Europe's #3 lightbulb maker by 1900. It adopted the name Philips Gloeilampenfabrieken (lightbulb factory) in 1912.

The Netherlands' neutrality during WWI allowed Philips to expand into glass manufacturing (1915) and X-ray and radio tubes (1918). The company set up its first foreign sales office in Belgium in 1919; then in the 1930s it started building plants abroad to avoid trade barriers and tariffs.

During WWII Philips created US and British trusts to control majority interests in North American Philips (NAP) and in Philips' British operations. Following the war, the company established hundreds of subsidiaries worldwide. It repurchased its British businesses in 1955; NAP operated independently until it was reacquired in 1987.

The company started marketing televisions and appliances in the 1950s. Philips introduced audiocassette, VCR, and laser disc technology in the 1960s but had limited success with computers and office equipment. Despite its development of new technologies, in the 1970s Philips was unable to maintain market share against an onslaught of inexpensive goods from Japan. Meanwhile, NAP acquired Magnavox (consumer electronics, US) in 1974. NAP also purchased GTE Television in 1981 and Westinghouse's lighting business in 1983. It provided $60 million in seed money in 1986 to start Taiwan Semiconductor Manufacturing with the Taiwanese government.

Philips' successful PolyGram unit (formed in 1972) went public in 1989 and bought record companies Island (UK) that year and A&M (US) the next. In 1991 the company changed its name to Koninklijke ("Royal") Philips Electronics.

Ill-timed product introductions contributed to huge losses in the early 1990s. Philips cut some 60,000 jobs and sold money-losing businesses, including its computer business. Cor Boonstra, a former Sara Lee executive, was named chairman and president in 1996. Philips took a $478 million restructuring hit that year as it changed gears. The company sold its cellular communications business in 1996 to AT&T and merged its systems integration unit with BSO/Origin to form Origin B.V.

Continuing to focus on core businesses, it sold its 75% stake in PolyGram to booze and entertainment giant Seagram for $10.2 billion and bought US-based medical instruments maker ATL Ultrasound in 1998. Also that year, Philips sold its optoelectronics unit to Uniphase Corp. (now JDS Uniphase) in exchange for stock (which it divested in 2000), and announced plans with Taiwan Semiconductor to build a $1.2 billion semiconductor plant in Singapore (set to open in 2001).

The company formed an alliance with Sun Microsystems and Sony in early 1999 to develop appliances that use the Internet. Philips then launched a hostile takeover of microchip maker VLSI Technology and, after negotiations, bought VLSI for nearly $1 billion. In mid-1999 it bought a 50% stake in flat-panel display maker LG LCD, a subsidiary of LG Group, for $1.6 billion; it was renamed LG.Philips LCD Co.

In March 2000 the company formed TriMedia Technologies with Sony to create embedded processor core designs and software. Also that month, Philips began divesting its 24% stake ($3.8 billion) in semiconductor equipment maker ASM Lithography, in which it first invested in 1988. In June 2000 Philips bought 60% of top medical transcription service MedQuist.

Chairman and President: Cor Boonstra, age 61,
$1,157,139 pay
COO: Gerard Kleisterlee
EVP and CFO: Jan H.M. Hommen, age 56, $790,485 pay
EVP; President and CEO Consumer Electronics:
Adri Baan, age 57, $605,191 pay
EVP; President and CEO Semiconductors:
Arthur P. M. van der Poel, age 51, $654,956 pay
EVP; President and CEO Lighting: John W. Whybrow,
age 52, $751,610 pay
EVP; President and CEO Components:
Gerard Kleisterlee
EVP Human Resources: Tjerk Hooghiemstra
Secretary and Chief Legal Officer: Arie Westerlaken
Auditors: KPMG Accountants N.V.

LOCATIONS

HQ: The Rembrandt Tower, Amstelplein 1,
1096 HA Amsterdam, The Netherlands
Phone: +31-20-59-77-777   **Fax:** +31-20-59-77-070
US HQ: 1251 Avenue of the Americas,
New York, NY 10020
US Phone: 212-536-0500   **US Fax:** 212-536-0827
Web site: http://www.philips.com

1999 Sales

	% of total
US	24
Germany	9
UK	7
China (including Hong Kong)	6
France	6
The Netherlands	5
Other countries	43
Total	**100**

PRODUCTS/OPERATIONS

1999 Sales

	% of total
Consumer products	40
Professional	17
Lighting	14
Semiconductors	12
Components	12
Origin	3
Other	2
Total	**100**

Selected Products and Services

Advanced ceramics and modules	Flat-display systems
Business electronics	Lighting electronics
Consumer electronics	Managed services
Display components	Medical systems
Domestic appliances and personal care products	Optical storage
Enterprise solutions	Professional services
	Semiconductors
	Telecom terminals

COMPETITORS

Alcatel	LG Electronics	Samsung
AMD	Marconi	SANYO
Bose	Matsushita	Sharp
Canon	Mitsubishi	Siemens
Daewoo	Electric	Solectron
Ericsson	Motorola	Sony
Fujitsu	Moulinex	STMicro-
GE	NEC	electronics
Gillette	Nokia	Texas
Harman	Oki Electric	Instruments
International	Pioneer	THOMSON
Hitachi	Rockwell	multimedia
Intel	International	Toshiba

HISTORICAL FINANCIALS & EMPLOYEES

NYSE: PHG FYE: December 31	Annual Growth	12/90	12/91	12/92	12/93	12/94	12/95	12/96	12/97	12/98	12/99
Sales ($ mil.)	(0.5%)	33,074	33,382	32,172	30,283	35,129	40,115	39,725	37,737	35,521	31,748
Net income ($ mil.)	—	(2,684)	704	(495)	1,012	1,224	1,654	(339)	2,830	7,059	1,816
Income as % of sales	—	—	2.1%	—	3.3%	3.5%	4.1%	—	7.5%	19.9%	5.7%
Earnings per share ($)	—	(2.28)	0.49	(0.41)	0.81	0.95	1.15	(0.26)	2.04	5.02	1.35
Stock price - FY high ($)	—	6.44	5.06	5.64	5.64	8.73	13.76	11.08	22.91	26.52	35.18
Stock price - FY low ($)	—	2.84	2.90	2.48	2.80	5.41	7.64	7.41	10.05	10.83	17.17
Stock price - FY close ($)	31.2%	3.03	4.51	2.77	5.32	7.57	9.25	10.31	15.59	17.45	34.80
P/E - high	—	—	10	—	7	9	11	—	19	42	26
P/E - low	—	—	6	—	3	6	6	—	8	17	13
Dividends per share ($)	0.5%	0.23	0.00	0.00	0.00	0.06	0.18	0.26	0.22	0.26	0.24
Book value per share ($)	5.8%	6.80	5.77	3.71	5.42	6.33	6.51	6.58	7.62	11.78	11.32
Employees	(2.0%)	272,787	240,001	257,671	252,214	253,000	263,554	272,270	264,685	233,686	226,874

STOCK PRICE HISTORY

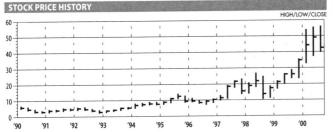

HIGH/LOW/CLOSE

1999 FISCAL YEAR-END

Debt ratio: 15.6%
Return on equity: 11.4%
Cash ($ mil.): 2,352
Current ratio: 1.55
Long-term debt ($ mil.): 2,762
No. of shares (mil.): 1,316
Dividends
  Yield: 0.7%
  Payout: 17.8%
Market value ($ mil.): 45,781

PINAULT-PRINTEMPS-REDOUTE

OVERVIEW

Pinault-Printemps-Redoute (PPR) might have its roots in timber, but its branches are spreading far and wide. The Paris-based company sells to businesses and consumers through four divisions that operate worldwide.

PPR's retail division accounts for about half of sales. It includes the world's #3 catalog merchant, Redcats, with catalogs (Brylane, La Redoute) in the US and Europe. The division also operates three large retail chains: Conforama, France's #1 home furniture and appliance retailer; Printemps, Paris' #1 department store; and Fnac books and music stores.

The company's other major division distributes directly to businesses. It includes Rexel (electrical equipment), Pinault Bois & Matériaux (building materials), and Guilbert (office supplies). Its financial division provides store credit cards.

Billionaire founder François Pinault has a cache of prestigious businesses, including auction house Christie's and, through PPR, a 42% stake in Italian fashion house Gucci Group. Pinault, through his holding company, Artemis, owns about 59% of PPR's voting shares.

HISTORY

Sixteen-year-old François Pinault left school in 1952 to join the family timber business, taking over the firm when his father died in 1963 (that year the company was renamed Pinault Group). Pinault diversified the company into wood importing and retailing and eventually built a flourishing enterprise. In 1973 Pinault began to show his talent for the art of the deal. Sensing the demand for timber was peaking, he sold 80% of the business, buying it back two years later at an 85% discount.

During the 1970s Pinault bought struggling timber businesses and turned them around. (He was helped, in part, by French government policies that subsidized purchases of failing companies in order to preserve jobs.) Pinault purchased bankrupt wood panel manufacturer Isoroy in 1986 for a token fee. In 1987 he purchased the ailing paper company Chapelle Darblay, selling it three years later at a 40% profit. By 1988, when it filed to go public on the Paris exchange, Pinault Group was a vertically integrated timber manufacturing, trading, and distribution company.

Pinault began to diversify outside the timber industry in the 1990s. In 1990 it acquired CFAO (Compagnie Française de l'Afrique Occidentale), an electrical equipment distributor. The next year the company moved into retailing with its purchase of the Conforama furniture chain from Bernard Arnault, head of luxury goods giant LVMH. In 1992 Pinault purchased Au Printemps (owner of Printemps stores and 54% of catalog company Redoute). The firm then became the Pinault-Printemps Group. The purchase of Au Printemps left the company heavily in debt, and it sold some of its noncore assets during the early 1990s.

In 1993 the group reorganized into four divisions: retail, business-to-business, financial services, and international trade. That year

Pinault-Printemps bought a majority stake in Groupelec and merged it with electrical equipment subsidiary CDME, forming Rexel. In 1994 the company completed its acquisition of Redoute. After renaming itself Pinault-Printemps-Redoute (PPR), it bought a majority stake in French book and music retailer Fnac (buying the rest in 1995). In 1995 Rexel head Serge Weinberg took over the company after CEO Pierre Blayau ran afoul of Pinault over strategy. PPR added West African pharmaceuticals distributor SCOA in 1996. While Rexel gobbled up 11 companies in Europe and the US that year, PPR launched a new chain of women's lingerie stores called Orcanta and started its own venture capital fund.

PPR acquired Becob, France's #3 building materials distributor, in 1997. Expanding globally, Redcats (Redoute's new name) launched the Vertbaudet (children's wear) and Cyrillus (sportswear) catalogs in the UK that year.

In 1998 PPR bought a majority stake in Guilbert, the European leader in office supplies and furniture, and a 44% stake in Brylane, the US's #4 mail-order company. International expansion continued as Rexel moved into Australia and New Zealand, and Fnac opened stores in Portugal and Spain. PPR also opened a new store format in France called Made in Sport (sporting goods). In addition, it began offering phone cards through subsidiary Kertel.

PPR bought the remainder of Brylane in 1999 and then moved into luxury goods with the purchase of 42% of Gucci. The company also launched a new division to oversee the online efforts of its various businesses. In early 2000 PPR bought France's largest computer retailer, Surcouf.

Chairman of the Management Board and CEO:
Serge Weinberg, age 49
Deputy CEO e-commerce; Chairman and CEO, Fnac:
François-Henri Pinault, age 38
VP Corporate Communications: Vincent de La Vaissière
VP Human Resources: François Potier
VP Strategy and Planning: Jean François Nebel
Corporate Secretary and CFO: Patrice Marteau
Chairman and CEO, REDCATS: Hartmut Krämer,
age 53
Chairman and CEO, Rexel: Alain Redheuil, age 52
Chairman of the Management Board; CEO, Conforama:
Jean-Claude Darrouzet, age 52
**Chairman of the Management Board; CEO,
France-Printemps:** Per Kaufmann, age 44
Chairman of the Management Board, Guilbert:
Jean Charles Pauze
Auditors: Deloitte Touche Tohmatsu;
KPMG Fiduciaire de France

HQ: 18, place Henri-Bergson, 75008 Paris, France
Phone: +33-1-44-90-61-00   **Fax:** +33-1-44-90-62-77
Web site: http://www.pprgroup.com

1999 Sales

	% of total
France	52
Europe	22
Americas	17
Africa	4
Oceania	3
Asia	2
Total	**100**

1999 Sales

	% of total
Electrical equipment	28
Apparel & accessories	23
Leisure & culture	16
Household equipment	14
Office equipment	6
Construction materials	5
Services	3
Automobiles	2
Pharmaceuticals	2
Food	1
Total	**100**

Selected Operations
CFAO (93%; distribution of automobiles, motorcycles,
pharmaceuticals, and consumer goods)
Conforama (furniture and appliances)
Credit and Financial Services (credit cards)
Fnac (electronics, books, music)
Gucci Group N.V. (42%, leather goods and apparel)
Guilbert (92%; distribution of office products and
furniture)
Pinault Bois & Matériaux (distribution of lumber and
building supplies)
Printemps (department stores in France)
Redcats (catalogs)
Rexel (72%; distribution of electrical equipment)

Carrefour	Kingfisher
Casino Guichard	LVMH
Consolidated Electrical	METRO AG
Galeries Lafayette	Otto Versand
Graybar Electric	Virgin Group
IKEA	

Euronext Paris: PP FYE: December 31	Annual Growth	12/90	12/91	12/92	12/93	12/94	12/95	12/96	12/97	12/98	12/99
Sales (€ mil.)	16.9%	4,625	5,535	10,707	9,650	10,793	11,860	12,256	13,595	16,515	18,912
Net income (€ mil.)	33.0%	48	77	89	78	185	231	315	435	508	626
Income as % of sales	—	1.0%	1.4%	0.8%	0.8%	1.7%	1.9%	2.6%	3.2%	3.1%	3.3%
Earnings per share (€)	24.1%	—	—	—	—	1.80	2.10	2.80	3.60	4.30	5.30
Stock price - FY high (€)	—	—	—	—	—	30.64	35.52	64.61	99.58	166.47	264.80
Stock price - FY low (€)	—	—	—	—	—	23.93	27.44	29.82	61.31	97.90	134.40
Stock price - FY close (€)	55.4%	—	—	—	—	28.90	29.79	62.75	97.90	162.82	262.00
P/E - high	—	—	—	—	—	17	17	23	28	39	50
P/E - low	—	—	—	—	—	13	13	11	17	23	25
Dividends per share (€)	20.5%	—	—	—	—	0.70	0.70	1.00	1.20	1.40	1.78
Book value per share (€)	21.9%	—	—	—	—	19.84	22.47	24.16	27.12	31.57	53.50
Employees	5.5%	—	—	53,914	50,586	60,843	59,299	57,241	59,501	69,690	78,540

HIGH/LOW/CLOSE

Debt ratio: 38.4%
Return on equity: 12.4%
Cash (€ mil.): 4,349
Current ratio: 2.71
Long-term debt (€ mil.): 3,964
No. of shares (mil.): 119
Dividends
  Yield: 0.0%
  Payout: 0.3%
Market value ($ mil.): 31,273
Sales ($ mil.): 19,002

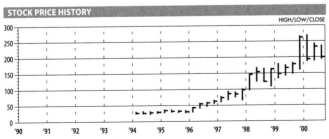

PIONEER CORPORATION

OVERVIEW

Trailblazing Pioneer (formerly Pioneer Electronic) is setting a course for a brave new world of "digital convergence." The Tokyo-based company — Pioneer Kabushiki Kaisha in Japanese — was the first to give us the laser disc (LD), car CD players, and car navigation devices that use a satellite-based global positioning system (GPS). A leading maker of consumer and commercial electronics, its products include car audio and navigation systems (about 45% of sales), DVD products, projection TVs, karaoke systems, cellular phones, CD-ROM drives, home stereo equipment, and various formats of entertainment software (some of which feature Pioneer-produced music and animation).

Pioneer is placing more energy on newer products, especially in the DVD arena (an area expected to have long-term growth). The company is also focusing efforts on its new plasma display technology and the development of digital networking hardware and related services. It believes its future lies in digital convergence — products that blend home entertainment, digital technology, and system networking. To meet its goal of doubling revenues by 2005, Pioneer is streamlining its manufacturing operations and trimming its workforce some 10% by 2002.

HISTORY

Nozomu Matsumoto, son of a Christian missionary, first heard high-fidelity speakers in 1932; nothing made in Japan compared in quality. In 1938 he founded Fukuin Shokai Denki Seisakusho (Gospel Electric Works) in Osaka to repair radios and speakers. It later began making these items. Matsumoto designed the company's trademark — a tuning fork overlaying the symbol for the ohm (a unit for measuring electrical resistance) — and chose the brand name Pioneer to reflect the company's spirit.

The firm introduced turntables and amplifiers in 1955 and hi-fi receivers in 1958. By the 1960s Pioneer Electronic was Japan's #1 audio equipment maker. It introduced the world's first stereo with speakers separate from the control unit in 1962 and the world's first car stereo in 1963. Subsidiaries opened in the US and Europe in 1966.

Convinced that laser disc (LD) technology was the wave of the future, Pioneer started work on an LD video player in 1972. Pioneer was listed on the NYSE four years later. It partnered with DiscoVision Associates (DVA, a partnership between IBM and Music Corporation of America) in 1977 to form Universal Pioneer Corporation (UPC). Home LD players appeared in the US in 1980 and in Japan in 1981. But consumers wanted machines that could record, not just play, and demand for LDs remained sluggish; Pioneer's competitors let it have the LD business to itself.

Matsumoto's eldest son, Seiya, became president in 1982. Two years later Pioneer introduced the world's first car CD system; it also created an LD/CD player, perhaps hoping customers would react better to LD products if they were combined with other features. Pioneer branched into office automation, introducing the Write-Once Read-Many (WORM) optical memory disk in 1985. In 1989 it bought DVA, by then a leading optical-disk research firm with more than 1,400 patents. Also that year it formed Pioneer Trimble with US-based Trimble Navigation to develop a computerized car navigation system.

Pioneer sold record company joint venture Warner-Pioneer to partner Warner — now Time Warner — in 1989, but it took another stab at the US entertainment business the next year when it bought 10% of theatrical film-maker Carolco Pictures (*Basic Instinct*). But like many high-profile Japanese investments in the US, Carolco turned sour: It filed for Chapter 11 bankruptcy protection in 1995, leading Pioneer to write off its investment.

With sales not meeting expectations, in 1996 Pioneer replaced Seiya as president with his in-law Kaneo Ito (former head of Pioneer's Europe sales network); Seiya became chairman and his brother Kanya was made VC. The company reentered the entertainment business with the 1996 launch of Pioneer Music Group. In 1997 Pioneer restructured itself into three separate operating units: Home Entertainment, Mobile Entertainment, and Business Systems; it added a Display Products unit the following year.

In 1999 the company opted for a simpler moniker, removing the word "electronic" from its name. Chairman Seiya died that year and was replaced by brother Kanya. With price wars and slow sales in its software business eroding profits, Pioneer announced in late 1999 that it would cut more than 2,500 jobs. (It cut 1,500 jobs in 1996.)

Chairman: Kanya Matsumoto
President: Kaneo Ito
EVP: Yoshimichi Inada
Senior Managing Director: Katsuhiro Abe
Managing Director: Takashi Kobayashi
Managing Director: Akira Niijima
Managing Director: Shoichi Yamada
Director: Hiroshi Aiba
Director: Toshihisa Koga
Director: Hiroshi Kuribayashi
Director: Satoshi Matsumoto
Director: Tadahiro Yamaguchi
Director: Shinji Yasuda
Auditors: Deloitte Touche Tohmatsu

LOCATIONS

HQ: 4-1, Meguro 1-chome, Meguro-ku,
Tokyo 153-8654, Japan
Phone: +81-3-3494-1111   **Fax:** +81-3-3495-4431
US HQ: 2265 E. 220th St., Long Beach, CA 90810
US Phone: 213-746-6337   **US Fax:** 310-952-2943
Web site: http://www.pioneer.co.jp

Pioneer has about 40 manufacturing facilities in Asia,
Europe, and North America. Its products are sold
around the world.

2000 Sales

	$ mil.	% of total
Japan	1,963	35
North America	1,712	30
Europe	1,281	23
Other regions	671	12
Total	**5,627**	**100**

PRODUCTS/OPERATIONS

2000 Sales

	$ mil.	% of total
Car electronics	2,320	41
Audio/video products	1,793	32
Audio/video software	450	8
Other software	1,064	19
Total	**5,627**	**100**

Selected Products

Amplifiers	Factory automation
AV receivers	systems
Cable TV systems	Laser disc players
equipment	Laser karaoke systems
Car navigation systems	Minidisc players
Car stereos	Multiscreen video systems
CD players	Online karaoke systems
CD recorders	Optical memory
CD-ROM drives	disk drives
Cellular phones	Plasma displays
Digital direct-broadcast	Prerecorded videotapes
satellite decoders	Projection TVs
DVD players	Speaker systems
	Stereo systems

COMPETITORS

Aiwa	Nokia
Bose	Philips Electronics
Fujitsu	Samsung Electronics
Harman International	SANYO
Hitachi	Sharp
LG Electronics	Siemens
Matsushita	Sony
Motorola	THOMSON multimedia
NEC	Toshiba

HISTORICAL FINANCIALS & EMPLOYEES

NYSE: PIO FYE: March 31	Annual Growth	3/91	3/92	3/93	3/94	3/95	3/96	3/97	3/98	3/99	3/00
Sales ($ mil.)	3.1%	4,265	4,618	5,135	4,973	5,728	4,779	4,456	4,241	4,701	5,627
Net income ($ mil.)	(7.3%)	244	215	94	64	(13)	(94)	20	47	10	123
Income as % of sales	—	5.7%	4.6%	1.8%	1.3%	—	—	0.5%	1.1%	0.2%	2.2%
Earnings per share ($)	(7.3%)	1.36	1.19	0.52	0.35	(0.08)	(0.52)	0.11	0.26	0.05	0.69
Stock price - FY high ($)	—	43.38	37.50	30.63	29.75	30.13	21.88	23.88	27.25	21.25	34.75
Stock price - FY low ($)	—	26.50	23.00	17.13	20.13	20.13	15.63	16.00	15.06	14.88	16.13
Stock price - FY close ($)	(2.0%)	35.00	28.00	20.88	24.00	20.25	21.00	16.75	16.19	18.63	29.19
P/E - high	—	32	32	71	331	—	—	217	105	425	50
P/E - low	—	19	19	40	224	—	—	145	58	298	23
Dividends per share ($)	(5.3%)	0.13	0.17	0.17	0.19	0.21	0.12	0.02	0.00	0.04	0.08
Book value per share ($)	3.3%	12.30	13.83	15.50	16.79	18.47	15.55	14.07	13.93	14.42	16.41
Employees	6.7%	15,307	16,574	17,340	18,341	18,341	19,378	19,962	20,470	23,647	27,414

STOCK PRICE HISTORY

HIGH/LOW/CLOSE

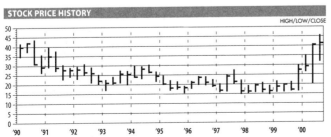

2000 FISCAL YEAR-END

Debt ratio: 13.1%
Return on equity: 4.5%
Cash ($ mil.): 1,432
Current ratio: 1.93
Long-term debt ($ mil.): 444
No. of shares (mil.): 180
Dividends
  Yield: 0.3%
  Payout: 11.6%
Market value ($ mil.): 5,242

PIRELLI S.P.A.

OVERVIEW

Pirelli can transport you down the information superhighway as swiftly as the autobahn. Milan, Italy-based Pirelli S.p.A. is a holding company best known for tires — but its cables (power, telecommunications, and fiber optic) account for 60% of sales. Pirelli tires are made for cars, motorcycles, trucks, and farm machinery. Pirelli complements its businesses with geographic diversity: Italy accounts for just over 10% of sales.

Pirelli has sold its terrestrial fiber-optic systems business to Cisco Systems and has agreed to sell its fiber-optic telecommunications business to Corning. Meanwhile, Pirelli is positioning itself to become the world's #1 maker of power cable, surpassing current leader France-based Alcatel by acquiring US-based General Cable's Bicc General division. The deal is waiting for approval from the European Commission.

HISTORY

After fighting for the unification of Italy with Garibaldi in the 1860s, Giovanni Battista Pirelli observed that France, not Italy, was providing rubber tubes for an Italian ship salvage attempt. The young patriot reacted by founding Pirelli & Co. in Milan, Italy, in 1872 to manufacture rubber products. In 1879 Pirelli began making insulated cables for the rapidly growing telegraph industry, and by 1890 he was making bicycle tires. Pirelli introduced his first air-filled automobile tire in 1899.

Foreign expansion began when the company opened cable factories in Spain (1902), the UK (1914), and Argentina (1917). It set up Societe Internationale Pirelli (SIP) in Switzerland in 1937 and consolidated all non-Italian operations within it. After WWII the group expanded along with the growth in worldwide auto sales. Pirelli began production in Turkey and Greece in 1962, and then six years later it set up cable plants in Peru.

Pirelli's first radial tires (early 1970s) backfired when they wore out too quickly. In 1971 the company swapped stock with tire maker Dunlop (UK). Although the firms engaged in joint research and development (R&D), they never consolidated production.

Pirelli S.p.A., the Italian operating company, and SIP became holding companies in 1982 by transferring their operating units into jointly owned Pirelli Societe Generale (Switzerland). That year Pirelli started producing fiber-optic cables.

Heavy spending on R&D and new equipment bolstered the newly unified tire business, and the 1986 purchase of Metzeler Kautscuk of Germany made Pirelli one of the world's largest motorcycle tire manufacturers.

Pirelli S.p.A. became an operating company in 1988 when it bought SIP's Pirelli Societe Generale holdings. It launched a hostile bid for Firestone through Pirelli Tyre, but was outbid by Bridgestone. Pirelli settled for the much smaller Armstrong Tire. In 1989 Pirelli sold nearly 24% of Pirelli Tyre to the public.

In 1990 Pirelli proposed an unusually complex and convoluted merger with Continental AG (Germany) designed to leave Pirelli in control. Continental declined, but negotiations continued throughout 1991 until Continental terminated the talks after learning of Pirelli's deteriorating financial condition.

The company won a contract in 1996 to install New Zealand's first long-distance photonic systems and in 1997 began a three-year, $170 million plant expansion in Gravatai, Brazil. Pirelli became a top power-cable maker with operations in more than 20 countries in 1998 by acquiring Germany-based Siemens' power cable unit in a $277 million deal.

In 1999 Pirelli agreed to ally with Cooper Tire and Rubber, including an arrangement whereby Cooper would distribute and sell Pirelli tires for passenger cars and light trucks in the US, Canada, and Mexico. In return, Pirelli agreed to sell Cooper tires in South America. Additionally, Pirelli Cables Australia acquired Metal Manufacturers Ltd's energy cable business to strengthen its market share down under.

In 1999 Pirelli unveiled a compact, computerized manufacturing system designed to cut the cost of tire production about 25%, while raising tire quality. (A pilot plant using the system is slated to begin producing tires in 2000.) Pirelli sold its terrestrial optical systems business to Cisco Systems for about $2.15 billion; Cisco agreed to invest $100 million in Pirelli's optical components and undersea cable transmissions divisions. The next year Pirelli agreed to buy General Cable's European, African, and Asian energy cable businesses for $216 million. Also in 2000, the company agreed to sell its fiber-optic telecommunications business to Corning for about $3.6 billion.

OFFICERS

Chairman and CEO: Marco Tronchetti Provera
Deputy Chairman: Alberto Pirelli
General Manager, Cables and Systems Sector:
Giuseppe Morchio
General Manager, Finance and Administration:
Carlo Buora
General Manager, Tyre Sector: Giovanni Ferrario
Secretary: Sergio Lamacchia
Auditors: PricewaterhouseCoopers

LOCATIONS

HQ: Viale Sarca, 222, 20126 Milan, Italy
Phone: +39-02-6442-4688   **Fax:** +39-02-6442-4686
US HQ: 300 George St., New Haven, CT 06511
US Phone: 203-784-2200   **US Fax:** 203-784-2408
Web site: http://www.pirelli.com

1999 Sales

	% of total
Europe	
Italy	12
Other countries	46
North America	15
Central & South America	17
Australia, Africa & Asia	10
Total	**100**

PRODUCTS/OPERATIONS

1999 Sales

	% of total
Cables & systems	60
Tires	40
Total	**100**

Selected Subsidiaries
Aberdare Cables Ltd. (UK, cables and systems)
Bergmann Kabel und Leitungen GmbH (cables and
systems, Germany)
Cables Pirelli SA (France)
Central Tyre Ltd. (UK)
CPK Auto Products Ltd. (UK, tires)
Desco Fabrica Portuguesa de Material Electrico e
Electronico SA (71%, cables and systems, Portugal)
Fercable SA (cable and systems)
Fibre Ottiche Sud FOS SpA (optical fibers)
Fipla SA (67%, cables and systems, Argentina)
Metzeler Motorcycle Tire North America Corp. (US)
MKM Magyar Kabel Muvek RT. (cables and systems,
Hungary)
Pirelli Cables and Systems Inc. (Canada)
Pirelli Construction Services Inc. (cables and systems,
US)
Pirelli Deutchland AG (99%, Germany)
Pirelli Gesellschaft mbH (tires, Austria)
Pirelli Informatica SpA (information systems)
Pirelli Productos Especiais Ltda (cables and systems,
Brazil)
Pirelli Tyres Belux SA (tires, Belgium)
Pirelli Tire Inc (Canada)

COMPETITORS

Alcatel	Marmon Group
Balfour Beatty	Michelin
Bridgestone	Nokia
Cable Design Technologies	Nortel Networks
CIENA	Pacific Dunlop
Continental AG	Sime Darby
Corning	Southwire
Goodyear	Superior TeleCom
Lucent	

HISTORICAL FINANCIALS & EMPLOYEES

Italian: P FYE: December 31	Annual Growth	12/90	12/91	12/92	12/93	12/94	12/95	12/96	12/97	12/98	12/99
Sales (€ mil.)	2.2%	5,351	5,316	4,370	4,884	5,056	5,626	5,288	5,818	5,608	6,482
Net income (€ mil.)	21.7%	52	(321)	(54)	(32)	57	133	200	238	276	305
Income as % of sales	—	1.0%	—	—	—	1.1%	2.4%	3.8%	4.1%	4.9%	4.7%
Earnings per share (€)	(14.3%)	0.60	(0.50)	(0.04)	(0.02)	0.03	0.09	0.14	0.14	0.13	0.15
Stock price - FY high (€)	—	1.64	1.04	0.77	1.17	1.75	1.39	2.07	2.77	3.69	3.08
Stock price - FY low (€)	—	0.75	0.48	0.51	0.56	0.99	0.92	0.98	1.44	1.80	1.88
Stock price - FY close (€)	12.3%	0.86	0.55	0.58	1.11	1.12	1.06	1.45	2.44	2.73	2.45
P/E - high	—	3	—	—	—	58	15	15	20	28	21
P/E - low	—	1	—	—	—	33	10	7	10	14	13
Dividends per share (€)	2.8%	0.08	0.05	0.00	0.00	0.00	0.00	0.05	0.06	0.07	0.10
Book value per share (€)	(4.0%)	1.86	1.40	0.97	0.86	1.00	1.13	1.18	1.31	1.29	1.29
Employees	(3.2%)	53,540	51,572	45,726	42,132	40,588	38,106	36,534	36,211	38,209	40,103

STOCK PRICE HISTORY   HIGH/LOW/CLOSE

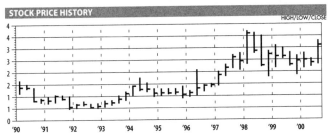

1999 FISCAL YEAR-END
Debt ratio: 37.6%
Return on equity: 12.4%
Cash (€ mil.): 502
Current ratio: 1.68
Long-term debt (€ mil.): 1,480
No. of shares (mil.): 1,897
Dividends
  Yield: 0.0%
  Payout: 0.7%
Market value ($ mil.): 4,669
Sales ($ mil.): 6,513

PLACER DOME INC.

OVERVIEW

When an Ontario prospector slipped and fell in 1909, he dislodged a clump of moss to reveal a dome-shaped rock sparkling with gold. Thus began the chain of events that led to the creation of Placer Dome. Vancouver-based Placer Dome, among the world's largest gold-mining companies, produces about 3.1 million ounces of gold a year. The company also produces silver (10.8 million ounces in 1999) and copper (about 267 million pounds in 1999). It has about 66 million ounces in gold reserves. Placer Dome owns and operates seven mines and owns interests in nine mines in Australia, Canada, Papua New Guinea, South Africa, South America, and the US.

The company paid a pricey $1 billion for the Nevada-based Getchell Gold mine, for which production has been pushed back to 2005. CEO Jay Taylor has been persuading shareholders to hang onto their stakes in Placer Dome, even as the company plans closures of its Australia, Papua New Guinea, and Montana mines. He's banking on the success of Getchell and another acquisition, the South Deep mine in South Africa.

HISTORY

Placer Dome was formed by the 1987 amalgamation of three Canadian mining firms: Dome Mines Ltd. (the famed gold-studded dome of rock that gave the company its name was found in 1909 and the company incorporated in 1910), Placer Development Ltd. (1926), and Campbell Red Lake Mines (1944). The merger formed North America's largest gold-mining firm. When Australian mining companies moved to take over Placer and Dome in the 1980s, Placer engineered the merger.

After consolidation, Placer Dome began acquiring new operations using gold loans, in which the company borrowed gold from its lenders' reserves to make acquisitions and then repaid the loans in gold obtained from its mining operations. It bought Consolidated TVX Mining Corp. in the late 1980s. The company increased its interest in Nevada's Cortez Gold Mine Joint Venture in 1991 and bought half of Chile's Compañía Minera Zaldívar in 1992. That year Placer Dome's sales topped $1 billion for the first time.

In 1993 mining veteran John Willson became president and CEO and melded the company into an organization focused on regional operations. He also narrowed Placer Dome's primary focus to mining gold.

The company began production at two new mines in 1996, the Musselwhite Mine in northern Ontario and the Pipeline Mine in Nevada. Despite this high note, the company ran into trouble. A major spill of 4 million tons of mine tailings at the company's 40%-owned Marcopper Mine in the Philippines led to a $43 million charge (the company sold its stake in Marcopper in 1997). In addition, Placer Dome began protracted battles, one to acquire Papua New Guinea-based Highlands Gold, the other to operate the Las Cristinas Mine in Venezuela.

The Highlands Gold acquisition evolved into a hostile takeover bid. In Venezuela, Crystallex International Corporation disputed Placer Dome's claim to Las Cristinas, believed to be one of the richest gold deposits in South America. (The court battle, which Placer Dome won, put development of the mine on hold for a few months in 1998.)

Also in 1997 both the Pipeline and Musselwhite mines in North America began producing their first gold within a week of each other. That year Placer Dome completed its takeover of Highlands Gold, including a 50% stake in Papua New Guinea's Porgera Mine.

Weak gold prices and writedowns for mining interests led to a big loss for Placer Dome in 1997. Despite the loss, the company continued to add mining properties. In 1998 it bought 51% of the Aldebaran copper-gold property in Chile, as well as the Can Can Mine (also in Chile) with joint venture partner PVX Gold. The next year Placer Dome bought a 50% share in the undeveloped South Deep gold deposit in South Africa (Western Areas Ltd. would own the rest) and Getchell Gold (two mines in central Nevada) for about $1 billion. Low metal prices caused Placer Dome to put operations at its Las Cristinas mine on hold, although later that year a promise by 15 European central banks to limit the sale of gold reserves raised gold prices.

Willson retired and Jay Taylor, an EVP and 20-year veteran of Placer Dome, replaced him as president and CEO in 2000. To shareholder dismay, the company announced that the Getchell mine might not produce gold until 2005.

Chairman Emeritus: Fraser M. Fell
Chairman: Robert M. Franklin
VC: John M. Willson, $644,098 pay
(prior to title change)
President and CEO: Jay K. Taylor, $417,283 pay
(prior to promotion)
EVP and CFO: Rex J. McLennan
EVP Asia/Pacific: Dignus W. Zandee
EVP Exploration: Eliseo Gonzalez-Urien, $318,000 pay
EVP Strategic Development: Ian G. Austin,
$345,437 pay
EVP United States and Latin America:
William M. Hayes, $324,558 pay
VP and Controller: Bruce B. Nicol
VP and Treasurer: Stephen J. Smith, age 44
VP Corporate Relations: David S. Smith
VP Human Resources: Jennifer Quaggin
VP, Secretary, and General Counsel: J. Donald Rose
Auditors: Ernst & Young LLP

LOCATIONS

HQ: 1055 Dunsmuir St., Ste. 1600, Bentall IV,
Vancouver, British Columbia V7X 1L3, Canada
Phone: 604-682-7082   **Fax:** 604-682-7092
Web site: http://www.placerdome.com

PRODUCTS/OPERATIONS

1999 Sales

	% of total
Gold	94
Copper	4
Silver	1
Other	1
Total	**100**

Selected Properties

Australia
Granny Smith Mine (60%, gold)
Kidston Mine (70%, gold)
Osborne Mine (copper and gold)

Canada
Campbell Mine (gold)
Dome Mine (gold)
Musselwhite Mine (68%, gold)

Chile
La Coipa (50%, gold and silver)Zaldivar Mine (copper)

Papua New Guinea
Misima Mine (80%, gold and silver)
Porgera Mine (50%, gold)

South Africa
South Deep (50%, gold)

US
Bald Mountain (gold)
Cortez Mine (60%, gold)
Getchell Mine (gold)
Golden Sunlight Mine (gold)

Venezuela
Las Cristinas (70%, gold)

COMPETITORS

Anglo American	Freeport-	Peñoles
Barrick Gold	McMoRan	Phelps Dodge
Battle Mountain	Copper & Gold	Pittston Minerals
Gold	Grupo Mexico	Rio Algom
BHP	Harmony Gold	Rio Tinto
Brascan	Homestake	Limited
Carso	Mining	Rio Tinto plc
Codelco	METALEUROP	Trelleborg
CVRD	Newmont	UM
	Mining	WMC Limited

HISTORICAL FINANCIALS & EMPLOYEES

NYSE: PDG FYE: December 31	Annual Growth	12/90	12/91	12/92	12/93	12/94	12/95	12/96	12/97	12/98	12/99
Sales ($ mil.)	3.9%	931	969	1,020	917	899	1,029	1,157	1,209	1,279	1,315
Net income ($ mil.)	(10.6%)	165	(236)	111	107	105	74	(65)	(249)	105	60
Income as % of sales	—	17.7%	—	10.9%	11.7%	11.7%	7.2%	—	—	8.2%	4.6%
Earnings per share ($)	(20.3%)	1.24	(1.00)	0.47	0.45	0.44	0.31	(0.27)	(1.06)	0.36	0.16
Stock price - FY high ($)	—	21.50	16.75	12.38	12.38	25.63	28.25	29.50	22.38	17.88	17.50
Stock price - FY low ($)	—	13.38	9.63	8.50	11.25	18.13	18.38	21.00	10.50	7.88	9.19
Stock price - FY close ($)	(5.0%)	17.00	11.00	11.63	24.88	21.75	24.13	21.75	12.69	11.50	10.75
P/E - high	—	80	—	26	57	64	95	—	—	50	109
P/E - low	—	50	—	18	25	41	59	—	—	22	57
Dividends per share ($)	(11.5%)	0.30	0.26	0.26	0.22	0.27	0.30	0.30	0.30	0.05	0.10
Book value per share ($)	0.4%	7.45	6.26	6.15	6.36	6.41	6.45	7.24	6.52	6.79	7.73
Employees	9.5%	5,305	5,305	4,690	6,231	6,231	8,000	8,300	8,400	7,300	12,000

STOCK PRICE HISTORY

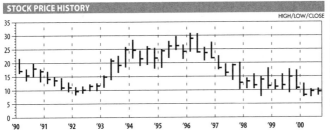

HIGH/LOW/CLOSE

1999 FISCAL YEAR-END

Debt ratio: 19.8%
Return on equity: 3.3%
Cash ($ mil.): 192
Current ratio: 1.83
Long-term debt ($ mil.): 624
No. of shares (mil.): 327
Dividends
 Yield: 0.9%
 Payout: 62.5%
Market value ($ mil.): 3,520

POHANG IRON & STEEL CO., LTD.

OVERVIEW

Pohang Iron & Steel Co. (POSCO) steeled itself against unfavorable market conditions in its neck of the woods, but things are looking up. The Pohang City, South Korea-based company is the world's #1 steel company, ahead of Nippon Steel of Japan. It makes hot- and cold-rolled steel products, stainless steel, and other value-added products for industries such as shipbuilding and construction. POSCO has the capability to produce 28 million tons of steel per year, but the late 1990s economic slowdown in Asia and excessive world supply caused the company to suspend or halt projects in China and Indonesia while reducing steel shipments to the US, the latter in an effort to reduce trade frictions. The price of

steel has rebounded, however, as Asia — except for Japan — recovers and steel demand increases. POSCO also has interests in engineering and construction.

POSCO plans to reduce or sell its low-profit operations, such as its minimills, and concentrate on higher-margin specialized products needed by automotive, electrical, and electronic manufacturers. POSCO is also preparing for the end of its 30-year monopoly in primary steelmaking in Korea as the government privatizes its ownership. The company has also formed an alliance with long-time rival Nippon Steel. The South Korean government holds a 9.8% stake in POSCO through its state-run Korea Development Bank.

HISTORY

After the Korean War, South Korea, the US, and its allies wanted to rebuild South Korea's infrastructure as quickly as possible. Steel was given a high priority, and before long about 15 companies were making various types of steel, including sheet, bar, rod, and pipe. Quality was a problem, though, as the companies used dated production processes.

With the backing of Korean president Chung Hee Park, momentum for a large steel plant grew in the late 1960s. In 1967 the South Korean government and Korean International Steel Associates (KISA) — a consortium of seven Western steelmakers — signed an agreement that called for the completion of an integrated mill by 1972. Pohang Iron & Steel, the operating company, was incorporated in 1968. Efforts to raise the necessary capital failed, however, and KISA was dissolved in 1969.

Undaunted, the Koreans turned to the Japanese, who arranged loans covering most of the mill's costs and the early phases of planning and construction. The Japanese also transferred the technology needed to run such a plant. Slow and deliberate planning resulted in a plant far away from Seoul (part of a plan to locate industries throughout the country) and a design that lent itself to future expansion. The first stage, including a blast furnace and two steel converters, was completed in 1973. By the time the fourth stage of construction began in 1979, the Koreans had gained enough confidence to take over many of the tasks. When the last stage was completed in 1981, the plant had an annual capacity of 8.5 million tons.

To ensure steel of acceptable quality, POSCO focused first on plain high-carbon steel for general construction, rather than on specialized

(and difficult to produce) varieties. It gradually broadened its specialized offerings.

By 1987 POSCO was exporting almost 3 million tons of steel a year and using its knowledge to assist in plant construction projects in other countries. Unfortunately for POSCO, South Korea has little native iron ore, and the company has had to look for iron elsewhere. To that end, the company has developed about 18 joint ventures in 10 countries, including six in China, as well as operations in Australia, Brazil, Canada, Indonesia, Myanmar, Thailand, the US, and Venezuela.

The South Korean government sold a 5% stake in POSCO to the public in 1998 and vowed to open up the primary steelmaking industry to competition. However, facing a severe downturn in steel demand that year because of sluggishness in Asian and domestic markets, the company canceled two projects in China, suspended two in Indonesia, and announced that it would sell POSVEN, its Venezuelan affiliate. POSCO also planned to integrate POSAC (design and appraisal) into POSCO Engineering & Construction Co., Ltd., and it will merge Pohang Coated Steel Co. with Pohang Steel Industries Co. The South Korean government continued selling off its 13% stake in 1999.

In 2000 POSCO sold its 51% stake in telecommunications company Shinsegi Telecom to SK Telecom in exchange for cash and a 6.5% stake in SK Telecom. It also formed a strategic alliance — exploration of joint ventures, shared research, and joint procurement — with Nippon Steel, the world's #2 steel maker. The deal also calls for each to take increased (to two or three percent) equity stakes in the other.

OFFICERS

Chairman and Co-CEO: Yoo Sang-Boo
President and Co-CEO: Lee Ku-Taek
SEVP Strategic Planning, PR, General Administration, Human Resources, Finance, Raw Materials, Procurement and Investment Finance, and Public Policy: Kim Yong-Woon
SEVP and General Superintendent, Marketing: Park Moon-Soo
EVP and General Superintendent, Pohang Works: Kang Chang-Oh
EVP and General Superintendent, Kwangyang Works: Han Soo-Yang
EVP and General Superintendent, Technical Research Laboratories: Lee Won-Pyo
EVP Corporate Strategic Planning Dept. I, II: Choi Kwang-Woong
SVP Human Resources Administration, Labor Relations, and Education and Training Center: Park Jung-Woo
SVP Finance Dept. and Finance Management Dept.: Hwang Tae-Hyun

LOCATIONS

HQ: Pohang Jehchul Chusik Hoesa,
1, Koedong-dong, Nam-ku, Pohang City,
Kyongsangpuk 790-600, South Korea
Phone: +82-562-220-0114   **Fax:** +82-562-220-6000
US HQ: Pohang Steel America Corp.,
Woodcliff Lake, NJ 07675
US Phone: 201-782-9200   **US Fax:** 201-782-9210
Web site: http://www.posco.co.kr

POSCO operates subsidiary companies in Australia, Brazil, Canada, China, Germany, Hong Kong, Indonesia, Japan, Myanmar, Russia, Singapore, South Africa, South Korea, Thailand, Turkey, the UK, the US, and Vietnam.

PRODUCTS/OPERATIONS

Selected Subsidiaries and Affiliates
Changwon Specialty Steel Co., Ltd. (99%, specialty steel)
Dalian POSCO-CFM Coated Steel Co., Ltd. (59%, coated-steel manufacturing, China)
Davey Distington Ltd. (54%, engineering)
IBC Corporation (58%, rent)
Pohang Steel America Corp. (99.9%, steel trading, US)
Pohang Steel Industries Co., Ltd. (coated steel)
POSCO Asia Co., Ltd. (57%, steel trading, Hong Kong)
POSCO Engineering & Construction Co., Ltd. (97%)
POSEC-Europe, Ltd. (97%, engineering, UK)
POS-Energy Co., Ltd. (99.9%)
POSLILAMA Steel Structure Co., Ltd. (68%, Vietnam)
Seung Kwang Co., Ltd. (94%, athletic facilities)
Shanghai POSEC Real Estate Development Co., Ltd. (97%, rent, China)
Zhangjiagang Pohang Stainless Steel Co., Ltd. (80%, China)

COMPETITORS

Bechtel	Mannesmann AG
Bethlehem Steel	Marubeni
Corus Group	Mitsubishi
Fluor	Mitsui
Hitachi	Nippon Steel
Hyundai	Samsung
Kawasaki Steel	Sumitomo
Kobe Steel	ThyssenKrupp
LTV	USX-U.S. Steel

HISTORICAL FINANCIALS & EMPLOYEES

NYSE: PKX FYE: December 31	Annual Growth	12/90	12/91	12/92	12/93	12/94	12/95	12/96	12/97	12/98	12/99
Sales ($ mil.)	5.2%	—	—	7,860	8,564	10,561	11,140	11,381	6,795	11,288	11,181
Net income ($ mil.)	28.6%	—	—	235	365	472	1,222	698	430	790	1,368
Income as % of sales	—	—	—	3.0%	4.3%	4.5%	11.0%	6.1%	6.3%	7.0%	12.2%
Earnings per share ($)	70.2%	—	—	—	—	0.25	3.25	1.88	1.15	2.10	3.57
Stock price - FY high ($)	—	—	—	—	—	37.88	35.50	28.25	35.00	25.19	42.19
Stock price - FY low ($)	—	—	—	—	—	25.00	20.00	18.75	14.13	10.00	13.81
Stock price - FY close ($)	3.7%	—	—	—	—	29.25	21.88	20.25	17.44	16.88	35.00
P/E - high	—	—	—	—	—	0	11	15	30	12	12
P/E - low	—	—	—	—	—	0	6	10	12	5	4
Dividends per share ($)	—	—	—	—	—	0.21	0.04	0.25	0.00	0.00	0.00
Book value per share ($)	(0.1%)	—	—	—	—	—	20.78	20.66	11.56	17.99	20.73
Employees	(2.3%)	—	—	—	—	—	—	—	29,161	28,500	—

STOCK PRICE HISTORY

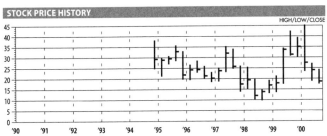

HIGH/LOW/CLOSE

1999 FISCAL YEAR-END

Debt ratio: 29.2%
Return on equity: 18.5%
Cash ($ mil.): 456
Current ratio: 1.32
Long-term debt ($ mil.): 3,292
No. of shares (mil.): 386
Dividends
  Yield: —
  Payout: —
Market value ($ mil.): 13,507

DR. ING. H. C. F. PORSCHE AG

OVERVIEW

Q: What auto designer was sought after by both Stalin and Hitler and also created the Mercedes S-class and the Volkswagen Beetle? (Hint: His last name often precedes 911, 928, 944, 956, and Boxster.)

A: Ferdinand Porsche.

Headquartered in Stuttgart, Germany, Dr.Ing.h.c.F.Porsche makes sports cars that have achieved legendary status among automotive aficionados. Newly streamlined, the company produces only two models: the rear-engine 911 and the Boxster. If you can't afford to shell out $40,000 for the "budget-priced" Boxster, then you can buy Porsche-designed watches, luggage, and tennis rackets. Porsche also offers consulting services to auto and furniture manufacturers and engineering and construction companies.

Since his arrival in the early 1990s, CEO Wendelin Wiedeking has transformed Porsche from a money-loser into a profitable carmaker by streamlining both the company's operations and its product line. The popular Boxster Roadster was followed-up with the souped-up Boxster S. With Volkswagen, Porsche is designing a luxury sport utility vehicle (SUV) for sale in 2002. Descendants of the Porsche family control the company.

HISTORY

Ferdinand Porsche was 25 when a battery-powered car with a motor he had designed was unveiled at the Paris Exposition in 1900. Six years later, Porsche was hired by Daimler Motor. During his rise to chief engineer at Daimler, he designed the famous Mercedes-Benz S-series.

Frustrated by the conservative nature of his employer, Porsche quit and opened an engine-design company bearing his name in 1931. The next year Josef Stalin offered to make Porsche the head of the Soviet Union's auto industry. Porsche turned Stalin down.

In 1933 Hitler announced his intention to build a widely affordable "volkswagen" (people's car). Soon Porsche was designing the vehicle that would become the Volkswagen Beetle. During WWII Porsche continued work on the Volkswagen project and also provided advice on increasing Germany's factory production. After the war, Ferdinand and his son Ferry were imprisoned for two years in France for allegedly abusing French laborers. Father and son were compelled to work on the Renault line of automobiles. After his release, Ferdinand reportedly burst into tears and exclaimed, "My Beetle!" when he saw his Volkswagen cars populating the streets in Germany.

By 1948 Ferdinand and Ferry had developed a Porsche sports-car prototype based on the Volkswagen. It was named the 356 because it was the 356th project undertaken at the Porsche design office. In 1950 the first Porsche 356 rolled off the assembly line in Stuttgart. Ferdinand Porsche lived just long enough to see his sports cars become highly sought by the rich and famous. He died in 1951, the same year the 1,000th Porsche was produced.

In 1952 Ferry designed the Porsche emblem, which combined the Porsche name and the Stuttgart and Wurttemberg coats of arms.

Porsches won hundreds of races during the 1950s, and the car's popularity grew. (James Dean was driving his brand-new Porsche when he was killed in a car wreck in 1955.)

By the 1960s Ferry Porsche decided to build an entirely new Porsche model that didn't rely so heavily on the Beetle's design. The company unveiled the Type 911 Porsche in 1964 and discontinued the 356 the next year. In 1973 the company went public under the Porsche AG name.

The company flourished in the 1980s, due largely to its cars' popularity in the US. By 1986 Porsche was producing almost 50,000 cars a year, with about 60% of them destined for the US market. Models introduced in the late 1980s included the 912 and 924, as well as the venerable 928.

Porsche's fortunes crashed in the early 1990s, when the company faced tough competition and a recession priced many consumers out of the sports-car market. In 1992 the company sold only 23,060 cars — 4,100 of those in the US. That year Wendelin Wiedeking, an engineering and manufacturing expert, was brought in as CEO. He cut costs, in part, by convincing most workers to reduce the number of hours they worked each day and eliminating overtime. Wiedeking also updated the 911 and initiated development of the Boxster.

Introduced in 1996, the Boxster was an instant hit — its first year of production sold out in advance. In 1998 the company initiated plans to produce a luxury SUV in partnership with Volkswagen. Porsche launched the Boxster S, featuring a 250-hp engine, in 1999. The next year Porsche announced that its Cayenne SUV — which shares a platform with Volkswagen's SUV — would hit the market in 2002.

Chairman of the Supervisory Board: Helmut Sihler
Deputy Chairman of the Supervisory Board: Hans Baur
President and CEO: Wendelin Wiedeking
CFO: Holger P. Haerter
Director Human Resources: Harro Harmel
Director, Production and Logistics: Michael Macht
Director, Research and Development: Horst Marchart
Director, Sales and Marketing: Hans Riedel
Auditors: Ernst & Young

LOCATIONS

HQ: 70432 Stuttgart, Germany
Phone: +49-711-911-0   **Fax:** +49-711-911-5777
US HQ: 980 Hammond Dr., Ste. 1000,
        Atlanta, GA 30328
US Phone: 770-290-3500   **US Fax:** 770-290-3706
Web site: http://www.porsche.com

Porsche operates main production facilities in
Zuffenhausen, Germany, and in Finland.

1999 Sales

	% of total
North America	35
Germany	30
Other regions	35
Total	**100**

PRODUCTS/OPERATIONS

1999 Sales

	% of total
Vehicles	79
Spare parts & accessories	7
Other	14
Total	**100**

Selected Vehicles
Porsche 911 (rear-engine)
  Carrera (Coupe and Cabriolet)
  Carrera 4 (Coupe and Cabriolet; four-wheel drive)
  GTE (water-cooled engine)
  Turbo
Porsche Boxster and Porsche Boxster S
  (mid-engine roadsters)

COMPETITORS

BMW
DaimlerChrysler
Fiat
Ford
General Motors
Honda
Mazda
Mitsubishi
Nissan
Peugeot
Renault
Saab Automobile
Volkswagen

HISTORICAL FINANCIALS & EMPLOYEES

Frankfurt: POR3 FYE: July 31	Annual Growth	7/90	7/91	7/92	7/93	7/94	7/95	7/96	7/97	7/98	7/99
Sales (€ mil.)	10.4%	1,293	1,570	1,373	978	1,194	1,333	1,438	2,093	2,520	3,161
Net income (€ mil.)	28.9%	28	35	(36)	(122)	(77)	1	24	71	142	276
Income as % of sales	—	2.2%	2.2%	—	—	—	0.1%	1.7%	3.4%	5.6%	8.7%
Earnings per share (€)	—	—	—	—	—	(52.66)	0.51	10.74	41.41	93.57	129.87
Stock price - FY high (€)	—	—	—	—	—	454.03	487.73	472.94	1,503.20	2,914.36	4,000.00
Stock price - FY low (€)	—	—	—	—	—	365.54	256.16	301.66	421.82	1,186.20	1,750.00
Stock price - FY close (€)	41.3%	—	—	—	—	419.26	337.45	434.60	1,452.07	2,479.77	2,360.00
P/E - high	—	—	—	—	—	—	956	44	36	31	31
P/E - low	—	—	—	—	—	—	502	28	10	13	13
Dividends per share (€)	81.3%	—	—	—	—	1.28	1.28	1.28	7.67	12.78	25.05
Book value per share (€)	6.1%	—	—	—	—	249.39	240.63	273.23	340.72	242.97	335.66
Employees	0.1%	—	—	8,431	7,133	6,970	6,970	7,107	7,959	8,151	8,506

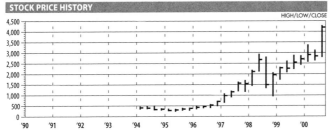

STOCK PRICE HISTORY — HIGH/LOW/CLOSE

1999 FISCAL YEAR-END
Debt ratio: 0.0%
Return on equity: —
Cash (€ mil.): 549
Current ratio: 1.55
Long-term debt (€ mil.): 0
No. of shares (mil.): 2
Dividends
  Yield: 0.0%
  Payout: 0.2%
Market value ($ mil.): 4,425
Sales ($ mil.): 3,387

PREUSSAG AG

OVERVIEW

Not long ago the only travel assistance you could get out of Preussag might have been a trip down a mineshaft. But this German conglomerate, based in Hanover, has reforged itself from a mining, shipbuilding, and steel-making firm into the top European tourism group. The Preussag group is welding together more than 350 companies into a new business entity focused on building engineering, energy and commodities, logistics, and tourism. The logistics and tourism units account for more than 60% of sales.

Preussag's restructuring has parked its tourism activities (including the former Hapag Touristik Union) under the TUI Group, which oversees some 3,600 travel agencies, some 190 hotels, more than 60 aircraft, and about 40 tour operators. The company's tourism business has expanded with the acquisition of UK tour operator Thomson Travel Group. To gain regulatory clearance for the Thomson deal, Preussag has agreed to sell its majority stake in Thomas Cook, another UK tour operator. Preussag's Hapag-Lloyd Group operates container shipping lines and cruise ships, chemicals transport specialist VTG-Lehnkering, and ALGECO, a portable buildings and logistics group.

Industrial holdings include energy and commodities firms, which produce oil and gas and trade steel and nonferrous metals. Its building engineering firms manufacture various products, including construction materials and fire protection systems.

State-owned Westdeutsche Landesbank owns 33% of Preussag, which is planning to sell off most of its nontourism businesses by 2002.

HISTORY

Preussag was founded in Berlin in 1923 as Preussische Bergwerks-und Hutten-Aktiengesellschaft (Prussian Mine and Foundry Company) to operate former state-owned mining companies, saltworks, and smelters. Despite outmoded equipment and a war-shattered economy, the company prospered. So in 1929 the Prussian parliament combined Preussag with Hibernia and Preussischen Elektrizitats to form the state-run VEBA group, hoping to stimulate foreign investment. It didn't.

Germany's military expansion of the 1930s saved Preussag from the global depression. But WWII left Preussag a shell of its former self. In 1952, as restrictions on steel production were lifted and industry rebounded, Preussag relocated to Hanover. After taking steps to re-establish itself, Preussag made a public offering in 1959; VEBA kept about 22%.

A worldwide steel glut that lasted through the 1960s forced Preussag to diversify. Acquisitions included railroad tank car and transport agent VTG and shipbuilding and chemical companies. The company also formed oil exploration unit Preussag Energie in 1968. In 1969 VEBA finally sold its remaining stake in Preussag to Westdeusche Landesbank (WestLB).

When the 1970s oil crisis drove up steel costs, Preussag began international ventures to counter falling revenues at home, and in 1981 the firm enjoyed its best postwar year. But the 1980s brought PR disasters. The European Commission fined Preussag and five other zinc producers for antitrust violations in 1984. In 1988 the US alleged that Preussag and other firms had built a poison gas plant in Libya and a chemical arms factory in Iraq. German prosecutors charged some Preussag employees with selling equipment to the Iraqi chemical weapons program.

In 1989 Preussag reorganized into a holding company with four independent units: coal, oil, natural gas, and plant construction. But it was about to take a sharp business turn. Michael Frenzel, who had managed WestLB's industry holdings, became CEO in 1994 in the midst of another steel recession. Frenzel was determined to shift Preussag away from its rusting past and toward services and technology. In 1997 it acquired container shipping and travel firm Hapag-Lloyd, which had a 30% stake in Touristik Union International (TUI). By the end of 1998 it was Europe's top tourism group after buying the rest of TUI, First Reisebuero Management, and a 25% stake in the UK's Thomas Cook (raised to 50.1% in 1999).

As part of its restructuring, Preussag traded its plant engineering units and half of its shipbuilding unit (HDW) to Babcock Borsig for a 33% stake in that company in 1999. Preussag then made plans to transfer another 25% of HDW to Sweden's Celsius in a deal (along with Babcock Borsig) to merge Celsius' Kockums submarine shipyards with HDW.

In 2000 the company announced plans to spin off its building, engineering, and energy and commodities businesses as Preussag Industrie, a separate company, in 2002. Also that year Preussag bought UK tour operator Thomson Travel Group for $2.7 billion.

Chairman, Preussag, Hapag-Lloyd, Hapag Touristik Union, TU Holding, VTG-Lehnkering, Transportmittel, Thomas Cook Holdings, and Preussag North America; Deputy Chairman, Algeco: Michael Frenzel

Executive Board, Finance and Accounting; Chairman, Wolf, Metaleurop, and Preussag Finance: Rainer Feuerhake

Executive Board, Personnel and Legal Affairs; Chairman, Preussag BKK: Wolfgang Schultze

Executive Board, Controlling; Chairman, Amalgamated Metal: Helmut Stodieck

Divisional Executive Energy: Günter Krallmann

Divisional Executive Trading: Harold Sher

Divisional Executive Building Engineering: Jens Schneider

Divisional Executive Logistics: Bernd Wrede

Divisional Executive Tourism: Ralf Corsten

Auditors: PwC Deutsche Revision

HQ: Karl-Wiechert Allee 4, D-30625 Hanover, Germany
Phone: +49-511-566-00   **Fax:** +49-511-566-1098
US HQ: 55 Railroad Ave., Greenwich, CT 06830
US Phone: 203-629-4400   **US Fax:** 203-863-0700
Web site: http://www.preussag.de

1999 Sales

	% of total
Europe	
Germany	24
Other EC	46
Other countries	6
US	13
Other regions	11
Total	**100**

1999 Sales

	% of total
Tourism	43
Energy & commodities	27
Logistics	18
Building engineering	11
Other	1
Total	**100**

Selected Subsidiaries

Amalgamated Metal Corporation PLC (AMC, 99.4%, metals trading, UK)
Deutsche Tiefbohr-AG (Deutag Group, oil and gas drilling services)
Delta Steel, Inc. (steel sales, US)
FELS-WERKE GmbH (Fels, building materials)
Feralloy Corporation (steel sales, US)
Hapag-Lloyd AG (logistics, 99.6%)
Preussag Energie GmbH (crude oil production and storage)
TUI Group GmbH (travel, 99.6%)

A.P. Moller	Deutsche Post	Lufthansa
Airtours	Evergreen	Mitsui O.S.K.
American	Marine	Lines
Express	Exxon Mobil	Nippon Yusen
APL	First Choice	KK
Bollore	Hanson	Overseas
BP	Heidelberger	Shipholding
BT Shipping	Zement	Royal Caribbean
Carlson	Hepworth	Cruises
Carnival	Karstadt	RWE-DEA
Club Med	Kvaerner	Stinnes
Crowley	Lafarge SA	Teekay
Maritime	LTU	ThyssenKrupp

German: 695200 FYE: September 30	Annual Growth	9/90	9/91	9/92	9/93	9/94	9/95	9/96	9/97	9/98	9/99
Sales (€ mil.)	6.8%	9,738	13,015	12,513	11,908	11,867	13,474	12,805	13,630	17,972	17,593
Net income (€ mil.)	8.9%	160	255	240	121	145	190	128	185	276	345
Income as % of sales	—	1.6%	2.0%	1.9%	1.0%	1.2%	1.4%	1.0%	1.4%	1.5%	2.0%
Earnings per share (€)	14.1%	—	—	—	—	0.92	1.43	0.87	1.23	1.64	1.78
Stock price - FY high (€)	—	—	—	—	—	25.46	24.08	22.60	29.45	39.32	55.90
Stock price - FY low (€)	—	—	—	—	—	20.50	19.83	17.38	17.49	23.16	38.80
Stock price - FY close (€)	19.8%	—	—	—	—	22.65	21.68	19.58	25.31	29.57	55.80
P/E - high	—	—	—	—	—	28	17	26	24	24	31
P/E - low	—	—	—	—	—	22	14	20	14	14	22
Dividends per share (€)	8.6%	—	—	—	—	0.51	0.61	0.61	0.61	0.77	0.77
Book value per share (€)	6.7%	—	—	—	—	11.36	11.25	10.67	10.55	9.75	15.72
Employees	1.0%	—	—	73,680	73,319	69,712	65,227	66,226	62,601	66,563	79,142

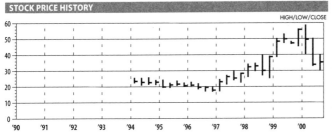

HIGH/LOW/CLOSE

Debt ratio: —
Return on equity: —
Cash (€ mil.): 3,324
Current ratio: 0.79
Long-term debt (€ mil.): —
No. of shares (mil.): 173
Dividends
  Yield: 0.0%
  Payout: 0.4%
Market value ($ mil.): 10,281
Sales ($ mil.): 18,747

PRICEWATERHOUSECOOPERS

OVERVIEW

After putting it all together, now they're taking it apart. PricewaterhouseCoopers (PwC), formed in the 1998 merger of the fourth- and sixth-largest accounting firms and now the world's largest professional services company, is splitting its auditing and consulting operations into separate businesses. The split follows the lead of rivals Andersen Worldwide, Deloitte Touche Tohmatsu, and KPMG after strong words from the SEC claiming an inherent conflict of interest between performing fiscal assurance and consulting services for the same clients.

The New York City-based partnership provides accounting, auditing, and other business services from more than 850 offices in about 150 countries. Its consulting operations are particularly strong in technology and e-commerce.

HISTORY

In 1850 Samuel Price founded an accounting firm in London and in 1865 took on partner Edwin Waterhouse. The firm and the industry grew rapidly, thanks to the growth of stock exchanges that required uniform financial statements from listees. By the late 1800s Price Waterhouse (PW) had become the world's best-known accounting firm.

US offices were opened in the 1890s, and in 1902 United States Steel chose the firm as its auditor. PW benefited from tough audit requirements instituted after 1929's market crash. The firm was given the prestigious job in 1935 of handling Academy Awards balloting. In 1946 it started a management consulting service.

PW's dominance slipped in the 1960s as it gained a reputation as the most traditional and formal of the major firms.

Acting as bankruptcy liquidator, in 1992 the UK arm of Deloitte Touche Tohmatsu sued PW for $11 billion to recover losses from the failure of Bank of Credit & Commerce International. The amount was later reduced.

Coopers & Lybrand, the product of a 1957 transatlantic merger, wrote the book on auditing. Lybrand, Ross Bros. & Montgomery was formed in 1898 by William Lybrand, Edward Ross, Adam Ross, and Robert Montgomery. In 1912 Montgomery wrote *Montgomery's Auditing,* the bible of accounting.

Cooper Brothers was founded in 1854 in London by William Cooper, eldest son of a Quaker banker. The company added additional branches in the 20th century.

In 1957 Lybrand joined up to form Coopers & Lybrand. During the 1960s the firm expanded into employee benefits and internal control consulting, building its technology capabilities in the 1970s as it studied ways to automate the audit process.

Coopers & Lybrand lost market share as mergers reduced the Big Eight to the Big Six. After the savings and loan debacle of the 1980s, investors and the government wanted accounting firms held liable not only for the form of audited financial statements, but for their veracity. In 1992 the firm paid $95 million to settle claims of defrauded investors in MiniScribe, a failed disk-drive maker. Other hefty payments followed, including a $108 million settlement relating to the late Robert Maxwell's defunct media empire.

In 1998 Price Waterhouse and Coopers & Lybrand combined PW's strength in the media, entertainment, and utility industries, and Coopers & Lybrand's focus on telecommunications and mining. But the merger brought some expensive legal baggage involving Coopers & Lybrand's performance of audits related to a bid-rigging scheme involving former Arizona governor Fife Symington.

Plans to grow even larger fell through in 1999 when merger talks between PwC and Grant Thornton International failed. Feeling the pinch of competition and the aftereffects of its megamerger, PwC announced it would cut 1,000 jobs and replace obsolete positions with e-business consultants to cut costs. The year 2000 began on a sour note: An SEC conflict-of-interest probe turned up more than 8,000 alleged violations, most involving PwC partners owning stock in their firm's audit clients.

As the SEC grew ever more shrill in its denunciation of the potential conflict of interest arising from auditing companies that the firm hoped to recruit or retain as consulting clients, PwC saw the writing on the wall and in 2000 began making plans to split the two operations. As part of this move, the company downsized and reorganized many of its operations, and retained Morgan Stanley to advise on the separation process.

That year the company announced it would start a subsidiary called BeTrusted, to provide Internet security software to corporations. It also said it would enter the emerging digital certificate business (which ensures the identity of businesses trading online).

OFFICERS

Chairman: Nicholas G. Moore
US Chairman and Senior Partner: Samuel A. Diapazza
CEO: James J. Schiro
COO: Tom O'Neill
Global CFO: Marcia Cohen
Global Service Line Leader: Willard W. Brittain
Global Geography Leader: Rolf Windmöller
Global Industries Leader: Peter A. Smith
Global Human Capital Leader: William K. O'Brien
Global Operations Leader: Geoffrey E. Johnson
Global Risk Management Leader: Ian Brindle
Global Consumer and Industrial Products Leader: Thomas W. Cross
Global Financial Services Leader: Rocco J. Maggiotto
Global Energy and Mining Leader: James G. Crump
Global Technology, Information, Communications, and Entertainment Leader: Francis A. Doyle
Global Services Leader: Bruce W. Hucklesby
Global Assurance and Business Advisory Services Leader: Amyas C.E. Morse
Global Business Process Outsourcing Leader: John C. Barnsley
Global Financial Advisory Services Leader: Raymond A. Ranelli
Global Human Resources Solutions Leader: Reed A. Keller

LOCATIONS

HQ: 1301 Avenue of the Americas, New York, NY 10019
Phone: 212-596-7000 **Fax:** 212-259-1301
Web site: http://www.pwcglobal.com

PricewaterhouseCoopers has more than 850 offices in about 150 countries.

PRODUCTS/OPERATIONS

Selected Services
Audit, assurance and business advisory
Business process outsourcing
Financial advisory
Human resources
Management consulting services
Tax services

Representative Clients
Alcoa
American International Group
Anheuser-Busch
AT&T
Avon
Bristol-Myers Squibb
Campbell Soup
Caterpillar
Chase Manhattan
CIGNA
Compaq
Dun & Bradstreet
DuPont
Eastman Kodak
Ericsson
Exxon Mobil
Fiat
Ford
Goodyear
Hewlett-Packard
IBM
Johnson & Johnson
J.P. Morgan
Kmart
3M
New York Life
NIKE
Nippon Telegraph and Telephone
Philip Morris
Shell Oil
Toshiba
Unilever
United Technologies
Walt Disney
W. R. Grace

COMPETITORS

American Management
Andersen Worldwide
Atos Origin
Bain & Company
BDO International
Booz-Allen
Boston Consulting
Deloitte Touche Tohmatsu
EDS
Ernst & Young
Getronics
H&R Block
Hewitt Associates
IBM
ICL
KPMG
Marsh & McLennan
McKinsey & Company
Perot Systems
Towers Perrin
Watson Wyatt

HISTORICAL FINANCIALS & EMPLOYEES

Partnership FYE: June 30	Annual Growth	6/91	6/92	6/93	6/94	6/95	6/96	6/97	6/98	6/99	6/00
Sales ($ mil.)	19.0%	3,603	3,781	3,890	3,980	4,460	5,020	5,630	15,000	15,300	17,300
Employees	13.9%	49,461	48,600	48,781	50,122	53,000	56,000	60,000	140,000	155,000	160,000

SALES HISTORY

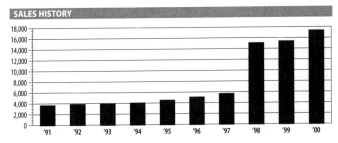

PRUDENTIAL PLC

OVERVIEW

Prudence pays off for Prudential, one of the UK's biggest insurers. London-based Prudential (no relation to the US's Prudential Insurance) offers life insurance and savings products to customers in the UK, Europe, the US, and Asia. The company's UK businesses include life insurer Scottish Amicable and its Prudential Banking division. Products include pensions, investment bonds, home and car insurance, and personal loans.

The bank's publicly listed Egg offers telephone and Internet banking services, as well as mortgages and VISA credit cards; Egg is expanding into online brokerage, and Prudential is planning an Asian version.

Prudential operates in the US through Jackson National Life, which offers annuities and life insurance. Asian operations are headed by Prudential Corporation Asia. Other businesses include fund management (PPM Worldwide) and real estate.

The firm has been remaking itself in the image of a company that can be all things financial to all people; it has divested noncore operations to concentrate on life insurance, retirement savings, and, through Prudential Bank, savings accounts and mortgages. To further streamline operations, Prudential has cut about 5,000 jobs. The company is considering launching another Egg geared toward the Asian market.

HISTORY

Actually, prudence almost killed Prudential before it ever got started. Founded in 1848 as Prudential Mutual Assurance Investment and Loan Association, the firm initially insured middle-class customers. The Dickensian conditions of the working poor made them too risky for insurers. Unfortunately the company found few takers of the right sort, and by 1852 Prudential was in peril.

Two events saved Prudential: The House of Commons pressed for insurance coverage for all classes, and Prudential's own agents pushed for change. The company expanded into industrial insurance, a modest coverage for the working poor. In 1864, to quell criticism of the insurance industry, Prudential brought in independent auditors to confirm its soundness. This soon became a marketing tool and business took off. The Pru, as it came to be known, became the leading industrial insurer by the 1880s. It covered half the country's population by 1905. The firm was known for its customer relations (the "Man from the Pru" became a ubiquitous icon in the 1940s and was revived in 1997) and its personal collections.

During the two world wars Prudential boosted its reputation by honoring the policies of war victims when it could have legally denied them. Between wars the company added fire and accident insurance in Europe.

In 1969 it bought Mercantile and General Reinsurance Company from Swiss Re.

In 1982, under the direction of CEO Brian Corby, the Pru reorganized product lines and in 1985 entered the real estate business. In 1986 it entered the US market by buying US-based Jackson National Life. The 1980s were volatile for insurance companies, especially in the wake of Britain's financial deregulation in 1986.

Prudential, which had considered selling Mercantile and General Reinsurance in the early 1990s, sold the reinsurer back to Swiss Re in 1996. It also formed Prudential Bank and created an Asian emerging-market investment fund that year.

In 1997 Prudential bought Scottish Amicable. Insurance regulators reprimanded the company for mis-selling financial products that year.

In 1998 Jackson National bought a California savings and loan, enabling it to sell investment products in the US. Also that year, the Pru sold its Australian and New Zealand businesses, and Prudential Bank launched its Internet bank Egg (now larger than any US online bank). In 1999 Prudential bought investment manager M & G Group and announced plans to cut more than 5,000 jobs by 2002 to reduce costs.

The company changed its name to Prudential plc and began talks with the Prudential Insurance Company of America to resolve confusion of their similar names as they expand into new markets. The Pru in 1999 joined forces with the Bank of China to offer pension and asset management in Hong Kong.

In 2000 the company announced plans to sell a chunk of its institutional fund management business as well as its traditional balanced pension business to Deutsche Bank. That year the company spun off 20% of Egg. Also in 2000 the company agreed to start an insurance joint venture in China with state-owned investment vehicle CITIC Group, and it agreed to buy Highland Bancorp, a Los Angeles bank.

Chairman: Sir Martin Jacomb, age 70, $175,000 pay
Deputy Chairman: Michael Abrahams, age 62, $65,000 pay
Chief Executive: Jonathan Bloomer, age 45, $626,000 pay
Group Finance Director: Philip Broadley, age 39
International Development Director; Chairman Prudential Europe: Keith Bedell-Pearce, age 53, $443,000 pay
Group Human Resources Director: Jane Kibbey
Group Legal Services Director: Peter Maynard
Director Corporate Relations and Group Marketing: Jan Shawe
Chairman Prudential Portfolio Managers: Derek Higgs, age 55, $612,000 pay
Chief Executive Egg and Prudential Banking: Mike Harris, age 51
Chief Executive Scottish Amicable: Roy Nicolson
Chief Executive Prudential Retail Financial Services: John Elbourne
Chief Executive The M&G Group: Michael McLintock, age 39
CEO Jackson National Life: Bob Saltzman, age 57
Chief Executive Prudential Asia: Mark Tucker, age 42, $205,000 pay
Managing Director Prudential Annuities: Kim Lerche-Thomsen
Managing Director Prudential Group Pensions: Rodney Baker-Bates
Auditors: KPMG Audit Plc

HQ: Laurence Pountney Hill, London EC4R 0HH, United Kingdom
Phone: +44-20-7220-7588   **Fax:** +44-20-7548-3850
US HQ: 5901 Executive Dr., Lansing, MI 48911
US Phone: 517-394-3400   **US Fax:** 517-394-0129
Web site: http://www.prudential.co.uk

Selected Subsidiaries
Jackson National Life Insurance Co. (life insurance, annuities; US)
Prudential Annuities Ltd. (insurance)
The Prudential Assurance Co. Ltd.
Prudential Assurance Co. Singapore (Pte) Ltd. (insurance)
Prudential Banking plc (banking)
  Egg (82%, Internet bank)
Prudential Finance BV (The Netherlands)
Prudential Portfolio Managers Limited (investment management)
Scottish Amicable Life plc (insurance)

Aachener und Münchener	MetLife
Abbey National	Mitsui Marine & Fire
AEGON	Munich Re
AIG	New York Life
Alliance & Leicester	Nippon Life Insurance
Allianz	Norwich Union
Allstate	Prudential
AXA	Royal & Sun Alliance
Britannic	Insurance
Canada Life	State Farm
CGNU plc	Sumitomo Marine & Fire
Citigroup	Tokio Marine and Fire
ERGO	Winterthur
Generali	Woolwich
Halifax	Yasuda Fire & Marine
ING	Insurance
Legal & General Group	Zurich Financial Services

NYSE: PUK FYE: December 31	Annual Growth	12/90	12/91	12/92	12/93	12/94	12/95	12/96	12/97	12/98	12/99
Assets ($ mil.)	21.9%	—	—	—	—	—	—	134,444	178,043	196,890	243,514
Net income ($ mil.)	(28.7%)	—	—	—	—	—	—	2,412	1,377	1,461	876
Income as % of assets	—	—	—	—	—	—	—	1.8%	0.8%	0.7%	0.4%
Earnings per share ($)	—	—	—	—	—	—	—	—	—	—	0.89
Stock price - FY high ($)	—	—	—	—	—	—	—	—	—	—	39.32
Stock price - FY low ($)	—	—	—	—	—	—	—	—	—	—	30.40
Stock price - FY close ($)	—	—	—	—	—	—	—	—	—	—	39.32
P/E - high	—	—	—	—	—	—	—	—	—	—	44
P/E - low	—	—	—	—	—	—	—	—	—	—	34
Dividends per share ($)	—	—	—	—	—	—	—	—	—	—	0.74
Book value per share ($)	—	—	—	—	—	—	—	—	—	—	5.67
Employees	0.6%	—	—	—	—	—	—	—	22,120	22,834	22,372

HIGH/LOW/CLOSE

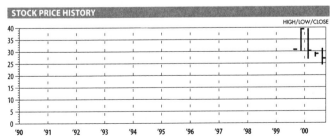

Equity as % of assets: 2.3%
Return on assets: 0.4%
Return on equity: 16.0%
Long-term debt ($ mil.): 2,500
No. of shares (mil.): 977
Dividends
  Yield: 0.0%
  Payout: 0.8%
Market value ($ mil.): 38,414
Sales ($ mil.): 41,845

PUBLICIS GROUPE S.A.

OVERVIEW

Paris-based Publicis may have once been *l'enfant* in the advertising world, but now it is *un du plus grand*. The French firm is the largest advertising company in Europe, spanning more than 80 countries with operations in creative services, direct marketing, media buying, and public relations. Publicis operates in France through its flagship agency Publicis Conseil, while its Publicis Worldwide network spans the globe. Its media-buying unit Optimedia operates in 27 countries. Publicis boasts such worldwide clients as Nestlé, Coca-Cola, British Airways, and Hewlett-Packard.

The company has been particularly focused on the US market (almost 25% of billings), buying up several small firms, including San Francisco-based Hal Riney, Chicago's Frankel & Co., and Fallon Worldwide. It also owns 49% of Burrell Communications Group — one of the largest African-American-owned marketing firms in the US — and a 10% stake in True North Communications. The company also bought US health care marketer Nelson Communications in 2000. In addition, Publicis is focused on new media services, combining its interactive units to form Publicis.Net in 2000. (The company has said it may take the new unit public.)

Publicis made a big splash on the world stage when it acquired UK-based Saatchi & Saatchi in a $1.9 billion takeover. The move vaulted the company into the top five advertising conglomerates. Elisabeth Badinter, supervisory board chair and daughter of late founder Marcel Bleustein-Blanchet, has about 46% voting control.

HISTORY

Marcel Bleustein, then 19 years old, founded Publicis, France's first advertising agency, in Paris in 1926 (the name was a takeoff on "publicity" and "six"). Two years later Bleustein ventured into radio advertising and eventually became the exclusive agent for all of France's government-run radio stations. In 1934, however, the French government banned all advertising on state-run stations, and Bleustein responded by creating his own, Radio Cite, the next year. By 1939 he had expanded into film distribution and movie theaters, but with the outbreak of WWII, Bleustein fled to London to serve with the Free French Forces.

He returned to France following the liberation, having adopted the name Bleustein-Blanchet, and proceeded to relaunch his advertising business. In 1958 he bought the former Hotel Astoria on the Champs-Elysees and opened the first Le Drugstore. The original structure burned in a 1972 fire, and legend has it that Bleustein-Blanchet tapped employee Maurice Levy (now CEO) after he found Levy salvaging records amid the ruins.

In 1988 Publicis and Chicago-based Foote, Cone & Belding Communications (FCB) formed an alliance that would sour five years later when Publicis acquired France's Groupe FCA. FCB declared the acquisition of the competing agency a breach of contract, but Publicis refused to cancel the deal. FCB countered by establishing a new holding company for itself, True North Communications. Bleustein-Blanchet died in 1996, and his daughter, Elisabeth Badinter, was named chair of the supervisory board. That year Publicis acquired ad agencies in Brazil, Canada, the Philippines, and Singapore, and opened agencies in Greece and Croatia.

In 1997 Publicis and True North divided their joint network, Publicis Communications, with True North getting the European offices and Publicis getting Africa, Asia, and Argentina. Later that year Publicis attempted a $700 million hostile bid for the 81.5% of True North it didn't already own to stop True North's acquisition of Bozell, Jacobs, Kenyon & Eckhardt. The bid failed, and Publicis' stake in True North was reduced to 11%.

The company gained new ground in the US through its acquisitions of Hal Riney & Partners and Evans Group in 1998. Levy also helped soothe a bitter feud among the descendants of Marcel Bleustein that year. Elisabeth Badinter had battled with her sister Michele Bleustein-Blanchet over Bleustein-Blanchet's desire to sell her stake in Publicis' holding company. Levy's solution allowed Bleustein-Blanchet to sell her shares and left Badinter with a 41% equity ownership.

Continuing its US expansion, in 1999 Publicis bought a 49% stake in Burrell Communications Group (#2 US African-American focused ad agency). In 2000 the company bought advertising outfit Fallon McElligott (now Fallon Worldwide), marketing firm Frankel & Co., and media buyer DeWitt Media (which was merged into Optimedia). It also announced completion of the powerhouse acquisition of Saatchi & Saatchi for about $1.9 billion.

In 2000 Publicis bought US health care marketing company Nelson Communications.

OFFICERS

Chairwoman: Elisabeth Badinter
VC: Sophie Dulac
CEO: Maurice Levy
CFO: Jean-Michel Etienne, age 48
EVP: Gerard Pedraglio
VP Communication and New Business: Joanna Baldwin
CEO, Media and Media Sales Division:
Bruno Desbarats-Bollet
Manager Administration: Fran Class
Auditors: Mazars & Guerard; Pierre Loeper

LOCATIONS

HQ: 133, avenue des Champs-Elysees,
75008 Paris, France
Phone: +33-1-44-43-73-00   **Fax:** +33-1-44-43-75-25
US HQ: 304 E. 45th St., New York, NY 10017
US Phone: 212-370-1313   **US Fax:** 212-949-0499
Web site: http://www.publicis.fr

Publicis has offices in 76 countries.

1999 Billings

	% of total
US	24
France	22
Germany	12
UK	7
Netherlands	4
Australia	3
Canada	3
Italy	3
Spain	3
Switzerland	2
Other	17
Total	**100**

PRODUCTS/OPERATIONS

Selected Services
Corporate communications
Direct marketing
Events and conventions marketing
Financial communications
Human resources communications
Media conception
Media planning and buying
Media space sales
Multimedia and new media services
Public relations
Sales promotion and incentive marketing
Strategic planning and consulting

Selected Clients

ABC	Hoover's, Inc.
Ariba	L'Oréal
Bombardier	Long John Silver's
British Airways	Restaurants
Cellular One	MTV Networks
Coca-Cola	Nestlé
Ebel	Procter & Gamble
Ericsson	Renault
European Central Bank	Siemens
Hewlett-Packard	Toyota

COMPETITORS

Aegis Group	Havas Advertising
Bcom3	Interpublic Group
Cordiant Communications	Omnicom
Group	Saatchi & Saatchi
Dentsu	True North
Grey Global	WPP Group
Hakuhodo	

HISTORICAL FINANCIALS & EMPLOYEES

Euronext Paris: PUB FYE: December 31	Annual Growth	12/90	12/91	12/92	12/93	12/94	12/95	12/96	12/97	12/98	12/99
Sales (€ mil.)	10.0%	—	—	536	479	524	556	571	663	850	1,042
Net income (€ mil.)	18.3%	—	—	23	19	23	23	28	35	47	74
Income as % of sales	—	—	—	4.3%	4.0%	4.4%	4.1%	4.9%	5.3%	5.5%	7.1%
Earnings per share (€)	19.8%	—	—	0.29	0.25	0.28	0.29	0.35	0.44	0.71	1.04
Stock price - FY high (€)	—	—	—	4.96	7.49	7.46	5.84	7.50	9.71	16.48	38.30
Stock price - FY low (€)	—	—	—	3.03	3.22	4.88	3.98	4.26	6.88	7.29	11.70
Stock price - FY close (€)	41.3%	—	—	3.29	7.27	5.59	4.41	6.89	7.49	15.25	37.00
P/E - high	—	—	—	17	31	26	20	21	22	23	37
P/E - low	—	—	—	10	13	17	14	12	16	10	11
Dividends per share (€)	15.8%	—	—	0.06	0.08	0.08	0.09	0.11	0.12	0.12	0.17
Book value per share (€)	7.7%	—	—	2.51	2.74	2.49	4.10	4.51	3.94	3.99	4.21
Employees	9.5%	—	—	5,500	4,690	5,540	6,000	6,038	7,363	8,709	10,362

STOCK PRICE HISTORY

HIGH/LOW/CLOSE

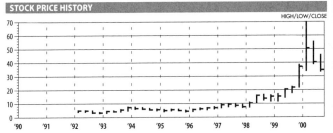

1999 FISCAL YEAR-END

Debt ratio: 0.0%
Return on equity: 19.7%
Cash (€ mil.): 349
Current ratio: 1.03
Long-term debt (€ mil.): 0
No. of shares (mil.): 94
Dividends
  Yield: 0.0%
  Payout: 0.2%
Market value ($ mil.): 3,504
Sales ($ mil.): 1,047

QANTAS AIRWAYS LIMITED

OVERVIEW

If there's a Kangaroo on your tail, you're probably flying Qantas. Based in Mascot, New South Wales, Qantas Airways is Australia's #1 airline and one of the top carriers operating international flights to and from Australia. With its core fleet of about 100 aircraft, Qantas carries passengers and transports cargo to about 65 destinations in 35 countries (including code-sharing flights), primarily in the Asia/Pacific region, Europe, and North America (where its main hub is Los Angeles). The airline also provides catering and tourism services, and it's developing e-commerce operations devoted to travel and transport.

Qantas' Australian regional subsidiaries — Airlink, Eastern Australia, Southern Australia,

and Sunstate — have more than kangaroos on their tail. The group, which flies its 40 planes to about 55 domestic destinations, is facing stiff competition. Besides Ansett Australia, Qantas faces an Aussie low-fare carrier being set up by Richard Branson's Virgin Atlantic just in time for the Olympics in Sydney.

Alliances are sweeping the airline industry, and Qantas is no exception. The carrier is 25%-owned by British Airways, and the pair have extensive code-sharing agreements; coordinate their scheduling, sales, and marketing; and share facilities such as airport lounges. They are also part of the Oneworld global marketing alliance, which includes American Airlines, among others.

HISTORY

Ex-WWI pilots Wilmot Hudson Fysh and Paul McGinness and stockman Fergus McMaster founded Queensland and Northern Territory Aerial Services (Qantas) in 1920 to provide an air link between Darwin in the Northern Territory and the railheads in Queensland. In 1922 Qantas began carrying airmail over a 577-mile route between Charleville and Cloncurry, and by 1930 it covered northeastern Australia with air routes. Qantas moved its headquarters to Sydney in 1938.

Qantas and Imperial Airways (predecessor of British Airways, or BA) formed Qantas Empire Airways in 1934 to fly the last leg of a London-to-Australia mail route (Singapore to Brisbane). Qantas bought the British share of Qantas Empire in 1947 (when Qantas made its first Sydney-London flight) and was subsequently nationalized.

By 1950 the airline served most major cities in the Pacific Rim. Qantas inaugurated a route to Johannesburg (1952) and opened the Southern Cross route, previously operated by British Commonwealth Pacific Airlines, to San Francisco and Vancouver via Honolulu (1953).

In 1958 Qantas offered the first complete round-the-world service. (Pan Am had started a similar service in 1957 but was barred by the US government from crossing North America.) It bought 29% of Malayan Airways in 1959 and added several European destinations in the 1960s, including Frankfurt (1966) and Amsterdam (1967). In 1966, Fysh retired as chairman and the airline took its present name in 1967.

Tourism in Australia boomed in the 1970s. Competition from foreign (especially US) airlines initially hurt Qantas, contributing to a

$4 million loss in 1971 (its second since 1924). But in 1973 annual boardings jumped 28%. Qantas' Aussie passengers flew some 4,217 miles per journey — the longest average trip of any airline.

In 1987 Qantas bought a stake in Fiji's Air Pacific. Later acquisitions included Australia-Asia Airlines (1989) and 20% of Air New Zealand (1990, sold in 1997). Qantas enjoyed record profits in 1989, but a strike by domestic pilots paralyzed Australia's tourist industry that year, hurting Qantas in 1990.

The Australian airline industry was deregulated in the early 1990s, and Qantas formed regional carrier Airlink in 1991. The next year it merged with Australia Airlines, and in 1993 the Australian government sold BA a 25% stake in Qantas. Still, the airlines' 1994 attempt to set prices and services together was rejected by Australian authorities.

Because Australian privatizations had deluged the stock exchange with issues, Qantas delayed its IPO until 1995. Also that year Qantas and BA got approval for a joint service agreement that allowed them to operate some facilities together. The carrier began code-sharing with American Airlines in 1995; three years later Qantas joined the Oneworld global marketing alliance, led by American and BA.

In 1998 and 1999, Qantas and BA began combining their operations in Hong Kong, Singapore, Thailand, Malaysia, and Indonesia. The airline expanded its code-sharing with affiliate Air Pacific in 2000, even as it braced for competition at home from Virgin Atlantic's new Australian low-fare carrier.

Chairman: Margaret Jackson, age 47
Chief Executive and Managing Director: James Strong,
  age 56
Deputy CEO: Geoff Dixon, age 60
CFO: Peter Gregg
Executive General Manager Aircraft Operations:
  David Forsyth
Executive General Manager Corporate Services:
  David Burden
Executive General Manager Strategic Planning:
  Steve Mann
Group General Manager Commercial Business:
  Denis Adams
**Group General Manager Commercial Strategy and
  Policy:** Paul Edwards
Group General Manager Human Resources:
  George Elsey
**Group General Manager Corporate Finance and
  Financial Planning:** Grant Fenn
General Counsel and Company Secretary: Brett Johnson
Deputy CFO: Adam Moroney
Auditors: KPMG

LOCATIONS

HQ: Qantas Centre, Level 9, Bldg. A, 203 Coward St.,
  Mascot, New South Wales 2020, Australia
Phone: +61-2-9691-3636   **Fax:** +61-2-9691-3339
US HQ: 841 Apollo St., Ste. 400, El Segundo, CA 90245
US Phone: 310-726-1400   **US Fax:** 310-726-1484
Web site: http://www.qantas.com.au

Qantas serves 56 destinations in Australia and 64 more
in some 35 other countries in Africa, the Americas, the
Asia/Pacific region, Europe, and the Middle East.

PRODUCTS/OPERATIONS

Selected Airline Operations
Air Pacific (46%)
Australian Regional Airlines Pty. Ltd.
  Airlink Pty. Ltd.
  Eastern Australia Airlines Pty. Ltd.
  Southern Australia Airlines Pty. Ltd.
  Sunstate Airlines (Qld) Pty. Ltd.

Selected Partners

Air Pacific	Cathay Pacific Airways
American Airlines	Japan Airlines
Asiana	LanChile
British Airways	Swissair
Canadian Airlines	Vietnam Airlines

COMPETITORS

Air New Zealand	Lufthansa
All Nippon Airways	Northwest Airlines
Ansett	SAS
Continental Airlines	Singapore Airlines
Delta	Swire Pacific
DHL	UAL
FedEx	UPS
KLM	Virgin Atlantic Airways

HISTORICAL FINANCIALS & EMPLOYEES

Australian: QAN FYE: June 30	Annual Growth	6/91	6/92	6/93	6/94	6/95	6/96	6/97	6/98	6/99	6/00
Sales (A$ mil.)	10.0%	3,861	4,158	5,832	6,602	7,163	7,600	7,834	8,132	8,449	9,107
Net income (A$ mil.)	31.4%	44	138	(377)	156	180	247	253	305	422	517
Income as % of sales	—	1.1%	3.3%	—	2.4%	2.5%	3.2%	3.2%	3.7%	5.0%	5.7%
Earnings per share (A$)	15.5%	—	—	—	—	—	0.24	0.24	0.27	0.35	0.43
Stock price - FY high (A$)	—	—	—	—	—	—	2.47	3.15	3.21	5.00	5.40
Stock price - FY low (A$)	—	—	—	—	—	—	2.03	1.79	2.13	2.27	3.07
Stock price - FY close (A$)	15.3%	—	—	—	—	—	2.15	3.10	2.43	4.99	3.80
P/E - high	—	—	—	—	—	—	10	13	12	14	13
P/E - low	—	—	—	—	—	—	8	8	8	6	7
Dividends per share (A$)	46.0%	—	—	—	—	—	0.13	0.13	0.14	0.33	0.59
Book value per share (A$)	0.2%	—	—	—	—	—	2.35	2.40	2.52	2.54	2.37
Employees	4.1%	20,430	17,646	25,159	26,791	28,565	29,627	30,080	28,934	28,226	29,217

STOCK PRICE HISTORY

HIGH/LOW/CLOSE

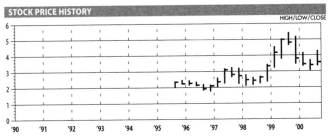

2000 FISCAL YEAR-END

Debt ratio: 52.1%
Return on equity: 17.5%
Cash (A$ mil.): 118
Current ratio: 0.49
Long-term debt (A$ mil.): 2,531
No. of shares (mil.): 1,211
Dividends
  Yield: 0.2%
  Payout: 1.4%
Market value ($ mil.): 2,773
Sales ($ mil.): 5,487

QUEBECOR INC.

OVERVIEW

Montréal-based Quebecor World has one hand on the printing press; the other on the Web. The company's Quebecor Printing subsidiary's purchase of rival World Color Press in 1999 pushed it into position as the world's largest commercial printer. The company makes advertising inserts, books, and magazines, as well as catalogs for North American retailers. Quebecor sold its stake in market pulp, lumber, and newsprint producer Donohue to rival Abitibi-Consolidated in 2000.

Meanwhile, Quebecor's newly created New Media subsidiary is getting a lot of press, operating an Internet portal (canoe.com) as well as several other Web sites (icimontreal.com). The company also has pushed into the Internet consulting realm through its purchase of a

58% stake in Nurun (formerly Informission Group). In addition, the conglomerate's 70%-owned Sun Media is the second-largest newspaper publisher in Canada (after Southam) with about 180 newspapers including eight major dailies. Its other operations include Canadian TV network TQS; book publication (literature, textbooks, legal); distribution of CD-ROMs, books, and newsstand publications; and music retail (Archambault superstores). Intent on expanding its media operations, Quebecor, with Caisse de Dépôt et Placement du Québec (Québec's public-pension agency), acquired Canada's #3 cable televison operator, Le Groupe Vidéotron, for $3.6 billion.

The Péladeau family controls about 60% of the voting shares.

HISTORY

In 1950 law student Pierre Péladeau borrowed $1,500 from his mother so he could buy a small Montréal newspaper called *Le Journal de Rosemont*. This became the base for Péladeau's publishing empire. Within a few years he had established five other weekly newspapers and his first printing firm.

In 1964 Péladeau seized the opportunity presented to him by a strike at the major Montréal paper *La Presse*. He assembled a team from his various weeklies and, according to company legend, had the tabloid *Le Journal* on the streets within three days.

Quebecor went public in 1972 and expanded beyond Québec, branching out into a variety of communication concerns. But by the late 1980s, the company had refocused on its core printing businesses.

In 1985 Quebecor got a foothold in the US with the purchase of printing plants in New Jersey and Michigan. Péladeau teamed with Robert Maxwell in 1987 to form Mircor to buy a stake in forestry concern Donohue. The company took a major step into the international arena when it bought the printing group BCE PubliTech in 1988, making the company the #1 commercial printer in Canada.

In 1990 Maxwell sold his US printing plants (with state-of-the-art printing presses) to Péladeau, who formed Quebecor Printing (USA) around the new assets. Maxwell subsequently bought a 26% stake in the new company for $100 million.

When Maxwell's mysterious death in 1991 was followed by revelations of deceptive finances and shady business dealings by the Maxwell empire, Péladeau was able to buy back all of

Maxwell's shares in Quebecor at bargain-basement prices.

In the 1990s Quebecor continued expanding, buying a bookbinding and publishing company in Mexico (Gráficas Monte Alban, 1991), three US printing plants (1993), France's largest commercial printer (Group Jean Didier, 1995), and a UK printer (1995). Quebecor Printing went public in 1995, which reduced the parent company's interest to less than 50%.

In 1997 a Quebecor-controlled consortium acquired Télévision Quatre Saisons, which operates three Canadian TV stations and the Quatre Saisons TV network license. Péladeau died from heart failure that year.

In 1999 Quebecor bought Sun Media, which vaulted the company to the #2 Canadian newspaper publisher. It later sold a 30% stake in Sun Media to a group of private investors. In 1999 Quebecor Printing acquired World Color Press. Also that year Pierre Karl Péladeau, the founder's second son, took over as president and CEO. Péladeau family members have filed a flood of lawsuits against one another and the executor of Pierre Péladeau's estate in an increasingly bitter battle for control of family assets, including the company.

In 2000 the company made a bid for Québec's largest cable firm, Le Groupe Vidéotron. Also that year Quebecor Printing changed its name to Quebecor World. Later in 2000, Quebecor and Caisse de Dépôt et Placement du Québec (Quebec's public-pension agency) won a bidding war with Rogers Communications for the acquisition of Le Groupe Vidéotron, Canada's #3 cable TV operator, with an offer of $3.6 billion.

Chairman; Chairman Quebecor Printing: Jean Neveu,
$459,182 pay (prior to title change)
VC; Chairman Quebecor Communications:
Érik Péladeau, $445,074 pay
President and CEO; Chairman Informission Group
Inc.; VC Quebecor Printing and Sun Media
Corporation: Pierre Karl Péladeau, $1,470,214 pay
(prior to title change)
EVP and CFO: François R. Roy, $459,305 pay
EVP and Chief Information Officer: Jacques Malo
Chairman and Interim CEO, Sun Media Corporation:
Brian Mulroney
President and CEO, Quebecor Communications: Jean-
François Douville
President and CEO, Quebecor Printing:
Charles G. Cavell, $1,814,458 pay
(prior to title change)
VP Human Resources Quebecor Communications:
Julie Tremblay
Auditors: KPMG LLP

HQ: 612 Saint-Jacques St.,
Montréal, Québec H3C 4M8, Canada
Phone: 514-877-9777   Fax: 514-877-9757
US HQ: 980 Washington St., Ste. 222,
Dedham, MA 02026
US Phone: 781-410-2000   US Fax: 781-410-2192
Web site: http://www.quebecor.com

1999 Sales

	% of total
United States	46
Canada	40
Europe & other	14
Total	**100**

1999 Sales

	% of total
Printing	68
Forest products	23
Newspapers	7
Books, magazines, music	2
Broadcasting	—
New media	—
Total	**100**

Selected Operations

Quebecor Media Inc.
Le Groupe Vidéotron (cable TV)
Nurun Inc. (58%, Web development and e-commerce
consulting)
Quebecor Communications Inc. (television
broadcasting; book and magazine publishing;
entertainment retailing)
Quebecor New Media (Internet holdings)
Sun Media Corporation (70%, newspaper publishing)
Quebecor World Inc. (commercial printing)

ACG Holdings	Pearson
Banta	Quad/Graphics
Big Flower Holdings	R. R. Donnelley
Courier	Southam
Dai Nippon Printing	Thomson Corporation
Hachette Filipacchi Médias	Treasure Chest Advertising
Hollinger	Valassis Communications
Mead	Wallace Computer

Toronto: QBR.A FYE: December 31	Annual Growth	12/90	12/91	12/92	12/93	12/94	12/95	12/96	12/97	12/98	12/99
Sales (C$ mil.)	23.0%	—	—	2,549	3,902	3,976	4,067	6,253	7,013	8,425	10,835
Net income (C$ mil.)	27.7%	—	—	87	75	89	137	147	143	173	481
Income as % of sales	—	—	—	3.4%	1.9%	2.2%	3.4%	2.4%	2.0%	2.1%	4.4%
Earnings per share (C$)	26.5%	—	—	1.43	1.15	1.34	2.83	2.23	2.18	2.64	7.43
Stock price - FY high (C$)	—	—	—	17.00	21.00	21.88	21.75	25.00	32.35	33.00	39.50
Stock price - FY low (C$)	—	—	—	10.38	16.75	15.38	16.25	20.20	22.60	23.60	31.25
Stock price - FY close (C$)	12.3%	—	—	16.88	18.13	17.75	20.38	22.90	25.70	32.90	38.10
P/E - high	—	—	—	12	18	16	8	11	15	13	5
P/E - low	—	—	—	7	15	11	6	9	10	9	4
Dividends per share (C$)	18.1%	—	—	0.15	0.20	0.24	0.33	0.40	0.40	0.44	0.48
Book value per share (C$)	14.3%	—	—	10.50	11.41	12.42	14.83	16.58	18.58	22.00	26.73
Employees	20.3%	—	—	16,500	20,600	25,900	28,900	33,700	37,000	39,000	60,000

HIGH/LOW/CLOSE

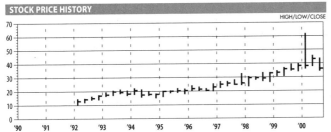

Debt ratio: 77.9%
Return on equity: —
Cash (C$ mil.): 53
Current ratio: 0.22
Long-term debt (C$ mil.): 5,860
No. of shares (mil.): 65
Dividends
 Yield: 0.0%
 Payout: 0.1%
Market value ($ mil.): 1,695
Sales ($ mil.): 7,462

RACAL ELECTRONICS PLC

OVERVIEW

Racal Electronics can help you fight a war, shop, or communicate, depending on how your day is going. The Bracknell, UK-based subsidiary of France's Thomson-CSF has about 90 subsidiaries that make defense and industrial electronics (including point-of-sale terminals) as well as commercial voice and data communication network equipment. The UK accounts for about three-fourths of Racal's sales.

Racal's defense operations segment (35% of sales) makes command information systems, electronic warfare radar, and avionic equipment; its industrial electronics operations range from

testing instrumentation and recording equipment to secure payment systems and survey services. Racal's information systems and logistics interests include data networks, satellite-based communications equipment, and communications recording equipment.

After exiting most of its money-losing data communications operations, the company sold its telecommunications business to Global Crossing of the US. Racal was acquired by France-based Thomson-CSF — which plans to restructure — in 2000

HISTORY

Ray Brown and Calder Cunningham merged their names and talents to form Racal (a consulting firm) in 1950. The company introduced its first proprietary product, the RA 17 radio receiver, seven years later. Cunningham died in 1958, but Brown stayed at the helm and launched Racal's IPO in 1961. The company developed the Squadcal, a lightweight military backpack radio, in 1966. That year Brown handed the reins over to Ernest Harrison, who started with the company as an accountant.

Racal bolstered its tactical radio business by acquiring British Communications Corp. in 1969. That year Racal formed a partnership with US data communications firm Milgo Electronic Corp. In 1977 Racal bought out Milgo for $60 million, then acquired modem manufacturer Vadic Corp. Racal made another lateral move in 1980 by acquiring Decca Ltd. (avionics, marine electronics, and radar) for $250 million. By 1982 the company's sales had reached $1 billion, but profits were uneven.

Racal then began to diversify in earnest. It won a UK cellular telephone license in 1983 and entered the building security business with its purchase of Chubb and Son in 1984. Harrison worked on a nationwide cellular phone network and by 1988 the cellular business was accounting for about a third of the company's profits.

Amid takeover rumors in 1990, Harrison announced plans to spin off the Chubb and Telecom units and organize a management buyout of Racal. Angry shareholders forced him off the idea of taking Racal private.

In August of 1991 Racal spun off its cellular business as Vodafone Group PLC. A day later British industrial conglomerate Williams Holdings PLC launched a hostile takeover bid for Racal. Shareholders refused to sell, however,

and the attempt failed. Racal spun off its security business as Chubb Security PLC in 1992.

Racal went on a shopping spree in 1994, buying Canadian radio equipment maker Spilsbury Communications, information technology security firm ACS Ventures, and Singapore-based submersibles manufacturer Techno Transfer. That year Racal's Camelot Group joint venture was selected to run the UK National Lottery.

In 1995 Racal bought the sensors division (radar and other electronic systems) from THORN EMI and acquired British Rail Telecommunications. The following year the company's Hermes Europe Railtel BV joint venture got permission to build a telecommunications network along railway lines throughout Europe. Racal also planned to provide a managed Internet business service through another joint venture.

Racal formed Archer Communications Systems, a joint venture with ITT Industries and Siemens, to work on a $2.4 billion project for the UK military in 1997. In 1998 Racal sold its Health & Safety Group to 3M. It also unloaded the bulk of its unprofitable data communications unit on investment firm Platinum Equity Holdings for a meager $47.5 million — and swallowed a write-off of more than $350 million.

The speculated 1999 spin-off of the company's telecommunications division was delayed by the sector's disappointing results. Racal completed the integration of its defense businesses under Racal Defense Electronics Limited in 1999. Later in 1999, Racal sold its ailing telecommunications business to Global Crossing of the US for $1.65 billion.

In 2000 the company was acquired by France's Thomson-CSF for about $2.2 billion.

Chairman: Ernest Harrison
Chief Executive: David C. Elsbury
General Counsel and Secretary: D. Whittaker
Director Finance: Andrew R. Wood
Director Defense Electronics: Barton J. Clarke
Director Defense Electronics: Richard J. Moon
Director Industrial Electronics: Martin J. Richardson
Director Corporate Communications: Richard Poston
Director Marketing Communication Development:
Clive O'Donnell
Director Marketing Communication Services:
Richard Vincent
Auditors: Deloitte & Touche

LOCATIONS

HQ: Western Rd., Bracknell, Berkshire RG12 1RG,
United Kingdom
Phone: +44-1344-481-222   **Fax:** +44-1344-454-119
US HQ: 1601 N. Harrison Pkwy., Bldg. A, Ste. 100,
Sunrise, FL 33323
US Phone: 954-846-4600   **US Fax:** 954-846-5026
Web site: http://www.racal.com

PRODUCTS/OPERATIONS

Selected Operations

Defense Electronics (Racal Defence Electronics)
Avionics
Command information systems
Electronic surveillance
Navigation systems
Radar
Radio communications

Industrial Electronics
Point-of-sale terminals
Recording products
Secure payment systems
Survey services
Testing instrumentation

Telecommunications Services
Racal Fieldforce (communication system installation,
repair, and maintenance)
Racal Translink (infrastructure services, information
systems, and project support for rail and transport
customers)

Selected Associated Companies
Archer Communications Systems Limited (30%, radio
communications)
Camelot Group plc (27%, lotteries)
China Nanhai Racal Positioning and Survey Company
Ltd. (50%; survey and positioning services; China)
Global Telematics Plc (50%, vehicle telematic
products/services)
International Optical Network LLC (50%;
telecommunications services; US)
Satellite Information Services (Holdings) Limited. (22%,
satellite communications)

COMPETITORS

Adaptive Broadband	Lockheed Martin
Alcatel	Marconi
Alliant Techsystems	Motorola
Andrew Corporation	Northrop Grumman
Banner Aerospace	Raytheon
Boeing	Rockwell International
Cubic	Smiths Industries
Ericsson	Tadiran
General Dynamics	Thomson-CSF

HISTORICAL FINANCIALS & EMPLOYEES

Subsidiary FYE: March 31	Annual Growth	3/91	3/92	3/93	3/94	3/95	3/96	3/97	3/98	3/99	3/00
Sales ($ mil.)	(2.2%)	—	—	1,434	1,359	1,541	1,615	1,865	1,857	1,698	1,229
Employees	(4.5%)	—	—	—	—	11,325	12,855	14,320	12,914	11,500	9,000

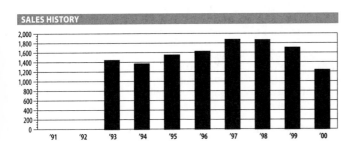

SALES HISTORY

THE RANK GROUP PLC

OVERVIEW

The Rank Group is freshening the foul odor of weak financial performance that has permeated the London-based leisure and entertainment conglomerate. Best known for its Hard Rock Cafe chain (with more than 100 owned and franchised restaurants around the world), Rank's leisure operations also include more than 30 Grosvenor Casinos and more than 130 Mecca Bingo clubs. Aside from leisure businesses, Rank provides film processing, video duplication, and DVD manufacturing services through Deluxe.

Restructuring efforts from new CEO Mike Smith have helped Rank reduce its debt load and increase profits. The company has already sold off its nightclub business (Rank Entertainment, 1999) and Odeon theater chain and Pinewood Studios (both in 2000). Furthermore, Rank has agreed to sell its 50% stake in Seagram's Universal Studios Escape theme park (Orlando, FL) and is trying to sell its holiday and resort operations (Haven, Butlins, Warner, and Oasis) and 89 Tom Cobleigh pubs.

Rank's divestiture of Universal Studios Escape does not include its stake in three hotels near the theme parks, nor its 10%-stake in Universal Studios Japan. Rank is also building three Hard Rock hotels, including a hotel and casino in Biloxi, Mississippi.

HISTORY

The Rank Group grew out of a sense of strong conviction. Joseph Arthur Rank was a devout Methodist who saw films as a way to spread the message of his religion. Leaving the successful family milling business, he started a production company in 1934 called British National Films. Later Rank amassed General Film Distributors, Pinewood Studios, and the Odeon theater chain. By 1941, Rank's entertainment holdings were so vast that many saw Rank as a monopolist. But after WWII the British film business deteriorated as American films flooded into the country. Television and an emerging leisure industry also took their toll in the 1950s.

With the holding company recast as The Rank Organisation in 1955, J. Arthur Rank and his managing director, John Davis, set about searching for alternative businesses. Rank formed a joint venture with the Haloid Company (now Xerox) in 1956 to market photocopying equipment. Later called Rank Xerox, the joint venture eventually dwarfed the profits of Rank's other operating units. Davis became chairman in 1962 (Rank died in 1972) and invested in a diverse but underperforming group of businesses, including bingo parlors, hotels, dance halls. The pitiful results of his efforts were exposed in the late 1970s as Rank Xerox's earnings receded under growing competition in the copier market. Investors forced Davis to step down in 1977.

Michael Gifford was installed as chief executive in 1983 and immediately began cutting overhead and dumping businesses, which increased profits. Rank joined with MCA to create the Universal Studios Florida (later renamed Escape) theme park in 1988 and acquired Mecca Leisure Group's bingo parlors, casinos, hotels, and clubs in 1990. It also bought the rights to a number of Hard Rock Cafes (originally established in London in 1971).

Rank named former ICI chief Sir Denys Henderson as its new chairman in 1994, and two years later Andrew Teare became Rank's new CEO. Teare led Rank's buyout of Hard Rock co-founder Peter Morton that year and installed former schoolteacher Jim Berk as Hard Rock's CEO. Teare also restructured Rank into four divisions (Film and Entertainment Services, Hard Rock, Holidays, and Leisure) and changed its name from The Rank Organisation to the Rank Group. The group sold its Rank Xerox stake back to Xerox (which renamed it Xerox Limited) for about $1.5 billion in 1997.

The following year Rank announced its Hard Rock Cafe unit would build a chain of 10 restaurants (six in foreign cities) in conjunction with the NBA (the first NBA City opened in Florida in 1999). After reporting more disappointing results, however, Teare left the company. Mike Smith, former head of Ladbroke's (now Hilton Group) betting and gaming division, came in as CEO in 1999, Peter Beaudrault replaced Berk at Hard Rock.

Rank sold its nightclub business to Northern Leisure in 1999 and followed that in 2000 by selling its Odeon theater chain to UK buyout specialist Cinven for $450 million and Pinewood Studios (where the James Bond films are made) for about $100 million. Rank also agreed to sell its 50% stake in Universal Studios Escape to Blackstone Capital Partners for $275 million and started shopping its holiday resorts and Tom Cobleigh pubs.

Chairman: Sir Denys Henderson, age 67, $275,000 pay
CEO: Mike Smith, age 53, $487,000 pay
(partial-year salary)
Finance Director: Ian Dyson, age 37, $146,000 pay
(partial-year salary)
President and COO, Hard Rock Cafe International:
Peter J. Beaudrault, age 45
Managing Director Deluxe: Philip Clement, age 55
Managing Director Holidays: Jerry Fowden, age 43
Company Secretary: Charles Cormick, age 48
Managing Director Gaming: David Boden, age 43
Auditors: PricewaterhouseCoopers

1999 Sales

	$ mil.	% of total
Deluxe	1,028	31
Holidays	755	23
Gaming	656	20
Hard Rock	388	12
Other	94	3
Eliminations	377	11
Total	**3,298**	**100**

Selected Operations
Butlins (3 family entertainment resorts, UK)
Deluxe Laboratories (film processing)
Deluxe Optical Services (DVD manufacturing
and authoring)
Deluxe Video Services (video duplication)
Grosvenor Casinos (Belgium and UK)
Hard Rock Cafe (104 restaurants in 36 countries)
Hard Rock Hotels
Hard Rock Live (concert arenas; Indonesia, Mexico, US)
Haven (103 RV parks; France, Italy, Spain, UK)
Mecca Bingo (Spain and UK)
Portofino Bay Hotel
Rank Leisure Machine Services (gaming machines, UK)
Resorts USA (campgrounds, timeshares, and real estate)
Royal Pacific Resort Hotel
Warner (13 hotels and resorts for adults, UK)

HQ: 6 Connaught Place, London W2 2EZ,
United Kingdom
Phone: +44-20-7706-1111   **Fax:** +44-20-7262-9886
Web site: http://www.rank.com

1999 Sales

	$ mil.	% of total
UK	1,527	47
North America	1,190	36
Other regions	204	6
Eliminations	377	11
Total	**3,298**	**100**

Allied Digital Technologies	Planet Hollywood
Camelot Group	Rainforest Cafe
Granada Compass	Stanley Leisure
Hilton Group	Video Services
HOB Entertainment	Virgin Group
Laser-Pacific Media	Whitbread
liberty livewire	

Nasdaq (SC): RANKY FYE: December 31	Annual Growth	10/90	10/91	10/92	10/93	10/94	*12/95	12/96	12/97	12/98	12/99
Sales ($ mil.)	2.6%	—	2,677	3,264	3,121	3,597	4,054	3,569	3,323	3,414	3,298
Net income ($ mil.)	(9.5%)	—	245	211	249	275	814	(58)	319	(181)	110
Income as % of sales	—	—	9.1%	6.5%	8.0%	7.6%	20.1%	—	9.6%	—	3.3%
Earnings per share ($)	(8.3%)	—	0.54	0.47	0.55	0.59	1.90	(0.23)	0.35	(0.44)	0.27
Stock price - FY high ($)	—	—	11.70	11.00	10.30	13.75	14.63	16.75	15.25	14.13	9.75
Stock price - FY low ($)	—	—	8.00	6.60	7.00	9.80	11.50	13.25	10.75	7.00	5.50
Stock price - FY close ($)	(4.7%)	—	9.00	7.30	10.00	13.13	14.63	15.00	11.25	7.50	6.13
P/E - high	—	—	22	23	19	23	8	—	44	—	15
P/E - low	—	—	15	14	13	17	6	—	31	—	9
Dividends per share ($)	2.3%	—	0.50	0.49	0.67	0.14	0.30	0.62	0.69	0.52	0.60
Book value per share ($)	(2.9%)	—	6.27	5.19	5.31	6.15	7.57	7.35	5.99	5.65	4.95
Employees	(0.3%)	—	—	—	—	—	—	43,478	43,698	45,600	43,081

* Fiscal year change

HIGH/LOW/CLOSE

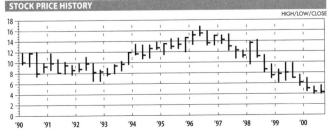

Debt ratio: 49.1%
Return on equity: 5.6%
Cash ($ mil.): 152
Current ratio: 1.22
Long-term debt ($ mil.): 1,845
No. of shares (mil.): 387
Dividends
  Yield: 9.8%
  Payout: 222.2%
Market value ($ mil.): 2,371

RECKITT BENCKISER PLC

OVERVIEW

With a cart full of well-known products, Reckitt Benckiser is cleaning up. Created by the merger of UK-based Reckitt & Colman and the Netherlands' Benckiser, the company is the world's leading household products company. Its household cleaners, home care products, and laundry products include Lime-A-Way, Lysol, Easy-Off, Vanish, Air Fresh, Air Wick, Mop & Glo, and Woolite. Its dishwashing products include the Electrasol and Calgonit brands. It also concocts French's mustard (US); over-the-counter drugs (such as Gaviscon gastrointestinal products); depilatories; pest control products (d-Con); and denture care products (Steradent, Kukident).

The company sells products in 180 countries worldwide. Reckitt Benckiser plans to divest about 75 minor brands (8% of sales), allowing the company to focus on its key brands in the fabric care, surface care, dishwasher products, health and personal, and home care products categories.

HISTORY

Reckitt & Colman's roots can be traced to Jeremiah Colman, who bought a flour mill near Norwich, England, in 1804. In 1823 his nephew James joined the company, and their business was incorporated as J. and J. Colman. Jeremiah died in 1851 and James' son, also named Jeremiah, became a partner, taking over the operations when his father died in 1854. The company moved to Carrow that year.

Colman worked to make the Carrow facilities as self-sufficient and waste-free as possible. The factory had its own foundry, print shop, paper mill (to make containers), and fire brigade. By-products from the milling process were sold to farmers for cattle feed and fertilizer. The company continued to expand, adding wheat flour and using the leftover starch from milling operations to make laundry bluing.

In 1903 the mill acquired Keen, Robinson & Co., a manufacturer of spices. J. and J. Colman got a lock on British mustard sales in 1912 when it acquired its only major competitor, Joseph Farrow & Company. A year later it joined another rival, starch maker Reckitt & Sons, in a joint venture in South America. The joint venture between Colman and Reckitt was a success, and in 1921 they pooled their overseas operations.

The two companies created Reckitt & Colman Ltd. in 1938 to manage their operations, although each company maintained a separate listing on the London Stock Exchange. In 1954 they formally merged into a single entity and acquired Chiswick Products (soap and polish).

Reckitt & Colman formed its US subsidiary in 1977, and during the 1980s it made a number of acquisitions (Airwick air fresheners, Durkee's Famous Foods, and Gold Seal bath products) to expand its presence in the US.

In 1990 the firm picked up such brands as Black Flag (insecticide), Woolite (fabric care), Old English (furniture polish), and Easy-Off (oven cleaner) when it bought Boyle-Midway from American Home Products. Reckitt & Colman exited the US spice business in 1992, selling its Durkee-French US seasonings operations.

The company gained the Lysol brand in 1994 when it bought L&F Household from Eastman Kodak. To help finance the $1.6 billion deal, Reckitt & Colman sold its flagship Colman Mustard unit to Unilever. Its French's operations in the US (mustard, Worcestershire sauce) were its only remaining food business.

Michael Colman, the last active family member, stepped down as chairman in 1995. That year the company sold Black Flag, and it sold its US personal products unit the next year.

In 1998 Reckitt & Colman bought certain cleaning products brands, including Spray'n Wash and Glass Plus, from S.C. Johnson & Son for about $160 million. CEO Vernon Sankey resigned in 1999, and Michael Turrell became the acting chief executive.

Johann A. Benckiser founded Benckiser in 1823 in the Netherlands to make industrial chemicals. The company launched Calgon Water Softener in 1956 and released Calgonit automatic dishwashing detergent in 1964. From 1982 to 1992 a number of acquisitions expanded the company's market in Central Europe and North America. By 1999 Benckiser's products were sold in 45 countries, including Eastern Europe, Asia, and the Middle East.

After the merger in December 1999, Alan Dalby, former chairman of Reckitt & Colman, was named chairman of Reckitt Benckiser. Bart Becht, previously CEO of Benckiser, was named CEO of the new company. In March 2000 Reckitt Benckiser announced plans to unload 75 brands to focus on more growth-oriented brands.

OFFICERS

Chairman: Alan J. Dalby, age 63
Deputy Chairman: Peter Harf, age 53, $82,000 pay
CEO: Bart Becht, age 43, $438,000 pay
CFO: Colin Day, age 45
EVP Americas: Ken Stokes, age 43
EVP Category Development: Marcello Bottoli, age 37
EVP Rest of World: Freddy Caspers, age 38
EVP Supply: Alain Le Goff, age 47
EVP Western Europe: Erhard Schoewel, age 50
SVP Human Resources: Frank Ruether, age 46
SVP Information Services: Tony Gallagher, age 43
SVP Investor Relations and Corporate Communications: Tom Corran
VP Human Resources (US): Bev Wilen
Company Secretary: P. David Saltmarsh
Category Group Director Health & Personal Care: Brian Bentley
Auditors: PricewaterhouseCoopers

LOCATIONS

HQ: 67 Alma Rd., Windsor,
Berkshire SL4 3HD, United Kingdom
Phone: +44-1753835835   **Fax:** +44-1753835830
US HQ: 1655 Valley Rd., Wayne, NJ 07474
US Phone: 973-633-3600   **US Fax:** 973-633-3633
Web site: http://www.reckittbenckiser.com

1999 Sales

	% of total
Western Europe	45
North America	29
Asia/Pacific	11
Latin America	6
Other regions	9
Total	**100**

PRODUCTS/OPERATIONS

1999 Sales

	% of total
Household & personal care	94
Food	6
Total	**100**

Selected Brands

Dishwashing	Health & Personal Care	Home Care
Calgonit	Dettol	Aerogard
Electrasol	Disprin	Air Wick
Finish	Gaviscon	Bom ar
Jet-Dry	Fybogel	d-Con
	Immac	Haze
Fabric Care	Lemsip	Mortein
Ava	Steradent	
Calgon	Veet	**Surface Care**
Colon		Brasso
Dosia		Dettox
Napisan		Easy Off
Resolve		Harpic
Spray'n Wash		Lime-A-Way
Vanish		Lysol
		Old English

COMPETITORS

Alticor	Henkel
Bestfoods	Johnson & Johnson
Blyth, Inc.	Mallinckrodt
Boots Company	Nabisco Holdings
Carter-Wallace	National Service Industries
Chattem	Pfizer
Church & Dwight	Procter & Gamble
Clorox	S.C. Johnson
Colgate-Palmolive	SmithKline Beecham
Dial	Unilever

HISTORICAL FINANCIALS & EMPLOYEES

London: RB. FYE: Saturday nearest Jan. 1	Annual Growth	12/90	12/91	12/92	12/93	12/94	12/95	12/96	12/97	12/98	12/99
Sales (£ mil.)	6.3%	1,764	1,987	1,904	2,096	2,071	2,306	2,295	2,197	2,202	3,054
Net income (£ mil.)	—	130	141	94	169	82	326	326	216	165	(37)
Income as % of sales	—	7.4%	7.1%	4.9%	8.0%	4.0%	14.1%	14.2%	9.8%	7.5%	—
Earnings per share (p)	—	35.00	37.90	25.20	43.60	21.30	76.80	57.70	53.10	39.70	(5.40)
Stock price - FY high (p)	—	562.00	775.00	755.00	765.00	747.00	758.00	777.00	1,054.00	1,333.00	907.00
Stock price - FY low (p)	—	462.00	507.00	546.00	551.00	553.00	614.00	649.00	696.00	780.00	500.00
Stock price - FY close (p)	0.8%	545.00	679.00	655.00	760.00	618.00	751.00	724.00	955.00	794.00	584.00
P/E - high	—	16	20	30	18	35	10	13	20	34	—
P/E - low	—	13	13	22	13	26	8	11	13	20	—
Dividends per share (p)	—	13.60	15.10	16.20	17.60	18.70	20.20	23.40	24.00	25.50	0.00
Book value per share (p)	(1.2%)	—	—	165.00	188.00	183.00	212.00	192.00	224.00	237.00	152.00
Employees	(1.8%)	23,800	22,500	21,000	21,000	18,700	18,739	17,425	16,500	15,900	20,200

STOCK PRICE HISTORY

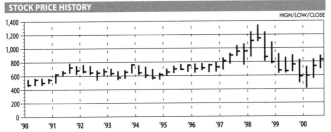

HIGH/LOW/CLOSE

1999 FISCAL YEAR-END

Debt ratio: 43.8%
Return on equity: —
Cash (£ mil.): 89
Current ratio: 0.99
Long-term debt (£ mil.): 426
No. of shares (mil.): 620
Dividends
 Yield: —
 Payout: —
Market value ($ mil.): 586,086
Sales ($ mil.): 4,940

REED ELSEVIER PLC

OVERVIEW

Looking for legal, business, or scientific information? With Reed Elsevier around, there's no need to go elsewhere. Formed in 1993 when Reed International and Elsevier combined their publishing empires, the London-based company offers information primarily in North America and Europe.

Generating more than 40% of Reed Elsevier's revenue, the company's business publishing operations span US business information publisher Cahners Business Information, Reed Business Information (UK magazines and directories), Elsevier Business Information (European business and reference publisher), and event organizer Reed Exhibition Companies.

Reed Elsevier's legal publishing operations bring in more than a third of the company's revenue and include legal, corporate, and government information provider LEXIS-NEXIS; the Reed Elsevier Legal Division (legal, tax, and regulatory information); and Reed Educational & Professional Publishing. No slouch in scientific publishing, Reed Elsevier issues more than 1,200 subscription-based journals such as *The Lancet* and operates Internet scientific information service ScienceDirect.

Hoping to reverse its sagging fortunes, Reed Elsevier is intensifying its focus on providing information via the Web. The company also is focusing on its business, legal, and scientific publishing operations and jettisoning noncore assets. Reed International and Elsevier each own about 50% of Reed Elsevier.

The company has agreed to purchase Harcourt General for $5.6 billion and sell some of its business to The Thomson Corporation.

HISTORY

Albert E. Reed & Co. was named after the man who founded the company as a newsprint manufacturer in 1894. It went public in 1903. For the next 50 years, Reed grew by buying UK pulp and paper mills. In the 1930s Reed began making packaging materials and in 1954 added building products. The company expanded into New Zealand (1955), Australia (1960), and Norway (1962).

Chairman Sir Don Ryder radically altered the company in the 1960s and 1970s, leading Reed into other paper-related products and into the wallpaper, paint, and interior-decorating and do-it-yourself markets. In 1970 Reed bought International Publishing, Mirror Group Newspapers, and 29% of Cahners Publishing (buying the remaining 71% in 1977). However, coordinating so many companies was difficult, and, strapped for cash, Reed dumped most of its Australian businesses in 1978.

The company sold the Mirror Group to Robert Maxwell in 1984 and divested the remainder of its nonpaper and nonpublishing companies by 1987 to focus on publishing. It bought Octopus Publishing (1987), the UK's *TV Times* (1989), News Corp.'s Travel Information Group (1989), and Martindale-Hubbell (1990).

Reed merged with Elsevier, the world's leading scholarly journal publisher in 1993. Elsevier was founded by five booksellers and publishers in Rotterdam in 1880. It took its name from a famous Dutch family publishing company, which had operated from the late 16th century to the early 18th century.

Elsevier entered the scientific publishing market in the 1930s, and following WWII diversified into trade journals and consumer manuals. In 1979 the company made its first US acquisition, Congressional Information Service.

In 1988 the company fended off a takeover bid by Maxwell by planning a merger with UK publisher Pearson; Maxwell was thwarted, the merger ultimately failed, and Elsevier later sold its Pearson stock. In 1991 Elsevier bought Maxwell's Pergamon Press.

In 1994 Reed International and Elsevier both were listed on the NYSE. Reed Elsevier also built its US presence that year with its purchase of Mead's LEXIS-NEXIS online service. In 1996 the company acquired Tolley, a UK tax and legal publisher, and a 50% interest in Shepard's, a US legal citation service.

Reed Elsevier bought the Chilton business magazine unit from Disney in 1997. The company sold IPC Magazines (now IPC Media, 69 general-interest titles) for $1.4 billion in early 1998 to an investment group led by venture capitalists Cinven. Reed Elsevier later terminated its agreement to buy Wolters Kluwer. Later that year the company bought the remaining 50% of Shepard's from Times Mirror.

In 1999 the company welcomed new CEO Crispin Davis, the former head of media-buying firm Aegis Group. It also reorganized Cahners, laying off several hundred employees and consolidating magazine operations. The company hoped to boost its scientific publishing profile by unveiling Web-based scientific information service ScienceDirect.

In 2000 the company has agreed to purchase Harcourt General and sell some of its business to The Thomson Corporation.

Chairman: Morris Tabaksblat, age 62
CEO: Crispin Davis, age 50, $525,000 pay
CFO: Mark Armour, age 45, $372,398 pay
Executive Director: Derk Haank, age 46, $32,668 pay
Director of Human Resources: Onno Laman Trip, age 53, $200,443 pay
CEO Cahners Business Information: Marc Teren
CEO Global Legal Publishing and Information Division: Andrew Prozes
President, Martindale Hubbel: Lou Andreozzi
President, Lexis-Nexis: Bill Pardue
COO Lexis Publishing: Nick Emrick
Auditors: Deloitte & Touche

LOCATIONS

HQ: 25 Victoria St., London SW1H 0EX, United Kingdom
Phone: +44-20-7222-8420   **Fax:** +44-20-7227-5799
US HQ: 2 Park Ave., 7th Fl., New York, NY 10016
US Phone: 212-448-2300   **US Fax:** 212-448-2196
Web site: http://www.reed-elsevier.com

Reed Elsevier has operations in the Asia/Pacific region, Europe, and North America.

1999 Sales

	$ mil.	% of total
North America	3,081	56
Europe		
UK	782	14
The Netherlands	383	7
Other countries	676	13
Other regions	558	10
Total	**5,480**	**100**

PRODUCTS/OPERATIONS

1999 Sales

	$ mil.	% of total
Business	2,376	43
Legal	2,050	38
Scientific	1,054	19
Total	**5,480**	**100**

Selected Operations
Business publishing
  Cahners Business Information
  Elsevier Business Information
  Reed Business Information
  Reed Exhibition Companies
Legal publishing
  LEXIS-NEXIS
  Reed Educational & Professional Publishing
  Reed Elsevier Legal Division
Scientific Publishing
  Editions Scientifiques et Médicales Elsevier
  Elsevier Science
  Excerpta Medic Communications

COMPETITORS

Advance Publications	Pearson
American Lawyer Media	Penton Media
Axel Springer	PRIMEDIA
Bertelsmann	Reuters
Bright Station	Thomson Corporation
Dow Jones	Time Warner
Gruner + Jahr	United News & Media
Havas	VNU
International Data Group	W.W. Norton
John Wiley	West Group
McGraw-Hill	Wolters Kluwer
News Corp.	

HISTORICAL FINANCIALS & EMPLOYEES

Joint venture FYE: December 31	Annual Growth	12/90	12/91	12/92	12/93	12/94	12/95	12/96	12/97	12/98	12/99
Sales ($ mil.)	6.0%	—	3,438	3,990	4,861	4,703	5,247	5,744	5,637	5,293	5,480
Net income ($ mil.)	—	—	382	501	661	700	794	1,028	343	1,281	(102)
Income as % of sales	—	—	11.1%	12.6%	13.6%	14.9%	15.1%	17.9%	6.1%	24.2%	—
Employees	5.5%	—	18,000	18,100	25,700	30,000	30,400	25,800	27,600	26,100	27,700

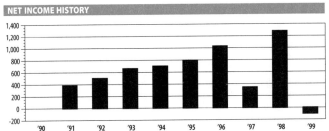

NET INCOME HISTORY

1999 FISCAL YEAR-END
Debt ratio: 25.1%
Return on equity: —
Cash ($ mil.): 711
Current ratio: 0.51
Long-term debt ($ mil.): 1,002

RENAULT S.A.

Not all Renault vehicles are built for speed, but the company has zipped past fellow rival Peugeot Citroën to become France's leading carmaker. Boulogne-Billancourt, France-based Renault S.A. produces a range of small to midsize cars, heavy trucks, and commercial vehicles, including buses, vans, and military vehicles. The company is also a leading heavy-truck maker (Mack Trucks) in the US. Renault also makes agricultural machinery.

With the purchase of 37% of Nissan and

51% of Automobile Dacia (Romania's leading car-maker), Renault made it clear that it doesn't intend to be left in the international slow lane. The company has agreed to buy a controlling (70%) stake in South Korea-based Samsung Motors' automobile business; it has also agreed to sell its Renault V.I. subsidiary and its Mack truck unit to Volvo in return for a 15% stake in the Swedish company. Formerly state-owned, the French government has reduced its stake to 44%.

In the Paris suburb of Billancourt in 1898, 21-year-old Louis Renault assembled a motorized vehicle with a transmission box of his own design. Louis and his brothers, Marcel and Fernand, established Renault Freres and produced the world's first sedan in 1899. Marcel died in a racing accident (1903) and Fernand left the business (1908), leaving Louis in sole possession of the company. He renamed it La Société Louis Renault in 1908.

In 1914 a fleet of 600 Paris taxis shuttled French troops to fight the Germans in the Battle of the Marne. Renault also built light tanks and airplane engines. Between world wars Renault expanded into trucks, tractors, and aircraft engines. Renault sustained heavy damage in WWII, but Louis Renault operated the remaining Paris facilities for the Germans during their occupation of France. After the liberation of Paris, he was accused of collaboration and died in prison while awaiting trial in 1944. The de Gaulle government nationalized Renault in 1945 and gave the company its present name.

Worldwide economic growth aided Renault's postwar comeback. The company achieved its greatest success in high-volume, low-cost cars such as the 4 CV in the late 1940s and 1950s, the Renault 4 in the 1960s and 1970s, and the Renault 5 in the 1970s and 1980s.

In 1979 Renault acquired 46% of American Motors Corporation (AMC). In the early 1980s AMC fared poorly, and Renault suffered from a worldwide slump in auto sales, an aging product line, and stiff competition from Japanese carmakers. Decreasing sales, an unwieldy bureaucracy, and above-average wages contributed to a $1.5 billion loss in 1984.

Georges Besse took over Renault in 1985, and trimmed employment by 20,000. When Besse was assassinated by terrorists in 1986, Raymond Levy assumed his role and continued

his policies, laying off 30,000 more workers and selling AMC to Chrysler (1987).

Renault and Volvo agreed to extensive cross-ownership and cooperation in 1990. In 1994 Renault swapped its 25% stake in Volvo's car division for the latter's 45% stake in Renault's troubled truck unit. (Volvo sold its remaining 11% stake in 1997.)

The French government reduced its share of the firm from 80% to 52% in 1995 and to 46% the following year. In 1997 it shut down a Belgian plant that employed more than 3,000 workers and fired a similar number of employees in France. Renault paid a $13 million civil penalty to the EPA in 1998 to settle allegations that its Mack unit cheated on its diesel engine emissions tests.

Renault and Fiat struck several deals in 1999. They combined their bus-making operations under the name Irisbus and their foundry operations into jointly owned Teksid. Renault sold a 51% stake in Renault Automation to Fiat's Comau robotics unit. Also that year Renault bought a 51% stake in Romanian automaker, Automobile Dacia SA, and paid $5.4 billion for a 37% stake in Nissan, and a 15% (later increased to 23%) stake in truck affiliate Nissan Diesel Motor.

Early in 2000 the company announced that it would spend around $100 million to build an SUV factory in Brazil and announced plans to trim almost $3 billion in costs between 2001 and 2003. The same year Renault agreed to buy a 70% stake in Samsung Motors' automobile business for around $550 million. It also inked a deal to sell its Mack truck unit to Volvo in exchange for a 15% stake in Volvo. Renault plans to buy another 5% of Volvo on the open market. Renault and Nissan also announced plans to save about $1 billion by combining their European sales and marketing operations.

Chairman and CEO: Louis Schweitzer
SVP and CFO: Christian Dor
EVP: Shemaya Levy
EVP Product and Strategic Planning and International Operations: Georges Douin
EVP Research, Engineering, Manufacturing, and Purchasing: Pierre-Alain de Smedt
EVP Sales and Marketing: François Hinfray
Chairman and CEO, Renault Credit International: Philippe Gamba
Chairman and CEO, Renault V.I.: Patrick Faure
Corporate Secretary General and Group Human Resources: Michel de Virville
Auditors: Deloitte Touche Tohmatsu

LOCATIONS

HQ: 13-15 Quai Le Gallo,
92100 Boulogne-Billancourt Cedex, France
Phone: +33-1-41-04-04-04   **Fax:** +33-1-41-04-51-49
US HQ: Mack Trucks Inc., Allentown, PA 18103
US Phone: 610-709-3011   **US Fax:** 610-709-2405
Web site: http://www.renault.com

Renault has manufacturing operations in Argentina, Australia, Brazil, France, Portugal, Slovenia, Spain, Turkey, and the US.

1999 Sales

	€ mil.	% of total
Europe		
France	13,731	37
Other EU countries	17,528	47
Other countries	6,333	16
Total	**37,592**	**100**

PRODUCTS/OPERATIONS

1999 Sales

	€ mil.	% of total
Automobiles	29,738	79
Commercial vehicles	6,474	17
Financing	1,380	4
Total	**37,592**	**100**

Selected Products

Automobiles

Clio	Safrane
Espace	Scenic
Kangoo	Spider
Laguna	Twingo
Megane	

Commercial Vehicles
Coaches
Construction trucks (Mack, Renault)
Long-haul trucks (Mack, Magnum, and Premium)
Military vehicles
Public service vehicles (fire trucks, garbage trucks, and snowplows)
Regional transport trucks (Mid-Liner, Premium)

COMPETITORS

BMW	Isuzu	Peugeot Motors
Daewoo	Kia Motors	of America, Inc.
DaimlerChrysler	Kubota	Saab Automobile
Fiat	Mazda	Suzuki
Ford	Mitsubishi	Tata Enterprises
General Motors	Navistar	Toyota
Grupo Dina	PACCAR	Volkswagen
Honda	Peugeot	Volvo
Hyundai		

HISTORICAL FINANCIALS & EMPLOYEES

Euronext Paris: RNO FYE: December 31	Annual Growth	12/90	12/91	12/92	12/93	12/94	12/95	12/96	12/97	12/98	12/99
Sales (€ mil.)	4.7%	24,944	25,303	28,089	25,884	27,218	28,061	28,063	31,696	37,187	37,592
Net income (€ mil.)	12.5%	184	469	866	163	554	326	(800)	827	1,337	534
Income as % of sales	—	0.7%	1.9%	3.1%	0.6%	2.0%	1.2%	—	2.6%	3.6%	1.4%
Earnings per share (€)	(1.4%)	—	—	—	—	2.39	1.38	(3.36)	3.47	5.64	2.23
Stock price - FY high (€)	—	—	—	—	—	28.07	28.14	24.07	28.63	60.96	55.00
Stock price - FY low (€)	—	—	—	—	—	26.31	20.12	15.70	16.17	25.61	30.53
Stock price - FY close (€)	14.9%	—	—	—	—	23.91	21.50	17.00	25.81	38.26	47.86
P/E - high	—	—	—	—	—	12	20	—	8	11	25
P/E - low	—	—	—	—	—	11	15	—	5	5	14
Dividends per share (€)	7.5%	—	—	—	—	0.53	0.53	0.00	0.53	0.53	0.76
Book value per share (€)	4.5%	—	—	—	—	27.40	28.13	25.30	30.75	32.78	34.13
Employees	0.2%	157,378	147,185	146,604	139,733	138,279	139,950	140,905	141,315	138,321	159,608

STOCK PRICE HISTORY

HIGH/LOW/CLOSE

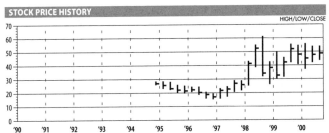

1999 FISCAL YEAR-END

Debt ratio: 45.8%
Return on equity: 6.7%
Cash (€ mil.): 1,046
Current ratio: 1.08
Long-term debt (€ mil.): 6,930
No. of shares (mil.): 240
Dividends
  Yield: 0.0%
  Payout: 0.3%
Market value ($ mil.): 11,532
Sales ($ mil.): 37,772

REPSOL YPF, S.A.

OVERVIEW

Repsol YPF, formerly Repsol, is not Spain's sole rep in the oil and gas industry, but it is the country's largest. Spain's #1 oil company, Madrid-based Repsol YPF is a fully integrated oil and gas enterprise. The company acquired its new name and expanded its reserves significantly with the 1999 purchase of YPF, Argentina's leading oil company.

With the merger, the company has proved reserves of 4.2 billion barrels of oil equivalent. It explores for and produces oil and gas primarily in Latin America, the Middle East, and North Africa. In Spain it operates five refineries and sells gasoline under the brands Campsa, Petronor, and Repsol through a network of more than 3,400 service stations. The company has expanded its European retail operations into Portugal and the UK.

Outside of Spain the company operates more than 3,760 gas stations, including some 3,000 in Argentina. But to comply with its agreement with Argentina's government to divest 11% of the company's refining and marketing assets in Argentina, Repsol YPF is shedding 700 of its stations and a refinery in a $1 billion asset swap with Brazil's Petrobras.

In other operations, Repsol YPF produces basic and derivative petrochemicals, and in Spain it dominates the market for liquefied petroleum gas.

Through 45%-owned subsidiary Gas Natural, the company controls Spanish natural gas supplier Enagas, although deregulation is forcing Repsol YPF to reduce its Enagas stake and open up 72% of the gas sold in Spain to competition. For growth, Repsol YPF has targeted Latin America. Besides YPF, the company owns a 99% stake in Argentine oil company Astra and has interests in oil and gas assets (including refineries) in other Latin American countries.

HISTORY

Repsol YPF, officially created as Repsol in 1987, is actually the result of efforts that began as early as the 1920s to organize Spain's fragmented energy industry.

Following an era of dependency on foreign investment prior to and during Francisco Franco's dictatorship (1939-75), Spain began reorganizing its energy industry. In 1979 it set up the Instituto Nacional de Hidrocarburos, which in 1981 incorporated all public-sector firms involved in gas and oil under one government agency.

Repsol was formed six years later to provide central management to a Spanish oil company that could compete in the unified European market. The government chose the name Repsol, after a well-known brand of Spanish lubricant products.

In 1989 Repsol offered 26% of the firm on the Madrid and New York stock exchanges, raising over $1 billion. That year Repsol increased its marine fleet with the purchase of the Naviera Vizcaina shipping company and bought Carless Refining & Marketing, a UK business with a chain of 500 service stations operating mainly under the Anglo brand. Although Spain was opening its doors to foreign investment, the Spanish government maintained control over the country's energy industry, including a tightly guarded distribution network under state-controlled Campsa. Campsa oversaw a marketing/logistics system of pipelines, storage terminals, and sales outlets.

The European Community demanded that Spain open its markets to other EC members, forcing Campsa in 1991 to divide its 3,800 gasoline stations among its four major shareholders: Cepsa (Spain's largest private refiner), Petromed, Ertoil, and Repsol. Repsol gained 66% of the logistical network and use of the Campsa brand name.

Repsol and Spanish bank La Caixa merged their interests in natural gas in 1992 to create Gas Natural, a new gas distributor. That year the Spanish government began reducing its majority holding, and by 1996 its stake had dwindled to 10%. (It sold its remaining stock in 1997).

Expanding its South American operations, Repsol acquired control of Argentinian oil company Astra and a Peruvian oil refinery in 1996. That year Repsol purchased a 30% stake in the Tin Fouye Tabankort field in Algeria.

In 1999 Repsol paid $2 billion for a 15% stake in giant oil company YPF, which was auctioned off by Argentina's government. After acquiring another 83% of YPF for $13.2 billion, Repsol changed its name to Repsol YPF. To help pay down debt incurred in the acquisition, Repsol YPF sold its UK North Sea oil and gas operations to US independent Kerr-McGee for $555 million in 2000. That year the company (as part of its commitment to Argentina's government after acquiring YPF) agreed to swap some of its Argentine refining and marketing assets for Brazilian oil and gas operations owned by Petrobras.

Chairman and CEO, Repsol YPF and YPF:
Alfonso Cortina de Alcocer
VC: Antonio Hernandez-Gil Alvarez Cienfuegos
VC: Emilio de Ybarra y Churruca
VC: Jose Vilarasau Salat
EVP Chemicals: Antonio Gonzalez-Adalid Garcia-Zozaya
EVP Exploration and Production: Roberto Monti
EVP Gas and Electricity: Guzman Solana Gomez
EVP Refining and Marketing: Juan Sancho Rof
SVP Planning, Control, and Strategic Development:
Miguel Angel Remon Gil
Director Finance: Carmelo de las Morenas Lopez
Director Human Resources:
Jesus Fernandez de la Vega Sanz
Director Legal Affairs: Rafael Piqueras Bautista
Auditors: Arthur Andersen

HQ: Paseo de la Castellana, 278, 28046 Madrid, Spain
Phone: +34-91-348-81-00   **Fax:** +34-91-348-28-21
Web site: http://www.repsol-ypf.com

Repsol YPF has operations in 27 countries in Africa, the Caribbean, Europe, Latin America, the Middle East, and the Far East.

1999 Sales

	% of total
Europe	
Spain	65
Other countries	4
Latin America	25
North Africa & Middle East	3
Far East	1
Other regions	2
Total	**100**

1999 Sales

	% of total
Refining & marketing	71
Exploration & production	13
Gas & electricity	11
Petrochemicals	5
Total	**100**

Selected Subsidiaries and Affiliates
Astra C.A.P S. A. (99%, oil and gas exploration and production, Argentina)
Repsol Comercial de Productos Petroliferos, SA (96%, marketing)
Repsol Exploracion, SA (oil and gas exploration and production)
Repsol YPF Peru (91%; refining, marketing, and LPG)
Repsol Petroleo, SA (refining)
Repsol Quimica, SA (chemicals)
YPF (99%, integrated oil company, Argentina)

A.G. Spanos	Enron	PETROBRAS
Anadarko	Exxon Mobil	Phillips
Petroleum	Iberdrola	Petroleum
Apco Argentina	Imperial Oil	Pioneer Natural
BHP	Kerr-McGee	Resources
BP	Koch	Royal
Caltex	Murphy Oil	Dutch/Shell
Chevron	Noble Affiliates	Texaco
Coastal	Norsk Hydro	TOTAL FINA
Conoco	Occidental	ELF
Devon Energy	PDVSA	Unión Fenosa
Endesa (Spain)	PEMEX	Unocal
Eni	Perez Companc	USX-Marathon

NYSE: REP FYE: December 31	Annual Growth	12/90	12/91	12/92	12/93	12/94	12/95	12/96	12/97	12/98	12/99
Sales ($ mil.)	6.7%	14,829	17,511	16,602	15,140	18,019	20,962	21,344	21,057	21,740	26,537
Net income ($ mil.)	4.1%	709	727	626	560	735	970	918	827	1,025	1,020
Income as % of sales	—	4.8%	4.1%	3.8%	3.7%	4.1%	4.6%	4.3%	3.9%	4.7%	3.8%
Earnings per share ($)	3.7%	0.79	0.81	0.70	0.63	0.82	1.00	1.00	0.92	1.13	1.10
Stock price - FY high ($)	—	10.11	9.07	10.24	10.45	11.66	11.41	13.03	15.15	19.15	24.25
Stock price - FY low ($)	—	6.70	6.91	6.95	7.41	8.66	8.78	10.49	12.36	13.55	15.44
Stock price - FY close ($)	14.0%	7.16	8.33	7.99	10.28	9.07	10.95	12.70	14.17	18.19	23.25
P/E - high	—	13	11	15	17	14	11	13	16	17	22
P/E - low	—	8	9	10	12	11	9	10	13	12	14
Dividends per share ($)	9.6%	0.21	0.22	0.26	0.21	0.21	0.28	0.40	0.44	0.44	0.48
Book value per share ($)	9.4%	4.72	5.17	4.65	4.09	4.96	6.02	7.25	6.73	7.85	10.64
Employees	3.6%	21,284	20,848	19,632	18,797	18,797	18,878	19,560	21,440	23,762	29,262

HIGH/LOW/CLOSE

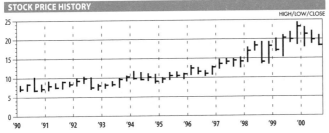

Debt ratio: 44.9%
Return on equity: 10.3%
Cash ($ mil.): 337
Current ratio: 0.60
Long-term debt ($ mil.): 10,317
No. of shares (mil.): 1,188
Dividends
  Yield: 2.1%
  Payout: 43.6%
Market value ($ mil.): 27,621

REUTERS GROUP PLC

Reuters rhymes with loiters, yet this company does anything but. The London-based firm is the world's largest provider of financial information. Its Reuters Financial division collects information from some 260 exchanges and over-the-counter markets, as well as contributing subscribers, and disseminates it to more than 521,000 users worldwide through products such as Markets 3000 (information on money, equity, and fixed income markets) and Reuters Television (for financial markets).

Through its Reuterspace unit, it provides news to more than 900 Web sites and operates the Greenhouse Fund, which invests in high-tech startups. Subsidiary Instinet, the world's #1 electronic agency brokerage, provides information on equities and fixed income markets. Reuters is planning to spin off Instinet in 2001.

In early 2000 the company announced plans to invest $800 million over four years in services delivered via the Internet. This long-awaited move represents a significant change for Reuters — its products will be targeted toward the individual investor instead of focusing on institutional clients. The Reuters Digital Dashboard (Reuters' personal portal) is the first of several planned products. The company has teamed with rival Dow Jones in the Dow Jones Reuters Business Interactive joint venture (operating under the name Factiva) and also with Microsoft to develop joint Internet initiatives.

Reuters is controlled by the Reuters Founders Share Company, an organization created in 1984 to ensure Reuters' independence.

In 1849 German news correspondent Paul Julius Reuter seized the chance to scoop his competitors by using carrier pigeons to bridge the telegraph gap between Aachen, Germany, and Brussels. He moved to London in 1851 and began telegraphing stock quotes between Paris and London. Six years later Reuter's Telegram Co. was organized as a limited company.

Reuter ceded management to his son Herbert in 1878 and died in 1899. Herbert made the disastrous decision to establish Reuter's Bank in 1913. Two years later, under the strain of WWI anti-German sentiment and the death of his wife, Herbert committed suicide. Successor Roderick Jones changed the company's name to Reuters Ltd. and took it private in 1916 to avoid a hostile takeover. Reuters advanced into new technology by using radios and teleprinters in the 1920s. By 1925 The Press Association owned a majority of the company; it ousted Jones in 1941, displeased with his relationship to the British government. In an attempt to uphold Reuters' independence, The Reuters Trust was created that year.

Reuters established international bureaus during the 1940s and 1950s, but its owners' focus on the bottom line limited the scale of expansion. The company partnered with Ultronic Systems Corporation in 1964 to launch Stockmaster, a financial data transmission system. Nine years later Reuters introduced its Monitor electronic marketplace to track the foreign exchange market. Monitor Dealing, introduced in 1981, enabled dealers to trade currencies online.

The company went public in 1984 as Reuters

Holdings PLC, and with the new capital, it accelerated acquisitions. It bought Visnews (now Reuters Television, 1985), Instinet (1986), TIBCO (1994), and Quotron (1994). The company also acquired a new CEO during this time when Peter Job, a journalist who joined Reuters in 1963, was named to the top spot in 1991. In 1994 the company launched Reuters Television for financial markets. The following year it agreed to make its information available on the Internet via IBM's infoMarket service.

With competition from the Internet nipping at its heels, Reuters restructured in 1998 to refocus along product lines (which led to the creation of holding company Reuters Group PLC). Its acquisition of Lipper Analytical Services' mutual fund business that year extended its financial information reach. In 1999 Reuters and Dow Jones & Company launched a joint venture combining their online news databases. Reuters also established the Reuters New Media International unit to oversee its Internet operations.

In 2000 Reuters and telecommunications firm Equant launched Radianz, a joint venture (51%-owned by Reuters) to offer secure business-to-business Internet and telecommunications service. It also announced joint ventures with online investment information provider Multex (to launch an Internet portal for European investors) and wireless communications firm Aether Systems (to provide wireless data application in Europe) and allied with Microsoft to develop a series of online products. It also purchased The Yankee Group from fellow financial information provider Primark.

Chairman: Sir Christopher A. Hogg, age 63,
$203,000 pay
Chief Executive: Peter Job, age 58, $878,000 pay
Finance Director: David Grigson, age 45
**Executive Director, Group Technical Strategy Reuters
Trading Systems:** David G. Ure, age 52, $496,000 pay
**Executive Director, Group Marketing Director;
Chairman, Reuters Information:**
Jean-Claude Marchand, age 53, $558,000 pay
Executive Director; CEO Reuters Trading Solutions:
Philip Green, age 46
Chairman Instinet: Andre-Francois H. Villeneuve,
age 55, $496,000 pay
Chairman Lipper: A. Michael Lipper
Chairman and CEO TIBCO: Vivek Ranadive
Co-CEO Greenhouse Fund: David Lockwood
Co-CEO Greenhouse Fund: John Taysom
CEO Reuters Information: Tom H. Glocer
CEO Reuterspace: Robert O. Rowley, age 50,
$539,000 pay (prior to title change)
Director of Human Resources: Geoffrey A. Weetman
Auditors: PricewaterhouseCoopers LLP

1999 Sales

	$ mil.	% of total
Reuters Financial	3,910	77
Instinet	848	17
Reuterspace	304	6
Adjustments	(13)	—
Total	**5,049**	**100**

Selected Products
AdValue Media Technologies (media buying and selling)
Markets 3000 (real-time data, news, and television
service covering money, equity, and fixed income
markets)
Reuters Broker Research (fixed income and economic
research from more than 600 contributors worldwide)
Reuters Business Network (business, consumer, and
finance reports for television affiliates)
Reuters Television (television service delivering live
coverage of financial markets)
Reuters World Service (24-hour coverage of global news)
Securities 3000 (news and television service covering
global equities markets)

HQ: 85 Fleet St., London EC4P 4AJ, United Kingdom
Phone: +44-20-7250-1122   **Fax:** +44-20-7542-4064
US HQ: 1700 Broadway, New York, NY 10019
US Phone: 212-603-3300   **US Fax:** 212-247-0346
Web site: http://www.reuters.com

1999 Sales

	$ mil.	% of total
Europe, Middle East & Africa	2,654	53
The Americas	1,582	31
Asia/Pacific	813	16
Total	**5,049**	**100**

ADP	Datastream	NASD
Agence France-	Systems	NYSE
Presse	Dow Jones	Pearson
Algorithmics	Dun &	Quick Corp.
Associated Press	Bradstreet	Quote.com
Bloomberg	Financial Times	SunGard Data
Bridge	Hoover's	Systems
Information	LEXIS-NEXIS	Telekurs
Bright Station	MarketWatch.com	Thomson
BT	McGraw-Hill	Corporation
CDA/Weisenberger	Misys	UPI
CSK	Morningstar	Value Line

Nasdaq: RTRSY FYE: December 31	Annual Growth	12/90	12/91	12/92	12/93	12/94	12/95	12/96	12/97	12/98	12/99
Sales ($ mil.)	7.5%	2,642	2,742	2,374	2,773	3,614	4,198	4,990	4,760	5,032	5,049
Net income ($ mil.)	6.2%	400	429	358	442	543	643	841	644	637	687
Income as % of sales	—	15.1%	15.7%	15.1%	16.0%	15.0%	15.3%	16.8%	13.5%	12.7%	13.6%
Earnings per share ($)	8.0%	1.44	1.54	1.28	1.60	1.02	2.40	3.12	2.40	2.65	2.88
Stock price - FY high ($)	—	35.56	29.06	34.56	42.56	48.38	58.88	76.88	76.75	74.75	100.00
Stock price - FY low ($)	—	16.06	17.88	27.19	27.69	38.94	38.38	54.63	56.00	42.13	50.25
Stock price - FY close ($)	16.6%	20.25	28.88	31.88	39.50	43.88	55.13	76.50	66.25	63.38	80.81
P/E - high	—	25	19	25	27	47	25	25	32	28	34
P/E - low	—	11	12	19	17	38	16	18	23	16	17
Dividends per share ($)	16.1%	0.41	0.45	0.54	0.56	0.66	0.99	1.04	1.48	1.21	1.57
Book value per share ($)	1.2%	3.68	4.65	4.49	3.47	4.02	5.26	7.67	9.72	2.61	4.10
Employees	4.9%	10,731	10,450	10,393	11,306	12,718	14,348	15,478	16,119	16,938	16,546

HIGH/LOW/CLOSE

Debt ratio: 30.3%
Return on equity: 86.5%
Cash ($ mil.): 192
Current ratio: 0.86
Long-term debt ($ mil.): 422
No. of shares (mil.): 237
Dividends
  Yield: 1.9%
  Payout: 54.5%
Market value ($ mil.): 19,161

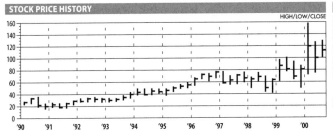

RICOH COMPANY, LTD.

OVERVIEW

Ricoh's copiers won't sort your mail for you — yet. The Tokyo-based company is counting on its history as an innovator to confront dizzying change in the markets for its products. A leading maker of copiers and supplies (60% of sales), Ricoh also makes fax machines, PCs, and printers, as well as digital cameras, semiconductors, and recordable and rewritable CD drives.

Environmentally conscious Ricoh, which has more than 320 subsidiaries and affiliates worldwide, is focusing product development on digital office machine convergence. Its digi-

tal copiers link to PCs and computer networks that allow access on the road, at home, or linking from another office. The company has upgraded its fax machines to connect to PCs and to incorporate e-mail and scanner functions. Japan accounts for 60% of sales.

Ricoh is counting on growing demand for digital cameras and data storage to spur growth. It is developing application-specific integrated circuits (ASICs) and application-specific standard products, including CD drive and PC card controllers for notebook computers.

HISTORY

Ricoh began in 1936 as the Riken Kankoshi Company making photographic paper. With Kiyoshi Ichimura at the helm, the company soon became the leader in Japan's sensitized-paper market. It changed its name to Riken Optical Company in 1938 and started making cameras. Two years later it produced its first Ricoh-brand camera.

Following WWII the company was allowed to reconstitute itself with Ichimura still at its head. By 1954 Ricoh cameras were Japan's #1 sellers and were also popular abroad. The next year the company entered the office machine market with its compact mimeograph machine. Ricoh followed that in 1960 with an offset duplicator.

Ricoh built its business in the 1960s with a range of office machines, including reproduction and data processing equipment and retrieval systems. The company began establishing operations overseas, including US subsidiary Ricoh Industries U.S.A. in 1962. (The subsidiary became Ricoh of America, Inc., in 1970; in 1984 all US production subsidiaries consolidated as Ricoh Corporation.) The US unit started marketing cameras but found greener pastures in the copier industry where Ricoh's products were sold under the Pitney Bowes and Savin brand names. The company name was changed to Ricoh Company in 1963. Two years later Ricoh entered the emerging field of office computers and introduced an electrostatic copier.

During the 1970s Ricoh debuted the first high-speed fax machine and began consolidating its network outside Japan. Ricoh established a second US subsidiary in 1973 — Ricoh Electronics — to assemble copier supplies and parts, becoming the first Japanese company to produce copiers in the US. It released a plain-paper copier in 1975, followed the next year by

a daisy wheel printer and its first word processor. Rapicom was established in 1978 in Japan to develop fax products.

Through the decade Savin and Pitney Bowes continued to brand and sell Ricoh-made products in the US, but in the early 1980s Ricoh started marketing products under its own name. It introduced a PC and its first laser printer in 1983. By the next year Ricoh had 7% of the US copier market. Other products introduced in the 1980s included a color copier, minicomputers developed with AT&T, and (in Japan) a digital copier that could also be used as an input/output station for electronic filing systems. Ricoh's overseas sales continued to grow in the late 1980s and for a while exceeded its domestic sales.

Ricoh founded Tailien Optical (Shenzhen) Co. Ltd. in 1992 to make compact camera parts. As the 1990s progressed, the company pushed digital-based products.

Ricoh won licensing fees from Samsung Electronics in a 1995 dispute over fax machine patents. Seeking to boost international sales, it bought marketing firms Savin in the US and Gestetner Holdings in Europe that year.

The company's push during the mid-1990s to increase overseas sales paid off. Amid an Asian economic crisis, Ricoh's overall sales remained relatively stable, while sales of its copiers outside Japan increased 20% and 9% for 1998 and 1999, respectively.

In 2000 the company made plans to launch its largest advertising campaign ever, as well as a reorganization of its US operations, and a consolidation of European distribution centers.

Chairman and CEO: Hiroshi Hamada
President and COO: Masamitsu Sakurai
Executive Managing Director and EVP:
 Haruo Kamimoto
Executive Managing Director and EVP:
 Tatsuo Hirakawa
Executive Managing Director and EVP: Noato Shibata
Executive Managing Director and EVP: Koichi Endo
Managing Director and EVP: Masaaki Iida
Managing Director and EVP: Masami Takeiri
Managing Director and EVP: Makoto Hashimoto
Managing Director and EVP: Masayuki Matsumoto
Human Resources (US): Lori Chrepta
Auditors: Arthur Andersen

LOCATIONS

HQ: 15-5, Minami-Aoyama 1-chome, Minato-ku,
 Tokyo 107-8544, Japan
Phone: +81-3-3479-3111   **Fax:** +81-3-3403-1578
US HQ: 5 Dedrick Place, W. Caldwell, NJ 07006
US Phone: 973-882-2000   **US Fax:** 973-882-2506
Web site: http://www.ricoh.co.jp

Ricoh has more than 320 subsidiaries and affiliates
worldwide. The company has more than 25 manufacturing
plants in China, France, Japan, the UK, and the US.

2000 Sales

	% of total
Japan	60
Europe	18
Americas	16
Other regions	6
Total	**100**

PRODUCTS/OPERATIONS

2000 Sales

	% of total
Office equipment	
Copiers & supplies	60
Communications systems	27
Other	13
Total	**100**

Selected Products

Copiers and Supplies
Copier/fax machines
Digital copiers
Wide-format copiers

Communications and Information Systems
Computers
Fax machines
Printers
Scanners
Word processors

Other
Digital cameras
Recordable and rewritable compact discs
Semiconductors

COMPETITORS

3M	IKON	Pitney Bowes
A.B.Dick	Lanier	SANYO
Canon	Worldwide	Sharp
Casio Computer	Matsushita	Siemens
Danka	Minolta	Toshiba
Eastman Kodak	NEC	Xerox
Fuji Photo	Nikon	
Hewlett-Packard	Corporation	
Hitachi	Oki Electric	

HISTORICAL FINANCIALS & EMPLOYEES

OTC: RICOY FYE: March 31	Annual Growth	3/91	3/92	3/93	3/94	3/95	3/96	3/97	3/98	3/99	3/00
Sales ($ mil.)	7.5%	7,136	7,654	8,896	9,424	11,789	10,377	10,631	10,546	11,972	13,716
Net income ($ mil.)	17.1%	96	15	44	93	215	204	234	226	257	397
Income as % of sales	—	1.3%	0.2%	0.5%	1.0%	1.8%	2.0%	2.2%	2.1%	2.1%	2.9%
Earnings per share ($)	15.6%	0.73	0.12	0.34	0.71	1.49	1.55	1.55	1.68	1.71	2.70
Stock price - FY high ($)	—	38.52	26.22	29.02	40.48	50.28	56.63	62.50	81.38	58.50	112.50
Stock price - FY low ($)	—	25.36	17.44	15.44	28.16	39.84	38.52	48.00	48.50	38.00	44.00
Stock price - FY close ($)	17.3%	26.73	18.34	27.91	39.80	47.09	53.83	58.50	51.50	52.37	112.50
P/E - high	—	53	219	85	57	34	37	40	48	34	42
P/E - low	—	35	145	45	40	27	25	31	29	22	16
Dividends per share ($)	5.2%	0.35	0.40	0.45	0.45	0.50	0.56	0.46	0.50	0.41	0.46	0.55
Book value per share ($)	8.2%	19.81	20.66	23.49	26.08	32.58	30.08	27.30	27.12	31.87	40.25
Employees	4.3%	46,000	47,000	48,000	48,000	50,000	50,000	60,200	63,600	65,000	67,300

STOCK PRICE HISTORY — HIGH/LOW/CLOSE

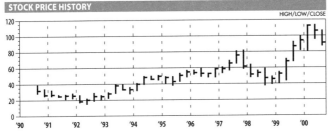

2000 FISCAL YEAR-END
Debt ratio: 43.8%
Return on equity: 8.0%
Cash ($ mil.): 1,060
Current ratio: 1.32
Long-term debt ($ mil.): 2,919
No. of shares (mil.): 138
Dividends
 Yield: 0.0%
 Payout: 0.2%
Market value ($ mil.): 15,572

RIO TINTO PLC

OVERVIEW

The world is just one big sandbox for Rio Tinto plc. The London-based enterprise and its sister company, Australia's Rio Tinto Limited, make up one of the world's leading metals and mining companies. Industrial minerals (borax, silica, talc) account for 25% of sales; coal and aluminum, 18% each; and the rest is copper, gold, and iron ore. The sister companies hold more than 57 mining projects worldwide, mostly in politically stable regions such as North America, Australia, and New Zealand. Both Rio Tintos trade independently but operate as a single unit.

By focusing on large-scale, long-life mining operations and improving operating efficiencies at its mines, the company has weathered commodity prices that have dipped and risen over several years. Although its tight-fisted tactics have turned around profits, they have also drawn the ire of unions who claim the company has a record of employment and environmental abuses. The company has upped its interest in Australia by acquiring Australia-based mining and forestry group North Ltd.; it has also won a bidding war (against De Beers) for Australia's Ashton Mining.

HISTORY

Rio Tinto, a British company, began life with mining operations in Spain in 1873. It sold most of its Spanish holdings in 1954 and branched out to Australia, Africa, and Canada. In 1962 Rio Tinto and Australia's Consolidated Zinc merged to form RTZ. The companies merged their Australian interests as a partially owned subsidiary, CRA (from Conzinc Riotinto of Australia).

Consolidated Zinc began in 1905 as the Zinc Corporation to recover zinc from the tailings of the silver and lead mines around Australia's mineral-rich Broken Hill area. The company discovered the world's largest deposit of bauxite in 1955 and formed Hamersley Holdings with Kaiser Steel in 1962 to mine iron ore.

In 1968 RTZ bought U.S. Borax, built on one of the earth's few massive boron deposits. The use of boron in cleansers became widespread in the late 19th century. A 1927 discovery in the Mojave Desert led to development of a large boron mine. Until its Turkish mine was nationalized, RTZ controlled the world's boron supply. It sold U.S. Borax's consumer products to Greyhound (later Dial Corporation) in 1988.

In 1969 RTZ opened a large copper mine at Bougainville in Papua New Guinea. Subsidiary CRA discovered diamonds in Western Australia's Argyle region in 1972. CRA, in 1984, opened Australia's largest thermal-coal development at Blair Athol.

RTZ bought Kennecott Corporation in 1989 and expanded its copper operations. Kennecott, formed by Stephen Birch and named for Robert Kennicott (a typo altered the spelling of the company's name), had begun mining at Bingham Canyon, Utah, in 1904. Kennicott died in Alaska while trying to establish an intercontinental telegraph line. Backed by J. P. Morgan and the Guggenheims, Birch also built a railroad to haul the ore. Kennecott merged its railroad and mine operations in 1915. Kennecott consolidated its hold on Chile's Braden copper mine (1925) and on the Utah Copper Company (1936) and other US mining properties. When copper prices slumped, British Petroleum's Standard Oil of Ohio subsidiary bought Kennecott in 1981. In 1989 RTZ purchased British Petroleum's US mineral operations, including Kennecott.

By the 1990s RTZ and CRA (by then 49%-owned by RTZ) were increasingly competing for mining rights to recently opened areas of Asia and Latin America. In 1995 RTZ brought CRA back and combined operations. The companies' names were changed to Rio Tinto plc and Rio Tinto Limited, respectively, in 1997. Rio Tinto bought a Wyoming coal mine from Kerr-McGee for about $400 million in 1998.

The company suffered its worst industrial accident in 1998, when 10 members of a rescue team were killed at an Austrian mine. In 1999 Rio Tinto bought 80% of Kestrel and increased its ownership of Blair Athol from 57% to 71%, both Australian-based coal mines. It increased its stake in Comalco (aluminum) to 72%.

In 2000 CEO Leon Davis retired, and his position passed to energy group executive Leigh Clifford. In a move that sparked an outcry from union officials, Davis accepted a position as nonexecutive deputy chairman. The same year a mine collapse at the Indonesia-based Grasberg project (a joint venture with Freeport-McMoran) killed four miners. Also in 2000 the company acquired Australian mining and forestry group North Ltd. Late in the year — after apparently giving up and ceding Australia-based Ashton Mining to rival bidder De Beers — Rio Tinto upped its bid which was then accepted by Ashton.

Chairman: Robert P. Wilson, age 56, $983,000 pay
Non-Executive Deputy Chairman: Richard V. Giordano, age 65, $50,000 pay
CEO: R. Leigh Clifford, age 52, $722,000 pay
Finance Director: Christopher R. H. Bull, age 57, $547,000 pay
CEO Copper Group: Oscar L. Groeneveld, age 46, $568,000 pay
CEO Gold and Other Minerals: Jonathan C. A. Leslie, age 49, $437,000 pay
CEO Industrial Minerals: Gordon H. Sage, age 52, $424,000 pay
Director of Planning and Development: Robert Adams, age 54, $558,000 pay
Auditors: PricewaterhouseCoopers

LOCATIONS

HQ: 6 St. James's Sq., London SW1Y 4LD, United Kingdom
Phone: +44-20-7930-2399   **Fax:** +44-20-7930-3249
Web site: http://www.riotinto.com

Rio Tinto operates mines in Africa, the Americas, the Asia/Pacific region, Australia, and Europe.

1999 Sales

	$ mil.	% of total
Australia & New Zealand	3,423	37
North America	2,937	32
Africa	943	10
Indonesia	840	9
Europe & other regions	612	7
South America	555	5
Adjustment	(2,113)	—
Total	**7,197**	**100**

PRODUCTS/OPERATIONS

1999 Sales

	$ mil.	% of total
Industrial minerals	2,300	25
Coal	1,672	18
Aluminum	1,644	18
Copper	1,324	14
Iron ore	985	10
Gold	847	9
Other	538	6
Adjustment	(2,113)	—
Total	**7,197**	**100**

COMPETITORS

Alcan	Mitsubishi
Alcoa	Mitsui
Anglo American	Newmont Mining
ASARCO	Noranda
BHP	Peter Kiewit Sons'
Carso	Phelps Dodge
Codelco	Placer Dome
CVRD	RAG
Freeport-McMoRan	Royal Dutch/Shell
Copper & Gold	Southern Peru Copper
Homestake Mining	Sumitomo
ITOCHU	Trelleborg
Kaiser Aluminum	UM
Marubeni	WMC Limited
METALEUROP	Zambia Copper

HISTORICAL FINANCIALS & EMPLOYEES

NYSE: RTP FYE: December 31	Annual Growth	12/90	12/91	12/92	12/93	12/94	12/95	12/96	12/97	12/98	12/99
Sales ($ mil.)	(0.4%)	7,463	6,641	6,986	4,711	3,581	4,112	7,076	7,717	7,112	7,197
Net income ($ mil.)	3.0%	979	383	377	425	958	1,247	1,183	1,358	884	1,282
Income as % of sales	—	13.1%	5.8%	5.4%	9.0%	26.7%	30.3%	16.7%	17.6%	12.4%	17.8%
Earnings per share ($)	(0.7%)	3.97	1.56	2.10	1.60	3.59	1.22	3.13	3.15	3.15	3.74
Stock price - FY high ($)	—	41.75	41.50	48.50	49.25	58.50	60.00	67.63	73.13	60.75	95.13
Stock price - FY low ($)	—	30.00	31.50	35.50	37.63	48.25	45.50	54.25	47.31	37.44	46.13
Stock price - FY close ($)	11.9%	34.38	35.00	41.38	48.88	52.63	57.50	64.00	51.75	45.31	94.75
P/E - high	—	11	18	23	31	16	49	22	13	19	25
P/E - low	—	8	14	17	24	13	37	17	8	12	12
Dividends per share ($)	5.1%	1.43	1.51	2.09	1.74	1.02	1.85	1.18	1.49	2.07	2.23
Book value per share ($)	3.7%	19.23	18.96	17.50	17.74	20.23	20.44	28.21	27.39	25.31	26.75
Employees	(8.3%)	73,612	73,495	—	—	36,271	34,763	31,876	35,425	34,809	33,786

STOCK PRICE HISTORY

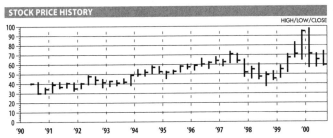

HIGH/LOW/CLOSE

1999 FISCAL YEAR-END

Debt ratio: 17.1%
Return on equity: 18.6%
Cash ($ mil.): 635
Current ratio: 1.09
Long-term debt ($ mil.): 1,459
No. of shares (mil.): 265
Dividends
  Yield: 2.4%
  Payout: 59.6%
Market value ($ mil.): 25,138

ROBERT BOSCH GMBH

It's stop and go at Robert Bosch, one of the world's leading makers of antilock braking equipment, fuel-injection systems, starters and alternators, and on-board electronics. The Stuttgart, Germany-based company makes electronic, mechanical, and hydraulic auto parts for OEMs and the automotive aftermarket.

More than 60% of Bosch's sales are from auto parts, which include car audio equipment made by its Blaupunkt unit. Bosch also makes telecom equipment (it is selling that unit to UK-based Marconi), handheld power tools, and industrial machinery, and owns 50% of Bosch-Siemens Hausgerate, a European appliance maker.

Bosch tends to spend heavily on R&D (8% of Sales in 1999). Recent innovations include high-pressure injection systems for gasoline and diesel engines, as well as vehicle navigation systems. Bosch (with joint-venture partner Siemens) has purchased Mannesmann's engineering and auto division, Atec. The Robert Bosch Foundation, a charitable organization, owns 92% of the company; the Bosch family owns 8%.

Self-taught electrical engineer Robert Bosch opened a Stuttgart workshop in 1886 and the following year produced the world's first alternator for a stationary engine. In 1897 his company built the first automobile alternator. Later electrical automotive product launches included spark plugs (1902), starters (1912), and regulators (1913). Bosch believed in treating employees well and shortened their workday to eight hours (extraordinary for 1906).

US operations begun in 1909 were confiscated during WWI as part of a trade embargo against Germany. Bosch survived the German depression of the 1920s, introduced power tools (1928) and appliances (1933), and bought Blaupunkt (car radios, 1933). Industrial and military demand for the company's products continued from the 1930s until WWII. Bosch died in 1942 and left 90% of his company to charity.

Bosch suffered severe damage in WWII, and its US operations were again confiscated. It rebuilt after the war and enjoyed growing demand for its appliances and automotive products as postwar incomes increased worldwide. In 1963 Hans Merkle took the helm. Believing fuel efficiency and pollution control would be important issues in the future, Bosch invested heavily to develop automotive components that would raise gas mileage and lower emissions. The company made the world's first electronic fuel-injection (EFI) system in 1967. That year Bosch and Siemens (West Germany) formed Bosch-Siemens Hausgerate to make home appliances.

The oil crisis of the 1970s increased awareness of fuel efficiency and benefited sales of EFI systems. Buying a plant in Charleston, South Carolina, Bosch re-entered the US in 1974 to make fuel-injection systems. It introduced the first antilock braking system in 1978.

A 1984 strike against Bosch in Germany disrupted automobile production throughout Europe. In the late 1980s the company developed technology for multiplexing (employing one wire to replace many by using semiconductor controllers) in automobiles, established it as an industry standard, and licensed it to chip makers Intel (US), Philips (the Netherlands), and Motorola (US). Throughout the 1980s and into the 1990s, Bosch acquired various telecommunications companies.

In 1993 Bosch's sales dropped for the first time since 1967. In response, the company cut its workforce. In 1996 Bosch bought Emerson's half of joint venture S-B Power Tool Co., which makes Bosch, Dremel, and Skil brand tools. Further consolidating its position as a world leader in braking systems, Bosch also purchased AlliedSignal's struggling light-vehicle braking unit. The company sold its private mobile radio business to Motorola in 1997 and, to speed its business for mobile phones, bought Dancall Telecom (a maker of mobile-phone handsets) from UK-based Amstrad.

In 1998 the company's Bosch-Siemens Hausgerate joint venture opened a plant in the US and bought Masco's Thermador unit (cooktops, ovens, and ranges). In 1999 Bosch agreed to sell its US-based telecom unit to a joint venture of Motorola and Cisco Systems. UK-based General Electric Company then agreed to buy the German operations of the telecom unit for $153 million. Bosch also allied with Fiat subsidiary Magneti Marelli and bought a controlling stake in Japan-based Zexel (fuel-injection pumps).

Early in 2000 the company sold its mobile-phone business to Siemens AG. The same year the company's joint venture with Siemens bought Atec, Mannesmann AG's automotive and engineering group, for about $9.2 billion.

Chairman Supervisory Council:
Ing. Wolfgang Eychmuller
Deputy Chairman Supervisory Council:
Walter Bauer Kohlberg
Chairman Management Board: Hermann Scholl
Deputy Chairman Management Board:
Tilman Todenhöfer
Director Management Board: Seigfried Dais
Director Management Board: Rainer Hahn
Director Management Board: Claus Dieter Hoffmann
Director Management Board: Stephan Rojahn
Director Management Board: Gotthard Romberg
Director Management Board; Chairman, President, and CEO, Robert Bosch Corporation: Robert S. Oswald
Deputy Director Management Board: Bernd Bohr
Deputy Director Management Board: Wolfgang Chur
Deputy Director Management Board: Franz Fehrenbach
Auditors: Ernst & Young Deutsche Allgemeine Treuhand AG

HQ: Robert-Bosch-Platz 1,
D-70839 Gerlingen-Schillerhöhe, Germany
Phone: +49-711-811-0   **Fax:** +49-711-811-6630
US HQ: 2800 S. 25th Ave., Broadview, IL 60155
US Phone: 708-865-5200   **US Fax:** 708-865-6430
Web site: http://www.bosch.com

1999 Sales

	$ mil.	% of total
Europe		
EU	19,381	69
Other countries	1,232	4
US	5,588	20
Asia, Africa, & Australia	1,902	7
Total	**28,103**	**100**

1999 Sales

	$ mil.	% of total
Automotive equipment	18,264	65
Consumer goods	6,053	21
Communications technology	2,708	10
Capital goods	1,078	4
Total	**28,103**	**100**

Selected Products
ABS and braking systems
Aerospace engineering
Automation technology
Body electrics
Bodywork electrics
Broadband networks
Engine management systems - gasoline
Fuel-injection technology - diesel
Household appliances
Mobile communications
Packaging machinery
Power tools
Security systems
Semiconductors and control units
Starters and alternators
Thermotechnology

American	Ford	Pioneer
Standard	GE	Siemens
Black & Decker	General Motors	Snap-on
BorgWarner	Honeywell	Stanley Works
BREED	International	Tenneco
Technologies	Hughes	Automotive
DaimlerChrysler	Electronics	Textron
Dana	Ingersoll-Rand	ThyssenKrupp
Donnelly	ITT Industries	TRW
Eaton	Lucent	Valeo
Electrolux AB	Mannesmann AG	Whirlpool
Emerson	Maytag	Yamaha
Federal-Mogul	Motorola	
Fiat	Nokia	

Private FYE: December 31	Annual Growth	12/90	12/91	12/92	12/93	12/94	12/95	12/96	12/97	12/98	12/99
Sales ($ mil.)	3.1%	21,259	22,105	21,239	18,674	22,251	24,930	26,490	26,143	30,029	28,103
Net income ($ mil.)	2.4%	374	355	316	245	330	383	322	926	507	463
Income as % of sales	—	1.8%	1.6%	1.5%	1.3%	1.5%	1.5%	1.2%	3.5%	1.7%	1.6%
Employees	0.9%	179,636	181,498	177,183	164,506	156,464	156,771	176,481	180,639	188,017	194,889

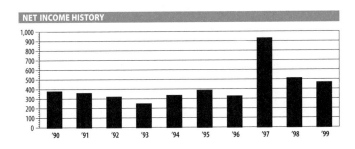

ROCHE HOLDING LTD.

OVERVIEW

Roche refuses to be rocked by waves that might swamp a lesser company. Despite heavy seas (the company agreed to a $500 million fine to settle price-fixing allegations), Roche ("rock" in French) remains one of the world's top drug firms, focusing on pharmaceuticals, diagnostics, and vitamins and fine chemicals. Nearly 60% of sales come from such prescription drugs as injectable antibiotic Rocephin (a US leader), AIDS drug Invirase, and severe acne treatment Roaccutan/Accutane. Basel, Switzerland-based Roche's OTC products include analgesic Aleve and antacid Rennie.

Roche has invested heavily in diagnostics,

including advanced DNA tests. Diagnostics was traditionally the company's smallest unit, but that changed with Roche's purchase of Corange, which made it the #1 diagnostics company in the world, ahead of Abbott Laboratories.

Roche spun off Givaudan, a world leader in the production of fragrances and flavors used in such products as cosmetics, soap, and household goods. The company also plans to spin off BASILEA Pharmaceutica, its infectious disease treatment division, in order to focus on its core products. Roche is also 58% owner of Genentech, one of the world's largest biotech companies.

HISTORY

Fritz Hoffmann-La Roche, backed by family wealth, began making pharmaceuticals in a lab in Basel, Switzerland, in 1894. At the time, drug compounds were mixed at pharmacies and lacked uniformity. Hoffmann was not a chemist, but saw the potential for mass-produced, standardized, branded drugs.

By WWI, Hoffman had become successful, selling Thiocal (cough medicine), Digalen (digitalis extract), and other products on four continents. During the war, the Bolsheviks seized the firm's St. Petersburg, Russia, facility, and its Warsaw plant was almost destroyed. Devastated, Hoffmann sold company shares outside the family in 1919 and died in 1920.

As WWII loomed, Roche divided its holdings between F. Hoffman-La Roche and Sapac, which held many of Roche's foreign operations. Roche synthesized vitamins C, A, and E (eventually becoming the world's top vitamin maker) and built plants and research centers worldwide.

Roche continued to develop such successful products as tranquilizers Librium (1960) and Valium (1963), the world's best-selling prescription drug prior to antiulcer successors Tagamet (SmithKline Beecham) and Prilosec (AstraZeneca). Roche made its first fragrance and flavor buy, Givaudan, in 1963.

In the 1970s, after several governments accused it of price-gouging on Librium and Valium, Roche agreed to price restraints. The company was fined for vitamin price-fixing in 1976. It was also rapped that year for its slow response to an Italian factory dioxin leak that killed thousands of animals and forced hundreds of families to evacuate.

Roche became one of the first drugmakers to sell another's products when it agreed to sell Glaxo's Zantac ulcer treatment in the US in 1982. The move let Roche maintain its large

US sales force at a time when Valium was about to go off patent, decimating the company's drug sales.

Roche acquired a product pipeline when it bought a majority stake in genetic engineering firm Genentech in 1990. In 1994 Roche bought the struggling Syntex, solidifying its position in North America. Roche gained Aleve and other products in 1996 when it bought out its joint venture with Procter & Gamble. It also spent an estimated $1 billion on Cincinnati-based flavors and fragrances firm Tastemaker.

In its biggest acquisition ever, Roche bought Corange in 1998 for $10.2 billion; its subsidiary Boehringer Mannheim was renamed Roche Molecular Biochemicals. In 1999 Roche announced it had located the gene that causes osteoarthritis. The company began to market anti-obesity pharmaceutical Xenical in the US that year, despite reports of some unpleasant side effects.

Also in 1999 Roche agreed to a record-setting fine to end a US Justice Department investigation into Roche's role in an alleged vitamin price-fixing cartel; in 2000 it agreed to pay out again (to 22 states) to settle a lawsuit regarding the cartel. A European Union probe into the price-fixing is ongoing. In 1999 and 2000 Roche squeezed cash out of its high-flying biotech progeny; it bought the 33% of Genentech it didn't own in 1999, then resold 42% of the company in three offerings in 1999 and 2000, raising a total of almost $8 billion.

Influenza drug Tamiflu failed to win European Union approval in 2000, but breast cancer drug Herceptin was OK'd there. Also that year, the company spun off its fragrances and flavors unit Givaudan SA, and announced that two long-time Roche leaders, chairman Fritz Gerber and CFO Henri Meier, would retire.

Chairman: Fritz Gerber
VC: Andres F. Leuenberger
VC: Rolf Hänggi
CEO, Chairman of the Executive Committee, and Head of Pharmaceuticals Division: Franz B. Humer
Member Executive Committee, Head of Finance, and CFO: Henri B. Meier
Member Executive Committee and Head of Global Pharmaceutical Research: Jonathan Knowles
President and CEO, Hoffmann-La Roche (US): Patrick J. Zenner
VP Human Resources Hoffman-La Roche (US): Steve Grossman
Auditors: PricewaterhouseCoopers AG

HQ: Grenzacherstrasse 124, Postfach CH-4070 Basel, Switzerland
Phone: +41-61-688-1111   **Fax:** +41-61-691-9391
US HQ: 340 Kingsland St., Nutley, NJ 07110
US Phone: 973-235-5000   **US Fax:** 973-235-7605
Web site: http://www.roche.com

1999 Sales

	$ mil.	% of total
Europe		
European Union	5,861	34
Switzerland	286	2
Other countries	685	4
North America	6,367	37
Asia	1,954	11
Latin America	1,620	9
Africa, Australia & Oceania	553	3
Total	**17,326**	**100**

1999 Sales

	$ mil.	% of total
Pharmaceuticals	10,362	60
Diagnostics	3,320	19
Vitamins & fine chemicals	2,293	13
Fragrances & flavors	1,351	8
Total	**17,326**	**100**

Selected Products

Aleve (analgesic)
Bepanthen (skin care)
Diabetes monitoring meters & strips
Dilatrend/Coreg (cardiovascular)
Dormicum/Versed (anesthesia)
Fine chemicals
Herceptin (breast cancer)
Invirase/Fortovase (HIV)
Lexotan (anxiety)
Madopar (Parkinson's disease)
Reagents & analytical systems
Rennie (antacid)
Roaccutan/Accutane (acne)
Rocaltrol (osteoporosis)
Rocephin (antibiotic)
Roferon-A (hepatitis B & C, cancer)
Tamiflu (influenza)
Viracept (HIV)
Xeloda (breast cancer)
Xenical (obesity)
Vitamins

Abbott Labs
American Home Products
Amgen
AstraZeneca
Aventis
BASF AG
Bayer AG
Bristol-Myers Squibb
Bush Boake Chiron
Dade Behring
Diagnostic Products
Elf Aquitaine
Eli Lilly
Glaxo Wellcome
IFF
Johnson & Johnson
Merck
Novartis
Pfizer
Schering-Plough
Sensient
SmithKline Beecham

OTC: ROHHY FYE: December 31	Annual Growth	12/90	12/91	12/92	12/93	12/94	12/95	12/96	12/97	12/98	12/99
Sales ($ mil.)	9.6%	7,572	8,411	8,827	9,617	11,270	12,754	11,902	12,838	17,932	17,326
Net income ($ mil.)	19.3%	742	1,089	1,306	1,665	2,186	2,921	2,906	(1,389)	3,193	3,623
Income as % of sales	—	9.8%	12.9%	14.8%	17.3%	19.4%	22.9%	24.4%	—	17.8%	20.9%
Earnings per share ($)	13.9%	—	—	1.68	1.93	2.23	3.39	3.37	(1.61)	3.70	4.18
Stock price - FY high ($)	—	—	—	27.11	44.58	50.55	79.78	79.75	101.75	123.25	133.00
Stock price - FY low ($)	—	—	—	25.75	25.75	39.25	48.30	74.75	76.63	97.00	102.50
Stock price - FY close ($)	23.6%	—	—	27.00	39.75	47.00	79.78	75.25	99.50	123.25	119.00
P/E - high	—	—	—	16	23	23	24	24	—	33	32
P/E - low	—	—	—	15	13	18	14	22	—	26	25
Dividends per share ($)	13.9%	—	—	0.25	0.32	0.36	0.55	0.56	0.57	0.63	0.62
Book value per share ($)	6.5%	—	—	12.67	13.95	14.55	17.63	17.96	14.47	18.26	19.64
Employees	2.8%	52,685	55,134	56,335	56,082	61,381	50,497	48,972	51,643	66,707	67,695

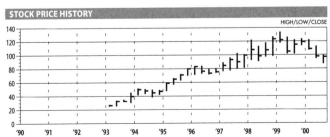

HIGH/LOW/CLOSE

Debt ratio: 44.6%
Return on equity: 22.2%
Cash ($ mil.): 11,857
Current ratio: 2.33
Long-term debt ($ mil.): 10,032
No. of shares (mil.): 863
Dividends
 Yield: 0.0%
 Payout: 0.1%
Market value ($ mil.): 102,645

ROGERS COMMUNICATIONS INC.

OVERVIEW

This Mr. Rogers is redrawing the lines of his neighborhood. Canada's #1 cable TV operator, Toronto-based Rogers Communications has more than 2.2 million subscribers in British Columbia and Ontario. The company is swapping its western systems for rival Shaw Communications' eastern ones.

In fact, Rogers is looking to become a one-stop communications shop for many of its neighbors. The company's cable unit provides high-speed Internet access (Rogers@Home) to almost 200,000 customers, and its networks are being upgraded for telephony services. The company owns 51% of Rogers Wireless, one of Canada's top wireless phone companies (along with BCE's wireless unit). Rogers Wireless provides cellular, digital PCS, paging, and wireless data services to 2.7 million Canadians under

the brand Rogers AT&T Wireless. (AT&T and British Telecommunications took a 33% stake in the wireless unit in 1999.) Rogers also owns a chain of more than 225 video stores, and it plans to roll out a video-on-demand service.

On the content side, Rogers Media operates 30 radio stations and two TV stations, and it produces 15 consumer magazines (including *Maclean's*) and some 45 business information products. Jumping into the Web, it invests in interactive media and Internet initiatives, including financial portal Quicken.ca. Rogers is also combining its 50% stake in Excite Canada with Shaw's @Home Canada to form an Excite@Canada portal.

President and CEO Ted Rogers owns 37% of the company and controls 91% of the vote. Microsoft owns 9% of the company.

HISTORY

Edward Rogers, at the age of 21, transmitted Canada's first radio signal across the Atlantic in 1921. He invented the first alternating current (AC) radio tube in 1925, which revolutionized the home-receiver industry. Son of a wealthy businessman, Rogers founded Rogers Majestic in Toronto in the mid-1920s to make his radio tubes. He also established several radio stations, including CFRB ("Canada's First Rogers Batteryless"), which later commanded the country's largest audience.

In 1931 Rogers won the first experimental license to broadcast TV, but his businesses were sold when he died in 1939. His son Ted Rogers Jr. was only five at the time, but even as a youngster he showed business acumen, buying up shares of Standard Broadcasting. In his twenties he bought CHFI, a Toronto radio station that pioneered FM broadcasting.

Rogers moved into cable TV and in 1967 was awarded licenses for Toronto, Brampton, and Leamington. Rogers Cable TV expanded when it bought Canadian Cablevision (1979) and Premier Cablevision (1980). With the takeover of UA-Columbia Cablevision in 1981, Rogers became Canada's largest cable company.

The firm also began pushing cellular phone service through subsidiary Rogers Cantel in 1985. (The carrier won a license for nationwide coverage in 1992.) In 1986 all of Rogers' holdings were combined under the name Rogers Communications.

Rogers acquired a stake in telecom company Unitel in 1989. When it received permission to sell long-distance in 1992, Unitel geared up to take on monopoly Bell Canada. However, the

venture wasn't successful, and Rogers walked away from its 32% stake in 1995.

Meanwhile, in 1994 Rogers acquired rival cable TV and publishing firm Maclean-Hunter. The next year it acquired Shaw Communications' Vancouver cable system and began providing Internet access. After selling its 62% stake in Toronto Sun Publishing to management in 1996, Rogers extended its Internet content operations, including a partnership with Intuit to develop a financial Web site.

Expenses related to cable network upgrades and Cantel's development created operating losses for several years. To raise cash, in 1998 Rogers sold subsidiary Rogers Telecom to local phone startup MetroNet Communications and sold its home-security unit to Protection One. That year it turned its first profit in the 1990s.

In 1999 Microsoft paid $400 million for a 9% stake in the company; Rogers agreed to use Microsoft set-top box software and offer Microsoft's Web services to its customers. Also in 1999 AT&T and British Telecommunications together bought a 33% stake in Cantel; Rogers' stake fell to 51%.

The next year Rogers agreed to buy Quebec cable operator Videotron. But media firm Quebecor, backed by pension fund manager Caisse, weighed in with a rival bid, and Rogers collected a breakup fee of about $160 million when Videotron terminated the companies' deal.

Also in 2000 Rogers agreed to pay $112 million for an 80% stake in the Toronto Blue Jays baseball team.

Chairman; VC Rogers Cantel Mobile Communications:
H. Garfield Emerson
VC: Philip B. Lind, $515,000 pay
President and CEO; Chairman, Rogers Cantel Mobile Communications: Edward S. Rogers, $3,200,000 pay
SVP Cable Communications; President and CEO, Rogers Cable: John H. Tory, $975,000 pay
SVP Wireless Communications; President and CEO, Rogers Cantel Mobile Communications:
Charles E. Hoffman, $2,979,298 pay
SVP Media; President and CEO, Rogers Media and Rogers Broadcasting: Anthony P. Viner,
$1,126,450 pay
Chief Information Officer; President, Rogers Shared Services: Ronan D. McGrath
VP E-Business: Ron J. McKerlie
VP Finance and CFO: Alan D. Horn
VP Financial Planning and Investor Relations:
David A. Robinson
VP Human Resources: Donald B. Burt
VP Marketing Administration and Procurement:
Frank A. DiMatteo
VP Technology and Strategic Planning: Roger D. Keay
Auditors: KPMG LLP

LOCATIONS

HQ: 333 Bloor St. East,
Toronto, Ontario M4W 1G9, Canada
Phone: 416-935-7777   **Fax:** 416-935-3538
Web site: http://www.rogers.com

Rogers Communications has cable TV operations in British Columbia and Ontario; video retail stores in Alberta, British Columbia, Manitoba, Ontario, and Saskatchewan; and broadcast, print, and Internet content operations across Canada.

PRODUCTS/OPERATIONS

1999 Sales

	% of total
Wireless	
Cellular services	36
Equipment sales	6
Messaging & data services	2
Cable systems	
Cable TV	31
Video stores	6
Media	
Broadcasting	10
Publishing	9
New media	—
Total	**100**

COMPETITORS

Aliant	Microcell
Alliance Atlantis	Telecommunications
Communications	Moffat Communications
Astral Media	Nextel
AT&T	Quebecor
BCE	Regional Cablesystems
Call-Net Enterprises	Shaw Communications
Cancom	Southam
CanWest Global	Tele-Metropole
Communications	Teleglobe
CBC	Telemedia
CHUM	TELUS
Clearnet Communications	Thomson Corporation
Cogeco Cable	Torstar
COGECO Inc.	Viacom
Corus Entertainment	Videotron
Fundy Communications	WebLink Wireless
G.T.C. Transcontinental	

HISTORICAL FINANCIALS & EMPLOYEES

NYSE: RG FYE: December 31	Annual Growth	12/90	12/91	12/92	12/93	12/94	12/95	12/96	12/97	12/98	12/99
Sales ($ mil.)	11.9%	781	875	923	1,008	1,604	1,975	1,812	1,885	1,834	2,148
Net income ($ mil.)	—	(92)	(52)	(142)	(217)	(120)	(208)	(203)	(377)	410	581
Income as % of sales	—	—	—	—	—	—	—	—	—	22.4%	27.0%
Earnings per share ($)	—	—	—	—	—	—	—	(1.26)	(2.22)	1.89	2.55
Stock price - FY high ($)	—	—	—	—	—	—	—	11.75	7.94	9.25	26.50
Stock price - FY low ($)	—	—	—	—	—	—	—	6.00	4.25	3.38	8.56
Stock price - FY close ($)	51.4%	—	—	—	—	—	—	7.13	4.88	8.88	24.75
P/E - high	—	—	—	—	—	—	—	—	—	4	9
P/E - low	—	—	—	—	—	—	—	—	—	2	3
Dividends per share ($)	—	—	—	—	—	—	—	0.00	0.00	0.00	0.00
Book value per share ($)	200.3%	—	—	—	—	—	—	0.19	(2.03)	(0.15)	5.05
Employees	10.0%	—	—	—	6,540	13,300	14,000	16,425	10,300	10,010	11,612

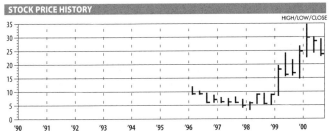

STOCK PRICE HISTORY   HIGH/LOW/CLOSE

1999 FISCAL YEAR-END
Debt ratio: 70.9%
Return on equity: 381.3%
Cash ($ mil.): 10
Current ratio: 0.58
Long-term debt ($ mil.): 2,485
No. of shares (mil.): 202
Dividends
  Yield: —
  Payout: —
Market value ($ mil.): 5,012

ROLLS-ROYCE PLC

OVERVIEW

Like a little Grey Poupon with that engine? London-based Rolls-Royce, the world's second-largest aircraft engine maker (behind the US's General Electric Company) shares its name with the luxury auto, but the two parted ways when the British government split them in 1971 (Volkswagen now makes the cars).

Rolls-Royce's aerospace business makes gas turbine engines for commercial and military aircraft worldwide. Customers include armed forces, airlines, and corporate aircraft operators. In the US the company makes engines for regional and corporate jets, helicopters, and turboprop aircraft. Rolls-Royce also constructs and installs power generation systems and is #1 in marine propulsion systems. About 80% of Rolls-Royce's sales are outside the UK.

The company, which is reducing its workforce as part of a restructuring plan to improve efficiency, wants to divest its materials handling division to better concentrate on power transmission and aerospace ventures. German carmaker BMW owns 10% of Rolls-Royce.

HISTORY

In 1906 automobile and aviation enthusiast Charles Rolls and engineer Henry Royce unveiled the Silver Ghost, an automobile that earned Rolls-Royce a reputation as maker of the best car in the world.

A year after Rolls' 1910 death in a biplane crash, Royce suffered a breakdown. He continued to design Rolls-Royce engines from his home, such as the Eagle, the first Rolls-Royce aircraft engine, in 1914, and other engines used to power airplanes during WWI — but management of the company fell to Claude Johnson, who remained chief executive until 1926.

Although the company returned to primarily making cars after WWI, its engines were used in several history-making flights and, in 1931, set world speed records for land, sea, and air. Rolls-Royce bought the Bentley Motor Company that year. In 1933 it introduced the Merlin engine, which powered the Spitfire, Hurricane, and Mustang fighters of WWII. Rolls-Royce began designing a jet engine in 1938 and over the years it pioneered the turboprop engine, turbofan, and vertical takeoff engine.

Realizing that it had to break into the lucrative US airliner market to stay alive, Rolls-Royce bought its main British competitor, Bristol-Siddley Engines in 1966. With Bristol-Siddley came its contract to build the engine for the Anglo-French Concorde in 1976 and a US presence.

Lockheed ordered the company's RB211 engine for its TriStar in 1968, but Rolls-Royce underestimated the project's technical and financial challenges and entered bankruptcy in 1971. The British government stepped in and nationalized the aerospace division and sold the auto group. The RB211 entered service on the TriStar in 1972 and on the Boeing 747 in 1977.

Rolls-Royce was reprivatized in 1987. In a diversification effort two years later, the company bought mining, marine, and power plant specialist Northern Engineering Industries. In the early 1990s the aerospace market was hurt by military spending cutbacks and a recession; the company cut more than 18,000 jobs.

A joint venture with BMW launched the BR710 engine for Gulfstream and Canadair's long-range business jets in 1990. The company bought Allison Engine in 1995. The company's biggest contract ever came in 1996 when Singapore Airlines ordered engines for 61 Boeing 777s.

The company sold Parsons Power Generation Systems to Siemens in 1997. Also that year it won a contract to supply Trent 892 engines for Boeing 777 jets being built for American Airlines in a deal worth $1 billion.

In 1998 the British government approved a repayable investment of about $335 million in the company to develop a new model of Trent aircraft engines. The company entered a joint venture with American Airlines to service Rolls-Royce engines.

Rolls-Royce pumped up its gas and oil equipment business in 1999 by buying the rotating compression equipment unit of Cooper Cameron, and it surged to #1 in marine propulsion by acquiring Vickers. The company then bought the aero and industrial engine repair service of First Aviation Services and announced it would take full control of its aircraft-engine joint venture with BMW; in return BMW bought a 10% stake in Rolls.

In 2000 subsidiary Rolls-Royce Energy Systems India Private was awarded its first order: producing a Bergen gas engine for Garden Silk Mills for powering a textile plant in India. That year Rolls-Royce won a contract to supply engines for Israel's El Al airline's Boeing 777s. Late in 2000 it was reported that the company would cut about 5,000 jobs over three years.

OFFICERS

Chairman: Ralph Robins, age 67
Chief Executive: John E. V. Rose, age 47
President and CEO, Rolls-Royce North America:
James M. Guyette, age 54
President, Marine Business: Saul Lanyado
Engineering and Technology Director: Philip C. Ruffles, age 60
Finance Director: Paul Heiden, age 43
Group Marketing Director: Richard T. Turner, age 57
Operations Director: Colin H. Green, age 51
Company Secretary: Charles E. Blundell, age 48
Auditors: KPMG Audit Plc

LOCATIONS

HQ: 65 Buckingham Gate,
London SW1E 6AT, United Kingdom
Phone: +44-20-7222-9020   **Fax:** +44-20-7227-9178
US HQ: 11911 Freedom Dr., Ste. 600, Reston, VA 20190
US Phone: 703-834-1700   **US Fax:** 703-709-6087
Web site: http://www.rolls-royce.com

Rolls-Royce sells its products in 135 countries.

1999 Sales

	$ mil.	% of total
UK	5,921	77
Other countries	1,748	23
Total	**7,669**	**100**

PRODUCTS/OPERATIONS

1999 Sales

	$ mil.	% of total
Civil aerospace	4,290	56
Defense	1,840	24
Energy	779	10
Marine systems	622	8
Financial services	60	1
Discontinued operations	78	1
Total	**7,669**	**100**

Selected Products and Services
Aircraft engines
Diesel engines
Engine support services
Gas turbine systems
Industrial power plants
Marine equipment
Nuclear submarine propulsion systems
Overhaul and repair services
Shiplift systems

COMPETITORS

AAR	Ishikawajima-Harima
Asea Brown Boveri	Kawasaki Heavy Industries
Bechtel	Mannesmann AG
Cummins Engine	Marubeni
DaimlerChrysler	McDermott
Emerson	Mitsubishi
Fiat	Peter Kiewit Sons'
Fluor	Siemens
GE	SNECMA
Halliburton	Textron
Hitachi	United Technologies
Honeywell International	Volvo

HISTORICAL FINANCIALS & EMPLOYEES

OTC: RYCEY FYE: December 31	Annual Growth	12/90	12/91	12/92	12/93	12/94	12/95	12/96	12/97	12/98	12/99
Sales ($ mil.)	0.9%	7,083	6,576	5,380	5,198	4,949	5,574	7,355	7,130	7,463	7,669
Net income ($ mil.)	6.6%	259	45	(305)	93	127	220	(81)	369	428	459
Income as % of sales	—	3.7%	0.7%	—	1.8%	2.6%	3.9%	—	5.2%	5.7%	6.0%
Earnings per share ($)	(2.1%)	1.83	0.75	(1.66)	0.44	0.55	0.79	(0.27)	1.25	1.43	1.51
Stock price - FY high ($)	—	21.38	16.52	15.80	12.92	15.61	15.38	22.25	22.00	24.50	24.63
Stock price - FY low ($)	—	14.44	10.75	6.97	8.16	11.25	11.77	14.25	17.00	15.50	15.75
Stock price - FY close ($)	1.9%	15.44	11.84	8.77	11.83	14.03	14.66	22.25	19.38	21.50	18.25
P/E - high	—	12	22	—	29	28	19	—	18	17	16
P/E - low	—	8	14	—	19	20	15	—	14	11	10
Dividends per share ($)	(2.0%)	0.70	0.68	0.38	0.37	0.39	0.39	0.45	0.49	0.54	0.59
Book value per share ($)	(1.2%)	11.68	10.94	6.87	7.39	7.90	7.13	7.57	8.02	9.40	10.47
Employees	(4.9%)	64,200	57,100	51,800	45,800	41,000	43,300	42,600	42,600	42,000	40,900

STOCK PRICE HISTORY

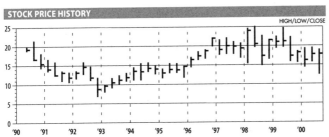

HIGH/LOW/CLOSE

1999 FISCAL YEAR-END

Debt ratio: 45.6%
Return on equity: 15.1%
Cash ($ mil.): 842
Current ratio: 1.37
Long-term debt ($ mil.): 2,055
No. of shares (mil.): 309
Dividends
  Yield: 0.0%
  Payout: 0.4%
Market value ($ mil.): 5,639

ROYAL AHOLD N.V.

Like its Dutch ancestors, Royal Ahold has taken to the high seas to find new opportunities outside its small home. The Zaandam, Netherlands-based company is one of the world's largest retailers; it owns or has interests in about 7,000 supermarkets and specialty stores in nearly 25 countries.

In the Netherlands, Royal Ahold owns or franchises the Albert Heijn supermarket chain (the country's largest, with nearly 700 stores), as well as almost 500 liquor stores, some 400 health and beauty care stores, and 135 candy shops. It also owns institutional food supplier GVA. Its other European holdings include a 50% stake in ICA, Scandinavia's top food retailer with 3,100 outlets.

The US accounts for more than 55% of Royal Ahold's sales. Mostly located in eastern US, its chains include BI-LO, Tops, Stop & Shop, and two unrelated Giant chains (Giant-Landover and Giant-Carlisle). The company fortified its US operations by buying #2 food service distributor U.S. Foodservice and a 51% stake in online grocer Peapod. Nearly doubling its presence in Spain, Royal Ahold is buying a 69% stake in Spanish grocery chain Superdiplo (300 stores).

Often working with local partners, Royal Ahold is also developing grocery chains in South America. The company dumped stakes in unprofitable grocery operations in China and Singapore to focus on Thailand and Malaysia.

Albert Heijn and his wife took over his father's grocery store in Ootzaan, Netherlands, in 1887. By the end of WWI, the company had 50 Albert Heijn grocery stores in Holland, and by the end of WWII, it had almost 250 stores. In 1948 the company went public.

It opened its first self-service store in 1952 and its first supermarket in 1955. Growing into the #1 grocer in the Netherlands, Albert Heijn opened liquor and cosmetic stores in 1973. (It changed its name to Ahold that year to better reflect its range of businesses.) Ahold expanded outside the Netherlands in 1976 when it founded supermarket chain Cadadia in Spain (sold to British Dee, 1985).

Ahold entered the US in 1977 by purchasing BI-LO and furthered its expansion in 1981 by adding Pennsylvania-based Giant Food Stores. In 1987, in honor of its 100th anniversary, Ahold was granted the title Koninklijke (Dutch for "royal"). In 1988 it bought a majority stake in Dutch food wholesaler Schuitema.

The company gained control of First National Supermarkets (Finast and Edwards supermarket chains, US) and added New York-based Tops Markets in 1991. That year Royal Ahold founded Euronova (now called Ahold Czech Republic), a food retailer and distributor in the Czech Republic, and in 1992 it acquired 49% of Jeronimo Martins Retail, a Portuguese food retailer. In 1993 Cees van der Hoeven was promoted to chief executive, and the firm bought the Jamin candy chain. Royal Ahold was listed on the NYSE in 1993.

In 1994 it bought the Red Food Stores chain (converted to the BI-LO banner); it acquired New England grocery giant The Stop & Shop Companies in 1996. In 1996 Royal Ahold

initiated a three-year trend of joint ventures, starting with Asian retailer Kuok Group, to open stores in Singapore and Malaysia. It formed a joint venture in 1998 with Argentina's Velox Retail Holdings that owns about 90% of supermarket operators DISCO and Santa Isabel. Royal Ahold then added Maryland-based grocer Giant Food Inc. (unrelated to Royal Ahold's Giant Food Stores) in 1998.

Royal Ahold's moves in 1999 included the purchase of Spanish supermarket chains Dialco, Dumaya, Guerrero, Castillo del Barrio, Mercasol, and Las Postas (with a total of about 200 stores); the purchase of Dutch institutional food wholesaler Gastronoom; the sale of its Dutch Meester and Nistria meat processing operations (to consumer products giant Sara Lee); and the acquisition of 50% of Sweden's top food seller, ICA AB.

Also in 1999 the company ended unprofitable joint ventures in Asia but expanded in South America through DISCO's acquisition of the Supamer and Gonzales chains. In Central America it acquired half of La Fragua, an operator of supermarkets and discount stores. North American expansion plans hit a snag when Royal Ahold backed out of a deal to buy Pathmark Stores.

In 2000 Royal Ahold acquired Spanish food retailer Kampio; #2 food service distributor U.S. Foodservice; US convenience store chains Sugar Creek and Golden Gallon; and the 50% of Brazilian retailer Bompreço that it didn't own. In June the firm bought a 51% stake in online grocer Peapod. Three months later, Royal Ahold announced it would aquire a 69% stake in food retailer Superdiplo, which runs 300 stores in Spain (and the Canary Islands).

OFFICERS

Chairman: H. de Ruiter, age 66
VC: R.J. Nelissen, age 68
President and CEO: Cees H. van der Hoeven, age 52
EVP Administration, Finance, Internal Audit, and Business Development: A. Michael Meurs, age 49
EVP European Business Development: Maarten J. Dorhout Mees
EVP European Operations: Jan G. Andreae, age 53
EVP European Sourcing: Harry Bruijniks
EVP, Latin American and Asia/Pacific Operations: Allan S. Noddle, age 59
SVP Finance and Fiscal Affairs: Andre Buitenhuis
President and CEO, BI-LO: Jon Wilken
President and CEO, Giant Food Inc.: Richard A. Baird
President and CEO, Giant Food Stores: Anthony Schiano
Auditors: Deloitte & Touche LLP

LOCATIONS

HQ: Koninklijke Ahold N.V.,
Albert Heijnweg 1,
1500 HB Zaandam, The Netherlands
Phone: +31-75-659-9111   **Fax:** +31-75-659-8350
US HQ: 14101 Newbrook Dr., Chantilly, VA 20151
US Phone: 703-961-6000   **US Fax:** 703-961-6077
Web site: http://www.ahold.com

1999 Stores

	No.
Europe	2,442
US	1,063
Latin America	408
Asia/Pacific	80
Total	**3,993**

PRODUCTS/OPERATIONS

Selected Subsidiaries and Joint Ventures
Ahold Czech Republic (99%, supermarkets, Czech Republic)
Ahold Polska (supermarkets and discount stores, Poland)
Ahold Real Estate Co. (US)
Ahold Supermercados (supermarkets, Spain)
Ahold Vastgoed (real estate, the Netherlands)
Bompreço (supermarkets and hypermarkets, Brazil)
Disco-Ahold International Holdings (50%, with Velox Retail Holdings, Argentina)
Grootverbruik Ahold BV (GVA, institutional food supply, the Netherlands)
ICA AB (50%, food retailer in Scandinavia)
Jeronimo Martins Retail (49%, supermarkets and hypermarkets, Portugal)
La Fragua (80%, supermarkets and discount stores, Central America)
Marvelo (food manufacturer, the Netherlands)
Peapod (51%, online food retailing)
Royal Ahold-Perlis (Tops) (65%, with Kuok Group, Malaysia)
Santa Isabel (69%, supermarkets, Chile)
Schuitema (73%, grocery wholesaler, the Netherlands)
U.S. Foodservice (food distribution, US)

COMPETITORS

A&P	IGA	Safeway
Albertson's	Kroger	Shaw's
ALDI	Laurus	Tengelmann
Carrefour	Lidl & Schwarz	Group
Delhaize	Stiftung	Wal-Mart
Golub	Meijer	Webvan
Grand Union	METRO AG	Winn-Dixie
Hannaford Bros.	Red Apple Group	

HISTORICAL FINANCIALS & EMPLOYEES

NYSE: AHO FYE: Sunday nearest Dec. 31	Annual Growth	12/90	12/91	12/92	12/93	12/94	12/95	12/96	12/97	12/98	12/99
Sales ($ mil.)	14.4%	10,036	11,788	11,870	13,947	16,694	18,431	20,891	24,961	30,946	33,811
Net income ($ mil.)	20.2%	145	162	168	177	236	284	362	461	639	758
Income as % of sales	—	1.4%	1.4%	1.4%	1.3%	1.4%	1.5%	1.7%	1.8%	2.1%	2.2%
Earnings per share ($)	9.8%	—	0.54	0.55	0.51	0.65	0.78	0.82	0.87	1.09	1.14
Stock price - FY high ($)	—	—	7.68	8.37	9.10	10.24	13.69	21.35	31.93	37.31	41.88
Stock price - FY low ($)	—	—	6.39	7.03	7.33	7.99	9.87	13.28	19.69	24.81	25.63
Stock price - FY close ($)	18.6%	—	7.66	8.12	8.28	10.20	13.69	20.56	26.13	37.00	29.94
P/E - high	—	—	14	15	18	16	18	26	37	34	36
P/E - low	—	—	12	13	14	12	13	16	23	23	22
Dividends per share ($)	19.3%	—	0.09	0.00	0.00	0.00	0.00	0.00	0.26	0.00	0.37
Book value per share ($)	3.5%	—	2.52	2.64	3.15	3.55	3.74	2.73	2.92	2.89	3.31
Employees	15.0%	87,978	103,069	110,654	119,027	127,668	139,839	191,267	218,446	235,248	309,000

STOCK PRICE HISTORY

HIGH/LOW/CLOSE

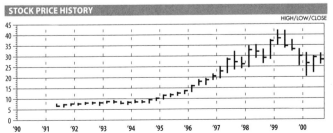

1999 FISCAL YEAR-END

Debt ratio: 62.7%
Return on equity: 39.0%
Cash ($ mil.): 894
Current ratio: 0.84
Long-term debt ($ mil.): 3,601
No. of shares (mil.): 646
Dividends
  Yield: 1.2%
  Payout: 32.5%
Market value ($ mil.): 19,356

ROYAL BANK OF CANADA

OVERVIEW

Royal Bank of Canada (RBC) is fighting the good fight for banking supremacy.

RBC, Canada's #1 bank, offers personal, commercial, corporate, and investment banking services at more than 1,400 offices nationwide. Subsidiaries include investment dealer RBC Dominion Securities and discount brokerage services Royal Bank Action Direct and Bull & Bear Securities. Internationally, RBC provides foreign exchange services and corporate, private, and investment banking for multinational clients in about 30 countries.

Recognizing it has to do *something* to remain competitive (barring mergers with its Canadian Big Five banking rivals), the bank has set out to become a leader in wealth management, acquiring and adding services to attract high-net-worth clients (and the fees it can charge them for handling their assets). RBC is also looking to increase its presence outside Canada, particularly in the US. To this end, it is buying US brokerage firm Dain Rauscher Corporation.

HISTORY

Royal Bank of Canada (RBC) has looked south of the border ever since its 1864 creation as Merchants Bank in Halifax, Nova Scotia, a port city bustling with trade spawned by the US Civil War. After incorporating in 1869 as Merchants Bank of Halifax, the bank added branches in eastern Canada. Merchants opened a branch in Bermuda in 1882. Gold strikes in Canada and Alaska in the late 1890s pushed it into western Canada.

Merchants opened offices in New York and Cuba in 1899 and changed its name to Royal Bank of Canada in 1901. Its initial success in Cuba led it to buy Banco de Oriente (1903) and Banco del Comercio (1904). RBC moved into new Montréal headquarters in 1907 and continued buying banks, including Union Bank of Canada (1925).

The bank faltered during the Depression but recovered during WWII. After the war RBC financed the expanding minerals and oil and gas industries. When Castro seized power in Cuba, RBC initially tried to operate its branches under communist rule but sold out to Banco Nacional de Cuba in 1960.

RBC opened offices in the UK in 1979 and in West Germany, Puerto Rico, and the Bahamas in 1980. Under CEO Rowland Frazee, the bank also beefed up New York subsidiary Royal Bank and Trust. As Canada's banking rules relaxed, RBC bought Dominion Securities in 1987.

Allan Taylor, an insider who became CEO in 1986, sought to expand further into the US. The US Federal Reserve approved RBC's brokerage arm for participation in stock underwriting in 1991. RBC acquired Québec-based McNeil Mantha (investment banking) the same year.

In 1992 the bank faced a $650 million loss after backing the Reichmann family's Olympia & York property development company, which failed under the weight of its UK projects. The next year, to diversify its operations, RBC bought Royal Trustco, Canada's #2 trust company, and Voyageur Travel Insurance, its largest retail supplier of travel insurance. A management shakeup in late 1994 ended with John Cleghorn, president of the bank, replacing Taylor.

RBC continued to strike out into new areas. In 1995 it listed on the New York Stock Exchange. It began offering PC home banking in 1996 and Internet banking in 1997. That year RBC became one of the world's largest securities-custody service providers with its acquisition of The Bank of Nova Scotia's institutional and pension custody operations.

The company and Bank of Montréal agreed to merge in 1998, but regulators, fearing the concentration of banking power, rejected the merger. In response, the bank began trimming its workforce to cut costs and orchestrated a sale-leaseback of its property portfolio (1999).

In the late 1990s RBC grew its online presence through such purchases as the Internet banking operations of Security First Network Bank (now Security First Technologies, 1998); the online trading division of Bull & Bear Group (1999); and 20% of AOL Canada (1999). It targeted its wealth management services for growth with plans to launch an online unit and to buy several trust and fiduciary services businesses from Ernst & Young.

In 2000 it bought US mortgager Prism Financial and the Canadian retail credit card business of BANK ONE. RBC also agreed to sell its commercial credit portfolio to U.S. Bancorp and agreed to buy the insurance subsidiaries of The Liberty Corporation to increase its US operations. The company agreed to pay a substantial fine after its RT Capital Management subsidiary came under scrutiny from the Ontario Securities Commission, which alleged that the firm was involved in illegal pension fund stock manipulation.

Chairman and CEO: John E. Cleghorn, age 58,
$1,978,333 pay
Deputy Chairman: Gordon J. Feeney, $745,833 pay
**Deputy Chairman; Chairman RBC Dominion
Securities:** Anthony S. Fell, $270,542 pay
VC and CFO: Peter W. Currie, $724,167 pay
VC and Chief Information Officer: Martin J. Lippert
VC and Chief Risk Officer: Suzanne B. Labarge
VC Personal and Commercial Banking: James T. Rager
**VC Wealth Management; Chairman and CEO Royal
Trust:** W. Reay Mackay, $762,500 pay
EVP Human Resources: Elisabetta Bigsby
EVP Sales: Anne Lockie
SVP and General Counsel: E. K. Weir
VC and CEO, RBC Dominion Securities:
Gordon M. Nixon
Auditors: Deloitte & Touche LLP;
PricewaterhouseCoopers LLP

LOCATIONS

HQ: 1 Place Ville Marie, Montréal,
Québec H3B 3A9, Canada
Phone: 514-874-2110 **Fax:** 514-874-6582
US HQ: 1 Liberty Plaza, New York, NY 10006
US Phone: 212-428-6200 **US Fax:** 212-428-2329
Web site: http://www.royalbank.com

Royal Bank of Canada operates more than 1,400
branches in Canada and some 100 offices in about 30
other countries.

1999 Sales

	% of total
Canada	82
Other countries	18
Total	**100**

PRODUCTS/OPERATIONS

1999 Assets

	$ mil.	% of total
Cash & equivalents	15,662	8
Trading account	23,985	13
Canadian government securities	5,277	3
Mortgage-backed securities	2,733	1
Bonds	3,118	2
Net loans	103,427	56
Other assets	31,559	17
Total	**185,761**	**100**

Selected Subsidiaries

RBC Finance B.V. (the Netherlands)
RBC Holdings (USA) Inc.
RBC Investment Management (Asia) Limited
(Hong Kong)
Royal Bank Mortgage Corporation
Royal Bank of Canada Financial Corporation
Royal Mutual Funds Inc.
The Royal Trust Company

COMPETITORS

Bank of America	J.P. Morgan
Bank of Montreal	Laurentien Bank
BANK ONE	Mellon Financial
Barclays	Merrill Lynch
BCE	National Bank of Canada
Bear Stearns	Nomura Securities
Canadian Imperial	Paine Webber
Chase Manhattan	Salomon Smith Barney
Citigroup	Holdings
Deutsche Bank	Scotiabank
FMR	Toronto-Dominion Bank
Goldman Sachs	UBS
HSBC Holdings	

HISTORICAL FINANCIALS & EMPLOYEES

NYSE: RY FYE: October 31	Annual Growth	10/90	10/91	10/92	10/93	10/94	10/95	10/96	10/97	10/98	10/99
Assets ($ mil.)	6.2%	107,842	117,856	111,584	124,889	127,957	137,206	163,011	173,814	177,783	185,761
Net income ($ mil.)	4.0%	826	875	86	227	864	943	1,069	1,192	1,182	1,173
Income as % of assets	—	0.8%	0.7%	0.1%	0.2%	0.7%	0.7%	0.7%	0.7%	0.7%	0.6%
Earnings per share ($)	6.6%	—	—	—	—	—	1.31	1.53	1.75	1.72	1.69
Stock price - FY high ($)	—	—	—	—	—	—	11.69	16.50	27.19	32.19	28.00
Stock price - FY low ($)	—	—	—	—	—	—	10.25	10.94	16.56	18.50	20.00
Stock price - FY close ($)	17.7%	—	—	—	—	—	11.25	16.50	26.84	23.00	21.59
P/E - high	—	—	—	—	—	—	9	11	15	18	16
P/E - low	—	—	—	—	—	—	8	7	9	11	12
Dividends per share ($)	—	—	—	—	—	—	0.00	0.25	0.69	0.85	0.85
Book value per share ($)	6.2%	—	—	—	—	—	10.74	12.44	11.96	12.48	13.65
Employees	0.6%	56,889	50,547	49,628	52,745	49,208	49,011	54,700	50,719	60,035	60,168

STOCK PRICE HISTORY

HIGH/LOW/CLOSE

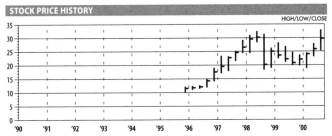

1999 FISCAL YEAR-END

Equity as % of assets: 4.5%
Return on assets: 0.6%
Return on equity: 17.5%
Long-term debt ($ mil.): 3,124
No. of shares (mil.): 618
Dividends
Yield: 3.9%
Payout: 50.3%
Market value ($ mil.): 13,338
Sales ($ mil.): 13,384

ROYAL DUTCH/SHELL GROUP

OVERVIEW

Once and future oil king Royal Dutch/Shell Group is making king-sized changes in the face of a consolidating industry. The Anglo/Dutch entity, based in London and The Hague, is the world's second-largest oil and gas group after losing the crown to Exxon Mobil. Royal Dutch/Shell — of which holding company Royal Dutch Petroleum owns 60% and "Shell" Transport and Trading, 40% — is cutting its $8 billion exploration budget and restructuring to stay competitive. Gone are the decentralized committees that ruled the company's byzantine monarchy; they have been replaced by divisional chiefs that report to CEO Mark Moody-Stuart.

The oil giant has operations in more than 135 countries. It has proved reserves of 9.8 million barrels of oil (most of the group's crude is produced in Nigeria, Oman, the UK, and the US) and 58.5 trillion cu.ft. of natural gas. Royal Dutch/Shell owns or has interests in about 50 refineries worldwide and sells fuel through more than 46,000 service stations. The company also has oil transportation and solar power development businesses.

Royal Dutch/Shell is selling off underperforming assets, including its coal operations. The group is trimming chemical assets to concentrate on major cracker products, petrochemical building blocks, and large-volume polymers. It is combining some of its petrochemical assets with those of BASF to form a massive plastics producer.

HISTORY

In 1870 Marcus Samuel inherited an interest in his father's London trading company, which imported seashells from the Far East. He expanded the business and, after securing a contract for Russian oil, began selling kerosene in the Far East.

Standard Oil underpriced competitors to defend its Asian markets. Samuel secretly prepared his response and in 1892 unveiled the first of a fleet of tankers. Rejecting Standard's acquisition overtures, Samuel created Shell Transport and Trading in 1897.

Meanwhile, a Dutchman, Aeilko Zijlker, struck oil in Sumatra and formed Royal Dutch in 1890 to exploit the oil field. Young Henri Deterding joined the firm in 1896 and established a sales force in the Far East.

Deterding became Royal Dutch's head in 1900 amid the battle for the Asian market. In 1903 Deterding, Samuel, and the Rothschilds created Asiatic Petroleum, a marketing alliance. With Shell's non-Asian business eroding, Deterding engineered a merger between Royal Dutch and Shell in 1907. Royal Dutch shareholders got 60% control; "Shell" Transport and Trading, 40%.

After the Standard Oil breakup in 1911, Deterding entered the US, building refineries and buying producers, so that by 1929 Shell products were available in every state. Royal Dutch/Shell joined the 1928 "As Is" cartel that fixed prices for most of two decades.

The post-WWII Royal Dutch/Shell profited from worldwide growth in oil consumption. It acquired 100% of Shell Oil, its US arm, in 1985, but shareholders sued, maintaining Shell Oil's assets had been undervalued in the deal. They were awarded $110 million in 1990.

After 1990's Persian Gulf crisis, Shell sold a major California refinery to Unocal in 1991 and its US coal mining unit to Zeigler Coal in 1992.

Management's slow response to two 1995 crises — environmentalists' outrage over the planned sinking of an oil platform and human rights activists' criticism of the company's role in Nigeria — spurred a major shakeup. It moved away from its decentralized structure and adopted a policy of corporate openness.

Shell Oil joined Texaco in 1998 to form Equilon Enterprises, combining US refining and marketing operations in the West and Midwest. Similarly, Shell Oil, Texaco, and Saudi Arabia's Aramco combined downstream operations on the US's East Coast and Gulf Coast as Motiva Enterprises.

As the oil industry slumped and rivals merged, Royal Dutch/Shell cut costs and closed its head offices in the UK, the Netherlands, France, and Germany in 1998. It also began cutting its chemical business by 40%, and in 1999 it laid plans with BASF to combine the two companies' petrochemical assets into a giant plastics producer.

That year Royal Dutch/Shell and the UK's BG plc acquired a controlling stake in Comgas, a unit of Companhia Energetica de São Paulo and the largest natural gas distributor in Brazil, for about $1 billion.

In 2000 the company agreed to sell its coal business to UK-based mining giant Anglo American for more than $850 million. To gain a foothold in the US power marketing scene, Royal Dutch/Shell formed a joint venture with construction giant Bechtel (called InterGen) and will transfer most of subsidiary Coral Energy's assets to the new company.

Chairman and Group Managing Director; Chairman and Managing Director, The "Shell" Transport and Trading Company: Mark Moody-Stuart, age 59, $969,872 pay
VC and Group Managing Director; President and Managing Director, Royal Dutch Petroleum: Maarten A. van den Bergh, $1,339,492 pay
Group Managing Director; Managing Director, Royal Dutch Petroleum: Jereon van der Veer, $1,032,041 pay
Group Managing Director and CEO Exploration and Production; Managing Director, The "Shell" Transport and Trading Company: Phil B. Watts, age 54, $690,872 pay
Group Managing Director and CEO Oil Products; Managing Director, The "Shell" Transport and Trading Company: Paul D. Skinner
Group Managing Director; Managing Director, Royal Dutch Petroleum: Harry J. M. Roels, $619,468 pay
Chairman, President, and CEO, Shell Oil: Steve L. Miller
Group Director Legal: Pieter L. Folmer
Group Director Human Resources: John D. Hofmeister
Group Controller: Rupert M. Cox
CEO Chemicals: Evert Henkes
CEO Renewables: Karen de Segundo
CEO Shell Hydrogen: Don Huberts
CEO Shell Capital: Mike Treanor
CEO Downstream Gas and Power: Linda Cook
CEO Coal: Bob Scharp
Auditors: KPMG Accountants N.V.; PricewaterhouseCoopers

LOCATIONS

HQ: N.V. Koninklijke Nederlandsche Petroleum Maatschappij (Royald Dutch Petroleum Company) 30 Carel van Bylandtlaan, 2596 HR The Hague, The Netherlands
Phone: +31-70-377-6655   **Fax:** +31-70-377-3115
HQ: The "Shell" Transport and Trading Company, p.l.c., Shell Centre, London SE1 7NA, UK
Phone: +44-20-7934-1234   **Fax:** +44-20-7934-3702
US HQ: 1 Shell Plaza, Houston, TX 77002
US Phone: 713-241-6161   **US Fax:** 713-241-4044
Web site: http://www.shell.com

Royal Dutch/Shell operates in more than 135 countries.

1999 Sales

	$ mil.	% of total
Eastern Hemisphere		
Europe	51,820	49
Other regions	21,068	20
Western Hemisphere		
US	17,306	16
Other regions	15,172	15
Total	**105,366**	**100**

PRODUCTS/OPERATIONS

1999 Sales

	$ mil.	% of total
Oil products	72,450	69
Chemicals	12,886	12
Downstream gas & power generation	9,729	9
Exploration & production	9,474	9
Other	827	1
Total	**105,366**	**100**

COMPETITORS

7-Eleven	Exxon Mobil	Shanghai
Amerada Hess	Huntsman	Petrochemical
Ashland	ICI	Sunoco
BHP	Imperial Oil	Texaco
BP	Kerr-McGee	Tosco
Celanese	Koch	TOTAL FINA
Chevron	Lyondell	ELF
Coastal	Chemical	Ultramar
Conoco	Norsk Hydro	Diamond
Dow Chemical	Occidental	Shamrock
DuPont	PDVSA	Union Carbide
Eastman	PEMEX	Unocal
Chemical	PETROBRAS	USX-Marathon
Eni	Phillips	
Enron	Petroleum	

HISTORICAL FINANCIALS & EMPLOYEES

Joint venture FYE: December 31	Annual Growth	12/90	12/91	12/92	12/93	12/94	12/95	12/96	12/97	12/98	12/99
Sales ($ mil.)	(0.1%)	106,479	102,697	96,625	95,173	94,830	109,872	128,313	128,115	93,692	105,366
Net income ($ mil.)	3.1%	6,533	4,288	5,369	4,497	6,267	6,919	8,886	7,753	350	8,584
Income as % of sales	—	6.1%	4.2%	5.6%	4.7%	6.6%	6.3%	6.9%	6.1%	0.4%	8.1%
Employees	(3.9%)	137,000	133,000	127,000	117,000	106,000	106,000	104,000	105,000	102,000	96,000

NET INCOME HISTORY

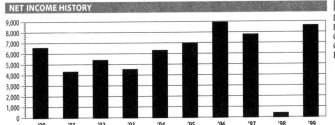

1999 FISCAL YEAR-END

Debt ratio: 9.2%
Return on equity: —
Cash ($ mil.): 4,043
Current ratio: 0.91
Long-term debt ($ mil.): 6,009

ROYAL KPN N.V.

Royal KPN's phone lines run throughout the Netherlands and keep on going. Based in The Hague, KPN sprang from the Dutch PTT — one of Europe's state-owned postal and telephone monopolies. The PTT's postal operation has taken its own path, and, thanks to deregulation, KPN is no longer a monopoly, though it is still 43%-owned by the state. The company remains the dominant telecom operator in the Netherlands, where it operates 9 million fixed telephone lines.

On top of traditional phone services, KPN benefits from the trend toward mobility and the Internet-driven demand for bandwidth and data services. Subsidiary KPN Mobile, which KPN plans to spin off as a public company, operates a digital GSM (global system for mobile communications) network and has some 3.6 million subscribers at home. It also has stakes in mobile phone providers in Belgium, Germany, Hungary, Indonesia, and the Ukraine. Japanese wireless operator NTT DoCoMo has taken a 15% stake in KPN Mobile, and the two companies, along with Hutchison Whampoa, are looking to bring next-generation wireless services to Europe.

Moving online, the company is a leading Internet access provider through its ownership of several European ISPs. It also provides such business data services as dedicated lines and frame relay, and it's adding to its domestic fiber-optic backbone to handle data traffic. The firm's KPNQwest venture is expanding its fiber network to stretch nearly 12,000 miles throughout Europe. KPN also owns 18% of Infonet, which provides data communications services to multinationals in more than 70 countries.

Royal KPN is a descendant of the Dutch PTT — a traditional European state-owned postal, telegraph, and telephone monopoly. The PTT traces its roots to the 1700s, when the Dutch provinces began taking over postal operations from the cities. Under Napoleonic rule in 1799, mail delivery was organized under one national service.

In 1877 postal and telegraph services were assigned to the new Ministry for Water, Commerce, and Industry. The operation became an independent administration, called Postal Services and Telegraphy (P&T), in 1893.

The telephone made its Dutch debut in 1881 with Netherlands Bell Telephone, and several private operators and the P&T soon entered the business. After building its first local phone exchange in 1911, the P&T became the Staats Bedrijf der Posterijen, Telegraphie & Telephony (PTT) in 1928. In 1941 during the Nazi occupation, all independent phone operators were folded into the PTT.

After WWII, business began to boom for the PTT, which had fully automated its phone systems by 1962. Despite inflation and the government's practice of siphoning off PTT funds in the 1970s, the company stuck to a course of investment and new services. It launched a packet data network in 1982 and an analog mobile phone network in 1985.

Following years of debate, the PTT became an independent corporation called PTT Netherland NV in 1989, but the state was its only shareholder. Momentum had been building within Europe for liberalizing telecom services, and the door was opened to competition for some postal and telecom services. Fearing competition from the likes of British Telecom, PTT joined Sweden's Televerket (renamed Telia in 1993) to form Unisource, a global communications provider. Swisscom joined Unisource in 1993, and AT&T began working with the venture the next year.

Meanwhile, KPN launched a digital GSM (global system for mobile communications) mobile phone network in 1994, and Dutch mobile use began to take off. The company, now called Koninklijke PTT Nederland NV (or KPN; *Koninklijke* means "royal") launched its long-awaited IPO that year; the state sold a 30% share. Also in 1995 the firm began offering Internet access.

KPN's mail delivery and logistics businesses were finally spun off in 1998 as TNT Post Group (KPN had bought express carrier TNT in 1996). The company began to focus squarely on telecom and adopted the name Royal KPN. AT&T abandoned the unsuccessful Unisource venture that year, and the others decided to sell its assets.

In 1999 KPN and Qwest teamed up to build a pan-European fiber-optic network. KPN also formed wireless subsidiary KPN Mobile, which then took a 77% interest in German GSM operator E-Plus (BellSouth bought the remaining 23%). The next year KPN held merger talks with Telefonica, but the Spanish government killed the deal. Also that year KPN teamed up with NTT DoCoMo (which took a 15% stake in KPN Mobile) and Hutchison Whampoa to develop wireless services in Europe. KPN announced it would take KPN Mobile public.

Chairman and CEO: Paul Smits
CFO: J. Maarten Henderson
Chief Technology Officer: Patrick Morley
Chief International Officer: Joop G. Drechsel
Head of Asia: Hans van Moorsel
Head of Business Communications: Cees P. Bosman
Head of Carrier Services: Theo R. Varaar
Head of Corporate Networks: Eelco Blok
Head of European Operations: Marten Pieters
Head of Fixed Telephony: Leo Roobeol
Head of Telecommerce: Rob G. L. Langezaal
President, KPN US: Peter Ritsema
Corporate Secretary: Joost F. E. Farwerck
Director Human Resources: Rudy Nieuwenhoven
Auditors: PricewaterhouseCoopers LLP

LOCATIONS

HQ: Koninklijke KPN N.V.,
Maanplein 5, 2516 CK The Hague, The Netherlands
Phone: +31-70-332-34-26   **Fax:** +31-70-332-44-85
US HQ: 1270 Avenue of the Americas, Ste. 2212,
New York, NY 10020
US Phone: 212-246-1818   **US Fax:** 212-246-1905
Web site: http://www.kpn.com

Royal KPN N.V. operates primarily in the Netherlands, but it also owns stakes in telecom operators in Belgium, the Czech Republic, Germany, Hungary, Indonesia, and the Ukraine. The company's KPNQwest venture operates a network serving 10 European cities in Belgium, France, Germany, the Netherlands, and the UK.

PRODUCTS/OPERATIONS

1999 Sales

	% of total
Fixed telephony, equipment & other	67
International activities	16
Mobile - domestic	16
Mobile - international	1
Total	**100**

Selected Subsidiaries, Joint Ventures, and Affiliates
Cesky Telecom (20%, Czech Republic)
E-Plus (77%, Germany)
Infonet Services Corporation (18%, US)
KPN Belgium
KPN Orange Belgium (50%)
KPNQwest NV (44%)
Pannon GSM (45%, Hungary)
PanTel (75%, Hungary)
  Euroweb Hungary Rt. (51%)
SNT Group N.V. (51%)
Telkomsel (17%, Indonesia)
UMC (16%, Ukraine)
Utel (10%, Ukraine)

COMPETITORS

Belgacom	NetCom
BT	SBC Communications
Casema	Tele Danmark
COLT Telecom	Telia
Deutsche Telekom	United Pan-Europe
Energis	VersaTel Telecom
Equant	International
France Telecom	Viatel
Getronics	Vodafone
Global TeleSystems	World Online
MATÁV	WorldCom

HISTORICAL FINANCIALS & EMPLOYEES

NYSE: KPN FYE: December 31	Annual Growth	12/90	12/91	12/92	12/93	12/94	12/95	12/96	12/97	12/98	12/99
Sales ($ mil.)	0.1%	—	—	9,110	9,001	10,720	12,344	12,246	15,191	9,377	9,177
Net income ($ mil.)	(1.2%)	—	—	908	912	1,173	1,403	1,413	1,328	802	832
Income as % of sales	—	—	—	10.0%	10.1%	10.9%	11.4%	11.5%	8.7%	8.5%	9.1%
Earnings per share ($)	(17.2%)	—	—	—	—	—	—	1.53	1.41	0.85	0.87
Stock price - FY high ($)	—	—	—	—	—	—	—	11.59	11.94	25.16	49.19
Stock price - FY low ($)	—	—	—	—	—	—	—	9.56	9.59	11.15	19.34
Stock price - FY close ($)	—	—	—	—	—	—	—	10.61	11.62	25.13	48.00
P/E - high	—	—	—	—	—	—	—	8	8	30	57
P/E - low	—	—	—	—	—	—	—	6	7	13	22
Dividends per share ($)	(8.9%)	—	—	—	—	—	—	0.74	0.27	0.21	0.56
Book value per share ($)	(12.3%)	—	—	—	—	—	—	9.90	9.26	7.24	6.67
Employees	—	—	—	—	—	—	—	—	—	—	38,550

STOCK PRICE HISTORY

HIGH/LOW/CLOSE

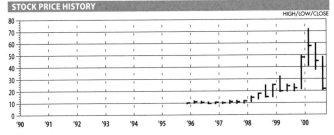

1999 FISCAL YEAR-END

Debt ratio: 45.9%
Return on equity: 13.0%
Cash ($ mil.): 2,638
Current ratio: 1.24
Long-term debt ($ mil.): 5,431
No. of shares (mil.): 959
Dividends
  Yield: 1.2%
  Payout: 64.4%
Market value ($ mil.): 46,019

RWE AKTIENGESELLSCHAFT

OVERVIEW

Rules, schmules! As Germany's old industrial controls continue to tumble like Berlin's famous wall in the face of European Union-wide deregulation, RWE is doing its best to cope with the chaos of a new order. Based in Essen, Germany, the holding company for some 120 energy and industrial interests is restructuring its regional energy businesses to do battle in an increasingly competitive utility industry.

About half of RWE's profits come from utility RWE Energie, Germany's #1 electricity supplier. The company provides electricity, gas, and water to German consumers and businesses. RWE Energie has lost its regional monopoly status because of deregulation; it has responded by acquiring stakes in Swiss, Hungarian, and other European utilities. It is buying German utility holding company VEW and UK-based water utility Thames Water to gain more strength.

Other businesses include integrated petroleum and petrochemical operations (RWE-DEA), industrial systems (LAHMEYER), mining (Rheinbraun), and construction and civil engineering (HOCHTIEF). RWE holds 56% of Heidelberger Druckmaschinen, one of the world's largest printing-press makers, and 68% of top US coal producer CONSOL Energy.

RWE has sold its slumping cranes business, as well as 40 subsidiaries in its underperforming waste-management operation. It has disconnected some telecommunications businesses as well. The company's joint venture with rival conglomerate VEBA has sold its fixed-line telephone business (o.tel.o), its cable business (Tele Columbus), and its 60% stake in mobile phone company E-Plus.

City governments in Germany own 26% of RWE; insurer Allianz owns 13%.

HISTORY

Founded at the end of the 19th century, RWE mirrored the industrialization of Germany in its growth. It was formed as Rheinisch-Westfalisches Elektrizitatswerk in 1898 by Erich Zweigert, the mayor of Essen, and Hugo Stinnes, an industrialist from Mulheim, to provide electricity to Essen and surrounding areas. The company began supplying power in 1900.

Stinnes persuaded other cities — Gelsenkirchen and Mulheim — to buy shares in RWE in 1905. In 1908 RWE and rival Vereinigte Elektrizitatswerk Westfalen (VEW) agreed to divide up the territories that each would supply.

Germany's coal shortages, caused by WWI, prompted RWE to expand its coal operations, and it bought Rheinische Aktiengesellschaft fur Braunkohlenbergbau, a coal producer, in 1932. RWE also built a power line network, completed in 1930, to connect the populous north Germany with the south. By 1939, as WWII began, the company had plants throughout most of western Germany. However, the war destroyed much of the company's infrastructure, and RWE had to rebuild.

RWE continued to rely on coal for most of its fuel needs in the 1950s, but in 1961 RWE and Bayern Atomkraft sponsored the construction of a demonstration nuclear reactor, the first of several such projects, at Gundremmingen. The Gundremmingen plant was shut down in 1977, and to replace it RWE built two 1,300-MW reactors that began operation in 1984.

RWE began to diversify, and in 1988 it acquired Texaco's German petroleum and petro-

chemical unit, which became RWE-DEA. By 1990 RWE's operations also included waste management and construction. RWE reorganized, creating RWE Aktiengesellschaft as a holding company for group operations.

RWE-DEA acquired the US's Vista Chemical in 1991, and RWE's Rheinbraun mining unit bought a 50% stake in Consolidation Coal from DuPont. (The mining venture went public in 1999 as CONSOL Energy.) RWE led a consortium that acquired major stakes in three Hungarian power companies in 1995.

Hoping to play a role in Germany's telecommunications market, RWE teamed with VEBA in 1997 to form the o.tel.o joint venture, and RWE and VEBA gained control of large German mobile phone operator E-Plus. The nation's telecom market was deregulated in 1998, but Mannesmann and former monopoly Deutsche Telekom proved to be formidable competitors. In 1999 RWE and VEBA sold o.tel.o's fixed-line business (along with the o.tel.o brand name) and cable TV unit Tele Columbus. The next year the companies sold their joint stake in E-Plus.

In 1998, faced with deregulating German electricity markets, RWE Energie began restructuring, and in 1999 it agreed to buy fellow German power company VEW in a $20 billion deal. RWE also joined with insurance giant Allianz and France's Vivendi in a successful bid for a 49.9% stake in state-owned water distributor Berliner Wasserbetriebe.

CEO: Dietmar Kuhnt, age 61
CFO: Klaus Sturany
EVP Corporate Development and Mergers and Acquisitions: Richard R. Klein, age 55
EVP Human Resources and Law: Jan Zilius, age 53
EVP Multi-Utility: Manfred Remmel, age 53
Auditors: PwC Deutsche Revision AG

HQ: Opernplatz 1, D-45128 Essen, Germany
Phone: +49-201-1200   **Fax:** +49-201-1215199
US HQ: 900 Threadneedle, Houston, TX 77079
US Phone: 281-588-3000   **US Fax:** 281-588-3183
Web site: http://www.rwe.de/english

RWE operates in Europe, mainly in Germany. It also has a presence in Africa, Asia, Australia, and the US.

2000 Sales

	% of total
Petroleum & chemicals	38
Energy	28
Construction & civil engineering	17
Industrial systems	14
Environmental services	3
Total	**100**

Selected Operations

Building services	Medical technology
Chemicals	Petrochemicals
Crude oil production	Petroleum products
Electrical plant engineering	Power components
Electricity distribution	Printing machines
Engineering services and plant construction	Recycling management
	Refining
	Waste disposal
Environmental consulting	Wastewater
Gas distribution	Water distribution
Hard coal	Water management
Lignite	

ABB	E.ON	Royal
AGIV	Enel	Dutch/Shell
BASF AG	Exxon Mobil	Schneider
Bechtel	Fluor	Siemens
Bewag	Mannesmann AG	ThyssenKrupp
BP	MDU Resources	Vivendi
Deutsche	Philipp	Waste
Telekom	Holzmann	Management

OTC: RWEOY FYE: June 30	Annual Growth	6/91	6/92	6/93	6/94	6/95	6/96	6/97	6/98	6/99	6/00
Sales ($ mil.)	5.8%	27,506	33,948	31,076	35,105	46,059	42,936	41,345	40,230	41,792	45,618
Net income ($ mil.)	10.3%	476	576	516	581	787	785	747	1,223	1,187	1,154
Income as % of sales	—	1.7%	1.7%	1.7%	1.7%	1.7%	1.8%	1.8%	3.0%	2.8%	2.5%
Earnings per share ($)	4.9%	1.38	1.67	1.41	1.43	1.94	1.94	1.83	2.10	2.14	2.13
Stock price - FY high ($)	—	31.61	27.41	27.95	30.86	35.42	42.16	46.25	61.88	60.63	47.75
Stock price - FY low ($)	—	21.70	20.95	22.75	22.98	26.00	34.17	35.50	40.63	43.00	30.00
Stock price - FY close ($)	5.0%	21.91	27.31	22.86	26.02	34.70	38.94	43.25	57.25	46.00	34.02
P/E - high	—	23	16	20	22	18	22	25	29	28	22
P/E - low	—	16	13	16	16	13	18	19	19	20	14
Dividends per share ($)	0.0%	0.95	1.23	1.00	1.26	1.45	1.40	1.67	1.88	1.47	0.95
Book value per share ($)	(0.7%)	12.34	12.74	12.85	14.88	9.45	9.64	8.72	15.60	18.65	11.58
Employees	4.8%	102,190	105,572	113,642	117,958	137,331	132,658	136,115	145,467	155,576	155,697

HIGH/LOW/CLOSE

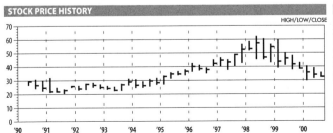

Debt ratio: 23.7%
Return on equity: 14.1%
Cash ($ mil.): 2,677
Current ratio: 1.72
Long-term debt ($ mil.): 172
No. of shares (mil.): 523
Dividends
  Yield: 0.0%
  Payout: 0.4%
Market value ($ mil.): 17,803

SAAB AUTOMOBILE AB

OVERVIEW

The tale of one of the world's smallest carmakers is a Saab story. Trollhattan, Sweden-based Saab Automobile makes the three-door, five-door, and convertible Saab 9-3 (formerly the 900); the Saab 9-5 luxury sedan and wagon (formerly the 9000). The 9-5 features a charcoal air filter, refrigerated glove compartment, and ventilated front seats.

Saab is a wholly owned subsidiary of General Motors (GM). GM bought the 50% of Saab it didn't already own from Investor AB early in 2000. As joint owner, GM had been leery of making large investments in the Swedish carmaker, but it is now pouring $3 billion into the company toward doubling production. GM wants Saab to produce five to eight new models over the next five years. GM has seen its share of the European luxury-car market shrivel in the shadow of Ford's four European luxury brands: Lincoln, Volvo, Jaguar, and Aston Martin. Under GM's full control, Saab will have the manufacturing, R&D, and distribution resources of the world's #1 carmaker at its disposal. And GM will gain inroads to European markets for its struggling Cadillac division, which traditionally has been eschewed by Europeans.

Unprofitable throughout most of the 1990s, Saab is hoping to turn things around with its new models, increased production, revamped marketing efforts, and a strengthened dealership network.

HISTORY

Companies controlled by Axel Wenner-Gren, head of Swedish conglomerate Electrolux, created Svenska Aeroplan AB (Saab) in 1937 because of the Swedish government's need for a military aircraft producer. The government wanted Saab to work with an aircraft manufacturer controlled by Marcus Wallenberg, but intercompany feuding slowed progress. Wallenberg joined the Saab board in 1939 when the government arranged for Saab to buy his enterprise. The first Saab-designed plane took off in 1940.

Swedish neutrality in WWII lessened the need for weaponry, and as the war's end approached, Saab began planning small-car production. It introduced a prototype, the Saab 92, in 1946 and began production in 1949 of two-cylinder, 25-horsepower cars — originally available only in green. The basic styling of Saab autos did not change until a 1967 redesign. At that time the cars became popular in Sweden but failed to catch on in the US.

Saab benefited from massive Swedish rearmament in the 1960s, building satellites, missiles, and computers. In 1969 Saab merged with Swedish truck maker Scania-Vabis to form Saab-Scania. Saab-Scania then bought arms makers Malmo Flygindustri and Nordarmatur. However, the mid-1970s recession and a lessened need for missiles took their toll on the company's auto, computer, and aerospace segments. Saab-Scania's future got brighter with its introduction of the upscale Saab 900 in 1979. Sales grew rapidly as the car quickly won a loyal following, especially in the US, where Saab customers were among the best-educated and most-affluent car buyers.

In the 1980s Saab-Scania introduced a popular line of trucks and began developing commuter aircraft. The company launched the Saab 9000 car series and its first convertible in 1986. But when the 9000 didn't sell as well as expected, and the 900 needed to be updated, the company sought a partner.

GM, seeking a prestigious European nameplate, bought 50% of Saab Automobile, Saab-Scania's passenger car business, in 1990. Restructuring and redesign costs led to losses of more than $800 million that year. Swedish property developer Sven Olof Johansson bought a 22% interest in Saab-Scania in 1990, but Peter Wallenberg's Investor AB bought back the stock in 1991 to take the company private.

The redesigned Saab 900 debuted in 1994, with the company offering a six-cylinder version for the first time, and the joint venture posted its first profit. The next year Saab-Scania was split into separate companies to better focus on each group: Saab Automobile and Saab AB (civil and military aerospace business).

In 1996 GM and Investor AB agreed to ante up another $262 million each to bring new models on line. That year GM veteran Robert Hendry took over as CEO and trimmed Saab's workforce — a move that raised eyebrows in a country where jobs practically come with a lifetime guarantee.

Saab released its new 9-5 series in 1997 and the 9-3 the following year. The company announced that the two models would replace the 9000 and 900 models, respectively. Saab unveiled a 9-5 wagon in Europe in 1998 and in the US the next year.

GM bought from Investor AB the 50% of Saab it didn't already own in 2000.

President and CEO: Peter Augustsson
VP and CFO, Finance, Product and Business Plan, and Legal: Frederick D. Stickel
VP, Technical Development, Vehicle: Lars Olsson
VP, Manufacturing, Vehicle: Lars Danielson
VP Powertrain: Jell Bergstrom
VP Sales and Marketing: Mikael Eliasson
Executive Director, After Sales and Service: Allan Smith
Executive Director Chief Information Officer: Urban Jansson
Executive Director, Corporate and Product Communications: Olle Axelson
Executive Director, Customer Satisfaction and Quality: Joseph M. Mazzeo
Executive Director, Personnel and Support Service: Allan Rothlind
Executive Director Portfolio Management: Anders Hellman
Executive Director Purchasing: Michael Lapinski
Executive Director Vehicle Line Executive Future Products: Alan Kennedy
Executive Director, Vehicle Line Executive Saab 9-5 and 9-3 Series: Kjell-Ake Ericsson
Deputy Executive Director, Corporate and Product Communications: Niklas Andersson

LOCATIONS

HQ: S-46180 Trollhattan, Sweden
Phone: +46-520-85000   **Fax:** +46-520-35016
US HQ: 4405-A International Blvd., Norcross, GA 30093
US Phone: 770-279-0100   **US Fax:** 770-279-6499
Web site: http://www.saab.com

Saab Automobile has subsidiaries and associated companies in Australia, Canada, Denmark, Finland, France, Germany, Italy, Japan, Norway, South Korea, Sweden, the UK, and the US.

1999 Sales

	$ mil.	% of total
Europe		
Sweden	679	19
Other Scandinavian countries	188	5
Other countries	1,274	37
US	1,136	33
Asia/Pacific	201	6
Other regions	13	—
Total	**3,491**	**100**

PRODUCTS/OPERATIONS

1999 Car Sales

	No.	% of total
Saab 9-5	58,459	45
Saab 9-3	55,348	42
Saab 9-3 convertible	17,341	13
Saab 9000	92	—
Total	**131,240**	**100**

Selected Subsidiaries and Affiliates
Oy Saab-Auto, Finland (50%)
Saab Automobile Australia Pty Ltd
Saab Automobile Investering AB
Saab Automobile Italia SpA
Saab Automobile Korea Ltd.
Saab Canada Inc.
Saab Cars Holdings Corp. (US)
Saab Danmark A/S (Denmark)
Saab Deutschland GmbH (Germany)
Saab France SA
Saab Great Britain Ltd
Saab Japan Inc
Saab Norge A/S (Norway)
Saab Opel Sverige AB

COMPETITORS

BMW	Mitsubishi
DaimlerChrysler	Nissan
Fiat	Peugeot
Ford	Renault
Honda	Toyota
Hyundai Motor	Volkswagen
Mazda	

HISTORICAL FINANCIALS & EMPLOYEES

Subsidiary FYE: December 31	Annual Growth	12/90	12/91	12/92	12/93	12/94	12/95	12/96	12/97	12/98	12/99
Sales ($ mil.)	2.0%	2,928	2,704	2,069	1,928	2,600	2,999	2,889	2,829	3,507	3,491
Net income ($ mil.)	—	—	—	—	—	77	1	(35)	(241)	(77)	(55)
Income as % of sales	—	—	—	—	—	3.0%	0.0%	—	—	—	—
Employees	(5.4%)	14,940	12,596	11,247	7,902	7,830	8,092	8,549	9,482	9,974	9,071

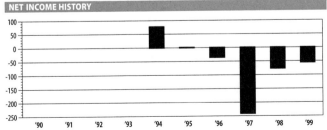

NET INCOME HISTORY

1999 FISCAL YEAR-END
Debt ratio: 100.0%
Return on equity: —
Cash ($ mil.): 39
Current ratio: 1.12
Long-term debt ($ mil.): 596

SAATCHI & SAATCHI PLC

OVERVIEW

Clients love what Saatchi & Saatchi does for them. The New York City-based advertising company, a unit of French ad giant Publicis Groupe has a long roster of loyal clients, including Toyota (for which it developed the "I Love What You Do For Me" campaign in 1990), American Home Products, and Johnson & Johnson. S&S offers its creative services through its eponymous agency network, which has more than 150 offices in 90 countries. Its largest clients, Toyota and Procter & Gamble, account for about 20% and 14% of sales, respectively.

In addition to advertising, S&S offers its clients communication and public relations services through its Rowland Worldwide agency, which has nearly 40 offices in the US, Europe, and Asia. S&S also provides technical and creative services through 70%-owned Facilities Group as well as media buying and planning through 50%-owned Zenith Media Worldwide. (S&S shares ownership in both units with UK-based Cordiant Communications Group.)

After being spun off from Cordiant in 1997, S&S tried to eschew the merger-manic strategies of its über-rivals WPP Group and Omnicom. Instead, the company banked on its tradition of quality work to gain and retain clients. Nevertheless, the company lost almost a dozen accounts in 1999, totaling more than $320 million. In 2000 these developments brought on the firm's acquisition by Publicis for $1.9 billion. Publicis is seeking greater penetration into the US market (North America accounts for almost 50% of Saatchi's sales).

HISTORY

In 1947 Nathan Saatchi, a prosperous Jewish merchant, emigrated from Iraq to London with his wife and sons, David, Charles, and Maurice. Charles left school at 17 and eventually became a junior copywriter at an advertising agency. Feeling creatively confined, he opened his own consultancy in 1967. Younger brother Maurice finished college and went to work for a publisher that wrote about the advertising industry.

Charles and Maurice opened their own ad agency in 1970. Despite an industry recession, the agency prospered and began to make acquisitions in 1973. The Saatchis bought the much larger, publicly held Compton UK Partners in 1975. In 1978 the firm was thrust into world view with an ad for Margaret Thatcher's campaign using the slogan, "Labour's Not Working." With further acquisitions, Saatchi & Saatchi became the largest agency in the UK by 1979. That year the company went public.

During the 1980s the Saatchis went on a huge buying spree, nabbing the much larger Compton Advertising (New York City) in 1982. That year it won the British Airways account. The company next acquired public relations firm Rowland and sales promotion company Howard Marlboro in 1985. The next year the firm bought ad agency Ted Bates Worldwide for $450 million, vaulting the firm to #1 in the world. However, several key clients left S&S because of perceived conflicts of interest. The acquisitions also left the firm riddled with debt, a burden exacerbated by a recession in the early 1990s.

In response, Robert Louis-Dreyfus was appointed CEO in 1990. He began selling non-core assets, including market researcher Yankelovich Clancy Shulman in 1992 and in-store marketer Howard Marlboro Group in 1993. Dreyfus managed a turnaround on the balance sheet, but key investors forced Maurice out in 1995 after a messy boardroom brawl. Maurice later started the M&C Saatchi Agency, taking along several top executives, brother Charles, and key clients such as British Airways.

The company recast itself as Cordiant in 1995, and consumer products executive Bob Seelert became CEO. After two years Cordiant spun off S&S as a separate company along with Rowland Worldwide and a stake in Zenith Media. New Zealand brewing executive Kevin Roberts was named CEO. S&S added Audi and Maple Leaf Foods, among others, to its client roster in 1998. Also that year the company sold its strategic marketing firm Siegel & Gale.

In 1999 Saatchi & Saatchi reorganized its European operations, closing offices in Barcelona, Spain; Dublin, Ireland; Munich, Germany; and Oslo, Norway. It also sold its Cliff Freeman & Partners agency to management. Later that year, in a closely watched case, the company was sued by shoe retailer Just For Feet for an allegedly racist TV spot that depicted a Kenyan runner drugged by hunters; the ad was seen by an estimated 175 million households during the 1999 Super Bowl. In 2000 Saatchi & Saatchi was bought for $1.9 billion by French ad firm Publicis. Following the buyout, Saatchi & Saatchi moved its global operations to New York City.

CEO: Kevin Roberts, age 50, $894,000 pay
Finance Director: Bill Cochrane, age 48, $316,000 pay
Deputy Finance Director: David I.C. Weatherseed, age 48
Company Secretary: Fiona Evans, age 34
Group Treasurer: Susan Day, age 44
Director Human Resources: Kate Morrin
Auditors: KPMG Audit Plc

LOCATIONS

HQ: 83/89 Whitfield Street,
London W1A 4XA
Phone: +44 20 7436 4000   **Fax:** +44 20 7436 2102
US HQ: 375 Hudson St., New York, NY 10014
US Phone: 212-463-2000   **US Fax:** 212-463-9855
Web site: http://www.saatchi-saatchiplc.com

Saatchi & Saatchi has about 150 offices in more than 90 countries.

1999 Sales

	% of total
North America	49
Europe, Africa & Middle East	18
UK	15
Asia/Pacific	13
Latin America	5
Total	**100**

PRODUCTS/OPERATIONS

Selected Operating Companies
The Facilities Group (70%, technical and creative services)
Rowland Communications Worldwide (communications consulting)
Zenith Media Worldwide (50%, media buying)

Selected Clients
American Home Products
DuPont
General Mills
Hewlett-Packard
Johnson & Johnson
Pharmacia Upjohn
Procter & Gamble
Sony
Toyota
VISA

COMPETITORS

Aegis Group
Bcom3
Cordiant Communications Group
Dentsu
Edelman Public Relations
Grey Global
Havas Advertising
Interpublic Group
Omnicom
SFM/Media
Tempus Group PLC
True North
WPP Group

HISTORICAL FINANCIALS & EMPLOYEES

Division FYE: December 31	Annual Growth	12/90	12/91	12/92	12/93	12/94	12/95	12/96	12/97	12/98	12/99
Sales ($ mil.)	70.1%	—	—	—	—	—	—	643	625	3,138	3,164
Net income ($ mil.)	17.6%	—	—	—	—	—	—	23	1,301	42	38
Income as % of sales	—	—	—	—	—	—	—	3.6%	208.2%	1.3%	1.2%
Employees	4.1%	—	—	—	—	—	—	4,692	5,256	5,206	5,289

NET INCOME HISTORY

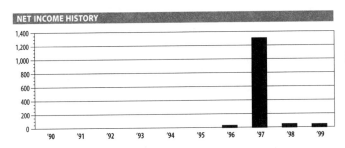

SAATCHI & SAATCHI

COMPAGNIE DE SAINT-GOBAIN

OVERVIEW

One of Europe's oldest and largest industrial corporations, Compagnie de Saint-Gobain controls more than 1,000 companies. The Paris-based materials mega-group operates in three business segments: glass, housing products, and high-performance materials. Its glass sector (44% of sales) includes flat glass, insulation and reinforcements, and containers; the housing products segment (36% of sales) includes building materials distribution and manufacturing and pipe; high-performance materials operations include ceramics, plastics, and abrasives. Most of the company's operations rank at or near the top of their respective markets worldwide. For example, Saint-Gobain's glass subsidiaries produce more than 30 billion bottles a year.

Saint-Gobain grows primarily through acquisitions; it has targeted Eastern Europe and Latin America as emerging areas ripe for growth. Internal growth also is important in Saint-Gobain's goal to achieve annual sales growth of 8%. The company has opened a large-scale research laboratory in France to help develop new products.

HISTORY

Originally called Dunoyer, Saint-Gobain (named after the factory location) was founded in 1665 by order of the Sun King, Louis XIV, who needed mirrors to adorn his palaces. Because Venice had the monopoly on glass, Louis lured Venetian artisans to Paris. Some were poisoned by Italian assassins, but enough remained to teach Parisians their secrets. Saint-Gobain glass decorates the Palace of Versailles' Hall of Mirrors.

With its decreed glass monopoly in France, the company grew steadily until the French Revolution interrupted its prosperity. By the early 1800s, however, Saint-Gobain was shining again. It set up a sales office in New York in 1830 and its first foreign subsidiary in Germany in 1857. Under chemist Joseph Gay-Lussac's direction, Saint-Gobain began dabbling in chemicals in the mid-1800s.

Expanding to Italy (1889) and Spain (1904), the firm was Europe's leading glassmaker by 1913. Saint-Gobain pioneered the production of tempered security glass in the 1920s; it diversified into glass fiber in the 1930s.

Pilkington, a UK competitor, developed a glassmaking method in 1959 that obviated the need for polishing and therefore slashed production costs. Saint-Gobain refit its factories to use the Pilkington method to keep its 50% EC market share. In 1968 the shareholding Suez Group forced Saint-Gobain to merge with Pont-à-Mousson (now Saint-Gobain Canalisations), then the world's leading iron pipe maker. The merger led to a much-needed restructuring that included selling Saint-Gobain's chemical interests.

The company acquired a majority interest in US building material maker CertainTeed in 1976. In 1982 it was forced to divest some of its interests when it was nationalized by the new socialist government of France. Despite nationalization the company grew steadily during the 1980s, investing in Compagnie Generale des Eaux, the world's largest drinking water distributor.

In 1986, after a change in France's political climate, Saint-Gobain became the first company to be reprivatized. Three years later it purchased Generale Francaise de Ceramique (clay tile) and controlling interests in ISP (51%, flat glass, Yugoslavia) and Vetri (79%, glass containers, Italy).

Saint-Gobain bought Norton (the world's leader in abrasives) and UK glassmaker Solaglas in 1990. With the 1991 purchases of German glassmakers GIAG and Oberland, Saint-Gobain became the world's #1 glass manufacturer within a year.

After the recession of the early 1990s, Saint-Gobain sold its paper and packaging interests to Jefferson Smurfit in 1994, raising more than $1 billion for acquisitions. With Ball Corporation, it formed a glass container joint venture, Ball-Foster Glass, in 1995; the next year it bought Ball's stake. Acquisitions in 1997 included industrial ceramics firms in Germany and France and UK abrasives maker Unicorn International. In 1998 the company bought Bird Corp. (roofing materials, US) and CALMAR (plastic pump sprayers, US). The next year Saint-Gobain bought US-based Furon, which was absorbed into a new unit, Saint-Gobain Performance Plastics.

Saint-Gobain acquired Meyer International, a UK building materials supplier, for about $1.7 billion in 2000. It also bought Raab Karcher, a German building materials distributor with about 300 outlets, and acquired polymer specialist Chemfab (US) in a $171 million takeover. To fund a share buyback program, the company announced its intention to sell its 32% stake in Essilor SA, a lens maker.

OFFICERS

Chairman and CEO: Jean-Louis Beffa
Adviser to the Chairman: Robert Pistre
SVP, COO: Gianpolo Caccini
SVP; President and CEO, Saint-Gobain Corporation:
Jean-François Phelizon
SVP; President Building Materials Distribution:
Emile François
SVP; President Containers Division: Claude Picot
Corporate Secretary: Bernard Field
VP Corporate Planning: Hervé Gastinel
VP Human Resources: Jean-Paul Gelly
VP International Development: Paul Neeteson
VP Research: Jean-Claude Lehmann
President, Abrasives Division:
Pierre-Andre de Chalendar
President, Building Materials Division: Giles Colas
President, Flat Glass Division: Jacques Aschenbroich
President, Industrial Ceramics Division:
Phillippe Crouzet
President, Insulation Division: Peter Dachowski
President, Pipe Division: Christian Streiff
President, Reinforcements Division: Roberto Caliari
Auditors: Befec-Price Waterhouse; SECEF

LOCATIONS

HQ: Les Miroirs, 18 avenue d'Alsace,
92096 Paris La Défense Cedex, France
Phone: +33-1-47-62-30-00 **Fax:** +33-1-47-78-45-03
US HQ: 750 E. Swedesford Rd., Valley Forge, PA 19482
US Phone: 610-341-7000 **US Fax:** 610-341-7797
Web site: http://www.saint-gobain.com/anglais

Saint-Gobain has more than 1,000 subsidiaries in 45
countries worldwide.

1999 Sales

	% of total
France	33
Other Europe	34
The Americas/Asia	33
Total	**100**

PRODUCTS/OPERATIONS

1999 Sales

	% of total
Glass	
Flat glass	16
Containers	16
Insulation & reinforcements	12
Housing products	
Building distribution	18
Building materials	11
Pipe	7
High-performance materials	
Ceramics, plastics & abrasives	13
Essilor	7
Total	**100**

COMPETITORS

Armstrong	Gerresheimer	Mitsubishi
Holdings	Glas	Owens Corning
Asahi Glass	Glaverbel Group	Owens-Illinois
Ball Corporation	Guardian	PPG
Corning	Industries	Preussag
Danone	Hanson	Sandvik
Deutsche	Hutschenreuther	Tetra Laval
Steinzeug	Johns Manville	USG
Dynamit Nobel	Kyocera	Vitro
Flachglas	Lafarge SA	
Franz Haniel	3M	

HISTORICAL FINANCIALS & EMPLOYEES

Euronext Paris: SGO FYE: December 31	Annual Growth	12/90	12/91	12/92	12/93	12/94	12/95	12/96	12/97	12/98	12/99
Sales (€ mil.)	9.0%	10,531	11,444	11,282	10,906	11,357	10,719	13,931	16,324	17,821	22,952
Net income (€ mil.)	10.2%	512	382	362	200	553	642	659	858	1,097	1,226
Income as % of sales	—	4.9%	3.3%	3.2%	1.8%	4.9%	6.0%	4.7%	5.3%	6.2%	5.3%
Earnings per share (€)	6.6%	7.93	5.64	5.18	2.70	7.15	7.91	7.60	9.62	12.40	14.05
Stock price - FY high (€)	—	107.17	100.46	74.70	92.08	90.71	111.90	104.28	116.62	182.48	189.90
Stock price - FY low (€)	—	82.93	48.02	49.85	64.49	69.06	87.66	78.82	81.87	99.70	103.10
Stock price - FY close (€)	7.4%	97.87	53.51	66.47	75.53	88.12	93.60	82.63	111.90	120.28	186.70
P/E - high	—	14	18	14	34	13	14	14	12	15	14
P/E - low	—	10	9	10	24	10	11	10	9	8	7
Dividends per share (€)	6.9%	1.98	2.21	2.21	2.21	2.36	2.52	2.59	2.82	3.19	3.60
Book value per share (€)	8.0%	65.71	69.36	70.28	72.26	72.71	82.99	102.37	94.30	97.12	131.19
Employees	5.2%	104,987	104,653	100,373	92,348	80,909	89,852	111,701	107,968	117,287	165,000

STOCK PRICE HISTORY

HIGH/LOW/CLOSE

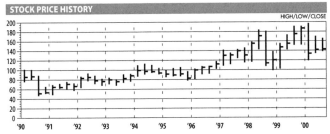

1999 FISCAL YEAR-END

Debt ratio: 41.5%
Return on equity: 12.3%
Cash (€ mil.): 729
Current ratio: 1.19
Long-term debt (€ mil.): 4,139
No. of shares (mil.): 85
Dividends
 Yield: 0.0%
 Payout: 0.3%
Market value ($ mil.): 15,946
Sales ($ mil.): 23,062

SAMSUNG GROUP

OVERVIEW

Samsung Group has traditionally been the kind of gambler the house hates, a high-rolling risk-taker with a neverending source of chips. One of South Korea's five largest *chaebol* (industrial groups), Seoul-based Samsung Group's biggest company is Samsung Electronics, one of the world's leading makers (along with Hyundai and Micron Technology) of dynamic random-access memory (DRAM) chips and a leading manufacturer of consumer appliances. The group also includes financial firms such as credit card company Samsung Card and Samsung Life Insurance, manufacturers such as Samsung Heavy Industries, and Samsung Corporation, the group's trading arm.

Lately, however, the tables have turned. A slump in the notoriously volatile memory-chip

market has eroded Samsung Electronics' profits. In the wake of the Korean economic crisis, the government has ordered the debt-burdened *chaebol* to sell more than half of their member companies and stop bailing each other out.

The *chaebol* are swapping businesses among themselves so that just a few remain in each industry sector. Samsung plans to concentrate on electronics (chips, information technology — including home multimedia — and telecommunications technology) finance, and services, while unloading some $5 billion in assets, and reducing its affiliate companies from 61 to 44. Lee Kun-Hee, son of Samsung's founder, has dissolved much of the central management structure, including his post as the group's chairman. He now chairs Samsung Electronics.

HISTORY

In 1936 Japan-educated Lee Byung-Chull began operating a rice mill in Korea, then under Japanese rule. By 1938 Lee had begun trading in dried fish and had incorporated as Samsung (Korean for "three stars"). WWII left Korea fairly unscathed, and by war's end Samsung had transportation and real estate adjuncts.

The Korean War, however, destroyed nearly all of Samsung assets. Left with a brewery and an import business for UN personnel, Lee reconstructed Samsung in South Korea. He formed the highly profitable Cheil Sugar Company, then the country's only sugar refiner, in 1953. Textile, banking, and insurance ventures followed.

A 1961 coup brought Park Chung Hee to power in South Korea. Lee, wealthy and tied to the former government, was accused of illegal profiteering. A 1966 smuggling case involving one of Lee's sons led to another scandal, but charges were dropped when Lee gave the government an immense fertilizer plant. Despite the political change, Samsung still grew, diversifying into paper, department stores, and publishing.

In 1969, with help from SANYO, Lee established Samsung Electronics, which benefited from the government's export drive and low wage rates. By disassembling Western-designed electronics Samsung Electronics figured out how to produce inexpensive black-and-white TVs and, later, color TVs, VCRs, and microwave ovens under private labels for corporations such as General Electric and Sears. In concert with the government's industrialization push, the *chaebol* also began making ships (1974),

petrochemicals (1977), and aircraft engines (1977). By the 1980s Samsung was exporting electronics under its own name.

When Lee died in 1987, his son Lee Kun-Hee assumed control. After years of importing technology and spending freely on R&D, in 1990 Samsung became a world leader in chip production. Encouraged by the government, Samsung agreed to cooperate with fellow *chaebol* Goldstar (now LG Group) to obtain foreign technology to develop liquid crystal displays. Lee, a longtime car lover, announced plans in 1994 to form Samsung Motors.

In 1996 Lee was caught in a corruption scandal and got a two-year suspended sentence for bribery. The next year Asian financial markets crashed. Nonetheless Samsung bought the remaining 50.1% of struggling PC maker AST (it bought a 49.9% share in 1996), but exited from the US consumer PC market. Even as the bottom fell out of the Korean auto market, Samsung Motors began delivering its first cars in 1998. To lessen its debt, Samsung's Heavy Industries unit sold its construction-equipment business to Sweden's Volvo and Samsung Electronics' power-device unit to Fairchild Semiconductor. Also in 1998 the company was one of several *chaebol* fined a collective $93 million for illegally funneling money to weaker subsidiaries.

Samsung sold the ailing AST to Beny Alagem, former head of Packard Bell NEC, in 1999. The following year Samsung sold a 70% stake in its struggling Samsung Motors to France-based Renault.

Vice Chairman and CEO, Samsung Corporation:
Hyun Myung-Kwan, age 58
President and COO Construction, Samsung
Corporation: Song Yong-Ro
CFO Samsung Corporation: Cho Jae-Yearl
VP and COO Housing, Samsung Corporation:
Lee Sang-Dae
VP and COO Trading, Samsung Corporation:
Jung Woo-Taik
Executive Director and COO Internet, Samsung
Corporation: Harry Lim
Human Resources Executive Managing Director
Samsung Corporation: Kim Chang-Soo
Chairman Samsung Electronics: Lee Kun-Hee, age 58
President and CEO, Cheil Industries: Won Dae-Yun
President and CEO, Samsung Electronics:
Yun Jong-Yong
President and CEO, Samsung Heavy Industries:
Lee Hai-Kyoo, age 60
President and CEO, Samsung SDI: Kim Soon-Taek
President and CEO, Samsung Techwin: Lee Joong-Koo
CEO Samsung Corning: Park Young-Koo
CEO Samsung Electro-Mechanics: Lee Hyung-Do

LOCATIONS

HQ: Samsung Main Bldg., 250 Taepyung-ro 2-ka,
Chung-ku, Seoul 100-742, South Korea
Phone: +82-2-727-7114   Fax: +82-2-751-2083
US HQ: 105 Challenger Rd., Ridgefield Park, NJ 07660
US Phone: 201-229-4000   US Fax: 201-229-5739
Web site: http://www.samsungcorp.com

PRODUCTS/OPERATIONS

Selected Operations

Chemicals
Samsung Fine Chemicals Co., Ltd.
Samsung General Chemicals Co., Ltd.
Samsung Petrochemical Co., Ltd.
Samsung-BP Chemicals Co., Ltd.

Electronics
Samsung Corning Co., Ltd. (TV picture-tube glass)
Samsung Electro-Mechanics Co., Ltd. (electronic
components)
Samsung Electronics Co., Ltd. (semiconductors,
consumer electronics)
Samsung SDS Co., Ltd. (systems integration,
telecommunications)

Financial and Insurance
Samsung Card Co., Ltd. (loans, cash
advances, financing)
Samsung Fire & Marine Insurance Co., Ltd.
Samsung Life Insurance Co., Ltd.
Samsung Life Investment Trust Management Co., Ltd.
Samsung Securities Co., Ltd.

Other
Cheil Communications, Inc. (advertising)
Cheil Industries Inc. (textiles)
S1 Corporation (security systems)
Samsung Corporation (general trading)
Samsung Engineering Co., Ltd.
Samsung Heavy Industries Co., Ltd.
(machinery, vehicles)
Samsung Lions (pro baseball team)

COMPETITORS

Compaq	Marubeni	Samsung
Daewoo	Matsushita	SANYO
DuPont	Micron	Sharp
Hitachi	Technology	SK Group
Hyundai	Mitsubishi	Sony
IBM	Mitsui	Ssangyong
ITOCHU	NEC	Sumitomo
LG Group	OR Technology	Tokio Marine
Litton Industries	Philips	and Fire
Marconi	Electronics	Toshiba

HISTORICAL FINANCIALS & EMPLOYEES

Group FYE: December 31	Annual Growth	12/90	12/91	12/92	12/93	12/94	12/95	12/96	12/97	12/98	12/99
Sales ($ mil.)	9.6%	40,900	43,900	48,900	51,300	63,900	87,000	94,654	57,199	72,000	93,500
Net income ($ mil.)	23.5%	330	348	375	521	1,681	3,802	164	173	201	2,200
Income as % of sales	—	0.8%	0.8%	0.8%	1.0%	2.6%	4.4%	0.2%	0.3%	0.3%	2.4%
Employees	(1.4%)	182,000	183,000	189,000	191,000	206,000	233,000	256,000	267,000	193,000	161,000

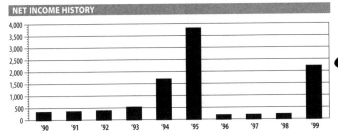

NET INCOME HISTORY

SAN MIGUEL CORPORATION

OVERVIEW

Filipinos who want their kicks in 12-oz. bottles often come to San Miguel. Manila-based San Miguel Corporation (SMC) is the Philippines' top beverage, food, and packaging firm. SMC sells more than 100 product lines in some 25 countries across Southeast Asia. The company makes beer, including San Miguel Pale Pilsen, its flagship brand that corners 80% of the domestic beer market. SMC also pours bottled and mineral water, fruit juice drinks, and spirits. In addition, SMC manages real estate and owns 21.5% of Australia's Coca-Cola Amatil.

The company's food and agribusiness subsidiaries make a variety of meat products, animal feeds, coconut products, and dairy goods,

while its packaging operations produce glass containers, aluminum cans, corrugated cartons, metal caps and crowns.

A 47% stake in the company has been held since the mid-1980s by the Filipino government, which seized the shares from tycoon Eduardo Cojuangco — a so-called naturalist who breeds fighting cocks — and the United Coconut Planters Bank after the fall of Ferdinand Marcos. Now back in political favor, Cojuangco was reinstalled as SMC's chief in 1998. In 2000 President Joseph Estrada said the government would sell a 27% stake in SMC.

HISTORY

La Fabrica de Cerveza de San Miguel, a brewery, was opened by Don Enrique Barretto y de Ycaza in Manila in 1890. Don Pedro Pablo Roxas joined Don Enrique and, to ensure European-style brewing, hired German Ludwig Kiene as technical director. By 1900 San Miguel was outselling imported brands five to one. Upon the death of Don Pedro Roxas in 1913, the company became a corporation. By WWI the brewery was selling beer in Hong Kong, Shanghai, and Guam.

Andres Soriano y Roxas joined San Miguel in 1918 and in the 1920s established the Royal Soft Drinks Plant (1922), the Magnolia Ice Cream Plant (1925), and the first non-US national Coca-Cola bottling and distribution franchise (1927). After WWII, the company added another brewery; more soft-drink facilities; a power plant; a poultry and livestock feed plant; and glass, carbon dioxide, and packaging factories.

In the 1960s the firm changed its name to San Miguel Corporation (SMC). After the death of Andres in 1964, his son Andres Soriano Jr. became president. He modernized and decentralized operations into product segments. SMC continued to diversify in the 1970s.

A family feud erupted in 1983 when members of the two families controlling SMC (the Sorianos and their cousins, the Zobels) engaged in a proxy battle. Enrique Zobel realized that he could not win and sold all of his shares (about 20% of SMC) to Eduardo Cojuangco, a Ferdinand Marcos crony and president of United Coconut Planters Bank. Upon Soriano's death in 1984, Cojuangco became chairman, thus securing the company within Marcos' sphere of influence.

During the 1986 election, Cojuangco ordered

all company employees to vote for Marcos. Cojuangco's estranged cousin Corazon Aquino won, and her government seized assets associated with Marcos and his followers, including Cojuangco's share of SMC. Cojuangco fled the country with Marcos, and Andres Soriano III became CEO. Cojuangco returned to the Philippines in 1989 to reclaim his share of the company.

As high ad valorem taxes in the 1990s (to help pay the nation's huge foreign debt) cut into its alcohol sales, SMC continued to expand into other areas. In 1991 it set up glass and brewing joint ventures. The company launched VIVA!-brand mineral water the next year.

SMC sold Coca-Cola Bottlers Philippines to Coca-Cola Amatil (CCA) of Sydney in 1995 in exchange for a 25% stake in CCA. In mid-1998, immediately following Cojuangco-backed Joseph Estrada's election as president of the Philippines, Andres Soriano III stepped down and Cojuangco returned to SMC's helm. (Earlier in the year a Philippines court allowed Cojuangco to install three people on SMC's board and vote 20% of his stake in the company.) Also in 1998 SMC sold its 45% stake in Philippines Nestlé back to Nestlé for $680 million and said it would start selling San Miguel-brand beer on the US West Coast. Coconut oil sales fell by more than 60% during 1998 due to a lack of copra (coconut meat).

In 1999 SMC withdrew plans to sell its remaining 21.5% of CCA, but in April 2000 again decided to divest its stake. The company also bought Filipino juice maker Sugarland. SMC bought Australian brewer J. Boag & Son in June 2000 and the next month Filipino President Joseph Estrada announced the government's plans to sell a 27% stake in San Miguel.

Chairman and CEO: Eduardo M. Cojuangco Jr.
VC: Ramon S. Ang
President and COO: Francisco C. Eizmendi Jr.
CFO and Treasurer: Alberto M. de Larrazabal
SVP and General Counsel: Francis H. Jardeleza
SVP Corporate Affairs: Alberto A. Manlapit
SVP Corporate Technical Services:
Alberto O. Villa-Abrille Jr.
VP Corporate Planning and Development:
Ma. Bellen C. Buensuceso
VP Corporate Human Resources:
Emiliano B. Canonigo Jr.
President, San Miguel Food Group: Arnaldo L. Africa
President, San Miguel Beer Division:
Faustino F. Galang
President, San Miguel Packaging Products:
Enrique A. Gomez Jr.
President, La Tondena Distillers:
Paulino A. Mediarito Jr.
Corporate Secretary: Jose Y. Feria
Auditors: SyCip Gorres Velayo & Co.

HQ: 40 San Miguel Ave., PO Box 271, Mandaluyong City,
Metro Manila 1550, Philippines
Phone: +63-2-632-3000 **Fax:** +63-2-632-3099
Web site: http://www.sanmiguel.com.ph

San Miguel Corporation has some 60 plants in China,
Hong Kong, Indonesia, the Philippines, Vietnam, and
other countries in Southeast Asia. The company's beers
are sold in some 20 countries in the Americas, Asia,
and Australia.

Selected Products and Brands
Beer, Multinational
  Ander Bir (licensed)
  Blue Ice
  Cerveza Negra
  Gold Eagle
  Miller Genuine Draft (licensed)
  Red Horse
  San Miguel Light
  San Miguel (Draft Beer, Pale Pilsen, Super Dry)
Beer, Regional
  China (Blue Star, Double Happiness Beer, Dragon
    Beer, Guang's Draft, Kirin, Pineapple Beer, Valor)
  Hong Kong (Bruck, Eagle High, San Miguel Dark)
  Indonesia (Anker Stout — licensed)
  Vietnam (Bock)
Bottled Water
Dairy products
Gin (Ginebra San Miguel, Oxford London Dry Gin —
  licensed)
Juice Drinks
Meat products (beef, chicken, pork)
Nonalcoholic malt beverages
Rum (Añejo, Tondeña, San Miguel)

Amcor	Carlsberg	International
Anheuser-Busch	CBR Brewing	Paper
Asahi Breweries	ConAgra Foods	Kirin
Asia Brewery	Danone	Lion Nathan
Bacardi USA	Diageo	Nestlé
Benguet	Foster's Brewing	PepsiCo
Cadbury	Heineken	Tsingtao
Schweppes	Hormel	Tyson Foods
Cargill	Interbrew	

OTC: SMGBY FYE: December 31	Annual Growth	12/90	12/91	12/92	12/93	12/94	12/95	12/96	12/97	12/98	12/99
Sales ($ mil.)	1.3%	1,682	2,047	2,297	2,209	2,790	3,027	3,232	1,699	1,911	1,881
Net income ($ mil.)	9.0%	69	108	141	146	484	223	232	75	629	150
Income as % of sales	—	4.1%	5.3%	6.2%	6.6%	17.3%	7.4%	7.2%	4.4%	32.9%	8.0%
Earnings per share ($)	(10.8%)	—	—	—	—	—	0.99	1.02	0.33	2.78	0.63
Stock price - FY high ($)	—	—	—	—	—	—	33.80	36.77	36.36	17.27	22.73
Stock price - FY low ($)	—	—	—	—	—	—	23.29	23.97	10.00	7.73	12.73
Stock price - FY close ($)	(13.2%)	—	—	—	—	—	24.88	34.70	10.45	16.36	14.14
P/E - high	—	—	—	—	—	—	34	36	110	6	36
P/E - low	—	—	—	—	—	—	24	24	30	3	20
Dividends per share ($)	4.5%	—	—	—	—	—	0.26	0.26	0.20	0.21	0.31
Book value per share ($)	(0.5%)	—	—	—	—	—	7.33	7.48	5.46	7.65	7.19
Employees	(9.5%)	35,694	36,060	33,136	32,832	30,965	31,485	28,544	18,444	15,923	14,511

HIGH/LOW/CLOSE

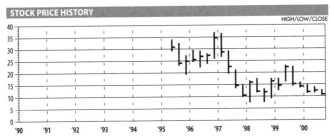

Debt ratio: 31.5%
Return on equity: 9.0%
Cash ($ mil.): 1,158
Current ratio: 1.87
Long-term debt ($ mil.): 544
No. of shares (mil.): 226
Dividends
  Yield: 0.0%
  Payout: 0.5%
Market value ($ mil.): 3,193

SANYO ELECTRIC CO., LTD.

OVERVIEW

After 50 years of experience, SANYO Electric is still green. The Moriguchi City, Japan-based electronics powerhouse encompasses nearly 150 subsidiaries in more than 25 countries. Group companies manufacture a variety of electrical devices and appliances, including industrial and commercial equipment (refrigerated supermarket cases, vending machines), video and audio equipment (CD players, TVs, VCRs), semiconductors and integrated circuits, information systems (wireless phones, computers), batteries, motor-assisted bicycles, and appliances (microwave ovens, air conditioners, washers, toasters).

SANYO is focused on developing environment-friendly products such as solar cells, rechargeable batteries, and CFC-free refrigerators and air-conditioning units. The company is also placing particular emphasis on the development of multimedia products such as digital cameras and LCD products.

To remain competitive in the explosive high-tech environment, the company is forming alliances with leading technology developers. It has separate pacts with IBM and Philips to work on semiconductors, and an alliance with Eastman Kodak to develop next-generation flat-panel displays.

HISTORY

"Sanyo" means "three oceans" in Japanese. Toshio Iue, SANYO's first CEO, had the Pacific, Atlantic, and Indian Oceans in mind — he wanted to turn the company into an international enterprise. SANYO was formed after WWII when the Allies broke Matsushita Electric into two companies. Toshio, brother-in-law to Matsushita founder Konosuke Matsushita, took charge of SANYO, which then made bicycle lamps.

By 1949 the company was producing radios, and in the 1950s it diversified into refrigerators, fans, and washing machines. In 1953 a Japanese household appliances rush began, and SANYO led washing machine sales. By the end of the decade, the company was Japan's leading exporter of transistor radios.

To raise money, in 1959 SANYO created Tokyo SANYO Electric, in which it took a 20% stake. The company established its first factory abroad, in Hong Kong, in 1961 and created Cadnica, a durable rechargeable battery.

The 1970s oil crisis drew SANYO into alternative energy development, and the company continued its energy research when the crisis had passed. In 1973 SANYO joined forces with Emerson Electric (US) to bail out Emerson's Fisher electronics subsidiary (in 1978 SANYO bought Fisher). SANYO began shifting its focus from appliances to high-tech products in the mid-1970s. It started making color TVs in the US in 1976. Although sales slowed when SANYO initially opted to develop VCRs using the ill-fated Betamax format, they rose tremendously in the 1970s, from $71 million in 1972 to $855 million in 1978.

SANYO and Tokyo SANYO Electric merged in 1986. A high yen forced the company to move much of its manufacturing outside Japan; that year it made more products abroad than any other Japanese company. By then the country's leading TV maker, SANYO formed a joint venture with Sears to manufacture TVs. SANYO also developed the world's first CFC-free refrigeration system (a version of which was installed in New York's Guggenheim Museum).

In 1993 SANYO set a world record for solar energy conversion efficiency. The company strengthened its electronic components and solar businesses two years later by establishing SANYO Electronic Components and SANYO Solar Industries. In 1997 SANYO introduced the highest-output home-use solar cells, capable of producing 160 watts of electricity.

Sanyo in 1998 formed a pact with IBM to make semiconductors using Big Blue's energy-saving copper circuit technology. The next year it allied with Philips to develop semiconductors and related products. Weakness in the Asian economy, a slowdown in US sales, and overall decreased demand hammered SANYO's earnings for fiscal 1999, followed by an announcement that it would cut 6,000 jobs (about 10% of its workforce) over the next three years.

Also in 1999 SANYO teamed up with Eastman Kodak to develop flat-panel displays based on next-generation organic electroluminescent technology. The company announced several product developments, including an advanced battery for hybrid-fuel vehicles and an air-conditioning and refrigeration compressor that uses carbon dioxide instead of freon. It signed a deal with TurboLinux to equip 20,000 medical workstations with the company's version of the Linux operating system — the largest enterprise deployment of Linux thus far.

Chairman and CEO: Satoshi Iue
President and COO: Sadao Kondo
Executive Director: Masaho Sugimoto
EVP and CFO: Yoshio Shimoda
Executive Director: Motoharu Iue
Executive Officer: Yasusuke Tanaka
Executive Officer: Junichiro Yano
Executive Officer: Yukinori Kuwano
Executive Officer: Toshimasa Iue
Executive Officer: Sunao Okubo
Senior Officer: Hiromoto Sekino
Senior Officer: Akiyoshi Takano
Senior Officer: Hitoshi Komada
Senior Officer: Masabumi Kawano
Auditors: PricewaterhouseCoopers

LOCATIONS

HQ: San'yo Denki Kabushiki Kaisha,
5-5 Keihan-Hondori, 2-chome, Moriguchi City,
Osaka 570-8677, Japan
Phone: +81-6-6991-1181   **Fax:** +81-6-6991-6566
US HQ: 2055 Sanyo Ave., San Diego, CA 92154
US Phone: 619-661-1134   **US Fax:** 619-661-6795
Web site: http://www.sanyo.co.jp/koho/index_e.html

2000 Sales

	$ mil.	% of total
Asia		
Japan	13,231	70
Other countries	2,188	12
North America	2,253	12
Other regions	1,330	6
Total	**19,002**	**100**

PRODUCTS/OPERATIONS

2000 Sales

	$ mil.	% of total
Audio, video, information & communications equipment	6,557	35
Electronic devices	3,705	19
Home appliances	2,845	15
Batteries	2,406	13
Industrial & commercial equipment	2,267	12
Other	1,222	6
Total	**19,002**	**100**

Selected Products
Audio equipment
Batteries
Home appliances
Industrial and commercial equipment
Information systems and electronic devices
Video equipment

COMPETITORS

AMD	Kyocera	Philips
Apple Computer	Lanier	Electronics
Black & Decker	Worldwide	Pioneer
Canon	LG Group	Pitney Bowes
Casio Computer	Marconi	Ralston Purina
Compaq	Matsushita	Ricoh
Dell Computer	Maytag	Samsung
Electrolux AB	National	Seiko Epson
Fujitsu	Semiconductor	Sharp
GE	NCR	Siemens
Gillette	NEC	Sony
Hewlett-Packard	Nokia	THOMSON
Hitachi	Oki Electric	multimedia
IBM	Olivetti	Toshiba
Intel		Whirlpool

HISTORICAL FINANCIALS & EMPLOYEES

Nasdaq (SC): SANYY FYE: March 31	Annual Growth	11/91	11/92	11/93	11/94	11/95	*3/96	3/97	3/98	3/99	3/00
Sales ($ mil.)	4.8%	12,444	12,559	14,292	17,124	17,081	4,949	14,889	14,581	15,687	19,002
Net income ($ mil.)	5.2%	130	(10)	(14)	115	153	(35)	143	93	(216)	205
Income as % of sales	—	1.0%	—	—	0.7%	0.9%	—	1.0%	0.6%	—	1.1%
Earnings per share ($)	—	0.33	(0.03)	(0.04)	0.29	0.39	(0.09)	0.37	0.24	(0.56)	0.54
Stock price - FY high ($)	—	25.25	21.25	22.00	30.50	30.00	31.50	31.88	23.50	17.00	30.88
Stock price - FY low ($)	—	16.75	13.25	13.88	18.00	23.38	23.38	18.13	11.00	11.56	16.44
Stock price - FY close ($)	5.0%	19.50	14.13	18.13	29.50	26.00	29.13	19.13	13.50	16.63	30.25
P/E - high	—	77	—	—	105	77	—	86	98	—	57
P/E - low	—	51	—	—	62	60	—	49	46	—	30
Dividends per share ($)	(0.5%)	0.23	0.24	0.17	0.19	0.21	0.12	0.06	0.19	0.11	0.22
Book value per share ($)	1.4%	14.75	15.04	16.89	18.62	20.18	19.58	16.03	14.57	15.22	16.77
Employees	4.5%	56,079	56,156	—	58,417	57,120	56,612	67,827	67,887	77,071	83,519

* Fiscal year change

STOCK PRICE HISTORY

HIGH/LOW/CLOSE

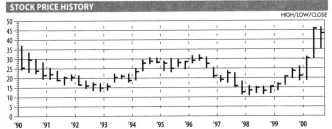

2000 FISCAL YEAR-END

Debt ratio: 47.8%
Return on equity: 3.4%
Cash ($ mil.): 3,221
Current ratio: 1.30
Long-term debt ($ mil.): 5,759
No. of shares (mil.): 374
Dividends
  Yield: 0.7%
  Payout: 40.7%
Market value ($ mil.): 11,326

SAP AKTIENGESELLSCHAFT

Die US ist das Mutterland der Datenverarbeitung — the US is the motherland of data processing. That may be true, but it's Walldorf, Germany-based SAP (pronounced by spelling out the letters) that makes the mother of all bookkeeping programs. The company's market-leading enterprise resource planning (ERP) software is used by Volkswagen, Eastman Chemical, Microsoft, and another 12,500 companies to coordinate production, distribution, financial, human resource, and other back-office processes. About 80% of its sales come from outside Germany.

In a weakening market, SAP is protecting itself through a move to the Internet. It offers front- and back-office software and services for rent or purchase through its mySAP.com exchange, which hosts transactions between SAP clients and their vendors. To catch up with rivals in this lucrative sector, SAP has launched a US subsidiary to build online marketplaces for large companies and their suppliers.

SAP is far from the traditional German company. An entrepreneurial sense pervades its small-town headquarters, giving it an almost California feel. While most German employees wear suits to work, many SAP employees don sandals and choose their own schedules. A competitive job market that has seen SAP lose hundreds of managers to rivals and startups has left the company instituting that most American of perks — a stock-option plan.

Three of SAP's founders — co-chairman and co-CEO Hasso Plattner, Dietmar Hopp, and Klaus Tschira — control about 60% of the company.

Software engineers Hasso Plattner, Hans-Werner Hector, Dietmar Hopp, and Klaus Tschira started SAP in 1972 when the project they were working on for IBM was moved to another unit. The four agreed to write a program for IBM customer Imperial Chemical Industries, and SAP (named for the IBM project they left — Systems, Applications, and Projects) was formed.

Set up in a cornfield, the group worked nights on borrowed computers until business picked up. While rival software companies made many products to automate the various parts of a company's operations, these engineers decided to make a single system that would tie a corporation together. In 1973 they launched an instantaneous accounting transaction processing program called R/1. By 1981, with 200 customers already on board, they had adapted the program to create R/2, mainframe software that linked external databases and communication systems.

The company went public in 1988. That year Plattner began a project to create software for the computer network market. In 1992, as sales of its R/2 mainframe software lagged, SAP introduced its R/3 software.

Still basically a stranger outside Europe, SAP built a technology development center that year in California to attract attention from Silicon Valley. To support its push into the US, the company launched a $2 million advertising campaign in 1993 (though it wasn't supported by the board). The gamble paid off as sales soared past projections, making SAP the world's leading developer of network computing software.

Also in 1993 SAP allied with Microsoft to make R/3 Windows NT-compatible.

By 1995 the US had become SAP's largest market. Charismatic and competitive Plattner instilled an Americanized way of running the company (open-door policies, mingling with employees in the cafeteria at lunch) that was emulated across Europe. That year SAP teamed with Microsoft, Netscape (now part of AOL), and Sun Microsystems to make R/3 software Internet-compatible.

SAP opened an office in Singapore in 1996 to boost its presence in Asia. That year Hector unwittingly signed away control of about 10% of SAP's common shares, possibly undermining takeover barriers, and left the company after a dispute with Hopp.

The next year SAP moved to the NYSE; longtime executive Henning Kagermann was named co-chairman along with Plattner. In 1999 the company expanded on the Internet, unveiling an e-commerce Web exchange (mySAP.com) supporting business-to-business transactions and other services. The company's long-standing resistance to employee stock options weakened in 2000 when SAP approved an option program to offset the loss of more than 200 key US managers in an 18-month period.

Later that year SAP launched a US subsidiary (SAPMarkets) to compete against American rivals in the market for business-to-business e-commerce services. It also increased its minority stake in software maker Commerce One. The two companies plan to jointly develop online marketplaces.

OFFICERS

Co-Chairman and Co-CEO: Hasso Plattner
Co-Chairman and Co-CEO: Henning Kagermann
Executive Board, Industry Solutions, Customer Relationship Management, E-Business and Global Research: Peter Zencke
Executive Board, R/3 Corporate Services and IT Infrastructure: Gerhard Oswald
Executive Board, R/3 Development and Supply Chain Management: Claus E. Heinrich
Extended Management Board and CFO: Dieter Matheis
Extended Management Board, Basis and mySAP.com Development: Karl-Heinz Hess
Head of Worldwide Marketing: Martin Homlish
CEO SAP America: Wolfgang Kemna
President, SAP America: Christopher Larsen
COO SAP America: Eric Rubino
Manager, Human Resources, SAP America: Larry Kleinman
Auditors: Arthur Andersen

LOCATIONS

HQ: Neurottstrasse 16, 69190 Walldorf, Germany
Phone: +49-6227-74-7474   **Fax:** +49-6227-75-7575
US HQ: 3999 West Chester Pike,
New Town Square, PA 19073
US Phone: 610-661-1000   **US Fax:** 610-355-3106
Web site: http://www.sap.com

1999 Sales

	% of total
Americas	43
Europe, Middle East & Africa	
Germany	21
Other countries	26
Asia/Pacific	10
Total	**100**

PRODUCTS/OPERATIONS

1999 Sales

	$ mil.	% of total
Products	3,116	60
Consulting	1,558	30
Training	397	9
Other	75	1
Total	**5,146**	**100**

Software
Business intelligence
Customer relationship management
E-commerce
Enterprise resource planning
Financials and accounting
Human resources management
Logistics
Product life cycle management
Supply chain management

Services
Business consulting
Implementation
Maintenance
Training

COMPETITORS

Ariba	i2 Technologies	Progress
Baan	IBM	Software
Clarus	Intentia	PSDI
Commerce One	J.D. Edwards	QAD
Computer	Lawson Software	SAS Institute
Associates	Manugistics	Siebel Systems
Epicor Software	Group	System Software
Geac Computer	MAPICS	Associates
Great Plains	Oracle	
Software	PeopleSoft	

HISTORICAL FINANCIALS & EMPLOYEES

NYSE: SAP FYE: December 31	Annual Growth	12/90	12/91	12/92	12/93	12/94	12/95	12/96	12/97	12/98	12/99
Sales ($ mil.)	35.5%	333	465	513	634	1,182	1,875	2,415	3,345	5,073	5,146
Net income ($ mil.)	31.1%	53	81	78	84	181	281	367	513	629	605
Income as % of sales	—	15.8%	17.4%	15.2%	13.2%	15.3%	15.0%	15.2%	15.3%	12.4%	11.8%
Earnings per share ($)	92.0%	—	—	—	—	—	—	—	—	0.50	0.96
Stock price - FY high ($)	—	—	—	—	—	—	—	—	—	60.13	55.00
Stock price - FY low ($)	—	—	—	—	—	—	—	—	—	29.69	23.75
Stock price - FY close ($)	44.4%	—	—	—	—	—	—	—	—	36.06	52.06
P/E - high	—	—	—	—	—	—	—	—	—	120	57
P/E - low	—	—	—	—	—	—	—	—	—	59	25
Dividends per share ($)	—	—	—	—	—	—	—	—	—	0.00	0.00
Book value per share ($)	14.7%	—	—	—	—	—	—	—	—	5.36	6.15
Employees	29.4%	2,138	2,685	3,157	3,648	5,229	6,857	9,202	12,856	17,323	21,699

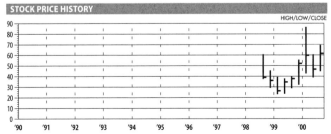

STOCK PRICE HISTORY — HIGH/LOW/CLOSE

1999 FISCAL YEAR-END
Debt ratio: 0.1%
Return on equity: 25.1%
Cash ($ mil.): 716
Current ratio: 1.97
Long-term debt ($ mil.): 1
No. of shares (mil.): 419
Dividends
Yield: —
Payout: —
Market value ($ mil.): 21,814

SCANDINAVIAN AIRLINES SYSTEM

Blast the horn — Scandinavian Airlines System (SAS) is fighting to send its competitors to Valhalla. Stockholm-based SAS carries passengers and cargo to more than 100 destinations in Scandinavia and the rest of Europe. Its Radisson SAS Hotels Worldwide operates about 125 hotels in 36 countries.

SAS is owned by parent companies SAS Danmark (two-sevenths ownership), SAS Norge (two-sevenths), and SAS Sverige (three-sevenths); each parent is in turn 50%-owned by the governments of Denmark, Norway, and Sweden, respectively.

European airline deregulation in 1997 ended SAS's 50-year monopoly in Scandinavia, but the company has responded strongly to the resulting increased competition from low-cost airlines by paring jobs and cutting noncore businesses. SAS has also

been optimizing its fleet, phasing out older aircraft as it buys new Boeing 737s and widebody airliners from Airbus.

Key to its continued success in the deregulated skies is the formation of the Star Alliance, whose members include Air Canada, All Nippon Airway, Lufthansa, Thai Airways, United Airlines, and VARIG of Brazil. The code-sharing alliance allows the carriers to pool frequent-flier programs and share booking and airport facilities. The Star Alliance extends SAS's offerings to more than 800 destinations in more than 130 countries worldwide.

SAS hasn't neglected local markets: The company has taken ownership stakes in regional airlines Cimber Air (Denmark), Skyways (Sweden), Wideroe (Norway), and Air Botnia (Finland).

The national airlines of Sweden (ABA), Norway (DNL), and Denmark (DDL) first met in 1938 to negotiate joint service to New York. The plan was delayed by WWII but kept alive in Sweden, where banker Marcus Wallenberg founded Svensk Interkontinental Luftrafik (SILA), a private airline that in 1943 replaced ABA as Sweden's international carrier. With SILA's financial backing, the yet-to-be-formed Scandinavian Airlines System (SAS) obtained the necessary landing concessions to open a Stockholm-New York air route in 1945. SAS was formed in 1946.

After opening service to South America (1946), Southeast Asia (1949), and Africa (1953), SAS inaugurated the world's first commercial polar route in 1954. It formed charter airline Scanair in 1961 and Danish domestic carrier Danair, through a joint venture, in 1971.

Deregulation of US airlines (1978) signaled the demise of nationally protected airlines. SAS seemed ill-equipped to adapt and reported its first loss in 18 years in 1980. Jan Carlzon, former head of Swedish airline Linjeflyg, became SAS's president in 1981. By targeting businessmen as the airline's most stable market and substituting an economy-rate business class for first-class service on European flights, Carlzon had turned SAS's losses into profits by the end of 1982.

The company bought about 25% of Airlines of Britain Holdings in 1988, gaining a foothold at London's Heathrow Airport. Another purchase that year brought SAS nearly 10% of Continental Airlines Holdings. In 1989 the

airline signed agreements that provided route coordination and hub-sharing with Swissair, Finnair, LanChile, and Canadian Airlines International.

SAS tried in the early 1990s to merge with KLM, Swissair, and Austrian Airlines to create a new international carrier, but that effort failed in 1993, leading to the replacement of Carlzon. New CEO Jan Stenberg consolidated the group, shed noncore businesses, and cut 15,000 jobs. By late 1994 SAS had sold SAS Service Partner (catering, its largest nonairline unit), Diners Club Nordic, and most of the SAS Leisure Group. By spinning off its 42% stake in LanChile and creating a new Latvian airline with Baltic International, SAS focused its air routes in Scandinavia, Western Europe, and the Baltic region.

The SAS trading subsidiary was folded into the airline unit in 1994. Through its hotel unit, SAS allied itself with Radisson Hotels to expand its presence in Europe, the Middle East, and Asia. In 1997 the company joined UAL's United Airlines, Lufthansa, VARIG, and others to form the Star Alliance. In 1998 SAS acquired Finland's Air Botnia.

New code-sharing agreements in 1999 included deals with Singapore Airlines and Icelandair. SAS agreed to sell half of its 40% stake in British Midlands (BM) to Lufthansa, paving the way for BM to join the Star Alliance.

SAS boosted its cargo services in 2000 when it partnered with giants Lufthansa Cargo and Singapore Airlines to harmonize their cargo handling and information technology services.

Chairman: Hugo Schrøder, age 68
First VC: Bo Berggren, age 64
Second VC: Bjørn Eidem, age 58
President and CEO; President, SAS Danmark, SAS Norge, and SAS Sverige: Jan Stenberg, age 61
EVP and CFO: Gunnar Reitan, age 46
SVP Business Systems Division: Vagn Sorensen, age 41
SVP Human Resources: Bernhard Rikardsen, age 44
SVP Information Strategies and Processes and CIO: Claes Broström, age 44
SVP Marketing and Sales Division: Erik Strand, age 49
SVP Operation Division: Jan Forsberg, age 49
SVP Public Relations and Government Affairs: Henry Sténson, age 45
SVP Station Services Division: Marie Ehrling, age 45
SVP Technical Division: Ørnulf Myrvoll, age 54
VP Corporate Finance: Johan Törngren
Director Investor Relations: Sture Stølen
Auditors: Deloitte & Touche LLP

LOCATIONS

HQ: Frösundaviks Allé 1, Solna,
S-195 87 Stockholm, Sweden
Phone: +46-8-797-00-00   **Fax:** +46-8-797-12-10
US HQ: 9 Polito Ave., Lyndhurst, NJ 07071
US Phone: 201-896-3600   **US Fax:** 201-896-3725
Web site: http://www.scandinavian.net

Scandinavian Airlines System serves about 100 destinations in 31 countries; with Star Alliance partners it serves more than 800 destinations in more than 130 countries. The company also operates hotels in about 36 countries.

PRODUCTS/OPERATIONS

1999 Sales

	% of total
Traffic	
Passengers	68
Freight	5
Mail	1
Other	3
SAS International Hotels	7
SAS Trading	6
Other	10
Total	**100**

Selected Operations
AirBaltic (34%)
British Midland plc (40%, British airline)
Commercial Aviation Leasing Ltd. (47%)
Gronlandsfly A/S (37%)
Oy Air Botnia Ab
Polygon Group Ltd (31%)
SAS International Hotels (Radisson SAS Hotels)
Spanair S.A. (49%, Spanish airline)
Wideroe's Flyveselskap (63%, Norwegian airline)

COMPETITORS

Accor	Granada Compass
Aer Lingus	Hilton Group
Air France	Hyatt
Air Portugal	Iberia
Alitalia	KLM
AMR	Marriott International
Austrian Airlines	Ryanair
Braathens SAFE	SAirGroup
British Airways	Starwood Hotels & Resorts
Cathay Pacific	Worldwide
Continental Airlines	TWA
Delta	Virgin Atlantic Airways
Finnair	

HISTORICAL FINANCIALS & EMPLOYEES

Consortium FYE: December 31	Annual Growth	12/90	12/91	12/92	12/93	12/94	12/95	12/96	12/97	12/98	12/99
Sales ($ mil.)	(1.7%)	5,660	5,812	4,851	4,679	4,968	5,318	5,166	4,919	5,054	4,869
Net income ($ mil.)	—	(12)	(33)	(123)	(71)	294	355	261	282	349	198
Income as % of sales	—	—	—	—	—	5.9%	6.7%	5.0%	5.7%	6.9%	4.1%
Employees	(3.8%)	40,830	38,940	40,140	37,330	28,425	22,731	23,607	25,057	27,071	28,863

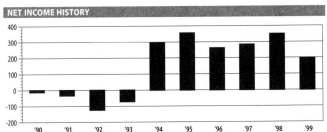

NET INCOME HISTORY

1999 FISCAL YEAR-END
Debt ratio: 33.4%
Return on equity: —
Cash ($ mil.): 150
Current ratio: 0.96
Long-term debt ($ mil.): 1,004

SCHNEIDER ELECTRIC SA

OVERVIEW

If Schneider Electric sees a light at the end of the tunnel, the company probably put it there. The company, based in Boulogne-Billancourt, France, is one of the world's largest electrical engineering companies. It specializes in electrical distribution and industrial control and automation, serving the electric power, industrial, infrastructure, and construction markets.

Schneider Electric helps power generators distribute electricity. It also designs automation systems for the automobile and water-treatment industries; builds infrastructure for airports, road and rail networks, and port facilities; and manages electric power in residential, industrial, and commercial buildings. Subsidiary Square D conducts Schneider Electric's North American operations.

Schneider Electric entered the consumer low-voltage market (visible products such as sockets, switches, and baseboards) with the purchase of Lexel (Norway). The company is also working with THOMSON multimedia S.A. to develop powerline communication technologies (PLC). PLCs use a dwelling's electrical wiring to transmit digital data to and from devices such as DVD and MP3 players.

HISTORY

Schneider Electric's predecessor was founded in 1782 to make industrial equipment. After the upheavals of the French Revolution and the Napoleonic Wars, the company came under the control of brothers Adolphe and Eugene Schneider in 1836. Within two years they had built the first French locomotive (the country's first rail line had opened in 1832).

The company became one of France's most important heavy-industry companies, branching into a variety of machinery and steel operations. However, the country's industrial development continued to trail that of Britain and Germany due to recurrent political strife, including the revolutions of 1848 and the Franco-Prussian War. France also possessed fewer coal and iron deposits.

During WWI Schneider was a key part of France's war effort. It entered the electrical contracting business in 1929 and fought off nationalization attempts in the mid-1930s.

The blitzkrieg of 1939 brought much of France under Nazi occupation, and those Schneider factories that were not destroyed were commandeered by the Germans. After the war, the company rebuilt, aided by the French government. It was restructured as a holding company, and its operating units were split into three subsidiaries: civil and electrical engineering, industrial manufacturing, and construction. Charles Schneider, the last family member to lead the company, died in 1950.

In 1963 Schneider concluded an alliance with the Empain Group of Belgium, and by 1969, three years after Schneider went public, the two companies merged to become Empain-Schneider. During this period the company made numerous noncore acquisitions, entering such fields as ski equipment, fashion, publishing, and travel.

Schneider began reorganizing in 1980. This effort entered its final phase in 1993 with a major recapitalization that saw the merger of its former parent company, Société Parisienne d'Entreprises et de Participations, with Schneider SA and the issue of new stock to existing stockholders. The company also streamlined operations. Merlin Gerin (acquired in 1975) and Telemecanique (1988) became Schneider Electric in Europe, and their North American operations were merged into Square D after its acquisition in 1991.

Schneider's 1994 takeover of two Belgian subsidiaries led Belgium's government to charge CEO Didier Pineau-Valencienne with fraud in the valuation of the stock.

In 1996 Schneider sold EPE Technologies, a maker of uninterruptible power supplies, to management. It also established the Schneider Electric (China) Investment Co. in Beijing, China's first totally French-owned firm. The next year the company sold Spie Batignolles, its electrical contracting subsidiary. Also in 1997 Charles Denny was named to the newly created post of chairman and CEO of Schneider North America. Cost-cutting measures and strong sales in France and North America combined to boost the company's 1998 income.

In 1999 Schneider agreed to pay $1.1 billion for Lexel, a joint venture owned by Finland's Ahlstrom and Denmark's NKT Holding, to broaden its electrical equipment offerings for the household. Also that year the company changed its name to Schneider Electric and changed its main subsidiary's name to Schneider Electric Industries. Looking to add more machinery makers to its list of customers, the company announced plans to acquire the electro-mechanical components business of Thomson-CSF and Switzerland-based Positec in 2000.

Honorary Chairman: Didier Pineau-Valencienne, age 69
Chairman and CEO: Henri Lachmann, age 61
VC and COO: Jean-Paul Jacamon, age 52
EVP Activities and Technologies: Jean-Paul Saas
EVP European Division: Christian Wiest, age 50
EVP Finance and Control: Antoine Giscard d'Estaing, age 39
EVP French Division: Marcel Torrents
EVP Human Resources and Corporate Communication: Jean-François Pilliard, age 51
EVP International Division: Jean-Louis Andreu
EVP North American Division: Chris C. Richardson, age 55
EVP Subsidiaries Department: Jean-Claude Perrin
Auditors: Arthur Andersen; Barbier Frinault & Autres; Befec-Price Waterhouse

LOCATIONS

HQ: 43-45, Blvd. Franklin-Roosevelt, F-92500 Rueil-Malmaison, France
Phone: +33-1-41-29-7000   **Fax:** +33-1-41-29-7100
Web site: http://www.schneider-electric.com

Schneider Electric has about 150 manufacturing and marketing facilities in 130 countries.

1999 Sales

	% of total
Europe	
France	18
Other countries	35
North America	30
Other regions	17
Total	**100**

PRODUCTS/OPERATIONS

1999 Sales

	% of total
Electrical distribution	71
Industrial control & automation	29
Total	**100**

COMPETITORS

ABB	Legris
Alcatel	MAN
Alstom	Mannesmann AG
Eaton	Mitsubishi Electric
EDF	OMRON
Eiffage	Peter Kiewit Sons'
EMCOR	Rockwell International
Finmeccanica	RWE
Fluor	Siemens
Foster Wheeler	Tractebel
GE	UNOVA
Internatio-Muller	VINCI
Johnson Controls	Vivendi
Legrand	

HISTORICAL FINANCIALS & EMPLOYEES

Euronext Paris: SU FYE: December 31	Annual Growth	12/90	12/91	12/92	12/93	12/94	12/95	12/96	12/97	12/98	12/99
Sales (€ mil.)	1.1%	7,605	7,626	9,367	8,595	8,532	9,059	9,397	7,226	7,626	8,378
Net income (€ mil.)	14.6%	141	42	46	62	104	125	201	335	409	481
Income as % of sales	—	1.9%	0.5%	0.5%	0.7%	1.2%	1.4%	2.1%	4.6%	5.4%	5.7%
Earnings per share (€)	15.9%	—	—	—	1.33	1.67	1.27	1.48	2.13	2.63	3.23
Stock price - FY high (€)	—	—	—	—	67.08	80.65	41.92	41.22	59.15	80.65	76.85
Stock price - FY low (€)	—	—	—	—	41.62	35.37	19.97	25.34	35.67	39.10	44.40
Stock price - FY close (€)	2.8%	—	—	—	66.16	40.40	25.46	36.57	49.82	51.68	77.95
P/E - high	—	—	—	—	50	48	33	28	28	31	24
P/E - low	—	—	—	—	31	21	16	17	17	15	14
Dividends per share (€)	3.8%	—	—	—	1.07	1.14	0.61	0.76	0.99	1.15	1.34
Book value per share (€)	(9.4%)	—	—	—	47.79	49.23	25.74	20.59	25.08	24.12	26.46
Employees	(2.3%)	83,600	101,100	97,451	91,458	89,762	92,700	63,000	61,499	60,780	67,510

STOCK PRICE HISTORY

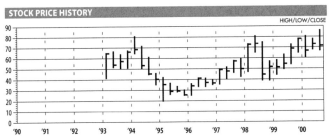

HIGH/LOW/CLOSE

1999 FISCAL YEAR-END

Debt ratio: 34.3%
Return on equity: 12.2%
Cash (€ mil.): 1,051
Current ratio: 1.41
Long-term debt (€ mil.): 1,522
No. of shares (mil.): 161
Dividends
  Yield: 0.0%
  Payout: 0.4%
Market value ($ mil.): 12,610
Sales ($ mil.): 8,418

SCOTTISH POWER PLC

With more power in England than Bonnie Prince Charlie, Scottish Power is a hero in the UK's deregulated energy market. The Glasgow-based company, with 5.5 million customers, is one of the largest multi-utilities in the country. Now Scottish Power is taking advantage of deregulation in the US to add to its empire: The firm has gained 1.5 million customers in the western US through its purchase of PacifiCorp.

At home Scottish Power provides everything from gas to Internet access. With a generating capacity of 6,000 MW, it provides electricity to 1.9 million customers in Scotland, and its Manweb subsidiary serves another 1.4 million in northwestern England and Wales. Another unit, Southern Water, provides water and wastewater services to 2.7 million customers in southern England. Moving into the telecommunications arena, Scottish Power's 50.1%-owned Thus (formerly Scottish Telecom) offers telecom services for businesses; one of the UK's top ISPs, it has more than 260,000 customers.

With its purchase of Oregon-based PacifiCorp, completed in 1999, Scottish Power became the first non-US entity to acquire a US utility. PacifiCorp (8,700-MW capacity) sells electricity in the western US. To absorb PacifiCorp and prepare for regulatory price cuts in the UK, Scottish Power has been divesting noncore businesses, cutting staff, and expanding telecom services. It has sold Australian assets owned by PacifiCorp.

The UK power industry was nationalized in 1947, and two regional state-controlled boards were charged with generating, transmitting, and distributing electricity in Scotland. The two monopolies were the North of Scotland Hydro-Electric Board (formed in 1943) and the South of Scotland Electricity Board (SSEB, formed in 1955). In keeping with the deregulation trend that swept the UK in the 1980s, Scottish Power was formed in 1989 to assume the non-nuclear operations of SSEB, and Hydro-Electric (now part of Scottish and Southern) took the northern board's assets. Scottish Power had to prepare for competition, which began in a limited form in 1990.

Scottish Power's initial assets included six coal, gas, and hydropower plants that served southern Scotland and Northumberland, including Glasgow and much of Scotland's industrial base. The company, which went public in 1991, also inherited 73 retail outlets that sold consumer electronic and electrical goods. It expanded this retail business across the UK in the 1990s.

The company teamed with SeaWest of the US and Japan's Toman in the early 1990s to set up Europe's largest wind farm, in Wales. It set up other wind-energy plants in Northern Ireland, Scotland, and in England; by the mid-1990s Scottish Power was the largest wind-farm operator in the UK.

In 1993 the company moved into telecommunications. Running fiber-optic lines alongside its high-voltage power lines between Glasgow and Edinburgh, the company's Scottish Telecom unit (established in 1994) provided high-speed voice and data services to several major business firms.

With opportunities for growth limited by the relatively small population base in southern Scotland, the company sought to expand through geographic and business diversification. In 1995 it became the first UK power firm to buy a rival when it acquired Manweb, a regional electricity company that served northwestern England and North Wales. The next year the company became the first British electricity firm to buy a water company when it acquired Southern Water, a water supply and wastewater services firm based in England's South Coast. Scottish Power disposed of many of Southern Water's noncore businesses in 1997.

In 1998 Scottish Power boosted its telecom business with the purchase of Demon Internet, then the UK's largest independent ISP. Also that year, after merger talks with two US electric utilities failed, Scottish Power agreed to acquire PacifiCorp, a major utility in the US Pacific Northwest. The deal was completed in 1999.

With the BBC, Scottish Telecom launched a free Internet service, Freebeeb.net, in 1999. That year Scottish Telecom's name was changed to Thus, and the company floated a 49.9% stake in the unit. The company also announced a restructuring plan that would cut jobs and divest noncore businesses. In 2000 Scottish Power announced plans to join the Royal Bank of Scotland in offering bundled services, including banking, utilities, and telecommunications, to its UK customers. Also in 2000 it divested PacifiCorp's Australian assets, including Powercor Australia.

OFFICERS

Chairman: Charles Miller Smith, age 60,
$41,333 pay (partial-year salary)
Deputy Chairman: Keith McKennon, age 66,
$21,511 pay (partial-year salary)
Chief Executive: Ian Robinson, age 58, $669,000 pay
Deputy Chief Executive: Ian M. Russell, age 47,
$603,792 pay
CEO PacifiCorp: Alan Richardson, age 53,
$293,667 pay (partial-year salary)
Finance Director: David Nish, age 39,
$86,407 pay (partial-year salary)
Executive Director Customer Sales and Services:
Charles Berry, age 48, $259,000 pay (partial-year salary)
Executive Director UK Power Operations: Ken L. Vowles,
age 58, $356,125 pay
Director Corporate Affairs: Sue Clark, age 35
Director Corporate Strategy: Julian Brown, age 50
Group Human Resources Director: Paul Pagliari, age 40
Group Commerical and Legal Director: James Stanley,
age 50
Group Secretary: Andrew Mitchell, age 48
Auditors: PricewaterhouseCoopers

LOCATIONS

HQ: 1 Atlantic Quay, Glasgow G2 8SP, United Kingdom
Phone: +44-141-248-8200　　**Fax:** +44-141-248-8300
US HQ: 825 N.E. Multnomah, Portland, OR 97232
US Phone: 503-813-5000　　**US Fax:** 503-813-7247
Web site: http://www.scottishpower.plc.uk

Scottish Power's three core areas of business are
southern Scotland (ScottishPower), northern Wales
and northwestern England (Manweb), and southern
England (Southern Water). Subsidiary PacifiCorp
operates in the western US.

PRODUCTS/OPERATIONS

Selected Subsidiaries
Manweb (electricity supply and distribution)
PacifiCorp (electricity generation and distribution)
Southern Water (water and wastewater operations)
Thus (50.1%, telecommunications services)

COMPETITORS

AWG
British Energy
Centrica
Edison International
Energis
Enron
Freeserve
Hyder
International Power
MidAmerican Energy
PG&E
Portland General Electric
PowerGen
Scottish and Southern Energy
Severn Trent
Thames Water
TXU Europe
United Utilities

HISTORICAL FINANCIALS & EMPLOYEES

NYSE: SPI FYE: March 31	Annual Growth	3/91	3/92	3/93	3/94	3/95	3/96	3/97	3/98	3/99	3/00
Sales ($ mil.)	17.3%	—	—	—	—	—	3,465	4,821	5,229	5,225	6,557
Net income ($ mil.)	35.0%	—	—	—	—	—	452	690	284	810	1,502
Income as % of sales	—	—	—	—	—	—	13.0%	14.3%	5.4%	15.5%	22.9%
Earnings per share ($)	111.4%	—	—	—	—	—	—	—	0.96	2.71	4.29
Stock price - FY high ($)	—	—	—	—	—	—	—	—	38.50	44.81	39.25
Stock price - FY low ($)	—	—	—	—	—	—	—	—	27.13	34.13	22.00
Stock price - FY close ($)	(8.6%)	—	—	—	—	—	—	—	37.94	35.19	31.69
P/E - high	—	—	—	—	—	—	—	—	14	16	16
P/E - low	—	—	—	—	—	—	—	—	10	13	9
Dividends per share ($)	—	—	—	—	—	—	—	—	0.00	1.73	2.83
Book value per share ($)	51.7%	—	—	—	—	—	—	—	9.54	10.46	21.95
Employees	—	—	—	—	—	—	—	—	—	—	—

STOCK PRICE HISTORY

HIGH/LOW/CLOSE

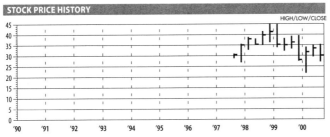

2000 FISCAL YEAR-END

Debt ratio: 40.5%
Return on equity: 22.6%
Cash ($ mil.): 295
Current ratio: 0.85
Long-term debt ($ mil.): 6,907
No. of shares (mil.): 462
Dividends
　Yield: 8.9%
　Payout: 66.0%
Market value ($ mil.): 14,638

THE SEAGRAM COMPANY LTD.

OVERVIEW

Seagram is sobering up and getting married. Montréal-based Seagram has morphed from one of the world's largest distillers into an entertainment company. The company is transforming itself again through its 2000 agreement to be acquired by French utility and media firm Vivendi for about $34 billion. The new Vivendi Universal will consist of the assets of Vivendi, Seagram, as well as Vivendi's Canal+ pay-TV unit.

Most of Seagram's sales come from its 92% interests in Universal Music Group (UMG) and Universal Studios. UMG is the world's largest music company, housing several popular record labels such as A&M, Geffen, Interscope, and Motown.

Universal Studios, in addition to film and television production, operates several theme parks (some are co-owned by Rank Group, which wants to sell its share) and more than 600 Spencer Gifts retail outlets. It also owns

45% of Barry Diller's USA Networks and 26% of movie house Loews Cineplex Entertainment.

With its move into entertainment, Seagram is giving up on its libations. The company's drinks business makes rum (Captain Morgan), whiskeys (Chivas Regal, Crown Royal), and other hard liquors, as well as wines, wine coolers, and mixers. It does so profitably, which is more than can be said for its Universal Studios division. That operation's struggles (as well as fallout from the AOL-Time Warner mega-merger) was one of the main factors that prompted Seagram to accept the acquisition deal with Vivendi. Once it is completed, Vivendi Universal plans to sell Seagram's liquor business to British liquor giant Diageo and French distiller Pernod Ricard for $8.15 billion.

CEO Edgar Bronfman Jr.'s family controls the company through its 25% stake. Philips Electronics owns 11% of Seagram.

HISTORY

Sam Bronfman bought the Bonaventure Liquor Store Company in Montréal in 1916 and started selling liquor by mail order, the only legal way during Canadian Prohibition (which lasted until the early 1920s). With the help of his brother Allan, Bronfman opened the first family distillery in neighboring La Salle as Distillers Corporation Ltd. in 1924. Bronfman purchased the larger Joseph E. Seagram & Sons in 1928, went public, and changed the company's name to Distillers Corporation-Seagrams Ltd.

Bronfman established a lucrative bootlegging operation throughout the 1920s to smuggle whiskey into the "dry" US. Anticipating the end of Prohibition in the US, Bronfman began stockpiling whiskey in 1928 and accumulated the world's largest supply of aged rye and sour mash whiskeys when Prohibition ended in 1933. The company introduced Seagram's 7 Crown in 1934 and Crown Royal in 1939. Expanding its liquor line, the company acquired Mumm and Perrier-Jouët (champagne), Barton & Guestier (wine), and Chivas Brothers (scotch) after WWII.

Edgar Bronfman succeeded his father as company president in 1957 and expanded the company's wine and spirits lines substantially. The Bronfman family also diversified into areas as varied as Israeli supermarkets and Texas gas fields in the late 1950s. The company adopted its present name in 1975 and acquired a major stake in DuPont in 1980 when DuPont bought

Seagram's interest in Conoco (Seagram later sold its DuPont shares in 1995, a move that many still decry as foolish). It later acquired Tropicana fruit juices in 1988.

Seagram started buying up shares of Time Warner in 1993 (accumulating more than 50 million shares). Edgar Jr. succeeded his father as CEO the next year and orchestrated the purchase of Universal Studios' parent MCA from Matsushita Electric for $5.7 billion in 1995. He followed that mega-deal with the $1.7 billion purchase from Viacom of the 50% of USA Networks it didn't already own. Then it shifted most of its TV assets into a joint venture with Home Shopping Network (led by TV mogul Barry Diller) in exchange for stock and cash worth more than $4 billion. Seagram got a 45% stake in Diller's company (renamed USA Networks).

Still not through with major deal making, Seagram bought PolyGram for $10.2 billion in 1998. To help pay for the deal, Seagram sold the last of its stock in Time Warner, sold most of PolyGram's film library to MGM for $250 million, and sold Tropicana to PepsiCo for $3.3 billion. PolyGram's leftover music assets, mixed with those of Universal Studios, became Universal Music Group.

In 2000 Seagram agreed to be acquired by France-based Vivendi for $34 billion. The combined Vivendi Universal plans to sell Seagram's liquor business.

Chairman: Edgar M. Bronfman, age 70, $1,563,255 pay
Co-Chairman; Chairman Executive Committee:
Charles R. Bronfman, age 68, $1,250,598 pay
President and CEO: Edgar Bronfman Jr., age 44,
$3,730,000 pay
EVP and CFO: Brian Mulligan, age 40
EVP; President and CEO, Seagram Spirits and Wine:
Steven J. Kalagher
EVP Human Resources: John D. Borgia, age 51,
$873,120 pay
EVP Legal and Environmental Affairs:
Daniel R. Paladino, age 56
EVP Corporate Communications and Public Policy:
Tod R. Hullin
Chairman and CEO, Universal Music: Doug Morris
**Chairman, Seagram Beverage; President, Seagram
Chateau and Estate Wines:** Samuel Bronfman II
Chairman, Seagram Spirits and Wine: John Hunter
Chairman Universal Television & Networks:
Blair Westlake
Auditors: PricewaterhouseCoopers LLP

HQ: 1430 Peel St., Montréal, Québec H3A 1S9, Canada
Phone: 514-849-5271   **Fax:** 514-987-5224
US HQ: 375 Park Ave., New York, NY 10152
US Phone: 212-572-7000   **US Fax:** 212-572-1080
Web site: http://www.seagram.com

Selected Operations and Brands

Spirits and Wine
Captain Morgan (rum)
Chivas Regal (whisky)
Crown Royal (whiskey)
Glenlivet (whisky)
Godiva (liqueur)
Martell (cognac)
Sandeman (sherry/port)
Seagram's 7 Crown
(whiskey)
Seagram's Extra Dry (gin)
Sterling Vinyards (wine)

Universal Music Group
A&M Records

Decca Records
Geffen Records
Interscope Records
MCA Records
Motown Record Company

Universal Studios
Spencer Gifts
Universal Pictures
Universal Studios
Recreation Group
(theme parks)
Universal Television &
Networks
USA Networks (45%)

Allied Domecq
Anheuser-Busch
Bacardi USA
BMG
Entertainment
Brown-Forman
constellation
brands

Diageo
EMI Group
Fortune Brands
Fox
Entertainment
Gallo
MGM
Pernod Ricard

Remy Cointreau
Six Flags
Sony
Time Warner
Viacom
Walt Disney

Subsidiary FYE: June 30	Annual Growth	1/92	1/93	1/94	1/95	1/96	*6/96	6/97	6/98	6/99	6/00
Sales ($ mil.)	10.6%	6,345	6,101	6,038	6,399	9,747	5,013	12,560	9,714	12,312	15,686
Net income ($ mil.)	(1.4%)	727	474	379	736	3,406	85	502	946	686	40
Income as % of sales	—	11.5%	7.8%	6.3%	11.5%	34.9%	1.7%	4.0%	9.7%	5.6%	0.3%
Employees	40.5%	17,700	16,800	15,800	15,800	16,100	30,000	30,000	24,200	34,000	34,000

* Fiscal year change

Debt ratio: 37.6%
Return on equity: 0.3%
Cash ($ mil.): 1,230
Current ratio: 1.16
Long-term debt ($ mil.): 7,378

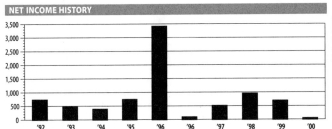

SEGA CORPORATION

OVERVIEW

SEGA wants to be the nightmare on Sony and Nintendo's street. With its 128-bit video game console, Dreamcast, Tokyo-based SEGA (formerly SEGA Enterprises) has visions of reclaiming the #1 spot from those rival video game makers. The company, a distant #3 in video game consoles, developed Dreamcast with high-tech partners such as Microsoft and NEC. It has realistic graphics and allows players to compete over the Internet. Sony has also introduced a 128-bit system and Nintendo plans to introduce a system more powerful than its current N64.

In addition to video game hardware, the company runs entertainment centers (arcades and theme parks), mostly in Japan, and makes arcade games. (Each account for about a third of sales.) It has been developing entertainment complexes that offer movie theaters, karaoke rooms, bowling, and shops. The company also produces video and computer games and Pico multimedia educational games.

SEGA is about 20%-owned by one of Japan's largest information services firms, CSK Corporation.

HISTORY

One of the originators of the Japanese electronic games industry was born in New York. David Rosen returned to Japan following a military stint there during the Korean War. He started an art export business, Rosen Enterprises, in 1951. However, Rosen recognized the need for a quick method of making ID cards, which were used for numerous purposes in Japan, and in 1954 he began importing instant photo booths made in the US. When the Japanese became concerned about the US company and its advanced technology, Rosen offered to license his machines to Japanese operators — perhaps the first franchise operation in Japan.

With Japan's economy improving, in 1957 Rosen imported coin-operated games into the country. In 1965, after becoming dissatisfied with US amusement game quality, he acquired a US company that made jukeboxes in Japan. The combined companies were renamed SEGA Enterprises (short for SErvice GAmes). It developed the popular game Periscope and began challenging US games.

Conglomerate Gulf + Western Industries acquired SEGA in 1970. It introduced the first laser disc game and SEGA's first consumer video game console but sold off SEGA's US operations as the video game industry floundered in the early 1980s. In 1984 a group led by Isao Okawa, chairman of Japan's CSK Corporation, bought SEGA. It went public in 1986, the year it established SEGA of America.

Initially SEGA was eclipsed by Nintendo's 8-bit system, released in Japan in 1985. However, SEGA beat its rival in Europe with its own 8-bit game player. SEGA introduced Genesis, the 16-bit game player, in 1989. By 1991, when Nintendo finally came out with a 16-bit system, SEGA had already sold more than a million Genesis systems. SEGA's

no-holds-barred version of the game *Mortal Kombat,* released in 1993, allowed players to rip off heads and pull out hearts and outsold Nintendo's sanitized version two to one.

SEGA released its 32-bit SegaSaturn system in 1995 and teamed up with software developer SOFTBANK to distribute PC software and hardware in the US. Even though SEGA tried new innovations for SegaSaturn (like NetLink, letting users link to the Internet), the console was an overall disappointment. In 1996 it set up a joint venture with US entertainment powers MCA (now Universal Studios) and DreamWorks SKG to develop family-oriented amusement centers in the US.

The next year its planned $1.1 billion merger with Japanese toy maker Bandai fell through after a near revolt by Bandai's middle managers (citing "cultural differences" between the companies and fears that Bandai would lose its identity). Also in 1997 SEGA and game maker Atlus brought their hugely popular (in Japan) Print Club photo-sticker machines to the US. Writeoffs and slumping Asian economies caused a loss for fiscal 1998; the year was also marked by the release in Japan of the 128-bit Dreamcast video game console.

Dreamcast was launched in the US in September 1999 and flew off the shelves (selling over 500,000 units its first month). In November 1999 Sega said it planned to split its video game software and arcade divisions into separate companies and intended to take a few of its software subsidiaries public. Working to boost its Internet stategy, in June 2000 the company announced plans with Motorola to develop wireless phones, pagers, personal digital assistants, and related software that will access Sega games online. In November 2000 SEGA Enterprises changed its name to SEGA Corporation.

Chairman and President: Isao Okawa
EVC: Shoichiro Irimajiri
Corporate EVP: Toshiro Kezuka
Corporate EVP and Human Resources:
Shunichi Nakamura
Corporate VP and CFO: Shoichi Yamazaki
Public Relations Representative: Nana Takahashi
Auditors: Chuo Audit Corporation

LOCATIONS

HQ: 1-2-12 Haneda, Ohta-ku, Tokyo 144-8531, Japan
Phone: +81-3-5736-7034   **Fax:** +81-3-5736-7059
US HQ: Townsend Center, 650 Townsend St., Ste. 650,
San Francisco, CA 94103
US Phone: 415-701-6000   **US Fax:** 415-701-6001
Web site: http://www.sega.co.jp

SEGA has subsidiaries and affiliates in Australia, Bulgaria,
the Czech Republic, France, Germany, Hungary, Japan,
Poland, Singapore, Spain, the UK, and the US.

1999 Sales

	$ mil.	% of total
Japan	1,759	79
Europe	282	13
North America	181	8
Other regions	13	—
Total	**2,235**	**100**

PRODUCTS/OPERATIONS

1999 Sales

	$ mil.	% of total
Amusement center operations	782	35
Amusement machines	742	33
Consumer products	711	32
Total	**2,235**	**100**

Selected Products

Video Game Consoles
Dreamcast
SegaSaturn (retired)

Video Games and Amusement Machines
Aerowings
Bass Fishing
Centipede
Crazy Taxi
House of the Dead
Mortal Kombat
NBA Showtime
Ready 2 Rumble
Zombie Revenge

Other
Activity booths (Print Club photo-sticker dispensing
machine)
Pico (educational games)
Theme parks (Club SEGA, GameWorks, Joypolis, Sega
City, SEGA Entertainment Universe, SEGAWORLD)

COMPETITORS

Anheuser-Busch	Nintendo
Electronic Arts	Sanrio
Hasbro	Six Flags
Havas	Sony
Midway Games	Walt Disney

HISTORICAL FINANCIALS & EMPLOYEES

OTC: SEGNY FYE: March 31	Annual Growth	3/90	3/91	3/92	3/93	3/94	3/95	3/96	3/97	3/98	3/99
Sales ($ mil.)	18.2%	498	758	1,863	3,623	4,054	4,432	3,588	3,496	2,492	2,235
Net income ($ mil.)	—	31	59	94	268	109	59	39	16	(268)	(360)
Income as % of sales	—	6.2%	7.8%	5.0%	7.4%	2.7%	1.3%	1.1%	0.5%	—	—
Earnings per share ($)	—	—	—	—	0.33	0.57	0.39	0.10	0.40	(0.67)	(0.89)
Stock price - FY high ($)	—	—	—	—	21.38	27.38	25.00	14.50	13.00	9.25	6.25
Stock price - FY low ($)	—	—	—	—	20.25	16.36	11.44	8.25	6.13	3.75	3.70
Stock price - FY close ($)	(21.0%)	—	—	—	20.50	18.58	12.14	11.31	6.38	4.63	5.00
P/E - high	—	—	—	—	65	48	51	145	33	—	—
P/E - low	—	—	—	—	61	29	29	83	15	—	—
Dividends per share ($)	54.0%	—	—	—	0.06	0.09	0.11	0.09	0.08	0.07	0.80
Book value per share ($)	(10.1%)	—	—	—	3.20	3.77	4.47	3.67	3.16	2.28	1.69
Employees	9.9%	1,695	1,786	2,324	3,034	3,492	3,758	3,764	3,872	3,982	3,974

STOCK PRICE HISTORY

HIGH/LOW/CLOSE

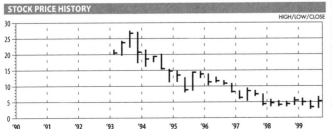

1999 FISCAL YEAR-END

Debt ratio: 72.7%
Return on equity: —
Cash ($ mil.): 846
Current ratio: 2.05
Long-term debt ($ mil.): 1,802
No. of shares (mil.): 403
Dividends
Yield: 0.2%
Payout: —
Market value ($ mil.): 2,013

SEIKO CORPORATION

OVERVIEW

Seiko has been an Olympic champion for more than three decades. Tokyo-based Seiko Corporation, one of the world's largest marketers of watches and clocks, was the official timekeeper for the 1964 Tokyo Olympics (under former name K. Hattori & Co.) and the 1998 Nagano Olympics. It will be the official timekeeper again for the 2002 Games in Utah. The company markets the watches made by other Seiko companies, including luxury watches made by Seiko Epson (which also makes printers, semiconductors, and LCDs) and mass-market watches made by Seiko Instruments (which makes electronic dictionaries, musical instruments, computer peripherals, and electronic components). The Hattori family controls Seiko.

The company sells thousands of styles of watches, including the no-battery Kinetic that is recharged by wrist movement and watches with features such as PC file storage and solar power. In addition to Seiko-brand watches, it sells luxury watches under the Credor and Lassale names and mass-market watches under the brands Pulsar, Lorus, and Alba. Seiko's other timepieces range from small bedside alarm clocks to large-scale public clocks; it also markets ophthalmic lenses, golf clubs, and jewelry.

Facing competition and ailing Asian economies, the company has formed a marketing venture with watch rival Fossil (called SII Marketing International) and reorganized its corporate structure to become more efficient.

HISTORY

Kitaro Hattori started in the jewelry business at age 13. In 1881, at age 21, he set up K. Hattori & Co. in Tokyo's Ginza district to import clocks. As increasing railroad traffic created a demand for accurate timepieces, Hattori started manufacturing wall clocks at his Seikosha factory in 1892. Pocket watches followed in 1895, alarm clocks in 1899, and table clocks in 1902. Hattori began exporting clocks to China and opened his first foreign branch, in Shanghai, in 1913.

Hattori first used the name "Seiko" — Japanese for "precision" — on a watch in 1924. The Seikosha plant started producing camera shutters six years later. Daini Seikosha, the predecessor to Seiko Instruments, was set up as an independent watch manufacturer in 1937. Production shifted during WWII from timepieces to time fuses and ammunition. In 1942 Daiwa Kogyo, which later became Seiko Epson, was established.

By 1953 K. Hattori had restored itself to its prewar position in the Japanese watch market, with a 55% market share. The company attacked the US market in the 1960s by initially offering jewel-lever watches in the midrange market with an average price of $50 and then expanding to the upper and lower ends of the market. This expansion was aided by K. Hattori's selection as the official timekeeper for the 1964 Tokyo Olympics. The company launched the world's first quartz wall clock in 1968 and the first analog quartz watch (the Seiko Astron) the following year.

During the 1970s K. Hattori expanded globally, establishing subsidiaries in Asia, Europe, and North and South America. The company broadened its quartz technology by offering the world's first women's quartz watch in 1972 and the first digital watch with an LCD the next year. K. Hattori introduced the first black-and-white TV watch in 1982. To promote the Seiko brand, the company changed its name to Hattori Seiko Co. the following year. In 1984 it marketed the world's first computer wristwatches and the first battery-operated LCD pocket color television.

The company changed its name to Seiko Corporation in 1990. The next year it introduced the Seiko Perpetual Calendar, a watch capable of tracking dates for more than 1,000 years. Also in 1991 Seiko acquired American Telephone and Electronics (AT&E) — its partner in a wristwatch pager joint venture — after AT&E filed for bankruptcy. Also that year Seiko and DEC established a joint venture to market PCs in Japan.

The official timekeeper for the Olympics in 1992 (Barcelona, Spain) and 1994 (Lillehammer, Norway), Seiko was outbid by rival SMH (Swatch watchmaker) for the 1996 Olympics. The company began marketing diamonds (produced by stonecutter Lazare Kaplan International) in Japan that year. In 1997 it secured the timekeeping position for the 2002 Utah Olympics; it also was timekeeper for the Nagano, Japan, Olympics in 1998. Also in 1998 Seiko began selling the Ruputer, a wristwatch/PC that exchanges data with a PC and stores files.

In 1999 the company formed SII Marketing International with Fossil to sell the companies' lower-priced watches in Wal-Marts and other discount outlets.

Chairman: Reijiro Hattori
President: Chushichi Inoue
Director Finance and Information Systems:
  Kunio Maeda
EVP Marketing and Sales: Hiroshi Harigaya
EVP Administration and Personnel: Koichi Murano
Auditors: Asahi & Co.

LOCATIONS

HQ: 15-1, Kyobashi 2-chome, Chuo-ku,
  Tokyo 104-8331, Japan
Phone: +81-3-3563-2111   **Fax:** +81-3-3563-9556
US HQ: 1111 MacArthur Blvd., Mahwah, NJ 07430
US Phone: 201-529-5730   **US Fax:** 201-529-0132
Web site: http://www.seiko-corp.co.jp

PRODUCTS/OPERATIONS

Selected Watch Brands
Alba
Credor
Kinetic
Lassale
Lorus
Pulsar
Ruputer
Seiko

COMPETITORS

Bausch & Lomb
Casio Computer
Citizen Watch
E. Gluck
Fossil
Gucci
Loews
Luxottica
Movado Group
Swatch
Timex

HISTORICAL FINANCIALS & EMPLOYEES

Tokyo: 8050 FYE: March 31	Annual Growth	3/90	3/91	3/92	3/93	3/94	3/95	3/96	3/97	3/98	3/99
Sales (¥ mil.)	(3.7%)	421,781	428,002	427,965	378,019	334,725	330,864	342,011	380,299	350,997	300,999
Net income (¥ mil.)	—	1,938	694	(2,266)	(5,222)	(6,295)	(9,385)	(11,151)	951	6,739	(13,537)
Income as % of sales	—	0.5%	0.2%	—	—	—	—	—	0.3%	1.9%	—
Earnings per share (¥)	—	18.35	6.57	(21.46)	(49.54)	(59.61)	(88.88)	(105.60)	9.00	63.82	(128.00)
Stock price - FY high (¥)	—	6,100	5,610	3,700	1,340	1,450	1,130	929	1,310	893	805
Stock price - FY low (¥)	—	2,103	1,770	1,180	770	795	691	620	655	401	415
Stock price - FY close (¥)	(23.1%)	5,400	3,510	1,200	1,080	933	778	878	666	600	510
P/E - high	—	332	854	—	—	—	—	—	146	14	—
P/E - low	—	115	269	—	—	—	—	—	73	6	—
Dividends per share (¥)	(7.4%)	10.00	10.00	10.00	10.00	10.00	10.00	10.00	7.50	7.50	5.00
Book value per share (¥)	(12.7%)	291.95	314.50	292.31	279.08	246.89	110.71	157.33	171.19	231.11	85.72
Employees	(7.3%)	—	1,528	1,488	1,470	1,458	1,360	1,182	1,023	898	—

STOCK PRICE HISTORY
HIGH/LOW/CLOSE

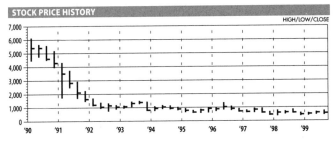

1999 FISCAL YEAR-END
Debt ratio: 46.3%
Return on equity: —
Cash (¥ mil.): 27,548
Current ratio: 0.67
Long-term debt (¥ mil.): 7,819
No. of shares (mil.): 106
Dividends
  Yield: 0.0%
  Payout: —
Market value ($ mil.): 511
Sales ($ mil.): 2,854

SEIKO EPSON CORPORATION

OVERVIEW

For Seiko Epson, timing isn't everything, but it's important. The privately held Suwa, Japan-based company is one of the two manufacturing arms of the Seiko Group, the internationally known watchmaker (Seiko Instruments is the group's other manuacturer). In addition to watches (which a third sister company, Seiko Corp., markets under the Seiko and Pulsar brand names), Seiko Epson (sometimes called Epson) makes information-related products such as desktop and portable computers; electronic devices and components, including semiconductors and LCDs (the company produces 60% of the LCDs used in cellular phones); and a variety of other products, such as lenses, motors, and magnets. Seiko Epson, a top printer manufacturer, produces dot matrix, ink jet,

laser, and thermal printers, as well as printer components. The company has about 17% of the market for low-end printers, plus about 5% of the world's scanner market.

Seiko Epson's factories tick off enough clock movements annually to make the company the world's largest watch producer. And although watchmaking is now the company's smallest segment (5% of sales), Seiko Epson has no plans to wind down its most dated business — the skills gleaned from watchmaking, including miniaturization and precision timing, have given rise to the company's other, more profitable lines.

Heirs of Seiko's founder, including Seiko Epson chairman Reijiro Hattori and VC Yasuo Hattori, control the company.

HISTORY

In 1881, 21-year-old Kitaro Hattori, who had begun working in the jewelry trade at age 13, opened a Tokyo watch shop and called it K. Hattori & Co. In 1892 Hattori started a factory in Seikosha to manufacture wall clocks and, later, watches and alarm clocks. K. Hattori & Co. went public in 1917. In 1924 it began using the Seiko brand on its timepieces. Kitaro's son Ganzo formed Daini Seikosha Co., precursor of Seiko Instruments, in 1937.

The company formed Daiwa Kogyo Ltd., a maker of mechanical watches, in 1942; it would later become Seiko Epson. Developments included self-winding watches (1955) and transistorized table clocks (1959).

A big break came for the company in 1964, when it developed crystal chronometers and printing timers for the Tokyo Olympics' official timekeepers. It was the first time a precision timepiece and a printer had been combined. Based on that technology, in 1968 Seiko Epson debuted the EP-101, the first commercially successful miniature printer (used primarily with calculators).

During the late 1960s Seiko Epson entered the semiconductor field when it began developing LSIs (large-scale integrated circuits) for its watches. The company introduced the world's first quartz watch in 1969 and the first quartz digital watch in 1973. It soon expanded into liquid crystal display (LCD) technology. It formed its US affiliate, Epson America, in 1975. With the advent of the PC in the 1970s, Seiko Epson also began working on computer printers. It released its first dot matrix model in 1978. The next year the company introduced the Alba and Pulsar watch brands.

The company's European headquarters, in the Netherlands, opened in 1980. Seiko Epson debuted the first laptop computer, the HX-20, in 1982; a high-quality daisy wheel printer and LCD color TVs in 1983; and an ink jet printer in 1984. In 1985 it began making contact lenses. Reijiro Hattori, grandson of the company's founder, took the company helm in the late 1980s.

In 1990 Seiko baptized the Scubamaster, a computerized divers' watch featuring a dive table. The next year it introduced a wristwatch/pager. The company in 1994 started marketing IBM-compatible PCs, made by Digital Equipment (now part of Compaq), in Japan. That year it added color printers to its line. Seiko Epson unveiled digital cameras for use with PCs and Macs in 1996. The next year Lattice Semiconductor invested $150 million with Seiko Epson to build a new semiconductor wafer factory.

In 1998 the company made its US semiconductor manufacturing subsidiary, Epson Electronics America, an independent firm. It also formed an ink jet printer joint venture in China. That year the company entered the personal digital assistant (PDA) market with a line of PDAs that use the satellite-based Global Positioning System.

In 1999 Seiko Epson acquired Pacific Metals Co.'s metal powder operations, a complement to metal injection molding subsidiary Injex. Seiko Epson that year announced its intention to go public in 2001.

Chairman: Reijiro Hattori
VC: Yasuo Hattori
President: Hideaki Yasukawa
EVP: Yuji Yamazaki
EVP: Saburo Kusama
EVP: Kokichi Kaneko
Senior Managing Director: Toyomitsu Hirasawa
Senior Managing Director: Toshio Kimura
Managing Director: Yoshifumi Gomi
Managing Director: Norio Niwa
Managing Director: Katsuya Iwaya
Managing Director: Seiji Hanaoka
Managing Director: Masayoshi Omae
Managing Director: Minoru Ozawa
Managing Director: Masayoshi Shindo

HQ: 3-3-5 Owa, Suwa-shi, Nagano-ken 392-8502, Japan
Phone: +81-266-52-3131   **Fax:** +81-266-53-4844
US HQ: 20770 Madrona Ave., Torrance, CA 90503
US Phone: 310-782-0770   **US Fax:** 310-782-5220
Web site: http://www.epson.co.jp

Seiko Epson has more than a dozen plants in Japan, as well as manufacturing and sales operations in the Americas, Asia, Australia, Europe, and New Zealand. The company's regional headquarters are in China, the Netherlands, and the US.

Products
Computers (desktop and laptop)
Contact lenses
Electronic devices (including quartz devices
  and magnets)
Engineering plastics moldings
LCD color TVs
LCD panels and modules
LCD video projectors
Plastic corrective lenses
Precision assembly robots
Printer mechanisms
Printers (dot matrix, ink jet, laser, and thermal)
Semiconductors (LSIs)
Watches

Acer	Lexmark International
Apple Computer	LSI Logic
Bausch & Lomb	Matsushita
Bulova	Minolta
Canon	NEC
Casio Computer	Océ
Citizen Watch	Oki Electric
Compaq	Olivetti
Dell Computer	Ricoh
Fossil	Samsung
Fujitsu	SANYO
Gateway	Sony
Guess?	Swatch
Hewlett-Packard	Timex
Hitachi	Toshiba
IBM	Xerox
Kyocera	

Private FYE: March 31	Annual Growth	3/91	3/92	3/93	3/94	3/95	3/96	3/97	3/98	3/99	3/00
Sales ($ mil.)	16.6%	—	—	3,755	4,327	5,903	5,603	5,032	6,125	8,760	10,994
Employees	11.1%	—	—	—	—	—	—	31,000	44,000	41,500	42,500

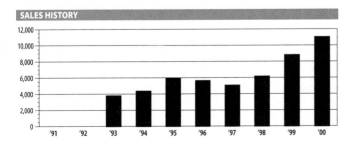

SEMA GROUP PLC

OVERVIEW

Sema is mobilizing. The Anglo-French, London-based Sema Group generates 90% of sales providing technology systems integration, technology management outsourcing, and consulting services. The company also offers disaster recovery support and develops mobile telephony and electronic payment software. Europe's #2 technology services company (behind Cap Gemini), Sema caters to customers in the finance (20% of sales), public (20%), telecommunications, transportation, and industrial sectors; clients include Gaz de France, Vivendi, and Vodafone AirTouch. More than 50% of Sema's sales come from France and the UK.

Sema has shifted to the booming financial services and telecommunications realms — developing custom software products for these markets — from the flattening energy and defense sectors. It is also expanding its global presence, particularly through the acquisition of LHS Group, which will boost its US mobile communications acumen. Sema is also moving into India and China.

France Telecom owns 22% of Sema; France-based financial services group Paribas owns 10%.

HISTORY

Sema Group was formed in 1988 from the merger of French information technology specialist Sema Metra — which traces itself back to Societe d'Economie et de Mathematiques Appliquees, established in 1958 — and the UK's Computer Analysts and Programmers (Cap) Group, formed in 1962. Harvard-educated Pierre Bonelli (CEO) left an engineering post at Texas Instruments in 1976 (colleagues included former Compaq CEO Eckhard Pfeiffer and Intel co-founder Robert Noyce) for Sema Metra and an eventual chairmanship, then later was named head of the merged entity.

Bonelli expanded Sema into the 1990s through acquisitions. Purchases included German services firm ADV/ORGA (1989); 49% of stock management services specialist Tibet (1990; increased to 100% in 1995); and the outsourcing, consulting, and systems integration operations of Swedish state-owned firm SKD Foretagen (1993).

Embracing the profitable defense technology market, Sema in 1991 forged a joint venture with British Aerospace (now BAE SYSTEMS) called BAeSEMA. In 1992 Sema added France Telecom as a major shareholder through a holding company controlled by France's Paribas. France Telecom during the next two years formed a civil telecommunications joint venture with Sema (Sema bought France Telecom's chunk in 1997) and purchased 24% of Sema (since reduced to 22%).

Bonelli eschewed marketing as a waste of potential shareholder return, and built a management hierarchy that many found odd. Besides himself, only one other executive served on the executive committee. The other seats were filled by non-board members. In 1994 Sema bought Contact Group, a Spanish company involved with card-based payment systems, and Aero, a France-based defense computer modeling company.

Cap Gemini in 1995 sold a 28% stake in Sema. That year Sema bought a large stake in France Telecom's outsourcing subsidiary, TS-FM, and a percentage of South Africa-based Paradigm Systems Technology (sold 1998).

Acquisitions intensified in the next two years, when Sema bought the computer assistance and backup systems unit of Sogeris (1996), Olivetti's Italian outsourcing division Syntax Processing (1996), 75% of Spanish systems integrator Infoservicios (1996; Sema now owns it in full), and UK database specialist BR Business Systems (1997).

US regulators had long viewed Sema as a subsidiary of Paribas, controller of the holding company that owned more than 40% of Sema. As a result Sema had been restricted from making US acquisitions because of a rule that prohibited financial companies from selling nonfinancial products. In 1997 Bonelli led a reorganization of Sema's shareholding structure, reducing Paribas' stake. The revamping gave Sema, which that year had already continued its drive into regions like Spain and Asia, a chance to push into the huge US services market.

When the defense technology markets grew more sluggish, Sema in 1998 sold its interest in BAeSEMA to British Aerospace. The company got a boost that year when it beat out IBM for an eight-year contract to be the official technology services provider at the Olympics beginning in 2002. Acquisitions in 1999 included Irish data recovery specialist Business Protection Services and Argentinian outsourcing company Informatica Technologia Servicios.

The purchases continued in 2000 when Sema bought Spanish integrator DSI and telecom software maker LHS Group.

Chairman: Julian Oswald
CEO: Pierre S. E. Bonelli
CFO: William H. Bitan
EVP: Frank S. Jones
SVP Corporate Development: Y.N. Tidu Maini
Secretary: N. Deeming
Human Resources: Patrick Semtob
Auditors: PricewaterhouseCoopers

LOCATIONS

HQ: 233 High Holborn,
  London WC1V 7DJ, United Kingdom
Phone: +44-20-7830-4444   **Fax:** +44-20-7830-1830
US HQ: 4170 Ashford Dunwoody Rd., Ste. 460,
  Atlanta, GA 30319
US Phone: 404-256-1447   **US Fax:** 404-256-2775
Web site: http://www.semagroup.com

Sema Group operates globally in 140 locations.

1999 Sales

	% of total
UK	31
France	24
Scandinavia	14
Italy	6
Spain	6
Americas	5
Asia	3
Benelux	3
Germany	3
Other regions	5
Total	**100**

PRODUCTS/OPERATIONS

1999 Sales

	% of total
Services	
Outsourcing	45
Systems integration	44
Products	11
Total	**100**

Selected Products and Services
Banking customer relationship management software
Consulting
Customer requirement analysis
Disaster recovery
Installation and maintenance
Mobile telephony software (SemaVision)
Systems integration
Telecommunications billing and pricing software
Telecommunications electronic payments software
Web development

COMPETITORS

ADC Telecom	Convergys	Kingston
ALLTEL	Daleen	Communications
Amdocs	Technologies	Logica
Andersen	Delphi Group	Lucent
Consulting	EDS	MetaSolv
Architel Systems	F.I. GROUP	Software
Atos Origin	Finsiel	Misys
Billing Concepts	Getronics	Parity
Bull	Hewlett-Packard	Portal Software
Cap Gemini	ICL	Serco Group
Capita	Intasys	Siemens
CMG	IBM	Ulticom
Compaq	ITDS	Unisys
Computer	ITNET	
Sciences		

HISTORICAL FINANCIALS & EMPLOYEES

London: SEM FYE: December 31	Annual Growth	12/90	12/91	12/92	12/93	12/94	12/95	12/96	12/97	12/98	12/99
Sales (£ mil.)	18.8%	—	—	—	—	596	678	927	1,130	1,250	1,410
Net income (£ mil.)	28.1%	—	—	—	—	20	23	32	44	69	69
Income as % of sales	—	—	—	—	—	3.4%	3.4%	3.5%	3.9%	5.5%	4.9%
Earnings per share (p)	23.1%	—	—	—	—	5.20	6.10	7.70	9.80	12.40	14.70
Stock price - FY high (p)	—	—	—	—	—	103.00	131.00	278.00	373.00	849.00	1,500.00
Stock price - FY low (p)	—	—	—	—	—	79.00	89.00	132.00	270.00	365.00	510.00
Stock price - FY close (p)	61.8%	—	—	—	—	100.00	131.00	271.00	371.00	591.00	1,108.00
P/E - high	—	—	—	—	—	20	21	36	38	68	102
P/E - low	—	—	—	—	—	15	15	17	28	29	35
Dividends per share (p)	22.1%	—	—	—	—	1.03	1.25	1.50	1.83	2.30	2.80
Book value per share (p)	17.9%	—	—	—	—	22.60	21.40	25.00	28.45	41.58	51.40
Employees	12.4%	—	—	—	—	—	—	—	15,308	17,428	19,349

STOCK PRICE HISTORY

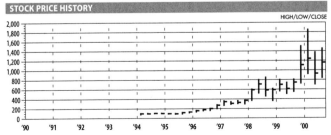

HIGH/LOW/CLOSE

1999 FISCAL YEAR-END

Debt ratio: 18.8%
Return on equity: 24.9%
Cash (£ mil.): 76
Current ratio: 1.18
Long-term debt (£ mil.): 37
No. of shares (mil.): 463
Dividends
  Yield: 0.0%
  Payout: 0.2%
Market value ($ mil.): 8,125
Sales ($ mil.): 2,281

SHANGHAI PETROCHEMICAL

The Chinese government didn't have to shanghai foreign companies to create a petrochemical company — it created one on its own. Shanghai Petrochemical Company is one of China's leading producers of ethylene, a crucial ingredient in the company's downstream (from parent to subsidiary) manufacture of synthetic fibers, resins, and plastics. The company also produces diesel fuel and gasoline, synthetic fibers (polyester and acrylic staple), and intermediate petrochemicals such as benzene, which it sells exclusively in China.

In anticipation of China's admission to the World Trade Organization, Shanghai Petrochemical Company is overhauling its production facilities. The upgrades, scheduled for completion in early 2002, will enable the company to process 10 million tons of crude oil per year, along with 1 million tons of ethylene and other synthetic fiber materials. The current quality of Chinese ethylene is generally inferior to that produced in developed countries. The upgrades will allow the company to produce world-class polyethylene and polypropylene which it can use domestically and sell on the world market. The Chinese government's China Petrochemical, or Sinopec, owns 56% of Shanghai Petrochemical; HKSCC (Nominees) Limited (Hong Kong) owns about 26%.

The Mao-inspired Cultural Revolution of the 1960s restored the aging leader's political grip, but it also caused immense economic disruptions in China, including a virtual shutdown of foreign trade. In the early 1970s party reformists led by Zhou Enlai and Deng Xiaoping advocated improved contact with the outside world and the restoration of foreign trade, giving the Chinese economy access to much-needed technology. In 1972, the year President Nixon's visit to China restored Sino-US ties, China began contracting for plant and equipment imports, especially in the petrochemical areas of chemical fertilizers for agriculture and artificial fibers for industrial use. That year Shanghai Petrochemical Company was founded as China's first large petrochemical enterprise, using imported equipment and technology.

Under Sinopec's control, Shanghai Petrochemical fit squarely into the government's Four Modernizations policy (agriculture, industry, technology, and defense). Other factors in the firm's growth were the booming economies of the coastal cities in the east and south, made possible by economic liberalization policies that encouraged foreign investment. The Guangdong province in the south led the way as Hong Kong enterprise migrated there in the 1980s in search of lower wages and overhead. The expansion of industrial output there and in other provinces resulted in greatly increased demand for petrochemicals.

Emboldened by growth and further reforms in the oil industry, Sinopec restructured Shanghai Petrochemical in 1993 and listed it on the Hong Kong and New York stock markets. (It was the first Chinese company listed on the New York Stock Exchange.) The company formed a joint venture with US-based agribusiness giant Continental Grain in 1995 to build a liquid petroleum gas plant and teamed up with British Petroleum (now BP Amoco) to build an acrylonitrile plant.

The company entered a joint venture with Union Carbide in 1996 to build a polymer emulsion plant in China. Shanghai Petrochemical increased its market share for acrylics with its 1997 purchase of the Zhejiang Acrylic Fibre Plant, then a producer of about 40% of China's total acrylic-fiber output. Annual production grew to 130,000 tons by 1999.

Three broad-reaching events have hammered the company's profits: the Asian economic crisis, the decrease of Sinopec's subsidy on crude oil, and a global oversupply of petrochemicals. In 1997 Shanghai Petrochemical's product-mix adjustments, combined with cost cutting, offset some of the increased crude costs and lower prices.

The company announced in 1998 that the Chinese government planned to crack down on the smuggling of foreign petrochemicals and help the domestic market. The firm remains vulnerable to policy changes, however. Additionally, consolidation of the Chinese petrochemical industry could translate into lost jobs.

The company continued to modernize its facilities and increase its capacity in 2000 when it moved to upgrade operations in order to become a world-class production base for petrochemicals and derivatives.

Chairman and President: Lu Yiping, age 54
CFO: Han Zhihao, age 50
VP Management, Personnel, and Education and Secretary: Rong Guangdao, age 44
VP Operations and Foreign Trade: Feng Jianping, age 46
VP Production: Zhang Zhiliang, age 46
VP Research and Development: Liu Xunfeng, age 35
Chairman of the Trade Union: Jiang Baoxing, age 55
Secretary: Zhang Jingming, age 43
Auditors: KPMG Peat Marwick Huazhen

LOCATIONS

HQ: Shanghai Shiyou Huagong Gufen Youxien Gongsi (Shanghai Petrochemical Company Limited)
2 Wei Er Rd., Jinshanwei, Shanghai 200540, China
Phone: +86-21-5794-3143   **Fax:** +86-21-5794-0050
Web site: http://www.spc.com.cn/English

Shanghai Petrochemical Company operates exclusively in China.

PRODUCTS/OPERATIONS

Selected Products

Intermediate Petrochemicals	Resins and Plastics
Benzene	LDPE film and pellets
Butadiene	Polyester chips
Ethylene	PP pellets
Ethylene glycol	PVA
Ethylene oxide	
	Synthetic Fibers
	Acrylic staple fiber
Petroleum Products	Acrylic top
Diesel	Polyester filament-DTY
Gasoline	Polyester filament-POY
Jet oil	Polyester staple
Residual oil	Polypropylene
	PVA fiber

COMPETITORS

DuPont
Elf Aquitaine
ExxonMobil Chemical
Formosa Plastics
ICI Americas
Jilin Chemical
Marubeni
Mitsubishi
Mitsui
Royal Dutch/Shell
Tianjin Bohai Chemical
Union Carbide
Yizheng Chemical
Zhenhai Refining & Chemical

HISTORICAL FINANCIALS & EMPLOYEES

NYSE: SHI FYE: December 31	Annual Growth	12/90	12/91	12/92	12/93	12/94	12/95	12/96	12/97	12/98	12/99
Sales ($ mil.)	4.5%	—	—	—	1,305	1,111	1,423	1,434	1,429	1,294	1,696
Net income ($ mil.)	(11.2%)	—	—	—	150	177	256	122	88	29	73
Income as % of sales	—	—	—	—	11.5%	15.9%	18.0%	8.5%	6.1%	2.2%	4.3%
Earnings per share ($)	(17.1%)	—	—	—	3.11	2.54	3.90	1.80	1.20	0.40	1.01
Stock price - FY high ($)	—	—	—	—	49.25	43.00	34.25	34.75	45.50	17.44	25.50
Stock price - FY low ($)	—	—	—	—	18.25	22.00	22.13	24.13	15.00	5.31	7.00
Stock price - FY close ($)	(15.8%)	—	—	—	42.25	28.88	28.50	29.38	15.56	8.50	15.06
P/E - high	—	—	—	—	16	17	9	19	38	44	25
P/E - low	—	—	—	—	6	9	6	13	13	13	7
Dividends per share ($)	—	—	—	—	0.00	1.04	2.54	1.56	0.00	0.00	0.36
Book value per share ($)	0.6%	—	—	—	20.47	16.69	17.55	19.68	20.82	20.80	21.22
Employees	(1.4%)	—	—	—	39,000	39,000	38,000	38,000	38,000	38,000	35,826

STOCK PRICE HISTORY

HIGH/LOW/CLOSE

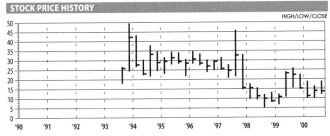

1999 FISCAL YEAR-END

Debt ratio: 16.3%
Return on equity: 4.8%
Cash ($ mil.): 308
Current ratio: 1.11
Long-term debt ($ mil.): 298
No. of shares (mil.): 72
Dividends
  Yield: 2.4%
  Payout: 35.6%
Market value ($ mil.): 1,084

SHARP CORPORATION

OVERVIEW

Sharp's screen presence appears to be out of focus. The Osaka-based company generates about a third of its sales from digital copiers, PCs, fax machines, and other communications and information equipment. But the company built its reputation as a leading maker of liquid crystal displays (LCDs), used in everything from airplane cockpits and air conditioners to PCs and pinball machines. Sharp also makes TVs and other home electronics equipment, refrigerators and other

home appliances, and integrated circuits and other electronic components.

The LCD market has been tapped by a slew of competitors that have deflated prices, leaving Sharp a little dull. The company as a result is honing its LCD technology (it wants to replace all of Japan's TV sets with LCD products by 2005) and pushing data storage media application technologies and digital electronic devices.

Sharp, which generates about 60% of its sales within Asia, has moved production outside Japan to level costs.

HISTORY

In 1912 Tokuji Hayakawa established a metal works in Tokyo called Hayakawa Electric Industry to make a type of belt buckle he had designed. Three years later he invented the first mechanical pencil, named the Ever-Sharp, which was a commercial success.

When an earthquake leveled much of Tokyo in 1923, including Hayakawa's business, he moved to Osaka and sold the rights to his pencil to finance a new factory. He introduced Japan's first crystal radio sets in 1925 and four years later debuted a vacuum tube radio.

After WWII, Hayakawa Electric developed an experimental TV, which it started to mass-produce in 1953 when Japan aired its first TV broadcasts. The company was ready with color TVs when Japan initiated color broadcasts in 1960. Through innovation, Hayakawa Electric grew tremendously during the 1960s, launching mass-produced microwave ovens (1962), mass-produced solar cells (1963), the first electronic desktop all-transistor-diode calculator (1964), and the first gallium arsenide LED (1969). The firm opened a US office in 1962.

In 1970 the company began to make its own microchips, and it changed its name to Sharp Corporation, a nod to the name of its first product. It began mass production of LCDs in 1973. Sharp then introduced the electronic calculator with an LCD (1973), solar-powered calculators (1976), and a credit card-sized calculator (1979).

The company began producing VCRs in the early 1980s and in 1984 released its color copier. That year Sharp introduced a fax machine and concentrated marketing efforts on small businesses (meanwhile, its competitors were scrambling for large corporate accounts).

Haruo Tsuji became president in 1986. He restructured the company and concentrated research on LCDs. Sharp blitzed the market with a new line of creative products in the late

1980s, including a high-definition LCD color TV (1987) and a notebook-sized PC (1988).

Sharp introduced a cordless pocket telephone in 1992 that operated continuously for more than five hours, plus a simplified high-definition television (HDTV) priced under $8,000, less than one-fourth of competitors' prices. That year the company announced strategic alliances with Apple to build the Newton personal digital assistant (which flopped) and with the Shanghai Radio and Television (Group) Company to make air conditioners, fax machines, copiers, and printers (Shanghai Sharp Electronics began production in 1994). During the mid-1990s Sharp had hits with its ViewCam camcorder and Zaurus personal digital assistant.

To protect its technology, Sharp began forming joint ventures with other big industry players. These included partnerships in 1996 with China's second-largest TV maker, Nanjing Panda Electronics; communications equipment maker Alcatel; electronics giant Fujitsu; semiconductor maker Advanced Micro Devices; and leading chip maker Intel, for flash memory chips.

More joint ventures followed in 1997, including a partnership with Sony to develop flat-panel displays and another with Fuji Xerox to create a technology that connects printers and fax machines with Sharp's handheld computer devices.

Katsuhiko Machida became president in 1998 as the company attempted to pump younger blood into its veins; Tsuji became company adviser. The company that year split itself into three separate business areas: home appliances and consumer electronics; information and communications; and devices. A restructuring of its LCD operations caused Sharp's profits to fall 80% for fiscal 1999.

President: Katsuhiko Machida
SEVP: Magohiro Aramoto
SEVP: Shigeo Misaka
SEVP: Isamu Washizuka
Senior Executive Director: Seiji Shiotsu
Senior Executive Director: Sueyuki Hirooka
Senior Executive Director: Buheita Fujiwara
Senior Executive Director and CFO: Hiroshi Saji
Senior Executive Director: Akihiko Kumagai
Auditors: Arthur Andersen

LOCATIONS

HQ: 22-22 Nagaike-cho, Abeno-ku,
   Osaka 545-8522, Japan
Phone: 6-6621-1221   **Fax:** 6-6627-1759
US HQ: Sharp Plaza, Mahwah, NJ 07430
US Phone: 201-529-8200   **US Fax:** 201-529-8425
Web site: http://sharp-world.com

Sharp has operations in Australia, Austria, Belgium, Canada, China, France, Germany, Greece, Hong Kong, India, Indonesia, Italy, Japan, Malaysia, Mexico, the Netherlands, New Zealand, the Philippines, Russia, Singapore, South Korea, Spain, Sweden, Switzerland, Taiwan, Thailand, the UK, the United Arab Emirates, the US, and Vietnam.

2000 Sales

	% of total
Asia	
Japan	52
Other countries	13
North America	22
Europe	10
Other regions	3
Total	**100**

PRODUCTS/OPERATIONS

2000 Sales

	% of total
Electronic components	33
Communication & information	
equipment	32
Audio/video equipment	22
Home appliances	13
Total	**100**

Selected Products

Compact disc players	Liquid crystal displays
Digital cameras	Microwave ovens
Digital copiers	Mobile business tools
DVD players	Radio-frequency
Flash memory	components
High-definition televisions	Refrigerators
Integrated circuits	Solar cells and other
Laser diodes and other	photovoltaic devices
optoelectronic devices	Video cameras

COMPETITORS

AMD	Intel	Pioneer
Bose	IBM	Ricoh
Canon	Konica	Samsung
Casio Computer	LG Electronics	SANYO
Compaq	Matsushita	Seiko Epson
Dell Computer	Maytag	Siemens
Eastman Kodak	Minolta	Sony
Electrolux AB	Mitsubishi	Thomson-CSF
Ericsson	Motorola	Toshiba
Fuji Photo	NEC	Whirlpool
Fujitsu	Nokia	White
GE	Oki Electric	Consolidated
Hewlett-Packard	Philips	Xerox
Hitachi	Electronics	

HISTORICAL FINANCIALS & EMPLOYEES

OTC: SHCAY FYE: March 31	Annual Growth	3/91	3/92	3/93	3/94	3/95	3/96	3/97	3/98	3/99	3/00
Sales ($ mil.)	5.7%	10,641	11,698	13,130	14,775	18,690	15,390	14,464	13,456	14,655	17,580
Net income ($ mil.)	(2.4%)	334	294	258	309	514	432	392	186	39	267
Income as % of sales	—	3.1%	2.5%	2.0%	2.1%	2.8%	2.8%	2.7%	1.4%	0.3%	1.5%
Earnings per share ($)	(3.0%)	3.15	2.76	2.41	2.83	4.63	3.87	3.49	1.65	0.35	2.40
Stock price - FY high ($)	—	125.00	118.58	103.44	168.09	191.23	171.50	175.00	141.50	105.00	257.50
Stock price - FY low ($)	—	81.13	87.05	66.73	90.16	135.47	133.03	117.00	61.00	59.00	105.20
Stock price - FY close ($)	8.4%	103.27	88.73	93.05	160.58	163.19	160.11	120.00	67.00	105.00	214.00
P/E - high	—	40	43	43	59	41	44	50	86	304	107
P/E - low	—	26	32	28	32	29	34	34	37	171	44
Dividends per share ($)	3.9%	0.78	0.83	0.96	1.07	1.39	1.12	0.97	0.90	1.00	1.10
Book value per share ($)	5.8%	48.58	53.27	62.50	72.02	88.61	75.00	67.95	64.29	71.14	80.65
Employees	3.5%	36,539	41,029	41,836	42,883	43,949	44,789	46,900	47,981	57,521	49,748

STOCK PRICE HISTORY

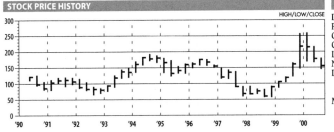

HIGH/LOW/CLOSE

2000 FISCAL YEAR-END

Debt ratio: 33.4%
Return on equity: 3.1%
Cash ($ mil.): 1,685
Current ratio: 1.44
Long-term debt ($ mil.): 2,286
No. of shares (mil.): 113
Dividends
   Yield: 0.0%
   Payout: 0.5%
Market value ($ mil.): 24,109

SHISEIDO COMPANY, LIMITED

OVERVIEW

Shiseido, Japan's largest beauty products firm, has applied a new face. For years it focused on the high end of the cosmetics market, selling the same merchandise in every store and insisting that all items be sold by in-store consultants. Tokyo-based Shiseido now offers different lines to different types of stores. Besides cosmetics (which it sells in about 60 countries), Shiseido makes professional salon hair care products, pharmaceuticals, nutritional supplements, and fine

chemicals. The company also owns the Ginza chain of upscale boutiques; various specialty fragrance, hair, and skin care salons; and Shiseido Parlour restaurants and food shops.

With domestic sales lagging, the company hopes to boost international business, now 15% of sales, to at least 25% of sales by fiscal 2003. Part of Shiseido's expansion plan is a multibrand approach that targets specific customer categories; the company is also seeking growth through mergers and acquisitions.

HISTORY

Yushin Fukuhara, former head pharmacist for the Japanese admiralty, established Japan's first modern drugstore, Shiseido Pharmacy, in 1872. Shiseido, a name derived from Confucian philosophy, implies "richness of life." Attracted by the store's Western-style products and format, the customers were the nobility and the rich. Shiseido manufactured Japan's first toothpaste in 1888 and introduced its first cosmetics product (Eudermine, a skin lotion) in 1897. Fukuhara opened the country's first soda fountain in 1902, importing everything from soda glasses to ice cream.

After studying art in New York, Yushin's third son, Shinzo, returned to Tokyo and began working for his father. Shinzo created Shiseido's first extensive makeup lines, introducing flesh-toned face powder in 1906 and a fragrance line in 1918. When he brought a Western beautician to Tokyo, her *mimi-kakushi* (or "ear hiding") hairstyle created a sensation. Under Shinzo's influence, cosmetics replaced drugs as Shiseido's mainstay.

Shiseido began franchise operations in 1923 and business boomed. The firm went public that year; in 1927 Shinzo became president. During WWII the company couldn't make cosmetics, only medicines, and many of Shiseido's factories were destroyed. This led to near-bankruptcy in 1945, but Shiseido rebounded the next year, thanks to nail enamel.

During the 1950s and 1960s, Shiseido sparked fashion movements. In 1951 it introduced its de Luxe high-end cosmetics line, and by 1956 it had become the #1 Japanese cosmetics firm. With a 1962 move into Hong Kong, Shiseido began overseas operations. It steadily expanded its international business by setting up subsidiaries across the world (including one in New York City in 1965).

In the 1970s Shiseido failed at marketing its products in the US, and at home its market share was slipping. Seen as being out of touch

with the young, it was also hampered by strict product development laws, dating back to the 1880s, which caused delays in getting products to market. Shiseido segmented its cosmetics line into five age groups and began producing more lines, in smaller quantities, in the early 1980s. In the mid-1980s it developed a successful US marketing strategy that included selling exclusive product lines in high-end department stores such as Macy's; it also made several acquisitions, including Zotos (hair products, US, 1988).

The firm's first prescription-only drug, an ophthalmological treatment used in certain types of cataract surgery and cornea transplants, was launched in 1993. In 1996 the company bought the Helene Curtis salon hair care business in the US and Canada from Unilever. In 1997 Shiseido bought Helene Curtis Japan salon hair operations.

Also in 1997 Akira Gemma (a Shiseido veteran of nearly four decades) became CEO, and the company expanded to Croatia, the Czech Republic, Hungary, and Vietnam.

Shiseido opened a New York City flagship store in 1998 and began selling cosmetics in Russia in 1999. It also began selling soap, shampoo, and baby powder in 1999 under the wildly popular Hello Kitty name, licensed from Japanese media firm Sanrio. Late that year Shiseido introduced Cle de Peau Beaute to international markets as its top-of-the-line beauty brand.

Looking to expand its foreign brands portfolio, in June 2000 Shiseido bought the Sea Breeze line of facial products from Bristol-Myers Squibb; it also acquired 75% of French cosmetics firm and aromatherapy specialists Laboratoires Decleor. In September the company announced an agreement with Intimate Brands (owner of Victoria's Secret and Bath & Body Works) to develop a new prestige beauty products line.

Chairman: Yoshiharu Fukuhara
President and CEO: Akira Gemma
EVP: Morio Ikeda
Senior Executive Director: Sadao Abe
Senior Executive Director: Osamu Hosokawa
Senior Executive Director: Shigeo Shimizu
Executive Director: Yoshimaru Kumano
Executive Director: Tadakatsu Saito
Auditors: ChuoAoyama Audit Corporation

LOCATIONS

HQ: 7-5-5, Ginza, Chuo-ku, Tokyo 104-8010, Japan
Phone: +81-3-3572-5111   **Fax:** +81-3-3574-8380
US HQ: 900 3rd Ave., New York, NY 10022
US Phone: 212-805-2300   **US Fax:** 212-688-0109
Web site: http://www.shiseido.co.jp

2000 Sales

	$ mil.	% of total
Japan	4,826	85
Other countries	829	15
Total	**5,655**	**100**

PRODUCTS/OPERATIONS

2000 Sales

	$ mil.	% of total
Cosmetics	4,184	74
Toiletries	868	15
Other	603	11
Total	**5,655**	**100**

Selected Brands and Operations

Cosmetics and Fragrances	New category 5S	Salon products
Mass market	Ettusais	Helene Curtis
Fine Toiletry	stila	Lamaur
(by Shiseido)	Prestige	Zotos RX
Sea Breeze	Aupres	
Middle Market	Ayura	**Toiletries**
Cosmenity	Carita	Aquair
Free Soul	Cle de Peau	Naturgo
Picadilly	Beaute	Neue
Za	D'ici la	Super Mild
	Elixir	Tessera
	Ipsa	
	Shiseido	

Other Operations

"Beauty" food products
Chromatography products (chemical analysis equipment)
Fine chemicals (photochromic titanium dioxide pigment)
Ginza fashion boutiques
Laboratoires Decleor (French cosmetics and aromatherapy)
Pharmaceuticals
Restaurants
  Shiseido Parlour restaurants and food shops

COMPETITORS

Alberto-Culver	Estée Lauder	Revlon
Avon	Henkel	Shu Uemura
Beiersdorf	Kao	Unilever
Body Shop	L'Oréal	Wella
Chanel	Mary Kay	Yves Saint-
Colgate-	Procter &	Laurent
Palmolive	Gamble	

HISTORICAL FINANCIALS & EMPLOYEES

OTC: SSDOY FYE: March 31	Annual Growth	3/91	3/92	3/93	3/94	3/95	3/96	3/97	3/98	3/99	3/00
Sales ($ mil.)	4.9%	3,679	4,163	4,888	5,345	6,243	5,229	4,754	4,666	5,073	5,655
Net income ($ mil.)	2.8%	113	120	116	143	131	163	155	127	87	145
Income as % of sales	—	3.1%	2.9%	2.4%	2.7%	2.1%	3.1%	3.3%	2.7%	1.7%	2.6%
Earnings per share ($)	1.7%	0.30	0.31	0.29	0.36	0.33	0.41	0.38	0.30	0.21	0.35
Stock price - FY high ($)	—	14.28	14.70	11.63	14.11	12.72	12.77	13.38	18.50	13.75	16.75
Stock price - FY low ($)	—	10.83	10.92	10.19	10.45	10.52	11.00	11.00	11.13	10.00	11.25
Stock price - FY close ($)	0.7%	12.80	11.13	11.55	11.38	12.72	11.78	13.00	12.00	13.75	13.60
P/E - high	—	48	47	40	39	39	31	35	62	67	48
P/E - low	—	36	35	35	29	32	24	29	37	49	32
Dividends per share ($)	7.2%	0.08	0.08	0.10	0.11	0.14	0.12	0.10	0.10	0.12	0.15
Book value per share ($)	4.4%	6.82	6.49	7.72	8.91	10.72	8.92	8.08	7.92	8.71	10.07
Employees	1.0%	—	—	—	—	23,355	22,305	22,045	22,718	23,688	24,495

STOCK PRICE HISTORY

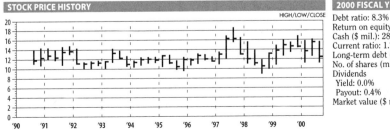

HIGH/LOW/CLOSE

2000 FISCAL YEAR-END

Debt ratio: 8.3%
Return on equity: 3.7%
Cash ($ mil.): 282
Current ratio: 1.72
Long-term debt ($ mil.): 57
No. of shares (mil.): 415
Dividends
  Yield: 0.0%
  Payout: 0.4%
Market value ($ mil.): 5,645

SIEMENS AG

OVERVIEW

Able-bodied Siemens is working to stay shipshape by revamping its fleet of businesses. The Munich, Germany-based global electronics giant has operations in the energy, industry, information and communications, health care, transportation, lighting (Osram), and components sectors; it also provides financing and real estate management services. Captained by CEO Heinrich von Pierer, Siemens is navigating through a major restructuring: It has cut 40,000 jobs and added new management to underperforming divisions.

As part of the restructuring effort, Siemens has spun off its semiconductor operations into Infineon Technologies, which went public in 2000, and spun off its passive components and

electron tubes unit into EPCOS, which went public in 1999. Siemens has sold its Nixdorf retail- and banking-systems unit and its optical cable business.

Siemens is also forming joint ventures: It has pooled its nuclear power activities with those of France's Framatome to create Nuclear Power International (NPI); Siemens owns a 34% stake in the new company. As part of a worldwide cooperation pact, Siemens and Japan's Fujitsu have combined most of their European computer operations in a joint venture. And Siemens is joining with Robert Bosch to buy Atecs Mannesmann, which includes Mannesmann's engineering and automotive parts businesses.

HISTORY

In 1847 electrical engineer Werner von Siemens and craftsman Johann Halske formed Siemens & Halske to make telegraphs in Germany. The firm's first major project linked Berlin and Frankfurt with the first long-distance telegraph system in Europe (1848). In 1870 the company completed the 6,600-mile India Line running from London to Calcutta, and in 1874 it made the first transatlantic cable to connect Ireland and the US.

Siemens' history of firsts includes Europe's first electric power transmission system (1876), the world's first electrified railway (1879), and one of the first elevators (1880). In 1896 it patented the world's first X-ray tube and completed the first European subway, in Budapest, Hungary.

The company formed German lightbulb cartel Osram with AEG and Auer (1919) and created a venture with Furukawa Electric called Fuji Electric (1923). It developed radios and traffic lights in the 1920s and began producing electron microscopes in 1939.

Siemens played a critical role in Germany's war effort in WWII and suffered heavy losses after the war. (In 1999 Siemens and other German companies agreed to pay reparations to victims of forced labor in WWII.) The 1950s brought quick recovery to Siemens as it developed data processing equipment, silicates for semiconductors, and the first implantable pacemaker. It formed joint ventures with Bosch (Bosch-Siemens Hausgerate, appliances, 1967) and AEG (Kraftwerk Union, nuclear power, 1969), among others.

In 1981 Karlheinz Kaske became the first CEO from outside the Siemens family. Under his lead the firm entered joint ventures with

Philips, Intel, and Advanced Micro Devices. In 1988 and 1989 it made several purchases, including Bendix Electronics (US). Siemens bought Rolm's development and manufacturing arm outright, and went halves with IBM in Rolm's marketing business. Siemens bought the rest of Rolm in 1992.

Siemens and German computer maker Nixdorf combined computer businesses to form Siemens Nixdorf Informationssysteme (SNI) in 1990.

For Siemens, 1998 was the Year of the Deal. It sold its defense electronics operations to British Aerospace (now BAE SYSTEMS) and Daimler-Benz (now DaimlerChrysler). In a $1.17 billion deal with partner GEC (now Marconi), Siemens swapped its 40% stake in GPT Holdings (the UK's #1 telecom equipment supplier) for GEC's 50% stake in Siemens GEC Communications Systems. Siemens also bought CBS's power generation business (formerly Westinghouse Electric).

Siemens spun off its semiconductor operations into Infineon Technologies and sold its electromechanical components business to Tyco International for $1.1 billion in 1999. It sold its worldwide optical cable and hardware business, plus its stakes in its Siecor joint ventures, to Corning in a $1.4 billion deal that closed in 2000.

Siemens sold 30% of Infineon to the public that year. A Siemens-Robert Bosch joint venture agreed to purchase Atecs Mannesmann, Mannesmann's engineering and automotive parts unit, for $9.2 billion. Later in 2000 Siemens announced plans for an IPO of its US subsidiary Unisphere, part of the company's information and communication division.

Chairman Supervisory Board: Karl-Hermann Baumann
President and CEO: Heinrich von Pierer
Member Managing Board: Roland Koch
Member Managing Board: Edward G. Krubasik
Member Managing Board: Jürgen Radomaski
Member Managing Board: Günter Wilhelm
Member Managing Board: Klaus Wucherer
**Member Managing Board; Chairman, Supervisory
Board, Infineon:** Volker Jung
Member Managing Board, Finance and CFO:
Heinz-Joachim Neubürger
**Member Managing Board, Human Resources;
Chairman, Siemens Corporation:** Peter Pribilla
Member Managing Board, Technology: Claus Weyrich
Auditors: KPMG Deutsche Treuhand-Gesellschaft

LOCATIONS

HQ: Wittelsbacherplatz 2, D-80333 Munich, Germany
Phone: +49-89-636-3300   **Fax:** +49-89-636-342-42
US HQ: 1301 Avenue of the Americas,
New York, NY 10019
US Phone: 212-258-4000   **US Fax:** 212-767-0580
Web site: http://www.siemens.de

Siemens operates in more than 190 countries.

1999 Sales

	$ mil.	% of total
Europe		
Germany	19,892	28
Other countries	22,903	31
The Americas	17,892	24
Asia/Pacific	8,819	12
Other regions	3,543	5
Total	**73,049**	**100**

PRODUCTS/OPERATIONS

Operating Units
Automation and Drives
Automotive Systems
Bosch-Siemens Hausgerate GmbH (household
appliances, BSH, joint venture with Robert Bosch)
EPCOS AG (components, 12.5%)
Industrial Projects and Technical Services
Infineon Technologies AG (components, 70%)
Information and Communication Products
Medical Engineering
Osram GmbH (lighting)
Power Generation
Power Transmission and Distribution
Production and Logistics Systems
Siemens Building Technologies AG
Siemens Business Services GmbH & Co. OHG
Siemens Financial Services
Siemens Real Estate Management
Transportation Systems

COMPETITORS

ABB	Hewlett-Packard	Olivetti
Agilent	Hitachi	Philips
Technologies	IBM	Electronics
Alcatel	Intel	Raytheon
AT&T	ITT Industries	Robert Bosch
Bull	Koor	Rolls-Royce
Compaq	Mannesmann AG	Samsung
Cooper	Matsushita	SANYO
Industries	Maytag	Sharp
Eni	Motorola	Texas
Ericsson	NEC	Instruments
GE	Nokia	ThyssenKrupp
Harris	Nortel Networks	Toshiba
Corporation	Oki Electric	

HISTORICAL FINANCIALS & EMPLOYEES

OTC: SMAWY FYE: September 30	Annual Growth	9/90	9/91	9/92	9/93	9/94	9/95	9/96	9/97	9/98	9/99
Sales ($ mil.)	6.8%	40,335	43,915	55,597	49,953	54,571	62,181	61,796	60,718	70,551	73,049
Net income ($ mil.)	8.1%	988	1,112	1,271	1,103	1,141	1,460	1,960	1,481	550	1,987
Income as % of sales	—	2.4%	2.5%	2.3%	2.2%	2.1%	2.3%	3.2%	2.4%	0.8%	2.7%
Earnings per share ($)	(3.2%)	1.92	2.17	2.27	1.96	2.06	2.32	2.67	2.40	0.94	1.43
Stock price - FY high ($)	—	46.88	42.81	44.73	41.44	46.89	53.00	57.00	71.38	74.50	88.25
Stock price - FY low ($)	—	39.00	32.83	36.08	34.28	38.97	38.05	49.75	45.50	52.13	47.62
Stock price - FY close ($)	8.6%	39.00	38.41	40.19	40.81	40.95	49.61	52.75	67.38	54.75	82.00
P/E - high	—	24	20	20	21	23	23	21	30	79	62
P/E - low	—	20	15	16	17	19	16	19	19	55	33
Dividends per share ($)	4.7%	0.70	0.78	0.92	0.80	0.84	0.91	0.98	0.85	0.90	1.06
Book value per share ($)	4.6%	20.56	20.03	22.80	20.92	23.80	28.65	30.02	28.71	31.01	30.79
Employees	1.9%	373,000	402,000	413,000	391,000	382,000	373,000	379,000	386,000	416,000	443,000

STOCK PRICE HISTORY

HIGH/LOW/CLOSE

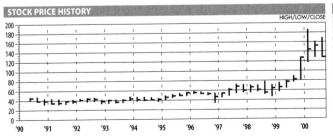

1999 FISCAL YEAR-END

Debt ratio: 29.7%
Return on equity: 10.9%
Cash ($ mil.): 2,611
Current ratio: 10.25
Long-term debt ($ mil.): 4,345
No. of shares (mil.): 595
Dividends
  Yield: 0.0%
  Payout: 0.7%
Market value ($ mil.): 48,790

SINGAPORE AIRLINES LIMITED

Passengers sing the praises of Singapore Airlines (SIA). Rated #1 by readers of *Travel & Leisure* and *Condé Nast Traveler* magazines, the airline is renowned for gourmet meals, free bubbly, and indulgent service. Its fleet of 91 aircraft, one of the youngest among international carriers, serves more than 110 destinations in some 40 countries (including code-sharing agreements). SIA is a member of the global Star Alliance airline marketing network, which includes UAL's United Airlines, Deutsche Lufthansa, and Scandinavian Airlines System.

The company's Singapore Airport Terminal Services (SATS) subsidiary provides catering, security, and cargo handling to other airlines, and it owns stakes in similar ventures outside Singapore. SIA plans to float SATS, as well as subsidiary SIA Engineering, the firm's maintenance and repair unit. Other SIA operations include regional airline SilkAir, a flying college, and property investment.

SIA has remained a relative bright spot during Asia'a economic downturn, continuing to invest in its operations and aircraft. With a rich balance sheet, the firm has been itching to take a stake in a foreign airline; after aborted attempts to buy into South African Airways and Ansett Australia, SIA has acquired 49% of UK carrier Virgin Atlantic.

The Singapore government, through Temasek Holdings, owns about 54% of SIA.

HISTORY

Singapore Airlines (SIA) was formed as Malayan Airways in 1937 but did not begin scheduled service until 1947, when the Mansfield & Co. shipping line used it to link Singapore with other Malayan cities. The airline added service to Vietnam, Sumatra, and Java by 1951 and opened routes to Borneo, Brunei, Burma, and Thailand by 1958.

Meanwhile, British Overseas Airways Corporation (BOAC, predecessor of British Airways) bought 10% of Malayan in 1948 and raised its stake to 30% in 1959. Australia's Qantas Airways also took a 30% stake in Malayan that year. In 1963 the governments of Singapore, Malaya, Sarawak, and Sabah merged to form Malaysia, inspiring Malayan to change its name to Malaysian Airways. Singapore seceded from the federation in 1965 but joined Malaysia to buy control of the airline from BOAC and Qantas in 1966, changing the name to Malaysia-Singapore Airlines.

The carrier extended service to Bombay, Melbourne, Rome, and London in 1971 and then to Osaka, Athens, Zurich, and Frankfurt in 1972. That year managerial disagreements led Malaysia and Singapore to dissolve the company to form two separate national airlines: The domestic network went to the Malaysian Airline System, and international routes went to SIA. Joe Pillay of Singapore's ministry of finance became SIA's first chairman. The government owned 82% and employees held 17%.

SIA had become famous for its service and served 25 cities worldwide by 1974. It added flights to Auckland and Paris in 1976, Tehran and Copenhagen in 1977, and San Francisco, its first US destination, in 1978.

In 1985 the government reduced its stake in SIA to 63%. The company joined Cathay Pacific and Thai International in 1988 to form Abacus, a computer reservation system for Asia/Pacific carriers.

The next year SIA bought stakes in Delta Air Lines and Swissair; the three created a coordinated route network reaching 82 countries. The Singapore airline also snagged a 40% stake in Royal Air Cambodge from the Cambodian government in 1993. In 1995 SIA ordered 77 Boeing 777s for delivery between 1997 and 2004.

The US and Singapore governments signed an "open skies" agreement in 1997 (the first between the US and an Asian nation), allowing unlimited flights between the two countries, but SIA canceled its alliance with Delta and Swissair in favor of one with Germany's Lufthansa.

A December 1997 crash of a new SilkAir 737 killed all 104 people on board; investigators speculated that the crash was an act of suicide by the pilot. (Two years later SIA agreed to pay each family settlements of up to $195,000.) The Asian crisis added to the airline's woes, but it was able to cut costs when the government reduced contributions to the national pension plan and the Singapore airport lowered landing fees.

In 1999 SIA implemented code-sharing with Scandinavian Airlines System, and soon SIA announced it would join SAS in the global Star Alliance marketing network. After failed attempts to buy into South African Airways and Ansett Australia, SIA bought a 49% stake in UK carrier Virgin Atlantic for some $960 million in 2000. The company also joined the Star Alliance that year.

Chairman: Michael Y. O. Fam
Deputy Chairman and CEO: Cheong Choong Kong, age 59
SVP Finance and Administration: Cedric Foo Chee Keng
EVP Administration: Chew Choon Seng
EVP Commercial: Michael T. J. Ngee
SVP Management Services: Tan Chik Quee
SVP Flight Operations: Maurice de Vaz
SVP Engineering: William Tan Seng Koon
SVP Marketing Planning: Huang Cheng Eng
SVP Cargo: Hwang Teng Aun
SVP Cabin Crew: J. E. Jesudason
SVP Personnel: Loh Meng See
SVP Corporate Affairs and Secretary: Mathew Samuel
CEO, Singapore Airport Terminal Services: Prush Nadaison
CEO, SIA Engineering: Chew Leng Seng
Chief Executive, SATS Catering: Joseph Chew
Chief Executive, SATS Airport Services: Karmijit Singh
SVP Europe: Sim Kay Wee
SVP Southeast Asia: Syn Chung Wah
SVP North Asia: Teh Ping Choon
Auditors: Ernst & Young

LOCATIONS

HQ: Airline House, 25 Airline Rd., 819829, Singapore
Phone: +65-542-3333 **Fax:** +65-542-1321
US HQ: 5670 Wilshire Blvd., Ste. 1800, Los Angeles, CA 90036
US Phone: 323-934-8833 **US Fax:** 323-934-4482
Web site: http://www.singaporeair.com

Singapore Airlines primarily operates in the Asia/Pacific regions; in total it serves more than 110 cities in over 40 countries on five continents.

PRODUCTS/OPERATIONS

2000 Sales

	% of total
Passenger	73
Cargo	23
Mail	1
Other	3
Total	**100**

Major Subsidiaries and Affiliates
Asia Airfreight Terminal Company Ltd. (25%, cargo handling, Hong Kong)
Beijing Airport Inflight Kitchen Limited (40%, catering services, China)
Eagle Services Asia Private Limited (49%, engine repair and overhaul)
SIA Engineering Company Private Limited (engine maintenance and repair)
SIA Properties (Pte) Ltd. (building services)
SilkAir (Singapore) Private Limited (regional airline)
Singapore Airport Terminal Services Private Limited
    SATS Airport Services Pte. Ltd.
    SATS Catering Pte. Ltd.
    SATS Security Services Private Ltd.
Singapore Aviation and General Insurance Company (Pte) Limited (aviation insurance)
Singapore Flying College Pte. Ltd. (pilot training)
Virgin Atlantic Limited (49%, holding company for Virgin Atlantic Airways, UK)

COMPETITORS

AMR	Delta
British Airways	JAL
Cathay Pacific	KLM
China Airlines	Korean Air
China Eastern Airlines	Malaysian Airlines
China Southern Airlines	Northwest Airlines
Continental Airlines	Qantas

HISTORICAL FINANCIALS & EMPLOYEES

Singapore: SIA FYE: March 31	Annual Growth	3/91	3/92	3/93	3/94	3/95	3/96	3/97	3/98	3/99	3/00
Sales (S$ mil.)	6.7%	4,948	5,421	5,648	6,236	6,556	6,890	7,222	7,724	7,796	8,899
Net income (S$ mil.)	2.7%	913	912	851	801	918	1,025	1,032	1,035	1,033	1,164
Income as % of sales	—	18.5%	16.8%	15.1%	12.8%	14.0%	14.9%	14.3%	13.4%	13.3%	13.1%
Earnings per share (S$)	2.6%	0.72	0.73	0.66	0.63	0.72	0.80	0.80	0.81	0.81	0.91
Stock price - FY high (S$)	—	7.30	6.90	7.45	8.60	9.00	8.60	7.15	9.65	9.30	20.80
Stock price - FY low (S$)	—	4.90	5.90	5.95	6.50	7.05	7.50	7.00	6.40	4.78	8.30
Stock price - FY close (S$)	10.9%	6.30	6.25	6.85	7.20	8.50	8.10	7.05	9.30	8.50	16.00
P/E - high	—	10	9	11	14	13	11	9	12	11	23
P/E - low	—	7	8	9	10	10	9	9	8	6	9
Dividends per share (S$)	0.0%	0.20	0.23	0.23	0.23	0.23	0.23	0.23	0.23	0.25	0.20
Book value per share (S$)	6.7%	4.88	5.48	5.99	6.46	7.01	7.64	8.22	8.87	9.50	8.78
Employees	3.3%	20,592	21,891	23,117	24,337	24,722	26,326	27,241	27,516	27,906	27,513

STOCK PRICE HISTORY
HIGH/LOW/CLOSE

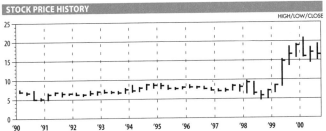

2000 FISCAL YEAR-END

Debt ratio: 20.7%
Return on equity: —
Cash (S$ mil.): 1,142
Current ratio: 0.94
Long-term debt (S$ mil.): 567
No. of shares (mil.): 1,250
Dividends
  Yield: 0.0%
  Payout: 0.2%
Market value ($ mil.): 11,646
Sales ($ mil.): 5,182

SMITHKLINE BEECHAM PLC

OVERVIEW

If the Rolling Stones are still touring, they may have SmithKline Beecham (SB) to thank. Maker of products such as Geritol, the Brentford, UK-based SB is one of the top two drug firms (Glaxo Wellcome is the other) in its home country; it will be one of the largest in the world after its planned merger with Glaxo. It develops prescription and OTC medicines, vaccines, and consumer care items. SB operates in 39 countries and sells its products worldwide.

SmithKline Beecham's pharmaceuticals unit accounts for about 60% of sales. Leading the pack is antidepressant Paxil/Seroxat (its #1 drug), followed by antibiotic Augmentin, and vaccines for diphtheria, tetanus, and hepatitis. Consumer products include top-selling smoking cessation aids NicoDerm CQ and Nicorette gum, Contac cold treatments, Tums antacid, and Aquafresh toothpaste. Its planned acquisition of Block Drug Company will add the Polident and Poli-Grip brands to its consumer lines.

SB has a large stake in genetic diagnostics through its collaboration with Human Genome Sciences and its diaDexus joint venture with Incyte Genomics.

HISTORY

Thomas Beecham established an apothecary in England in 1847, opened the world's first drug-making factory in 1859, and began advertising for Beecham's Pills, a laxative. By the early 1900s, output surpassed 1 million pills per day.

In 1924 land developer Philip Hill purchased the Beecham estate, including the pill business. He changed the name to Beecham's Pills Ltd. in 1928 and began buying other consumer products. In 1938 he bought US toothpaste firm Macleans and high-energy drink Lucozade, which produced about half of the company's profit within 15 years.

Beecham founded a research lab in 1943; its investment paid off in 1959 when the company introduced the first partly synthetic penicillin and again in 1961 when it developed the first broad-spectrum antibiotic.

Beecham continued buying consumer health companies with strong positions in foreign markets, including Massengill (1971), Calgon (1977), Jovan (1979), J.B. Williams (Aqua Velva, Sominex, Geritol; 1982), and Norcliff Thayer (Tums; 1985). After years of poor earnings, Beecham sold off nondrug companies between 1987 and 1990 and merged with troubled SmithKline Beckman in 1989.

SmithKline started in 1830 as a small Philadelphia apothecary and became a major pharmaceuticals company. It developed the first timed-release capsule (Dexedrine, 1944) and the first all-day cold remedy (Contac, 1960). But ulcer medication Tagamet, introduced in 1976, transformed the company; by 1981 Tagamet was the world's best-selling drug. However, poor results from diversification and low R&D productivity had reversed the company's fortunes by the time of the merger.

A 1993 collaboration gave SB exclusive rights to Human Genome Sciences' (HGS) gene database. In 1994 former Danish tennis star Jan Leschly became CEO and SB went on a spending spree, buying Diversified Pharmaceutical Services (a US marketer of discount drugs to managed care companies, sold at a loss in 1999) and Sterling Winthrop's nonprescription business from Kodak. It sold its animal health division and Sterling's North American consumer lines (including Bayer aspirin).

Tagamet's sales plummeted when it went off patent in 1994, prodding SB to boost R&D to avoid future over-reliance on a single drug. The firm bounced back with FDA approval in 1996 for such drugs as Hycamtin (for ovarian cancer) and NicoDerm (a nicotine patch).

In 1997 the company's Clinical Laboratories division settled fraudulent billing claims with Medicare and other government programs; health insurers filed similar claims. Looking for cheaper ways to develop drugs and expand capacity for leads from HGS, SB started eyeing merger mates; talks with both American Home Products (1997) and Glaxo Wellcome (1998) failed.

In 1999 SB renewed its focus on core operations, selling sideline units to Express Scripts and Quest Diagnostics. That year the company introduced the first approved vaccine for Lyme disease, LYMErix.

In 2000 the company talked merger again with Glaxo Wellcome, this time successfully. To appease regulators, SmithKline sold or made plans to sell herpes treatment Famvir and chemotherapy nausea drug Kytril. The merger was delayed while regulators eyed the companies' smoking-cessation products. In the meantime, SB made plans to buy Block Drug Company, a health and oral products company, to enhance its position in the consumer health products arena.

Chairman: Peter Walters, age 68, $276,000 pay
Chief Executive: Jan Leschly, age 59, $2,147,000 pay
COO: Jean-Pierre Garnier, age 52, $1,407,000 pay
CFO: Andrew R. J. Bonfield, age 37, $456,000 pay
SVP, Secretary, and General Counsel: James Beery,
age 58
SVP and Human Resources Director: Daniel J. Phelan
Chairman International: Mitch Cybulski
Chairman Research and Development,
Pharmaceuticals: Tadataka Yamada, age 54,
$581,000 pay
President Worldwide Supply Operations:
Peter S. Jensen
President Consumer Healthcare: Jack B. Ziegler
President Pharmaceuticals: Howard Pien
Auditors: PricewaterhouseCoopers

LOCATIONS

HQ: New Horizons Ct., Brentford,
Middlesex TW8 9EP, United Kingdom
Phone: +44-20-8975-2000   **Fax:** +44-20-8975-2090
US HQ: 1 Franklin Plaza, Philadelphia, PA 19100
US Phone: 215-751-4000   **US Fax:** 215-751-3400
Web site: http://www.sb.com

SmithKline Beecham has operations in about 40
countries and sells its products throughout the world.

1999 Sales

	% of total
US	51
Europe	
UK	8
Other countries	21
Other regions	20
Total	**100**

PRODUCTS/OPERATIONS

1999 Sales

	% of total
Pharmaceuticals	62
Consumer Healthcare	30
Healthcare Services	8
Total	**100**

Selected Products

Prescription
Augmentin (antibiotic)
Dexedrine (stimulant)
Paxil (antidepressant)
Requip (Parkinson's
disease therapy)
Seroxat (paroxetine, UK)
Tagamet (histamine H2-
receptor antagonist)
Thorazine (antipsychotic,
antiemetic, tranquilizer)

Consumer
Aquafresh (oral
health care)
Contac (cold treatment)

Geritol (vitamins and
natural remedies)
NicoDerm CQ (nicotine
patches)
Nicorette (nicotine gum)
Sucrets (cold treatment)
Tagamet HB (antacid)
Tums (antacid)

Vaccines
Fluarix (influenza vaccine)
LYMErix (Lyme disease
vaccine)
Polio Sabin (polio vaccine)
Priorix (measles, mumps,
and rubella vaccine)

COMPETITORS

Abbott Labs
American Home
Products
AstraZeneca
Bayer AG
Bristol-Myers
Squibb
Colgate-
Palmolive

Corning
Eli Lilly
Express Scripts
Glaxo Wellcome
Johnson
& Johnson
Laboratory
Corporation of
America

Merck
Mylan Labs
Novartis
Pfizer
Procter
& Gamble
Roche Holding
Schering-Plough
Unilever

HISTORICAL FINANCIALS & EMPLOYEES

NYSE: SBH FYE: December 31	Annual Growth	12/90	12/91	12/92	12/93	12/94	12/95	12/96	12/97	12/98	12/99
Sales ($ mil.)	4.4%	9,195	8,759	7,904	9,120	10,020	10,874	13,572	12,875	13,412	13,542
Net income ($ mil.)	1.0%	1,635	1,238	1,103	1,203	111	1,542	1,836	1,862	1,089	1,781
Income as % of sales	—	17.8%	14.1%	13.9%	13.2%	1.1%	14.2%	13.5%	14.5%	8.1%	13.2%
Earnings per share ($)	5.0%	0.99	1.13	1.04	1.13	1.40	1.40	1.63	1.63	0.90	1.53
Stock price - FY high ($)	—	15.19	21.69	24.00	19.31	18.44	27.69	34.69	53.63	71.88	76.38
Stock price - FY low ($)	—	9.44	14.06	17.59	13.75	13.19	17.63	24.31	32.56	48.06	56.06
Stock price - FY close ($)	17.4%	15.19	21.56	18.88	14.94	17.88	27.63	34.00	51.44	69.50	64.13
P/E - high	—	15	19	23	17	35	20	21	33	43	41
P/E - low	—	10	12	17	12	25	13	15	20	29	30
Dividends per share ($)	11.7%	0.30	0.37	0.41	0.40	0.48	0.43	0.76	0.26	0.22	0.81
Book value per share ($)	14.2%	1.43	2.06	2.28	2.50	1.58	2.49	3.54	4.07	3.98	4.73
Employees	(0.2%)	54,100	54,000	53,000	51,900	52,700	52,400	53,800	55,400	58,300	53,300

STOCK PRICE HISTORY

HIGH/LOW/CLOSE

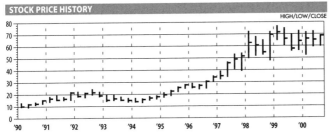

1999 FISCAL YEAR-END

Debt ratio: 16.2%
Return on equity: 53.5%
Cash ($ mil.): 585
Current ratio: 1.06
Long-term debt ($ mil.): 1,029
No. of shares (mil.): 1,123
Dividends
  Yield: 1.3%
  Payout: 52.9%
Market value ($ mil.): 72,033

SODEXHO ALLIANCE

OVERVIEW

Sodexho Alliance serves up its business piping hot (unless, of course, it's supposed to be cold). With operations in 66 countries, the global caterer from Montigny-le-Bretonneux, France, is the largest contract food service provider in the world. The company's clients include colleges, large corporations, hospitals, and prisons. It also provides facility management services (groundskeeping, laundry) and remote site management (including offshore rigs). In addition, the company owns 48% of Sodexho Marriott Services — one of the largest food service providers in the US and a product of the merger between the North American food service branches of Marriott International and Sodexho in 1998.

Through its Sodexho Pass subsidiary, the company supplies service vouchers (passes, coupons, and smart cards used for food, transportation, medical care, and employee and social benefits) in Europe and Latin America. It also operates river and harbor dinner cruises on a fleet of more than 40 boats in cities such as Boston, Chicago, London, New York, Paris, Philadelphia, Seattle, and Washington, DC.

While Sodexho has turned its focus toward organic growth after years of acquisitions (it hopes to lure new clients and keep current ones with its move into facilities management), the company still pursues international alliances, reflecting the addition of "Alliance" to the company name in 1997. Founder, chairman, and CEO Pierre Bellon and his family own about 42% of Sodexho Alliance.

HISTORY

The Bellon family had been luxury ship hospitality specialists since the turn of the century, 60 years before Pierre Bellon founded Sodexho in 1966. By 1971 Bellon had his first contract outside of France to provide food service to a Brussels hospital. Sodexho continued to expand its services into the late 1970s, entering remote site management in Africa and the Middle East in 1975 and starting its service vouchers segment in Belgium and Germany in 1978.

Sodexho jumped the pond in 1980, expanding its businesses to North and South America. The company went public on the Paris Bourse exchange in 1983. Two years later it bought Seiler, a Boston vending machine company-turned-restaurateur. Sodexho then bought San Francisco's Food Dimensions in 1987. After beefing up its American operations with four other US acquisitions, the company merged Food Dimensions and Seiler in 1989. Sodexho's US river cruise company, Spirit Cruises — an echo of the Bellon family's original calling — was also included in the merger. The merged US companies were renamed Sodexho USA in 1993.

The 1990s proved an era of growth and acquisitions for Sodexho. The company expanded into Japan, Africa, Russia, and five Eastern European countries in 1993. The company acquired a 20% stake in Corrections Corporation of America the following year and virtually doubled its size with the acquisition of the UK's Gardner Merchant in 1995. The largest catering company in that region, Gardner Merchant's holdings spanned Australia, the Far East, northern Europe, the UK, and the US — generally markets where Sodexho did not have a strong presence. That year the company also acquired Partena, a Swedish security and care company, from Volvo's Fortos.

Gardner Merchant's US business was officially merged with Sodexho USA in 1996 to make it the #4 food service company in the US. Also that year Sodexho acquired Brazilian service voucher company Cardapio. After a year of legal wrangling, Sodexho also lost a fight for control of Accor's Eurest France to rival caterer Compass Group (now Granada Compass), selling off its minority interest. The next year Sodexho acquired 49% of Universal Ogden Services, renamed Universal Services, an American remote site manager. To signify its efforts to maintain the individuality of the companies it acquires, Sodexho changed its name to Sodexho Alliance in 1997.

Marriott International merged its food service branch with Sodexho's North American food service operations in 1998. Sodexho Alliance,with a 48% stake, became the largest shareholder; stockholders in Marriott International took the remainder, with the Marriott family controlling 9%. Sodexho USA had been less than one-fourth the size of Marriott International's food service division before the merger.

Sodexho acquired GR Servicios Hoteleros in 1999, thereby becoming the largest caterer in Spain. The following year it agreed to merge its remote site management operations with Universal Services and rename it Universal Sodexho.

OFFICERS

Chairman and CEO: Pierre Bellon
SVP Corporate Human Resources: Elisabeth Carpentier
CFO; SVP Sodexho Group: Bernard Carton
Managing Director South America, Service Vouchers and Cards: Antonino Cirrincione
VP Planning, Innovation and Quality: Nicolas Crowley
President, River & Harbor Cruises, Penitentiary Institutions, Sodexho Food & Management Services, and French Overseas Possessions: Jean-Pierre Cuny
Group COO, Sodexho Food and Management Services and Worldwide Healthcare Market Champion: Jean-Michel Dhenain
Group COO, Sodexho Food and Management Services and Worldwide Remote Site Management Market Champion: Patrice Douce
General Counsel and Investor Relations: Raphael Dubrule
Chief Executive UK and Ireland, Gardner Merchant Food & Management Services, and Worldwide Business & Industry Market Champion: David Ford
COO, Sodexho Pass, Service Vouchers and Cards: Albert George
President, Central and Eastern Europe, Sodexho Food and Management Services: Petr Hlista
Auditors: Befec-Price Waterhouse

LOCATIONS

HQ: 3, avenue Newton, 78180 Montigny-le-Bretonneux, France
Phone: +33-1-30-85-75-00 **Fax:** +33-1-30-43-09-58
US HQ: 9801 Washingtonian Blvd., Gaithersburg, MD 20878
US Phone: 301-987-4431 **US Fax:** 301-987-4068
Web site: http://sodexho.com

Sodexho Alliance has operations in 66 countries.

1999 Sales

	$ mil.	% of total
North America	4,548	48
Europe		
UK & Ireland	1,568	16
France	1,147	12
Other countries	1,569	16
South America	344	4
Middle East, Asia		
& Pacific	272	3
Africa	73	1
Total	**9,521**	**100**

PRODUCTS/OPERATIONS

1999 Sales

	$ mil.	% of total
Food & management	8,949	94
Remote site management	296	3
Service vouchers & cards	169	2
River & harbor cruises	107	1
Total	**9,521**	**100**

Selected Services
Food and Management
  Business and industry
  Education
  Health care
  Prestige (conference halls and centers)
River and harbor cruises
Sodexho Pass (service vouchers and cards)

COMPETITORS

Accor	Granada Compass
ARAMARK	HDS Services
Delaware North	HMSHost
Fine Host	Host America

HISTORICAL FINANCIALS & EMPLOYEES

Euronext Paris: SW FYE: August 31	Annual Growth	8/90	8/91	8/92	8/93	8/94	8/95	8/96	8/97	8/98	8/99
Sales (€ mil.)	26.2%	1,173	1,360	1,388	1,618	1,713	2,797	3,805	4,497	6,261	9,521
Net income (€ mil.)	22.1%	23	29	33	35	97	43	104	82	111	139
Income as % of sales	—	2.0%	2.1%	2.4%	2.2%	5.7%	1.5%	2.7%	1.8%	1.8%	1.5%
Earnings per share (€)	12.5%	1.44	1.42	1.55	1.63	4.46	1.72	3.57	2.71	2.50	4.14
Stock price - FY high (€)	—	28.94	27.18	39.17	39.31	43.46	46.72	88.72	119.88	199.56	200.00
Stock price - FY low (€)	—	17.28	13.34	27.15	31.91	31.87	27.14	44.17	86.10	97.33	135.10
Stock price - FY close (€)	28.8%	18.06	26.97	35.09	37.06	34.34	44.32	86.61	102.76	160.07	175.70
P/E - high	—	20	19	25	24	10	27	25	44	80	48
P/E - low	—	12	9	18	20	7	16	12	32	39	33
Dividends per share (€)	17.7%	0.43	0.46	0.51	0.75	0.82	0.82	0.82	0.97	1.34	1.87
Book value per share (€)	19.6%	9.99	11.06	11.33	12.95	16.38	19.10	22.97	28.13	35.18	49.97
Employees	32.3%	—	—	—	50,339	55,000	115,669	141,118	152,000	250,000	269,973

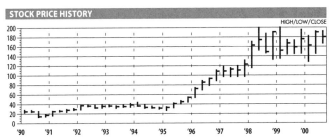

STOCK PRICE HISTORY HIGH/LOW/CLOSE

1999 FISCAL YEAR-END
Debt ratio: 55.7%
Return on equity: —
Cash (€ mil.): 385
Current ratio: 1.47
Long-term debt (€ mil.): 1,835
No. of shares (mil.): 34
Dividends
  Yield: 0.0%
  Payout: 0.5%
Market value ($ mil.): 6,300
Sales ($ mil.): 10,041

SOFTBANK CORP.

Full-throttle investing by founder, president, and CEO Masayoshi Son, who is hailed by many as the Bill Gates of Japan, has put SOFTBANK at the forefront of the Internet age. Under his tutelage, the Tokyo-based holding company has extended its investment reach across Internet infrastructure, e-commerce, financial services, information technology-related distribution services, publishing and marketing, and technology services.

SOFTBANK's portfolio is bulging with direct or indirect investments in more than 400 Internet-related companies. The bedrock of its Internet holdings is its nearly 22% stake in Yahoo!, but SOFTBANK's Internet investments also include stakes in E*TRADE Japan, Nasdaq Japan, VerticalNet Japan, and trade show company Key3Media (the producer of the COMDEX trade show, Key3Media was a spinoff of Ziff-Davis, now part of CNET.)

In 2000 SOFTBANK made its presence felt in banking when it became part of a consortium that purchased Japan's failed Nippon Credit Bank (later renamed Aozora). SOFTBANK owns nearly 49% of the bank.

Although SOFTBANK's stock price took a beating in 2000, Son remained steadfast in his determination to continue expanding the company's investment portfolio. SOFTBANK abandoned plans to float several of its holdings in 2000. Son owns 38% of the company.

Ethnic Korean Masayoshi Son grew up in Japan using the name Yasumoto to conform with the Japanese policy of assimilation. In the early 1970s, the 16-year-old came to the US and began using his Korean name. Son entered the University of California at Berkeley and, while there, invented the prototype for the Sharp Wizard handheld organizer.

Bankrolled by the nearly $1 million that Sharp paid him for his patent, Son returned to Japan and founded software distributor SOFTBANK in 1981. The company got its first big break when it inked a distribution agreement with Joshin Denki, one of Japan's largest consumer electronics retailers, that year. Son used this agreement to gain exclusive distribution rights for much of the software he distributed.

SOFTBANK went public in 1994. That year, as part of an evolving plan to control digital data delivery, Son purchased the trade show division of Ziff-Davis Publishing, augmenting it in 1995 with the purchase of COMDEX, the trade show operations of the Interface Group. The next year SOFTBANK purchased the rest of Ziff-Davis. It also bought 80% of Kingston Technology and a stake in Yahoo! — which laid the cornerstone for its Internet empire.

SOFTBANK accelerated its Internet investment pace in 1997, taking stakes in dozens of Web-related companies. That year it filed a lawsuit against Yell Publishing, the Japanese publisher of a book accusing SOFTBANK of issuing phony financial statements, among other improprieties.

In 1998 the company moved into financial services by entering a joint venture with E*Trade Group to offer online stock trading in Japan. SOFTBANK also took Ziff-Davis public (it retained a majority stake).

Internal change marked 1999 as SOFTBANK merged with MAC, Son's private asset management company, and transformed itself into a holding company. The company also sold its stake in Kingston Technology and announced its plans to focus investments on Internet-related companies. It teamed with the National Association of Securities Dealers to create a Japanese version of the Nasdaq stock market (launched in 2000). SOFTBANK also partnered with Microsoft and Tokyo Electric Power to launch SpeedNet, a Japanese Internet service provider.

In 2000 the nearly decimated Ziff-Davis announced it would transform its online arm, ZDNet, from a tracking stock into a stand-alone company and adopt the ZDNet name; later CNET Networks bought both companies instead. That year SOFTBANK formed venture capital funds focusing on areas such as Latin America, Japan, Europe, the UK, and emerging markets.

The company reorganized in 2000 and placed most of its non-Japan-based holdings under a new unit called SOFTBANK Global Ventures. Sharpening its focus on Internet investments, SOFTBANK sold its stake in anti-virus software maker Trend Micro. Branching into banking, a consortium headed by SOFTBANK paid $932 million for Japan's failed Nippon Credit Bank. SOFTBANK's share of the bank stood at nearly 49%; the bank was renamed Aozora. SOFTBANK's stock price tumbled in 2000, and the company called off plans to take several of its holding companies public.

President and CEO: Masayoshi Son
EVP and CFO; President and CEO, SOFTBANK
  Finance Corp.: Yoshitaka Kitao
President and CEO, SOFTBANK E-Commerce:
  Ken Miyauchi
CEO SOFTBANK Global Ventures: Ronald D. Fisher
President and Executive Managing Director,
  SOFTBANK International Ventures; Chairman and
  CEO, Ziff-Davis: Eric Hippeau
President and Executive Managing Director,
  SOFTBANK Venture Capital: Gary E. Rieschel
Auditors: ChuoAoyama Audit Corporation

HQ: 24-1, Nihonbashi Hakozakicho, Chuo-ku,
  Tokyo 103-8501, Japan
Phone: +81-3-5642-8005   Fax: +81-3-5641-3401
US HQ: 10 Langley Rd., Ste. 403,
  Newton Center, MA 02159
US Phone: 617-928-9300   US Fax: 617-928-9301
Web site: http://www.softbank.co.jp

SOFTBANK has operations in Asia, Australia, Europe,
Latin America, and the US.

2000 Sales

	¥ mil.	% of total
Japan	289,531	66
North America	111,229	26
Europe	11,126	3
Other regions	23,050	5
Adjustments	(11,716)	—
Total	**423,220**	**100**

2000 Sales

	¥ mil.	% of total
E-commerce	231,527	53
Media & marketing	118,884	28
Internet culture	17,911	4
E-finance	18,649	4
International venture funds	2,604	1
Other	43,934	10
Adjustments	(10,289)	—
Total	**423,220**	**100**

Selected Operations
SOFTBANK Broadmedia
SOFTBANK E-Commerce
SOFTBANK Finance
SOFTBANK Global Ventures (for investments outside
  Japan)
SOFTBANK Media & Marketing
SOFTBANK Networks
SOFTBANK Technology (63%)

Accel Partners	Internet Capital
Alloy Ventures	Internet Initiative Japan
Benchmark Capital	Kleiner Perkins
CMGI	Liberty Digital
CSK	Safeguard Scientifics
Flatiron Partners	Sequoia Capital
Fujitsu	Shikoku Electric Power
Hummer Winblad	Trinity Ventures
idealab	

Tokyo: 9984 FYE: March 31	Annual Growth	3/91	3/92	3/93	3/94	3/95	3/96	3/97	3/98	3/99	3/00
Sales (¥ mil.)	30.5%	38,619	43,821	51,627	64,090	96,808	171,101	359,742	513,364	528,159	423,220
Net income (¥ mil.)	51.0%	207	131	607	938	2,052	5,794	9,092	10,303	37,538	8,446
Income as % of sales	—	0.5%	0.3%	1.2%	1.5%	2.1%	3.4%	2.5%	2.0%	7.1%	2.0%
Earnings per share (¥)	20.6%	—	—	—	—	29.85	69.22	95.58	100.77	365.38	76.05
Stock price - FY high (¥)	—	—	—	—	—	5,186	12,143	12,308	8,450	14,010	198,000
Stock price - FY low (¥)	—	—	—	—	—	1,998	2,495	5,846	1,670	4,630	12,500
Stock price - FY close (¥)	104.5%	—	—	—	—	2,559	1,978	7,850	5,360	13,280	91,500
P/E - high	—	—	—	—	—	174	175	129	84	38	2,604
P/E - low	—	—	—	—	—	67	36	61	17	13	164
Dividends per share (¥)	5.9%	—	—	—	—	15.00	15.00	20.00	40.00	15.00	20.00
Book value per share (¥)	35.3%	—	—	—	—	764.21	1,759.47	2,980.33	2,484.96	3,191.06	3,461.27
Employees	50.5%	—	—	590	630	909	4,375	5,600	7,743	6,865	—

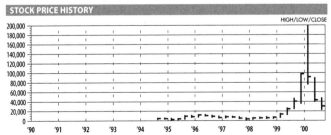

HIGH/LOW/CLOSE

2000 FISCAL YEAR-END
Debt ratio: 52.6%
Return on equity: 2.3%
Cash (¥ mil.): 254,708
Current ratio: 1.50
Long-term debt (¥ mil.): 336,463
No. of shares (mil.): 110
Dividends
  Yield: 0.0%
  Payout: 0.3%
Market value ($ mil.): 95,435
Sales ($ mil.): 4,013

SONY CORPORATION

OVERVIEW

Sony goes full circle — producing entertainment and the devices to experience it.

Tokyo-based Sony is a consumer electronics and multimedia entertainment giant. Electronics, including stereos, TVs, VCRs, and digital cameras, account for nearly two-thirds of sales (it is #2 worldwide, behind Matsushita). Its most profitable product ever, its PlayStation home video game system (#1 worldwide), alone brings in about 11% of sales. Its entertainment assets include Columbia TriStar (movies and TV shows) and the Columbia and Epic record labels.

The company also makes semiconductors and computer equipment and hot sellers such as digital camcorders, laptop computers, MiniDisc systems, and its Walkman personal stereos. In addition, Sony operates insurance and finance businesses.

It is developing digital networks for distribution of music and movies along with insurance and financial services. Columbia House (Sony's 50-50 joint venture with Time Warner) will expand its online presence by forming deals with CDnow. The company is also developing digital TVs and broadcasting equipment and has introduced its 128-bit PlayStation2 to rival SEGA's Dreamcast.

Sony plans to cut 10% of its worldwide workforce and eliminate 15 of its 70 plants by the year 2003, mainly to cut costs among its electronics businesses.

HISTORY

Akio Morita, Masaru Ibuka, and Tamon Maeda (Ibuka's father-in-law) started Tokyo Telecommunications Engineering in 1946 with funding from Morita's father's sake business. The company produced the first Japanese tape recorder in 1950. Three years later Morita paid Western Electric (US) $25,000 for transistor technology licenses, which sparked a consumer electronics revolution in Japan. His firm launched one of the first transistor radios in 1955, followed by the first Sony-trademarked product, a pocket-sized radio, in 1957. The next year the company changed its name to Sony (from "sonus," Latin for "sound," and "sonny," meaning little man). It beat the competition to newly emerging markets for transistor TVs (1959) and solid-state videotape recorders (1961).

Sony launched the first home video recorder in 1964 and, in 1965, a solid-state condenser microphone. Its 1968 introduction of the Trinitron color TV tube began another decade of explosive growth. The company bet wrong on its Betamax VCR (1976), which lost to rival Matsushita's VHS as the industry standard. However, 1979 brought another success, the Walkman personal stereo.

Pressured by adverse currency rates and competition worldwide, Sony used its technology to diversify beyond consumer electronics and began to move production to other countries. In the 1980s it introduced Japan's first 32-bit workstation and became a major producer of computer chips and floppy disk drives. The purchases of CBS Records in 1988 ($2 billion) and Columbia Pictures in 1989 (a $4.9 billion deal, which included TriStar Pictures) made Sony a major force in the entertainment industry.

The firm manufactured Apple's wildly successful PowerBook, but its portable CD player, Data Discman, was only successful in Japan (1991). In the early 1990s Sony joined Nintendo to create a new kind of game console, combining Sony's CD-ROM drive with the graphic capabilities of a workstation. Athough Nintendo pulled out in 1992, Sony released PlayStation in Japan (1994) and in the US (1995) to great success. Two years later, in a joint venture with Intel, it developed a line of PC desktop systems.

In 1998 Sony shipped its first digital, high-definition TV to the US; folded TriStar into Columbia Pictures; and merged its Loews Theatres unit with Cineplex Odeon. In addition, the company successfully launched its Wega flat-screen TV.

Philips, Sun Microsystems, and Sony formed a joint venture in early 1999 to develop networked entertainment products. Also in 1999 Sony introduced its $2,000 robotic dog, AIBO; Nobuyuki Idei became CEO; and on the heels of the Walkman's 20th anniversary, the company introduced a Walkman with the capability to download music from the Internet.

In early 2000 Sony formed PlayStation.com Japan to sell its game consoles (including the PlayStation2) and software online. It also introduced its 128-bit PlayStation2, which can play DVD movies and connects to the Internet. In April 2000 Sony said it would acquire a 15% stake in Fujitsu Hitachi Plasma Display, a joint venture with Fujitsu and Hitachi to develop and produce thinner plasma display panels for television screens. The company later restructured, placing all of its US entertainment holdings under a new umbrella company called Sony Broadband Entertainment.

Chairman: Norio Ohga
Chairman and CEO: Nobuyuki Idei
President and COO: Kunitake Ando
Executive Deputy President and CFO:
 Teruhisa Tokunaka
VC and Executive Representative, Technology:
 Minoru Morio
VC, Finance and Insurance Business: Tamotsu Iba
**SEVP Legal Matters and Telecommunications
 Business:** Teruo Masaki
Chairman and CEO, Sony Corporation of America:
 Howard Stringer
**Corporate SEVP Corporate Human Resources and
 General Affairs:** Kenichi Oyama
**Corporate SEVP Public Relations and Investor
 Relations:** Masayoshi Morimoto
Corporate EVP Legal and Intellectual Property:
 Kenichiro Yonezawa
Auditors: PricewaterhouseCoopers

HQ: 7-35, Kitashinagawa, 6-chome, Shinagawa-ku,
 Tokyo 141-0001, Japan
Phone: +81-3-5448-2111   **Fax:** +81-3-5448-2244
US HQ: 550 Madison Ave., 9th Fl.,
 New York, NY 10022
US Phone: 212-833-6800   **US Fax:** 212-833-6938
Web site: http://www.world.sony.com

2000 Sales

	$ mil.	% of total
Japan	20,012	32
US	19,124	30
Europe	13,872	22
Other regions	10,074	16
Total	**63,082**	**100**

2000 Sales & Operating Income

	$ mil.	% of total	$ mil.	% of total
Electronics	44,525	64	1,119	42
Music	6,669	10	268	10
Games	6,177	9	730	27
Motion pictures	4,642	7	364	14
Insurance	3,588	5	197	7
Other	3,435	5	(122)	—
Adjustments	(5,954)	—	(286)	—
Total	**63,082**	**100**	**2,270**	**100**

Selected Operations
Consumer electronics (audio systems, computer
 systems, video equipment, video game systems)
Loews Cineplex Entertainment Corporation (39.5%)
Movies (Columbia Pictures, Columbia TriStar, Sony
 Pictures Classics, Sony)
Recorded music (Epic, Columbia, Sony Classical)
Television (Columbia TriStar Television Group)

Amazon.com	Hitachi	Pioneer
BASF	Intel	Robert Bosch
Bertelsmann	IBM	Samsung
Bose	LG Electronics	SANYO
Canon	Matsushita	SEGA
Compaq	3M	Sharp
Daewoo	Motorola	Time Warner
Dell Computer	News America	Toshiba
EMI Group	Nintendo	Universal
Fuji Photo	Nokia	Studios
Fujitsu	Oki Electric	Viacom
Harman	Philips	Walt Disney
International	Electronics	

NYSE: SNE FYE: March 31	Annual Growth	3/91	3/92	3/93	3/94	3/95	3/96	3/97	3/98	3/99	3/00
Sales ($ mil.)	10.2%	26,249	29,495	34,766	36,250	44,758	43,326	45,670	51,178	57,109	63,082
Net income ($ mil.)	3.7%	832	905	316	149	(3,296)	512	1,125	1,682	1,505	1,149
Income as % of sales	—	3.2%	3.1%	0.9%	0.4%	—	1.2%	2.5%	3.3%	2.6%	1.8%
Earnings per share ($)	3.2%	0.93	1.11	0.40	0.21	(3.92)	0.63	1.25	1.83	1.65	1.24
Stock price - FY high ($)	—	27.95	22.90	19.50	30.88	31.63	33.13	37.13	51.84	50.38	157.38
Stock price - FY low ($)	—	18.29	14.44	14.13	19.13	21.25	22.75	29.44	34.75	30.13	44.63
Stock price - FY close ($)	23.1%	21.65	15.38	19.19	28.19	24.44	30.38	34.56	42.53	45.66	140.06
P/E - high	—	30	21	49	147	—	53	30	24	27	115
P/E - low	—	20	13	35	91	—	36	24	16	16	33
Dividends per share ($)	4.0%	0.14	0.15	0.17	0.20	0.22	0.12	0.10	0.00	0.10	0.20
Book value per share ($)	4.3%	15.49	15.52	16.66	17.27	15.14	14.74	15.32	16.90	18.67	22.70
Employees	5.9%	112,900	119,000	126,000	130,000	138,000	151,000	163,000	173,000	177,000	189,700

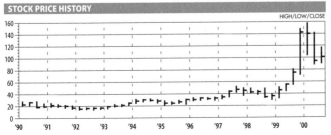

HIGH/LOW/CLOSE

Debt ratio: 27.2%
Return on equity: 6.4%
Cash ($ mil.): 5,906
Current ratio: 1.45
Long-term debt ($ mil.): 7,678
No. of shares (mil.): 907
Dividends
 Yield: 0.1%
 Payout: 16.1%
Market value ($ mil.): 127,073

SOUTH AFRICAN BREWERIES PLC

OVERVIEW

Monopoly is the favorite drinking game at South African Breweries (SAB). The company, based in Johannesburg, is the country's largest brewer, with a dominant — if not oppressive — 98% share of the market. It is also the #4 brewer worldwide, after Anheuser-Busch, Heineken, and AmBev. SAB's Castle Lager brand is tops in Africa; other local brews include Hansa Pilsener and Ohlsson's Lager, among about a dozen others. SAB also bottles Coca-Cola and Schweppes soft drinks and produces wine and spirits, fruit drinks, and mineral water.

Apartheid kept SAB from investing overseas in the 1980s, so it grew by purchasing a diverse range of businesses at home. After sanctions were lifted in the early 1990s, the company bulked up on foreign breweries; it now has interests in brewers in Europe, Russia, and Asia. SAB shed most of its non-brewing units, and it might sell its hotels (most under the Holiday Inn and Formule 1 banners), primarily in South Africa, and three casinos. SAB is looking to acquire other brewers.

HISTORY

British sailor Frederick Mead purchased the Castle Brewery in Johannesburg in 1892, about 15 years after gold was discovered in South Africa. Mead took his brewing operation public as South African Breweries (SAB) in 1895. The company began making its flagship Castle Lager three years later and survived the Anglo-Boer War (1899-1902) as South Africa's fastest growing nonindustrial firm. Mead died in 1915.

The brewer acquired the Grand Hotel in Cape Town in 1921 and a stake in Schweppes (carbonated drinks) in 1925. SAB and main rival Ohlsson's, having cooperated in hops production as far back as 1912, formed a joint venture for that pursuit in 1935 and teamed up again ten years later to grow barley.

In the late 1940s SAB began an extensive expansion program involving its breweries, small hotels, and pubs. In 1951 it acquired the Hotel Victoria in Johannesburg. An increase in beer taxes during the 1950s led SAB to start producing liquors. With beer demand slackening, South Africa's three largest brewers — SAB, Ohlsson's, and United Breweries — merged in 1956. Although SAB was the smallest of the three, it headed the merger and the company's name was retained. The new company controlled about 90% of the beer market.

Beer taxes continued to pressure sales, and in 1960 SAB acquired control of Stellenbosch Farmers' Winery to extend its product range. Blacks in South Africa had been prohibited from drinking alcohol, but in 1962 that restriction was lifted, opening an enormous market. SAB continued to extend its range of beer brands during the 1960s by adding licenses to brew Amstel and Carling Black Label.

Further diversifying, SAB formed Barsab (an investment venture with Thomas Barlow & Sons) in 1966. The company launched its hotel division, Southern Sun Hotels, three years later by merging its hotels with those owned by the

Sol Kerzner family. The Barsab venture was dissolved in 1973, leaving SAB with furniture and footwear businesses. The following year it added discount food retailer OK Bazaars and acquired the South African bottling business of Pepsi (converted to Coca-Cola in 1977). The company added the beer interests of the Rembrandt Group and a 49% stake in Appletiser, a fruit drinks company, in 1979. (It gained control of it in 1982.)

SAB moved into apparel retailing with its purchase of the Scotts Stores group (1981) and Edgars stores (1982). Antiapartheid sanctions forced the company to grow at home. After forming a joint venture with Ceres Fruit Juices (1986), SAB made a number of investments in South Africa, including Lion Match Company (1987), Da Gama Textiles (1989), and Plate Glass (1992).

As sanctions eased in the 1990s, the company expanded internationally. It acquired stakes in breweries in Hungary (1993), Tanzania and China (1994), and Poland and Romania (1996). Graham Mackay (now CEO) became managing director in 1996. As SAB refocused on brewing, it sold noncore operations, including OK Bazaars (1997) and Da Gama Textiles (1998).

Before moving its main listing to the London Stock Exchange in 1999, SAB sold its Amalgamated Retail unit (furniture, appliances), Lion Match Company, and a large stake in Edgars. It then bought controlling interests in Czech brewers Pilsner Urquell and Radegast to become the largest brewer in Central Europe, and sold its 68% interest in Plate Glass to Dibelco (a D'Ieteren and Copeba joint venture). Bevcon (a consortium of three South African companies) sold its 27% interest in SAB in 1999.

OFFICERS

Chairman: Jacob Meyer Kahn, age 60, $92,500 pay
Chief Executive; Chairman ABI:
Ernest Arthur Graham Mackay, age 50, $435,696 pay
Financial Director: Nigel Geoffrey Cox, age 52,
$245,519 pay
Corporate Finance and Development Director:
Malcolm Ian Wyman, age 53, $260,800 pay
Head of Organizational Development:
Richard Llewellyn Lloyd, age 56, $57,300 pay
Managing Director SAB Europe: Michael Hugh Simms,
age 51, $72,481 pay
Managing Director Beers South Africa:
Norman Joseph Adami, age 45, $71,250 pay
Chief Executive SAB's Soft Drinks: Alan Clark
President and CEO, SAB USA: Barry Smith
Auditors: PricewaterhouseCoopers

LOCATIONS

HQ: 25 Grosvenor St., London, W1X 9FE,
United Kingdom
Phone: +44-207-659-0100   **Fax:** +44-207-659-0111
Web site: http://www.sab.co.za

South African Breweries has brewing operations in sub-
Saharan Africa, Asia, and Europe. It also owns 75 hotels
and three casinos in Africa.

PRODUCTS/OPERATIONS

Selected Brands

Beers South Africa
Amstel (licensed from
Heineken)
Carling Black Label
Castle
Dakota Ice
Dooley's
Hansa Pilsener
Heineken (imported)
Hofbrau
Ohlsson's Lager
Redd's

SAB International (beer)
Bohlinger's (Africa)
Chairmans ESB (Africa)
Chibuku (Africa, sorghum
beer)
Club (Africa)
Dorada (Canary Islands)
Dreher (Hungary)
Keller (China)
Kilimanjaro (Africa)

Lech (Poland)
Ndovu (Africa)
Nile (Africa)
Pilsner Urquell (Czech
Republic)
Radegast (Czech Republic)
Safari (Africa)
Saris (Slovakia)
Smadny Mnich
Snowflake (China)
Tropical (Canary Islands)
Tyskie (Poland)
Ursus (Romania)
Zambesi Export (Africa)

Soft Drinks
Appletiser
Coca-Cola brands
Grapetiser
Just Juice
Schweppes brands

Other
Valpre (spring water)

COMPETITORS

Accor
Anadolu
Anheuser-Busch
Asahi Breweries
Asia Pacific
Breweries
Bass Brewers
Brauerei BECK
Budvar

Carlsberg
China Internet
Global Alliance
Danone
Grolsch
Guinness/UDV
Heineken
Interbrew
Kirin

Lion Nathan
Marriott
International
MGM Mirage
Miller Brewing
Nestlé
PepsiCo
Tsingtao
Yanjing

HISTORICAL FINANCIALS & EMPLOYEES

London: SAB FYE: March 31	Annual Growth	3/91	3/92	3/93	3/94	3/95	3/96	3/97	3/98	3/99	3/00
Sales (£ mil.)	(0.3%)	—	—	—	—	—	2,782	2,839	2,860	2,905	2,751
Net income (£ mil.)	(1.9%)	—	—	—	—	—	206	227	215	189	191
Income as % of sales	—	—	—	—	—	—	7.4%	8.0%	7.5%	6.5%	6.9%
Earnings per share (p)	55.7%	—	—	—	—	—	—	—	—	25.80	40.16
Stock price - FY high (p)	—	—	—	—	—	—	—	—	—	586.00	668.00
Stock price - FY low (p)	—	—	—	—	—	—	—	—	—	433.00	430.00
Stock price - FY close (p)	(9.6%)	—	—	—	—	—	—	—	—	539.00	487.50
P/E - high	—	—	—	—	—	—	—	—	—	23	17
P/E - low	—	—	—	—	—	—	—	—	—	17	11
Dividends per share (p)	—	—	—	—	—	—	—	—	—	0.00	15.00
Book value per share (p)	38.3%	—	—	—	—	—	—	—	—	14.98	20.71
Employees	(30.0%)	—	—	—	—	—	—	—	—	49,099	34,365

STOCK PRICE HISTORY

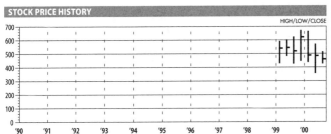

HIGH/LOW/CLOSE

2000 FISCAL YEAR-END

Debt ratio: 19.0%
Return on equity: —
Cash (£ mil.): 123
Current ratio: 0.63
Long-term debt (£ mil.): 184
No. of shares (mil.): 774
Dividends
  Yield: 0.0%
  Payout: 0.4%
Market value ($ mil.): 602,543
Sales ($ mil.): 4,390

STMICROELECTRONICS N.V.

OVERVIEW

STMicroelectronics (ST) makes semiconductors with a continental flair. The Geneva, Switzerland-based company is the second-largest semiconductor maker based in Europe (after Siemens spinoff Infineon). ST is a leading global supplier of discrete devices (such as transistors and diodes) and integrated circuits (ICs), including analog chips (half of sales), microprocessors, memory chips, and application-specific and custom ICs. The company, formerly SGS-THOMSON, sells its chips to manufacturers in the telecommunications (27% of sales), computer, consumer electronics, industrial, and automotive markets. Customers include Ford, Hewlett-Packard, IBM, Nokia, and Scientific-Atlanta.

Aggressive product development focusing on key customers is central to ST's business strategy. The company is focusing on differentiated ICs (such as dedicated products and semi-custom devices; nearly two-thirds of sales) for fast-growing market segments, including digital consumer, smart cards, wireless networking, and automotive electronics. ST's product breadth also enables it to meet the demand of system-on-a-chip ICs and to develop cross-licensing relationships with other leading chip companies.

French-government-controlled companies — CEA-Industrie and France Telecom — together own 22% of ST. The Italian government and Italy's Comitato SIR also own 22%.

HISTORY

SGS-THOMSON (ST) was formed through the 1987 merger of SGS Microelettronica, a state-owned Italian chipmaker, and the non-military electronics arm of Thomson-CSF. Included in the merger were two US operations: SGS Semiconductor in Phoenix and Texas-based Thomson Components-Mostek, which was purchased by Thomson from United Technologies in 1986.

Microelettronica was part of Finmeccanica, formed in 1948 as the engineering subsidiary of the (now liquidated) Italian state industrial holding company IRI.

Thomson SA got its start shortly before the turn of the 20th century, when a group of French businessmen acquired patents from General Electric predecessor Thomson-Houston Electric and created a company, Compagnie Française Thomson-Houston, to produce power-generation equipment.

Both Thomson and Microelettronica were struggling at the time of their merger. Pasquale Pistorio, a Motorola veteran who became head of SGS in 1980, was named president of the new company. To jump-start the organization, he began shutting and selling factories, trimming management, and shifting jobs to the Mediterranean and Asia. During the 1980s the company joined Jessi (the Joint European Semiconductor Silicon research program), which offered funding and tax incentives to European semiconductor companies.

ST lost $300 million in its first two years of operation, made a small profit in 1989, then stumbled again as recession spread across Europe. To secure ST's market presence, Pistorio began making acquisitions. In 1989 the company acquired 32-bit microprocessor technology when it bought UK-based INMOS from British conglomerate THORN EMI. Pistorio also forged alliances with major chip buyers, including Alcatel, Hewlett-Packard, and Sony. In 1992 ST started making x86 microprocessors for Cyrix. By 1993 ST had become the world's #1 maker of erasable programmable read-only memories (EPROMs). Profits soared to $160 million, and the company bought Tag Semiconductors, a maker of low-cost chips, from US conglomerate Raytheon. ST went public in 1994.

ST opened its largest software design center outside Europe, near New Delhi, India, in 1995. The next year the company shipped its billionth smart card integrated circuit (IC) and its 5 millionth MPEG (video) decoder IC. Thomson sold off its stake in ST in 1997 and SGS-THOMSON changed its name to STMicroelectronics in 1998. The company formed development deals with Philips Electronics (for advanced chip manufacturing processes) in 1997 and with Mitsubishi (for flash memory chips) in 1998.

In 1999 ST bought Adaptec's Peripheral Technology Solutions group, which makes chips for disk drives; Vision Group, a developer of complementary metal-oxide semiconductor (CMOS) image sensors; and Arithmos, a maker of ICs for digital displays. In 2000 ST acquired the semiconductor production operations of Nortel Networks for about $100 million. The deal includes a six-year supply agreement worth at least $2 billion.

OFFICERS

Chairman: Jean-Pierre Noblanc
VC: Bruno Steve
President and CEO: Pasquale Pistorio, age 64
VP and CFO: Maurizio Ghirga, age 62
VP and Treasurer: Piero Mosconi, age 60
VP America Region: Richard Pieranunzi, age 61
VP Asia/Pacific: Jean-Claude Marquet, age 58
VP Central Research and Development: Joel Monnier
VP European Region: Enrico Villa, age 59
VP Japan Region: Keizo Shibata, age 63
VP Strategic Planning and Human Resources:
Alain Dutheil, age 55
Auditors: PricewaterhouseCoopers N.V.

LOCATIONS

HQ: Technoparc du Pays de Gex,
165 rue Edouard Branly,
01637 Saint Genis Pouilly, France
Phone: +33-4-50-40-26-40   **Fax:** +33-4-50-40-25-80
US HQ: 1310 Electronics Dr., Carrollton, TX 75006
US Phone: 972-466-6000   **US Fax:** 972-466-8130
Web site: http://www.st.com

STMicroelectronics' facilities include manufacturing operations in Canada, China, France, Italy, Malaysia, Malta, Morocco, Singapore, and the US. The company has more than 70 sales offices in 26 countries.

1999 Sales

	$ mil.	% of total
Europe	1,834	36
North America	1,156	23
Asia/Pacific		
Japan	240	5
Other countries	1,658	33
Other regions	168	3
Total	**5,056**	**100**

PRODUCTS/OPERATIONS

1999 Sales

	$ mil.	% of total
Telecommunications, peripherals		
& automotive	2,306	46
Discrete & standard ICs	928	18
Consumer & microcontrollers	882	17
Memory products	836	17
New Ventures Group & other	104	2
Total	**5,056**	**100**

Selected Products

Application-specific chips	Metal oxide semiconductor
Battery-backed memories	field effect transistors
Bipolar transistors	Microcontrollers
Electrically erasable	Microprocessors
programmable read-only	Multimedia accelerators
memories	Power switches and
Erasable programmable	amplifiers
read-only memories	Smart card products
Flash memories	Static random-access
	memories

COMPETITORS

AMD	LSI Logic
Analog Devices	Lucent
Atmel	Mitsubishi
Cirrus Logic	Motorola
Cypress Semiconductor	National Semiconductor
Fairchild Semiconductor	NEC
Hitachi	ON Semiconductor
Infineon Technologies	Philips Electronics
Integrated Device	Samsung
Technology	Texas Instruments
Intel	Toshiba
International Rectifier	Vishay Intertechnology

HISTORICAL FINANCIALS & EMPLOYEES

NYSE: STM FYE: December 31	Annual Growth	12/90	12/91	12/92	12/93	12/94	12/95	12/96	12/97	12/98	12/99
Sales ($ mil.)	15.8%	1,355	1,374	1,568	2,038	2,640	3,554	4,122	3,970	4,248	5,056
Net income ($ mil.)	—	(97)	(103)	3	160	363	527	626	407	411	547
Income as % of sales	—	—	—	0.2%	7.9%	13.8%	14.8%	15.2%	10.2%	9.7%	10.8%
Earnings per share ($)	(1.9%)	—	—	—	—	—	0.67	0.75	0.49	0.48	0.62
Stock price - FY high ($)	—	—	—	—	—	—	9.57	12.09	16.49	15.28	51.28
Stock price - FY low ($)	—	—	—	—	—	—	3.75	4.75	8.57	5.97	13.40
Stock price - FY close ($)	65.6%	—	—	—	—	—	6.70	11.66	10.17	13.00	50.43
P/E - high	—	—	—	—	—	—	14	16	34	32	80
P/E - low	—	—	—	—	—	—	6	6	17	12	21
Dividends per share ($)	—	—	—	—	—	—	0.00	0.00	0.00	0.00	0.00
Book value per share ($)	13.1%	—	—	—	—	—	3.21	3.91	3.96	4.77	5.24
Employees	8.9%	—	17,730	17,813	19,898	21,800	25,523	25,468	28,728	29,182	35,000

STOCK PRICE HISTORY

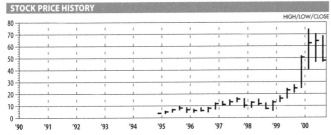

HIGH/LOW/CLOSE

1999 FISCAL YEAR-END

Debt ratio: 22.8%
Return on equity: 12.7%
Cash ($ mil.): 1,823
Current ratio: 2.24
Long-term debt ($ mil.): 1,349
No. of shares (mil.): 870
Dividends
Yield: —
Payout: —
Market value ($ mil.): 43,889

SUEZ LYONNAISE DES EAUX

OVERVIEW

Having dredged up success from the Suez to the sewers, Suez Lyonnaise des Eaux is channeling its efforts into infrastructure development around the world. The Franco-Belgian conglomerate, based in Paris, was formed by the 1997 merger of Compagnie de Suez (builder of the Suez Canal) and water treatment and engineering giant Lyonnaise des Eaux.

Suez Lyonnaise operates private infrastructure services in more than 120 countries, focusing on energy, water services, waste treatment, and communications. The company owns more than 42,000 MW of electric generating capacity and moves more than 100 billion cubic meters (3,500 billion cu. ft.), of natural gas per year; operations include Tractebel, Belgium's #1 utility. Through Lyonnaise des Eaux and

Degrémont, Suez Lyonnaise is the world's #2 water company, behind Vivendi; its water business has expanded with the purchase of Nalco Chemical, a producer of water treatment chemicals, and water utility operator United Water Resources, both US companies.

The conglomerate's businesses also include cable TV, heavy construction and operation of toll roads, airports, and other concessions.

Suez Lyonnaise is divesting most of its noncore assets, including its real estate, banking, insurance, and other financial services; at the same time, the company has been expanding internationally, primarily in the US, through acquisitions. Plans are to boost its revenues for core businesses outside of France and Belgium from 42% to 50%.

HISTORY

The first canal in Egypt was dug in the 13th century BC, but it was Napoleon who revived the idea of a shorter trade route to India: a canal through Egypt linking the Gulf of Suez with the Mediterranean. Former French diplomat and engineer Ferdinand de Lesseps formed Compagnie Universelle du Canal Maritime de Suez in 1858 to build and eventually operate the canal, which opened 11 years later. Egypt's modernization had pushed it into debt and increased its ties to the British government, which, by 1875, had acquired a 44% stake in the company.

For more than 80 years the Suez Canal was a foreign enclave, protected by the British Army since 1936. After Egypt's puppet government fell, and as Gamal Abd Al-Nasser assumed power in 1956, British troops exited the Canal Zone, which Egypt quickly nationalized. Israel, Britain, and France attacked, but the United Nations arranged a truce and foreign forces withdrew, leaving the Suez in Egypt's control.

With no canal to operate, Universelle du Canal Maritime de Suez became Compagnie Financiere de Suez in 1958. A year later it created a bank (which became Banque Indosuez in 1974).

In 1967 Financiere de Suez became the largest shareholder in Societe Lyonnaise des Eaux et de L'Eclairage, a leading French water company. Formed in 1880, Lyonnaise des Eaux had stakes in water (Northumbrian Water) and energy (Elyo). After France's energy firms were nationalized in 1946, Lyonnaise des Eaux dipped deeper into the water industry by acquiring Degrémont in 1972. It also purchased

stakes in waste management (SITA, 1970) and heating systems (Cofreth, 1975).

In the 1980s Lyonnaise des Eaux expanded in Spain, the UK, and the US, and diversified into cable TV (1986) and broadcast TV (1987). It merged with construction firm Dumez in 1990.

Meanwhile, Financiere de Suez became a financial power when it won a controlling stake in Société Générale de Belgique (SGB) in 1988 and bought Groupe Victoire in 1989. But the two buys left the firm (renamed Compagnie de Suez in 1990) deeply in debt.

Losing money, Compagnie de Suez disposed of Victoire (1994) and then the valuable Banque Indosuez (1996). In 1996 the company bought a controlling stake in Belgium's top utility, Tractebel. Compagnie de Suez and Lyonnaise des Eaux merged in 1997 to create Suez Lyonnaise des Eaux. The following year the company acquired the rest of SGB and bought the European and Asian operations of waste management giant Browning-Ferris Industries; it also began divesting oncore operations.

Suez Lyonnaise in 1999 expanded its core businesses, primarily in the US. The company bought Calgon (water treatment, US) and Nalco Chemical (water treatment chemicals, US), then merged Calgon into Nalco.

In 2000 Suez Lyonnaise bought United Water Resources and acquired the rest of SITA. Through its Elyo subsidiary, Suez Lyonnaise bought out minority shareholders in US-based Trigen Energy. It also merged its construction and concessions unit, Groupe GTM, with French construction rival VINCI.

OFFICERS

Honorary Supervisory Chairman: Jérôme Monod, age 69
Supervisory Chairman: Jean Gandois, age 69
Executive Chairman, President, and CEO:
Gérard Mestrallet
Executive VC: François Jaclot, age 51
Executive VC: Philippe Brongniart, age 61
SVP Finance, and Acting Director Planning, Control, and Accounts Management: Didier Retali
SEVP: Bernard Prades
EVP Development and Strategy: Patrick Buffet
SVP Corporate Marketing: Vincent Matteoli
SVP, General Counsel, and Committee Secretary:
Philippe de Margerie
SVP Human Resources: Dominique Fortin
Chairman and CEO, Nalco: Christian Maurin
Auditors: Barbier Frinault & Autres; Mazars & Guerard; Deloitte Touche Tohmatsu - Audit

LOCATIONS

HQ: 1, rue d'Astorg, 75008 Paris, France
Phone: +33-1-40-06-66-29   **Fax:** +33-1-40-06-67-33
Web site: http://www.suez-lyonnaise-eaux.com

1999 Sales

	% of total
Europe	
France	33
Belgium	25
Other EU countries	18
Other countries	4
The Americas	11
Asia & Oceania	5
Africa	4
Total	**100**

PRODUCTS/OPERATIONS

1999 Sales

	% of total
Core businesses	
Energy	41
Water	20
Waste services	13
Communications	2
Other	
Construction	24
Financial services	—
Total	**100**

SelectedOperations

Energy	Communications
Elyo	Lyonnaise Câble (77%)
Tractebel (98%, Belgium)	M6 (35%)
Trigen Energy (US)	Paris Première (53%)

Water	Concessions Management,
Degrémont	Construction and
Lyonnaise des Eaux	Industrial Contracting
Nalco (US)	VINCI (24%)
United Water Resources (US)	

Waste Services	Financial and Industrial Businesses
SITA	Fortis B (20%)
Tractebel (98%)	Suez Industrie
	Union Minière (25%)

COMPETITORS

American Water Works	CANAL+	United Utilities
Azurix	EDF	Vivendi
Bouygues	France Telecom	Waste
Brambles Industries	National Grid	Management
	Ogden	
	Severn Trent	

HISTORICAL FINANCIALS & EMPLOYEES

Euronext Paris: SZE FYE: December 31	Annual Growth	12/90	12/91	12/92	12/93	12/94	12/95	12/96	12/97	12/98	12/99
Sales (€ mil.)	12.6%	10,775	13,337	13,775	14,263	15,240	15,034	13,967	29,029	31,361	31,462
Net income (€ mil.)	23.5%	217	178	58	123	162	138	206	612	1,005	1,453
Income as % of sales	—	2.0%	1.3%	0.4%	0.9%	1.1%	0.9%	1.5%	2.1%	3.2%	4.6%
Earnings per share (€)	4.8%	6.22	3.85	1.21	2.40	2.92	2.41	3.50	4.92	7.41	9.46
Stock price - FY high (€)	—	115.10	98.33	89.03	89.03	95.13	82.17	81.26	109.15	178.67	196.50
Stock price - FY low (€)	—	64.18	61.74	64.46	59.47	65.25	62.28	66.48	71.04	98.33	145.00
Stock price - FY close (€)	8.9%	73.94	66.32	74.85	88.57	71.06	71.88	73.62	101.53	175.01	159.10
P/E - high	—	19	26	74	37	33	34	23	22	24	21
P/E - low	—	10	16	53	25	22	26	19	14	13	15
Dividends per share (€)	3.9%	2.12	2.29	2.29	2.29	2.52	2.63	2.63	2.74	2.70	3.00
Book value per share (€)	(3.1%)	—	—	—	68.84	74.61	71.71	78.06	136.68	122.13	56.92
Employees	8.2%	—	—	127,552	120,038	151,873	118,770	116,290	175,000	210,100	222,000

STOCK PRICE HISTORY

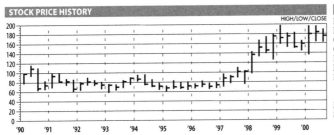

HIGH/LOW/CLOSE

1999 FISCAL YEAR-END

Debt ratio: 69.4%
Return on equity: 9.9%
Cash (€ mil.): 4,812
Current ratio: 1.04
Long-term debt (€ mil.): 17,845
No. of shares (mil.): 198
Dividends
  Yield: 0.0%
  Payout: 0.3%
Market value ($ mil.): 31,653
Sales ($ mil.): 31,612

SUMITOMO GROUP

OVERVIEW

Sumitomo Group has more operations than a M*A*S*H unit, and like a field hospital, it has been operating in a war zone — Asia's troubled economies. The Tokyo-based *keiretsu* (group of firms linked by cross-ownership) is led by Sumitomo Bank, one of the world's largest banks; Sumitomo Life Insurance, the world's #3 mutual life insurance firm (after Nippon Life and Dai-ichi Mutual Life); and Sumitomo Corporation, a leading *sogo shosha,* or integrated trading company. Other operations include mining, construction, and the manufacture of steel, wire and cable, chemicals, lumber, tires, ships, electronic components, glass, cement, and machinery.

Japan's push to deregulate its financial industries and the depletion of Sumitomo Bank's resources by the Asian economic crisis have prompted the bank and rival Sakura Bank to announce plans to merge by 2002.

Sumitomo Corporation has suffered heavy losses from a 1996 copper market fraud by one of its traders. Still, the *keiretsu* has recovered enough to make capital investments in emerging regions, such as Southeast Asia and China, offering such things as financing, insurance, industrial construction, and building materials. Its metals division continues to be one of the world's largest traders of nonferrous metals.

HISTORY

Around 1630 Masatomo Sumitomo, a Buddhist priest from the Kyoto area, opened a medicine shop/bookstore after the dissolution of his sect. His descendants preserved his writings on business ethics, and he is considered the spiritual founder of the Sumitomo Group. The *keiretsu's* commercial founder, however, was Riemon Soga, Masatomo's brother-in-law. Soga researched and duplicated a Western copper-smelting technique that enabled him to build a prosperous copper company. After Soga died in 1636, his son, Tomomochi, married into the Sumitomo family and became its head.

Tomomochi Soga combined the families' businesses and moved to Osaka. By 1693 the family had turned a dilapidated copper mine into one of Japan's top producers. By the mid-1800s, however, the company's biggest mine was aging and output had dropped. The family mortgaged its assets to modernize the mine, imported French technology, and bought ships for copper transport. Production soared.

Sumitomo Bank was created from existing family operations in 1895. A copper wire business, founded in 1897, evolved into Sumitomo Electric and Sumitomo Metal Industries. The family formed Sumitomo Chemical in 1913 and in 1925 began selling life insurance.

Nippon Electric Company (NEC) was managed by Sumitomo from 1932 until post-WWII occupation forces split the *zaibatsu* (family-run conglomerate) into numerous independent pieces. Employees of the old Sumitomo group migrated to a real estate and trading company, today's Sumitomo Corporation. Sumitomo companies began regrouping in the 1950s at the behest of the Japanese government.

Sumitomo companies went on a buying spree during the "bubble economy" of the

1980s and early 1990s. Purchases included Dunlop's tire operations, investments in Phelps Dodge's Candelaria copper and gold mine in Chile, and one-third of Satellite Japan. The Sumitomo Bank bought 13% of US investment house Goldman Sachs. In 1990, however, bank chairman Ichiro Isoda resigned in an illegal-loan scandal.

Sumitomo Metal Industries invested about $200 million in LTV in 1993 to shore up its US supply of high-quality steel. Ironically, LTV was one of several US steel companies that campaigned against Japanese steel imports in 1998.

In its first loss in 50 years, Sumitomo Bank took a $2.8 billion hit in 1995 from bad loans (the legacy of the 1992 bursting of the bubble economy). The next year Sumitomo Corporation announced that its head copper trader, Yasuo Hamanaka, had engaged in unauthorized trading over the previous decade, first attempting to corner the market, then trying to cover his own deficit. Hamanaka pleaded guilty and went to jail. Sumitomo Corporation chairman Tomiichi Akiyama resigned in 1997. By 1998 the company had suffered $3 billion in trading losses, fines, and restitutions. (Sumitomo Corporation sued four investment banks, alleging they had aided Hamanaka; separately, Merrill Lynch settled a dispute over its role in the scandal by agreeing in 2000 to pay the company $275 million.)

In 1999 Sumitomo Rubber Industries and Goodyear Tire formed an alliance: Sumitomo Rubber got cash and control of Goodyear's Japanese operations, and Goodyear gained control of Sumitomo Rubber's business in the US and Europe. Sumitomo Bank in 1999 announced plans to merge with Sakura Bank by 2002.

President and CEO, Sumitomo Corporation:
Kenji Miyahara
EVP, Internal Auditing Division, Finance and
Accounting Division, and Risk Management Division,
Sumitomo Corporation: Takashi Nomura
General Manager, Personnel and General Affairs
Division, Sumitomo Corporation: Susumu Kato
Auditors: Arthur Andersen

LOCATIONS

HQ: Sumitomo Corporation, 2-2, Hitotsubashi 1-chome,
Chiyoda-ku, Tokyo 100-8601, Japan
Phone: +81-3-3217-5000   Fax: +81-3-5658-3070
US HQ: Sumitomo Corporation of America
600 3rd Ave., New York, NY 10016
US Phone: 212-207-0700   US Fax: 212-207-0456
Web site: http://www.sumitomocorp.co.jp/about/group

Sumitomo Group has operations worldwide. Its Sumitomo
Corporation unit has offices in 89 countries.

PRODUCTS/OPERATIONS

2000 Sumitomo Corporation Sales

	% of total
Machinery, electronics & media	35
Retail & consumer services	21
Chemicals & fuels	19
Metals	9
Other	16
Total	**100**

COMPETITORS

Aventis
Compaq
Daewoo
Dai-Ichi Kangyo
Dai-ichi Mutual Life
DuPont
E.ON
Exxon Mobil
Fuji Bank
Hewlett-Packard
Hitachi
Hyundai
Industrial Bank of Japan
Intel
IBM
ITOCHU
Kanematsu
Komatsu
Marubeni
Mitsubishi
Mitsui
Motorola
Nichimen
Nippon Steel
Nissho Iwai
Peter Kiewit Sons'
RAG
Royal Dutch/Shell
Samsung
Sanwa Bank
Tokio Marine and Fire
TOMEN
Toshiba
Toyota

HISTORICAL FINANCIALS & EMPLOYEES

Tokyo: 8053* FYE: March 31	Annual Growth	3/91	3/92	3/93	3/94	3/95	3/96	3/97	3/98	3/99	3/00
Sales (¥ bil.)	(6.8%)	20,019	19,937	18,027	17,000	16,139	16,170	13,435	12,569	11,379	10,672
Net income (¥ bil.)	(6.3%)	47	37	20	7	7	20	(146)	26	(13)	26
Income as % of sales	—	0.2%	0.2%	0.1%	0.0%	0.0%	0.1%	—	0.2%	—	0.2%
Earnings per share (¥)	(3.4%)	44.00	34.32	19.23	6.86	6.83	19.09	(136.80)	24.19	(12.28)	32.31
Stock price - FY high (¥)	—	1,380	1,190	925	1,060	1,100	1,170	1,260	1,160	869	1,401
Stock price - FY low (¥)	—	948	896	662	774	730	731	795	600	481	692
Stock price - FY close (¥)	1.0%	1,140	930	785	999	790	1,130	880	867	777	1,244
P/E - high	—	31	35	48	155	161	61	—	48	—	43
P/E - low	—	22	26	34	113	107	38	—	25	—	21
Dividends per share (¥)	0.0%	8.00	8.00	8.00	8.00	8.00	8.00	8.00	8.00	8.00	8.00
Book value per share (¥)	(0.7%)	636.00	660.00	668.00	662.00	689.67	703.18	559.76	582.55	535.16	595.79
Employees	(1.1%)	—	8,959	9,215	9,212	9,240	9,071	8,804	9,000	8,500	8,192

* Information is for Sumitomo Corporation only.

STOCK PRICE HISTORY

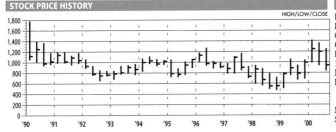

2000 FISCAL YEAR-END

Debt ratio: 75.4%
Return on equity: 0.0%
Cash (¥ mil.): 211,385
Current ratio: 1.09
Long-term debt (¥ mil.):
1,942,900
No. of shares (mil.): 1,065
Dividends
Yield: 0.0%
Payout: 0.2%
Market value ($ mil.): 12,544
Sales ($ mil.): 101,088

SUZUKI MOTOR CORPORATION

OVERVIEW

How did Suzuki Motor become so successful? Fruit of the looms. From its beginnings as Suzuki Loom Works, the Hamamatsu, Japan-based manufacturer has emerged as its country's #1 minicar maker, as well as a worldwide leader in motorcycle sales.

Suzuki is striving for product and market diversity. Its nonvehicle product lines (21% of sales) include electric wheelchairs, generators, prefabricated houses, and outboard motors. General Motors, the world's #1 carmaker, owns a 10% stake in Suzuki, and it is increasing its share to 20%. GM's added participation not only brings an influx of $600 million, it will also strengthen cooperation between the two companies in the development of small cars and contribute to Suzuki's product diversification.

HISTORY

In 1909 Michio Suzuki started Suzuki Loom Works in Hamamatsu, Japan. The company went public in 1920 and continued producing weaving equipment until the onset of WWII, when it began to make war-related products.

Suzuki began developing inexpensive motor vehicles in 1947, and in 1952 it introduced a 36cc engine to motorize bicycles. The company changed its name to Suzuki Motor and launched its first motorcycle in 1954. Suzuki's entry into the minicar market came in 1955 with the Suzulight, followed by the Suzumoped (1958), a delivery van (1959), and the Suzulight Carry FB small truck (1961).

Suzuki's triumph in the 1962 50cc-class Isle of Man TT motorcycle race started a string of racing successes that brought international prominence to the Suzuki name. The company established its first overseas plant in Thailand in 1967.

In the 1970s Suzuki met market demand for motorcycles with large engines. Meanwhile, a mid-1970s recession and falling demand for low-powered cars in Japan led the minicar industry there to produce two-thirds fewer minicars in 1974 than in 1970. Suzuki responded by pushing overseas, beginning auto exports, and expanding foreign distribution. In 1975 it started producing motorcycles in Taiwan, Thailand, and Indonesia.

Suzuki boosted capacity internationally throughout the 1980s through joint ventures. Motorcycle sales in Japan peaked in 1982, then tapered off, but enjoyed a modest rebound in the late 1980s. In 1988 the company agreed to handle distribution of Peugeot cars in Japan.

Suzuki and General Motors began their longstanding relationship in 1981 when GM bought a small stake in Suzuki. The company began producing Swift subcompacts in 1983 and sold them through GM as the Chevy Sprint and, later, as the Geo Metro. In 1986 Suzuki and GM of Canada jointly formed CAMI Automotive to produce vehicles, including Sprints, Metros, and Geo Trackers (Suzuki Sidekicks), in Ontario. Production began in 1989.

Although sales via GM increased through 1990, US efforts with the Suzuki nameplate faltered shortly after Suzuki formed its US subsidiary in Brea, California, in 1986. A 1988 *Consumer Reports'* claim that the company's Samurai SUV was prone to rolling over devastated US sales. The next year Suzuki's top US executives quit, apparently questioning the company's commitment to the US market.

Suzuki established Magyar Suzuki, a joint venture with Hungarian automaker Autokonszern Rt., C. Itoh & Co., and International Finance Corporation in 1991 to begin producing the Swift sedan in Hungary. The company expanded a licensing agreement with a Chinese government partner in 1993, becoming the first Japanese company to take an equity stake in a Chinese carmaking venture. The next year Suzuki introduced the Alto van, Japan's cheapest car, at just over $5,000, and the Wagon R miniwagon, which quickly became one of Japan's top-selling vehicles.

In a case that was later overturned, a woman was awarded $90 million from Suzuki after being paralyzed in a Samurai rollover in 1990. The company sued Consumers Union, publisher of *Consumer Reports*, in 1996, charging it had intended to fix the results in the 1988 Samurai testing.

In 1997 Suzuki accused the Indian government of stacking the board of directors of their Maruti Udyog joint venture (India's most successful car company) with government officials. GM raised its 3% stake in Suzuki to 10% in 1998; in 1999 GM and Suzuki announced that in 2001 they would begin producing a small car for the Asian market, reportedly to be made in India. In 2000 the company decided to team up with GM and Fuji Heavy Industries (Subaru) to develop compact cars for the European market. It was also announced that GM would spend about $600 million to double its stake in Suzuki to 20%.

Chairman and CEO: Osamu Suzuki
President and COO: Masao Toda
EVP: Akira Tsutsui
EVP: Sokichi Nakano
Senior Managing Director: Keiji Yamauchi
Senior Managing Director: Yuichi Nakamura
Senior Managing Director: Chuichi Mizuguchi
Senior Managing Director: Kotaro Naito
Managing Director: Katsuhiro Yokota
Managing Director: Chosuke Sato
Managing Director: Kouhei Murata
Managing Director: Toshitaka Suzuki
Managing Director: Tsuneo Kobayashi
Managing Director: Takahira Kiriyama
Managing Director: Osamu Matsuoka
Managing Director: Hiroshi Tsuda
Auditors: Seimei Audit Corporation

HQ: 300 Takatsuka-cho, Hamamatsu-shi,
Shizuoka 432-91, Japan
Phone: +81-53-440-2061 **Fax:** +81-53-440-2776
US HQ: 3251 E. Imperial Hwy., Brea, CA 92821
US Phone: 714-996-7040 **US Fax:** 714-524-8499
Web site: http://www.suzuki.co.jp

Suzuki Motor Corporation operates more than 60
manufacturing facilities in nearly 30 countries.

2000 Sales

	% of total
Japan	71
Europe	15
Other regions	14
Total	**100**

2000 Sales

	% of total
Automobiles	65
Motorcycles	14
Other products	21
Total	**100**

Selected Products

Cars, Minicars, and SUVs	GS series500	QuadRunner
Alto	Intruder series	series
Baleno	JRseries	
Grand Vitara	Katana 750	**Other Products**
Ignis	Marauder	Electro-scooters
Jimny	RM series	General-purpose
Swift	Savage	engines
Wagon R	**All Terrain**	Generators
	Vehicles	Motorized
Motorcycles	King Quad	wheelchairs
Bandit	QuadMaster	Outboard motors
DR series		Prefabricated
		houses

BMW	Honda	Peugeot Motors
Bombardier	Hyundai	of America, Inc.
Brunswick	Invacare	Piaggio
DaimlerChrysler	Isuzu	Renault
Delco Remy	Kawasaki Heavy	Saab Automobile
Dover	Industries	Toyota
Ek Chor China	Kohler	Triumph
Motorcycle	Mazda	Motorcycles
Fiat	Mitsubishi	Volkswagen
Ford	Nissan	Volvo
General Motors	Outboard Marine	Yamaha Motor
Harley-Davidson		

Tokyo: 7269 FYE: March 31	Annual Growth	3/91	3/92	3/93	3/94	3/95	3/96	3/97	3/98	3/99	3/00
Sales (¥ bil.)	2.6%	1,210	1,249	1,259	1,227	1,258	1,381	1,502	1,489	1,456	1,521
Net income (¥ bil.)	5.9%	16	20	19	15	20	27	34	30	24	27
Income as % of sales	—	1.3%	1.6%	1.5%	1.2%	1.6%	2.0%	2.3%	2.0%	1.6%	1.8%
Earnings per share (¥)	3.9%	39.00	48.00	45.00	34.00	45.00	59.00	75.00	67.00	52.00	55.00
Stock price - FY high (¥)	—	1,020	775	951	1,460	1,520	1,390	1,510	1,520	1,650	2,265
Stock price - FY low (¥)	—	520	580	598	879	826	828	1,010	1,010	1,064	1,435
Stock price - FY close (¥)	9.2%	710	628	919	1,250	929	1,320	1,200	1,250	1,571	1,565
P/E - high	—	26	16	21	43	34	24	20	23	32	41
P/E - low	—	13	12	13	26	18	14	13	15	20	26
Dividends per share (¥)	1.4%	7.50	7.50	7.50	7.50	7.50	8.50	8.50	7.50	7.50	8.50
Book value per share (¥)	8.2%	500.00	538.00	579.00	624.00	610.00	717.00	785.00	853.00	906.00	1,018.00
Employees	1.0%	13,561	12,757	13,013	13,218	13,455	14,650	13,873	13,820	14,760	14,800

HIGH/LOW/CLOSE

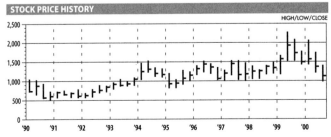

Debt ratio: 24.1%
Return on equity: —
Cash (¥ mil.): 209,427
Current ratio: 1.08
Long-term debt (¥ mil.): 26,914
No. of shares (mil.): 489
Dividends
  Yield: 0.0%
  Payout: 0.2%
Market value ($ mil.): 7,249
Sales ($ mil.): 14,407

SWIRE PACIFIC LIMITED

OVERVIEW

A scion of British Hong Kong, Swire Pacific, the venerable Hong Kong *hong* (general trading company), still wields power in Hong Kong under the sovereignty of China. Swire Pacific owns and develops prime real estate in Hong Kong, including its flagship Cityplaza shopping center. Despite the collapse of the local property market, about 68% of the company's operating profits come from real estate dealings. Other holdings include about 45% of international carrier Cathay Pacific Airways and interests in regional carrier Dragonair and an airfreight company. The company is also involved in apparel, sugar, and manufacturing operations, and in marine services.

Swire, which has holdings in Europe, North America, and other parts of Asia, has assiduously allied itself with Chinese interests through joint ventures in Hong Kong and Taiwan and on the mainland. These businesses include Coca-Cola soft drink operations and a 49% stake in brewer Carlsberg's operations in the region. It also has joint ventures with Allied Waste (waste services), Crown Cork & Seal (aluminum cans), ICI (paint), and Tate & Lyle (sugar). Swire is controlled from the UK by its founding family. Privately held John Swire & Sons owns about 28% of Swire Pacific and more than 50% of its voting shares.

HISTORY

John Swire began a Liverpool trading company in 1816. By the time he died in 1847, the company, John Swire & Sons, derived much of its revenues from the US cotton trade. One of Swire's sons, John Samuel Swire, refocused the company on Chinese tea and textiles during the US Civil War. Unhappy with his representatives in Asia, Swire went to Shanghai and in 1866 partnered with customer Richard Butterfield. Butterfield & Swire (B&S) took *Taikoo* ("great and ancient") as a Chinese name. Butterfield soon left, but his name lived on with the company until 1974.

By 1868 B&S had offices in New York and Yokohama, Japan; it added a Hong Kong office two years later. The firm created China Navigation Company in 1872 to transport goods on the Yangtze River; the shipping line served all the major Pacific Rim ports by the late 1880s. Hong Kong-based Taikoo Sugar Refinery began operations in 1884.

The third John Swire took over B&S in 1898 and built the Taikoo Dockyard in Hong Kong. The company's Chinese operations were eventually devastated by the Japanese attack on China in 1937, WWII, and the Communist takeover in 1949. However, the company had rebuilt in Hong Kong, and in 1948 it bought control of Cathay Pacific, a Hong Kong airline with six DC-3s.

In the 1950s and 1960s the Swire family expanded the airline and established airport and aircraft service companies. Swire Pacific, the holding company for most of the family's Hong Kong interests, went public in 1959. It won the Coca-Cola bottling franchise for Hong Kong in 1965. The fifth generation of Swires, John and Adrian, took command of parent company John Swire & Sons in 1968 (Adrian became chairman in 1987). The Taikoo Dockyard merged with Hongkong & Whampoa Dockyard in 1972.

The 1984 agreement to return Hong Kong to Chinese control in 1997 plunged the colony into uncertainty. Capital flight and free-falling real estate values gave Swire an opportunity to pick up properties at bargain prices.

Meanwhile, Cathay Pacific had become a major Pacific carrier. In 1987 Swire sold about 12% of the airline to CITIC, China's state-owned overseas investment company. (CITIC later increased its share.) Three years later Swire bought 35% of Hong Kong's Dragonair, also partly owned by CITIC, and gave it Cathay Pacific's Shanghai and Beijing routes.

In the 1990s Swire's financial results and property values fluctuated along with confidence about the consequences of China's takeover. In 1997 Swire expanded its Chinese operations, acquiring the rights to distribute Volvo cars in China and Hong Kong. As Asian financial markets collapsed, Swire sold its insurance-underwriting businesses to focus on core operations. Adrian Swire stepped down that year, relinquishing the John Swire & Sons chairmanship to a nonfamily member, Edward Scott.

To expand its dwindling undeveloped property base, in 1998 a Swire-led consortium bought a reclaimed waterfront site on Hong Kong Island. Reflecting a rebounding economy, in 1999 the company sold more than 274,000 sq. ft. of Hong Kong office space to Time Warner and Cable & Wireless HKT.

In 2000 Swire sold its health care and medical products trading unit Swire Loxley to diversified Chinese company CITIC Pacific.

OFFICERS

Chairman, Swire Pacific, Cathay Pacific Airways, and Swire Properties: J. W. J. Hughes-Hallett, age 50
Finance Director: M. Cubbon, age 42
Executive Director, Aviation Division; VC and CEO, Cathay Pacific Airways; Chairman, Hong Kong Aircraft Engineering: D. M. Turnbull, age 44
Executive Director, Property Division; Managing Director, Swire Properties: K. G. Kerr, age 47
Executive Director; Chairman Taiwan Operations: D. Ho, age 52
Executive Director; Staff Director John Swire & Sons: Michael J. Bell, age 52
Secretary: P. A. Moore, age 42
Auditors: PricewaterhouseCoopers

LOCATIONS

HQ: 35th Fl., 2 Pacific Place,
88 Queensway, Hong Kong
Phone: +852-2840-8098   **Fax:** +852-2526-9365
Web site: http://www.swirepacific.com

1999 Sales

	% of total
Asia	
Hong Kong	53
Other countries	15
North America	23
Europe	4
Shipowning & other revenues	5
Total	**100**

PRODUCTS/OPERATIONS

1999 Sales

	% of total
Property	42
Beverages	27
Trading	22
Marine services	5
Industrial	4
Total	**100**

Selected Operations
AHK Air Hong Kong Ltd. (34%, cargo airline)
Carlsberg Brewery Hong Kong Ltd. (49%)
Cathay Pacific Airways Ltd. (45%)
Crown Can Hong Kong Ltd. (40%)
ICI Swire Paints Ltd. (40%)
Swire Beverages Holdings Ltd.
Swire Coca-Cola HK Ltd. (88%, soft drink production and distribution)
Swire Pacific Holdings Inc. (property, US)
Swire Pacific Ship Management Ltd. (ship personnel management)
Swire Properties Ltd.
Swire Resources Ltd (general trading and retailing)
Taikoo Motors Ltd. (automobile distribution)
Tate & Lyle Swire Ltd. (33%)
Waylung Waste Collection Ltd. (50%)

COMPETITORS

AMR	Hyundai	Northwest
China Southern	ITOCHU	Airlines
Airlines	JAL	PepsiCo
Hopewell	Jardine	Qantas
Holdings	Matheson	Sime Darby
HSBC Holdings	Kumagai Gumi	Singapore
Hutchison	Marks & Spencer	Airlines
Whampoa	Mitsubishi	UAL

HISTORICAL FINANCIALS & EMPLOYEES

OTC: SWRAY FYE: December 31	Annual Growth	12/90	12/91	12/92	12/93	12/94	12/95	12/96	12/97	12/98	12/99
Sales ($ mil.)	(6.6%)	3,996	4,321	5,027	5,278	6,155	6,939	4,847	3,163	2,182	2,170
Net income ($ mil.)	6.9%	314	396	571	603	719	835	990	862	228	571
Income as % of sales	—	7.9%	9.2%	11.4%	11.4%	11.7%	12.0%	20.4%	27.2%	10.4%	26.3%
Earnings per share ($)	6.7%	0.20	0.25	0.36	0.38	0.45	0.53	0.62	0.55	0.15	0.36
Stock price – FY high ($)	—	2.88	3.11	4.94	9.05	8.99	8.27	10.13	9.88	6.75	10.63
Stock price – FY low ($)	—	1.80	1.89	2.95	3.72	5.50	4.94	7.50	4.50	2.15	3.63
Stock price – FY close ($)	13.8%	1.88	3.00	3.77	8.98	6.22	7.75	9.50	5.50	4.38	6.00
P/E – high	—	14	12	14	24	20	16	16	18	46	30
P/E – low	—	9	8	8	10	12	9	12	8	15	10
Dividends per share ($)	3.8%	0.10	0.11	0.13	0.15	0.18	0.21	0.23	0.23	0.11	0.14
Book value per share ($)	16.9%	2.30	2.82	3.73	4.98	5.78	5.82	8.22	12.56	8.53	9.38
Employees	6.9%	—	36,300	—	30,000	35,000	37,000	56,000	60,000	58,000	—

STOCK PRICE HISTORY   HIGH/LOW/CLOSE

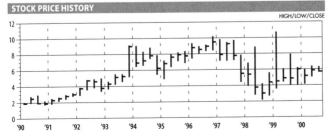

1999 FISCAL YEAR-END
Debt ratio: 20.4%
Return on equity: 6.8%
Cash ($ mil.): 70
Current ratio: 0.66
Long-term debt ($ mil.): 1,762
No. of shares (mil.): 940
Dividends
 Yield: 0.0%
 Payout: 0.4%
Market value ($ mil.): 5,640

TATA ENTERPRISES

OVERVIEW

From the Bay of Bengal to Kashmir, Indians know the Tata name. Based in Mumbai, Tata Enterprises is India's largest industrial conglomerate, with more than 80 subsidiaries and affiliates. The group's biggest businesses have traditionally been steel and automobiles — Tata Iron and Steel Company and Tata Engineering and Locomotive Company. Although a recessionary economy has taken its toll on India's heavy industries, Tata has had better success with its information technology and other growth businesses led by Tata Consultancy Services.

The group has holdings in chemicals and pharmaceuticals, metals, agribusiness, consumer products, power, heavy construction, import/export, shipping, financial services, hotels, information technology and communications networks, and business services. The company has alliances with numerous major foreign companies, including DaimlerChrysler, Johnson Controls, Microsoft, and Thyssen Krupp.

The Tata family's ownership stakes are managed through Tata Sons Ltd., the group's principal holding company, of which the family owns about 3%. Much of the remainder is held by charitable trusts established by the Tata family; about 66% of Tata Sons' profits are channeled into philanthropic trusts. Tata Sons generally holds only minority stakes in the group's companies, but maintains control with the support of other investors, including state-owned financial institutions.

Tata Sons chairman CEO Ratan Tata is overseeing a major restructuring of the group, aimed at paring down its bureacracy, pulling out of noncore businesses, and making individual companies more cost-efficient and customer-responsive.

HISTORY

Jamsetji Tata, a Parsi (Zoroastrian) from Bombay, started a textile trading company in 1868. He began manufacturing textiles, then embarked on a mission to industrialize India. Before his death in 1904 Tata had built the Taj Mahal Hotel in Bombay and set in motion plans to create a hydroelectric power plant, a forum for technical education and research in India, and a steel mill (and workers' town) to supply rapidly expanding railroads.

Jamsetji's son, Dorabji, carried on. Dorabji found a jungle site for the steel mill, renamed the area Jamshedpur after his father, and in 1907 established Tata Iron and Steel. Three years later Tata Hydro-Electric Power went on line. By 1911 Jamsetji's plans were realized when the Indian Institute of Science opened.

The British chairman of the Railway Board promised "to eat every pound of steel rail" Tata made. Dorabji lamented the man's probable indigestion after the mill shipped 1,500 miles of rail to British troops in Mesopotamia during WWI.

Six years after Dorabji's death in 1932, J. R. D. Tata, the son of Dorabji's cousin, took over the family empire. India's first licensed pilot, J. R. D. had started Tata Airlines, later nationalized as part of Air India. He started Tata Chemicals in 1939. After WWII and Indian independence, the government built a state-owned steel industry but allowed Tata's mills to operate through a grandfather clause. Inefficient government operations led to high fixed prices for steel, and Tata profited.

Tata Engineering and Locomotive, founded in 1945 to make steam locomotives, entered truck production in 1954 by collaborating with Daimler-Benz (now DaimlerChrysler). With help from Swiss firm Volkart Brothers, the company also started the Voltas manufacturing conglomerate. In 1962 Tata teamed with James Finlay of Scotland to create Tata-Finlay, now Tata Tea.

For a long time India's socialist government and unwieldy bureaucracy hampered Tata. The group was reluctant to pay bribes for licenses to enter new fields, and red tape and trade restrictions discouraged international expansion. A 1970 antitrust law ended the "managing agency" system, in which Tata Sons had held interests in subsidiary companies and Tata Industries managed them for a fee. The subsidiaries became independently managed.

J. R. D. retired as chairman in 1991, and his cousin Ratan Tata became head of the company. In 1994 Tata formed a major alliance with Daimler-Benz to assemble cars. A Tata IBM joint venture in 1997 launched the first computer operating system in Hindi, India's national language (Tata sold its IBM stake in 1999).

Not every new venture flew. In 1998 Tata dropped a proposal to start a Indian airline that hadn't won government approval after three years. But tea and sympathy weren't necessary. In 2000 Tata Tea bought UK tea bag maker Tetley in one of the largest overseas takeovers by an Indian company.

Chairman, Tata Sons Limited, Tata Industries, Tata Engineering, Tata Electric Companies, and The Indian Hotels Company: Ratan N. Tata
Director, Tata Sons Limited: N. A. Soonawala
Managing Director, Tata Industries: Kishor Chaukar
Chairman, Nelco Limited: K. M. Gherda
Chairman, Voltas International: A. H. Tobaccowala
Deputy Chairman, Tata Consultancy Services: Faqir C. Kohli
Managing Director, Voltas: Nawshir Khurody
CEO, Tata Consultancy Services: S. Ramadorai
Managing Director, Indian Hotels: R. K. Krishna Kumar
Managing Director, Tata Asset Management: K. N. Atmaramani
Managing Director, Tata Chemicals: Manu Sheth
Managing Director, Tata Infotech: Nirmal Jain
Managing Director, Tata Iron and Steel: J. J. Irani
Managing Director, Tata Tea: S. M. Kidwai
EVP, Tata Consultancy Services: S. Mahalingam
VP, Tata Tea: S. S. Dogra
Director Human Resources: Manab Bose
Auditors: A.F. Ferguson & Co.

HQ: Tata Sons Limited,
Bombay House, 24 Homi Mody St.,
Fort Mumbai, Mumbai 400 001, India
Phone: +91-22-204-9131   **Fax:** +91-22-204-8187
US HQ: 101 Park Ave. , New York, NY 10178
US Phone: 212-557-7979   **US Fax:** 212-557-7987
Web site: http://www.tata.com

Besides having a strong presence in India, Tata Enterprises has several operations in the following countries: Algeria, Iran, Iraq, Kuwait, Laos, Liberia, Malaysia, Oman, the Philippines, Saudi Arabia, Singapore, Tanzania, and Uzbekistan. The Indian Hotels Company Ltd. has hotels in India, Oman, the UK, the United Arab Emirates, the US, Yemen, and Zambia.

Major Areas of Operation
Agribusinesses
Automobiles
Chemicals and pharmaceuticals
Consumer products
Energy
Engineering
Exports
Finance and investment
Information technology and consultancy services
Metals and associated industries
Services

Selected Group Companies
Hitech Drilling Services India Ltd.
The Indian Hotels Company Ltd.
The National Radio and Electronics Co. Ltd.
Tata Chemicals Ltd.
Tata Consultancy Services
Tata Electric Cos.
Tata Engineering and Locomotive Co. Ltd.
  (commercial vehicles)
Tata Finance Ltd.
Tata Honeywell Ltd. (joint venture)
Tata Industries Ltd.
Tata Infotech Ltd.
Tata Iron and Steel Co. Ltd.
Tata Lucent Technologies Ltd. (joint venture)
Tata Sons Ltd.
Tata Tea Ltd. (tea and spices)
Tata Telecom Ltd.
Voltas Ltd. (commercial and industrial products)

Accor	Indian Oil
Caterpillar	James Finlay
Compaq	Mitsubishi
Daewoo	Mitsui
Fluor	Nippon Steel
Ford	Procter & Gamble
Four Seasons Hotels	Ritz Carlton
GE	Sumitomo
General Motors	Suzuki
Hilton	Toyota
Hyatt	Unilever
Hyundai	

Group FYE: March 31	Annual Growth	3/90	3/91	3/92	3/93	3/94	3/95	3/96	3/97	3/98	3/99
Sales ($ mil.)	(10.3%)	—	—	—	—	—	—	—	—	8,407	7,541
Employees	(2.7%)	—	—	—	—	—	—	—	—	262,000	255,000

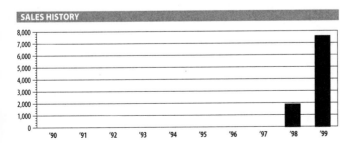

SALES HISTORY

TATE & LYLE PLC

OVERVIEW

If bread helps us sustain life, Tate & Lyle helps us enjoy it. The London-based company is one of the world's largest sweetener and starch processing groups, with operations on five continents. Tate & Lyle processes sugar beets and cane into white and raw sugar, as well as sugar by-products such as molasses (used in animal feed). The company takes wheat and corn and makes citric acids (used in foods and beverages), starches (used in foodstuffs and packaging), and sweeteners (corn syrup, fructose, and others used in

beverages, baked goods, and pharmaceuticals). Tate & Lyle also offers Sucralose, a low-calorie sweetener made from sugar and sold under the name Splenda.

The company has a bevy of top national sugar brands. Domino Sugar holds about 20% of the US market. In the UK, its flagship Tate & Lyle is one of the UK's best-known brands. Other prominent brands include Alcantara in Portugal and Redpath in Canada. Archer Daniels Midland (corn and wheat processor, US) owns about 6% of Tate & Lyle.

HISTORY

Henry Tate founded Henry Tate & Sons in 1869 and the next year began building a sugar refinery in Liverpool. Tate was noted for his philanthropy, and in 1896 he provided the money to found the Tate Gallery. When he died three years later, he left the business to his sons. In 1903 William Henry Tate took the company public, although only 17 investors, primarily family members, put up money for the company.

Abram Lyle founded his sugar company in 1881 when he bought Odam's and Plaistow Wharves, on the River Thames, to build a sugar refinery. While Tate focused on sugar cubes, Lyle concentrated on a sugary concoction called Golden Syrup.

WWI saw an interruption in raw beet sugar imports from Germany and Austria, and in 1918 the two companies began discussing a merger. Although they combined, creating Tate & Lyle in 1921, they kept separate sales organizations into the 1940s. Seeking new sources of sugar, Tate & Lyle began investing abroad. In 1937 it created the West Indies Sugar Company and built a processing plant in Jamaica.

Although WWII brought sugar rationing (1940) and both of Tate & Lyle's London factories were severely damaged by bombs, there was great demand for the company's inexpensive syrup. Following the war, a movement to nationalize Tate & Lyle failed, thanks in part to a campaign featuring a cartoon character named "Mr. Cube" who spouted slogans such as "Only the State will make my price jump!"

In the 1950s Tate & Lyle expanded, buying Rhodesian Sugar Refineries (1953, now ZSR) and Canada & Dominion Sugar Company (1959, later Redpath Industries). It added United Molasses in 1965.

Tate & Lyle acquired the only other independent British cane refiner, Manbre and Garton, in 1976. That year it entered the US

market when it bought Refined Sugars. A collapse in sugar prices led Tate & Lyle to close its original Liverpool plant and lay off many third-generation workers.

As the company rebounded, it began to expand, adding Portugese sugar refiner Alcantara in 1983; US beet refiner Great Western Sugar Company in 1985; and Staley Continental (now A E Staley Manufacturing), a major producer of high-fructose corn syrup, in 1988. That year it sold Staley's food service business to SYSCO for $700 million and bought Amstar Sugar Corporation (which became Domino Sugar) for about $300 million. Tate & Lyle launched Sucralose, a low-calorie sweetener, in 1991 in cooperation with Johnson & Johnson.

The company began investing millions in emerging markets in 1990 through acquisitions and joint ventures, including Mexico's Occidente in 1995. Although operations in Ukraine and Bulgaria were abandoned the next year, Tate & Lyle continued with new ventures in Vietnam and India.

Larry Pillard became CEO in 1996. Sucralose was approved for use in the US in 1998. Also in 1998 Tate & Lyle purchased the food ingredients division of Bayer AG's Haarmann & Reimer unit for about $219 million, renaming it Tate & Lyle Citric Acid. The deal made Tate & Lyle the only global producer of citric acid.

In 1999 Tate & Lyle sold its 61% share of Industrias de Maiz SA (Argentina) for almost $81 million. Sugar prices in the US remained low due to bumper harvests, which affected the company's 1999 bottom line. Tate & Lyle put its UK animal feed units up for sale in 1999 to streamline its portfolio.

In June 2000 Tate & Lyle sold Bundaberg, its Australian sugar company, to Société Financière de Sucres for more than $250 million. It also attained full ownership of Europe's Amylum (sweeteners and starches).

Non-Executive Chairman: David Lees, age 63, $300,000 pay
Chief Executive: Larry G. Pillard, age 53, $540,000 pay
Group Finance Director: Simon Gifford, age 54, $540,000 pay
President, Group Operations: Loren Luppes
President, AE Staley Manufacturing, and Tate & Lyle Citric Acid: D Lynn Grider
President, Tate & Lyle North American Sugars: Clive Rutherford
CEO, Tate & Lyle Europe: Stanley Musesengwa
Managing Director, European Division: John H. W. Walker, $426,000 pay
Managing Director, International Division: Walker Stuart Strathdee, age 49, $363,000 pay
Director Group Human Resources: Chris Moynihan
Company Secretary: John Hunter
General Counsel: Robert Gibber
Auditors: PricewaterhouseCoopers LLP

LOCATIONS

HQ: Sugar Quay, Lower Thames St., London EC3R 6DQ, United Kingdom
Phone: +44-20-7626-6525   **Fax:** +44-20-7623-5213
US HQ: 2200 E. El Dorado St., Decatur, IL 62521
US Phone: 217-423-4411   **US Fax:** 217-421-2216
Web site: http://www.tate-lyle.co.uk

Tate & Lyle has plants in more than 50 countries in Africa, Asia, Europe, and North and South America.

PRODUCTS/OPERATIONS

Selected Brands
Alcantara (Portugal)
Domino Sugar (US)
Lyle's Golden Syrup
Redpath (Canada)
Splenda (low-calorie sweetener)
Tate & Lyle (UK)
Whitespoon (Africa)

Selected Products
Animal feed (molasses)
Corn sweeteners (dextrose, fructose, glucose, high fructose corn syrup, maltodextrin)
Fermentation products (amino acid, citric acid, ethanol, monosodium glutamate, polyols, potable alcohol)
Starches and starch derivatives
Sugar (beet, cane, raw, white)

COMPETITORS

ADM
Ag Processing
American Crystal Sugar
Associated British Foods
Cargill
Corn Products International
CSM
Eridania Béghin-Say
Genesee
Imperial Sugar
Onex
Penford
Pharmacia
PPB Group
Südzucker AG
U.S. Sugar

HISTORICAL FINANCIALS & EMPLOYEES

OTC: TATYY FYE: March 31	Annual Growth	9/90	9/91	9/92	9/93	9/94	9/95	9/96	9/97	9/98	*3/00
Sales ($ mil.)	3.9%	6,349	5,640	5,854	5,532	6,427	6,577	8,063	7,514	7,588	8,987
Net income ($ mil.)	(1.4%)	332	252	206	223	270	307	272	164	211	293
Income as % of sales	—	5.2%	4.5%	3.5%	4.0%	4.2%	4.7%	3.4%	2.2%	2.8%	3.3%
Earnings per share ($)	1.7%	2.19	2.31	1.86	1.96	2.34	2.66	2.39	1.44	1.84	2.56
Stock price - FY high ($)	—	22.00	28.41	31.80	26.06	28.34	29.45	30.30	33.25	36.50	31.00
Stock price - FY low ($)	—	17.63	17.69	22.03	21.56	21.72	24.92	27.19	26.00	21.63	13.00
Stock price - FY close ($)	(2.6%)	17.63	27.73	24.27	22.38	28.02	28.41	29.22	28.75	21.63	13.95
P/E - high	—	10	12	17	13	12	11	13	23	20	12
P/E - low	—	8	8	12	11	9	9	11	18	12	5
Dividends per share ($)	9.6%	0.75	0.78	0.85	0.78	0.91	0.99	1.06	1.17	1.15	1.72
Book value per share ($)	3.5%	11.21	12.09	12.09	13.51	15.96	16.76	16.93	12.71	16.18	15.34
Employees	2.8%	—	16,159	15,834	15,450	15,450	17,743	21,281	21,435	21,494	20,085

*Fiscal year change

STOCK PRICE HISTORY

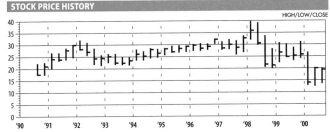

HIGH/LOW/CLOSE

2000 FISCAL YEAR-END

Debt ratio: 49.2%
Return on equity: 16.3%
Cash ($ mil.): 81
Current ratio: 1.32
Long-term debt ($ mil.): 1,006
No. of shares (mil.): 114
Dividends
  Yield: 0.1%
  Payout: 0.7%
Market value ($ mil.): 1,594

TATUNG CO.

OVERVIEW

Tatung's far flung. The Taipei, Taiwan-based electronics giant manufactures more than 300 products that it sells in more than 100 countries. Its Computers and Communications segment makes PCs, workstations, and servers, as well as peripherals such as CD-ROM drives. Tatung's Consumer Products segment produces appliances ranging from rice cookers to refrigerators. The company's Industrial Products operations manufacture cable and wire, transformers, and motors, among other products.

The company has subsidiaries in nearly a dozen countries. Taiwan-based subsidiaries include Tatung OTIS Elevator (a joint venture with US-based elevator maker Otis), Chunghwa

Picture Tubes (cathode-ray tube and LCD products), and San Chih Semiconductor (silicon wafers). Its US operations include Tatung Co. of America (computers and peripherals), Tatung Science and Technology (SPARC workstations and servers), and Tatung Telecom Corporation (telecommunications equipment). Tatung also has operations in Canada, Mexico, Europe, and other areas of Asia.

Tatung promotes its partnership with two schools, Tatung University and Tatung Senior High School, endowed by Tatung's founder. Tatung is currently overseen by chairman Lin Tingsheng (T.S.), the son, and president Lin Weishan (W.S.), the grandson, of its founder.

HISTORY

In 1918 Shan-Chih Lin founded a construction company, the Shan-Chih Business Association. Projects complete during its 30-year lifespan included the Taiwanese government's Building of the Executive Yuan, which houses the country's ministry offices.

The company entered heavy industry in 1946 when it began repairing railway cars. It diversified into electric products in 1949 with fans, which it started exporting five years later. In 1950 the company changed its name to Tatung ("great harmony").

Because he believed strongly in the importance of education, when Lin retired in 1942, he donated 80% of his assets to the Hsieh-Chih Association for the Development of Industry, which went on to administer scholarships, awards, the Tatung Institute of Technology, and the Hsieh-Chih Industrial Publishing Company. The philanthropist's bequest established the Tatung Schools-Company, made up of the Institute of Technology and Tatung High School. This education-industry cooperative provides hands-on training in Tatung factories and offices. The Institute of Technology was founded in 1956.

During the 1960s Tatung expanded further into home appliances and electronics, adding refrigerators (1961), air conditioners (1964), and televisions (1964) to its product line. Taiwan Telecommunication was formed in 1966.

Lin died in 1971. In 1972 Lin's grandson, Lin Weishan (W. S.) was named president; he began expanding Tatung's operations overseas. Tatung established US subsidiary Tatung Co. of America that year, initially to make electric fans. In 1973 Tatung formed a joint venture with Japanese computer maker Fujitsu. Tatung would go on

that decade to establish offices in Japan (1975) and Korea (1979).

The company formed a joint venture with the US's Otis Elevator in 1983. Tatung continued to expand overseas during the 1980s, establishing subsidiaries in the UK (1981) and Germany (1985). During that period the company continued to move production overseas, shipping finished goods back to Taiwan as imports.

Tatung's profits slipped in the early 1990s as Taiwan's economy slowed, but the company rebounded, signing a deal with Packard Bell (folded into NEC) in 1991 to supply the computer marketer with 100,000 PCs a month. In 1994 the company formed an alliance with telecommunications company QUALCOMM to develop cellular phone systems for Taiwan.

The following year Tatung subsidiary Chunghwa Picture Tubes began making large picture tubes for Toshiba. Tatung started making computer motherboards in 1996.

To keep pace with Internet use, the company in 1997 introduced an Internet access set-top box. Sales were down that fiscal year, a result of the Asian economic crisis and falling cathode-ray tube prices. In 1998 Tatung unveiled a DVD player and its PC Cinema, a PC combining TV, computer, and telephone functions with Internet access.

In 1999 Chunghwa Picture Tubes opened Taiwan's first factory to build thin-film transistor LCDs. The subsidiary's chairman was indicted later that year for allegedly investing foreign capital to manipulate parent Tatung's stock. In 2000 Tatung spun off its information and communications department as a separate company, Tatung System Technologies.

Chairman: Lin Tingsheng
President: Lin Weishan
Chairman, President, and CEO, Tatung Co. of America: Lun Kwan Lin
CFO, Tatung Co. of America: Michael Lai
Secretary: Frank D. Lin
Manager Human Resources, Tatung Co. of America: Albert Peres

LOCATIONS

HQ: 22 Chungshan North Rd., Sec. 3, Taipei, Taiwan
Phone: +886-22-592-5252   **Fax:** +886-22-598-4509
US HQ: 2850 El Presidio St., Long Beach, CA 90810
US Phone: 310-637-2105   **US Fax:** 310-637-8484
Web site: http://www.tatung.com.tw

Tatung has operations in Canada, Hong Kong, Japan, Mexico, the Netherlands, Singapore, South Korea, Taiwan, Thailand, the UK, and the US.

PRODUCTS/OPERATIONS

Selected Products

Computers and Communications
Cable set-top boxes
CD-ROM drives
Internet services (TSINet, Chinese-language Tatung Internet Service Network)
Monitors
PCs
Servers
Silicon wafers
Workstations

Consumer
Air conditioners and dehumidifiers
Appliances
Components
Office furniture and office furniture systems
Televisions and video displays
Watt-hour meters

Industrial
Copper rods
Cyclos
Elevators
Industrial castings
Motors
Switch gears
Transformers
Varnishes and varnish thinners
Wire and cable (including communications and power cable)

COMPETITORS

Acer	Kyocera	Sagem
Aiwa	Lennox	Samsung
Casio Computer	LG Group	SANYO
Compaq	Marconi	Sharp
Daewoo	Marubeni	Siemens
Dell Computer	Matsushita	Sony
Dover	Maytag	Sun
Electrolux AB	Mitsumi Electric	Microsystems
Emerson	NEC	Toshiba
Fujitsu	Nokia	United
GE	Oki Electric	Technologies
Hewlett-Packard	Philips	Whirlpool
Hitachi	Electronics	Yamaha
IBM	Pioneer	Zenith

HISTORICAL FINANCIALS & EMPLOYEES

Taiwan: 2371 FYE: December 31	Annual Growth	12/90	12/91	12/92	12/93	12/94	12/95	12/96	12/97	12/98	12/99
Sales (T$ mil.)	19.7%	27,767	44,808	52,042	54,431	64,842	84,698	83,573	70,313	94,110	140,160
Net income (T$ mil.)	40.6%	216	405	1,216	3,509	5,391	6,606	7,408	4,003	(438)	4,630
Income as % of sales	—	0.8%	0.9%	2.3%	6.4%	8.3%	7.8%	8.9%	5.7%	—	3.3%
Earnings per share (T$)	12.3%	—	—	0.52	1.52	2.02	2.37	2.61	1.38	(0.11)	1.17
Stock price - FY high (T$)	—	—	—	8.84	26.80	35.03	32.35	47.43	45.35	34.40	43.90
Stock price - FY low (T$)	—	—	—	5.92	6.07	19.35	23.12	39.09	25.93	16.28	25.00
Stock price - FY close (T$)	31.1%	—	—	6.41	26.80	30.21	30.09	43.88	31.06	30.60	42.70
P/E - high	—	—	—	17	18	17	14	18	33	—	38
P/E - low	—	—	—	11	4	10	10	15	19	—	21
Dividends per share (T$)	—	—	—	0.00	0.00	0.43	0.53	0.83	0.50	0.00	0.00
Book value per share (T$)	6.2%	—	—	7.45	9.05	11.85	13.57	16.06	18.22	10.28	11.33
Employees	(1.1%)	21,300	20,552	26,550	26,000	17,869	19,491	20,671	19,750	—	—

STOCK PRICE HISTORY

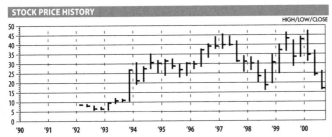
HIGH/LOW/CLOSE

1999 FISCAL YEAR-END

Debt ratio: 34.6%
Return on equity: 10.8%
Cash (T$ mil.): 22,003
Current ratio: 1.24
Long-term debt (T$ mil.): 23,788
No. of shares (mil.): 3,971
Dividends
  Yield: —
  Payout: —
Market value ($ mil.): 5,403
Sales ($ mil.): 4,467

TDK CORPORATION

OVERVIEW

TDK remains a fountain of ferrite — a ceramic material with countless uses in electronics — but it has expanded far beyond its roots as a materials supplier.

The company is a major manufacturer of electronics products from cassette tapes to disk drive components to multilayer chip capacitors. Tokyo-based TDK manufactures a broad array of devices including magnetoresistive heads for computer drives and other recording devices, recording media such as audio- and videotapes, capacitors and other ceramic and assembled components, magnetic products such as ferrite cores, and semiconductor products.

The company has stepped up R&D efforts by establishing two internal research organizations focused on new technologies for telecommunications and data storage applications. TDK's growth strategy calls for a focus on the recording and communications markets. The company also plans to augment its traditional core strengths in discrete passive components and recording media with enhanced lines of products that incorporate integrated circuits.

Japanese consumer electronics giant Matsushita owns 5% of TDK.

HISTORY

Japan's Yogoru Kato is credited with inventing ferrite, a type of ceramic (made mainly from iron oxide) that was believed to hold promise for electronics applications. In 1935 Kanzo Saito, who seven years before had been raising rabbits for their fur, took out a patent on ferrite and founded Tokyo Denkikagaku Kogyo K.K. (TDK) to pioneer its mass production. TDK's ferrite output swiftly rose as developers found countless new uses for the substance. Saito handed over the presidency of the company in 1946 to Teiichi Yamazaki, who expanded TDK's portfolio into products such as magnetic recording tape (1952).

The company's global thrust started when it opened a Los Angeles office in 1959. Two years later it was listing shares on the Tokyo Stock Exchange. TDK branched into cassette tapes in 1966 and electromagnetic wave absorbers in 1968. Also in 1968 the company opened its first overseas manufacturing center, in Taiwan.

Expansion in the 1970s included the establishment of operations in Australia, Europe, and South America. TDK began listing its shares on the New York Stock Exchange in 1982. That year it also introduced a solar battery. In 1983 TDK officially changed its name to TDK Corporation, and was named a supplier to the International Track and Field World Championships in Helsinki, Finland. (The company has been a major sponsor of the event ever since.)

Operations thrived, and in 1986 the company established a plant in West Germany for the production of audio- and videocassettes, and another in the US for making electronic components. In 1987 Hiroshi Sato was appointed president of the company.

TDK bought integrated circuits maker Silicon Systems in 1989 (sold in 1996 to Texas Instruments) as Sato began modernizing the company's offerings and organization. His management style was conservative: He'd wait to see how other companies did in new markets before committing TDK, prompting the industry to label him as the "gambler who follows someone else." During his tenure, Sato gave the company solid footholds in niches such as optical disks, high-density heads, and cellular phone components.

To reverse falling profits in 1992, Sato made plans to eliminate managers by playing on the Japanese sense of honor — he asked them to accept pay cuts and work on standby at home until their retirement, expecting that they would simply resign. Sato was forced to scuttle the plans amid international outcries and depleted morale.

The company revamped its organization in 1994 around four operating divisions. That year it began production in China of high-end magnetic heads, but poor demand and a weakened yen caused sales and profit drops. By then TDK was the global leader in magnetic tape manufacturing.

The company bought UK-based communications equipment maker Grey Cell Systems in 1997. The purchase gave TDK a European presence in the market for data transmissions using the Global System for Mobile telephone system standard.

In 1998 Sato and Yamazaki retired; Sato was replaced by Hajime Sawabe. The next year TDK established a mobile communications development unit in Ireland. A sluggish Japanese economy helped cause a decline in earnings for fiscal 1999. TDK restructured its product lines again in 2000 and acquired California-based Headway Technologies, a maker of giant magnetoresistive heads used in computer disk drives.

President and CEO: Hajime Sawabe
EVP Sales: Motoyuki Kurihara
EVP, Technology and General Manager, Telecom Technology Development: Shunjiro Saito
Executive Managing Director and General Manager, Electronic Components Sales and Marketing: Hirokazu Nakanishi
Executive Director, Patent and Licensing and General Manger, Corporate Research and Development: Suguru Takayama
Executive Director and General Manager, Materials Research Center: Takeshi Nomura
Director Human Resources: Robin McConnell
Auditors: KPMG

LOCATIONS

HQ: 1-13-1 Nihonbashi, Chuo-ku, Tokyo 103-8272, Japan
Phone: +81-3-5201-7102   **Fax:** +81-3-5201-7114
US HQ: 12 Harbor Park Dr., Port Washington, NY 11050
US Phone: 516-625-0100   **US Fax:** 516-625-0651
Web site: http://www.tdk.co.jp

TDK has manufacturing plants in Brazil, China, Germany, Hong Kong, Hungary, Ireland, Japan, Luxembourg, Malaysia, Mexico, the Philippines, Singapore, South Korea, Taiwan, Thailand, the UK, and the US.

2000 Sales

	$ mil.	% of total
Asia & Oceania		
Japan	4,153	46
Other Asia	2,901	33
Americas	1,103	12
Europe	824	9
Adjustment	(2,618)	—
Total	**6,363**	**100**

PRODUCTS/OPERATIONS

2000 Sales

	% of total
Electronic materials & components	
Recording devices	30
Electronic materials	26
Electronic devices	19
Semiconductors & other	4
Recording media	21
Total	**100**

Selected Products

Audiotapes	Floppy disks
Capacitors	Hard disk drive
Coils	magnetoresistive heads
Deflection yoke cores that create TV and computer screen pictures	Integrated circuits
	MiniDiscs
	Modems
DVD-RAMs	Noise reduction
Factory automation equipment	components
	Optical and other disks
Fax and computer networking cards	PC cards
	Power supplies
Ferrite cores	Tape-based data
Filters	storage media
Floppy disk drive heads	Thermistors

COMPETITORS

AVX	Kyocera	Solectron
California Micro Devices	Matsushita	Sony
Control Devices	Philips Electronics	Toshiba
EPCOS	Pioneer	Vishay Intertechnology
Fuji Photo	Read-Rite	Yamaha
Fujitsu	Samsung	
Hitachi	SanDisk	

HISTORICAL FINANCIALS & EMPLOYEES

NYSE: TDK FYE: March 31	Annual Growth	3/91	3/92	3/93	3/94	3/95	3/96	3/97	3/98	3/99	3/00
Sales ($ mil.)	5.8%	3,840	4,029	4,583	4,507	5,605	5,108	5,006	5,278	5,589	6,363
Net income ($ mil.)	10.0%	203	163	160	54	150	261	486	442	380	479
Income as % of sales	—	5.3%	4.0%	3.5%	1.2%	2.7%	5.1%	9.7%	8.4%	6.8%	7.5%
Earnings per share ($)	9.6%	1.57	1.23	1.21	0.42	1.14	1.97	3.65	3.32	2.85	3.59
Stock price - FY high ($)	—	51.25	46.38	34.25	44.00	49.50	54.50	68.63	95.00	91.25	143.50
Stock price - FY low ($)	—	29.88	28.25	24.88	30.75	39.00	41.00	51.50	68.25	58.00	74.25
Stock price - FY close ($)	14.3%	39.63	28.50	32.38	41.75	45.13	51.88	67.25	76.75	80.75	131.50
P/E - high	—	33	38	28	110	43	28	19	29	32	40
P/E - low	—	19	23	21	77	34	21	14	21	20	21
Dividends per share ($)	8.5%	0.25	0.32	0.34	0.39	0.43	0.23	0.23	0.45	0.18	0.52
Book value per share ($)	7.9%	20.13	22.15	25.59	28.09	32.62	28.84	28.71	29.63	33.02	39.91
Employees	4.2%	—	—	—	26,830	27,276	29,070	28,055	29,747	31,305	34,321

STOCK PRICE HISTORY

HIGH/LOW/CLOSE

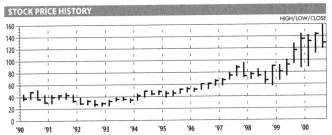

2000 FISCAL YEAR-END

Debt ratio: 0.0%
Return on equity: 9.9%
Cash ($ mil.): 1,646
Current ratio: 3.14
Long-term debt ($ mil.): 0
No. of shares (mil.): 133
Dividends
  Yield: 0.4%
  Payout: 14.5%
Market value ($ mil.): 17,514

TELECOM ITALIA S.P.A.

OVERVIEW

Italy's one-time state phone company, Telecom Italia is surviving in the arena of competition. The Rome-based former monopoly is still the nation's largest fixed-line phone company, having more than 26.5 million access lines in service.

Telecom Italia also holds 60% of Italy's leading wireless operator Telecom Italia Mobile (TIM), which has 18 million subscribers. The group plans to place its international mobile carrier holdings, concentrated largely in Europe and Latin America, under the control of TIM.

To strengthen its Internet operations, the group is combining its ISP, Tin.it, with yellow page publisher and Web portal SEAT. Telecom Italia also provides satellite communications (through subsidiary Telespazio) and information technology services. To focus on core activities, Telecom Italia is selling its 49% stake in cable-laying unit Sirti and 81% of telecom equipment maker Italtel. Olivetti, through funding vehicle Tecnost, controls 55% of Telecom Italia.

HISTORY

After gaining political power in Italy, Benito Mussolini began a program of nationalization, focusing first on three major banks and their equity portfolios. Included were three local phone companies that became the core of Società Finanziaria Telefonica (STET), created in 1933 to handle Italy's phone services under the state's industrial holding company, Istituto per La Ricostruzione Industriale (IRI).

Germany and Italy grew closer in the years leading up to WWII, and Italian manufacturers entered a venture with Siemens to make phone equipment. STET came through the war with most of its infrastructure intact and a monopoly on phone service in Italy. Siemens' properties, along with those of other equipment makers, were taken over by another company, TETI, which was nationalized and put under STET's control in 1958. This expanded STET's monopoly to include equipment manufacturing.

Italy's industries were increasingly nationalized under IRI. Companies within the IRI family forged alliances with each other and with independent companies, which frequently were absorbed into STET.

STET's scope expanded during the 1960s and 1970s to include satellite and data communications, but its monopoly was undermined by new technologies such as faxes, PCs, and teleconferencing. In the technology race among equipment makers, STET fell behind. And in a satellite communications era, STET's status as a necessary long-distance carrier was threatened. Despite these pressures, change did not come easily to STET. State monopolies maintained popular support, not only on nationalistic grounds but also because of labor's strong anticompetitive stance.

Anticipating privatization, however, IRI reorganized STET in 1994 and poured new capital into the company. STET's five telecom companies — SIP (domestic phone operator), Italcable (intercontinental), Telespazio (satellite), SIRM (maritime), and Iritel (domestic long distance) — were merged into one, Telecom Italia. Its mobile phone business was spun off as Telecom Italia Mobile (TIM) in 1995.

To end political feuding, the government abruptly replaced the heads of STET and Telecom Italia in 1997. Telecom Italia was merged with STET, which took the Telecom Italia name and was privatized that year. Berardino Libonati became chairman, and Franco Bernabe, formerly CEO of oil company ENI, took the helm as CEO. The company had begun taking stakes in foreign telecom companies, including Mobilkom Austria, Spanish broadcaster Retevision, and — as European Union competition began in 1998 — Telekom Austria.

Erstwhile rival Olivetti launched a hostile takeover bid for Telecom Italia in 1999. Though Telecom Italia tried to fend off the smaller firm with various maneuvers, including a proposed merger with Deutsche Telekom, Olivetti gained 55% of Telecom Italia. Olivetti CEO Roberto Colaninno took over as chairman and CEO.

That year Telecom Italia sold 65% of Stream, its pay-TV unit, to an investor group led by News Corp. And in a venture with Lockheed Martin and TRW, Telecom Italia planned to develop a $3.5 billion global broadband satellite system called Astrolink.

The company also announced plans to spin off and sell a stake in its ISP, Tin.it. In 2000, however, Telecom Italia said it would instead combine Tin.it with SEAT Pagine Gialle, a yellow page publisher and Internet portal operator. SEAT PG is a former Telecom Italia subsidiary in which the company still holds a minority stake. Also that year the company agreed to sell off 81% of its telecom equipment unit, Italtel, and its 49% stake in installations firm Sirti.

OFFICERS

Honorary Chairman; Chairman, Tecnost and Olivetti: Antonio Tesone
Chairman and CEO; Chairman, Olivetti, Tecnost, and Telecom Italia Mobile: Roberto Colaninno, age 56
Deputy Chairman: Sergio Erede
VP Corporate Communications and Image: Vittorio Meloni
VP Corporate Development: Giulia Nobili
VP Finance and Control: Massimo Brunelli
VP Human Resources: Mario Rosso
VP International Operations: Oscar Cicchetti
VP Internet: Lorenzo Pellicioli
VP Mobile Service; CEO Telecom Italia Mobile: Marco De Benedetti
VP Public and Regulatory Affairs: Andrea Camanzi
VP Satellite Services; CEO Telespazio: Enzo Badalotti
VP Venture Capital: Andrea Granelli
VP Wireline Services: Rocco Sabelli
VP and General Secretariat: Vittorio Nola
Auditors: Arthur Andersen S.p.A.

LOCATIONS

HQ: 34 Via Bertola, 20122 Turin, Italy
Phone: +39-01-1551-41   **Fax:** +39-01-1532-269
US HQ: 499 Park Ave., New York, NY 10022
US Phone: 212-755-5280   **US Fax:** 212-755-5766
Web site: http://www.telecomitalia.it

Telecom Italia operates principally in Italy but has interests in subsidiaries and affiliates in Argentina, Austria, Bolivia, Brazil, Canada, Chile, Costa Rica, Cuba, Czech Republic, Ecuador, France, Germany, Greece, Hong Kong, Hungary, India, Ireland, Israel, Kenya, Luxembourg, Mexico, the Netherlands, Nigeria, Poland, Portugal, Romania, Russia, San Marino, Spain, Switzerland, the UK, Ukraine, the US, and Yugoslavia.

PRODUCTS/OPERATIONS

1999 Sales

	% of total
Domestic wireline telecommunications	59
Domestic mobile telecommunications	24
International telecommunications	5
Information technology activities	5
Manufacturing	3
Installation	2
Satellite telecommunications	2
Total	**100**

Selected Subsidiaries and Affiliates
Finsiel - Consulenza e Applicazioni Informatiche S.p.A. (77%, information technology applications)
Sodalia S.p.A. (operating software for telecommunications networks)
STET International S.p.A. (88%, investments in foreign telecommunications companies)
Telecom Italia Mobile S.p.A. (60%, mobile phone operations)
Telespazio S.p.A. (satellite telecommunications services)
Telemedia International Italia S.p.A. (TMI, international telecommunications)
Telesoft S.p.A. (60%, IT software and services)

COMPETITORS

AT&T	Cable and	Italgas
Autostrade	Wireless	NTL
Belgacom	Cegetel	Omnitel
BellSouth	Deutsche	Sprint
Corporation —	Telekom	Swisscom
Latin America	e.Biscom	Telefónica
Group	Enel	Tiscali
BT	France Telecom	Verizon
	Infostrada	WorldCom

HISTORICAL FINANCIALS & EMPLOYEES

NYSE: TI FYE: December 31	Annual Growth	12/90	12/91	12/92	12/93	12/94	12/95	12/96	12/97	12/98	12/99
Sales ($ mil.)	4.4%	17,667	20,144	18,393	17,325	20,822	23,588	24,153	24,203	29,302	25,989
Net income ($ mil.)	7.8%	848	852	653	590	719	921	1,033	1,475	2,317	1,666
Income as % of sales	—	4.8%	4.2%	3.6%	3.4%	3.5%	3.9%	4.3%	6.1%	7.9%	6.4%
Earnings per share ($)	2.2%	—	—	—	—	—	1.74	1.80	1.98	3.12	1.90
Stock price - FY high ($)	—	—	—	—	—	—	33.13	45.25	68.56	90.88	143.63
Stock price - FY low ($)	—	—	—	—	—	—	25.63	27.38	41.75	53.00	82.50
Stock price - FY close ($)	49.7%	—	—	—	—	—	27.88	44.38	64.00	87.00	140.00
P/E - high	—	—	—	—	—	—	19	25	35	29	76
P/E - low	—	—	—	—	—	—	15	15	21	17	43
Dividends per share ($)	—	—	—	—	—	—	0.00	0.57	0.00	0.00	1.08
Book value per share ($)	1.7%	—	—	—	—	—	20.54	19.73	22.78	25.80	22.01
Employees	(0.7%)	—	129,492	134,136	136,184	139,346	132,548	126,381	127,451	122,300	122,662

STOCK PRICE HISTORY
HIGH/LOW/CLOSE

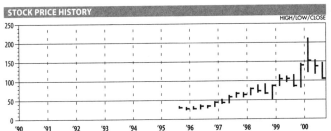

1999 FISCAL YEAR-END
Debt ratio: 23.3%
Return on equity: 9.4%
Cash ($ mil.): 650
Current ratio: 0.71
Long-term debt ($ mil.): 4,953
No. of shares (mil.): 743
Dividends
  Yield: 0.8%
  Payout: 56.8%
Market value ($ mil.): 103,966

TELECOMUNICACIONES DE CHILE

OVERVIEW

Compañía de Telecomunicaciones de Chile (known as Telefónica CTC Chile) metes out most of that country's telecommunications services. Based in Santiago, the former state monopoly is 44%-owned by Telefónica Internacional, a unit of Spain's national phone company.

Telefónica CTC Chile maintains about 2.6 million phone lines (almost 90% of the market) and handles more than a third of the long-distance market through subsidiaries Telefónica Mundo 188 and Globus (formerly VTR Larga Distancia).

Having one of the world's first all-digital networks, CTC is well equipped to handle Chile's telecom needs, though competition is fierce. There is a lot of room for growth in Chile, where the lack of phone lines has aided the wireless market: Telefónica CTC Chile's mobile subsidiary is the leading Chilean wireless operator with more than 1 million cellular customers.

Telefónica CTC Chile also provides data transmission, directory services, public phones, telecom equipment, and owns 60% of SONDA, Chile's principal information systems provider.

HISTORY

Telecommunications in Chile began in 1880, four years after Alexander Graham Bell's invention of the telephone, with the establishment of Compañía de Telefonos de Edison in Valparaiso.

The International Telephone and Telegraph Corporation (ITT) bought the company's 26,205 phones in 1927. Three years later the Compañía de Telefonos de Chile S.A. (CTC) was formed to acquire local phone companies. CTC became ITT's largest phone company in South America by gaining a 50-year concession that controlled 92% of Chile's phones. CTC became very valuable to ITT; by 1962 it provided about 12% of ITT's total profits. CTC was ITT's last phone property in South America to escape nationalization. In 1970 ITT CEO Harold Geneen, fearing that the election of Marxist Salvador Allende as president would lead to CTC's nationalization, met clandestinely with CIA officials to discuss how to prevent Allende's inauguration.

Allende won the election. The Chilean government assumed management control of CTC in 1971 but to delay having to compensate ITT, did not formally expropriate CTC. During sensitive negotiations over compensation, internal ITT memos that discussed the anti-Allende plans came to light. Allende offered a mere $12 million for CTC, about $141 million less than CTC was worth.

Allende was killed in a 1973 coup led by General Augusto Pinochet, who was to run Chile under a military dictatorship for the next 17 years. Pinochet agreed to pay ITT's price for CTC, and in 1974 the Corporacion de Fomento de la Produccion (CORFO, or Corporation for the Promotion of Production) bought the 80% of the company that had been owned by ITT.

CORFO sold 30% of its CTC shares to Bond Corporation Chile in 1988. A subsidiary of Telefónica de España (today Telefónica S.A.), the Spanish telephone monopoly, bought Bond Chile stock in 1990 and changed Bond Chile's name to Telefónica Internacional Chile. Later that year CTC became the first South American company to be listed on the NYSE.

In 1994 Chile became the first Latin American country to allow all comers to offer fixed-line phone service. Although deregulation increased competition and slashed long-distance prices in 1994, other regulatory changes expanded CTC's protected local calling areas. CTC increased local call prices as much as 70%. That year CTC acquired 80% of Intercom, Chile's largest cable TV company.

The company changed its name to Compañía de Telecomunicaciones de Chile S.A. in 1995 and won the right to expand service to all regions of Chile. In 1996 CTC merged its cable operations with those of Metropolis to form Metropolis-Intercom, a cable TV company with over 40% of the market; it also merged its cellular operations with those of VTR-Celular, forming Startel, to achieve national coverage. That year CTC joined a Telefónica-led consortium that won a 35% stake in telecom company Companhia Riograndense de Telecomunicaçoes in Brazil's first privatization auction.

In 1998, the year Pinochet retired, CTC received government approval to acquire VTR Larga Distancia, Chile's #4 long-distance carrier, despite regulatory concerns over the possible stifling of competition. A year later CTC sold its Internet division to Telefónica (as part of that company's Terra Networks subsidiary) and acquired 60% of SONDA, Chile's largest information systems provider. It also began using the brand name Telefónica CTC Chile. The next year the company announced the sale of its cable TV assets.

Chairman: Javier Aguirre Nogués
VC: Hans Eben Oyanedel
General Manager and CEO: Claudio Muñoz Zuniga
VP Administration and Finance and CFO:
Julio Covarrubias Fernandez
VP Corporate Develoment: Paul Fontaine
VP Organization and Human Resources:
Jose Victor Nunez
VP Planning and Control: Rafael Zamora
VP Regulation and Development:
Raimundo Beca Infante
VP Information Systems and Chief Information
Officer: Oscar Márquez
General Manager Ateno Chile: Felipe Tomic E. Anteno
General Manager, E-Solutions and Telefonica Movil:
Ismael Vásquez
General Manager Istel: Inés Naddaf
General Manager InfoEra: Pedro Gutierrez
General Manager Multimedia Network:
Ramón Castañeda
General Manager SONDA and Telefonica Empresas:
Ricardo Majluf
General Manager SONDA: Mario Pavón
General Manager Telefonica Larga Distancia and
Telefonica Mundo 188: Velko Petric
General Manager Telefonica Residencial: Diego Barros
General Manager Telefonica Movil: José Molés
General Manager Telefonica Network Services:
Franco Faccilongo
Auditors: Arthur Andersen-Langton Clarke

LOCATIONS

HQ: Compañiá de Telecomunicaciones de Chile S.A.,
Providencia 111, Piso 2, Santiago, Chile
Phone: +56-2-691-2020   Fax: +56-2-699-1032
Web site: http://www.ctc.cl

PRODUCTS/OPERATIONS

1999 Sales

	$ mil.	% of total
Local services	646	40
Mobile communications	199	12
Equipment	130	8
Long-distance phone service	118	7
Interconnections	93	6
Public telephones	39	3
Installations & connections	30	2
Directory advertising	28	2
Other	321	20
Total	**1,604**	**100**

Selected Services
Data transmission
Directory advertising
Domestic and international long distance
Equipment sales
Information technology systems
Interconnections
Line installations and connections
Local phone service
Mobile communications
Paging
Public telephones
Radio trunking

COMPETITORS

AT&T Latin America
BellSouth Corporation —
 Latin America Group
Entel
SBC Communications
TELECOM (Colombia)
Telecom Argentina
Telecom Italia
Telefónica de Argentina
Telefónica del Peru
Telex-Chile
WorldCom

HISTORICAL FINANCIALS & EMPLOYEES

NYSE: CTC FYE: December 31	Annual Growth	12/90	12/91	12/92	12/93	12/94	12/95	12/96	12/97	12/98	12/99
Sales ($ mil.)	15.1%	453	493	663	967	1,014	1,037	1,274	1,439	1,602	1,604
Net income ($ mil.)	—	131	142	186	235	226	268	354	312	237	(115)
Income as % of sales	—	28.9%	28.8%	28.0%	24.3%	22.3%	25.9%	27.8%	21.6%	14.8%	—
Earnings per share ($)	—	0.04	0.68	0.85	1.03	0.88	1.64	1.65	1.40	1.00	(0.48)
Stock price - FY high ($)	—	4.02	11.40	14.75	24.44	31.43	21.94	24.14	38.13	30.00	28.38
Stock price - FY low ($)	—	3.03	3.64	8.69	13.81	17.62	11.28	18.77	22.75	12.13	15.13
Stock price - FY close ($)	19.2%	3.76	9.34	13.98	23.94	18.50	19.47	23.76	29.88	20.69	18.25
P/E - high	—	101	17	17	22	30	13	15	26	29	—
P/E - low	—	76	5	10	13	17	7	11	16	12	—
Dividends per share ($)	—	0.04	0.16	0.06	0.36	0.78	0.41	0.59	0.00	0.00	0.00
Book value per share ($)	8.2%	4.53	4.40	5.31	6.25	6.90	7.93	8.98	9.57	10.68	9.21
Employees	2.4%	7,994	7,991	8,000	9,000	9,354	9,170	8,982	8,802	8,985	9,933

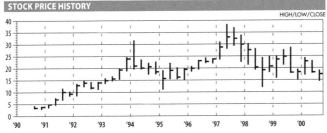

STOCK PRICE HISTORY   HIGH/LOW/CLOSE

1999 FISCAL YEAR-END
Debt ratio: 51.8%
Return on equity: —
Cash ($ mil.): 93
Current ratio: 1.38
Long-term debt ($ mil.): 2,368
No. of shares (mil.): 239
Dividends
 Yield: —
 Payout: —
Market value ($ mil.): 4,367

TELEFÓNICA, S.A.

OVERVIEW

Like a latter-day conquistador, Madrid-based Telefónica is seeking its fortune in Latin America. Spain's dominant phone company is also the leading communications provider among Spanish- and Portuguese-speaking populations; its international unit operates about 21 million fixed lines and serves more than 9 million mobile phone subscribers outside Spain. Telefónica is also part of a venture with Tyco International that is building an undersea fiber-optic cable to connect the US and Latin America.

At home, Telefónica de España provides phone and data transmission services and is participating in European auctions for third-generation wireless licenses. In Spain it maintains about 20 million fixed lines and its mobile service has more than 11 million subscribers. Other operations include directory publishing, pay TV, and public telephony.

Telefónica is the largest shareholder in Terra Lycos, which was formed when the company's ISP, Terra Networks, bought the US-based Lycos Internet portal.

HISTORY

When a 1923 military coup brought General Miguel Primo de Rivera to power in Spain, the government-run phone system was in shambles. More than half of the country's 90,000 lines did not work. With little cash in the government coffers, Primo de Rivera sought foreign assistance.

Supported by National City Bank (now Citicorp), US-based ITT bought three private Spanish phone companies, later combining them to form Compañía Telefónica Nacional de España. The ITT unit gained the state phone concession in 1924, and the government agreed not to reclaim the system for 20 years. But when Franco came to power in 1939, he froze Telefónica's assets. ITT tried to sell the company to German buyers in 1941 but backed out when the US State Department objected. The Spanish government nationalized Telefónica in 1945, keeping 41% of its shares.

Long-distance service was introduced in 1960, satellite communications in 1967, and international service in 1971. Still, when Spain entered the European Union (EU) in 1986, Telefónica was unprepared for the increase in demand for services, and complaints rose.

The firm purchased a minority stake in Compañía de Telefonos de Chile in 1990 (now Compañía de Telecomunicaciones de Chile), and a Telefónica-led consortium won a bid to manage the southern half of ENTEL, Argentina's former state phone system. The company acquired a majority stake in Peru's telecom monopoly in 1994 and a year later joined Unisource, a European telecom consortium.

The Spanish government at first defied the EU's directive to break up its telecom monopoly. But in 1994 the government announced that it would meet the EU's 1998 deadline for opening telecom markets; in exchange Telefónica won permission to begin new businesses when competition arrived.

Flamboyant former investment banker Juan Villalonga took over as chairman in 1996. The boyhood friend of Spain's prime minister began expanding Telefónica's presence in Latin America with several acquisitions in 1997. They included 35% of Brazil's Companhia Riograndense de Telecomunicaçoes (CRT); a large stake in Multicanal, Argentina's #1 cable company (sold in 1998 to Grupo Clarin); and 35% of satellite TV service Via Digital.

That year Telefónica broke off with Unisource and allied with British Telecom and MCI, only to have the alliance break up when MCI agreed to be bought by WorldCom (1998). Meanwhile, the Spanish government had finished divesting its interest in the company in 1997 (retaining a golden share), and competition came to Spain the next year. The company revamped its corporate structure, cut 10,000 jobs, and became Telefónica S.A. It also won fixed-line phone company Telesp and a cellular company in Brazil's auction of the former national phone company, Telebras.

In 1999 Telefónica sold to the public part of its Internet unit, Terra Networks (formerly Telefónica Interactiva). The next year it took near-total ownership of four of its Latin American units: Telefónica de Argentina, Telefónica del Peru, Telesp, and Tele Sudeste Celular (it later sold its stake in CRT to meet regulatory approval) and separated the mobile and data operations to reorganize by business units.

Telefónica, to expand its multimedia offerings, bought Netherlands-based independent TV producer Endemol for $5.3 billion in 2000. After dropping out of the UK wireless license auction, it teamed up with Finland's Sonera to win a license in the German auction. But when merger talks with Dutch telecom carrier Royal KPN broke down, Villalonga resigned over disagreements on the direction of the company.

Chairman: Cesar Alierta
VC: Jose Maria Concejo Alvarez
VC: Isidro Faine Casas
VC: Francisco Gomez Roldan
CEO: Fernando Abril-Martorell
Member of the Executive Committee and General Director Finances and Control: Jose Maria Alvarez-Pallete Lopez
Member of the Executive Committee; Advisor Telefonica Datacorp: Guillermo Fernandez Vidal
Member of the Executive Committee; CEO Telefonica de Espana: Julio Linares Lopez
Member of the Executive Committee; CEO Telefonica Moviles: Luis Lada Diaz
Member of the Executive Committee; CEO Telefonica Datacorp: Antonio Vinana-Baptista
Secretary: Jose Maria Mas Millet
Vice Secretary: Diego L. Lozano Romeral
Director Human Resources: Federico Castellanos Martinez
Auditors: Arthur Andersen

HQ: Gran Via 28, 28013 Madrid, Spain
Phone: +34-91-584-47-00   **Fax:** +34-91-531-93-47
Web site: http://www.telefonica.es

In addition to Spain, Telefónica's areas of operation include Argentina, Austria, Brazil, Chile, El Salvador, Guatemala, Italy, Morocco, Peru, Puerto Rico, Portugal, the Netherlands, Russia, Venezuela, and the US.

1999 Sales

	% of total
Basic telephony (domestic)	
Basic telephone service	21
Public telephony	3
Lease of circuits	3
ISDN lines	3
Interconnection fees	1
Other	6
International business	37
Mobile services	14
Data transmission & Internet services	3
Directory publishing & media services	2
Call center operations	1
Other	6
Total	**100**

AT&T
BCI
BellSouth Corporation — Latin America Group
BT
Cable and Wireless
Deutsche Telekom
Ericsson
France Telecom
Global Crossing
Grupo Prisa
IFX Corporation
Jazztel
Nortel Inversora

PSINet
Retevisión
SBC Communications
Sprint
StarMedia Network
Telecom Argentina
Telecom Italia
Telex-Chile
Telmex
Universo Online International
Vodafone
WorldCom

NYSE: TEF FYE: December 31	Annual Growth	12/90	12/91	12/92	12/93	12/94	12/95	12/96	12/97	12/98	12/99
Sales ($ mil.)	11.2%	8,924	12,203	8,924	12,203	13,162	14,297	15,288	15,601	20,476	23,168
Net income ($ mil.)	9.7%	793	1,079	793	1,079	856	1,094	1,222	1,255	1,533	1,821
Income as % of sales	—	8.9%	8.8%	8.9%	8.8%	6.5%	7.7%	8.0%	8.0%	7.5%	7.9%
Earnings per share ($)	8.2%	0.82	1.13	0.84	1.15	0.87	1.12	1.24	1.17	1.46	1.67
Stock price - FY high ($)	—	9.39	12.14	9.58	12.39	14.74	14.06	22.28	30.51	50.52	79.88
Stock price - FY low ($)	—	7.07	7.87	7.21	8.03	10.70	10.62	13.50	21.61	27.96	40.34
Stock price - FY close ($)	28.2%	8.43	11.98	8.60	12.23	11.22	13.38	22.12	29.09	44.13	78.81
P/E - high	—	11	11	0	4	17	13	18	26	35	48
P/E - low	—	9	7	0	2	12	9	11	18	19	24
Dividends per share ($)	—	0.39	0.39	0.40	0.40	1.67	0.38	0.43	0.36	0.00	0.00
Book value per share ($)	(0.3%)	13.83	14.05	14.11	14.33	11.72	12.96	14.49	13.41	15.12	13.44
Employees	5.2%	75,350	75,499	74,437	74,340	72,207	69,570	92,148	92,022	101,809	118,778

HIGH/LOW/CLOSE

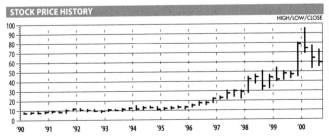

Debt ratio: 53.5%
Return on equity: 12.0%
Cash ($ mil.): 188
Current ratio: 0.71
Long-term debt ($ mil.): 16,824
No. of shares (mil.): 1,088
Dividends
  Yield: —
  Payout: —
Market value ($ mil.): 85,714

TELÉFONOS DE MÉXICO, S.A. DE C.V.

OVERVIEW

After a decade of competition, Teléfonos de México (Telmex) is holding on to its top spot in Mexico's telecommunications market. But rivals are crying foul. Based in Mexico City, the company still controls about 75% of Mexico's long-distance market but competitors — and the US government — have sought an end to what they claim are monopolistic practices by the telecom giant. The company maintains more than 11 million phone lines, and wireless subsidiary TELCEL has more than 7 million cellular subscribers.

Looking beyond Mexico, Telmex is expanding its presence in Latin America. The company plans to spin off TELCEL and its international investments to form America

Movil, a new company and one of the region's largest wireless operators. Telmex sells phone lines to US customers for installation in Mexico and resells long-distance to Hispanic communities in the US. It has also acquired US companies that provide prepaid local and cellular phone service.

Telmex has a minority stake in US ISP Prodigy and those customers are automatically signed up with the new Spanish-language portal, T1msn.com, a partnership with US software giant Microsoft.

Mexican billionaire Carlos Slim Helu's holding company Grupo Carso Telecom holds a controlling stake in Telmex. Texas-based SBC Communications has a minority stake.

HISTORY

Mexican Telephone and Telegraph, backed by investors allied with AT&T, received a government concession to operate in Mexico City in 1903. Two years later a Swedish consortium led by equipment maker Ericsson also won a concession, and it became Empresa de Teléfonos Ericsson in 1909.

In 1915 Mexican Telephone and Telegraph was nationalized. The company languished after WWI, but the Ericsson enterprise thrived. In 1925 International Telephone and Telegraph (ITT), led by telecom pioneer Sosthenes Behn, won the concession to operate Mexican Telephone and Telegraph. ITT expanded operations nationwide and linked to AT&T's system in the US. In 1932 ITT won control of Ericsson.

Teléfonos de México (Telmex) was created after WWII to buy the ITT and Ericsson subsidiaries in Mexico. Private investors bought Telmex in 1953, but it remained under close state regulation until the government bought 51% of the voting shares in 1972. Phone service grew slowly, and the government continually raised the long-distance tax until it accounted for half of Telmex's revenues. By the 1980s the government was using Telmex funds for unrelated programs.

The 1985 earthquakes heavily damaged Telmex's facilities, and it was forced to modernize and expand in the rebuilding stage. To improve the inefficient enterprise, President Carlos Salinas announced in 1989 that Telmex would be privatized. The following year a consortium that included Grupo Carso, SBC Communications, and France Telecom won voting control of Telmex. (France Telecom sold its stake in 2000.)

Telmex bought a 49% stake in Empresas

Cablevision's Mexican cable business in 1995, and the next year it teamed with Sprint to offer business telecom services in the US and Mexico. After long-distance competition began in 1997, Telmex surrendered about a quarter of its market share. Many customers, angered over years of unexplained hang-ups and incorrect billings, switched providers. Also that year Telmex and Sprint formed another venture to resell long-distance service to Mexican Americans. However, the venture had to gain approval from the FCC, and regulators insisted that Telmex lower the high termination fees charged to US long-distance providers. Telmex agreed to do so, and the venture won approval in 1998. Telmex also invested in US ISP Prodigy in 1998.

Meanwhile, Telmex maintained a de facto monopoly over local service until 1999 when MAXCOM, backed by Grupo Radio Centro, entered the market. Telmex gained strength in other communications arenas, receiving additional radio spectrum for mobile and PCS wireless services, joining SBC to buy Cellular Communications of Puerto Rico, and buying Miami-based Topp Telecom (prepaid cellular service) and Dallas-based CommSouth (prepaid local service). It bought out Sprint's share of their joint venture and took a 1% stake ($100 million) in Williams Communications, the US-based fiber-optic firm. It also began managing Guatemalan phone company TELGUA and the next year acquired a controlling stake.

Also in 2000 Telmex and Microsoft introduced the T1msn.com Spanish-language Internet portal. It also formed a joint venture with Bell Canada and SBC to expand operations in South America.

Chairman, Telefonos de Mexico and Carso Global Telecom: Carlos Slim Helu, age 59
CEO: Jaime Chico Pardo
Director Finance and Administration and CFO: Adolfo Cerezo Perez
Director Commercial: Isidoro Ambe Attar
Director Human Resources: Javier Elguea Solis
Director Internet, Regulation, and Communication: Arturo Elias Ayub
Director Legal Affairs: Javier Mondragon Alarcon
Director Operational Support: Hector Slim Seade
Director Strategic Development: Andres R. Vazquez del Mercado Benshimol
Director Technical and Long Distance: Eduardo Gomez Chibli
Director Telecommunications Operators, Systems, and Processes: Oscar Von Hauske Solis
Director Wireless and Affiliates: Daniel Hajj Aboumrad
Director Telnor: Miguel A. Gonzalez Arriaga
Director Center Division: Jorge L. Suastegui Esquivel
Director East Metro Division: Jose Covarrubias Bravo
Director Gulf-Pacific Division: Javier Coca Muniz
Director North Division: Miguel A. Vera Garcia
Director Northeast Division: Facundo Alonso Garcia
Director Northwest Division: Raymundo Paulin Velasco
Director South Metro Division: Gerardo Leal Garza
Auditors: Mancera, S.C.

LOCATIONS

HQ: Parque Via 190, Colonia Cuauhtemoc, 06599 Mexico, D.F., Mexico
Phone: +52-5-703-3990   **Fax:** +52-5-545-5550
Web site: http://www.telmex.com.mx

Telmex operates primarily in Mexico and has interests in other operations in Latin America and the US.

PRODUCTS/OPERATIONS

1999 Sales

	$ mil.	% of total
Local service	5,396	53
Long-distance service		
Domestic	2,342	23
International	1,222	12
Interconnection service	509	5
Other	713	7
Total	**10,182**	**100**

Selected Services
Calling cards
Cellular phone service
Internet access
Local service
National/international long distance
Pay phones
Telephone directories

COMPETITORS

Alestra	IMPSAT
ALFA, S.A. de C.V.	Leap Wireless
America Online	quepasa.com
AT&T	Radio Centro
Avantel	StarMedia Network
Biper	Telefónica
Global Light Telecommunications	Telscape International
Grupo Iusacell	Verizon
	Yahoo!

HISTORICAL FINANCIALS & EMPLOYEES

NYSE: TMX FYE: December 31	Annual Growth	12/90	12/91	12/92	12/93	12/94	12/95	12/96	12/97	12/98	12/99
Sales ($ mil.)	12.4%	3,556	4,773	6,644	7,923	5,914	5,428	6,714	7,529	7,903	10,182
Net income ($ mil.)	10.4%	1,087	1,877	2,559	2,900	1,591	1,209	1,478	1,593	1,657	2,656
Income as % of sales	—	30.6%	39.3%	38.5%	36.6%	26.9%	22.3%	22.0%	21.2%	21.0%	26.1%
Earnings per share ($)	6.4%	—	2.10	2.40	2.73	1.51	1.25	1.61	1.90	2.10	3.44
Stock price - FY high ($)	—	—	24.13	30.06	33.94	38.06	20.75	19.13	28.41	29.22	56.94
Stock price - FY low ($)	—	—	12.13	20.19	21.81	18.50	11.50	13.94	16.25	16.38	19.94
Stock price - FY close ($)	11.6%	—	23.38	28.00	33.75	20.50	15.94	16.50	28.03	24.34	56.25
P/E - high	—	—	11	13	12	25	17	12	15	14	16
P/E - low	—	—	6	8	8	12	9	9	9	8	6
Dividends per share ($)	28.6%	—	0.08	0.24	0.48	0.74	0.46	0.46	0.22	0.62	0.60
Book value per share ($)	12.3%	—	6.78	9.40	11.25	10.62	10.64	12.80	13.48	13.85	17.20
Employees	1.5%	63,400	61,800	62,350	62,977	63,246	62,777	62,317	54,758	54,425	72,321

HIGH/LOW/CLOSE

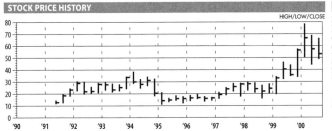

1999 FISCAL YEAR-END
Debt ratio: 16.6%
Return on equity: 22.6%
Cash ($ mil.): 3,000
Current ratio: 1.84
Long-term debt ($ mil.): 2,552
No. of shares (mil.): 747
Dividends
  Yield: 1.1%
  Payout: 17.4%
Market value ($ mil.): 42,044

TELEGLOBE INC.

OVERVIEW

Spinning on the axis of its Internet network, Teleglobe is one of the world's leading providers of global broadband services. Canada's longtime telecommunications link to the outside world, Montreal-based Teleglobe — a "carrier's carrier" that caters to broadcasters, carriers, content providers, ISPs, and more than 60,000 businesses — has been acquired by the Bell Canada unit of leading Canadian phone company BCE.

Subsidiary Teleglobe Communications operates the global network with full carrier status in the world's five largest telecom markets (France, Germany, Japan, the UK, and the US) and the authority to operate in 27 countries. It also has a network of cable systems and satellites that reaches into more than 100 countries. Subsidiary EXCEL Communications, one of the top long-distance companies in the US, has introduced its multilevel marketing tactics in Canada, with plans for expansion to Europe.

Teleglobe has begun a five-year, $5 billion initiative, GlobeSystem, to provide scalable broadband service platforms linking 160 cities with a seamless data network. Subsidiary Teleglobe World Mobility is engaged in mobile satellite communications; it has a 66% stake in ORBCOMM, a commercial low-earth-orbit satellite system. Teleglobe Enterprises handles holdings in five cable-laying ships and broadcast distributor Look Communications.

HISTORY

After World War II, the Canadian government saw the need to control the telecommunications industry by nationalizing Cable & Wireless and Canadian Marconi. The result was the Canadian Overseas Telecommunication Corporation (COTC), formed in 1950 to provide wireless telegraph and radiotelephone service. COTC soon acquired the submarine telegraph cable terminals and overseas high-frequency radio circuits to begin operations as a telecom carrier. In 1953 COTC became a partner in TAT-1, the first transatlantic coaxial cable (completed in 1956).

Its network of submarine cables quickly grew, linking Canada with Australia, Greenland, Iceland, Japan, New Zealand, and the UK. In 1965 it participated in the launching of Early Bird, the first commercial communications satellite.

In 1975 the COTC changed its name to Teleglobe Canada. In the early 1980s, Canada began privatization and soon Teleglobe was the subject of a bidding war. To everyone's surprise, the winning bid — $488 million (Canadian) — belonged to a little known systems developer, Memotec Data. As a wholly owned subsidiary of Memotec, Teleglobe fell under government regulation, with a mandate to operate Canada's international telecom services. In 1987 Bell Canada's parent company, BCE, bought a one-third stake in Memotec.

In another milestone, Teleglobe became co-owner in 1988 of TAT-8, the first transatlantic fiber-optic cable. Work on the first transpacific fiber-optic cable, TPC-4, began a year later. Teleglobe formed a 50-50 joint venture with IDB Communications in 1990 to provide mobile satellite communications.

Charles Sirois, the founder of BCE Mobile Communications, engineered a boardroom coup in 1992, buying a 12% stake in Teleglobe and allying with other investors. Already considered a visionary, Sirois was named Teleglobe's CEO and provided a new mission: to become the world's #3 international carrier by moving into foreign markets.

The company joined with Orbital Sciences in 1993 to develop ORBCOMM, the low-earth-orbit satellite system. It became the sole promoter of CANTAT 3, a new cable link with Europe. CANUS 1, linking CANTAT 3 with the US, went online in 1995. Teleglobe added to its network of fiber-optic cables with an investment in the China-US Cable Network.

Facing deregulation and looking for new markets, Teleglobe in 1998 joined forces with US long-distance company EXCEL Communications in a $3.6 billion merger that gave Teleglobe entry into the US long-distance market. Teleglobe continued its global expansion in 1999 with the GlobeSystem initiative to connect 160 cities in a single network.

Sirois stepped down in 2000 and was replaced by BCE's Jean Monty, who took over as Teleglobe's chairman. BCE acquired Teleglobe later that year in a stock deal worth more than $7 billion.

Chairman; President and CEO, BCE: Jean C. Monty
VC; Chairman Excel Communications: Kenny A. Troutt,
$445,187 pay (prior to title change)
CEO: Terry Jarman
CFO: Michael T. Boychuk
EVP Global Development: Guthrie J. Stewart
VP, Chief Legal Officer, and Corporate Secretary:
Andre Bourbonnais
VP and Corporate Treasurer: Jacques Deforges
**VP Corporate Human Resources and Employee
Communications:** Brigitte Bourque
VP Finance and Corporate Controller: François Laurin
President and COO, Excel Communications:
Selby Shaver, $401,153 pay
President, Global Markets, Teleglobe Communications:
Serge Fortin
Auditors: Arthur Andersen & Cie

LOCATIONS

HQ: 1000 de la Gauchetiere St. West,
Montreal, Quebec H3B 4X5, Canada
Phone: 514-868-7272   **Fax:** 514-868-7234
US HQ: 11480 Commerce Park Dr., Reston, VA 20191
US Phone: 703-755-2000   **US Fax:** 703-755-2600
Web site: http://www.teleglobe.com

Teleglobe has operations in Argentina, Australia, Austria,
Belgium, Brazil, Canada, China, Colombia, Costa Rica,
the Czech Republic, Denmark, the Dominican Republic,
Egypt, El Salvador, France, Germany, Hong Kong, India,
Indonesia, Ireland, Israel, Italy, the Ivory Coast, Japan,
Malaysia, Mexico, the Netherlands, New Zealand, Norway,
Panama, the Philippines, Poland, Puerto Rico, Romania,
Russia, Singapore, South Africa, South Korea, Spain,
Sweden, Switzerland, Taiwan, Thailand, the United Arab
Emirates, the UK, and the US.

1999 Sales

	% of total
North America	
US	61
Canada	12
Europe	11
Other	16
Total	**100**

PRODUCTS/OPERATIONS

1999 Sales

	% of total
Telephony - US	48
Telephony - global	25
Telephony - Canada	15
Transmission & data services	8
Marketing services	2
Other	2
Total	**100**

Selected Services

Business
ATM (asynchronous
transfer mode) switches
Direct international
outbound calls
ISDN
International private lines
International toll free
Operator services

Carriers
ATM (asynchronous
transfer mode) services
Carrier leases
Frame relay
International dedicated
access

International switched
transit
International toll free
Operator services/
collect calling
Prepaid calling card
service
Roaming signaling service

Content Distribution
Internet
Video transmission

Internet
Access
Colocation
Web hosting

COMPETITORS

360networks	Concert	Sprint
Aliant	Equant	STAR Telecom
ALLTEL	France Telecom	Teledesic
AT&T	Global Crossing	Telmex
BCE	Globalstar	TELUS
BellSouth	Level 3	Verizon
Broadwing	Communications	Williams
BT	Pacific Gateway	Communications
Cable and	Exchange	Group
Wireless	PanAmSat	WorldCom
Call-Net	Primus Telecom	
Enterprises	Qwest	
Carrier1	SBC	
International	Communications	

HISTORICAL FINANCIALS & EMPLOYEES

Subsidiary FYE: December 31	Annual Growth	12/90	12/91	12/92	12/93	12/94	12/95	12/96	12/97	12/98	12/99
Sales ($ mil.)	26.4%	348	379	345	410	459	527	1,251	1,391	3,389	2,873
Net income ($ mil.)	(0.3%)	7	22	(40)	57	65	70	82	98	15	7
Income as % of sales	—	2.0%	5.9%	—	13.9%	14.1%	13.3%	6.6%	7.1%	0.4%	0.2%
Employees	8.7%	2,500	2,340	2,082	2,128	1,899	1,619	1,882	1,204	5,351	5,295

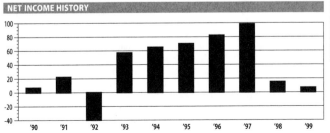

NET INCOME HISTORY

1999 FISCAL YEAR-END
Debt ratio: 27.2%
Return on equity: 0.2%
Cash ($ mil.): 118
Current ratio: 1.29
Long-term debt ($ mil.): 1,518

GRUPO TELEVISA, S.A.

OVERVIEW

Grupo Televisa is the head honcho in the Latin media world, with diverse holdings in television, radio, publishing, music, film, and satellite broadcasting. The Mexico City-based company owns more than 250 TV stations and four networks that capture about 80% of the audience, ranking Televisa as Mexico's #1 TV broadcaster. It also produces a number of programs for its networks and licenses distribution to more than 70 countries. (It supplies much of the programming for Univision Communications, the US-based Hispanic broadcaster in which Televisa has a 7% stake.) The company also reaches audiences through its cable joint venture Cablevisión (51%-owned), as well as through its direct-to-home satellite venture Innova (60%-owned with News Corp. and Liberty Media), which operates SKY.

Off the small screen, Televisa is one of the leading publishers of Spanish-language magazines. Its wholly owned Edivisa unit (formerly Editorial Televisa) publishes more than 30 titles that cover entertainment, science, music, and culture. It also produces Spanish versions of such titles as *Cosmopolitan* and *Elle*. Televisa also plans to dominate the radio market through an announced merger of its Radiopolis unit (17 stations) with rival Grupo Acir (40%-owned by US-based Clear Channel Communications) to create a broadcasting giant with 116 stations. (Televisa will own just more than 50% of the operation.) Other businesses include sports and entertainment (Mexico City's Azteca Stadium and two soccer teams), paging systems (51%-owned Skytel), film production and distribution, and music recording.

While a leader in many of its business segments, Televisa has been moving to strengthen its position on the balance sheet. Cost cutting and payroll reduction efforts have proved successful, and in 2000 the company refinanced much of its outstanding debt. It also is expanding its operations into cyberspace, launching the Spanish-language portal EsMas.com in 2000. Chairman Emilio Azcárraga Jean owns 51% of holding company Televicentro, which in turn controls 51% of Televisa.

HISTORY

Credited with launching the Golden Age of Mexican cinema in the 1940s via his Churrubusco Studios, Emilio Azcárraga Vidaurreta was a radio pioneer who also owned one of Mexico's first TV channels. He joined fellow TV channel owners Romulo O'Farrill (a newspaper publisher) and Guillermo Camarena (an inventor) to form one network, Telesistema Mexicana, in 1954. When Azcárraga Vidaurreta died in 1972, his son Emilio Azcárraga Milmo took the reins of the company, redubbed it Grupo Televisa, and began his long stint as chairman. His aggressive style earned him the nickname "El Tigre" (The Tiger).

Azcárraga Milmo saw Mexican television as an escape for the nation's middle and lower classes. He nurtured stars for soap operas (called *telenovelas*) and variety shows and insisted upon the actors' loyalty in return. Grupo Televisa started producing feature films for markets in Mexico and abroad in 1978. It also ran cable TV and music recording businesses, and a regional TV network that it bought in 1982. The company used its news programs to support Mexico's Institutional Revolutionary Party (PRI).

A 1990 attempt to start a sports newspaper in the US (*The National*) met with failure (it closed after a year, leaving the company with heavy debts). Azcárraga Milmo bought out the other principal investors in 1990 and reorganized Televisa into a holding company, taking it public in 1991. The company launched its Skytel paging service in Mexico in 1992 and bought a minority stake in US-based Univision. The Mexican government privatized the Television Azteca network in 1993, giving Televisa its first taste of competition in the TV broadcast market. The company got the legal go-ahead to develop 67 new TV stations throughout Mexico in 1994.

Televisa joined Brazil's Organizações Globo and TCI (now AT&T Broadband) in 1995 to develop direct-to-home (DTH) satellite television. (News Corp. joined the venture, now called SKY, in 1997.) The company also sold 49% of its cable TV businesses to telephone giant Teléfonos de México (Telmex).

A month before Azcárraga Milmo passed away in 1997, he installed his 29-year-old son, Emilio Azcárraga Jean, as president of the company. The company sold half of its stake in Univision the next year and slashed more jobs. Holding company Grupo Televicentro sold a 9% stake in Televisa in 2000 and used the proceeds to pay off debt. Later that year, Televisa consolidated its ownership of publishing unit Editorial Televisa (changing its name to Edivisa) and agreed to merge its radio stations with Grupo Acir.

Chairman, President, and CEO: Emilio Azcárraga Jean
VC: Alejandro Burillo Azcárraga
EVP and COO: Jaime Dávila Urcullu
EVP and CFO: Gilberto Perezalonso Cifuentes
EVP Corporate Planning: Alfonso de Angoitia Noriega
VP Finance: Guillermo Nava Gómez Tagle
VP Human Resources and Administrative Services: Guillermo Jimenez Rivas
VP Sales and Marketing: Alejandro Quintero Iñiguez
CEO Cablevisión: Pablo Vázquez Oria
CEO Innova: Jorge Alvarez Hoth
CEO Radio: Eugenio Bernal Macouzet
President, Music Recording: Guillermo R. Santiso
President, Publishing: Laura Diez Barroso de Laviada
Auditors: PricewaterhouseCoopers

LOCATIONS

HQ: Avenida Chapultepec 28, 06724 México, D.F., Mexico
Phone: +52-5-709-3333   **Fax:** +52-5-261-2019
Web site: http://www.televisa.com

PRODUCTS/OPERATIONS

1999 Sales

	% of total
Television broadcasting	59
Publishing	9
Music recording	7
Programming licensing	6
Publishing distribution	4
Cable television	4
Radio	2
Programming for pay TV	2
Other	7
Total	**100**

Selected Operations and Subsidiaries

Music Recording and Distribution Labels
Fonovisa
Melody

Paging Systems
Skytel (51%)

Publishing and Distribution
Edivisa

Radio and Television
Cable television
  Cablevisión (51%)
Direct-to-home satellite
  Innova (60%)
  SKY (Latin America and Caribbean basin, 30%)
Pay-per-view programming
Radio stations
Television broadcasting stations and networks
  Channel 2 (154 affiliate stations, 147 company-owned)
  Channel 4 (48 affiliate stations, 17 company-owned)
  Channel 5 (84 affiliate stations, 74 company-owned)
  Channel 9 (37 affiliate stations, 21 company-owned)
  Red Televisiva Megavisión (Chile, 30%)
  Univision Communications (US, 7%)
Television production

Sports and Entertainment
Azteca Stadium (Mexico City)
Soccer teams

COMPETITORS

Bertelsmann
Cisneros Group
Corporacion
  Interamericana de
  Entretenimiento
DIRECTV
MVS
Radio Centro
Telemundo
Time Warner
TV Azteca

HISTORICAL FINANCIALS & EMPLOYEES

NYSE: TV FYE: December 31	Annual Growth	12/90	12/91	12/92	12/93	12/94	12/95	12/96	12/97	12/98	12/99
Sales ($ mil.)	10.8%	750	923	1,355	1,926	1,982	1,147	1,460	1,756	1,699	1,892
Net income ($ mil.)	—	(163)	106	608	261	167	122	(76)	740	77	112
Income as % of sales	—	—	11.5%	44.9%	13.6%	8.4%	10.7%	—	42.1%	4.5%	5.9%
Earnings per share ($)	(14.7%)	—	—	—	0.57	0.40	0.30	(0.16)	1.59	0.16	0.22
Stock price - FY high ($)	—	—	—	—	72.00	73.75	32.38	34.63	40.50	43.25	72.25
Stock price - FY low ($)	—	—	—	—	63.50	29.00	12.13	22.38	22.00	14.88	18.25
Stock price - FY close ($)	(0.4%)	—	—	—	70.00	31.75	22.50	25.63	38.69	24.69	68.25
P/E - high	—	—	—	—	126	184	108	—	25	270	328
P/E - low	—	—	—	—	111	73	40	—	14	93	83
Dividends per share ($)	—	—	—	—	0.00	0.36	0.07	0.00	0.00	0.00	0.00
Book value per share ($)	10.3%	—	—	—	2.56	3.54	2.56	2.55	4.14	4.30	4.61
Employees	1.6%	—	17,500	21,200	23,600	21,600	20,700	20,700	19,900	15,400	19,900

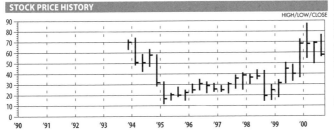

STOCK PRICE HISTORY
HIGH/LOW/CLOSE

1999 FISCAL YEAR-END
Debt ratio: 30.9%
Return on equity: 5.3%
Cash ($ mil.): 136
Current ratio: 4.71
Long-term debt ($ mil.): 911
No. of shares (mil.): 442
Dividends
  Yield: —
  Payout: —
Market value ($ mil.): 30,165

TELIA AB

OVERVIEW

Bolstered by its Scandinavian roots, Telia is taking its telecommunications offerings around the globe. Farsta-based Telia is the former telecom monopoly in Sweden, where it's still on top of the competition. The company also is reaching out to other countries with a fiber-optic network that is expected to span some 18,600 miles in Europe and the US by 2001. The company's Internet protocol (IP) backbone connects Europe, the Americas, and Asia; Telia has investments in telecom ventures in some 30 countries.

Telia provides fixed telephony services to 6 million subscribers, but most of the company's growth is driven by mobile phone service and Internet traffic. It provides wireless phone service over its GSM (global system for mobile communications) networks to some 2.5 million subscribers in Sweden and another 200,000 in Denmark and Finland. The company also is pulling its wireless customers online using SMS (short messaging service) and WAP (wireless application protocol) technologies. The leading ISP in Sweden, Telia provides Internet access to more than 620,000 customers, and it's expanding its broadband access services. Other Telia activities include directory publishing and telecom equipment sales, and it sells wholesale capacity on its networks to other carriers.

After Telia's proposed merger with Norway's Telenor fell through in 1999, the company has been tweaking its strategy to become a strong global player. The Swedish government has floated 30% of the company, with plans to reduce its stake to 51% in 2001. Telia also is narrowing its focus and shedding noncore operations, including its Swedish cable TV business, its consulting and software arm, and its telecom holdings in Africa, Asia, and Brazil.

HISTORY

Telia's wires go back to 1853 when the Swedish government created Kongl. Elektriska Telegraf-Verket to operate a telegraph line linking Stockholm and Uppsala. The next year it opened a line that reached the main European continent; the company became Telegrafverket in 1860.

Just a year after the telephone was invented in 1876, the firm installed its first phone line. The 1880s saw private phone companies sprout up in Sweden's larger cities, and by 1900 Telegrafverket had installed some 62,000 telephones. Even though Sweden was open to telecom competition, the company became a de facto monopoly in 1918 when it bought the country's largest exchange, Stockholms Allmanna Telefon. In 1921 Telegrafverket began laying its first long-distance cable.

Telegrafverket began automating its phone systems in the 1930s. After WWII, the company entered a major growth period: More than 110,000 new telephone users were connected in 1947 alone. Also in the mid-1940s, Telegrafverket launched one of the world's first mobile phone networks (closed radio).

Renamed Televerket, the firm continued to grow rapidly in the 1960s and 1970s and introduced data communications services in 1965. It teamed up with equipment maker Ericsson in 1970 to form Ellemtel, an R&D concern that developed the first all-digital public switching system. (Ellemtel ceased operations in 1999.) Televerket began moving into satellite services in 1970, when INTELSAT installed an earth station in the Nordic region. In the early 1980s it rolled out several new services, including cable TV, cellular, and international packet switching.

Meanwhile, the company began losing its monopoly status in the 1980s and lost its government funding in 1984. Fearing competition from giants such as AT&T and British Telecom, the company in 1991 joined the Netherlands' Royal KPN to form Unisource, a global telecommunications provider; Swisscom joined the group two years later. Sweden's telecom deregulation was completed in 1993, and the firm became Telia. That year it ventured into the Baltic states.

AT&T teamed up with Unisource in 1994 to provide services to multinationals. In 1995 Telia began providing Internet access and announced it was installing an overlay Internet protocol (IP) backbone. Moving into the Americas in 1997, Telia led a consortium that secured rights to offer cellular service in Brazil.

Unisource never took off, and, after AT&T jumped ship in 1998, Telia and its partners began divesting the venture's assets. In another global play, Telia agreed to merge with Norway's Telenor in 1999. But Telia's plan failed once again when the two couldn't agree to terms and scrapped the deal. In 2000 the Swedish government floated 30% of Telia, and the company bought 51% of Netcom, a Norwegian mobile phone operator.

Chairman: Lars-Eric Petersson
Acting President and CEO: Marianne Nivert
CFO: Bo Jacobsson
EVP Human Resources; VP Group Business Development: Lars Harenstam
EVP; President Telia Nara: Jan Rudberg
Business Solutions: Anders Glyder
Enterprises Business Area: Anders Bruse
President, Telia Globalcast: Raymond Jennersjo
President, Telia Mobile: Kenneth Karlberg
Auditors: Ernst & Young AB

HQ: Marbackagatan 11, SE-123 86 Farsta, Sweden
Phone: +46-8-713-10-00   **Fax:** +46-8-713-33-33
Web site: http://www.telia.se

Telia operates primarily in Denmark, Finland, Sweden, and Norway. It also has telecom interests in about 30 other countries, including Belarus, Estonia, France, Germany, Italy, Latvia, Lithuania, the Netherlands, Poland, Russia, the UK, Ukraine, and the US.

1999 Sales

	% of total
Consumer services	34
Business services	22
Enterprise services	19
Mobile	16
Carrier & networks	9
Total	**100**

Selected Subsidiaries

Belfakta SP (75%, directory services, Belarus)
China (Nantong) Skycell (13%, mobile telephony, Hong Kong)
Digitel (10%, mobile telephony, Philippines)
Eesti Telekom (25%, Estonia)
Eircom (14%, telephony, Ireland)
Infonet Services Corporation (21%, data carrier, US)
Lietuvos Telekomas (30%, telephony services, Lithuania)
MNT Uganda Ltd (30%, mobile telephony)
MTC Ltd (26%, mobile telephony, Namibia)
Netcom ASA (51%, mobile telephony, Norway)
Netia Holdings (29%, public telephony, Poland)
Punwire Paging Services Ltd (49%, India)
Si.Mobil (25%, mobile telephony, Slovenia)
SIA Televizijas Koomunikaciju Centers (49%, cable TV systems, Latvia)
Suntel Ltd, Colombo (55%, fixed telephony, Sri Lanka)
TELEConsultores LDA (50%, training and consulting, Mozambique)
Telia A/S (communications services, Denmark)
Telia Electronic Commerce AB (business communications services)
Telia Finland Oy (communications services)
Telia Iberia (ISP, Spain)
Telia UK Ltd (public telephony)
Tess S.A. (45%, mobile telephony, Brazil)

AT&T	IBM	Tele Danmark
BT	Infonet Services	Telenor
Cable and	NetCom	United Pan-
Wireless	Rostelecom	Europe
chello	RSL	Vodafone
Deutsche	Communications	World Online
Telekom	Sema Group	WorldCom
Equant	Sonera	
France Telecom	Sprint	

Stockholm: TLIA FYE: December 31	Annual Growth	12/90	12/91	12/92	12/93	12/94	12/95	12/96	12/97	12/98	12/99
Sales (SEK mil.)	7.6%	—	—	—	—	—	38,953	42,430	45,665	49,569	52,121
Net income (SEK mil.)	14.2%	—	—	—	—	—	2,484	2,337	2,222	5,011	4,222
Income as % of sales	—	—	—	—	—	—	6.4%	5.5%	4.9%	10.1%	8.1%
Employees	(1.9%)	—	—	—	—	—	33,065	34,192	32,549	30,593	30,643

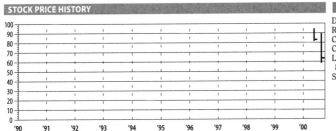

Debt ratio: 30.9%
Return on equity: 23.6%
Cash (SEK mil.): 313
Current ratio: 1.08
Long-term debt (SEK mil.): 8,841
Sales ($ mil.): 6,116

TELSTRA CORPORATION LIMITED

OVERVIEW

Telstra is on a tear. Based in Melbourne, the former monopoly still dominates telecommunications in Australia, providing a full suite of telecom services — fixed and mobile phone service, Internet access, and business data communications. Telstra provides local phone service to almost all of Australia's residential market with almost 7 million access lines in operation; it has more than 3 million business lines. It's also the country's leading provider of long-distance and international phone service. Deregulation has crashed over the Great Barrier Reef: Telstra now offers wholesale services to 30 licensed telecom operators, 50 phone service resellers, and 700 ISPs. With competition in every arena, the company is focusing on the Internet and mobile phone markets. Telstra is Australia's largest wireless operator, with 3.8 million customers. Online, the carrier provides Internet access to almost 500,000 subscribers and has developed remote access via satellite. The firm also owns 50% of pay TV operator Foxtel.

Branching out beyond Australia, Telstra is moving to offer telecom services to multinational customers: It operates facilities in Hong Kong, Japan, the UK, and New Zealand, where it is combining its operations with those of cable TV operator Austar United to form Telstra Saturn. Telstra has agreed to invest $3 billion in upstart Pacific Century CyberWorks, which is buying Cable & Wireless HKT, and the companies plan Internet backbone and mobile phone joint ventures.

The Australian government plans to sell its remaining 50.1% stake in the company.

HISTORY

When Australia became independent in 1901, telecommunications were assigned to the new Postmaster-General's Department (PMG), a state-owned monopoly. Engineer H. P. Brown, who had managed the UK's telegraph and telephone system, became head of PMG in 1923. He set up research labs that year, oversaw the first overseas call to London in 1930, and streamlined operations until his reign ended in 1939.

During WWII Australia quickly expanded its communications infrastructure to assist the Allied Front in the South Pacific. Following the war, the Australian government formed the Overseas Telecommunications Commission (OTC) in 1946 to handle international telecommunications independent of PMG.

Even as new telecom technology connected the continent and boosted PMG's productivity, its postal operations steadily recorded losses in the postwar era. In 1974 a Royal Commission recommended that postal and telecom services be split. Australian Telecommunications Commission (Telecom Australia) was launched in 1975 (OTC retained overseas services); it turned a profit in its first year.

Looking to connect residents in the outback, the firm signed Japan's Nippon Electric (now NEC) in 1981 to set up a digital radio transmission system; by the next decade it connected some 50,000 outback users. Also in 1981 Telecom Australia took a 25% stake in government-owned satellite operator AUSSAT and launched nationwide paging and mobile phone service in Melbourne and Sydney. Renamed Australian Telecommunications in 1989, the carrier got its first whiff of competition as others were allowed to provide phone equipment. Two years later Optus Communications (now Cable & Wireless Optus) began competing with Telecom Australia; for that privilege it was forced to buy the unsuccessful AUSSAT. Long-distance competition began in 1991, and a year later, mobile phone competition began. In response, Telecom Australia merged with OTC to become the Australian and Overseas Telecommunications Corporation (AOTC). AT&T's Frank Blount became CEO to lead the transition.

AOTC became Telstra Corporation in 1993 and launched a digital wireless GSM-based network. It joined with Rupert Murdoch's News Corp. to form pay TV operator Foxtel in 1995. That year Telstra teamed with Microsoft to create ISP On Australia. Microsoft dropped out in 1996, but Telstra kept the service and its portal, naming it Big Pond (renamed Telstra.com in 1999). The government fully deregulated telecommunications and sold a third of Telstra to the public in 1997.

Kerry Packer's Publishing and Broadcasting bought a 25% stake in Foxtel in 1998. The next year Telstra posted an Australian record-setting profit, former Optus CEO Ziggy Switkowski succeeded Blount, and the government floated an additional 16.6% stake. In 2000 the company announced plans to trim 10,000 jobs, despite being on pace for record profits. It also agreed to partner with UnitedGlobalCom's Austar unit in building a major telecom competitor in New Zealand.

Chairman: Robert C. Mansfield, age 49, $106,630 pay
Deputy Chairman: John T. Ralph, age 67, $89,775 pay
CEO and Managing Director: Zygmunt E. Switkowski, age 52
Group Managing Director, Finance and Administration: Paul Rizzo
Group Managing Director, Commercial and Consumer Business Unit: Peter Shore
Group Managing Director Telstra Business Solutions: Lindsay Yelland
Group Managing Director, Wholesale and International: Doug Campbell
Group Managing Director Employee Relations: Robert Cartwright
Group Managing Director, Network and Technology Group: Gerry Moriarty
Group Director, Public Affairs and Corporate Marketing: Graeme Ward
Group Managing Director Convergent Business: Ted Pretty
Group Managing Director, Mobile and Wireless Communication: Dick Simpson
Group Managing Director, Legal and Regulatory: Bruce Akhurst
Auditors: Ernst & Young; Auditor General of Melbourne

LOCATIONS

HQ: Level 41, 242 Exhibition St., Melbourne, Victoria 3000, Australia
Phone: +61-3-9634-6400   **Fax:** +61-3-9632-3215
Web site: http://telstra.com

Telstra operates primarily in Australia. It also has sales and service operations in Asia, Europe, and North America, and it has telecom facilities in Hong Kong, Japan, New Zealand, and the UK.

PRODUCTS/OPERATIONS

2000 Sales

	% of total
Mobile phone service	15
Data, text & Internet services	15
Local calls	14
Long-distance	14
Basic access	11
Fixed to mobile service	7
Directory services	6
Intercarrier services	4
Inbound calling	2
Customer premises equipment	2
Facilities management	1
Other	9
Total	**100**

Selected Brands

Conferlink (audio, video, and Internet conferencing)
DialConnect (corporate Internet access)
Easymail (e-mail)
FaxStream (enhanced fax products and services)
Freecall (toll-free 1-800 phone service)
MobileNet (cellular phone service)
OnRamp (ISDN service)
Phoneaway (prepaid calling card)
Telstra.com (Internet access and data services)

COMPETITORS

AAPT	Hutchison	Telecom
America Online	Whampoa	New Zealand
Cable & Wireless	IDT	UIH Asia/Pacific
Optus	New Tel	UnitedGlobalCom
Communication	NTT	Vodafone
Telesystems	One.Tel	Williams Group
Energis	Pacific Internet	WorldCom
	Primus	

HISTORICAL FINANCIALS & EMPLOYEES

NYSE: TLS FYE: June 30	Annual Growth	6/91	6/92	6/93	6/94	6/95	6/96	6/97	6/98	6/99	6/00
Sales ($ mil.)	3.4%	—	—	—	—	10,001	12,009	12,051	10,740	12,057	11,844
Net income ($ mil.)	12.0%	—	—	—	—	1,245	1,816	1,219	1,865	2,307	2,195
Income as % of sales	—	—	—	—	—	12.4%	15.1%	10.1%	17.4%	19.1%	18.5%
Earnings per share ($)	—	—	—	—	—	—	—	—	—	—	0.85
Stock price - FY high ($)	—	—	—	—	—	—	—	—	—	—	29.69
Stock price - FY low ($)	—	—	—	—	—	—	—	—	—	—	18.38
Stock price - FY close ($)	—	—	—	—	—	—	—	—	—	—	20.69
P/E - high	—	—	—	—	—	—	—	—	—	—	35
P/E - low	—	—	—	—	—	—	—	—	—	—	22
Dividends per share ($)	—	—	—	—	—	—	—	—	—	—	0.55
Book value per share ($)	—	—	—	—	—	—	—	—	—	—	2.69
Employees	(9.8%)	—	—	—	—	76,522	66,109	57,234	52,840	50,761

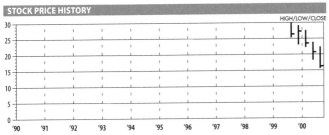

STOCK PRICE HISTORY

HIGH/LOW/CLOSE

(Chart with y-axis 0–30, x-axis years '90 through '00)

2000 FISCAL YEAR-END

Debt ratio: 45.8%
Return on equity: 32.0%
Cash ($ mil.): 448
Current ratio: 0.52
Long-term debt ($ mil.): 3,883
No. of shares (mil.): 2,577
Dividends
  Yield: 0.0%
  Payout: 0.6%
Market value ($ mil.): 53,316

TENGELMANN GROUP

OVERVIEW

If Tengelmann Group took out a personal ad, it might read: Tight-lipped billionaire who enjoys travel seeks (financially) uninhibited shopper with a healthy appetite. The Mulheim, Germany-based company is one of the largest food retailers in the world, along with German rivals METRO AG and Rewe. Its more than 7,900 supermarkets, drugstores, and specialty and discount stores cover Europe under an assortment of names, including Tengelmann and Kaiser's (grocery and drugstores), Obi (do-it-yourself supply stores), and Plus (a discount chain). In addition, Tengelmann makes chocolate and candy and is a wholesaler to German

retailers. It owns 55% of The Great Atlantic & Pacific Tea Company (A&P), which operates about 750 stores in the US and Canada.

Billionaire chairman and CEO Erivan Haub and his family own the private company and run a tight ship, rarely speaking publicly. Haub still runs the show, but his offspring are not slacking off: His youngest son, Christian, runs A&P, and the eldest, Karl Erivan, leads Tengelmann's European operations.

While Tengelmann is expanding its Plus and Obi chains, the company is closing or selling at least 600 of its Tenglemann and Kaiser's supermarkets.

HISTORY

William and Louise (Scholl) Schmitz founded Wilh. Schmitz Scholl in Mulheim, Germany, in 1867, importing goods and processing coffee. In 1893 the Schmitz's sons opened their first retail store, selling groceries, sweets, coffee, tea, and cocoa. The family called the store Tengelmann, after employee Emil Tengelmann, to avoid the social stigma then attached to grocers in Germany.

The company rebuilt after WWII left many of its stores in ruins. The man who would guide the company through much of its growth was still a youngster at this time. In 1952 Erivan Haub, the great-grandson of William and Louise Schmitz, was 20 when he was sent to the US for three years to learn the ropes at supermarkets in California and Illinois. He saw that US grocery stores, unlike most in Germany, let consumers serve themselves. Haub passed this practice along to his relatives, and Tengelmann Group opened its first self-serve stores in Germany soon afterward. Haub developed a fondness for the US during this trip that has not faded: His children were born in America to give them citizenship; St. Joseph's University in Philadelphia named its business school after Haub to recognize the family's contributions.

Haub took over as head of the company in 1969 after his uncle's death. First on his shopping list was acquisitions. He bought Kaiser's Kaffee-Geschaft, a troubled German supermarket chain, two years later, then converted some of the stores into the discount Plus format. Tengelmann came to the rescue in 1979 when it agreed to buy more than half of the troubled US supermarket chain Great Atlantic & Pacific Tea Company (A&P). Haub turned the grocer around by focusing on acquisitions and revamping older store formats.

International expansion marked the tone

of Tengelmann in the 1990s. Using its Plus discount chain as a vehicle, Tengelmann branched out into East Germany and other countries once part of the communist bloc, such as Hungary and Poland. Germany, with its stiff competition and strict laws limiting acquisitions and requiring shops to close early on weeknights, paled in comparison as a growth opportunity to the hungry environments in the East.

Tengelmann enraged Holocaust survivors in 1991 when it proposed building a Kaiser's supermarket on part of the Ravensbrueck Nazi concentration camp site, where approximately 92,000 women and children were killed. The company canceled its plans after worldwide protests, although the local community, in need of jobs, had supported the idea.

Heavy competition among German retailers (including pressure from warehouse-style stores) hammered profits in 1995. Haub announced plans to cut costs and restructure the company. The changes included modifying the Plus store format from discounter to neighborhood convenience store; Haub continued to back new deep-discount chain Ledi. Tengelmann entered a partnership in 1998 with the Pam group of Venice, merging its Italian supermarkets with Pam's and taking a stake in the venture. It also bought 165 German Tip discount stores from competitor Metro. The youngest Haub son, Christian, was promoted to CEO of A&P in 1998.

In the midst of a restructuring, in early 2000 the company announced its would sell or close at least 600 of the poorly performing Tengelmann and Kaiser's stores.

Chairman and CEO: Karl Erivan W. Haub
Managing Director of Finance: Jens-Juergen Boeckel
Personnel Director (HR): Bernd Ahlers

LOCATIONS

HQ: Wissollstrasse 5-43,
45478 Mulheim an der Ruhr, Germany
Phone: +49-208-5806-662   **Fax:** +49-208-5806-6401
Web site: http://www.tengelmann.de

Tengelmann Group has stores in Austria, Canada, the
Czech Republic, France, Germany, Hungary, Italy,
Latvia, the Netherlands, Poland, Slovenia, Spain,
Switzerland, and the US.

PRODUCTS/OPERATIONS

Selected Store Operations
The Great Atlantic & Pacific Tea Company (55%,
A&P grocery store chain)
Grosso/Magnet (grocery store chain)
Hermans Group (grocery store chain, Netherlands)
Kaiser's (grocery and drugstore chain)
Kik (discount stores)
Lowa (supermarkets, Austria)
Obi (do-it-yourself supply retailer)
Plus (grocery and goods discount store chain)
Skala Co-Op (department stores and mass-market stores)
Tengelmann (grocery store chain)
TIH (wholesaler)
WISSOLL (chocolate and candy maker)

COMPETITORS

ALDI
AVA AG
Carréfour
Casino Guichard
Delhaize
Edeka Zentrale
ITM Entreprises
METRO AG
Rewe-Zentral
Royal Ahold
SPAR Handels
Tesco
Vendex
Wal-Mart

HISTORICAL FINANCIALS & EMPLOYEES

Private FYE: June 30	Annual Growth	6/91	6/92	6/93	6/94	6/95	6/96	6/97	6/98	6/99	6/00
Sales ($ mil.)	(5.5%)	—	—	—	—	36,116	33,000	30,005	29,430	28,820	22,000
Employees	0.0%	—	—	—	—	200,000	200,000	200,000	200,000	200,000	200,000

SALES HISTORY

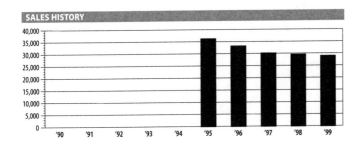

TESCO PLC

OVERVIEW

Having fed Britain its fill of food outlets, Tesco is taking its larder to new lands. The Cheshunt, UK-based company's bread and butter is its 640 or so supermarkets, superstores, and convenience stores in the UK, where it holds the crown as the country's #1 food retailer (leading rival J Sainsbury). But since 1993 the company has grown significantly outside the UK: It has about 180 stores (including hypermarkets) in Asia, Central Europe, and Ireland, where it is also the largest food retailer. Its expanding online division sells groceries in London and southern England.

Nearly half of Tesco's stores are superstores that offer food and nonfood items, including gasoline. The mature UK market has also led Tesco to bolster its sales through newer formats, including small urban stores (Tesco Metro), combination convenience stores and gasoline stations (Tesco Express), and Tesco Extra hypermarkets. Its private-label products account for about 40% of sales.

Tesco offers financial services in a joint venture with the Royal Bank of Scotland.

HISTORY

With WWI behind him, in 1919 Jack Cohen invested his serviceman's gratuity in a grocery stall in London's East End. In 1924 Cohen introduced his first private-label product, Tesco Tea; the name was the combination of the initials of his tea supplier (T. E. Stockwell) and the first two letters of Cohen's last name. By the late 1920s Cohen was operating stores in other areas of London, and in 1929 Cohen opened his first lock-up shop in Edgeware, London, under the Tesco name.

Cohen founded Tesco Stores Limited in 1932. During the remainder of the decade, the company added more than 100 stores, mainly in the London area. At the invitation of several suppliers, Cohen visited the US in 1935, studying its self-service supermarkets, and returned to England with a plan of using a similar "pile it high and sell it cheap" format. Thwarted by WWII, Tesco finally opened its first American-styled store in 1947 and went public that year as Tesco Stores Holdings. By 1950 the company operated 20 self-service stores.

During the 1950s and 1960s, Tesco grew primarily through acquisitions, including 70 Williamsons stores in 1957, 200 Harrow Stores in 1959, 212 Irwin's outlets in 1960, 97 Charles Phillips stores in 1964, and the Victor Value chain of discount stores in 1968 (sold to the Bejam Group in 1986).

By the early 1970s, however, aggressive competition and a recession battered Tesco. Managing director Ian MacLaurin initiated radical changes, including abandoning Green Shield trading stamps (introduced in 1963) and, to shed its down-market image, refurbishing stores with a more upscale decor. As a result of a price-slashing initiative in 1977, Tesco dramatically increased market share within a year. Because cheap brands were best-sellers, Tesco began creating its own private-label brands. (In

1978 private-label brands accounted for less than a fifth of sales; today they account for 40%.) The company also began closing about 500 unprofitable stores while opening superstores, some with gas stations.

In 1979, the year Sir Jack Cohen died, Tesco entered Ireland by buying Three Guys (abandoning the effort in 1986). In 1983 the company became Tesco, and two years later it named MacLaurin as chairman. In 1987 it added the 40 Yorkshire stores of Hillards. By 1991 Tesco was the largest independent retailer of gasoline in the UK.

Looking for new growth opportunities, in 1992 Tesco introduced small urban stores called Tesco Metro. The next year it acquired 97 grocery stores in France from Catteau (sold to Promodes in 1997). In 1994 Tesco acquired 57 stores in Scotland and Northern England from William Low and purchased an initial 51% stake in Global, a 43-store grocery chain in Hungary. That year it also opened Tesco Express, combination convenience stores and gas stations.

Tesco acquired 31 stores in Poland from Savia in 1995. Tesco returned to Ireland in 1997 by acquiring 109 stores in Northern Ireland and the Republic of Ireland from Associated British Food. It also launched its financial services division that year and named John Gardiner as chairman (replacing the retiring MacLaurin) and Terry Leahy as CEO. In 1998 the retailer purchased 75% of food retailer Lotus, with 13 stores in Thailand. The following year Tesco partnered with Samsung to develop Homeplus hypermarkets in South Korea.

In spring 2000 the company announced plans to expand into Taiwan and said it would triple its number of hypermarkets in the Czech Republic and Slovakia. Tesco also said it would separate its online shopping business into a wholly owned subsidiary, tesco.com.

OFFICERS

Chairman: John A. Gardiner, age 63, $300,000 pay
Deputy Chairman: David Reid, age 53, $557,000 pay
Chief Executive: Terry Leahy, age 44, $648,000 pay
Finance Director: Andrew Higginson, age 42,
$378,000 pay
Secretary: Rowley Ager, age 54, $379,000 pay
Human Resources Director: Clare Chapman
Information Technology and Logistics Director:
Philip Clarke, age 39, $249,000 pay
Commercial and Trading Director: John Gildersleeve,
age 55, $504,000 pay
Marketing and E-Commerce Director: Tim Mason,
age 42, $381,000 pay
Retail Director: Michael Wemms, age 60, $422,000 pay
Head of Operations in Northern Ireland and the
Republic of Ireland: David Potts, age 42, $314,000 pay
Auditors: PricewaterhouseCoopers

LOCATIONS

HQ: Tesco House, Delamare Rd., Cheshunt,
Hertfordshire EN8 9SL, United Kingdom
Phone: +44-1992-632-222   **Fax:** +44-1992-630-794
Web site: http://www.tesco.co.uk

Tesco operates stores in the Czech Republic, France,
Hungary, Ireland, Poland, Slovakia, South Korea,
Thailand, and the UK.

2000 Sales

	$ mil.	% of total
Europe		
UK	29,225	90
Other countries	2,434	8
Asia	792	2
Adjustment	(2,785)	—
Total	**29,666**	**100**

PRODUCTS/OPERATIONS

Stores
Global (Hungary)
Homeplus (81%, South Korea)
Lotus (75%, Thailand)
Tesco
Tesco Express
Tesco Extra
Tesco Metro

COMPETITORS

ALDI
ASDA Group
Boots Company
BP
Budgens
Carréfour
Exxon Mobil
J Sainsbury
John Lewis Partnership
Marks & Spencer
METRO AG
Royal Ahold
Royal Dutch/Shell
Safeway plc
Somerfield
Wm Morrison
Supermarkets

HISTORICAL FINANCIALS & EMPLOYEES

OTC: TSCDY FYE: Last Saturday in February	Annual Growth	2/91	2/92	2/93	2/94	2/95	2/96	2/97	2/98	2/99	2/00
Sales ($ mil.)	10.4%	12,140	12,745	10,807	12,775	15,998	18,502	24,403	29,277	27,451	29,666
Net income ($ mil.)	7.0%	579	695	563	443	602	713	847	832	970	1,064
Income as % of sales	—	4.8%	5.5%	5.2%	3.5%	3.8%	3.9%	3.5%	2.8%	3.5%	3.6%
Earnings per share ($)	9.0%	—	—	—	—	—	0.34	0.38	0.40	0.43	0.48
Stock price - FY high ($)	—	—	—	—	—	—	5.38	6.25	9.13	10.38	9.63
Stock price - FY low ($)	—	—	—	—	—	—	3.94	3.88	5.44	2.92	5.75
Stock price - FY close ($)	19.4%	—	—	—	—	—	4.00	5.38	8.50	8.75	8.12
P/E - high	—	—	—	—	—	—	16	16	23	24	20
P/E - low	—	—	—	—	—	—	12	10	14	7	12
Dividends per share ($)	9.3%	—	—	—	—	—	0.15	0.17	0.19	0.20	0.21
Book value per share ($)	6.5%	—	—	—	—	—	2.57	2.91	2.90	3.10	3.31
Employees	(6.4%)	—	—	—	—	—	—	98,440	124,172	131,031	80,650

STOCK PRICE HISTORY

HIGH/LOW/CLOSE

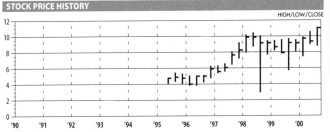

2000 FISCAL YEAR-END

Debt ratio: 51.4%
Return on equity: 14.6%
Cash ($ mil.): 139
Current ratio: 0.38
Long-term debt ($ mil.): 2,470
No. of shares (mil.): 2,274
Dividends
  Yield: 0.0%
  Payout: 0.4%
Market value ($ mil.): 18,468

THE THOMSON CORPORATION

OVERVIEW

The Thomson Corporation can help with everything from portfolio management to prescription drug information to math homework. The Toronto-based company provides specialized information through online services, CD-ROMs and computer software, and printed materials. It provides legal and regulatory data, as well as educational, financial, health care, reference, and scientific information. Thomson also publishes some 130 newspapers in North America, including Toronto's *The Globe and Mail.*

The company is concentrating on electronically delivered products and has announced its intention to dramatically increase Internet-related sales. As part of that strategy, it has agreed to buy rival information provider Primark for about $1 billion, and has acquired

investor research firm Carson Group. Thomson's online products include legal directory lawoffice.com and research service investext.com. It also is forming a powerhouse media venture with Canadian telecommunications firm BCE with $2.7 billion in assets. The yet-to-be-named company will consist of Thomson assets *The Globe and Mail;* sister Web site Globe Interactive; and the company's 50% stake in ROBTV, a business television channel. BCE plans to contribute its CTV national TV network and Sympatico Internet portal to the venture. Thomson will own 20% of the new firm.

Thomson has agreed to buy some Harcourt General businesses (worth $2.6 billion), after Harcourt is purchased by Reed Elsevier. The Thomson family owns 73% of the company.

HISTORY

Having failed at farming and auto parts distribution, Roy Thomson left Toronto for the hinterlands of Ontario and started a radio station in 1930. He purchased the *Timmons Press,* a gold-mining town newspaper, in 1934. Thomson bought other town papers, venturing outside Ontario in 1949 and into the US in 1952.

The Thomson Newspaper empire grew rapidly during the 1950s. Thomson moved to the UK in 1953, where he bought the *Scotsman* (Edinburgh). When commercial TV broadcasting began in the UK, Thomson started Scottish Television (1957) and merged it with the UK's Kemsley Newspapers, publisher of the *Sunday Times,* to create the International Thomson Organization in 1959.

International Thomson bought the *Times* of London (1967) and entered the travel business. Queen Elizabeth II conferred the title of Lord upon Thomson in 1970. The next year J. Paul Getty invited International Thomson into a North Sea oil drilling venture. The consortium struck oil in 1973, just as the OPEC oil embargo took hold. Oil accounted for the bulk of International Thomson's profits by 1976, when Lord Thomson died. His son, Kenneth, took over as chairman. In 1978 a public holding company was created to house International Thomson's operations.

Using oil earnings to expand and diversify its publishing interests, the company sold the *Times* in 1981 and began shopping for specialty publishers with subscription-based revenues, which would be less vulnerable to recession. Purchases included American Banker and Bond Buyer (financial publications, 1983),

Gale Research (library reference materials, 1985), Lawyers Cooperative Publishing (1989), and several online information providers. The company completed the sale of its oil and gas holdings a year later.

Thomson Newspapers and International Thomson merged to become The Thomson Corporation in 1989, and in 1991 it bought Maxwell's Macmillan Professional and Business Reference Publishing. The company grouped its newspapers in regional clusters, and by the end of 1996 it had sold 74 Canadian and US newspapers.

In 1998 Thomson veteran Richard Harrington became CEO. Also that year Thomson bought tax return software maker Computer Language Research for $325 million. It also bought Knight Ridder's Technimetrics financial information unit and spun off its travel group business. The next year Thomson bought reference book publisher Macmillan Library Reference USA from Pearson.

In 2000 Thomson announced it would sell its newspapers (excluding *The Globe and Mail*) to focus on the Internet. It bought Sylvan Learning Systems' Prometric division, which provides computer-based testing services, and Wave Technologies International, a provider of multimedia instructional products. Thomson also bought the online data services division of Dialog (now Bright Station). Thomson also bought rival financial data provider Primark for $1 billion and investor relations firm Carson Group, and it agreed to purchase Brazil's IOB regulatory publisher and acquiring Argentinian legal publisher La Ley.

Chairman: Kenneth R. Thomson, $1,214,458 pay
President and CEO: Richard J. Harrington,
$2,772,000 pay
EVP and CFO: Robert D. Daleo
EVP and COO: David H. Schaffer, $2,110,500 pay
EVP and Human Resources Officer: Theron S. Hoffman
EVP; President and CEO, Thomson Learning:
Robert S. Christie
**EVP; President and CEO, Thomson Scientific,
Reference, and Healthcare:** Ronald H. Schlosser
**EVP; President and CEO, Thomson Legal &
Regulatory:** Brian H. Hall, $1,759,968 pay
EVP; President and CEO, Thomson Financial:
Patrick J. Tierney
SVP; President and CEO, Newspaper Group:
Stuart M. Garner, $1,653,372 pay
SVP, General Counsel, and Secretary: Michael S. Harris
Auditors: PricewaterhouseCoopers LLP

LOCATIONS

HQ: Toronto Dominion Bank Tower, Ste. 2706,
Toronto-Dominion Center,
Toronto, Ontario M5K 1A1, Canada
Phone: 416-360-8700   **Fax:** 416-360-8812
US HQ: Metro Center 1 Station Place, 6th Fl.,
Stamford, CT 06902
US Phone: 203-328-9400   **US Fax:** 203-328-8398
Web site: http://www.thomcorp.com

1999 Sales

	% of total
US	83
UK	8
Canada	5
Other countries	4
Total	**100**

PRODUCTS/OPERATIONS

Selected Operations
Thomson Financial
First Call (real-time broker research)
The Globe and Mail (Canadian newspaper)
Primark
EDGAR Direct (electronic delivery of SEC
filings & documents)
I/B/E/S (analytic estimates)
Thomson Learning
Brooks/Cole (math, science, engineering, and
statistics course materials)
Wave Technologies International (information
technology instruction products)
Thomson Legal & Regulatory
Lawoffice.com (online legal directory)
West Group (legal information)
Thomson Scientific, Reference & Healthcare
Dialog (online professional information)
Macmillan Reference USA (school and library
reference material)
Physician's Desk Reference (healthcare directory)

COMPETITORS

Addison-Wesley	Grolier	Pearson
Bell & Howell	Harcourt	Reed Elsevier
Berkshire	General	Reuters
Hathaway	HCIA	Southam
Bloomberg	Hollinger	Torstar
Bridge	Hoover's	Tribune
Information	Hungry Minds	United News &
Dow Jones	IHS Group	Media
Dun &	infoUSA	W.W. Norton
Bradstreet	John Wiley	Wolters Kluwer
Encyclopaedia	LEXIS-NEXIS	
Britannica	McGraw-Hill	

HISTORICAL FINANCIALS & EMPLOYEES

Toronto: TOC FYE: December 31	Annual Growth	12/90	12/91	12/92	12/93	12/94	12/95	12/96	12/97	12/98	12/99
Sales (C$ mil.)	3.3%	6,261	6,407	7,226	7,546	8,687	9,909	10,579	12,532	9,643	8,357
Net income (C$ mil.)	5.2%	490	367	220	357	584	1,082	796	828	2,796	773
Income as % of sales	—	7.8%	5.7%	3.0%	4.7%	6.7%	10.9%	7.5%	6.6%	29.0%	9.2%
Earnings per share (C$)	4.8%	0.82	0.61	0.36	0.62	1.01	1.84	1.30	1.30	4.57	1.25
Stock price - FY high (C$)	—	17.00	18.25	17.63	16.88	19.00	19.50	31.30	40.50	45.65	51.00
Stock price - FY low (C$)	—	12.50	14.00	12.13	13.75	16.38	16.38	18.25	26.25	29.05	35.50
Stock price - FY close (C$)	9.3%	17.00	16.00	14.50	16.25	19.00	19.00	30.25	39.25	35.90	38.00
P/E - high	—	21	30	49	27	19	11	24	31	10	41
P/E - low	—	15	23	34	22	16	9	14	20	6	28
Dividends per share (C$)	7.3%	0.51	0.52	0.55	0.58	0.64	0.70	0.76	0.84	0.97	0.96
Book value per share (C$)	11.6%	6.08	6.23	6.23	6.62	7.52	9.02	10.55	11.59	16.85	16.36
Employees	(3.5%)	44,800	45,800	46,000	46,400	48,250	48,600	47,800	48,400	48,000	32,500

STOCK PRICE HISTORY

1999 FISCAL YEAR-END

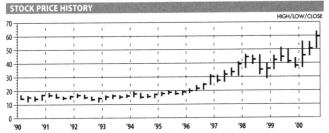
HIGH/LOW/CLOSE

Debt ratio: 21.6%
Return on equity: —
Cash (C$ mil.): 478
Current ratio: 0.89
Long-term debt (C$ mil.): 2,774
No. of shares (mil.): 621
Dividends
  Yield: 0.0%
  Payout: 0.8%
Market value ($ mil.): 16,263
Sales ($ mil.): 5,756

THYSSENKRUPP AG

OVERVIEW

You can bet the receptionist at Fried. Krupp AG Hoesch-Krupp jumped for joy when the company announced that it was merging with Thyssen (pronounced "TISS-in") to form Düsseldorf, Germany-based ThyssenKrupp. Besides creating a much shorter name, the marriage of the two leading German industrial and engineering firms created Germany's fifth-largest company.

The largest of ThyssenKrupp's businesses is the steel division, ThyssenKrupp Stahl. Specializing in carbon and stainless steel, the unit was created as a joint venture of both companies' steel units in 1997. ThyssenKrupp's automotive unit makes bodies, chassis, power-trains, and suspension systems. ThyssenKrupp Industries makes elevators, machine tools, plastics machinery, and bearings and other components; it also builds merchant and naval ships. The engineering division builds chemical and cement plants and makes waste-treatment and surface-mining systems. The materials and services division handles project management and industrial and building services.

Weak economic conditions in Asia, Europe, and Latin America and dropping steel prices have damaged steel companies worldwide. ThyssenKrupp had planned to spin off its steel division to focus on its engineering business, but is reconsidering its options in light of its falling stock price. Meanwhile, the company offered to buy the engineering businesses of Mannesmann AG for $8.4 billion. The Krupp Foundation owns 17% of the new company; the government of Iran owns nearly 8%.

HISTORY

Formed separately in the 1800s, both Thyssen and Krupp flourished under family control and then enjoyed a resurgence after nearly falling into ruin following WWII. Friedrich Krupp opened his steel factory in 1811. He died in 1826 and left the nearly bankrupt factory to his 14-year-old son Alfred, who turned the firm around. At the first World's Fair in 1851, Alfred unveiled a steel cannon that was far superior to older bronze models.

Twenty years later, August Thyssen founded a puddling and rolling mill near Mulheim. He bought up small factories and mines and, by the beginning of WWI, ran Germany's largest iron and steel company.

The years after WWII were tough for both companies. Thyssen was split up by the Allies, and when it began production again in 1953, it consisted of one steel plant. In the Krupp camp Alfred's great grandson Alfried was convicted in 1948 of using slave labor during WWII. Released from prison in 1951, Alfried rebuilt Krupp. Both companies prospered and expanded as the German economy began recovering in the 1950s.

By the 1980s Thyssen's businesses included ships, locomotives, offshore oil rigs, specialty steel, and metals trading and distribution. Iran acquired 25% of Krupp in 1976. Krupp continued to grow, and in 1992 it took over Hoesch AG, an engineering and steelmaking firm only slightly smaller than itself. (Eberhard Hoesch began making railroad tracks in the 1820s. The company grew and expanded into infrastructure and building products.)

The new Fried. Krupp AG Hoesch-Krupp bought Italian specialty steelmaker Acciai Speciali Terni, chemical plant builder Uhde, and South African shipper J.H. Bachmann. Its automotive division formed a joint venture in Brazil and added production sites in China, Mexico, Romania, and the US.

In 1997 Thyssen expanded in North America with its $675 million acquisition of US machine-tool maker Giddings & Lewis. Also in 1997 Thyssen agreed to merge its shipbuilding unit with Preussag AG's to create Germany's largest shipbuilder.

Krupp attempted a hostile takeover of Thyssen in 1997. The takeover failed, but the companies soon agreed to merge their quality steel operations to form Thyssen Krupp Stahl. Bigger plans were in the works, and in 1998 the two firms agreed to merge.

In 1999 Krupp's Krupp Hoesch Automotive division agreed to buy Cummins' Atlas Crankshaft subsidiary. Thyssen also bought US-based Dover's elevator business for $1.1 billion. Krupp and Thyssen completed their merger in 1999. The company planned to enter the Chinese metals industry by building a $295 million stainless-steel mill in Shanghai in a joint venture with Shanghai Baosteel Group.

ThyssenKrupp offered to buy the engineering businesses of Mannesmann AG the following year. It also sold its Krupp Kunststofftechnik unit (plastic molding machines) for about $183 million. Also in 2000 ThyssenKrupp's Budd Company subsidiary bought Stahl Specialty Company (aluminum foundry).

Executive Board Co-Chairman; Executive Board Chairman Thyssen Krupp Automotive: Gerhard Cromme
Executive Board Co-Chairman; Executive Board Chairman Thyssen Krupp Steel: Ekkehard Schulz
Executive Board Chairman Thyssen Krupp Materials & Services: Hans-Erich Forster
Executive Board Chairman Thyssen Krupp Industries: Eckhard Rohkamm
Controller and Director, Mergers and Acquisitions: Ulrich Middelmann
Director of Accounting, Taxes, Foreign Organization, Materials Management, and Information Technology: Gerhard Jooss
Director of Finance, Investor Relations, Group Investments, and Insurance: Heinz-Gerd Stein
Human Resources; Labor Director Thyssen Krupp Steel: Dieter Hennig

HQ: August-Thyssen-Strasse 1, D-40221 Düsseldorf, Germany
Phone: +49-211-824-1000   Fax: +49-211-824-6000
Web site: http://www.thyssenkrupp.com/eng

Selected Subsidiaries
The Budd Company (auto components, US)
Copper and Brass Sales, Inc. (US, copper and brass plate, rod, bar, wire, coil, and sheet)
Giddings & Lewis, Inc. (machine tools, US)
Krupp Bilstein (suspension components)
Krupp Fordertechnik (mining, processing, and handling equipment)
Krupp Uhde GmbH (design and construction of chemical and industrial plants)
Mediagate Gesellschaft fur (information services)
Thyssen Krupp Stahl AG (lightweight steel)

Allegheny Technologies	Magna International
ARBED	MAN
Bechtel	Mannesmann AG
Bethlehem Steel	Marubeni
Cargill	mg technologies
Corus Group	Mitsubishi
Daewoo	Mitsui
Dana	Nippon Steel
E.ON	Robert Bosch
Franz Haniel	Rolls-Royce
GE	RWE
HBG	Siemens
Hyundai	Tenneco Automotive
Ingersoll-Rand	Tower Automotive
Ispat International	TRW
ITOCHU	Usinor
LTV	USX-U.S. Steel

Frankfurt: TKA FYE: September 30	Annual Growth	9/90	9/91	9/92	9/93	9/94	9/95	9/96	9/97	9/98	9/99
Sales (€ mil.)	5.4%	18,502	18,694	18,281	17,129	17,869	20,003	19,773	20,837	22,260	29,794
Net income (€ mil.)	(3.1%)	353	266	179	(508)	46	396	179	1,115	1,120	267
Income as % of sales	—	1.9%	1.4%	1.0%	—	0.3%	2.0%	0.9%	5.4%	5.0%	0.9%
Earnings per share (€)	—	—	—	—	—	—	—	—	—	—	0.55
Stock price - FY high (€)	—	—	—	—	—	—	—	—	—	—	24.50
Stock price - FY low (€)	—	—	—	—	—	—	—	—	—	—	17.25
Stock price - FY close (€)	—	—	—	—	—	—	—	—	—	—	18.55
P/E - high	—	—	—	—	—	—	—	—	—	—	45
P/E - low	—	—	—	—	—	—	—	—	—	—	31
Dividends per share (€)	—	—	—	—	—	—	—	—	—	—	0.00
Book value per share (€)	—	—	—	—	—	—	—	—	—	—	16.64
Employees	2.1%	152,708	148,250	148,272	141,009	131,863	126,987	122,659	127,873	116,174	184,770

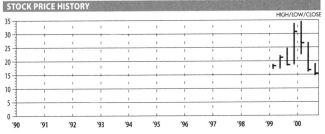

HIGH/LOW/CLOSE

Debt ratio: 8.0%
Return on equity: —
Cash (€ mil.): 768
Current ratio: 11.12
Long-term debt (€ mil.): 562
No. of shares (mil.): 484
Dividends
  Yield: —
  Payout: —
Market value ($ mil.): 9,567
Sales ($ mil.): 31,749

TOKIO MARINE AND FIRE

OVERVIEW

The Big Bang is lighting a fire under Tokio Marine and Fire Insurance, Japan's oldest and largest property/casualty insurance company (Yasuda Fire and Marine is #2).

The company provides commercial marine, fire, property/casualty, flight coverage, personal accident, liability, and auto insurance through more than 500 offices nationwide. It also has offices in 16 other countries; its foreign non-life operations have been consolidated and moved to business-friendly Dublin, Ireland. The firm is allied with the Mitsubishi industrial group.

The ailing Japanese economy has hurt Tokio Marine, but it hopes to draw more customers by selling on the Internet and offering extended hours and express service for accidents. It is also expanding its lines to include such products as long-term-care insurance for Japan's growing elderly population and coverage for bacterial food poisoning. The company has slashed premiums to draw new consumers (Japan's insurance rates were strictly regulated before the Big Bang). Tokio Marine is also entering the brokerage business in Japan through a joint venture with Charles Schwab.

Deregulation has allowed Tokio Marine to add a life insurance subsidiary; the company has also begun to insure companies and governments against adverse weather. On the downside, the dismantling of Japan's *keiretsu* is allowing more vigorous consolidation: The pending merger of insurers Mitsui Marine & Fire, Nippon Fire & Marine, and Koa Fire & Marine could dethrone Tokio Marine as Japan's largest property/casualty insurer. However, the company is strengthening itself by forming a partnership with Asahi Mutual Life Insurance and Nichido Fire & Marine Insurance.

HISTORY

After the US forced Japan to open to trade in 1854, Western marine insurers began operating there. In 1878 Japan's government organized backers for a Japanese marine insurance firm. Tokio Marine and Fire was founded the next year.

Tokio grew quickly, insuring trading companies like Mitsubishi and Mitsui; it soon had offices in London, Paris, and New York. Increased competition in the 1890s forced it to curtail its foreign operations and begin using brokers in most other countries.

Victory in the Russo-Japanese War of 1904-05 buoyed the country, but the economy slowed as it demobilized. Businesses responded by forming cooperative groups known as *zaibatsu*. Tokio Marine and Fire was allied with the Mitsubishi group.

Before WWI, Tokio expanded by adding fire, personal accident, theft, and auto insurance; it continued to buy new foreign sales brokers. Japan's insurance industry consolidated in the 1920s, and the company bought up smaller competitors. The 1923 Tokyo earthquake hit the industry hard, but Tokio's new fire insurance operations had little exposure.

Most of Tokio Marine's foreign operations were seized during WWII. In 1944 Tokio merged with Mitsubishi Marine Insurance and Meiji Fire Insurance. Business grew in WWII, but wartime destruction left Tokio with nothing to insure and no money to pay claims.

After the war, Tokio slowly recovered and resumed overseas operations. Although the US had dismantled the *zaibatsu* during occupation, Tokio Marine allied once again with Mitsubishi when Japan's government rebuilt most of the old groups as *keiretsu*.

During the 1950s and 1960s, the company grew its personal lines, adding homeowners coverage. Domestic business slowed during the 1970s and 1980s, and Tokio boosted operations overseas. It added commercial property/casualty insurer Houston General Insurance (a US company sold in 1997), Tokio Reinsurance, and interests in insurance and investment management firms.

In the 1980s the firm invested heavily in real estate through *jusen* (mortgage companies). In the early 1990s Japan's overheated real estate market collapsed, dumping masses of nonperforming assets on *jusen* and their investors (Japan's major banks and insurers, including Tokio Marine).

Deregulation began in 1996; economic recession soon followed. In 1998 Tokio Marine joined other members of the Mitsubishi group, including Bank of Tokyo-Mitsubishi and Meiji Life Insurance, to form investment banking, pension, and trust joint ventures. The firm also formed its own investment trust and allied with such foreign financial companies as BANK ONE to develop new investment products. Brokerage Charles Schwab Tokio Marine Securities, a joint venture, was launched in 1999. Also that year Tokio consolidated its foreign reinsurance operations into Tokio Marine Global Re in Dublin, Ireland, and kicked off a business push that included reorganizing its agent force and planning for online sales.

OFFICERS

Chairman: Shunji Kono
President: Koukei Higuchi
Senior Managing Director: Yukio Hayama
Senior Managing Director: Takehisa Kikuchi
Senior Managing Director: Akihiko Mori
Senior Managing Director: Hirotada Seyama
Senior Managing Director: Shoji Ueno
Senior Managing Director: Makoto Akutsu
Senior Managing Director: Kunio Ishihara
Senior Managing Director: Toshikazu Kakudai
Auditors: KPMG

LOCATIONS

HQ: Tokyo Kaijo Kasai Hoken Kabushiki Kaisha
(The Tokio Marine and Fire Insurance
Company, Limited)
2-1, Marunouchi 1-chome, Chiyoda-ku,
Tokyo 100-8050, Japan
Phone: +81-3-3212-6211   **Fax:** +81-3-5223-3100
US HQ: 101 Park Ave., New York, NY 10178
US Phone: 212-297-6600   **US Fax:** 212-986-6898
Web site: http://www.tokiomarine.co.jp

PRODUCTS/OPERATIONS

2000 Premiums

	% of total
Voluntary & compulsory auto	60
Fire & allied	12
Personal accident	10
Marine	4
Other	14
Total	**100**

Selected Subsidiaries and Affiliates

America Latina Companhia de Seguros (Brazil,
property/casualty and life insurance)
P.T. Asuransi Tokio Marine Indonesia (property/casualty
insurance)
Charles Schwab Tokio Marine Securities (joint venture,
brokerage)
Morita & Co., Inc. (US, property/casualty and life
insurance)
TM Claims Service, Inc. (US, product liability and cargo
insurance)
TM Management Services Ltd. (UK, administration)
The Tokio Marine and Fire Insurance Co. (Singapore)
Pte. Limited (property/casualty insurance)
The Tokio Marine and Fire Insurance Co. (Hong Kong)
Limited (property/casualty insurance)
Tokio Marine Asset Management New York Co., Ltd. (US,
investments)
Tokio Marine Investment Services, Limited. (Hong
Kong, investment services)
Tokio Marine Realty Co., Ltd. (US, real estate
investments)
Tokio Re Corporation (US, property/casualty insurance)
Trans Pacific Insurance Company (US, property/casualty
insurance)
Vietnam International Assurance Company
(property/casualty insurance)

COMPETITORS

AEGON	GeneralCologne	Nippon Life
AIG	Re	Insurance
Allianz	HCC Insurance	Sumitomo
AXA	ING	Marine & Fire
CGNU plc	Kemper	The Hartford
Chiyoda Mutual	Insurance	Travelers
Life	Mitsui Marine &	Yasuda Fire &
CIGNA	Fire	Marine
CNA Financial		Insurance

HISTORICAL FINANCIALS & EMPLOYEES

Nasdaq: TKIOY FYE: March 31	Annual Growth	3/91	3/92	3/93	3/94	3/95	3/96	3/97	3/98	3/99	3/00
Assets ($ mil.)	3.9%	54,150	50,283	59,496	70,904	79,361	73,235	61,077	58,158	64,451	76,146
Net income ($ mil.)	4.7%	526	155	519	1,933	1,021	806	952	1,138	1,225	794
Income as % of assets	—	1.0%	0.3%	0.9%	2.7%	1.3%	1.1%	1.6%	2.0%	1.9%	1.0%
Earnings per share ($)	4.8%	1.68	0.50	1.66	6.25	3.30	2.60	3.07	3.60	3.89	2.56
Stock price - FY high ($)	—	56.50	55.25	53.50	67.00	66.00	69.25	69.00	66.00	62.81	67.00
Stock price - FY low ($)	—	34.50	36.50	32.25	49.25	49.88	50.88	42.00	41.25	39.00	45.00
Stock price - FY close ($)	1.3%	46.50	37.88	53.25	59.75	58.36	65.00	50.75	56.00	56.13	52.44
P/E - high	—	34	111	32	11	20	27	22	18	16	26
P/E - low	—	21	73	19	8	15	20	14	11	10	18
Dividends per share ($)	4.0%	0.21	0.25	0.27	0.32	0.34	0.38	0.32	0.32	0.30	0.30
Book value per share ($)	4.5%	54.59	44.76	52.50	68.45	73.74	73.63	60.09	57.27	66.31	81.03
Employees	0.5%	12,995	14,054	14,500	14,900	14,000	14,000	14,029	15,294	13,751	13,616

STOCK PRICE HISTORY

HIGH/LOW/CLOSE

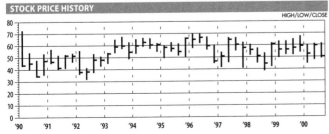

2000 FISCAL YEAR-END

Equity as % of assets: 33.0%
Return on assets: 1.1%
Return on equity: 3.5%
Long-term debt ($ mil.): 472
No. of shares (mil.): 310
Dividends
  Yield: 0.0%
  Payout: 0.1%
Market value ($ mil.): 16,251
Sales ($ mil.): 14,304

TOKYO ELECTRIC POWER

Tokyo residents might see their country's currency fluctuate, but they can count on constant current from The Tokyo Electric Power Company (TEPCO). One of the world's largest electric utilities, the Tokyo-based company serves 26 million customers in Japan's Kanto region.

TEPCO has a generating capacity of 56,800 MW, produced at fossil fuel (56%), nuclear (30%), and hydroelectric (14%) power plants. Although public confidence has been shaken by a rash of accidents and cover-ups within Japan's nuclear industry, the firm has been reducing its dependency on oil by developing nuclear, hydroelectric, and gas-fired power plants. In the wake of the liberalization of

Japan's electric industry in 1995, TEPCO also purchases electricity generated by independent power producers.

Deregulation is shaking up the Japanese power market in 2000: Large customers (accounting for 30% of TEPCO's sales) are now allowed to choose their suppliers. In response, the company is moving into telephony and Internet services. TEPCO owns a major stake in Tokyo Telecommunication Network (TTNet), which provides local and long-distance phone service. It's also teaming up with SOFTBANK and Microsoft in a joint venture called SpeedNet. The venture provides Internet access via fiber-optic cables strung alongside TEPCO power lines.

The Tokyo Electric Power Company (TEPCO) traces its heritage to Tokyo Electric Light, formed in 1883. It switched on Japan's first power plant in 1887, a 25-KW fossil fuel generator that supplied many customers with their first electric power. Fossil fuels were the primary source of electricity in Japan until 1912, when long-distance transmission techniques became more efficient, making hydroelectric power considerably cheaper.

In 1938 the Japanese government nationalized electric utilities, despite strong objections from Yasuzaemon Matsunaga, a leader in Japan's utility industry and former president of the Japan Electric Association. After WWII Matsunaga championed public ownership of Japan's power companies, helping in 1951 to establish the current system of 10 regional companies, each with a service monopoly. Of these 10 companies, Tokyo Electric Power was the largest. That year it was listed on the Tokyo Stock Exchange. The Ministry of International Trade and Industry has regulated electric utilities since 1965.

Fossil fuel plants made a comeback in Japan in the postwar era because they could be built more economically than hydroelectric plants. When the OPEC oil embargo of the 1970s highlighted Japan's dependence on foreign oil, TEPCO increased its use of liquefied natural gas (LNG) and nuclear energy sources. (It brought its first nuke online in 1971.) In 1977 it formed the Energy Conservation Center to promote conservation and related legislation. The next year it opened an office in Washington, DC, to exchange data with the US government and utility industry.

In 1982 TEPCO joined other US and

Japanese firms in building a coal gasification plant in California's Mojave Desert, to further reduce its oil dependence. Two years later TEPCO announced it would begin building its first coal-burning generator since the oil crisis. It established Tokyo Telecommunication Network (TTNet), a partnership to provide telecommunications services, in 1986 and TEPCO Cable TV in 1989.

As part of its interest in alternative energy systems, TEPCO established a global environment department in 1990 to conduct R&D on energy and the environment (such as global warming studies). Its environmental program has included growing beech trees for reforestation and demonstrating the use of phosphoric acid fuel cells as an alternative to standard fuel generation.

Liberalization in 1995 allowed Japan's electric utilities to buy power from independent power producers (IPPs); TEPCO quickly lined up 10 suppliers. The company proceeded with energy experimentation in 1996, trying a 6,000-KW sodium-sulfur battery at a Yokohama transformer station.

To gain experience in deregulating markets, TEPCO and trading house Mitsubishi Corporation agreed to invest in US power generating company Orion Power in 1999. At home the firm joined Microsoft and SOFTBANK to form joint venture SpeedNet, which provides Internet access over TTNet's fiber-optic network. In 2000 it announced joint ventures to build cogeneration systems for businesses and to provide digital cable TV. TEPCO also got its first taste of deregulation when large customers (accounting for about a third of the utility's sales) began choosing their electricity suppliers.

Chairman: Hiroshi Araki
President: Nobuya Minami
EVP: Tsunehisa Katsumata
EVP: Shigemi Tamura
EVP: Takeshi Taneichi
EVP: Masaru Yamamoto
EVP: Ryoichi Shirato
EVP: Katsumasa Ishige
Managing Director: Takashi Aoki
Managing Director: Toshiaki Enomoto
Managing Director: Hidehiko Haru
Managing Director: Teruaki Masumoto
Managing Director: Masakatsu Ikawa
Managing Director: Tsuneo Futami
General Manager Finance: Norimitsu Muramatsu
**General Manager Employee Relations and Human
  Resources:** Hisao Naito
Auditors: Showa Ota & Co.

PRODUCTS/OPERATIONS

2000 Electricity sales

	% of total
Commercial & industrial	42
Residential	30
Deregulated	28
Total	**100**

Major Subsidiaries
Japan COM Company, Limited
Toden Kogyo Co., Ltd.
Tokyo Densetsu Services Co., Ltd.
The Tokyo Electric Generation Company, Incorporated
Tokyo Electric Power Environmental Engineering
  Company, Incorporated
Tokyo Electric Power Home Service Company, Limited
The Tokyo Electric Power Real Estate Maintenance
  Co., Inc.
Tokyo Electric Power Services Company, Limited

LOCATIONS

HQ: Tokyo Denryoku Kabushiki Kaisha
(The Tokyo Electric Power Company, Incorporated)
1-3, Uchisaiwai-cho 1-chome,
Chiyoda-ku, Tokyo 100-0011, Japan
Phone: +81-3-4216-1111   **Fax:** +81-3-4216-6220
US HQ: 1901 L St. NW, Ste. 720, Washington, DC 20036
US Phone: 202-457-0790   **US Fax:** 202-457-0810
Web site: http://www.tepco.co.jp

The Tokyo Electric Power Company serves Japan's Kanto
region, which includes Tokyo and Yokohama. It also has
interests in power plants in China, India, Indonesia,
Malaysia, and Thailand.

COMPETITORS

BT	ORIX
Enron	Pacific Gateway Exchange
Global One	PSINet
Internet Initiative Japan	Showa Shell Sekiyu
Japan Telecom	Texaco
Kansai Electric	Tohoku Electric Power
KDDI	Tokyo Gas
Mitsui	UUNET
NTT	WorldCom

HISTORICAL FINANCIALS & EMPLOYEES

Tokyo: 7951 FYE: March 31	Annual Growth	3/91	3/92	3/93	3/94	3/95	3/96	3/97	3/98	3/99	3/00
Sales (¥ bil.)	1.7%	4,384	4,597	4,700	4,721	5,002	5,054	5,039	5,278	5,088	5,092
Net income (¥ bil.)	4.4%	59	75	74	62	87	52	82	135	97	87
Income as % of sales	—	1.3%	1.6%	1.6%	1.3%	1.7%	1.0%	1.6%	2.6%	1.9%	1.7%
Earnings per share (¥)	6.3%	44.00	56.00	55.00	46.00	60.00	36.00	60.00	100.00	72.00	—
Stock price - FY high (¥)	—	5,050	3,980	3,386	4,406	3,317	2,830	2,880	2,550	3,000	3,110
Stock price - FY low (¥)	—	2,653	2,713	2,178	2,782	2,485	2,505	2,120	2,080	2,350	2,020
Stock price - FY close (¥)	(5.7%)	3,802	2,851	3,297	3,129	2,693	2,740	2,250	2,520	2,550	2,250
P/E - high	—	115	71	62	96	55	79	48	26	42	—
P/E - low	—	60	48	40	60	41	70	35	21	33	—
Dividends per share (¥)	2.0%	50.00	50.00	50.00	50.00	50.00	50.00	50.00	50.00	50.00	60.00
Book value per share (¥)	3.1%	1,037.00	1,043.00	1,049.00	1,045.00	1,122.00	1,100.00	1,159.00	1,180.00	1,180.12	1,367.21
Employees	(0.1%)	39,640	40,081	40,789	41,967	43,122	43,448	43,166	42,672	42,700	39,334

STOCK PRICE HISTORY

HIGH/LOW/CLOSE

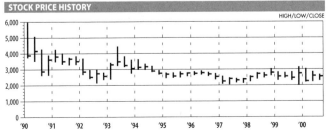

2000 FISCAL YEAR-END

Debt ratio: 84.5%
Return on equity: 0.0%
Cash (¥ mil.): 73,229
Current ratio: 0.22
Long-term debt (¥ mil.):
  8,540,871
No. of shares (mil.): 1,353
Dividends
  Yield: 0.0%
  Payout: —
Market value ($ mil.): 29,805
Sales ($ mil.): 49,858

TOKYO ELECTRON LIMITED

OVERVIEW

To tell the truth, Tokyo-based Tokyo Electron Limited (TEL) is the world's #2 manufacturer of semiconductor production equipment (well behind #1 Applied Materials). TEL's products include systems for such chip making processes as chemical vapor deposition, diffusion, etching, cleaning, and testing. The company also makes equipment for manufacturing liquid crystal displays. Production equipment accounts for more than four-fifths of sales. Other operations include distribution of other companies' chip making equipment, computer systems, networking equipment, and software. Subsidiary Tokyo Electron Device distributes chips made by companies such as Advanced Micro Devices and Motorola. Another subsidiary, Tokyo Electron EE Limited, refurbishes and upgrades chip making equipment.

In the competitive global chip market, local manufacturing and customer support have become increasingly important to TEL. The company is concentrating its expansion efforts on the dominant semiconductor manufacturing markets in Asia and the US. Since 1993 the company has formed subsidiaries throughout Asia and the US, as well as in Europe and the Middle East. TEL is made up of 30 companies in 14 countries.

HISTORY

Frustrated by the unreliable semiconductor production equipment their employer, Nissho Trading Co. (now Nissho Iwai), was importing from the US, Tokuo Kubo and Toshio Kodada quit their jobs at Nissho in 1963 and founded Tokyo Electron Laboratories (TEL). Tokyo Broadcasting System provided some initial backing.

At first about half of the company's sales came from importing US semiconductor equipment. The other half came from exporting Japanese electronics such as car radios. In 1968 TEL and US-based diffusion furnace maker Thermco Systems (later acquired by Allegheny International) formed TEL-Thermco Engineering Co. (now Tokyo Electron Tohoku Ltd. Sagami Plant). TEL followed with other joint ventures, paying royalties to manufacture other companies' products in Japan.

The company's US unit, TEL America (now Tokyo Electron America), was established in 1972. In 1978 Tokyo Electron Laboratories was renamed Tokyo Electron Limited (also TEL).

TEL went public in 1980. In 1981 the company formed a joint venture with GenRad to make test systems in the US. The next year TEL started a joint venture with Varian Associates, called Tel-Varian, to make and customize Varian equipment in Japan. In 1988 TEL acquired Thermco's stake in their joint venture. Also that year TEL and Varian expanded their agreement, giving Varian exclusive distribution rights for TEL products in the US and Europe.

The company began a major international expansion in 1993, setting up shop in South Korea. In 1994 TEL formed subsidiaries in Germany, Italy, and the UK. The company formed Tokyo Electron Oregon in 1995. Its Taiwanese and Swiss operations were started in 1996. Also in 1996 TEL managing director Tetsuro Higashi was named president.

TEL formed subsidiaries in Spain and the Netherlands in 1997. That year TEL and Varian ended their long-standing alliance, leaving Varian to handle its own sales and maintenance in Japan. Also in 1997 TEL delivered the first of its 300mm wafer-production equipment. That year TEL joined Nintendo and Fuji Photo Film to develop software for some Nintendo game machines.

In 1998 TEL completed construction of its Process Technology Center in Japan, designed to speed mass production of 300mm wafer-making equipment. It also acquired the semiconductor equipment division (now part of Tokyo Electron Arizona) of Sony's Material Research Corp. That year TEL formed Tokyo Electron EE Limited to refurbish and upgrade semiconductor manufacturing equipment. The two-headed dragon of a chip industry slump and the Asian economic crisis lowered the company's sales that year.

The company formed its French subsidiary in 1999. That year TEL and AlliedSignal (now Honeywell International, being acquired by General Electric) formed a joint venture to develop chip making equipment. Also in 1999 rival Tegal won a permanent injunction against TEL to stop US sales of some of TEL's wafer etching equipment; legal wrangling over patent issues continued between the two companies through 2000.

Thanks to a general recovery in the semiconductor industry and Asian financial markets, sales rebounded strongly in 2000 on increased demand for semiconductor production equipment and distributed electronic components.

President and CEO: Tetsuro Higashi
EVP: Tetsuo Tsuneishi
SVP: Takeo Tanaka
SVP: Mitsutaka Yoshida
Executive Manager Accounting, Finance, Order Process and Information Systems: Yuichi Honda
General Manager General Affairs, Personnel, and Global Operations of Administration: Kousuke Ishii
General Manager Sales Promotion, North America and Europe: Kiyoshi Sunohara
General Manager Corporate Marketing: Ryuichi Komatsubara
Corporate Technology Strategist: Takaaki Matsuoka
President, Tokyo Electron Tohoku: Kengo Kuroiwa
President, Tokyo Electron Yamanashi: Yasuo Inoue
Auditors: Masatoshi Yoshino, Eiji Miyashita, Fumihiko Sugiura

LOCATIONS

HQ: TBS Broadcast Center, 3-6 Akasaka 5-chome, Minato-ku, Tokyo 107-8481, Japan
Phone: +81-3-5561-7000   **Fax:** +81-3-5561-7400
US HQ: 2400 Grove Blvd., Austin, TX 78741
US Phone: 512-424-1000   **US Fax:** 512-424-1001
Web site: http://www.tel.co.jp

Tokyo Electron Limited has operations in China, France, Germany, Ireland, Israel, Italy, Japan, the Netherlands, South Korea, Spain, Switzerland, Taiwan, the UK, and the US.

2000 Sales

	% of total
Japan	42
Other countries	58
Total	**100**

PRODUCTS/OPERATIONS

2000 Sales

	% of total
Semiconductor & LCD production equipment	81
Electronic components	16
Computer systems	3
Other	—
Total	**100**

Selected Products

Production Equipment
Liquid-crystal displays
Semiconductors

Electronic Components
Semiconductors and board-level products
Software

Computer Systems
Board testers
Data management software
Network systems

COMPETITORS

Amtech Systems	CVC	Novellus
Applied Materials	Electroglas	Systems
ASM	EMCORE	Semitool
International	FSI International	Silicon Valley
ASM	GaSonics	Group
Lithography	International	SpeedFam-IPEC
Brooks	Genus	Tegal
Automation	Lam Research	Teradyne
Cerprobe	Mattson	Trikon
CFM	Technology	Veeco
Technologies		Instruments

HISTORICAL FINANCIALS & EMPLOYEES

Tokyo: 8035 FYE: March 31	Annual Growth	3/91	3/92	3/93	3/94	3/95	3/96	3/97	3/98	3/99	3/00
Sales (¥ mil.)	10.6%	—	196,335	153,724	189,716	251,853	402,407	432,784	455,584	313,820	440,728
Net income (¥ mil.)	11.6%	—	8,273	3,172	3,904	7,711	24,532	29,974	30,009	1,866	19,847
Income as % of sales	—	—	4.2%	2.1%	2.1%	3.1%	6.1%	6.9%	6.6%	0.6%	4.5%
Earnings per share (¥)	38.7%	—	8.10	5.33	31.16	59.11	188.06	181.96	174.68	10.70	110.64
Stock price - FY high (¥)	—	—	3,582	2,227	3,145	3,082	4,291	4,200	8,670	6,630	18,000
Stock price - FY low (¥)	—	—	1,673	1,182	2,018	2,136	2,118	2,545	3,920	2,755	6,080
Stock price - FY close (¥)	31.8%	—	1,700	2,136	2,973	2,400	3,318	4,100	4,490	6,130	15,500
P/E - high	—	—	442	418	101	52	23	23	50	620	163
P/E - low	—	—	207	222	65	36	11	14	22	257	55
Dividends per share (¥)	1.2%	—	12.72	12.72	14.55	21.81	25.45	30.00	30.00	12.00	14.00
Book value per share (¥)	9.0%	—	—	853.00	864.00	898.00	1,029.00	1,177.00	1,495.00	1,476.00	1,558.00
Employees	10.6%	—	—	—	4,896	5,410	6,148	6,988	8,242	8,576	8,946

STOCK PRICE HISTORY

HIGH/LOW/CLOSE

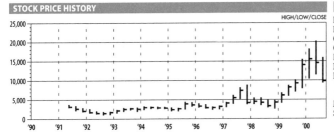

2000 FISCAL YEAR-END

Debt ratio: 31.2%
Return on equity: —
Cash (¥ mil.): 79,519
Current ratio: 2.56
Long-term debt (¥ mil.): 67,278
No. of shares (mil.): 176
Dividends
  Yield: 0.0%
  Payout: 0.1%
Market value ($ mil.): 25,823
Sales ($ mil.): 4,179

TOMEN CORPORATION

TOMEN is dealing with a common situation in Japan. Too many companies, not enough profit. One of Japan's largest *sogo shosha* (general trading companies), TOMEN deals in everything from produce to textiles and apparel to metals and machinery. Begun as a spinoff of the Mitsui Group, the Osaka-based company has grown to more than 460 subsidiaries and affiliates worldwide.

Chemicals and energy operations together account for about a third of the firm's sales. TOMEN trades fine chemicals, particularly agrochemicals such as feed additives and pesticides, acting as a distributor and purchasing the business rights to develop some chemicals. The company also builds power plants worldwide.

TOMEN installs fiber-optic communications networks, exports semiconductors, and trades electronics components between Japan, North America, and Europe. TOMEN is one of Japan's top grain traders; the *sogo shosha's* food-related businesses run the gamut from soy importing to eel processing.

Pummeled by the Asian financial crisis, TOMEN is shedding 130 companies in a major two-year restructuring program, focusing its resources on chemicals, utilities, information and communications, foodstuffs and textiles. The company also has identified businesses related to the environment (such as wind power projects and batteries for electric cars), media and healthcare as candidates for future expansion.

Japanese business is a small world. In 1897 Sakichi Toyoda (father of the founder of Toyota) perfected the nation's first power-driven loom. Developed over the next three decades with the backing of the Mitsui *zaibatsu* (a group of affiliated companies), the new looms had a voracious appetite that sent Mitsui scrambling for cotton supplies.

But because raw cotton was a highly volatile commodity, Mitsui spun off its cotton trading business in 1920 as Toyo Menka Kaisha (Oriental Cotton Trading). Toyo Menka soon had a healthy share of the market in Japan, and Japan, thanks to the lightning-quick looms, grabbed market share from other nations' cotton weavers. In 1924 it established a US subsidiary in Dallas and by the 1930s was able to buy up Brazil's entire cotton crop and later expand it by sponsoring Japanese emigrants to grow there. By the mid-1930s the company's markets for finished cotton included India, Indonesia, and Europe, and it was Japan's largest cotton importer.

Success had a dark side. The firm's dominance was due partly to cotton mills that had been seized in Shanghai and other cities in the wake of Japan's 1932 invasion of China. When WWII came, Japanese trade was restricted to its fast-expanding empire (known as the Greater East Asia Co-Prosperity Sphere). Thus, Toyo Menka was also cut off from most world cotton-growing regions. As the war dragged on, what remained of the company's production was diverted to the war effort.

US occupation forces broke up the *zaibatsu* after WWII, and Toyo Menka was forced to survive without the backing of Mitsui. As Japan

rebuilt, the company expanded its trading activities into metals, machinery, and food. It also was assisted by the formation of new, less formal, business combinations, known as *keiretsu*, along the lines of the old *zaibatsu*.

Toyo Menka grew throughout the 1950s and 1960s, merging with other specialized trading companies and expanding its heavy industry-related businesses. It also established a web of international offices. In 1970 the company shortened its name to TOMEN. During the 1970s it expanded into energy and targeted Asian markets more strongly.

Buoyed by the Japanese economic boom of the 1980s, TOMEN moved into communications, power supply, and high tech, and in 1990 it spun off its cotton operations. With the advent of a Japanese recession, however, sales fell steadily. TOMEN slashed costs, streamlined operations, and began building overseas.

TOMEN in 1997 joined a consortium to build power plants in Thailand, but the Asian financial crisis placed large infrastructure projects there in jeopardy. Romania was the next stop: In 1998 TOMEN and UDI of Israel signed a $100 million contract to renovate one of Romania's major power plants. At home, TOMEN completed Japan's first full-scale wind power plant in 1999.

Still struggling in 1999, TOMEN made plans to withdraw from its trading operations in less profitable commodities, such as steel and paper. That year the company launched the first commercially operated wind power generating plant in Japan.

OFFICERS

President: Morihiko Tashiro
EVP: Yasumasa Nishi
EVP Textile Materials, Apparel, Produce, Foodstuff, Organic Chemicals and Plastics, Specialty and Inorganic Chemicals, and Osaka Head Office: Yoshiaki Ueki
Senior Managing Director, Business Promotion and Portfolio Management, Metals and Energy, and Industrial Project and Automobile: Yuzo Takeshige
Senior Managing Director, IT Promotion and Coordination, Information and Communications, Power and Utility Projects, New Business Research and Development, Nagoya Office, Domestic Branches, Overseas Branches, Offices and Trading Subsidiaries, and Chief Representative in China: Kazuhiko Otsuka
Senior Managing Director, Corporate Staff and Administration: Noriaki Akatsuka
Senior Managing Director: Michio Ishidate
Managing Director: Yoshio Tadano
Managing Director: Yoji Yoshikawa
Managing Director: Minoru Kano
Managing Director: Kenzo Inoue
Managing Director: Toshio Hori
Auditors: Mizuho Audit Corporation

LOCATIONS

HQ: Tomen Marunouchi Bldg.,
8-1, Marunouchi 3-chome, Chiyoda-ku,
Tokyo 100-8623, Japan
Phone: +81-3-5288-2111   **Fax:** +81-3-5288-9100
US HQ: 1285 Avenue of the Americas,
New York, NY 10019
US Phone: 212-397-4600   **US Fax:** 212-397-3342
Web site: http://www.tomen.co.jp

TOMEN has operations in more than 50 countries worldwide.

PRODUCTS/OPERATIONS

2000 Sales

	% of total
Chemicals & energy	35
Machinery	21
Textiles	15
Produce & provisions	13
Metals	10
Construction, lumber & general merchandise	6
Total	**100**

Selected Subsidiaries and Affiliates
Alexandria National Iron and Steel Co., SAE (steel mill, Egypt)
Alpha Industries Bhd. (copper wire and rods, Malaysia)
Casio, Inc. (sales of Casio products, US)
Chikasha Cotton Oil Co. (cottonseed oil products, US)
Eastern Chemical Co., Ltd. (production of ethyl alcohol from molasses, Thailand)
Grand Biotechnology Co., Ltd. (agricultural genetics, Taiwan)
Kohinoor Energy Ltd. (energy generation, Pakistan)
Nutri-Tomen SA (sales of animal feed additives, veterinary medicines, and agricultural chemicals; France)
Tomen Power (Europe) B.V. (power generation projects, the Netherlands)
Wuxi Advanced Chemical Co. Ltd. (dyestuffs, China)
Zhong Shan Zhonglong Aquatic Co., Ltd. (eel processing, China)

COMPETITORS

Bechtel	Kanematsu	Nippon Steel
Daewoo	Marubeni	Nissho Iwai
Dow Chemical	Mitsubishi	Sumitomo
DuPont	Mitsui	
ITOCHU	Nichimen	

HISTORICAL FINANCIALS & EMPLOYEES

Tokyo: 8003 FYE: March 31	Annual Growth	3/91	3/92	3/93	3/94	3/95	3/96	3/97	3/98	3/99	3/00
Sales (¥ bil.)	(10.1%)	7,458	7,957	7,676	6,974	6,944	6,540	5,238	5,328	3,954	2,867
Net income (¥ bil.)	—	7	5	4	2	1	5	5	(22)	3	(95)
Income as % of sales	—	0.1%	0.1%	0.1%	0.0%	0.0%	0.1%	0.1%	—	0.1%	—
Earnings per share (¥)	—	11.00	8.00	5.00	2.00	2.00	7.00	7.00	(33.00)	4.00	(141.00)
Stock price - FY high (¥)	—	869	614	438	445	439	410	443	309	143	176
Stock price - FY low (¥)	—	413	370	361	320	305	280	268	55	80	84
Stock price - FY close (¥)	(14.3%)	592	381	497	385	330	410	294	120	111	148
P/E - high	—	79	77	88	223	220	59	63	—	36	—
P/E - low	—	38	46	72	160	153	40	38	—	20	—
Dividends per share (¥)	—	5.50	5.50	5.50	5.50	5.50	5.00	5.00	0.00	2.50	0.00
Book value per share (¥)	(25.8%)	—	175.62	177.63	176.29	178.08	175.67	179.33	140.57	144.19	16.15
Employees	—	—	—	—	—	—	—	—	—	—	—

STOCK PRICE HISTORY

HIGH/LOW/CLOSE

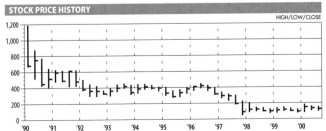

2000 FISCAL YEAR-END

Debt ratio: 99.1%
Return on equity: —
Cash (¥ mil.): 140,941
Current ratio: 0.90
Long-term debt (¥ mil.): 485,532
No. of shares (mil.): 670
Dividends
  Yield: —
  Payout: —
Market value ($ mil.): 939
Sales ($ mil.): 27,157

TOMKINS PLC

OVERVIEW

There was a time when, whether you want to pack some heat or merely pack some lunch, multinational conglomerate Tomkins had a subsidiary that could make your day. But the London-based company, which is considering selling subsidiary Smith & Wesson (the world's top handgun maker), is in the midst of divesting its food manufacturing businesses in order to reshape itself as a global engineering group.

Tomkins companies make and distribute automotive products; industrial power systems; plumbing components, windows, doors, valves, and other construction products. More than half of the company's sales come from the US, where Tomkins' marquee names

include Gates (automotive belts and hoses) and Trico (wiper blades).

Former CEO Gregory Hutchings transformed Tomkins from a local buckle maker into a global conglomerate. He was known for buying poorly managed manufacturing companies and streamlining their operations. But Hutchings came under fire for his generous paychecks in light of the underperformance of several subsidiaries, and he resigned in 2000 after Tomkins began investigating the use of corporate jets and apartments and the presence of Hutchings' wife and housekeeper on the company payroll.

HISTORY

Tomkins was founded in 1925 as the F. H. Tomkins Buckle Company, a maker of buckles and fasteners. Tomkins continued to develop within this niche market for the next six decades. In 1983 Gregory Hutchings acquired a 23% stake in the company. Hutchings, who at age 24 had started his own construction business, had won a reputation as a go-getter when he caught the eye of Lords Hanson and White; he was hired by the Hanson Group in 1980 as its chief acquisition scout. In 1984 Hutchings became Tomkins' CEO and set about acquiring manufacturing companies in the UK and the US.

The company acquired Ferraris Piston Service (auto components) and Hayters (a garden tool manufacturer) that year, followed by Pegler-Hattersley (plumbing fixtures) in 1986, Smith & Wesson (guns) in 1987, and Murray Ohio (lawn mowers and bicycles) the next year. In 1992 the company acquired Rank Hovis McDougall, a leading UK baker and food manufacturer.

Tomkins made only eight major purchases between 1983 and 1993, as Hutchings worked to put his acquisitions on a sound financial footing, upgrading plants and equipment and giving each company the autonomy to become efficient.

In 1994 Tomkins bought Outdoor Products and Dynamark Plastics from Noma Industries of Canada: Outdoor Products complemented the Murray Ohio operations, and injection molder Dynamark Plastics fit into Tomkins' industrial products portfolio.

Two years later the company acquired Gates, a US maker of belts and hoses, with operations in 15 countries; the move gave Tomkins access to new markets in Latin America and Southeast

Asia. That year Tomkins acquired the hose operations of Nationwide Rubber Enterprises, making Gates the leading manufacturer of curved hose in Australia. In 1997 Tomkins acquired US firm Stant Corp., a leading maker of windshield wipers, fuel tank caps, and other auto accessories, to further complement Gates' product lines.

Besides acquisitions, Tomkins regularly disposed of companies that no longer fit its strategic plan. It sold Inchbrook Printers in 1996 and Ferraris Piston Service, the first business purchased by Tomkins under Hutchings' leadership, in 1997. In a symbolic break with its past, Tomkins sold F. H. Tomkins Buckle in 1998.

That year Tomkins made another automotive equipment acquisition when it bought US-based Schrader-Bridgeport; it also bought Martine Spécialités, a supplier of frozen patisserie products. In 1999 the company acquired ACD Tridon, a Canadian manufacturer of automotive parts.

In 2000 Smith & Wesson settled more than a dozen lawsuits with US cities attempting to collect damages for handgun violence cases. Breaking rank with other handgun makers, the company agreed to install child-safety locks on its guns and ensure that gun sellers conduct background checks.

Tomkins moved to exit the food manufacturing business in 2000, selling Red Wing and agreeing to sell the European operations of Ranks Hovis McDougall. Hutchings resigned that year in the midst of an investigation of his spending practices, and chairman David Newlands took over. That year the company sold its bicycle, snowblower, and mowing machinery businesses (Hayter and Murray).

Chairman and CEO: David Newlands, age 53,
$15,000 pay (partial-year salary)
COO: David J. Snowden, age 55, $419,000 pay
Finance Director: Ken Lever, age 46, $176,000 pay
(partial-year salary)
Chairman, Tomkins Corporation: Anthony J. Reading,
age 56, $397,000 pay
Administration Director and Company Secretary:
Richard N. Marchant, age 54, $147,000 pay
Auditors: Arthur Andersen

HQ: East Putney House, 84 Upper Richmond Rd.,
London SW15 2ST, United Kingdom
Phone: +44-20-8871-4544   **Fax:** +44-20-8877-9700
Web site: http://www.tomkins.co.uk

2000 Sales

	% of total
US	51
Europe	
UK	34
Other countries	6
Other regions	9
Total	**100**

2000 Sales

	% of total
Industrial & automotive engineering	34
Food manufacturing	34
Construction components	22
Professional, garden & leisure products	10
Total	**100**

Selected Subsidiaries and Affiliates
Air System Components (heating, ventilation, and
air-conditioning components, US)
British Bakeries (bakery products)
Dearborn Mid-West Conveyor Company (heavy-duty
conveyor systems, US)
Fedco (automotive heaters)
Gates (UK) Ltd. (belts, couplings, carpet underlay,
conveyor belting, and footwear)
Gates Rubber Company (auto belts and hoses, US)
J A Sharwood & Co. Ltd. (international foods)
Rank Hovis Ltd. (wheat flour)
Smith & Wesson Corp. (handguns, handcuffs, and
the Identi-Kit system; US)

Applied	Continental AG	Sturm, Ruger
Industrial	Glock	SYSCO
Technologies	Goodyear	Tenneco
Beretta	Hi-Point	Automotive
Bestfoods	Firearms	Topco Associates
Blount	Huffy	Trek
Bridgestone	LESCO	United
Brunswick	Nash Finch	Technologies
Carrier	Navegar	
Colt's	Remington Arms	

NYSE: TKS FYE: Saturday nearest April 30	Annual Growth	4/91	4/92	4/93	4/94	4/95	4/96	4/97	4/98	4/99	4/00
Sales ($ mil.)	19.2%	1,799	2,263	3,239	4,931	6,006	5,431	7,451	8,442	8,600	8,722
Net income ($ mil.)	2.2%	135	165	188	273	335	338	459	545	491	164
Income as % of sales	—	7.5%	7.3%	5.8%	5.5%	5.6%	6.2%	6.2%	6.5%	5.7%	1.9%
Earnings per share ($)	(7.1%)	0.91	0.98	0.83	0.92	1.13	1.14	1.34	1.52	1.42	0.47
Stock price - FY high ($)	—	12.06	18.00	19.13	17.25	16.38	18.38	20.25	26.63	24.00	19.50
Stock price - FY low ($)	—	7.69	11.13	12.63	13.00	12.88	14.13	14.75	16.50	12.88	9.75
Stock price - FY close ($)	1.1%	11.00	17.75	15.25	15.75	15.38	17.00	18.00	23.06	17.63	12.19
P/E - high	—	11	17	22	18	14	16	14	16	16	10
P/E - low	—	7	10	14	14	11	12	11	10	9	5
Dividends per share ($)	2.5%	1.13	0.41	0.92	0.42	0.55	0.59	0.73	0.94	0.94	1.41
Book value per share ($)	7.0%	2.41	2.86	4.51	4.88	5.38	5.57	7.81	5.71	3.99	4.45
Employees	6.4%	—	—	45,496	43,714	46,096	46,096	54,496	65,300	66,927	70,039

HIGH/LOW/CLOSE

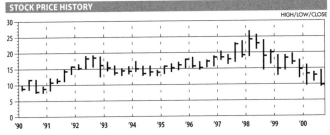

Debt ratio: 62.7%
Return on equity: 36.6%
Cash ($ mil.): 724
Current ratio: 1.52
Long-term debt ($ mil.): 1,778
No. of shares (mil.): 238
Dividends
  Yield: 11.6%
  Payout: 300.0%
Market value ($ mil.): 2,896

THE TORONTO-DOMINION BANK

OVERVIEW

What do you do when your megamerger plans are spurned? Score a major acquisition coup.

Canada's #5 bank (Royal Bank of Canada is #1), Toronto-Dominion Bank (TD) provides consumer, corporate, and government banking services. Offerings include deposit accounts, credit cards, mortgages, trusts, estate planning, and investment services. TD offers financial and advisory services to businesses. Its TD Waterhouse Group is one of the top online brokers (Charles Schwab's eSchwab is #1.) Other operations include TD Asset Management (mutual funds) and TD Securities (investment banking, equities, and foreign exchange).

TD Waterhouse Group's IPO helped spur the bank's 1999 income, while its purchase of CT Financial Services (including #1 trust company Canada Trust) catapulted it into the lead in the retail banking sector. As competition at home heats up, Toronto-Dominion is invading the US by linking its online trading customers to its online Waterhouse National Bank, cross-selling deposit, loan, and other banking services.

HISTORY

The Bank of Toronto was established in 1855 by flour traders who wanted their own banking facilities; its growth encouraged another group of businessmen to found the Dominion Bank in 1869. Dominion emphasized commercial banking and invested heavily in railways and construction.

As the new nation expanded westward, both banks established branch networks. They helped fund Canada's primary industries — dairy, mining, oil, pulp, and textiles. WWI transformed the country from debtor to creditor, and true to its pioneering spirit, a Bank of Toronto official claimed to be the first to have set up a branch office with the help of aviation (in Manitoba in the 1920s).

The demand for agricultural products and commodities dropped after the war, but production continued full throttle, creating a world grain glut that helped trigger the stock market crash of 1929. Canada suffered along with the US in the Depression; both the Bank of Toronto and Dominion Bank contracted during the 1930s. After growing during and after World War II, The Bank of Toronto and Dominion Bank decided to increase their capital base, merging into a 450-branch bank in 1955.

In the 1970s TD opened offices in Bangkok, Beirut, and Frankfurt, among others. During the 1980s it was active in making loans to less-developed countries. After the deregulation of the Canadian securities industry in 1987, CEO Richard Thomson (chairman since 1976) reduced international lending and began focusing on brokerage activities. Thus, when several Latin American countries fell behind on their loans in 1987, TD eked out a profit while its four Maple Leaf rivals lost money.

As the North American economy slowed in the early 1990s, TD's nonperforming loans increased and, with it, its loan loss reserves. The bank still made acquisitions, including Central Guaranty Trust (1993) and Lancaster Financial Holdings (1995, investment banking). It worked to build its financial services, expanding its range of service offerings and geographic coverage and buying New York-based Waterhouse Investor Services (1996); 97% of Australia-based Pont Securities (1997); and California-based Kennedy, Cabot & Co. (1997).

In 1998 the bank sold its payroll services to Ceridian, and its Waterhouse Securities unit bought US discount brokerage Jack White & Co.

That year the government nixed TD's merger with Canadian Imperial on the same day it voided the Royal Bank of Canada/Bank of Montreal deal. The banks believed the consolidation necessary to stave off foreign banks' encroachment into Canada, but the government had domestic anticompetition concerns: Though Canada has one-tenth the population of the US, its five top banks all ranked in the top 15 in North America.

In 1999 TD bought Trimark Financial's retail trust banking business and spun off part of Waterhouse Investor Services (now TD Waterhouse Group). That year the bank ramped up its focus on Internet banking (TD Waterhouse is already a top online brokerage); the company's Web site sells competitors' products as well as TD's.

TD has not given up on acquisition-fueled growth. In 2000 the company bought CT Financial Services from British American Tobacco. As a condition of government approval for the acquisition, TD had to sell its MasterCard credit portfolio (sold to Citibank Canada) and a dozen southern Ontario branches (to Bank of Montreal). TD is also shopping for a US bank and has teamed up with Commerce One to launch TDMarketSite, a business-to-business (B2B) Web site.

OFFICERS

Chairman and CEO; Chairman, TD Waterhouse:
A. Charles Baillie, age 60, $3,266,164 pay
VC Commercial Banking: J. Duncan Gibson
VC Group Administration; Deputy Chairman and CEO,
TD Waterhouse: Stephen D. McDonald, age 43,
$1,564,880 pay
VC: Donald A. Wright, $6,538,390 pay
EVP Group Human Resources: Allen W. Bell
EVP Retail Banking: Jeffrey R. Carney
EVP and CFO: Daniel A. Marinangeli
EVP, General Counsel, and Secretary:
Christopher A. Montague
EVP: Michael P. Mueller
EVP: Thomas R. Spencer
President and COO, TD Waterhouse:
Frank J. Petrelli, age 49
Auditors: Ernst & Young LLP; KPMG LLP

LOCATIONS

HQ: Toronto-Dominion Centre,
King St. West and Bay St.,
Toronto, Ontario M5K 1A2, Canada
Phone: 416-982-8222   **Fax:** 416-982-5671
US HQ: 909 Fannin St. , Houston, TX 77010
US Phone: 713-653-8200   **US Fax:** 713-951-9921
Web site: http://www.tdbank.ca

The Toronto-Dominion Bank has operations in Asia and
the Pacific Rim, Europe, and North and South America.

1999 Sales

	% of total
Canada	60
US	34
Other countries	6
Total	**100**

PRODUCTS/OPERATIONS

1999 Assets

	$ mil.	% of total
Cash & equivalents	21,706	15
Securities	46,962	32
Net loans	59,463	41
Other assets	17,608	12
Total	**145,739**	**100**

Selected Subsidiaries
First Nations Bank of Canada (89%)
TD Asset Management Inc.
TD Investment Management Inc.
TD Ireland
TD Mortgage Corporation
TD Realty Limited
TD Reinsurance (Barbados) Inc.
TD Securities Inc.
TD Trust Company
TD Waterhouse Holdings, Inc. (US)
  TD Waterhouse Bank, N.A. (US)
  TD Waterhouse Group, Inc. (89%, US)
Toronto Dominion General Insurance Company
Toronto Dominion International Inc.
Toronto Dominion Life Insurance Company

COMPETITORS

Ameritrade
Bank of Montreal
Canadian
  Imperial
Charles Schwab
Credit Suisse
First Boston
(USA), Inc.
Datek Online

Desjardins
E*TRADE
FleetBoston
FMR
Jones Financial
  Companies
Laurentian Bank
Morgan Stanley
Dean Witter

National Bank of
  Canada
Quick &
  Reilly/Fleet
Royal Bank of
  Canada
Scotiabank

HISTORICAL FINANCIALS & EMPLOYEES

NYSE: TD FYE: October 31	Annual Growth	10/90	10/91	10/92	10/93	10/94	10/95	10/96	10/97	10/98	10/99
Assets ($ mil.)	10.9%	57,287	61,358	59,816	64,368	73,718	80,930	93,919	116,351	117,808	145,739
Net income ($ mil.)	17.8%	465	403	303	186	475	591	683	773	726	2,026
Income as % of assets	—	0.8%	0.7%	0.5%	0.3%	0.6%	0.7%	0.7%	0.7%	0.6%	1.4%
Earnings per share ($)	44.2%	—	—	—	—	—	—	1.11	1.26	1.18	3.33
Stock price - FY high ($)	—	—	—	—	—	—	—	11.69	18.91	26.13	30.50
Stock price - FY low ($)	—	—	—	—	—	—	—	9.44	11.56	12.06	13.81
Stock price - FY close ($)	25.4%	—	—	—	—	—	—	11.69	18.25	15.00	23.06
P/E - high	—	—	—	—	—	—	—	11	15	22	9
P/E - low	—	—	—	—	—	—	—	9	9	10	4
Dividends per share ($)	66.5%	—	—	—	—	—	—	0.13	0.56	0.66	0.60
Book value per share ($)	15.3%	—	—	—	—	—	—	8.25	8.73	9.30	12.64
Employees	2.5%	24,560	24,003	23,514	25,603	25,705	25,413	26,815	28,001	29,236	30,636

STOCK PRICE HISTORY   HIGH/LOW/CLOSE

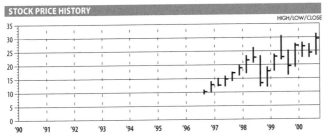

1999 FISCAL YEAR-END

Equity as % of assets: 5.4%
Return on assets: 1.5%
Return on equity: 33.1%
Long-term debt ($ mil.): 2,187
No. of shares (mil.): 620
Dividends
  Yield: 2.6%
  Payout: 18.0%
Market value ($ mil.): 14,305
Sales ($ mil.): 10,660

TOSHIBA CORPORATION

OVERVIEW

Another falling son in the land of the rising sun. Tokyo-based Toshiba makes a range of products from portable computers (#1 in the world) and consumer appliances to liquid-crystal displays and semiconductors. Information and communication products account for about 40% of sales. The company's industrial units build elevators, power generating plants, and medical systems, among others. Toshiba sells three-quarters of its products in Asia.

CEO Tadashi Okamura oversees a company defined by change. Weak private-sector demand, growing competition from agile rivals, and declining semiconductor memory prices have stifled profitability in recent years. Chairman and former CEO Taizo Nishimuro, a marketing and multimedia specialist in a country that typically fills its top high-tech executive positions from engineering ranks, spent more than a decade building Toshiba's US presence. He has cut directors, streamlined units, and touted an autonomy among the new core product groups that gives managers quicker decision-making responsibilities. Nishimuro handed the CEO spot to Okamura in mid-2000.

Toshiba is shifting to logic devices and other high-growth fields, and striking deals with companies such as Carrier and GE to help product development.

HISTORY

Two Japanese electrical equipment manufacturers came together in 1939 to create Toshiba. Tanaka Seizo-sha, Japan's first telegraph equipment manufacturer, was founded in 1875 by Hisashige Tanaka, the so-called Edison of Japan. In the 1890s the company started making heavier electrical equipment such as transformers and electric motors, adopting the name Shibaura Seisakusho Works in 1893. Seisakusho went on to pioneer the production of hydroelectric generators (1894) and X-ray tubes (1915) in Japan.

The other half of Toshiba, Hakunetsusha & Company, was founded by Ichisuke Fujioka and Shoichi Miyoshi as Japan's first incandescent lamp maker (1890). Renamed Tokyo Electric Company (1899), the company developed the coiled filament lightbulb (1921), Japan's first radio receiver and cathode-ray tube (1924), and the internally frosted glass lightbulb (1925). In 1939 it merged with Shibaura Seisakusho to form Tokyo Shibaura Electric Company (Toshiba).

Toshiba was the first company in Japan to make fluorescent lamps (1940), radar systems (1942), broadcasting equipment (1952), and digital computers (1954). Production of black-and-white televisions began in 1949. Even so, through the 1970s the company was considered an also-ran, trailing other Japanese *keiretsu* (business groups), partly because of its bureaucratic management style.

Electrical engineer Shoichi Saba became president in 1980. Saba invested heavily in Toshiba's information and communications segments. The company became the first in the world to produce the powerful one-megabit DRAM chip (1985). That year it unveiled its first laptop PC. In the meantime Saba (named chairman 1986) pushed Toshiba into joint ventures to exchange technology with companies such as Siemens and Motorola.

But in 1987 Toshiba incurred the wrath of the US government. A subsidiary sold submarine sound-deadening equipment to the USSR, resulting in threats of US sanctions and a precipitous decline in its stock price and in US sales. Chairman Saba and president Sugichiro Watari resigned in shame.

Toshiba in 1992 bought a $500 million stake in Time Warner (reduced in 1998). In 1996 the company appointed Taizo Nishimuro as president, breaking its tradition of filling the position with an engineer from its heavy electrical operations.

In 1997 Toshiba and IBM formed joint venture Dominion Semiconductor to develop memory chips. (IBM sold its stake to Toshiba in 1999.) The next year the company looked to boost earnings by cutting its workforce and allying with other manufacturers such as GE and Fujitsu in development deals. But continued semiconductor price declines, and sluggish demand in Japan, caused the company to record its first annual loss in more than two decades.

Toshiba in 1999 agreed to take a $1 billion charge to settle a class-action lawsuit alleging some manufacturers supplied potentially corrupt disk drives in its portable computers — even though no Toshiba customer complaints were filed. That year the company made plans to spin off its industrial equipment operations in 2000.

In 2000 Nishimuro stepped down as CEO. SVP and Information and Industrial Systems subsidiary president Tadashi Okamura assumed the post. Nishimuro filled the vacant chairman's seat.

OFFICERS

Chairman: Taizo Nishimuro
President and CEO: Tadashi Okamura
SEVP: Kiyoaki Shimagami
SEVP: Akinobu Kasami
EVP; President and CEO, Digital Media Equipment and Services: Tetsuya Mizoguchi
EVP; President and CEO, Semiconductor: Yasuo Morimoto
SVP; President and CEO, Home Appliances: Makoto Nakagawa
SVP; President and CEO, Display Devices and Components: Tadashi Matsumoto
Auditors: PricewaterhouseCoopers

LOCATIONS

HQ: 1-1, Shibaura 1-chome, Minato-ku, Tokyo 105-8001, Japan
Phone: +81-3-3457-2096   **Fax:** +81-3-3455-9202
US HQ: 1251 6th Ave., 41st Fl., New York, NY 10020
US Phone: 212-596-0600   **US Fax:** 212-593-3875
Web site: http://www.toshiba.co.jp

2000 Sales

	$ mil.	% of total
Asia		
Japan	41,961	67
Other countries	6,168	10
North America	8,696	14
Europe	4,880	8
Other regions	594	1
Adjustments	(7,806)	—
Total	**54,493**	**100**

PRODUCTS/OPERATIONS

2000 Sales

	$ mil.	% of total
Information & communication	17,531	28
Digital media	14,318	23
Electronic devices & materials	13,937	23
Home appliances	6,525	10
Power systems	5,384	9
Other	4,466	7
Adjustments	(7,668)	—
Total	**54,493**	**100**

COMPETITORS

Acer	Lucent
Alcatel	Matsushita
Canon	Minolta
Casio Computer	Mitsubishi Electric
Compaq	NEC
Daewoo	Nokia
Dell Computer	Oki Electric
Electrolux AB	Philips Electronics
Emerson	Pioneer
Ericsson	Ricoh
Fuji Photo	Rolls-Royce
Fujitsu	Samsung
Gateway	SANYO
GE	Seiko
Hewlett-Packard	Sharp
Hitachi	Siemens
Ingersoll-Rand	Sony
Intel	SPX
IBM	Sun Microsystems
Kyocera	Unisys

HISTORICAL FINANCIALS & EMPLOYEES

OTC: TOSBF FYE: March 31	Annual Growth	3/91	3/92	3/93	3/94	3/95	3/96	3/97	3/98	3/99	3/00
Sales ($ mil.)	5.2%	34,645	36,866	41,705	45,070	56,199	48,410	44,605	41,020	44,504	54,493
Net income ($ mil.)	—	857	297	179	118	516	843	542	55	(117)	(265)
Income as % of sales	—	2.5%	0.8%	0.4%	0.3%	0.9%	1.7%	1.2%	0.1%	—	—
Earnings per share ($)	—	0.25	0.09	0.06	0.04	0.15	0.25	0.16	0.02	(0.04)	(0.08)
Stock price - FY high ($)	—	6.69	6.30	5.83	7.64	8.42	8.22	8.00	6.80	7.44	10.19
Stock price - FY low ($)	—	4.66	4.03	4.05	5.48	6.05	5.86	5.20	3.80	3.55	6.00
Stock price - FY close ($)	6.2%	5.91	4.38	5.66	7.16	6.80	7.59	5.52	4.05	7.33	10.19
P/E - high	—	27	70	97	191	56	33	50	340	—	—
P/E - low	—	19	45	68	137	40	23	33	190	—	—
Dividends per share ($)	(9.0%)	0.07	0.08	0.09	0.10	0.11	0.09	0.08	0.10	0.05	0.03
Book value per share ($)	2.5%	2.61	2.77	3.11	3.77	4.31	3.67	3.35	2.95	3.06	3.26
Employees	(3.2%)	162,000	168,000	173,000	175,000	190,000	186,000	186,000	186,000	198,000	121,000

STOCK PRICE HISTORY

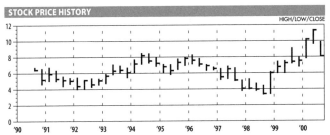

HIGH/LOW/CLOSE

2000 FISCAL YEAR-END

Debt ratio: 69.8%
Return on equity: —
Cash ($ mil.): 4,410
Current ratio: 1.10
Long-term debt ($ mil.): 16,187
No. of shares (mil.): 3,219
Dividends
  Yield: 0.0%
  Payout: —
Market value ($ mil.): 32,802

TOTAL FINA ELF S.A.

TOTAL FINA ELF has grown into one of the world's largest integrated oil companies by adding to its TOTAL. The Paris-based company, formerly just TOTAL, has expanded by making back-to-back acqusitions of European rivals PetroFina and Elf Aquitaine.

The combined TOTAL FINA ELF explores for, develops, and produces crude oil and natural gas; refines and markets petroleum products; and trades and transports both crude and finished products in more than 100 countries. The company has proved reserves of almost 10.5 billion barrels of oil equivalent; its 29 refineries have a capacity of 2.6 million barrels per day. TOTAL FINA ELF operates some 20,000 service stations, primarily in Europe and Africa, under the Premier, FINA, and Elf brands.

The company's chemical unit, ATOFINA, produces monomers, polymers, and specialty chemicals such as adhesives, inks, paints, resins, and rubbers. TOTAL FINA ELF also owns 33% of drugmaker Sanofi-Synthelabo, gained in the Elf acquisition.

The old TOTAL had been exiting mature markets in favor of high-growth regions when it joined the industry consolidation (Exxon and Mobil, BP and Amoco) spurred by the slump in oil prices. The combined company is integrating the operations of its acquisitions and looking to cut costs where there are overlaps.

A French consortium formed the Compagnie Française des Pétroles (CFP) in 1924 to develop an oil industry for the country. Lacking reserves within its borders, France had a 24% stake in the Turkish Petroleum Company (TPC), acquired from Germany in 1920 as part of the spoils from WWI. When oil was discovered in Iraq in 1927, the TPC partners (CFP; Anglo-Persian Oil, later British Petroleum; Royal Dutch/Shell; and a consortium of five US oil companies) became major players in the oil game.

In 1929 France acquired a 25% stake in CFP (raised to 35% in 1931) but ensured the company's independence from government control. CFP began establishing refining and transporting capabilities, and by the start of WWII it was a vertically integrated petroleum company.

With France's occupation by Germany during WWII, CFP was effectively blocked from further expansion, and its stake in Iraq Petroleum (formerly the TPC) was held by its partners until the end of the war. In 1948, over French protests, the US partners ended the "Red Line" agreement, a pact that limited members' competition in that Middle Eastern region.

After WWII, CFP diversified its sources for crude, opening a supply in 1947 from the Venezuelan company Pantepec and making several major discoveries in colonial Algeria in 1956. It also began supplying crude to Japan, South Korea, and Taiwan in the 1950s. To market its products in North Africa and France and other European areas, it introduced the brand name TOTAL in 1954. It began making petrochemicals in 1956.

Algeria in 1971 became North Africa's first major oil-producing country to nationalize its petroleum industry. This was not as dire a blow to CFP as it could have been; by that time the company got only about 20% of its supplies from Algeria. Exploration had paid off, with discoveries in Indonesia in the 1960s and, in the early 1970s, the North Sea.

CFP joined Elf Aquitaine in 1980 to buy Rhône-Poulenc's petrochemical segment. Ten years later it purchased state-owned Orkem's coating business (inks, resins, paints, and adhesives).

In 1985 the company had adopted its brand name as part of its new name, TOTAL Compagnie Française des Pétroles, shortened in 1991 to TOTAL. The firm was listed on the NYSE that year. The French government began reducing its stake in TOTAL in 1992 (ultimately to less than 1%). The company expanded reserves with stakes in fields in Argentina, the Caspian Sea, and Colombia.

In 1995, the year Thierry Desmarest became CEO, TOTAL contracted to develop two large oil and gas fields in Iran, despite US pressure not to do business there. The next year TOTAL led a consortium (including Russia's Gazprom and Malaysia's Petronas) in a $2 billion investment in Iran's gas sector, just days after selling its 55% stake in its North American arm, Total Petroleum, to Ultramar Diamond Shamrock — insulating TOTAL from the threat of US sanctions.

TOTAL bought Belgium's Petrofina, an integrated oil and gas company, for $11 billion in 1999 and became TOTAL FINA. Within days the new TOTAL FINA launched a $43 billion hostile bid for rival Elf Aquitaine. Elf made a counterbid, but TOTAL FINA wound up acquiring 95% of Elf in 2000 for $48.7 billion and became TOTAL FINA ELF. The new company gained control of the remainder of Elf later that year.

OFFICERS

Chairman and CEO, TOTAL FINA ELF and Elf Aquitaine; Chairman, TOTAL: Thierry Desmarest, age 54
VC, EVP, and President, Trading, Gas and Power; Chairman, ATOFINA: François Cornélis
VC, EVP and President, Trading, Gas and Power; EVP, Refining, Marketing, and Trading, Elf Aquitaine: Bernard de Combret
EVP, Finance and CFO: Robert Castaigne
EVP and SEVP, Exploration and Production: Chrisophe de Margerie
EVP and President, Exploration and Production; EVP, Exploration and Production, Elf Aquitaine: Jean-Luc Vermeulen
EVP and President, Refining and Marketing: Jean-Paul Vettier
EVP and President, Strategy and Risk Management; EVP, Finance, Elf Aquitaine: Bruno Weymuller
President, Chemicals: Jean-Pierre Seeuws
President, Strategy and Finance: Alain Madec
Deputy Human Resources and Internal Communications: R. Taverne
Auditors: KPMG

LOCATIONS

HQ: 2 place de la Coupole, 92400 Courbevoie La Defense 6, France
Phone: +33-1-47-44-45-46   **Fax:** +33-1-47-44-78-78
US HQ: 1585 Broadway, 26th Fl., New York, NY 10036
US Phone: 212-969-2810   **US Fax:** 212-969-2979
Web site: http://www.totalfinaelf.com

TOTAL FINA ELF has operations in more than 100 countries.

PRODUCTS/OPERATIONS

1999 Sales

	$ mil.	% of total
Downstream	29,599	62
Chemicals	9,929	21
Upstream	8,043	17
Corporate	236	—
Adjustments	(5,241)	—
Total	**42,566**	**100**

Selected Subsidiaries and Affiliates
ATOFINA
   ATOFINA Chemicals, Inc. (US)
   ATOFINA Petrochemicals, Inc. (US)
   Ato Findley (adhesives)
   Bostik (adhesives)
   Hutchinson (seals, gaskets, and other rubber products)
Elf Aquitaine
FINA, Inc. (refining and marketing, chemicals, US)
Sanofi-Synthelabo (pharmaceuticals, 33%)

COMPETITORS

Akzo Nobel	Kerr-McGee
Anglo American	Lyondell Chemical
Ashland	Norsk Hydro
BASF AG	Occidental
BHP	PDVSA
BP	PEMEX
Chevron	PETROBRAS
Conoco	PPG
Devon Energy	Royal Dutch/Shell
DuPont	Texaco
Eni	Unocal
Exxon Mobil	

HISTORICAL FINANCIALS & EMPLOYEES

NYSE: TOT FYE: December 31	Annual Growth	12/90	12/91	12/92	12/93	12/94	12/95	12/96	12/97	12/98	12/99
Sales ($ mil.)	6.0%	25,185	27,530	24,732	23,037	25,612	27,696	34,062	31,720	28,507	42,566
Net income ($ mil.)	7.5%	797	1,118	515	504	634	458	1,089	1,263	1,038	1,534
Income as % of sales	—	3.2%	4.1%	2.1%	2.2%	2.5%	1.7%	3.2%	4.0%	3.6%	3.6%
Earnings per share ($)	8.6%	—	—	1.22	1.14	1.37	0.98	2.27	2.58	2.12	2.18
Stock price - FY high ($)	—	—	—	25.75	28.63	33.00	34.00	41.50	59.44	67.13	72.63
Stock price - FY low ($)	—	—	—	19.50	20.00	25.38	25.50	31.00	38.88	46.69	49.88
Stock price - FY close ($)	18.8%	—	—	20.75	27.13	29.50	34.00	40.25	55.75	49.75	69.25
P/E - high	—	—	—	21	25	24	35	18	23	32	33
P/E - low	—	—	—	16	18	19	26	14	15	22	23
Dividends per share ($)	8.1%	—	—	0.51	0.00	0.51	0.61	0.64	0.00	0.00	0.88
Book value per share ($)	(1.0%)	—	—	21.97	20.47	21.97	23.34	24.13	23.14	25.27	20.45
Employees	12.0%	46,024	49,365	51,139	49,772	49,772	53,000	57,555	54,391	57,166	127,252

STOCK PRICE HISTORY

HIGH/LOW/CLOSE

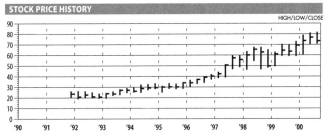

1999 FISCAL YEAR-END

Debt ratio: 26.5%
Return on equity: 7.7%
Cash ($ mil.): 3,977
Current ratio: 1.13
Long-term debt ($ mil.): 10,266
No. of shares (mil.): 1,395
Dividends
   Yield: 1.3%
   Payout: 40.4%
Market value ($ mil.): 96,607

TOYOTA MOTOR CORPORATION

OVERVIEW

Whether you're struggling with teen acne or a midlife crisis, Toyota Motor Corporation wants you in its cars. The Toyota City, Japan-based company is Japan's largest automaker (#4 worldwide behind General Motors, Ford, and DaimlerChrysler). Its models include the Camry, Celica, Corolla, Sienna, RAV4, and Land Cruiser, as well as the luxury Lexus line.

Toyota is expanding its vehicle offerings. For a growing population of "green" enthusiasts, Toyota has introduced the Prius, a hybrid gas- and electric-powered car, and the Echo, a small, high-mileage, low-cost car. Aiming to cash in on the SUV and pickup craze, Toyota has also introduced the V-8 powered Tundra. The company's other businesses include cellular telephone services and the manufacture of industrial equipment.

While enjoying strong sales in Europe and the US, Toyota has begun to increase production in emerging markets such as India and China. It is diversifying into products and services indirectly related to cars such as cellular phones and credit cards, and it is expanding its financial services operations.

HISTORY

In 1926 Sakichi Toyoda founded Toyoda Automatic Loom Works. In 1930 he sold the rights to the loom he invented and gave the proceeds to his son Kiichiro Toyoda to begin an automotive business. Kiichiro opened an auto shop within the loom works in 1933. When protectionist legislation (1936) improved prospects for Japanese automakers, Kiichiro split off the car department, took it public (1937), and changed its name to Toyota.

During WWII the company made military trucks, but financial problems after the war caused Toyota to reorganize in 1950. Its postwar commitment to R&D paid off with the launch of the four-wheel-drive Land Cruiser (1951); full-sized Crown (1955); and the small Corona (1957).

Toyota Motor Sales, U.S.A., debuted the Toyopet Crown in the US in 1957, but it proved underpowered for the US market. Toyota had better luck with the Corona in 1965 and with the Corolla (which became the best-selling car of all time) in 1968. By 1970 Toyota was the world's fourth-largest carmaker.

Toyota expanded rapidly in the US. During the 1970s the oil crisis caused demand for fuel-efficient cars, and Toyota was there to grab market share. In 1975 Toyota displaced Volkswagen as the US's #1 auto importer. Toyota began production in the US in 1984 through NUMMI, its joint venture with GM. The Lexus was launched in the US in 1989.

Because of the European Community's restrictions on Japanese auto imports until the year 2000, Toyota's European expansion slowed. Toyota responded in 1992 by agreeing to distribute cars in Japan for Volkswagen and also by establishing an engine plant (later moved to full auto production) in the UK.

The sport utility vehicle (SUV) mania of the 1990s spurred Toyota's introduction of luxury minivans and light trucks. Hiroshi Okuda, a 40-year veteran with Toyota and the first person from outside the Toyoda family to run the firm, succeeded Tatsuro Toyoda as president in 1995. The next year it consolidated North American production units into Toyota Motor Manufacturing North America with headquarters in Cincinnati.

In 1997 Toyota introduced the Prius, a hybrid electric- and gas-powered car. The next year the company boosted its stake in affiliate Daihatsu (minivehicles) to about 51% and started Toyota Mapmaster (51%-owned), to make map databases for car navigation systems.

Okuda became chairman in 1999, replacing Shoichiro Toyoda, and Fujio Cho became president. Also that year Toyota agreed to form a joint venture with Isuzu to manufacture buses, and it announced plans to invest $800 million to boost US auto production by 200,000 vehicles a year (16%) to about 1.45 million.

In 2000 Toyota launched the WiLL Vi, a sedan aimed at young people. It announced that it was building an online replacement parts marketplace with i2 Technology. Toyota also stated that it was buying a 5% stake in Yamaha (the world's #2 motorcycle maker), and that it would raise its stake in truck maker Hino Motors from about 20% to almost 34%. Toyota announced that it was forming a financial services company (Toyota Financial Service) and a brokerage firm (Toyota Financial Services Securities Corp.). International developments included Toyota's agreement with the Chinese government to produce passenger cars for sale in China. The cars are to be built by Tianjin Toyota Motor Corp., a joint venture between Chinese carmaker Tianjin Automobile Xiali and Toyota.

OFFICERS

Honorary Chairman: Shoichiro Toyoda
Chairman: Hiroshi Okuda
VC: Iwao Isomura
President: Fujio Cho
EVP Government and Public Affairs, Domestic Sales, Overseas: Kosuke Yamamoto
EVP Production: Kosuke Ikebuchi
EVP Development Group, Quality Control, Design: Shinichi Kato
EVP Corporate Planning, Business Development, Information Systems: Tadaaki Jagawa
EVP Housing Group: Noritaka Shimizu
Senior Managing Director: Yoshio Uesaka
Senior Managing Director: Akihiko Saito
Senior Managing Director: Ryuji Araki
Senior Managing Director: Yoshio Ishizaka
Senior Managing Director: Kosuke Shiramizu
Senior Managing Director: Katsuaki Watanabe
Senior Managing Director: Koichiro Noguchi
Senior Managing Director: Susumu Miyoshi
Senior Managing Director: Kazushi Iwatsuki
Senior Managing Director: Akiyoshi Morita
Director Global Human Resources, Secretarial, General Administration: Mitsuo Kinoshita
Auditors: Itoh Audit Corporation; PricewaterhouseCoopers

LOCATIONS

HQ: Toyota Jidosha Kabushiki Kaisha,
   1, Toyota-cho, Toyota City, Aichi 471-8571, Japan
Phone: +81-565-28-2121   **Fax:** +81-565-23-5800
US HQ: 9 W. 57th St., Ste. 4900, New York, NY 10019
US Phone: 212-223-0303   **US Fax:** 212-759-7670
Web site: http://www.global.toyota.com

Toyota Motor has manufacturing facilities in 26 countries.

2000 Sales

	$ mil.	% of total
Japan	88,980	59
North America	43,889	29
Europe	10,388	7
Other regions	7,788	5
Adjustments	(31,389)	—
Total	**119,656**	**100**

PRODUCTS/OPERATIONS

2000 Sales

	$ mil.	% of total
Automotive	104,903	86
Finance	5,032	4
Other	11,521	10
Adjustments	(1,800)	—
Total	**119,656**	**100**

COMPETITORS

BMW	Komatsu
Caterpillar	Kubota
Daewoo	Marubeni
DaimlerChrysler	Mazda
Deere	Mitsubishi
Fiat	Nissan
Ford	Peugeot Motors of
General Motors	America, Inc.
Honda	Renault
Hyundai	Saab Automobile
Ingersoll-Rand	Suzuki
Isuzu	Volkswagen
Kia Motors	Volvo

HISTORICAL FINANCIALS & EMPLOYEES

NYSE: TM FYE: March 31	Annual Growth	6/91	6/92	6/93	6/94	*3/95	3/96	3/97	3/98	3/99	3/00
Sales ($ mil.)	5.9%	71,598	80,809	95,338	95,032	95,828	101,120	98,741	88,473	105,832	119,656
Net income ($ mil.)	4.2%	3,135	1,891	1,648	1,277	1,557	2,424	3,112	3,442	3,747	4,540
Income as % of sales	—	4.4%	2.3%	1.7%	1.3%	1.6%	2.4%	3.2%	3.9%	3.5%	3.8%
Earnings per share ($)	4.6%	1.62	0.98	0.86	0.68	0.81	1.24	1.62	1.80	1.98	2.42
Stock price - FY high ($)	—	28.52	24.75	31.88	44.63	45.13	44.75	57.88	65.00	58.75	104.00
Stock price - FY low ($)	—	22.27	18.88	21.50	28.00	34.75	35.50	43.25	50.50	40.94	52.38
Stock price - FY close ($)	17.8%	23.75	23.00	28.75	44.63	39.75	44.50	50.50	52.75	57.25	104.00
P/E - high	—	18	25	37	66	56	36	36	36	30	43
P/E - low	—	14	19	25	41	43	29	27	28	21	22
Dividends per share ($)	6.7%	0.19	0.21	0.24	0.29	0.28	0.27	0.33	0.16	0.37	0.34
Book value per share ($)	6.5%	19.69	20.17	23.90	26.33	31.70	26.74	24.15	23.98	29.37	34.73
Employees	8.6%	102,423	108,167	109,279	110,534	142,645	146,855	150,736	159,035	183,879	214,631

* Fiscal year change

STOCK PRICE HISTORY

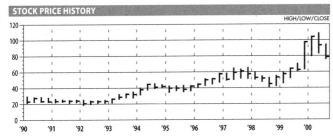

HIGH/LOW/CLOSE

2000 FISCAL YEAR-END

Debt ratio: 29.7%
Return on equity: —
Cash ($ mil.): 14,407
Current ratio: 1.22
Long-term debt ($ mil.): 27,450
No. of shares (mil.): 1,875
Dividends
   Yield: 0.3%
   Payout: 14.0%
Market value ($ mil.): 194,969

HOOVER'S HANDBOOK OF WORLD BUSINESS 2001   **617**

UBS AG

OVERVIEW

Toppled from its spot at the summit of Europe's financial Matterhorn by Germany's Deutsche Bank, UBS AG isn't content to be #2. The company operates through three units. UBS Switzerland includes its top-ranked domestic retail and commercial banking operations, as well as its onshore and offshore private banking services. UBS Asset Management encompasses its individual and institutional investment management services and mutual funds, while UBS Warburg (formerly Warburg Dillon Read) oversees the company's securities and investment banking businesses, including its corporate finance, private equity

(through UBS Capital), fixed income, and other products.

UBS has offices around the world, concentrated in Europe and North America.

UBS is looking to catapult itself higher into the echelons of global finance. One growth target is its laggard asset management segment. It lost clients after its 1998 merger with Swiss Bank, and its aversion to "New Economy" stocks hurt its performance. Another sore spot is the US: UBS, making good on plans to use its NYSE listing to buy its way to a bigger presence in that important market, bought US investment broker Paine Webber.

HISTORY

Businessmen in Winterthur, Switzerland, formed the Bank of Winterthur in 1862 to serve trading interests, finance railroads, and operate a warehouse. In 1912 the bank merged with the Bank of Toggenburg (formed in 1863) to create Schweizerische Bankgesellschaft — Union Bank of Switzerland (UBS).

It expanded in Switzerland, buying smaller banks and adding branches. After a post-WWI growth period, it was hit hard by the Depression. UBS benefited from Switzerland's neutrality in WWII, gaining deposits from both Jews and Nazis. In 1946 the bank opened an office in New York. Expansion in Switzerland continued after the war with the purchase of Eidgenossische Bank of Zurich.

UBS continued its acquisitions in the 1950s; by 1962 it had 81 branches. Other purchases included Interhandel, a cash-rich Swiss financial concern (1967), and four savings banks (1968). In 1967 it opened a full-service office in London, and during the 1970s established several securities underwriting subsidiaries abroad.

International financial markets became supercharged in the 1980s, and UBS resolved to catch up with its domestic peers in international operations. As London prepared for financial deregulation in 1986, UBS bought brokerage house Phillips & Drew.

The firm's UK brokerage business was hit hard by the 1987 US stock market crash; over the next two years losses continued, prompting an overhaul of the London operations. Then its US operations were jarred by the collapse of the junk bond market in 1990. The next year UBS set up offices in Paris, Singapore, and Hong Kong and took over Chase Manhattan's New York money management unit.

Meanwhile, the firm continued to expand within Switzerland, buying five more banks to

boost market share and fill in gaps in its branch network. These buys left UBS with overlapping operations and a bloated infrastructure when recession hit. Falling real estate values left the bank with a heavy load of nonperforming loans.

In 1994 profits plummeted. Stockholder Martin Ebner, dissatisfied with the performance of president Robert Studer, tried to gain control of UBS; failing that, he sought to have Studer charged with criminal fraud. In 1996 he almost thwarted Studer's election to the chairmanship.

UBS launched a multiyear reorganization in 1994 by consolidating its consumer credit operations. The next year it joined with Swiss Life/Rentenanstalt to offer insurance products through its bank network.

In 1996, after rebuffing Credit Suisse Group's merger bid, UBS began an even more draconian reorganization, cutting domestic branches and writing down billions of francs in bad loans, leading to UBS' first loss ever (with another the next year). In 1998 the company merged with Swiss Bank Corp. then cut 23% of its staff. Later that year the bank lost $1.6 billion in the stumbling Long-Term Capital Management hedge fund, prompting chairman Mathis Cabiallavetta to resign.

As UBS struggled to swallow Swiss Bank in 1999, it retreated somewhat from riskier markets. The company began selling some $2 billion in real estate and sold its 25% stake in Swiss Life/Rentenanstalt. Looking to bulk up, the firm that year bought Bank of America's European and Asian private banking operations and Allegis Realty Investors, a US real estate investment management firm.

In 2000 UBS reorganized yet again and bought US broker Paine Webber Inc.

Chairman: Alex Krauer, age 69
VC: Markus Kundig
VC: Alberto Togni
Group CEO: Marcel Ospel, age 50
CFO: Lugman Arnold
Chairman and Chief Investment Officer, UBS Asset Management: Gary P. Brinson
CEO Private Banking: Georges Gagnebin
CEO, UBS Asset Management: Peter A. Wuffli
CEO, UBS Capital: Pierre de Weck
CEO, UBS Switzerland: Stephan Haeringer
CEO, UBS Warburg: Markus J. Granziol
CEO, Philips & Drew London, UBS Asset Management: Crispian Collins
CEO, UBS Brinson/Brinson Partners, UBS Asset Management: Benjamin F. Lenhardt Jr.
CEO, Warburg Dillon Read Asia/Pacific, UBS Warburg: Clive Standish
Deputy CEO and Head Products, Services and Logistics, UBS Private Banking: Arthur Decurtins
COO and Global Head Fixed Income and Treasury Products, UBS Warburg: John Costas
Group Chief Credit Officer: Marco Suter
Group Chief Risk Officer: Marcel Rohner
Group Controller: Hugo Schaub
Auditors: ATAG Ernst & Young Ltd.

HQ: Bahnhofstrasse 45, CH-8098 Zurich, Switzerland
Phone: +41-1-234-4100   **Fax:** +41-1-234-3415
US HQ: 10 E. 50th St., New York, NY 10022
US Phone: 212-574-3000   **US Fax:** 212-574-5499
Web site: http://www.ubs.com

UBS has 385 branches in Switzerland and subsidiaries in more than 50 countries.

1999 Assets

	$ mil.	% of total
Cash & equivalents	136,791	22
Trading portfolio	136,252	22
Net loans	147,465	24
Other investments	4,419	1
Other assets	191,403	31
Total	**616,330**	**100**

Selected Operations

UBS Asset Management
Individual asset management
Institutional asset management
Mutual funds
Research

UBS Switzerland
Consumer banking in Switzerland
Corporate banking in Switzerland
Private banking

UBS Warburg
Corporate finance
Equities
Fixed income
Investment banking
Treasury

Bank of America
Bank of Tokyo-Mitsubishi
Barclays
Canadian Imperial
Chase Manhattan
Citigroup
Credit Lyonnais
Credit Suisse
Dai-Ichi Kangyo
Deutsche Bank
HSBC Holdings
Royal Bank of Canada

NYSE: UBS FYE: December 31	Annual Growth	12/90	12/91	12/92	12/93	12/94	12/95	12/96	12/97	12/98	12/99
Assets ($ mil.)	14.4%	183,229	183,100	181,774	209,106	249,417	335,081	324,091	396,564	684,673	616,330
Net income ($ mil.)	21.2%	702	893	915	1,524	1,233	1,458	(258)	(89)	2,197	3,956
Income as % of assets	—	0.4%	0.5%	0.5%	0.7%	0.5%	0.4%	—	—	0.3%	0.6%
Employees	6.7%	27,470	27,677	27,280	27,500	28,882	29,071	29,153	27,611	48,011	49,058

Equity as % of assets: 3.5%
Return on assets: 0.6%
Return on equity: 17.2%
Long-term debt ($ mil.): 35,371
Sales ($ mil.): 26,085

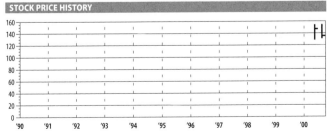

UNILEVER

If any one company can move the Earth, it's Unilever. One of the world's top packaged consumer goods companies, Unilever has leveraged its brand-name food, cleaning, and personal care products into market dominance worldwide. Dually headquartered in London and Rotterdam, the Netherlands, it is operated by two different holding companies, Unilever PLC (UK) and Unilever N.V. (the Netherlands), which have separate stock listings but an identical board of directors.

Unilever's food products (about half of sales) include frozen foods (Gorton's, Birds Eye in the UK), ice cream (Breyers, Popsicle), margarine (Country Crock, Promise), tea (Lipton), Ragu sauces, salad dressings (Wishbone in the US), and Slim-Fast diet foods. The company has also purchased Bestfoods (Hellmann's, Knorr, Skippy), making it one of the top three

food companies worldwide, after Nestlé and Kraft. Unilever added ice-cream maker Ben & Jerry's Homemade to its icebox as well.

Unilever is one of the industry leaders in deodorants (Degree, Sure), hair care products (Suave, ThermaSilk), prestige fragrances (Calvin Klein, Lagerfeld), and soap (Dove, Lever 2000). Other familiar goods include Q-Tips, Vaseline, Pepsodent and Mentadent toothpastes, and laundry and cleaning products such as all, Wisk, and Surf. Unilever also makes institutional cleaning products.

Unilever is undergoing major restructuring, including cutting 1,200 of its 1,600 brands and 25,000 jobs over a five-year period. To simplify its operations, the company is splitting into two global divisions, one focused on food, the other on household and personal care items.

After sharpening his sales skills in the family wholesale grocery business, Englishman William Lever formed a new company in 1885 along with his brother James. Lever Brothers introduced Sunlight, the world's first packaged, branded laundry soap. Sunlight was a success in Britain, and within 15 years Lever Brothers was selling soap worldwide. Between 1906 and 1915 it grew mostly through acquisitions. Needing vegetable oil to make soap, the company established plantations and trading companies around the world. During WWI Lever began using its vegetable oil to make margarine.

Rival Dutch butter makers Jurgens and Van den Berghs were pioneers in margarine production. In 1927 they created the Margarine Union, a cartel that owned the European market. The Margarine Union and Lever Brothers merged in 1930, but for tax reasons formed two separate entities: Unilever PLC in London and Unilever N.V. in Rotterdam, the Netherlands.

Despite the Depression and WWII, Unilever expanded, acquiring US companies Thomas J. Lipton (1937) and Pepsodent (1944). However, its domination of the US market ended after Procter & Gamble's (P&G) 1946 introduction of Tide, the first synthetic detergent. Unilever benefited from the postwar boom in Europe, the increasing use of margarine, new detergent technologies, and the growing use of personal care products.

Although product development fueled some growth, acquisitions (at one time running at the rate of one per week) played a major role in shaping Unilever. These included Birds Eye

Foods in the UK (1957) and, in the US, Good Humor (1961), Lawry's Foods (1979), Ragu (1986), Chesebrough-Ponds (1987), Calvin Klein Cosmetics (1989), Faberge/Elizabeth Arden (1989), and Breyers ice cream (1993).

In 1995 Unilever began cutting its global workforce by 7,500. The following year it bought hair care and deodorant maker Helene Curtis. Also in 1996 Niall FitzGerald became co-chairman. Unilever shed its specialty chemicals operations in 1997 (resulting in an $8.1 billion special dividend to shareholders in 1999).

In 1999 Antony Burgmans was appointed co-chairman. That year Unilever agreed to buy Amora Maille (mustard, France) for about $743 million. Also in 1999 the company announced plans to eliminate 1,200 brands, keeping the 400 brands that are #1 or #2 in their respective markets.

Unilever bought US weight-management firm Slim-Fast Foods for $2.3 billion in May 2000 and superpremium ice-cream maker Ben & Jerry's Homemade that August. As part of its previously announced brand-reduction strategy, Unilever agreed in July 2000 to sell its European bakery supplies business (with operations in 13 countries) to CSM NV for $672 million.

In October 2000 Unilever bought Bestfoods for $20.3 billion; to gain regulatory approval, the company agreed to sell off some brands, including Lesieur, Oxo, and Royco. The company also agreed that month to sell its Elizabeth Arden fragrance and skin care business to prestige perfume marketer French Fragrances for about $225 million.

Chairman, Unilever PLC; VC, Unilever N.V.:
Niall W. A. FitzGerald, age 54
Chairman, Unilever N.V.; VC, Unilever PLC:
Antony Burgmans, age 53
Financial Director: Patrick J. Cescau, age 51
Personnel Director: Jan Peelen, age 60
Strategy and Technology Director: Rudy Markham, age 54
Category Director Foods: Alexander Kemner, age 60
Category Director Home and Personal Care: Clive Butler, age 53
Business Group President Food and Beverages, Europe: Roy Brown, age 53
Business Group President Ice Cream and Frozen Foods, Europe: Robert Polet, age 44
Business Group President Home and Personal Care, Europe: John Sharpe, age 58
Business Group President Home and Personal Care, North America; President and CEO, Unilever United States: Charles B. Strauss, age 57
Business Group President Africa: Manfred Stach, age 57
Business Group President Central Asia and Middle East: Jeff Fraser, age 56
Business Group President Central and Eastern Europe: Jean Martin, age 55
Business Group President China: Bruno Lemagne, age 53
Business Group President Latin America: Ralph Kugler, age 44
Joint Secretary and General Counsel: Stephen Williams
Joint Secretary and Head of Taxation: Jos Westerburgen
Auditors: PricewaterhouseCoopers

LOCATIONS

HQ: Unilever PLC, PO Box 68, Unilever House, Blackfriars, London EC4P 4BQ, United Kingdom
Phone: +44-20-7822-5252   **Fax:** +44-20-7822-5951
HQ: Unilever N.V., Weena 455, 3000 DK Rotterdam, The Netherlands
Phone: +31-10-217-4000   **Fax:** +31-10-217-4798
US HQ: 390 Park Ave., New York, NY 10022
US Phone: 212-888-1260   **US Fax:** 212-906-4666
Web site: http://www.unilever.com

1999 Sales & Operating Income

	Sales $ mil.	Sales % of total	Operating Income $ mil.	Operating Income % of total
Europe	20,009	46	2,410	50
North America	9,411	22	1,036	21
Asia/Pacific	7,160	16	703	14
Latin America	4,609	10	453	9
Africa & Middle East	2,447	6	267	6
Total	**43,636**	**100**	**4,869**	**100**

PRODUCTS/OPERATIONS

1999 Sales & Operating Income

	Sales $ mil.	Sales % of total	Operating Income $ mil.	Operating Income % of total
Foods				
Oil- & dairy-based & bakery	7,751	18	829	17
Ice cream & beverage	7,068	16	632	13
Culinary & frozen	7,017	16	705	14
Personal care	11,367	26	1,681	35
Home & professional care	9,696	22	909	19
Trading operations	737	2	113	2
Total	**43,636**	**100**	**4,869**	**100**

COMPETITORS

Alberto-Culver	Dial	Nestlé
Alticor	Estée Lauder	Pillsbury
Avon	Gillette	Procter
Beiersdorf	Hillsdown	& Gamble
Campbell Soup	Holdings	Reckitt
Carter-Wallace	Hormel	Benckiser
Church	Interbake Foods	Revlon
& Dwight	Johnson	S.C. Johnson
Clorox	& Johnson	Sara Lee
Coca-Cola	Kao	Shiseido
Colgate-	Kraft Foods	SmithKline
Palmolive	L'Oréal	Beecham
ConAgra Foods	LVMH	Tata Enterprises
Dairy Farmers	Mars	Uniq plc
of America	McBride	USA Detergents
Danone	Nabisco	
Del Monte	Holdings	

HISTORICAL FINANCIALS & EMPLOYEES

Joint venture FYE: December 31	Annual Growth	12/90	12/91	12/92	12/93	12/94	12/95	12/96	12/97	12/98	12/99
Sales ($ mil.)	5.1%	27,784	44,777	42,091	39,962	47,580	48,881	50,403	46,693	47,532	43,636
Net income ($ mil.)	9.1%	1,442	2,228	2,200	1,860	2,500	2,285	2,420	5,568	3,432	3,165
Income as % of sales	—	5.2%	5.0%	5.2%	4.7%	5.3%	4.7%	4.8%	11.9%	7.2%	7.3%
Employees	(1.9%)	304,000	298,000	287,000	294,000	304,000	308,000	306,000	270,000	265,000	255,000

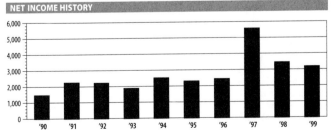

NET INCOME HISTORY

1999 FISCAL YEAR-END
Debt ratio: 15.2%
Return on equity: —
Cash ($ mil.): 4,015
Current ratio: 1.51
Long-term debt ($ mil.): 2,845

UNITED NEWS & MEDIA PLC

OVERVIEW

United News & Media is tossing its eggs into fewer baskets. The London-based media company is primarily active in business service and consumer publishing. United generates about 60% of its profits through its business services division, which includes CMP Media (one of the world's largest high-tech publishers), PR Newswire, and market research firms NOP Research Group and Audits & Surveys. It also owns Miller Freeman, the world's top trade show group, but is combining Miller's UK operations with other units and has been selling the rest.

The company owns a 35% ownership interest in Channel 5, a UK commercial TV broadcaster. Its string of UK newspapers includes *The Express* and *Daily Star.* The company also owns 50% of Internet service provider LineOne.

United had agreed to merge with rival broadcaster Carlton Communications as commercial television consolidation in the UK is at a fever pitch. The recent relaxing of rules governing Independent Television (ITV) ownership jeopardized the United/Carlton transaction; in the end, it was called off. As a result, United instead sold its ITV business to rival Granada Media. The company then began streamlining its operations through the sale of US-based United Advertising Publications (consumer magazines) and most of Miller Freeman. As part of its new focus on business publishing and exhibitions, United News & Media plans to change its name to United Business Media. The company is also seeking to expand its Web activities through newly formed unit Xilerate.

HISTORY

United Newspapers was formed in 1918 after British Prime Minister David Lloyd George, stung by criticism of his war strategy in the *Daily Chronicle*, persuaded a group of Liberal Party supporters to buy the newspaper. The company also acquired *Lloyd's Weekly News* (founded in 1842). It went public in 1925. William Harrison later bought a controlling interest and merged United with his Provincial Newspapers.

Burdened by debt, United merged the *Daily Chronicle* with the *Daily News* in 1930 to produce the *Daily News and Chronicle,* and sold 50% of it to News and Westminster. United later sold its stake in the paper.

Harold Drayton bought a third of the company in 1946 and became chairman in 1948. After persevering through the UK's postwar recovery period of the 1950s, the company accelerated its acquisitions, buying regional newspapers, weekly papers, and periodicals.

After a period of consolidation in the 1970s, David Stevens took over the leadership and launched an expansion drive in 1981. United made several acquisitions, including Gralla (a US publisher and promoter of trade shows), Miller Freeman, and PR Newswire, as well as newspaper group Fleet Holdings and the Hong Kong International Trade Fair Group. Reflecting its expanded interests, the company changed its name to United News & Media in 1995.

In 1996 United News & Media merged with financial services group MAI. MAI was founded in 1974 as the J.H. Vavasseur Group and was headed by Clive Hollick (later Lord Hollick), who had helped the struggling company turn its fortunes around. MAI brought several operations to United News & Media, including NOP Research Group, two Independent Television broadcast licenses, and interests in financial services. Following the merger, Hollick became United's chief executive and Stevens continued as chairman.

Acquisitions and disposals followed the merger. In 1996 the company acquired conference organizer Blenheim. The next year it sold its stake in Yorkshire Tyne-Tees Television and acquired HTV (the ITV license in Wales and western England) and Telecom Library (US magazines and trade shows). In 1998 it finished disposing of its regional newspapers and also became an equal partner in LineOne, an Internet venture.

A renewed focus on its media businesses led United to spin off its financial services unit (Garban) in late 1998. The next year the company bought high-tech publisher CMP Media. Sir Ronald Hampel succeeded Stevens as chairman in 1999. Also that year United News agreed to merge with rival broadcasting firm Carlton Communications in a $12.6 billion deal that fell apart when ITV ownership rules were relaxed.

In 2000 the company sold UAP, its consumer magazine business, to Trader Publishing for $520 million. United also agreed to sell most of Miller Freeman, in parts, to VNU and Reed Elsevier. Also that year it sold its ITV assets to UK broadcaster Granada Media for about $2.6 billion.

OFFICERS

Chairman: Sir Ronald Hampel, age 67
Deputy Chairman: Sir James McKinnon, age 70
Group Chief Executive: Clive Hollick, age 54,
$927,000 pay
Finance Director: Charles Stern, age 49, $386,250 pay
Executive Director Business Information:
Charles Gregson, age 52, $165,830 pay
Chairman and CEO, United Advertising Publications,
Inc.: Nigel Donaldson, age 55, $337,971 pay
CEO, Miller Freeman: Tony Tillin, age 54, $387,524 pay
CEO, UIG: Simon Chadwick
President and CEO, Mediamark Research:
Kathleen D. Love
Chief Executive, UBE: Malcolm Wall
Chief Executive, United Productions: John Willis
President, PR Newswire (US): Ian Capps
President and CEO, CMP Media Inc.: Gary Marshall
Managing Director, Express: Andrew Jonesco
Managing Director, UAP plc: Tony Thomas
Editor, Express: Rosie Boycott
Secretary: Anne Siddell
Personnel and Human Resources Director: Nicky Gray
Auditors: PricewaterhouseCoopers

LOCATIONS

HQ: Ludgate House, 245 Blackfriars Rd.,
London SE1 9UY, United Kingdom
Phone: +44-20-7921-5000 **Fax:** +44-20-7928-2717
US HQ: 32 Union Sq. East, New York, NY 10003
US Phone: 212-358-6750 **US Fax:** 212-358-6755
Web site: http://www.unm.com

United News & Media generates most of its sales in
North America and the UK; it also operates in other
parts of Europe and the Asia/Pacific region.

PRODUCTS/OPERATIONS

1999 Sales

	% of total
Business services	59
Broadcasting & entertainment	23
Consumer publishing	18
Total	**100**

Selected Business Services Operations
Audits & Surveys Worldwide (market research)
CMP Media (high tech publishing)
NOP Research Group (market research)
PR Newswire (press release service)
United Business Media (UK magazine publishing and
trade show services)

COMPETITORS

ACNielsen	Johnston Press
Advanstar	Key3Media
BBC	News Corp.
Bristol Evening Post	Newsquest
BSkyB	Penton Media
Carlton Communications	PGI
Daily Mail and General	Reed Elsevier
Trust	Reuters
Flextech	RTL
Granada Media	Town Pages
Hollinger International	Trinity Mirror
Information Resources	VNU
International Data Group	

HISTORICAL FINANCIALS & EMPLOYEES

Nasdaq: UNEWY FYE: December 31	Annual Growth	12/90	12/91	12/92	12/93	12/94	12/95	12/96	12/97	12/98	12/99
Sales ($ mil.)	9.1%	1,600	1,519	1,259	1,345	1,591	1,659	3,409	3,728	3,659	3,508
Net income ($ mil.)	—	120	94	121	148	151	106	261	539	516	(170)
Income as % of sales	—	7.5%	6.2%	9.6%	11.0%	9.5%	6.4%	7.7%	14.5%	14.1%	—
Earnings per share ($)	—	1.23	0.94	1.21	1.34	1.24	0.87	1.07	1.84	2.03	(0.69)
Stock price - FY high ($)	—	15.13	14.50	16.50	19.75	21.63	17.75	23.38	26.50	31.25	26.13
Stock price - FY low ($)	—	9.88	10.75	14.63	14.63	15.38	14.75	17.50	21.13	16.38	16.00
Stock price - FY close ($)	9.3%	11.50	11.75	16.25	19.50	15.50	17.00	23.38	23.75	18.13	25.50
P/E - high	—	12	12	14	15	17	20	22	18	22	—
P/E - low	—	8	9	10	11	12	17	16	15	11	—
Dividends per share ($)	(0.5%)	0.86	0.80	0.83	0.98	0.73	0.51	0.85	0.79	1.13	0.82
Book value per share ($)	1.2%	3.71	5.41	2.52	5.07	3.95	2.83	(1.89)	(3.59)	5.70	4.14
Employees	2.0%	12,550	12,020	11,860	11,850	13,333	13,573	18,318	18,150	15,096	15,000

STOCK PRICE HISTORY

HIGH/LOW/CLOSE

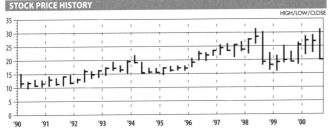

1999 FISCAL YEAR-END

Debt ratio: 67.1%
Return on equity: —
Cash ($ mil.): 110
Current ratio: 0.81
Long-term debt ($ mil.): 2,120
No. of shares (mil.): 251
Dividends
 Yield: 3.2%
 Payout: —
Market value ($ mil.): 6,394

VIRGIN GROUP LTD.

OVERVIEW

Virgin sacrifices little as the parent of more than 200 entertainment, media, and travel companies worldwide. Flamboyant owner and entrepreneur Sir Richard Branson has made the London-based Virgin Group name one of the most recognizable brands in the world by plastering it on everything from airplanes to cola (he tactfully refrained from placing it on a line of condoms).

Virgin Group's travel operations are its biggest breadwinner. Virgin Atlantic Airways (second in the UK to British Airways; the company sold 49% of the airline to Singapore Airlines in 2000) flies to dozens of destinations around the world and is complemented regionally by its pan-European low-fare cousin, Virgin Express. Branson's eccentricities apply to his businesses as well: Branson's attempts to travel the globe by hot-air balloon are well-documented, and his company operates passenger balloon flights. On the ground, Virgin Group gets around by rail with two train lines, puts up guests in more than 30 hotels in seven countries, operates tours, and even owns an island in the Caribbean. Branson's next pie in the sky is commercial space travel under the name Virgin Galactic Airways, with plans to launch, literally, in 2007.

Virgin Entertainment is the group's other major moneymaker. It sells music, movies, and computer games from more than 350 Megastore and Our Price locations. Extra Virgin Group operations include beverages, book publishing, clothing, financial services, health clubs, Internet services, a modeling agency, mobile phone services, radio, record labels, and TV production.

HISTORY

Always one to revel in competition, Richard Branson got his start in the business world at the age of 17, dropping out of boarding school to pursue his magazine, *Student*, in 1968. Two years later he was on to a new challenge when he started Virgin — a mail-order record company named for his lack of experience at such things. After a postal strike the next year put a damper on that enterprise, Branson opened the first Virgin record store. Continued success led to a recording studio and record label that went on to sign several popular British rock bands in the 1970s, including the Sex Pistols, Genesis, and the Rolling Stones.

With his entertainment businesses flourishing in the early 1980s, Branson sought a new adventure and found it in the airline industry, another business he knew very little about. Virgin Atlantic Airways took off in 1984 with one plane and one transatlantic route. Growing steadily, Virgin Atlantic became one of the world's most profitable airlines in the 1980s. The company added Virgin Holidays (tours) to its travel group in 1985.

Branson collected all his businesses (except the travel operations) into a new company called Virgin Group and took it public in 1986. Despite the company's continued growth and profits, the market slashed its value after the crash of 1987, and a frustrated Branson bought it all back the following year. Virgin sold its smaller UK record stores in 1988 to focus on the development of its Megastores concept. It also entered the hotel business that year.

Virgin started Britain's first national commercial rock radio station in 1992.

Branson sold the Virgin Music Group (a decision he still regrets) to THORN EMI that year for about $1 billion, using the proceeds to build Virgin Atlantic.

The company debuted Virgin Cola in 1994 and bought 25% of the Our Price record store chain with WH Smith (it purchased the rest in 1998). Virgin acquired MGM Cinemas (the UK's largest theater operator) and introduced its financial services business in 1995. Meanwhile it added dozens of new Megastores around the world in the mid-1990s. Virgin got back into the recording business in 1996 when it launched the V2 record label. It also bought low-fare Euro Belgian Airlines (renamed Virgin Express).

Virgin looked to keep itself on the right track in 1997 when it got into the rail business. Realizing that the right track might be the Internet, Branson has pushed the group towards the age of e-commerce and online services with Virgin.com. Mobile phone sales (at its existing retail locations) entered the company's cornucopia in 1999, and Branson is rumored to be considering a public offering again. In late 1999 Virgin agreed to sell its cinema chain to Vivendi, raising funds for other online and retail ventures. It also announced plans to launch a major Australian airline.

With billionaire Bill Gates as a partner, Branson in early 2000 threw his hat into the ring for the UK's national lottery license. However, the UK's National Lottery Commission has rejected his offer, as well as that of current lottery contract holder Camelot Group.

OFFICERS

Chairman and President: Sir Richard Branson
Director Finance: Stephen Murphy
Managing Director, Virgin Retail Group: Simon Wright
Managing Director, Virgin Media Group: Kenneth Ibbett
Managing Director, Virgin Hotels Group:
Michael Herriot

LOCATIONS

HQ: 120 Campden Hill Rd.,
London W8 7AR, United Kingdom
Phone: +44-20-7229-1282   **Fax:** +44-20-7727-8200
US HQ: 15 Haskel Dr., Princeton Junction, NJ 08550
US Phone: 609-897-7865   **US Fax:** 609-275-1769
Web site: http://www.virgin.com

Virgin Group has operations worldwide, including Virgin Megastores in Austria, Belgium, Canada, France, Ireland, Italy, Japan, the Netherlands, Norway, Spain, the UK, and the US; hotels in Australia, France, Italy, South Africa, Spain, the UK, and the US; and movie theaters in Ireland and the UK.

PRODUCTS/OPERATIONS

Selected Operations

Entertainment
London Broncos (professional rugby club)
Our Price (music stores)
V2 Music (record labels)
  V2 Music Publishing
  V2 Records
Virgin Cinemas (more than 30 multiplex theaters in the UK and Ireland)
Virgin Cola (beverage brands)
  Virgin Cola
  Virgin Ginger Beer
  Virgin Hi-Energy
  Virgin Lips
Virgin Megastores (retail music, movies, and computer games)
Virgin Publishing (book publishing)
Virgin Radio (UK rock radio station and Internet broadcasts)

Financial Businesses
Virgin Direct (financial services)
Virgin One (banking services)

Lifestyle Businesses
The Roof Gardens (nightclub and restaurant)
Virgin Active (health clubs)
Virgin Bride (bridal emporium)
Virgin Clothing (men's and women's apparel in the UK)
Virgin Cosmetics (more than 500 products for men and women available in the UK)
Virgin Net (Internet access and online services)

Media Businesses
525 Post Production (editing, graphics, and special effects)
Rapido TV (TV and film production)
Rushes Postproduction (special effects and postproduction house)
Virgin Arcadia Productions (video production)
Virgin Digital Studio Services (postproduction facility development)
West One TV (TV and video postproduction)

Travel Businesses
Necker Island (privately owned resort in British Virgin Islands)
The Trainline (train schedules and reservations)
Virgin Atlantic Airways (51%, international airline)
Virgin Balloon Flights (passenger balloons)
Virgin Express (pan-European low-fare airline)
Virgin Holidays (UK-based tour operator)
Virgin Hotels (more than 35 in seven countries)
Virgin Limobike (motorcycle passenger service)
Virgin Limousines (Northern California limo service)
Virgin Trains (passenger trains)
  Cross Country Trains
  West Coast Trains

COMPETITORS

Accor	News Corp.
Air France	Pearson
Airtours	PepsiCo
AMR	Rank
Bertelsmann	Seagram
British Airways	Sony
Coca-Cola	Starwood Hotels & Resorts
EMI Group	Worldwide
JAL	Time Warner
KLM	UAL
Lufthansa	Viacom
Marriott International	Walt Disney
MTS	

HISTORICAL FINANCIALS & EMPLOYEES

| Private
FYE: October 31 | Annual
Growth | 10/90 | 10/91 | 10/92 | 10/93 | 10/94 | 10/95 | 10/96 | 10/97 | 10/98 | 10/99 |
|---|---|---|---|---|---|---|---|---|---|---|---|
| Estimated sales ($ mil.) | 13.9% | 1,500 | 2,000 | 1,600 | 1,800 | 2,500 | 2,800 | 3,254 | 4,181 | 500 | 4,832 |
| Employees | 16.3% | — | 7,450 | — | — | 9,000 | 10,000 | — | 20,000 | 24,000 | 25,000 |

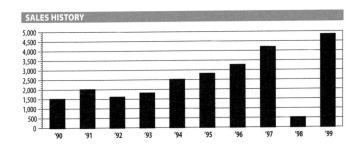

SALES HISTORY

VIVENDI

Vivendi vends its watery wares worldwide with vim and vigor, but the Paris-based company is shifting its emphasis to filling entertainment pipelines. The company has agreed to acquire Canada's Seagram (owner of Universal Music Group and Universal Studios; it is selling Seagram's drinks business) and the 51% of French pay-TV provider CANAL+ that it doesn't already own. The new company, to be known as Vivendi Universal, will be a global media giant. The company plans to integrate its new prizes with its existing media and communications businesses. Through its Havas unit and other affiliates, Vivendi is involved in publishing, advertising, and software. It owns 44% of Cegetel, which provides fixed-line and mobile telecom services in France. Shaking up its Internet operations, the company is selling its 55% stake in AOL France, and, with partner Vodafone, it is rolling out the Vizzavi Internet

portal, designed to be accessible from wireless phones, cable TV, and computers. The company is also looking to dive into the free Internet access market.

However, Vivendi's water operations aren't dried up: It became the world's #1 water company (ahead of Suez Lyonnaise) after swallowing USFilter. Vivendi's water and wastewater services reach 100 million customers in about 100 countries. It also provides waste management services worldwide.

Besides handling water and waste, the company's environmental unit is involved in energy activities, including independent power projects through its stake in Sithe Energies. It also has stakes in road and rail transportation concerns in Europe. Vivendi has sold a minority stake in Vivendi Environnement to the public, and it has been selling off its construction operations and real estate holdings.

Authorized by an imperial decree, Compagnie Générale des Eaux was founded in 1853 by investors who included the Rothschild family and Napoleon III's half-brother to irrigate French farmland and supply water to towns. It won contracts to serve Lyons (in 1853), Nantes (1854), Paris (1860), and Venice (1880).

After WWI Générale des Eaux created Société Auxiliaire de Distribution d'Eau (Sade, 1918), a water engineering firm, and extended its water distribution network to several areas of France. By 1953 the company had added trash collection to its services. In the 1960s it began managing district heating networks and waste incineration/composting plants. The company moved into construction in 1972, building an office tower (and later hotels and houses) in Paris. By the time Guy Dejouany became chairman in 1976, water distribution accounted for less than half of the company's sales.

Dejouany began an expansion drive in the 1980s. In 1980 Générale des Eaux became France's #1 private energy management firm when it bought Générale de Chauffe. Also that year it expanded its wastewater and waste management businesses and moved into transportation, buying Compagnie Générale d'Entreprises Automobiles (CGEA). The company also entered communications in the 1980s; it took a 15% stake in pay-TV provider CANAL+ (1983) and created a mobile telephone unit, Société Francaise de Radiotelephonie (SFR, 1987).

Générale des Eaux's water services seeped into the Asia/Pacific region, Latin America, the

UK, and the US in the 1990s. Dejouany stepped down in 1996, and the new helmsman, Jean-Marie Messier, dumped noncore businesses. In 1997 the company launched fixed-line and mobile telecom provider Cegetel and increased its stake in publisher Havas to 30%. In 1998 the firm bought the rest of Havas (upping ownership in Canal+) and took the name Vivendi — representing vivacity and mobility.

Its purchase of USFilter in 1999 made Vivendi the world's largest water company; it also bought US waste management company Superior Services. It joined German giants Allianz and RWE to grab a 49.9% stake in state-owned water company Berliner Wasserbetriebe.

Bulking up its media holdings, it added US firm Cendant Software (educational software and games) and bought French film producer Pathé. Vivendi sold most of Pathé's assets but kept stakes in BSkyB and CANAL+'s digital-TV unit. The company sold $985 million in real estate to Unibail and its hotel and restaurant businesses to Accor, the French hotels group.

In 2000 Vivendi and Vodafone launched an Internet portal, Vizzavi. Later that year Vivendi agreed to buy Seagram and the portion of CANAL+ that it didn't already own in a $55 billion deal. To gain European Commission approval for the Seagram acquisition, Vivendi agreed to sell its stake in BSkyB. Also that year Vivendi brought its environmental services businesses together under the name Vivendi Environnement and agreed to sell Seagram's drinks business to Diageo and Pernod Ricard.

OFFICERS

Chairman and CEO: Jean-Marie Messier, age 43
Honorary President: Guy Dejouany
COO; Chairman and CEO, Havas: Eric Licoys, age 61
SEVP, Vivendi Environment: Henri Proglio
SEVP, Vivendi Communications: Philippe Germond
EVP Finance: Guillaume Hannezo
EVP Human Resources: Jean-François Colin
EVP: Daniel Caille
VP Corporate Communication: Christine Delavennat
VP International Affairs: Thierry de Beaucé
VP Strategy and Business Development: Agnès Audier
Company and Board Secretary: Jean-François Dubos
Auditors: Deloitte Touche Tohmatsu - BMA;
Salustro Reydel; Barbier Frinault & Cie

LOCATIONS

HQ: 42 avenue de Friedland,
75380 Paris Cedex 08, France
Phone: +33-1-71-71-10-00   **Fax:** +33-1-71-71-10-01
US HQ: 800 3rd Ave., New York, NY 10012
US Phone: 212-753-2000   **US Fax:** 212-753-9301
Web site: http://www.vivendi.com

1999 Sales

	% of total
Europe	
France	57
UK	8
Germany	6
Spain	5
Benelux	1
Other countries	6
Americas	13
Africa & the Middle East	2
Asia/Pacific	2
Total	**100**

PRODUCTS/OPERATIONS

1999 Sales

	% of total
Environmental services	
Water	26
Energy	9
Waste management	8
Transport	6
Other	5
Construction	21
Telecommunications	10
Media	9
Property	4
Audiovisual	2
Total	**100**

COMPETITORS

American States Water	Kelda Group
American Water Works	Lagardère
Azurix	Mannesmann AG
Bechtel	Pennon Group
Bertelsmann	Publicis
Bouygues	RWE
EDF	Suez Lyonnaise des Eaux
Eiffage	Technip
Enron	Thames Water
France Telecom	Waste Recycling

HISTORICAL FINANCIALS & EMPLOYEES

NYSE: V FYE: December 31	Annual Growth	12/90	12/91	12/92	12/93	12/94	12/95	12/96	12/97	12/98	12/99
Sales ($ mil.)	7.6%	21,757	24,823	25,376	24,395	28,985	32,713	31,884	27,894	33,933	41,914
Net income ($ mil.)	14.2%	435	503	526	541	627	(751)	376	900	1,198	1,441
Income as % of sales	—	2.0%	2.0%	2.1%	2.2%	2.2%	—	1.2%	3.2%	3.5%	3.4%
Earnings per share ($)	—	—	—	—	—	—	(2.20)	1.05	1.85	2.15	2.70
Stock price - FY high ($)	—	—	—	—	—	—	40.42	43.13	55.63	86.67	101.67
Stock price - FY low ($)	—	—	—	—	—	—	27.29	31.25	35.00	41.88	66.25
Stock price - FY close ($)	28.4%	—	—	—	—	—	33.54	40.43	45.83	85.42	91.25
P/E - high	—	—	—	—	—	—	—	41	30	40	38
P/E - low	—	—	—	—	—	—	—	30	19	19	25
Dividends per share ($)	7.5%	—	—	—	—	—	0.75	0.75	0.85	0.85	1.00
Book value per share ($)	(4.3%)	—	—	—	—	—	21.95	21.75	24.65	18.65	18.41
Employees	5.1%	—	—	—	204,307	215,281	221,157	217,300	193,300	234,800	275,000

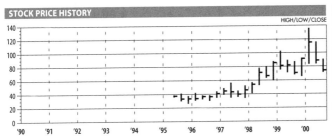

STOCK PRICE HISTORY

HIGH/LOW/CLOSE

1999 FISCAL YEAR-END

Debt ratio: 75.8%
Return on equity: 14.9%
Cash ($ mil.): 7,158
Current ratio: 0.96
Long-term debt ($ mil.): 19,188
No. of shares (mil.): 596
Dividends
  Yield: 0.0%
  Payout: 0.4%
Market value ($ mil.): 54,353

VNU N.V.

OVERVIEW

If you're an information junkie, VNU is a Dutch treat. Based in Haarlem, The Netherlands, VNU is a leading publisher of consumer magazines in Europe. Its portfolio includes women's and men's titles, TV and puzzle magazines, and general interest publications. It also publishes telephone directories in six countries and educational materials in Belgium and The Netherlands, and operates several business, consumer, and education Web sites.

VNU is making acquisitions to solidify its US and European business information operations (nearly 45% of sales), which include business magazine publishing, trade show and conference hosting, and market research. The company acquired US-based TV ratings firm Nielsen Media Research in 1999 and has agreed to buy United News & Media's trade show unit Miller Freeman and the European business magazine unit of Ziff-Davis (acquired by CNET in 2000). Through Nielsen Media Research, VNU owns about 59% of Internet traffic analyst NetRatings.VNU is developing a financial portal in a push to increase its online business.

HISTORY

VNU was formed by the 1964 merger of two of The Netherlands' largest mass-market consumer publishing companies: Cebema, based in 'sHertogenbosch, and De Spaarnestad, headquartered in Haarlem. The new company added to its empire through a series of acquisitions during the late 1960s. In 1967 it bought book publisher Het Spectrum and regional newspaper publisher Het Nieuwsblad van het Zuiden. The next year it acquired magazine publisher NRM and Smeets, one of the largest offset printers in Europe.

The company's buying spree pumped up sales and profits but also created an unwieldy organization. During the early 1970s VNU hired US management consultant McKinsey & Company to help streamline its operations.

VNU continued to add companies to the fold, including trade journal publisher Intermediair (1973), Belgian bookbinder Reliure Industrielle de Barchon (1974), and trade journal publisher Diligentia (1975). In the late 1970s the company began moving into professional publishing, and in 1980 VNU acquired the publishing portions of Computing Publications and of Business and Career Publications.

During the 1980s VNU began to focus on expanding its US business. It bought financial information provider Disclosure (1985) and New Jersey-based Hayden Publishing (1986). Hayden's publications, which included *Computer Decisions* and *Personal Computing*, were hit by a decline in the computer business during the late 1980s, and in 1989 VNU began selling them off.

With its US prospects not particularly rosy, VNU continued expanding elsewhere. Its 1988 acquisition of Audet made it the #1 publisher of regional newspapers in The Netherlands. The next year the company made its first foray into television when it bought an 11% stake in VTM (later raised to 44%; sold in 1998), a commercial Belgian TV station. VNU also acquired a 19% interest in Dutch TV station RTL 4 (later raised to 38%; also sold in 1998).

The company entered the eastern European market in 1990, launching *Moscow Magazine*. As part of a plan to focus on its publishing operations, VNU sold its printing operations to Koninklijke De Boer Boekhoven in 1993. It acquired US-based BPI Communications, publisher of *Billboard* and *Adweek,* in 1994. The next year the company sold Disclosure and bought SRDS, a business information provider, as part of its strategy to increase its US market share of business information services (professional newsletters, magazines, directories, trade shows).

In 1997 VNU acquired Kwety Ceske, the largest consumer magazine publisher in the Czech Republic. Also that year it acquired 50% of RCV Entertainment (later boosted to full-ownership), a Netherlands-based film, video, and TV program distributor. Early in 1998 VNU paid $2.1 billion for a directories unit of ITT. Later that year the company bought three US food industry magazines to strengthen its market position in US food products publishing. In 1999 the company bought the venerable *Editor & Publisher Magazine* and made its biggest US investment, buying TV ratings firm Nielsen Media Research for $2.5 billion. It also established an Internet unit.

In 2000 Rob van den Bergh, a 20-year company veteran, was appointed chairman of VNU. Also that year the company sold its VNU Dagbladen newspaper publishing division. In addition, it entered into a joint venture with Germany's Gatrixx to create localized financial portals in Europe and bought Netherlands-based Internet portal Startpagina (starting page).

Chairman Supervisory Board: P.A.W. Roef
Chairman Executive Board: R.F. van den Bergh
Business Development: R. J. Goedkoop
Controlling: F. L. Dombrée
Corporate Communications: M.M. A. Schikker
Human Resources: G. Abendanon
Information & Communication Technology: E. LeGrand
Legal Department: T.C.M. van Kampen
Operational Audit: J.J. Schilder
Tax Department: D. J. W. van Neutegem
Treasury: R. de Meel
Secretary of the Executive Board:
  M. M. I. Cohen de Lara
President/CEO, BPI Communications: J. B. Babcock Jr.
Management-Music Group, BPI Communications:
  H. Lander
Management-Film Group, BPI Communications:
  R. J. Dowling
Auditors: Ernst & Young

HQ: Ceylonpoort 5-25,
  2037 AA Haarlem, The Netherlands
Phone: +31-23-546-34-63   Fax: +31-23-546-39-38
US HQ: 1515 Broadway, New York, NY 10036
US Phone: 212-536-6700   US Fax: 212-536-5243
Web site: http://www.vnu.com

1999 Sales

	% of total
The Netherlands	44
US	30
Belgium	13
UK	6
Other countries	7
Total	**100**

1999 Sales

	$ mil.	% of total
Advertising	1,293	46
Circulation	599	21
Database services	532	19
Distribution	135	5
Miscellaneous	270	9
Total	**2,829**	**100**

Selected Operating Groups and Subsidiaries

Bill Communications (organizes conferences; publishes
  professional magazines)
BPI Communications (publishes consumer magazines)
Claritas (marketing)
L.C.G. Malmberg bv (educational publishing)
Nielsen Media Research (TV ratings measurement in the
  US and Canada)
NetRatings (59%, Internet audience measurement)
RCV Entertainment (distribution of filmed
  entertainment in the Netherlands)
Uitgeverij Van In (educational publishing)
VNU Business Information Europe
VNU Magazines
VNU USA
VNU World Directories (telephone directories and
  information services)

Advance Publications	International Data Group
Axel Springer	McGraw-Hill
Bertelsmann	News Corp.
Crain Communications	Reader's Digest
EMAP PLC	Reed Elsevier
Gruner + Jahr	Time Warner
Hachette Filipacchi Médias	Viacom
Hearst	Wolters Kluwer

OTC: VNUVY FYE: December 31	Annual Growth	12/90	12/91	12/92	12/93	12/94	12/95	12/96	12/97	12/98	12/99
Sales ($ mil.)	6.5%	1,609	1,597	1,195	1,186	1,600	1,897	1,949	1,935	2,848	2,829
Net income ($ mil.)	12.4%	87	68	26	74	119	268	186	207	294	247
Income as % of sales	—	5.4%	4.3%	2.2%	6.3%	7.4%	14.1%	9.5%	10.7%	10.3%	8.7%
Earnings per share ($)	9.4%	—	—	—	—	—	0.90	0.98	1.04	1.43	1.29
Stock price - FY high ($)		—	—	—	—	—	15.05	21.00	28.75	43.88	53.00
Stock price - FY low ($)		—	—	—	—	—	11.78	7.40	18.75	24.38	32.50
Stock price - FY close ($)	39.7%	—	—	—	—	—	13.84	20.50	27.75	37.00	52.75
P/E - high		—	—	—	—	—	17	21	28	31	41
P/E - low		—	—	—	—	—	13	8	18	17	25
Dividends per share ($)	12.5%	—	—	—	—	—	0.30	0.32	0.29	0.51	0.48
Book value per share ($)	29.8%	—	—	—	—	—	2.96	3.09	2.31	3.58	8.40
Employees	2.6%	11,594	11,448	10,971	8,367	9,919	9,285	10,462	12,123	12,059	14,591

HIGH/LOW/CLOSE

Debt ratio: 64.0%
Return on equity: 19.6%
Cash ($ mil.): 621
Current ratio: 0.54
Long-term debt ($ mil.): 1,368
No. of shares (mil.): 220
Dividends
  Yield: 0.0%
  Payout: 0.4%
Market value ($ mil.): 11,605

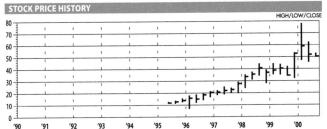

VODAFONE GROUP PLC

OVERVIEW

Customers have voted with their phones to make Vodafone Group the world's top wireless phone service provider (by subscribers). The Newbury, UK-based company, formerly known as Vodafone AirTouch, serves more than 65 million customers through its subsidiaries and affiliates in Europe, the US, the Asia/Pacific region, the Middle East, and Africa.

The company has advanced toward its goal of creating a pan-European wireless network with the acquisition of Germany's Mannesmann, which controlled the #1 network in Germany (D2) and the #2 network in Italy (Omnitel). Overall, Vodafone affiliates serve more than 37 million European mobile phone users. To satisfy regulators' concerns, Vodafone has agreed to open its European networks to rivals and sold Orange, the UK mobile phone operator acquired by Mannesmann in 1999.

In the UK, where Vodafone is the #1 wireless carrier, the company has built on the success of its Vodafone Retail outlets by launching a virtual Web store and by distributing prepaid service. Features available through the company's GSM (global system for mobile communications) network include popular messaging services and access to the Internet.

On the other side of the Atlantic, Vodafone has combined its US wireless operations (acquired when the company bought AirTouch in 1999) with those of Bell Atlantic and GTE to form Verizon Wireless. Verizon Wireless is 45%-owned by Vodafone and 55%-owned by Verizon Communications (formed when Bell Atlantic bought GTE).

Vodafone is expanding its wireless data offerings, and the company has partnered with France's Vivendi to develop the Vizzavi Internet portal, which is designed to be accessible from mobile phones, computers, and TV sets.

HISTORY

Vodafone was formed in 1983 as a joint venture between Racal Electronics (a UK electronics firm) and Millicom (a US telecom company), and was granted one of two mobile phone licenses in the UK. It launched service in 1985 as a Racal subsidiary. Vodafone and Cellnet, the other licensee, were swamped with demand. In 1988 Racal offered 20% of Vodafone to the public; three years later the rest of the firm was spun off to become Vodafone Group.

Vodafone moved beyond the UK in the 1990s. By 1993 it had interests in mobile phone networks in Australia, Greece, Hong Kong, Malta, and Scandinavia.

For a time Vodafone and Cellnet (a joint venture of British Telecom and Securicor) enjoyed a duopoly in the UK. Regulators elected not to impose price controls, and the pounds rolled in. But in 1993 a new wireless provider, One 2 One, launched a digital network in London. Vodafone countered that year with its own GSM (global system for mobile communications) digital network.

With increasing competition at home, Vodafone continued to expand in 1994. It launched or bought stakes in operations in Fiji, Germany, South Africa, and Uganda.

Digital service began to take on a larger role in Vodafone's UK business, and by 1997 some 85% of new subscribers were opting for digital GSM. In 1998 Vodafone sold its French service provider, Vodafone SA, and bought digital cellular carrier BellSouth New Zealand. It also expanded into Egypt by buying a minority stake in Misrfone, marking the largest British investment in Egypt since the Suez Canal.

In 1999 Vodafone prevailed in a brief bidding war with Bell Atlantic to buy AirTouch Communications for about $60 billion. Vodafone's Chris Gent took over as CEO of the new company, Vodafone AirTouch. The prize for Vodafone: entry into the lucrative US market, plus the opportunity to consolidate minority interests in European wireless carriers.

Vodafone AirTouch moved to significantly boost its European footprint in 1999 by launching a $131 billion hostile takeover bid for Germany's Mannesmann. The company acquired Mannesmann for about $180 billion in stock in 2000 and agreed to sell the conglomerate's engineering operations and its UK mobile phone unit, Orange. (France Telecom bought Orange for $37.5 billion later that year.) Vodafone AirTouch also announced plans for an IPO for Italian fixed-line carrier Infostrada, acquired in the Mannesmann deal, but then the company instead agreed to sell Infostrada to Italian utility giant Enel.

Also in 2000 Vodafone AirTouch expanded its presence in the US, buying CommNet Cellular for $1.4 billion, then combining its US wireless operations with those of Bell Atlantic and GTE to form Verizon Wireless. That year the company dropped AirTouch from its name and became Vodafone Group once again.

Chairman: Lord MacLaurin of Knebworth, age 63,
$204,000 pay (prior to title change)
Deputy Chairman: Paul Hazen, age 58
CEO: Christopher C. Gent, age 52, $1,162,000 pay
Financial Director: Kenneth J. Hydon, age 55,
$649,000 pay
CEO, UK, Middle East, and Africa Region:
Peter R. Bamford, age 46, $451,000 pay
(prior to title change)
CEO, European Region; Chairman, Mannesman:
Julian Horn-Smith, age 51, $600,000 pay
(prior to title change)
President, Americas and Asia Region: Bill Keever
Group Personnel Director: Phillip Williams
Investor Relations Director: Tim Brown
Corporate Affairs Director: Terry Barwick
Corporate Communications Director: Mike Caldwell
Secretary: S. R. Scott
Auditors: Deloitte & Touche

LOCATIONS

HQ: The Courtyard, 2-4 London Rd., Newbury,
Berkshire RG14 1JX, United Kingdom
Phone: +44-1635-33-251   **Fax:** +44-1635-45-713
Web site: http://www.vodafone.com

2000 Sales

	% of total
US and Asia/Pacific region	44
UK	33
Europe, Middle East, and Africa	23
Total	**100**

PRODUCTS/OPERATIONS

Selected Subsidiaries and Affiliates

Mobile Telephone Interests
Airtel Movil (22%, Spain)
Belgacom Mobile (25%, Belgium)
Celtel (37%, Uganda)
D2 (Germany)
Europolitan (71%, Sweden)
J-Phone Kansai Co., Ltd. (20%, Japan)
J-Phone Tokai Co., Ltd. (20%, Japan)
J-Phone Tokyo Co., Ltd. (20%, Japan)
Libertel NV (70%, The Netherlands)
Misrfone (60%, Egypt)
MobiFon (20%, Romania)
Omnitel Pronto Italia S.p.A (76%)
Panafon (55%, Greece)
Polkomtel (20%, Poland)
Shinsegi Mobile Telecommunications Company Inc.
(12%, South Korea)
Societe Francaise du Radiotelephone (20%, France)
Telecel (51%, Portugal)
tele.ring (75%, Austria)
Verizon Wireless (45%, US)
Vodacom (32%, South Africa)
Vodafone Holdings Australia Pty Limited (91%)
Vodafone Hungary (50.1%)
Vodafone Malta (80%)

COMPETITORS

Asia Pacific	France Telecom
Wire & Cable	KPN
AT&T Wireless	Nextel
Belgacom	NTT DoCoMo
BT	Sprint PCS
Cingular	Telstra
Debitel	TIM
Deutsche Telekom	

HISTORICAL FINANCIALS & EMPLOYEES

NYSE: VOD FYE: March 31	Annual Growth	3/91	3/92	3/93	3/94	3/95	3/96	3/97	3/98	3/99	3/00
Sales ($ mil.)	33.4%	939	1,016	1,005	1,263	1,868	2,140	2,868	4,130	5,415	12,545
Net income ($ mil.)	11.4%	295	320	336	364	385	473	597	700	1,026	776
Income as % of sales	—	31.4%	31.5%	33.4%	28.8%	20.6%	22.1%	20.8%	16.9%	18.9%	6.2%
Earnings per share ($)	3.8%	0.20	0.21	0.22	0.24	0.25	0.31	0.39	0.46	0.66	0.28
Stock price - FY high ($)	—	4.50	4.90	4.75	6.31	7.05	9.00	9.75	20.90	39.55	64.38
Stock price - FY low ($)	—	2.84	3.64	3.55	3.88	4.86	5.93	6.60	8.60	18.80	33.84
Stock price - FY close ($)	33.1%	4.25	3.73	3.92	5.15	6.63	7.50	8.83	20.78	37.55	55.56
P/E - high	—	23	23	22	26	28	29	25	45	60	222
P/E - low	—	14	17	16	16	19	19	17	19	28	117
Dividends per share ($)	16.1%	0.06	0.14	0.08	0.08	0.10	0.13	0.17	0.10	0.13	0.23
Book value per share ($)	61.7%	0.48	0.52	0.60	0.68	0.87	1.02	0.82	0.31	0.85	36.59
Employees	58.0%	—	—	—	—	—	4,728	6,051	9,640	12,642	29,465

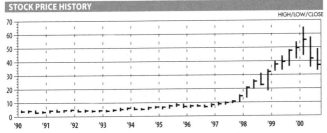

HIGH/LOW/CLOSE

2000 FISCAL YEAR-END
Debt ratio: 4.1%
Return on equity: 0.7%
Cash ($ mil.): 253
Current ratio: 0.57
Long-term debt ($ mil.): 9,621
No. of shares (mil.): 6,133
Dividends
  Yield: 0.4%
  Payout: 82.1%
Market value ($ mil.): 340,772

VOLKSWAGEN AG

OVERVIEW

Volkswagen (VW) caught the nostalgia bug. The Wolfsburg, Germany-based automaker added a revamped version of its classic Beetle (last sold in the US in 1979) to a broadening range of models. Europe's #1 carmaker, VW makes about 4.9 million cars annually in Africa, the Asia/Pacific region, Europe, and North and South America.

Its cars include its namesake Volkswagen, Audi (luxury models, Germany), Lamborghini (luxury sports cars, Italy), Rolls-Royce (super-luxury models, UK), SEAT (family cars, Spain), and SKODA (family cars, the Czech Republic).

VW also makes pickup trucks and vans. It offers consumer financing through its Volkswagen Financial Services subsidiary and owns Europcar, a European car rental company. The German state of Lower Saxony owns 16% of the company.

Boosting its truck making business and expanding its market, VW has agreed to purchase a 19% stake in Swedish commercial truck maker Scania. Its Rio de Janeiro plant will be building a new truck, the 1.5 ton Robust; the bulk of its projected 80,000-truck production will be bound for the US market.

HISTORY

Since the early 1920s auto engineer Ferdinand Porsche (whose son later founded the Porsche car company) had wanted to make a small car for the masses. He found no backers until he met Adolf Hitler in 1934. Hitler formed the Gesellschaft zur Vorbereitung des Volkswagens (Company for the Development of People's Cars) in 1937 and built a factory in Wolfsburg, Germany.

No cars were delivered during WWII, as the company produced military vehicles using the slave labor of Jews and Russian prisoners of war.

Following WWII British occupation forces oversaw the rebuilding of the bomb-damaged plant and initial production of the odd-looking "people's car" (1945). The British appointed Heinz Nordhoff to manage Volkswagen (1948) and then turned the company over to the German government (1949).

In the 1950s VW launched the Microbus and built foreign plants. Although US sales began slowly, by the end of the decade acceptance of the little car had increased. Advertising that coined the name "Beetle" helped carve VW's niche in the US.

VW sold stock to the German public in 1960. In 1966 it purchased Auto Union (AUDI) from Daimler-Benz. The Beetle became a counterculture symbol in the 1960s, and US sales took off. By Nordhoff's death in 1968, the Beetle had become the best-selling car in history.

In the 1970s the Beetle was discontinued in every country except Mexico. VW lost heavily during the model-changeover period.

VW agreed to several deals in the 1980s, including a car venture in China (1984), the purchase of 75% of SEAT (1986; it bought the rest in 1990), and the merger of its suddenly faltering Brazilian unit with Ford's ailing Argentine operations to form Autolatina (1987). In 1990 the company began building China's largest

auto plant and acquired a 70% stake in Czech auto company SKODA. After suffering a $1.1 billion loss, the company put Ferdinand Piech in the driver's seat in 1993. Under his leadership the company cut costs and boosted sales by resuscitating the SEAT and SKODA brands and launching the Passat sedan in 1997.

VW acquired Rolls-Royce Motor Cars, Vickers' Cosworth auto engines subsidiary, Italian sports-car maker Bugatti, and Italy's Automobili Lamborghini—all in 1998. Although less luxurious than VW's other pursuits, the New Beetle helped boost US sales that year. Also in 1998 VW established a $12 million fund to compensate the surviving 2,000 concentration-camp inmates forced to work as slave labor during WWII. However, the company was hit with a class-action lawsuit filed on behalf of Holocaust survivors anyway. VW also faced a $109 million fine from the European Commission for preventing new car sales across the borders of the 15 nations in the European Union.

In 1999 chairman Ferdinand Piech announced an end to VW's acquisition binge, saying that growth would be driven from within; VW announced it would pour $31.5 billion into modernizing its factories through 2004. VW hoped to tap the market in China after getting approval in 1999 to sell a newly developed minicar there. That year it announced plans to invest $1 billion in its Mexico plant over the next five years.

The company expanded into heavy commercial vehicles by agreeing to buy a 19% stake in Swedish truck maker Scania (from holding company Investor). That year it bought the 30% of SKODA that it didn't already own. Later in 2000 Volkswagen entered into talks with Volvo to discuss buying that company's stake in Scania. The deal could lead to Volkswagen controlling Scania.

Chairman Supervisory Board: Klaus Liesen, age 68
Deputy Chairman Supervisory Board: Klaus Zwickel, age 60
Chairman Management Board: Ferdinand Piech, age 62
Member of Management Board and Director Controlling and Accounting: Bruno Adelt, age 60
Member of Management Board and Director Group Strategy, Treasury, Legal Matters, and Organization: Jens Neumann, age 54
Member of Management Board and Director Human Resources: Peter Hartz, age 58
Member of Management Board and Director Sales and Marketing: Robert Buchelhofer, age 57
Director Communications: Klaus Kocks, age 47
Auditors: PwC Deutsche Revision Aktiengesellschaft

HQ: Brieffach 1848-2, D-38436 Wolfsburg, Germany
Phone: +49-53-61-90   **Fax:** +49-53-61-92-82-82
US HQ: 3800 Hamlin Rd., Auburn Hills, MI 48326
US Phone: 248-340-5000   **US Fax:** 248-340-5540
Web site: http://www2.vw-online.de

1999 Sales

	$ mil.	% of total
Europe		
Germany	24,401	32
Other countries	31,650	42
North America	12,463	17
South America	3,981	5
Asia/Pacific	2,385	3
Africa	817	1
Total	**75,697**	**100**

Selected Makes and Models

AUDI	Inca Kombi	LT
A3	Leon	LT Kombi
A4	Marbella	Octavia
A6	Polo	Passat
A8	Classic/Variant	Polo
Cabriolet	Toledo	Skoda pickup
TT Coupe	**SKODA**	Transporter
TT Roadster	Caddy pickup	**Volkswagen**
Lamborghini	Fabia	**Passenger**
Diablo	Felicia	**Vehicles**
Rolls-	Octavia	Alhambra
Royce/Bentley	Pickup	Beetle
Bentley Arnage	**Volkswagen**	Bora
Bentley Azure	**Commercial**	Golf
Bentley	**Vehicles**	Jetta/Bora/Vento
Continental	Audi A6	Lupo
Rolls-Royce	Caddy delivery	New Beetle
SEAT	van	Parati
Arosa	Caravelle/Kombi	Passat, Santana
Caddy Kombi	Cordoba	Polo
Cordoba	Felicia	Sharan
Ibiza	Inca delivery van	Toledo

BMW	Honda	Nissan
Daewoo	Hyundai	Peugeot
DaimlerChrysler	Isuzu	Renault
Fiat	Kia Motors	Saab
Ford	Mazda	Suzuki
General Motors	Mitsubishi	Toyota

OTC: VLKAY FYE: December 31	Annual Growth	12/90	12/91	12/92	12/93	12/94	12/95	12/96	12/97	12/98	12/99
Sales ($ mil.)	5.8%	45,465	50,207	52,679	44,048	51,656	61,287	64,952	62,959	80,547	75,697
Net income ($ mil.)	2.1%	704	726	48	(1,172)	96	246	428	757	1,346	850
Income as % of sales	—	1.5%	1.4%	0.1%	—	0.2%	0.4%	0.7%	1.2%	1.7%	1.1%
Earnings per share ($)	66.4%	—	—	—	—	—	0.14	0.24	0.38	0.66	—
Stock price - FY high ($)	—	—	—	—	—	—	6.77	8.45	17.50	20.30	16.38
Stock price - FY low ($)	—	—	—	—	—	—	5.45	6.67	8.16	11.50	9.50
Stock price - FY close ($)	12.6%	—	—	—	—	—	6.77	8.17	11.17	15.63	10.87
P/E - high	—	—	—	—	—	—	47	36	46	31	—
P/E - low	—	—	—	—	—	—	38	28	22	17	—
Dividends per share ($)	73.9%	—	—	—	—	—	0.04	0.08	0.10	0.18	0.39
Book value per share ($)	2.6%	—	—	—	—	—	4.37	4.16	3.52	4.72	—
Employees	1.5%	267,997	267,009	259,696	253,108	243,638	259,342	260,811	279,892	297,916	306,275

HIGH/LOW/CLOSE

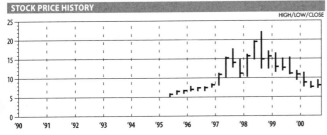

Debt ratio: 33.7%
Return on equity: 8.6%
Cash ($ mil.): 3,026
Current ratio: 1.54
Long-term debt ($ mil.): 5,031
No. of shares (mil.): 1,560
Dividends
  Yield: 3.6%
  Payout: 72.2%
Market value ($ mil.): 16,955

AB VOLVO

OVERVIEW

What do Fords and fjords have in common? Both can be found in Sweden. Goteborg, Sweden-based Volvo has sold its Volvo auto brand and auto-manufacturing operations to #2 automaker Ford Motor Company. The sale allows Volvo to focus on its remaining operations — heavy trucks (#4 in worldwide production behind DaimlerChrysler, Navistar, and PACCAR), buses, engines (marine, aerospace, and industrial), and construction equipment.

Although cars accounted for almost 50% of the company's sales, independent Volvo — one of Europe's smallest automakers — realized that it couldn't successfully compete in a consolidating auto industry. By selling off a unit in which it would never be a leader, Volvo has pocketed enough cash to increase its more profitable trucks and buses business. Already a 45% owner of rival Swedish truck maker Scania, Volvo attempted to buy another 28% from Investor AB, but was thwarted by the EU Commission. Volvo is looking to ink an alliance with Renault in order to assume that company's truck-making activities, and, through a deal with Mitsubishi, it will own almost 20% of a truck and bus concern to be formed by the Japanese giant in 2001.

HISTORY

Swedish ball bearing maker SKF formed Volvo (Latin for "I roll") as a subsidiary in 1915. Volvo began building cars in 1926, trucks in 1928, and bus chassis in 1932 in Goteborg. Sweden's winters and icy roads made the company keenly attentive to engineering and safety. Volvo bought an engine maker in 1931. In 1935 Volvo became an independent company led by Assar Gabrielsson and Gustaf Larson.

Sweden's neutrality during World War II allowed Volvo to grow and move into component manufacturing and tractor production. Output in 1949 exceeded 100,000 units, 80% of which were sold in Sweden. The purchase of Bolinder-Munktell (farm machinery, diesel engines; Sweden; 1950) enhanced Volvo's position in the Swedish tractor market. Volvo introduced turbocharged diesel truck engines and windshield defrosters and washers in the 1950s. By 1956 car production had outstripped truck and bus output.

Aware that it was too small to compete in global markets, Volvo diversified (energy, industrial products, food, finance, and trading). Volvo increased its market share by purchasing several trucking and construction equipment companies that included White Motors' truck unit (US, 1981) and Leyland Bus (UK, 1986). In the 1980s Volvo acquired Pharmacia (drugs, biotechnology; Sweden) and Custos (investments, Sweden). The company consolidated its food and drug units with state-controlled holding company Procordia in 1990.

At that time, however, Volvo was facing stagnant sales. It embarked on the largest industrial undertaking in Swedish history, spending more than $2 billion to modernize plants and develop a series of high-performance family sedans, which it introduced in 1991. Still, high costs and persistent recession in Europe kept the company in the red during the early 1990s.

Adding to its troubles, there was public outcry against a planned merger with French automaker Renault. The plan was abandoned in 1993, and the company sold its drug and consumer product interests (which had landed back in Volvo's lap when the government divested Procordia in 1993). These sales brought Volvo back into the black.

In 1997 Volvo sold its 11% stake in Renault left over from the abandoned merger. The next year the company strengthened its line of excavators and its Far Eastern presence by buying Samsung Heavy Industries' construction equipment unit. Volvo also bought Mexico's bus maker Mexicana de Autobuses and GM's share in Volvo GM Heavy Truck (now Volvo Trucks North America).

Anticipating a lower demand for cars, Volvo closed an assembly plant in Canada in 1998, and in 1999 Volvo acquired a 13% stake (later upped to 25%) in rival truck maker Scania. To pay for its new focus on making heavy trucks, Volvo sold its auto brand and manufacturing operations in Sweden, Belgium, and the Netherlands to Ford Motor Company for $6.45 billion in 1999. Volvo then agreed to take a 20% stake in the truck and construction equipment operations of Japan's Mitsubishi Motors — a deal that could make the alliance the world's #1 truck maker when it's completed in late 2001 or 2002.

In 2000 Volvo boosted its stake in Scania to 46%, but its hope of acquiring a majority interest died when the EU rejected the $7.53 billion deal. Volvo then turned to France's Renault, agreeing to buy the company's Mack truck unit for a 15% stake in Volvo. Later in the year Volvo entered into talks with Volkswagen AG concerning the possible sale of Volvo's stake in Scania.

Chairman: Lars Ramqvist
President, AB Volvo; CEO, Volvo Group: Leif Johansson
Deputy CEO and EVP: Lennart Jeansson
EVP: Arne Wittlov
SVP and CFO: Stefan Johnsson
**SVP Legal Matters, Taxes, and Group Security and
Secretary:** Eva Persson
**SVP Corporate Communications and Investor
Relations:** Per Lojdquist
**SVP Environment, Brand Management, and Public
Affairs:** Lars Anell
President, Volvo Truck: Tryggve Stherr
President, Volvo Construction Equipment:
Tony Helsham, age 46
President, Volvo Bus: Jan Engstrom
President, Volvo Aero: Fred Bodin
President, Volvo Penta: Staffan Jufors
Auditors: PricewaterhouseCoopers

1999 Sales

	$ mil.	% of total
Trucks	8,158	56
Construction equipment	2,263	15
Buses	1,778	12
Aero	1,168	8
Marine & industrial engines	676	5
Other	622	4
Total	**14,665**	**100**

Selected Business Units
Volvo Aero (aircraft engines)
Volvo Bus (city, intracity, and special applications)
Volvo Construction Equipment (articulated haulers,
excavators, motor graders, and wheel loaders)
Volvo Penta (marine and other engines)
Volvo Truck (primarily trucks weighing more than
16 tons)

HQ: S-405 08 Goteborg, Sweden
Phone: +46-31-59-66-00   **Fax:** +46-31-54-57-72
US HQ: 570 Lexington Ave., 20th Fl.,
New York, NY 10022
US Phone: 212-418-7400   **US Fax:** 212-418-7435
Web site: http://www.volvo.com

1999 Sales

	$ mil.	% of total
Europe	8,101	55
North America	5,044	35
Asia	707	5
South America	462	3
Other regions	351	2
Total	**14,665**	**100**

Cummins Engine
Freightliner
Fuji Heavy Industries
General Motors
Hino Motors
Isuzu
MAN
Mayflower
Mitsubishi

Navistar
Nissan
Outboard Marine
PACCAR
Renault
Rolls-Royce
Scania
Toyota

Nasdaq: VOLVY FYE: December 31	Annual Growth	12/90	12/91	12/92	12/93	12/94	12/95	12/96	12/97	12/98	12/99
Sales ($ mil.)	(0.1%)	14,765	13,954	11,728	13,339	15,649	25,641	22,676	23,229	26,276	14,665
Net income ($ mil.)	—	(181)	385	(469)	(416)	1,328	1,385	1,813	1,310	1,066	3,780
Income as % of sales	—	—	2.8%	—	—	8.5%	5.4%	8.0%	5.6%	4.1%	25.8%
Earnings per share ($)	—	(0.01)	0.32	(1.21)	(1.07)	3.19	3.02	3.91	2.90	2.42	8.56
Stock price - FY high ($)	—	14.98	12.35	15.50	13.08	20.53	25.38	24.38	30.63	35.50	32.25
Stock price - FY low ($)	—	7.10	7.08	7.35	9.15	12.95	16.50	18.38	21.63	19.25	23.75
Stock price - FY close ($)	14.5%	7.45	11.38	9.80	12.93	18.75	20.59	21.75	27.00	23.31	25.25
P/E - high	—	—	39	—	—	6	8	6	11	15	40
P/E - low	—	—	22	—	—	4	5	5	7	8	29
Dividends per share ($)	3.7%	0.44	0.43	0.45	0.18	0.17	0.46	0.60	0.00	0.00	0.61
Book value per share ($)	5.4%	16.14	15.77	10.82	8.38	9.80	16.51	18.14	17.31	19.02	25.95
Employees	(2.7%)	68,797	63,582	60,115	73,641	75,549	79,050	70,330	79,050	79,820	53,600

HIGH/LOW/CLOSE

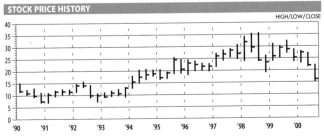

Debt ratio: 24.8%
Return on equity: 38.1%
Cash ($ mil.): 975
Current ratio: 1.87
Long-term debt ($ mil.): 3,780
No. of shares (mil.): 442
Dividends
Yield: 2.4%
Payout: 7.1%
Market value ($ mil.): 11,148

WAL-MART DE MEXICO

OVERVIEW

In Mexico City, the shop around the corner probably belongs to Wal-Mart de Mexico (formerly Cifra). Mexico's largest retailer, the company operates about 200 stores (Aurrera, Bodega Aurrera, and Superama supermarkets and discount food warehouses, as well as clothing stores Suburbia and Liquidaciones) and about 200 restaurants. Although Wal-Mart de Mexico has operations throughout the country, most of its outlets are clustered in or around Mexico City, where its headquarters is located. The company once had a joint venture with

giant US retailer Wal-Mart Stores that operated Wal-Mart and Sam's Club outlets; Wal-Mart has since acquired control of the company (it holds about 60%). As a result, then-named Cifra assumed control of Wal-Mart's Mexican operations. It now runs more than 60 Sam's Club membership warehouse outlets and Wal-Mart Supercenters, which combine for about 40% of Wal-Mart de Mexico's total sales.

Cifra was the first Mexican retailer to sell generic brands, go public, and combine clothing, food, and hardware in a single store.

HISTORY

Spanish-born Jeronimo Arango Arias studied art and literature at several American universities without graduating. In his twenties he wandered around Spain, Mexico, and the US. He struck upon an idea after seeing a crowd waiting in line at the E. J. Korvette discount department store in New York City. Jeronimo called his two brothers, Placido and Manuel, and convinced them to join him in a new business venture.

Borrowing about $250,000 from their father, a Spanish immigrant to Mexico successful in textiles, the three brothers opened their first Aurrera Bolivar discount store in downtown Mexico City in 1958. Offering goods and clothing well below manufacturers' list prices, the store was an immediate hit with consumers but encountered hostility from competing retailers. When local retailers threatened to boycott the Arangos' suppliers, the company turned to suppliers in Guadalajara and Monterrey.

In 1965 the Arango brothers formed a joint venture with Jewel Cos. of Chicago to open new Aurrera stores. Jewel bought a 49% interest in the business a year later. Placido and Manuel left the business with their portion of the money, but Jeronimo stayed as head of the company, taking it public in 1976.

By 1981 almost a third of Jewel's earnings came from its operations in Mexico. But the next year the peso crashed, obliterating its earnings there. American Stores took over Jewel in 1984, and Jeronimo bought back Jewel's stake in the company (which was renamed Cifra that year).

With the Mexican economy staggering from the peso devaluation, weak oil markets, and a huge debt crisis, Jeronimo was taking a major risk. Although no new stores were opened, none were closed. Employees were expected to work longer, and those who left were not replaced. With Mexico's middle class hit hard,

Jeronimo emphasized the Bodega Aurrera no-frill warehouses, which discounted all kinds of nonperishable merchandise, from canned chili to VCRs.

Cifra and Wal-Mart Stores formed a joint venture in 1991 to open Club Aurrera membership clubs similar to Sam's Club outlets. The two companies expanded the venture the next year to include the development of Sam's Club and Wal-Mart Supercenters in Mexico. Remodeling began on Cifra's stores in 1992. The work was completed two years later, and the company was poised to take advantage of Mexico's much-improved economy.

However, devaluation struck again late in 1994. The resulting contraction of credit and rise in prices hit Mexican consumers hard, and Cifra's 1995 sales declined 15%. But again it kept on as many employees as possible, transferring them to new stores that had been in development. Despite the hard times, Cifra opened 27 new stores (including 15 restaurants). The company was able to withstand the difficulties in part because it stayed debt-free.

Wal-Mart consolidated its joint venture into Cifra in 1997 in exchange for about 34% of that company; Wal-Mart later raised its stake to 51%. The cost-conscious companies combined the joint venture stores and Cifra's separate stores under one umbrella. Cifra opened 11 stores and eight restaurants that year.

Cifra opened nine stores and 17 restaurants in 1998; the next year it opened about 20 stores and nearly 25 restuarants. In early 2000 Cifra was renamed Wal-Mart de Mexico. Shortly thereafter, Wal-Mart upped its stake in Wal-Mart de Mexico to almost 60%.

Chairman: Cesareo Fernandez
VC: Hector M. De Uriarte
Director of Suburbia: Sergio Amescua
Director of Aurrera: Alejandro Bustos
Director of Bodega Aurrera: Antonio Echebarrena
Director of Superama: Eduardo Juarez
Director of Distribution: Jose Angel Gallegos
Director of Sam's Club: Jose Luis Laparte
Director of Vips: Sergio Larraguivel
Director of Wal-Mart Supercenter: Eduardo Solorzano
Director of Global Purchasing: Francisco Casado
Director of Public Relations: Mercedes Aragones
Director of Internal Audit: Jesus Corona
Director of Real Estate: Xavier del Rio
CFO: Rafael Matute
Director of Human Resources: Ignacio Perez-Lizaur
Secretary: Enrique Ponzanelli
Auditors: Mancera, S.C.

LOCATIONS

HQ: Wal-Mart de Mexico, S.A. de C.V.
Blvd. Manuel Avila Camacho 647,
Delegacion Miguel Hidalgo,
11220 Mexico, D.F., Mexico
Phone: +52-5-283-0100   **Fax:** +52-5-387-9240
Web site: http://www.walmartmexico.com.mx

Wal-Mart de Mexico operates about 460 stores and restaurants in Mexico.

PRODUCTS/OPERATIONS

1999 Sales

	% of total
Sam's Club	26
Bodega Aurrera	23
Wal-Mart Supercenters	16
Aurrera	15
Superama	8
Suburbia	7
Restaurants	4
Liquidaciones	1
Total	**100**

Selected Stores
Aurrera (medium-sized hypermarkets)
Bodega Aurrera (large discount warehouses)
El Porton (restaurants)
Liquidaciones (discount apparel stores)
Ragazzi (restaurants)
Sam's Club (membership-only warehouse outlets)
Suburbia (apparel stores)
Superama (supermarkets)
Vips (restaurants)
Wal-Mart Supercenters (discount hypermarkets)

COMPETITORS

Carrefour	J. C. Penney
Carso	Safeway
Comerci	Sears Roebuck de Mexico
Costco Wholesale	Soriana
Gigante	TRICON
H-E-B	

HISTORICAL FINANCIALS & EMPLOYEES

OTC: WMMVY FYE: December 31	Annual Growth	12/90	12/91	12/92	12/93	12/94	12/95	12/96	12/97	12/98	12/99
Sales ($ mil.)	11.2%	2,463	2,765	3,690	4,580	3,165	2,623	2,947	4,086	6,009	6,406
Net income ($ mil.)	8.9%	173	211	301	333	236	202	257	432	281	374
Income as % of sales	—	7.0%	7.6%	8.2%	7.3%	7.5%	7.7%	8.7%	10.6%	4.7%	5.8%
Employees	9.3%	31,635	34,178	35,321	39,934	46,898	47,129	49,510	57,649	61,145	70,700

STOCK PRICE HISTORY

1999 FISCAL YEAR-END
Debt ratio: 0.0%
Return on equity: 12.6%
Cash ($ mil.): 980
Current ratio: 1.51
Long-term debt ($ mil.): 0

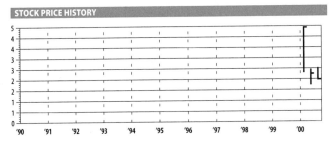

WATERFORD WEDGWOOD PLC

OVERVIEW

Not every company has a great-great-great-great-grandson of its founder sitting on the board of directors. And although Waterford Wedgwood has just that in Alan Wedgwood, it's Heinz ketchup king Tony O'Reilly who has given the Dublin, Ireland-based firm its luster. Waterford Wedgwood is the world's premier maker of luxury crystal and fine china, and its predecessors have been at it for centuries.

The company's Waterford Crystal Group makes Waterford and Stuart premium-quality crystal stemware, giftware, and lamps. Its Wedgwood Group makes fine bone china tableware and giftware. Waterford Wedgwood also owns a 85% stake in German porcelain maker

Rosenthal, German ceramics brand Hutschenreuther, a 15% stake in UK ceramics maker Royal Doulton, and all of US premium cookware maker All-Clad.

Chairman O'Reilly and deputy chairman Peter Goulandris, his brother-in-law, own about 25% of the company. O'Reilly helped turn the company around after years of losses in the late 1980s and early 1990s. He outsourced product lines to cheaper manufacturers and licensed its popular brands to makers of products such as linens and writing instruments. Most of the company's sales are through department stores and specialty retailers.

HISTORY

Waterford Wedgwood traces its roots back to two companies more than 200 years old. Josiah Wedgwood, an 18th-century English artisan, got his start as a potter bridging the gap between wooden bowls for the common people and fine porcelain for the rich. He developed a way of making ordinary clay look like porcelain and later created fine ceramicware incorporating neoclassical figures applied in a white cameo relief on a colored background, which became the signature product of Josiah Wedgwood and Sons.

Wedgwood operated as a family business for the next 176 years and may have indirectly contributed to Darwin's theory of evolution. Charles Darwin married into the Wedgwood clan and thus gained the financial security to pursue his scientific research on a full-time basis. Wedgwood did not have a non-family director on its board until 1945.

Around the same time that Wedgwood was gaining recognition in England, Quakers George and William Penrose founded a crystal glassmaking business in 1783 in the Irish port city of Waterford. The two companies shared a reputation for quality and for exquisite craftsmanship. However, they both experienced the vagaries of fashion and financial difficulties.

Waterford went bankrupt in 1851 and remained inactive until its revival, aided by WWII refugees. With this new base of skilled artisans from Central Europe, it started operations again in 1947. The company quickly reestablished the Waterford reputation. Profits rose steadily in the 1970s and early 1980s, with the US emerging as Waterford's primary market. In addition to consumer products, Waterford glassware has been used for the Boston Marathon Trophy and to hold President Reagan's jelly beans.

In 1986 Waterford borrowed heavily to acquire Wedgwood for $360 million, a move designed to allow both companies to cut costs by sharing marketing operations and by streamlining production. Waterford Wedgwood was still struggling in 1990 when Tony O'Reilly (the Irish-born chairman of US-based H.J. Heinz and a former rugby star) and Morgan Stanley bought a 30% stake worth $125 million. That year the company launched its first new brand of crystal in 200 years, Marquis by Waterford, and sold it at 20% below traditional Waterford prices. The line was a success, and by 1993 Waterford Wedgwood had returned to profitability.

The company acquired Stuart & Sons, the leading UK maker of premium crystal, in 1995 and introduced a best-seller, its Cornucopia fine bone china pattern. In 1996 Waterford Wedgwood also launched new licensed gift lines — pens and linens — and formed a strategic alliance with German luxury ceramics maker Rosenthal, in which it owned a 26% stake. In 1997, in a departure from tradition, the company introduced a line of china under the Waterford name.

In 1998 Waterford Wedgwood increased its stake in Rosenthal to nearly 85%, making it the world's #1 producer of fine porcelain, and began cutting some 1,500 jobs to reduce costs. In 1999 the company purchased US premium cookware-maker All-Clad for $110 million. Also in 1999 the company bought a 15% stake in ceramics maker Royal Doulton. Expanding its European presence, the company acquired German ceramics brand Hutschenreuther in August 2000.

OFFICERS

Chairman: Anthony J. F. O'Reilly
Deputy Chairman; Executive Chairman Ceramics:
Peter John Goulandris
Group President and COO: P. Redmond O'Donoghue,
age 57
Group Finance Director: Richard A. Barnes
VP Human Resources (USA): Brian Smith
Co-Chairman and CEO, All-Clad: Sam Michaels
CEO, Rosenthal: Ottmar C. Kusel
CEO, Waterford Wedgwood USA:
Christopher J. McGillivary
CEO, Waterford: John Foley, age 48
CEO, Wedgwood: Brian D. Patterson
Secretary: Patrick T. Dowling
Auditors: PricewaterhouseCoopers

LOCATIONS

HQ: 1-2 Upper Hatch St., Dublin 2, Ireland
Phone: +353-51-37-33-11   **Fax:** +353-14-78-48-63
US HQ: 1330 Campus Pkwy., Wall, NJ 07719
US Phone: 732-938-5800   **US Fax:** 732-938-6915
Web site: http://www.wwreview.com

1999 Sales

	% of total
US	44
Europe	41
Australasia	
(including Japan)	12
Other regions	3
Total	**100**

PRODUCTS/OPERATIONS

Selected Operations
All-Clad Inc.

Rosenthal AG
Bvlgari (licensed)
Hutschenreuther
Rosenthal
Versace (licensed)

Waterford Crystal Group
John Rocha at Waterford Crystal
Marquis by Waterford Crystal
Stuart
Waterford

Wedgwood Group
Coalport
Sarah's Garden
Wedgwood

COMPETITORS

Brown-Forman
Carlsberg
CRISAL
Fitz and Floyd, Silvestri
Lancaster Colony
Mikasa
Newell Rubbermaid
Noritake
Oneida
Royal Doulton
Taittinger
Tiffany

HISTORICAL FINANCIALS & EMPLOYEES

Nasdaq: WATFZ FYE: December 31	Annual Growth	12/90	12/91	12/92	12/93	12/94	12/95	12/96	12/97	12/98	12/99
Sales ($ mil.)	5.5%	549	510	414	450	509	551	623	596	856	888
Net income ($ mil.)	—	(50)	(9)	(29)	13	32	39	48	9	19	58
Income as % of sales	—	—	—	—	2.8%	6.3%	7.0%	7.7%	1.5%	2.2%	6.5%
Earnings per share ($)	—	(0.79)	(0.13)	(0.12)	0.18	0.20	0.54	0.66	0.12	0.26	0.79
Stock price - FY high ($)	—	9.63	7.00	6.50	6.38	9.75	9.88	13.50	14.13	17.00	12.00
Stock price - FY low ($)	—	3.00	3.50	2.25	3.13	6.38	8.13	9.13	11.38	8.13	7.50
Stock price - FY close ($)	12.1%	3.50	5.88	3.50	6.13	9.25	9.25	12.13	12.63	9.00	9.75
P/E - high	—	—	—	—	35	49	18	20	21	22	15
P/E - low	—	—	—	—	17	32	15	14	17	11	9
Dividends per share ($)	—	0.00	0.00	0.00	0.00	0.00	0.14	0.27	0.00	0.07	0.26
Book value per share ($)	—	0.00	3.50	2.16	2.42	2.92	3.28	3.90	3.09	2.94	3.23
Employees	(7.2%)	—	—	8,352	7,668	7,415	7,405	7,903	8,036	9,271	4,944

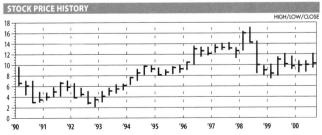

STOCK PRICE HISTORY — HIGH/LOW/CLOSE

1999 FISCAL YEAR-END
Debt ratio: 62.7%
Return on equity: 25.3%
Cash ($ mil.): 88
Current ratio: 2.44
Long-term debt ($ mil.): 401
No. of shares (mil.): 74
Dividends
  Yield: 2.7%
  Payout: 32.9%
Market value ($ mil.): 720

WHITBREAD PLC

OVERVIEW

Whitbread has climbed on the wagon and given up beer. The London-based concern was one of the largest brewers in the UK before selling that business to Belgium's Interbrew in 2000. Whitbread still serves suds at its about 2,800 pubs across the UK (1,700 are leased through the company's Whitbread Pub Partnership division, and the rest are operated by the company). One of the UK's top restaurateurs, the company operates more than 1,500 restaurants (Beefeater, Bella Pasta, Café Rouge, Pizza Hut, T.G.I. Friday's) at home and in Austria and Germany. It is also a leading UK hotel operator, with some 310 properties, including Marriott, Swallow, and Travel Inn brands. For those who spend a little too much time at its pubs and restaurants, the company owns about 55 fitness clubs (David Lloyd Leisure, Curzons The Gym) across the UK. In addition, it operates about 2,600 wine and spirits shops with Allied Domecq.

Whitbread is transforming itself from a traditional British brewer into a leisure company focused on restaurants, lodging, and fitness clubs. Following the sale of its brewing operations, it has announced that it will also sell its pub holdings.

HISTORY

Samuel Whitbread became a brewer's apprentice in 1734 and learned his lessons well; in 1742 he began brewing beer at his own brewery. By 1750 he had built a new brewery and began producing porter in bulk. He had a head for business as well as beer, acquiring other breweries and investing in new brewing techniques to increase the quality of his beers. The company prospered, despite an unlucky venture into politics by Samuel II; he opposed the war with Napoleon and committed suicide after Waterloo.

In the 1880s beer drinking declined, and Whitbread began buying up sinking pubs. But by WWI, the company started to concentrate on bottled beer sales in order to reduce its dependence on the tied pubs.

In 1944 W. H. Whitbread became chairman (the first Whitbread since founder Samuel) and took advantage of the aftermath of WWII to snap up less-robust rivals. The company first absorbed smaller breweries into its production and distribution operations but later made a living from taking over breweries and keeping their tied houses. The company went public in 1948 and had 10,000 pubs by 1970.

In the 1970s beer consumption fell yet again, and Whitbread started streamlining operations. The company closed its original brewery in 1976 and began its shift from beer to other businesses, including acquiring a Pizza Hut franchise. It sold its wines and spirits business at the end of the 1980s.

The company continued to remake itself the next decade under the leadership of CEO Peter Jarvis. As more Britons began to eat out instead of going to the local pub for entertainment, Whitbread shifted with them, buying and developing restaurant concepts including its Beefeater Restaurant and Pub and family-friendly Brewers Fayre (complete with Charlie Chalk Fun Factories for kids). In 1995, even as it divested 400 underperforming pubs, it went shopping, buying David Lloyd Leisure and 16 Marriott Hotels. Whitbread continued to refine its strategy, selling its Australian and Canadian Keg steak houses in 1995 and 1996, respectively, buying the 180-store BrightReasons pizza and pasta restaurant chain, and expanding its number of Pizza Hut restaurants from 350 to 500 in 1996.

Whitbread bought Busy Bees day care centers and put them under its David Lloyd Leisure unit in 1997. That year Jarvis stepped down and was succeeded by David Thomas. A renewed focus on its core business that year also prompted the company to dispose of all pubs that served beer not brewed by Whitbread.

In 1998 Whitbread and Allied Domecq agreed to merge their retail beer and wine stores into a new company called First Quench. It also sold one of its five breweries, put another brewery on the market, and in the wake of the declining popularity of old-fashioned pubs, sold 253 of its pubs and 40 of its Beefeaters Restaurant & Pubs.

Whitbread's 1999 attempt to buy more than 3,500 UK pubs and restaurants from Allied Domecq for $3.8 billion failed. (Rival Punch Taverns had the winning bid.) In 1999 the company sold off 75 pubs to Alehouse Company and is trying to sell its children's nursery unit. In early 2000 the company bought Swallow Group, a hotel and pub operator. Also that year Whitbread exited the brewing business by selling its beer operations to Belgium-based Interbrew for about $590 million and later announced that it would sell all its pub holdings.

Chairman: John Bahnam, age 59
Deputy Chairman: Lord MacLaurin, age 63
Chief Executive: David Thomas, age 56
Finance Director: Alan S. Perelman, age 52
Director Strategic Planning: David H. Richardson, age 48
Director Legal Affairs and Company Secretary: Simon Barratt, age 39
Director Human Resources: Chris Bulmer
Managing Director, Whitbread Restaurants: Bill F. C. Shannon, age 50
Auditors: Ernst & Young

LOCATIONS

HQ: Chiswell St., London EC1Y 4SD, United Kingdom
Phone: +44-20-7606-4455   **Fax:** +44-20-7615-1000
Web site: http://www.whitbread.co.uk

Whitbread has operations in Austria, Germany, and the UK.

PRODUCTS/OPERATIONS

2000 Sales

	% of total
Beer	28
Inns	22
Restaurants	19
Hotels	7
Pub partnerships	4
Health & fitness	3
Other beverages	17
Total	**100**

Selected Operations

Hotels	Restaurants	Retail beer and wine stores (in joint venture with Allied Domecq)
Courtyard by Marriott	Beefeater	
Marriott Hotels	Bella Pasta	
Swallow Hotels	Café Rouge	
Travel Inn	Churrasco	Bottoms Up
	Costa	Drinks Cabin
Leisure clubs	Dôme	Haddows
Curzons:	Dragon Inn	Huttons
The Gym	Mamma Amalfi	Thresher
David Lloyd Leisure	Pelican	Wine Shop
	Pizza Hut	Victoria Wine
	Tascaria	Wine Rack
Pubs	Maredo	
Brewers Fayre	T.G.I. Friday's	
Family Inn		
Hogshead		
Wayside Inn		

COMPETITORS

Bass	Granada	Rank
City Centre Restaurants	Compass	Scottish & Newcastle
De Vere Group	Greene King	Thistle Hotels
Enterprise Inns	J D Wetherspoon	Wolverhampton
Esporta	PizzaExpress	& Dudley
First Leisure	Punch Taverns Group	Breweries

HISTORICAL FINANCIALS & EMPLOYEES

London: WTB FYE: February 28	Annual Growth	2/91	2/92	2/93	2/94	2/95	2/96	2/97	2/98	2/99	2/00
Sales (£ mil.)	4.1%	2,060	3,794	3,305	2,360	2,472	2,750	3,027	3,198	2,966	2,951
Net income (£ mil.)	1.9%	152	108	153	166	205	223	247	299	249	180
Income as % of sales	—	7.4%	2.8%	4.6%	7.0%	8.3%	8.1%	8.2%	9.3%	8.4%	6.1%
Earnings per share (p)	11.6%	—	22.30	27.90	34.50	42.80	46.10	50.80	61.00	50.00	53.79
Stock price - FY high (p)	—	—	482	499	618	587	732	819	998	998	1,187
Stock price - FY low (p)	—	—	426	347	447	492	521	676	606	592	400
Stock price - FY close (p)	1.7%	—	460	459	565	538	721	784	980	981	526
P/E - high	—	—	22	18	18	14	16	16	16	20	22
P/E - low	—	—	19	12	13	11	11	13	10	12	7
Dividends per share (p)	13.5%	—	—	—	13.80	20.50	21.85	23.70	26.02	27.78	29.50
Book value per share (p)	0.9%	—	—	—	458.40	472.00	464.00	462.00	504.00	533.00	484.00
Employees	2.7%	—	—	—	62,389	65,238	70,594	80,074	81,375	76,100	73,058

STOCK PRICE HISTORY   HIGH/LOW/CLOSE

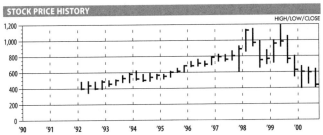

2000 FISCAL YEAR-END
Debt ratio: 42.0%
Return on equity: —
Cash (£ mil.): 123
Current ratio: 0.37
Long-term debt (£ mil.): 1,120
No. of shares (mil.): 526
Dividends
  Yield: 0.1%
  Payout: 0.5%
Market value ($ mil.): 441,665
Sales ($ mil.): 4,706

WMC LIMITED

OVERVIEW

WMC gets a lot out of the Outback. The Australian mining giant, headquartered in Southbank, Victoria, is the third-largest miner of nickel in the world, behind #1 Inco and #2 Norilsk Nickel. WMC also ranks as the third-largest-producer of gold in Australia. It owns Olympia Dam, a leading source of uranium for power generators throughout the world. WMC also owns 50% of Mondo Minerals Oy, the second-largest producer of talc in Europe, an industrial mineral used in the manufacture of paper, plastic, and paint. The company owns a 40% stake in Alcoa World Alumina & Chemicals, an Alcoa subsidiary. WMC has worldwide mining operations, including exploration projects in Australia, Brazil, Canada, China, French Guiana, and Indonesia.

To reduce its exposure to commodity prices, WMC seeks to maintain a diversified portfolio of mining properties. By driving down costs and improving productivity, the company believes it can remain globally competitive.

HISTORY

William Sydney Robinson and his older brother helped finance the western Australia gold boom of the late 1800s and early 1900s. The brothers moved to London where William made a name as a stockbroker. When William returned to Australia in 1930, he formed Gold Mines of Australia. He also formed Western Mining Corp. (WMC) in 1933. WMC began production at Kalgoorlie in 1936, on Australia's Golden Mile. By the start of WWII, WMC had 10 mines in operation.

Most of the company's mines closed during WWII, but mining resumed in 1945. With gold prices fixed due to the war and with inflation high, WMC began exploring for copper, aluminum, iron ore, and nickel. The company formed Western Aluminum NL (WANL) in 1958 to develop a bauxite reserve in the Darling Range near Perth.

In 1960 WMC bought 50% of Three Springs Talc Pty. Ltd., and in 1961 WMC, Alcoa of America, and WMC's partners in WANL formed Alcoa of Australia Ltd. (later AWAC) to mine bauxite and refine aluminum. The company discovered nickel at Kambalda in 1966. Nickel smelting operations started at nearby Kalgoorlie in 1972.

WMC acquired a stake in the Hill 50 Gold Mine NL at Mount Magnet in 1974 (sold 1996) and discovered the Olympic copper-uranium-gold body at Roxby Downs in southern Australia in 1975. With gold prices up, expansion began at Kalgoorlie, Mount Magnet, and Norseman in 1976. The company expanded its interest in petroleum in 1978 with increased production at Durham Downs, Queensland, and Poolawanna, South Australia. The following year WMC's various interests were consolidated as Western Mining Corp. Holdings.

WMC acquired Queensland Phosphate in 1980. The company's operations expanded to Brazil in 1983 through a joint venture with Alcoa of America. In 1985 WMC bought a 50% stake in fertilizer importer and distributor Hi-Fert (it acquired the remainder in 1988). Development of the Olympic Dam deposit began in 1985 in a joint venture with British Petroleum (now BP Amoco). WMC sold its interest in Kalgoorlie in 1987 and acquired the part of Mount Magnet that it didn't yet own. It also bought interests in several North American mines in 1988. WMC's gold production topped a million ounces for the first time in 1989. That year it bought the Agnew Nickel Mine.

In 1992 WMC acquired the Mount Keith nickel deposit, and the next year it purchased British Petroleum's stake in Olympic Dam. During 1995-96 the company built the Goldfields Gas Transmission pipeline to supply natural gas to WMC power stations in southwestern Australia.

The company produced its 20 millionth ounce of gold in 1996. That year AWAC formed a 30-year agreement to supply China's Sino Mining Alumina with 400,000 tons of alumina annually. Also, WMC initiated a plan to develop a major fertilizer project at Phosphate Hill (Queensland). In 1997 WMC sold its petroleum operations (other than the Goldfields pipeline), expanded its alumina production in Texas and Brazil, and it began production at an aluminum refinery in the US Virgin Islands.

Depressed metals prices continued to affect revenues in 1998 as the company sold its interest in the Goldfields Gas Transmission project. WMC also sold its Nifty Copper Operation and its Hill 50 Gold Mine NL, which slightly lowered gold production for the year.

The company completed a major expansion of its Olympic Dam uranium mine and Queensland fertilizer facilities in 1999. The next year, environmental protesters moved onto Olympic Dam property, blocked access roads, and sabotaged equipment in an effort to shut down the mine.

Chairman: Ian G. R. Burgess, $137,258 pay
CEO and Managing Director: Hugh M. Morgan,
$1,021,400 pay
Director Finance: Donald M. Morley, $598,270 pay
Executive General Manager Copper Uranium:
Pearce M. Bowman, $390,100 pay
Executive General Manager, Corporate Human
Resources and Development: Greg Travers,
$298,500 pay
Executive General Manager Exploration: John R. Parry,
$493,711 pay
Executive General Manager Gold: Anthony O'Neill
Executive General Manager Industrial Minerals and
Fertilizers: Andrew G. Michelmore, $395,600 pay
Executive General Manager Nickel: Peter B. Johnston,
$437,900 pay
Executive General Manager Projects: Ross P. McCann,
$403,475 pay
Auditors: PricewaterhouseCoopers LLP

LOCATIONS

HQ: Level 16, IBM Centre, 60 City Rd.,
Southbank, Victoria 3006, Australia
Phone: +61-3-9685-6000   Fax: +61-3-9686-3569
US HQ: 8008 E. Arapahoe Ct., Ste. 110,
Englewood, CO 80112
US Phone: 303-268-8300   US Fax: 303-268-8370
Web site: http://www.wmc.com.au

WMC has mining, refining, and exploration
operations worldwide.

PRODUCTS/OPERATIONS

Selected Products
Alumina and aluminum
Copper
Fertilizer
Gold
Nickel
Talc
Uranium

COMPETITORS

Alcan
Alcoa
Anglo American
Barrick Gold
BHP
Billiton
Cameco
Carso
COGEMA
Cominco
Freeport-McMoRan Copper & Gold
Gold Fields Limited
Great Central Mines
Homestake Mining
Inco Limited
Kaiser Aluminum
Newmont Mining
Noranda
Norilsk Nickel
Phelps Dodge
Placer Dome
Rio Algom
Rio Tinto plc

HISTORICAL FINANCIALS & EMPLOYEES

NYSE: WMC FYE: December 31	Annual Growth	6/91	6/92	6/93	6/94	6/95	6/96	6/97	*12/97	12/98	12/99
Sales ($ mil.)	1.7%	1,180	1,435	886	1,093	1,457	1,846	1,620	643	1,054	1,374
Net income ($ mil.)	(4.2%)	267	(35)	50	81	212	308	222	64	104	181
Income as % of sales	—	22.6%	—	5.6%	7.4%	14.5%	16.7%	13.7%	10.0%	9.8%	13.2%
Earnings per share ($)	(7.7%)	1.32	(0.16)	0.21	0.32	0.76	1.11	0.79	0.23	0.36	0.64
Stock price - FY high ($)	—	18.50	17.50	16.25	24.63	25.50	31.25	28.75	26.75	15.00	22.00
Stock price - FY low ($)	—	11.50	12.63	10.25	12.75	19.00	21.88	23.38	11.75	9.63	11.50
Stock price - FY close ($)	4.3%	15.00	15.50	15.63	21.00	22.00	28.75	25.63	13.63	12.00	21.88
P/E - high	—	14	—	77	77	34	28	36	116	42	34
P/E - low	—	9	—	49	40	25	20	30	51	27	18
Dividends per share ($)	(18.3%)	0.93	0.52	0.22	0.30	0.82	0.33	0.53	0.00	0.00	0.15
Book value per share ($)	1.2%	9.69	—	8.47	9.49	9.81	11.22	11.73	10.52	9.93	10.78
Employees	1.3%	—	—	4,704	6,694	6,885	7,225	—	—	5,541	5,143

* Fiscal year change

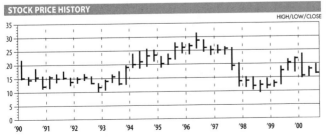

STOCK PRICE HISTORY   HIGH/LOW/CLOSE

1999 FISCAL YEAR-END
Debt ratio: 32.5%
Return on equity: 6.1%
Cash ($ mil.): 40
Current ratio: 1.15
Long-term debt ($ mil.): 1,492
No. of shares (mil.): 288
Dividends
  Yield: 0.7%
  Payout: 23.4%
Market value ($ mil.): 6,296

WOLTERS KLUWER NV

OVERVIEW

Wolters Kluwer will clue you in. The publisher, based in Amsterdam, produces information in print and electronic formats for professionals in 26 countries, primarily in Europe and North America. Its publications cover business, education, legal and tax affairs, and medical and scientific information. Wolters Kluwer's London-based professional training division offers management and employee training through Krauthammer International (Belgium) and Blessing/White (US), among other subsidiaries.

The firm is making the adjustment from its role as a content provider to an information services provider. It is expanding into online publishing, software and product development, and conference management through various acquisitions. Wolters Kluwer also announced it would spend some $240 million over the next serveral years on Internet-based initiatives.

HISTORY

Wolters Kluwer was formed in 1987 when venerable Dutch publisher Wolters Samson merged with fellow publisher Kluwer.

Wolters, Samson, and Kluwer were all pioneers in the Dutch publishing industry in the 19th century. J. B. Wolters founded a publishing house in 1836 to provide instructional material for Netherlands schools. The company later merged with educational publisher Noordhoff, founded in 1858. J. B. Wolters had no children, and the business went to his brother-in-law E. B. Horst in 1860.

Dutch academic Anthony Schepman took over the management of Wolters-Noordhoff in 1917 and led it on a major expansion drive. In 1920 it opened an office in the Dutch colony of Indonesia.

Wolters-Noordhoff and Information and Communication Union (ICU) merged in 1972. ICU had been formed by the 1970 merger of Samson (founded by Nicholaas Samson in 1883 to print government publications) and publisher A. W. Sijthoff. After the Wolters-Noordhoff-ICU merger, the resulting company initially took the ICU name, but in 1983 it became the Wolters Samson Group. That year it began exploring a merger with Kluwer.

Abele Kluwer, a former assistant schoolteacher, became a publisher in 1889. His publishing house specialized in educational products and children's books. The company expanded its range in the 1920s with a growing number of up-to-date publications regarding new laws, regulations, court decisions, and scholarly texts. Kluwer hired its first nonfamily managing director, J. M. Gorter, in 1957 and went public in 1967.

Reed Elsevier, jointly owned by publishing titans Reed International (UK) and Elsevier (the Netherlands), made a bid to acquire Kluwer in 1987, buying a minority stake in the company. The Anglo-Dutch concern was rebuffed by the subsequent merger of Wolters Samson with Kluwer, however, and was left with about a third of the shares in the new Wolters Kluwer.

Despite Reed Elsevier's repeated advances to work closely with Wolters Kluwer, the company pursued an independent growth strategy. In 1990 it acquired J.B. Lippincott, a US health care publisher. That year Reed Elsevier sold its 33% stake in the firm.

In the early 1990s Wolters Kluwer acted on its strategy of buying several medium-sized European companies. In 1995 the company acquired Commerce Clearing House (CCH), which was founded in 1892 to publish import/export and income tax guides. By the 1980s CCH was so well-versed in tax law that its largest customer was the US Internal Revenue Service.

Wolters Kluwer agreed in 1997 to be bought by Reed Elsevier for $8.8 billion, but the deal fell apart in 1998 as both companies blamed regulatory hurdles for the pact's failure. Meanwhile, Wolters Kluwer bought Waverly, a publisher of medical and scientific books and magazines, and Plenum Publishing, a scientific and technical trade book and journal publisher. Consistent with the goal of upgrading its electronic publishing offerings, Wolters Kluwer also bought Ovid Technologies, which provides electronic information retrieval services to the academic, medical, and scientific markets.

The following year it acquired US professional information publisher Bureau of Business Practice (Waterford, Connecticut) and search and retrieval service Accusearch (Houston). In late 1999 internal candidate Casper van Kempen replaced C.J. Brakel as chairman; he was out six months later, having clashed with the board over the company's Web strategy. The company named deputy chairman Robert Pieterse to replace him. Also in 2000 Wolters Kluwer announced that it would devote about $240 million to Internet-related operations.

OFFICERS

Chairman; Managing Director, Wolters Kluwer Scandinavia: R. Pieterse
CFO and Corporate Director Finance and Acquisitions/ Investor Relations: J. E. M. van Dinter
Member Executive Board: J. M. Detailleur
Member Executive Board: P. W. van Wel
Member Executive Board: Hugh J. Yarrington
Corporate Director Human Resources: M. H. Sanders
Corporate Director Strategy and Competence Development: A. S. F. Kuipers
Corporate Director Technology: C. Seigle
Corporate Director Accounting and Operations Control: P.C. Kooijmans
Secretary Executive Board: Patrick C. J. Hendricks
Auditors: KPMG Accountants N.V.

LOCATIONS

HQ: Apollolaan 153, P.O.Box 75248,
NL-1070 AE Amsterdam, The Netherlands
Phone: +31-20-607-0400 **Fax:** +31-20-607-0490
US HQ: 161 N. Clark St., 48th Fl., Chicago, IL 60601
US Phone: 312-425-7000 **US Fax:** 312-425-7023
Web site: http://www.wolters-kluwer.com

Wolters Kluwer publishes in 26 countries, primarily in Europe and North America.

1999 Sales

	$ mil.	% of total
Europe	1,694	55
US & Canada	1,302	42
Asia/Pacific & other regions	107	3
Total	**3,103**	**100**

PRODUCTS/OPERATIONS

1999 Sales

	$ mil.	% of total
Legal,tax & business publishing	2,075	68
International health & science	603	19
Educational publishing	290	9
Professional training	135	4
Total	**3,103**	**100**

Selected Operating Units
Akademische Arbeitsgemeinschaft Verlagsgesellschaft (tax publishing, Germany; 72%)
Aspen Publishers (legal publishing, US)
Blessing/White (performance improvement courses, US)
CCH (law and tax publishing, US)
Croner (business and educational publishing, UK)
Educatieve Partners Nederland (educational publishing)
Krauthammer International (professional training, Belgium)
Lamy (electronic legal database, France)
Liber (educational publishing, Sweden)
Lippincott Williams & Wilkins (medical and health information services, US)
Ovid Technologies (electronic information retrieval services for research and medical markets, US)
Teleroute (European electronic road transport information system, Belgium)

COMPETITORS

BNA	McGraw-Hill
Cadmus Communications	Pearson
Equifax	Reed Elsevier
Havas	Thomson Corporation
Hearst	Tribune
Houghton Mifflin	VNU
IHS Group	W.W. Norton
John Wiley	

HISTORICAL FINANCIALS & EMPLOYEES

OTC: WTKWY FYE: December 31	Annual Growth	12/90	12/91	12/92	12/93	12/94	12/95	12/96	12/97	12/98	12/99
Sales ($ mil.)	9.6%	1,365	1,390	1,295	1,343	1,577	1,830	2,497	2,931	3,214	3,103
Net income ($ mil.)	15.0%	102	125	142	163	220	281	277	326	363	361
Income as % of sales	—	7.5%	9.0%	11.0%	12.2%	14.0%	15.4%	11.1%	11.1%	11.3%	11.6%
Earnings per share ($)	5.5%	—	—	—	—	—	1.05	1.02	1.19	1.31	1.30
Stock price - FY high ($)		—	—	—	—	—	23.44	33.25	34.38	53.50	55.50
Stock price - FY low ($)		—	—	—	—	—	19.44	22.94	28.25	32.13	30.00
Stock price - FY close ($)	9.6%	—	—	—	—	—	23.25	32.50	32.00	53.50	33.50
P/E - high		—	—	—	—	—	22	33	29	41	43
P/E - low		—	—	—	—	—	19	22	24	25	23
Dividends per share ($)	13.2%	—	—	—	—	—	0.28	0.31	0.35	0.47	0.46
Book value per share ($)	33.0%	—	—	—	—	—	1.70	2.54	3.73	4.24	5.31
Employees	9.3%	7,842	8,732	8,089	8,052	8,693	8,993	14,948	15,385	17,431	17,452

STOCK PRICE HISTORY

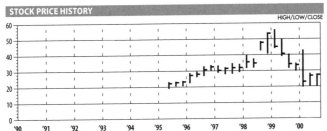

HIGH/LOW/CLOSE

1999 FISCAL YEAR-END

Debt ratio: 63.9%
Return on equity: 26.9%
Cash ($ mil.): 109
Current ratio: 0.67
Long-term debt ($ mil.): 2,380
No. of shares (mil.): 282
Dividends
  Yield: 0.0%
  Payout: 0.4%
Market value ($ mil.): 9,447

WOOLWORTHS LIMITED

Australians looking to stock up on Vegemite stop most often at supermarkets owned by Woolworths. The Sydney-based retail group is the #1 food retailer in Australia, running about 600 supermarkets and liquor stores under names including its flagship Woolworths (known as "Woolies" down under) as well as Food for Less, Purity, Roelf Vos, and Safeway. Supermarkets and liquor stores (Mac's Liquor, Cheaper Liquor) account for nearly 85% of the company's total sales. The #2 retailer in Australia (behind Coles Myer), Woolworths also runs general merchandise stores (Big W, Crazy Prices, and Woolworths Variety) and electronics stores (Dick Smith Electronics). In addition, it has about 120 Plus Petrol gas stations. The

company's Australian Independent Wholesalers subsidiary supplies goods to its own stores and independent food retailers.

Woolworths is trying not to choke on its own success. Instead of adding more supermarkets to its full cart (and cannibalizing its market share), the company has been trying new ventures as well as selling off unprofitable ones. It has added gas pumps and banking to some supermarket locations and has opened Woolworths Metro, which offers convenience foods. Woolworths sold its Rockmans women's clothing shops and plans to divest its Chisholm Manufacturing meat processing plants.

Woolworths has no relation to the five-and-dime chain once operated in the US.

Harold Percival Christmas first tried a mail-order dress business before opening the popular Frock Salon retail store. Christmas and his partners opened a branch store in the Imperial Arcade in Sydney in 1924, renaming it "Woolworths Stupendous Bargain Basement" and luring customers with advertisements calling it "a handy place where good things are cheap . . . you'll want to live at Woolworths." The company borrowed the name from Frank Woolworth's successful US chain, after determining that chain had no plans to open stores in Australia. Woolworths was listed on the Australian stock exchange in 1924.

Food sales came more than 30 years later. Woolworths opened its first freestanding, full-line supermarket in 1960, then diversified into specialty retail, buying the Rockmans women's clothing store chain the next year. It expanded into discounting with the Big W chain in 1976 and further diversified when it bought 60% of the Dick Smith Electronics store chain in 1981 (buying the remainder in 1983).

The purchase of the Safeway grocery chain (the Australian operations of the US-based chain) put Woolworths on the top of the supermarket heap in 1985. But the company was hurting (it lost $13 million in 1985-86) because of a restructuring in the early 1980s that had weakened management by bulking up the front offices and dividing responsibilities. Woolworths got a shot in the arm from Paul Simons, who returned to the company in 1987 after running competitor Franklins. Simons cleaned house in the front offices, closed

unprofitable stores, and began the successful "Fresh Food People" marketing strategy.

Industrial Equity Limited (IEL) bought the company in 1989; IEL then became part of the Adelaide Steamship group. Woolworths was spun off as a public company in 1993. The following year career Woolworths manager Reg Clairs took over as CEO, following the untimely death (on a golf course) in 1993 of Harry Watts, who was being groomed for the job. As a result, the company has an unwritten rule of avoiding CEOs older than 60.

Clairs took the company in a variety of new directions. Woolworths began supplying fresh food to neighbor Asia in 1995. The company added Plus Petrol outlets adjacent to Woolworths Supermarkets in 1996. It also started a superstore concept for its Dick Smith Electronics chain (Power House) that year. In 1997 the company launched its Woolworths Metro store chain, which targets commuters and other on-the-run shoppers in urban areas, and it aggressively jumped into wholesaling to independent grocers.

In late 1998 Clairs stepped down and Roger Corbett took over as CEO. (Clairs turned 60 in 1999.) Woolworths also struck an alliance with Commonwealth Bank of Australia to offer banking services to its customers and bought Dan Murphy, a Victoria-based liquor chain, in 1998.

In early 2000 Woolworths sold underperforming women's apparel chain Rockmans to retailer Pretty Girl.

Chairman: John C. Dahlsen, age 64
Deputy Chairman: Mervyn J. Philips, age 69
Group Managing Director and CEO: Roger C.
Corbett, age 57, $1,016,775 pay
CFO: Bill Wavish
Group Financial Controller and Manager Investor
Relations: David Freiman
Group Taxation Manager: Bridget Gay
Group Manager Executive Planning & Development and
Corporate Human Resources Manager: Judy Howard
Corporate Manager IT: Stephen Bradley
Chief General Manager Supermarket Buying and
Marketing: Bernie Brookes
Chief General Manager General Merchandise; Chief
General Manager General Merchandise, Big W:
K. R. McMorron, $729,951 pay
Chief General Manager Supermarket Operations:
Naum J. Onikul, $531,843 pay
Managing Director, Dick Smith Electronics:
Jeff I. P. Grover, $579,999 pay
General Manager, Chisholm Manufacturing:
Gerry Andersen
General Manager, AIW/Wholesale: Brian Edwards
General Manager, Victoria: Tom Flood
General Manager, Variety/Crazy Prices Stores:
Simon Grigg
General Manager Corporate Services, and Secretary:
Rohan K. S. Jeffs
General Manager, Queensland: Marty Hamnett
General Manager, Tasmania: Michael Kent
Auditors: BDO Nelson Parkhill

HQ: 540 George St., 5th Fl., Sydney 2000, Australia
Phone: +61-2-9323-1555   Fax: +61-2-9323-1599
Web site: http://www.woolworths.com.au

2000 Sales

	A$ mil.	% of total
Supermarkets	16,671	81
General merchandise	2,768	13
Wholesale	580	3
Adjustments	548	3
Total	20,567	100

Selected Operations

Food Stores
BCC
Flemings
Food for Less
Jack the Slasher
Philip Leong
Purity
Roelf Vos
Safeway
Woolworths Metro
Woolworths Supermarkets

General Merchandise Stores
Big W
Crazy Prices
Woolworths Variety

Liquor Outlets
Cheaper Liquor
Dan Murphy
Mac's Liquor
Safeway Liquor

Specialty Retail
Dick Smith Electronics
Dick Smith Electronics
Power House

Other
Australian Independent
Wholesalers (wholesale
division)
Plus Petrol (gas stations)

ALDI
BP
Caltex
Coles Myer
Davids Limited

Franklins Holdings
Harris Scarfe Holdings
Harvey Norman Holdings
Royal Dutch/Shell

Australian: WOW FYE: June 30	Annual Growth	6/91	6/92	6/93	6/94	6/95	6/96	6/97	6/98	6/99	6/00
Sales (A$ mil.)	10.6%	—	9,183	10,489	11,482	12,790	13,986	15,574	16,482	18,465	20,567
Net income (A$ mil.)	17.1%	—	84	171	200	234	234	258	279	257	296
Income as % of sales	—	—	0.9%	1.6%	1.7%	1.8%	1.7%	1.7%	1.7%	1.4%	1.4%
Earnings per share (A$)	5.4%	—	—	—	0.19	0.22	0.21	0.25	0.25	0.22	0.26
Stock price - FY high (A$)	—	—	—	—	3.32	3.10	3.45	4.36	6.24	6.10	6.33
Stock price - FY low (A$)	—	—	—	—	2.60	2.57	2.75	2.72	3.66	4.76	4.63
Stock price - FY close (A$)	13.5%	—	—	—	2.89	2.92	3.07	4.29	5.35	5.03	6.17
P/E - high	—	—	—	—	17	14	16	17	25	28	24
P/E - low	—	—	—	—	14	12	13	11	15	22	18
Dividends per share (A$)	0.0%	—	—	—	0.13	0.14	0.15	0.16	0.17	0.18	0.13
Book value per share (A$)	12.7%	—	—	—	0.75	0.91	1.04	1.09	1.20	1.29	1.54
Employees	7.7%	—	69,000	72,000	79,000	87,000	95,000	100,000	100,000	120,000	125,000

HIGH/LOW/CLOSE

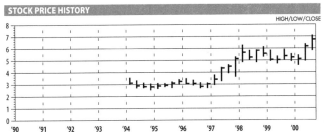

Debt ratio: 20.9%
Return on equity: —
Cash (A$ mil.): 350
Current ratio: 0.90
Long-term debt (A$ mil.): 302
No. of shares (mil.): 1,060
Dividends
  Yield: 0.0%
  Payout: 0.5%
Market value ($ mil.): 3,940
Sales ($ mil.): 12,392

WPP GROUP PLC

OVERVIEW

For WPP Group, it takes three to be #1. The London-based company has become the world's largest advertising conglomerate, surpassing US-based rivals Omnicom and Interpublic (now #2 and #3, respectively) following its $4.7 billion acquisition of Young & Rubicam. The addition gives WPP a third major advertising agency network (joining Ogilvy & Mather and J. Walter Thompson) as well as new business services units and access to new clients. WPP serves such clients as Ford, IBM, and American Express through its 950 offices in more than 90 countries.

The road to becoming the world's top advertising and marketing concern has been paved with acquisitions, especially in the high-growth business services segment. WPP has built a cache of public relations firms, direct marketing

businesses, brand consulting units, and niche marketers. Some of its top brands include The Kantar Group (market research), Hill and Knowlton (public relations), and MindShare (media buying). Cementing its position in the US, WPP has also acquired or invested in several small firms, like Dallas-based Brierley & Partners (direct marketing) and New York City's UniWorld (49%-owned), the largest African-American-owned ad firm in the US.

But don't expect WPP to rest on its laurels now that the Y&R acquisition has put it over the top. The company is focused on improving margins, increasing organic growth, and keeping its debt under control. It also is investing in a growing list of new media and start-up technology companies through its wpp.com unit (formed in 1999).

HISTORY

WPP Group began as Wire and Plastic Products, a maker of grocery baskets and other goods founded in 1958 by Gordon Sampson (now CEO of WPP's manufacturing division). Investors led by former Saatchi & Saatchi advertising executive (and current WPP CEO) Martin Sorrell bought the company in 1985 and shortened its name to WPP. Under Sorrell's leadership, the company acquired several marketing firms. In 1987 Sorrell used revenues from these businesses (and a sizable loan) to buy US advertising warhorse J. Walter Thompson (JWT).

JWT was founded by William James Carlton as the Carlton & Smith agency in 1864. The New York City-based firm was bought by James Walter Thompson in 1877. The agency later was responsible for Prudential Insurance's Rock of Gibraltar symbol (1896) and began working for Ford (which is still a client) in 1943. JWT went public in 1969.

Following its acquisition of JWT, WPP formed European agency Conquest in 1988. The company (and its debt) grew the next year when it bought the Ogilvy Group (founded by David Ogilvy in 1948) for $860 million, making WPP the world's largest advertising company. But its acquisition frenzy also positioned the company for a fall in 1991, when depressed economies in the US and the UK slowed advertising spending. Saddled with debt, WPP nearly went into receivership before recovering the next year.

WPP entered a period of controlled growth with no major acquisitions in 1993. Instead, the company expanded internationally in 1994, opening new offices in South America, Europe,

the Middle East, and Asia. Winning IBM's $500 million international advertising contract that year also aided WPP's financial recovery. However, this led to the loss of business from IBM's rivals, including AT&T, Compaq's European division, and Microsoft.

By 1997 the company was again ready to flex its acquisition muscle. The firm bought 21 companies that year, including a stake in IBOPE (a market research firm in Latin America) and a share of Batey Holdings (the majority owner of Batey Ads, a prominent ad agency in the Asia/Pacific region). That year WPP also created its media planning unit MindShare.

More acquisitions followed in 1998, including a 20% stake in Asatsu (the #3 advertising agency in Japan) and a 30% interest in the AGB Italia Group (an Italian market research company, now part of WPP's Kantar Group). The next year the company bought Texas-based market research firm IntelliQuest Information Group, which was merged into WPP's Millward Brown unit. Along with its acquisitions, WPP snagged some significant new accounts in 1998 and 1999, lining up business with Kimberly-Clark, Merrill Lynch, and the embattled International Olympic Committee.

In 2000 the company bought US-based rival Young & Rubicam for about $4.7 billion — one of the largest advertising mergers ever. The move catapulted WPP to the top spot among the world's advertising firms. Also that year it took a 49% stake in UniWorld Group, the largest African-American-owned ad agency in the US.

OFFICERS

Chairman: Hamish Maxwell, age 73
Group Chief Executive: Martin S. Sorrell, age 55,
$2,210,000 pay
Group Finance Director: Paul Richardson, age 42
Chief Human Resources Officer: Brian Brooks, age 44
Group Director of Strategy; CEO, wpp.com:
Eric Salama, age 39
Group Communications Director: Feona McEwan
Chief Executive Manufacturing: Gordon Sampson
Chairman and CEO, Hill and Knowlton: Howard Paster,
$894,000 pay
Chairman and CEO, Ogilvy & Mather Worldwide:
Shelly Lazarus, $1,488,000 pay
Chairman and CEO, Mindshare.com: Irwin Gotlieb,
$219,000 pay
Chairman, J. Walter Thompson: Charlotte Beers
Chairman, Young & Rubicam: Thomas D. Bell Jr.
Joint Chairman, The Kantar Group: Martin Goldfarb
Joint Chairman, The Kantar Group: Phil Barnard
Chairman, Conquest: Dominique Simonin
President and CEO, Ogilvy Public Relations Worldwide:
Robert Seltzer, $818,000 pay
CEO, J. Walter Thompson: Chris Jones, $975,000 pay
CEO, Conquest: Luca Linder
CEO, The Kantar Group: David Jenkins
CEO Branding & Identity, Healthcare, and Specialist
Communications: John Zweig
Auditors: Arthur Andersen

LOCATIONS

HQ: 27 Farm St., London W1X 6RD, United Kingdom
Phone: +44-20-7408-2204   **Fax:** +44-20-7493-6819
US HQ: 309 W. 49th St., New York, NY 10019
US Phone: 212-632-2200   **US Fax:** 212-632-2222
Web site: http://www.wpp.com

1999 Sales

	$ mil.	% of total
US	1,479	42
Europe		
UK	703	20
Other countries	688	20
Other regions	641	18
Total	**3,511**	**100**

PRODUCTS/OPERATIONS

1999 Sales

	$ mil.	% of total
Media advertising	1,637	47
Specialist communications	906	26
Information & consultancy	679	19
Public relations	289	8
Total	**3,511**	**100**

COMPETITORS

ACNielsen	Havas Advertising
Aegis Group	Interpublic Group
Bcom3	M&C Saatchi
Cordiant Communications	marchFIRST
Group	Omnicom
Dentsu	Publicis
Edelman Public Relations	Taylor Nelson
Grey Global	Tempus Group PLC
Hakuhodo	True North
Harte-Hanks	

HISTORICAL FINANCIALS & EMPLOYEES

Nasdaq: WPPGY FYE: December 31	Annual Growth	12/90	12/91	12/92	12/93	12/94	12/95	12/96	12/97	12/98	12/99
Sales ($ mil.)	4.1%	2,440	2,252	1,929	2,117	2,233	2,412	2,896	2,885	3,184	3,511
Net income ($ mil.)	12.4%	98	58	(18)	34	74	107	171	192	233	279
Income as % of sales	—	4.0%	2.6%	—	1.6%	3.3%	4.4%	5.9%	6.6%	7.3%	8.0%
Earnings per share ($)	(13.7%)	6.88	2.60	1.02	1.26	2.55	0.71	1.14	1.19	1.56	1.82
Stock price - FY high ($)	—	60.31	20.63	10.31	8.59	9.84	13.44	21.69	24.94	38.63	83.13
Stock price - FY low ($)	—	4.22	3.13	2.50	3.05	6.41	7.81	11.94	19.56	17.38	29.00
Stock price - FY close ($)	31.9%	6.88	4.69	3.59	6.41	8.44	12.69	21.47	22.56	30.88	83.13
P/E - high	—	8	8	10	5	3	18	18	19	24	45
P/E - low	—	1	1	2	2	2	11	10	15	11	16
Dividends per share ($)	(22.0%)	2.33	1.48	0.00	0.95	0.08	0.08	0.14	0.18	0.21	0.25
Book value per share ($)	—	(291.50)	(288.76)	(40.21)	(97.04)	(6.07)	(0.68)	0.13	(0.28)	1.02	3.32
Employees	2.3%	22,590	21,218	20,717	20,416	19,198	19,138	21,166	22,909	25,589	27,711

STOCK PRICE HISTORY

HIGH/LOW/CLOSE

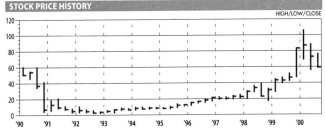

1999 FISCAL YEAR-END

Debt ratio: 53.6%
Return on equity: 67.6%
Cash ($ mil.): 981
Current ratio: 0.88
Long-term debt ($ mil.): 593
No. of shares (mil.): 155
Dividends
  Yield: 0.3%
  Payout: 13.7%
Market value ($ mil.): 12,877

YAMAHA CORPORATION

OVERVIEW

Electronic equipment is music to Yamaha's ears. Hamamatsu, Japan-based Yamaha is the world's largest maker of musical instruments, such as pianos, electronic keyboards, synthesizers, wind instruments, drums, and guitars. It makes "silent" instruments, including drums, cellos, and violins. (The user tunes in with headphones.)

Although musical instruments and audio products (mixing boards, stereo systems) account for about 70% of sales, Yamaha also

makes CD recorders, semiconductors, furniture, specialty metals, and golf clubs. Yamaha also operates music schools around the world and resorts in Japan.

Affiliate Yamaha Motor, 33%-owned by Yamaha, is the world's second-largest motorcycle manufacturer (after Honda). A specialist in small-engine technologies, the company also makes outboard motors, snowmobiles, and WaveRunners.

HISTORY

Torakusu Yamaha, a Japanese watchmaker and medical equipment repairman, tinkered with his first reed organ in 1885. Captivated, he decided to build one himself, completing it in 1887; two years later he established Yamaha Organ Manufacturing Company to make reed organs. In 1897, as production grew, he incorporated the company as Nippon Gakki (Japan Musical Instruments). Nippon Gakki began producing upright pianos in 1900 and grand pianos in 1902.

In 1920 the company diversified into the production of wooden airplane propellers (based on woodworking skills used in making pianos) and added pipe organs (1932) and guitars (1946) to its line of musical instruments. Genichi Kawakami, whose father had managed the company since 1927, took over in 1950. He moved the business into motorcycle production in 1954, transferring the motorcycle business to Yamaha Motor, a separate but affiliated company, the next year.

The company formed its first overseas subsidiary, Yamaha de Mexico, in 1958. Under Kawakami's leadership, Nippon Gakki became the world's largest producer of musical instruments, developing Japan's first electronic organ, the Electone, in 1959. Kawakami spearheaded the company's move into wind instruments (1965), stereos (1968), microchips (1971), and furniture (1975). He established the Yamaha Music Foundation in 1966, which oversees the company's popular music schools. By 1982 musicians in the Americas, Europe, and Asia could buy Yamaha-brand products locally.

Nippon Gakki undertook further diversification, particularly into customized chips for CD players. In 1983 it unveiled a powerful synthesizer cheap enough to appeal to a mass market.

The company changed its name to Yamaha in 1987. It opened a facility in China two years later. Yamaha emphasized exports of

electronic instruments and the production of integrated circuits. Meanwhile, Yamaha Motor's sales were revived in 1991, powered by demand for big bikes by aging baby boomers.

Until 1992 three successive generations of the Kawakami family dominated Yamaha. After a failed attempt by heir apparent Hiroshi Kawakami to cut back Yamaha's workforce through early retirement, the manufacturer's in-house labor union revolted. Kawakami was replaced by Seisuke Ueshima, a 36-year Yamaha veteran who set out to work on a combination of product innovation and corporate restructuring. Ueshima made a pact with the unions to keep most factory workers, lay off 30% of Japanese administrative staff, and cut overseas employees.

Yamaha and Western Digital formed a partnership in 1995 to develop 3-D technology for PCs. Two years later Kazukiyo Ishimura was named Yamaha's president, and the company launched a joint licensing program with Stanford University for the Sondius-XG sound synthesis technology; the two institutions share royalties from the technology, which provides realistic sound quality for musical instruments and computer games.

Undergoing sluggish sales of electronic parts, in 1999 Yamaha stopped producing magnetic heads for hard disk drives, shut down a semiconductor plant, and trimmed its workforce by giving 11% of its employees early retirement.

In 2000 Yamaha introduced a CD player-equipped "singing" player piano, the Disklavier Mark III. The piano includes a feature that allows the user to hear artists, including Frank Sinatra, singing their hit songs along with piano accompaniment provided automatically or by the user.

OFFICERS

President: Shuji Ito
Senior Managing Director: Katsuhiro Kishida
Managing Director: Kunihiro Maejima
Managing Director: Masatada Wachi
President, Yamaha Corporation of America:
M. Umemura
President, Yamaha Motor: Takehiko Hasegawa
Auditors: Century Ota Showa & Co.

LOCATIONS

HQ: 10-1, Nakazawa-cho, Hamamatsu,
   Shizuoka 430-8650, Japan
Phone: +81-53-460-2211 **Fax:** +81-53-460-2525
US HQ: 6600 Orangethorpe Ave., Buena Park, CA 90620
US Phone: 714-522-9011 **US Fax:** 714-522-9235
Web site: http://www.yamaha.co.jp

2000 Sales

	% of total
Japan	66
North America	14
Europe	10
Other regions	10
Total	**100**

PRODUCTS/OPERATIONS

2000 Sales

	% of total
Musical instruments & audio	72
Electronic equipment & metals	12
Lifestyle-related products	9
Recreation	4
Other	3
Total	**100**

Selected Products and Services

Musical Instruments and Audio
Audio products (home theater systems, stereo
   equipment, CD recorders)
Digital musical instruments
Educational musical instruments
Guitars
Mixing boards and related equipment
Music schools
Percussion instruments
Pianos (Yamaha, Disklavier)
Telecommunications equipment
Wind instruments

Electronic Equipment and Metals
Electronic alloys
Large-scale integration chips (LSIs)
Thin-film heads

Lifestyle-Related Products
Bathtubs and washstands
Furniture
Parts for housing facilities
Sound equipment for housing
System kitchens

COMPETITORS

Allen Organ Company	Marshall Amplification
Baldwin Piano	Matsushita
C. F. Martin & Company	NEC
Casio Computer	Philips Electronics
Fender Musical	Pioneer
Instruments	Roland
Fujitsu	Seiko Epson
Gibson Musical	Sony
Intel	Steinway
Kaman	

HISTORICAL FINANCIALS & EMPLOYEES

Tokyo: 7951 FYE: March 31	Annual Growth	3/91	3/92	3/93	3/94	3/95	3/96	3/97	3/98	3/99	3/00
Sales (¥ mil.)	0.4%	509,149	512,591	483,457	446,025	482,845	531,111	604,554	608,990	563,751	527,897
Net income (¥ mil.)	—	7,639	5,740	1,827	(3,985)	5,339	9,430	14,066	13,475	(15,879)	(40,777)
Income as % of sales	—	1.5%	1.1%	0.4%	—	1.1%	1.8%	2.3%	2.2%	—	—
Earnings per share (¥)	—	39.65	29.58	9.41	(20.53)	27.51	48.51	71.96	65.25	(76.89)	(197.45)
Stock price - FY high (¥)	—	2,090	1,830	1,380	1,310	1,430	1,980	2,520	2,630	1,429	1,609
Stock price - FY low (¥)	—	1,340	1,250	720	861	999	922	1,670	1,220	1,010	620
Stock price - FY close (¥)	(7.9%)	1,740	1,340	1,060	1,090	1,020	1,950	2,290	1,300	1,254	832
P/E - high	—	53	62	147	—	52	41	35	40	—	—
P/E - low	—	34	42	77	—	36	19	23	19	—	—
Dividends per share (¥)	—	10.00	10.00	6.00	6.00	7.00	8.00	9.00	10.00	6.00	0.00
Book value per share (¥)	2.8%	834.00	847.00	835.00	797.00	810.00	884.00	1,078.00	1,140.00	1,041.00	1,074.00
Employees	6.5%	12,241	11,647	11,000	10,676	10,812	9,872	9,324	9,281	9,044	21,599

STOCK PRICE HISTORY

HIGH/LOW/CLOSE

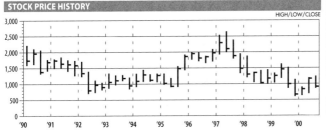

2000 FISCAL YEAR-END

Debt ratio: 28.5%
Return on equity: —
Cash (¥ mil.): 33,796
Current ratio: 1.16
Long-term debt (¥ mil.): 34,002
No. of shares (mil.): 207
Dividends
   Yield: —
   Payout: —
Market value ($ mil.): 1,629
Sales ($ mil.): 5,005

YPF, S.A.

No swords were involved, but a modern-day Spanish conquistador has gained control of Argentina's integrated oil company YPF. Spain's Repsol, now Repsol YPF, bought 98% of Buenos Aires-based YPF, the largest company in Argentina, in 1999 (which Repsol YPF upped to 99% in 2000).

YPF is involved in petroleum exploration, production, refining, marketing, transportation, and distribution; it also produces petrochemicals. YPF has proved reserves of 3.3 billion barrels of oil equivalent; the company accounts for 44% of Argentina's oil reserves and 40% of its natural gas reserves. It operates more than 2,200 gas stations in Argentina (about 35% of the nation's total number of service stations).

YPF has transformed itself from an inefficient state-owned firm into a streamlined international player, and it has benefited from the Mercosur agreement, which set up an economic union in South America to promote regional trade. Strong demand in Brazil and Chile have promoted YPF's natural gas export business; it already has pipelines in Chile and will build more in Bolivia and Brazil (marked as having South America's largest potential natural gas market).

The company has turned around its formerly loss-making US-based Maxus Energy subsidiary, the core unit of its international exploration and production arm, YPF International. YPF International also has holdings in Brazil, Ecuador, Indonesia, and Venezuela.

An Argentine government team discovered oil while drilling for water in 1907. Determined to keep the oil under Argentine control, the government in 1922 formed Direccion Nacional de los Yacimientos Petroliferos Fiscales (YPF), the world's first state-owned oil company, to operate the newly discovered field. However, YPF lacked drilling equipment, capital, and staff; it found that the only way to increase domestic oil production was to allow in foreign oil companies. Although YPF's activities ebbed in the 1920s, it made major oil discoveries across Argentina in the 1930s.

A major turning point came with Juan Peron's rise to power in 1945. Peron extended state control over broad sections of the economy, including oil. He nationalized British and US oil holdings and gave YPF a virtual monopoly. In 1945 YPF accounted for 68% of the country's oil production; by 1955 it produced 84% of the national total. The company discovered a huge gas field two years later in western Argentina, making YPF — and Argentina — a major gas producer.

However, YPF's production failed to keep pace with the demands of the growing economy, and imports still dominated Argentina's oil market. Over the next 30 years, YPF experienced radical swings in government policy as ultranationalist military regimes alternated with liberal, reformist governments. YPF grew into a bloated and inefficient conglomerate. Between 1982 and 1989, despite a World Bank-financed program to modernize YPF's refineries, the firm lost more than $6 billion.

In 1989 Carlos Menem became Argentina's president, and YPF was privatized as part of his economic reform plan to cut loose 50 state-owned companies. To prepare YPF for its IPO, the president brought in a former head of Baker Hughes, Jose Estenssoro, to draft a plan for privatization. The plan was so impressive that Menem gave him the job as CEO of the company in 1990. Estenssoro cut 87% of YPF's staff and sold off $2 billion of noncore assets. By 1993 YPF was profitable and went public as YPF Sociedad Anonima, selling 45% of its shares to raise $3 billion.

A year later YPF began expanding beyond Argentina by shipping crude oil to Chile through a new 300-mile pipeline. It bought woebegone Texas oil company Maxus Energy in 1995 and turned it around at great expense. Estenssoro and three other YPF executives died in a plane crash that year; in 1997 YPF selected Roberto Monti, who had headed Maxus, to serve as its CEO.

In 1997 YPF and Astra C.A.P. S.A. — in which Spanish oil firm Repsol had a controlling stake — jointly purchased a 67% stake in Mexpetrol Argentina (affiliate of Mexican state oil company PEMEX). Repsol was aggressively moving overseas. In 1998 Repsol lobbied hard to buy part of YPF; Spain's King Juan Carlos himself phoned up Menem to promote Repsol's interests.

A year later the Argentine government auctioned off a 15% stake in YPF to Repsol for $2 billion; Repsol then bought another 83% for $13.2 billion. Repsol became Repsol YPF, and its chairman, Alfonso Cortina, took over as chairman and CEO of YPF, while Monti was named VC and COO (he retired in 2000).

In 2000 Repsol YPF increased its stake in YPF from 98% to 99%.

Chairman and CEO, Repsol YPF and YPF:
Alfonso Cortina de Alcocer, age 56
Director Finance, Repsol YPF:
Carmelo de las Morenas López
Director Human Resources, Repsol YPF:
Jesús Fernández de la Vega Sanz
Auditors: Arthur Andersen

LOCATIONS

HQ: Avenida Presidente Roque Sáenz Peña 777,
1364 Buenos Aires, Argentina
Phone: +54-11-4329-2000   Fax: +54-11-4329-2113
Web site: http://www.repsol-ypf.com

YPF has interests in Argentina, Bolivia, Brazil,
Colombia, Ecuador, Indonesia, the US, and Venezuela.

PRODUCTS/OPERATIONS

Major Activities
Refining, marketing, transportation, and distribution of
oil and a range of petroleum products, derivatives,
petrochemicals, and liquid petroleum gas
Oil and natural gas exploration and production
Electricity generation

COMPETITORS

BP
Brasileira de Petroleo Ipiranga
Chevron
Exxon Mobil
Imperial Oil
PDVSA
PEMEX
PETROBRAS
Compañia de Petróleos
Pioneer Natural Resources
Royal Dutch/Shell
Texaco
TOTAL FINA ELF
Unocal
Virginia Indonesia

HISTORICAL FINANCIALS & EMPLOYEES

NYSE: YPF FYE: December 31	Annual Growth	12/90	12/91	12/92	12/93	12/94	12/95	12/96	12/97	12/98	12/99
Sales ($ mil.)	5.5%	—	4,292	3,867	3,964	4,403	4,974	5,944	6,145	5,501	6,598
Net income ($ mil.)	7.9%	—	261	256	707	564	823	845	886	589	481
Income as % of sales	—	—	6.1%	6.6%	17.8%	12.8%	16.5%	14.2%	14.4%	10.7%	7.3%
Earnings per share ($)	(3.3%)	—	—	—	—	1.60	2.30	2.31	2.48	1.64	1.35
Stock price - FY high ($)	—	—	—	—	—	29.63	22.25	25.38	38.13	36.50	44.75
Stock price - FY low ($)	—	—	—	—	—	20.38	14.38	19.25	24.88	18.69	26.50
Stock price - FY close ($)	11.6%	—	—	—	—	21.38	21.63	25.25	34.19	27.94	36.94
P/E - high	—	—	—	—	—	19	10	11	15	22	33
P/E - low	—	—	—	—	—	13	6	8	10	11	20
Dividends per share ($)	(3.8%)	—	—	—	—	0.80	0.60	0.60	0.42	0.66	0.66
Book value per share ($)	6.7%	—	—	—	—	15.10	16.73	18.08	19.66	20.43	20.89
Employees	(16.0%)	—	32,117	10,600	7,500	6,750	9,350	9,750	10,000	9,500	—

STOCK PRICE HISTORY

HIGH/LOW/CLOSE

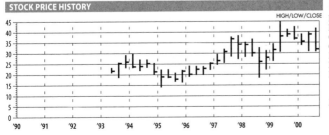

1999 FISCAL YEAR-END

Debt ratio: 21.7%
Return on equity: 6.6%
Cash ($ mil.): 81
Current ratio: 0.88
Long-term debt ($ mil.): 2,045
No. of shares (mil.): 353
Dividends
  Yield: 1.8%
  Payout: 48.9%
Market value ($ mil.): 13,039.8

ZURICH FINANCIAL SERVICES

The gnomes hard at work at Zurich Financial Services (ZFS) must know what they're doing. The firm is one of the top insurance firms in Europe, keeping company with such giants as AXA and Allianz.

The Zurich-based company offers life and property/casualty insurance, financial planning, asset management, reinsurance, and other financial services. Although it has operations in some 60 countries around the world, ZFS considers the US, the UK, and Switzerland its three "home" countries (together they account for almost 70% of its sales).

Since the merger that created it in 1998, ZFS has been working to simplify and expand its operations. The firm is streamlining its many brands in the UK and increasing its presence on the Internet. Its ownership structure has also been streamlined: Holding companies Zurich Allied and Allied Zurich (which owned 57% and 43% of the company, respectively) have merged and been absorbed into ZFS. The firm, with its sleeker new structure, hopes to list in the US as part of its expansion plans there.

The roots of Zurich Financial Services (ZFS) stretch back to the 1872 founding of a reinsurer for Switzerland Transport Insurance. The company soon branched out into accident, travel, and workers' compensation insurance and changed its name to Transport and Accident Insurance plc Zurich in 1875 to reflect the changes. It began moving into such German cities as Berlin (the jumping-off point for its expansion into Scandinavia and Russia) and Stuttgart. The company exited marine lines in 1880; it later left the reinsurance business. It expanded into liability insurance and in 1894 changed its name to Zurich General Accident and Liability Insurance.

In 1912 Zurich moved into the US. It agreed in 1925 to provide insurance for Ford cars at favorable terms. Zurich's business was hit hard during WWII, and its wartime conduct would later come back to haunt it. In 1955 the company changed its name to Zurich Insurance.

Starting in the 1960s, Zurich began buying other insurers, including Alpina (1965, Switzerland), Agrippina (1969, Germany), and Maryland Casualty Group (1989, US). It also bought the property liability operations of American General Corp.

In the early 1990s the company's strategy shifted. Being big wasn't enough; Zurich needed to find a focus. It began to specialize in such markets as life insurance in Switzerland, and to jettison such marginal or unprofitable business lines as commercial fire insurance in Germany.

In 1995 Zurich bought struggling Chicago-based asset manager Kemper, and in 1997 it bought Scudder Stevens & Clark, a lackluster mutual fund manager, creating Scudder Kemper. That year it also bought failed Hong Kong investment bank Peregrine Investment Holdings. In 1998 Zurich merged with the financial services businesses of B.A.T Industries.

The British-American Tobacco Co. was created in 1902 as a joint venture between UK-based Imperial Tobacco and American Tobacco.

As public disapproval of smoking grew in the 1970s, the company began diversifying; it changed its name to B.A.T Industries in 1976 and moved into insurance. In 1984 it rescued UK insurer Eagle Star from a hostile offer by German insurance giant Allianz. The next year it bought Hambro Life Assurance, renaming it Allied Dunbar. Moving into the large US market, B.A.T bought Farmers Insurance Group in 1988. (Farmers was founded in 1928 as an automobile insurer.)

While B.A.T battled the antismoking army of the 1990s, the insurance industry struggled with stagnant growth. The late 1990s were a bad time for Swiss insurance and banking firms as they, along with other European insurers, faced pressure to pay on insurance policies taken out by Holocaust victims. In 1998 Zurich became one of six Swiss insurers that agreed to pay on the life insurance policies.

That year Zurich and B.A.T's insurance units merged to create ZFS. The new company was immediately caught up in an investigation of insider trading relating to the merger. CFO Markus Rohrbasser resigned, disclosing that he had traded in Zurich Insurance stock before the merger. The firm reshuffled its holdings and sold Eagle Star Reinsurance. In 1999 ZFS spun off its real estate holdings into PSP Swiss Property. At the turn of the century, it focused on expanding, buying mobile home insurer Foremost Group and the new business of insurer Abbey Life, which it merged into Allied Dunbar.

In 2000, the holding companies formed to own ZFS when it was created (Zurich Allied and Allied Zurich) were merged into the firm.

Chairman and CEO, Zurich Financial Services and Zurich Allied; Deputy Chairman, Allied Zurich: Rolf Hüppi, age 56
VC, Zurich Financial Services and Zurich Allied; Chairman and CEO, Allied Zurich: Earl Cairns, age 60
Member Group Executive Board, North and Latin American Operations, Corporate/Industrial Insurance, Zurich International, and Risk Engineering: William H. Bolinder, age 56
Member Group Executive Board, Swiss and Liechtenstein Operations: Peter Eckert, age 55
Member Group Executive Board, Farmers Group Operations and US Personal Lines: Martin D. Feinstein, age 51
Member Group Executive Board, Northern and Eastern Europe Operations: Heinrich Focke, age 47
Member Group Executive Board and CFO; CFO, Zurich Allied and Allied Zurich; CEO, Zurich Life Insurance: Günther Gose, age 55
Member Group Executive Board, UK, Irish, and Southern African Operations: Alexander P. Leitch, age 52
Member Group Executive Board, Southern European, Asian, Australia, Middle Eastern, and Northern African Operations: Frank Schnewlin, age 49
Director of Human Resources: Barbara Zuber
CEO, Zurich US: Constantine Iordanou
Director of Human Resources, Zurich US: Jan Hahn
Auditors: PricewaterhouseCoopers AG

1999 Sales

	$ mil.	% of total
Premiums	24,836	65
Investment income	6,142	16
Capital gains	3,169	9
Asset management fees	1,450	4
Farmers Group management fee income	1,490	4
Other income	2,875	2
Total	**39,962**	**100**

AEGON	GeneralCologne	Nippon Life
AIG	Generali	Prudential
Allianz	ING	State Farm
Allstate	Liebherr	Sumitomo Life
AXA	Lloyd's of	Swiss Life
CGNU plc	London	Swiss Re
Citigroup	MetLife	Tokio Marine
CNA Financial	Mitsui Marine	and Fire
ERGO	& Fire	Winterthur
FMR	Munich Re	Yasuda Fire &
GEICO	New York Life	Marine

HQ: Mythenquai 2, 8002 Zurich, Switzerland
Phone: +41-1-625-2525   Fax: +41-1-625-3555
Web site: http://www.zurich.com

1999 Sales

	$ mil.	% of total
Europe		
UK	8,505	21
Switzerland	6,601	17
Other countries	8,456	21
US	11,578	29
Other regions	4,822	12
Total	**39,962**	**100**

Swiss: ZURN FYE: December 31	Annual Growth	12/90	12/91	12/92	12/93	12/94	12/95	12/96	12/97	12/98	12/99
Assets ($ mil.)	7.4%	—	—	—	—	—	—	—	191,807	214,651	221,178
Net income ($ mil.)	23.4%	—	—	—	—	—	—	—	2,142	802	3,260
Income as % of assets	—	—	—	—	—	—	—	—	1.1%	0.4%	1.5%
Employees	0.6%	—	—	—	—	—	—	—	68,000	68,876	68,785

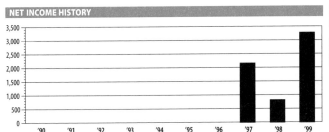

NET INCOME HISTORY

1999 FISCAL YEAR-END
Equity as % of assets: 10.8%
Return on assets: 1.5%
Return on equity: 14.4%
Long-term debt ($ mil.): 4,402
Sales ($ mil.): 39,962

Hoover's Handbook of World Business

THE INDEXES

HOOVER'S Company Capsules on CD-ROM

Business Press

This easy-to-use program is ideal for generating mailing lists. It features information on 11,000 major U.S. companies and includes 30,000 executive names. Each record includes company name, address, phone and fax numbers; Web site address; names of CEO, CFO, and chief human resources officer; sales and one-year sales change; fiscal year-end, stock exchange and symbol; industry; metro area; and a brief overview of operations.

Developed in Claris' FileMaker Pro, the program combines a simple, intuitive interface (no user manual required) with a powerful search engine.

- Sort and search by one or more fields, including company name, location, sales, industry and more
- Create mailing labels, merge letters and lists
- Import the information into your own database, word processing or spreadsheet programs
- Click on Web site address to connect to the company's Web site, or click on the stock symbol for a stock quote or chart (requires Internet access)

Requires Windows 3.1 or higher, 4MB RAM, and 20MB free hard-disk space. License permits use of information for creating letters and labels for individual use only. Information may not be disseminated to multiple users through company intranets or other means of distribution.

ITEM #HCCD1 • U.S. CD-ROM • $399.95

International Version

The international version of Hoover's CD-ROM contains information on more than 2,600 of the most important companies headquartered outside the United States. CEO names are included for all companies, and most list a CFO. Some of the companies also include a human resources executive.

ITEM #HCDF • International CD-ROM • $149.95

REGIONAL CD-ROMS

These regional versions of Hoover's Company Capsules on CD-ROM make easy, inexpensive mailing lists. The software is the same as described at left.

GREAT LAKES
1,559 capsules (IL, IN, MI, OH, WI).
ITEM #HEMGLCD • CD-ROM • $124.95

MIDDLE ATLANTIC
1,533 capsules (DE, DC, MD, NJ, PA, VA, WV).
ITEM #HEMMACD • CD-ROM • $124.95

NORTHEAST
2,019 capsules (CT, ME, MA, NH, NY, RI, VT).
ITEM #HEMNECD • CD-ROM • $124.95

NORTHWEST AND GREAT PLAINS
780 capsules (ID, IA, MN, MT, NE, ND, OR, SD, WA, WY).
ITEM #HEMNWCD • CD-ROM • $124.95

SOUTHEAST
1,389 capsules (AL, FL, GA, KY, MS, NC, SC, TN).
ITEM #HEMSECD • CD-ROM • $124.95

SOUTHWEST AND SOUTH CENTRAL
1,641 capsules (AR, CO, KS, LA, MO, NM, OK, TX).
ITEM #HEMSWCD • CD-ROM • $124.95

WEST
2,097 capsules (AZ, AK, CA, HI, NV, UT).
ITEM #HEMWCD • CD-ROM • $124.95

For a free catalog or to order, call 800-486-8666, or e-mail orders@hoovers.com

Hoover's, Inc. • 1033 La Posada Drive, Suite 250 • Austin, Texas 78752
Phone: 512-374-4500 • Fax: 512-374-4505 • e-mail: orders@hoovers.com

Business Press

Why Pay Big Bucks for Company Information?

Get vital information on thousands of top companies for just pennies a piece

Hoover's
$124.⁹⁵ MasterList of
hardcover **Major U.S.
Companies 2001**

This edition provides vital information on more than 5,600 of the largest U.S. public and private companies and other enterprises (government-owned, foundations, schools, partnerships, subsidiaries, joint ventures, cooperatives and not-for-profits) with sales of more than $125 million, plus public companies with a market capitalization of more than $500 million.

Entries include a description of operations and ownership; five years of financials including sales, net income, market cap and number of employees; address, telephone, fax and Web site; fiscal year-end; names of CEO, CFO and chief human resources officer; and, if public, stock exchange and symbol. Indexed by industry, headquarters location and stock symbol.

Seventh edition, October 2000.
Hardcover • $124.95 • ISBN 1-57311-062-0 • 8-1/2" x 11" • 1,034 pp.

Hoover's
$89.⁹⁵ MasterList of
hardcover **Major International
Companies 1998-99**

This resource covers the top 1,600 companies in countries around the globe and includes:
• non-U.S. companies with sales greater than $5 billion
• ADRs trading on the major U.S. exchanges, plus nearly 200 others traded OTC
• companies on the major indexes from stock markets worldwide (FTSE 100, Nikkei 225, TSE 100 and others)
• the top companies from more than 20 countries in Europe, Latin America, Africa, Asia and the Pacific Rim.

You'll get a description of operations and ownership; five years of financials including sales, net income and number of employees; address, telephone, fax and Web site; fiscal year-end; names of CEO and CFO; and stock exchange and stock symbol (if traded in the U.S.). All financial information is converted to U.S. dollars. Indexed by industry and country.

First edition, November 1998.
Hardcover • $89.95 • ISBN 1-57311-043-4 • 8-1/2" x 11" • 324 pp.

SAVE $70!
Get the U.S. and International MasterLists for just **$145** when you order directly from Hoover's. That's a 33% savings!

ITEM# HMS • $145

For a free catalog or to order, call 800-486-8666, or e-mail orders@hoovers.com

Hoover's, Inc. • 1033 La Posada Drive, Suite 250 • Austin, Texas 78752 • Phone: 512-374-4500 • Fax: 512-374-4505 • e-mail: orders@hoovers.com

Business Press

More is Better!

For information on even more companies, order the complete set of Hoover's Handbooks.

Complete Set of
Hoover's Handbooks

Get the complete set of four **Hoover's Handbooks** plus a FREE combined index (a $39.95 value) for only **$375** when you order directly from Hoover's. You save 25%! Make Hoover's Handbooks the cornerstone of your business information collection. Specify the "complete set" when ordering.

Hoover's Handbook of
American Business 2001

This two-volume set profiles 750 of the largest and most influential enterprises in America, with company histories and strategies, up to 10 years of key financial and employment data, lists of products and key competitors, names of key officers, addresses, and phone and fax numbers.
December 2000 • ISBN 1-57311-064-7

Hoover's Handbook of
World Business 2001

Within this book are profiles of 300 of the most influential companies based outside of the U.S., many of which have a profound impact on American life.
February 2001 • ISBN 1-57311-066-3

Hoover's Handbook of
Private Companies 2001

Here's that hard-to-find information on private companies. This book covers 750 of the largest nonpublic U.S. enterprises and includes in-depth profiles for 250 of those companies.
March 2001 • ISBN 1-57311-067-1

Hoover's Handbook of
Emerging Companies 2001

This title covers 500 of America's most exciting growth companies, with in-depth profiles of 125 of the companies.
January 2001 • ISBN 1-57311-065-5

**For a free catalog or to order, call 800-486-8666,
or e-mail orders@hoovers.com**

Hoover's, Inc. • 1033 La Posada Drive, Suite 250 • Austin, Texas 78752
Phone: 512-374-4500 • Fax: 512-374-4505 • e-mail: orders@hoovers.com